# Lecture Notes in Computer Science    11891

More information about this series at http://www.springer.com/series/7410

Dennis Hofheinz · Alon Rosen (Eds.)

# Theory
# of Cryptography

17th International Conference, TCC 2019
Nuremberg, Germany, December 1–5, 2019
Proceedings, Part I

 Springer

*Editors*
Dennis Hofheinz
Karlsruhe Institute of Technology
Karlsruhe, Germany

Alon Rosen
IDC Herzliya
Herzliya, Israel

ISSN 0302-9743            ISSN 1611-3349   (electronic)
Lecture Notes in Computer Science
ISBN 978-3-030-36029-0       ISBN 978-3-030-36030-6   (eBook)
https://doi.org/10.1007/978-3-030-36030-6

LNCS Sublibrary: SL4 – Security and Cryptology

This Springer imprint is published by the registered company Springer Nature Switzerland AG
The registered company address is: Gewerbestrasse 11, 6330 Cham, Switzerland

# Preface

The 17th Theory of Cryptography Conference (TCC 2019) was held during December 1–5, 2019, at the DB Museum in Nuremberg, Germany. It was sponsored by the International Association for Cryptologic Research (IACR). The general chair of the conference was Dominique Schröder.

The conference received 147 submissions, of which the Program Committee (PC) selected 43 for presentation. Each submission was reviewed by at least three PC members, often more. The 35 PC members (including PC chairs), all top researchers in our field, were helped by 171 external reviewers, who were consulted when appropriate. These proceedings consist of the revised version of the 43 accepted papers. The revisions were not reviewed, and the authors bear full responsibility for the content of their papers.

As in previous years, we used Shai Halevi's excellent Web-review software, and are extremely grateful to him for writing it, and for providing fast and reliable technical support whenever we had any questions. We made extensive use of the interaction feature supported by the review software, where PC members could anonymously interact with authors. This was used to ask specific technical questions, such as suspected bugs. We felt this approach helped us prevent potential misunderstandings and improved the quality of the review process.

This year's TCC was extended from three to four days of talks, and the lengths of the presentations were accordingly extended from 20 to 25 minutes.

This was the sixth year that TCC presented the Test of Time Award to an outstanding paper that was published at TCC at least eight years ago, making a significant contribution to the theory of cryptography, preferably with influence also in other areas of cryptography, theory, and beyond. This year the Test of Time Award Committee selected the following paper, published at TCC 2008: "Incrementally Verifiable Computation or Proofs of Knowledge Imply Time/Space Efficiency" by Paul Valiant. This paper was selected for demonstrating the power of recursive composition of proofs of knowledge and enabling the development of efficiently verifiable proofs of correctness for complex computations. The authors were invited to deliver a talk at TCC 2019. The conference also featured two other invited talks, by Rachel Lin and by Omer Reingold.

A Best Young Researcher Paper Award was given to Henry Corrigan-Gibbs and Dmitry Kogan for their paper "The Function-Inversion Problem: Barriers and Opportunities."

We are greatly indebted to many people who were involved in making TCC 2019 a success. First of all, a big thanks to the most important contributors: all the authors who submitted papers to the conference. Next, we would like to thank the PC members for their hard work, dedication, and diligence in reviewing the papers, verifying the correctness, and in-depth discussion. We are also thankful to the external reviewers for their volunteered hard work and investment in reviewing papers and answering questions, often under time pressure. For running the conference itself, we are very grateful to the general chair, Dominique Schröder. We appreciate the sponsorship from the IACR, Deloitte, Siemens, Syss, and HGS. We also wish to thank Friedrich-Alexander-Universität Erlangen-Nürnberg and Nuremberg Campus of Technology for their support. Finally, we are thankful to the TCC Steering Committee as well as the entire thriving and vibrant TCC community.

October 2019                                    Dennis Hofheinz
                                                    Alon Rosen

# TCC 2019

## The 17th Theory of Cryptography Conference

Nuremberg, Germany,
December 1–5, 2019

## General Chair

Dominique Schröder      University of Erlangen-Nuremberg, Germany

## Program Co-chairs

Dennis Hofheinz      Karlsruhe Institute of Technology
Alon Rosen      IDC Herzliya

## Program Committee

| | |
|---|---|
| Adi Akavia | Haifa University, Israel |
| Joël Alwen | Wickr, USA |
| Benny Applebaum | Tel Aviv University, Israel |
| Gilad Asharov | JP Morgan AI Research, USA |
| Nir Bitansky | Tel Aviv University, Israel |
| Chris Brzuska | Aalto University, Finland |
| Kai-Min Chung | Institute of Information Science, Academia Sinica, Taiwan |
| Ran Cohen | BU and Northeastern University, USA |
| Geoffroy Couteau | Karlsruhe Institute of Technology, Germany |
| Dana Dachman-Soled | University of Maryland, USA |
| Nico Döttling | CISPA, Saarbrücken, Germany |
| Marc Fischlin | Technische Universität Darmstadt, Germany |
| Siyao Guo | NYU Shanghai, China |
| Julia Hesse | Technische Universität Darmstadt, Germany |
| Pavel Hubáček | Charles University Prague, Czech Republic |
| Abhishek Jain | Johns Hopkins University, USA |
| Bhavana Kanukurthi | Indian Institute of Science, India |
| Eike Kiltz | Ruhr-Universität Bochum, Germany |
| Susumu Kiyoshima | NTT Secure Platform Laboratories, Japan |
| Venkata Koppula | Weizmann Institute of Science, Israel |
| Mohammad Mahmoody | University of Virginia, USA |
| Nikolaos Makriyannis | Technion, Israel |
| Pratyay Mukherjee | Visa Research, San Francisco, USA |
| Jörn Müller-Quade | Karlsruhe Institute of Technology, Germany |

Ryo Nishimaki              NTT Secure Platform Laboratories, Japan
Omer Paneth                MIT, USA
Antigoni Polychroniadou    JP Morgan AI Research, USA
Mariana Raykova            Google, Inc., New York, USA
Ron Rothblum               IDC Herzliya, Israel
Noah Stephens-Davidowitz   MIT, USA
Prashant Vasudevan         UC Berkeley, USA
Muthuramakrishnan          University of Rochester, USA
  Venkitasubramaniam
Yu Yu                      Shanghai Jiaotong University, China

## External Reviewers

Masayuki Abe
Hamza Abusalah
Divesh Aggarwal
Shashank Agrawal
Thomas Agrikola
Prabhanjan Ananth
Daniel Apon
Benedikt Auerbach
Marshall Ball
Laasya Bangalore
Carsten Baum
Amos Beimel
Wasilij Beskorovajnov
Dan Boneh
Zvika Brakerski
Anne Broadbent
Brandon Broadnax
Ran Canetti
Ignacio Cascudo
David Cash
Leo de Castro
Hubert Chan
Nishanth Chandran
Xing Chaoping
Yilei Chen
Yu Chen
Wutichai Chongchitmate
Arka Rai Choudhuri
Hao Chung
Michele Ciampi
Deepesh Data
Akshay Degwekar

Frédéric Dupuis
Naomi Ephraim
Xiong (Leo) Fan
Pooya Farshim
Serge Fehr
Ariel Gabizon
Tommaso Gagliardoni
Chaya Ganesh
Romain Gay
Federico Giacon
Aarushi Goel
Huijing Gong
Rishab Goyal
Vipul Goyal
Alex Bredariol Grilo
Adam Groce
Josh Grochow
Roland Gröll
Chun Guo
Iftach Haitner
Mohammad Hajiabadi
Carmit Hazay
Kuan-Yi Ho
Thibaut Horel
Shih-Han Hung
Vincenzo Iovino
Aayush Jain
Stanislaw Jarecki
Zhengfeng Ji
Haodong Jiang
Zhengzhong Jin
Seny Kamara

Shuichi Katsumata
Sam Kim
Fuyuki Kitagawa
Michael Klooss
Alexander Koch
Konrad Kohbrok
Lisa Kohl
Ilan Komargodski
Yashvanth Kondi
Mukul Kulkarni
Ashutosh Kumar
Sai Lakshmi
Rio LaVigne
Eysa Lee
Yi Lee
Max Leibovich
Xin Li
Xiao Liang
Tai-Ning Liao
Wei-Kai Lin
Qipeng Liu
Tianren Liu
Yi-Kai Liu
Zhen Liu
Alex Lombardi
Julian Loss
Steve Lu
Fermi Ma
Sven Maier
Monosij Maitra
Giulio Malavolta
Yacov Manevich

# Contents – Part I

# Contents – Part II

# Algebraically Structured LWE, Revisited

Chris Peikert[✉] and Zachary Pepin

Computer Science and Engineering, University of Michigan, Ann Arbor, USA
cpeikert@umich.edu

**Abstract.** In recent years, there has been a proliferation of *algebraically structured* Learning With Errors (LWE) variants, including Ring-LWE, Module-LWE, Polynomial-LWE, Order-LWE, and Middle-Product LWE, and a web of reductions to support their hardness, both among these problems themselves and from related worst-case problems on structured lattices. However, these reductions are often difficult to interpret and use, due to the complexity of their parameters and analysis, and most especially their (frequently large) blowup and distortion of the error distributions.

In this paper we unify and simplify this line of work. First, we give a general framework that encompasses *all* proposed LWE variants (over commutative base rings), and in particular unifies all prior "algebraic" LWE variants defined over number fields. We then use this framework to give much simpler, more general, and tighter reductions from Ring-LWE to other algebraic LWE variants, including Module-LWE, Order-LWE, and Middle-Product LWE. In particular, all of our reductions have easy-to-analyze and frequently small error expansion; in some cases they even leave the error unchanged. A main message of our work is that it is straightforward to use the hardness of the original Ring-LWE problem as a foundation for the hardness of all other algebraic LWE problems defined over number fields, via simple and rather tight reductions.

## 1  Introduction

### 1.1  Background

Regev's *Learning With Errors* (LWE) problem [15] is a cornerstone of lattice-based cryptography, serving as the basis for countless cryptographic constructions (see, for example, the surveys [12, 16]). One primary attraction of LWE is that it can be supported by worst-case to average-case reductions from conjectured hard problems on general lattices [4, 11, 14, 15]. But while constructions based on LWE can have reasonably good asymptotic efficiency, they are often not as practically efficient as one might like, especially in terms of key and ciphertext sizes.

Inspired by the early NTRU cryptosystem [6] and Micciancio's initial worst-case to average-case reductions for "algebraically structured" lattices over polynomial rings [10], Lyubashevsky, Peikert, and Regev [9] introduced *Ring-LWE* to

This material is based upon work supported by the National Science Foundation under Award CNS-1606362. The views expressed are those of the authors and do not necessarily reflect the official policy or position of the National Science Foundation.

D. Hofheinz and A. Rosen (Eds.): TCC 2019, LNCS 11891, pp. 1–23, 2019.
https://doi.org/10.1007/978-3-030-36030-6_1

improve the asymptotic and practical efficiency of LWE (see also [19]). Ring-LWE is parameterized by the ring of integers in a number field, and [9] supported the hardness of Ring-LWE by a reduction from conjectured worst-case-hard problems on lattices corresponding to *ideals* in the ring (see also [14]). Since then, several works have introduced and studied a host of other algebraically structured LWE variants—including Module-LWE [1,3,7], Polynomial-LWE [18,19], Order-LWE [2], and Middle-Product LWE [17]—relating them to each other and to various worst-case problems on structured lattices. Of particular interest is the work on Middle-Product LWE (MP-LWE) [17,18], which, building on ideas from [8], gave a reduction from Ring- or Poly-LWE over a *huge class* of rings to a *single* MP-LWE problem. This means that breaking the MP-LWE problem in question is at least as hard as breaking *all* of huge number of Ring-/Poly-LWE problems defined over unrelated rings.

Thanks to the above-described works, we now have a wide assortment of algebraic LWE problems to draw upon, and a thick web of reductions to support their respective hardness. However, these reductions are often difficult to interpret and use due to the complexity of their parameters, and most especially their effect on the *error distributions* of the problems. In particular, some reductions incur a rather large blowup and distortion in the error, which is often quite complicated to analyze and bounded loosely by large or even unspecified polynomials. Some desirable reductions, like the one from Ring-LWE to MP-LWE, even require composing multiple hard-to-analyze steps. Finally, some of the reductions require non-uniform advice in the form of special short ring elements that in general do not seem easy to compute.

All this makes it rather challenging to navigate the state of the art, and especially to draw conclusions about precisely which problems and parameters are supported by reductions and proofs. The importance of having a clear, precise view of the landscape is underscored by the fact that certain seemingly reasonable parameters of algebraic LWE problems have turned out to be insecure (ultimately for prosaic reasons); see, e.g., [5,13] for an overview. This work aims to provide such a view.

## 1.2   Contributions and Technical Overview

Here we give an overview of our contributions and how they compare to prior works. At a high level, we provide a general framework that encompasses all the previously mentioned LWE variants, and in particular unifies all prior "algebraic" LWE variants defined over number fields. We then use this framework to give much simpler, more general, and tighter reductions from Ring-LWE to other algebraic LWE variants, including Module-LWE, Order-LWE, and Middle-Product LWE. A main message of our work is that it is possible to use the hardness of Ring-LWE as a foundation for the hardness of all prior algebraic LWE problems (and some new ones), via simple and easy-to-analyze reductions.

**Generalized (Algebraic) LWE.** In Sect. 3 we define new forms of LWE that unify and strictly generalize all previously mentioned ones.

*Generalized LWE.* First, in Sect. 3.1 we describe a single general framework that encompasses *all* the previously mentioned forms of LWE, including plain, Ring-, Module-, Poly-, Order-, and Middle-Product LWE (in both "dual" and "primal" forms, where applicable), as well as the unified algebraic LWE we describe below. The key observation is that in all such problems, the secret $s$, public multipliers $a$, and their (noiseless) products $s \cdot a$ respectively belong to some *free modules* $M_s, M_a, M_b$ over some commutative ring $\mathcal{R}$. Moreover, the products are determined by a fixed $\mathcal{R}$-*bilinear map* $T \colon M_s \times M_a \to M_b$. An LWE problem involves some fixed choices of these parameters, along with an error distribution. By fixing some $\mathcal{R}$-bases of the modules, the map $T$ can be represented as an *order-three tensor* (i.e., a three-dimensional array) where $T_{ijk}$ is the $k$th coordinate of the product of the $i$th and $j$th basis elements of $M_s$ and $M_a$, respectively.

For example, plain LWE uses the $\mathbb{Z}_q$-modules $M_s = M_a = \mathbb{Z}_q^n$ and $M_b = \mathbb{Z}_q$, with the ordinary inner product as the bilinear map, which corresponds to the $n \times n \times 1$ "identity matrix" tensor. Ring-LWE uses the rank-1 $R_q$-modules $M_s = M_b = R_q^\vee$ and $M_a = R_q$ where $R = \mathcal{O}_K$ is the ring of integers in a number field $K$, with field multiplication as the bilinear map, which corresponds to the scalar unity tensor.

We also show how Middle-Product LWE straightforwardly fits into this framework. Interestingly, by a judicious choice of bases, the matrix "slices" $T_{i \cdot \cdot}$ of the middle-product tensor are seen to form the standard basis for the space of all *Hankel* matrices. (In a Hankel matrix, the $(j, k)$th entry is determined by $j + k$.) This formulation is central to our improved reduction from Ring-LWE over a wide class of number fields to Middle-Product LWE, described in Sect. 1.2 below.

*LWE over Number Field Lattices.* Next, in Sect. 3.2 we define a unified class of problems that strictly generalizes prior "algebraic" LWE variants defined over number fields, including Ring-, Module-, Poly-, and Order-LWE. A member $\mathcal{L}$-LWE of our class is parameterized by *any (full-rank) lattice* (i.e., discrete additive subgroup) $\mathcal{L}$ of a number field $K$. Define

$$\mathcal{O}^{\mathcal{L}} := \{x \in K : x\mathcal{L} \subseteq \mathcal{L}\}$$

to be the set of field elements by which $\mathcal{L}$ is closed under multiplication; this set is known as the *coefficient ring* of $\mathcal{L}$. Letting $\mathcal{L}^\vee = \{x \in K : \mathrm{Tr}_{K/\mathbb{Q}}(x\mathcal{L}) \subseteq \mathbb{Z}\}$ denote the *dual lattice* of $\mathcal{L}$, it turns out that $\mathcal{O}^{\mathcal{L}} = (\mathcal{L} \cdot \mathcal{L}^\vee)^\vee$, and it is an *order* of $K$, i.e., a subring with unity that is also a lattice. Note that if $\mathcal{L}$ itself is an order $\mathcal{O}$ of $K$ or its dual $\mathcal{O}^\vee$, then $\mathcal{O}^{\mathcal{L}} = \mathcal{O}$, but in general $\mathcal{L}$ can be any lattice, and $\mathcal{O}^{\mathcal{L}}$ is just the largest order of $K$ by which $\mathcal{L}$ is closed under multiplication.[1]

---

[1] We caution that $\mathcal{O}^{\mathcal{L}}$ is not "monotonic" in $\mathcal{L}$ under set inclusion, i.e., $\mathcal{L}' \subseteq \mathcal{L}$ does not imply any inclusion relationship between $\mathcal{O}^{\mathcal{L}'}$ and $\mathcal{O}^{\mathcal{L}}$, in either direction. In particular, $\mathcal{L}$ and $c\mathcal{L}$ have the same coefficient ring for any integer $c > 1$, but there can exist $\mathcal{L}'$ with $c\mathcal{L} \subsetneq \mathcal{L}' \subsetneq \mathcal{L}$ that has a different coefficient ring.

In all that follows, let $\mathcal{L}_q$ denote the quotient group $\mathcal{L}/q\mathcal{L}$ for any lattice $\mathcal{L}$ of $K$ and positive integer $q$. In $\mathcal{L}$-LWE, there is a secret $s \in \mathcal{L}_q^\vee$, and we are given noisy random products

$$(a \leftarrow \mathcal{O}_q^{\mathcal{L}}, \, b = s \cdot a + e \bmod q\mathcal{L}^\vee),$$

where $a$ is uniformly random, and $e$ is an error term that is drawn from a specified distribution (see below for discussion). Observe that the reduction modulo $q\mathcal{L}^\vee$ is well defined because the (noiseless) product $s \cdot a \in \mathcal{L}_q^\vee$, since $\mathcal{L}^\vee \cdot \mathcal{O}^{\mathcal{L}} \subseteq \mathcal{L}^\vee$ due to $\mathrm{Tr}(\mathcal{L}^\vee \cdot \mathcal{O}^{\mathcal{L}} \cdot \mathcal{L}) \subseteq \mathrm{Tr}(\mathcal{L}^\vee \cdot \mathcal{L}) \subseteq \mathbb{Z}$.

We now explain how $\mathcal{L}$-LWE strictly generalizes Ring-, Poly-, and Order-LWE. As already noted, when $\mathcal{L} = \mathcal{O}$ or $\mathcal{L} = \mathcal{O}^\vee$ for an order $\mathcal{O}$ of $K$, we have $\mathcal{O}^{\mathcal{L}} = \mathcal{O}$, so $\mathcal{L}$-LWE specializes to:

1. Ring-LWE [9] when $\mathcal{L} = \mathcal{O}_K$ is the full ring of integers of $K$;
2. Poly-LWE [18] when $\mathcal{L} = \mathbb{Z}[\alpha]^\vee$ for some $\alpha \in \mathcal{O}_K$; and
3. Order-LWE [2] when $\mathcal{L} = \mathcal{O}^\vee$ for some arbitrary order $\mathcal{O}$ of $K$.

Notice that in the latter two cases, $\mathcal{L}$ is the *dual* of some order, so the secret $s$ and product $s \cdot a$ belong to the order itself (modulo $q$). But as we shall see, for reductions it turns out to be more natural and advantageous to let $\mathcal{L}$ itself be an order, not its dual. Furthermore, $\mathcal{L}$-LWE also captures other cases that are not covered by the ones above, namely, those for which $\mathcal{L}$ is not an order or its dual. For $\mathcal{L}$-LWE, we just need the $\mathcal{O}^{\mathcal{L}}$-module structure of $\mathcal{L}^\vee$, not any ring structure.

As mentioned above, $\mathcal{L}$-LWE is also parameterized by an error distribution. For consistency across problems and with prior work, and without loss of generality, we always view the error distribution in terms of the *canonical embedding* of $K$. For concreteness, and following worst-case hardness theorems for Ring-LWE [9,14], the reader can keep in mind a spherical Gaussian distribution of sufficiently large width $r = \omega(\sqrt{\log \deg(K)})$ over the canonical embedding. While this differs syntactically from the kind of distribution often considered for Poly-LWE—namely, a spherical Gaussian over the *coefficient vector* of the error polynomial—the two views are interchangeable via some fixed linear transformation. For Gaussians, this transformation just changes the covariance, and if desired we can also add some independent compensating error to recover a spherical Gaussian. However, our results demonstrate some advantages of working exclusively with the canonical embedding, even for Poly-LWE.

**Error-Preserving Reduction for $\mathcal{L}$-LWE.** In Sect. 4 we give a simple reduction from $\mathcal{L}$-LWE to $\mathcal{L}'$-LWE for *any* lattices $\mathcal{L}' \subseteq \mathcal{L}$ of $K$ for which $\mathcal{O}^{\mathcal{L}'} \subseteq \mathcal{O}^{\mathcal{L}}$ and the index $|\mathcal{L}/\mathcal{L}'|$ is coprime with the modulus $q$. Essentially, the reduction transforms samples of the former problem (for an unknown secret $s$) to samples of the latter problem (for a related secret $s'$). Importantly, and unlike prior reductions of a similar flavor, our reduction is *error preserving*: the error distribution over the number field is exactly the same for the two problems. In addition, the reduction is *sample preserving*: it produces as many samples as it consumes.

The only loss associated with the reduction, which seems inherently necessary, is that when $\mathcal{L} \neq \mathcal{L}'$, the lattice $q(\mathcal{L}')^\vee$ by which the resulting noisy products $b' \approx s' \cdot a'$ are reduced is "denser" than the lattice $q\mathcal{L}^\vee \subsetneq q(\mathcal{L}')^\vee$ by which the original noisy products $b \approx s \cdot a$ are reduced. One can alternatively see this as the (unchanging) error distribution being "larger" relative to the target lattice than to the original one. This can have consequences for applications, where we typically need the accumulated error from some combined samples to be decodable modulo $q(\mathcal{L}')^\vee$. That is, we need to be able to efficiently recover $e'$ (or at least a large portion of it) from the coset $e' + q(\mathcal{L}')^\vee$; standard decoding algorithms require sufficiently short elements of $q^{-1}\mathcal{L}'$ to do this. So in general, the "sparser" we take $\mathcal{L}' \subseteq \mathcal{L}$ to be, the denser $(\mathcal{L}')^\vee$ is, and the larger we need $q$ to be to compensate. This weakens both the theoretical guarantees and concrete hardness of the original $\mathcal{L}$-LWE problem, and is reason to prefer denser $\mathcal{L}'$.

*Implications and Comparison to Prior Work.* Here we describe some of the immediate implications of our reduction, and compare to prior related reductions. Take $\mathcal{L} = \mathcal{O}_K$ to be the full ring of integers of $K$, which corresponds to the "master" problem of Ring-LWE, for which we have worst-case hardness theorems [9, 14]. Then these same hardness guarantees are immediately inherited by Order-LWE (and in particular, Poly-LWE) in its "dual" form, by taking $\mathcal{L}'$ to be an arbitrary order $\mathcal{O}$ of $K$, as long as $|\mathcal{L}'/\mathcal{L}|$ is coprime with $q$. These guarantees are qualitatively similar to the ones established in [2, 18], but are obtained in a much simpler and more straightforward way; in particular, we do not need to replicate all the technical machinery of the worst-case to average-case reductions from [9, 14] for arbitrary orders $\mathcal{O}$, as was done in [2].

Our reduction can also yield hardness for the "primal" form of Poly-LWE and Order-LWE via a different choice of $\mathcal{L}'$ (see the next paragraph); however, it is instructive to see why it is preferable to reduce to the "dual" form of these problems. The main reason is that the dual form admits quite natural reductions, both *from* Ring-LWE and *to* Middle-Product LWE and Module-LWE, whose effects on the error distribution are easy to understand and bound entirely in terms of certain known short elements of $\mathcal{O}$. (See Sect. 1.2 below for further details.)

By contrast, the reduction and analysis for "primal" Order-LWE over order $\mathcal{O}$—including Poly-LWE for $\mathcal{O} = \mathbb{Z}[\alpha]$, as in [18]—is much more complex and cumbersome. Because $\mathcal{O}^\vee \not\subseteq \mathcal{O}_K$ (except in the trivial case $K = \mathbb{Q}$), we cannot simply take $\mathcal{L}' = \mathcal{O}^\vee$. Instead, we need to apply a suitable "tweak" factor $t \in K$, so that $\mathcal{L}' = t\mathcal{O}^\vee \subseteq \mathcal{O}_K$ and hence $(\mathcal{L}')^\vee = t^{-1}\mathcal{O}$. Reducing to $\mathcal{L}'$-LWE preserves the error distribution, but to finally convert the samples to primal Order-LWE samples we need to multiply by $t$, which distorts the error distribution. It can be shown that $t$ must lie in the product of the *different ideal* of $\mathcal{O}_K$ and the *conductor ideal* of $\mathcal{O}$ (among other constraints), so the reduction requires non-uniform advice in the form of such a "short" $t$ that does not distort the error too much. The existence proof for such a $t$ from [18] is quite involved, requiring several pages of rather deep number theory. Finally, the decodability of the (distorted) error modulo $q\mathcal{O}$ is mainly determined by the known short vectors in $\mathcal{O}^\vee$, which also must be analyzed. (All these issues arise under slightly different guises in [18]; in fact, there the error is distorted by $t^2$, yielding an even lossier reduction.)

**Reduction from $\mathcal{O}$-LWE to MP-LWE.** In Sect. 5 we give a simple reduction from $\mathcal{O}$-LWE, for a *wide class* of number fields $K$ and orders $\mathcal{O}$ including polynomial rings of the form $\mathcal{O} = \mathbb{Z}[\alpha] \cong \mathbb{Z}[x]/f(x)$, to a *single* Middle-Product LWE problem. Together with the error-preserving reduction described above, this yields a Ring/MP-LWE connection similar to the one obtained in [17,18], which implies that breaking the MP-LWE problem in question is at least as hard as breaking *all* of a wide class of Ring-LWE problems over unrelated number fields. However, our result subsumes the prior one by being simpler, more general, and tighter: it drops certain technical conditions on the order, and the overall distortion in the error distribution (starting from Ring-LWE) is given entirely by the spectral norm $\|\vec{p}\|$ of a certain known basis $\vec{p}$ of $\mathcal{O}$. In particular, spherical Gaussian error over the canonical embedding of $\mathcal{O}$ translates to spherical Gaussian MP-LWE error (over the reals) that is just a $\|\vec{p}\|$ factor wider. These advantages arise from the error-preserving nature of our $\mathcal{L}$-LWE reduction (described above), and the judicious use of dual lattices in the definition of $\mathcal{O}$-LWE.

At heart, what makes our reduction work is the hypothesis that the order $\mathcal{O}$ has a "tweaked" power basis $\vec{p} = t \cdot (x^i)$ for some $t, x \in \mathcal{O}$; clearly any monogenic order $\mathcal{O} = \mathbb{Z}[\alpha]$ has such a basis (with tweak factor $t = 1$), but it seems plausible that some non-monogenic orders may have such bases as well.[2] Using our generalized LWE framework from Sect. 3.1 (described above in Sect. 1.2), we show that when using a tweaked power basis $\vec{p}$ and its dual $\vec{p}^\vee$ for $\mathcal{O}$ and $\mathcal{O}^\vee$ respectively, all the "slices" $T_{i\cdot\cdot}$ of the tensor $T$ representing multiplication $\mathcal{O}^\vee \times \mathcal{O} \to \mathcal{O}^\vee$ are *Hankel* matrices. So, using the fact that the slices $M_{i\cdot\cdot}$ of the middle-product tensor $M$ form the standard basis for the space of all Hankel matrices, we can transform $\mathcal{O}$-LWE samples to MP-LWE samples. The resulting MP-LWE error distribution is simply the original error distribution represented in the $\vec{p}^\vee$ basis, which is easily characterized using the geometry of $\vec{p}$.

The above perspective is helpful for finding other reductions from wide classes of LWE problems to a single LWE problem. Essentially, it suffices that all the slices $T_{i\cdot\cdot}$ of all the source-problem tensors $T$ over a ring $\mathcal{R}$ lie in the $\mathcal{R}$-span of the slices of the target-problem tensor. We use this observation in our final reduction, described next.

**Reduction from $\mathcal{O}'$-LWE to $\mathcal{O}$-Module-LWE.** Finally, in Sect. 6 we give a reduction establishing the hardness of Module-LWE over an order $\mathcal{O}$ of a number field $K$, based on the hardness of Ring-LWE over *any one* of a *wide class* of

---

[2] For example, consider the ring of integers $\mathcal{O}_K$ where $K = \mathbb{Q}(\alpha)$ for $\alpha^3 - \alpha^2 - 2\alpha - 8 = 0$. In a classical result, Dedekind showed that this order is non-monogenic, but it has $\vec{p} = (t, tx, tx^2)$ as a basis, where $x = (\alpha^2 - \alpha - 2)/4$ and $t = 1 - 2x$. We caution that $x \notin \mathcal{O}_K$, so this is actually not a tweaked power basis according to our definition, but it still suffices for a special case of our reduction that does not extend $\vec{p}$ by more powers of $x$.

orders $\mathcal{O}'$ of a number field extension $K'/K$. This is qualitatively analogous to what is known for Middle-Product LWE, but is potentially more beneficial because Module-LWE is easier to use in applications, and is indeed much more widely used in theory and in practice.

A bit more precisely, we give a simple reduction from $\mathcal{O}'$-LWE, for a wide class of orders $\mathcal{O}'$, to a *single* $\mathcal{O}$-LWE$^k$ problem, i.e., rank-$k$ Module-LWE over an order $\mathcal{O}$. (In $\mathcal{O}$-LWE$^k$, the secret $\vec{s}$ and public multipliers $\vec{a}$ are simply $k$-dimensional vectors over their respective domains from $\mathcal{O}$-LWE, and we are given their noisy inner products.) The only technical condition we require is that $\mathcal{O}'$ should be a rank-$k$ free $\mathcal{O}$-module. For example, this is easily achieved by defining $\mathcal{O} = \mathcal{O}[\alpha] \cong \mathcal{O}[x]/f(x)$ for some root $\alpha$ of an arbitrary degree-$k$ monic irreducible polynomial $f(x) \in \mathcal{O}[x]$. Once again, due to the use of duality in the definition of the problems, the reduction's effect on the error distribution is very easy to characterize: the output error is simply the trace (from $K'$ to $K$) of the input error. In particular, the typical example of spherical Gaussian error in the canonical embedding of $K'$ maps to spherical Gaussian error in the canonical embedding of $K$, because the trace just sums over a certain partition of the coordinates.

We point out that our result is reminiscent of, but formally incomparable to, the kind of worst-case hardness theorem given in [7]: there the worst-case problem involves arbitrary rank-$k$ *module lattices* over $\mathcal{O}$, whereas here our source problem is an average-case Order-LWE problem for an order that is a rank-$k$ module over $\mathcal{O}$.

## 2 Preliminaries

In this work, by "ring" we always mean a commutative ring with identity.

### 2.1 Algebraic Number Theory

*Number Fields.* An (algebraic) *number field* $K$ is a finite-dimensional field extension of the rationals $\mathbb{Q}$. More concretely, it can be written as $K = \mathbb{Q}(\zeta)$, by adjoining to $\mathbb{Q}$ some element $\zeta$ that satisfies the relation $f(\zeta) = 0$ for some irreducible polynomial $f(x) \in \mathbb{Q}[x]$. The polynomial $f$ is called the *minimal polynomial* of $\zeta$, and the degree of $f$ is called the *degree* of $K$, which is denoted by $n$ in what follows.

*Trace and Norm.* The (field) *trace* $\mathrm{Tr} = \mathrm{Tr}_{K/\mathbb{Q}} \colon K \to \mathbb{Q}$ and (field) *norm* $N = N_{K/\mathbb{Q}} \colon K \to \mathbb{Q}$ of $x \in K$ are the trace and determinant, respectively, of the $\mathbb{Q}$-linear transformation on $K$ (viewed as a vector space over $\mathbb{Q}$) representing multiplication by $x$. More concretely, fixing any $\mathbb{Q}$-basis of $K$ lets us uniquely represent every element of $K$ as a vector in $\mathbb{Q}^n$, and multiplication by any $x \in K$ corresponds to multiplication by a matrix $M_x \in \mathbb{Q}^{n \times n}$; the trace and norm of $x$ are respectively the trace and determinant of this matrix.

*Lattices and Duality.* For the purposes of this work, a *lattice* $\mathcal{L}$ in $K$ is a discrete additive subgroup of $K$ for which $\text{span}_{\mathbb{Q}}(\mathcal{L}) = K$. A lattice is generated as the integer linear combinations of $n$ *basis* elements $\vec{b} = (b_1, \ldots, b_n) \in K^n$, as $\mathcal{L} = \{\sum_{i=1}^{n} \mathbb{Z} \cdot b_i\}$; in other words, $\mathcal{L}$ is a free $\mathbb{Z}$-module of rank $n$. For convenience, we let $\mathcal{L}_q$ denote the quotient group $\mathcal{L}/q\mathcal{L}$ for any positive integer $q$.

For any two lattices $\mathcal{L}, \mathcal{L}' \subset K$, their product $\mathcal{L} \cdot \mathcal{L}'$ is the set of all integer linear combinations of terms $x \cdot x'$ for $x \in \mathcal{L}, x' \in \mathcal{L}'$. This set is itself a lattice, and given bases for $\mathcal{L}, \mathcal{L}'$ we can efficiently compute a basis for $\mathcal{L} \cdot \mathcal{L}'$ via the Hermite normal form.

For a lattice $\mathcal{L}$, its *dual lattice* $\mathcal{L}^{\vee}$ (which is indeed a lattice) is defined as

$$\mathcal{L}^{\vee} := \{x \in K : \text{Tr}(x\mathcal{L}) \subseteq \mathbb{Z}\}.$$

It is easy to see that if $\mathcal{L} \subseteq \mathcal{L}'$ are lattices in $K$, then $(\mathcal{L}')^{\vee} \subseteq \mathcal{L}^{\vee}$, and if $\vec{b}$ is a basis of $\mathcal{L}$, then its *dual basis* $\vec{b}^{\vee} = (b_1^{\vee}, \ldots, b_n^{\vee})$ is a basis of $\mathcal{L}^{\vee}$, where $\vec{b}^{\vee}$ is defined so that $\text{Tr}(b_i \cdot b_j^{\vee})$ is 1 when $i = j$, and is 0 otherwise. Observe that by definition, $x = \vec{b}^t \cdot \text{Tr}(\vec{b}^{\vee} \cdot x)$ for every $x \in K$.

*Orders.* An *order* $\mathcal{O}$ of $K$ is a lattice that is also a subring with unity, i.e., $1 \in \mathcal{O}$ and $\mathcal{O}$ is closed under multiplication. An element $\alpha \in K$ is an *algebraic integer* if there exists a monic integer polynomial $f$ such that $f(\alpha) = 0$. The set of algebraic integers in $K$, denoted $\mathcal{O}_K$, is called the *ring of integers* of $K$, and is its maximal order: every order $\mathcal{O} \subseteq \mathcal{O}_K$. For any order $\mathcal{O}$ of $K$, we have $\mathcal{O} \cdot \mathcal{O}^{\vee} = \mathcal{O}^{\vee}$ because $\mathcal{O}^{\vee} = 1 \cdot \mathcal{O}^{\vee} \subseteq \mathcal{O} \cdot \mathcal{O}^{\vee}$ and $\text{Tr}((\mathcal{O} \cdot \mathcal{O}^{\vee}) \cdot \mathcal{O}) = \text{Tr}(\mathcal{O}^{\vee} \cdot \mathcal{O}) \subseteq \mathbb{Z}$, since $\mathcal{O} \cdot \mathcal{O} = \mathcal{O}$.

*The Space $K_{\mathbb{R}}$.* In order to formally define Gaussian distributions (see Sect. 2.2 below) we define the field tensor product $K_{\mathbb{R}} = K \otimes_{\mathbb{Q}} \mathbb{R}$, which is essentially the "real analogue" of $K/\mathbb{Q}$, obtained by generalizing rational scalars to real ones. In general this is not a field, but it is a ring; in fact, it is isomorphic to the ring product $\mathbb{R}^{s_1} \times \mathbb{C}^{s_2}$, where $K$ has $s_1$ real embeddings and $s_2$ conjugate pairs of complex ring embeddings, and $n = s_1 + 2s_2$. Therefore, there is a "complex conjugation" involution $\tau \colon K_{\mathbb{R}} \to K_{\mathbb{R}}$, which corresponds to the identity map on each $\mathbb{R}$ component, and complex conjugation on each $\mathbb{C}$ component.

We extend the trace to $K_{\mathbb{R}}$ in the natural way, writing $\text{Tr}_{K_{\mathbb{R}}/\mathbb{R}}$ for the resulting $\mathbb{R}$-linear transform. It turns out that under the ring isomorphism with $\mathbb{R}^{s_1} \times \mathbb{C}^{s_2}$, this trace corresponds to the sum of the real components plus twice the sum of the real parts of the complex components. From this it can be verified that $K_{\mathbb{R}}$ is an $n$-dimensional real inner-product space, with inner product $\langle x, y \rangle = \text{Tr}_{K_{\mathbb{R}}/\mathbb{R}}(x \cdot \tau(y))$. In particular, $K_{\mathbb{R}}$ has some (non-unique) orthonormal basis $\vec{b}$, and hence $\vec{b}^{\vee} = \tau(\vec{b})$.

*Extension Fields.* For the material in Sect. 6 we need to generalize some of our definitions to number field extensions $K'/K$, where possibly $K \neq \mathbb{Q}$. The (field) *trace* $\text{Tr} = \text{Tr}_{K'/K} \colon K' \to K$ and (field) *norm* $N = N_{K'/K} \colon K' \to K$ of $x \in K'$ are the trace and determinant, respectively, of the $K$-linear transformation on $K'$ (viewed as a vector space over $K$) representing multiplication by $x$. We extend the trace to the real inner-product spaces $K'_{\mathbb{R}}$ and $K_{\mathbb{R}}$ in the natural way, writing $\mathrm{Tr}_{K'_{\mathbb{R}}/K_{\mathbb{R}}}$ for the resulting $\mathbb{R}$-linear transform.

Let $\vec{b} = (b_1, \ldots, b_k)$ be a $K$-basis of $K'$. Its *dual basis* $\vec{b}^{\vee} = (b_1^{\vee}, \ldots, b_k^{\vee})$ is defined so that $\mathrm{Tr}_{K'/K}(b_i \cdot b_j^{\vee})$ is 1 when $i = j$, and is 0 otherwise.

**Lemma 1.** *Let $K'/K$ be a number field extension with $K$-basis $\vec{b}$, and let $x = \langle \vec{b}^{\vee}, \vec{x} \rangle, y = \langle \vec{b}, \vec{y} \rangle$ for some $\vec{x}, \vec{y}$ over $K$. Then $\mathrm{Tr}_{K'/K}(x \cdot y) = \langle \vec{x}, \vec{y} \rangle$.*

*Proof.* Letting $\mathrm{Tr} = \mathrm{Tr}_{K'/K}$, by $K$-linearity of $\mathrm{Tr}$ we have

$$\mathrm{Tr}(x \cdot y) = \mathrm{Tr}(\langle \vec{b}^{\vee}, \vec{x} \rangle \cdot \langle \vec{b}, \vec{y} \rangle) = \mathrm{Tr}(\vec{x}^t \cdot (\vec{b}^{\vee} \cdot \vec{b}^t) \cdot \vec{y}) = \vec{x}^t \cdot \mathrm{Tr}(\vec{b}^{\vee} \cdot \vec{b}^t) \cdot \vec{y} = \vec{x}^t \cdot I \cdot \vec{y} = \langle \vec{x}, \vec{y} \rangle.$$

We also will need the following standard fact, whose proof is straightforward.

**Lemma 2.** *Let $K'/K$ be a number field extension, $\mathcal{O}$ be an order of $K$, and $\mathcal{O}'$ be an order of $K'$ that is a free $\mathcal{O}$-module with basis $\vec{b}$. Then $\vec{b}^{\vee}$ is an $\mathcal{O}^{\vee}$-basis of $(\mathcal{O}')^{\vee}$.*

### 2.2 Gaussians

Here let $H$ be an $n$-dimensional real inner-product space (e.g., $H = \mathbb{R}^n$ or $H = K_{\mathbb{R}}$) and fix an orthonormal basis, so that any element $x \in H$ may be uniquely represented as a real vector $\mathbf{x} \in \mathbb{R}^n$ relative to that basis.

**Definition 1.** *For a positive definite $\Sigma \in \mathbb{R}^{n \times n}$, called the covariance matrix, the Gaussian function $\rho_{\sqrt{\Sigma}}: H \to (0, 1]$ is defined as $\rho_{\sqrt{\Sigma}}(\mathbf{x}) := \exp(-\pi \mathbf{x}^t \cdot \Sigma^{-1} \cdot \mathbf{x})$, and the Gaussian distribution $D_{\sqrt{\Sigma}}$ on $H$ is the one having the normalized probability density function $\det(\Sigma)^{-1} \cdot \rho_{\sqrt{\Sigma}}$.*[3]

When $\Sigma = r^2 \cdot \mathbf{I}$ for some $r > 0$, we often write $\rho_r$ and $D_r$ instead, and refer to these as *spherical* Gaussians with parameter $r$. In this case, the choice of orthonormal basis for $H$ is immaterial, i.e., any orthonormal basis yields the same $\Sigma = r^2 \cdot \mathbf{I}$.

It is well known that the sum of two independent Gaussians having covariances $\Sigma_1, \Sigma_2$ (respectively) is distributed as a Gaussian with covariance $\Sigma_1 + \Sigma_2$. Therefore, a Gaussian of covariance $\Sigma$ can be transformed into one of any desired covariance $\Sigma' \succ \Sigma$, i.e., one for which $\Sigma' - \Sigma$ is positive definite, simply by adding an independent compensating Gaussian of covariance $\Sigma' - \Sigma$.

## 3 Generalized (Algebraic) Learning with Errors

In this section we define new forms of LWE that unify and strictly generalize previous ones. First, in Sect. 3.1 we give an overarching framework that encompasses

---

[3] Note that the covariance of $D_{\sqrt{\Sigma}}$ is actually $\Sigma/(2\pi)$, due to the normalization factor in the definition of $\rho_{\sqrt{\Sigma}}$.

all LWE variants (over commutative rings) that we are aware of. We employ this framework only in our reductions to MP-LWE and Module-LWE, but expect that it may be useful for other purposes in the future. Then, in Sect. 3.2 we generalize and unify *algebraic* forms of LWE like Ring-, Order-, and Poly-LWE into a single problem that is merely parameterized by a lattice in a number field.

## 3.1   Generalized LWE

Here we describe a general framework that captures all variants of Learning With Errors (over commutative rings) that we are aware of, and will be helpful in linking some of them together. Our starting point is the observation that in all such problems, the secret $s$, public multipliers $a$, and their "products" $s \cdot a$ (without noise) all belong to some respective *free modules* over a particular finite commutative ring $\mathcal{R}$. Moreover, the products are determined by a fixed $\mathcal{R}$-*bilinear map* from (the direct product of) the former two modules to the latter one. As a few examples:

- Ordinary LWE uses the inner-product map $\langle \cdot, \cdot \rangle \colon \mathbb{Z}_q^n \times \mathbb{Z}_q^n \to \mathbb{Z}_q$, where $\mathbb{Z}_q^n$ and $\mathbb{Z}_q$ are $\mathbb{Z}_q$-modules of ranks $n$ and 1, respectively.
- Ring-LWE uses the multiplication map $R_q^\vee \times R_q \to R_q^\vee$ where $R = \mathcal{O}_K$ is a number ring; here $R_q^\vee$ and $R_q$ can be seen as $R_q$-modules of rank one, or as $\mathbb{Z}_q$-modules of rank $n = \deg(R/\mathbb{Z})$.
- Module-LWE interpolates between the above two cases, using the inner-product map $(R_q^\vee)^d \times R_q^d \to R_q^\vee$, where here the input modules are of rank $d$ over $R_q$, or rank $dn$ over $\mathbb{Z}_q$.

In general, an LWE variant involves: (1) a finite commutative ring $\mathcal{R}$, (2) some finite-rank free $\mathcal{R}$-modules $M_s, M_a, M_b$, and (3) an $\mathcal{R}$-bilinear map $T \colon M_s \times M_a \to M_b$. The associated LWE problem is concerned with "noisy products" $(a \leftarrow M_a, b \approx T(s, a))$ for some fixed $s \in M_s$. Clearly, each bilinear map $T$ (and choice of error distribution) potentially yields a different distribution of noisy products.

By fixing bases for the modules, the map $T$ can be represented via a third-order *tensor* $T_{ijk}$ over $\mathcal{R}$. Specifically, if we fix bases $\vec{s}, \vec{a}, \vec{b}$ for $M_s, M_a, M_b$ (respectively), then $T_{ijk}$ is the coefficient of $b_k$ in $T(s_i, a_j) \in M_b$. By bilinearity, the coefficient vector of $T(a, s)$ is the product of the tensor $T$ with the coefficient vectors of $a, s$ along the appropriate dimensions. This naturally generalizes to fixed *generating sets* in place of bases for $M_s$ and $M_a$ (and even $M_b$, if we do not need a unique representation of the output).

Due to the generality of $\mathcal{R}$ and (often desirable) possibility of error distributions over supersets of $M_b \cong \mathcal{R}^l$ (for some $l$), we do not give a fully general formal definition of LWE problems in this framework. However, we remark that frequently $\mathcal{R} = \mathcal{O}_q$ for an order $\mathcal{O}$ of some number field $K$, in which case one would usually consider an error distribution over $K_{\mathbb{R}}^l$.

*Middle-Product LWE.* The Middle-Product LWE (MP-LWE) problem from [17] can be seen as an instance of the above framework, as follows. The middle-product operation $\odot_d$ takes two polynomials of fixed degree bounds, multiplies them together, and outputs only the "middle" $d$ coefficients of the product. More specifically, the product of two polynomials respectively having degrees $< n + d - 1$ and $< n$ has degree $< 2n + d - 2$; the middle-product discards the lowest and highest $n - 1$ coefficients, and outputs the remaining $d$ coefficients. Middle-Product LWE is concerned with random noisy middle products of a secret polynomial over $\mathbb{Z}_q$.

To see this in the above framework, define $M_s = \mathbb{Z}_q^{n+d-1}$ and $M_a = \mathbb{Z}_q^n$, which we respectively identify with the $\mathbb{Z}_q$-modules $\mathbb{Z}_q^{<n+d-1}[x]$ and $\mathbb{Z}_q^{<n}[x]$ of polynomials of degrees $< n + d - 1$ and $< n$, via the bases $\vec{s} = (1, x, \ldots, x^{n+d-2})$ and $\vec{a} = (x^{n-1}, x^{n-2}, \ldots, 1)$, respectively. (Basis $\vec{a}$ is in decreasing order by degree for reasons that will become clear shortly.) Define $M_b = \mathbb{Z}_q^d$, which we identify with the $\mathbb{Z}_q$-module $x^{n-1} \cdot \mathbb{Z}_q^{<d}[x]$ via the basis $\vec{b} = (x^{n-1}, x^n, \ldots, x^{n+d-2})$.

The middle-product bilinear form $M_s \times M_a \to M_b$ is then represented by the third-order tensor $M$ (which is indexed from zero in all dimensions) defined by

$$
M_{ijk} = \begin{cases} 1 & \text{if } i = j + k \\ 0 & \text{otherwise.} \end{cases} \tag{1}
$$

This is because $s_i \cdot a_j = x^i \cdot x^{n-1-j} = x^{(n-1)+(i-j)}$, which equals $b_{i-j}$ if $0 \leq i - j < d$, and vanishes under the middle product otherwise. Therefore, the "slice" matrix $M_{i\cdot\cdot}$, obtained by fixing the $i$ coordinate arbitrarily, is the $n \times d$ rectangular Hankel matrix defined by the standard basis vector $\mathbf{e}_i \in \mathbb{Z}^{n+d-1}$, which is 1 in the $i$th coordinate and zero elsewhere (again indexing from zero).[4] Importantly, these $M_{i\cdot\cdot}$ slices form the standard basis of all $n \times d$ Hankel matrices.

For the following definitions, let $M$ be the third-order tensor defined above in Eq. (1).

**Definition 2 (MP-LWE distribution).** *Let $n, d, q$ be positive integers and $\psi$ be a distribution over $\mathbb{R}^d$. For $\mathbf{s} \in \mathbb{Z}_q^{n+d-1}$, a sample from the MP-LWE distribution $C_{n,d,q,\psi}(\mathbf{s})$ over $\mathbb{Z}_q^n \times (\mathbb{R}/q\mathbb{Z})^d$ is generated by choosing $\mathbf{a} \leftarrow \mathbb{Z}_q^n$ uniformly at random, choosing $\mathbf{e} \leftarrow \psi$, and outputting $(\mathbf{a}, \mathbf{b} = M(\mathbf{s}, \mathbf{a}) + \mathbf{e} \bmod q\mathbb{Z})$.*

**Definition 3 (MP-LWE problem, decision).** *The decision MP-LWE$_{n,d,q,\psi,\ell}$ problem is to distinguish between $\ell$ samples from $C_{n,d,q,\psi}(\mathbf{s})$ for $\mathbf{s} \leftarrow U(\mathbb{Z}_q^{n+d-1})$, and $\ell$ samples from $U(\mathbb{Z}_q^n \times (\mathbb{R}/q\mathbb{Z})^d)$.*

**Definition 4 (MP-LWE problem, search).** *The search MP-LWE$_{n,d,q,\psi,\ell}$ problem is, given $\ell$ samples from $C_{n,d,q,\psi}(\mathbf{s})$ for some arbitrary $\mathbf{s} \in \mathbb{Z}_q^{n+d-1}$, find $s$.*

---

[4] Recall that a matrix $H$ is Hankel if each entry $H_{jk}$ is determined by $j + k$ (equivalently, it is an "upside down" Toeplitz matrix). So, an $n \times d$ Hankel matrix is defined by an $(n + d - 1)$-dimensional vector whose $i$th entry defines the entries $H_{jk}$ for $i = j + k$.

We remark that MP-LWE becomes no harder as $d$ decreases (and the corresponding final coordinate(s) of the error distribution are dropped), because the degree-$(n + d - 2)$ monomial of the secret can affect only the monomial of the same degree in the middle product. Therefore, dropping the latter just has the effect of dropping the former. In the tensor $M$, this corresponds to removing the "slices" $M_{(n+d-2)..}$ and $M_{..(d-1)}$, which yields the tensor for parameters $n$ and $d - 1$.

## 3.2    LWE over Number Field Lattices

We now define an algebraic form of LWE that strictly generalizes prior ones including Ring-, Module-, Order-, and Poly-LWE. The key observation is that all these problems arise simply from parameterizing by a suitable *lattice* in a given number field, and taking the public multipliers to be over the lattice's *coefficient ring* (modulo $q$), which we now define.

**Coefficient Ring.** For any lattice $\mathcal{L}$ in a number field $K$, an $x \in K$ for which $x\mathcal{L} \subseteq \mathcal{L}$ is called a *coefficient* of $\mathcal{L}$. It turns out that the set of coefficients of $\mathcal{L}$ is an order of $K$, and equals $(\mathcal{L} \cdot \mathcal{L}^\vee)^\vee$. For elucidation we recall the (easy) proofs of these facts.

**Definition 5 (Coefficient ring).** *For a lattice $\mathcal{L}$ in a number field $K$, its* coefficient ring *is defined as*

$$\mathcal{O}^{\mathcal{L}} := \{x \in K : x\mathcal{L} \subseteq \mathcal{L}\}.$$

**Lemma 3.** *We have $\mathcal{O}^{\mathcal{L}} = (\mathcal{L} \cdot \mathcal{L}^\vee)^\vee$. In particular, $\mathcal{L}$ and $\mathcal{L}^\vee$ have the same coefficient ring $\mathcal{O}^{\mathcal{L}} = \mathcal{O}^{\mathcal{L}^\vee}$, and if $\mathcal{L}$ is an order $\mathcal{O}$ of $K$ or its dual $\mathcal{O}^\vee$, then $\mathcal{O}^{\mathcal{L}} = \mathcal{O}$.*

*Proof.* For any $x \in K$, we have

$$x \in (\mathcal{L} \cdot \mathcal{L}^\vee)^\vee \iff \mathrm{Tr}(x(\mathcal{L} \cdot \mathcal{L}^\vee)) \subseteq \mathbb{Z} \iff \mathrm{Tr}((x\mathcal{L})\mathcal{L}^\vee) \subseteq \mathbb{Z} \iff x\mathcal{L} \subseteq (\mathcal{L}^\vee)^\vee = \mathcal{L}.$$

The final claim follows by recalling that $\mathcal{O} \cdot \mathcal{O}^\vee = \mathcal{O}^\vee$.

**Lemma 4.** *The coefficient ring $\mathcal{O}^{\mathcal{L}}$ is an order of $K$.*

*Proof.* It is clear that $\mathcal{O}^{\mathcal{L}} = (\mathcal{L} \cdot \mathcal{L}^\vee)^\vee$ is a lattice in $K$ (because $\mathcal{L} \cdot \mathcal{L}^\vee$ is), thus we only need to show that it is a subring of $K$ with unity. By definition of $\mathcal{O}^{\mathcal{L}}$, we clearly have $1 \in \mathcal{O}^{\mathcal{L}}$. Moreover, for any $x, y \in \mathcal{O}^{\mathcal{L}}$, we have $(xy)\mathcal{L} = x(y\mathcal{L}) \subseteq x\mathcal{L} \subseteq \mathcal{L}$, so $xy \in \mathcal{O}^{\mathcal{L}}$, as desired.

An immediate corollary is that $\mathcal{O}^{\mathcal{L}} \subseteq \mathcal{O}_K$, the ring of integers (i.e., maximal order) of $K$.[5]

---

[5] This can also be seen by using one of the characterizations of algebraic integers, that $x$ is an algebraic integer if and only if $x\mathcal{L} \subseteq \mathcal{L}$ for some nonzero finitely generated $\mathbb{Z}$-module $\mathcal{L} \subseteq \mathbb{C}$.

$\mathcal{L}$-LWE **Problem.** Using the coefficient ring, we now define a general algebraic LWE problem that is parameterized by an arbitrary number-field lattice $\mathcal{L}$.

**Definition 6 ($\mathcal{L}$-LWE distribution).** *Let $\mathcal{L}$ be a lattice in a number field $K$, $\mathcal{O}^{\mathcal{L}}$ be the coefficient ring of $\mathcal{L}$, $\psi$ be a distribution over $K_{\mathbb{R}}$, and $q, k$ be positive integers. For $\vec{s} \in (\mathcal{L}_q^{\vee})^k$, a sample from the $\mathcal{L}$-LWE distribution $A_{q,\psi}^{\mathcal{L},k}(\vec{s})$ over $(\mathcal{O}_q^{\mathcal{L}})^k \times K_{\mathbb{R}}/q\mathcal{L}^{\vee}$ is generated by choosing $\vec{a} \leftarrow (\mathcal{O}_q^{\mathcal{L}})^k$ uniformly at random, choosing $e \leftarrow \psi$, and outputting $(a, b = \langle \vec{s}, \vec{a} \rangle + e \bmod q\mathcal{L}^{\vee})$.*

**Definition 7 ($\mathcal{L}$-LWE problem, decision).** *The decision $\mathcal{L}$-LWE$_{q,\psi,\ell}^k$ problem is to distinguish between $\ell$ samples from $A_{q,\psi}^{\mathcal{L},k}(\vec{s})$ where $\vec{s} \leftarrow U((\mathcal{L}_q^{\vee})^k)$, and $\ell$ samples from $U((\mathcal{O}_q)^k \times K_{\mathbb{R}}/q\mathcal{L}^{\vee})$.*

**Definition 8 ($\mathcal{L}$-LWE problem, search).** *The search $\mathcal{L}$-LWE$_{q,\psi,\ell}^k$ problem is given $\ell$ samples from $A_{q,\psi}^{\mathcal{L},k}(\vec{s})$ for some arbitrary $\vec{s} \in (\mathcal{L}_q^{\vee})^k$, find $\vec{s}$*

For both of the above definitions, we often omit $k$ when $k = 1$. Notice that in this case, we have $s \in \mathcal{L}_q^{\vee}$, $a \in \mathcal{O}_q^{\mathcal{L}}$, and a sample from the distribution $A_{q,\psi}^{\mathcal{L}}(s)$ has the form $(a, b = s \cdot a + e \bmod q\mathcal{L}^{\vee})$.

The above definitions strictly generalize all prior algebraic LWE variants defined over number fields or polynomial rings. For simplicity, take $k = 1$ (taking $k > 1$ simply yields "Module" analogues of what follows). Recall that if $\mathcal{L}$ is an order $\mathcal{O}$ of $K$ or its dual $\mathcal{O}^{\vee}$, then $\mathcal{O}^{\mathcal{L}} = \mathcal{O}$. Therefore, by taking $\mathcal{L} = \mathcal{O}_K$ to be the full ring of integers, we get the Ring-LWE problem as originally defined in [9]. Alternatively, by taking $\mathcal{L} = \mathcal{O}^{\vee}$ we get the "primal" form of Order-LWE over $\mathcal{O}$ [2], which corresponds to the Poly-LWE problem [18] when $\mathcal{O} = \mathbb{Z}[\alpha]$ for some $\alpha \in \mathcal{O}_K$. By instead taking $\mathcal{L} = \mathcal{O}$, we get a natural "dual" variant of Order-LWE, where the secret $s$ and products $s \cdot a$ are in $\mathcal{O}^{\vee}/q\mathcal{O}^{\vee}$; this formulation has advantages in terms of simplicity and tightness of reductions. Finally, by taking $\mathcal{L}$ to be neither an order nor the dual of an order, we get other problems that are not covered by any of the prior ones.

## 4    Error-Preserving Reduction from $\mathcal{L}$-LWE to $\mathcal{L}'$-LWE

In this section, we present an efficient, deterministic reduction from $\mathcal{L}$-LWE$_{q,\psi,\ell}$ to $\mathcal{L}'$-LWE$_{q,\psi,\ell}$, where $\mathcal{L}' \subseteq \mathcal{L}$ are lattices in a number field $K$ such that $\mathcal{O}^{\mathcal{L}'} \subseteq \mathcal{O}^{\mathcal{L}}$ and the index $|\mathcal{L}/\mathcal{L}'|$ is coprime with $q$. We stress that the reduction preserves the error distribution $\psi$ and the number of samples $\ell$ exactly.

### 4.1    Helpful Lemmas

Before presenting the main theorem in Sect. 4.2 below, we introduce a couple of helpful lemmas. For any lattices $\mathcal{L}' \subseteq \mathcal{L}$ in $K$, the *natural inclusion map* $\mathcal{L}'_q \to \mathcal{L}_q$ sends $x + q\mathcal{L}'$ to $x + q\mathcal{L}$. (This can be seen as the composition of a natural homomorphism and an inclusion map.) The following lemmas give conditions under which maps of this kind are bijections.

**Lemma 5.** *Let $\mathcal{L}' \subseteq \mathcal{L}$ be lattices in a number field $K$ and let $q$ be a positive integer. Then the natural inclusion map $h\colon \mathcal{L}'_q \to \mathcal{L}_q$ is a bijection if and only if $q$ is coprime with the index $|\mathcal{L}/\mathcal{L}'|$; in this case, $h$ is efficiently computable and invertible given an arbitrary basis of $\mathcal{L}'$ relative to a basis of $\mathcal{L}$.*

Because $|\mathcal{L}/\mathcal{L}'| = |(\mathcal{L}')^\vee / \mathcal{L}^\vee|$, the same conclusions hold for the natural inclusion map $\mathcal{L}^\vee_q \to (\mathcal{L}')^\vee_q$.

*Proof.* Let $\vec{b}, \vec{b}'$ respectively be some $\mathbb{Z}$-bases of $\mathcal{L}, \mathcal{L}'$ (and hence $\mathbb{Z}_q$-bases of $\mathcal{L}_q, \mathcal{L}'_q$). Then $\vec{b}' = \mathbf{T} \cdot \vec{b}$ for some given square matrix $\mathbf{T}$. This $\mathbf{T}$ is integral because $\mathcal{L}' \subseteq \mathcal{L}$, and we have $|\det(\mathbf{T})| = |\mathcal{L}/\mathcal{L}'|$. Letting $\mathbf{x}'$ be the coefficient vector (over $\mathbb{Z}_q$) of some arbitrary $x' = \langle \vec{b}', \mathbf{x} \rangle \in \mathcal{L}'_q$, we have $x' = \langle \mathbf{T} \cdot \vec{b}, \mathbf{x}' \rangle = \langle \vec{b}, \mathbf{T}^t \cdot \mathbf{x}' \rangle$, so $\mathbf{x} = \mathbf{T}^t \cdot \mathbf{x}'$ is the coefficient vector (over $\mathbb{Z}_q$) of $h(x') \in \mathcal{L}_q$ relative to $\vec{b}$. Moreover, $\mathbf{x}$ and $\mathbf{x}'$ are in bijective correspondence if and only if $\mathbf{T}$ is invertible modulo $q$, i.e., if $|\det(\mathbf{T})| = |\mathcal{L}/\mathcal{L}'|$ is coprime with $q$, and we can efficiently evaluate and invert this bijection given $\mathbf{T}$.

**Lemma 6.** *Let $\mathcal{L}' \subseteq \mathcal{L}$ be lattices in a number field $K$, and let $q$ be a positive integer that is coprime with the index $|\mathcal{L}/\mathcal{L}'|$. If $\mathcal{O}^{\mathcal{L}'} \subseteq \mathcal{O}^{\mathcal{L}}$, then the natural inclusion map $g\colon \mathcal{O}^{\mathcal{L}'}_q \to \mathcal{O}^{\mathcal{L}}_q$ is a bijection.*

*Proof.* Let $h\colon \mathcal{L}'_q \to \mathcal{L}_q$ be the natural inclusion map, which by Lemma 5 is a bijection. First, notice that for any $a \in \mathcal{O}^{\mathcal{L}'}_q$ and $x \in \mathcal{L}'_q$, we have $h(a \cdot x) = g(a) \cdot h(x)$. This is because

$$g(a) \cdot h(x) = (a + q\mathcal{O}^{\mathcal{L}}) \cdot (x + q\mathcal{L}) = a \cdot x + q(\mathcal{O}^{\mathcal{L}} \cdot x + a \cdot \mathcal{L} + \mathcal{O}^{\mathcal{L}} \cdot \mathcal{L}) = a \cdot x + q\mathcal{L} = h(a \cdot x).$$

Now, let $a, b \in \mathcal{O}^{\mathcal{L}'}_q$ satisfy $g(a) = g(b)$. Then for all $x \in \mathcal{L}'$, we have

$$h(a \cdot x) = g(a) \cdot h(x) = g(b) \cdot h(x) = h(b \cdot x).$$

Since $h$ is a bijection, it follows that $a \cdot x = b \cdot x \pmod{q\mathcal{L}'}$ for all $x \in \mathcal{L}'$. Therefore,

$$(a - b) \cdot \mathcal{L}' \subseteq q\mathcal{L}' \Rightarrow a - b \in q\mathcal{O}^{\mathcal{L}'} \Rightarrow a = b \pmod{q\mathcal{O}^{\mathcal{L}'}}.$$

Thus, $g$ is injective. Since the sets $\mathcal{O}^{\mathcal{L}'}_q$ and $\mathcal{O}^{\mathcal{L}}_q$ have the same cardinality $q^{\deg(K/\mathbb{Q})}$, $g$ must bijective.

## 4.2   Reduction

**Theorem 1.** *Let $\mathcal{L}' \subseteq \mathcal{L}$ be lattices in a number field $K$, $\psi$ be a distribution over $K_{\mathbb{R}}$, and $q$ be a positive integer. If $\mathcal{O}^{\mathcal{L}'} \subseteq \mathcal{O}^{\mathcal{L}}$ and the natural inclusion map $g\colon \mathcal{O}^{\mathcal{L}'}_q \to \mathcal{O}^{\mathcal{L}}_q$ is an efficiently invertible bijection, then there is an efficient deterministic transform which:*

*1. maps distribution $U(\mathcal{O}^{\mathcal{L}}_q \times K_{\mathbb{R}}/q\mathcal{L}^\vee)$ to distribution $U(\mathcal{O}^{\mathcal{L}'}_q \times K_{\mathbb{R}}/q(\mathcal{L}')^\vee)$, and*

2. *maps distribution $A^{\mathcal{L}}_{q,\psi}(s)$ to distribution $A^{\mathcal{L}'}_{q,\psi}(s')$, where $s' = s \bmod q(\mathcal{L}')^{\vee} \in (\mathcal{L}')^{\vee}/q(\mathcal{L}')^{\vee}$.*

*Proof.* The claimed transform is as follows: for each given sample $(a, b) \in \mathcal{O}^{\mathcal{L}}_q \times K_{\mathbb{R}}/q\mathcal{L}^{\vee}$, output

$$(a' = g^{-1}(a), \; b' = b \bmod q(\mathcal{L}')^{\vee}).$$

It is clear that this transform sends uniformly random $a$ to uniformly random $a'$, because $g$ is a bijection. Also, since $\mathcal{L}' \subseteq \mathcal{L}$, we know that $q\mathcal{L}^{\vee} \subseteq q(\mathcal{L}')^{\vee}$. Therefore, the transform sends uniformly random $b$ to uniformly random $b'$.

It remains to show that if $b = a \cdot s + e \bmod q\mathcal{L}^{\vee}$, then $b' = a' \cdot s' + e \bmod q(\mathcal{L}')^{\vee}$. To see this, observe that $a = a' \pmod{q\mathcal{O}^{\mathcal{L}}}$, because $g$ is the natural inclusion map. Therefore,

$$
\begin{aligned}
a \cdot s &= a' \cdot s + q(\mathcal{O}^{\mathcal{L}} \cdot s) \\
&\subseteq a' \cdot s + q\mathcal{L}^{\vee} \\
&\subseteq a' \cdot (s' + q(\mathcal{L}')^{\vee}) + q\mathcal{L}^{\vee} \\
&\subseteq a' \cdot s' + q(\mathcal{L}')^{\vee},
\end{aligned}
$$

where in the first and third containments we have used $\mathcal{O}^{\mathcal{L}} \cdot \mathcal{L}^{\vee} \subseteq \mathcal{L}^{\vee}$ and $\mathcal{O}^{\mathcal{L}'} \cdot (\mathcal{L}')^{\vee} \subseteq (\mathcal{L}')^{\vee}$, respectively. The claim follows by adding $e$ to both sides.

**Corollary 1.** *Adopt the notation from Theorem 1, and assume that $|\mathcal{L}/\mathcal{L}'|$ is coprime with $q$, that $\mathcal{O}^{\mathcal{L}'} \subseteq \mathcal{O}^{\mathcal{L}}$, and that bases of $\mathcal{L}', \mathcal{O}^{\mathcal{L}'}$ relative to bases of $\mathcal{L}, \mathcal{O}^{\mathcal{L}}$ (respectively) are known. Then there is an efficient deterministic reduction from $\mathcal{L}$-$\mathsf{LWE}_{q,\psi,\ell}$ to $\mathcal{L}'$-$\mathsf{LWE}_{q,\psi,\ell}$ for both the search and decision versions.*

A main case of interest is when $\mathcal{L} = \mathcal{O}^{\mathcal{L}}$ and $\mathcal{L}' = \mathcal{O}^{\mathcal{L}'}$ are themselves orders, in which case the above coprimality hypothesis is implied by the *conductor* of $\mathcal{L}'$ in $\mathcal{L}$ being coprime with $q\mathcal{L}$, as ideals of $\mathcal{L}$. The latter hypothesis is used in [18], so our hypothesis is no stronger.

*Proof.* We first note that by Lemmas 5 and 6, the natural inclusion maps $h \colon \mathcal{L}'_q \to \mathcal{L}_q$ and $g \colon \mathcal{O}^{\mathcal{L}'}_q \to \mathcal{O}^{\mathcal{L}}_q$ are efficiently computable and invertible bijections. For the decision problems, use the deterministic transform from Theorem 1 to transform the input samples of the $\mathcal{L}$-$\mathsf{LWE}_{q,\psi,\ell}$ problem. This will produce the same number of samples for the $\mathcal{L}'$-$\mathsf{LWE}_{q,\psi,\ell}$ problem, where uniform samples map to uniform ones, and samples from $A^{\mathcal{L}}_{q,\psi}(s)$ map to samples from $A^{\mathcal{L}'}_{q,\psi}(s')$ for $s' = s \bmod q(\mathcal{L}')^{\vee}$. Also, because $h$ is a bijection, the uniformly random secret $s \in \mathcal{L}^{\vee}_q$ maps to a uniformly random secret $s' \in (\mathcal{L}')^{\vee}_q$, as needed. For the search problems, it suffices to also note that we can recover the original secret $s$ from $s'$ by computing $h^{-1}(s')$.

## 5    Reduction from $\mathcal{O}$-LWE to MP-LWE

Rosca *et al.* [17] introduced the Middle-Product LWE (MP-LWE) problem and gave a hardness theorem for it, by showing a reduction from a wide class of

Poly-LWE instantiations—and by extension, Ring-LWE instantiations [18]—over various polynomial rings of the form $\mathbb{Z}[\alpha] \cong \mathbb{Z}[x]/f(x)$ for $f(x)$ satisfying mild conditions. Here we give a reduction that, when combined with our error-preserving reduction from Sect. 4, subsumes the prior Ring/MP-LWE connection in the simplicity of its descriptions and analysis, and the tightness of its error distortion (or expansion). These advantages arise from our use of $\mathcal{O}$-LWE as an intermediate problem, and in particular its use of dual lattices (in contrast to the entirely "primal" nature of Poly-LWE).

### 5.1   Reduction

We start with a slight generalization of the notion of a power basis, by allowing a "tweak" factor.

**Definition 9.** *For an order $\mathcal{O}$ of a number field, a tweaked power basis of $\mathcal{L}$ is a $\mathbb{Z}$-basis $\vec{p}$ of $\mathcal{O}$ of the form $t \cdot (1, x, x^2, \ldots, x^{d-1})$ for some $t, x \in \mathcal{O}$.*

For simplicity, in the rest of this section the reader may wish to focus initially on the case $d = n$.

**Theorem 2.** *Let $d \leq n$ be positive integers, $\mathcal{O}$ be an order of a degree-$d$ number field $K$ with a tweaked power basis $\vec{p}$, $\psi$ be a distribution over $K_{\mathbb{R}}$, and $q$ be a positive integer. There is an efficient randomized transform which:*

1. *maps distribution $U(\mathcal{O}_q \times K_{\mathbb{R}}/q\mathcal{O}^{\vee})$ to distribution $U(\mathbb{Z}_q^n \times (\mathbb{R}/q\mathbb{Z})^d)$, and*
2. *maps the $\mathcal{O}$-LWE distribution $A_{q,\psi}^{\mathcal{O}}(s)$ to the MP-LWE distribution $C_{n,d,q,\psi'}(\mathbf{s}')$, where $\mathbf{s}'$ is some fixed linear function (depending only on $\vec{p}$) of $s$, and $\psi' = \mathrm{Tr}_{K_{\mathbb{R}}/\mathbb{R}}(\psi \cdot \vec{p})$.*

*In particular, there is an efficient randomized reduction from (search or decision) $\mathcal{O}\text{-LWE}_{q,\psi,\ell}$ to (search or decision, respectively) $\mathsf{MP\text{-}LWE}_{n,d,q,\psi',\ell}$.*

*Proof.* First, we extend the tweaked power basis $\vec{p} = t \cdot (x^i)_{i=0,\ldots,d-1}$ of $\mathcal{O}$ into a tweaked power *generating set* $\vec{p}' = t \cdot (x^i)_{i=0,\ldots,n-1}$ in the natural way, by including more powers of $x$ (if necessary).

The transform, given a sample $(a, b) \in \mathcal{O}_q \times K_{\mathbb{R}}/q\mathcal{O}^{\vee}$, computes and outputs the (coefficient) vectors

$$(\mathbf{a}, \mathbf{b} = \mathrm{Tr}_{K_{\mathbb{R}}/\mathbb{R}}(b \cdot \vec{p})) \in \mathbb{Z}_q^n \times (\mathbb{R}/q\mathbb{Z})^d.$$

where $\mathbf{a}$ is a uniformly random solution to $\langle \vec{p}', \mathbf{a} \rangle = a$. This can be generated by adding to any particular solution (e.g., the unique one using just the elements of $\vec{p}$) a uniformly random element of the subgroup $G = \{\mathbf{z} \in \mathbb{Z}_q^n : \langle \vec{p}', \mathbf{z} \rangle \in q\mathcal{O}\} \subseteq \mathbb{Z}_q^n$ (for which we can find a $\mathbb{Z}_q$-basis using standard methods). This transform sends uniformly random $a$ to uniformly random $\mathbf{a}$, since $a$ corresponds to a uniformly random coset of $G$. In addition, the transform sends uniformly random $b$ to uniformly random $\mathbf{b}$, because $\mathrm{Tr}_{K_{\mathbb{R}}/\mathbb{R}}(b \cdot \vec{p})$ is the coefficient vector of $b$ with respect to $\vec{p}^{\vee}$, which is a $\mathbb{Z}$-basis of $\mathcal{O}^{\vee}$, and thus an $\mathbb{R}$-basis of $K_{\mathbb{R}}$.

It remains to show that if $b = s \cdot a + e \bmod q\mathcal{O}^\vee$ for some $s \in \mathcal{O}_q^\vee$ and $e \leftarrow \psi$, then $(\mathbf{a}, \mathbf{b})$ is a properly distributed MP-LWE sample for secret $\mathbf{s}'$. To do this we use definition of MP-LWE in the generalized LWE framework from Sect. 3.1. Specifically, consider the $\mathbb{Z}_q$-bilinear multiplication map $T \colon \mathcal{O}_q^\vee \times \mathcal{O}_q \to \mathcal{O}_q^\vee$, and consider the generating sets $\vec{p}^\vee, \vec{p}'$ for the $\mathbb{Z}_q$-modules $\mathcal{O}_q^\vee, \mathcal{O}_q$, respectively. Then letting $\mathrm{Tr} = \mathrm{Tr}_{K/\mathbb{Q}}$, the third-order tensor representing $T$ relative to $\vec{p}^\vee, \vec{p}'$ is given by

$$T_{ijk} := \mathrm{Tr}(p_i^\vee \cdot p_j' \cdot p_k) \bmod q = \mathrm{Tr}(p_i^\vee \cdot g_{j+k}) \bmod q,$$

where $g_{j+k} = p_j' \cdot p_k = t^2 \cdot x^{j+k}$ depends only on $j + k$.

In particular, each "slice" $T_{i\cdot\cdot}$ for fixed $i$ is a Hankel matrix, so it can be written as a $\mathbb{Z}_q$-linear combination of the slices $M_{i\cdot\cdot}$ of the tensor for the middle-product bilinear form $M \colon \mathbb{Z}_q^{n+d-1} \times \mathbb{Z}_q^n \to \mathbb{Z}_q^d$, because these slices form the standard basis for the set of $n \times d$ Hankel matrices over $\mathbb{Z}_q$. In other words, there exists a matrix $\mathbf{P} \in \mathbb{Z}_q^{(n+d-1) \times d}$ such that $T_{i\cdot\cdot} = \sum_{i'} M_{i'\cdot\cdot} \mathbf{P}_{i'i}$ for all $i$; specifically, the $i$th column of $\mathbf{P}$ is simply the vector defining the Hankel matrix $T_{i\cdot\cdot}$. Therefore,

$$\mathrm{Tr}((s \cdot a) \cdot \vec{p}) = \mathrm{Tr}(T(s, a) \cdot \vec{p}) = M(\mathbf{Ps}, \mathbf{a}),$$

where $\mathbf{s} = \mathrm{Tr}(s \cdot \vec{p}) \in \mathbb{Z}_q^d$ is the coefficient vector of $s$ with respect to $\vec{p}^\vee$.

Finally, we address the error term. By linearity and the above, we have $\mathbf{b} = M(\mathbf{Ps}, \mathbf{a}) + \mathbf{e} \bmod q\mathbb{Z}^d$ where $\mathbf{e} = \mathrm{Tr}(e \cdot \vec{p})$, which has distribution $\psi'$ because $e$ has distribution $\psi$ over $K_\mathbb{R}$.

Notice that for the search and decision reductions, we cannot simply apply the claimed transformation to each input sample, because the resulting distribution on $\mathbf{s}'$ is not uniform. However, this is easily addressed by the standard technique of re-randomizing the secret, choosing a uniformly random $\mathbf{r} \in \mathbb{Z}_q^{n+d-1}$ and transforming each given sample $(\mathbf{a}, \mathbf{b})$ to $(\mathbf{a}, \mathbf{b} + M(\mathbf{r}, \mathbf{a}))$. This preserves the uniform distribution in the random case, and maps secret $\mathbf{s}$ to a uniformly random secret $\mathbf{s}' + \mathbf{r}$ in the LWE case.

To obtain the claimed search reduction, first apply the above transforms to each input sample of the $\mathcal{O}$-LWE$_{q,\psi,\ell}$ problem. This produces the same number of samples for the MP-LWE$_{n,d,q,\psi',\ell}$ problem. We can then compute the original secret $s$ from the transformed secret $\mathbf{s}' + \mathbf{r}$ via $\mathbf{s} = \mathbf{P}_L^{-1} \cdot \mathbf{s}'$, and $s = \langle \vec{p}^\vee, \mathbf{s} \rangle$ where $\mathbf{P}_L^{-1}$ is a left inverse of $\mathbf{P}$. For the claimed decision reduction, it suffices that the transform also maps uniform samples to uniform samples.

**Corollary 2.** *Adopt the notation from Theorem 2, and let $\mathcal{O}' \subseteq \mathcal{O}$ be a suborder which has a known tweaked power basis $\vec{p}$ and for which $|\mathcal{O}/\mathcal{O}'|$ is coprime with $q$. There is a randomized sample-preserving reduction from $\mathcal{O}$-LWE$_{q,\psi,\ell}$ to MP-LWE$_{n,d,q,\psi',\ell}$, where $\psi' = \mathrm{Tr}_{K_\mathbb{R}/\mathbb{R}}(\psi \cdot \vec{p})$.*

*Proof.* We can reduce $\mathcal{O}$-LWE$_{q,\psi,\ell}$ to $\mathcal{O}'$-LWE$_{q,\psi,\ell}$ by Corollary 1, and then to MP-LWE$_{n,d,q,\psi',\ell}$ by Theorem 2.

### 5.2 Managing the Error Distribution

The reduction described in Theorem 2 reduces $\mathcal{O}$-LWE with error distribution $\psi$ to MP-LWE with error distribution $\psi' = \mathrm{Tr}_{K_\mathbb{R}/\mathbb{R}}(\psi \cdot \vec{p})$ where $\vec{p}$ is some tweaked power basis of $\mathcal{O}$. However, we ultimately want a reduction from *many* $\mathcal{O}$-LWE problems to a *single* MP-LWE problem, so we need to further control the resulting error distribution. To this end, we consider the usual case where $\psi$ is a Gaussian distribution over $K_{\mathbb{R}}$, in which case it turns out that $\psi'$ is a Gaussian over $\mathbb{R}^n$ whose covariance is related to the Gram matrix of $\vec{p}$. Moreover, by a standard technique we can add some independent Gaussian error having a compensating covariance to arrive at any desired target covariance that is sufficiently large.

Throughout this section, we use the following notation. Let $\mathrm{Tr} = \mathrm{Tr}_{K_{\mathbb{R}}/\mathbb{R}}$, and given a tweaked basis $\vec{p}$ of $\mathcal{O}$, let $\mathbf{P} = \mathrm{Tr}(\vec{p} \cdot \tau(\vec{p})^t)$ denote the (positive definite) Gram matrix of $\vec{p}$, whose $(i,j)$th entry is $\langle p_i, p_j \rangle = \mathrm{Tr}(p_i \cdot \tau(p_j))$. Fix some orthonormal $\mathbb{R}$-basis $\vec{b} = \tau(\vec{b}^\vee)$ of $K_{\mathbb{R}}$, and let $\mathbf{P}_b = \mathrm{Tr}(\vec{b} \cdot \vec{p}^t)$. Then by $\mathbb{R}$-linearity of $\tau$ and trace, we have

$$\mathbf{P} = \mathrm{Tr}(\vec{p} \cdot \tau(\vec{p})^t) = \mathrm{Tr}\Big(\vec{p} \cdot \tau\big((\vec{b}^\vee)^t \cdot \mathrm{Tr}(\vec{b} \cdot \vec{p}^t)\big)\Big) = \mathrm{Tr}(\vec{p} \cdot \vec{b}^t) \cdot \mathrm{Tr}(\vec{b} \cdot \vec{p}^t) = \mathbf{P}_b^t \cdot \mathbf{P}_b \,.$$

For a real matrix $\mathbf{A}$, let

$$\|\mathbf{A}\| = \max_{\|\mathbf{u}\|_2=1} \|\mathbf{A}\mathbf{u}\|_2$$

denote the spectral (or operator) norm of $\mathbf{A}$; observe that by the above, we have $\|\mathbf{P}\| = \|\mathbf{P}_b\|^2$.

**Corollary 3.** *Let $d \leq n$ be positive integers, $\mathcal{O}$ be an order of a degree-$d$ number field $K$ with a tweaked power basis $\vec{p}$, $\Sigma \in \mathbb{R}^{d \times d}$ be a positive definite matrix, and $q$ be a positive integer. For any $\Sigma' \succ \mathbf{P}_b^t \cdot \Sigma \cdot \mathbf{P}_b$, there is an efficient randomized reduction from (search or decision) $\mathcal{O}$-LWE$_{q,D_{\sqrt{\Sigma}},\ell}$ to (search or decision, respectively) MP-LWE$_{n,d,q,D_{\sqrt{\Sigma'}},\ell}$.*

*In particular, for any $r' > r \cdot \sqrt{\|\mathbf{P}\|}$, there is an efficient randomized reduction from (search or decision) $\mathcal{O}$-LWE$_{q,D_r,\ell}$ to (search or decision, respectively) MP-LWE$_{n,d,q,D_{r'},\ell}$.*

*Proof.* By applying Theorem 2 we obtain an efficient randomized reduction from $\mathcal{O}$-LWE$_{q,D_{\sqrt{\Sigma}},\ell}$ to MP-LWE$_{n,d,q,\psi',\ell}$, where $\psi'$ is a distribution over $\mathbb{R}^d$ and is analyzed as follows. Let $D = D_{\sqrt{\Sigma}}$ be the original error distribution over $K_{\mathbb{R}}$, which (because $\vec{b}$ is an orthonormal basis of $K_{\mathbb{R}}$) has the form $D = \vec{b}^t \cdot C$ where the coefficient distribution $C = D_{\sqrt{\Sigma}}$ is a Gaussian over $\mathbb{R}^n$. Then by $\mathbb{R}$-linearity of the trace,

$$\psi' = \mathrm{Tr}(\vec{p} \cdot D) = \mathrm{Tr}(\vec{p} \cdot \vec{b}^t \cdot C) = \mathrm{Tr}(\vec{p} \cdot \vec{b}^t) \cdot C = \mathbf{P}_b^t \cdot C = D_{\sqrt{\Sigma_1}},$$

where $\Sigma_1 = \mathbf{P}_b^t \cdot \Sigma \cdot \mathbf{P}_b$.

Since $\Sigma' \succ \Sigma_1$ by assumption, we may transform the error distribution $D_{\sqrt{\Sigma_1}}$ to $D_{\sqrt{\Sigma'}}$ by adding (to the b-part of each MP-LWE sample) a fresh error term from the compensating Gaussian distribution of covariance $\Sigma' - \Sigma_1$. This yields the desired error distribution and completes the proof of the first claim.

For the second claim, notice that if $\Sigma = r^2 \cdot \mathbf{I}$, then $\Sigma' = (r')^2 \mathbf{I} \succ \mathbf{P}_b^t \cdot \Sigma \cdot \mathbf{P}_b = r^2 \cdot \mathbf{P}$, because $(r')^2 \mathbf{I} - r^2 \mathbf{P}$ is positive definite, since $\mathbf{x}^t \mathbf{P} \mathbf{x} \leq \|\mathbf{P}\| \cdot \|\mathbf{x}\|_2^2$ for any $\mathbf{x}$.

## 5.3    Example Instantiations

Corollary 3 bounds the expansion of the error distribution by the square root of the spectral norm of the Gram matrix $\mathbf{P}$ of a tweaked power basis $\vec{p}$ of $\mathcal{O}$. Here we show that there are large families of orders with well-behaved power bases (with tweak factor $t = 1$).

Let $\alpha$ be an algebraic integer with minimal polynomial $f(x) \in \mathbb{Z}[x]$ of degree $d$, and consider the order $\mathcal{O} = \mathbb{Z}[\alpha] \subset K = \mathbb{Q}(\alpha)$, which has power basis $\vec{p} = (1, \alpha, \ldots, \alpha^{d-1})$. Consider the Vandermonde matrix

$$\mathbf{V} = \begin{pmatrix} 1 & \alpha_1 & \alpha_1^2 & & \alpha_1^{d-1} \\ 1 & \alpha_2 & \alpha_2^2 & \cdots & \alpha_2^{d-1} \\ 1 & \alpha_3 & \alpha_3^2 & & \alpha_3^{d-1} \\ & \vdots & & \ddots & \vdots \\ 1 & \alpha_d & \alpha_d^2 & \cdots & \alpha_d^{d-1} \end{pmatrix}$$

where the $\alpha_i$ are the $d$ distinct roots of $f$, i.e., the conjugates of $\alpha$. This $\mathbf{V}$ represents the linear transform $\sigma$ that maps coefficient vectors with respect to $\vec{p}$ to the canonical (or Minkowski) embedding.

It is easy to see that the Gram matrix of $\vec{p}$ is $\mathbf{P} = \mathbf{V}^*\mathbf{V}$, where $\mathbf{V}^*$ denotes the conjugate transpose of $\mathbf{V}$, so $\sqrt{\|\mathbf{P}\|} = \|\mathbf{V}\|$. Therefore, we immediately have the bound $\sqrt{\|\mathbf{P}\|} \leq \|\mathbf{V}\|_2 \leq \sqrt{d} \cdot \max_i \|\sigma(\alpha^i)\|$, where the maximum is taken over $i \in \{0, 1, \ldots, d-1\}$. That is, the Frobenius and Euclidean norms of the power-basis elements (in the canonical embedding) yield bounds on the error expansion. The following lemma gives an alternative bound directly in terms of the minimal polynomial $f(x)$.

**Lemma 7.** *Adopt the above notation, and assume that the minimal polynomial $f(x) = x^d - g(x) \in \mathbb{Z}[x]$, where $g(x) = a_k x^k + \cdots + a_1 x + a_0$ has degree at most $k < d$. Then $\sqrt{\|\mathbf{P}\|} \leq d \cdot A^{d/(d-k)}$ where $A = \sum_{i=0}^k |a_i|$. In particular, if $k = (1-c)d$ for some $c \in (0,1)$, then $\sqrt{\|\mathbf{P}\|} \leq d \cdot A^{1/c}$.*

For example, if all the $|a_i| = \text{poly}(d)$ and $c < 1$ is any positive constant, then $\sqrt{\|\mathbf{P}\|} = \text{poly}(d)$. This enlarges the set of moduli $f(x)$ yielding polynomial error expansion from those considered in [17].

*Proof.* We bound $\|\mathbf{V}\|$ as follows. Let $\alpha_* = \max_i |\alpha_i| \geq 1$ be the maximum magnitude of any root of $f$. Then $\|\mathbf{V}\| \leq d \max |\mathbf{V}_{i,j}| \leq d \cdot \alpha_*^d$. Now, because the $\alpha_i$ satisfy $\alpha_i^d = g(\alpha_i)$, by the triangle inequality we have $\alpha_*^d \leq \alpha_*^k \cdot A$ and hence $\alpha_*^{d-k} \leq A$. The claim follows by raising to the $d/(d-k)$ power. $\quad\square$

## 6    Reduction from $\mathcal{O}'$-LWE to $\mathcal{O}$-LWE$^k$

In this section we give a simple reduction from $\mathcal{O}'$-LWE, for a *wide class* of orders $\mathcal{O}'$, to a *single* rank-$k$ Module-LWE problem over an order $\mathcal{O}$.

## 6.1  Reduction

**Theorem 3.** *Let $K'/K$ be a number field extension; $\mathcal{O}$ be an order of $K$; $\mathcal{O}'$ be an order of $K'$ that is a rank-$k$ free $\mathcal{O}$-module with known basis $\vec{b}$; $\psi'$ be a distribution over $K'_{\mathbb{R}}$; and $q$ be a positive integer. Then there is an efficient, deterministic transform which:*

1. *maps distribution $U(\mathcal{O}'_q \times K'_{\mathbb{R}}/q(\mathcal{O}')^{\vee})$ to $U(\mathcal{O}^k_q \times K_{\mathbb{R}}/q\mathcal{O}^{\vee})$, and*
2. *maps distribution $A^{\mathcal{O}'}_{q,\psi'}(s')$ to $A^{\mathcal{O},k}_{q,\psi}(\vec{s})$, for $\vec{s} = \mathrm{Tr}_{K'/K}(s' \cdot \vec{b}) \bmod q\mathcal{O}^{\vee}$ and $\psi = \mathrm{Tr}_{K'_{\mathbb{R}}/K_{\mathbb{R}}}(\psi')$.*

*It immediately follows that there is an efficient, deterministic reduction from (search or decision) $\mathcal{O}'\text{-}\mathsf{LWE}^1_{q,\psi',\ell}$ to (search or decision, respectively) $\mathcal{O}\text{-}\mathsf{LWE}^k_{q,\psi,\ell}$.*

*Proof.* Let $\mathrm{Tr} = \mathrm{Tr}_{K'_{\mathbb{R}}/K_{\mathbb{R}}}$, which coincides with $\mathrm{Tr}_{K'/K}$ on $K'$. The claimed transform is as follows. Given a sample $(a', b') \in \mathcal{O}'_q \times K'_{\mathbb{R}}/q(\mathcal{O}')^{\vee}$, output

$$\left( \vec{a} = \mathrm{Tr}(a' \cdot \vec{b}^{\vee}) , \, b = \mathrm{Tr}(b') \bmod q\mathcal{O}^{\vee} \right) \in \mathcal{O}^k_q \times K_{\mathbb{R}}/q\mathcal{O}^{\vee}.$$

Clearly, this transform sends uniformly random $a' \in \mathcal{O}'_q$ to uniformly random $\vec{a} \in \mathcal{O}^k_q$, because $\vec{b}$ is an $\mathcal{O}_q$-basis of $\mathcal{O}'_q$, and $\mathrm{Tr}(a' \cdot \vec{b}^{\vee})$ is the coefficient vector of $a$ with respect to this basis. Also, the transform sends uniformly random $b' \in K'_{\mathbb{R}}/q(\mathcal{O}')^{\vee}$ to uniformly random $b \in K_{\mathbb{R}}/q\mathcal{O}^{\vee}$, because $\mathrm{Tr} \colon K'_{\mathbb{R}} \to K_{\mathbb{R}}$ is a surjective $K_{\mathbb{R}}$-linear map and $\mathrm{Tr}((\mathcal{O}')^{\vee}) \subseteq \mathcal{O}^{\vee}$, since $\mathrm{Tr}((\mathcal{O}')^{\vee} \cdot \mathcal{O}) \subseteq \mathrm{Tr}((\mathcal{O}')^{\vee} \cdot \mathcal{O}') \subseteq \mathcal{O}^{\vee}_K$.

What remains to show is that if $b' = s' \cdot a' + e'$ then $b = \langle \vec{s}, \vec{a} \rangle + e$ for $\vec{s} = \mathrm{Tr}(s' \cdot \vec{b})$ and $e = \mathrm{Tr}(e')$. Observe that $s' = \langle \vec{b}^{\vee}, \vec{s} \rangle$ and $a' = \langle \vec{b}, \vec{a} \rangle$. Therefore, by Lemma 1, we know that $\mathrm{Tr}(s' \cdot a') = \langle \vec{s}, \vec{a} \rangle$. The claim then follows by linearity of $\mathrm{Tr}$.

To obtain the claimed search reduction, simply apply the above transform to the input samples for the $\mathcal{O}'\text{-}\mathsf{LWE}^1_{q,\psi',\ell}$ problem. This produces the same number of samples for the $\mathcal{O}\text{-}\mathsf{LWE}^k_{q,\psi,\ell}$ problem. It is clear that this maps the uniformly random secret $s' \in (\mathcal{O}')^{\vee}_q$ to uniformly random $\vec{s} \in (\mathcal{O}^{\vee}_q)^k$, because $\vec{b}^{\vee}$ is an $\mathcal{O}^{\vee}_q$-basis of $(\mathcal{O}')^{\vee}_q$ by Lemma 2, and $\mathrm{Tr}(s' \cdot \vec{b})$ is the coefficient vector of $s$ with respect to this basis. Furthermore, we can compute the original secret $s$ from the transformed secret $\vec{s}$, as $s = \langle \vec{b}^{\vee}, \vec{s} \rangle$. For the claimed decision reduction, it is suffices that the transform also maps uniform samples to uniform ones.

## 6.2  Managing the Error Distribution

Similarly to our reduction from $\mathcal{O}\text{-}\mathsf{LWE}$ to MP-LWE in Sect. 5, we want a reduction from many $\mathcal{O}'\text{-}\mathsf{LWE}$ problems to a single $\mathcal{O}\text{-}\mathsf{LWE}^k$ problem. To control the resulting error distribution, we consider the usual case where the original error distribution $\psi'$ is a Gaussian, in which case it turns out that the resulting error distribution $\psi$ is also a Gaussian. As in Sect. 5.2, we can add some independent Gaussian error with a compensating covariance to obtain any large enough desired target covariance. Alternatively, when $\psi'$ is a *spherical* Gaussian, then $\psi$ is one as well, with a covariance that is a $k$ factor larger, so no compensating error is needed. (Also note that $(\mathcal{O}')^\vee$ can be much denser than $\mathcal{O}^\vee$—or seen another way, $\mathcal{O}$ can have shorter vectors than $\mathcal{O}'$—so the increase in covariance does not necessarily represent a real loss.)

In what follows, let $K'/K$ be a number field extension, fix some orthonormal $\mathbb{R}$-bases $\vec{c}' = \tau((\vec{c}')^\vee)$ and $\vec{c} = \tau(\vec{c}^\vee)$ of $K'_\mathbb{R}$ and $K_\mathbb{R}$ (respectively) for defining Gaussian distributions, and let $\mathbf{A} = \mathrm{Tr}_{K'_\mathbb{R}/\mathbb{R}}(\vec{c}' \cdot \tau(\vec{c})^t)$ be the real matrix whose $(i,j)$th entry is $\langle c'_i, c_j \rangle$. The proof below shows that $\mathbf{A}^t \cdot \mathbf{A} = k\mathbf{I}$ where $k = \deg(K'/K)$; by choosing the bases appropriately we can obtain, e.g., $\mathbf{A} = \mathbf{1}_k \otimes \mathbf{I}$ where $\mathbf{1}_k \in \mathbb{Z}^k$ is the all-ones vector.

**Corollary 4.** *Adopt the notation and hypotheses of Theorem 3, with $\psi' = D_{\sqrt{\Sigma'}}$ over $K'_\mathbb{R}$ for some positive definite matrix $\Sigma'$. For any $\Sigma \succ \mathbf{A}^t \cdot \Sigma' \cdot \mathbf{A}$, there is an efficient, randomized reduction from (search or decision) $\mathcal{O}'\text{-}\mathsf{LWE}^1_{q,D_{\sqrt{\Sigma'}},\ell}$ to (search or decision, respectively) $\mathcal{O}\text{-}\mathsf{LWE}^k_{q,D_{\sqrt{\Sigma}},\ell}$.*

*Moreover, for $r = r'\sqrt{k}$, there is an efficient deterministic reduction from (search or decision) $\mathcal{O}'\text{-}\mathsf{LWE}^1_{q,D_{r'},\ell}$ to (search or decision, respectively) $\mathcal{O}\text{-}\mathsf{LWE}^k_{q,D_r,\ell}$.*

*Proof.* By Theorem 3, there exists an efficient, deterministic reduction from $\mathcal{O}'\text{-}\mathsf{LWE}^1_{q,D_{\sqrt{\Sigma'}},\ell}$ to $\mathcal{O}\text{-}\mathsf{LWE}^k_{q,\psi,\ell}$ where $\psi$ is a distribution over $K_\mathbb{R}$ and is analyzed as follows. Let $D' = D_{\sqrt{\Sigma'}}$ be the original error distribution over $K'_\mathbb{R}$, which has the form $D' = \vec{c}'^t \cdot C'$ where the coefficient distribution $C' = D_{\sqrt{\Sigma'}}$ is a Gaussian over $\mathbb{R}^{kn}$. Further, let $\Sigma_1 = \mathbf{A}^t \cdot \Sigma' \cdot \mathbf{A}$ and let $D = D_{\sqrt{\Sigma_1}}$ be a Gaussian over $K_\mathbb{R}$, which has the form $D = \vec{c}^t \cdot C$ where the coefficient distribution $C = D_{\sqrt{\Sigma_1}}$ is a Gaussian over $\mathbb{R}^n$. Then by linearity,

$$\psi = \mathrm{Tr}_{K'_\mathbb{R}/K_\mathbb{R}}(D') = \vec{c}^t \cdot \mathrm{Tr}_{K'_\mathbb{R}/\mathbb{R}}(\tau(\vec{c}) \cdot \vec{c}'^t \cdot C') = \vec{c}^t \cdot \mathbf{A}^t \cdot C' = \vec{c}^t \cdot C = D.$$

Since $\Sigma \succ \Sigma_1$ by assumption, we can transform the error distribution $D_{\sqrt{\Sigma_1}}$ to $D_{\sqrt{\Sigma'}}$ by adding (to the $b$-part of each Module-LWE sample) a fresh error term from the compensating Gaussian distribution of covariance $\Sigma' - \Sigma_1$. This yields the desired error distribution and completes the proof of the first claim.

For the second claim, observe that because $\vec{c}'$ and $\vec{c}$ are orthonormal,

$$\mathbf{A}^t \cdot \mathbf{A} = \mathrm{Tr}_{K'_\mathbb{R}/\mathbb{R}}(\vec{c} \cdot \tau(\vec{c})^t) = \mathrm{Tr}_{K_\mathbb{R}/\mathbb{R}}(\mathrm{Tr}_{K'_\mathbb{R}/K_\mathbb{R}}(1) \cdot \vec{c} \cdot \tau(\vec{c})^t) = \mathrm{Tr}_{K_\mathbb{R}/\mathbb{R}}(k \cdot \vec{c} \cdot \tau(\vec{c})^t) = k \cdot \mathbf{I}.$$

Therefore, if $\Sigma' = (r')^2 \cdot \mathbf{I}$ and $\Sigma = r^2 \cdot \mathbf{I}$, then $\Sigma_1 = \mathbf{A}^t \cdot \Sigma' \cdot \mathbf{A} = k(r')^2 \cdot \mathbf{I} = r^2 \cdot \mathbf{I} = \Sigma$, so no compensating error is needed, yielding a deterministic reduction.

## 6.3 Instantiations

It is straightforward to instantiate Theorem 3 and Corollary 4 to get reductions from a huge class of Order-LWE problems to a single Module-LWE problem.

Let $\mathcal{O}$ be an arbitrary order of a number field $K$, and let $\alpha$ denote some root of an arbitrary monic irreducible degree-$k$ polynomial $f(X) \in \mathcal{O}[X]$. Then we can satisfy the hypotheses of Theorem 3 by letting $K' = K(\alpha)$ and $\mathcal{O}' = \mathcal{O}[\alpha]$, so that $(1, \alpha, \ldots, \alpha^{k-1})$ is an $\mathcal{O}$-basis of $\mathcal{O}'$. (We emphasize that there are no restrictions on the choice of the algebraic integer $\alpha$, other than its degree over $\mathcal{O}$.) Letting, e.g., $\psi' = D_r$ be a spherical Gaussian over $K'_{\mathbb{R}}$ and $\psi = D_{r\sqrt{k}}$ be the corresponding spherical Gaussian over $K_{\mathbb{R}}$, we have an efficient, deterministic reduction from $\mathcal{O}'\text{-LWE}^1_{q,\psi',\ell}$ to $\mathcal{O}\text{-LWE}^k_{q,\psi,\ell}$.

# References

1. Albrecht, M.R., Deo, A.: Large modulus ring-LWE $\geq$ module-LWE. In: Takagi, T., Peyrin, T. (eds.) ASIACRYPT 2017. LNCS, vol. 10624, pp. 267–296. Springer, Cham (2017). https://doi.org/10.1007/978-3-319-70694-8_10
2. Bolboceanu, M., Brakerski, Z., Perlman, R., Sharma, D.: Order-LWE and the hardness of Ring-LWE with entropic secrets. Cryptology ePrint Archive, Report 2018/494 (2018). https://eprint.iacr.org/2018/494
3. Brakerski, Z., Gentry, C., Vaikuntanathan, V.: (Leveled) fully homomorphic encryption without bootstrapping. TOCT **6**(3), 13 (2014). Preliminary version in ITCS 2012
4. Brakerski, Z., Langlois, A., Peikert, C., Regev, O., Stehlé, D.: Classical hardness of learning with errors. In: STOC, pp. 575–584 (2013)
5. Castryck, W., Iliashenko, I., Vercauteren, F.: Provably weak instances of ring-LWE revisited. In: Fischlin, M., Coron, J.-S. (eds.) EUROCRYPT 2016. LNCS, vol. 9665, pp. 147–167. Springer, Heidelberg (2016). https://doi.org/10.1007/978-3-662-49890-3_6
6. Hoffstein, J., Pipher, J., Silverman, J.H.: NTRU: a ring-based public key cryptosystem. In: Buhler, J.P. (ed.) ANTS 1998. LNCS, vol. 1423, pp. 267–288. Springer, Heidelberg (1998). https://doi.org/10.1007/BFb0054868
7. Langlois, A., Stehlé, D.: Worst-case to average-case reductions for module lattices. Des. Codes Crypt. **75**(3), 565–599 (2015)
8. Lyubashevsky, V.: Digital signatures based on the hardness of ideal lattice problems in all rings. In: Cheon, J.H., Takagi, T. (eds.) ASIACRYPT 2016. LNCS, vol. 10032, pp. 196–214. Springer, Heidelberg (2016). https://doi.org/10.1007/978-3-662-53890-6_7
9. Lyubashevsky, V., Peikert, C., Regev, O.: On ideal lattices and learning with errors over rings. J. ACM **60**(6), 43:1–43:35 (2013). Preliminary version in Eurocrypt 2010
10. Micciancio, D.: Generalized compact knapsacks, cyclic lattices, and efficient one-way functions. Comput. Complex. **16**(4), 365–411 (2007). Preliminary version in FOCS 2002
11. Peikert, C.: Public-key cryptosystems from the worst-case shortest vector problem. In: STOC, pp. 333–342 (2009)
12. Peikert, C.: A decade of lattice cryptography. Found. Trends Theor. Comput. Sci. **10**(4), 283–424 (2016)
13. Peikert, C.: How (not) to instantiate ring-LWE. In: Zikas, V., De Prisco, R. (eds.) SCN 2016. LNCS, vol. 9841, pp. 411–430. Springer, Cham (2016). https://doi.org/10.1007/978-3-319-44618-9_22
14. Peikert, C., Regev, O., Stephens-Davidowitz, N.: Pseudorandomness of Ring-LWE for any ring and modulus. In: STOC, pp. 461–473 (2017)

15. Regev, O.: On lattices, learning with errors, random linear codes, and cryptography. J. ACM **56**(6), 1–40 (2009). Preliminary version in STOC 2005
16. Regev, O.: The learning with errors problem (invited survey). In: IEEE Conference on Computational Complexity, pp. 191–204 (2010)
17. Roşca, M., Sakzad, A., Stehlé, D., Steinfeld, R.: Middle-product learning with errors. In: Katz, J., Shacham, H. (eds.) CRYPTO 2017. LNCS, vol. 10403, pp. 283–297. Springer, Cham (2017). https://doi.org/10.1007/978-3-319-63697-9_10
18. Rosca, M., Stehlé, D., Wallet, A.: On the ring-LWE and polynomial-LWE problems. In: Nielsen, J.B., Rijmen, V. (eds.) EUROCRYPT 2018. LNCS, vol. 10820, pp. 146–173. Springer, Cham (2018). https://doi.org/10.1007/978-3-319-78381-9_6
19. Stehlé, D., Steinfeld, R., Tanaka, K., Xagawa, K.: Efficient public key encryption based on ideal lattices. In: Matsui, M. (ed.) ASIACRYPT 2009. LNCS, vol. 5912, pp. 617–635. Springer, Heidelberg (2009). https://doi.org/10.1007/978-3-642-10366-7_36

# Lattice Trapdoors and IBE
# from Middle-Product LWE

Alex Lombardi[1(✉)], Vinod Vaikuntanathan[1], and Thuy Duong Vuong[2]

[1] MIT, Cambridge, MA 02139, USA
alexjl@mit.edu
[2] Stanford University, Stanford, CA 94305, USA

**Abstract.** Middle-product learning with errors (MP-LWE) was recently introduced by Rosca, Sakzad, Steinfeld and Stehlé (CRYPTO 2017) as a way to combine the efficiency of Ring-LWE with the more robust security guarantees of plain LWE. While Ring-LWE is at the heart of *efficient* lattice-based cryptosystems, it involves the choice of an underlying ring which is essentially arbitrary. In other words, the effect of this choice on the security of Ring-LWE is poorly understood. On the other hand, Rosca et al. showed that a new LWE variant, called MP-LWE, is as secure as Polynomial-LWE (another variant of Ring-LWE) *over any of a broad class of number fields*. They also demonstrated the usefulness of MP-LWE by constructing an MP-LWE based public-key encryption scheme whose efficiency is comparable to Ring-LWE based public-key encryption. In this work, we take this line of research further by showing how to construct Identity-Based Encryption (IBE) schemes that are secure under a variant of the MP-LWE assumption. Our IBE schemes match the efficiency of Ring-LWE based IBE, including a scheme in the random oracle model with keys and ciphertexts of size $\tilde{O}(n)$ (for $n$-bit identities).

We construct our IBE scheme following the lattice trapdoors paradigm of [Gentry, Peikert, and Vaikuntanathan, STOC'08]; our main technical contributions are introducing a new leftover hash lemma and instantiating a new variant of lattice trapdoors compatible with MP-LWE.

This work demonstrates that the efficiency/security tradeoff gains of MP-LWE can be extended beyond public-key encryption to more complex lattice-based primitives.

**Keywords:** Middle-product LWE · Identity-Based Encryption · Lattice Trapdoors

## 1 Introduction

Cryptographic schemes based on the polynomial learning with errors problem (PLWE) [23] and the ring learning with errors problem (RLWE) [13] have the

---

Work done while at MIT.

D. Hofheinz and A. Rosen (Eds.): TCC 2019, LNCS 11891, pp. 24–54, 2019.
https://doi.org/10.1007/978-3-030-36030-6_2

advantage of having key size and algorithm runtime that are quasi-linear in the security parameter. However, their security guarantees are not as strong as that of the original learning with errors problem (LWE) [20].

One of the main differences between these two settings is that the PLWE problem parametrized by some (say, irreducible) polynomial $f$, denoted $\text{PLWE}^{(f)}$, is only known to be as hard as a worst-case problem on some class of lattices *that depends on the polynomial* $f$, which could possibly be easier to solve for some choices of $f$ as compared to others. In particular, we do not have a clear understanding of the relative hardness of $\text{PLWE}^{(f)}$ for different $f$, making it hard for a cryptosystem designer to pick the right $f$. In contrast, with the LWE problem, there is no such ambiguity. For essentially any choice of possible modulus $q$, LWE is as hard as worst-case problems on *arbitrary* lattices [17, 20]. In summary, the concrete efficiency gains of RLWE and PLWE have only been obtained through a trade-off involving making both quantitatively and qualitatively more questionable security assumptions.

Recently, following on an earlier work of Lyubashevsky [11] who initiated the study of ring-independent assumptions, Rosca et al. [21] introduced the "middle-product learning with errors" assumption (MP-LWE), a new variant of LWE that uses the "middle product" of polynomials modulo $q$. For any $f$ in a broad class of polynomials, they show a reduction from $\text{PLWE}^{(f)}$ to the MP-LWE problem, which is defined independently of any such $f$, freeing the cryptosystem designer from making an essentially arbitrary choice of $f$. They also describe a public key encryption (PKE) scheme that has quasi-linear (optimal) key size and algorithm runtime, while being IND-CPA secure under the MP-LWE assumption. Thus, they obtain a public-key encryption scheme with the same efficiency gains over LWE-based PKE as enjoyed by PLWE-based schemes, but prove security under a worst-case assumption on a comparatively broader class of lattices.

While the idea of using MP-LWE as an alternative to Ring-LWE, as proposed by [21], is intriguing, it is only currently known how to construct plain public-key encryption from MP-LWE. In this work, we consider and make progress on the following question.

*Can we instantiate more complex lattice-based primitives using middle-product LWE while maintaining the improved efficiency/security tradeoff?*

Indeed, it is explicitly left open by [21] to instantiate more complex lattice-based primitives, such as lattice trapdoors [8] and their applications, using MP-LWE.

## 1.1 Our Results

We construct an Identity-Based Encryption (IBE) scheme based on MP-LWE. This scheme is IND-CPA secure in the random oracle model under the MP-LWE assumption and has quasi-linear key size and algorithm runtime.

Our construction follows the "lattice trapdoors" paradigm of [8]. Specifically, we construct a "dual" of the public key encryption scheme in [21], then combine the dual scheme with Micciancio-Peikert style lattice trapdoors [15] to obtain the IBE scheme. In addition to our IBE scheme in the random oracle model, we sketch how techniques for constructing IBE schemes in the standard model [2,3,7] can also be adapted to the MP-LWE setting using our lattice trapdoors.

Our main IBE construction from MP-LWE can be stated informally as follows.

**Theorem 1 (Informal).** *For any $\epsilon \geq 2^{-\mathsf{poly}(\log n)}$, there is a $(T, \epsilon)$-secure IBE scheme (in the random oracle model) under the $(T', \epsilon')$ MP-LWE assumption with $T' \approx T$, $\epsilon' \approx \epsilon$. This scheme has quasi-linear $\tilde{O}(n)$ key size and encryption runtime.*

By $(T, \epsilon)$-security, we mean that any $T$-time adversary fails to break the primitive/assumption with advantage greater than $\epsilon$. In particular, assuming that MP-LWE is hard for $T(n) = 2^{\alpha n}$-time adversaries, we show that our IBE scheme is hard to break in time roughly $T$ with better than some inverse quasi-polynomial advantage.

Our IBE scheme demonstrates that the better efficiency/security trade-off obtained by [21] for public key encryption can be extended to more expressive cryptographic primitives such as IBE. Tables 1 and 2 compare the efficiency of our PKE and IBE schemes to prior works.

**Table 1.** Summary of parameters of our "dual Regev"-like public encryption scheme from MP-LWE versus prior ones.

| PKE scheme | LWE based [19] | RLWE based [13] | MP-LWE based ("primal"-[21], "dual"-this work) |
|---|---|---|---|
| pk size | $\tilde{O}(n^2)$ | $\tilde{O}(n)$ | $\tilde{O}(n)$ |
| sk size | $\tilde{O}(n)$ | $\tilde{O}(n)$ | $\tilde{O}(n)$ |
| Enc/Dec runtime per encrypted bit | $\tilde{O}(n)$-amortized | $\tilde{O}(1)$ | $\tilde{O}(1)$ |

### 1.2 Technical Overview

As mentioned before, we follow the "lattice trapdoors" paradigm of [8]. We first recall the approach of [8] for constructing IBE from LWE. The high-level idea is as follows: using a random oracle $H$, design a key pair (distribution) $(\mathsf{mpk}, \mathsf{msk})$ such that for any identity id, $\mathsf{pk_{id}} := (\mathsf{mpk}, H(\mathsf{id}))$ is a valid public key for some public key encryption scheme PKE. In order for this to yield an IBE scheme, it must be possible to derive a corresponding secret key $\mathsf{sk_{id}}$, using msk, from the public value $H(\mathsf{id})$. This is achieved in the following way.

**Table 2.** Summary of parameters of our identity-based encryption (IBE) scheme from MP-LWE versus prior ones that are from LWE and Ring-LWE.

| IBE scheme | LWE based [8, 15] | RLWE based [15] | MP-LWE based (this work) |
|---|---|---|---|
| mpk size | $\tilde{O}(n^2)$ | $\tilde{O}(n)$ | $\tilde{O}(n)$ |
| msk size | $\tilde{O}(n^2)$ | $\tilde{O}(n)$ | $\tilde{O}(n)$ |
| Enc/Dec runtime per encrypted bit | $\tilde{O}(n)$-amortized | $\tilde{O}(1)$ | $\tilde{O}(1)$ |

- **Step 1: Dual Regev Encryption.** First, [8] constructs a "dual" variant of Regev encryption [20] in which public keys are (statistically close to) uniformly random. In slightly more detail, public keys have the form $(A, u = Ar)$ for $A \xleftarrow{\$} \mathbb{Z}_q^{n \times m}$ and $r \xleftarrow{\$} \chi^m$ for some distribution $\chi$ of "small numbers." This step is done so that in an associated IBE scheme, $u = H(\text{id})$ can be interpreted as (part of) a dual Regev public key.
- **Step 2: Lattice Trapdoors.** The most technically complicated step in [8] is designing an alternative procedure TrapGen that outputs a (statistically close to) uniformly random matrix $A$ along with a *trapdoor* $T_A$ that allows for sampling, given an input $u \in \mathbb{Z}_q^n$, a random preimage $r \leftarrow \chi^m \mid Ar = u$. This step allows for efficient secret key extraction from a public key $(A, u)$.
- **Step 3: Constructing IBE.** As has been implicitly described already, [8] then write down an IBE scheme with a master key pair $(A, T_A)$ sampled using TrapGen, so that encryption for an identity id uses dual Regev encryption with public key $(A, u = H(\text{id}))$, and secret keys $\text{sk}_{\text{id}} = r$ can be extracted from $(A, u = H(\text{id}))$ using $\text{msk} = T_A$.

We now describe how we instantiate this framework using middle-product LWE.

*Step 1: MP-LWE Based Dual Regev.* Our first step is to develop an analogue of dual Regev encryption based on middle-product LWE. We first recall from [21] that the middle-product learning with errors assumption over $\mathbb{Z}_q$ with degrees $(n, d)$ is that the distribution

$$\{(a_i, a_i \odot_d s + e_i)_{i=1}^t\}$$

is computationally pseudorandom, where $s$ is a uniformly random degree $n$ polynomial,[1] each $a_i$ is a uniformly random degree $n - d$ polynomial, each $e_i$ is a random "small" degree $d$ polynomial, and $a_i \odot_d s$ is the "middle product" consisting of the $d$ "middle terms" of the polynomial product $a \cdot s$. [21] show that this assumption suffices to construct a "primal Regev" public key encryption scheme, and show that this assumption follows from the hardness of $\text{PLWE}^{(f)}$ for various polynomials $f$.

---

[1] The parameters are slightly simplified for exposition.

We would like to develop a "dual Regev" public-key encryption scheme similar to the PKE of [21], and a natural approach suggests itself (based on [21]): Let $a_1, \ldots, a_t$ be $t$ i.i.d. degree $n$ polynomials, let $r_1, \ldots, r_t$ be $t$ i.i.d. degree $k$ polynomials (for some additional parameter $k$), and set

$$\left( \mathsf{pk} = (a_1, \ldots, a_t, u = \sum a_i r_i), \mathsf{sk} = (r_1, \ldots, r_t) \right).$$

Encrypting a message $\mu$ then consists of sampling a random MP-LWE secret $s$ and outputting middle products[2] $(a_i \odot s, +2e_i)_{i \leq t}$ along with $u \odot s + 2e' + \mu$. We would then like to argue, as in [21], that the security of this scheme follows from MP-LWE (with secret $s$).

*Technical Challenges.* However, there are two main issues that arise from this approach to Step 1 (which both arise again when implementing Step 2):

- We need a new variant of the leftover hash lemma to argue that the polynomial $u = \sum a_i r_i$ is (statistically close to) uniformly random. The reason that previous leftover hash lemma variants seem insufficient is related to the fact that the map $r \mapsto \sum_i a_i r_i$ has a larger range (degree $n + k$ polynomials) than its domain (degree $k$ polynomials); this stands in contrast to the PLWE setting, where $r \mapsto \sum a_i r_i \pmod{f}$ is reduced modulo a degree $n$ polynomial $f$. Indeed, the hash function $h_{a_1, \ldots, a_t}(r_1, \ldots, r_t) = \sum a_i r_i$ is *not* 2-universal, unlike the hash function considered in [21], so we have to argue the desired statistical indistinguishability directly. We state and prove our new variant of the LHL in Sect. 4. We use techniques from [14] designed to prove a variant of the LHL in the *Ring-LWE* setting; however, these techniques must be substantially modified to handle the distinction between multiplication of bounded-degree polynomials in $\mathbb{Z}_q[x]$ (as in our setting) and multiplication over rings of the form $R_q = \mathbb{Z}_q[x]/f(x)$ (as in the RLWE/PLWE setting).
- Middle-product LWE as defined in [21] does not seem directly applicable to (the security of) our dual-Regev encryption scheme; the reason is that the "coefficient polynomials" $(a_1, \ldots, a_t, u)$ do not all have the same degree.[3] In order to prove security, we have to consider a new variant of MP-LWE in which "coefficient polynomials" $\{a_i\}$ can have different degrees; we consider a variant in which the adversary can specify a new degree $d_i$ for each sample in advance. In Sect. 3, we show that (a simple modification of) the [21] reduction from PLWE to MP-LWE carries over to our variant of MP-LWE, which we call "degree-parametrized MP-LWE."

After addressing these two difficulties, the approach outlined in Step 1 can be made to work, yielding a dual-Regev encryption scheme based on MP-LWE.

---

[2] We omit some details regarding degrees; it turns out that the middle products $a_i \odot s$ will have a different degree from the middle product $u \odot s$ in order to get decryption correctness.

[3] In fact, after introducing lattice trapdoors, our scheme will be modified so that *three* different degrees will be used rather than two (as it is currently written).

*Step 2: Lattice Trapdoors for MP-LWE.* Having developed a variant of dual Regev encryption, we next turn to constructing lattice trapdoors [8] that are compatible with this new encryption scheme. To do so, we make use of the work [15], which gives a highly general roadmap for constructing lattice trapdoors.

Following the basic idea of [15], our procedure TrapGen will produce polynomials $a_1, \ldots, a_t, a_{t+1}, \ldots, a_{t'}$ such that for $t < i \leq t'$,

$$a_i = c_i - \sum_{j=1}^{t} a_j w_{ij}$$

for random, small "trapdoor" polynomials $\{w_{ij}\}$ and specific polynomials $\{c_j = 2^u x^{dv}\}$ which are our analogue to the "$G$ matrix" in plain LWE-based constructions. Similarly to the Ring-LWE setting, we can think of these polynomials as "structured matrices" by associating a polynomial $g(x)$ with the "multiplication by $g(x)$" matrix acting on a vector space of bounded-degree polynomials. We show that with this choice of polynomials $\{c_j\}$, the matrix $A$ corresponding to $(a_1, \ldots, a_{t'})$ has a "$G$-trapdoor" (as defined in [15]) that can be efficiently described using our trapdoor $\{w_{ij}\}$. The preimage sampling algorithm of [15] can then be adapted to yield a corresponding preimage sampling algorithm for polynomial sum-products; moreover, we show that our preimage sampling algorithm has the same $\tilde{O}(n)$ efficiency gain over plain LWE that is enjoyed by Ring-LWE based constructions. See Sect. 5 for more details.

Finally, we note that we are implicitly relying on resolutions to both "technical challenges" mentioned above in this step; our leftover hash lemma is what guarantees that TrapGen outputs a distribution $\{(a_1, \ldots, a_{t'})\}$ that is statistically close to uniform, while our "degree-parametrized MP-LWE" allows us to redesign our dual Regev scheme to have public key $(a_1, \ldots, a_{t'}, u)$ such that $\{a_1, \ldots, a_t\}$ and $\{a_{t+1}, \ldots, a_{t'}\}$ have different degrees.

*Step 3: Constructing IBE Schemes.* Given our variant of dual Regev encryption from MP-LWE (Step 1) and our variant of lattice trapdoors compatible with this new encryption scheme (Step 2), constructing IBE is fairly straightforward given prior work. We describe constructions analogous to those of [8] (in the random oracle model) and [3] (in the standard model) using our new tools.

*Remark On Concrete Efficiency/Security.* As usual, some care is required when comparing the efficiency of various LWE-based cryptosystems to take into account their expected levels of security. We give an overview of the comparison of LWE/RLWE/MPLWE-based IBE schemes using concrete security [5].

The concrete security of all relevant lattice-based cryptosystems is based on assumptions of the following form.

**Definition 1 (($T, \epsilon$)-secure $X$-LWE, Informal).** *Any time $T$ adversary breaks the $X$-LWE assumption with advantage at most $\epsilon$.*

Our main IBE construction from MP-LWE (as stated in Theorem 1) constructs $(T, \epsilon)$-secure IBE from roughly $(T, \epsilon)$-secure LWE, *as long as $\epsilon \geq 2^{-\text{poly} \log n}$.*

This technical limitation is due to the achievable parameters of our leftover hash lemma (which was already implicitly noted in [21]) when used in a standard hybrid argument to prove security of the IBE scheme. This barrier also appears in the Ring-LWE context (see, e.g., the signature scheme of [15]) when quasi-linear efficiency is desired. However, these works (and ours) still attain a meaningful form of concrete security because security is proved against adversaries that run in exponential time (assuming that the LWE variants are exponentially secure).

In addition, with some more work, it is possible to improve Theorem 1 to hold for smaller values of $\epsilon$ (without sacrificing efficiency). This improved security proof is based on the use of Renyi divergence (as opposed to statistical distance), as demonstrated in [4], and will appear in the full version of this paper.

### 1.3 Organization

The rest of the paper is organized as follows. In Sect. 2, we review basic definitions and other preliminaries. In Sect. 3, we introduce and prove the hardness of our "degree-parametrized MP-LWE," a slight variant on the original definition. In Sect. 4, we prove our new leftover hash lemma for bounded degree polynomials. In Sect. 5, we use our new LHL in combination with [15] to develop lattice trapdoors for middle-product LWE. Finally, in Sect. 6, we combine our new tools to construct MP-LWE based dual Regev public-key encryption and IBE.

## 2    Preliminaries

*Negligible Functions.* We use $n$ to denote the security parameter. We use standard big-O notation to classify the growth of functions, and say that $f(n) = \tilde{O}(g(n))$ if $f(n) = O(g(n) \cdot \log^c n)$ for some fixed constant c. We let poly$(n)$ denote an unspecified function $f(n) = O(n^c)$ for some constant c. We say that a function $f(n)$ is negligible (denoted $f(n) = \mathsf{negl}(n)$) if $f(n) = o(n^{-c})$ for every fixed constant c. We say that a probability (or fraction) is overwhelming if it is $1 - \mathsf{negl}(n)$.

*Statistical and Computational Indistinguishability.* The statistical distance between two distributions $X$ and $Y$ over a countable domain $\Omega$ is defined to be $\Delta(X, Y) := \frac{1}{2} \cdot \sum_{d \in \Omega} |X(d) - Y(d)|$. We say that two distributions $X, Y$ (formally, two ensembles of distributions indexed by $n$) are statistically indistinguishable if $\Delta(X, Y) = \mathsf{negl}(n)$, and write $X \approx_s Y$.

Two ensembles of distributions $\{X_n\}$ and $\{Y_n\}$ are computationally indistinguishable if for every probabilistic poly-time machine $A$, $|\Pr[A(1^n, X_n) = 1] - \Pr[A(1^n, Y_n) = 1]| = \mathsf{negl}(n)$; we denote this relationship by $X \approx_c Y$.

*Polynomials.* Let $R$ be a ring. For any integer $d > 0$ and any set $S \subseteq R$, we let $S^{<d}[x]$ denote the set of polynomials in $R[x]$ of degree $< d$ whose coefficients are in $S$. For any distribution $\chi$ defined over $R$, let $\chi^d[x]$ denote the distribution on polynomials in $R^{<d}[x]$ where each coefficient is sampled independently according to $\chi$.

Given a polynomial $a = \sum_{j=0}^{d-1} a_i x^i \in R^{<d}[x]$, define the coefficient vector of $a$ as $\mathbf{a} := (a_0, \cdots, a_{d-1})^T \in R^d$. In particular, for any $0 \leq i \leq d-1$, $\mathbf{a}_i$ denotes the coefficient of $x^i$ in $a$.

*Probability.* For any distribution $X$ defined on a countable domain $\Omega$, we define the *collision probability*

$$\mathrm{CP}(X) := \Pr_{X,X' \text{ i.i.d.}}[X = X']$$

as well as the *Renyi entropy* of $X$,

$$H_2(X) := \log_2 \frac{1}{\mathrm{CP}(X)},$$

and the *min-entropy* of $X$,

$$H_\infty(X) := \log_2 \min_{x \in \Omega} \frac{1}{\Pr[X = x]}.$$

We remark that $H_2(X) \geq H_\infty(X)$ for all distributions $X$. For a finite set $\Omega$, we let $U(\Omega)$ denote the uniform distribution over $\Omega$, and we use the notation $X \xleftarrow{\$} \Omega$ to denote that $X$ is sampled uniformly at random from $\Omega$. For a distribution $\chi$ over $\mathbb{R}$, let $\chi^k$ denote the distribution over $\mathbb{R}^k$ where each coordinate is independently sampled from $\chi$. For a distribution $D$ over $\mathbb{R}^k$, let $D[x]$ be the distribution over $\mathbb{R}^{<k}[x]$ where the coefficient vector of polynomials is sampled from $D$.

## 2.1 Identity-Based Encryption

We recall the standard syntax and definition of security under chosen-plaintext and chosen-identity attack [1,6] for IBE. An IBE scheme consists of four algorithms.

- A setup algorithm IBESetup (on input $1^n$) outputs a master public key mpk and master secret key msk.
- A secret key extraction algorithm IBEExtract, given msk and an identity id, outputs a secret key $sk_{id}$.
- An encryption algorithm Enc, given the master public key mpk, an identity id, and a message $m$, outputs a ciphertext $c$.
- A decryption algorithm Dec, given the secret key sk and a ciphertext $c$, outputs a message $m$.

We require that an IBE scheme IBE = (IBESetup, IBEExtract, Enc, Dec) satisfies two properties.

- **Correctness:** For all identities id and messages $m$, we have

$$\Pr[\mathsf{Dec}(\mathsf{sk_{id}}, \mathsf{Enc}(\mathsf{mpk}, \mathsf{id}, m)) = m] = 1 - \mathsf{negl}(n),$$

where the probability is taken with respect to the randomness of IBESetup, IBEExtract, Enc, and Dec.
- **Security:** Security is defined by the following game (defined for a given PPT adversary $\mathcal{A}$).
  - $(\mathsf{mpk}, \mathsf{msk}) \leftarrow \mathsf{IBESetup}(1^n)$ is sampled. Define a (randomized) oracle $\mathcal{O}(\cdot)$ that on input id outputs $\mathsf{IBEExtract}(\mathsf{msk}, \mathsf{id})$.
  - $\mathcal{A}^{\mathcal{O}(\cdot)}(\mathsf{mpk})$ outputs a challenge $(\mathsf{id}^*, m_0, m_1)$.
  - $b \leftarrow U(\{0, 1\})$ is sampled uniformly at random.
  - $\mathsf{ct}^* \leftarrow \mathsf{Enc}(\mathsf{mpk}, \mathsf{id}^*, m_b)$ is sampled.
  - $\mathcal{A}^{\mathcal{O}(\cdot)}(\mathsf{ct}^*)$ outputs a bit $b'$ and wins if (1) $\mathcal{O}(\mathsf{id}^*)$ was not queried and (2) $b' = b$.

We say that the scheme is secure if every PPT adversary $\mathcal{A}$ wins the above game with probability at most $\frac{1}{2} + \mathsf{negl}(n)$

### 2.2   Middle Product of Polynomials [21]

**Definition 2** ([21], **Definition 3.1**). *Let $d_a, d_b, d, k$ be integers such that $d_a + d_b - 1 = d + 2k$. The middle product $\odot_d : R^{<d_a}[x] \times R^{<d_b}[x] \to R^{<d}[x]$ is defined to be the map*

$$(a, b) \mapsto a \odot_d b = \left\lfloor \frac{(a \cdot b) \mod x^{k+d}}{x^k} \right\rfloor = \sum_{k \leq i+j \leq k+d-1} (a_i b_j) x^{i+j},$$

*where $\boldsymbol{a}$ and $\boldsymbol{b}$ are the coefficient vectors of $a$ and $b$, respectively. In other words, $a \odot_d b$ is obtained by deleting the $k$ highest and $k$ lowest degree terms of the polynomial product $a \cdot b$, then dividing the remaining $d$ terms by $x^k$.*

Immediately from Definition 2, the middle product is commutative, i.e., $a \odot_d b = b \odot_d a$ for all polynomials $a, b$. The middle product also satisfies a "quasi-associative" property.

**Lemma 1** ([21]). *Let $d, k, n > 0$. For all $r \in R^{<k+1}[x], a \in R^{<n}[x], s \in R^{<n+d+k-1}[x]$, we have*

$$r \odot_d (a \odot_{d+k} s) = (r \cdot a) \odot_d s.$$

### 2.3   Lattices

An $n$-dimensional lattice $\Lambda$ is a discrete additive subgroup of $\mathbb{R}^n$. A lattice has rank $k \leq m$ if it is generated as the set of all $\mathbb{Z}$-linear combinations of some $k$ linearly independent *basis* vectors $\mathbf{B} = (\mathbf{b}_1, \cdots, \mathbf{b}_k)$; we say $\Lambda$ is full-rank if $k = m$. The dual lattice $\Lambda^*$ is the set of all $v \in \mathrm{Span}_{\mathbb{R}}(\Lambda)$ such that $\langle v, x \rangle \in \mathbb{Z}$

for every $x \in \Lambda$. If $\mathbf{B}$ is a basis of $\Lambda$, then $\mathbf{B}^* = B(B^t B)^{-1}$ is a basis of $\Lambda^*$. Note that when $\Lambda$ is full-rank, $\mathbf{B}$ is invertible and hence $\mathbf{B}^* = \mathbf{B}^{-1}$.

For any set $\mathbf{S} = (s_1, \cdots, s_k)$ of linearly independent vectors, let $\tilde{\mathbf{S}}$ denote its Gram-Schmidt orthogonalization, defined iteratively in the following way: $\tilde{s}_1 = s_1$, and for each $i = 2, \cdots, n$, $\tilde{s}_i$ is the component of $s_i$ orthogonal to span $(s_1, \cdots, s_{i-1})$.

For positive integers $n, q$ and any matrix $A \in \mathbb{Z}_q^{n \times m}$, let $\Lambda^{\perp}(A) := \{z \in \mathbb{Z}^m : Az = 0 \mod q\}$. For $u \in \mathbb{Z}_q^n$ such that $\exists t \in \mathbb{Z}_q^m$ satisfying $At = u$, let $\Lambda_u^{\perp}(A) := \{z \in \mathbb{Z}^m : Az = u \mod q\} = \Lambda^{\perp}(A) + t$.

## Gaussian Distributions

**Definition 3 (Continuous Gaussian distribution).** *For a positive semidefinite matrix $\Sigma \in \mathbb{R}^{n \times n}$, the continuous Gaussian distribution $D_\Sigma$ is the probability distribution over $\mathbb{R}^n$ whose density is proportional to $\rho_\Sigma(x) = \exp(-\pi x^T \Sigma^{-1} x)$.*

**Definition 4 (Discrete Gaussian distribution).** *Given countable set $S \subset \mathbb{R}^n$ and $s > 0$, the discrete Gaussian distribution $D_{S,\sigma,c}$ is the probability distribution over $S$ whose density is proportional to $\rho_{\sigma,c}(x) := \exp(-\pi \cdot ||x - c||^2 / \sigma^2)$. That is, for $x \in S : D_{S,\sigma,c} = \frac{\rho_{\sigma,c}(x)}{\rho_{\sigma,c}(S)}$. If $c = 0$, we can omit $c$ and write $D_{S,\sigma}$ instead.*

As usual, we will make use of various statistical properties of the discrete Gaussian $D_{\Lambda,\sigma}$ when $\sigma$ is large compared to the *smoothing parameter* of the lattice $\Lambda$, defined below.

**Definition 5 ([16]).** *For any $n$-dimensional lattice $\Lambda$ and real $\epsilon > 0$, the smoothing parameter $\eta_\epsilon(\Lambda)$ is defined to be the smallest real $s > 0$ such that $\rho_{1/s}(\Lambda^* \setminus \{0\}) \le \epsilon$.*

The following lemma gives an upper bound on the smoothing parameter of $\Lambda$ in terms of its Gram-Schmidt basis $\tilde{B}$.

**Lemma 2 ([8], Theorem 3.1).** *Let $\Lambda \subset \mathbb{R}^n$ be a lattice with basis $\mathbf{B}$ and real $\epsilon > 0$. Then,*

$$\eta_\epsilon(\Lambda) \le ||\tilde{\mathbf{B}}|| \cdot \sqrt{\ln(2n(1 + \epsilon^{-1}))/\pi}.$$

*where $\tilde{\mathbf{B}} = (\tilde{b}_1, \cdots, \tilde{b}_k)$ is the Gram-Schmidt orthogonalization of $\mathbf{B}$ as defined in Sect. 2.3, and $||\tilde{\mathbf{B}}|| = \max_{i \in [k]} ||\tilde{b}_i||$.*

We will make use of tail bounds on $D_{\Lambda,\sigma}$ (for $\sigma$ larger than the smoothing parameter).

**Lemma 3 ([8], Lemma 2.9).** *For any $\epsilon > 0$, any $\sigma \ge \eta_\epsilon(\mathbb{Z})$, and any $t > 0$, we have*

$$\Pr_{x \leftarrow D_{\mathbb{Z},\sigma,c}} [|x - c| \ge t \cdot \sigma] \le 2e^{-\pi t^2} \cdot \frac{1 + \epsilon}{1 - \epsilon}.$$

*In particular, for $\epsilon \in (0, 1/2)$ and $t \ge \omega(\sqrt{\log n})$, the probability that $|x - c| \ge t \cdot \sigma$ is negligible in $n$.*

In addition, we will make use of *entropy* bounds on $D_{\Lambda,\sigma}$ (again for $\sigma$ sufficiently large). In order to prove these bounds, we first recall the following approximation.

**Lemma 4** ([18], **Lemma 2.10**).   *Let $\Lambda \subset \mathbb{R}^d$ be a full-rank lattice. For any $s \geq \eta_\epsilon(\Lambda)$, we have*

$$s^d \det(\Lambda^*) \cdot (1 - \epsilon) \leq \rho_s(\Lambda) \leq s^d \det(\Lambda^*) \cdot (1 + \epsilon).$$

Using Lemma 4, we can bound $H_\infty(D_{\Lambda,\sigma})$ and $H_2(D_{\Lambda,\sigma})$.

**Lemma 5.** *For a full-rank lattice $\Lambda \subset \mathbb{R}^d$ and discrete Gaussian distribution $\chi = D_{\Lambda,\sigma}$ with parameters $\epsilon \in (0,1), \delta \in (0,1)$, and $\sigma \geq \max(\sqrt{2}, \delta^{-1}) \cdot \eta_\epsilon(\Lambda)$, we have*

$$2^{-H_\infty(\chi)} \leq \delta^d \frac{1 + \epsilon}{1 - \epsilon}$$

*and*

$$\mathrm{CP}(\chi) \leq \left(\frac{\delta}{\sqrt{2}}\right)^d (\frac{1 + \epsilon}{1 - \epsilon})^2.$$

*Proof.* Using Lemma 4, we obtain the bound

$$D_{\Lambda,\sigma}(\mathbf{x}) \leq \frac{1}{\sigma^d \det(\Lambda^*) \cdot (1 - \epsilon)}$$

for all $\mathbf{x} \in \Lambda$. Moreover, we assumed that $\sigma\delta \geq \eta_\epsilon(\Lambda)$, so by Lemma 4 we also have

$$1 \leq \rho_{\sigma\delta}(\Lambda) \leq (\sigma\delta)^d \det(\Lambda^*) \cdot (1 + \epsilon).$$

Combining this with the first inequality, we see that

$$D_{\Lambda,\sigma}(\mathbf{x}) \leq \delta^d \frac{1 + \epsilon}{1 - \epsilon},$$

yielding the desired bound on $2^{-H_\infty(\chi)}$. In order to bound $\mathrm{CP}(\chi)$, we write

$$\mathrm{CP}(\chi) = \sum_{x \in \Lambda} D_{\Lambda,\sigma}(x)^2 = \rho_\sigma(\Lambda)^{-2} \sum_{x \in \Lambda} \rho_\sigma(x)^2 = \rho_\sigma(\Lambda)^{-2} \cdot \rho_{\sigma/\sqrt{2}}(\Lambda),$$

where the last equality uses the identity $\rho_\sigma(x)^2 = \rho_{\sigma/\sqrt{2}}(x)$. Since we assumed that $\sigma > \delta\sigma \geq \eta_\epsilon(\Lambda)$, Lemma 4 (applied three times, to parameters $\sigma$, $\frac{\sigma}{\sqrt{2}}$ and $\sigma\delta$) tells us that

$$\rho_\sigma(\Lambda)^{-2} \rho_{\sigma/\sqrt{2}}(\Lambda) \leq \frac{(\sigma/\sqrt{2})^d \det(\Lambda^*)(1 + \epsilon)}{\sigma^{2d} \det^2(\Lambda^*)(1 - \epsilon)^2}$$

$$= \left(\frac{\delta}{\sqrt{2}}\right)^d \left(\frac{1 + \epsilon}{1 - \epsilon}\right)^2 \frac{1}{(\sigma\delta)^d \det(\Lambda^*)(1 + \epsilon)}$$

$$\leq \left(\frac{\delta}{\sqrt{2}}\right)^d (\frac{1 + \epsilon}{1 - \epsilon})^2,$$

completing the proof.   □

## 2.4   Polynomials and Matrices

For a vector $\mathbf{v} \in \mathbb{R}^n$, let $||v||, ||v||_\infty$ denote the Euclidean and sup norm respectively. We define the largest singular value of a matrix $A \in \mathbb{R}^{m \times n}$ as $\sigma_1(A) := \max_{||u||=1} ||Au||$.

**Lemma 6.** *For any matrix $A \in \mathbb{R}^{m \times n}$, we have $\sigma_1(A) \le \sqrt{mn} \max_{i,j} |A_{ij}|$.*

We will make use of the following matrix representation of polynomial multiplication.

**Definition 6.** *Let $R$ be a ring and $d, k, > 0$ be positive integers. For any polynomial $a \in R^{<k}[x]$ of degree less than $k$, let $T^{k,d}(a)$ denote the matrix in $R^{(k+d-1) \times d}$ whose $i$-th column, for $i = 1, \cdots, d$, is given by the coefficients of $x^{i-1} \cdot a$, listed from lowest to highest degree. In particular, $T^{k,1}(a)$ is the coefficient vector $\mathbf{a}$ of the polynomial $a$ (possibly with zeros appended).*

**Lemma 7.** *For $\ell, k, d > 0, a \in R^{<k}[x], b \in R^{<\ell}[x]$, $T^{k,\ell+d-1}(a) \cdot T^{\ell,d}(b) = T^{\ell+k-1,d}(a \cdot b)$.*

**Definition 7** ([21], from[12]). *Let $f \in \mathbb{Z}[x]$ have degree $m$. The expansion factor of $f$ is defined as*

$$\mathrm{EF}(f) := \max_{g \in \mathbb{Z}^{<2m-1}[x]} \frac{||g \mod f||_\infty}{||g||_\infty}.$$

For our purposes, we are interested in polynomials with $\mathrm{poly}(n)$-bounded expansion factors. One such class [12] is the family of all $f = x^m + h$ where $\deg(h) \le m/2$ and $||h||_\infty \le \mathrm{poly}(n)$.

**Definition 8.** *Let $f$ be a monic polynomial over a ring $R$ of degree $m$. Define the (Hankel) matrix $\mathbf{M}_f \in R^{m \times m}$ such that for $1 \le i, j \le m$, $(\mathbf{M}_f)_{i,j}$ is the constant coefficient of $x^{i+j-2} \mod f$.*

Under suitable conditions on $f$, the matrix $\mathbf{M}_f$ is guaranteed to be invertible.

**Lemma 8.** *If $f \in R[x]$ has constant coefficient $f_0$ which is invertible in $R$, then $\mathbf{M}_f$ is an invertible matrix.*

*Proof.* Rearranging the columns of $\mathbf{M}_f$ gives a triangular matrix whose diagonal is the constant coefficient of $f$.                                               □

Moreover, when $f \in \mathbb{Z}[x]$, we will make use of singular value bounds on $\mathbf{M}_f$ and related matrices in terms of the expansion factor of $f$. For a matrix $A \in \mathbb{R}^{m \times n}$ let $A^{(d)}$ denote the matrix whose rows are the first $d$ rows of $A$.

**Lemma 9.** *For any $f \in \mathbb{Z}[x]$, $\sigma_1(\mathbf{M}_f^{(d)}) \le \sqrt{d} \, \mathrm{EF}(f)$.*

*Remark 1.* This inequality generalizes and improves on [21, Theorem 2.8] by a factor of $\sqrt{d}$.

*Proof.* We want to show that for all nonzero vectors $u \in \mathbb{R}^m$, the following inequality holds:

$$\frac{||\mathbf{M}_f^{(d)} u||}{||u||} \leq \sqrt{d}\, \mathrm{EF}(f).$$

We first note that because $\mathbb{Q}$ is dense in $\mathbb{R}$, it suffices to show the same inequality for all nonzero $u \in \mathbb{Q}^n$. Moreover, since the inequality is scale-invariant, we may further reduce to the case where $u \in \mathbb{Z}^m$.

Given any nonzero vector $u \in \mathbb{Z}^m$, we define $v := \mathbf{M}_f u$. Then, letting $g \in \mathbb{R}^{<m}[x]$ denote the degree $< m$ polynomial with coefficient vector $u$, we know by [21, Lemma 2.4] that $v_i$ is the constant coefficient of $x^{i-1} \cdot g \bmod f$. Thus,

$$|v_i| \leq ||g \cdot x^{i-1} \bmod f||_\infty \leq \mathrm{EF}(f)||x^{i-1} \cdot g||_\infty = \mathrm{EF}(f)||u||_\infty.$$

We conclude that

$$\frac{||\mathbf{M}_f^{(d)} u||}{||u||} \leq \sqrt{d}\frac{||u||_\infty}{||u||}\, \mathrm{EF}(f) \leq \sqrt{d}\, \mathrm{EF}(f),$$

where the last inequality holds because $||u||_\infty \leq ||u||$. $\qquad\square$

# 3   Degree-Parametrized MP-LWE

In this section, we define and consider a variant of MP-LWE in which samples generated from a fixed secret $s$ (which are polynomials with coefficients in $\mathbb{Z}_q$) can have varying (pre-specified) degrees. This is in contrast to the variant considered in [21], in which all samples have the same degree. We then prove a hardness reduction relating polynomial LWE (PLWE) to our variant of MP-LWE, which we call *degree-parametrized* MP-LWE.

For the rest of the paper, we will let $\mathbb{R}_q$ denote $\mathbb{R}/q\mathbb{Z}$.

**Definition 9 (Degree-Parametrized MP-LWE).** *Let $n > 0, q \geq 2, m > 0, \mathbf{d} \in [\frac{n}{2}]^t$, and let $\chi$ be a distribution over $\mathbb{R}_q$. For $s \in \mathbb{Z}_q^{<n-1}[x]$, we define the distribution $\mathrm{MP}_{q,n,d,\chi}(s)$ over $\prod_{i=1}^t (\mathbb{Z}_q^{<n-d_i}[x] \times \mathbb{R}_q^{<d_i}[x])$ as follows.*

- *For each $i \in [t]$, sample $a_i \xleftarrow{\$} \mathbb{Z}_q^{<n-d_i}[x])$ and sample $e_i \leftarrow \chi^{d_i}$ (interpreted as a degree $< d_i$ polynomial).*
- *Output $(a_i, b_i := a_i \odot_{d_i} s + e_i)_{i \in [t]}$.*

*The (degree-parametrized) MP-LWE problem consists of distinguishing between arbitrarily many samples from $\mathrm{MP}_{q,n,d,\chi}(s)$ and the same number of samples from $\prod_{i=1}^t U(\mathbb{Z}_q^{<n-d_i}[x] \times \mathbb{R}_q^{<d_i}[x])$ with non-negligible probability over the choice of $s \xleftarrow{\$} \mathbb{Z}_q^{<n-1}[x]$.*

Following [21], we show that degree-parametrized MP-LWE is as hard as the polynomial-LWE problem $\mathrm{PLWE}_f$ for a wide class of polynomials $f$. The reduction is effectively the same as that of [21], although we obtain better parameters due to an improved singular value bound on the matrix $\mathbf{M}_f$ (Lemma 6). We recall the definition of $\mathrm{PLWE}_f$, taken from [21].

**Definition 10 (PLWE).** *Let $q \geq 2, m > 0$, $f$ a polynomial of degree $m$, $\chi$ a distribution over $\mathbb{R}[x]/f$. The decision problem $\mathsf{PLWE}_{q,\chi}^{(f)}$ consists in distinguishing between arbitrarily many samples*

$$\{a \xleftarrow{\$} \mathbb{Z}_q[x]/f, e \leftarrow \chi : (a, a \cdot s + e)\}$$

*and the same number of samples from $U(\mathbb{Z}_q[x]/f \times \mathbb{R}_q[x]/f)$ with non-negligible probability over choice of $s \xleftarrow{\$} \mathbb{Z}_q[x]/f$.*

**Theorem 2 (Hardness of MP-LWE).** *Let $n > 0, q \geq 2, t > 0, \boldsymbol{d} \in [\frac{n}{2}]^t$, and $\alpha \in (0,1)$. For $S > 0$, let $\mathcal{F}(S, \boldsymbol{d}, n)$ be the set of polynomials in $\mathbb{Z}[x]$ that are monic, have constant coefficient coprime with $q$, have degree $m$ in $\bigcap_{i=1}^{t}[d_i, n-d_i]$ and satisfy $\mathrm{EF}(f) < S$. Then, there exists a ppt reduction from $\mathsf{PLWE}_{D_{\alpha \cdot q}}^{(f)}$ for any $f \in \mathcal{F}(S, \boldsymbol{d}, n)$ to $\mathsf{MPLWE}_{q,n,d,D_{\alpha' \cdot q}}$ with $\alpha' = \alpha \cdot \sqrt{\frac{n}{2}} \cdot S$.*

*Proof.* For $d \in [n/2]$ and any polynomial $f$ of degree $m \in [d, n-d]$, we describe a ppt mapping

$$\phi_{n,d} : (a, b) \in \mathbb{Z}_q[x]/f \times \mathbb{R}_q[x]/f \mapsto (a', b') \in \mathbb{Z}_q^{<n-d}[x] \times \mathbb{R}_q^{<d}[x].$$

We will then show that $\phi$ maps $U(\mathbb{Z}_q[x]/f \times \mathbb{Z}_q[x]/f)$ to $U(\mathbb{Z}_q^{<n-d}[x] \times \mathbb{Z}_q^{<d}[x])$ and maps a random PLWE sample (with secret $s$) to a random MP-LWE sample with secret $s'$ depending on $s$. This mapping (with slightly different parameters) was previously defined in [21].

Let $(a, b) \in \mathbb{Z}_q[x]/f \times \mathbb{R}_q[x]/f$ be an input pair. Then, the pair $(a', b') \leftarrow \phi_{n,d}(a, b)$ is sampled by the following process.

- Define the matrix $\Sigma = (\alpha' q)^2 \mathbf{I}_d - (\alpha q)^2 \mathbf{J}_d \cdot \mathbf{M}_f^{(d)}$, where $\mathbf{I}_d$ denotes the $d \times d$ identity matrix and $\mathbf{J}_d$ denotes the $d \times d$ anti-diagonal matrix.
- Sample $h \xleftarrow{\$} \mathbb{Z}_q^{<n-d-m}[x]$ and $\epsilon \leftarrow D_\Sigma$.
- Set $a' = a + h \cdot f$ and set $b'$ to be the polynomial with coefficient vector $\mathbf{b}' = \mathbf{J}_d \cdot \mathbf{M}_f^{(d)} \cdot \mathbf{b} + \epsilon$.

We note that the matrix $\Sigma$ above is positive definite (and hence the distribution $D_\Sigma$ is well-defined) by the following calculation: using Lemma 9,

$$\sigma_1 \left( (\alpha q)^2 \mathbf{J}_d \cdot \mathbf{M}_f^{(d)} \right) \leq \alpha q \cdot \sigma_1(\mathbf{J}_d) \cdot \sigma_1(\mathbf{M}_f^{(d)}) \leq \alpha q \cdot 1 \cdot \sqrt{d}\, \mathrm{EF}(f) < \alpha' \cdot q.$$

We first show that if $(a, b) \xleftarrow{\$} \mathbb{Z}_q[x]/f \times \mathbb{R}_q[x]/f$, then $(a', b')$ is distributed uniformly on the set $\mathbb{Z}_q^{<n-d}[x] \times \mathbb{R}_q^{<d}[x]$. Since $a$ and $h$ are uniformly random distributed in $\mathbb{Z}_q^{<m}[x]$ and $\mathbb{Z}_q^{<n-d-m}[x]$ respectively, we see that $a'$ is uniformly distributed over $\mathbb{Z}_q^{<n-d}[x]$. Moreover, if $b$ is uniformly distributed in $\mathbb{R}_q[x]/f$, then its coefficient vector $\mathbf{b}$ is uniformly distributed in $\mathbb{R}_q^m$. Since $\mathbf{J}$ and $\mathbf{M}_f$ are invertible (see Lemma 8), $\mathbf{J}_d \cdot \mathbf{M}_f^{(d)} \cdot \mathbf{b}$ is therefore uniformly distributed (over $\mathbb{R}_q^d$), thus so is $\mathbf{b}'$ and its polynomial representation $b'$.

We next show that if $(a, b)$ is a PLWE-sample, then $(a', b')$ is a MP-LWE sample. Suppose that $b = a \cdot s + e$ for $s \in \mathbb{Z}_q[x]/f$ and error polynomial $e$ with coefficient vector $\mathbf{e} \leftarrow \chi^d$. Let $s' \in \mathbb{Z}_q^{<n-1}[x]$ be defined so that it has coefficient vector

$$\mathbf{s}' = \mathbf{J}_{n-1} \cdot (\mathbf{B}_{n-1,f} \cdot \mathbf{M}_f \cdot \mathbf{s}),$$

where $\mathbf{B}_{n-1,f} \in \mathbb{Z}_q^{n-1 \times m}$ is defined so that the $i$th row of $\mathbf{B}_{n-1,f}$ is the coefficient vector of $x^{i-1} \mod f$. Moreover, define $e' \in \mathbb{R}_q^{<d}[x]$ to have coefficient vector

$$\mathbf{e}' = \mathbf{J}_d \cdot \mathbf{M}_f^{(d)} \cdot \mathbf{e} + \epsilon.$$

We refer to [21] for a proof that $b' = a' \odot_d s' + e'$. Since $\epsilon$ is sampled independent of $\mathbf{e}$, the distribution of $\mathbf{e}'$ is $D_{\alpha' \cdot q}$ by standard (continuous) Gaussian distribution identities.

As in [21], the collection of maps $\phi_{n,d_i}$ (ranging over all $i \in [t]$) can be used to implement a MP-LWE oracle using a PLWE oracle, and hence immediately give a reduction from $\mathsf{PLWE}_{D_{\alpha \cdot q}}^{(f)}$ for any $f \in \mathcal{F}(S, \mathbf{d}, n)$ to $\mathsf{MPLWE}_{q,n,\mathbf{d},D_{\alpha' \cdot q}}$. $\square$

## 4   A Leftover Hash Lemma for Polynomials

In this section, we state and prove Theorem 3, a Leftover Hash Lemma for polynomials with bounded degree. The closest previous work is [14], in which the author proves a Leftover Hash Lemma for elements of the ring $R := \mathbb{Z}_q[\alpha]/[\alpha^n - 1]$; the proof technique in [14] inspires our proof of Theorem 3. However, we encounter some subtleties as a result of working with bounded-degree polynomials; specifically, difficulties arise due to the fact that the set of bounded-degree polynomials is not closed under multiplication.

Let $q = \mathsf{poly}(n)$ be a sequence of prime numbers, so that $\mathbb{Z}_q$ is a field for every $q = q(n)$. For polynomials $z_1, \cdots, z_t \in \mathbb{Z}_q[x]$, we adopt the convention that $\gcd(z_1, \cdots, z_t)$ is always monic.

Our goal is to prove that the hash function

$$h_{a_1,\ldots,a_t}(z_1, \ldots, z_t) = \sum_{i=1}^{t} a_i z_i,$$

with hash key $\vec{a} = (a_1, \ldots, a_t)$ consisting of $t$ polynomials drawn i.i.d. from $U(\mathbb{Z}_q^{<n}[x])$, extracts uniform randomness from high entropy sources of bounded-degree polynomials, in the special case of sources that are *product distributions*.

Following the approach of [14], we want to analyze, for any fixed input $\vec{z} = (z_1, \ldots, z_t)$, the distribution of outputs $H(\vec{z}) := h_{a_1,\ldots,a_t}(z_1, \ldots, z_t)$ over the choice of uniformly random hash key. In [14], the $a_i$ and $z_i$ are all elements of a ring $R$, so the set $\{h_{a_1,\cdots,a_t}(z_1, \cdots, z_t) | (a_1, \cdots, a_t) \in R^t\}$ is simply the ideal generated by $z_1, \cdots, z_t$. Moreover, a simple argument shows that $H(\vec{z})$ is uniform over this set. Here, however, we are working with bounded degree polynomials, so the characterization of $H(\vec{z})$ is not as immediate. Lemma 10 characterizes $H(\vec{z})$.

**Lemma 10 (Range of hash output).** *Consider $z_1, \cdots, z_t \in \mathbb{Z}_q^{<n}[x]$ that are not all zero polynomials. Let $I$ denote the set of degree-bounded linear combinations of $\{z_i\}$, that is,*

$$I = \left\{ \sum_{i=1}^{t} a_i z_i \,\middle|\, a_i \in \mathbb{Z}_q^{<n}[x] \right\}.$$

*Moreover, let $d = \max_i \deg(z_i)$, and let $g = \gcd(z_1, \ldots, z_t)$. Then,*

$$I = (g \cdot \mathbb{Z}_q[x]) \cap \mathbb{Z}_q^{<n+d}[x]$$

*Moreover, for polynomials $(a_1, \ldots, a_t)$ sampled i.i.d. from $U(\mathbb{Z}_q^{<n}[x])$, the distribution $\left\{ \sum_{i=1}^{t} a_i \cdot z_i \right\}$ is uniform on the set $I$.*

*Proof.* Recall that $g = \gcd(z_1, \cdots, z_t)$ is some monic polynomial in $\mathbb{Z}_q[x]$ dividing each $z_i$. Therefore, the inclusion

$$I \subset (g \cdot \mathbb{Z}_q[x]) \cap \mathbb{Z}_q^{<n+d}[x]$$

is immediate. For the rest of the proof, we aim to show the opposite inclusion. We assume without loss of generality that all $z_i$ are nonzero and prove the claim by induction on $t$.

We begin with a base case of $t = 2$ and further assume (at first) that $g = 1$. Fix polynomials $(z_1, z_2)$ with $\gcd(z_1, z_2) = 1$, and assume WLOG that $d = \deg(z_1)$. We want to show that for every $\alpha \in \mathbb{Z}_q^{<n+d}[x]$, there exists a key $(a_1, a_2)$ such that $h_{a_1, a_2}(z_1, z_2) = \alpha$. To do this, we write

$$\alpha = z_1 z_2 Q + R$$

for polynomials $(Q, R)$ satisfying $\deg(Q) < n + d - \deg(z_1 z_2) = n - \deg(z_2)$, $\deg(R) < \deg(z_1 z_2)$. By the Chinese remainder theorem, we know that there exist polynomials $s_1, s_2$ satisfying $\deg(s_1) < \deg(z_2)$, $\deg(s_2) < \deg(z_1)$, and

$$s_1 z_1 + s_2 z_2 = R.$$

Then, choosing $a_1 = Q z_2 + s_1$ and $a_2 = s_2$, we see that $\deg(a_1) < n$, $\deg(a_2) < n$, and

$$a_1 z_1 + a_2 z_2 = z_1 z_2 Q + (s_1 z_1 + s_2 z_2) = \alpha,$$

as desired.

In the case that $\gcd(z_1, z_2) = g \neq 1$, for any $\alpha \in g\mathbb{Z}_q[x] \cap \mathbb{Z}_q^{<n+d}[x]$ write $\alpha = g\alpha'$ with $\deg(\alpha') < n + d - \deg(g)$. Since $\gcd(\frac{z_1}{g}, \frac{z_2}{g}) = 1$, we just showed that there exist $a_1, a_2$ with $\deg(a_i) < n$ and $a_1 \frac{z_1}{g} + a_2 \frac{z_2}{g} = \alpha'$, which implies that $a_1 z_1 + a_2 z_2 = g\alpha' = \alpha$. This completes the base case.

For the inductive step, consider any $t \geq 3$ and any polynomials $(z_1, \ldots z_t)$ with $d = \max_i \deg(z_i)$ and $g = \gcd(z_1, \ldots, z_t)$. We want to show that for any $\alpha \in g\mathbb{Z}_q[x] \cap \mathbb{Z}_q^{<n+d}[x]$, there exist polynomials $(a_1, \ldots, a_t)$ with $\deg(a_i) < n$ and $\sum_i a_i z_i = \alpha$.

We suppose without loss of generality that $\deg(z_1) = d$. Then, let $g' = \gcd(z_2, \ldots, z_t)$, and note that by the base case, there exist polynomials $(a_1, a^*)$ such that $\deg(a_1) < n$, $\deg(a^*) < n$, and

$$a_1 z_1 + a^* g' = \alpha.$$

The base case applies because $\max(\deg(z_1), \deg(g')) = d$ and $\gcd(z_1, g') = g$. Now, further note that $\deg(a^* g') < n + \deg(g') \leq n + \max_{2 \leq i \leq t} \deg(z_i)$. Therefore, by the inductive hypothesis (applied to $(z_2, \ldots, z_t)$), there exist polynomials $(a_2, \ldots, a_t)$ such that $\deg(a_i) < n$ for all $i$, and

$$\sum_{i=2}^{n} a_i z_i = a^* g'.$$

This completes the inductive step.

Finally, we prove the distributional claim. Our reasoning follows the proof of ([14], Lemma 4.4). For every $\alpha \in I$, define the set

$$S_\alpha = \left\{ (a_1, \cdots, a_t) \in (\mathbb{Z}_q^{<n}[x])^t : \sum_{i=1}^{t} a_i z_i = \alpha \right\}.$$

By construction, the sets $S_\alpha$ for $\alpha \in I$ partition $(\mathbb{Z}_q^{<n}[x])^t$. In order to prove the distributional claim, we only need to show that $|S_0| = |S_\alpha|$ for all $\alpha \in I$. To see this, note that for a given $\alpha \in I$, we have already shown that $S_\alpha \neq \emptyset$, so there exist $a'_1, \cdots, a'_t$ such that $\deg(a'_i) < n$ and $\sum_{i=1}^{t} a'_i z_i = b$. Then, the function $(a_i)_{i \leq t} \mapsto (a_i - a'_i)_{i \leq t}$ is a bijection from $S_\alpha$ to $S_0$, proving that $|S_\alpha| = |S_0|$, as desired.                                                                 □

Having proved Lemma 10, we are ready to state and prove our variant of the leftover hash lemma.

**Theorem 3.** *Let $\chi$ be a distribution over $\mathbb{Z}_q$ and $\delta \in (0,1)$ be such that $H_\infty(\chi) \geq \log(\frac{1}{\delta})$. Define the distribution $V := (\vec{a}, h_{\vec{a}}(\vec{r}))$ over $S = (\mathbb{Z}_q^{<n}[x])^t \times \mathbb{Z}_q^{<n+n'-1}[x]$, where $\vec{a} = (a_1, \ldots a_t)$ consists of i.i.d. samples from $U(\mathbb{Z}_q^{<n}[x])$, and $\vec{r} = (r_1, \ldots, r_t)$ consists of i.i.d. samples from $\chi^{n'}[x]$.*

*Then, for $n' \leq n$, if $\delta^t q = o(1)$,*

$$\Delta(V, U(S)) = O\left( \delta^{\frac{t}{2}} q + \delta^{\frac{n't}{2}} q^{\frac{n+n'+1}{2}} \right).$$

*In particular, for any $q = \mathsf{poly}(n)$, if $\delta^{-1} = \omega(1)$ and $n't/n = \Omega(\log n)$, we have $V \approx_s U(S)$.*

*Proof.* By ([10], Claim 2) (i.e., by applying a generalized mean inequality), in order to prove that $\Delta(V, U(S)) \leq \epsilon$, it suffices to show that $\mathrm{CP}(V) \leq \frac{1+4\epsilon^2}{|S|}$; note that in our case, $|S| = q^{nt} \times q^{n+n'-1}$.

More precisely, let $\vec{a} = (a_i)_{i\in[t]}, \vec{a}' = (a_i')_{i\in[t]}, \vec{r} = (r_i)_{i\in[t]}, \vec{r}' = (r_i')_{i\in[t]}$ consist of i.i.d. samples from $U(\mathbb{Z}_q^{<n}[x])$ and $\chi^{n'}[x]$ respectively. We want to show that

$$\mathrm{CP}(V) = \Pr\left[\vec{a} = \vec{a}' \wedge \sum_{i=1}^{t} a_i r_i = \sum_{i=1}^{t} a_i' r_i'\right] \leq \frac{1 + 4\epsilon^2}{q^{nt+n+n'-1}}.$$

We first partially evaluate the left-hand side of this inequality:

$$\Pr\left[\vec{a} = \vec{a}' \wedge \sum_{i=1}^{t} a_i r_i = \sum_{i=1}^{t} a_i' r_i'\right] = \Pr\left[\vec{a} = \vec{a}' \wedge \sum_{i=1}^{t} a_i(r_i - r_i') = 0\right]$$

$$= q^{-nt} \Pr\left[\sum_{i=1}^{t} a_i(r_i - r_i') = 0\right]. \qquad (1)$$

Defining the random variable $\vec{v} = \vec{r} - \vec{r}'$, we then have

$$q^{-nt} \Pr\left[\sum_{i=1}^{t} a_i(r_i - r_i') = 0\right] = q^{-nt} \sum_{\vec{z}} \Pr[\vec{v} = \vec{z}] \Pr\left[\sum_{i=1}^{t} a_i z_i = 0\right]$$

$$\leq q^{-nt}\left(\mathrm{CP}(\chi)^{n't} + \sum_{\vec{z}\neq 0} \frac{\Pr[\vec{v} = \vec{z}]}{|I(\vec{z})|}\right), \qquad (2)$$

where $I(z) := \{\sum_{i=1}^{t} a_i z_i \mid a_i \in \mathbb{Z}_q^{<n}[x]\} = \gcd(z_1, \ldots, z_t)\mathbb{Z}_q[x] \cap \mathbb{Z}_q^{<n+\max_i \deg(z_i)}[x]$ as in Lemma 10. The last inequality follows from the distributional claim in Lemma 10.

To further simplify, we know by assumption that $\mathrm{CP}(\chi) \leq 2^{-H_\infty(\chi)} \leq \delta$. In addition, we group terms of the summation by the associated sets $I(z)$. That is, for every monic polynomial $g \in \mathbb{Z}_q^{<n'}[x]$ and degree $d < n'$, we define $I_{g,d} = g\mathbb{Z}_q[x] \cap \mathbb{Z}_q^{<n+d}[x]$ and obtain

$$q^{-nt}\left(\mathrm{CP}(\chi)^{n't} + \sum_{\vec{z}\neq 0} \frac{\Pr[\vec{v} = \vec{z}]}{|I(z)|}\right)$$

$$\leq q^{-nt}\left(\delta^{n't} + \sum_{\substack{g \text{ monic } \in \mathbb{Z}_q^{<n'}[x] \\ d<n'}} \Pr\left[I(\vec{v}) = I_{g,d}\right]\frac{1}{|I_{g,d}|}\right)$$

$$\leq q^{-nt}\left(\delta^{n't} + \sum_{g,d} \Pr\left[I(\vec{v}) \subset I_{g,d}\right]\frac{1}{|I_{g,d}|}\right). \qquad (3)$$

We next bound the probability that $I(\vec{v}) \subset I_{g,d}$ for any fixed $g, d$. To do this, we note by inspection that $I(\vec{v}) \subset I_{g,d}$ if and only if $v_i \in g\mathbb{Z}_q[x] \cap \mathbb{Z}_q^{<d+1}[x]$ for

all $i$. For a fixed $i$, this occurs with probability

$$\Pr\left[v_i \in g\mathbb{Z}_q[x] \cap \mathbb{Z}_q^{<d+1}[x]\right]$$

$$= \Pr\left[v_i \in \mathbb{Z}_q^{<d+1}[x]\right]\Pr\left[v_i \in g\mathbb{Z}_q[x] \mid v_i \in \mathbb{Z}_q^{<d+1}[x]\right]$$

$$= \mathrm{CP}(\chi)^{n'-d-1}\Pr\left[v_i \in g\mathbb{Z}_q[x] \mid v_i \in \mathbb{Z}_q^{<d+1}[x]\right]$$

$$\leq \delta^{n'-d-1}\Pr\left[v_i \in g\mathbb{Z}_q[x] \mid v_i \in \mathbb{Z}_q^{<d+1}[x]\right] \tag{4}$$

In order to bound this probability, we define random variables $w_i, w_i'$ to be drawn i.i.d. from $\chi^{d+1}[x]$ and compute

$$\Pr\left[v_i \in g\mathbb{Z}_q[x] \mid v_i \in \mathbb{Z}_q^{<d+1}[x]\right] = \Pr\left[w_i - w_i' \in g\mathbb{Z}_q[x]\right]$$

$$\leq \max_{\overline{w}\in\mathbb{Z}_q^{<\deg(g)}[x]}\Pr\left[w_i - \overline{w} \in g\mathbb{Z}_q[x]\right] \tag{5}$$

Fix an arbitrary $\overline{w}$. For a vector $v \in \mathbb{Z}_q^{d+1-\deg(g)}$ let $T_v$ be set of polynomials $w_i \in \mathbb{Z}_q^{<d+1}[x]$ whose $(d+1-\deg(g))$ highest order coefficients are fixed to match $v$. Then, the "reduction mod $g$" map is a bijection from $T_v$ to $\mathbb{Z}_q^{<\deg(g)}[x]$. Letting $\overline{w}^v$ denote the unique inverse of $\overline{w}$ in $T_v$ and making use of the fact that $H_\infty(\chi) \geq \log(\frac{1}{\delta})$, we compute

$$\Pr\left[w_i - \overline{w} \in g\mathbb{Z}_q[x]\right] = \sum_{v\in\mathbb{Z}_q^{d+1-\deg(g)}} \Pr[w_i \in T_v]\Pr[w_i = \overline{w}^v \mid w_i \in T_v]$$

$$\leq \sum_{v\in\mathbb{Z}_q^{d+1-\deg(g)}} \Pr[w_i \in T_v]\delta^{\deg(g)}$$

$$= \delta^{\deg(g)}. \tag{6}$$

Combining our calculations (Eqs. (1)–(6)), we conclude that

$$\mathrm{CP}(V) \leq q^{-nt}\delta^{n't} + q^{-nt}\delta^{(n'-1)t}\sum_{\substack{g \text{ monic } \in\mathbb{Z}_q^{<n'}[x] \\ d<n'}} \delta^{\deg(g)-d}\frac{1}{|I_{g,d}|}$$

$$= q^{-nt}\delta^{n't} + q^{-nt}\delta^{(n'-1)t}\sum_{\substack{g \text{ monic } \in\mathbb{Z}_q^{<n'}[x] \\ d<n'}} \delta^{(\deg(g)-d)t}\frac{1}{q^{n+d-\deg(g)}}$$

$$= q^{-nt}\delta^{n't} + q^{-nt-n}\delta^{(n'-1)t}\sum_{\substack{d'=\deg(g)<n' \\ d<n'}} q^{d'}\left(\delta^t q\right)^{d'-d}$$

$$= q^{-nt}\delta^{n't} + q^{-nt-n}\delta^{(n'-1)t}\sum_{\substack{d'<n' \\ d<n'}} \delta^{(d'-d)t}q^{2d'-d}$$

$$\leq q^{-nt}\delta^{n't} + q^{-nt-n-n'+1}(1+O(\delta^t q^2))$$

$$= q^{-nt-n-n'+1}\left(1+O(\delta^t q^2 + \delta^{n't}q^{n+n'-1})\right),$$

where the final inequality follows from the assumption that $\delta^t q^2 = o(1)$. This completes the proof of Theorem 3.                                                                    $\square$

For our application to IBE, we are interested in applying Theorem 3 in the case of a discrete Gaussian input distribution $D_{\mathbb{Z},\sigma}$. We now show that the hypothesis of Theorem 3 holds for sufficiently large $\sigma$.

**Lemma 11.** *Let* $\chi := D_{\mathbb{Z},\sigma}$ *and* $\chi_q := \chi \bmod q$. *For* $\sigma = \mathsf{poly}(n), q = \omega(\sigma \log^{1/2} n), \sigma = \omega(1)$, *we have* $H_\infty(\chi_q) \geq \log(\frac{\sigma}{c})$ *for some constant* $c$.

*Proof.* Since $q = \omega(\sigma \log^{1/2} n)$, only a negligible fraction of $\chi$'s probability mass "wraps around," i.e., is not contained in the interval $[-\frac{q}{2}, \frac{q}{2})$, so the min-entropy bound we proved about $\chi$ directly gives a min-entropy bound on $\chi_q$.

In more detail, fix $\epsilon \in (0, 1/2)$ to be a small constant. By Lemma 2, $n_\epsilon(\mathbb{Z}) \leq c' \log(1 + \epsilon^{-1})$ for some constant $c'$. By Lemma 3 and our hypothesis, we see that

$$\Pr_{x \sim \chi}[|x| \geq q/2] = \mathsf{negl}(n).$$

Given this, we can compute

$$2^{-H_\infty(\chi_q)} = \max_{z \in \mathbb{Z}_q} \Pr_{x \sim \chi}[x \equiv z \pmod q]$$

$$\leq \Pr_{x \sim \chi}[|x| \geq q/2] + \max_{z \in \mathbb{Z} \cap [-q/2, q/2]} Pr[x \equiv z \pmod q]$$

$$\leq 2^{-H_\infty(\chi)} + \mathsf{negl}(n).$$

The bound $2^{-H_\infty(\chi_q)} \leq \frac{c}{\sigma}$ then follows from Lemma 5 applied to parameter $\delta = \sigma^{-1} c' \log(1 + \epsilon^{-1}) < 1/\sqrt{2}$; this parameter setting is possible since $\sigma = \omega(1)$.                                                                    $\square$

## 5    Lattice Trapdoors for MP-LWE

In this section, we implement the "lattice trapdoors" paradigm of [8] for middle-product LWE. In particular, we show that the Micciancio-Peikert variant of lattice trapdoors [15] can be instantiated for MP-LWE.

In our setting, we want an algorithm TrapGen for generating random polynomials $(a_1, \ldots, a_{t'})$ along with a trapdoor td that allows for sampling polynomials $(r_i)$ satisfying

$$\sum_{i=1}^{t'} a_i r_i = u$$

given any polynomial $u$ (of the correct degree).

We briefly describe the method for generating $(a_i)$. Let $t \leq t', d, n$ and distribution $\chi$ over $\mathbb{Z}_q$ be parameters to be defined later. For $(i, j) \in [t] \times [t' - t]$, we sample $a_i \xleftarrow{\$} \mathbb{Z}_q^{<n}[x]$ and $w_{i,j} \leftarrow \chi^d[x]$, and construct $a_{t+j} = c_j - \sum_{i \leq t} a_i \cdot w_{i,j}$, where $(c_j)_{j \in [t'-t]}$ is an analogue of matrix $G$ in Definition 11. Note that

$(a_i)_{i \le t'} \in (\mathbb{Z}_q^{<n}[x])^t \times (\mathbb{Z}_q^{<n+d-1}[x])^{t'-t}$. We will choose $d$ according to Theorem 3 to ensure that the distribution of each $a_{t+j}$ is close to random. Finally, we will show that the trapdoor $\{w_{ij}\}$ can be used to implement the preimage sampling algorithm of [15] by considering the polynomials $(a_i)$ as structured matrices, similarly to the Ring-LWE setting.

For the rest of this section, let $\tau := \lceil \log_2 q \rceil$. We first recall the notion of a "$G$-trapdoor" from [15].

**Definition 11** ([15], **Definition 5.2**). *Let $G := I_k \otimes [1 \ 2 \ \cdots \ 2^{\tau-1}] \in \mathbb{Z}_q^{k \times k\tau}$. Then, given a matrix $A \in \mathbb{Z}^{k \times (m+k\tau)}$, we say that a matrix $R \in \mathbb{Z}^{m \times k\tau}$ is a **G-trapdoor** for $A$ if*

$$A \begin{bmatrix} R \\ I_{k\tau} \end{bmatrix} = G.$$

We make use of the following result in [15], Section 5.4, which states that $G$-trapdoors allow for efficient Gaussian preimage sampling in the style of [8].

**Theorem 4** ([15], **Theorem 5.5**). *Let $G := I_k \otimes [1 \ 2 \ \cdots \ 2^{\tau-1}] \in \mathbb{Z}_q^{k \times k\tau}$ and matrices $A \in \mathbb{Z}^{k \times (m+k\tau)}, R \in \mathbb{Z}^{m \times k\tau}$ be such that*

$$A \begin{bmatrix} R \\ I_{k\tau} \end{bmatrix} = G.$$

*There exists an efficient algorithm $\mathcal{C} = (\mathcal{C}_1, \mathcal{C}_2)$ that operates as follows:*

- *In the **offline phase**, $\mathcal{C}_1(A, R, \sigma)$ does some polynomial-time preprocessing on input $(A, R, \sigma)$ and outputs a state st.*
- *In the **online phase**, $\mathcal{C}_2(\mathsf{st}, u)$, additionally given a vector $u$, samples from $D_{\Lambda_u^\perp(A), \sigma}$, as long as $\sigma \ge \omega(\sqrt{\log k})\sqrt{7(\sigma_1(R)^2 + 1)}$.*

*Moreover, the runtime of $\mathcal{C}_2$ is the time to compute $Rz$ for $z \in \mathbb{Z}^{k\tau}$ plus $\tilde{O}(m + k\tau)$.*

We note that the proof of Theorem 4 given in [15] has a minor error that we correct in the Appendix. We now use Theorem 4 to instantiate lattice trapdoors for MP-LWE.

**Theorem 5.** *Suppose that $q = \mathsf{poly}(n), d \le n, dt/n = \Omega(\log n), \sigma = \omega(\log^2 n)\sqrt{ndt}$ and $\gamma = \frac{n+2d-2}{d}$ is an integer. Then, there exist ppt algorithms $(\mathsf{TrapGen}, \mathsf{SamplePre})$ with the following properties.*

- $\mathsf{TrapGen}(1^n)$ *generates polynomials*

$$(a_1, \cdots, a_t, a_{t+1}, \cdots, a_{t+\gamma\tau}) \approx_s U((\mathbb{Z}_q^{<n}[x])^t \times (\mathbb{Z}_q^{<n+d-1}[x])^{\gamma\tau})$$

  *together with a trapdoor td that can be stored in $O(n\tau t)$ space.*
- $\mathsf{SamplePre}(\mathsf{td}, u)$ *that operates as follow:*
  - *In the **offline** phase, does some polynomial-time preprocessing with trapdoor td and parameter $\sigma$, and output a state st.*

- *In the **online** phase, given state* st *and a syndrome* $u \in \mathbb{Z}_q^{<n+2d-2}[x]$, *outputs* $(r_i)_{i=1}^{t+\gamma\tau}$ *satisfying*

$$\sum_{i=1}^{t+\gamma\tau} a_i \cdot r_i = u$$

*in* $\tilde{O}(nt)$ *time. Moreover, the output distribution of* $(r_i)$ *is exactly the conditional distribution*

$$(D_{\mathbb{Z}^{2d-1},\sigma}[x])^t \times (D_{\mathbb{Z}^d,\sigma}[x])^{\gamma\tau} \mid \sum_{i=1}^{t+\gamma\tau} a_i \cdot r_i = u,$$

*Proof.* Let $\beta := \left\lceil \frac{\log_2 n}{2} \right\rceil$.

TrapGen*Algorithm:* We first describe TrapGen and prove that it outputs the right distribution of polynomials $(a_i)$.

- For $(i,j) \in [t] \times [\gamma\tau]$, sample $a_i \overset{\$}{\leftarrow} \mathbb{Z}_q^{<n}[x]$ and $w_{i,j} \leftarrow \chi^d[x]$ where $\chi = U(\{-\beta, \cdots, \beta\})$. Since $\beta \ll q/2$, we can interpret samples from $\chi$ as elements of $\mathbb{Z}_q$.
- For all $j \in [\gamma\tau]$, define polynomials

$$u_j = \sum_{i=1}^{t} a_i \cdot w_{i,j}$$

$$a_{t+j} = c_j - u_j$$

for $c_j \in \mathbb{Z}_q^{<n+d-2}[x]$ dependent only on $j$. Specifically, $c_j = 2^u x^{dv}$ for $j = v\tau + u + 1$ where $u \in \{0, \cdots, \tau - 1\}, v \in \{0, \cdots, \gamma - 1\}$.
- Output $(a_1, \ldots, a_{t+\gamma\tau})$ with associated trapdoor td $= (w_{i,j})$.

We first note that the amount of space required to store td $= (w_{i,j})$ is $O(d(\gamma\tau)t) = O(n\tau t)$, since $\gamma d = n + 2d - 2 \leq 3n$.

To see that the sampled polynomials $(a_1, \ldots, a_{t+\gamma\tau})$ are statistically close to uniform, we apply our Leftover Hash Lemma (Theorem 3). In particular, $H_\infty(\chi) = \log(\frac{1}{\beta}) \geq \log\log n - 1$. Therefore, by Theorem 3,

$$(a_1, \cdots, a_t, u_1, \cdots, u_{\gamma\tau}) \approx_s U(\mathbb{Z}_q^{<n}[x]^t \times \mathbb{Z}_q^{<n+d-1}[x]^{\gamma\tau}),$$

and so

$$(a_i)_{i=1}^{t+\gamma\tau} = (a_1, \cdots, a_t, c_1 - u_1, \cdots, c_{\gamma\tau} - u_{\gamma\tau}) \approx_s U(\mathbb{Z}_q^{<n}[x]^t \times \mathbb{Z}_q^{<n+d-1}[x]^{\gamma\tau}).$$

SamplePre *Algorithm:* We next describe SamplePre using the algorithm from Theorem 4.

- Implicitly define matrices $A, L$ by the following equations.

$$\tilde{A} = \left[T^{n,2d-1}(a_1)|\cdots|T^{n,2d-1}(a_t)\right]$$

$$\tilde{L} = \begin{bmatrix} T^{d,d}(w_{1,1}) & \cdots & T^{d,d}(w_{1,\gamma\tau}) \\ \vdots & & \vdots \\ T^{d,d}(w_{t,1}) & \cdots & T^{d,d}(w_{t,\gamma\tau}) \end{bmatrix}$$

$$\Gamma(h) = \left[T^{n+d-1,d}(h)|\cdots|T^{n+d-1,d}(h2^{\tau-1})\right]$$

$$G = \left[\Gamma(1)|\Gamma(x^d)|\cdots|\Gamma(x^{(\gamma-1)d})\right] \tag{7}$$

$$I = I_{\gamma d\tau} = \begin{bmatrix} T^{1,d}(1) & \cdots & \\ & \cdots & \cdots \\ & & T^{1,d}(1) \end{bmatrix}$$

$$A = [\tilde{A}|G - \tilde{A}\tilde{L}]$$

$$L = \begin{bmatrix} \tilde{L} \\ I \end{bmatrix}$$

so that $AL = G = I_{\gamma d} \otimes [1 \cdots 2^{\tau-1}]$, i.e., $L$ is a $G$-trapdoor for $A$.
- Let $\mathbf{u} = T^{n+2d-2}(u) \in \mathbb{Z}_q^{n+2d-2}$ be the coefficient vector of $u$.
- Apply the algorithm from Theorem 4 (for $k = \gamma d = n + 2d - 2$) to sample $\mathbf{y}$ from $D_{\Lambda_{\mathbf{u}}^{\perp}(A),\sigma}$ where

$$\sigma = \omega(\sqrt{\log(\gamma d)})\beta\sqrt{7((\gamma d\tau) \cdot d \cdot t + 1)} = c\omega(\log^2 n)\sqrt{n \cdot (dt)},$$

for some constant $c$.

- Write $\mathbf{y}$ as $\begin{bmatrix} T^{2d-1,1}(r_1) \\ \vdots \\ T^{2d-1,1}(r_t) \\ T^{d,1}(r_{t+1}) \\ \vdots \\ T^{d,1}(r_{t+\gamma\tau}) \end{bmatrix}$, where $\deg(r_i) \begin{cases} < 2d - 1 \text{ for } i \in [t] \\ < d \text{ for } i \in \{t+1, \cdots, t+\gamma\tau\} \end{cases}$

- Output $(r_1, \ldots, r_{t+\gamma\tau})$.

In order to analyze the correctness of SamplePre, we first note that by construction, $\max_{i,j}|\tilde{L}_{ij}| \leq \beta$, and so $\sigma_1(\tilde{L}) \leq \beta\sqrt{(\gamma d\tau) \cdot (2d-1)t}$ by Lemma 6. Combined with Theorem 4 (for $k = \gamma d = n + 2d - 2$), this tells us that $\mathbf{y}$ is sampled from from $D_{\Lambda_{\mathbf{u}}^{\perp}(A),\sigma}$ where

$$\sigma = \omega(\sqrt{\log(\gamma d)})\beta\sqrt{7((\gamma d\tau) \cdot d \cdot t + 1)} = c\omega(\log^2 n)\sqrt{n \cdot (dt)}$$

for some constant $c$. Theorem 4 applies because of our parameter settings of $\gamma d = n + 2d - 2 \leq 3n$ and $\tau = \theta(\log q) = \theta(\log n)$ for $q = \mathsf{poly}(n)$.

Moreover, by Lemma 7 and Eq. (7),

$$\tilde{A}\tilde{L} = \left[T^{n+d-1,d}(u_1)|\cdots|T^{n+d-1,d}(u_{\gamma\tau})\right], \text{ and}$$

$$A = \left[T^{n,2d-1}(a_1)|\cdots|T^{n,2d-1}(a_t)|T^{n+d-1,d}(a_{t+1})|\cdots|T^{n+d-1,d}(a_{t+\gamma\tau})\right], \tag{8}$$

and so by Eq. (8) and Lemma 7

$$Ay = T^{n+2d-2,1}\left(\sum_{i=1}^{t+\gamma\tau} a_i \cdot r_i\right). \tag{9}$$

Thus, $y \in \Lambda_u^\perp(A)$ if and only if $\sum_{i=1}^{t+\gamma\tau} a_i \cdot r_i = u$.

To prove the claim about distribution of $r = (r_i)$, we note that the columns of $A$ generate $\mathbb{Z}^{n+2d-2}$ since (1) the columns of $G$ generate $\mathbb{Z}^{n+2d-2}$ and (2) $AL = G$. Hence, there exists $y^*$ such that $Ay^* = u$. Then, Lemma 5.2 in [8] applies, allowing us to conclude that the distribution of $y$ sampled by our algorithm is exactly

$$D_{\Lambda_u^\perp(A),\sigma} \equiv y^* + D_{\Lambda^\perp(A),\sigma,-y^*} \equiv D_{\mathbb{Z},\sigma}^{(2d-1)t+d\gamma\tau} \mid Ay = u.$$

To see that the first equality of distributions holds, note that the two distributions have the same support (i.e., $t + \Lambda^\perp(A) = \Lambda_u^\perp(A)$), and for all $x \in \Lambda_u^\perp(A)$,

$$D_{\Lambda_u^\perp(A),\sigma}(x) = \frac{\rho_\sigma(x)}{\rho_\sigma(\Lambda_u^\perp(A))} = \frac{\rho_\sigma(x - t + t)}{\rho_\sigma(\Lambda^\perp(A)) + t} = D_{\Lambda^\perp(A),\sigma,-t}(x - t).$$

Thus, the conditional distribution of $r$ is as claimed. Finally, we analyze the runtime of SamplePre's online phase, which is precisely the runtime of $C_2$. Computing $\tilde{L}z$ for $z \in \mathbb{Z}_q^{d\gamma\tau}$ can be performed, using polynomial multiplication, in $O((d\log d)t\gamma\tau) = \tilde{O}(nt)$ time; this bound uses the fact that $\gamma d \leq 3n$, $\log d \leq \log n$ and $\tau = \Theta(\log n)$. $\qquad\square$

## 6   New Encryption Schemes from Middle-Product LWE

In this section, we describe how to build a "Dual Regev"-style public-key encryption scheme, as well as an identity-based encryption scheme, whose security is based on the hardness of MP-LWE. As in [8], our IBE scheme is constructed by combining the Dual Regev scheme with lattice trapdoors as constructed in Sect. 5.

### 6.1   Middle Product Dual Regev Encryption

Unless otherwise stated, the following parameters are positive integers.

Let $q = q(n)$ be a prime, $\tau := \lceil \log_2 q \rceil$, $n, d, k$ be such that $\gamma = \frac{n+2d-2}{d} \in \mathbb{N}$ and $2d + k \leq n$. Let $t > 0$, $t' = t + \gamma\tau$. Let $\chi := \lfloor D_{\alpha \cdot q} \rceil$ be the distribution over $\mathbb{Z}$ in which $\epsilon \leftarrow D_{\alpha \cdot q}$ is sampled and then rounded to the nearest integer.

Finally, let $\sigma \in \mathbb{R}_{>0}$ be a parameter to be specified later. We then define a public-key encryption scheme with message space $\mathcal{M} = \{0, 1\}^{<k+1}[x]$.

- **Key Generation**: KeyGen($1^n$) operates as follows.
  - For $1 \leq i \leq t$, sample $a_i \xleftarrow{\$} \mathbb{Z}_q^{<n}[x]$, $r_i \leftarrow D_{\mathbb{Z}^{2d-1},\sigma}[x]$;
  - For $t+1 \leq i \leq t'$, sample $a_i \xleftarrow{\$} \mathbb{Z}_q^{<n+d-1}[x]$, $r_i \leftarrow D_{\mathbb{Z}^d,\sigma}[x]$.
  - Compute $u = \sum_{i=1}^{t'} a_i r_i$ and output $\mathsf{pk} := (a_1, \ldots, a_{t'}, u)$; $\mathsf{sk} := (r_1, \ldots, r_{t'})$
- **Encryption**: Enc($\mathsf{pk} = ((a_i)_{i \leq t'}, u), \mu$) operates as follows.
  - Sample $s \xleftarrow{\$} \mathbb{Z}_q^{<n+2d+k-1}[x]$
  - For $1 \leq i \leq t$, sample $e_i \leftarrow \chi^{2d+k}[x]$, and compute $b_i = a_i \odot_{2d+k} s + 2e_i$
  - For $t+1 \leq i \leq t'$, sample $e_i \leftarrow \chi^{d+k+1}[x]$, and compute $b_i = a_i \odot_{d+k+1} s + 2e_i$
  - Sample $e' \leftarrow \chi^{k+1}[x]$, and compute $c_1 = \mu + u \odot_{k+1} s + 2e'$
  - Output $c = (c_1, (b_i)_{i \leq t'})$.
- **Decryption**: Dec($\mathsf{sk} = (r_i)_{i \leq t}, c = (c_1, (b_i)_{i \leq t'})$ outputs $(c_1 - \sum_{i=1}^{t'} b_i \odot_{k+1} r_i \mod q) \mod 2$.

**Lemma 12.** *For $\alpha^{-1} > (4\omega(\log n)\sigma K + 1)$ where $K := t(2d-1) + \gamma\tau d$, the scheme satisfies $(1 - \mathsf{negl}(n))$-correctness.*

*Proof.* We want to show that $\mathsf{Dec}(\mathsf{sk}, \mathsf{Enc}(\mathsf{pk}, \mu)) = 1$ with probability $1 - \mathsf{negl}(n)$ over the randomness of KeyGen and Enc. Consider a random key pair $(\mathsf{pk}, \mathsf{sk}) \leftarrow \mathsf{KeyGen}(1^n)$ and ciphertext $c = (c_1, (b_i)_{i \leq t'}) \leftarrow \mathsf{Enc}(\mathsf{pk}, \mu)$. By Lemma 1 (the quasi-associative law for middle products),

$$c_1 = \mu + \sum_{i=1}^{t'} (r_i \cdot a_i) \odot_{k+1} s + 2e'$$

$$= \mu + \sum_{i=1}^{t} r_i \odot_{k+1} (a_i \odot_{2d+k} s) + \sum_{i=t+1}^{t'} r_i \odot_{k+1} (a_i \odot_{d+k+1} s).$$

Therefore, we see that

$$c_1 - \sum_{i=1}^{t'} b_i \odot_{k+1} r_i = \mu + 2(e' - \sum_{i=1}^{t'} r_i \odot_{k+1} e_i).$$

We conclude that if $\left\| \mu + 2(e' - \sum_{i=1}^{t'} r_i \odot_{k+1} e_i) \right\|_{\infty} < q/2$, then $\mathsf{Dec}(\mathsf{sk}, c)$ will indeed output the message $\mu$.

To complete the proof of correctness, we want to bound the coefficients of $\sum_{i=1}^{t'} r_i \odot_{k+1} e_i$. The coefficient of $x^{\ell}$ in $r_i \odot_{k+1} e_i$ is

$$\sum_{w \in [0, \deg(r_i)] \cap [\ell+k-\deg(e_i), z+k]} (\mathbf{r}_i)_w (\mathbf{e}_i)_{\ell+k-w}.$$

Using our discrete Gaussian tail inequality (see Lemma 3) and a union bound, we obtain the following bounds on $\|\mathbf{r}_i\|_{\infty}$ and $\|\mathbf{e}_i\|_{\infty}$:

$$\Pr[\|\mathbf{r}_i\|_{\infty} > \omega(\sqrt{\log n})\sigma] = \mathsf{negl}(n).$$

$$\Pr[\|\mathbf{e}_i\|_\infty > \omega(\sqrt{\log n})\alpha q] = \mathsf{negl}(n).$$

Thus, again by union bound, except with $\mathsf{negl}(n)$ probability

$$\left\|\mathbf{e}' - \sum_{i=1}^{t'} r_i \odot_{k+1} \mathbf{e}_i\right\|_\infty < K(\omega(\sqrt{\log n})\sigma)(\omega(\sqrt{\log n})\alpha \cdot q) + (\omega(\sqrt{\log n})\alpha \cdot q).$$

for $K := t(2d-1) + \gamma\tau d \geq \sum_{i=1}^{t'}(\deg(r_i)+1)$. Picking $\alpha < (4\omega(\log n)\sigma K + 1)^{-1}$, the above is less than $q/4$ and so the scheme is $(1 - \mathsf{negl}(n))$-correct.    □

**Theorem 6.** *Assume that $\sigma = \omega(1), dt/n = \Omega(\log n)$, $q$ is a prime polynomial in $n$, $q = \Omega(\alpha^{-1}n^{1/2+1/2+c})$ and $q = \omega(\log^{1/2} n)\sigma$. The scheme is semantically secure assuming $\mathsf{PLWE}_{q,D_{\alpha'\cdot q}}^{(f)}$ is hard for some polynomial $f$ such that the constant coefficient of $f$ is coprime with $q, \deg(f) \in [2d+k,n], \mathrm{EF}(f) = O(n^c)$ and error $\alpha' = \Omega(\sqrt{\deg(f)/q})$.*

*Proof.* By Theorem 3, Lemma 11 and hypothesis on $\sigma$ and $dt$, we have:

$$\left((a_i)_{i=1}^t, \sum_{i=1}^t a_i \cdot r_i\right)_{\substack{a_i \xleftarrow{\$} \mathbb{Z}_q^{<n}[x] \\ r_i \leftarrow D_{\mathbb{Z}^{2d-1},\sigma}[x]}} \approx_s \left((a_i)_{i=1}^t, u'\right)_{\substack{a_i \xleftarrow{\$} \mathbb{Z}_q^{<n}[x] \\ u' \xleftarrow{\$} \mathbb{Z}_q^{<n+2d-2}[x]}}$$

Since an honestly generated public key has the form $\mathsf{pk} = (a_1 \ldots, a_{t'}, u)$ for $u = \sum_{i=1}^t a_i \cdot r_i + \sum_{i=t+1}^{t'} a_i \cdot r_i$, we see that $\mathsf{pk}$ is computationally indistinguishable from a public key $\widetilde{\mathsf{pk}}$ of the form

$$\widetilde{\mathsf{pk}} = (a_1, \ldots, a_{t'}, u), u \xleftarrow{\$} \mathbb{Z}_q^{<n+2d-2}[x].$$

Thus, we see that for any message $\mu$, we have

$$\left(\mathsf{pk}, \mathsf{Enc}(\mathsf{pk}, \mu)\right) \approx_s \left(\widetilde{\mathsf{pk}}, \mathsf{Enc}(\widetilde{\mathsf{pk}}, \mu)\right).$$

Moreover, we have

$$\left(\widetilde{\mathsf{pk}}, \mathsf{Enc}(\widetilde{\mathsf{pk}}, \mu)\right) \approx_c \left(\widetilde{\mathsf{pk}}, \mathsf{Enc}(\widetilde{\mathsf{pk}}, 0)\right)$$

assuming the hardness of (degree-parametrized) $\mathsf{MPLWE}_{q,n+2d+k,\mathbf{d},\lfloor D_{\alpha\cdot q}\rceil}$ with degree vector

$$\mathbf{d}_i = \begin{cases} 2d+k, & \text{if } i \in [t] \\ d+k+1, & \text{if } t+1 \leq i \leq t' \\ k+2, & \text{if } i = t'+1. \end{cases}$$

The hardness of $\mathsf{MPLWE}_{q,n+2d+k,\mathbf{d},\lfloor D_{\alpha\cdot q}\rceil}$ follows from the hardness of $\mathsf{MPLWE}_{q,n+2d+k,\mathbf{d},D_{\alpha\cdot q}}$ via a standard reduction that maps $(a,b) \in \mathbb{Z}_q[x] \times \mathbb{R}_q[x]$ to $(a, \lceil b \rfloor)$, where $\lceil b \rfloor$ is the polynomial obtained by rounding every coefficient of $b$ to the nearest integer. Finally, Theorem 2 tells us that $\mathsf{MPLWE}_{q,n+2d+k,\mathbf{d},D_{\alpha\cdot q}}$ is hard assuming the hardness of $\mathsf{PLWE}_{q,D_{\alpha'\cdot q}}^{(f)}$, for $\alpha \cdot q = \Omega(n^{1/2+1/2+c}) \geq \alpha' \cdot q\sqrt{\frac{n+2d+k}{2}}n^c$. This completes the proof of semantic security.    □

## 6.2  IBE in the Random Oracle Model

We construct an IBE scheme in the random oracle model by combining our "Dual Regev" scheme (Sect. 6.1) with our MP-LWE lattice trapdoors (Sect. 5). The IBE construction is essentially identical to that of [8]; we give an explicit description for completeness. Let the set of identity be $\mathcal{I} = \mathbb{Z}_q^{n+2d-2}$. We assume the parameters are chosen such that Theorem 5 holds. Use algorithm TrapGen to generate mpk:$= (a_i)_{i=1}^{t'}$ and msk:$= \tilde{L}$. Given an identity id, interpret it as an element $u \in \mathbb{Z}_q^{<n+2d-2}[x]$ and use algorithm SamplePre to generate sk$_{id}$ := $(r_i)_{i=1}^{t'}$ such that $\sum_{i=1}^{t'} a_i \cdot r_i = u$. Then use the Dual Regev scheme with public key pk $:= ((a_i)_{i=1}^{t'}, u)$ and secret key sk $:= (r_i)_{i=1}^{t'}$ for encryption/decryption of message.

- **Setup:** The setup algorithm IBESetup (on input $1^n$) calls TrapGen($1^n$), obtaining polynomials $(a_1, \ldots, a_{t'})$ along with a trapdoor td. It outputs master public key mpk $= (a_1, \ldots, a_{t'})$ and master secret key msk = td.
- **Key Extraction:** The secret key extraction algorithm IBEExtract, given msk and an identity id, calls SamplePre(td, $H(\text{id})$), where $H(\cdot)$ is modelled as a random oracle. It outputs sk$_{id} = (r_1, \ldots, r_{t'})$, the output of SamplePre.
- **Encryption:** The encryption algorithm Enc, given the master public key mpk $= (a_1, \ldots, a_{t'})$, an identity id, and a message $\mu$, computes $u = H(\text{id})$ and outputs a ciphertext $c \leftarrow$ DualRegev.Enc(pk$_{id}$, $\mu$) (using the Dual Regev encryption algorithm) for pk$_{id} = (a_1, \ldots, a_{t'}, u)$.
- **Decryption:** The decryption algorithm Dec, given the secret key sk$_{id}$ = $(r_1, \ldots, r_{t'})$ and a ciphertext $c$, outputs DualRegev.Dec(sk$_{id}$, $c$).

**Theorem 7.** *Assume the parameters are picked as in Theorems 5 and 6 (so that the Dual Regev Scheme is correct and semantically secure). Then the above IBE scheme is correct and CPA-secure in the random oracle model.*

*Proof.* See ([8], Theorem 7.2).  □

*Remark 2 (Efficiency).* Pick $d, k = \Theta(n), t = \log n$ and $\sigma, \alpha^{-1}, q$ satisfying bounds in Theorems 5 and 6. By construction, the schemes in Subsects. 6.1 and 6.2 have key size and ciphertext size $\tilde{O}(n)$. We show that encryption and decryption algorithms in these schemes take $\tilde{O}(n)$ time. As in [21], products and middle products of polynomials can be computed in $\tilde{O}(n)$ time using FFT-based techniques [9,22]. By doing some preprocessing, sampling from $\chi = \lfloor D_{\alpha \cdot q} \rceil$ can be done in quasi-constant time via table look-up as in [15]. Thus, encryption and decryption in our Dual-Regev like public key scheme and IBE scheme take $\tilde{O}(n)$ time; since the message is of size $k = \Theta(n)$, runtime per encrypted bit is $\tilde{O}(1)$.

## 6.3  IBE in the Standard Model

[2,7] present IBE schemes secure in the standard model from the same framework of lattice trapdoors and dual-Regev encryption. A simplified version of one

construction is presented in [3], Sect. 3. We give a brief summary of [3]'s IBE construction, and sketch how to adapt it to the MP-LWE setting.

Suppose we have an identity space $\{0,1\}^{\ell}$. Set $m = O(n \log n)$. In IBESetup, the [3] scheme samples a random matrix $A \in \mathbb{Z}_q^{n \times m}$ together with trapdoor $T_A$, as well as random matrices $H_{i,b} \in \mathbb{Z}_q^{n \times m}$ for $i \in [\ell]$ and $b \in \{0,1\}$. The public key is $(A, (H_{i,b})_{(i,b) \in [\ell] \times \{0,1\}}, u_0)$ where $u_0$ is a random vector in $\mathbb{Z}_q^n$. The master secret key is $T_A$. The key extraction algorithm IBEExtract, given an identity $\mathsf{id} = \mathsf{id}_1 \cdots \mathsf{id}_\ell$, assembles $H_{\mathsf{id}} = H_{1,\mathsf{id}_1} | \cdots | H_{\ell,\mathsf{id}_\ell} \in \mathbb{Z}_q^{n \times \ell m}$ as the concatenation of $\ell$ matrices. It then samples random vectors $r_i \in \mathbb{Z}_q^m$, and constructs a vector $r = (r_i)_{i \in \ell} \in \mathbb{Z}_q^{\ell m}$. Finally, the trapdoor $T_A$ is used to sample preimages $e \in \mathbb{Z}_q^m$ satisfying $A e = u_0 + H_{\mathsf{id}} r$, i.e. $\begin{bmatrix} A \,|\, - H_{\mathsf{id}} \end{bmatrix} \begin{bmatrix} e \\ r \end{bmatrix} = u_0$, yielding a secret key $\mathsf{sk}_{\mathsf{id}} = (e, r)$. Encryption and Decryption then proceed as in Dual Regev encryption.

[3] proves that their scheme is selective-ID secure in the standard model. Selective-ID security is defined by a game similar to that in Sect. 2.1, except that the adversary generates the challenge identity $\mathsf{id}^*$ *before* seeing the public parameters of the scheme. [2]'s proof of selective-ID security relies on replacing each random matrix $H_{i,b}$ with an indistinguishable matrix $H'_{i,b}$ equipped with trapdoor $T_{i,b}$. Then, given an extraction query $\mathsf{id}$ that differs from the challenge $\mathsf{id}^*$, letting $i$ denote an index on which $\mathsf{id}_i \neq \mathsf{id}_i^*$, the trapdoor $T_{i,\mathsf{id}_i}$ can be used to sample $r_i$ such that $H'_{i,\mathsf{id}_i} r_i = A e - \sum_{j \neq i} H'_{j,\mathsf{id}_j} r_j - u_0$, where $e$ and $r_j$ are sampled randomly from $\mathbb{Z}_q^m$, to produce a secret key $\mathsf{sk}_{\mathsf{id}} = (e, r)$. Crucially, sampling $(e, r)$ using trapdoor $T_{i,\mathsf{id}_i}$ is (statistically) indistinguishable from the honest key extraction procedure (that uses $T_A$).

Our MP-LWE Dual Regev encryption scheme, combined with the lattice trapdoors of Theorem 5, can be used to create a standard model IBE scheme analogous to the one just described. Specifically, we replace the matrix $A$ and its trapdoor $T_A$ with tuple $(a_j)_{j \leq t}$ of $t = \tilde{O}(1)$ polynomials and its trapdoor as generated by Theorem 5. We replace each matrix $H_{i,b}$ with tuple $\bar{h}^{(i,b)} = (h_j)_{j \leq t}^{(i,b)}$ of random polynomials, and replace random vector $u_0$ with a random polynomial. Theorem 5 allows us to replace any particular $\bar{h}^{(i,b)}$ with $\tilde{h}^{(i,b)}$ that is equipped with a trapdoor $T_{i,b}$, and our SamplePre algorithm guarantees the same $(T_A, T_{i,b})$ indistinguishability that was leveraged by [3].

To summarize, this allows for an IBE scheme in the standard model based on MP-LWE with efficiency gains of $\tilde{O}(n)$ over the [3] scheme.

# Appendix

We describe a minor correction to the proof of ([15], Theorem 5.5).

In [15], it is mistakenly claimed (see Sect. 2.1) that for positive semi-definite $B \geq A \geq 0$, the inequality $A^+ \geq B^+$ holds. This is not true in general. For example, when $B$ is positive definite (that is, $B > 0$), we have $B^+ = B^{-1} > 0$; if $A^+ \geq B^+$ then $A^+ > 0$ so $A > 0$ (a contradiction if $A$ is not invertible).

However, the proof of ([15], Theorem 5.5) can be modified to avoid using the mistaken claim. The relevant setting is as follows: consider a matrix of the form

$$\Sigma_3 = (\Sigma_y^+ + \Sigma_p^+)^+$$

such that $\Sigma_y = 2 \begin{bmatrix} R \\ I \end{bmatrix} [R^T\ I]$ and $\Sigma_p > 2 \begin{bmatrix} R \\ I \end{bmatrix} [R^T\ I].$[4] We want to prove that

$\Sigma_3 \geq \begin{bmatrix} R \\ I \end{bmatrix} [R^T\ I]$ (see p. 29)

To prove this, we write $2 \begin{bmatrix} R \\ I \end{bmatrix} [R^T\ I] = Q \begin{bmatrix} D & 0 \\ 0 & 0 \end{bmatrix} Q^T$ where $Q$ is orthogonal and $D$ is diagonal matrix of positive entries. Then, there exists some small $\epsilon > 0$ s.t. $\Sigma_p \geq Q \begin{bmatrix} D & 0 \\ 0 & \epsilon I \end{bmatrix} Q^T > 0$. Thus,

$$0 < \Sigma_p^+ = \Sigma_p^{-1} \leq Q \begin{bmatrix} D^{-1} & 0 \\ 0 & \epsilon^{-1}I \end{bmatrix} Q^T = \frac{1}{2} \left( \begin{bmatrix} R \\ I \end{bmatrix} [R^T\ I] \right)^+ + \begin{bmatrix} 0 & 0 \\ 0 & \epsilon^{-1}I \end{bmatrix}$$

and so

$$0 < \Sigma_p^+ + \Sigma_y^+ \leq \left( \begin{bmatrix} R \\ I \end{bmatrix} [R^T\ I] \right)^+ + \begin{bmatrix} 0 & 0 \\ 0 & \epsilon^{-1}I \end{bmatrix} = Q \begin{bmatrix} 2D^{-1} & 0 \\ 0 & \epsilon^{-1}I \end{bmatrix} Q^T.$$

We conclude that

$$(\Sigma_y^+ + \Sigma_p^+)^+ = (\Sigma_y^+ + \Sigma_p^+)^{-1} \geq Q \begin{bmatrix} \frac{1}{2}D & 0 \\ 0 & \epsilon I \end{bmatrix} Q^T \geq \begin{bmatrix} R \\ I \end{bmatrix} [R^T\ I].$$

# References

1. Abdalla, M., et al.: Searchable encryption revisited: consistency properties, relation to anonymous IBE, and extensions. In: Shoup, V. (ed.) CRYPTO 2005. LNCS, vol. 3621, pp. 205–222. Springer, Heidelberg (2005). https://doi.org/10.1007/11535218_13
2. Agrawal, S., Boneh, D., Boyen, X.: Efficient lattice (H)IBE in the standard model. In: Gilbert, H. (ed.) EUROCRYPT 2010. LNCS, vol. 6110, pp. 553–572. Springer, Heidelberg (2010). https://doi.org/10.1007/978-3-642-13190-5_28
3. Agrawal, S., Boyen, X.: Identity-based encryption from lattices in the standard model (2009)
4. Bai, S., Langlois, A., Lepoint, T., Stehlé, D., Steinfeld, R.: Improved security proofs in lattice-based cryptography: using the Rényi divergence rather than the statistical distance. In: Iwata, T., Cheon, J.H. (eds.) ASIACRYPT 2015. LNCS, vol. 9452, pp. 3–24. Springer, Heidelberg (2015). https://doi.org/10.1007/978-3-662-48797-6_1

---

[4] Our assumptions on $\Sigma_y$ and $\Sigma_p$ are slightly different from those of [15]; these minor modifications are without loss of generality with respect to the application to Gaussian sampling but necessary for the proof to go through.

5. Bellare, M., Desai, A., Jokipii, E., Rogaway, P.: A concrete security treatment of symmetric encryption. In: Proceedings 38th Annual Symposium on Foundations of Computer Science, pp. 394–403. IEEE (1997)
6. Boneh, D., Franklin, M.: Identity-based encryption from the weil pairing. In: Kilian, J. (ed.) CRYPTO 2001. LNCS, vol. 2139, pp. 213–229. Springer, Heidelberg (2001). https://doi.org/10.1007/3-540-44647-8_13. http://dl.acm.org/citation.cfm?id=646766.704155
7. Cash, D., Hofheinz, D., Kiltz, E., Peikert, C.: Bonsai trees, or how to delegate a lattice basis. In: Gilbert, H. (ed.) EUROCRYPT 2010. LNCS, vol. 6110, pp. 523–552. Springer, Heidelberg (2010). https://doi.org/10.1007/978-3-642-13190-5_27
8. Gentry, C., Peikert, C., Vaikuntanathan, V.: Trapdoors for hard lattices and new cryptographic constructions. In: Proceedings of the Fortieth Annual ACM Symposium on Theory of Computing, pp. 197–206. ACM (2008)
9. Hanrot, G., Quercia, M., Zimmermann, P.: The middle product algorithm I. Appl. Algebra Eng. Commun. Comput. **14**(6), 415–438 (2004)
10. Impagliazzo, R., Zuckerman, D.: How to recycle random bits. In: 30th Annual Symposium on Foundations of Computer Science, pp. 248–253. IEEE (1989)
11. Lyubashevsky, V.: Digital signatures based on the hardness of ideal lattice problems in all rings. In: Cheon, J.H., Takagi, T. (eds.) ASIACRYPT 2016. LNCS, vol. 10032, pp. 196–214. Springer, Heidelberg (2016). https://doi.org/10.1007/978-3-662-53890-6_7
12. Lyubashevsky, V., Micciancio, D.: Generalized compact knapsacks are collision resistant. In: Bugliesi, M., Preneel, B., Sassone, V., Wegener, I. (eds.) ICALP 2006. LNCS, vol. 4052, pp. 144–155. Springer, Heidelberg (2006). https://doi.org/10.1007/11787006_13
13. Lyubashevsky, V., Peikert, C., Regev, O.: On ideal lattices and learning with errors over rings. In: Gilbert, H. (ed.) EUROCRYPT 2010. LNCS, vol. 6110, pp. 1–23. Springer, Heidelberg (2010). https://doi.org/10.1007/978-3-642-13190-5_1
14. Micciancio, D.: Generalized compact knapsacks, cyclic lattices, and efficient one-way functions from worst-case complexity assumptions. In: Proceedings of the 43rd Symposium on Foundations of Computer Science, FOCS 2002, pp. 356–365. IEEE Computer Society, Washington, DC, USA (2002). http://dl.acm.org/citation.cfm?id=645413.652130
15. Micciancio, D., Peikert, C.: Trapdoors for lattices: simpler, tighter, faster, smaller. In: Pointcheval, D., Johansson, T. (eds.) EUROCRYPT 2012. LNCS, vol. 7237, pp. 700–718. Springer, Heidelberg (2012). https://doi.org/10.1007/978-3-642-29011-4_41
16. Micciancio, D., Regev, O.: Worst-case to average-case reductions based on Gaussian measures. SIAM J. Comput. **37**(1), 267–302 (2007)
17. Peikert, C., Regev, O., Stephens-Davidowitz, N.: Pseudorandomness of ring-LWE for any ring and modulus. In: Proceedings of the 49th Annual ACM SIGACT Symposium on Theory of Computing, pp. 461–473. ACM (2017)
18. Peikert, C., Rosen, A.: Efficient collision-resistant hashing from worst-case assumptions on cyclic lattices. In: Halevi, S., Rabin, T. (eds.) TCC 2006. LNCS, vol. 3876, pp. 145–166. Springer, Heidelberg (2006). https://doi.org/10.1007/11681878_8
19. Peikert, C., Vaikuntanathan, V., Waters, B.: A framework for efficient and composable oblivious transfer. In: Wagner, D. (ed.) CRYPTO 2008. LNCS, vol. 5157, pp. 554–571. Springer, Heidelberg (2008). https://doi.org/10.1007/978-3-540-85174-5_31

20. Regev, O.: On lattices, learning with errors, random linear codes, and cryptography. In: Proceedings of the Thirty-Seventh Annual ACM Symposium on Theory of Computing, pp. 84–93. ACM (2005)
21. Roşca, M., Sakzad, A., Stehlé, D., Steinfeld, R.: Middle-product learning with errors. In: Katz, J., Shacham, H. (eds.) CRYPTO 2017. LNCS, vol. 10403, pp. 283–297. Springer, Cham (2017). https://doi.org/10.1007/978-3-319-63697-9_10
22. Shoup, V.: Efficient computation of minimal polynomials in algebraic extensions of finite fields. In: Proceedings of the 1999 International Symposium on Symbolic and Algebraic Computation, Vancouver, BC (1999). Citeseer
23. Stehlé, D., Steinfeld, R., Tanaka, K., Xagawa, K.: Efficient public key encryption based on ideal lattices. In: Matsui, M. (ed.) ASIACRYPT 2009. LNCS, vol. 5912, pp. 617–635. Springer, Heidelberg (2009). https://doi.org/10.1007/978-3-642-10366-7_36

# Matrix PRFs: Constructions, Attacks, and Applications to Obfuscation

Yilei Chen[1]([⊠]), Minki Hhan[2], Vinod Vaikuntanathan[3], and Hoeteck Wee[4]

[1] Visa Research, Palo Alto, USA
yilchen@visa.com
[2] Seoul National University, Seoul, South Korea
hhan_@snu.ac.kr
[3] MIT, Cambridge, USA
vinodv@csail.mit.edu
[4] CNRS, ENS, PSL, Paris, France
wee@di.ens.fr

**Abstract.** We initiate a systematic study of pseudorandom functions (PRFs) that are computable by simple matrix branching programs; we refer to these objects as "matrix PRFs". Matrix PRFs are attractive due to their simplicity, strong connections to complexity theory and group theory, and recent applications in program obfuscation.

Our main results are:
- We present constructions of matrix PRFs based on the conjectured hardness of computational problems pertaining to matrix products.
- We show that any matrix PRF that is computable by a read-$c$, width $w$ branching program can be broken in time $\text{poly}(w^c)$; this means that any matrix PRF based on constant-width matrices must read each input bit $\omega(\log(\lambda))$ times. Along the way, we simplify the "tensor switching lemmas" introduced in previous IO attacks.
- We show that a subclass of the candidate local-PRG proposed by Barak et al. [Eurocrypt 2018] can be broken using simple matrix algebra.
- We show that augmenting the CVW18 IO candidate with a matrix PRF provably immunizes the candidate against all known algebraic and statistical zeroizing attacks, as captured by a new and simple adversarial model.

## 1 Introduction

Pseudorandom functions (PRFs), defined by Goldreich, Goldwasser, and Micali [29], are keyed functions that are indistinguishable from truly random functions given black-box access. In this work we focus on pseudorandom functions that can be represented by simple matrix branching programs; we refer to these objects as "matrix PRFs". In the simplest setting, a matrix PRF takes a key specified by $\ell$ pairs of $w \times w$ matrices $\{\mathbf{M}_{i,b}\}_{i\in[\ell], b\in\{0,1\}}$ where

$$\text{PRF}(\{\mathbf{M}_{i,b}\}_{i\in[\ell], b\in\{0,1\}}, \mathbf{x} \in \{0,1\}^{\ell}) := \prod_{i=1}^{\ell} \mathbf{M}_{i,x_i}$$

© International Association for Cryptologic Research 2019
D. Hofheinz and A. Rosen (Eds.): TCC 2019, LNCS 11891, pp. 55–80, 2019.
https://doi.org/10.1007/978-3-030-36030-6_3

Matrix PRFs are attractive due to their simplicity, strong connections to complexity theory and group theory [1,12,44], and recent applications in program obfuscation [11,27].

*Existing Constructions.* First, we note that the Naor-Reingold PRF [37] (extended to matrices in [34]) and the Banerjee-Peikert-Rosen PRF [7] may be viewed as matrix PRFs with post-processing, corresponding to group exponentiation and entry-wise rounding respectively. However, the applications we have in mind do not allow such post-processing. Instead, we turn to a more general definition of read-$c$ matrix PRFs, where the key is specified by $h := c \cdot \ell$ pairs of $w \times w$ matrices $\{\mathbf{M}_{i,b}\}_{i \in [h], b \in \{0,1\}}$ where

$$\mathsf{PRF}(\{\mathbf{M}_{i,b}\}_{i \in [h], b \in \{0,1\}}, \mathbf{x}) := \mathbf{u}_L \cdot \prod_{i=1}^{h} \mathbf{M}_{i, x_i \bmod \ell} \cdot \mathbf{u}_R$$

Here, $\mathbf{u}_L, \mathbf{u}_R$ correspond to fixed vectors independent of the key. This corresponds exactly to PRFs computable by read-$c$ matrix branching programs. By applying Barrington's theorem on the existing PRFs in $\mathsf{NC}^1$, such as the two PRFs we just mentioned [7,37], we obtain read-poly($\ell$) matrix PRFs based on standard assumptions like DDH and LWE.

*This Work.* In this work, we initiate a systematic study of matrix PRFs.

- From the constructive perspective, we investigate whether there are "simpler" constructions of matrix PRF, or hardness assumptions over matrix products that can be used to build matrix PRFs. Here "simpler" means the matrices $\mathbf{M}_{i,b}$'s are drawn from some "natural" distribution, for instance, independently at random from the same distribution. Note that the constructions obtained by apply Barrington's theorem [10] on PRFs in $\mathsf{NC}^1$ yield highly correlated and structured distributions.
- From the attacker's perspective, the use of matrices opens the gate for simple linear algebraic attacks in breaking the hardness assumptions. We would like to understand what are the characteristics that a matrix PRF could or could not have, by trying different linear algebraic attacks. These characteristics include the distribution of the underlying matrices, as well as the complexity of the underlying branching program.
- Finally, we revisit the application of matrix PRFs to program obfuscation as a mechanism for immunizing against known attacks.

## 1.1  Our Contributions

Our contributions may be broadly classified into three categories, corresponding to the three lines of questions mentioned above.

**Constructions.** We show how to build a matrix PRF starting from simple assumptions over matrix products via the Naor-Reingold paradigm [37], and we present candidates for these assumptions. Concretely, we consider the assumption

$$\left(\{\mathbf{A}_{i,b}\}_{i\in[k],b\in\{0,1\}}, \prod_{i=1}^{k}(\mathbf{A}_{i,0}\mathbf{B}), \prod_{i=1}^{k}(\mathbf{A}_{i,1}\mathbf{B})\right) \approx_c \left(\{\mathbf{A}_{i,b}\}_{i\in[k],b\in\{0,1\}}, \mathbf{B}_0, \mathbf{B}_1\right)$$

(1)

where the matrices $\mathbf{A}_{i,b}$, $\mathbf{B}$, $\mathbf{B}_0$ and $\mathbf{B}_1$ are uniformly random over some simple matrix groups. We clarify that the ensuing matrix PRF while efficiently computable, requires a product of $O(k^\ell)$ matrices where $\ell$ is the length of the PRF input.

**Attacks.** We show that any matrix PRF that is computable by a read-$c$, width-$w$ branching program can be broken in time poly$(w^c)$; this means that any matrix PRF based on constant-width matrices must read each input bit $\omega(\log(\lambda))$ times. Our attack and the analysis are inspired by previous zeroizing attacks on obfuscation [6,18,23]; we also provide some simplification along the way. We note that the case of $c = 1$ appears to be folklore.

*The Attack.* The attack is remarkably simple: given oracle access to a function $F : \{0,1\}^\ell \to R$,

1. pick any $L := w^{2c}$ distinct strings $x_1, \ldots, x_L \in \{0,1\}^{\ell/2}$;
2. compute $\mathbf{V} \in R^{L\times L}$ whose $(i,j)$'th entry is $F(x_i\|x_j)$;
3. output rank$(\mathbf{V})$

If $F$ is a truly random function, then $\mathbf{V}$ has full rank w.h.p. On the other hand, if $F$ is computable by a read-$c$, width $w$ branching program, then we show that $F(x_i\|x_j)$ can be written in the form $\langle\mathbf{u}_i, \mathbf{v}_j\rangle$ for some fixed $\mathbf{u}_1, \ldots, \mathbf{u}_L, \mathbf{v}_1, \ldots, \mathbf{v}_L \in R^{w^{2c-1}}$. This means that we can write

$$\mathbf{V} = \underbrace{\begin{pmatrix} \leftarrow \mathbf{u}_1 \rightarrow \\ \vdots \\ \leftarrow \mathbf{u}_L \rightarrow \end{pmatrix}}_{L\times w^{2c-1}} \underbrace{\begin{pmatrix} \uparrow & & \uparrow \\ \mathbf{v}_1 & \cdots & \mathbf{v}_L \\ \downarrow & & \downarrow \end{pmatrix}}_{w^{2c-1}\times L}$$

which implies rank$(\mathbf{V}) \le w^{2c-1}$.

Next, we sketch how we can decompose $F(x_i\|x_j)$ into $\langle\mathbf{u}_i, \mathbf{v}_j\rangle$. This was already shown in [23, Section 4.2], but we believe our analysis is simpler and more intuitive. Consider a read-thrice branching program of width $w$ where

$$\mathbf{M}_{x\|y} = \mathbf{u}_L \mathbf{M}_x^1 \mathbf{N}_y^1 \mathbf{M}_x^2 \mathbf{N}_y^2 \mathbf{M}_x^3 \mathbf{N}_y^3 \mathbf{u}_R$$

Suppose we can rewrite $\mathbf{M}_{x\|y}$ as

$$\hat{\mathbf{u}}_L \cdot (\mathbf{M}_x^1\mathbf{N}_y^1) \otimes (\mathbf{M}_x^2\mathbf{N}_y^2) \otimes (\mathbf{M}_x^3\mathbf{N}_y^3) \cdot \hat{\mathbf{u}}_R$$
$$= \underbrace{\hat{\mathbf{u}}_L \cdot (\mathbf{M}_x^1 \otimes \mathbf{M}_x^2 \otimes \mathbf{M}_x^3)}_{1 \times w^3} \cdot \underbrace{(\mathbf{N}_y^1 \otimes \mathbf{N}_y^2 \otimes \mathbf{N}_y^3) \cdot \hat{\mathbf{u}}_R}_{w^3 \times 1}$$

for some suitable choices of $\hat{\mathbf{u}}_L, \hat{\mathbf{u}}_R$. Unfortunately, such a statement appears to be false. Nonetheless, we are able to prove a similar decomposition where we replace $\hat{\mathbf{u}}_L \cdot (\mathbf{M}_x^1 \otimes \mathbf{M}_x^2 \otimes \mathbf{M}_x^3)$ on the left with

$$\underbrace{\mathsf{flat}\big(\overbrace{\mathbf{u}_L\mathbf{M}_x^1 \otimes \mathbf{M}_x^2 \otimes \mathbf{M}_x^3}^{w^2 \times w^3}\big)}_{1 \times w^5}$$

where $\mathsf{flat}$ "flattens" a $n \times m$ matrix into a $1 \times nm$ row vector by concatenating the rows of the input matrix.

**Applications to IO.** We show that augmenting the CVW18 GGH15-based IO candidate with a matrix PRF provably immunizes the candidate against known algebraic and statistical zeroizing attacks, as captured by a new and simple adversarial model.

*Our IO Candidate.* Our IO candidate on a branching program for a function $f : \{0,1\}^\ell \to \{0,1\}$ samples random Gaussian matrices $\{\mathbf{S}_{i,b}\}_{i\in[h],b\in\{0,1\}}$, a random vector $\mathbf{a}_h$ over $\mathbb{Z}_q$ and a random matrix PRF $\mathsf{PRF}_{\mathbf{M}} : \{0,1\}^\ell \to [0,2^\tau]$ where $2^\tau \ll q$, and outputs

$$\mathbf{A}_J, \{\mathbf{D}_{i,b}\}_{i\in[h],b\in\{0,1\}}$$

The construction basically follows that in [18], with the matrix PRF embedded along the diagonal. By padding the programs, we may assume that the input program and the matrix PRF share the same input-to-index function $\varpi : \{0,1\}^h \to \{0,1\}^\ell$. Then, we have

$$\mathbf{A}_J\mathbf{D}_{\varpi(\mathbf{x})} \bmod q \approx \begin{cases} 0 \cdot \mathbf{S}_{\varpi(\mathbf{x})}\mathbf{a}_h + \mathsf{PRF}_{\mathbf{M}}(\mathbf{x}) & \text{if } f(\mathbf{x}) = 1 \\ (\neq 0) \cdot \mathbf{S}_{\varpi(\mathbf{x})}\mathbf{a}_h + \mathsf{PRF}_{\mathbf{M}}(\mathbf{x}) & \text{if } f(\mathbf{x}) = 0 \end{cases}$$

where $\approx$ captures an error term which is much smaller than $2^\tau$. Functionality is straight-forward: output 1 if $\|\mathbf{A}_J\mathbf{D}_{\varpi(\mathbf{x})}\| < 2^\tau$ and 0 otherwise.

*Our Attack Model.* We introduce the *input-consistent evaluation model* on GGH15-based IO candidates, where the adversary gets oracle access to

$$O_r(\mathbf{x}) := \mathbf{A}_J\mathbf{D}_{\varpi(\mathbf{x})} \bmod q$$

instead of $\mathbf{A}_J, \{\mathbf{D}_{i,b}\}_{i\in[h],b\in\{0,1\}}$. Basically, all known attacks on GGH15-based IO candidates (including the rank attack and statistical zeroing attacks [18, 19] can be implemented in this model. In fact, many of these attacks only make use of the low-norm quantities $\{O_r(\mathbf{x}) : f(\mathbf{x}) = 1\}$, which are also referred to as encodings of zeros, and hence the name zeroing attacks.

Note that our model allow the adversary to perform arbitrary polynomial-time computation on the output of $O_r(\cdot)$, whereas the "weak multi-linear map model" in [11] only allows for algebraic computation of these quantities. The latter does not capture computing the norm of these quantities, as was done in the recent statistical zeroing attacks [19]. In fact, we even allow the adversary access to $\{\mathbf{A}_J\mathbf{D}_{\varpi(\mathbf{x})} \bmod q : f(\mathbf{x}) = 0\}$, quantities which none of the existing attack takes advantage of except the some attacks [18, 21] for a simple GGH15 obfuscation [31]. In fact, the class of adversaries that only does such evaluations appears to capture all known attacks for GGH15-based obfuscation.

We clarify that our attack model does not capture so-called mixed-input attacks, where the adversary computes $\mathbf{A}_J\mathbf{D}_{\mathbf{x}'} \bmod q$ for some $\mathbf{x}' \notin \varpi(\{0,1\}^\ell)$. As in prior works, we make sure that such quantities do not have small norm, but pre-processing the branching program to reject all $\mathbf{x}' \notin \varpi(\{0,1\}^\ell)$ (see Construction of Subprograms in Sect. 6.1 for details).

*Analysis.* We show that for our IO candidate, we can simulate oracle access to $O_r(\cdot)$ given oracle access to $f(\cdot)$ under the LWE assumption (which in particular implies the existence of matrix PRFs). This basically says that our IO candidate achieves "virtual black-box security" in the input-consistent evaluation model.

The proof strategy is quite simple: we hide the lower bits by using the embedded matrix PRFs, and hide the higher bits using lattice-based PRFs [7, 14]. In more detail, observe that the lower $\tau$ bits of of $O_r(\cdot)$ are pseudorandom, thanks to pseudorandomness of $\mathsf{PRF}_\mathbf{M}(\cdot)$. We can then simulate the higher $\log q - \tau$ bits exactly as in [18]:

- if $f(\mathbf{x}) = 1$, then these bits are just 0.
- if $f(\mathbf{x}) = 0$, then we can just rely on the pseudorandomness of existing LWE-based PRFs [7, 14], which tells us that the higher $\log q - \tau$ bits of $\mathbf{S}_{\varpi(\mathbf{x})}\mathbf{a}_h$ are pseudorandom.

Note that the idea of embedding a matrix PRF into an IO candidate already appeared in [27, Section 1.3]; however, the use of matrix PRF for "noise flooding" the encodings of zeros and the lower-order bits as in our analysis –while perfectly natural in hindsight– appears to be novel to this work. In prior works [11, 27], the matrix PRF is merely used to rule out non-trivial algebraic relations amongst the encodings of zeros, namely that there is no low-degree polynomial that vanishes over a large number of pseudorandom values.

## 1.2 Discussion

*Implications for IO.* Our results demonstrate new connections between matrix PRFs and IO in this work and shed new insights into existing IO constructions and candidates:

- Many candidates for IO follow the template laid out in [26]: start out with a branching program $\{\mathbf{M}_{i,b}\}_{i\in[h],b\in\{0,1\}}$, perform some pre-processing, and encode the latter using graded encodings. To achieve security in the generic group model [9] or to defeat against the rank attack [18], the pre-processing would add significant redundancy or blow up the length of the underlying branching program. In particular, even if we start out with a read-once branching program as considered in [31], the program we encode would be a read-$\ell$ (e.g. for so-called dual-input branching programs) or read-$\lambda$ branching program. But, why read-$\ell$ or read-$\lambda$? Our results –both translating existing IO attacks to attacks on matrix PRFs, and showing how to embed a matrix PRF to achieve resilience against existing attacks– suggest that the blow-up is closely related to the complexity of computing matrix PRFs.
- A recent series of works demonstrated a close connection between building functional encryption (and thus IO) to that of low-degree pseudorandom generators (PRG) over the *integers* [2,5,35], where the role of the PRGs is to flood any leakage from the error term during FHE decryption [30]. Here, we show to exploit matrix PRFs –again over the *integers*– to flood any leakage from the error term in the GGH15 encodings (but unlike the setting of PRGs, we do not require the output of the PRFs to have polynomially bounded domain). Both these lines of works point to understanding pseudorandomness over the integers as a crucial step towards building IO.
- Our results suggest new avenues for attacks using input-inconsistent evaluations, namely to carefully exploit the quantities $\{\mathbf{A}_J\mathbf{D}_{\mathbf{x}'} \bmod q : \mathbf{x}' \notin \varpi(\{0,1\}^\ell)\}$ instead of the input-consistent evaluations.

We note that our attacks also play a useful pedagogical role: explaining the core idea of existing zeroizing attacks on IO in the much simpler context of breaking pseudorandomness of matrix PRFs.

*Additional Related Works.* Let us remark that recently Boneh et al. [13] also look for (weak) PRFs with simple structures, albeit with a different flavor of simplicity. Their candidates in fact use the change of modulus, which is what we are trying to avoid.

## 2    Preliminaries

*Notations and Terminology.* Let $\mathbb{R}, \mathbb{Z}, \mathbb{N}$ be the set of real numbers, integers and positive integers. Denote $\mathbb{Z}/(q\mathbb{Z})$ by $\mathbb{Z}_q$. For $n \in \mathbb{N}$, let $[n] := \{1, ..., n\}$. A vector in $\mathbb{R}^n$ (represented in column form by default) is written as a bold lower-case letter, e.g. $\mathbf{v}$. For a vector $\mathbf{v}$, the $i^{th}$ component of $\mathbf{v}$ will be denoted by $v_i$. A matrix is written as a bold capital letter, e.g. $\mathbf{A}$. The $i^{th}$ column vector of $\mathbf{A}$ is denoted $\mathbf{a}_i$.

Subset products (of matrices) appear frequently in this article. For a given $h \in \mathbb{N}$, a bit-string $\mathbf{v} \in \{0,1\}^h$, we use $\mathbf{X}_{\mathbf{v}}$ to denote $\prod_{i\in[h]} \mathbf{X}_{i,v_i}$ (it is implicit that $\{\mathbf{X}_{i,b}\}_{i\in[h],b\in\{0,1\}}$ are well-defined).

The tensor product (Kronecker product) for matrices $\mathbf{A} \in \mathbb{R}^{\ell \times m}$, $\mathbf{B} \in \mathbb{R}^{n \times p}$ is defined as

$$\mathbf{A} \otimes \mathbf{B} = \begin{bmatrix} a_{1,1}\mathbf{B}, \ldots, a_{1,m}\mathbf{B} \\ \ldots, \ldots, \ldots \\ a_{\ell,1}\mathbf{B}, \ldots, a_{\ell,m}\mathbf{B} \end{bmatrix} \in \mathbb{R}^{\ell n \times mp}. \tag{2}$$

For matrices $\mathbf{A} \in \mathbb{R}^{\ell \times m}$, $\mathbf{B} \in \mathbb{R}^{n \times p}$, $\mathbf{C} \in \mathbb{R}^{m \times u}$, $\mathbf{D} \in \mathbb{R}^{p \times v}$,

$$(\mathbf{AC}) \otimes (\mathbf{BD}) = (\mathbf{A} \otimes \mathbf{B}) \cdot (\mathbf{C} \otimes \mathbf{D}). \tag{3}$$

*Matrix Rings/Groups.* Let $M_n(R)$ denote a matrix ring, i.e., the ring of $n \times n$ matrices with coefficients in a ring $R$. When $M_n(R)$ is called a matrix group, we consider matrix multiplication as the group operation. By default we assume $R$ is a commutative ring with unity. The rank of a matrix $\mathbf{M} \in M_n(R)$ refers to its $R$-rank.

Let $\mathsf{GL}(n, R)$ be the group of units in $M_n(R)$, i.e., the group of invertible $n \times n$ matrices with coefficients in $R$. Let $\mathsf{SL}(n, F)$ be the group of $n \times n$ matrices with determinant 1 over a field $F$. When $q = p^k$ is a prime power, let $\mathsf{GL}(n, q)$, $\mathsf{SL}(n, q)$ denote the corresponding matrix groups over the finite field $\mathbb{F}_q$.

*Cryptographic Notions.* In cryptography, the security parameter (denoted as $\lambda$) is a variable that is used to parameterize the computational complexity of the cryptographic algorithm or protocol, and the adversary's probability of breaking security. An algorithm is "efficient" if it runs in (probabilistic) polynomial time over $\lambda$.

When a variable $v$ is drawn randomly from the set $S$ we denote as $v \xleftarrow{\$} S$ or $v \leftarrow U(S)$, sometimes abbreviated as $v$ when the context is clear. We use $\approx_s$ and $\approx_c$ as the abbreviations for statistically close and computationally indistinguishable.

**Definition 2.1 (Pseudorandom function [29]).** *A family of deterministic functions* $\mathcal{F} = \{F_k : D_\lambda \to R_\lambda\}_{\lambda \in \mathbb{N}}$ *is pseudorandom if there exists a negligible function* $\mathrm{negl}(\cdot)$ *for any probabilistic polynomial time adversary* $\mathsf{Adv}$*, such that*

$$\left| \Pr_{k,\mathsf{Adv}}[\mathsf{Adv}^{F_k(\cdot)}(1^\lambda) = 1] - \Pr_{O,\mathsf{Adv}}[\mathsf{Adv}^{O(\cdot)}(1^\lambda) = 1] \right| \leq \mathrm{negl}(\lambda),$$

*where* $O(\cdot)$ *denotes a truly random function.*

## 3   Direct Attacks on Matrix PRFs

In this section we stand from the attacker's point of view to examine what are the basic characteristics that a matrix PRF should (or should not) have. Let $\mathbb{G} = M_w(R)$, $h = c \cdot \ell$. We consider read-$c$ matrix PRFs of the form:

$$F : \{0,1\}^\ell \to R, \quad x \mapsto \mathbf{u}_L \cdot \prod_{i=1}^{h} \mathbf{M}_{i, x_i \bmod \ell} \cdot \mathbf{u}_R \tag{4}$$

where $\mathbf{u}_L, \mathbf{u}_R$ denote the left and right bookend vectors. The seed is given by

$$\mathbf{u}_L, \{\mathbf{M}_{i,b} \in \mathbb{G}\}_{i \in [h], b \in \{0,1\}}, \mathbf{u}_R.$$

### 3.1  Rank Attack

We describe the rank attack which runs in time and space $w^{O(c)}$, where $w$ is the dimension of the $\mathbf{M}$ matrices, $c$ is the number of repetitions of each input bits in the branching program steps. The attack is originated from the zeroizing attack plus tensoring analysis in the obfuscation literature [6,18,23].

The main idea of the attack is to form a matrix from the evaluations on different inputs. We argue that the rank of such a matrix is bounded by $w^{O(c)}$, whereas for a truly random function, the matrix is full-rank with high probability.

**Algorithm 3.1 (Rank attack).** *The algorithm proceeds as follows.*

1. *Let $\rho > w^{2c-1}$. Divide the $\ell$ input bits into 2 intervals $[\ell] = \mathcal{X} \mid \mathcal{Y}$ such that $|\mathcal{X}|, |\mathcal{Y}| \geq \lceil \log \rho \rceil$.*
2. *For $1 \leq i, j \leq \rho$, evaluate the function $F$ on $\rho^2$ different inputs of the form $u^{(i,j)} = x^{(i)} \mid y^{(j)} \in \{0,1\}^\ell$. Let $v^{(i,j)} \in R$ be the evaluation result on $u^{(i,j)}$:*

$$v^{(i,j)} := F(u^{(i,j)})$$

3. *Output the rank of matrix $\mathbf{V} = (v^{(i,j)}) \in R^{\rho \times \rho}$.*

**Analysis for Read-Once Branching Programs.** First we analyze the case where $c = 1$, i.e. the function is read-once. For a truly random function, the $R$-rank of $\mathbf{V}$ is $\rho$ with non-negligible probability.

However, for the function $F$ in Eq. (4), the $R$-rank of $\mathbf{V}$ is bounded by $w$, since

$$\mathbf{V} = \begin{pmatrix} v^{(1,1)} & \dots & v^{(1,\rho)} \\ \dots & \dots & \dots \\ v^{(\rho,1)} & \dots & v^{(\rho,\rho)} \end{pmatrix} = \underbrace{\begin{pmatrix} \mathbf{u}_L \cdot \mathbf{M}_{x^{(1)}} \\ \dots \\ \mathbf{u}_L \cdot \mathbf{M}_{x^{(\rho)}} \end{pmatrix}}_{:=\mathbf{X} \in R^{\rho \times w}} \cdot \underbrace{\left( \mathbf{M}_{y^{(1)}} \cdot \mathbf{u}_R \ \dots \ \mathbf{M}_{y^{(\rho)}} \cdot \mathbf{u}_R \right)}_{:=\mathbf{Y} \in R^{w \times \rho}}. \qquad (5)$$

Here we abuse the subset product notation at $\mathbf{M}_{y^{(j)}}$ by assuming the index of the string $y^{(j)}$ starts at the $(|\mathcal{X}| + 1)^{th}$ step, for $j \in [\rho]$.

**Analysis for Matrix PRFs with Multiple Repetitions.** The analysis for read-once width $w$ branching programs simply uses the fact that $\mathbf{M}_{x \| y}$ can be written as an inner product of two vectors of length $w$ which depend only on $x$ and $y$ respectively. Here, we show that for read-$c$ width $w$ branching programs, $\mathbf{M}_{x \| y}$ can be written as an inner product of two vectors of length $w^{2c-1}$. Note that this was already shown in [23, Section 4.2], but we believe our analysis is simpler and more intuitive.

*Flattening Matrices.* For a matrix $\mathbf{A} = \begin{pmatrix} \mathbf{a}_1 \mid \dots \mid \mathbf{a}_m \end{pmatrix} \in \mathbb{R}^{n \times m}$, let $\mathsf{flat}(\mathbf{A}) \in \mathbb{R}^{1 \times nm}$ denote the row vector formed by concatenating the rows of $\mathbf{A}$. As it turns out, we can write

$$\mathbf{a}\mathbf{B}_1\mathbf{B}_2 \dots \mathbf{B}_c = \mathsf{flat}(\mathbf{a}\mathbf{B}_1 \otimes \mathbf{B}_2 \otimes \dots \otimes \mathbf{B}_c)\mathbf{J} \qquad (6)$$

where $\mathbf{J}$ is a fixed matrix over $\{0,1\}$ independent of $\mathbf{a}, \mathbf{B}_1, \mathbf{B}_2, \ldots, \mathbf{B}_c$.[1] The intuition for the identity is that each entry in the row vector $\mathbf{aB}_1 \cdots \mathbf{B}_c$ is a linear combination of terms, each a product of entries in $\mathbf{aB}_1, \ldots, \mathbf{B}_c$, which appears as an entry in $\mathbf{aB}_1 \otimes \cdots \otimes \mathbf{B}_c$.

In addition, we also have the identity

$$\mathsf{flat}(\mathbf{AB}) = \mathsf{flat}(\mathbf{A}) \cdot (\mathbf{I}_n \otimes \mathbf{B}) \tag{7}$$

where $n$ is the height of $\mathbf{A}$.[2]

*Decomposing Read-Many Branching Programs.* Given a read-$c$ branching program of width $w$, we can write $\mathbf{M}_{x\|y}$ as

$$
\begin{aligned}
\mathbf{M}_{x\|y} &= \mathbf{u}_L \mathbf{M}_x^1 \mathbf{N}_y^1 \cdots \mathbf{M}_x^c \mathbf{N}_y^c \mathbf{u}_R \\
&= \mathsf{flat}\big((\mathbf{u}_L \mathbf{M}_x^1 \mathbf{N}_y^1) \otimes \cdots \otimes (\mathbf{M}_x^c \mathbf{N}_y^c \mathbf{u}_R)\big) \cdot \mathbf{J} \quad \text{via (6)} \\
&= \mathsf{flat}\big(\underbrace{(\mathbf{u}_L \mathbf{M}_x^1 \otimes \cdots \otimes \mathbf{M}_x^c)}_{w^{c-1} \times w^c} \cdot \underbrace{(\mathbf{N}_y^1 \otimes \cdots \otimes \mathbf{N}_y^c \mathbf{u}_R)}_{w^c \times w^{c-1}}\big) \cdot \mathbf{J} \quad \text{via mixed-product} \\
&= \mathsf{flat}\big(\underbrace{(\mathbf{u}_L \mathbf{M}_x^1 \otimes \cdots \otimes \mathbf{M}_x^c)}_{1 \times w^{2c-1}}\big) \cdot \underbrace{(\mathbf{I}_{w^{c-1}} \otimes \mathbf{N}_y^1 \otimes \cdots \otimes \mathbf{N}_y^c \mathbf{u}_R)}_{w^{2c-1} \times 1} \cdot \mathbf{J} \quad \text{via (7)}
\end{aligned}
$$

That is, $\mathbf{M}_{x\|y}$ can be written as an inner product of two vectors of length $w^{2c-1}$. Therefore, the rank of $\mathbf{V}$ is at most $w^{2c-1}$.

*Comparison With* [6,23]. We briefly mention that the previous analysis in [6,23] works by iterating applying the identity

$$\mathsf{flat}(\mathbf{A} \cdot \mathbf{X} \cdot \mathbf{B}) = \mathsf{flat}(\mathbf{X}) \cdot (\mathbf{A}^\top \otimes \mathbf{B})$$

$c$ times along with the mixed-product property to switch the order of the matrix product. (The papers refer to "vectorization" $\mathsf{vec}$, which is the column analogue of $\mathsf{flat}$.) Our analysis is one-shot and avoids this iterative approach, and also avoids keeping track of matrix transposes.

---

[1] Here's a concrete example:

$$
(a_1\ a_2) \begin{pmatrix} b_1 \\ b_2 \end{pmatrix} = \underbrace{\mathsf{flat}\Big((a_1\ a_2) \otimes \begin{pmatrix} b_1 \\ b_2 \end{pmatrix}\Big)}_{=(a_1 b_2\ a_2 b_1\ a_1 b_2\ a_2 b_2)} \begin{pmatrix} 1 \\ 0 \\ 0 \\ 1 \end{pmatrix}.
$$

[2] Here's a concrete example:

$$
\mathsf{flat}\Big(\begin{pmatrix} a_1 \\ a_2 \end{pmatrix} (b_1\ b_2)\Big) = (a_1 b_1\ a_1 b_2\ a_2 b_1\ a_2 b_2) = (a_1\ a_2) \begin{pmatrix} b_1\ b_2 & \\ & b_1\ b_2 \end{pmatrix}.
$$

*Open Problem.* Can we prove the following generalization of the rank attack? Let $g$ be a polynomial of total degree at most $d$ in the variables $x_1, \ldots, x_n, y_1, \ldots, y_n$ over $\mathbb{F}_q$ (or even $\mathbb{Z}$), which computes a function $\{0,1\}^n \times \{0,1\}^n \to \mathbb{F}_q$. Now, pick some arbitrary $X_1, \ldots, X_L, Y_1, \ldots, Y_L \in \{0,1\}^n$, and consider the matrix

$$\mathbf{V} := (g(X_i, Y_j)) \in \mathbb{F}_q^{L \times L}$$

Conjecture:

$$\mathsf{rank}(\mathbf{V}) \leq \max\{L, n^{O(d)}\}$$

If the conjecture is true, then we obtain an attack that works not only for matrix products, but basically any low-degree polynomial.

Here's a potential approach to prove the conjecture (based on the analysis of the rank attack). Write $g$ as a sum of monomials $g_k$. We can write $\mathbf{V}$ as a sum of matrices $\mathbf{V}_k$ where $\mathbf{V}_k := (g_k(X_i, Y_j))$. Each $\mathbf{V}_k$ can be written as a product of two matrices, which allows us to bound the rank of $\mathbf{V}_k$. Then, use the fact that $\mathsf{rank}(\mathbf{V}) \leq \sum_k \mathsf{rank}(\mathbf{V}_k)$. A related question is, can we use this approach to distinguish $g$ from random low-degree polynomials? A related challenge appears here in [1].

## 3.2 Implication of the Rank Attack

We briefly discuss the implication of the rank attack to two relevant proposals (or paradigms) of constructing efficient PRFs [12] and cryptographic hash functions [43,44]. Both proposals use the group operations over a sequence of group elements as the evaluation functions. The rank attack implies when the underlying group $\mathbb{G}$ admits an efficiently computable homomorphism to a matrix group $M_n(R)$, and when each input bit chooses a constant number of steps in the evaluation, then the resulting function is not a PRF (resp. the resulting hash function cannot be used as a random oracle).

Let us remark that our attack does not refute any explicit claims in those two proposals. It mainly serves as a sanity check for the future proposals of instantiating PRFs (resp. hash functions) following those two paradigms. Let us also remark that the rank attack is preventable by adding an one-way extraction function at the end of the evaluation. But when the PRF (resp. hash function) is used inside other applications, an extraction function that is compatible with the application may not be easy to construct. As an example, when the matrix PRFs are used in safeguarding the branching-program obfuscator like [26,27], it is not clear how to apply an extraction function that is compatible with the obfuscator.

**Efficient PRF Based on the Conjugacy Problem.** In the conference on mathematics of cryptography at UCI, 2015, Boneh proposed a simple construction of PRF based on the hardness of conjugacy problem, and suggested to look for suitable non-abelian groups for which the conjugacy problem is hard [12]. If such a group is found, it might lead to a PRF that is as efficient as AES.

However, even without worrying about efficiency, it is not clear how to find a group where the decisional conjugacy problem is hard.

Here is a brief explanation of the conjugacy problem and the PRF construction [12]. Let $K$ be a non-abelian group, $G$ be a subset of $K$, $H$ be a subgroup of $K$. Given $g \xleftarrow{\$} G$, $z = h \circ g \circ h^{-1}$ where $h \xleftarrow{\$} H$, the search conjugacy problem asks to find $h$.

The PRF construction relies on the following decision version of the conjugacy problem. Let $m$ be a polynomial. For $h \xleftarrow{\$} H$, $g_1, g_2, ..., g_m \xleftarrow{\$} G^m$. The decisional problem asks to distinguish

$$g_1, h \circ g_1 \circ h^{-1}, ..., g_m, h \circ g_m \circ h^{-1}$$

from $2m$ random elements in $G$.

Let the input be $x \in \{0,1\}^\ell$, the key be $k = g, \{h_{i,b}\}_{i\in[\ell], b\in\{0,1\}}$. Then the following construction is a PRF assuming the decisional conjugacy problem is hard.

$$F_k(x) := h_{\ell,x_\ell} \circ h_{\ell-1,x_{\ell-1}} \circ ... \circ h_{1,x_1} \circ g \circ h_{1,x_1}^{-1} \circ ... \circ h_{\ell,x_\ell}^{-1}$$

The proof follows the augmented cascade technique of [15].

Note that $F$ only has $2\ell - 1$ steps, with each index in the input repeating for at most 2 times. So if $G$ admits an efficient homomorphism to a matrix group, then the rank attack applies.

Finally, let us remark that there are candidate group for which the search conjugacy problem is hard, e.g. the braid group [33]. But the decisional conjugacy problem over the braid group is broken exactly using a representation as a matrix group [22].

**Cryptographic Hash Functions Based on Cayley Graphs.** We first recall the hard problems on Cayley graphs and their applications in building cryptographic hash functions [41]. Let $\mathbb{G}$ be a finite non-abelian group, and $S = \{s_0, ..., s_m\}$ be a small generation set. The Cayley graph with respect to $(\mathbb{G}, S)$ is defined as follows: each element $v \in \mathbb{G}$ defines a vertex; there is an edge between two vertices $v_i$ and $v_j$ if $v_i = v_j \circ s$ for some $s \in S$. The factorization problem asks to express an element of the group $\mathbb{G}$ as a "short" product of elements from $S$. For certain groups and generation sets, the factorization problem is conjectured to be hard.

In 1991, Zémor [44] introduced a cryptographic hash function based on a Cayley graph with respect to the group $\mathbb{G} = \mathsf{SL}(2, \mathbb{F}_p)$ and the set $S = \left\{ s_0 = \begin{pmatrix} 1, & 1 \\ 0, & 1 \end{pmatrix}, s_1 = \begin{pmatrix} 1, & 0 \\ 1, & 1 \end{pmatrix} \right\}$. Let the input of the hash function be $x \in \{0,1\}^\ell$. The evaluation of the hash function is simply

$$H(x) := \prod_{i=1}^{\ell} s_{x_i}.$$

The collision resistance of this function is based on the hardness of the factorization problem.

The factorization problem with respect to the original proposal of Zémor was solved by [43]. Then alternative proposals of the group $\mathbb{G}$ and generation set $S$ have since then been given (see the survey of [41]). Most of the groups in these proposals are still matrix groups.

We observe that since $H$ is read-once, if the underlying group $\mathbb{G}$ is a matrix group, then the rank attack is able to distinguish the hash function from a random oracle.

Finally, let us clarify that the original authors of the Cayley hash function proposals do not claim to achieve the random-oracle like properties, and most of the analyses of the Cayley graph-based hash function focus on its collision resistance (which is directly related to the factorization problem). Still, many applications of cryptographic hash functions require random-oracle like properties (e.g. in the Fiat-Shamir transformation), so we think it is worth to point out that the Cayley graph-based hash function does not achieve those strong properties when instantiated with matrix groups.

# 4    PRFs from Hard Matrix Problems

In this section, we propose plausibly hard problems related to matrix products, from which we can build a matrix PRF using the Naor-Reingold paradigm. We start from a few simple problems and explain how these problems can be solved efficiently. Then we generalize the attack methodology. Finally, we conclude with the final assumptions which survive our cryptanalytic attempts.

## 4.1    The Initial Attempts

*First Take and the Determinant Attack.* Our first assumption sets $\mathbb{G}$ to be the group $\mathsf{GL}(n, p)$ where we think of $n$ as being the security parameter. Let $m$ be an arbitrarily polynomially large integer. The assumption says that the following two distributions are computationally indistinguishable:

$$(\mathbf{A}_1, ..., \mathbf{A}_m, (\mathbf{A}_1\mathbf{B})^k, ..., (\mathbf{A}_m\mathbf{B})^k) \approx_c (\mathbf{A}_1, ..., \mathbf{A}_m, \mathbf{U}_1, ..., \mathbf{U}_m) \qquad (8)$$

where all the matrices are chosen uniformly at random from $\mathsf{GL}(n, p)$.

Let us explain the choice of $k$. When $k = 1$, the assumption is trivially broken since we can just compute $\mathbf{B}$ on the LHS. When $k$ is a constant, we are still able to break the assumption using a linear algebraic technique detailed in Sect. 3. So we set $k$ to be as large as the security parameter.

Unfortunately, even with a large $k$ the assumption is broken, since on the LHS we have

$$\det((\mathbf{A}_2\mathbf{B})^k) \cdot \det(\mathbf{A}_1)^k = \det((\mathbf{A}_1\mathbf{B})^k) \cdot \det(\mathbf{A}_2)^k$$

In general, any group homomorphism from $\mathbb{G}$ to an Abelian group $\mathcal{H}$ allows us to carry out this attack.

*Second Take and the Order Attack.* The easy fix for this is to take the group to be $\mathsf{SL}(n,p)$, the group of $n$-by-$n$ matrices with determinant 1. It is known that *for several choices of $n$ and $p$*, $\mathsf{SL}(n,p)$ is simple, namely, it has no normal subgroups. Consequently, it admits no non-trivial group homomorphisms to any Abelian group.

**Fact 1 (see, e.g., [32]).** *The following are true about the special linear group* $\mathsf{SL}(n,p)$.

1. *The projective special linear group* $\mathsf{PSL}(n,p)$ *defined as the quotient* $\mathsf{SL}(n,p)/Z(\mathsf{SL}(n,p))$ *is simple for any $n$ and $p$, except when $n = 2$ and $p = 2, 3$. Here, $Z(G)$ denotes the center of group $G$, the set of elements in $G$ that commute with any other element of $G$.*
2. *For $n$ and $p$ where $\gcd(n, p-1) = 1$, the center of $\mathsf{SL}(n,p)$ is trivial. Namely,* $Z(\mathsf{SL}(n,p)) = \{I_n\}$.
3. *As a consequence of (1) and (2) above, for $n \geq 3$ and $p$ such that $\gcd(n, p - 1) = 1$, $\mathsf{SL}(n,p)$ is simple.*

In particular, we will pick $p = 2$ and $n \geq 3$ to be a large number.

However, we notice that there is a way to break the assumption simply using the group order.

**Fact 2 (see, e.g., [32]).** *The order of* $\mathsf{SL}(n,p)$ *is easily computable. It is*

$$r := |\mathsf{SL}(n,p)| = p^{n(n-1)/2} \cdot (p^n - 1) \cdot (p^{n-1} - 1) \cdot \ldots \cdot (p^2 - 1)$$

Therefore, when $k$ is relatively prime to $r$, we can compute $\mathbf{A}_1\mathbf{B}$ from $(\mathbf{A}_1\mathbf{B})^k$ as follows: let $s = k^{-1} \bmod r$ and compute $\left((\mathbf{A}_1\mathbf{B})^k\right)^s = \mathbf{A}_1\mathbf{B}$. Consequently, the similar assumption for group $\mathsf{SL}(n,p)$ is also broken easily.

One may hope that the assumption holds for certain subgroup of $\mathbb{G} \subset \mathsf{GL}(n,p)$. To rule out the order attack, however, we should choose either (1) to hide the order of group $\mathbb{G}$ or (2) fix the order of group to have many divisors, but neither is a nontrivial. We instead seek another way as follows.

*Summary.* From the first two attempts we rule out some choices of the group and parameters. Here is a quick summary.

- $k$ has to be as large as the security parameter $\lambda$ to avoid the rank attack.
- The determinant attack can be generalized to the case when there is an (efficiently computable) homomorphism $f$ from $\mathbb{G}$ to an abelian group $H$, since it crucially relies on the fact that $f((\mathbf{A}_2\mathbf{B})^k) \cdot f(\mathbf{A}_1)^k = f((\mathbf{A}_1\mathbf{B})^k) \cdot f(\mathbf{A}_2)^k$ for $f = \det$. To rule out this class of attacks, we fix $\mathbb{G}$ to be non-abelian simple group.
- The order attack heavily relies on the fact that one can cancel out $\mathbf{A}_1$ in the left-end of the product. We thus use multiple $\mathbf{A}$'s to avoid this canceling with non-abelian group.

## 4.2 The First Formal Assumption and Construction

Let $\mathbb{G}$ be a non-commutative simple group where the group elements can be efficiently represented by matrices (for example, the alternating group $A_n$ for a polynomially large $n \geq 5$). Let $k$ be as large as the security parameter $\lambda$. Our assumption is

$$\left( \{\mathbf{A}_{i,b}\}_{i\in[k],b\in\{0,1\}}, \prod_{i=1}^{k}(\mathbf{A}_{i,0}\mathbf{B}), \prod_{i=1}^{k}(\mathbf{A}_{i,1}\mathbf{B}) \right) \approx_c \left( \{\mathbf{A}_{i,b}\}_{i\in[k],b\in\{0,1\}}, \mathbf{B}_0, \mathbf{B}_1 \right)$$

$$(9)$$

where the matrices $\{\mathbf{A}_{i,b}\}_{i\in[k],b\in\{0,1\}}$, $\mathbf{B}$, $\mathbf{B}_0$ and $\mathbf{B}_1$ are chosen from $U(\mathbb{G})$.

*The PRF Construction.* The family of pseudorandom functions is defined iteratively as follows.

**Construction 4.1** *The construction is parameterized by matrices* $\mathbf{A}_{1,0}$, $\mathbf{A}_{1,1}, \ldots, \mathbf{A}_{k,0}, \mathbf{A}_{k,1}$ *sampled uniformly random from* $\mathbb{G}$.

$$\mathsf{PRF}^{(i)}(x_1 x_2 \ldots x_i) = \prod_{j=1}^{k}(\mathbf{A}_{j,x_i} \cdot \mathsf{PRF}^{(i-1)}(x_1 x_2 \ldots x_{i-1}))$$

$$\mathsf{PRF}^{(0)}(\epsilon) = \mathbf{I}$$

*where* $\epsilon$ *is the empty string and* $\mathbf{I}$ *is the identity matrix.*

The proof follows a Naor-Reingold style argument and proceeds by showing, inductively, that $\mathsf{PRF}^{(i-1)}(x_1 x_2 \ldots x_{i-1})$ is pseudorandom. If we now denote this matrix by $\mathbf{B}$,

$$\left( \mathsf{PRF}^{(i)}(x_1 x_2 \ldots 0), \mathsf{PRF}^{(i)}(x_1 x_2 \ldots 1) \right) = \left( \prod_{j=1}^{k}(\mathbf{A}_{j,0} \cdot \mathbf{B}), \prod_{j=1}^{k}(\mathbf{A}_{j,1} \cdot \mathbf{B}) \right)$$

which, by Assumption 9, is pseudorandom.

## 4.3 Another Assumption and the Synthesizer-Based PRF Construction

In the second assumption, we still choose $\mathbb{G}$ as a non-commutative simple group where the group elements can be efficiently represented by matrices. Let $m_1, m_2$ be arbitrarily polynomially large integers, $k = O(\lambda)$. Let $\{\mathbf{A}_{i,1}, ..., \mathbf{A}_{i,k} \leftarrow U(\mathbb{G}^k)\}_{i\in[m_1]}$, $\{\mathbf{B}_{j,1}, ..., \mathbf{B}_{j,k} \leftarrow U(\mathbb{G}^k)\}_{j\in[m_2]}$. Our assumption is

$$\left( \prod_{v=1}^{k}(\mathbf{A}_{i,v}\mathbf{B}_{j,v}) \right)_{i\in[m_1],j\in[m_2]} \approx_c \left( \mathbf{U}_{i,j} \leftarrow U(\mathbb{G}) \right)_{i\in[m_1],j\in[m_2]}$$

$$(10)$$

*The Synthesizer-Based PRF Construction.* To assist the construction of a synthesizer-based matrix PRF from Assumption (9), let us first define the lists of indices used in the induction.

Let $k = O(\lambda)$, $v = \lceil \log k \rceil$. Let $\ell \in \text{poly}(\lambda)$ be the input length of the PRF. Let $\epsilon$ denote the empty string. Let $||$ be the symbol of list concatenation. For any list $S$ of length $t$, let $S^L$ denote the sublist of the $\lfloor t/2 \rfloor$ items from the left, let $S^R$ denote the sublist of the $t - \lfloor t/2 \rfloor$ items from the right.

Define the initial index list as $S_\epsilon := \{i_1, i_2, ..., i_\ell\}$. Define the "counter" list as $C := \{a_1, ..., a_v\}$. Let $r \in \{0,1\}^* \cup \epsilon$, iteratively define $S_{r0}$ and $S_{r1}$ as:

$$\text{if } S_r \text{ is defined and } |S_r| \geq 4v, \quad S_{r0} := S_r^L || C, \ S_{r1} := S_r^R || C$$
$$\text{if } S_r \text{ is defined and } |S_r| < 4v, \quad \perp.$$

Let $d \in \mathbb{Z}$ be the depth of the induction, i.e., any defined list $S_r$ has $|r| \leq d$. We have $2^d \geq \ell \geq \left(\frac{4-1}{3-1}\right)^d = 1.5^d$. Since $\ell \in \text{poly}(\lambda)$, we have $2^d \in \text{poly}(\lambda)$.

**Construction 4.2** *The PRF is keyed by $2^{4v} \cdot 2^d \in \text{poly}(\lambda)$ random matrices $\{\mathbf{A}_{i,S_r} \leftarrow U(\mathbb{G})\}_{i \in \{0,1\}^{4v}, r \in \{0,1\}^d}$. The evaluation formula $\text{PRF}(x) := \text{PRF}_{S_\epsilon}(x_1 x_2 \ldots x_\ell)$ is defined inductively as*

$$\text{if } |S_r| \geq 4v \quad \text{PRF}_{S_r}(x_1 x_2 \ldots x_t) = \prod_{j=1}^{k} \left( \text{PRF}_{S_{r0}}(x_1 x_2 \ldots x_{\lfloor t/2 \rfloor} \tilde{j}) \cdot \text{PRF}_{S_{r1}}(x_{\lfloor t/2 \rfloor + 1} \ldots x_t \tilde{j}) \right)$$

$$\text{if } |S_r| < 4v \quad \text{PRF}_{S_r}(x_1 x_2 \ldots x_t) = \mathbf{A}_{x_1 x_2 \ldots x_t, S_r}.$$

*where $\tilde{j}$ denotes the bit-decomposition of $j$.*

### 4.4 Open Problems

*Open Problem 1.* In both of our PRF constructions, the numbers of steps in the final branching program (i.e., the number of matrices in each product) are super-polynomial. In Construction 4.1 it takes roughly $O(k^\ell)$ steps; in Construction 4.2 it takes roughly $O(k^d)$ steps. Although those PRFs are efficiently computable (the key is to reuse intermediate products), the numbers of steps are enormous. Is there a way to obtain a matrix PRF with polynomial number of steps from inductive assumptions?

*Open Problem 2.* Any PRF in $\mathsf{NC}^1$ gives rise a matrix PRF, with a possibly different order of products. Is there a *canonical order* and a *canonical group* such that the security of any $\mathsf{NC}^1$ PRF can be reduced to one construction? This would possibly give us a (nice) universal PRF.

## 5 Matrix Attacks for the Candidate Block-Local PRG from BBKK18

A pseudorandom generator $f : \{0,1\}^{bn} \to \{0,1\}^m$ is called $\ell$-block-local if the input can be separated into $n$ blocks, each of size $b$ bits, such that every output bit of $f$ depends on at most $\ell$ blocks. When roughly $m \geq \tilde{\Omega}(n^{\ell/2})^3$, there is a generic attack on $\ell$-block-local PRGs [8]. Specific to 3-block-local PRGs, no generic attack is known for $m < n^{1.5}$.

In [8], the authors propose a simple candidate $\ell$-block-local PRG from group theory, where $m$ can be as large as $n^{\ell/2-\epsilon}$. Let us recall their candidate, with $\ell = 3$ for the simplicity of description. Let $\mathbb{G}$ be a finite group that does not have any abelian quotient group. Choose $3m$ random indices $\left\{ i_{j,k} \overset{\$}{\leftarrow} [n] \right\}_{j \in [m], k \in [3]}$. The 3-block-local-PRG $f$ is mapping from $\mathbb{G}^n$ to $\mathbb{G}^m$ as

$$f_j(x_1, ..., x_n) = x_{j,1} \circ x_{j,2} \circ x_{j,3}.$$

In particular, the authors mentioned that $\mathbb{G}$ can be a non-commutative simple group.

We show that when $\mathbb{G}$ admits an efficiently computable homomorphism to a matrix group $M_w(R)$ (e.g. when $\mathbb{G}$ is an alternating groups $A_w$ with $w \geq 5$), then there is an attack that rules out certain choices of combinations of indices in $f$. In particular, we show that when $\mathbb{G}$ is chosen as the alternating group, then a non-negligible fraction of the candidates (where the randomness is taken over the choices of the indices) are not PRGs.

The attack uses the fact that for any two matrices $\mathbf{A}, \mathbf{B} \in R^{w \times w}$, $\chi(\mathbf{AB}) = \chi(\mathbf{BA})$, where $\chi$ denotes the characteristic polynomial. For simplicity let us assume the group $\mathbb{G}$ is super-polynomially large (e.g. $\mathbb{G} = A_w$ where $w = O(\lambda)$). The distinguisher trys to find four output bits whose indices are of the pattern

$$(a, b, c), (d, e, f), (b, c, d), (e, f, a) \tag{11}$$

where the same letter denote the same index.

Then for these four output group elements represented by matrices $\mathbf{M}_1, \mathbf{M}_2, \mathbf{M}_3, \mathbf{M}_4$, we always have $\chi(\mathbf{M}_1\mathbf{M}_2) = \chi(\mathbf{M}_3\mathbf{M}_4)$ in the real case. In the random case, since we assume $\mathbb{G}$ is super-polynomially large, the characteristic polynomials are unlikely to be equal.

Now we bound the probability for the existence of Pattern (11) if the indices are chosen randomly. The total number $N$ of different layouts of the indices is:

$$N = n^{3m}$$

The total number $M$ of different layouts of the indices such that Pattern (11) occurs can be lower bounded by fixing Pattern (11) over 4 output bits, and choose the rest arbitrarily. I.e.

$$M \geq n^{3(m-4)}$$

So $M/N \geq n^{-12}$, which means as long as $m \geq 4$, a non-negligible fraction of all the candidate 3-block-local-PRGs can be attacked when instantiated with $\mathbb{G}$ as a matrix group.

The attack can be generalized to smaller $\mathbb{G}$, and larger $\ell$. On the positive side, the attack also seem to be avoidable by not choosing the indices that form Pattern (11).

---

[3] More precisely, $m = \Omega(2^{\ell b})(n + 2\ell b)^{\lceil \ell/2 \rceil}$ for the size of each block $b$.

# 6   Candidate Indistinguishability Obfuscation

In this section we give a candidate construction of indistinguishability obfuscation $\mathcal{O}$, following [11, 18, 27].

*Preliminaries.* A branching program $\Gamma$ is a set

$$\Gamma = \left\{ \mathbf{u}_L^P \in \{0,1\}^{1 \times w}, \left\{ \mathbf{P}_{i,b} \in \{0,1\}^{w \times w} \right\}_{i \in [h], b \in \{0,1\}}, \mathbf{u}_R, \varpi : \{0,1\}^\ell \to \{0,1\}^h \right\}$$

where $w$ is called width of branching program and $\varpi$ an input-to-index function. We write

$$\Gamma(\mathbf{x}') := \begin{cases} \mathbf{u}_L \mathbf{P}_{\mathbf{x}'} \mathbf{u}_R & \text{if } \mathbf{x}' \in \{0,1\}^h \\ \mathbf{u}_L \mathbf{P}_{\mathbf{x}'} & \text{if } \mathbf{x}' \in \{0,1\}^{<h} \end{cases}$$

We say that a branching program $\Gamma$ computes a function $f : \{0,1\}^\ell \to \{0,1\}$ if

$$\forall \mathbf{x} \in \{0,1\}^\ell : \Gamma(\varpi(\mathbf{x})) = 0 \iff f(\mathbf{x}) = 1$$

We particularly consider a simple input-to-index function $\varpi : \{0,1\}^\ell \to \{0,1\}^h$ that outputs $h/\ell$ copies of $\mathbf{x}$, i.e. $\varpi(\mathbf{x}) = \mathbf{x}|\mathbf{x}| \cdots |\mathbf{x}$. We denote $c := h/\ell$ and call this branching program $c$-input-repeating. We define an index-to-input function $\iota : [h] \to [\ell]$ so that $\iota : x \mapsto (x \bmod \ell) + 1$. For a string $\mathbf{x} \in \{0,1\}^*$, we denote the length of $\mathbf{x}$ by $|\mathbf{x}|$. We say $\mathbf{x}' \in \varpi(\{0,1\}^\ell)$ input-consistent or simply consistent.

*Lattice Basics.* We briefly describe the basic facts in the lattice problems and trapdoor functions. For more detailed discussion and review we refer [18] to readers. What we need for the construction is, roughly speaking, that there is an algorithm, given matrices $\mathbf{A}$ and $\mathbf{B}$ and a trapdoor $\tau_{\mathbf{A}}$, to sample a (random) matrix $\mathbf{D}$ whose entries follow the discrete Gaussian distribution with small variance such that $\mathbf{A}\mathbf{D} = \mathbf{B} \bmod q$. We denote this random small-norm Gaussian $\mathbf{D}$ by $\mathbf{A}^{-1}(\mathbf{B})$ following [18]. Readers who are not interested in the details may skip the detailed definitions and lemmas described here, since they are only used for technical details such as set parameters, etc.

We denote the discrete Gaussian distribution over $\mathbb{Z}^n$ with parameter $\sigma$ by $D_{\mathbb{Z}^n, \sigma}$. Given matrix $\mathbf{A} \in \mathbb{Z}_q^{n \times m}$, the kernel lattice of $\mathbf{A}$ is denoted by

$$\Lambda^{\perp}(\mathbf{A}) := \{ \mathbf{c} \in \mathbb{Z}^m : \mathbf{A} \cdot \mathbf{c} = \mathbf{0}^n \bmod q \}.$$

Given $\mathbf{y} \in \mathbb{Z}_q^n$ and $\sigma > 0$, we use $\mathbf{A}^{-1}(\mathbf{y}, \sigma)$ to denote the distribution of a vector $\mathbf{d}$ sampled from $D_{\mathbb{Z}^m, \sigma}$ conditioned on $\mathbf{A}\mathbf{d} = \mathbf{y} \bmod q$. We sometimes omit $\sigma$ when the context is clear.

**Definition 6.1 (Decisional learning with errors (LWE) [42]).** *For $n, m \in \mathbb{N}$ and modulus $q \geq 2$, distributions for secret vector, public matrices, and error vectors $\theta, \pi\chi \subset \mathbb{Z}_q$. An LWE sample w.r.t. these parameters is obtained by sampling $\mathbf{s} \leftarrow \theta^n$, $\mathbf{A} \leftarrow \pi^{n \times m}$, $\mathbf{e} \leftarrow \chi^m$ and outputting $(\mathbf{A}, \mathbf{s}^T \mathbf{A} + \mathbf{e}^T \bmod q)$.*

*We say that an algorithm solves $\mathsf{LWE}_{n,m,q,\theta,\pi,\chi}$ if it distinguishes the LWE sample from a random sample distributed as $\pi^{n \times m} \times U(\mathbb{Z}_q^{1 \times m})$ with probability bigger than $1/2$ plus non-negligible.*

**Lemma 6.2 (Standard form** [16,38,39,42]**).** *For $n \in \mathbb{N}$ and for any $m = \text{poly}(n)$, $q \leq 2^{\text{poly}(n)}$. Let $\theta = \pi = U(\mathbb{Z}_q)$ and $\chi = D_{\mathbb{Z},\sigma}$ where $\sigma \geq 2\sqrt{n}$. If there exist an efficient (possibly quantum) algorithm that solves $\mathsf{LWE}_{n,m,q,\theta,\pi,\chi}$, then there exists an efficient (possibly quantum) algorithm for approximating $\mathsf{SIVP}$ and $\mathsf{GapSVP}$ in $\ell_2$ norm, in the worst case, within $\tilde{O}(nq/\sigma)$ factors.*

**Lemma 6.3 (LWE with small public matrices** [14]**).** *If $n, m, q, \sigma$ are chosen as Lemma 6.2, then $\mathsf{LWE}_{n',m,q,U(\mathbb{Z}_q),D_{\mathbb{Z},\sigma},D_{\mathbb{Z},\sigma}}$ is as hard as $\mathsf{LWE}_{n,m,q,\theta,\pi,\chi}$ for $n' \geq 2n \log q$.*

**Lemma 6.4** ([3,4,28,36]**).** *There is a p.p.t. algorithms $\mathsf{TrapSamp}(1^n, 1^m, q)$ that, given modulus $q \geq 2$ and dimension $m, n$ such that $m \geq 2n \log q$, outputs $\mathbf{A} \approx_s U(\mathbb{Z}_q^{n \times m})$ with a trapdoor $\tau$. Further, if $\sigma \geq 2\sqrt{n \log q}$, there is a p.p.t. algorithm that, given $(\mathbf{A}, \tau) \leftarrow \mathsf{TrapSam}(1^n, 1^m, q)$ and $\mathbf{y} \in \mathbb{Z}_q^n$, outputs a sample from $\mathbf{A}^{-1}(\mathbf{y}, \sigma)$. Further, it holds that*

$$\{\mathbf{A}, \mathbf{x}, \mathbf{y} : \mathbf{y} \leftarrow U(\mathbb{Z}_q^n), \mathbf{x} \leftarrow \mathbf{A}^{-1}(\mathbf{y}, \sigma)\} \approx_s \{\mathbf{A}, \mathbf{x}, \mathbf{y} : \mathbf{x} \leftarrow D_{\mathbb{Z}^m, \sigma}, \mathbf{y} = \mathbf{A}\mathbf{x}\}.$$

### 6.1   Construction

*Input.* The obfuscation algorithm takes as input a $c$-input-repeating branching program $\Gamma = \{\mathbf{u}_L \in \{0,1\}^{1 \times w}, \{\mathbf{P}_{i,b} \in \{0,1\}^{w \times w}\}_{i \in [h], b \in \{0,1\}}, \mathbf{u}_R\}$ computing a function $f : \{0,1\}^\ell \to \{0,1\}$.

We modify $\Gamma$ to a new functionally equivalent branching program $\Gamma'$ so that it satisfies $\Gamma'(\mathbf{x}') \neq 0$ for all $\mathbf{x}' \notin \varpi(\{0,1\}^h)$ (as well as $\mathbf{x}' \in \{0,1\}^{<h}$). This can be done by padding an input-consistency check program in the right-bottom diagonal of $\mathbf{P}$, which only slightly increases $w$ and the bound of entries. Concretely we follow Construction 6.1. For brevity, we just assume that the input program is of the form

$$\Gamma = \{\mathbf{u}_L \in \{0, 1, \cdots, T\}^{1 \times w}, \{\mathbf{P}_{i,b} \in \{0, 1, \cdots, T\}^{w \times w}\}_{i \in [h], b \in \{0,1\}}, \mathbf{u}_R\}$$

and assume that it satisfies the condition above without loss of generality. In particular, $|\Gamma(\varpi(\mathbf{x}))| \leq T$ in this construction.

*Obfuscation Procedure*

- Set parameters $n, m, q, \tau, \nu, B \in \mathbb{N}$ and $\sigma \in \mathbb{R}^+$ as in Parameter (Sect. 6.1). Let $d := wn + 5\tau + 3\ell$ be a dimension of pre-encoding.
- Sample a matrix PRF $\{\mathbf{u}_L^{\mathsf{M}} \in \{0,1\}^{1 \times 5\tau}, \{\mathbf{M}_{i,b} \in \{0,1\}^{5\tau \times 5\tau}\}_{i \in [h], b \in \{0,1\}}, \mathbf{u}_R^{\mathsf{M}} \in \mathbb{Z}^{5\tau \times 1}\}$ with input length $\ell$ and $c$-repetition whose range is $[0, 2^\tau - 1]$. Concretely, we follow Construction 6.1. By padding the programs, we may assume that the input program and the matrix PRF share the same input-to-index function $\varpi : \{0,1\}^h \to \{0,1\}^\ell$.

– Sample $\left\{ \mathbf{S}_{i,b} \leftarrow D_{\mathbb{Z},\sigma}^{n \times n} \right\}_{i \in [h], b \in \{0,1\}}$ and $\mathbf{a}_h \leftarrow U(\mathbb{Z}_q^{n \times 1})$, and compute pre-encodings as follows:

$$\mathbf{J} := \left( \mathbf{u}_L \otimes \mathbf{1}^{1 \times n} \| \mathbf{u}_L^M \right), \quad \mathbf{L} := \begin{pmatrix} \mathbf{u}_R \otimes \mathbf{a}_h \\ \mathbf{u}_R^M \end{pmatrix},$$

$$\hat{\mathbf{S}}_{i,b} := \begin{pmatrix} \mathbf{P}_{i,b} \otimes \mathbf{S}_{i,b} & \\ & \mathbf{M}_{i,b} \end{pmatrix} \quad \text{for } i \in [h]$$

For brevity we write $\mathbf{S}(\mathbf{x}') := \mathbf{1}^{1 \times n} \cdot \mathbf{S}_{\mathbf{x}'} \cdot \mathbf{a}_h$. In particular, for all $\mathbf{x}' \in \{0,1\}^h$,

$$\mathbf{J} \cdot \hat{\mathbf{S}}_{\mathbf{x}'} \cdot \mathbf{L}$$
$$= \Gamma(\mathbf{x}') \cdot \mathbf{S}(\mathbf{x}') + \mathbf{u}_L^M \cdot \mathbf{M}_{\mathbf{x}'} \cdot \mathbf{u}_R^M$$
$$= \begin{cases} \mathsf{PRF}_{\mathbf{M}}(\mathbf{x}) & \text{if } \mathbf{x}' = \varpi(\mathbf{x}) \text{ and } f(\mathbf{x}) = 1 \\ (\neq 0) \cdot \mathbf{S}(\mathbf{x}') + \mathbf{u}_L^M \mathbf{M}_{\mathbf{x}'} \mathbf{u}_R^M & \text{otherwise} \end{cases}$$

Note that $\Gamma(\mathbf{x}')$ is a scalar, thus $\otimes$ is just a multiplication.

– Sample error matrices $\mathbf{E}_{i,b}$ from $D_{\mathbb{Z},\sigma}$ with the corresponding dimension and computes

$$\mathbf{A}_J = \mathbf{J} \cdot \mathbf{A}_0 \in \mathbb{Z}^{1 \times m}$$
$$\mathbf{D}_{i,b} \leftarrow \mathbf{A}_{i-1}^{-1} \left( \hat{\mathbf{S}}_{i,b} \cdot \mathbf{A}_i + \mathbf{E}_{i,b} \right) \in \mathbb{Z}^{m \times m}, i = 1, 2, \cdots, h-1$$
$$\mathbf{D}_{h,b} \leftarrow \mathbf{A}_{h-1}^{-1} \left( \hat{\mathbf{S}}_{h,b} \cdot \mathbf{L} + \mathbf{E}_{h,b} \right) \in \mathbb{Z}^{m \times 1}$$

*Output.* The obfuscation algorithms outputs $\{\mathbf{A}_J, \{\mathbf{D}_{i,b}\}_{i \in [h], b \in \{0,1\}}\}$ as an obfuscated program.

*Evaluation.* For input $\mathbf{x} \in \{0,1\}^\ell$, returns 1 if $|\mathbf{A}_J \cdot \mathbf{D}_{\varpi(\mathbf{x})} \bmod q| < B$, and 0 otherwise.

*Correctness.* For $\mathbf{x} \in \{0,1\}^{\leq h}$ with length $h'$,

$$\mathbf{A}_J \cdot \mathbf{D}_{\mathbf{x}'} = \mathbf{J} \cdot \hat{\mathbf{S}}_{\mathbf{x}'} \cdot \mathbf{A}_{h'} + \mathbf{J} \cdot \sum_{j=1}^{h'} \left( \left( \prod_{i=1}^{j-1} \hat{\mathbf{S}}_{i,x_i} \right) \cdot \mathbf{E}_{j,x_j} \cdot \prod_{k=j+1}^{h'} \mathbf{D}_{k,x_k} \right) \bmod q \tag{12}$$

where $\mathbf{A}_h := \mathbf{L}$. Note that all entries following the discrete Gaussian distribution is bounded by $\sqrt{m}\sigma$ with overwhelming probability. The latter term, GGH15 errors, can be bounded, with all but negligible probability, as follows:

$$\left\| \mathbf{J} \cdot \sum_{j=1}^{h'} \left( \left( \prod_{i=1}^{j-1} \hat{\mathbf{S}}_{i,x_i} \right) \cdot \mathbf{E}_{j,x_j} \cdot \prod_{k=j+1}^{h'} \mathbf{D}_{k,x_k} \right) \right\|_\infty \leq (2wd) \cdot h' \cdot (m\sqrt{m}\sigma \cdot wT)^{h'}$$

In particular, for $\mathbf{x}' = \varpi(\mathbf{x})$ and $f(\mathbf{x}) = 1$, the first term is $\mathsf{PRF_M}(\mathbf{x})$, which is bounded by $2^\tau - 1$. We set $B \geq 2^\tau + (2wd) \cdot h \cdot (m\sqrt{m}\sigma \cdot wT)^h$ so that for every $\mathbf{x}$ satisfying $f(\mathbf{x}) = 1$ the obfuscation outputs correctly.

We also note that, if we set $q > B \cdot \omega(\mathrm{poly}(\lambda))$,

$$\Gamma(\mathbf{x}') = \mathbf{0} \iff \mathbf{x}' = \varpi(\mathbf{x}) \wedge f(\mathbf{x}) = 1$$

holds for any $\mathbf{x}' \in \{0,1\}^{\leq h}$ since we pad the input-consistency check program at the beginning. This implies that the random matrix $\mathbf{A}'_h$ the (partial) evaluation $\mathbf{A}_J \cdot \mathbf{D}_{\mathbf{x}'}$ is not canceled. That is, the probability that the evaluation of obfuscation outputs 1 is negligible for an incomplete, inconsistent input $\mathbf{x}'$ or an input $\mathbf{x}' = \varpi(\mathbf{x})$ satisfying $f(\mathbf{x}) = 0$.

**Parameters.** Our parameter settings follow [11,18], which matches to the current existing safety mechanisms. Let $\lambda$ be a security parameter of construction and $\lambda_{\mathsf{LWE}} = \mathrm{poly}(\lambda)$ a security parameter of underlying LWE problem. Let $d := wn + 5\tau$ be a dimension of pre-encodings. For trapdoor functionalities, $m = \Omega(d\log q)$ and $\sigma = \Omega(\sqrt{z\log q})$ by Lemma 6.4. Set $n = \Omega(\lambda_{\mathsf{LWE}}\log q)$ and $\sigma = \Omega(\sqrt{\lambda_{\mathsf{LWE}}})$ for the security of LWE as in Lemmas 6.2 and 6.3. Set $q \leq (\sigma/\lambda_{\mathsf{LWE}}) \cdot 2^{\lambda_{\mathsf{LWE}}^{1-\epsilon}}$ for an $\epsilon \in (0,1)$. Also for the security proof in our model, we set $2^\tau \geq (2wd) \cdot h \cdot (m\sqrt{m}\sigma \cdot wT)^h \cdot \omega(\mathrm{poly}(\lambda))$. On the other hand, we set $B \geq 2^\tau + (2wd) \cdot h \cdot (m\sqrt{m}\sigma \cdot wT)^h$ and $q \geq B \cdot \omega(\mathrm{poly}(\lambda))$ for the correctness.[4]

### Construction of Subprograms

*Input-Consistency Check Program.* We describe a read-once branching program for checking whether $\mathbf{x}' \in \varpi(\{0,1\}^\ell)$; this plays the role of so-called "bundling scalars" or "bundling matrices" in prior constructions. For $i \in [h]$ and $b \in \{0,1\}$, compute $\mathbf{C}_{i,b} \in \mathbb{Z}^{3\ell \times 3\ell}$ as the $\mathrm{diag}(\mathbf{C}_{i,b}^{(1)}, \cdots, \mathbf{C}_{i,b}^{(\ell)})$ where

$$\mathbf{C}_{i,b}^{(k)} = \begin{cases} \mathbf{I}^{3\times3} & \text{if } \iota(i) \neq k \\ \mathrm{diag}(1,0,1) & \text{if } \iota(i) = k \text{ and } i \leq (c-1)\ell \\ \mathrm{diag}(0,1,1) & \text{if } \iota(i) = k \text{ and } i > (c-1)\ell \end{cases}$$

Let $\mathbf{u}_L^{\mathbf{C}} = B \cdot \mathbf{1}^{1\times3\ell}$ and $\mathbf{u}_R^{\mathbf{C}} = (1,1,-1)^T \otimes \mathbf{1}^{\ell\times1}$, where $T$ is an integer satisfying $\|\mathbf{P}(\mathbf{x}')\|_\infty < T$ for all $\mathbf{x}' \in \{0,1\}^{\leq h}$.

Then $\{\mathbf{u}_L^{\mathbf{C}}, \{\mathbf{C}_{i,b}\}_{i\in[h]b\in\{0,1\}}, \mathbf{u}_R^{\mathbf{C}}\}$ is an input-consistency check program, and further $\mathbf{C}(\mathbf{x}') + \mathbf{P}(\mathbf{x}') \neq \mathbf{0}$ for all $\mathbf{x}' \notin \varpi(\{0,1\}^\ell)$ and $\mathbf{x}' \in \{0,1\}^{<h}$. That is, we concretely consider

$$\Gamma' = \left\{\mathbf{u}'_L = (\mathbf{u}_L\|\mathbf{u}_L^{\mathbf{C}}), \{\mathbf{P}'_{i,b} = \mathrm{diag}(\mathbf{P}_{i,b}, \mathbf{C}_{i,b})\}_{i\in[h],b\in\{0,1\}}, \mathbf{u}'_R = \begin{pmatrix} \mathbf{u}_R \\ \mathbf{u}_R^{\mathbf{C}} \end{pmatrix}\right\}.$$

---

[4] Note that by adjusting $\lambda_{\mathsf{LWE}}$ appropriately large, all constraint can be satisfied as in [11, Section 4.3].

In particular, this gives $w_{\mathsf{new}} = w + 3\ell$ and the bound of entry $T = 2w$. Also we note that $\Gamma'(\varpi(\mathbf{x})) = \Gamma(\varpi(\mathbf{x}))$, thus this is bounded by $T$.

*Remark 6.5.* Usual construction of branching programs have a property that $\mathbf{u}_L \cdot \mathbf{P}'_{\mathbf{x}} \in \{0,1\}^{1 \times w}$ for all $\mathbf{x}' \in \{0,1\}^{<h}$ and $|\mathbf{P}(\mathbf{x}')| \leq w$, thus we can set $T := 2w$; or set $T = w^h$ safely. In our parameter setting, we used $T = 2w$.

*Matrix PRFs.* For concreteness we provide the construction of matrix PRFs used in the obfuscation given in [27, Section 4.2]. By Barrington's theorem [10], we know that there exist matrix PRFs that output a random binary value. WLOG, we assume that it is $c$-input-repetition branching program. We write this as $\{\mathbf{u}_L^{(j)}, \{\mathbf{M}_{i,b}^{(j)}\}_{i \in [h], b \in \{0,1\}}, \mathbf{u}_R^{(j)}\}_{j \in [\tau]}$ that are independent to each others. Note that all entries are binary. We concatenate them as

$$\mathbf{u}_L^{\mathbf{M}} = (\mathbf{u}_L^{(1)} \| \cdots \| \mathbf{u}_L^{(\tau)}), \quad \mathbf{M}_{i,b} = \mathsf{diag}(\mathbf{M}_{i,b}^{(1)}, \cdots, \mathbf{M}_{i,b}^{(\tau)}), \quad \mathbf{v}_R^{\mathbf{M}} = \begin{pmatrix} \mathbf{v}_R^{(1)} \\ 2 \cdot \mathbf{v}_R^{(2)} \\ \cdots \\ 2^{\tau-1} \cdot \mathbf{v}_R^{(\tau)} \end{pmatrix}$$

then $\mathsf{PRF}_{\mathbf{M}} : \mathbf{x} \mapsto \mathbf{u}_L^{\mathbf{M}} \cdot \mathbf{M}_{\varpi(\mathbf{x})} \cdot \mathbf{u}_R^{\mathbf{M}} \in [0, 2^\tau - 1]$ is a pseudorandom function, which is the desired construction. Note that the width of this program is $5\tau$.

## 6.2  Security

*Security Model.* We note that almost all known attacks including the recently reported *statistical zeroizing attack* [19], *rank attack* and *subtraction attack* [18] only exploit the evaluations of $\mathbf{x}' \in \varpi(\{0,1\}^\ell)$. While some attacks called *mixed-input attack* are considered in the literature (e.g. [26]), however, there is only one actual attack [17] in such class for GGH15-based obfuscation so far, which only exploits several input-consistent evaluations as well in the first phase to extract the information to run mixed-input attack. Some attack that indeed use the mixed-inputs for other multilinear maps [24, 25], but the first step either uses the valid inputs [40] or decodes the multilinear map using known weakness of the NTRU problem [20].

From this motivation, we consider a restricted class of adversary which can gets oracle access to an input-consistent evaluation oracle

$$O_r : \mathbf{x} \mapsto \mathbf{A}_J \mathbf{D}_{\varpi(\mathbf{x})} \bmod q, \ \forall \mathbf{x} \in \{0,1\}^\ell$$

In our model that we call *input-consistent evaluation model* the purpose of adversary is to obtain any meaningful information of the implementation of $\Gamma$ beyond the input-output behavior. More concretely, we say that the obfuscation procedure is VBB-secure in the input-consistent evaluation model if any p.p.t. adversary cannot distinguish the oracle $O_r$ from the following oracle

$$F_r(\mathbf{x}) = \begin{cases} U([0, 2^\tau - 1]) & \text{if } f(\mathbf{x}) = 0 \\ U(\mathbb{Z}_q) & \text{otherwise} \end{cases} \tag{13}$$

with non-negligible probability, i.e. $O_r(\cdot) \approx_c F_r(\cdot)$.

**Theorem 6.6.** *The obfuscation construction $\mathcal{O}$ is VBB-secure in the input-consistent evaluation models.*

The main strategy is to hide the lower bits by embedded matrix PRFs, and hide the higher bits using lattice-based PRFs [7,14] stated as follows.

**Lemma 6.7** ([18, **Lemma 7.4**]). *Let $h, n, q, b \in \mathbb{N}$ and $\sigma, \sigma^* \in \mathbb{R}$ s.t. $n = \Omega(\lambda \log q)$, $\sigma = \Omega(\sqrt{\lambda \log q})$, $b \geq h \cdot (\sqrt{n}\sigma)^h$, $\sigma^* > \omega(\mathrm{poly}(\lambda)) \cdot b$, $q \geq \sigma^* \omega(\mathrm{poly}(\lambda))$. Define a function family $\mathcal{F} = \{f_\mathbf{a} : \{0,1\}^h \to \mathbb{Z}_q^n\}$, for which the key generation algorithm samples $\mathbf{a} \leftarrow U(\mathbb{Z}_q^n)$ as the private key, $\left\{ \mathbf{S}_{i,b} \leftarrow D_{\mathbb{Z},\sigma}^{n \times n} \right\}$ as the public parameters. The evaluation algorithm takes input $\mathbf{x}' \in \{0,1\}^h$ and computes*

$$f_\mathbf{a}(\mathbf{x}') = \left( \prod_{i=1}^{h} \mathbf{S}_{i,x_i} \right) \cdot \mathbf{a} + \mathbf{e}_{\mathbf{x}'} = \mathbf{S}_{\mathbf{x}'} \cdot \mathbf{a} + \mathbf{e}_{\mathbf{x}'} (\mathrm{mod} q)$$

*where $\mathbf{e}_{\mathbf{x}'} \leftarrow D_{\mathbb{Z},\sigma^*}^n$ is freshly sampled for every $\mathbf{x}' \in \{0,1\}^h$. Then, for $d = \mathrm{poly}(\lambda)$, the distribution of evaluations $\{f_\mathbf{a}(\mathbf{x}_1'), \cdots, f_\mathbf{a}(\mathbf{x}_d')\}$ over the choice of $\mathbf{a}$ and errors is computationally indistinguishable from $d$ independent uniform random vectors from $\mathbb{Z}_q^n$, assuming the hardness of $\mathsf{LWE}_{n,\mathrm{poly},q,U(\mathbb{Z}_q),D_{\mathbb{Z},\sigma},D_{\mathbb{Z},\sigma}}$.*

The proof of the main theorem is as follows.

*Proof (Proof of Theorem 6.6).* We will show that the sequence of $d = \mathrm{poly}(\lambda)$ queries to $O_r$ are indistinguishable to the corresponding queries to $F_r$ as follows.

$$\{O_r(\cdot)\} = \{\mathbf{x} \mapsto \Gamma(\varpi(\mathbf{x})) \cdot \mathbf{S}(\varpi(\mathbf{x})) + \mathsf{PRF}_\mathbf{M}(\varpi(\mathbf{x})) + (\text{GGH15 errors})\}_{k \in [d]}$$
$$\approx_c \{\mathbf{x} \mapsto \Gamma(\varpi(\mathbf{x})) \cdot \mathbf{S}(\varpi(\mathbf{x})) + U([0, 2^\tau - 1]) + (\text{GGH15 errors})\}_{k \in [d]}$$
$$\approx_s \{\mathbf{x} \mapsto \Gamma(\varpi(\mathbf{x})) \cdot (\mathbf{S}(\varpi(\mathbf{x})) + \mathbf{e}_{\varpi(\mathbf{x})}) + U([0, 2^\tau - 1]))\}_{k \in [d]}$$
$$\approx_s \{\mathbf{x} \mapsto \Gamma(\varpi(\mathbf{x})) \cdot U(\mathbb{Z}_q) + U([0, 2^\tau - 1]))\}_{k \in [d]}$$
$$\approx_s \{F_r(\cdot)\}$$

Here, we are using noise-flooding applied to $\Gamma(\varpi(\mathbf{x})) e_{\varpi(\mathbf{x})} +$ (GGH15 errors). More precisely, to invoke Lemma 6.7, it should hold that $2^\tau \geq h \cdot (\sqrt{n}\sigma)^h \cdot \omega(\mathrm{poly}(\lambda))$ and $2^\tau \geq (2wd) \cdot h \cdot (m\sqrt{m}\sigma \cdot wT)^h \cdot \omega(\mathrm{poly}(\lambda))$ to neglect GGH15 errors.

*Remark 6.8 (weakening PRF requirements).* We note that we only use the matrix PRF for noise-flooding, and therefore it suffices to relax pseudorandomness of $F : \{0,1\}^\ell \to [0, 2^\tau - 1]$ to the following: for any efficiently computable $B$-bounded function $g : \{0,1\}^\ell \to [B, -B]$ where $B \ll 2^\tau$, we have

$$\{\mathbf{x} \mapsto F(\mathbf{x})\} \approx_c \{\mathbf{x} \mapsto F(\mathbf{x}) + g(\mathbf{x})\}$$

where $+$ is computed over $\mathbb{Z}$. A similar relaxation has been considered in the context of weaker pseudorandom generators for building IO [5]. For this notion, one could potentially have candidates where each $\mathbf{M}_{i,b}$ is drawn uniformly at random from a Gaussian distribution but where $\mathbf{v}_R^\mathbf{M}$ is the same as in Sect. 6.1.

## 6.3   Comparison

In this section we compare our model to the previous security model in [11].

First, we briefly review the security model in [11]. This model gives a stronger oracle to the adversary that allows the adversary to query a *polynomial* (or circuit) rather than an input $\mathbf{x}$. More precisely, the adversary chooses a circuit $C$ described by $\left\{\beta_{i,b}^{(k)}\right\}_{i\in[h],b\in\{0,1\},k\in K}$ and queries

$$T = \mathbf{A}_J \sum_{k\in K} \prod_{i=1}^{h} (\beta_{i,0}^{(k)}\mathbf{D}_{i,0} + \beta_{1,1}^{(k)}\mathbf{D}_{i,1}) \bmod q$$

to a zero-testing oracle, and learns the value $T$ only if it is sufficiently small compared to $q$. We index the zerotesting values obtained by the adversary by $u$, thus $T_u$ is the adversary's $u$-th successful zerotesting value. The purpose of adversary is to find any non-trivial algebraic relation between $T_u$'s and pre-encodings $\hat{\mathbf{S}}$.[5] Despite the generality of oracle inputs, the statistical zeroizing attacks in [19] do not fall into this class; the adversary using the statistical zeroizing attacks is to check if an inequality holds.

On the other hand, our model gives an input-consistent oracle to adversary which is much weaker. Instead, the purpose of adversary is to find any information beyond input-output behavior of the program. That is, we do not restrict the goal of adversary to computing a nontrivial algebraic relations. This freedom allows us to capture almost all existing attacks.

An interesting question is to design a model that embrace both models, and construct a secure obfuscation procedure in such model. A candidate model is to allow the adversary to access both oracles described above. Note that [11, Lemma 8] states that the set of adversary's successful zerotest is essentially a set of polynomially-many linear sum of input-consistent evaluations. With this lemma in mind, an obfuscation procedure satisfying the corresponding lemma as well as the VBB security in the input-consistent evaluation model may satisfy a meaningful security in this model.

**Acknowledgments.** We would like to thank Jiseung Kim, Alex Lombardi, Takashi Yamakawa and Mark Zhandry for helpful discussions.

The research of Yilei Chen was conducted while the author was at Boston University supported by the NSF MACS project and NSF grant CNS-1422965. Minki Hhan is supported by Institute for Information & communication Technology Promotion (IITP) grant funded by the Korea government (MSIT) (No. 2016-6-00598, The mathematical structure of functional encryption and its analysis), and the ARO and DARPA under Contract No. W911NF-15-C-0227. Vinod Vaikuntanathan is supported in part by NSF Grants CNS-1350619 and CNS-1414119, Alfred P. Sloan Research Fellowship, Microsoft Faculty Fellowship, the NEC Corporation and a Steven and Renee Finn

---

[5] The original model is more general. For example, they considered GGH15 maps over general graphs instead of source-to-sink path, and allows the adversary to query much general polynomials. Still every adversary's query in this model is essentially of the described form.

Career Development Chair from MIT. This work was also sponsored in part by the Defense Advanced Research Projects Agency (DARPA) and the U.S. Army Research Office under contracts W911NF-15-C-0226 and W911NF-15-C-0236. Hoeteck Wee is supported by ERC Project aSCEND (H2020 639554).

# References

1. Aaronson, S.: Arithmetic natural proofs theory is sought (2008). https://www.scottaaronson.com/blog/?p=336. Accessed 27 Feb 2018
2. Agrawal, S.: Indistinguishability obfuscation without multilinear maps: new methods for bootstrapping and instantiation. In: Ishai, Y., Rijmen, V. (eds.) EUROCRYPT 2019, Part I. LNCS, vol. 11476, pp. 191–225. Springer, Cham (2019). https://doi.org/10.1007/978-3-030-17653-2_7
3. Ajtai, M.: Generating hard instances of the short basis problem. In: Wiedermann, J., van Emde Boas, P., Nielsen, M. (eds.) ICALP 1999. LNCS, vol. 1644, pp. 1–9. Springer, Heidelberg (1999). https://doi.org/10.1007/3-540-48523-6_1
4. Alwen, J., Peikert, C.: Generating shorter bases for hard random lattices. Theory Comput. Syst. **48**(3), 535–553 (2011)
5. Ananth, P., Jain, A., Lin, H., Matt, C., Sahai, A.: IO without multilinear maps: New paradigms via low-degree weak pseudorandom generators and security amplification. In: CRYPTO (2019)
6. Apon, D., Döttling, N., Garg, S., Mukherjee, P.: Cryptanalysis of indistinguishability obfuscations of circuits over GGH13. In: ICALP, LIPIcs, vol. 80, pp. 38:1–38:16. Schloss Dagstuhl - Leibniz-Zentrum fuer Informatik (2017)
7. Banerjee, A., Peikert, C., Rosen, A.: Pseudorandom functions and lattices. In: Pointcheval, D., Johansson, T. (eds.) EUROCRYPT 2012. LNCS, vol. 7237, pp. 719–737. Springer, Heidelberg (2012). https://doi.org/10.1007/978-3-642-29011-4_42
8. Barak, B., Brakerski, Z., Komargodski, I., Kothari, P.K.: Limits on low-degree pseudorandom generators (or: sum-of-squares meets program obfuscation). In: Nielsen, J.B., Rijmen, V. (eds.) EUROCRYPT 2018, Part II. LNCS, vol. 10821, pp. 649–679. Springer, Cham (2018). https://doi.org/10.1007/978-3-319-78375-8_21
9. Barak, B., Garg, S., Kalai, Y.T., Paneth, O., Sahai, A.: Protecting obfuscation against algebraic attacks. In: Nguyen, P.Q., Oswald, E. (eds.) EUROCRYPT 2014. LNCS, vol. 8441, pp. 221–238. Springer, Heidelberg (2014). https://doi.org/10.1007/978-3-642-55220-5_13
10. Mix Barrington, D.A.: Bounded-width polynomial-size branching programs recognize exactly those languages in $nc^1$. In: STOC, pp. 1–5 (1986)
11. Bartusek, J., Guan, J., Ma, F., Zhandry, M.: Return of GGH15: provable security against zeroizing attacks. In: Beimel, A., Dziembowski, S. (eds.) TCC 2018, Part II. LNCS, vol. 11240, pp. 544–574. Springer, Cham (2018). https://doi.org/10.1007/978-3-030-03810-6_20
12. Boneh, D.: The dan and craig show (2015). https://www.youtube.com/watch?v=m4lv0lXI5uU. Accessed 17 May 2019
13. Boneh, D., Ishai, Y., Passelègue, A., Sahai, A., Wu, D.J.: Exploring crypto dark matter: new simple PRF candidates and their applications. In: Beimel, A., Dziembowski, S. (eds.) TCC 2018. LNCS, vol. 11240, pp. 699–729. Springer, Cham (2018). https://doi.org/10.1007/978-3-030-03810-6_25

14. Boneh, D., Lewi, K., Montgomery, H., Raghunathan, A.: Key homomorphic PRFs and their applications. In: Canetti, R., Garay, J.A. (eds.) CRYPTO 2013, Part I. LNCS, vol. 8042, pp. 410–428. Springer, Heidelberg (2013). https://doi.org/10.1007/978-3-642-40041-4_23
15. Boneh, D., Montgomery, H.W., Raghunathan, A.: Algebraic pseudorandom functions with improved efficiency from the augmented cascade. In: ACM Conference on Computer and Communications Security, pp. 131–140 (2010)
16. Brakerski, Z., Langlois, A., Peikert, C., Regev, O., Stehlé, D.: Classical hardness of learning with errors. In: Symposium on Theory of Computing Conference, STOC 2013, Palo Alto, CA, USA, 1–4 June 2013, pp. 575–584 (2013)
17. Chen, Y., Gentry, C., Halevi, S.: Cryptanalyses of candidate branching program obfuscators. In: Coron, J.-S., Nielsen, J.B. (eds.) EUROCRYPT 2017, Part III. LNCS, vol. 10212, pp. 278–307. Springer, Cham (2017). https://doi.org/10.1007/978-3-319-56617-7_10
18. Chen, Y., Vaikuntanathan, V., Wee, H.: GGH15 beyond permutation branching programs: proofs, attacks, and candidates. In: Shacham, H., Boldyreva, A. (eds.) CRYPTO 2018, Part II. LNCS, vol. 10992, pp. 577–607. Springer, Cham (2018). https://doi.org/10.1007/978-3-319-96881-0_20
19. Cheon, J.H., Cho, W., Hhan, M., Kim, J., Lee, C.: Statistical zeroizing attack: cryptanalysis of candidates of bp obfuscation over GGH15 multilinear map. In: Boldyreva, A., Micciancio, D. (eds.) CRYPTO 2019, Part III. LNCS, vol. 11694, pp. 253–283. Springer, Cham (2019). https://doi.org/10.1007/978-3-030-26954-8_9
20. Cheon, J.H., Hhan, M., Kim, J., Lee, C.: Cryptanalyses of branching program obfuscations over GGH13 multilinear map from the NTRU problem. In: Shacham, H., Boldyreva, A. (eds.) CRYPTO 2018, Part III. LNCS, vol. 10993, pp. 184–210. Springer, Cham (2018). https://doi.org/10.1007/978-3-319-96878-0_7
21. Cheon, J.H., Hhan, M., Kim, J., Lee, C.: Cryptanalysis on the HHSS obfuscation arising from absence of safeguards. IEEE Access 6, 40096–40104 (2018)
22. Cheon, J.H., Jun, B.: A polynomial time algorithm for the braid Diffie-Hellman conjugacy problem. In: Boneh, D. (ed.) CRYPTO 2003. LNCS, vol. 2729, pp. 212–225. Springer, Heidelberg (2003). https://doi.org/10.1007/978-3-540-45146-4_13
23. Coron, J.-S., Lee, M.S., Lepoint, T., Tibouchi, M.: Zeroizing attacks on indistinguishability obfuscation over CLT13. In: Fehr, S. (ed.) PKC 2017, Part I. LNCS, vol. 10174, pp. 41–58. Springer, Heidelberg (2017). https://doi.org/10.1007/978-3-662-54365-8_3
24. Coron, J.-S., Lepoint, T., Tibouchi, M.: Practical multilinear maps over the integers. In: Canetti, R., Garay, J.A. (eds.) CRYPTO 2013, Part I. LNCS, vol. 8042, pp. 476–493. Springer, Heidelberg (2013). https://doi.org/10.1007/978-3-642-40041-4_26
25. Garg, S., Gentry, C., Halevi, S.: Candidate multilinear maps from ideal lattices. In: Johansson, T., Nguyen, P.Q. (eds.) EUROCRYPT 2013. LNCS, vol. 7881, pp. 1–17. Springer, Heidelberg (2013). https://doi.org/10.1007/978-3-642-38348-9_1
26. Garg, S., Gentry, C., Halevi, S., Raykova, M., Sahai, A., Waters, B.: Candidate indistinguishability obfuscation and functional encryption for all circuits. In: FOCS, pp. 40–49 (2013)
27. Garg, S., Miles, E., Mukherjee, P., Sahai, A., Srinivasan, A., Zhandry, M.: Secure obfuscation in a weak multilinear map model. In: Hirt, M., Smith, A. (eds.) TCC 2016, Part II. LNCS, vol. 9986, pp. 241–268. Springer, Heidelberg (2016). https://doi.org/10.1007/978-3-662-53644-5_10
28. Gentry, C., Peikert, C., Vaikuntanathan, V.: Trapdoors for hard lattices and new cryptographic constructions. In: STOC, pp. 197–206 (2008)

29. Goldreich, O., Goldwasser, S., Micali, S.: How to construct random functions. J. ACM **33**(4), 792–807 (1986)
30. Gorbunov, S., Vaikuntanathan, V., Wee, H.: Predicate encryption for circuits from LWE. In: Gennaro, R., Robshaw, M. (eds.) CRYPTO 2015. LNCS, vol. 9216, pp. 503–523. Springer, Heidelberg (2015). https://doi.org/10.1007/978-3-662-48000-7_25
31. Halevi, S., Halevi, T., Shoup, V., Stephens-Davidowitz, N.: Implementing BP-obfuscation using graph-induced encoding. In: ACM CCS, pp. 783–798 (2017)
32. Igusa, K.: Notes on the special linear group. http://people.brandeis.edu/~igusa/Math131b/SL.pdf. Accessed 08 Feb 2018
33. Ko, K.H., Lee, S.J., Cheon, J.H., Han, J.W., Kang, J., Park, C.: New public-key cryptosystem using braid groups. In: Bellare, M. (ed.) CRYPTO 2000. LNCS, vol. 1880, pp. 166–183. Springer, Heidelberg (2000). https://doi.org/10.1007/3-540-44598-6_10
34. Lewko, A.B., Waters, B.: Efficient pseudorandom functions from the decisional linear assumption and weaker variants. In: ACM CCS, pp. 112–120 (2009)
35. Lin, H., Tessaro, S.: Indistinguishability obfuscation from trilinear maps and block-wise local PRGs. In: Katz, J., Shacham, H. (eds.) CRYPTO 2017, Part I. LNCS, vol. 10401, pp. 630–660. Springer, Cham (2017). https://doi.org/10.1007/978-3-319-63688-7_21
36. Micciancio, D., Peikert, C.: Trapdoors for lattices: simpler, tighter, faster, smaller. In: Pointcheval, D., Johansson, T. (eds.) EUROCRYPT 2012. LNCS, vol. 7237, pp. 700–718. Springer, Heidelberg (2012). https://doi.org/10.1007/978-3-642-29011-4_41
37. Naor, M., Reingold, O.: Number-theoretic constructions of efficient pseudo-random functions. In: FOCS, pp. 458–467. IEEE Computer Society (1997)
38. Peikert, C.: Public-key cryptosystems from the worst-case shortest vector problem: extended abstract. In: STOC, pp. 333–342 (2009)
39. Peikert, C., Regev, O., Stephens-Davidowitz, N.: Pseudorandomness of ring-LWE for any ring and modulus. In: STOC, pp. 461–473. ACM (2017)
40. Pellet-Mary, A.: Quantum attacks against indistinguishablility obfuscators proved secure in the weak multilinear map model. In: Shacham, H., Boldyreva, A. (eds.) CRYPTO 2018, Part III. LNCS, vol. 10993, pp. 153–183. Springer, Cham (2018). https://doi.org/10.1007/978-3-319-96878-0_6
41. Petit, C., Quisquater, J.-J.: Rubik's for cryptographers. IACR Cryptology ePrint Archive 2011, 638 (2011)
42. Regev, O.: On lattices, learning with errors, random linear codes, and cryptography. J. ACM **56**(6), 34:1–34:40 (2009)
43. Tillich, Jean-Pierre, Zémor, Gilles: Hashing with $SL_2$. In: Desmedt, Yvo G. (ed.) CRYPTO 1994. LNCS, vol. 839, pp. 40–49. Springer, Heidelberg (1994). https://doi.org/10.1007/3-540-48658-5_5
44. Zémor, G.: Hash functions and graphs with large girths. In: Davies, D.W. (ed.) EUROCRYPT 1991. LNCS, vol. 547, pp. 508–511. Springer, Heidelberg (1991). https://doi.org/10.1007/3-540-46416-6_44

# Obfuscated Fuzzy Hamming Distance and Conjunctions from Subset Product Problems

Steven D. Galbraith$^{(\boxtimes)}$ and Lukas Zobernig

Department of Mathematics, The University of Auckland, Auckland, New Zealand
{s.galbraith,lukas.zobernig}@auckland.ac.nz

**Abstract.** We consider the problem of obfuscating programs for fuzzy matching (in other words, testing whether the Hamming distance between an $n$-bit input and a fixed $n$-bit target vector is smaller than some predetermined threshold). This problem arises in biometric matching and other contexts. We present a virtual-black-box (VBB) secure and input-hiding obfuscator for fuzzy matching for Hamming distance, based on certain natural number-theoretic computational assumptions. In contrast to schemes based on coding theory, our obfuscator is based on computational hardness rather than information-theoretic hardness, and can be implemented for a much wider range of parameters. The Hamming distance obfuscator can also be applied to obfuscation of matching under the $\ell_1$ norm on $\mathbb{Z}^n$.

We also consider obfuscating conjunctions. Conjunctions are equivalent to pattern matching with wildcards, which can be reduced in some cases to fuzzy matching. Our approach does not cover as general a range of parameters as other solutions, but it is much more compact. We study the relation between our obfuscation schemes and other obfuscators and give some advantages of our solution.

## 1 Introduction

Program obfuscation is a major topic in cryptography. Since it was shown that *virtual black box (VBB) obfuscation* is impossible in general [3], a large amount of research has gone into constructing solutions in special cases. One special case that has attracted attention is evasive functions [2,37]. Evasive functions are programs for which it is hard to find an accepting input from black-box access to the program. There are some classes of evasive functions that are quite efficiently obfuscated, such as hyperplane membership [12], logical formulae defined by many conjunctions [9,10], pattern matching with wild cards [4,6], root of a polynomial system of low degree [2], compute-and-compare programs [26,44], and more [37].

More general obfuscation tools are less practical. For example, there are candidates for *indistinguishability obfuscation* [24], but the downside of all of these schemes is they are completely infeasible in terms of runtime and are only

© International Association for Cryptologic Research 2019
D. Hofheinz and A. Rosen (Eds.): TCC 2019, LNCS 11891, pp. 81–110, 2019.
https://doi.org/10.1007/978-3-030-36030-6_4

able to deal with very simple programs. While general-purpose and efficient obfuscation is a "holy grail", the hope is that by restricting to a narrow class of programs we are able to construct customised and practical solutions.

**Hamming Distance.** One very natural class of evasive functions is fuzzy matching for the Hamming metric. Define the program $P_x(y)$, parametrised by $x \in \{0,1\}^n$ and a threshold $0 < r < n/2$, that determines whether or not the $n$-bit input $y$ has Hamming distance at most $r$ from $x$. Let $D$ be a distribution on $\{0,1\}^n$. Then $D$ determines a program collection $\mathcal{P} = \{P_x : x \leftarrow D\}$. For $\mathcal{P}$ to be an evasive program collection it is necessary that the distribution $D$ has high Hamming ball min-entropy (see Definition 2.4; this notion is also known as fuzzy min-entropy in [23]). The uniform distribution on $\{0,1\}^n$ is an example of such a distribution.

We are interested in obfuscating the membership program $P_x(y)$, so that the description of $P_x$ does not reveal the value $x$. Note that once an accepting input $y \in \{0,1\}^n$ is known then one can easily determine $x$ by a sequence of chosen executions of $P_x$. Indeed, as with most other solutions to this problem, our scheme is essentially an error correcting code, and so the computation recovers the value $x$.

Fuzzy matching has already been treated by many authors and there is a large literature on it. For example, Dodis et al. [18–20] introduced the notion of *secure sketch* and a large number of works have built on their approach. They also show how to obfuscate proximity queries.

One drawback of the secure sketch approach is that the parameters are strongly constrained by the need for an efficient decoding algorithm. As discussed by Bringer et al. [11] this leads to "a trade-off between the correction capacity and the security properties of the scheme". In contrast, our scheme is based on computational hardness rather than information-theoretic hardness, and can be implemented for a much wider range of parameters.

A different solution to fuzzy matching was given by Karabina and Canpolat [33], based on computational assumptions related to the discrete logarithm problem. Note that they do not mention obfuscation or give a security proof. Wichs and Zirdelis [44] note that fuzzy matching can be obfuscated using an obfuscator for compute-and-compare programs.

**Our Contribution.** We give a full treatment of fuzzy matching based on computational assumptions. We present an extremely practical and efficient obfuscator, based on a natural number-theoretic computational assumption we call the *modular subset product problem*. In short, given $r < n/2$, distinct primes $(p_i)_{i=1,\dots,n}$, a prime $q$ such that $\prod_{i \in I} p_i < q$ for all subsets $I$ of $\{1,\dots,n\}$ of size $r$, and an integer $X = \prod_{i=1}^{n} p_i^{x_i} \bmod q$ for some secret vector $x \in \{0,1\}^n$, the problem is to find $x$. We call the decisional version of the problem the *decisional modular subset product problem*: Distinguish between a modular subset product instance and uniformly random element of $(\mathbb{Z}/q\mathbb{Z})^*$. If $q \leq 2^n$, we conjecture that the statistical distance of the distribution $\prod_{i=1}^{n} p_i^{x_i} \bmod q$ for uniform $x$

and the uniform distribution on $(\mathbb{Z}/q\mathbb{Z})^*$ is negligible. For $q > 2^n$ we conjecture that the distributions are computationally indistinguishable.

The modular subset product problem is similar to computational problems that have been used in previous works in cryptography [15].

In practice our scheme improves upon all previous solutions to this problem: It handles a wider range of parameters than secure sketches; it is 20 times faster than [33]; it is many orders of magnitude more compact than [13,44]; for full discussion see Sect. 7.5. Our solution is related to [33], but we think our approach is simpler and furthermore we give a complete security analysis.

We present two variants of our scheme. One is based only on the subset-product assumption but when $r$ is very small, it admits the possibility of accepting an input $y$ that is not within the correct Hamming ball. The second variant (and the one we present in the main body of this work) assumes the existence of a *dependent auxiliary input point function obfuscator* [5,7,8,37,43] and is perfectly correct. The key idea is to use the point function obfuscator to verify the Hamming ball center after error correction, see Sect. 7.3 for details. The auxiliary input in our case is the tuple $((p_i)_{i=1,\dots,n}, q, X)$.

The following theorems are both special cases of Theorem 8.1, which we will prove later. The first one shows that, under the subset product assumption, our scheme gives a secure obfuscator for the uniform distribution over $\{0,1\}^n$ when $n$ is sufficiently large.

**Theorem 1.1.** *Let $\lambda \in \mathbb{N}$ be a security parameter. Consider the family of parameters $(n,r) = (6\lambda, \lambda)$. Assuming the decisional modular subset product problem is hard and that there exists a dependent auxiliary input distributional VBB point function obfuscator, the Hamming distance obfuscator for a uniformly distributed $x \in \{0,1\}^n$ is distributional VBB secure.*

Taking $\lambda = 170$ gives parameters $(n,r) = (1020, 170)$, which are beyond the reach of practical secure sketches.

Under the further constraint $r < n/\log(n\log(n))$ we prove security under the discrete logarithm assumption. Taking $n = 1000$ this allows $r = 113$. This gives us the following

**Theorem 1.2.** *Let $\lambda > 20$ be a security parameter. Consider the family of parameters $(n,r) = (6\lambda, n/\log(n\log(n)))$. Under the discrete logarithm assumption and the assumptions of Theorem 5.1 and assuming that there exists a dependent auxiliary input distributional VBB point function obfuscator, the Hamming distance obfuscator for a uniformly distributed $x \in \{0,1\}^n$ is distributional VBB secure.*

**Conjunctions.** Another class of evasive functions are conjunctions. A conjunction on Boolean variables $b_1, \dots, b_n$ is $\chi(b_1, \dots, b_n) = \bigwedge_{i=1}^{k} c_i$ where each $c_i$ is of the form $b_j$ or $\neg b_j$ for some $1 \le j \le n$.

An alternative representation of a conjunction is called *pattern matching with wildcards*. Consider a vector $x \in \{0, 1, \star\}^n$ of length $n \in \mathbb{N}$ where $\star$ is a special *wildcard* symbol. Such an $x$ then corresponds to a conjunction $\chi : \{0,1\}^n \rightarrow \{0,1\}$ which, using Boolean variables $b_1, \ldots, b_n$, can be written as $\chi(b) = \bigwedge_{i=1}^{n} c_i$ where $c_i = \neg b_i$ if $x_i = 0$, $c_i = b_i$ if $x_i = 1$, and $c_i = 1$ if $x_i = \star$.

Conjunction obfuscators have been considered before [4,6,9,10]. It is clear that, if the number $r$ of wildcards is sufficiently smaller than $n/2$, one can reduce pattern matching with wildcards to fuzzy Hamming matching. Hence our solution also gives an alternative approach to obfuscating conjunctions that can be used for certain parameter ranges. We give a full security analysis and comparison to existing schemes.

**Applications.** Hamming distance obfuscators are interesting for a variety of applications. One major application is biometric matching, where a biometric reading is taken and matched with a stored template [32, 36, 41, 42]. Since biometric readings (e.g., fingerprints, iris scans, or facial features) are a noisy process, the binary string representing the extracted features may not be an exact match for the template string.

**Our Approach.** We give a short summary of our Hamming distance obfuscator. Let $r, n \in \mathbb{N}$ with $r < n/2$. We wish to "encode" an element $x \in \{0,1\}^n$ so that it is hidden, and yet we will be able to recognise if an input $y \in \{0,1\}^n$ is within Hamming distance $r$ of $x$. To do this we will sample a sequence of small distinct primes $(p_i)_{i=1,\ldots,n}$ (i.e., $p_i \neq p_j$ for $i \neq j$) and a small safe prime $q$ such that $\prod_{i \in I} p_i < q/2$ for all $I \subset \{1, \ldots, n\}$ with $|I| \leq r$. The encoding of $x \in \{0,1\}^n$ is

$$X = \prod_{i=1}^{n} p_i^{x_i} \mod q$$

along with the primes $(p_i)_{i=1,\ldots,n}$ and $q$. Given an input $y \in \{0,1\}^n$ anyone can compute the encoding $Y = \prod_{i=1}^{n} p_i^{y_i} \mod q$ and then compute

$$XY^{-1} \mod q \equiv \prod_{i=1}^{n} p_i^{x_i - y_i} \mod q = \prod_{i=1}^{n} p_i^{\epsilon_i} \mod q$$

for *errors* $\epsilon_i = x_i - y_i \in \{-1, 0, 1\}$. If $y$ is close to $x$ then almost all $\epsilon_i$ are zero, and so we are able to recover the errors $\epsilon_i$ using the continued fraction algorithm and factoring. We give the background theory and explanation in Sect. 6. In Remark 1 we explain that this technique also applies to matching vectors in $\mathbb{Z}^n$ under the $\ell_1$-norm.

Note that these ideas have also been used in [39] where they are used to construct a *number theoretic error correcting code*. Some major differences to our scheme are: In [39] the parameters $(p_i)_{i=1,\ldots,n}$ and $q$ are fixed for all messages; the encoding $X$ is appended to each message. A similar application is given in [21] to construct a lattice with efficient bounded distance decoding.

**Outline of This Work.** Sections 2, 3, and 4 introduce basic notions in hamming distance/fuzzy matching and obfuscation. Section 5 introduces our new computational assumption. Section 6 gives background on continued fractions. Section 7 presents the obfuscator for fuzzy matching in the Hamming distance, including parameters and performance. Section 8 proves that the obfuscator is VBB secure and input-hiding. Section 9 briefly discusses our solution to obfuscating conjunctions.

# 2   Hamming Distance

We want to obfuscate the function that determines if an input binary vector is close to a fixed target. In our setting, one of the input vectors will be a secret and the other an arbitrary input. Let us first state some key definitions.

A natural property of a binary vector is its *Hamming weight* which is the number of non-zero elements of the vector. For $x \in \{0,1\}^n$, we will denote this by $w_H(x)$. The *Hamming distance* between two binary vectors $x, y \in \{0,1\}^n$ is then given by $d_H(x,y) = w_H(x-y)$. Finally, a *Hamming ball* $B_{H,r}(x) \subset \{0,1\}^n$ of radius $r$ around a point $x \in \{0,1\}^n$ is the set of all points with Hamming distance at most $r$ from x. We denote by $B_{H,r}$ the Hamming ball around an unspecified point.

## 2.1   Hamming Ball Membership over Uniformly Chosen Centers

We are interested in programs that determine if an input binary vector $y \in \{0,1\}^n$ is contained in a Hamming ball of radius $r$ around some secret value $x$, i.e., if $y \in B_{H,r}(x)$. This problem is only interesting if it is hard for a user to determine such an input $y$, because if it is easy to determine values $y$ such that $y \in B_{H,r}(x)$ and also easy to determine values $y$ such that $y \notin B_{H,r}(x)$ then an attacker can easily learn $x$ by binary search. So the first task is to find conditions that imply it is hard to find a $y$ that is accepted by such a program. In other words, we need conditions that imply Hamming ball membership is an *evasive* problem. As we will see in Fig. 1, there are essentially three ways that this problem can become easy: if the Hamming balls are too big; if there are too few possible centers $x$; or if the centers $x$ are clustered together.

**Definition 2.1 (Evasive Program Collection).** *Let* $\mathcal{P} = \{\mathcal{P}_n\}_{n \in \mathbb{N}}$ *be a collection of polynomial-size programs such that every* $P \in \mathcal{P}_n$ *is a program* $P : \{0,1\}^n \to \{0,1\}$. *The collection* $\mathcal{P}$ *is called* evasive *if there exists a negligible function* $\epsilon$ *such that for every* $n \in \mathbb{N}$ *and for every* $y \in \{0,1\}^n$:

$$\Pr_{P \leftarrow \mathcal{P}_n} [P(y) = 1] \leq \epsilon(n).$$

In short, Definition 2.1 means that a random program from an evasive collection $\mathcal{P}$ evaluates to 0 with overwhelming probability. Finally, we call a member $P \in \mathcal{P}_n$ for some $n \in \mathbb{N}$ an *evasive program* or an *evasive function*.

**Hamming Ball Program Collection.** Let $r, n \in \mathbb{N}$ with $0 < r < n/2$. For every binary vector $x \in \{0,1\}^n$ there exists a polynomial size program $P_x :$ $\{0,1\}^n \to \{0,1\}$ that computes whether the input vector $y \in \{0,1\}^n$ is contained in a Hamming ball $B_{H,r}(x)$ and evaluates to 1 in this case, otherwise to 0. Any distribution on $\{0,1\}^n$ therefore gives rise to a distribution $\mathcal{P}_n$ of polynomial-size programs.

We first consider the uniform distribution on $\{0,1\}^n$, so that sampling $P \leftarrow \mathcal{P}_n$ means choosing $x$ uniformly in $\{0,1\}^n$ and setting $P = P_x$. Since the condition $y \in B_{H,r}(x)$ is equivalent to $x \in B_{H,r}(y)$ we need to determine the probability that a random element lies in a Hamming ball. This is done in the next two lemmas. Note that if $r \geq n/2$ then a random element lies in the Hamming ball with probability $\geq 1/2$, which is why we are always taking $r < n/2$.

**Lemma 2.1.** *Let $n \in \mathbb{N}$, $x \in \{0,1\}^n$. The number of elements in a Hamming ball $B_{H,r}(x) \subseteq \{0,1\}^n$ of radius $r$ is given by $h_r = |B_{H,r}| = \sum_{k=0}^{r} \binom{n}{k}$.*

*Proof.* This can be readily seen from the fact that for each $k \in [0, r]$ a vector has $\binom{n}{k}$ possible ways to be at Hamming distance of $k$ from the origin point. $\square$

Next we show that the probability for a randomly chosen element in $\{0,1\}^n$ to be contained in a Hamming ball $B_{H,r}$ is negligible if the parameters $r < n/2$ are chosen properly.

**Lemma 2.2.** *Let $\lambda \in \mathbb{N}$ be a security parameter and let $r, n \in \mathbb{N}$ such that $r \leq n/2 - \sqrt{n\lambda \log(2)}$. Fix a point $x \in \{0,1\}^n$. Then the probability that a randomly chosen vector $y \in \{0,1\}^n$ is contained in a Hamming ball of radius $r$ around $x$ satisfies $\Pr_{y \leftarrow \{0,1\}^n} [y \in B_{H,r}(x)] \leq 1/2^\lambda$.*

*Proof.* The total number of points in $\{0,1\}^n$ is given by $2^n$. By Lemma 2.1 we thus have the probability of a randomly chosen vector $y \in \{0,1\}^n$ to be contained in a Hamming ball of radius $r$ around a point $x$ given by $h_r/2^n = 2^{-n} \sum_{k=0}^{r} \binom{n}{k}$. On the other hand, consider the cumulative binomial distribution for probability $p$ which for $r \leq np$ is bounded[1] by

$$\Pr(X \leq r) = \sum_{k=0}^{r} \binom{n}{k} p^k (1-p)^{n-k} \leq \exp\left(-\frac{1}{2p}\frac{(np-r)^2}{n}\right).$$

Substitute $p = 1/2$ to find $\Pr(X \leq r) = h_r/2^n$. Hence, for $r < n/2 - \sqrt{n\lambda \log(2)}$ we have $h_r/2^n \leq \exp\left(-\left(n/2 - r\right)^2/n\right) \leq 1/2^\lambda$ and the result follows. $\square$

This result shows that Hamming ball membership over the uniform distribution is evasive when $r$ is small enough.

**Lemma 2.3.** *Let $\lambda(n)$ be such that the function $1/2^{\lambda(n)}$ is negligible. Let $r(n)$ be a function such that $r(n) \leq n/2 - \sqrt{\log(2)n\lambda(n)}$. Let $\mathcal{P}_n$ be the set of programs that tests Hamming ball membership in $B_{H,r(n)}(x) \subseteq \{0,1\}^n$ over uniformly sampled $x \in \{0,1\}^n$. Then $\mathcal{P}_n$ is an evasive program collection.*

---

[1] Chernoff bound for binomial distribution tail [1,14].

*Proof.* We need to show that, for every $n \in \mathbb{N}$ and for every $y \in \{0,1\}^n$, $\Pr_{P \leftarrow \mathcal{P}_n}[P(y) = 1]$ is negligible. Note that

$$\Pr_{P \leftarrow \mathcal{P}_n}[P(y) = 1] = \Pr_{x \leftarrow \{0,1\}^n}[y \in B_{H,r(n)}(x)] = \Pr_{x \leftarrow \{0,1\}^n}[x \in B_{H,r(n)}(y)]$$

and this is negligible by Lemma 2.2. $\qquad\square$

## 2.2 Hamming Ball Membership over General Distributions

Biometric templates may not be uniformly distributed in $\{0,1\}^n$, so it is important to have a workable theory for fuzzy matching without assuming that the input data is uniformly sampled binary strings. For example, in the worst case, there is only a small number of possible values $x \in \{0,1\}^n$ that arise, in which case taking $y$ to be one of these $x$-values will show that Hamming ball membership is not evasive. More generally, as pictured in the right hand panel of Fig. 1, one could have many centers but if they are too close together then there might be values for $y$ such that $\Pr_{P \leftarrow \mathcal{P}_n}[P(y) = 1]$ is not negligible.

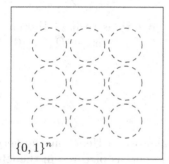 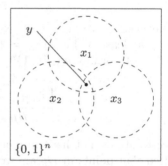

**Fig. 1.** Two example cases of Hamming ball distributions. The left side depicts the ideal distribution of Hamming ball centers. The right one shows what happens if the balls overlap.

Hence, for Hamming ball membership to be evasive, the centers $x$ must be chosen from a "reasonably well spread" distribution. Before treating this in detail we give some definitions related to entropy of distributions in the computational sense.

**Definition 2.2 (Min-Entropy).** *The* min-entropy *of a random variable $X$ is defined as* $\mathrm{H}_\infty(X) = -\log(\max_x \Pr[X = x])$. *The* (average) conditional min-entropy *of a random variable $X$ conditioned on a correlated variable $Y$ is defined as* $\mathrm{H}_\infty(X|Y) = -\log(\mathrm{E}_{y \leftarrow Y}[\max_x \Pr[X = x|Y = y]])$.

**Definition 2.3 (Computational Indistinguishability).** *We say that two ensembles of random variables $X = \{X_\lambda\}_{\lambda \in \mathbb{N}}$ and $Y = \{Y_\lambda\}_{\lambda \in \mathbb{N}}$ are computationally indistinguishable and write $X \overset{c}{\approx} Y$ if for every (non-uniform) PPT* *distinguisher $\mathcal{A}$ it holds that $\Pr[\mathcal{A}(X_\lambda) = 1] - \Pr[\mathcal{A}(Y_\lambda) = 1] \leq \epsilon(\lambda)$ where $\epsilon(\lambda)$ is some negligible function.*

Now suppose we have a distribution $D_n$ on $\{0,1\}^n$, which defines a distribution $P_n$ of Hamming ball membership programs. For the program collection to be evasive (i.e., to satisfy Definition 2.1), it is necessary that for any $y \in \{0,1\}^n$ we have $\Pr_{P \leftarrow P_n}[P(y) = 1]$ being negligible. But note that

$$\Pr_{P \leftarrow P_n}[P(y) = 1] = \Pr_{x \leftarrow D_n}[y \in B_{H,r}(x)] = \Pr_{x \leftarrow D_n}[x \in B_{H,r}(y)].$$

So the requirement for evasiveness is that this probability is negligible. In other words, we need that $D_n$ has large min-entropy in the following sense.

**Definition 2.4 (Hamming Ball Min-Entropy).** *(Also known as* fuzzy min-entropy *[23, Definition 3].) The* Hamming ball min-entropy *of a random variable $X$ on $\{0,1\}^n$ is defined to be*

$$H_{H,\infty(X)} = -\log\left(\max_{y \in \{0,1\}^n} \Pr[X \in B_{H,r}(y)]\right).$$

For convenience, we give some necessary conditions to have Hamming ball min-entropy at least $\lambda$. Let $|D_n| = \{x \in \{0,1\}^n : \Pr(x \leftarrow D_n) > 0\}$ be the support of $D_n$. If for any $y \in \{0,1\}^n$

$$\frac{\left|\bigcup_{x \in |D_n|} B_{H,r}(x)\right|}{|B_{H,r}(y)|} < 2^\lambda$$

then we certainly do not have min-entropy at least $\lambda$. Hence at the very least it is required that points in $D_n$ are well-spread-out, as pictured in the left-hand panel of Fig. 1.

Intuitively, we can say that if there are enough points in $|D_n|$ and if they are spread out such that the overlap between the Hamming balls is relatively small, then Hamming ball membership is an evasive problem.

**Definition 2.5 (Hamming Distance Evasive Distribution).** *Consider an ensemble of distributions $D_\lambda$ over $\{0,1\}^{n(\lambda)}$, call it $D = \{D_\lambda\}_{\lambda \in \mathbb{N}}$. Let $r(\lambda) < n(\lambda)/2$ be some function. We say that $D$ is* Hamming distance evasive *if the Hamming ball min-entropy of $D_\lambda$ for Hamming balls in $\{0,1\}^{n(\lambda)}$ of radius $r(\lambda)$ (as in Definition 2.4) is at least $\lambda$.*

## 3    Conjunctions

Similar to Sect. 2, we will first give basic definitions regarding conjunctions and then determine necessary conditions for a given conjunction to be evasive.

**Definition 3.1 (Conjunction/Pattern Matching With Wildcards).** *Let $n \in \mathbb{N}$ and let $x \in \{0, 1, \star\}^n$ where $\star$ is a special* wildcard *symbol. Such an $x$ then corresponds to a* conjunction $\chi : \{0, 1\}^n \to \{0, 1\}$ *which, using a vector of Boolean variables $b = (b_1, \ldots, b_n)$, can be written as $\chi(b) = \bigwedge_{i=1}^{n} c_i$ where $c_i = \neg b_i$ if $x_i = 0$, $c_i = b_i$ if $x_i = 1$, and $c_i = 1$ if $x_i = \star$. Denote by $W_x = \{i | x_i = \star\}$ the set of all wildcard positions and let $r = |W| \in \mathbb{N}$ be the number of wildcards.*

Note that a priori the input is considered a plaintext and directly visible to the evaluating party. The wildcard positions of an obfuscated conjunction are only secret as long as no matching input is known. Once such an input is presented to the evaluator, it is straightforward to work out all wildcard positions in time linear in the input length: Simply flip each input bit and check whether this changed input still matches, in which case the flipped position must be a wildcard.

**Lemma 3.1.** *Let $\lambda \in \mathbb{N}$ be a security parameter and let $r < n/2 \in \mathbb{N}$ such that $r \leq n - \lambda$. Fix a conjunction $\chi$ corresponding to a vector $x \in \{0, 1, \star\}^n$ such that $r = |\{i | x_i = \star\}|$. Then the probability that $\chi$ evaluates to true on a randomly chosen vector $y \in \{0, 1\}^n$ satisfies $\Pr_{y \leftarrow \{0,1\}^n} [\chi(y) = 1] \leq 1/2^\lambda$.*

*Proof.* The total number of points in $\{0, 1\}^n$ is given by $2^n$. We thus have the probability of a randomly chosen vector $y \in \{0, 1\}^n$ to be matched by $\chi$ to be $\Pr_{y \leftarrow \{0,1\}^n} [\chi(y) = 1] = 2^r / 2^n$. This probability is upper-bounded by $1/2^\lambda$ if $r \leq n - \lambda$.

Lemma 3.1 shows that all conjunctions which have their non-wildcard values uniformly distributed over $\{0, 1\}^{n-r}$ are evasive. For general distributions we need to consider the following

**Definition 3.2 (Conjunction Evasive Distribution).** *Consider an ensemble $D = \{D_\lambda\}_{\lambda \in \mathbb{N}}$ of distributions $D_\lambda$ over $\{0, 1, \star\}^{n(\lambda)}$ with $r(\lambda)$-many wildcards for functions $r(\lambda) < n(\lambda)$. We say that $D$ is* conjunction evasive *if the min-entropy of $D_\lambda$ is at least $\lambda$.*

# 4 Obfuscation Definitions

Our ultimate goal is to prove that our obfuscators are distributional *virtual black box* (VBB) secure. For this we first state the definition of such a distributional VBB obfuscator.

**Definition 4.1 (Distributional Virtual Black-Box Obfuscator [2,3]).** *Let $\mathcal{P} = \{\mathcal{P}_n\}_{n \in \mathbb{N}}$ be a family of polynomial-size programs with input size $n$ and let $\mathcal{O}$ be a PPT algorithm which takes as input a program $P \in \mathcal{P}$, a security parameter $\lambda \in \mathbb{N}$ and outputs a program $\mathcal{O}(P)$ (which itself is not necessarily in $\mathcal{P}$). Let $\mathcal{D}$ be a class of distribution ensembles $D = \{D_\lambda\}_{\lambda \in \mathbb{N}}$ that sample $P \leftarrow D_\lambda$ with $P \in \mathcal{P}$. The algorithm $\mathcal{O}$ is a VBB obfuscator for the distribution class $\mathcal{D}$ over the program family $\mathcal{P}$ if it satisfies the following properties:*

– *Functionality preserving: There exists a negligible function $\epsilon(\lambda)$ such that for all $P \in \mathcal{P}$*

$$1 - \Pr\left[\forall x \in \{0,1\}^n : P(x) = \mathcal{O}(P)(x)\right] \leq \epsilon(\lambda)$$

*where the probability is over the coin tosses of $\mathcal{O}$.*
– *Polynomial slowdown: For every $\lambda \in \mathbb{N}$ and $P \in \mathcal{P}$, we have $|\mathcal{O}(P)| \leq \mathrm{poly}(|P|, \lambda)$.*
– *Virtual black-box: For every (non-uniform) polynomial size adversary $\mathcal{A}$, there exists a (non-uniform) polynomial size simulator $\mathcal{S}$ with oracle access to $P$, such that for every $D = \{D_\lambda\}_{\lambda \in \mathbb{N}} \in \mathcal{D}$, and every (non-uniform) polynomial size predicate $\varphi : \mathcal{P} \to \{0,1\}$:*

$$\left| \Pr_{P \leftarrow D_\lambda, \mathcal{O}, \mathcal{A}}\left[\mathcal{A}(\mathcal{O}(P)) = \varphi(P)\right] - \Pr_{P \leftarrow D_\lambda, \mathcal{S}}\left[\mathcal{S}^P(|P|) = \varphi(P)\right] \right| \leq \epsilon(\lambda)$$

*where $\epsilon(\lambda)$ is a negligible function.*

In simple terms, Definition 4.1 states that a VBB obfuscated program $\mathcal{O}(P)$ does not reveal anything more than would be revealed from having black box access to the program $P$ itself.

A definition that is more convenient to work with is *distributional indistinguishability*.

**Definition 4.2 (Distributional Indistinguishability** [44]**).** *An obfuscator $\mathcal{O}$ for the distribution class $\mathcal{D}$ over a family of programs $\mathcal{P}$ satisfies distributional indistinguishability if there exists a (non-uniform) PPT simulator $\mathcal{S}$ such that for every distribution ensemble $D = \{D_\lambda\}_{\lambda \in \mathbb{N}} \in \mathcal{D}$ the following distributions are computationally indistinguishable*

$$(\mathcal{O}(P), \alpha) \stackrel{c}{\approx} (\mathcal{S}(|P|), \alpha) \tag{4.1}$$

*where $(P, \alpha) \leftarrow D_\lambda$. Here $\alpha$ denotes some auxiliary information.*

Note that the sampling procedure for the left and right side of Eq. (4.1) in Definition 4.2 is slightly different. For both we sample $(P, \alpha) \leftarrow D_\lambda$ and for the left side we simply output $(\mathcal{O}(P), \alpha)$ immediately. On the other hand, for the right side we record $|P|$, discard $P$ and finally output $(\mathcal{S}(|P|), \alpha)$ instead.

It can be shown that distributional indistinguishability implies VBB security under certain conditions. To see this, we first require the following.

**Definition 4.3 (Predicate Augmentation** [44]**).** *For a distribution class $\mathcal{D}$, its augmentation under predicates $\mathrm{aug}(\mathcal{D})$ is defined as follows: For any (non-uniform) polynomial-time predicate $\varphi : \{0,1\}^* \to \{0,1\}$ and any $D = \{D_\lambda\}_{\lambda \in \mathbb{N}} \in \mathcal{D}$, the class $\mathrm{aug}(\mathcal{D})$ indicates the distribution $D' = \{D'_\lambda\}_{\lambda \in \mathbb{N}}$ where $D'_\lambda$ samples $(P, \alpha) \leftarrow D_\lambda$, computes $\alpha' = (\alpha, \varphi(P))$ and outputs $(P, \alpha')$. Here $\alpha$ denotes some auxiliary information.*

**Theorem 4.1 (Distributional Indistinguishability Implies VBB** [10]**).**
*For any family of programs $P$ and a distribution class $D$ over $P$, if an obfus-cator satisfies distributional indistinguishability (Definition 4.2) for the class of distributions $\text{aug}(D)$ then it also satisfies distributional VBB security for the distribution class $D$ (Definition 4.1).*

Lastly, we also want to prove that our obfuscator is *input hiding*. For this we state the definition of an input hiding obfuscator.

**Definition 4.4 (Input Hiding Obfuscator** [2]**).** *An obfuscator $O$ for a col-lection of evasive programs $P$ is input hiding, if for every PPT adversary $A$ there exists a negligible function $\epsilon$ such that for every $n \in \mathbb{N}$ and for every auxiliary input $\alpha \in \{0, 1\}^{\text{poly}(n)}$ to $A$:*

$$\Pr_{P \leftarrow P_n} [P(A(\alpha, O(P))) = 1] \le \epsilon(n),$$

*where the probability is also over the randomness of $O$.*

To summarise, Definition 4.4 states that given the obfuscated program $O(P)$ it is hard to find an input that evaluates to 1.

# 5  Computational Assumptions

In this section we introduce our new computational assumptions. We start with the definition of a safe prime.

**Definition 5.1 (Safe Prime, Sophie Germain Prime).** *A prime $q$ is called a* safe prime *if $q$ is of the form $q = 2p + 1$ for a prime $p$. The prime $p$ is then called a* Sophie Germain prime.

**Problem 5.1 (Distributional Modular Subset Product Problem).** *Let $r < n \in \mathbb{N}$, $D$ be a distribution over $\{0, 1\}^n$. Given a sequence of distinct primes $(p_i)_{i=1,\ldots,n}$, a safe prime $q$ such that*

$$\prod_{i \in I} p_i < \frac{q}{2} < (1 + o(1)) \max\{p_i\}^r \text{ for all } I \subset \{1, \ldots, n\} \text{ with } |I| \le r \quad (5.1)$$

*and an integer*

$$X = \prod_{i=1}^{n} p_i^{x_i} \mod q \quad (5.2)$$

*for some vector $x \leftarrow D$, the $(r, n, D)$-distributional modular subset product problem ($MSP_{r,n,D}$) is to find $x$.*

We also state a decisional version of the problem.

**Problem 5.2 (Decisional Distrib. Modular Subset Product Problem).**
*Let $r < n \in \mathbb{N}$, $D$ be a distribution over $\{0,1\}^n$. Define the distribution*

$$\mathcal{D}_0 = ((p_i)_{i=1,\ldots,n}, q, X)$$

*where $(p_i)_{i=1,\ldots,n}$ are distinct primes, $q$ satisfies Eq. (5.1), and $X$ satisfies Eq. (5.2) for some vector $x \leftarrow D$. Define the distribution*

$$\mathcal{D}_1 = ((p_i)_{i=1,\ldots,n}, q, X')$$

*where $(p_i)_{i=1,\ldots,n}$ and $q$ are as in $\mathcal{D}_0$, but*

$$X' \leftarrow (\mathbb{Z}/q\mathbb{Z})^*.$$

*Then the $(r, n, D)$-decisional distributional modular subset product problem $(D\text{-}MSP_{r,n,D})$ is to distinguish $\mathcal{D}_0$ from $\mathcal{D}_1$. In other words, given a sample from $\mathcal{D}_b$ for uniform $b \in \{0,1\}$, the problem is to determine $b$.*

We believe these computational problems are hard whenever the fuzzy matching problem itself is evasive. Precisely we make the following conjecture that covers all possible distributions $D$.

*Conjecture 1.* Fix $r < n/2 \in \mathbb{N}$. If $D$ is a distribution on $\{0,1\}^n$ with Hamming ball min-entropy at least $\lambda$ (i.e. $D$ is a Hamming distance evasive distribution in the sense of Definition 2.5) then solving D-MSP$_{r,n,D}$ (Problem 5.2) requires $\Omega(\min\{2^\lambda, 2^{n/2}\})$ operations.

Note that Problem 5.2 only makes sense if the two distributions are different. In the case $2^n \gg q$ we conjecture that the values $X = \prod_{i=1}^{n} p_i^{x_i} \bmod q$ are distributed close to uniformly if $x$ is sampled uniformly, and so it makes no sense to ask for a distinguisher between this distribution and the uniform distribution. For the proof of Theorem 5.1 we need a more precise version of this statement, so we make the following conjecture that we believe is very reasonable.

*Conjecture 2.* Let $r, n, (p_i)_{i=1,\ldots,n}, q$ be as in Problem 5.1, with the extra condition that $q \leq 2^n$. Let $D$ be the uniform distribution on $\{0,1\}^n$. Then the statistical distance of the distribution $\prod_{i=1}^{n} p_i^{x_i} \bmod q$ over $x \leftarrow D$ and the uniform distribution on $(\mathbb{Z}/q\mathbb{Z})^*$ is negligible.

The situation is summarised in the following diagram. The left hand side is the *low-density* case. The right hand side is the *high-density* case where for every value $X$ there are likely (multiple) solutions. As can be seen in Fig. 2 our interest reaches over all density cases.

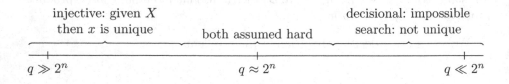

A "search-to-decision" reduction in the low-density or density one case (i.e., $2^n < q$) is possible by borrowing techniques from [31,38]. One can obtain the result that a decision oracle for Problem 5.2 in this case can be used to solve the search problem Problem 5.1 in polynomially many queries to the decision oracle. This gives further evidence that Problem 5.2 should be hard (recall that the assumption makes no sense in the high-density case).

## 5.1   Algorithms

We now consider algorithms for Problem 5.1. If the Hamming weight of $x$ is too small, or if $q$ is too large, then it might happen that $\prod_{i=1}^{n} p_i^{x_i} < q$ and hence Problem 5.1 can be solved by factoring $X$ over the integers. This is the low-density case. More generally, an approach to Problem 5.1 is to guess some $x_i$ for $i \in I$ and try to factor $X \prod_{i \in I} p_i^{-x_i} \mod q$. It can be shown that if $q = O((n \log(n))^r)$ and if $x$ is sampled from a distribution with large Hamming ball min-entropy then this approach does not lead to an efficient attack. In short, the requirement that the Hamming ball membership program is evasive already implies that such an attack requires exponential time.

We now consider algorithms that are appropriate in general. There is an obvious meet-in-the-middle algorithm: Let $m = \lfloor n/2 \rfloor$. Given $X$ we compute a list $L$ of pairs $(z, Z)$ where $Z = \prod_{i=1}^{m} p_i^{z_i} \mod q$ for all $z \in \{0,1\}^m$. Then for all $z' \in \{0,1\}^{n-m}$ compute $Z' = X \prod_{i=1}^{n-m} p_{m+i}^{-z'_i} \mod q$ and check if $Z'$ is in $L$. If there is a match then we have found $x = z \| z'$. This attack requires $O(2^{n/2})$ operations. It follows that $n$ must be sufficiently large for the problem to be hard.

## 5.2   Hardness

We now give evidence that Problems 5.1 and 5.2 are hard in the high-density case. Our argument is based on ideas from index calculus algorithms in finite fields. We prove that if one can solve Problem 5.1 (in the medium-/high-density case) in time $T$ then can solve the discrete logarithm problem (DLP) in $(\mathbb{Z}/q\mathbb{Z})^*$ in time $poly(T)$. Note that this result gives at best a subexponential hardness guarantee, and does not say anything about post-quantum security. A similar computational assumption (called the *very smooth number discrete log*) was considered in [15], where a similar reduction to the discrete logarithm problem is also given.

**Theorem 5.1.** *Fix $r, n \in \mathbb{N}$ such that $r < n/2$. Let $q$ be prime such that $q \leq 2^n$ and $(p_i)_{i=1,\ldots,n}$ be a sequence of distinct primes such that $p_i \in [2, O(n \log(n))]$. Assume Conjecture 2 holds and suppose $MSP_{r,n,D}$ (Problem 5.1) can be solved with probability 1 in time $T$. Then there is an algorithm to solve the DLP in $(\mathbb{Z}/q\mathbb{Z})^*$ with expected time $\tilde{O}(nT)$.*

*Proof.* Let $g, h \in \mathbb{Z}_q^*$ be a DLP instance and let $\mathcal{A}$ be an oracle for Problem 5.1 that runs in time $T$ and succeeds with probability 1. Let $g$ be a generator of $(\mathbb{Z}/q\mathbb{Z})^*$ so that its order is $M = q - 1$. Choose random $1 < a < q$ and compute

$C = g^a \mod q$. Call $\mathcal{A}$ on $C$. Due to the assumptions in the theorem, with probability bounded below by a constant, $\mathcal{A}$ succeeds and outputs a solution $x$. Store $(a, x)$. Note that each relation implies a linear relation $a \equiv \sum_{i=1}^{n} x_i \log_g(p_i) \mod M$. Repeat until we have $n$ linearly independent relation vectors $x$, and hence use linear algebra to solve for $\log_g(p_i)$. Finally, choose a random $b$ and set $C = hg^b \mod q$. Call $\mathcal{A}$ on $C$ to get, with high probability, one more relation $(b, y)$. Knowing $\log_g(p_i)$ we now compute $\log_g(h) = -b + \sum_i y_i \log_g(p_i)$.     □

The above proof can be generalised to any group whose order is known. When $q = (n \log(n))^r$ then the condition $2^n \geq q$ boils down to $r < n/\log_2(n \log(n))$. Hence, when $r < n/\log_2(n \log(n))$ the hardness of Problem 5.1 follows from the discrete log assumption.

It follows that Problem 5.1 has a spectrum of difficulty, ranging from easy in the extreme low-density case to hard in the medium-/high-density case. We visualise the situation below.

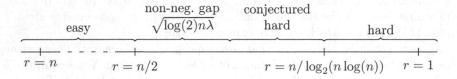

All index calculus algorithms for factoring and discrete logarithms are based on smoothness. A typical situation is to generate certain random elements $x$ modulo $N$ (or $p$), and check if they are *equal* to $\prod_i p_i^{e_i}$ for primes $p_i$ less than some bound. If one could efficiently compute a smooth product $\prod_i p_i^{e_i}$ that is *congruent* to $x$ modulo $N$ (or $p$) then factorization and discrete logarithm algorithms would be revolutionised (and classical public key crypto broken).

Our subset product problem is slightly different, since we impose the restriction $e_i \in \{0, 1\}$. But we still believe any fundamentally new algorithmic approach to the problem would likely lead to major advances. The only algorithms we know for this problem are "combinatorial" (in other words, requiring some kind of brute-force search), apart from when the density is extremely low and we can just factor. Note that our parameter choices (e.g. in Fig. 2) are very far from such low density (as we require $r < n/2$ by Lemma 2.3).

We briefly discuss the relation with lattice problems in the next section and in Sect. 7.3. Our feeling is that the subset product problem is not really a lattice problem but a number-theoretical problem. As evidence, references [21,39] use similar number theory ideas to solve coding/lattice type problems. Nevertheless, any new algorithms to solve Problem 5.1 would have implications in lattices, such as giving an improvement on the work of [21].

Ultimately, we are making a new assumption based on our experience and knowledge. A similar assumption was made in [15]. We hope this work will inspire further study of these problems.

## 5.3   Post-Quantum Security

To the best of our knowledge there exists no classical nor quantum algorithm that efficiently solves either of Problem 5.1 or Problem 5.2 in general.

Consider an adversary that has access to a quantum computer for computing discrete logarithms. Given an encoding $((p_i)_{i=1,\ldots,n}, q, X)$ of a secret $x \in \{0, 1\}^n$, the adversary may then turn it into a modular subset sum instance $\log_g(X) = \sum_i x_i \log_g(p_i) \mod q - 1$. Such a modular subset sum problem may be classified by its density $d$, see [16, 34]. In our case, when $x$ is chosen from the uniform distribution, the density is $d = n/\log_2(q)$.

There is a polynomial time algorithm for low-density subset sum instances where $d < 0.645$ [34] which was later improved to $d < 0.941$ [16]. This algorithm requires access to a perfect lattice oracle (just using LLL [35] is not enough). It is furthermore assumed that the lattice oracle is *perfect*.

In our case, we can give an estimate for when we expect post-quantum security. By the prime number theorem, we have $q \sim (n \log n)^r$. Thus we can estimate the density by $d \sim n/(r \log_2(n \log n))$. To ensure density of $d > 1$ we can require

$$r < \frac{n}{\log_2(n \log n)} = r_{\mathrm{PQ}}(n). \tag{5.3}$$

Hence we conjecture post-quantum hardness of the modular subset product problem when $r < r_{\mathrm{PQ}}(n)$, and potentially even for slightly larger values for $r$.

# 6   Continued Fractions

The background can be found in any number theory textbook, such as [27]. Consider a rational number $x \in \mathbb{Q}$. It has a finite *continued fraction* representation of the form

$$x = a_0 + \cfrac{1}{a_1 + \cfrac{1}{\ddots + \cfrac{1}{a_N}}}$$

for $a_i \in \mathbb{N}$. We define the notation $x = [a_0, a_1, a_2, \ldots, a_N]$ for such a representation. In the more general case of $x \in \mathbb{R}$ such a representation also exists, though it is not necessarily finite.

We call the fractions $h_i/k_i$ for an index $i \in \mathbb{N}$ defined by the recursion

$$\begin{aligned} h_i &= a_i h_{i-1} + h_{i-2}, & h_{-1} &= 1, & h_{-2} &= 0, \\ k_i &= a_i k_{i-1} + k_{i-2}, & k_{-1} &= 0, & k_{-2} &= 1 \end{aligned} \tag{6.1}$$

the *convergents* of $x$.

**Theorem 6.1 (Diophantine Approximation [30]).** *Let $\alpha \in \mathbb{R}$ then there exist fractions $p/q \in \mathbb{Q}$ such that $\left| \alpha - \frac{p}{q} \right| < \frac{1}{\sqrt{5}q^2}$. If, on the other hand, there exist $p/q \in \mathbb{Q}$ such that $\left| \alpha - \frac{p}{q} \right| < \frac{1}{2q^2}$, then $p/q$ is a convergent of $\alpha$.*

To find the continued fraction representation it is useful to review the extended Euclidean algorithm first.

**Extended Euclidean Algorithm.** For a pair of integers $a, b$, the extended euclidean algorithm finds integers $x, y$ such that $ax + by = \gcd(a, b)$. The algorithm proceeds as follows: First, it initialises variables $r_i, s_i, t_i$ for $i = 0, 1$ as

$$r_0 = a, \quad r_1 = b, \quad s_0 = 1, \quad s_1 = 0, \quad t_0 = 0, \quad t_1 = 1.$$

Then it iteratively produces the sequence

$$r_{i+1} = r_{i-1} - q_i r_i, \quad s_{i+1} = s_{i-1} - q_i s_i, \quad t_{i+1} = t_{i-1} - q_i t_i. \tag{6.2}$$

Here $r_{i+1}$ and $q_i$ are found using Euclidean division ($r_{i-1} = q_i r_i + r_{i+1}$) such that $0 \le r_{i+1} < |r_i|$. Finally, the algorithms stops when $r_{i+1} = 0$.

It can be shown that the worst-case runtime of the extended Euclidean algorithm is of the order $O(\log(b))$ assuming that $b < a$; the average runtime is of a similar order [17, 28].

**Finding Convergents.** Comparison of Equation (6.1) with Equation (6.2) shows that the convergents of a fraction $p/q \in \mathbb{Q}$ are exactly produced by the integers $s_i, t_i$ (up to signs) in the steps of the extended Euclidean algorithm applied to $p$ and $q$. Thus the runtime for computing the continued fraction representation is essentially the same as that of the extended Euclidean algorithm. Furthermore, we see that the number of convergents is linear in the input size.

## 7    Obfuscating Hamming Distance

In this section we will present our Hamming distance obfuscator in detail and then give some examples for parameter choices. The obfuscator is given in Sect. 7.1.

**The Hamming Distance Obfuscator.** Let $r, n \in \mathbb{N}$ with $r < n/2$. Choose a random sequence of small distinct primes $(p_i)_{i=1,\ldots,n}$ (i.e., $p_i \ne p_j$ for $i \ne j$). By the prime number theorem it suffices to randomly sample each $p_i$ from the interval $[2, O(n \log(n))]$. Choose then a safe prime $q$ such that $\prod_{i \in I} p_i < q/2$ for all $I \subset \{1, \ldots, n\}$ with $|I| \le r$. The prime $q$ should be sampled to satisfy the bound $q/2 < (1 + o(1)) \max\{p_i\}^r$ as in Eq. (5.1). We refer to the discussion regarding Eq. (9.3) to justify why we may assume that such a suitable safe prime exists.

To encode an element $x \in \{0, 1\}^n$, publish

$$X = \prod_{i=1}^{n} p_i^{x_i} \quad \bmod q \tag{7.1}$$

along with the list of primes $(p_i)_{i=1,\ldots,n}$ and $q$. Note that, for this encoding to hide $x$, we require that $w_H(x) > r$ and $\prod_{i=1}^{n} p_i^{x_i} > q$.

Given another element $y \in \{0,1\}^n$ we can now check if $y \in B_{H,r}(x)$ using the encoding $X$. First we compute $Y = \prod_{i=1}^n p_i^{y_i} \mod q$ from which we can find

$$E = XY^{-1} \mod q = \prod_{i=1}^n p_i^{x_i - y_i} \mod q = \prod_{i=1}^n p_i^{\epsilon_i} \mod q \qquad (7.2)$$

where $\epsilon_i \in \{-1, 0, 1\}$. We show in Lemma 7.1 that if $y \in B_{H,r}(x)$ then we are able to recover the errors $\epsilon_i$ using continued fraction decomposition and factoring.

**Legendre Symbol.** Recall that the *Legendre symbol* $\left(\frac{a}{q}\right)$ is $+1$ if $a$ is a non-zero square modulo $q$ and $-1$ if $a$ is a non-zero non-square. It is multiplicative in the sense that $\left(\frac{ab}{p}\right) = \left(\frac{a}{p}\right)\left(\frac{b}{p}\right)$. Thus for $X$ as in Eq. (7.1) the Legendre symbol $\left(\frac{X}{q}\right)$ is equal to the product $\prod_i \left(\frac{p_i}{q}\right)^{x_i}$, which reveals a linear equation in the secret $(x_i)_{i=1,\ldots,n}$. In other words, the encoding $X$ leaks one bit of information about $x$. Note that this does not violate the definition of VBB security: since the primes $p_i$ are chosen randomly by the obfuscator, we cannot fix in advance a predicate and compute it using the Legendre symbol.

**Why a Safe Prime.** As mentioned, the Legendre symbol leaks a linear equation in $(x_i)$. If there were other small prime divisors of $q - 1$ then one could extend this idea to get further linear equations. Hence we choose $q$ to be a safe prime to ensure that only the single bit of leakage arises. An alternative solution would be to square $X$, but this would mean we need to use larger parameters to do fuzzy matching with Hamming weight $r$, so we prefer to use the minimal parameters.

## 7.1   Obfuscator and Obfuscated Program

To be precise, for every pair of integers $r < n/2 \in \mathbb{N}$ and every binary vector $x \in \{0,1\}^n$ there exists a polynomial size program $P_x : \{0,1\}^n \to \{0,1\}$ that computes whether the input vector $y \in \{0,1\}^n$ is contained in a Hamming ball $B_{H,r}(x)$ and evaluates to 1 in this case, otherwise to 0. Denote the family of all such programs with $\mathcal{P}$.

The Hamming distance obfuscator $\mathcal{O}_H : \mathcal{P} \to \mathcal{P}'$ takes one such program $P_x \in \mathcal{P}$ and uses Algorithm 7.2 to output another polynomial size program in a different family denoted by $\mathcal{P}'$. In our case this is the decoding algorithm along with the polynomial size elements $(p_i)_{i=1,\ldots,n}$, $q$ and $X \in \mathbb{Z}/q\mathbb{Z}$.

We furthermore require a dependent auxiliary input point function obfuscator [7,8] that we call $\mathcal{O}_{PT}$. Let $R_z : \{0,1\}^n \to \{0,1\}$ be a program that takes an input $y \in \{0,1\}^n$ and outputs 1 if and only if $y = z$. The point function obfuscator outputs an obfuscated version $\mathcal{O}_{PT}(R_z)$ of $R_z$. In addition to the output of Algorithm 7.2, our obfuscator $\mathcal{O}_H$ also outputs $Q = \mathcal{O}_{PT}(R_x)$.

As the decoding algorithm is a universal algorithm, we will simply denote the *obfuscated program* $\mathcal{O}_H(P)$ with the tuple $((p_i)_{i=1,\ldots,n}, q, X, Q)$. During the execution of the obfuscated program, Algorithm 7.4 is run on $(n, (p_i)_{i=1,\ldots,n}, q, X, y)$

and returns either $\perp$ (in which case the program returns 0) or a candidate value $x'$. The obfuscated program then outputs $Q(x')$, which is 1 if and only if $x' = x$. Formally, the obfuscated program is given in Algorithm 7.1.

---

**Algorithm 7.1.** Obfuscated Program (with embedded data $(p_i)_{i=1,\dots,n}, q, X, Q$)

  **procedure** EXECUTE($y \in \{0,1\}^n$)
    $x' = \text{DECODE}(n, (p_i)_{i=1,\dots,n}, q, X, y)$
    **if** $x' = \perp$ **then return** 0
    **return** $Q(x')$
  **end procedure**

---

The encoder (Algorithm 7.2) receives as an input the distance threshold $r$, the vector size $n$ and the target vector $x$. It then outputs the encoding represented by a triple $((p_i)_{i=1,\dots,n}, q, X)$.

---

**Algorithm 7.2.** Encoding (Obfuscation)

  **procedure** ENCODE($r < n/2 \in \mathbb{N}$; $x \in \{0,1\}^n$)
    sample a random sequence of distinct primes $(p_i)_{i=1,\dots,n}$ from $[2, O(n\log(n))]$
    sample small safe prime $q$ such that $\forall I \subset \{1,\dots,n\}$ with $|I| \leq r$, $\prod_{i \in I} p_i < q/2$
    compute $X = \prod_{i=1}^n p_i^{x_i} \mod q$
    **return** $((p_i)_{i=1,\dots,n}, q, X)$
  **end procedure**

---

The constrained factoring algorithm (Algorithm 7.3) factors an input number using a fixed list of primes and outputs the factors respectively fails if the input is composite with factors that are not in the list of primes.

---

**Algorithm 7.3.** Constrained Factoring

  **procedure** CFACTOR($n, (p_i)_{i=1,\dots,n}, x \in \mathbb{N}$)
    set $F = \{\}$
    **for** $i = 1,\dots,n$ **do**
      **if** $p_i \mid x$ **then** append $p_i$ to $F$ and reduce $x \leftarrow x/p_i$
    **end for**
    **return** $F$ **if** $x = 1$ **else** $\perp$
  **end procedure**

---

The decoder (Algorithm 7.4) receives as an input an encoding in the form of a triple $((p_i)_{i=1,\dots,n}, q, X)$ and a test vector. It then attempts to decode the triple and outputs the original target vector or fails if the test vector was not within the required distance threshold.

---

**Algorithm 7.4.** Decoding (Executing the obfuscated program)

> **procedure** DECODE($n, (p_i)_{i=1,\ldots,n}, q \in \mathbb{N}; X \in \mathbb{Z}/q\mathbb{Z}; y \in \{0,1\}^n$)
>   compute $Y^{-1} = \prod_{i=1}^n p_i^{-y_i} \mod q$
>   compute $E = XY^{-1} \mod q$
>   compute the continued fraction representation of $E/q$, with convergents $C$
>   **for all** $h/k \in C$ **do**
>     $F \leftarrow$ CFACTOR$(n, (p_i)_{i=1,\ldots,n}, k)$, $F' \leftarrow$ CFACTOR$(n, (p_i)_{i=1,\ldots,n}, kE \mod q)$
>     **if** $F \neq \perp$ and $F' \neq \perp$ **then**
>       let $m = (0,\ldots,0) \in \{0,1\}^n$ be the zero vector
>       **for** $i = 1,\ldots,n$ **do**
>         **if** $p_i \in F \cup F'$ **then** set $m_i = 1$
>       **end for**
>       **return** $y \oplus m$
>     **end if**
>   **end for**
>   **return** $\perp$
> **end procedure**

---

## 7.2  Decoding

In this section we will analyse decoding complexity and efficiency. For decoding we have to factor the product Eq. (7.2). First, we note that it can be written as $ND^{-1}$ modulo $q$, or in other words $ED = N + sq$, $N = \prod_{i=1}^n p_i^{\mu_i}$, and $D = \prod_{i=1}^n p_i^{\nu_i}$ for some $s \in \mathbb{Z}$ and where now $\mu_i, \nu_i \in \{0,1\}$, $\mu_i \nu_i = 0$ for all $i$. By expanding $E/q$ into a continued fraction we are then able to recover $s/D$ from one of the convergents $h_i/k_i$ for some $i \in \mathbb{N}$ under the condition that $ND < q/2$. Hence decoding always succeeds since we have chosen the primes $(p_i)_{i=1,\ldots,n}$ and $q$ such that $ND = \prod_{i \in I} p_i < q/2$ for some $I \subset \{1,\ldots,n\}$ with $|I| \leq r$.

**Lemma 7.1 (Correctness).** *Consider the algorithms* ENCODE *(Algorithm 7.2) and* DECODE *(Algorithm 7.4). For every* $r < n/2 \in \mathbb{N}, x \in \{0,1\}^n$, *for every* $((p_i)_{i=1,\ldots,n}, q, X) \leftarrow$ ENCODE$(r, n, x)$ *and for every* $y \in \{0,1\}^n$ *such that* $d_H(x,y) < r$ *it holds that* DECODE$(n, (p_i)_{i=1,\ldots,n}, q, X, y) = x$.

*Proof.* To see why we require $ND < q/2$, note that there exists an $s \in \mathbb{Z}$ such that $ED - sq = N$. Therefore $\left|\frac{E}{q} - \frac{s}{D}\right| = \frac{N}{qD}$. Now Theorem 6.1 asserts us that $s/D$ is a convergent of $E/q$ if $\left|\frac{E}{q} - \frac{s}{D}\right| < \frac{1}{2D^2}$ and so we find the requirement $ND < q/2$.

For each convergent $h_i/k_i$ of $E/q$, $k_i$ respectively ($k_i E \mod q$) can be factored separately using the $p_i$ to recover the $\nu_i$ and $\mu_i$ from which $x \in \{0,1\}^n$ can then finally be recovered using $y \in \{0,1\}^n$. This all works assuming $y \in B_{H,r}(x)$ since then the factors of $N$ and $D$ will be unique (of multiplicity 1) and contained in the sequence $(p_i)_{i=1,\ldots,n}$. If now $y \notin B_{H,r}(x)$ then with high probability (dependent on $r, n$) the factors of $N$ and $D$ will not be unique and/or not contained in $(p_i)_{i=1,\ldots,n}$ in which case the decoding fails. $\qquad\square$

*Remark 1.* Note that our decoding algorithm can also be used to solve the problem of matching distance in $\mathbb{Z}^n$ under the $\ell_1$ norm. If $X = \prod_i p_i^{x_i} \mod q$ is an encoding of $\mathbf{x} \in \mathbb{Z}^n$ and if $\mathbf{y} \in \mathbb{Z}^n$ is such that $\|\mathbf{x} - \mathbf{y}\|_1 \leq r$ then by taking continued fractions and factoring still reveals the error vector $\mathbf{e} = \mathbf{x} - \mathbf{y} \in \mathbb{Z}^n$.

**Decoding Efficiency.** We will now argue that decoding $E$ is efficient. Assuming that $E = XY^{-1}$ for some $x, y \in \{0,1\}^n$ such that $d_H(x, y) < r$, one of the convergents $h_i/k_i$ will yield $s/D$. From Sect. 6 we know that in our case the number of convergents we have to factor is of the order $O(\log(q))$ in the worst case. Because we fixed a list of small primes $p_i$ beforehand, we can test for a proper convergent $h_i/k_i$ and simultaneously factor $N$ and $D$ efficiently. Thus decoding is of the order $O(n \log(q))$ in the number of (modular) multiplications/divisions. By the prime number theorem we may take $q \sim (n \log n)^r$ and thus decoding is also of the order $O(nr \log(n \log n))$.

### 7.3    Avoiding False Accepts

We define a *false accept* to be an input $y$ that is far from $x$ but such that $E$ has a smooth product representation. Recall that the obfuscator $\mathcal{O}_H$ defined in Sect. 7.1 additionally outputs $Q = \mathcal{O}_{PT}(R_x)$ which is used to prevent such false accepts. We will explain in this section that the additional step can be omitted if $r$ is chosen such that

$$r > \log(2\sqrt{2\pi e}) \frac{n}{\log(n \log(n))} = r_f(n). \tag{7.3}$$

Let $y$ be a false accept, which means $XY^{-1} \equiv \prod_i p_i^{\epsilon_i} \mod q$ as in Eq. (7.2), where $\epsilon_i \in \{-1, 0, 1\}$. Then $\prod_{i=1}^n p_i^{x_i - y_i - \epsilon_i} = 1 \mod q$ where $-2 \leq x_i - y_i - \epsilon_i \leq 2$. It follows that there is a non-zero vector in the lattice $\Lambda = \{x \in \mathbb{Z}^n \mid \prod_{i=1}^n p_i^{x_i} = 1 \mod q\}$ with norm bounded by $2\sqrt{n}$.

Treating the lattice $\Lambda$ as a random lattice, the Gaussian heuristic (see [29, Section 7.5.3]) estimates the size of the shortest non-zero vector in $\Lambda$ as $\lambda_1 \sim \sqrt{\frac{n}{2\pi e}} \mathrm{vol}(\Lambda)^{\frac{1}{n}} \leq \sqrt{\frac{n}{2\pi e}} (q-1)^{\frac{1}{n}}$, where equality holds if the $p_i$ generate $(\mathbb{Z}/q\mathbb{Z})^*$. We use this bound to argue that there is no vector of length bounded by $2\sqrt{n}$, and hence no false accept, Indeed, to have $\lambda_1 > 2\sqrt{n}$ we need $\sqrt{\frac{n}{2\pi e}} (n \log(n))^{\frac{r}{n}} > 2\sqrt{n}$ and so

$$(n \log(n))^{\frac{r}{n}} > 2\sqrt{2\pi e}. \tag{7.4}$$

Equation (7.4) assumes that $q \sim (n \log(n))^r$, i.e. the size of the primes $p_i$ is as small as possible. If we want to be able to use a smaller $r$ we may also choose the primes $p_i > n \log(n)$.

### 7.4    Example Parameters

The parameters of the Hamming distance obfuscator can be chosen fairly flexibly. We want to emphasize that a priori any vector size $n \in \mathbb{N}$ is possible. The actual security level of the obfuscator depends on the error parameter $r < n/2$ which we expect to be fixed by the demands of the application. Note that it is naturally bounded by Lemma 2.2. Assuming a uniform distribution of possible target vectors $x$, the bit-security (meaning logarithm to base 2 of the expected number of operations to find an accepting input) of a parameter set $(r, n)$ can be calculated using $\lambda_{r,n} = -\log_2(h_r/2^n)$ where $h_r$ is defined in Lemma 2.1. We give some example parameter sets along with their bit-security in Fig. 2.

| $r$ | $\lfloor \lambda_{r,n} \rfloor$ | $\lfloor \log_2(q) \rfloor$ |
| --- | --- | --- |
| 155 | 64 | 1804 |
| 128 | 102 | 1490 |
| 32 | 346 | 372 |

| $r$ | $\lfloor \lambda_{r,n} \rfloor$ | $\lfloor \log_2(q) \rfloor$ |
| --- | --- | --- |
| 306 | 128 | 3915 |
| 256 | 199 | 2546 |
| 64 | 686 | 818 |

(a) $n = 512$ ($r_f(n) = 134$, $r_{\mathrm{PQ}}(n) = 44$)    (b) $n = 1024$ ($r_f(n) = 244$, $r_{\mathrm{PQ}}(n) = 80$)

**Fig. 2.** Example parameter sets for obfuscated Hamming distance with $r < n/2$ and bit-security parameter $\lambda_{r,n}$. We estimate the size of $q$ by $q \sim (n \log n)^r$. When $r > r_f(n)$ (see Eq. (7.3)) we do not expect false accepts, and so do not need to use the point obfuscator. When $r < r_{\mathrm{PQ}}(n)$ (see Eq. (5.3)) then the scheme is conjectured to be post-quantum secure (as long as the point obfuscator is post-quantum secure).

## 7.5    Performance

For completeness, we have implemented (an unoptimised version of) the Hamming distance obfuscator using the C programming language and conducted experiments on a desktop computer (Intel(R) Core(TM) i7-4770 CPU 3.40 GHz). We take $n = 511$ and $r = 85$ (i.e. $\lfloor \lambda_{85,511} \rfloor = 185$ and $\lfloor \log_2(q) \rfloor = 989$) to allow comparison with [33,42]. We measured the time to produce and decode 1000 obfuscation instances. We found an average encoding time of 52 ms and an average decoding time of 14 ms. In comparison Karabina and Canpolat [33] found 100 ms for encoding and 350 ms for decoding respectively on a similar computer (Intel(R) Xeon(R) CPU E31240 3.30 GHz). It is possible to further speed up encoding by choosing a good safe prime generating algorithm and decoding can be parallelised in the factoring steps instead of attempting to factor after computing each new convergent. Note that the data $((p_i)_{i=1,\dots,n}, q, X)$ can be stored in less than one kilobyte.

An interactive model of program obfuscation called *token based obfuscation* was first considered by Goldwasser et al. [25] and an LWE based implementation was presented by Chen et al. [13]. They found experimentally that "For the case of the Hamming distance threshold of 3 and 24-bit strings, the TBO construction requires 213 GB to store the obfuscated program." Obfuscation took 72.6 min. Of course, the parameters $(n, r) = (24, 3)$ are much too small for the function to be evasive. Further, this problem is easily solved using a secure sketch. In comparison our scheme can be implemented with realistic parameters like $(n, r) = (511, 85)$ and requires less than a kilobyte of storage and less than a second to run. Clearly the ring-LWE approach in [13] is orders of magnitude worse than in our scheme. Also for comparison, the scheme of Bishop et al. [6]

(using the optimised variant in [4]) requires $n + 1$ elements of a group with a hard discrete logarithm problem. With $n = 511$ and a group of size $2^{256}$ this would require at least 16 kilobytes to store the program.

### 7.6   Polynomial Ring Variant

There is a variant of our Hamming distance obfuscator that uses a polynomial ring over a finite field to encode binary vectors. Note that this variant works analogously for the conjunction obfuscator.

Let $k$ be a field and let $R = k[z]$. The idea is to replace $\mathbb{Z}/q\mathbb{Z}$ by $R/Q$ where the ideal $Q = (q(z))$ is generated by some suitable irreducible polynomial $q \in R$ of sufficiently large degree. For the ground field we may take a finite field of suitable order.

Given $r < n/2 \in \mathbb{N}$, encoding a target vector $x \in \{0,1\}^n$ follows the same process as before. We choose a random sequence of small distinct irreducible polynomials $(p_i)_{i=1,\dots,n}$ in $R$ and an irreducible polynomial $q$ such that

$$\sum_{i \in I} \deg(p_i) < \deg(q)$$

for all $I \subset \{1, \dots, n\}$ with $|I| \leq r$. To encode $x \in \{0,1\}^n$, publish $X = \prod_{i=1}^{n} p_i^{x_i}$ mod $q$ along with the polynomials $(p_i)_{i=1,\dots,n}$ and $q$. Given another element $y \in \{0,1\}^n$ we can check if $y \in B_{H,r}(x)$ using the encoding $X$. Again, to recover the errors $\epsilon_i$ we use continued fraction decomposition and factoring, though now in $R$. We refer to the full version of this work for details.

**Comparison to $\mathbb{Z}/q\mathbb{Z}$ Case.** Using polynomials has several advantages: The ground field $k$ can be of small order since the order of $R/Q$ is given by $|R/Q| = |k|^{\deg(q)}$ and thus controllable by the size of $q \in R$. We may furthermore choose a compact representation of the irreducibles $(p_i)_{i=1,\dots,n}$ and $q$ to shrink encoding size and speed up computation. Working out an exact comparisons of parameters, encoding sizes, and computational aspects we leave as a future open question.

## 8   Security

Here we analyse the security of our Hamming distance obfuscator. We will show distributional VBB security and that the obfuscator is input-hiding. Our results will depend on the hardness of the *distributional modular subset product problem* that was introduced in Sect. 5.

### 8.1   Security of the Obfuscator

To show that the Hamming distance obfuscator is a distributional VBB obfuscator, we need to show that it satisfies all the properties of Definition 4.1. Note that Definition 4.1 for VBB obfuscation is given in asymptotic terms with respect to a security parameter $\lambda$. On the other hand, Problems 5.1 and 5.2 are given in terms of explicit parameters $r, n \in \mathbb{N}$. Thus in the following, let the parameters $r, n \in \mathbb{N}$ be implicitly dependent on the security parameter $\lambda$, i.e. $r = r(\lambda), n = n(\lambda)$. Taking $(n(\lambda), r(\lambda)) = (16\lambda, \lambda)$ gives Theorem 1.1 of the introduction.

**Theorem 8.1.** *Let $(n(\lambda), r(\lambda))$ be a sequence of parameters for $\lambda \in \mathbb{N}$. Let $D = \{D_\lambda\}_{\lambda \in \mathbb{N}}$ be an ensemble of Hamming distance evasive distributions (as in Definition 2.5). Suppose that D-$MSP_{r,n,D}$ (Problem 5.2) is hard and that $\mathcal{O}_{PT}$ is a dependent auxiliary input distributional VBB point function obfuscator. Then the Hamming distance obfuscator $\mathcal{O}_H$ is a distributional VBB obfuscator.*

*Proof.* The obfuscator is functionality preserving by Lemma 7.1. It is also clear that the obfuscator causes only a polynomial slowdown when compared to an unobfuscated Hamming distance calculation since the evaluation algorithm runs in time polynomial in all the involved parameters.

By Theorem 4.1 it is sufficient to show that there exists a (non-uniform) PPT simulator $\mathcal{S}$ such that, for every distribution ensemble $D = \{D_\lambda\}_{\lambda \in \mathbb{N}} \in \mathcal{D}$, it holds that (where $\alpha$ denotes any auxiliary information, if required)

$$(\mathcal{O}_H(P), \alpha) \stackrel{c}{\approx} (\mathcal{S}(|P|), \alpha).$$

Let $\mathcal{D}$ now be a class of distribution ensembles such that each $D \in \mathcal{D}$ is a Hamming distance evasive distribution as in Definition 2.5. We will construct the simulator $\mathcal{S}$. First the simulator $\mathcal{S}$ takes as input $|P|$ and determines the parameters $r, n \in \mathbb{N}$. Then it runs Algorithm 8.1 which will generate the first half of the eventual output.

---

**Algorithm 8.1.** Encoding Simulator

---

  **procedure** SIMULATEENCODE($r < n/2 \in \mathbb{N}$)
    sample random sequence of distinct primes $(p_i)_{i=1,\ldots,n}$ from $[2, O(n \log(n))]$
    sample small safe prime $q$ such that $\forall I \subset \{1, \ldots, n\}$ with $|I| \leq r$: $\prod_{i \in I} p_i < q/2$
    sample $X' \leftarrow \mathbb{Z}/q\mathbb{Z}$ uniformly
    **return** $((p_i)_{i=1,\ldots,n}, q, X')$
  **end procedure**

---

Lastly, the simulator $\mathcal{S}$ samples a uniformly random $Q'$ from the codomain of $\mathcal{O}_{PT}$ (using the simulator $\mathcal{S}_{PT}$ that exists due to the assumption of $\mathcal{O}_{PT}$ being a distributional VBB obfuscator). The simulator $\mathcal{S}_{PT}$ receives the auxiliary information $((p_i)_{i=1,\ldots,n}, q, X')$ as additional input, provided by the top-level simulator $\mathcal{S}$.

Denote the simulator output by the tuple $((p_i)_{i=1,\ldots,n}, q, X', Q')$. It is clear that $\mathcal{S}$ is polynomial-time since Algorithm 8.1 is too. Finally, assuming that Problem 5.2 is hard, a real obfuscation $((p_i)_{i=1,\ldots,n}, q, X, Q)$ obtained from the Hamming distance obfuscator $\mathcal{O}_H$ described in Sect. 7.1 and the simulator output are computationally indistinguishable:

$$((p_i)_{i=1,\ldots,n}, q, X, Q) \stackrel{c}{\approx} ((p_i)_{i=1,\ldots,n}, q, X', Q'). \tag{8.1}$$

This completes the proof. □

*Remark 2.* As noted in Sect. 7.3, the obfuscator $\mathcal{O}_H$ can be modified to omit the point obfuscation step. Hence Theorem 8.1 can be restated without requiring a distributional VBB obfuscator $\mathcal{O}_{PT}$ by assuming an ensemble of Hamming distance evasive distributions $\{D_\lambda\}_{\lambda \in \mathbb{N}}$ that satisfy Eq. (7.3).

Next, we will show that the Hamming distance obfuscator is input hiding according to Definition 4.4.

**Theorem 8.2.** *Let* $(n(\lambda), r(\lambda))$ *be parameters satisfying* $r > r_f(n)$ *(recall Eq. (7.3)). Let* $D = \{D_\lambda\}_{\lambda \in \mathbb{N}}$ *be an ensemble of Hamming distance evasive distributions (as in Definition 2.5). Suppose that* $MSP_{r,n,D}$ *(Problem 5.1) is hard. Then the Hamming distance obfuscator* $\mathcal{O}_H$ *is input hiding.*

*Proof.* The ensemble $\{D_\lambda\}_{\lambda \in \mathbb{N}}$ of Hamming distance evasive distributions induces an ensemble of programs $\{\mathcal{P}_n\}_{n \in \mathbb{N}}$ (see Sect. 7.1). Suppose there exists a PPT adversary $\mathcal{A}$ such that the success probability is bounded by

$$\Pr_{P \leftarrow \mathcal{P}_n} [P(\mathcal{A}(\alpha, \mathcal{O}_H(P))) = 1] \leq g(n)$$

for some function $g(n)$ (recall Definition 4.4 of an input hiding obfuscator).

We will now construct an algorithm $\mathcal{A}'$ that solves Problem 5.1 given $\mathcal{A}$ with success probability bounded by $g(n)$. Let $((p_i)_{i=1,\dots,n}, q, X)$ be an instance of Problem 5.1. Since $r > r_f(n)$, this instance uniquely defines $x \in \{0,1\}^n$ such that $X = \prod_{i=1}^{n} p_i^{x_i} \mod q$, and hence defines a program $P$. Then $((p_i)_{i=1,\dots,n}, q, X)$ is a correct obfuscation of $P$. The algorithm $\mathcal{A}'$ runs the adversary on $\mathcal{A}$ on $((p_i)_{i=1,\dots,n}, q, X)$ and $\mathcal{A}$ outputs a vector $y \in \{0,1\}^n$ that is accepted by $P$ with probability $g(n)$. Note that in Definition 4.4 the adversary outputs a valid input for $P$, not $\mathcal{O}_H(P)$. Hence, $y$ is close to $x$ as $r > r_f(n)$. Finally, $\mathcal{A}'$ decodes $X$ given $y$ using Algorithm 7.4 and thus outputs $x$ with probability $g(n)$.

But we assumed that Problem 5.1 is hard and hence $g(n)$ is negligible.     □

# 9    Obfuscating Conjunctions

In this section we describe a new obfuscator for conjunctions, based on the Hamming distance obfuscator of Sect. 7. Recall the notation $\chi(x)$ from Definition 3.1.

We first give a generic reduction of pattern matching with wildcards to hamming distance. Let $x \in \{0,1,\star\}^n$ be a pattern and let $r$ be the number of wildcards. Let $x' \in \{0,1\}^n$ be any string such that $x'_i = x_i$ for all non-wildcard positions $1 \leq i \leq n$. Then it is clear that any $y \in \{0,1\}^n$ that satisfies the pattern has Hamming distance at most $r$ from $x'$. The problem is that there are many other vectors $y$ that have Hamming distance at most $r$ from $x'$ but which do not satisfy the pattern. Further, pattern matching with wildcards can be evasive with $r$ as large as $n - \lambda$ where $\lambda$ is a security parameter (e.g., $n = 1000$ and $r = 900$), while Hamming distance is not evasive if $r > n/2$. So it is clear that this is not a general reduction of obfuscating conjunctions to fuzzy matching.

However, in certain parameter ranges (where $r < n/2$) one can consider using fuzzy matching to give an approach to obfuscating conjunctions. As we will explain in this section, our scheme has some advantages over the generic reduction because inputs $y$ that match the pattern are more easily identified than vectors $y$ that are close to $x'$ in the Hamming metric but do not match the pattern. Indeed, we will explain that, for certain parameter ranges, our approach is much more compact than other solutions to the conjunction problem.

**The Conjunction Obfuscator.** Let $n \in \mathbb{N}$ and $x \in \{0, 1, \star\}^n$. Choose a random sequence of small distinct primes $(p_i)_{i=1,\ldots,n}$ (i.e. $p_i \neq p_j$ for $i \neq j$). It suffices to randomly sample each $p_i$ from the interval $[(n \log(n))^2, ((n+1) \log(n+1))^2]$. Denote by $W_x = \{i \mid x_i = \star\}$ the set of indices such that $x_i$ is a wildcard. Assume we can choose a safe prime $q$ such that

$$\prod_{i \in W_x} p_i < \frac{q}{2} < \prod_{i \in W_x \cup \{j\}} p_i \qquad (9.1)$$

for all $j \in \{1, \ldots, n\} \setminus W_x$. Set $r = |W_x|$; we furthermore require that $r < n/2$ as we will see shortly.

To encode $x$, consider the map $\sigma : \{0, 1, \star\} \to \{-1, 0, 1\}$ that acts in the following fashion

$$0 \mapsto -1, \quad 1 \mapsto 1, \quad \star \mapsto 0.$$

Publish then

$$X = \prod_{i=1}^{n} p_i^{\sigma(x_i)} \mod q$$

along with the list of primes $(p_i)_{i=1,\ldots,n}$ and the modulus $q$. Note that, for this encoding to hide $x$, we require $\prod_{i=1}^{n} p_i^{\sigma(x_i)} > q$.

Given a vector $y \in \{0, 1\}^n$ such that $\chi(y) = 1$, we compute $Y = \prod_{i=1}^{n} p_i^{\sigma(y_i)}$ mod $q$ from which we can immediately find

$$E = XY^{-1} \mod q = \prod_{i=1}^{n} p_i^{\sigma(x_i) - \sigma(y_i)} \mod q = \prod_{i=1}^{n} p_i^{\epsilon_i} \mod q \qquad (9.2)$$

where $\epsilon_i \in \{-1, 0, 1\}$. We then recover the errors $\epsilon_i$ using continued fraction decomposition and factoring. The errors $\epsilon_i$ directly correspond to the wildcard positions $W_x$.

If $\chi(y) \neq 1$ then $y_i \neq x_i$ in some non-wildcard positions, i.e. Eq. (9.2) includes values $\epsilon_i \in \{-2, 2\}$ and so decoding fails with high probability. The fact that incorrect inputs give factors $p_i^{\pm 2}$ in the product (while wildcard positions introduce simply $p_i$) is a nice feature that makes our scheme more secure than the generic transformation of conjunctions to Hamming matching. It means we are not reducing conjunctions to Hamming distance, but to a weighted $\ell_1$-distance on $\mathbb{Z}$, where the non-wildcard positions are weighted double. Hence, even if an attacker guesses some wildcard positions (and so does not include the corresponding $p_i$ in their product $Y$), the value $XY^{-1}$ mod $q$ has $p_i^{\pm 2}$ terms for each incorrect non-wildcard position and so the attacker still needs to correctly guess the correct bits in most non-wildcard positions.

**Obfuscator and Obfuscated Program.** The conjunction obfuscator works as follows: For every conjunction $x \in \{0,1,\star\}^n$ with $|W_x| < n/2$ there exists a polynomial size program $P : \{0,1\}^n \to \{0,1\}$ that computes whether the input vector $y \in \{0,1\}^n$ matches $x$ and evaluates to 1 in this case, otherwise to 0. Denote the family of all such programs with $\mathcal{P}$.

The conjunction obfuscator $\mathcal{O}_C : \mathcal{P} \to \mathcal{P}'$ takes one such program $P \in \mathcal{P}$ and outputs another polynomial size program in a different family $\mathcal{P}'$. In our case this is the decoding algorithm along with the polynomial size elements $(p_i)_{i=1,\ldots,n}$, $q$ and $X \in \mathbb{Z}/q\mathbb{Z}$. The obfuscator also outputs $Q = \mathcal{O}_{PT}(R_{x'})$ where $x'$ denotes the vector $x$ with the wildcards replaced with 0.

We again identify the obfuscated program with the tuple $((p_i)_{i=1,\ldots,n}, q, X, Q)$. The obfuscated program outputs 1 if evaluation succeeds for an input $y \in \{0,1\}^n$ and if the program $Q$, when executed on the decoded conjunction with its wildcards replaced with 0, outputs 1, else the output is 0. See the full version of this work for details.

**Parameters.** The same considerations regarding the use of a safe prime and decoding efficiency as in Sect. 7 apply here. Let us now argue that a safe prime $q$ which is bounded as in Eq. (9.1) exists. We use the following heuristic: The density of Sophie Germain primes is given by $\pi_{SG}(n) \sim 2Cn/\log^2(n)$ for a constant $2C \approx 1.32032$ [40]. An asymptotic inverse is given by $n\log^2(n)$ and so we can expect the $m$-th Sophie Germain prime to be of size approximately $m\log^2(m)$. Hence, assuming that the $p_i$ are sampled from $[(n\log(n))^2, ((n+1)\log(n+1))^2]$, we require that there exists an index $m \in \mathbb{N}$ such that

$$((n+1)\log(n+1))^{2r} < m\log^2(m) < (n\log(n))^{2(r+1)} \tag{9.3}$$

which, heuristically, we may convince ourselves to hold by considering the exponential nature of the bounding expressions in $r$. We refer to the full version of this work for details.

## 9.1    Relation to Hamming Distance

Our conjunction obfuscator construction is related to our Hamming distance obfuscator (cf. Sect. 7) and thus exhibits several limitations.

Firstly, the construction limits the number of wildcards $|W_x| < n/2$.

Secondly, due to the construction, the problem of finding a match to $x \in \{0,1,\star\}^n$ reduces to the problem of finding a vector $y \in \{-1,0,1\}^n \subset \mathbb{Z}^n$ such that $\|\sigma(x) - y\|_1 < |W_x|$. Note that we took the representatives of $\mathbb{Z}/3\mathbb{Z}$ to be $\{-1,0,1\}$ such that the wildcard primes never appear as factors of $X$. We may compute the number of possible vectors in an $\ell_1$-ball of radius $r$ $(0 \le r \le n(q-1)$ for $\mathbb{Z}/q\mathbb{Z})$ using $|B_{1,q,r}| = \sum_{k=0}^{r} \left\langle {n \atop k} \right\rangle_q$ where $\left\langle {n \atop k} \right\rangle_q = \sum_{i=0}^{n}(-1)^i \binom{n}{i}\binom{k+n-1-iq}{n-1}$ is the $q$-*nomial triangle*. The upper limit of the sum may actually be taken as $\lfloor (k+n-1)/q \rfloor$ instead of $n$. The symbol $\left\langle {n \atop k} \right\rangle_q$ counts the number of compositions of $k$ into $n$ parts $p_i$ such that $0 \le p_i \le q-1$ for each $p_i$ [22].

Finally, an input conjunction $x \in \{0, 1, \star\}^n$ needs to be evasive. Assuming a uniform conjunction, this will be the case if $|B_{1,3,r}|/3^n < 1/2^\lambda$ is negligible.

## 9.2 Parameter Choices

In Sect. 9.1 we have learned that the possible parameter choices of the conjunction obfuscator are more limited. Assuming a uniform and evasive conjunction distribution, we find from Lemma 3.1 and Sect. 9.1 that the bit-security is given by $\lambda_{r,n} = \min\{n - r, -\log_2(|B_{1,3,r}|/3^n)\}$. On the other hand, the conjunction obfuscators given in [4,6] allow for a wider range of $r < n - O(\log(n))$ at the cost of assuming a generic group model.

Brakerski et al. [10] give no estimate of encoding size or security parameters for their graded coding scheme based obfuscator. Chen et al. [13] found experimentally that "The TBO of 32-bit conjunctions is close to being practical, with a total evaluation runtime of 11.6 ms, obfuscation runtime of 5.1 min, and program size of 11.6 GB for a setting with more than 80 bits of security." This program size and obfuscation time is orders of magnitude worse than the encoding size of our scheme or the schemes of [4,6].

## 9.3 Security

Showing security of the conjunction obfuscator works in essentially the same way as for the Hamming distance obfuscator in Sect. 8.1. Note that Problem 5.1 respectively Problem 5.2 also makes sense when the distribution $D$ is considered to be over $\{-1,0,1\}^n$ instead of $\{0,1\}^n$. Note that Remark 2 applies to Theorem 9.1 as well.

**Theorem 9.1.** *Let* $D = \{D_\lambda\}_{\lambda \in \mathbb{N}}$ *be an ensemble of conjunction evasive distributions (as in Definition 3.2). Suppose that D-MSP$_{r,n,D}$ (Problem 5.2) with the distribution $D$ over $\{-1,0,1\}^n$ is hard and that $\mathcal{O}_{PT}$ is a dependent auxiliary input distributional VBB point function obfuscator. Then the Conjunction obfuscator $\mathcal{O}_C$ is a distributional VBB obfuscator.*

**Theorem 9.2.** *Let* $D = \{D_\lambda\}_{\lambda \in \mathbb{N}}$ *be an ensemble of conjunction evasive distributions (as in Definition 3.2). Suppose that MSP$_{r,n,D}$ (Problem 5.1) with the distribution $D$ over $\{-1,0,1\}^n$ is hard for $r > r_f(n)$ (recall Eq. (7.3)). Then the Conjunction obfuscator $\mathcal{O}_C$ is input hiding.*

## 10  Conclusion

We have introduced a new special purpose obfuscator for fuzzy matching under Hamming distance as well as a new special purpose obfuscator for conjunctions. We have shown that our obfuscators are virtual-black-box secure and input hiding, based on the search and decision versions of the distributional modular subset product problem. We believe our obfuscators are post-quantum secure. The Hamming distance obfuscator can cover a wider range of parameters than previous solutions based on secure sketches.

Open problems include finding optimal parameters. More speculative open problems include obfuscating fuzzy matching with respect to edit distance or other metrics.

**Acknowledgements.** We thank Trey Li for several corrections and comments. We thank the Marsden Fund of the Royal Society of New Zealand for funding this research, and the reviewers for suggestions.

## References

1. Alon, N., Spencer, J.H.: The Probabilistic Method. Wiley, New York (1992)
2. Barak, B., Bitansky, N., Canetti, R., Kalai, Y.T., Paneth, O., Sahai, A.: Obfuscation for evasive functions. In: Lindell, Y. (ed.) TCC 2014. LNCS, vol. 8349, pp. 26–51. Springer, Heidelberg (2014). https://doi.org/10.1007/978-3-642-54242-8_2
3. Barak, B., et al.: On the (im)possibility of obfuscating programs. In: Kilian, J. (ed.) CRYPTO 2001. LNCS, vol. 2139, pp. 1–18. Springer, Heidelberg (2001). https://doi.org/10.1007/3-540-44647-8_1
4. Bartusek, J., Lepoint, T., Ma, F., Zhandry, M.: New techniques for obfuscating conjunctions. In: Ishai, Y., Rijmen, V. (eds.) EUROCRYPT 2019. LNCS, vol. 11478, pp. 636–666. Springer, Cham (2019). https://doi.org/10.1007/978-3-030-17659-4_22
5. Bellare, M., Stepanovs, I.: Point-function obfuscation: a framework and generic constructions. In: Kushilevitz, E., Malkin, T. (eds.) TCC 2016. LNCS, vol. 9563, pp. 565–594. Springer, Heidelberg (2016). https://doi.org/10.1007/978-3-662-49099-0_21
6. Bishop, A., Kowalczyk, L., Malkin, T., Pastro, V., Raykova, M., Shi, K.: A simple obfuscation scheme for pattern-matching with wildcards. In: Shacham, H., Boldyreva, A. (eds.) CRYPTO 2018. LNCS, vol. 10993, pp. 731–752. Springer, Cham (2018). https://doi.org/10.1007/978-3-319-96878-0_25
7. Bitansky, N., et al.: The impossibility of obfuscation with auxiliary input or a universal simulator. In: Garay, J.A., Gennaro, R. (eds.) CRYPTO 2014. LNCS, vol. 8617, pp. 71–89. Springer, Heidelberg (2014). https://doi.org/10.1007/978-3-662-44381-1_5
8. Bitansky, N., Paneth, O.: Point obfuscation and 3-round zero-knowledge. In: Cramer, R. (ed.) TCC 2012. LNCS, vol. 7194, pp. 190–208. Springer, Heidelberg (2012). https://doi.org/10.1007/978-3-642-28914-9_11
9. Brakerski, Z., Rothblum, G.N.: Obfuscating conjunctions. J. Cryptol. **30**(1), 289–320 (2017)

10. Brakerski, Z., Vaikuntanathan, V., Wee, H., Wichs, D.: Obfuscating conjunctions under entropic ring LWE. In: 2016 ACM Conference on Innovations in Theoretical Computer Science, pp. 147–156. ACM (2016)

11. Bringer, J., Chabanne, H., Cohen, G., Kindarji, B., Zemor, G.: Theoretical and practical boundaries of binary secure sketches. IEEE Trans. Inf. Forensics Secur. **3**(4), 673–683 (2008)

12. Canetti, R., Rothblum, G.N., Varia, M.: Obfuscation of hyperplane membership. In: Micciancio, D. (ed.) TCC 2010. LNCS, vol. 5978, pp. 72–89. Springer, Heidelberg (2010). https://doi.org/10.1007/978-3-642-11799-2_5

13. Chen, C., Genise, N., Micciancio, D., Polyakov, Y., Rohloff, K.: Implementing token-based obfuscation under (ring) LWE. Cryptology ePrint Archive, Report 2018/1222 (2018). https://eprint.iacr.org/2018/1222

14. Chernoff, H., et al.: A measure of asymptotic efficiency for tests of a hypothesis based on the sum of observations. Ann. Math. Stat. **23**(4), 493–507 (1952)

15. Contini, S., Lenstra, A.K., Steinfeld, R.: VSH, an efficient and provable collision-resistant hash function. In: Vaudenay, S. (ed.) EUROCRYPT 2006. LNCS, vol. 4004, pp. 165–182. Springer, Heidelberg (2006). https://doi.org/10.1007/11761679_11

16. Coster, M.J., Joux, A., LaMacchia, B.A., Odlyzko, A.M., Schnorr, C.P., Stern, J.: Improved low-density subset sum algorithms. Comput. Complex. **2**(2), 111–128 (1992)

17. Dixon, J.D.: The number of steps in the Euclidean algorithm. J. Number Theory **2**(4), 414–422 (1970)

18. Dodis, Y., Ostrovsky, R., Reyzin, L., Smith, A.: Fuzzy extractors: how to generate strong keys from biometrics and other noisy data. SIAM J. Comput. **38**(1), 97–139 (2008)

19. Dodis, Y., Reyzin, L., Smith, A.: Fuzzy extractors: how to generate strong keys from biometrics and other noisy data. In: Cachin, C., Camenisch, J.L. (eds.) EUROCRYPT 2004. LNCS, vol. 3027, pp. 523–540. Springer, Heidelberg (2004). https://doi.org/10.1007/978-3-540-24676-3_31

20. Dodis, Y., Smith, A.: Correcting errors without leaking partial information. In: STOC 2005, pp. 654–663. ACM (2005)

21. Ducas, L., Pierrot, C.: Polynomial time bounded distance decoding near minkowski's bound in discrete logarithm lattices. Des. Codes Crypt. **87**(8), 1737–1748 (2019)

22. Fielder, D.C., Alford, C.O.: Pascal's triangle: top gun or just one of the gang? In: Bergum, G.E., Philippou, A.N., Horadam, A.F. (eds.) Applications of Fibonacci Numbers, pp. 77–90. Springer, Dordrecht (1991). https://doi.org/10.1007/978-94-011-3586-3_10

23. Fuller, B., Reyzin, L., Smith, A.: When are fuzzy extractors possible? In: Cheon, J.H., Takagi, T. (eds.) ASIACRYPT 2016. LNCS, vol. 10031, pp. 277–306. Springer, Heidelberg (2016). https://doi.org/10.1007/978-3-662-53887-6_10

24. Garg, S., Gentry, C., Halevi, S., Raykova, M., Sahai, A., Waters, B.: Candidate indistinguishability obfuscation and functional encryption for all circuits. SIAM J. Comput. **45**(3), 882–929 (2016)

25. Goldwasser, S., Kalai, Y., Popa, R.A., Vaikuntanathan, V., Zeldovich, N.: Reusable garbled circuits and succinct functional encryption. In: STOC 2013, pp. 555–564. ACM (2013)

26. Goyal, R., Koppula, V., Waters, B.: Lockable obfuscation. In: FOCS 2017, pp. 612–621. IEEE (2017)

27. Hardy, G.H., Wright, E.M.: An Introduction to the Theory of Numbers, 4th edn. Oxford University Press, Oxford (1975)
28. Hensley, D.: The number of steps in the Euclidean algorithm. J. Number Theory **49**(2), 142–182 (1994)
29. Hoffstein, J., Pipher, J., Silverman, J.H.: An Introduction to Mathematical Cryptography. UTM. Springer, New York (2014). https://doi.org/10.1007/978-1-4939-1711-2
30. Hurwitz, A.: Über die angenäherte darstellung der irrationalzahlen durch rationale brüche. Math. Ann. **39**(2), 279–284 (1891)
31. Impagliazzo, R., Naor, M.: Efficient cryptographic schemes provably as secure as subset sum. J. Cryptol. **9**(4), 199–216 (1996)
32. Jain, A.K., Nandakumar, K., Nagar, A.: Biometric template security. EURASIP J. Adv. Signal Process. **2008**, 113 (2008)
33. Karabina, K., Canpolat, O.: A new cryptographic primitive for noise tolerant template security. Pattern Recogn. Lett. **80**, 70–75 (2016)
34. Lagarias, J.C., Odlyzko, A.M.: Solving low-density subset sum problems. J. ACM **32**(1), 229–246 (1985)
35. Lenstra, A.K., Lenstra, H.W., Lovász, L.: Factoring polynomials with rational coefficients. Math. Ann. **261**(4), 515–534 (1982)
36. Li, Q., Sutcu, Y., Memon, N.: Secure sketch for biometric templates. In: Lai, X., Chen, K. (eds.) ASIACRYPT 2006. LNCS, vol. 4284, pp. 99–113. Springer, Heidelberg (2006). https://doi.org/10.1007/11935230_7
37. Lynn, B., Prabhakaran, M., Sahai, A.: Positive results and techniques for obfuscation. In: Cachin, C., Camenisch, J.L. (eds.) EUROCRYPT 2004. LNCS, vol. 3027, pp. 20–39. Springer, Heidelberg (2004). https://doi.org/10.1007/978-3-540-24676-3_2
38. Micciancio, D., Mol, P.: Pseudorandom knapsacks and the sample complexity of LWE search-to-decision reductions. In: Rogaway, P. (ed.) CRYPTO 2011. LNCS, vol. 6841, pp. 465–484. Springer, Heidelberg (2011). https://doi.org/10.1007/978-3-642-22792-9_26
39. Brier, E., Coron, J.-S., Géraud, R., Maimuţ, D., Naccache, D.: A number-theoretic error-correcting code. In: Bica, I., Naccache, D., Simion, E. (eds.) SECITC 2015. LNCS, vol. 9522, pp. 25–35. Springer, Cham (2015). https://doi.org/10.1007/978-3-319-27179-8_2
40. Shoup, V.: A Computational Introduction to Number Theory and Algebra. Cambridge University Press, New York (2009)
41. Sutcu, Y., Li, Q., Memon, N.: Protecting biometric templates with sketch: theory and practice. IEEE Trans. Inf. Forensics Secur. **2**(3), 503–512 (2007)
42. Tuyls, P., Akkermans, A.H.M., Kevenaar, T.A.M., Schrijen, G.-J., Bazen, A.M., Veldhuis, R.N.J.: Practical biometric authentication with template protection. In: Kanade, T., Jain, A., Ratha, N.K. (eds.) AVBPA 2005. LNCS, vol. 3546, pp. 436–446. Springer, Heidelberg (2005). https://doi.org/10.1007/11527923_45
43. Wee, H.: On obfuscating point functions. In: Proceedings of the Thirty-Seventh Annual ACM Symposium on Theory of Computing, pp. 523–532. ACM, New York (2005)
44. Wichs, D., Zirdelis, G.: Obfuscating compute-and-compare programs under LWE. In: FOCS 2017, pp. 600–611. IEEE (2017)

# A Black-Box Construction of Fully-Simulatable, Round-Optimal Oblivious Transfer from Strongly Uniform Key Agreement

Daniele Friolo[1(✉)], Daniel Masny[2], and Daniele Venturi[1]

[1] Department of Computer Science, Sapienza University of Rome, Rome, Italy
friolo@di.uniroma1.it
[2] VISA Research, Palo Alto, CA, USA

**Abstract.** We show how to construct maliciously secure oblivious transfer (M-OT) from a strengthening of key agreement (KA) which we call *strongly uniform* KA (SU-KA), where the latter roughly means that the messages sent by one party are computationally close to uniform, even if the other party is malicious. Our transformation is black-box, almost round preserving (adding only a constant overhead of up to two rounds), and achieves standard simulation-based security in the plain model.

As we show, 2-round SU-KA can be realized from cryptographic assumptions such as low-noise LPN, high-noise LWE, Subset Sum, DDH, CDH and RSA—all with polynomial hardness—thus yielding a black-box construction of fully-simulatable, round-optimal, M-OT from the same set of assumptions (some of which were not known before).

**Keywords:** Oblivious transfer · Malicious security · LPN

## 1 Introduction

Oblivious transfer (OT) is a very simple functionality between two parties: a sender with input two strings $(s_0, s_1)$, and a receiver with input a choice bit $b$; the output for the receiver equals $s_b$, while the sender learns nothing (i.e., the receiver's choice bit remains hidden) [15,51]. The standard security definition for OT compares an execution of the protocol in the real world—where either the sender or the receiver might act maliciously—with an execution in the ideal

D. Friolo and D. Venturi—Supported in part by the research projects "PRIvacy-preserving, Security, and MAchine-learning techniques for healthcare applications (PRISMA)" and "Protect yourself and your data when using social networks", both funded by Sapienza University of Rome, and in part by the MIUR under grant "Dipartimenti di eccellenza 2018–2022" of the Computer Science Department of Sapienza University of Rome.

D. Masny—Part of the work was done at UC Berkeley, funded by the Center for Long-Term Cybersecurity (CLTC, UC Berkeley).

© International Association for Cryptologic Research 2019
D. Hofheinz and A. Rosen (Eds.): TCC 2019, LNCS 11891, pp. 111–130, 2019.
https://doi.org/10.1007/978-3-030-36030-6_5

world where a trusted third party simply implements the above functionality. Following previous work, we call *"fully simulatable"* an OT protocol that meets this notion.

Surprisingly, OT turned out to be sufficient for constructing secure multi-party computation (MPC) for *arbitrary* functionalities [6,20,32,33,38,53,54]. For this reason, constructing OT has been an important objective and received much attention. Nevertheless, previous constructions of fully-simulatable OT suffer from diverse shortcomings (cf. also Sect. 1.4): (i) They require *trusted setup*, or are based on *random oracles* (as, e.g., in [34,50]); (ii) They have *high round complexity* (as, e.g., in [27]), while the optimal number of rounds would be 4 [19,32]; (iii) They are *non-black-box*, in that they are obtained by generically transforming semi-honestly secure OT (SH-OT)—which in turn can be constructed from special types of PKE [21]—to fully-simulatable OT via (possibly interactive) zero-knowledge proofs (*á la* GMW [22]); (iv) They are tailored to *specific hardness assumptions* (as, e.g., in [7,41]).

One exception is the work of Ostrovsky, Richelson and Scafuro [49], that provide a black-box construction of 4-round, fully-simulatable OT in the plain model from *certified trapdoor permutations* (TDPs) [5,10,45], which in turn can be instantiated from the RSA assumption under some parameter regimes [10,35]. This draws our focus to the question:

*Can we obtain 4-round, fully-simulatable OT in a black-box way from minimal assumptions, without assuming trusted setup or relying on random oracles?*

## 1.1 Our Contribution

We give a positive answer to the above question by leveraging a certain type of key agreement (KA) protocols, which intuitively allow two parties to establish a secure channel in the presence of an eavesdropper. The influential work by Impagliazzo and Rudich [31] showed a (black-box) separation between secret-key cryptography and public-key cryptography and KA. Ever since, it is common sense that public-key encryption (PKE) requires stronger assumptions than the existence of one-way functions, and thus secure KA is the weakest assumption from which public-key cryptography can be obtained. More recent research efforts have only provided further confidence in this conviction [18].

In more details, our main contribution is a construction of fully-simulatable OT (a.k.a. *maliciously secure* OT, or M-OT) from a strengthening of KA protocols, which we term *strongly uniform* (SU); our protocol is fully *black-box* and essentially *round-preserving*, adding only a constant overhead of at most two rounds. In particular, we show:

**Theorem 1.** *For any odd $t \in \mathbb{N}$, with $t > 1$, there is a black-box construction of a $(t + 1)$-round, fully-simulatable oblivious transfer protocol in the plain model,* *from any t-round strongly uniform key agreement protocol and a perfectly binding commitment scheme.*[1]

Since, as we show, 2-round and 3-round SU-KA can be instantiated from several assumptions, including low-noise (ring) LPN, high-noise (ring) LWE, Subset Sum, CDH, DDH, and RSA—all with polynomial hardness—a consequence of our result is that we obtain round-optimal M-OT in the plain model under the same set of assumptions (in a black-box way). In particular, this yields the *first* such protocols from LPN, LWE (with modulus noise ratio $\sqrt{n}$), CDH, and Subset Sum.[2] Note that our LWE parameter setting relates to an approximation factor of $n^{1.5}$ for SIVP in lattices of dimension $n$ [52], which is the weakest LWE assumption known to imply PKE.

In our construction, we use a special kind of *"commit-and-open"* protocols which were implicitly used in previous works [39,49]. As a conceptual contribution, we formalize their security properties, which allows for a more modular presentation and security analysis.

## 1.2 Technical Overview

We proceed to a high level overview of the techniques behind our main result, starting with the notion of strong uniformity and the abstraction of commit-and-open protocols, and landing with the intuition behind our construction of M-OT (cf. Fig. 1).

*Strong Uniformity.* As an important stepping stone to our main result, in Sect. 3, we introduce the notion of strong uniformity. Recall that a KA protocol allows Alice and Bob to share a key over a public channel, in such a way that the shared key is indistinguishable from uniform to the eyes of a passive eavesdropper. Strong uniformity here demands that, even if Bob is malicious, the messages sent by Alice are computationally close to uniform over an efficiently sampleable group.[3] This flavor of security straightforwardly translates to SH-OT and PKE, yielding so-called SUSH-OT and SU-PKE. In the case of SUSH-OT, it demands that all messages of the receiver have this property (even if the sender is malicious).

---

[1] Statistically binding commitment schemes are implied by perfectly-correct KA protocols [44]. Both LWE and low-noise LPN implied statistically binding commitment schemes as well [25].

[2] We can also base our construction on Factoring when relying on the hardness of CDH over the group of signed quadratic residues [30], but this requires a trusted setup of this group which is based on a Blum integer.

[3] We call a group efficiently sampleable if we can efficiently sample uniform elements from the group and, given a group element, we can simulate this sampling procedure. A reverse sampleable group [23] would suffice. In the context of public-key encryption a similar property is called oblivious key generation [14]. In our construction, we require a stronger property where the public keys are additionally computationally indistinguishable from uniform.

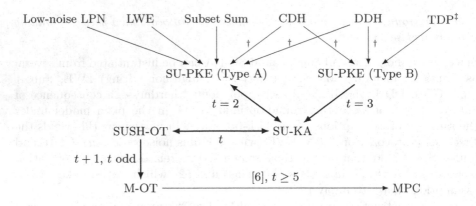

**Fig. 1.** Overview over equivalence and implications of the notion of strong uniformity. The value $t \in \mathbb{N}$ denotes the round complexity. [†] This holds over efficiently sampleable groups. [‡] We need an enhanced certified TDP.

For SU-PKE, we distinguish two types, which are a strengthening of the types defined by Gertner *et al.* [21].[4]

- **Type-A PKE:** The distribution of the public key is computationally indistinguishable from uniform. This type of PKE is known to exist under DDH [17] and CDH [24] over efficiently sampleable groups,[5] LWE [52], low-noise LPN [2], and Subset Sum [46].
- **Type-B PKE:** The encryption of a uniformly random message w.r.t. a maliciously chosen public key is computationally close to the uniform distribution over the ciphertext space. This type of PKE is harder to obtain, and can be constructed from enhanced certified TDPs, and from CDH and DDH over efficiently sampleable groups. In case of a TDP $f$, a ciphertext has the form $(f(r), h(r) \oplus m)$, where $h$ is a hardcore predicate for $f$, and $r$ is a random element from the domain of $f$. Under CDH or DDH, a ciphertext is defined as $g^r$ and $h(g^{xr}) \cdot m$, $g^{xr} \cdot m$ respectively, where $g^r$ is a uniform group element, and $g^x$ is the public key. Clearly, for a uniform message $m$, these ciphertexts are uniform even under maliciously chosen public keys.

In Sect. 3, we show that SU Type-A and SU Type-B PKE imply, respectively, 2-round and 3-round SU-KA, whereas 2-round SU-KA implies SU Type-A PKE.

---

[4] The difference is that the notions in [21] only ask for oblivious sampleability, rather than our stronger requirement of computational uniformity over efficiently sampleable groups.

[5] These are groups for which one can directly sample a group element without knowing the discrete logarithm with respect to some generator. The latter requires non black-box access to the group, which is also needed when using ElGamal with messages that are encoded as group elements and not as exponents. Though we need the stronger property of sampleability of elements that are computationally close to uniform.

Further, we prove that SU-KA is equivalent to SUSH-OT. The latter implies that strong uniformity is a sufficiently strong notion to bypass the black-box separation between OT and KA, in a similar way as Type-A and Type-B PKE bypass the impossibility of constructing OT from PKE [21].

*Commit-and-Open Protocols.* A 1-out-of-2 commit-and-open (C&O) protocol is a 3-round protocol with the following structure: (1) In the first round, the prover, with inputs two messages $m_0, m_1$ and a bit $d$, sends a string $\gamma$ (called "commitment") generated with $m_d$ but independent of $m_{1-d}$ to the verifier; (2) In the second round, the verifier sends a value $\beta$ to the prover (called "challenge"); (3) In the third round, the prover sends a tuple $(\delta, m_0, m_1)$ to the verifier (called "opening"). Security requires two properties. The first property, called *existence of a committing branch*, demands that a malicious prover must be committed to at least one message, i.e. $m_d$, already after having sent $\gamma$. The second property, called *committing branch indistinguishability*, asks that a malicious verifier cannot learn the committing branch, i.e. $d$, of an honest prover.

A construction of C&O protocols for single bits is implicit in Kilian [39]. This has been extended to strings by Ostrovsky *et al.* [49]. Both constructions make black-box use of a statistically binding commitment scheme, and allow a prover to equivocally open one of the messages.

*M-OT from SUSH-OT: A Warm Up.* In order to explain the main ideas behind our construction of M-OT, we describe below a simplified version of our protocol for the special case of $t = 2$, i.e. when starting with a 2-round SUSH-OT $(S', R')$; here, we denote with $\rho$ the message sent by the receiver, and with $\sigma$ the message sent by the sender, and further observe that for the case of 2 rounds the notion of strong uniformity collapses to standard semi-honest security with the additional property that the distribution of $\rho$ is (computationally close to) uniform to the eyes of an eavesdropper. We then construct a 4-round OT protocol $(S, R)$, as informally described below:

1. $(R \rightarrow S)$: The receiver picks a uniformly random value $m_{1-b} \in \mathcal{M}$, where $b$ is the choice bit, and runs the prover of the C&O protocol upon input $m_{1-b}$, obtaining a commitment $\gamma$ that is forwarded to the sender.
2. $(S \rightarrow R)$: The sender samples a challenge $\beta$ for the C&O protocol, as well as uniformly random elements $r_0, r_1 \in \mathcal{M}$. Hence, it forwards $(\beta, r_0, r_1)$ to the receiver.
3. $(R \rightarrow S)$: The receiver runs the receiver $R'$ of the underlying 2-round OT protocol with choice bit fixed to 0, obtaining a value $\rho_b$ which is used to define the message $m_b = \rho_b - r_b$ required to complete the execution of the C&O protocol in the non-committing branch $b$. This results in a tuple $(\delta, m_0, m_1)$ that is forwarded to the sender.
4. $(S \rightarrow R)$: The sender verifies that the transcript $T = (\gamma, \beta, (\delta, m_0, m_1))$ is accepting for the underlying C&O protocol. If so, it samples $u_0, u_1 \in \mathcal{M}$ uniformly at random, and runs the sender $S'$ of the underlying 2-round OT protocol twice, with independent random tapes: The first run uses input strings

$(s_0, u_0)$ and message $m_0 + r_0$ from the receiver, resulting in a message $\sigma_0$, whereas the second run uses input strings $(s_1, u_1)$ and message $m_1 + r_1$ from the receiver, resulting in a message $\sigma_1$. Hence, it sends $(\sigma_0, \sigma_1)$ to the receiver.

5. Output: The receiver runs the receiver $\mathsf{R}'$ of the underlying 2-round OT protocol, upon input message $\sigma_b$ from the sender, thus obtaining $s_b$.

Correctness is immediate. In order to prove simulation-based security we proceed in two steps. In the first step, we show the above protocol achieves a weaker security flavor called *receiver-sided simulatability* [48,49] which consists of two properties: (1) The existence of a simulator which by interacting with the ideal OT functionality can fake the view of any efficient adversary corrupting the receiver in a real execution of the protocol (i.e., standard simulation-based security w.r.t. corrupted receivers); (2) Indistinguishability of the protocol transcripts with choice bit of the receiver equal to zero or one, for any efficient adversary corrupting the sender in a real execution of the protocol (i.e., game-based security w.r.t. corrupted senders). In the second step, we rely on a *round-preserving* black-box transformation given in [49], which allows to boost receiver-sided simulatability to fully-fledged malicious security. To show (1), we consider a series of hybrid experiments:

- In the first hybrid, we run the first 3 rounds of the protocol, yielding a partial transcript $\gamma, (\beta, r_0, r_1), (\delta, m_0, m_1)$. Hence, after verifying that $T = (\gamma, \beta, (\delta, m_0, m_1))$ is a valid transcript of the C&O protocol, we rewind the adversary to the end of the first round and continue the execution of the protocol from there using a fresh challenge $(\beta', r_0', r_1')$, except that after the third round we artificially abort if there is no value $\hat{b} \in \{0, 1\}$ such that $m_{\hat{b}} = m_{\hat{b}}'$, where $(\delta', m_0', m_1')$ is the third message sent by the adversary after the rewinding.

  Notice that an abort means that it is not possible to identify a committing branch for the C&O protocol, which however can only happen with negligible probability; thus this hybrid is computationally close to the original experiment.

- In the second hybrid, we modify the distribution of the value $r_{1-b}'$ (right after the rewinding) to $r_{1-b}'' = \rho_{1-b} - m_{1-b}$, where we set $1 - b \stackrel{\text{def}}{=} \hat{b}$ from the previous hybrid, and where $\rho_{1-b}$ is obtained by running the receiver $\mathsf{R}'$ of the underlying 2-round OT protocol with choice bit fixed to 1.

  To argue indistinguishability, we exploit the fact that the distribution of $m_{1-b}$ is independent from that of $r_{1-b}'$, and thus by strong uniformity we can switch $r_{1-b}' + m_{1-b}$ with $\rho_{1-b}$ from the receiver $\mathsf{R}'$.

- In the third hybrid, we use the simulator of the underlying 2-round SH-OT protocol to compute the messages $\sigma_{1-b}$ sent by the sender. Note that in both the third and the second hybrid the messages $(\rho_{1-b}, \sigma_{1-b})$ are computed by the honest sender, and thus any efficient algorithm telling apart the third and the second hybrid violates semi-honest security of $(\mathsf{S}', \mathsf{R}')$.

In the last hybrid, a protocol transcript is independent of $s_{1-b}$ but still yields a well distributed output for the malicious receiver, which immediately implies a simulator in the ideal world.

To show (2), we first use the strong uniformity property of $(S', R')$ to sample $m_b$ uniformly at random at the beginning of the protocol. Notice the this implies that the receiver cannot recover the value $s_b$ of the sender anymore. Finally, we use the committing branch indistinguishability of the C&O protocol to argue that the transcripts with $b = 0$ and $b = 1$ are computationally indistinguishable.

*M-OT from SUSH-OT: The General Case.* There are several difficulties when trying to extend the above protocol to the general case where we start with a $t$-round SUSH-OT. In fact, if we would simply iterate sequentially the above construction, where one iteration counts for a message from R' to S' and back, the adversary could use different committing branches from one iteration to the other. This creates a problem in the proof, as the simulator would need to be consistent with both choices of possible committing branches from the adversary, which however requires knowing both inputs from the sender.

We resolve this issue by having the receiver sending all commitments $\gamma_i$ for the C&O protocol in the first round, where each value $\gamma_i$ is generated including a random message $m_{1-b}^i$ concatenated with the full history $m_{1-b}^{i-1}, \ldots, m_{1-b}^1$. Hence, during each iteration, the receiver opens one commitment as before. As we show, this prevents the adversary from switching committing branch from one iteration to the next one. We refer the reader to Sect. 4 for a formal description of our protocol, and for a somewhat detailed proof intuition.

## 1.3   Application to Round-Efficient MPC

Since M-OT implies maliciously secure MPC [6,20] and very recently, the work of Choudhuri et al. [11], a direct consequence of Theorem 1 is the following:

**Corollary 1.** *For any odd $t \in \mathbb{N}$, there is a non-black-box construction of a $(t + 1)$-round maliciously secure multi-party computation protocol in the plain model, from any $t$-round strongly uniform key agreement protocol.*

Corollary 1 yields 4-round maliciously secure MPC from any of low-noise LPN, high-noise LWE, Subset Sum, CDH, DDH, and RSA, all with polynomial hardness. Previously to our work, it was known how to get maliciously secure MPC in the plain model, for arbitrary functionalities:

- Using 5 rounds, via interactive ZK proofs and SH-OT [6], assuming polynomially-hard LWE with super-polynomial noise ratio and adaptive commitments [8], polynomially-hard DDH [3], and enhanced certified trapdoor permutations (TDP) [6,49];
- Using 4 rounds, assuming sub-exponentially-hard LWE with super-polynomial noise ratio and adaptive commitments [8], polynomially-hard LWE with a SIVP approximation factor of $n^{3.5}$ [7], sub-exponentially-hard DDH and one-way permutations [3], polynomially-hard DDH/QR/DCR [4],

and either polynomially-hard QR or QR together with any of LWE/D-DH/DCR (all with polynomial hardness) [29].

## 1.4   Related Work

*Maliciously Secure OT.* Jarecki and Shamtikov [34], and Peikert, Vaikuntanathan, and Waters [50], show how to construct 2-round M-OT in the common reference string model.

A result by Haitner *et al.* [27,28] gives a black-box construction of M-OT from SH-OT. While being based on weaker assumptions (i.e., plain SH-OT instead of SUSH-OT), assuming the starting OT protocol has round complexity $t$, the final protocol requires 4 additional rounds for obtaining an intermediate security flavor known as "defensible privacy", plus 4 rounds for cut and choose, plus 2 times the number of rounds required for running coin tossing, plus a final round to conclude the protocol. Assuming coin tossing can be done in 5 rounds [37], the total accounts to $t + 19$ rounds, and thus yields 21 rounds by setting $t = 2$.

Lindell [41] gives constructions of M-OT with 7 rounds, under the DDH assumption, the $N$th residuosity assumption, and the assumption that homomorphic PKE exists. Camenish, Neven, and shelat [9], and Green and Hohenberger [26], construct M-OT protocols, some of which even achieve adaptive security, using computational assumptions over bilinear groups.

There are also several efficient protocols for OT that guarantee only privacy (but not simulatability) in the presence of malicious adversaries, see, e.g. [1,7, 36,40,47].

*Round-Optimal MPC.* Katz and Ostrovsky [37] proved that 5 rounds are necessary and sufficient for realizing general-purpose two-party protocols, without assuming a simultaneous broadcast channel (where the parties are allowed to send each other messages in the same round). Their result was later extended by Garg *et al.* [19] who showed that, assuming simultaneous broadcast, 4 rounds are optimal for general-purpose MPC. Together with a result by Ishai *et al.* [32]—yielding *non-interactive* maliciously secure two-party computation for arbitrary functionalities, in the OT-hybrid model—the latter implies that 4 rounds are optimal for constructing fully-simulatable M-OT in the plain model.

Ciampi *et al.* [13] construct a special type of 4-round M-OT assuming certified TDPs,[6] and show how to apply it in order to obtain (fully black-box) 4-round two-party computation with simultaneous broadcast. In a companion paper [12], the same authors further give a 4-round MPC protocol for the specific case of multi-party coin-tossing.

---

[6] They also claim [13, Footnote 3] that their OT protocol can be instantiated using PKE with special properties, however no proof of this fact is provided.

# 2 Preliminaries

## 2.1 Standard Notation

We use $\lambda \in \mathbb{N}$ to denote the security parameter, sans-serif letters (such as A, B) to denote algorithms, caligraphic letters (such as $\mathcal{X}$, $\mathcal{Y}$) to denote sets, and bold-face letters (such as $\mathbf{v}$, $\mathbf{A}$) to denote vectors and matrices; all vectors are by default row vectors, and $\mathbf{v}^\top$ denotes a column vector. An algorithm is *probabilistic polynomial-time* (PPT) if it is randomized, and its running time can be bounded by a polynomial in its input length. By $y \leftarrow_\$ \mathsf{A}(x)$, we mean that the value $y$ is assigned to the output of algorithm A upon input $x$ and fresh random coins. We implicitly assume that all algorithms are given the security parameter $1^\lambda$ as input.

A function $\nu : \mathbb{N} \to [0,1]$ is negligible in the security parameter (or simply negligible) if it vanishes faster than the inverse of any polynomial in $\lambda$, i.e. $\nu(\lambda) \in O(1/p(\lambda))$ for all positive polynomials $p(\lambda)$. We often write $\nu(\lambda) \in \mathsf{negl}(\lambda)$ to denote that $\nu(\lambda)$ is negligible.

For a random variable $X$, we write $\mathbb{P}[X = x]$ for the probability that $X$ takes on a particular value $x \in \mathcal{X}$ (with $\mathcal{X}$ being the set where $X$ is defined). The statistical distance between two random variables $X$ and $X'$ defined over the same set $\mathcal{X}$ is defined as $\Delta(X; X') = \frac{1}{2} \sum_{x \in \mathcal{X}} |\Pr[X = x] - \Pr[X' = x]|$. Given two ensembles $X = \{X_\lambda\}_{\lambda \in \mathbb{N}}$ and $Y = \{Y_\lambda\}_{\lambda \in \mathbb{N}}$, we write $X \equiv Y$ to denote that they are identically distributed, $X \approx_s Y$ to denote that they are statistically close (i.e., $\Delta(X_\lambda; Y_\lambda) \in \mathsf{negl}(\lambda)$), and $X \approx_c Y$ to denote that they are computationally indistinguishable—i.e., for all PPT distinguishers D there exists a negligible function $\nu : \mathbb{N} \to [0,1]$ such that $|\Pr[\mathsf{D}(X_\lambda) = 1] - \Pr[\mathsf{D}(Y_\lambda) = 1]| \leq \nu(\lambda)$.

We call a group efficiently sampleable if and only if there is a PPT sampling procedure Samp for the uniform distribution over the group, and moreover there exists a PPT simulator SimSamp that given an element of the group, outputs the randomness used by Samp. More precisely, $(r, \mathsf{Samp}(1^\lambda, r)) \approx_c (r', \mathsf{Samp}(1^\lambda, r'))$ where $r' \leftarrow_\$ \mathsf{SimSamp}(1^\lambda, \mathsf{Samp}(1^\lambda; r))$ and $r \leftarrow_\$ \{0,1\}^*$.[7] A group that is efficiently reverse sampleable (as in [23]) suffices.

## 2.2 Oblivious Transfer

An interactive protocol $\Pi$ for the Oblivious Transfer (OT) functionality, features two interactive PPT Turing machines S, R called, respectively, the sender and the receiver. The sender S holds a pair of strings $s_0, s_1 \in \{0,1\}^\lambda$, whereas the receiver R is given a choice bit $b \in \{0,1\}$. At the end of the protocol, which might take several rounds, the receiver learns $s_b$ (and nothing more), whereas the sender learns nothing.

Typically, security of OT is defined using the real/ideal paradigm. Specifically, we compare a real execution of the protocol, where an adversary might

---

[7] The existence of a simulator is crucial for constructing SUSH-OT from SU-KA; we solely use it for this purpose.

corrupt either the sender or the receiver, with an ideal execution where the parties can interact with an ideal functionality. The ideal functionality, which we denote by $\mathcal{F}_{OT}$, features a trusted party that receives the inputs from both the sender and the receiver, and then sends to the receiver the sender's input corresponding to the receiver's choice bit. We refer the reader to Fig. 2 for a formal specification of the $\mathcal{F}_{OT}$ functionality.

In what follows, we denote by $REAL_{\Pi, \mathsf{R}^*(z)}(\lambda, s_0, s_1, b)$ (resp., $REAL_{\Pi, \mathsf{S}^*(z)}(\lambda, s_0, s_1, b)$)) the distribution of the output of the malicious receiver (resp., sender) during a real execution of the protocol $\Pi$ (with $s_0, s_1$ as inputs of the sender, $b$ as choice bit of the receiver, and $z$ as auxiliary input for the adversary), and by $IDEAL_{\mathcal{F}_{OT}, \mathsf{Sim}^{\mathsf{R}^*(z)}}(\lambda, s_0, s_1, b)$ (resp., $IDEAL_{\mathcal{F}_{OT}, \mathsf{Sim}^{\mathsf{S}^*(z)}}(\lambda, s_0, s_1, b)$) the output of the malicious receiver (resp., sender) in an ideal execution where the parties (with analogous inputs) interact with $\mathcal{F}_{OT}$, and where the simulator is given black-box access to the adversary.

### Ideal Functionality $\mathcal{F}_{OT}$:

The functionality runs with Turing machines $(\mathsf{S}, \mathsf{R})$ and adversary $\mathsf{Sim}$, and works as follows:

- Upon receiving message $(\mathsf{send}, s_0, s_1, \mathsf{S}, \mathsf{R})$ from $\mathsf{S}$, where $s_0, s_1 \in \{0,1\}^\lambda$, store $s_0$ and $s_1$ and answer $\mathsf{send}$ to $\mathsf{R}$ and $\mathsf{Sim}$.
- Upon receiving a message $(\mathsf{receive}, b)$ from $\mathsf{R}$, where $b \in \{0,1\}$, send $s_b$ to $\mathsf{R}$ and $\mathsf{receive}$ to $\mathsf{S}$ and $\mathsf{Sim}$, and halt. If no message $(\mathsf{send}, \cdot)$ was previously sent, do nothing.

**Fig. 2.** Oblivious transfer ideal functionality

**Definition 1 (OT with full simulation).** *Let $\mathcal{F}_{OT}$ be the functionality from Fig. 2. We say that a protocol $\Pi = (\mathsf{S}, \mathsf{R})$ securely computes $\mathcal{F}_{OT}$ with full simulation if the following holds:*

*(a) For every non-uniform PPT malicious receiver $\mathsf{R}^*$, there exists a non-uniform PPT simulator $\mathsf{Sim}$ such that*

$$\left\{ REAL_{\Pi, \mathsf{R}^*(z)}(\lambda, s_0, s_1, b) \right\}_{\lambda, s_0, s_1, b, z} \approx_c \left\{ IDEAL_{\mathcal{F}_{OT}, \mathsf{Sim}^{\mathsf{R}^*(z)}}(\lambda, s_0, s_1, b) \right\}_{\lambda, s_0, s_1, b, z}$$

*where $\lambda \in \mathbb{N}$, $s_0, s_1 \in \{0,1\}^\lambda$, $b \in \{0,1\}$, and $z \in \{0,1\}^*$.*

*(b) For every non-uniform PPT malicious sender $\mathsf{S}^*$, there exists a non-uniform PPT simulator $\mathsf{Sim}$ such that*

$$\left\{ REAL_{\Pi, \mathsf{S}^*(z)}(\lambda, s_0, s_1, b) \right\}_{\lambda, s_0, s_1, b, z} \approx_c \left\{ IDEAL_{\mathcal{F}_{OT}, \mathsf{Sim}^{\mathsf{S}^*(z)}}(\lambda, s_0, s_1, b) \right\}_{\lambda, s_0, s_1, b, z}$$

*where $\lambda \in \mathbb{N}$, $s_0, s_1 \in \{0,1\}^\lambda$, $b \in \{0,1\}$, and $z \in \{0,1\}^*$.*

*Game-Based Security.* One can also consider weaker security definitions for OT, where simulation-based security only holds when either the receiver or the sender is corrupted, whereas when the other party is malicious only game-based security is guaranteed. Below, we give the definition for the case of a corrupted sender, which yields a security notion known as *receiver-sided* simulatability. Intuitively, the latter means that the adversary cannot distinguish whether the honest receiver is playing with choice bit 0 or 1.

**Definition 2 (OT with receiver-sided simulation).** *Let $\mathcal{F}_{OT}$ be the functionality from Fig. 2. We say that a protocol $\Pi = (S, R)$ securely computes $\mathcal{F}_{OT}$ with receiver-sided simulation if the following holds:*

*(a) Same as property (a) in Definition 1.*
*(b) For every non-uniform PPT malicious sender $S^*$ it holds that*

$$\left\{ VIEW^{R}_{\Pi, S^*(z)}(\lambda, s_0, s_1, 0) \right\}_{\lambda, s_0, s_1, z} \approx_c \left\{ VIEW^{R}_{\Pi, S^*(z)}(\lambda, s_0, s_1, 1) \right\}_{\lambda, s_0, s_1, z}$$

*where $\lambda \in \mathbb{N}$, $s_0, s_1 \in \{0,1\}^\lambda$, and $z \in \{0,1\}^*$, and where $VIEW^{R}_{\Pi, S^*(z)}$ $(\lambda, s_0, s_1, b)$ is the distribution of the view of $S^*$ (with input $s_0, s_1$ and auxiliary input $z$) at the end of a real execution of protocol $\Pi$ with the honest receiver $R$ given $b$ as input.*

Receiver-sided simulatability is a useful stepping stone towards achieving full simulatability. In fact, Ostrovsky *et al.* [49] show how to compile any 4-round OT protocol with receiver-sided simulatability to a 4-round OT protocol with full simulatability. This transformation can be easily extended to hold for any $t$-round protocol, with $t \geq 3$; the main reason is that the transform only relies on an extractable commitment scheme, which requires at least 3 rounds.

**Theorem 2. (Adapted from [49]).** *Assuming $t \geq 3$, there is a black-box transformation from $t$-round OT with receiver-sided simulation to $t$-round OT with full simulation.*[8]

## 2.3 Commit-and-Open Protocols

We envision a 3-round protocol between a prover and a verifier where the prover takes as input two messages $m_0, m_1 \in \mathcal{M}$ and a bit $d \in \{0, 1\}$. The prover speaks first, and the protocol is public coin, in the sense that the message of the verifier consists of uniformly random bits. Intuitively, we want that whenever the prover manages to convince the verifier, he must be committed to at least one of $m_0, m_1$ already after having sent the first message.

More formally, a 1-out-of-2 commit-and-open (C&O) protocol is a tuple of efficient interactive Turing machines $\Pi_{c\&o} \stackrel{\text{def}}{=} (P = (P_0, P_1), V = (V_0, V_1))$ specified as follows. (i) The randomized algorithm $P_0$ takes $m_d$ and returns a string

---

[8] They also need the existence of one-way functions. Since OT implies OT extension which implies one-way functions [42,43], OT implies one-way functions.

$\gamma \in \{0,1\}^*$ and auxiliary state information $\alpha \in \{0,1\}^*$; (ii) The randomized algorithm $V_0$ returns a random string $\beta \leftarrow_\$ \mathcal{B}$; (iii) The randomized algorithm $P_1$ takes $(\alpha, \beta, \gamma, m_{1-d})$ and returns a string $\delta \in \{0,1\}^*$; (iv) The deterministic algorithm $V_1$ takes a transcript $(\gamma, \beta, (\delta, m_0, m_1))$ and outputs a bit.

We write $\langle P(m_0, m_1, d), V(1^\lambda) \rangle$ for a run of the protocol upon inputs $(m_0, m_1, d)$ to the prover, and we denote by $T \stackrel{\text{def}}{=} (\gamma, \beta, (\delta, m_0, m_1))$ the random variable corresponding to a transcript of the interaction. Note that the prover does not necessarily need to know $m_{1-d}$ before computing the first message. We say that $\Pi_{c\&o}$ satisfies completeness if honestly generated transcripts are always accepted by the verifier, i.e. for all $m_0, m_1 \in \mathcal{M}$ and $d \in \{0,1\}$, we have $\Pr[V_1(T) = 1 : T \leftarrow_\$ \langle P(m_0, m_1, d), V(1^\lambda) \rangle] = 1$, where the probability is over the randomness of $P_0, V_0$, and $P_1$.

*Security Properties.* Roughly, a C&O protocol must satisfy two security requirements. The first requirement is that at the end of the first round, a malicious prover is committed to at least one message. This can be formalized by looking at a mental experiment where we first run the protocol with a malicious prover, yielding a first transcript $T = (\gamma, \beta, (\delta, m_0, m_1))$; hence, we rewind the prover to the point it already sent the first message, and give it a fresh challenge $\beta'$ which yields a second transcript $T' = (\gamma, \beta', (\delta', m'_0, m'_1))$. The security property now states that, as long as the two transcripts $T$ and $T'$ are valid, it shall exist at least one "committing branch" $\hat{d} \in \{0,1\}$ for which $m_{\hat{d}} = m'_{\hat{d}}$. The second requirement says that no malicious verifier can learn any information on the committing branch of the prover. See the full version [16] for formal definitions.

# 3    Strong Uniformity at a Glance

This section contains a brief overview over the notion of strongly uniform OT and KA. We refer to the full version [16] for detailed definitions and for the implications of these notions.

In KA, Alice and Bob interact with the goal of establishing a shared key which remains hidden to an eavesdropper. We strengthen this notion by asking that Alice's messages are computationally close to uniform over an efficiently sampleable group, even when Bob is malicious. We call this security feature *strong uniformity.*

Strong uniformity straightforwardly translates to OT. We call an OT protocol strongly uniform if the receiver's messages are computationally close to uniform over an efficiently sampleable group, even when the sender is malicious. An important consequence of strong uniformity is that strongly uniform secure KA and strongly uniform semi-honestly secure OT are equivalent.

**Theorem 3.** *There is a black-box construction of strongly uniform semi-honestly secure OT from strongly uniform secure KA and vice versa, with the same round complexity.*

Intuitively, one can construct a KA protocol from OT by using the first of the sender's inputs as key, and setting the receiver's choice bit to 0, such that the receiver learns this key. Gertner *et al.* [21] already described this protocol, and it turns out that it preserves strong uniformity.

To construct strongly uniform semi-honestly secure OT from strongly uniform secure KA, one can use strong uniformity to let the receiver sample uniform messages rather than follow the KA protocol. More precisely, the sender and receiver will run two instances of the KA protocol, and the sender will use the two shared keys as one-time pad masks for his inputs. The receiver, depending on his choice bit, will run one of the two KA instances according to the protocol description, whereas, for the other one, he will sample uniform messages. Hence, the receiver will learn only one of the shared keys and inputs of the sender.

## 4   From SUSH-OT to M-OT

Let $\Pi_{c\&o} = (P_0, P_1, V_0, V_1)$ be a 1-out-of-2 C&O protocol and $\Pi' = (S', R')$ be a $(2t'+1)$-round OT protocol, where the first message $\sigma^1$ might be the empty string. Our OT protocol $\Pi = (S, R)$ is depicted in Fig. 3 on page 19. The protocol consists of $(2t'+2)$ rounds as informally described below.

1. The receiver samples $m_{1-b,i} \in \mathcal{M}$ for all $i \in [t']$, where $b$ is the choice bit. Then he runs the prover of the C&O protocol upon input $(m_{1-b,j})_{j\in[i]}$ for all $i \in [t']$, obtaining $(\gamma_i)_{i\in[t']}$ which are forwarded to the sender.
2. The sender samples uniform values $u_0, u_1 \leftarrow_\$ \mathcal{M}$. Then, he runs the underlying $(2t'+1)$-round OT twice with inputs $(s_0, u_0)$ and $(s_1, u_1)$ to generate the first messages $\sigma_0^1$ and $\sigma_1^1$. Further, the sender samples a challenge $\beta_1$ for the C&O protocol, as well as two uniformly random group elements $r_{0,1}, r_{1,1}$ from $\mathcal{M}$, and forwards $(\beta_1, r_{0,1}, r_{1,1})$ to the receiver together with the first messages of the OTs (i.e. $\sigma_0^1$ and $\sigma_1^1$).
3. Repeat the following steps for each $i \in [t']$:
   (a) (R → S): The receiver runs the receiver R' of the underlying $(2t'+1)$-round OT protocol with choice bit fixed to 0, and upon input message $\sigma_b^i$ from the sender, obtaining a message $\rho_b^i$ which is used to define the message $m_{b,i} = \rho_b^i - r_{b,i}$ required to complete the execution of the C&O protocol in the non-committing branch $b$. This results in a tuple $(\delta_i, m_{0,i}, m_{1,i})$ that is forwarded to the sender.
   (b) (S → R): The sender verifies that the transcript $T_i = (\gamma_i, \beta_i, (\delta_i, (m_{0,j})_{j\in[i]}, (m_{1,j})_{j\in[i]}))$ is accepting for the underlying C&O protocol. If so, he continues the two runs of the sender S' for the underlying $(2t'+1)$-round OT protocol. The first run uses state $\alpha_{S,0}^i$ and message $m_{0,i} + r_{0,i}$ from the receiver resulting in a message $\sigma_0^{i+1}$ and state $\alpha_{S,0}^{i+1}$, whereas the second run uses state $\alpha_{S,1}^i$ and message $m_{1,i} + r_{1,i}$ from the receiver resulting in a message $\sigma_1^{i+1}$ and state $\alpha_{S,1}^{i+1}$. Finally, the sender samples a challenge $\beta_{i+1}$ for the C&O protocol, as well as another two uniformly random group elements $r_{0,i+1}, r_{1,i+1}$ from $\mathcal{M}$, and forwards $(\sigma_0^{i+1}, \sigma_1^{i+1})$ and $\beta_{i+1}, r_{0,i+1}, r_{1,i+1}$ to the receiver.

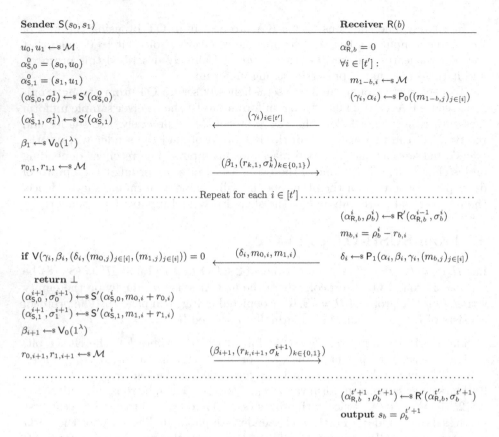

| Sender $S(s_0, s_1)$ | | Receiver $R(b)$ |
|---|---|---|

**Fig. 3.** $(2t'+2)$-round OT protocol achieving receiver-sided simulatability from $(2t'+1)$-round strongly uniform semi-honestly secure OT. Note that the initial state information $\alpha_{S,0}^0, \alpha_{S,1}^0$ and $\alpha_{R,b}^0$ is set to be equal, respectively to the inputs used by the sender and the receiver during the runs of the underlying OT protocol $(S', R')$. The values $\beta_{t'+1}, r_{0,t'+1}, r_{1,t'+1}$ are not needed and can be removed, but we avoided to do that in order to keep the protocol description more compact.

4. Output: The receiver runs the receiver $R'$ of the underlying $(2t' + 1)$-round OT protocol, upon input the $(t' + 1)$-th message $\sigma_b^{t'+1}$ from the sender, thus obtaining an output $\rho_b^{t'+1}$.

Correctness follows by the fact that, when both the sender and the receiver are honest, by correctness of the C&O protocol the transcripts $T_i$ are always accepting, and moreover the messages produced by the sender $\sigma_b^i$ are computed using message $m_{b,i} + r_{b,i} = \rho_b^i$ from the receiver, so that each pair $(\rho_b^i, \sigma_b^i)$ corresponds to the $i$-th interaction of the underlying $(2t' + 1)$-round OT protocol with input strings $(s_b, u_b)$ for the sender and choice bit 0 for the receiver, and thus at the end the receiver outputs $s_b$. As for security, we have:

**Theorem 4. (Receiver-sided simulatability of $\Pi$).** *Assuming that $\Pi'$ is a $(2t'+1)$-round strongly uniform semi-honestly secure OT protocol, and that $\Pi_{c\&o}$ is a secure 1-out-of-2 commit-and-open protocol, then the protocol $\Pi$ from Fig. 3 securely realizes $\mathcal{F}_{OT}$ with receiver-sided simulation.*

We give a detailed proof in the full version [16], and here provide some intuition. In order to show receiver-sided simulatability we need to prove two things: (1) The existence of a simulator Sim which by interacting with the ideal functionality $\mathcal{F}_{OT}$ can fake the view of any efficient adversary corrupting the receiver in a real execution of the protocol; (2) Indistinguishability of the protocol transcripts with choice bit of the receiver equal to zero or one, for any efficient adversary corrupting the sender in a real execution of the protocol.

To show (1), we consider a series of hybrid experiments that naturally lead to the definition of a simulator in the ideal world. In order to facilitate the description of the hybrids, it will be useful to think of the protocol as a sequence of $t'$ iterations, where each iteration consists of 2 rounds, as depicted in Fig. 3 on page 19.

- In the first hybrid, we run a malicious receiver twice after he has sent his commitments. The purpose of the first run is to learn a malicious receiver's input bit, i.e. on which branch he is not committed. If he is committed on both branches, simulation will be easy since he will not be able to receive any of the sender's inputs. We use the second run to learn the output of a malicious receiver. We describe the two runs now.
  1. The first round of each iteration yields an opening $(\delta_i, m_{0,i}, m_{1,i})$. Hence, after verifying that the opening is valid, we rewind the adversary to the end of the first round of the $i$-th iteration to receive another opening $(\delta'_i, m'_{0,i}, m'_{1,i})$.
     Now, let $b \in \{0,1\}$ such that $m_{b,i} \neq m'_{b,i}$. By the security of the C&O protocol, there can be at most one such $b$. If there is no $b$ we continue the first run. Otherwise, if there is such a $b$, we have learned the equivocal branch and start the second run.
  2. We execute the second run according to the protocol with the difference that we now know the equivocal branch, i.e. $b$, from the very beginning, which will help us later to simulate correctly right from the start. Notice that by the security of the C&O protocol, a malicious receiver cannot change the equivocal branch in the second run. Obviously, he cannot change it during the same iteration since then he would be equivocal on both branches and contradict the security of the C&O protocol. He can also not change the equivocal branch of one of the later rounds $j > i$, since in the $j$-th commitment $\delta_j$ he cannot be committed to both $m_{b,i}$ and $m'_{b,i}$, so he needs to equivocally open $\delta_j$ as well. Thus, he needs to be committed on the other branch, i.e. branch $1 - b$.
- The values $m'_{k,i}$ (right after the rewinding) of each iteration of the first run for $k \in \{0,1\}$, and second run for $k = 1 - b$, are identical to $m_{k,i}$. Moreover, $m'_{k,i} \neq m_{k,i}$ holds only for the second run for branch $k = b$. Therefore, in the second hybrid, we can change the distribution of $r'_{k,i}$ to $r'_{k,i} = \rho^i_k - m_{k,i}$ for

$k \in \{0, 1\}$, and both runs except branch $k = b$ during the second run. The value $\rho_k^i$ is obtained by running the simulator for the receiver of the underlying strongly uniform semi-honest OT protocol with choice bit 1 and input $u_k$. We can use the messages generated by this simulator on the sender's side as well.

We will use the strong uniformity of the OT to argue that a malicious receiver cannot distinguish $r'_{k,i} = \rho_k^i - m_{k,i}$ from uniform. By the semi-honest security, the messages generated by the simulator are indistinguishable from the actual semi-honest OT. At the same time this simulator is independent of the sender's inputs $s_0$ and $s_1$. Note that in this hybrid, we only need to known $s_b$ for the second run after having learned $b$.

In the last hybrid, a protocol transcript is independent of $s_{1-b}$ but still yields a well distributed output for the malicious receiver, which directly yields a simulator in the ideal world.

To show (2), we first use the strong uniformity of the underlying OT protocol to sample $m_{b,i}$ uniformly at random at the beginning of the protocol. Notice that this implies that the receiver cannot recover the value $s_b$ of the sender anymore. Further, we need the strong uniformity property here, since the receiver is interacting with a malicious sender who could influence the distribution of $m_{b,i}$ sent by the receiver. Once both messages, $m_{0,i}$ and $m_{1,i}$ for all iterations are known before the start of the protocol, we can challenge the choice bit indistinguishability of the C&O protocol. As a consequence, we can argue that the transcripts with $b = 0$ and $b = 1$ are computationally indistinguishable, which implies game-based security against a malicious sender.

## 5   Conclusions

We have shown a construction of maliciously secure oblivious transfer (M-OT) protocol from a certain class of key agreement (KA) and semi-honestly secure OT (SH-OT) protocols that enjoy a property called *strong uniformity* (SU), which informally means that the distribution of the messages sent by one of the parties is computationally close to uniform, even in case the other party is malicious.

When starting with 2-round or 3-round SUSH-OT or SU-KA, we obtain 4-round M-OT, and thus, invoking [11], 4-round maliciously secure MPC from standard assumptions including low-noise LPN, LWE, Subset Sum, CDH, DDH, and RSA (all with polynomial hardness).

Also, it is a natural question to see whether SU-KA with $t \geq 4$ rounds can be instantiated from concrete assumptions that do not imply PKE.

**Acknowledgments.** We would like to thank Silas Richelson for a discussion on their commit-and-open protocol. We also thank the anonymous reviewers who helped removing wrong claims and clarifying the presentation of our results.

# References

1. Aiello, B., Ishai, Y., Reingold, O.: Priced oblivious transfer: how to sell digital goods. In: Pfitzmann, B. (ed.) EUROCRYPT 2001. LNCS, vol. 2045, pp. 119–135. Springer, Heidelberg (2001). https://doi.org/10.1007/3-540-44987-6_8
2. Alekhnovich, M.: More on average case vs approximation complexity. In: IEEE FOCS, pp. 298–307 (2003)
3. Ananth, P., Choudhuri, A.R., Jain, A.: A new approach to round-optimal secure multiparty computation. In: Katz, J., Shacham, H. (eds.) CRYPTO 2017. LNCS, vol. 10401, pp. 468–499. Springer, Cham (2017). https://doi.org/10.1007/978-3-319-63688-7_16
4. Badrinarayanan, S., Goyal, V., Jain, A., Kalai, Y.T., Khurana, D., Sahai, A.: Promise zero knowledge and its applications to round optimal MPC. In: Shacham, H., Boldyreva, A. (eds.) CRYPTO 2018. LNCS, vol. 10992, pp. 459–487. Springer, Cham (2018). https://doi.org/10.1007/978-3-319-96881-0_16
5. Bellare, M., Yung, M.: Certifying cryptographic tools: the case of trapdoor permutations. In: Brickell, E.F. (ed.) CRYPTO 1992. LNCS, vol. 740, pp. 442–460. Springer, Heidelberg (1993). https://doi.org/10.1007/3-540-48071-4_31
6. Benhamouda, F., Lin, H.: $k$-round multiparty computation from $k$-round oblivious transfer via garbled interactive circuits. In: Nielsen, J.B., Rijmen, V. (eds.) EUROCRYPT 2018. LNCS, vol. 10821, pp. 500–532. Springer, Cham (2018). https://doi.org/10.1007/978-3-319-78375-8_17
7. Brakerski, Z., Döttling, N.: Two-message statistically sender-private OT from LWE. In: Beimel, A., Dziembowski, S. (eds.) TCC 2018. LNCS, vol. 11240, pp. 370–390. Springer, Cham (2018). https://doi.org/10.1007/978-3-030-03810-6_14
8. Brakerski, Z., Halevi, S., Polychroniadou, A.: Four round secure computation without setup. In: Kalai, Y., Reyzin, L. (eds.) TCC 2017. LNCS, vol. 10677, pp. 645–677. Springer, Cham (2017). https://doi.org/10.1007/978-3-319-70500-2_22
9. Camenisch, J., Neven, G., Shelat, A.: Simulatable adaptive oblivious transfer. In: Naor, M. (ed.) EUROCRYPT 2007. LNCS, vol. 4515, pp. 573–590. Springer, Heidelberg (2007). https://doi.org/10.1007/978-3-540-72540-4_33
10. Canetti, R., Lichtenberg, A.: Certifying trapdoor permutations, revisited. In: Beimel, A., Dziembowski, S. (eds.) TCC 2018. LNCS, vol. 11239, pp. 476–506. Springer, Cham (2018). https://doi.org/10.1007/978-3-030-03807-6_18
11. Choudhuri, A.R., Ciampi, M., Goyal, V., Jain, A., Ostrovsky, R.: Round optimal secure multiparty computation from minimal assumptions. Cryptology ePrint Archive, Report 2019/216 (2019). https://eprint.iacr.org/2019/216
12. Ciampi, M., Ostrovsky, R., Siniscalchi, L., Visconti, I.: Delayed-input non-malleable zero knowledge and multi-party coin tossing in four rounds. In: Kalai, Y., Reyzin, L. (eds.) TCC 2017. LNCS, vol. 10677, pp. 711–742. Springer, Cham (2017). https://doi.org/10.1007/978-3-319-70500-2_24
13. Ciampi, M., Ostrovsky, R., Siniscalchi, L., Visconti, I.: Round-optimal secure two-party computation from trapdoor permutations. In: Kalai, Y., Reyzin, L. (eds.) TCC 2017. LNCS, vol. 10677, pp. 678–710. Springer, Cham (2017). https://doi.org/10.1007/978-3-319-70500-2_23
14. Damgård, I., Nielsen, J.B.: Improved non-committing encryption schemes based on a general complexity assumption. In: Bellare, M. (ed.) CRYPTO 2000. LNCS, vol. 1880, pp. 432–450. Springer, Heidelberg (2000). https://doi.org/10.1007/3-540-44598-6_27

15. Even, S., Goldreich, O., Lempel, A.: A randomized protocol for signing contracts. In: Chaum, D., Rivest, R.L., Sherman, A.T. (eds.) Advances in Cryptology, pp. 205–210. Springer, Boston, MA (1983). https://doi.org/10.1007/978-1-4757-0602-4_19

16. Friolo, D., Masny, D., Venturi, D.: A black-box construction of fully-simulatable, round-optimal oblivious transfer from strongly uniform key agreement. Cryptology ePrint Archive, Report 2018/473 (2018). https://eprint.iacr.org/2018/473

17. ElGamal, T.: A public key cryptosystem and a signature scheme based on discrete logarithms. In: Blakley, G.R., Chaum, D. (eds.) CRYPTO 1984. LNCS, vol. 196, pp. 10–18. Springer, Heidelberg (1985). https://doi.org/10.1007/3-540-39568-7_2

18. Garg, S., Mahmoody, M., Masny, D., Meckler, I.: On the round complexity of OT extension. In: Shacham, H., Boldyreva, A. (eds.) CRYPTO 2018. LNCS, vol. 10993, pp. 545–574. Springer, Cham (2018). https://doi.org/10.1007/978-3-319-96878-0_19

19. Garg, S., Mukherjee, P., Pandey, O., Polychroniadou, A.: The exact round complexity of secure computation. In: Fischlin, M., Coron, J.-S. (eds.) EUROCRYPT 2016. LNCS, vol. 9666, pp. 448–476. Springer, Heidelberg (2016). https://doi.org/10.1007/978-3-662-49896-5_16

20. Garg, S., Srinivasan, A.: Two-round multiparty secure computation from minimal assumptions. In: Nielsen, J.B., Rijmen, V. (eds.) EUROCRYPT 2018. LNCS, vol. 10821, pp. 468–499. Springer, Cham (2018). https://doi.org/10.1007/978-3-319-78375-8_16

21. Gertner, Y., Kannan, S., Malkin, T., Reingold, O., Viswanathan, M.: The relationship between public key encryption and oblivious transfer. In: IEEE FOCS, pp. 325–335 (2000)

22. Goldreich, O., Micali, S., Wigderson, A.: Proofs that yield nothing but their validity for all languages in NP have zero-knowledge proof systems. J. ACM **38**(3), 691–729 (1991)

23. Goldreich, O., Rothblum, R.D.: Enhancements of trapdoor permutations. J. Cryptology **26**(3), 484–512 (2013)

24. Goldwasser, S., Micali, S.: Probabilistic encryption. J. Comput. Syst. Sci. **28**(2), 270–299 (1984)

25. Goyal, R., Hohenberger, S., Koppula, V., Waters, B.: A generic approach to constructing and proving verifiable random functions. In: Kalai, Y., Reyzin, L. (eds.) TCC 2017. LNCS, vol. 10678, pp. 537–566. Springer, Cham (2017). https://doi.org/10.1007/978-3-319-70503-3_18

26. Green, M., Hohenberger, S.: Blind identity-based encryption and simulatable oblivious transfer. In: Kurosawa, K. (ed.) ASIACRYPT 2007. LNCS, vol. 4833, pp. 265–282. Springer, Heidelberg (2007). https://doi.org/10.1007/978-3-540-76900-2_16

27. Haitner, I.: Semi-honest to malicious oblivious transfer—the black-box way. In: Canetti, R. (ed.) TCC 2008. LNCS, vol. 4948, pp. 412–426. Springer, Heidelberg (2008). https://doi.org/10.1007/978-3-540-78524-8_23

28. Haitner, I., Ishai, Y., Kushilevitz, E., Lindell, Y., Petrank, E.: Black-box constructions of protocols for secure computation. SIAM J. Comput. **40**(2), 225–266 (2011)

29. Halevi, S., Hazay, C., Polychroniadou, A., Venkitasubramaniam, M.: Round-optimal secure multi-party computation. In: Shacham, H., Boldyreva, A. (eds.) CRYPTO 2018. LNCS, vol. 10992, pp. 488–520. Springer, Cham (2018). https://doi.org/10.1007/978-3-319-96881-0_17

30. Hofheinz, D., Kiltz, E.: The group of signed quadratic residues and applications. In: Halevi, S. (ed.) CRYPTO 2009. LNCS, vol. 5677, pp. 637–653. Springer, Heidelberg (2009). https://doi.org/10.1007/978-3-642-03356-8_37

31. Impagliazzo, R., Rudich, S.: Limits on the provable consequences of one-way permutations. In: Goldwasser, S. (ed.) CRYPTO 1988. LNCS, vol. 403, pp. 8–26. Springer, New York (1990). https://doi.org/10.1007/0-387-34799-2_2

32. Ishai, Y., Kushilevitz, E., Ostrovsky, R., Prabhakaran, M., Sahai, A.: Efficient non-interactive secure computation. In: Paterson, K.G. (ed.) EUROCRYPT 2011. LNCS, vol. 6632, pp. 406–425. Springer, Heidelberg (2011). https://doi.org/10. 1007/978-3-642-20465-4_23

33. Ishai, Y., Prabhakaran, M., Sahai, A.: Founding cryptography on oblivious transfer – efficiently. In: Wagner, D. (ed.) CRYPTO 2008. LNCS, vol. 5157, pp. 572–591. Springer, Heidelberg (2008). https://doi.org/10.1007/978-3-540-85174-5_32

34. Jarecki, S., Shmatikov, V.: Efficient two-party secure computation on committed inputs. In: Naor, M. (ed.) EUROCRYPT 2007. LNCS, vol. 4515, pp. 97–114. Springer, Heidelberg (2007). https://doi.org/10.1007/978-3-540-72540-4_6

35. Kakvi, S.A., Kiltz, E., May, A.: Certifying RSA. In: Wang, X., Sako, K. (eds.) ASIACRYPT 2012. LNCS, vol. 7658, pp. 404–414. Springer, Heidelberg (2012). https://doi.org/10.1007/978-3-642-34961-4_25

36. Kalai, Y.T.: Smooth projective hashing and two-message oblivious transfer. In: Cramer, R. (ed.) EUROCRYPT 2005. LNCS, vol. 3494, pp. 78–95. Springer, Heidelberg (2005). https://doi.org/10.1007/11426639_5

37. Katz, J., Ostrovsky, R.: Round-optimal secure two-party computation. In: Franklin, M. (ed.) CRYPTO 2004. LNCS, vol. 3152, pp. 335–354. Springer, Heidelberg (2004). https://doi.org/10.1007/978-3-540-28628-8_21

38. Kilian, J.: Founding cryptography on oblivious transfer. In: ACM STOC, pp. 20–31 (1988)

39. Kilian, J.: A note on efficient zero-knowledge proofs and arguments (extended abstract). In: ACM STOC, pp. 723–732 (1992)

40. Kushilevitz, E., Ostrovsky, R.: Replication is NOT needed: SINGLE database, computationally-private information retrieval. In: IEEE FOCS, pp. 364–373 (1997)

41. Lindell, Y.: Efficient fully-simulatable oblivious transfer. Chicago J. Theor. Comput. Sci. **2008** (2008). Article no 6

42. Lindell, Y., Zarosim, H.: On the feasibility of extending oblivious transfer. In: Sahai, A. (ed.) TCC 2013. LNCS, vol. 7785, pp. 519–538. Springer, Heidelberg (2013). https://doi.org/10.1007/978-3-642-36594-2_29

43. Lindell, Y., Zarosim, H.: On the feasibility of extending oblivious transfer. J. Cryptology **31**(3), 737–773 (2018)

44. Lombardi, A., Schaeffer, L.: A note on key agreement and non-interactive commitments. Cryptology ePrint Archive, Report 2019/279 (2019). https://eprint.iacr.org/2019/279

45. Lysyanskaya, A., Micali, S., Reyzin, L., Shacham, H.: Sequential aggregate signatures from trapdoor permutations. In: Cachin, C., Camenisch, J.L. (eds.) EUROCRYPT 2004. LNCS, vol. 3027, pp. 74–90. Springer, Heidelberg (2004). https://doi.org/10.1007/978-3-540-24676-3_5

46. Lyubashevsky, V., Palacio, A., Segev, G.: Public-key cryptographic primitives provably as secure as subset sum. In: Micciancio, D. (ed.) TCC 2010. LNCS, vol. 5978, pp. 382–400. Springer, Heidelberg (2010). https://doi.org/10.1007/978-3-642-11799-2_23

47. Naor, M., Pinkas, B.: Efficient oblivious transfer protocols. In: SODA, pp. 448–457 (2001)

48. Naor, M., Pinkas, B.: Computationally secure oblivious transfer. J. Cryptology **18**(1), 1–35 (2005)
49. Ostrovsky, R., Richelson, S., Scafuro, A.: Round-optimal black-box two-party computation. In: Gennaro, R., Robshaw, M. (eds.) CRYPTO 2015. LNCS, vol. 9216, pp. 339–358. Springer, Heidelberg (2015). https://doi.org/10.1007/978-3-662-48000-7_17
50. Peikert, C., Vaikuntanathan, V., Waters, B.: A framework for efficient and composable oblivious transfer. In: Wagner, D. (ed.) CRYPTO 2008. LNCS, vol. 5157, pp. 554–571. Springer, Heidelberg (2008). https://doi.org/10.1007/978-3-540-85174-5_31
51. Rabin, M.O.: How to exchange secrets by oblivious transfer. Technical report, Harvard University (1981)
52. Regev, O.: On lattices, learning with errors, random linear codes, and cryptography. In: ACM STOC, pp. 84–93 (2005)
53. Yao, A.C.: Protocols for secure computations (extended abstract). In: IEEE FOCS, pp. 160–164 (1982)
54. Yao, A.C.: How to generate and exchange secrets (extended abstract). In: IEEE FOCS, pp. 162–167 (1986)

# Synchronous Consensus with Optimal Asynchronous Fallback Guarantees

Erica Blum[1], Jonathan Katz[2(✉)], and Julian Loss[1,3]

[1] Department of Computer Science, University of Maryland, College Park, USA
erblum@cs.umd.edu
[2] Department of Computer Science, George Mason University, Fairfax, USA
jkatz2@gmail.com
[3] Ruhr University Bochum, Bochum, Germany
julian.loss@rub.de

**Abstract.** Typically, protocols for Byzantine agreement (BA) are designed to run in either a *synchronous* network (where all messages are guaranteed to be delivered within some known time $\Delta$ from when they are sent) or an *asynchronous* network (where messages may be arbitrarily delayed). Protocols designed for synchronous networks are generally insecure if the network in which they run does not ensure synchrony; protocols designed for asynchronous networks are (of course) secure in a synchronous setting as well, but in that case tolerate a lower fraction of faults than would have been possible if synchrony had been assumed from the start.

Fix some number of parties $n$, and $0 < t_a < n/3 \leq t_s < n/2$. We ask whether it is possible (given a public-key infrastructure) to design a BA protocol that is resilient to (1) $t_s$ corruptions when run in a synchronous network and (2) $t_a$ faults even if the network happens to be asynchronous. We show matching feasibility and infeasibility results demonstrating that this is possible if and only if $t_a + 2 \cdot t_s < n$.

## 1 Introduction

*Byzantine agreement* (BA) [24,35] is a classical problem in distributed computing. Roughly speaking, a BA protocol allows a group of $n$ parties, each holding some initial input value, to agree on their outputs even in the presence of some threshold of corrupted parties. Such protocols are used widely in practice for ensuring consistency among a set of distributed processors [6,21,23,30], and have received renewed interest in the context of blockchain protocols. They also serve as a core building block for more complicated protocols, e.g., for secure multiparty computation. There is an extensive literature on Byzantine agreement, and many different models in which it can be studied. We focus here on the setting in which a *public-key infrastructure* (PKI) is available.

---

J. Katz—Portions of this work were done while at the University of Maryland.
J. Loss—Work was done while at Ruhr University Bochum.

D. Hofheinz and A. Rosen (Eds.): TCC 2019, LNCS 11891, pp. 131–150, 2019.
https://doi.org/10.1007/978-3-030-36030-6_6

Typically, protocols for Byzantine agreement are designed and analyzed assuming either a *synchronous network*, where messages are guaranteed to be delivered within some known time bound $\Delta$, or an *asynchronous network*, where messages can be delayed arbitrarily. Existing results precisely characterize when the problem can be solved in each case [5,8,10,24,35]: in a synchronous network, it is possible if and only if $t_s < n/2$ parties are corrupted, while in an asynchronous network it can be achieved only when there are $t_a < n/3$ corruptions. In each case, protocols tolerating the optimal threshold and running in expected *constant* rounds are known [5,20].

In real-world deployments of Byzantine agreement, the network conditions in which a protocol are run may be unclear; for example, the network may generally be synchronous but intermittently experience congestion that prevents messages from being delivered in a timely fashion. This results in the following dilemma when deciding what protocol to use:

- Protocols designed for a synchronous network are, in general, insecure if the assumption of network synchrony fails.
- Protocols designed for an asynchronous network will (of course) be secure when the network is synchronous. But in this case the fraction of faults that can be tolerated is *lower* than what could have been tolerated if the protocol were designed for the synchronous setting.

Fix some thresholds $t_a, t_s$ with $0 < t_a < n/3 \leq t_s < n/2$. We ask the following question: is it possible to design a BA protocol that is (1) resilient to any $t_s$ (adaptive) corruptions when run in a synchronous network and also (2) resilient to $t_a$ (adaptive) corruptions even if the network happens to be asynchronous? We completely resolve this question by showing matching feasibility and infeasibility results demonstrating that this is possible if and only if $t_a + 2 \cdot t_s < n$.

**Positive Result.** The protocol achieving our positive result is constructed by combining two sub-protocols $\Pi_{\mathsf{SBA}}, \Pi_{\mathsf{ABA}}$ for Byzantine agreement, where $\Pi_{\mathsf{SBA}}$ is secure in a synchronous network and $\Pi_{\mathsf{ABA}}$ is secure in an asynchronous network. The key to our analysis is to separately analyze the validity, consistency, and liveness guarantees of these sub-protocols. Specifically, we design $\Pi_{\mathsf{SBA}}$ so that it also satisfies a certain validity guarantee *even when run in an asynchronous network*. We also design $\Pi_{\mathsf{ABA}}$ so that it achieves validity (in an asynchronous network) *even beyond $n/3$ corruptions*. We then use these properties to prove security of our main protocol, for different thresholds, when run in either a synchronous or asynchronous network.

**Impossibility Result.** We also show that our positive result is *tight*, namely, that if $t_a + 2 \cdot t_s \geq n$ then there is no protocol that is simultaneously resilient to $t_s$ corruptions when run in a synchronous network and also resilient to $t_a$ faults in an asynchronous network. In fact, we show a result that is slightly stronger: it is not possible to achieve validity for $t_s$ static faults in the synchronous setting while also achieving a weak notion of consistency for $t_a$ static faults in an asynchronous network.

## 1.1   Related Work

The question of designing protocols that remain secure when run in various network conditions is natural, and so it is somewhat surprising that it has only recently begun to draw attention in the literature. Recent work by Malkhi et al. [28] is most closely related to our own. Among other things, they consider protocols with certain guarantees when run in synchronous or *partially synchronous* networks. In contrast, we consider the case of synchronous or *fully asynchronous* networks. Liu et al. [25] design a protocol that is resilient to a minority of malicious corruptions in a synchronous network, and a minority of *fail-stop* faults in an asynchronous network. Our work can be viewed as extending theirs to consider malicious corruptions in both settings. Guo, Pass, and Shi [16] consider a model motivated by eclipse attacks [18] on blockchain protocols, whereby an attacker temporarily disconnects some subset $S$ of honest parties from the rest of the network $S'$, e.g., by delaying or dropping messages between $S$ and $S'$. Parties in $S$ may not be able to reach agreement with honest parties in $S'$; nevertheless, as observed by Guo et al., it may be possible to provide certain guarantees for the parties in $S'$ if their network is well-behaved (i.e., synchrony continues to hold for messages sent between parties in $S'$). Guo et al. gave BA protocols tolerating the optimal corruption threshold in this model, and Abraham et al. [2] extended their work to achieve similar guarantees for state-machine replication. The main difference between these works and ours is that they continue to assume synchrony in part of the network, and their protocols fail completely if the all communication channels in the network may be asynchronous.

Kursawe [22] shows a protocol for asynchronous BA that reaches agreement more quickly in case the network is synchronous. In contrast to our work, that protocol does not achieve better fault tolerance (and, in particular, cannot tolerate $n/3$ or more faults) in the synchronous case.

Other recent work has looked at designing protocols for synchronous BA that achieve good *responsiveness* when the network latency is low. That is, these protocols ensure that if the actual message-delivery time is $\delta < \Delta$ then the time to reach agreement is proportional to $\delta$ rather than the upper bound $\Delta$. This problem was considered by Pass and Shi [31,32], who gave protocols that rely on a leader and are therefore not adaptively secure, as well as by Loss and Moran [27], who avoid the use of a leader. The work of Loss and Moran was extended by Liu-Zhang et al. [26] to the case of general secure computation. None of these works provides security in case the synchrony assumption fails altogether.

Several prior works [3,7,12,34] consider a model in which synchrony is assumed to be available for some (known) limited period of time, and asynchronous afterward. Fitzi et al. [11] and Loss and Moran [27] study trade-offs between the validity, consistency, and liveness properties of BA that inspired our asynchronous BA protocol in Sect. 4 and our lower bound in Sect. 6.

## 1.2  Paper Organization

We introduce our model as well as definitions for Byzantine agreement and related tasks in Sect. 2. In Sects. 3 and 4 we describe two protocols for Byzantine agreement and prove various properties about them. Those protocols are used, in turn, as sub-protocols of our main protocol in Sect. 5 that achieves security (for different thresholds) in both synchronous and asynchronous networks. Finally, in Sect. 6 we show that the bounds we achieve are tight.

## 2  Model and Definitions

Throughout, we consider a network of $n$ parties $P_1, \ldots, P_n$ who may communicate over point-to-point authenticated channels. We also assume that the parties have established a public-key infrastructure in advance of the protocol execution. This means that all parties hold the same vector $(pk_1, \ldots, pk_n)$ of public keys for a digital signature scheme, where each honest party $P_i$ holds the honestly generated secret key $sk_i$ associated with $pk_i$. (Malicious parties may choose their keys arbitrarily.) A *valid* signature $\sigma$ on $m$ from $P_i$ is one for which $\mathsf{Verify}_{pk_i}(m, \sigma) = 1$. We make the standard convention of treating signatures as idealized objects; i.e., throughout our analysis, signatures are assumed to be perfectly unforgeable. When the signature scheme used is existentially unforgeable under chosen-message attacks we thus obtain security against computationally bounded adversaries, with a negligible probability of failure. We implicitly assume that parties use domain separation when signing (e.g., via unique session IDs) to ensure that signatures generated for one purpose will be considered invalid if used in another context.

When we say a protocol tolerates $t$ corrupted parties we always mean that it is secure against an adversary who may *adaptively* corrupt up to $t$ parties during execution of the protocol and coordinate the actions of those parties as they deviate from the protocol in an arbitrary manner. An honest party is one who is not corrupted by the end of the protocol. We stress that our claims about adaptive security are only with respect to the "property-based" definitions we give here; we do not consider adaptive security with respect to a simulation-based definition [13,19].

We are interested in protocols running in one of two possible settings. When a protocol is run in a *synchronous* network, we assume all messages are delivered within a known time bound $\Delta$ after they are sent. We allow the adversary to arbitrarily schedule delivery of messages subject to this bound, which implies in particular that we consider a *rushing* adversary who may obtain messages sent to it before sending messages of its own. In the synchronous case, we also assume all parties begin running the protocol at the same time, and all parties have local clocks that progress at the same rate. When we refer to a protocol running in an *asynchronous* network, we allow the adversary to arbitrarily schedule delivery of messages without any upper bound on their delivery time. We do, however, require that all messages that are sent are eventually delivered. Importantly, honest parties do not know *a priori* which type of network the protocol is running in.

We may view executions in a synchronous network as proceeding in a series of *rounds*, where execution begins at time 0 and the $r$th round refers to the period of time from $(r-1) \cdot \Delta$ to $r \cdot \Delta$. When we say a party receives a message in round $r$ we mean that it receives a message in that time interval; when we say it sends a message in round $r$ we means it sends that message at the beginning of that round, i.e., at time $(r-1) \cdot \Delta$. Thus, in a synchronous network all messages sent in round $r$ are received in round $r$ (but in an asynchronous network this need not be the case).

We assume a *coin-flip mechanism* CoinFlip available as an atomic primitive. This can be viewed as an ideal functionality, parameterized by a value $t$, that upon receiving input $k$ from $t+1$ parties generates an unbiased coin $\mathsf{Coin}_k \in \{0,1\}$ and sends $(k, \mathsf{Coin}_k)$ to all parties. (When run in an asynchronous network, messages to and from CoinFlip can be arbitrarily delayed.) The key property this ensures is that, if at most $t$ parties are corrupted, at least one honest party must send $k$ to CoinFlip before the adversary can learn $\mathsf{Coin}_k$. Several protocols for realizing such a coin flip[1] in an asynchronous network, based on general assumptions, are known [1,5,29,33]. For our purposes, we need a protocol that is secure for $t < n/3$ faults, and that *terminates* for $t' < n/2$ faults. Such protocols can be constructed using a threshold unique signature scheme [4,14,17,27].

## 2.1  Definitions

We are ultimately interested in *Byzantine agreement*, but we find it useful to define the related notions of *broadcast* and *graded consensus*. Relevant definitions follow.

**Byzantine Agreement.** Byzantine agreement allows a set of parties who each hold some initial input to agree on their output. We consider several security properties that may hold for such protocols. For simplicity, we consider the case of agreement on a bit; this is without loss of generality as one can run any such protocol $\ell$ times to agree on a string of length $\ell$.

We consider Byzantine agreement protocols where, in some cases, parties may not terminate immediately upon generating output, or may never terminate. For that reason, we treat termination separately in the definition that follows. By convention, any party that terminates generates output before doing so; however, we allow parties to output the special symbol $\perp$.

**Definition 1 (Byzantine agreement).** *Let $\Pi$ be a protocol executed by parties $P_1, \ldots, P_n$, where each party $P_i$ begins holding input $v_i \in \{0,1\}$.*

---

[1] Some of these realize a $p$-weak coin flip, where honest parties agree on the coin only with probability $p < 1$. We can also rely on such protocols, at an increase in the expected round complexity by a factor of $O(1/p)$.

- **Weak validity:** $\Pi$ *is* $t$-weakly valid *if the following holds whenever at most* $t$ *of the parties are corrupted: if every honest party's input is equal to the same value* $v$, *then every honest party outputs either* $v$ *or* $\perp$.
- **Validity:** $\Pi$ *is* $t$-valid *if the following holds whenever at most* $t$ *of the parties are corrupted: if every honest party's input is equal to the same value* $v$, *then every honest party outputs* $v$.
- **Validity with termination:** $\Pi$ *is* $t$-valid with termination *if the following holds whenever at most* $t$ *of the parties are corrupted: if every honest party's input is equal to the same value* $v$, *then every honest party outputs* $v$ *and terminates.*
- **Weak consistency:** $\Pi$ *is* $t$-weakly consistent *if the following holds whenever at most* $t$ *of the parties are corrupted: there is a* $v \in \{0,1\}$ *such that every honest party outputs either* $v$ *or* $\perp$.
- **Consistency:** $\Pi$ *is* $t$-consistent *if the following holds whenever at most* $t$ *of the parties are corrupted: there is a* $v \in \{0,1,\perp\}$ *such that every honest party outputs* $v$.
  *(In the terminology of Goldwasser and Lindell [15], weak consistency might be called "consistency with abort" and consistency might be called "consistency with unanimous abort.")*
- **Liveness:** $\Pi$ *is* $t$-live *if whenever at most* $t$ *of the parties are corrupted, every honest party outputs a value in* $\{0,1\}$.
- **Termination:** $\Pi$ *is* $t$-terminating *if whenever at most* $t$ *of the parties are corrupted, every honest party terminates.* $\Pi$ *has* guaranteed termination *if it is* $n$-*terminating.*

If $\Pi$ *is* $t$-*valid,* $t$-*consistent,* $t$-*live, and* $t$-*terminating, then we say* $\Pi$ *is* $t$-secure.

While several of the above definitions are not entirely standard, our notion of security matches the standard one. In particular, $t$-liveness and $t$-consistency imply that whenever at most $t$ parties are corrupted, there is a $v \in \{0,1\}$ such that every honest party outputs $v$. Note that $t$-validity with termination is weaker than $t$-validity plus $t$-termination, as the former does not require termination in case the inputs of the honest parties do not agree.

**Broadcast.** Protocols for *broadcast* allow a set of parties to agree on a value chosen by a designated sender. We only consider broadcast protocols with guaranteed termination, and so do not mention termination explicitly when defining the various properties.

**Definition 2 (Broadcast).** *Let* $\Pi$ *be a protocol executed by parties* $P_1, \ldots,$ $P_n$, *where a sender* $P^* \in \{P_1, \ldots, P_n\}$ *begins holding input* $v^* \in \{0,1\}$ *and all parties are guaranteed to terminate.*

- **Weak validity:** $\Pi$ *is* $t$-weakly valid *if the following holds whenever at most* $t$ *of the parties are corrupted: if* $P^*$ *is honest, then every honest party outputs either* $v^*$ *or* $\perp$.
- **Validity:** $\Pi$ *is* $t$-valid *if the following holds whenever at most* $t$ *of the parties are corrupted: if* $P^*$ *is honest, then every honest party outputs* $v^*$.

- **Weak consistency:** $\Pi$ *is $t$-weakly consistent if the following holds whenever at most $t$ of the parties are corrupted: there is a $v \in \{0, 1\}$ such that every honest party outputs either $v$ or $\perp$.*
- **Consistency:** $\Pi$ *is $t$-consistent if the following holds whenever at most $t$ of the parties are corrupted: there is a $v \in \{0, 1, \perp\}$ such that every honest party outputs $v$.*
- **Liveness:** $\Pi$ *is $t$-live if whenever at most $t$ of the parties are corrupted, every honest party outputs a value in $\{0, 1\}$.*

*If $\Pi$ is $t$-valid, $t$-consistent, and $t$-live, then we say $\Pi$ is $t$-secure.*

**Graded consensus.** As a stepping stone to Byzantine agreement, it is also useful to define *graded consensus* [9]. Here, each party outputs both a value $v \in \{0, 1, \perp\}$ as well as a *grade* $g \in \{0, 1, 2\}$. As in the case of Byzantine agreement, we consider protocols that may not terminate; however, parties terminate upon generating output.

**Definition 3 (Graded consensus).** *Let $\Pi$ be a protocol executed by parties $P_1, \ldots, P_n$, where each party $P_i$ begins holding input $v_i \in \{0, 1\}$ and each party terminates upon generating output.*

- **Graded validity:** $\Pi$ *achieves $t$-graded validity if the following holds whenever at most $t$ of the parties are corrupted: if every honest party's input is equal to the same value $v$, then all honest parties output $(v, 2)$.*
- **Graded consistency:** $\Pi$ *achieves $t$-graded consistency if the following hold whenever at most $t$ of the parties are corrupted: (1) If two honest parties output grades $g, g'$, then $|g - g'| \le 1$. (2) If two honest parties output $(v, g)$ and $(v', g')$ with $g, g' \ge 1$, then $v = v'$.*
- **Liveness:** $\Pi$ *is $t$-live if whenever at most $t$ of the parties are corrupted, every honest party outputs $(v, g)$ with either $v \in \{0, 1\}$ and $g \ge 1$, or $v = \perp$ and $g = 0$.*

*If $\Pi$ achieves $t$-graded validity, $t$-graded consistency, and $t$-liveness then we say $\Pi$ is $t$-secure.*

## 3   Synchronous BA with Fallback (Weak) Validity

In this section we show a protocol that is secure for some threshold $t_s$ of corrupted parties when run in a synchronous network, and achieves weak validity (though liveness and weak consistency may not hold) for a lower threshold $t_a$ even when run in an asynchronous network.

Our protocol relies on a variant of the Dolev-Strong broadcast protocol [8] as a subroutine. Since we use a slightly non-standard version of that protocol, we describe it in Fig. 1 for completeness. In the protocol, we say that $(v, \mathsf{SET})$ is an *$r$-correct message* (from the point of view of a party $P_i$) if $\mathsf{SET}$ contains valid signatures on $v$ from $P^*$ and $r - 1$ additional, distinct parties other than $P_i$.

---

**Protocol $\Pi_{\mathsf{DS}}$**

**Round 1:** $P^*$ signs its input $v^*$ to obtain a signature $\sigma^*$. It sets $\mathsf{SET} := \{\sigma^*\}$ and sends $(v^*, \mathsf{SET})$ to all parties.

**Rounds 1 to n − 1:** Each $P_i$ begins with $\mathsf{ACC}_i = \emptyset$, and then acts as follows: upon receiving an $r$-correct message $(v, \mathsf{SET})$ in round $r$, add $v$ to $\mathsf{ACC}_i$. If $r < n - 1$, then also compute a signature $\sigma_i$ on $v$, let $\mathsf{SET} := \mathsf{SET} \cup \{\sigma_i\}$, and send $(v, \mathsf{SET})$ to all parties in the following round. (This is done at most once for each $(v, r)$ pair.)

**Output determination:** At time $(n - 1) \cdot \Delta$, if $\mathsf{ACC}_i$ contains one value, then output that value and terminate. In any other case, output $\bot$ and terminate.

---

**Fig. 1.** The Dolev-Strong broadcast protocol $\Pi_{\mathsf{DS}}$.

**Lemma 1.** *Broadcast protocol $\Pi_{\mathsf{DS}}$ satisfies the following properties:*

1. *When run in a synchronous network, it is n-consistent and n-valid.*
2. *When run in an asynchronous network, it is n-weakly valid.*

*Proof.* The standard analysis of the Dolev-Strong protocol shows that, when run in a synchronous network with any number of corrupted parties, $\mathsf{ACC}_i = \mathsf{ACC}_j$ for any honest parties $P_i, P_j$. This implies $n$-consistency. Since an honest $P^*$ sends a 1-correct message to all honest parties, and the attacker cannot forge signatures of the honest sender, $n$-validity holds.

The second claim follows because an attacker cannot forge the signature of an honest $P^*$.

We now define a BA protocol using $\Pi_{\mathsf{DS}}$ as a sub-routine. This protocol is parameterized by a value $t_a$ which determines the security thresholds the protocol satisfies.

---

**Protocol $\Pi_{\mathsf{SBA}}^{t_a}$**

Each $P_i$ initially holds a bit $v_i$. The protocol proceeds as follows:

- Each party $P_i$ broadcasts $v_i$ by running $\Pi_{\mathsf{DS}}$ as the sender.
- Let $v_j^i$ denote the output of $P_i$ in the $j$th execution of $\Pi_{\mathsf{DS}}$.
- Each $P_i$ does: if there are at least $2t_a + 1$ values $v_j^i$ that are in $\{0, 1\}$, output the majority of those values (with a tie broken arbitrarily) and terminate. Otherwise, output $\bot$ and terminate.

---

**Fig. 2.** A Byzantine agreement protocol, parameterized by $t_a$.

**Theorem 1.** *For any $t_a, t_s$ with $t_a < n/3$ and $t_a + 2 \cdot t_s < n$, Byzantine agreement protocol $\Pi_{\mathsf{SBA}}^{t_a}$ satisfies the following properties:*

1. *When the protocol is run in a synchronous network, it is $t_s$-secure.*
2. *When the protocol is run in an asynchronous network, it is $t_a$-weakly valid.*

*Moreover, the protocol has guaranteed termination in both cases, and when run in a synchronous network every honest party terminates in time at most $n \cdot \Delta$.*

*Proof.* The claim about termination is immediate.

When run in a synchronous network with $t_s$ corrupted parties, at least $n - t_s > 2t_a$ of the executions of $\Pi_{\mathsf{DS}}$ result in boolean output for all honest parties (by $n$-validity of $\Pi_{\mathsf{DS}}$) and so all honest parties generate boolean output in $\Pi_{\mathsf{SBA}}^{t_a}$; this proves $t_s$-liveness. By $n$-consistency of $\Pi_{\mathsf{DS}}$, all honest parties agree on the $\{v_j\}$ values they obtain and hence $\Pi_{\mathsf{SBA}}^{t_a}$ is $t_s$-consistent (in fact, it is $n$-consistent). Finally, $n$-validity of $\Pi_{\mathsf{DS}}$ implies that when all honest parties begin holding the same input $v \in \{0, 1\}$, then all honest parties will have $v$ as their majority value. This proves $t_s$-validity (in fact, the protocol is $t$-valid for any $t < n/2$).

For the second claim, assume all honest parties begin holding the same input $v$, and $t_a$ parties are corrupted. Any honest party $P_i$ who generates boolean output must have at least $2t_a + 1$ boolean values $\{v_j^i\}$, of which at most $t_a$ of these can be equal to $\bar{v}$. Hence, any honest party who generates boolean output will in fact output $v$.

## 4 Validity-Optimized Asynchronous BA

Here we show a protocol that is secure for some threshold when run in an asynchronous network, and achieves validity for a higher threshold. Throughout this section we only consider protocols running in an asynchronous network, and so drop explicit mention of this fact for the remainder of this section.

**Theorem 2.** *For any $t_a, t_s$ with $t_a < n/3$ and $t_a + 2 \cdot t_s < n$, there is an $n$-party protocol for Byzantine agreement that, when run in an asynchronous network, is $t_a$-secure and also achieves $t_s$-validity with termination.*

Our proof of Theorem 2 proceeds in a number of steps. In Sect. 4.1 we describe a "validity-optimized" protocol $\Pi_{\mathsf{GC}}^{t_s}$ for graded consensus that is $t_a$-secure and also achieves $t_s$-graded validity. Then, in Sect. 4.2, we show a Byzantine agreement protocol $\Pi_{\mathsf{ABA}}^{t_s}$ using $\Pi_{\mathsf{GC}}^{t_s}$ as a subroutine. This protocol illustrates our main ideas, and achieves all the properties claimed in Theorem 2 except termination. We then discuss how termination can be added using existing techniques.

Our protocol is based on the work of Mostéfaoui et al. [29], but allows for variable thresholds. Also, our description simplifies theirs by presenting the protocol in a modular fashion.

## 4.1   Validity-Optimized Graded Consensus

Our graded consensus protocol relies on a sub-protocol $\Pi_{\text{prop}}^{t_s}$ for proposing values, shown in Fig. 3. This protocol is parameterized by a value $t_s$ that determines its security thresholds. We begin by proving some properties of $\Pi_{\text{prop}}^{t_s}$. Throughout, we let $n$ denote the number of parties.

---

**Protocol $\Pi_{\text{prop}}^{t_s}$**

We describe the protocol from the point of view of a party with input $v \in \{0, 1, \lambda\}$.

1. Set vals $:= \emptyset$.
2. Send (prepare, $v$) to all parties.
3. Upon receiving the message (prepare, $b$), for some $b \in \{0, 1, \lambda\}$, from strictly more than $t_s$ parties, do: If (prepare, $b$) has not been sent, then send (prepare, $b$) to all parties.
4. Upon receiving the message (prepare, $b$), for some $b \in \{0, 1, \lambda\}$, from at least $n - t_s$ parties, set vals $:=$ vals $\cup \{b\}$.
5. Upon adding the first value $b \in \{0, 1, \lambda\}$ to vals, send (propose, $b$) to all parties.
6. Once at least $n - t_s$ messages (propose, $b$) have been received on values $b \in$ vals, let prop $\subseteq$ vals be the set of values carried by those messages. Output prop and terminate.

---

**Fig. 3.** A sub-protocol for proposing values, parameterized by $t_s$.

**Lemma 2.** *Assume $t_a < n - 2 \cdot t_s$ parties are corrupted in an execution of $\Pi_{\text{prop}}^{t_s}$. If two honest parties $P_i, P_j$ output $\{b\}$, $\{b'\}$, respectively, then $b = b'$.*

*Proof.* Since $P_i$ outputs $\{b\}$, it must have received at least $n - t_s$ messages (propose, $b$), of which at least $n - t_s - t_a$ of those were sent by honest parties. Similarly, $P_j$ must have received at least $n - t_s - t_a$ messages (propose, $b'$) that were sent by honest parties. If $b \neq b'$, then because $2 \cdot (n - t_s - t_a)$ is strictly greater than the number of honest parties $n - t_a$, this would mean that some honest party sent propose messages on two different values, which is impossible.

**Lemma 3.** *Assume $t_a \leq t_s$ parties are corrupted in an execution of $\Pi_{\text{prop}}^{t_s}$. If no honest party has input $v$, then no honest party outputs prop containing $v$.*

*Proof.* If $v$ was not input by any honest party, then at most $t_a \leq t_s$ messages (prepare, $v$) are sent in step 2. Thus, no honest party ever sends a message (prepare, $v$), and consequently no honest party ever sends a message (propose, $v$). It follows that no honest party ever adds $v$ to vals, and so no honest party outputs prop containing $v$.

**Lemma 4.** *Assume $t_a$ parties are corrupted in an execution of $\Pi_{\text{prop}}^{t_s}$, where $t_a < n - 2 \cdot t_s$ and $t_a \le t_s$. If an honest party sends a message (propose, $b$), all honest parties add $b$ to vals.*

*Proof.* Suppose some honest party $P_i$ sends (propose, $b$). Then $P_i$ must have received at least $n - t_s$ messages (prepare, $b$). At least $n - t_s - t_a > t_s$ of these must have been sent by honest parties, and so eventually all other honest parties also receive strictly more than $t_s$ messages (prepare, $b$). We thus see that every honest party will eventually send (prepare, $b$). Therefore, every honest party will eventually receive at least $n - t_a \ge n - t_s$ messages (prepare, $b$), and consequently every honest party will add $b$ to vals.

Note that whenever parties in $\Pi_{\text{prop}}^{t_s}$ generate output, they terminate. While honest parties do not necessarily terminate (for example, if honest parties are split evenly among 0, 1, and $\lambda$), we show they do terminate as long as honest parties hold at most two different input values.

**Lemma 5.** *Assume $t_a$ parties are corrupted in an execution of $\Pi_{\text{prop}}^{t_s}$, where $t_a < n - 2 \cdot t_s$ and $t_a \le t_s$. If all honest parties hold one of two different inputs, then all honest parties terminate.*

*Proof.* We first argue that every honest party sends a propose message. Indeed, there are $n - t_a$ honest parties, so at least $\frac{1}{2}(n - t_a) > t_s$ honest parties must have the same input $v$. Therefore, all honest parties receive strictly more than $t_s$ messages (prepare, $v$). Consequently, all honest parties will eventually send (prepare, $v$). Thus, every honest party receives $n - t_a \ge n - t_s$ messages (prepare, $v$) and adds $v$ to vals. In particular, vals is nonempty and so every honest party sends a propose message.

Each honest party thus receives at least $n - t_a \ge n - t_s$ propose messages sent by honest parties. By Lemma 4, for any $b$ proposed by an honest party, all honest parties eventually have $b \in$ vals. Thus, every honest party eventually receives at least $n - t_s$ propose messages for values in their set vals, and therefore all honest parties terminate.

$\Pi_{\text{prop}}^{t_s}$ satisfies a notion of validity even for $t_s$ corrupted parties.

**Lemma 6.** *Assume $t_s < n/2$ parties are corrupted in an execution of $\Pi_{\text{prop}}^{t_s}$. If all honest parties hold the same input $v$, then all honest parties output prop $= \{v\}$.*

*Proof.* Suppose $t_s$ parties are corrupted, and all honest parties hold the same input $v$. In step 2, all $n - t_s$ honest parties send (prepare, $v$), and so all honest parties add $v$ to vals. Any prepare messages on other values in step 2 are sent by the $t_s < n - t_s$ corrupted parties, and so no honest party ever adds a value other than $v$ to vals. Thus, all $n - t_s$ honest parties send their (single) propose message (propose, $v$) in step 5. It follows that every honest party outputs prop $= \{v\}$ in step 6.

---

**Protocol $\Pi_{\mathsf{GC}}^{t_s}$**

We describe the protocol from the point of view of a party with input $v \in \{0, 1\}$.

- Set $b_1 := v$.
- Run protocol $\Pi_{\mathsf{prop}}^{t_s}$ using input $b_1$, and let $\mathsf{prop}_1$ denote the output.
- If $\mathsf{prop}_1 = \{b\}$, then set $b_2 := b$. Otherwise, set $b_2 := \lambda$.
- Run protocol $\Pi_{\mathsf{prop}}^{t_s}$ using input $b_2$, and let $\mathsf{prop}_2$ denote the output.
- If $\mathsf{prop}_2 = \{b'\}$ for $b' \neq \lambda$, then output $(b', 2)$ and terminate. If $\mathsf{prop}_2 = \{b', \lambda\}$ for $b' \neq \lambda$, then output $(b', 1)$ and terminate. If $\mathsf{prop}_2 = \{\lambda\}$, then output $(\bot, 0)$ and terminate.

---

**Fig. 4.** A protocol for graded consensus, parameterized by $t_s$.

In Fig. 4 we show a graded consensus protocol $\Pi_{\mathsf{GC}}^{t_s}$ that relies on $\Pi_{\mathsf{prop}}^{t_s}$ as a subroutine. Note that parties terminate upon generating output. We now analyze the protocol.

**Lemma 7.** *If* $t_s < n/2$, *then* $\Pi_{\mathsf{GC}}^{t_s}$ *achieves* $t_s$-*graded validity.*

*Proof.* Suppose $t_s$ parties are corrupted, and every honest party's input is equal to the same value $v$. By Lemma 6, all honest parties have $\mathsf{prop}_1 = \{v\}$ following the first execution of $\Pi_{\mathsf{prop}}^{t_s}$, and so use $v$ as the input for the second execution of $\Pi_{\mathsf{prop}}^{t_s}$. By the same reasoning, all honest parties have $\mathsf{prop}_2 = \{v\}$ after the second execution of $\Pi_{\mathsf{prop}}^{t_s}$. Thus, all honest parties output $(v, 2)$. $\qquad\blacksquare$

**Lemma 8.** *Assume* $t_a \leq t_s$ *and* $t_a + 2 \cdot t_s < n$. *Then* $\Pi_{\mathsf{GC}}^{t_s}$ *achieves* $t_a$-*graded consistency.*

*Proof.* Suppose $t_a$ parties are corrupted. First, we show that the grades output by two honest parties $P_i, P_j$ differ by at most 1. The only way this can possibly fail is if one of the parties (say, $P_i$) outputs a grade of 2. $P_i$ must then have received $\mathsf{prop}_2 = \{b\}$, for some $b \in \{0, 1\}$, as its output from the second execution of $\Pi_{\mathsf{prop}}^{t_s}$. It follows from Lemma 2 that $P_j$ could not have received $\mathsf{prop}_2 = \{\lambda\}$. Therefore, it is not possible for $P_j$ to output grade 0.

Next, we show that any two honest parties that output nonzero grades must output the same value. Observe first that there is a bit $b$ such that the inputs of all the honest parties to the second execution of $\Pi_{\mathsf{prop}}^{t_s}$ lie in $\{b, \lambda\}$. (Indeed, if all honest parties set $b_2 := \lambda$ this claim is immediate. On the other hand, if some honest party sets $b_2 := b \in \{0, 1\}$ then they must have $\mathsf{prop}_1 = \{b\}$; but then Lemma 2 implies that any other honest party who sets $b_2$ to anything other than $\lambda$ will set it equal to $b$ as well.) Lemma 3 thus implies that no honest party outputs a set $\mathsf{prop}_2$ after the second execution of $\Pi_{\mathsf{prop}}^{t_s}$ that contains a value other than $b$ or $\lambda$. Thus, any two honest parties that output a nonzero grade must output the same value $b$.

**Lemma 9.** *Assume $t_a \leq t_s$ and $t_a + 2 \cdot t_s < n$. Then $\Pi_{GC}^{t_s}$ achieves $t_a$-liveness.*

*Proof.* All honest parties hold input in $\{0,1\}$ in the first execution of $\Pi_{prop}^{t_s}$, so Lemma 5 shows that all honest parties terminate that execution. As in the proof of the previous lemma, there is a bit $b$ such that the inputs of all the honest parties to the second execution of $\Pi_{prop}^{t_s}$ lie in $\{b, \lambda\}$; so, using Lemma 5 again, that execution also terminates. Moreover, by Lemma 3, the set $prop_2$ output by any honest party is a nonempty subset of $\{b, \lambda\}$, i.e., is either $\{b\}, \{b, \lambda\}$, or $\{\lambda\}$. Thus, every honest party generates output and terminates in $\Pi_{GC}^{t_s}$.

## 4.2 Validity-Optimized Byzantine Agreement

We present a Byzantine agreement protocol $\Pi_{ABA}^{t_s}$ in Fig. 5. Recall from Sect. 2 that we assume an atomic primitive CoinFlip that allows all parties to generate and learn an unbiased value $Coin_k \in \{0,1\}$ for $k = 1, \ldots$. We refer there for a discussion as to how it can be realized.

---

**Protocol $\Pi_{ABA}^{t_s}$**

We describe the protocol from the point of view of a party with input $v \in \{0,1\}$.

Set $b := v$, done $:=$ false, and $k := 1$. Then repeat the following steps forever:

1. Run $\Pi_{GC}^{t_s}$ on input $b$, and let $(b, g)$ denote the output.
2. $Coin_k \leftarrow$ CoinFlip$(k)$.
3. If $g < 2$ then set $b := Coin_k$.
4. Run $\Pi_{GC}^{t_s}$ on input $b$, and let $(b, g)$ denote the output.
5. If $g = 2$ and done $=$ false, then output $b$ and set done $:=$ true.
6. Set $k := k + 1$.

---

**Fig. 5.** A Byzantine agreement protocol, parameterized by $t_s$.

**Lemma 10.** *If $t_s < n/2$, then protocol $\Pi_{ABA}^{t_s}$ satisfies $t_s$-validity. Moreover, if all honest parties initially hold $v$, then all honest parties output $v$ at the end of the first iteration of $\Pi_{ABA}^{t_s}$.*

*Proof.* Suppose there are at most $t_s$ corrupted parties and all honest parties initially hold $v \in \{0,1\}$. All honest parties use input $v$ in the first execution of $\Pi_{GC}^{t_s}$ in the first iteration; $t_s$-graded validity of $\Pi_{GC}^{t_s}$ (cf. Lemma 7) implies they all output $(v, 2)$ from that execution. Thus, all honest parties ignore the result of the coin flip and run a second instance of $\Pi_{GC}^{t_s}$ using input $v$, again unanimously obtaining $(v, 2)$ as output. Thus, all honest parties output $v$ in the first iteration.

**Lemma 11.** *Assume $t_a \leq t_s$ and $t_a + 2 \cdot t_s < n$. Then $\Pi_{\mathsf{ABA}}^{t_s}$ satisfies $t_a$-liveness and $t_a$-consistency. Moreover: (1) if an honest party generates generates output for the first time in iteration $k$, then every other honest party generates output in iteration $k$ or $k+1$, and (2) all honest parties generate output in an expected constant number of iterations.*

*Proof.* Assume $t_a$ parties are corrupted. Consider an iteration $k$ of the protocol by which no honest party has yet generated output. Let Agree be the event that all honest parties use the same input to the second execution of $\Pi_{\mathsf{GC}}^{t_s}$ in that iteration. If Agree occurs, then $t_s$-graded validity of $\Pi_{\mathsf{GC}}^{t_s}$ implies that all honest parties will obtain a grade of 2 in that execution and hence generate output in iteration $k$. We show that Agree occurs with probability at least $1/2$. We distinguish two cases:

- Say some honest party outputs $(b, 2)$ in the first execution of $\Pi_{\mathsf{GC}}^{t_s}$ in iteration $k$. By $t_a$-graded consistency of $\Pi_{\mathsf{GC}}^{t_s}$, all honest parties output either $(b, 2)$ or $(b, 1)$ in that execution of $\Pi_{\mathsf{GC}}^{t_s}$. Since $\mathsf{Coin}_k$ is not revealed until the first honest party terminates that execution of $\Pi_{\mathsf{GC}}^{t_s}$, this means $b$ is chosen independently of $\mathsf{Coin}_k$. If $\mathsf{Coin}_k = b$, which occurs with probability $1/2$, then all parties will use the same input in the second execution of $\Pi_{\mathsf{GC}}^{t_s}$ in iteration $k$.
- If no honest party outputs $(b, 2)$ after the first execution of $\Pi_{\mathsf{GC}}^{t_s}$, then all honest parties will use $\mathsf{Coin}_k$ as their input in the second execution of $\Pi_{\mathsf{GC}}^{t_s}$ in iteration $k$.

The above implies that in expected constant rounds *some* honest party generates boolean output. We next show that if some honest party $P_i$ outputs $b \in \{0, 1\}$ in iteration $k$, then all other honest parties output $b$ in iteration $k$ or $k+1$. Since $P_i$ output $b$ in iteration $k$, it must have seen $(b, 2)$ as the output of the second execution of $\Pi_{\mathsf{GC}}^{t_s}$ in iteration $k$. By $t_a$-graded consistency of $\Pi_{\mathsf{GC}}^{t_s}$, every honest party obtains either $(b, 1)$ or $(b, 2)$ as output from that execution of $\Pi_{\mathsf{GC}}^{t_s}$. Clearly, all honest parties in the second situation output $b$ in iteration $k$. We argue that all honest parties in the first situation (namely, who obtain output $(b, 1)$) will output $b$ in iteration $k+1$. This can be seen as follows. Since all honest parties use input $b$ in the first execution of $\Pi_{\mathsf{GC}}^{t_s}$ in iteration $k+1$, all honest parties output $(b, 2)$ in that execution (by $t_s$-validity of $\Pi_{\mathsf{GC}}^{t_s}$). All honest parties then participate in the coin flip but ignore the result, and use input $b$ in the next execution of $\Pi_{\mathsf{GC}}^{t_s}$. Thus, all honest parties obtain output $(b, 2)$ from the second execution of $\Pi_{\mathsf{GC}}^{t_s}$ in iteration $k+1$, and any honest party that did not output $b$ in the previous iteration will output it now.

**Corollary 1.** *For any $t_a, t_s$ with $t_a < n/3$ and $t_a + 2 \cdot t_s < n$, there is an $n$-party protocol for Byzantine agreement that, when run in an asynchronous network, achieves $t_s$-validity, $t_a$-consistency, and $t_a$-liveness.*

*Proof.* We may assume $t_s \geq t_a$ since, if not, we can set $t_s = t_a$ and $t_a + 2 \cdot t_s < n$ will still hold. Note also that the stated conditions imply $t_s < n/2$. The corollary thus follows from Lemmas 10 and 11.

**Adding Termination.** Corollary 1 proves all the claims of Theorem 2 except for termination and, indeed, parties in $\Pi_{\mathsf{ABA}}^{t_s}$ participate indefinitely and so the protocol does not terminate. However, we can obtain a terminating protocol $\Pi_{\mathsf{ABA}*}^{t_s}$ (and hence complete the proof of Theorem 2) using existing techniques [29]. We refer to the appendix for further discussion.

## 5    Main Protocol

Fix $n, t_a, t_s$ with $t_a < n/3$ and $t_a + 2 \cdot t_s < n$. As in the proof of Corollary 1 we may assume $t_a \leq t_s$. Our main protocol $\Pi_{\mathsf{HBA}}^{t_a, t_s}$ is given in Fig. 6. It relies on the following sub-protocols:

- $\Pi_{\mathsf{SBA}}^{t_a}$ is an $n$-party BA protocol that is $t_s$-secure when run in a synchronous network, and $t_a$-weakly valid when run in an asynchronous network. Moreover, the protocol has guaranteed termination regardless of the network, and when run in a synchronous network all honest parties terminate by time $n \cdot \Delta$. The existence of such a protocol is guaranteed by Theorem 1.
- $\Pi_{\mathsf{ABA}*}^{t_s}$ is an $n$-party BA protocol that is $t_a$-secure and $t_s$-valid with termination when run in an asynchronous network. (Of course, these properties also hold if the protocol is run in a synchronous network.) The existence of such a protocol is guaranteed by Theorem 2.

---

### Protocol $\Pi_{\mathsf{HBA}}^{t_a, t_s}$

Each $P_i$ initially holds a bit $v_i$. The protocol proceeds as follows:

- Each party $P_i$ runs $\Pi_{\mathsf{SBA}}^{t_a}$ using input $v_i$ for time $n \cdot \Delta$. Let $b_i$ denote the output of $P_i$ from this protocol, with $b_i = \bot$ denoting no output.
- Each party $P_i$ does the following: if $b_i \neq \bot$, set $v_i^* := b_i$; otherwise set $v_i^* := v_i$. Then run $\Pi_{\mathsf{ABA}*}^{t_s}$ using input $v_i^*$, output the result, and terminate.

---

**Fig. 6.** A Byzantine agreement protocol, parameterized by $t_a, t_s$.

**Theorem 3.** *Let $n, t_a, t_s$ be as above. Then protocol $\Pi_{\mathsf{HBA}}^{t_a, t_s}$ satisfies the following properties:*

1. *When the protocol is run in a synchronous network, it is $t_s$-secure.*
2. *When the protocol is run in an asynchronous network, it is $t_a$-secure.*

*Proof.* First consider the case when $\Pi_{\mathsf{HBA}}^{t_a, t_s}$ is run in a synchronous network, and at most $t_s$ parties are corrupted. By $t_s$-security of $\Pi_{\mathsf{SBA}}^{t_a}$, after running $\Pi_{\mathsf{SBA}}^{t_a}$ there is a value $b \neq \bot$ such that $b_i = b$ for every honest $P_i$. Moreover, if every honest party's input was equal to the same value $v$, then $b = v$. Thus, all honest parties set $v_i^*$ to the same value $b$ and, if every party's input was the same value $v$, then $v_i^* = v$. By $t_s$-validity with termination of $\Pi_{\mathsf{ABA}^*}^{t_s}$, all honest parties terminate and agree on their output from $\Pi_{\mathsf{HBA}}^{t_a,t_s}$, proving $t_s$-consistency, $t_s$-liveness, and $t_s$-termination. Moreover, if every honest party's original input was equal to the same value $v$, then the output of $\Pi_{\mathsf{ABA}^*}^{t_s}$ (and thus of $\Pi_{\mathsf{HBA}}^{t_a,t_s}$) is equal to $v$. This proves $t_s$-validity.

Next consider the case when $\Pi_{\mathsf{HBA}}^{t_a,t_s}$ is run in an asynchronous network, and at most $t_a$ parties are corrupted. The protocol inherits $t_a$-consistency, $t_a$-liveness, and $t_a$-termination from $t_a$-security of $\Pi_{\mathsf{ABA}^*}^{t_s}$, and so it only remains to argue $t_a$-validity. Assume every honest party's initial input is equal to the same value $v$. Then $t_a$-weak validity of $\Pi_{\mathsf{SBA}}^{t_a}$, plus the fact that it always terminates, imply that $b_i \in \{v, \bot\}$, and hence $v_i^* = v$, for every honest $P_i$. It follows from $t_s$-validity (note $t_a \leq t_s$) of $\Pi_{\mathsf{ABA}^*}^{t_s}$ that all honest parties output $v$.

# 6    Impossibility Result

We show here that our positive result from the previous section is tight. That is:

**Theorem 4.** *For any $n$, if $t_a \geq n/3$ or $t_a + 2 \cdot t_s \geq n$ there is no $n$-party protocol for Byzantine agreement that is $t_s$-secure in a synchronous network and $t_a$-secure in an asynchronous network.*

The case of $t_a \geq n/3$ follows from existing impossibility results for asynchronous consensus, so the interesting case is when $t_a < n/3$ but $t_a + 2 \cdot t_s \geq n$. Theorem 4 follows from the lemma below.

**Lemma 12.** *Fix $n, t_a, t_s$ with $t_a + 2t_s \geq n$. If an $n$-party Byzantine agreement protocol is $t_s$-valid in a synchronous network, then it cannot also be $t_a$-weakly consistent in an asynchronous network.*

*Proof.* The proof is similar to that of [36]. Assume $t_a + 2t_s = n$ and fix a BA protocol $\Pi$. Partition the $n$ parties into sets $S_0, S_1, S_a$ where $|S_0| = |S_1| = t_s$ and $|S_a| = t_a$, and consider the following experiment:

- Parties in $S_0$ run $\Pi$ using input 0, and parties in $S_1$ run $\Pi$ using input 1. All communication between parties in $S_0$ and parties in $S_1$ is blocked (but all other messages are delivered within time $\Delta$).
- Create virtual copies of each party in $S_a$, call them $S_a^0$ and $S_a^1$. Parties in $S_a^0$ run $\Pi$ using input 0, and communicate only with each other and parties in $S_0$. Parties in $S_a^1$ run $\Pi$ using input 1, and communicate only with each other and parties in $S_1$.

Consider an execution of $\Pi$ in a synchronous network where parties in $S_1$ are corrupted and simply abort, and all remaining (honest) parties use input 0. The views of the honest parties in this execution are distributed identically to the views of $S_0 \cup S_a^0$ in the above experiment. In particular, $t_s$-validity of $\Pi$ implies that all parties in $S_0$ output 0. Analogously, all parties in $S_1$ output 1.

Next consider an execution of $\Pi$ in an asynchronous network where parties in $S_a$ are corrupted, and run $\Pi$ using input 0 when interacting with $S_0$ while running $\Pi$ using input 1 when interacting with $S_1$. Moreover, all communication between the (honest) parties in $S_0$ and $S_1$ is delayed indefinitely. The views of the honest parties in this execution are distributed identically to the views of $S_0 \cup S_1$ in the above experiment, yet the conclusion of the preceding paragraph shows that weak consistency is violated.

**Acknowledgments.** Julian Loss was supported by ERC Project ERCC (FP7/ 615074).

# Appendix

Protocol $\Pi_{\mathsf{ABA}}^{t_s}$ has the property that parties never terminate. It is worth noting that the naive way to address this drawback—in which honest parties participate in one more iteration after generating output, and then terminate—is not sufficient to allow the remaining honest parties to terminate. To see why, suppose that some honest party $P_i$ receives $(b, 2)$ as output from the second instance of $\Pi_{\mathsf{GC}}^{t_s}$ in iteration $k$, and some other honest party $P_j$ receives $(b, 1)$. Now $P_i$ will participate in iteration $k + 1$, helping $P_j$ to output $(b, 2)$ in that iteration. However, $P_i$ then terminates and does not participate in iteration $k+2$, while $P_j$ still needs to complete iteration $k + 2$ in order to terminate. $P_j$ will not receive messages from $P_i$ when running $\Pi_{\mathsf{GC}}^{t_s}$, and (since the network may be asynchronous) has no way of knowing whether $P_i$ has terminated or is sending messages that have been delayed. Thus, $P_j$ may never terminate its execution of $\Pi_{\mathsf{GC}}^{t_s}$.

Nevertheless, we can obtain a terminating protocol $\Pi_{\mathsf{ABA}*}^{t_s}$ using existing techniques [29]. The basic idea is that when an honest party generates output, it announces that fact to all other parties and terminates; the remaining honest parties can then simulate its behavior for the rest of their execution. Specifically, we modify $\Pi_{\mathsf{ABA}}^{t_s}$ as follows: when an honest party $P_i$ outputs $b^*$, it sends (notify, $b^*$) to all parties. Upon receiving such a message, the remaining parties each locally simulate the behavior of $P_i$ in the rest of the protocol, and specifically simulate receiving (prepare, $b^*$) and (propose, $b^*$) from $P_i$ in each execution of the $\Pi_{\mathsf{prop}}^{t_s}$ subroutines. The following lemma shows that this is sufficient to simulate the behavior of honest parties who have already terminated.

**Lemma 13.** *Let $t_a, t_s$ be such that $t_a \leq t_s$ and $t_a + 2 \cdot t_s < n$, and assume at most $t_a$ parties are corrupted in an execution of $\Pi_{\mathsf{ABA}}^{t_s}$. If an honest party outputs $b^*$, then in every future execution of $\Pi_{\mathsf{prop}}^{t_s}$ within $\Pi_{\mathsf{ABA}}^{t_s}$ that party will send exactly the messages* (prepare, $b^*$) *and* (propose, $b^*$).

*Proof.* Say honest party $P_i$ outputs $b^* \in \{0, 1\}$ in some iteration $k$. Then $P_i$ must have received $(b^*, 2)$ as the output of the second execution of $\Pi_{\mathsf{GC}}^{t_s}$ in iteration $k$. By $t_a$-graded consistency of $\Pi_{\mathsf{GC}}^{t_s}$, every honest party obtained $(b^*, 1)$ or $(b^*, 2)$

as output from the second execution of $\Pi_{\mathsf{GC}}^{t_s}$ in iteration $k$. Therefore, in the first execution of $\Pi_{\mathsf{GC}}^{t_s}$ in iteration $k+1$, all honest parties use input $b^*$. Using the same argument as in the proof of Lemma 3, observe that no value other than $b^*$ receives enough prepare messages to be echoed (and therefore proposed) in this execution of $\Pi_{\mathsf{prop}}^{t_s}$. Therefore every honest party sends (prepare, $b^*$) in that execution of $\Pi_{\mathsf{prop}}^{t_s}$, and hence every honest party sends (propose, $b^*$) as in the proof of Lemma 5. This establishes that honest parties send exactly the messages (prepare, $b^*$) and (propose, $b^*$) in the first execution of $\Pi_{\mathsf{prop}}^{t_s}$ (as a subroutine of the first execution of $\Pi_{\mathsf{GC}}^{t_s}$). Since, by Lemma 6, all honest parties terminate with $\{b^*\}$ in that execution, they all use input $b^*$ in the second execution of $\Pi_{\mathsf{prop}}^{t_s}$ (still in the first execution of $\Pi_{\mathsf{GC}}^{t_s}$), and we can repeat the argument. Moreover, $t_s$-graded validity of $\Pi_{\mathsf{GC}}^{t_s}$ ensures that all parties output $(b^*, 2)$ from the first execution of $\Pi_{\mathsf{GC}}^{t_s}$. Therefore, all honest parties input $b^*$ to the second execution of $\Pi_{\mathsf{GC}}^{t_s}$ in iteration $k+1$ and we can apply the same argument to show that during iteration $k+1$ of $\Pi_{\mathsf{ABA}}^{t_s}$, all honest parties send exactly the messages (prepare, $b^*$) and (propose, $b^*$). Now, $t_s$-graded validity of $\Pi_{\mathsf{GC}}^{t_s}$ ensures that all honest parties output $(b^*, 2)$ in the second execution of $\Pi_{\mathsf{GC}}^{t_s}$ in iteration $k+1$ as well, and hence set $b = b^*$ for iteration $k+2$. We can therefore repeat the same argument inductively for any iteration $k' > k+1$.

Putting everything together, we have:

**Lemma 14.** *For any $t_a, t_s$ with $t_a \leq t_s$ and $t_a + 2 \cdot t_s < n$, protocol $\Pi_{\mathsf{ABA}^*}^{t_s}$ is $t_a$-secure and also achieves $t_s$-validity with termination.*

*Proof.* Protocol $\Pi_{\mathsf{ABA}^*}^{t_s}$ inherits $t_a$-validity, $t_a$-consistency, and $t_a$-liveness directly from $\Pi_{\mathsf{ABA}}^{t_s}$. In addition, $t_a$-liveness of $\Pi_{\mathsf{ABA}}^{t_s}$ implies $t_a$-termination of $\Pi_{\mathsf{ABA}^*}^{t_s}$.

It remains only to show that $\Pi_{\mathsf{ABA}^*}^{t_s}$ is $t_s$-valid with termination. Suppose at most $t_s$ parties are corrupted during an execution of $\Pi_{\mathsf{ABA}^*}^{t_s}$, and all honest parties hold input $v \in \{0, 1\}$. The execution proceeds exactly as described in Lemma 10, and so all honest parties output $v$ in the first iteration and terminate.

**Realizing CoinFlip within $\Pi_{\mathsf{ABA}^*}^{t_s}$.** Both Mostéfaoui et al. [29] and the above analysis treat the coin flip as an atomic primitive that outputs the $k$th coin when the first honest party invokes CoinFlip($k$), even if some honest parties have terminated. When the coin flip is realized by an interactive protocol, however, this may no longer hold. When realizing the coin flip via a threshold unique signature scheme, however, there is a simple way to fix this issue: When an honest party terminates in iteration $k$, it appends its share of the signature for iteration $k+1$ to its notify message. Then, all honest parties who have not yet terminated will be able to compute the coin in iteration $k+1$ as needed. It is crucial here to note that since an honest party terminated in iteration $k$, the value of the coin in iteration $k+1$ will be ignored by all honest parties anyway, so it does not matter if the adversary learns it in advance.

# References

1. Abraham, I., Dolev, D., Halpern, J.Y.: An almost-surely terminating polynomial protocol for asynchronous Byzantine agreement with optimal resilience. In: 27th Annual ACM Symposium on Principles of Distributed Computing (PODC), pp. 405–414. ACM Press (2008)
2. Abraham, I., Malkhi, D., Nayak, K., Ren, L., Yin, M.: Sync HotStuff: simple and practical synchronous state machine replication (2019). http://eprint.iacr.org/2019/270
3. Beerliová-Trubíniová, Z., Hirt, M., Nielsen, J.B.: On the theoretical gap between synchronous and asynchronous MPC protocols. In: 29th Annual ACM Symposium on Principles of Distributed Computing (PODC), pp. 211–218. ACM Press (2010)
4. Cachin, C., Kursawe, K., Shoup, V.: Random oracles in Constantinople: practical asynchronous Byzantine agreement using cryptography. J. Cryptology 18(3), 219–246 (2005)
5. Canetti, R., Rabin, T.: Fast asynchronous Byzantine agreement with optimal resilience. In: 25th Annual ACM Symposium on Theory of Computing (STOC), pp. 42–51. ACM Press (1993)
6. Castro, M., Liskov, B.: Practical Byzantine fault tolerance and proactive recovery. ACM Trans. Comput. Syst. 20(4), 398–461 (2002)
7. Damgård, I., Geisler, M., Krøigaard, M., Nielsen, J.B.: Asynchronous multiparty computation: theory and implementation. In: Jarecki, S., Tsudik, G. (eds.) PKC 2009. LNCS, vol. 5443, pp. 160–179. Springer, Heidelberg (2009). https://doi.org/10.1007/978-3-642-00468-1_10
8. Dolev, D., Strong, H.R.: Authenticated algorithms for Byzantine agreement. SIAM J. Comput. 12(4), 656–666 (1983)
9. Feldman, P., Micali, S.: An optimal probabilistic protocol for synchronous Byzantine agreement. SIAM J. Comput. 26(4), 873–933 (1997)
10. Fischer, M.J., Lynch, N.A., Paterson, M.: Impossibility of distributed consensus with one faulty process. J. ACM 32(2), 374–382 (1985)
11. Fitzi, M., Hirt, M., Holenstein, T., Wullschleger, J.: Two-threshold broadcast and detectable multi-party computation. In: Biham, E. (ed.) EUROCRYPT 2003. LNCS, vol. 2656, pp. 51–67. Springer, Heidelberg (2003). https://doi.org/10.1007/3-540-39200-9_4
12. Fitzi, M., Nielsen, J.B.: On the number of synchronous rounds sufficient for authenticated byzantine agreement. In: Keidar, I. (ed.) DISC 2009. LNCS, vol. 5805, pp. 449–463. Springer, Heidelberg (2009). https://doi.org/10.1007/978-3-642-04355-0_46
13. Garay, J.A., Katz, J., Kumaresan, R., Zhou, H.-S.: Adaptively secure broadcast, revisited. In: 30th Annual ACM Symposium on Principles of Distributed Computing (PODC), pp. 179–186. ACM Press (2011)
14. Gilad, Y., Hemo, R., Micali, S., Vlachos, G., Zeldovich, N.: Algorand: scaling Byzantine agreements for cryptocurrencies (2017). http://eprint.iacr.org/2017/454
15. Goldwasser, S., Lindell, Y.: Secure multi-party computation without agreement. J. Cryptology 18(3), 247–287 (2005)
16. Guo, Y., Pass, R., Shi, E.: Synchronous, with a chance of partition tolerance. In: Boldyreva, A., Micciancio, D. (eds.) CRYPTO 2019. LNCS, vol. 11692, pp. 499–529. Springer, Cham (2019). https://doi.org/10.1007/978-3-030-26948-7_18
17. Hanke, T., Movahedi, M., Williams, D.: Dfinity technology overview series consensus system, rev. 1 (2018). https://dfinity.org/faq

18. Heilman, E., Kendler, A., Zohar, A., Goldberg, S.: Eclipse attacks on Bitcoin's peer-to-peer network. In: 24th USENIX Security Symposium, pp. 129–144. USENIX Association (2015)
19. Hirt, M., Zikas, V.: Adaptively secure broadcast. In: Gilbert, H. (ed.) EURO-CRYPT 2010. LNCS, vol. 6110, pp. 466–485. Springer, Heidelberg (2010). https://doi.org/10.1007/978-3-642-13190-5_24
20. Katz, J., Koo, C.-Y.: On expected constant-round protocols for Byzantine agreement. J. Comput. Syst. Sci. **75**(2), 91–112 (2009)
21. Kotla, R., Alvisi, L., Dahlin, M., Clement, A., Wong, E.L.: Zyzzyva: speculative Byzantine fault tolerance. ACM Trans. Comput. Syst. **27**(4), 7:1–7:39 (2009)
22. Kursawe, K.: Optimistic Byzantine agreement. In: 21st Symposium on Reliable Distributed Systems (SRDS), pp. 262–267. IEEE Computer Society (2002)
23. Lamport, L.: The part-time parliament. Technical Report 49, DEC Systems Research Center (1989)
24. Lamport, L., Shostak, R.E., Pease, M.C.: The Byzantine generals problem. ACM Trans. Program. Lang. Syst. **4**(3), 382–401 (1982)
25. Liu, S., Viotti, P., Cachin, C., Quéma, V., Vukolic, M.: XFT: practical fault tolerance beyond crashes. In: 12th USENIX Symposium on Operating Systems Design and Implementation (OSDI), pp. 485–500. USENIX Association (2016)
26. Liu-Zhang, C.-D., Loss, J., Moran, T., Maurer, U., Tschudi, D.: Robust MPC: asynchronous responsiveness yet synchronous security (2019). http://eprint.iacr.org/2019/159
27. Loss, J., Moran, T.: Combining asynchronous and synchronous Byzantine agreement: the best of both worlds (2018). http://eprint.iacr.org/2018/235
28. Malkhi, D., Nayak, K., Ren, L.: Flexible Byzantine fault tolerance (2019). https://arxiv.org/abs/1904.10067
29. Mostéfaoui, A., Moumen, H., Raynal, M.: Signature-free asynchronous binary Byzantine consensus with $t < n/3$, $O(n^2)$ messages, and $O(1)$ expected time. J. ACM **62**(4), 31:1–31:21 (2015)
30. Ongaro, D., Ousterhout, J.K.: In search of an understandable consensus algorithm. In: USENIX Annual Technical Conference, pp. 305–319. USENIX Association (2014)
31. Pass, R., Shi, E.: Hybrid consensus: efficient consensus in the permissionless model. In: 31st International Symposium on Distributed Computing (DISC), volume 91 of LIPIcs, pp. 39:1–39:16. Schloss Dagstuhl–Leibniz-Zentrum fuer Informatik (2017)
32. Pass, R., Shi, E.: Thunderella: blockchains with optimistic instant confirmation. In: Nielsen, J.B., Rijmen, V. (eds.) EUROCRYPT 2018. LNCS, vol. 10821, pp. 3–33. Springer, Cham (2018). https://doi.org/10.1007/978-3-319-78375-8_1
33. Patra, A., Choudhary, A., Pandu Rangan, C.: Simple and efficient asynchronous byzantine agreement with optimal resilience. In: 28th Annual ACM Symposium on Principles of Distributed Computing (PODC), pp. 92–101. ACM Press (2009)
34. Patra, A., Ravi, D.: On the power of hybrid networks in multi-party computation. IEEE Trans. Inf. Theory **64**(6), 4207–4227 (2018)
35. Pease, M., Shostak, R.E., Lamport, L.: Reaching agreement in the presence of faults. J. ACM **27**(2), 228–234 (1980)
36. Toueg, S.: Randomized Byzantine agreements. In: 3rd Annual ACM Symposium on Principles of Distributed Computing (PODC), pp. 163–178. ACM Press (1984)

# Predicate Encryption from Bilinear Maps and One-Sided Probabilistic Rank

Josh Alman[✉] and Robin Hui

MIT CSAIL and EECS, Cambridge, USA
{jalman,ctunoku}@mit.edu

**Abstract.** In predicate encryption for a function $f$, an authority can create ciphertexts and secret keys which are associated with 'attributes'. A user with decryption key $K_y$ corresponding to attribute $y$ can decrypt a ciphertext $CT_x$ corresponding to a message $m$ and attribute $x$ if and only if $f(x,y) = 0$. Furthermore, the attribute $x$ remains hidden to the user if $f(x,y) \neq 0$.

We construct predicate encryption from assumptions on bilinear maps for a large class of new functions, including sparse set disjointness, Hamming distance at most $k$, inner product mod 2, and any function with an efficient Arthur-Merlin communication protocol. Our construction uses a new probabilistic representation of Boolean functions we call 'one-sided probabilistic rank,' and combines it with known constructions of inner product encryption in a novel way.

**Keywords:** Predicate encryption · Bilinear maps · Probabilistic rank

## 1 Introduction

In this paper, we study Predicate Encryption (PE), a variant of functional encryption. In PE for a Boolean function $f : \{0,1\}^{2n} \to \{0,1\}$, an authority can create ciphertexts and secret keys which are labeled with values, or "attributes", from $\{0,1\}^n$. An authorized user with a decryption key $K_y$ (with label $y \in \{0,1\}^n$) can decrypt a ciphertext $CT_x$ (with label $x \in \{0,1\}^n$) if and only if $f(x,y) = 0$. Furthermore (in contrast to the related, weaker notion of attribute-based encryption), the attribute $x$ is hidden unless the user can decrypt the message[1].

Predicate encryption was first introduced by Boneh and Waters [10] and is a natural cryptographic primitive with a number of applications throughout cryptography and security [10,22]. For instance, an executive may issue a secret

---

J. Alman—Supported in part by NSF CCF-1651838 and NSF CCF-1741615.
R. Hui—Supported by an NSF Graduate Research Fellowship.

[1] Predicate encryption is sometimes alternatively defined with the ciphertexts corresponding to attributes $x_i$ and the secret keys being labeled with *predicates* $f_j$, where a ciphertext can be decrypted if $f_j(x_i) = 0$. These formulations are equivalent; we can go from one to the other by considering the single function $f(x,j) := f_j(x)$ or vice versa.

© International Association for Cryptologic Research 2019
D. Hofheinz and A. Rosen (Eds.): TCC 2019, LNCS 11891, pp. 151–173, 2019.
https://doi.org/10.1007/978-3-030-36030-6_7

key that allows her assistant to read only her emails that are labeled with certain business-related keywords, without revealing any of the keywords of any other emails. A credit card company may issue a secret key that allows an intermediary to check whether a transaction should be flagged for suspicious activity (based on attributes such as amount, home address, and location of purchase), without revealing bulk information for all transactions. A bank may issue a secret key that allows a credit-reporting company to learn complete information about certain statuses, such as late payments, but not about all of them.

In these examples, the metadata (i.e. attributes) of messages may carry sensitive information and should not be revealed en masse, while revealing only a limited or targeted set of attributes may be acceptable, especially if the number of decrypted messages is small relative to the total number of messages (as in the credit-card example).

## 1.1 Constructing PE

A long line of work [10,17,18,22] has shown how to construct PE for certain classes of functions based on various cryptographic assumptions. [10] first constructed PE for some simple functions such as wildcard-matching (i.e. $s \in \{0,1\}^n$ matches $p \in \{0,1,*\}^n$ if $p[i] = s[i]$ whenever $p[i] \neq *$) with relatively standard assumptions on bilinear maps. However, the known bilinear maps-based constructions typically can only support functions that can be essentially expressed as inner products. The one known exception is [22], which shows how to construct PE for the greater-than function (which cannot be expressed as a succinct inner product) using a different approach.

Some recent work has shown how to achieve better results using other assumptions. [13] showed how the stronger multilinear maps assumption can be used to construct PE for any $f$ with polynomial-size circuits. [17] showed how to construct PE for polynomial-size circuits using assumptions on learning with errors (LWE).

In this work, we return to the question of constructing PE based only on bilinear maps. We will show how to do so for a large class of functions whose 'one-sided probabilistic rank' is low.

## 1.2 One-Sided Rank

Consider a Boolean function $f : \{0,1\}^{2n} \to \{0,1\}$ where we think of 0 as 'true' and 1 as 'false'. The *one-sided rank* of $f$ over a ring $\mathcal{R}$ is the minimum integer $d$ such that there are two maps $g, h : \{0,1\}^n \to \mathcal{R}^d$ so that for any two $x, y \in \{0,1\}^n$ we have:

- If $f(x, y) = 0$ then $\langle g(x), h(y) \rangle = 0$, and
- If $f(x, y) = 1$ then $\langle g(x), h(y) \rangle \neq 0$.

One-sided rank is a generalization of the notion of matching vector families (in the case when $f$ is the equality function), and was recently studied in a cryptographic context by Bauer, Vihrovs, and Wee [8]. As first described by [18], if $f$ has one-sided rank $d$, then $f$ has ciphertexts of length $O(d \log |\mathcal{R}|)$ for a number of different cryptographic primitives, including PE, given assumptions on bilinear maps. The idea is that $g$ and $h$ give an embedding of $f$ into the *inner product* function, for which PE is already known from assumptions on bilinear maps [20] (specifically, from a variant on the Decisional Diffie-Hellman assumption; see Sect. 4.4 for more details).

This remark leads to PE for some functions with surprisingly low one-sided rank. For instance, over any ring with sufficiently large characteristic, Bauer et al. show that the equality function $\mathsf{EQ}_n : \{0,1\}^{2n} \to \{0,1\}$, where $\mathsf{EQ}_n(x,y)$ tests whether $x = y$, has one-sided rank only 2, by picking $g(x) = (x,1)$ and $h(y) = (-1,y)$. However, for a number of other functions $f$ of interest, including the greater-than function, the not-equals function, threshold functions, and or-of-equality functions, Bauer et al. show *one-sided rank lower bounds*, i.e. that the one-sided rank must be exponentially large in $n$. Hence, this one-sided rank approach is insufficient to construct PE with poly($n$) size ciphertexts for these functions.

## 1.3 One-Sided Probabilistic Rank

In this paper, we nonetheless achieve predicate encryption for these aforementioned functions and more. Our approach is to consider a new variant on one-sided rank, which we call *one-sided probabilistic rank*[2], which combines one-sided rank with the notion of *probabilistic rank* introduced by Alman and Williams [3]. We say $f : \{0,1\}^{2n} \to \{0,1\}$ has one-sided probabilistic rank $d$ if there is a joint distribution $\mathcal{D}$ on pairs of functions $g, h : \{0,1\}^n \to \mathcal{R}^d$ such that for any two $x, y \in \{0,1\}^n$ we have

- If $f(x,y) = 0$ then $\Pr_{g,h \sim \mathcal{D}}[\langle g(x), h(y) \rangle = 0] \geq 1/\mathrm{poly}(n)$, and
- If $f(x,y) = 1$ then $\Pr_{g,h \sim \mathcal{D}}[\langle g(x), h(y) \rangle = 0] \leq \varepsilon(n)$ for a negligible function $\varepsilon$.

Note in particular that, in contrast with the usual notion of probabilistic rank, or other related notions like matching vector families, the error in the $f(x,y) = 0$ case may be very large in our definition; the success probability must only be polynomially bounded away from 0.

In a surprisingly simple construction, we show that PE can be constructed given assumptions about bilinear maps for any function with polynomially-low one-sided probabilistic rank, despite the high error.

**Theorem 1 (Informal).** Suppose the Boolean function $f : \{0,1\}^{2n} \to \{0,1\}$ has one-sided probabilistic rank $d$ over the ring $\mathcal{R}$. Then, assuming the existence of PE for inner product over $\mathcal{R}$, there is a PE scheme for $f$ with ciphertexts of length $O(d \log |\mathcal{R}|)$.

---

[2] Bauer et al. [8] also briefly considered a different probabilistic version of one-sided rank, but their two-sided error seems insufficient to achieve PE; see Sect. 5 for more details.

Loosely, the nonnegligible probability of outputting 0 in the $f(x,y) = 0$ case of one-sided probabilistic rank will lead to the *correctness* of the PE scheme, and the negligible probability $\varepsilon$ in the $f(x,y) = 1$ case will be crucial for the *security*, since the scheme will leak information with probability $\varepsilon$. Theorem 1 can then be combined with the aforementioned bilinear maps-based PE for inner product, or with any other construction of PE for inner product.

We use Theorem 1 to give a number of new constructions of predicate encryption for various functions. We show that by taking advantage of the allowed error, we can achieve $\mathrm{poly}(n)$ one-sided probabilistic rank upper bounds for many functions $f : \{0,1\}^{2n} \to \{0,1\}$ of interest, including:

**Functions with $O(\log n)$ Arthur-Merlin (AM) Communication Complexity.** In a AM communication protocol for inputs $x, y$, first a public random string $z$ is drawn, then Merlin, who sees $x, y$, and $z$, picks a proof $\varphi$. Alice and Bob, who are each given access to $z$, $\varphi$, and their own input, independently decide to accept or reject. The protocol is correct if there is always a proof $\varphi$ which makes both players accept when $f(x,y) = 0$, but there is unlikely to be one when $f(x,y) = 1$.

We show that if $\neg f$ has such a protocol where the proof $\varphi$ can be described by $O(\log n)$ bits, then $f$ has $\mathrm{poly}(n)$ one-sided probabilistic rank. Such protocols, which take advantage of both randomness and a nondeterministic proof, are very powerful, and despite decades of work, there are no explicit functions for which $\omega(\log n)$ AM communication lower bounds are known [2,6,12,14,15]. Moreover, we will be able to use AM communication protocols where the probability that there is a proof which makes both players accept when $f(x,y) = 1$ only has to be $\leq 1 - 1/\mathrm{poly}(n)$; this is even stronger than normal AM communication, and hence harder to prove lower bounds for.

To complement this result, we give $O(\log n)$ AM communication protocols, and hence $\mathrm{poly}(n)$ one-sided probabilistic rank constructions, for some functions of interest, including:

- The greater-than function $\mathsf{GEQ}_n : \{0,1\}^{2n} \to \{0,1\}$ where $\mathsf{GEQ}_n(x,y)$ tests whether $x \geq y$ when interpreted as $n$-bit integers in the range $[0, 2^n - 1]$. We show its one-sided probabilistic rank is $\mathrm{poly}(n)$, whereas Bauer et al. showed a $2^n$ lower bound on its one-sided rank.

  Range checking (even multidimensional) can be implemented by using two or more greater-than functions. This supports, for example, the use case of police stations being permitted to view emergency reports originating within a fixed area surrounding their precincts.

- Sparse Set Disjointness, the function which, for two subsets $S_1, S_2 \subseteq U$ of a universe $U$ with $|S_1|, |S_2| \leq \mathrm{poly}(n)$ and $|U| \leq 2^{\mathrm{poly}(n)}$, outputs 0 if $S_1$ and $S_2$ are disjoint. Using one-sided probabilistic rank allows us to handle universe sizes that are exponentially larger than is allowed by one-sided rank (which can only handle $|U| \leq \mathrm{poly}(n)$).

  As described in the introduction, this can be used in the example where a CEO wants to give her assistant the ability to decrypt all of her emails, *except* those which are labeled with any of a set of keywords, e.g. "personal", "receipts" or "legal".

Our result is not the first to relate AM communication with variants on PE: conditional disclosure of secrets (CDS) is known to capture a weaker version of PE called attribute-based encryption, and is related to several communication models including AM [4,5].

**Polynomial-size SYM ∘ SYM Circuits.** Here, SYM refers to the set of symmetric Boolean functions (i.e. functions which only depend on the number of 1s in their input), and SYM ∘ SYM is the set of depth-2 circuits of SYM gates. This is a very expressive circuit class for which proving lower bounds is a notoriously open problem (the best known lower bounds are only against quadratic size SYM ∘ SYM circuits; see e.g. [1]).

It includes, as a simple example, for any $0 \leq k \leq n$, the function which on input $x, y \in \{0,1\}^n$ tests whether the Hamming distance from $x$ to $y$ is at most $k$. It is known that the one-sided rank of this function, as well as the usual probabilistic rank of this function, must be exponential in $n$ [3,8], but we show that its one-sided probabilistic rank is only poly($n$). PE for this function can be thought of as PE for the 'approximately equal' function, and thus generalizes Identity-Based Encryption [9]. This is applicable, for example, in *approximate matching* for online dating [17], where users may want to find other users that are sufficiently similar to their target profile.

Interestingly, our one-sided probabilistic rank construction for SYM ∘ SYM circuits seemingly cannot be converted into an AM communication protocol, ostensibly showing that one-sided probabilistic rank is a more expressive notion than just AM communication (although, as mentioned, no $\omega(\log n)$ AM communication lower bound is known for SYM ∘ SYM).

**Constant-size, polynomial fan-in AND-OR circuits of low one-sided probabilistic rank functions.** It is not hard to see that one can construct PE for the OR of polynomially many functions for which PE is already known (one way is to simultaneously use an independent copy of the PE scheme for each function). We show that if the functions have PE because they have low one-sided probabilistic rank (such as in the examples above), then one may use any constant-size AND-OR circuit with polynomial fan-in gates rather than just a single OR gate. (There are some additional properties we require of the low one-sided probabilistic rank functions; see Sect. 3.5 for more details.)

Finally, we show that for $m \leq$ poly($n$), **functions with low one-sided probabilistic rank over $\mathbb{Z}_m$ also have low one-sided probabilistic rank over any ring of sufficiently large characteristic.** Known bilinear maps-based constructions of PE for inner product, including the aforementioned construction by [20], only seem to work over $\mathbb{Z}_M$ for $M > n^{\omega(1)}$. It is thus not evident, a priori, that low one-sided probabilistic rank expressions over, say, $\mathbb{F}_2$, lead to PE via our construction. We nonetheless show that such a low rank expression over $\mathbb{F}_2$, or any $\mathbb{Z}_m$ for $m \leq$ poly($n$), also leads to one over $\mathbb{Z}_M$, and hence to PE. This seems surprising: by comparison, many other notions of rank can change drastically depending on the underlying ring (e.g. [7,16]).

This construction implies, for instance, that we can construct PE for the inner product mod 2 given assumptions about bilinear maps, which was not previously known to the best of our knowledge.

## 1.4  Outline

In Sect. 2 we introduce the relevant notation and the formal notions of AM communication and PE we will be using. Then, in Sect. 3 we give our new one-sided probabilistic rank constructions, and in Sect. 4 we show how to construct PE using probabilistic one-sided rank and PE for inner product.

## 2    Preliminaries

### 2.1  Notation

For $n \in \mathbb{N}$, we write $[n]$ to denote the set $\{1, 2, \ldots, n\}$. For a $r$-dimensional vector $x$ and any $i \in [r]$, we write $x[i]$ for the $i$th entry of $x$. For an $r_1$-dimensional vector $x_1$ and an $r_2$-dimensional vector $x_2$, we write $x_1 \| x_2$ to denote the $(r_1 + r_2)$-dimensional vector resulting from concatenating the two. For a ring $\mathcal{R}$, $n \in \mathbb{N}$, and length-$n$ vectors $a, b \in \mathcal{R}^n$, we write $\langle a, b \rangle_{\mathcal{R}}$ for their inner product over $\mathcal{R}$, and we simply write $\langle a, b \rangle$ when the ring is clear from context. For $m \in \mathbb{N}$, we write $\mathbb{Z}_m$ for the ring of integers mod $m$, and if $m$ is a power of a prime, we write $\mathbb{F}_m$ to denote the finite field of order $m$.

A function $f : \mathbb{N} \to [0, 1]$ is *negligible* if it is smaller than any inverse polynomial, i.e. for any positive constant $c$, there is a $\Lambda > 0$ such that $f(\lambda) < \frac{1}{\lambda^c}$ for all $\lambda > \Lambda$.

### 2.2  Boolean Functions

For Boolean functions $f : \{0, 1\}^n \to \{0, 1\}$, we think of 0 as 'true' and 1 as 'false'. Hence, the function $\mathsf{AND}_n : \{0, 1\}^n \to \{0, 1\}$ has $\mathsf{AND}_n(x) = 1$ unless $x$ is all all-0s vector, in which case $\mathsf{AND}_n(x) = 0$, and $\mathsf{OR}_n : \{0, 1\}^n \to \{0, 1\}$ is defined similarly. For any $f : \{0, 1\}^n \to \{0, 1\}$, we write $\neg f$ for the function $\neg f : \{0, 1\}^n \to \{0, 1\}$ given by $\neg f(x) = 1 - f(x)$.

Define $\mathsf{EQ}_n, \mathsf{NEQ}_n : \{0, 1\}^{2n} \to \{0, 1\}$ by $\mathsf{EQ}_n(x, y) = 0$ if $x = y$ and $\mathsf{EQ}_n(x, y) = 1$ otherwise, and $\mathsf{NEQ}_n(x, y) = \neg\mathsf{EQ}_n(x, y)$. Further define $\mathsf{GEQ}_n : \{0, 1\}^{2n} \to \{0, 1\}$ by $\mathsf{GEQ}_n(x, y) = 0$ if $x \geq y$ when interpreted as binary representations of integers between 0 and $2^n - 1$, and $\mathsf{GEQ}_n(x, y) = 1$ otherwise.

A Boolean function $f : \{0, 1\}^n \to \{0, 1\}$ is *symmetric* if it only depends on the Hamming weight of its input, i.e. $f(x) = f(y)$ for any $x, y \in \{0, 1\}^n$ with $\sum_{i=1}^n x_i = \sum_{i=1}^n y_i$. We write $\mathsf{SYM}$ for the set of such functions. For $x, y \in \{0, 1\}^n$, write $\mathsf{HAM}(x, y)$ for the Hamming distance between $x$ and $y$.

For $k, n \in \mathbb{N}$, let $B_{n,k} \subseteq 2^{[n]}$ denote the set of subsets $X \subseteq [n]$ with size $|X| \leq k$. Define $\mathsf{DISJ}_{n,k} : B_{n,k} \times B_{n,k} \to \{0, 1\}$ by $\mathsf{DISJ}_{n,k}(X, Y) = 0$ if $|X \cap Y| = 0$ and $\mathsf{DISJ}_{n,k}(X, Y) = 1$ otherwise. Note that elements of $B_{n,k}$ can be described using only $k \log n$ bits.

## 2.3  AM Communication Protocols

An Efficient Arthur-Merlin Communication Protocol $\Pi$ with success probability $p$ for a Boolean function $f : \{0,1\}^{2n} \rightarrow \{0,1\}$ proceeds as follows:

1. Initially Alice has an input $x \in \{0,1\}^n$ and Bob has an input $y \in \{0,1\}^n$.
2. A uniformly random $z \in \{0,1\}^r$ for some $r \in \mathbb{N}$ is publicly sampled and given to Alice, Bob, and Merlin.
3. Merlin observes $x$, $y$, and $z$, and then selects a proof $\varphi \in \{0,1\}^t$ for some $t \in \mathbb{N}$, and sends $\varphi$ to both Alice and Bob.
4. Alice and Bob each look at $z$, $\varphi$, and their own input, and independently decide to accept or reject in deterministic polynomial time.

The communication cost of $\Pi$ is $t$. $\Pi$ is said to be correct for $f$ if for every $x, y \in \{0,1\}^n$:

- If $f(x,y) = 0$ then there is a $\varphi$ that Merlin can send to make both Alice and Bob accept no matter what $z$ is.
- If $f(x,y) = 1$ then with probability at least $p$ over the choice of $z$, there is no $\varphi$ which makes both Alice and Bob accept.

Past work using AM communication protocols has typically assumed that $p$ is a constant greater than 0; here we will be able to use the protocol to design a one-sided probabilistic rank expression in the much more powerful setting where we only require $p \geq 1/\text{poly}(n)$. One could amplify such a low $p$ to a constant by repetition, but this would increase $t$ by a factor which will be prohibitive in our constructions below.

## 2.4  Cryptographic Definitions

We now formally define the various notions of secure encryption we use. We follow the notation of [21].

**Secret-Key Predicate Encryption.** Let $\Sigma$ be a finite set, denoting the set of possible attributes; for our purposes, $\Sigma$ will typically be $\{0,1\}^n$. Let $f$ be a function $\Sigma \times \Sigma \rightarrow \{0,1\}$. We say that $x \in \Sigma$ satisfies a predicate $y \in \Sigma$ if $f(x,y) = 0$ (recall that 0 corresponds to 'true' and nonzero to 'false').

**Definition 1 (Secret-key predicate encryption).** A *secret-key predicate encryption (PE) scheme* for a function $f$ over the set of attributes $\Sigma$ consists of the following probabilistic polynomial time (PPT) algorithms.

Setup$(1^\lambda)$ : Takes as input a security parameter $1^\lambda$; outputs a secret key SK.
Enc$(SK, x, m)$ : Takes as input a secret key SK, an attribute $x \in \Sigma$, and a plaintext $m \in \{0,1\}$ and outputs a ciphertext CT.
KeyGen$(SK, y)$ : Takes as input a secret key SK and a predicate $y \in \Sigma$ and outputs a predicate key $SK_y$.

$\mathsf{Dec}(SK_y, CT)$ : Takes as input a predicate key $SK_y$ and a ciphertext CT (corresponding to attribute $x$ and plaintext $m$) and outputs a value in $\{0, 1, \perp\}$.

**Correctness.** For correctness, we require the following condition. For all $\lambda$, all $x \in \Sigma$, all $y \in \Sigma$, and all $m \in \{0, 1\}$, letting $SK \leftarrow \mathsf{Setup}(1^\lambda)$, $CT \leftarrow \mathsf{Enc}(SK, x, m)$, and $SK_y \leftarrow \mathsf{KeyGen}(SK, y)$:

- If $f(x, y) = 0$, then $\mathsf{Dec}(SK_y, CT) = m$ with all but negligible probability.
- If $f(x, y) = 1$, then $\mathsf{Dec}(SK_y, CT) = \perp$ with all but negligible probability.

We further define *partial* correctness as the same, except that in the case $f(x, y) = 0$, we only require that $\mathsf{Dec}(SK_y, CT) = m$ with at least $1/\mathrm{poly}(\lambda)$ (a much smaller probability), and $\mathsf{Dec}(SK_y, CT) = 1 - m$ with negligible probability (and otherwise $\mathsf{Dec}(SK_y, CT) = \perp$).

**Security.** We define security using the following game between an adversary $\mathcal{A}$ and a challenger.

**Setup:** The challenger runs $\mathsf{Setup}(1^\lambda)$ and keeps $SK$ to itself. The challenger chooses a random bit $b$.

**Queries:** $\mathcal{A}$ adaptively makes two types of queries:
- Ciphertext query. $\mathcal{A}$ submits attributes $x_i^0, x_i^1$ and messages $m_i^0, m_i^1$ and receives $CT_i \leftarrow \mathsf{Enc}(SK, x_i^b, m_i^b)$.
- Secret key query. $\mathcal{A}$ submits a predicate $y_j$ and receives $SK_{y_j} \leftarrow \mathsf{KeyGen}(SK, y_j)$.

These queries are subject to the restriction that for every $i, j$, $f(x_i^0, y_j) = f(x_i^1, y_j) = 1$.

**Guess:** $\mathcal{A}$ outputs a guess $b'$ of $b$.

The advantage of $\mathcal{A}$ is defined as $\mathrm{Adv}_\mathcal{A} = |\Pr[b' = b] - \frac{1}{2}|$.

A PE scheme is *secure* if, for all PPT adversaries $\mathcal{A}$, the advantage of $\mathcal{A}$ in winning the above game is negligible in $\lambda$.

*Remark 1.* A secure PE scheme that achieves the partial correctness definition described above can be generically transformed into a secure PE scheme with full correctness. By repeating the scheme $\mathrm{poly}(\lambda)$ times and taking the first non-$\perp$ result, the output is equal to $m$ with all but negligible probability. By a straightforward hybrid argument (with $\mathrm{poly}(\lambda)$ hybrids, where the $i$-th hybrid has $i - 1$ copies of the scheme hardcoded to 0, then one real copy of the scheme, then the rest hardcoded to 1), this will not affect security. See Appendix C for the full proof of this fact.

In light of this remark, in our proof we will only prove partial correctness. Similarly, although we consider the message here to be a single bit, we can replicate the scheme in order to allow arbitrary bitstrings as the message.

**Predicate Encryption for Inner Products** We will refer to the special case of predicate encryption for inner products as *inner product encryption*, or IPE. For any ring $\mathcal{R}$ and integer $n \in \mathbb{N}$, predicate encryption for inner products will be over the set of attributes $\mathcal{R}^n$, and the function $f$ will be the inner-product zero-testing function: if $\langle x, y \rangle = 0$ then $f(x, y) = 0$, and otherwise $f(x, y) = \bot$.

We note that we define PE (and hence IPE) that is not predicate-hiding (i.e. the key $K_y$ reveals the predicate $y$). In fact, we either need the IPE scheme to be predicate-hiding, or else that the probabilistic rank expression never output 0 in the $f(x, y) = 1$ case, for the full security of our construction; see the full version (https://eprint.iacr.org/2019/1045) for more details.

# 3  One-Sided Probabilistic Rank

## 3.1  Definitions

We begin by introducing the new notion of one-sided probabilistic rank which we will use in this paper. Most of our results in this section will hold over arbitrary rings $\mathcal{R}$ (often with a restriction on the characteristic of $\mathcal{R}$), although we will only need them in the case when $\mathcal{R} = \mathbb{Z}_m$ is the ring of integers mod $m$ in our application to PE below.

For positive integers $n, d$, values $p_1, p_2 \in [0, 1]$, ring $\mathcal{R}$, and a Boolean function $f : \{0, 1\}^{2n} \to \{0, 1\}$, we say $f$ has *Efficient $(p_1, p_2)$-Probabilistic Rank $d$ over $\mathcal{R}$* (or for short we will write "$(p_1, p_2)$-rank $d$ over $\mathcal{R}$" and sometimes omit $\mathcal{R}$ when it is clear from context) if there is a joint distribution $\mathcal{D}$ on pairs of functions $g, h : \{0, 1\}^n \to \mathcal{R}^d$ such that:

- $g$ and $h$ can be sampled from $\mathcal{D}$ and evaluated in poly$(nd)$ time,
- all $x, y \in \{0, 1\}^n$ with $f(x, y) = 0$ have $\Pr_{(g,h) \sim \mathcal{D}}[\langle g(x), h(y) \rangle = 0] \geq p_1$, and
- all $x, y \in \{0, 1\}^n$ with $f(x, y) = 1$ have $\Pr_{(g,h) \sim \mathcal{D}}[\langle g(x), h(y) \rangle = 0] \leq p_2$.

If $\{f_n\}_{n \in \mathbb{N}}$ is a family of Boolean functions with $f_n : \{0, 1\}^{2n} \to \{0, 1\}$, $\lambda : \mathbb{N} \to \mathbb{N}$ is any function, and $\mathcal{R}$ is any ring, we say $\{f_n\}_{n \in \mathbb{N}}$ has *Efficient One-sided Probabilistic Rank $\lambda$ over $\mathcal{R}$* if there are functions $p_1, p_2 : \mathbb{N} \to [0, 1]$ and $d : \mathbb{N} \to \mathbb{N}$ such that for all $n$, $f_n$ has $(p_1(n), p_2(n))$-rank $d(n)$ over $\mathcal{R}$, where

- $d(n) \leq \text{poly}(\lambda(n))$,
- $p_1(n) \geq 1/\text{poly}(\lambda(n))$, and
- $p_2(n) \leq \text{negl}(\lambda(n))$.

## 3.2  Construction from **AM** Communication Protocols

We now show that a number of functions $f : \{0, 1\}^{2n} \to \{0, 1\}$ of interest have efficient one-sided probabilistic rank poly$(n)$. We begin by showing this for any function whose co-AM communication complexity is $O(\log n)$:

**Lemma 1.** For any $n, t \in \mathbb{N}$, any $p \in [0, 1]$, any Boolean function $f : \{0, 1\}^{2n} \to \{0, 1\}$ such that $\neg f$ has an Arthur-Merlin communication protocol $\Pi$ with communication $t$ and success probability $p$, and any ring $\mathcal{R}$ of characteristic greater than $2^t$, the function $f$ has $(p, 0)$-rank at most $2^t$ over $\mathcal{R}$.

*Proof.* Our randomized construction of the required maps $g, h : \{0,1\}^n \to \mathcal{R}^{2^t}$ proceeds as follows. First, sample a uniformly random $z \in \{0,1\}^r$ (where $r$ is the length of the random string from $\Pi$). Then, for $x \in \{0,1\}^n$, the vector $g(x)$, whose $2^t$ entries are indexed by $\varphi \in \{0,1\}^t$, is given by:

$$g(x)[\varphi] := \begin{cases} 1 & \text{if Alice accepts in } \Pi \text{ on input } x, \text{ randomness } z, \text{ and proof } \varphi, \\ 0 & \text{otherwise.} \end{cases}$$

Similarly, for $y \in \{0,1\}^n$,

$$h(y)[\varphi] := \begin{cases} 1 & \text{if Bob accepts in } \Pi \text{ on input } y, \text{ randomness } z, \text{ and proof } \varphi, \\ 0 & \text{otherwise.} \end{cases}$$

Since Alice and Bob must make decisions in polynomial time in the definition of $\Pi$, these maps $g$ and $h$ can also be computed in polynomial time.

Now, for a given $x, y \in \{0,1\}^n$, the inner product $\langle g(x), h(y) \rangle$ counts the number of proofs $\varphi \in \{0,1\}^t$ that Alice and Bob would both accept given inputs $x, y$ and randomness $z$. If $f(x,y) = 0$, then since $\Pi$ has correctness $p$ for $\neg f$, there is no such $\varphi$, and hence $\langle g(x), h(y) \rangle = 0$, with probability at least $p$. If $f(x,y) = 1$, then there is always such a $\varphi$, and so $\langle g(x), h(y) \rangle \in \{1, 2, \ldots, 2^t\}$, which is always nonzero since the characteristic of $\mathcal{R}$ is greater than $2^t$.    □

Using Lemma 1, we can construct low one-sided probabilistic rank expressions for many functions of interest. Some examples include:

**Lemma 2 (GREATER THAN OR EQUALS).** For any $n \in \mathbb{N}$ and ring $\mathcal{R}$ with characteristic at least $n + 1$, and any $\varepsilon > 0$, $\mathsf{GEQ}_n$ has $(1 - \varepsilon, 0)$-rank $O(n^2/\varepsilon)$ over $\mathcal{R}$.

**Lemma 3 (SPARSE DISJOINTNESS).** For any $n, k \in \mathbb{N}$ and ring $\mathcal{R}$ with characteristic at least $k+1$, and any $\varepsilon > 0$, the function $\mathsf{DISJ}_{n,k}$ has $(1-\varepsilon, 0)$-rank $O(k^2/\varepsilon)$ over $\mathcal{R}$.

In Appendix A below, we give the AM communication protocols which prove these results when combined with Lemma 1.

### 3.3    Circuits of SYM Gates

We first use a technique from [23] for exactly representing SYM gates.

**Lemma 4.** For every $n \in \mathbb{N}$, every symmetric Boolean function $f : \{0,1\}^{2n} \to \{0,1\}$, and every ring $\mathcal{R}$, there are maps $g, h : \{0,1\}^n \to \mathcal{R}^{n+1}$ which can be computed in polynomial time, such that $\langle g(x), h(y) \rangle = f(x,y)$ for all $x, y \in \{0,1\}^n$.

*Proof.* Let $w : \{0,1\}^n \to \mathbb{Z}$ be the function which counts the number of 1s in its input, i.e. $w(x) = x[1] + \cdots + x[n]$. There is a set $S \subseteq \{0, 1, \ldots, 2n\}$ such that $f(x,y) = 1$ if and only if $w(x) + w(y) \in S$. We define $g$ and $h$ as follows, for $i \in [n+1]$:

$$g(x)[i] := \begin{cases} 1 & \text{if } w(x) = i - 1, \\ 0 & \text{otherwise,} \end{cases}$$

$$h(y)[i] := \begin{cases} 1 & \text{if } w(y) + i - 1 \in S, \\ 0 & \text{otherwise.} \end{cases}$$

In other words, $g(x)$ is 0 in every entry except 1 in a single entry, and $h(y)$ has a 1 in that entry if $f(x,y) = 1$ and a 0 otherwise. Hence, $\langle g(x), h(y) \rangle = f(x,y)$ for all $x, y \in \{0,1\}^n$. $\qquad\square$

**Lemma 5 (SYM ∘ SYM circuits).** Any function $f : \{0,1\}^{2n} \to \{0,1\}$ which can be written as a depth-2 circuit of SYM gates, with $m$ gates in the bottom layer, has $(1/m, 0)$-rank at most $nm + m + 1$ over any ring $\mathcal{R}$ of characteristic at least $m + 1$.

*Proof.* Let $p : \{0,1\}^m \to \{0,1\}$ be the symmetric function computed by the top gate, and let $S \subseteq \{0, \ldots, m\}$ be the set such that, for $z \in \{0,1\}^m$, $p(z) = 0$ if and only if $z[1] + \cdots + z[m] \in S$. For each $i \in [m]$, let $g_i, h_i : \{0,1\}^{2n} \to \mathcal{R}^{n+1}$ be the maps from Lemma 4 which exactly compute the $i$th SYM gate in the bottom layer of the circuit for $f$.

We now define the probabilistic rank expression for $f$. Pick a uniformly random $k \in S$. The rank expressions $g, h : \{0,1\}^n \to \mathcal{R}^{nm+1}$ are given by $g(x) = g_1(x)||g_2(x)|| \cdots ||g_m(x)||(1)$, and $h(y) = h_1(y)||h_2(y)|| \cdots ||h_m(y)||(-k)$. Hence,

$$\langle g(x), h(y) \rangle = \left( \sum_{i=1}^{m} \langle g_i(x), h_i(y) \rangle \right) - k,$$

which is the number of bottom-layer gates satisfied by $x$ and $y$, minus $k$. Since $\mathcal{R}$ has characteristic at least $m + 1$, this equals 0 if and only if exactly $k$ of the bottom layer gates are satisfied by $x$ and $y$. It follows that when $f(x,y) = 1$ we always have $\langle g(x), h(y) \rangle \neq 0$, and when $f(x,y) = 0$ we have $\langle g(x), h(y) \rangle = 0$ with probability $1/|S| \geq 1/m$, which happens when we pick the correct $k$. $\qquad\square$

**Corollary 1.** For any positive integer $n$, any map $p : \{0, 1, \ldots, n\} \to \{0,1\}$, and any ring $\mathcal{R}$ of characteristic at least $2n + 1$, the function $s : \{0,1\}^{2n} \to \{0,1\}$ given by $s(x,y) = p(\mathsf{HAM}(x,y))$ has $(1/n, 0)$-rank $O(n)$ over $\mathcal{R}$.

*Proof.* The function $s$ is of the form described by Lemma 5, where $m = n$, and the $i$th bottom layer gate is 1 if $x[i] \neq y[i]$ (equivalently, $x[i] + y[i] \in \{1\}$) and 0 otherwise. $\qquad\square$

## 3.4   Inner Products in Small Fields

We next show that one-sided probabilistic rank constructions over $\mathbb{Z}_m$ for $m \leq \text{poly}(\lambda)$ lead to one-sided probabilistic rank constructions over any ring of sufficiently large characteristic, with only a polynomial change in the error probabilities. This will be helpful in constructing PE later, since the known bilinear maps-based constructions of PE for inner products only work for certain rings of large characteristic.

**Lemma 6.** For any $m, d \in \mathbb{N}$ and $p_1, p_2 \in [0, 1]$, suppose $f : \{0,1\}^{2n} \to \{0,1\}$ is a Boolean function with $(p_1, p_2)$-rank $d$ over $\mathbb{Z}_m$. Then, $f$ also has $(p_1/(dm), p_2/(dm))$-rank $d + 1$ over any ring $\mathcal{R}$ of characteristic greater than $d(m-1)^2$.

*Proof.* Draw $g', h' : \{0,1\}^n \to \mathbb{Z}_m^d$ from the one-sided probabilistic rank expression over $\mathbb{Z}_m$. Interpreting $\mathbb{Z}_m$ as the set of integers $\{0, 1, 2, \ldots, m-1\} \subseteq \mathbb{Z}$, we have for any $x, y$ that $\langle g'(x), h'(y) \rangle_{\mathbb{Z}}$ is an integer in $\{0, 1, 2, \ldots, d(m-1)^2\}$, such that $\langle g'(x), h'(y) \rangle_{\mathbb{Z}_m} = 0$ if and only if $\langle g'(x), h'(y) \rangle_{\mathbb{Z}}$ is an integer multiple of $m$. Letting $m' \in \mathbb{N}$ be the largest multiple of $m$ which is at most $d(m-1)^2$, it follows since $\mathcal{R}$ has characteristic greater than $d(m-1)^2$ that $\langle g'(x), h'(y) \rangle_{\mathbb{Z}_m} = 0$ if and only if $\langle g'(x), h'(y) \rangle_{\mathcal{R}}$ is in the set $M := \{0, m, 2m, 3m, \ldots, m'\}$, and otherwise $\langle g'(x), h'(y) \rangle_{\mathcal{R}}$ is in the set $\{0, 1, 2, \ldots, d(m-1)^2\} \setminus M$.

We thus pick a uniformly random $k \in M$ and output $g(x) = g'(x) || (-1)$ and $h(y) = h'(y) || (k)$. Thus, we will have $\langle g(x), h(y) \rangle_{\mathcal{R}} = 0$ if and only if $\langle g'(x), h'(y) \rangle_{\mathbb{Z}_m} = 0$ (which happens with probability $p_1$ or $p_2$ in the true and false cases, respectively) and we pick the correct $k \in M$ (which happens with probability $1/|M| \leq 1/(dm)$). $\qquad\square$

## 3.5   Small Circuits of Low One-Sided Probabilistic Rank Functions

We next give low one-sided probabilistic rank expressions for AND and OR, which can be combined to give such expressions for small AND-OR circuits.

**Lemma 7.** Suppose $f_1, \ldots, f_m : \{0,1\}^{2n} \to \{0,1\}$ are Boolean functions, each of which has $(p_1, p_2)$-rank $d$ over field $\mathbb{F}$. Then, the AND of these functions, $f_1 \wedge f_2 \wedge \cdots \wedge f_m$, has $(p_1^m, 1/|\mathbb{F}| + p_2)$-rank $dm$ over $\mathbb{F}$.

*Proof.* For each $i \in [m]$, we draw $g_i, h_i : \{0,1\}^n \to \mathcal{F}^d$ from the assumed probabilistic rank expression for $f_i$, and draw a uniformly random $\alpha_i \in \mathbb{F}$. We then output $g, h : \{0,1\}^n \to \mathcal{F}^{dm}$ given by $g(x) = \alpha_1 g_1(x) || \alpha_2 g_2(x) || \cdots || \alpha_m g_m(x)$ and $h(x) = \alpha_1 h_1(x) || \alpha_2 h_2(x) || \cdots || \alpha_m h_m(x)$. Hence, for $x, y \in \{0,1\}^n$ we have

$$\langle g(x), h(y) \rangle = \sum_{i=1}^{m} \alpha_i \langle g_i(x), h_i(y) \rangle.$$

First, suppose that $f_i(x, y) = 0$ for all $i$. Thus, with probability $p_1^m$, we have $\langle g_i(x), h_i(y) \rangle = 0$ for all $i$, and thus $\langle g(x), h(y) \rangle = 0$ as desired.

Second, suppose that there is an $i$ such that $f_i(x, y) = 1$. Then in particular, $\langle g_i(x), h_i(y) \rangle \neq 0$ with probability at least $1 - p_2$. If it is nonzero, then $\langle g(x), h(y) \rangle$ is a sum of a positive number of uniformly random elements of $\mathbb{F}$, and so it is 0 with probability $1/|\mathbb{F}|$. In total, it is 0 with probability at most $1/|\mathbb{F}| + p_2$.    □

*Remark 2.* Although Lemma 7 only yields an efficient one-sided probabilistic rank $\lambda$ expression when $|\mathbb{F}|$ is superpolynomial in $\lambda$, we can assume this without loss of generality by first applying Lemma 6 to increase $|\mathbb{F}|$.

**Lemma 8.** Suppose $f_1, \ldots, f_m : \{0,1\}^{2n} \to \{0,1\}$ are Boolean functions, each of which has $(p_1, p_2)$-rank $d$ over ring $\mathcal{R}$. Then, the OR of these functions, $f_1 \vee f_2 \vee \cdots \vee f_m$, has $(p_1/m, p_2)$-rank $d$ over $\mathcal{R}$.

*Proof.* We draw a uniformly random $i^* \in [m]$, then draw $f_{i^*}, g_{i^*} : \{0,1\}^n \to \mathcal{F}^d$ from the assumed probabilistic rank expression for $f_{i^*}$, and simply output $g(x) = g_{i^*}(x)$ and $h(y) = h_{i^*}(y)$.

First, suppose there is an $i \in [m]$ such that $f_i(x, y) = 0$. Then, there is a $1/m$ probability that we select $i^* = i$, and a $p_1$ probability that $\langle g_i(x), h_i(y) \rangle = 0$, so there is at least a $p_1/m$ probability that $\langle g(x), h(y) \rangle = 0$.

Second, suppose that $f_i(x, y) = 1$ for all $i \in [m]$. Then, for whichever $i^*$ we pick, there is a $1 - p_2$ probability that $\langle g_{i^*}(x), h_{i^*}(y) \rangle \neq 0$, and so there is at most a $p_2$ probability that $\langle f(x), g(y) \rangle = 0$.    □

We can construct one-sided probabilistic rank expressions for many simple circuits by applying Lemmas 7 and 8 to all the AND and OR gates. To give two examples:

**Corollary 2.** Suppose there is a constant $c$ and Boolean functions $f_1, \ldots, f_c : \{0,1\}^{2n} \to \{0,1\}$ which all have efficient one-sided probabilistic rank $\lambda$ over a field $\mathbb{F}$ with $|\mathbb{F}| > \lambda^{\omega(1)}$. Then, any constant-sized AND-OR circuit with the $f_i$ as input also has $\lambda$-efficient one-sided probabilistic rank over $\mathbb{F}$.

**Corollary 3.** For any $m = \text{poly}(n)$, let $f_1, \ldots, f_m : \{0,1\}^{2n} \to \{0,1\}$ be any functions whose $(1 - 1/2m, 0)$-rank is $\text{poly}(n)$ over a field $\mathbb{F}$ with $|\mathbb{F}| > n^{\omega(1)}$. Then, any constant-sized AND-OR circuit, with unbounded fan-in AND and OR gates in the bottom layer, and with the $f_i$ as input, has $(1/n)$-efficient one-sided probabilistic rank over $\mathbb{F}$.

*Remark 3.* Recall from Lemma 2 that Corollary 3 applies when the $f_i$ are GEQ on subsets of the input bits.

## 4    Predicate Encryption Construction

We now construct secret-key predicate encryption for functions $f$ with Efficient One-sided Probabilistic Rank $\lambda$ (see the definition in Sect. 3.1). We will use inner product encryption as described in Sect. 2.4.

We will assume that our rank expression works over any $\mathbb{Z}_p$ with prime $p > \lambda^{\omega(1)}$,[3] and that the underlying inner product encryption takes inner products over one such $\mathbb{Z}_p$. Most constructions of inner product encryption, including the one we make use of below in Corollary 4, take the inner product over $\mathbb{Z}_M$, where either $M$ is itself a large prime, or else a product of a constant number of large primes, e.g. $M = pqr$, which contains $\mathbb{Z}_p$ as a subfield.

**Theorem 2.** Assuming a secure inner product encryption scheme (as described above), there is a secret-key predicate encryption scheme for any Boolean function $f$ with efficient one-sided probabilistic rank $\lambda$ (the time and space complexity of the PE scheme is polynomial in $\lambda$).

### 4.1   Construction

We now describe our construction for Theorem 2.

Let $g, h \leftarrow \mathcal{D}$ be functions sampled from the joint distribution $\mathcal{D}$ in the definition of one-sided probabilistic rank, in Sect. 3.1. In our construction, we only require a *predicate-only* IPE scheme, and as such we will always set the message $m$ to 0 in IPE.Enc$(SK, x, m)$.

---

**Setup$(1^\lambda)$:** The setup algorithm runs IPE.Setup$(1^\lambda)$ twice, one scheme for vectors of length $\lambda$ and one for vectors of length $\lambda + 1$, to get secret keys sk and sk$'$ respectively. It outputs

$$SK = (\text{sk}, \text{sk}').$$

**Enc$(SK, x, m)$:** The encryption algorithm outputs

$$CT = \big(\text{IPE.Enc}(\text{sk}, g(x), 0), \text{IPE.Enc}(\text{sk}', g(x)\|m, 0)\big).$$

**KeyGen$(SK, y)$:** The key generation algorithm outputs

$$SK_y = \big(\text{IPE.KeyGen}(\text{sk}, h(y)), \text{IPE.KeyGen}(\text{sk}', h(y)\|1)\big).$$

**Dec$(SK_y, CT)$:** The decryption algorithm takes $CT = (c_1, c_2)$ and $SK_y = (k_1, k_2)$ and runs IPE.Dec$(c_1, k_1)$. If this is $\bot$, then it outputs $\bot$. Otherwise, if IPE.Dec$(c_2, k_2) = 0$ it outputs 0, and if IPE.Dec$(c_2, k_2) = \bot$ it outputs 1.

---

**Fig. 1.** Predicate encryption construction

We prove correctness and security in the following subsections.

### 4.2   Proof of Correctness

Recall (from Remark 1) that it suffices to prove *partial* correctness, and then amplify to achieve all but negligible correctness.

---

[3] Recall that all our constructions above have this property, and that one can assume it without loss of generality by applying Lemma 6.

**Lemma 9.** The scheme in Sect. 4.1 achieves partial correctness.

*Proof.* Let $CT = (c_1, c_2)$ and $SK_y = (k_1, k_2)$ be as above.

- Suppose $f(x, y) = 1$. Then by the definition of $g, h$, $\langle g(x), h(y) \rangle \neq 0$ with all but negligible probability, and thus by the correctness of IPE, we have IPE.Dec$(c_1, k_1) = \bot$ and Dec$(SK_y, CT) = \bot$ as desired.
- Suppose $f(x, y) = 0$. Then by the definition of $g, h$, $\langle g(x), h(y) \rangle = 0$ with probability at least $1/\text{poly}(\lambda(n))$. In this case, IPE.Dec$(c_1, k_1) = 0$ and Dec$(SK_y, CT)$ proceeds to check IPE.Dec$(c_2, k_2)$. Then $\langle g(x)||m, h(y)||1 \rangle = 0 + m = m$ and hence, if $m = 0$, IPE.Dec$(c_2, k_2) = 0$ and Dec$(SK_y, CT) = 0$, and if $m = 1$, IPE.Dec$(c_2, k_2) = \bot$ and Dec$(SK_y, CT) = 1$. Thus Dec$(SK_y, CT) = m$, except when the decryption algorithm outputs $\bot$.

Therefore, in both cases, we satisfy the correctness requirement.     $\square$

## 4.3   Proof of Security

The security proof is given in Appendix B below.

## 4.4   Combining with Bilinear Maps

We have now proven Theorem 2. We can thus construct a predicate encryption scheme directly using an assumption on bilinear maps, the $n$-eDDH assumption (an extension of the bilinear decisional Diffie-Hellman assumption; see [20, Section 3.3] for more details), to instantiate the IPE scheme.

Although we use the construction of [20] in a completely black-box way and the details therefore do not impact our proofs, we will describe the basic idea here. A typical assumption describes three groups $\mathcal{G}_1, \mathcal{G}_2, \mathcal{G}_T$ and corresponding generators $g_1, g_2, g_T$ (not to be confused with the function $g$ elsewhere in this paper), as well as the bilinear map itself, a public function $e(g_1^x, g_2^y) = g_T^{xy}$. The assumption is that discrete log is hard in these groups, so that the exponents $x, y$ are hidden, *except* that the map allows an exponent in the first group to be multiplied with an exponent in the second group. The resulting elements of $g_T$ can then be multiplied to produce $g_T^{x_1 y_1 + x_2 y_2 + \ldots + x_n y_n}$, computing the inner product in the exponent, and if the exponent is zero this value will be equal to 1. Of course, this simple explanation is not secure, and the construction involves more details that we omit here.

**Corollary 4.** If the $n$-eDDH assumption holds, there is a secret-key predicate encryption scheme for any Boolean function $f$ with efficient one-sided probabilistic rank $\lambda$.

*Proof.* We can use the $n$-eDDH assumption to construct a fully secure inner product encryption scheme following [20], then apply Theorem 2 to construct the predicate encryption scheme.     $\square$

## 5    Conclusion

A natural question is whether this approach can be extended to the stronger notion of functional encryption (FE), where the attributes are hidden *even when the user can decrypt*. At first glance, our scheme seems to offer such a guarantee, as it only reveals the inner product and not the vectors $g(x), h(y)$. However, the inner products from one-sided probabilistic rank have an error probability, and those errors are necessarily correlated, so that an adversary observing a certain error pattern can make inferences about which $x, y$ pairs are consistent with that pattern. Furthermore, such an extension could be quite strong. FE for the greater-than function, also known as order-revealing encryption (ORE), is a desirable primitive and has potential applications beyond crypto [11, 19]; however, it is not known to be constructible using bilinear maps or any other standard cryptographic assumptions. An extension to FE would also allow surprising constructions if combined with degree-2 PRGs over $\mathbb{F}_2$.

One may hope to get around this possibility by designing probabilistic rank expressions whose error probability is negligible both when $f(x, y) = 0$ and when $f(x, y) = 1$. However, one can see that such a probabilistic rank expression could be used to construct a one-sided (deterministic) rank expression for $f$ with only a polynomial blow-up in the rank. It is known that many functions of interest, including GEQ, do not have such rank expressions, so for these functions, probabilistic rank expressions with negligible error are also impossible.

Another question is whether our approach can support rank expressions with polynomial error on both sides, such as those considered in Bauer et al. [8]. For example, if $f(x, y) = 0$ then $\langle g(x), h(y) \rangle = 0$ with probability at least $2/3$, and otherwise with probability at most $1/3$. One idea for attempting to use such an expression is to secret-share the message, making $2m$ shares where $m$ are required to decrypt, and then instantiate $2m$ distinct PE schemes to encrypt each share. However, if the adversary has multiple keys (none of which are authorized to decrypt $x$), she could try decrypting a share with each key, and decrypt any particular share with high probability (since any key works on any share with probability $1/3$).

**Acknowledgements.** We would like to thank Akshay Degwekar, Alex Lombardi, Dylan McKay, Hoeteck Wee, Lijie Chen, Lisa Yang, Prabhanjan Ananth, Ryan Williams, and Vinod Vaikuntanathan for useful discussions throughout this project, and anonymous reviewers for a number of helpful suggestions.

## A    AM Communication Protocols

We now present the aforementioned AM communication protocols, which can be combined with Lemma 1 to construct one-sided probabilistic rank expressions.

**Lemma 10 (EQUALITY).** For any $\varepsilon > 0$, there is an AM communication protocol for $\mathsf{EQ}_n$ with success probability $1 - \varepsilon$ and communication $O(\log(1/\varepsilon))$.

*Proof.* We use the well-known strategy for randomized communication protocols for EQ - simply hash the two inputs. Let $r = \lceil 1/\varepsilon \rceil$. Alice, Bob and Merlin use the public randomness to publicly pick a pairwise-independent random function $b : \{0,1\}^n \to [r]^4$. Merlin then sends a $\varphi \in [r]$, and Alice and Bob accept if $b(x) = \varphi$ and $b(y) = \varphi$, respectively.

For any $x, y \in \{0,1\}^n$, if $\mathsf{EQ}_n(x, y) = 0$, meaning $x = y$, then Merlin can send $\phi = b(x)$ and both Alice and Bob will accept. If $\mathsf{EQ}_n(x, y) \neq 0$, then the probability that $b(x) = b(y)$ is at most $1/r \leq \varepsilon$, and if this is not the case, there is no $\varphi$ that Merlin can send which both Alice and Bob would accept.
□

**Lemma 11 (GREATER-THAN-OR-EQUALS).** For any $\varepsilon > 0$, there is an AM communication protocol for $\neg\mathsf{GEQ}_n$ with success probability $1 - \varepsilon$ and communication $O(\log(n/\varepsilon))$.

*Proof.* Our construction is very similar to [3, Lemma D.2], and again uses a common strategy for communication protocols for GEQ. For $x \in \{0,1\}^n$, and $i \in \{0, 1, \ldots, n-1\}$, write $x[1 : i] \in \{0,1\}^i$ to denote the first $i$ entries of $x$. We use the following characterization of $\mathsf{GEQ}_n$: $\mathsf{GEQ}_n(x, y) = 1$ if and only if there is an $i \in [n]$ such that $y[i] = 1$, $x[i] = 0$, and $x[1 : i-1] = y[1 : i-1]$.

After the public randomness is sampled, Merlin sends an $i^* \in [n]$. Alice, Bob and Merlin then use the protocol from Lemma 10 with success probability $\varepsilon/n$ to test whether $x[1 : i^* - 1] = y[1 : i^* - 1]$. Alice accepts if this is the case and $x[i^*] = 0$; Bob accepts if this is the case and $y[i^*] = 1$.

For any $x, y \in \{0,1\}^n$, suppose first that $\mathsf{GEQ}_n(x, y) = 1$. Thus, Merlin can send the $i^* = i \in [n]$ such that $y[i] = 1$, $x[i] = 0$, and $x[1 : i-1] = y[1 : i-1]$. By Lemma 10, the equality test will always return that $x[1 : i-1] = y[1 : i-1]$, and so both will always accept.

Next, suppose $\mathsf{GEQ}_n(x, y) = 0$. Thus, for any $i^*$ that Merlin can send, there is at most a $\varepsilon/n$ probability that Merlin can send a proof in the protocol for Lemma 10 which will make Alice and Bob accept. By a union bound over all $n$ choices of $i$, there is at most an $\varepsilon$ probability that Merlin can send an $i^*$ and subsequent proof which will make Alice and Bob accept.
□

*Remark 4.* In general, for a Boolean function $f$, the two functions $f$ and $\neg f$ may have very different AM communication complexities. However, they are actually essentially equal for $f = \mathsf{GEQ}$ since $\neg\mathsf{GEQ}_n(x, y) = \mathsf{GEQ}_n(2^n - x, 2^n - 1 - y)$.

**Lemma 12 (SPARSE DISJOINTNESS).** For any $n, k \in \mathbb{N}$ and any $\varepsilon > 0$, there is an AM communication protocol for $\neg\mathsf{DISJ}_{n,k}$ with success probability $1 - \varepsilon$ and communication $O(\log(k/\varepsilon))$.

---

[4] There are standard constructions of such pairwise-independent functions which can be sampled and evaluated in polynomial time. For instance, we may pick uniformly random $c_1, c_2 \in \mathbb{F}_r$, and define $b(x) = c_1 x + c_2$.

*Proof.* Let $r = \lceil k^2/\varepsilon \rceil$. Similar to Lemma 10, Alice, Bob and Merlin first use the public randomness to publicly sample a random pairwise independent $b : [n] \to [r]$. Merlin then chooses a proof $\varphi \in [r]$ and sends it to both Alice and Bob. Alice accepts if there is an element of $x$ of her input $X$ with $b(x) = \varphi$, and Bob accepts if there is an element $y$ of his input $Y$ with $b(y) = \varphi$.

If $X$ and $Y$ are not disjoint, and both contain $c \in [n]$, then Merlin can send $\phi = b(c)$, and both Alice and Bob will always accept. If $X$ and $Y$ are disjoint, then for every pair $(x, y) \in X \times Y$, there is at most a $1/r$ probability that $b(x) = b(y)$. If this is not the case for all such pairs, which happens with probability at least $1 - k^2/r \geq 1 - \varepsilon$ by a union bound, then Merlin cannot send any message to make both Alice and Bob accept.     $\square$

*Remark 5.* The inputs to $\mathsf{DISJ}_{n,k}$ are bit-strings of length $O(k \log n)$. Lemmas 3 and 12 show that $\mathsf{DISJ}_{n,k}$ has poly($k$)-efficient one-sided probabilistic rank whenever $n \leq 2^{\mathrm{poly}(k)}$; note in particular that the rank is independent of $n$.

# B     Predicate Encryption Security Proof

We now present the proof of security for the predicate encryption scheme from Sect. 4.1.

*Remark 6.* We begin by making a small modification to our given probabilistic rank expression. Considering the $g, h$ corresponding to our function $f$, the definition of one-sided probabilistic rank guarantees that if $f(x, y) = 1$, then $\langle g(x), h(y) \rangle \neq 0$ with all but negligible probability. Our modification will ensure that also, $\langle g(x), h(y) \rangle \neq -1$ with all but negligible probability. Our modification is simple: we pick a uniformly random $r \in \mathbb{F}$ and replace $g$ with $g'(x) = rg(x)$. Thus, whenever $\langle g(x), h(y) \rangle \neq 0$, then $\langle g'(x), h(y) \rangle = r \cdot \langle g(x), h(y) \rangle$ is a uniformly random nonzero element of $\mathbb{F}$. Since $\mathbb{F}$ is superpolynomially large, this means it is $-1$ with only negligible probability.

**Lemma 13.** The scheme in Sect. 4.1 is secure.

*Proof.* Suppose towards a contradiction that an adversary $\mathcal{A}$ can win the PE security game with probability $1/2 + \varepsilon$. We will construct an adversary $\mathcal{A}'$ that wins the IPE security game with the same probability. $\mathcal{A}'$ will actually interact with two separate IPE challengers, with independently generated secret keys, with vectors of length $d$ and $d + 1$ respectively; by a hybrid argument, distinguishing the two combined instances also contradicts the IPE security guarantee. $\mathcal{A}'$ acts as the PE challenger to $\mathcal{A}$ and transforms each input query into two queries to the IPE challengers. The game proceeds as shown in Fig. 2.

First, we must prove that $\mathcal{A}'$ only outputs valid queries with all but negligible probability. Since $\mathcal{A}$ outputs only valid queries, for every $i, j$, we have $f(x_i^0, y_j) = f(x_i^1, y_j) = 1$. Then, since $g, h$ have one-sided error, with all but negligible probability, $\langle g(x), h(y) \rangle \neq 0$ and furthermore $\langle g(x), h(y) \rangle \neq -1$ (as described at the start of the proof). Therefore, for every $i, j$ and for $b \in \{0, 1\}$,

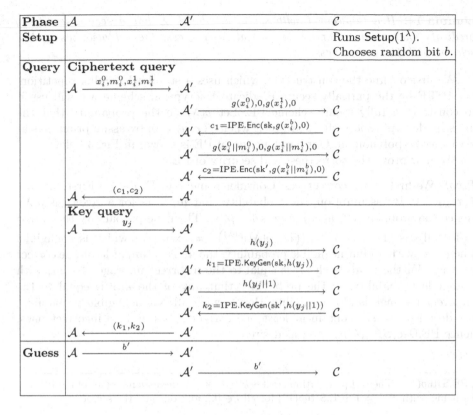

**Fig. 2.** IPE Security Game

$\langle g(x_i^b), h(y_j) \rangle \neq 0$ and $\langle g(x_i^b || b), h(y_j || 1) \rangle \neq 0$. That is, all of the inner products are nonzero, satisfying the IPE restriction. Now we prove that $\mathcal{A}'$ succeeds in the security game with almost the same probability as $\mathcal{A}$. $\mathcal{A}'$ responds to ciphertext query $x_i$ with $CT = \big(\mathsf{IPE.Enc}(\mathsf{sk}, g(x_i^b), 0), \mathsf{IPE.Enc}(\mathsf{sk}', g(x_i^b) || m_i^b), 0)\big)$, which is exactly the value $\mathsf{Enc}(SK, x_i^b, m_i^b)$ in the PE security game. Similarly, $\mathcal{A}'$ responds to secret key query $y_j$ with
$CT = \big(\mathsf{IPE.KeyGen}(\mathsf{sk}, g(y_j)), \mathsf{IPE.KeyGen}(\mathsf{sk}', g(y_j) || 1)\big)$, which is the value $\mathsf{KeyGen}(SK, y_j)$ in the PE security game. In other words, $\mathcal{A}$ is presented with the same interaction as in the real PE security game, and if it correctly guesses $b'$, then so does $\mathcal{A}$ in the IPE security game. The only case where $\mathcal{A}$ is correct but $\mathcal{A}'$ is not is the case when $\mathcal{A}'$ outputs an invalid query, which happens with negligible probability as described in the previous paragraph. Therefore, $\mathcal{A}'$ wins the IPE security game with non-negligible advantage, a contradiction.  □

# C    Partial Correctness to Full Correctness Proof

We now present the proof of security for Remark 1 in Sect. 2.4.

**Lemma 14.** *If a function $f$ with set of attributes $\Sigma$ has a secure secret-key predicate encryption scheme with partial correctness, then it also has such a scheme with full correctness.*

We first outline the construction, which uses a standard parallel repetition. Let PSPE be the partially secure Predicate Encryption scheme; we will use it to construct a fully secure scheme PE. Let $p(\lambda)$ be the probability that the message decrypts successfully in PSPE when $f(x, y) = 0$; by assumption, $p$ is at least inverse-polynomial. Our construction of PE is shown in Fig. 3 below.

We now prove the correctness and security of PE.

*Proof.* We first prove correctness. Consider some $x \in \Sigma, y \in \Sigma$. First suppose $f(x, y) = 0$. By assumption, the probability that $\tilde{m}_i = m$ for a given $i$ is $p(\lambda)$. Hence the probability that $\tilde{m}_i \neq m$ is $1 - p(\lambda)$. Then the probability that $\tilde{m}_i \neq m$ for all $i$ is $(1 - p(\lambda))^k = \left((1 - p(\lambda))^{p(\lambda)}\right)^\lambda = \exp(-\lambda)$, which is negligible. Therefore, with all but negligible probability, the $\tilde{m}_i$s contain at least one correct message. Furthermore, each $\tilde{m}_i$ is equal to the incorrect message $(1 - m)$ with negligible probability, so the probability that any of the $\tilde{m}_i$s is equal to the incorrect message is also negligible. Hence, with all but negligible probability, the decoded guesses contain at least one correct guess and no incorrect ones, hence $\text{PE.Dec}(SK_y, CT) = m$, as desired.

---

PE.Setup($1^\lambda$): The setup algorithm creates $k = \lambda \cdot p(\lambda)$ independent copies of the PSPE scheme, with $SK_i = \text{PSPE.Setup}(1^\lambda)$ for all $i \in [k]$, and outputs the secret key

$$SK \leftarrow (SK_1, \ldots, SK_k)$$

PE.Enc($SK, x, m$): The encryption algorithm takes the secret key $SK = (SK_1, \ldots, SK_k)$, attribute $x$, and plaintext $m$. It outputs a ciphertext

$$CT \leftarrow (\text{PE.Enc}(SK_1, x, m), \ldots, \text{PE.Enc}(SK_k, x, m))$$

PE.KeyGen($SK, y$): The key generation algorithm takes the secret key $SK = (SK_1, \ldots, SK_k)$ and outputs

$$SK_y \leftarrow (\text{PSPE.KeyGen}(SK_1, y), \ldots, \text{PSPE.KeyGen}(SK_k, y))$$

PE.Dec($SK_y, CT$): The decryption algorithm takes the predicate key $SK_y = (SK_{y,1}, \ldots, SK_{y,k})$ and a ciphertext $CT = (CT_1, \ldots, CT_k)$. It decrypts them to corresponding messages $\tilde{m}_i \leftarrow \text{PSPE.Dec}(SK_{y,i}, CT_i)$ for $i \in 1 \ldots k$. Then:

- If at least one $\tilde{m}_i$ is 0 and none are 1, it outputs 0.
- If at least one $\tilde{m}_i$ is 1 and none are 0, it outputs 1.
- Otherwise (if $\tilde{m}_i = \bot$ for every $i$, or there are both 0's and 1's), it outputs $\bot$.

---

**Fig. 3.** Fully correct predicate encryption construction.

Now suppose $f(x, y) = 1$. By assumption, PSPE.Dec$(SK_{y,i}, CT_i) = \bot$ with all but negligible probability. Hence with all but negligible probability, every one of the $\tilde{m}_i$s is equal to $\bot$ and therefore PE.Dec$(SK_y, CT)$ is also $\bot$, as desired.

Now we prove security. We construct a series of $k+1$ hybrids. The $l$-th hybrid proceeds as follows:

- The challenger runs PE.Setup$(1^\lambda)$ to produce $(SK_1, \ldots, SK_k)$ and chooses a random bit $b$.
- In a ciphertext query, the adversary $\mathcal{A}$ submits attributes $x_i^0, x_i^1$ and messages $m_i^0, m_i^1$ and receives

$$CT_i \leftarrow (\text{PSPE.Enc}(SK_1, x_i^0, m_i^0), \ldots, \text{PSPE.Enc}(SK_l, x_i^0, m_i^0),$$
$$\text{PSPE.Enc}(SK_{l+1}, x_i^1, m_i^1), \ldots, \text{PSPE.Enc}(SK_k, x_i^1, m_i^1) \quad (1)$$

- In a secret key query, the adversary $\mathcal{A}$ submits predicate $y_j$ and receives $SK_{y_j} \leftarrow \text{PE.KeyGen}(SK, y_j)$.
- After as many queries as desired, the adversary outputs a guess $b'$ of $b$.

Note that, when $l = 0$, this is the $b = 1$ case of the security game for PE, and when $l = k$, this is the $b = 0$ case. Hence, if an adversary $\mathcal{A}$ can win the security game for PE with non-negligible advantage, it distinguishes between two adjacent hybrids (say $l$ and $l + 1$) with non-negligible advantage. These two hybrids differ only in the $(l + 1)$-th index of the ciphertext query. Then we can create an adversary $\mathcal{A}'$ that wins the PSPE security game: it samples $SK_1, \ldots, SK_l, SK_{l+2}, \ldots, SK_k$, then answers queries using those keys and querying its own challenger in order to receive PSPE.Enc$(SK_{l+1}, x_i^b, m_i^b)$ and PSPE.KeyGen$(SK_{l+1}, y_j)$ as needed. The cases $b = 1$ and $b = 0$ correspond exactly to hybrids $l$ and $l + 1$ respectively, hence $\mathcal{A}'$ wins the security game with non-negligible advantage, a contradiction.  □

# References

1. Alman, J., Chan, T.M., Williams, R.: Polynomial representations of threshold functions and algorithmic applications. In: 57th Annual Symposium on Foundations of Computer Science (FOCS), pp. 467–476. IEEE (2016)
2. Alman, J., Chen, L.: Efficient construction of rigid matrices using an NP oracle. In: 60th Annual Symposium on Foundations of Computer Science (FOCS). IEEE (2019)
3. Alman, J., Williams, R.: Probabilistic rank and matrix rigidity. In: Proceedings of the 49th Annual ACM SIGACT Symposium on Theory of Computing, pp. 641–652. ACM (2017)
4. Applebaum, B., Raykov, P.: From private simultaneous messages to zero-information arthur-merlin protocols and back. J. Cryptology **30**(4), 961–988 (2017)
5. Applebaum, B., Vasudevan, P.N.: Placing conditional disclosure of secrets in the communication complexity universe. In: 10th Innovations in Theoretical Computer Science Conference (ITCS 2019). Schloss Dagstuhl-Leibniz-Zentrum fuer Informatik (2018)

6. Babai, L., Frankl, P., Simon, J.: Complexity classes in communication complexity theory. In: 27th Annual Symposium on Foundations of Computer Science (sfcs 1986), pp. 337–347. IEEE (1986)
7. Barrington, D.A.M., Beigel, R., Rudich, S.: Representing boolean functions as polynomials modulo composite numbers. Comput. Complex. **4**(4), 367–382 (1994)
8. Bauer, B., Vihrovs, J., Wee, H.: On the inner product predicate and a generalization of matching vector families. In: 38th IARCS Annual Conference on Foundations of Software Technology and Theoretical Computer Science (FSTTCS 2018). Schloss Dagstuhl-Leibniz-Zentrum fuer Informatik (2018)
9. Boneh, D., Franklin, M.: Identity-based encryption from the weil pairing. In: Kilian, J. (ed.) CRYPTO 2001. LNCS, vol. 2139, pp. 213–229. Springer, Heidelberg (2001). https://doi.org/10.1007/3-540-44647-8_13
10. Boneh, D., Waters, B.: Conjunctive, subset, and range queries on encrypted data. In: Vadhan, S.P. (ed.) TCC 2007. LNCS, vol. 4392, pp. 535–554. Springer, Heidelberg (2007). https://doi.org/10.1007/978-3-540-70936-7_29
11. Bun, M., Zhandry, M.: Order-revealing encryption and the hardness of private learning. In: Kushilevitz, E., Malkin, T. (eds.) TCC 2016. LNCS, vol. 9562, pp. 176–206. Springer, Heidelberg (2016). https://doi.org/10.1007/978-3-662-49096-9_8
12. Chen, L., Wang, R.: Classical algorithms from quantum and arthur-merlin communication protocols. In: 10th Innovations in Theoretical Computer Science (2019)
13. Garg, S., Gentry, C., Halevi, S., Raykova, M., Sahai, A., Waters, B.: Candidate indistinguishability obfuscation and functional encryption for all circuits. SIAM J. Comput. **45**(3), 882–929 (2016)
14. Göös, M., Pitassi, T., Watson, T.: The landscape of communication complexity classes. Comput. Complex. **27**(2), 245–304 (2015). https://doi.org/10.1007/s00037-018-0166-6
15. Göös, M., Pitassi, T., Watson, T.: Zero-information protocols and unambiguity in arthur-merlin communication. Algorithmica **76**(3), 684–719 (2016)
16. Gopalan, P., Shpilka, A., Lovett, S.: The complexity of boolean functions in different characteristics. Comput. Complex. **19**(2), 235–263 (2010)
17. Gorbunov, S., Vaikuntanathan, V., Wee, H.: Predicate encryption for circuits from LWE. In: Gennaro, R., Robshaw, M. (eds.) CRYPTO 2015. LNCS, vol. 9216, pp. 503–523. Springer, Heidelberg (2015). https://doi.org/10.1007/978-3-662-48000-7_25
18. Katz, J., Sahai, A., Waters, B.: Predicate encryption supporting disjunctions, polynomial equations, and inner products. In: Smart, N. (ed.) EUROCRYPT 2008. LNCS, vol. 4965, pp. 146–162. Springer, Heidelberg (2008). https://doi.org/10.1007/978-3-540-78967-3_9
19. Lewi, K., Wu, D.J.: Order-revealing encryption: new constructions, applications, and lower bounds. In: Proceedings of the 2016 ACM SIGSAC Conference on Computer and Communications Security, pp. 1167–1178. ACM (2016)
20. Lewko, A., Okamoto, T., Sahai, A., Takashima, K., Waters, B.: Fully secure functional encryption: attribute-based encryption and (hierarchical) inner product encryption. In: Gilbert, H. (ed.) EUROCRYPT 2010. LNCS, vol. 6110, pp. 62–91. Springer, Heidelberg (2010). https://doi.org/10.1007/978-3-642-13190-5_4
21. Shen, E., Shi, E., Waters, B.: Predicate privacy in encryption systems. In: Reingold, O. (ed.) TCC 2009. LNCS, vol. 5444, pp. 457–473. Springer, Heidelberg (2009). https://doi.org/10.1007/978-3-642-00457-5_27

22. Shi, E., Bethencourt, J., Chan, T.H., Song, D., Perrig, A.: Multi-dimensional range query over encrypted data. In: 2007 IEEE Symposium on Security and Privacy (SP 2007), pp. 350–364. IEEE (2007)
23. Williams, R.: New algorithms and lower bounds for circuits with linear threshold gates. In: Proceedings of the forty-sixth annual ACM symposium on Theory of computing, pp. 194–202. ACM (2014)

# Optimal Bounded-Collusion Secure Functional Encryption

Prabhanjan Ananth[1(✉)] and Vinod Vaikuntanathan[2]

[1] University of California, Santa Barbara, USA
prabhanjan@cs.ucsb.edu
[2] CSAIL, MIT, Cambridge, USA
vinodv@mit.edu

**Abstract.** We construct private-key and public-key functional encryption schemes in the bounded-key setting; that is, secure against adversaries that obtain an a-priori bounded number of functional keys (also known as the collusion bound).

An important metric considered in the literature on bounded-key functional encryption schemes is the dependence of the running time of the encryption algorithm on the collusion bound $Q = Q(\lambda)$ (where $\lambda$ is the security parameter). It is known that bounded-key functional encryption schemes with encryption complexity growing with $Q^{1-\varepsilon}$, for any constant $\varepsilon > 0$, implies indistinguishability obfuscation. On the other hand, in the public-key setting, it was previously unknown whether we could achieve encryption complexity growing linear with $Q$, also known as *optimal* bounded-key FE, based on well-studied assumptions.

In this work, we give the *first* construction of an optimal bounded-key public-key functional encryption scheme under the minimal assumption of the existence of any public-key encryption scheme. Moreover, our scheme supports the class of all polynomial-size circuits.

Our techniques also extend to the private-key setting. We achieve a construction of an optimal bounded-key functional encryption in the private-key setting based on the minimal assumption of one-way functions, instead of learning with errors as achieved in prior works.

## 1 Introduction

Functional Encryption [SW05, BSW11] (FE) is a powerful type of encryption where the owner of a secret key sk can generate special-purpose functional secret keys $sk_F$ which allow anyone to compute $F(x)$ given an encryption of $x$. The standard and demanding security notion for functional encryption is *collusion-resistance* which, informally stated, requires that an adversary who holds functional secret keys for an *arbitrary polynomial* number of boolean functions $F_1, F_2, \ldots, F_m$ of her choice should learn no more than $F_1(x), F_2(x), \ldots, F_m(x)$ given an encryption of $x$. Collusion-resistant functional encryption schemes are extremely powerful: [AJ15, BV15, AJS15] show that such FE schemes can be used to construct indistinguishability obfuscators and therefore, can be used to

© International Association for Cryptologic Research 2019
D. Hofheinz and A. Rosen (Eds.): TCC 2019, LNCS 11891, pp. 174–198, 2019.
https://doi.org/10.1007/978-3-030-36030-6_8

instantiate a vast majority of cryptographic primitives (see [SW14] and a large number of followup works.) It is no surprise then that collusion-resistant FE schemes are very hard to construct and indeed, to this date, we do not know constructions from well-established cryptographic assumptions.

In many uses of functional encryption, however, the weaker notion of *bounded-key setting* might suffice. Bounded-key setting permits the secret-key owner to release an a priori bounded number $Q = Q(\lambda)$ of functional keys. (Here and henceforth, $\lambda$ denotes the security parameter.) Thus, bounded-key setting is appropriate in scenarios where functional keys are tied to users, and a large colluding set of users is hard to form. Historically, bounded-collusion resistance has been well-studied with the goals of improving efficiency, reducing computational assumptions, and supporting a larger class of functions; see [DKXY02, HK04, CHH+07, GLW12, SS10, GVW12a, ISV+17, AR17, Agr17] and the references therein.

*Encryption Complexity.* An important complexity measure considered in the FE literature is encryption complexity (defined to be the size of the encryption circuit). Of particular interest in the setting of bounded-collusion resistance (referred as bounded-key FE) is the growth of the encryption complexity with the collusion bound $Q$. The importance of this measure stems from the recent results [BV15, AJ15, AJS15, GS16, LM16, BNPW16, KNT18], which tell us that, for any constant $\epsilon > 0$, bounded-key FE with encryption complexity $Q^{1-\epsilon} \cdot \mathsf{poly}(\lambda, s)$, where $s$ is the maximum size of the functions queried, is as powerful as collusion-resistant FE. Thus, achieving encryption complexity $Q^{1-\epsilon} \cdot \mathsf{poly}(\lambda, s)$ in bounded-key FE schemes from well-studied assumptions would be a breakthrough in cryptography.

On the other hand, we could still hope to base bounded-key FE schemes, in the public-key setting, with encryption complexity $Q \cdot \mathsf{poly}(\lambda, s)$ (henceforth, referred to as *optimal bounded-key FE*) on well-studied assumptions. Unfortunately, this question has remained unanswered so far. The best known result, by Agrawal and Rosen [AR17], managed to reduce the encryption complexity to $Q^2 + \mathsf{poly}(\lambda, s)$.

We ask the following question:

*Can we construct optimal bounded-key public-key FE for all functions in*
P/poly *based on well-studied assumptions?*

## 1.1   Our Results

In this work, we answer the above question in the affirmative and in fact, our construction can be based on minimal assumptions alone, i.e., existence of any public-key encryption scheme.

Specifically, we prove the following theorem.

**Theorem 1 (Informal).** *Assuming the existence of public-key encryption, there exists a bounded-key public-key FE scheme for* P/Poly *with encryption* *complexity* $Q \cdot \mathsf{poly}(\lambda, s)$, *where* $Q$ *is the collusion bound and* $s$ *is the maximum size of the functions queried.*

Additionally our scheme has many advantages. It satisfies simulation security and adaptive security, which is the best possible security notion that we can achieve in this setting. Moreover, our scheme makes only black box use of the underlying public-key encryption scheme. We note that even constructing optimal public-key attribute-based encryption, a weaker form of FE, based on minimal assumptions was unknown prior to our work.

*Private-Key Setting.* In the private-key setting, a recent work of Chen, Vaikuntanathan, Waters, Wee and Wichs [CVW+18] showed how to achieve optimal bounded-key FE based on the assumption of learning with errors. Moreover, their scheme was only selectively secure. Thus, constructing optimal bounded-key FE in the private-key setting based on the minimal assumption of one-way functions was open.

We show,

**Theorem 2 (Informal).** *Assuming the existence of one-way functions, there exists a bounded-key private-key FE scheme for* $\mathsf{P}/\mathsf{Poly}$ *with encryption complexity* $Q \cdot \mathsf{poly}(\lambda, s)$, *where* $Q$ *is the collusion bound and* $s$ *is the maximum size of the functions queried.*

Our private-key scheme has the same attractive features as our public-key scheme, that is, our private-key scheme satisfies simulation security, adaptive security and only makes black-box use of the underlying cryptographic primitive.

*Dichotomy in Bounded-Key Functional Encryption.* We see our work as establishing a dichotomy in bounded-key functional encryption (in both public-key and private-key settings): (i) for any constant $\varepsilon > 0$, any bounded-key FE scheme with encryption complexity $Q^{1-\varepsilon}\mathsf{poly}(\lambda, s)$ implies indistinguishability obfuscation and, (ii) the existence of bounded-key FE with encryption complexity $Q \cdot \mathsf{poly}(\lambda, s)$ can be based solely on minimal assumptions.

## 1.2    Prior Works on Bounded-Collusion FE

*Dichotomy in Bounded-Key IBE.* Early work by Dodis, Katz, Xu and Yung [DKXY02] showed how to construct a $Q$-bounded identity-based encryption (IBE) scheme, another special case of FE, where the public parameters had size $O(Q^2\lambda)$, and the ciphertexts and secret keys had size $O(Q\lambda)$, starting from any public-key encryption scheme. Goldwasser, Lewko and Wilson [GLW12] later showed a construction with public parameters of size $O(Q\lambda)$, and ciphertexts and secret keys of size $O(\lambda)$, albeit under more structured algebraic assumptions.

More recently, Döttling and Garg [DG17b] and followup works [BLSV18, DG17a] showed how to bootstrap any bounded collusion IBE with public parameters of size $Q^{1-\epsilon} \cdot \mathsf{poly}(\lambda)$, irrespective of ciphertext and secret-key length, into a full-fledged (i.e., fully collusion-resistant) IBE scheme.

This gives us a dichotomy for IBE: $Q$-bounded IBE with public parameters of size $\Omega(Q)$ exists under the minimal assumption of public-key encryption; and doing any better in terms of the size of public parameters is as hard as achieving unbounded-collusion IBE.

*Bounded-Key FE.* In the other extreme, the situation with general functional encryption (FE) is less clear-cut. The first construction of bounded-key FE for *Boolean functions*[1] in $NC^1$ was demonstrated by Gorbunov, Vaikuntanathan and Wee [GVW12a], who built on the work of Sahai and Seyalioglu [SS10]; the encryption complexity in their scheme was $Q^4 \cdot \text{poly}(\lambda, s)$. They also showed how to extend this to support all poly-time computable functions, but at the expense of an additional assumption, namely pseudorandom functions that can be computed in $NC^1$, an object that we currently know how to construct based only on algebraic assumptions such as factoring, DDH and LWE. (see Fig. 1 for a detailed comparison.) Agrawal and Rosen [AR17] showed how to reduce the ciphertext size to $Q^2 + \text{poly}(\lambda, s)$ under the LWE assumption. Chen, Vaikuntanathan, Waters, Wee and Wichs [CVW+18] very recently showed how to reduce the dependence even further to $Q \cdot \text{poly}(\lambda, d)$ under the LWE assumption, except they could only achieve private-key FE. The ciphertext size dependence on $Q$ in this last result is the best possible (without constructing IO) except that (a) they rely on LWE; and (b) they only achieve private-key FE. Even in the much weaker setting of public-key *attribute-based* encryption (ABE), the best known ciphertext size is $Q^2 \cdot \text{poly}(\lambda, s)$ in constructions that rely only on public-key encryption [ISV+17].

*Dependence on the Circuit Size.* We do caution the reader that our focus will be on the dependence of the ciphertext size on the collusion-bound $Q$. Ciphertexts in our scheme grow with the circuit-size of the functions that the scheme supports (denoted $s$ in Fig. 1). On the one hand, for constructions that rely only on the minimal assumption of public-key encryption, this dependence seems hard to remove; indeed, even the best 1-bounded FE with ciphertext size sublinear in the circuit-size of the (Boolean) functions assumes (subexponential) LWE [GKP+13]. On the other hand, we show how to translate any improvement in this state of affairs for 1-bounded FE into a corresponding improvement in $Q$-bounded FE with ciphertexts that grow *linearly* in the collusion bound $Q$. Concretely, applying our techniques to the 1-bounded FE of [GKP+13] gives us a $Q$-bounded FE from subexponential LWE where ciphertexts grow as $Q \cdot \text{poly}(\lambda, d)$ where $d$ is the circuit-depth, improving on [AR17] (who achieve a quadratic dependence in $Q$) and on [CVW+18] (who construct a private-key FE scheme with a linear dependence in $Q$).

---

[1] Handling functions with output size $\ell$ is morally the same as increasing the collusion bound and handling $\ell$ functions with Boolean output. Indeed, this is made precise in the results of [BV15, AJS15, GS16, LM16].

| | Ciphertext Size | Circuit Class | Assumptions | Remarks |
|---|---|---|---|---|
| [GVW12a] | $Q^4\text{poly}(\lambda,s)$ | $NC^1$ | PKE | Public-Key, Adaptive |
| | $Q^4\text{poly}(\lambda,s)$ | $NC^1$ | OWFs | Private-Key, Adaptive |
| | $Q^4\text{poly}(\lambda,s)$ | P/Poly | DDH/LWE | Public-Key, Adaptive |
| [AR17] | $Q^2+\text{poly}(\lambda,s)$ | P/Poly | LWE/Ring-LWE | Public-Key, Selective |
| [CVW+18] | $Q\cdot\text{poly}(\lambda,s)$ | P/Poly | LWE | Private-Key, Selective |
| **Our Work** | $Q\cdot\text{poly}(\lambda,s)$ | P/Poly | PKE | Public-Key, Adaptive |
| | $Q\cdot\text{poly}(\lambda,s)$ | P/Poly | OWFs | Private-Key, Adaptive |

**Fig. 1.** State of the art for bounded key functional encryption schemes in terms of query dependence. $Q$ denotes the number of circuit queries allowed in the security experiment and $s$ denotes the size of the circuits for which functional keys are issued.

## 1.3 Technical Overview

We give an overview of the techniques. For the current discussion, our focus will be on the public-key setting; the techniques carry over *mutatis mutandis* to the private-key setting as well. We show our result in two steps. In the first step, we construct a public-key bounded-key FE for P/Poly starting from any public-key encryption scheme. We will not worry about optimizing the ciphertext size; indeed, it will be a large polynomial in the collusion bound $Q$. In the second step, we show a general way to reduce the ciphertext size: we show how to transform an FE scheme, where the ciphertext complexity grows polynomial in the collusion bound, into a FE scheme with *linear complexity*.

We now describe an overview of the techniques involved in the two steps, in order. In the technical sections, we invert the order of presentation since the second step (see Sect. 4) is simpler than the first (see Sect. 5).

**First Step: Bounded-Key FE for p/poly.** Our starting point is the observation from [SS10, GVW12a] that secure multiparty computation protocols with certain properties can be used to construct FE schemes; for [SS10], it was Yao's two-party computation protocol [Yao86] and for [GVW12a], it was a non-interactive version of the BGW multi-party protocol [BOGW88]. Broadly speaking, our goal in this paper is to identify *the right* notion of MPC that can be turned into *optimal* bounded-collusion FE.

Towards this end, we define secure multiparty computation protocols in a client-server framework where there is a single client who wishes to delegate an a-priori bounded number $Q$ of computations to $N$ servers. We first describe the syntax of such protocols and then the security we require of them. A protocol in the client-server framework proceeds in two phases:

- An *offline phase* where the client encodes a private input $x$ into $N$ encodings, and the $i^{th}$ server gets the $i^{th}$ encoding.
- An *online phase* which is executed $Q$ times, once for every function that the client wishes to delegate. In the $j^{th}$ session, the client encodes a circuit $C_j$ into $N$ encodings, and sends each server an encoding. At this stage, only $n$ of the $N$ servers come online, perform some local computation on their encodings,

and output a single message each. (We call the local computation function Local.) A public decoding algorithm can then reconstruct the value $C_j(x)$ from these server messages. (We call the reconstruction function Decode.) Crucially, we require that the client does not keep any shared state between the online and offline phases.

As for security, we consider an adversary that corrupts an arbitrary size-$t$ subset of the servers (for some pre-determined $t$) and learns (a) the offline phase messages received by these $t$ servers and (b) the messages of *all the servers* in the online phase; that is, the adversary gets to see the entire communication between the client and the servers in the online phase. We require that such an adversary does not learn anything more about the client input $x$ other than $\{C_j(x)\}_{j \in [Q]}$. This requirement is captured through a simulation-based definition. Two aspects make it challenging to construct such protocols:

- *Reusability:* the input encodings generated by the client should be reusable across different computations; and
- *Dynamic Recovery:* the ability for only a subset of servers to come together in the online phase to recover the output.

For the current discussion, we call secure protocols that satisfy both the above properties as *reusable dynamic MPC* protocols. In the technical sections, we will not explicitly use the terminology of reusable dynamic MPC protocols and just refer to them as client-server protocols.

Implicit in [GVW12a] is a construction of a reusable dynamic MPC protocol, where the circuits delegated by the client are in $NC^1$. There is a fundamental barrier in extending their approach to handle circuits in P/Poly as they crucially use a two-round MPC protocol (derived from BGW) that securely computes polynomials. Circuits in P/Poly are believed to not have efficient polynomial representations. While several recent works [BL18, GS18, ACGJ18, GIS18, ABT18] demonstrate two-round MPC protocols that securely compute P/Poly, they fail to simultaneously satisfy reusability *and* dynamic recovery. Nonetheless, we will crucially use the construction of reusable dynamic MPC protocol for $NC^1$ [GVW12a], denoted by $\Pi_{NC^1}$, to build a protocol for P/Poly.

*From Client-Server Protocol for* P/Poly *to Bounded-Key FE for* P/Poly. Before we construct reusable dynamic MPC protocols for P/Poly, we first show how such protocols are useful in obtaining bounded-collusion FE for P/Poly. As an intermediate tool, we use a single-key FE scheme for P/Poly. This is a well studied object and can be based solely on the existence of public-key encryption [SS10]. We call such a scheme 1fe and we denote the bounded-collusion FE scheme that we wish to construct to be BFE. The construction of BFE, which follows along the lines of [GVW12a], proceeds as follows:

- The setup of BFE invokes $N = \text{poly}(Q)$ instantiations of 1fe. The $N$ public keys of 1fe form the master public key of BFE and similarly the $N$ secret keys of 1fe form the master secret key of BFE.

- To encrypt an input $x$ in BFE, run the offline phase of the client-server framework. Denote the output to be $(\widehat{x}^1, \ldots, \widehat{x}^N)$. Encrypt $\widehat{x}^u$ under the $u^{th}$ instantiation of 1fe. Output all the $N$ ciphertexts of 1fe.
- The key generation for a circuit $C$ in BFE is done as follows: run the client delegation procedure CktEnc on $C$ to obtain $(\widehat{C}^1, \ldots, \widehat{C}^N)$. Pick a random $n$-sized subset $\mathbf{S} \subseteq [N]$ and generate 1fe functional keys for $\mathsf{Local}(\widehat{C}^u, \cdot)$ (recall that Local is part of the online phase in client-server framework) for every $u$ in the set $\mathbf{S}$. Output all the $n$ functional keys of 1fe.

  Note that here we crucially use the fact that the client does not share state between the offline and online phases.
- The decryption proceeds by first decrypting the $u^{th}$ ciphertext of 1fe using the $u^{th}$ functional key to obtain the encoding $\widehat{y}^u$. Then run Decode to recover the answer.

The correctness of BFE follows from the correctness guarantees of 1fe and the reusable dynamic MPC framework. To argue security, as in [GVW12a], a simple combinatorial argument is first invoked to prove that the size of pairwise intersections of the sets chosen during the key-generation procedures of all the $Q$ functional keys is at most $t$. For this argument to work, we need to set $N$ to be a sufficiently large polynomial in $Q$. Using this observation, we can deduce that at most $t$ instantiations of 1fe can be rendered insecure. An 1fe instantiation being rendered insecure means that the corresponding server is corrupted in the client-server framework; note that there is a one-to-one correspondence between the number of instantiations of 1fe and the number of servers in the client-server framework. We can then use the property that the client-server protocol is secure even if at most $t$ servers are corrupted, to argue that the scheme BFE is secure.

Moreover, since 1fe can be based on public-key encryption (resp., one-way functions), we obtain a public-key (resp., secret-key) BFE for P/Poly from reusable dynamic MPC for P/Poly assuming only public-key encryption (resp., one-way functions).

*Reusable Dynamic MPC Protocol for* P/Poly. Now that we have shown that reusable dynamic MPC is useful for constructing bounded-key FE, we shift our focus to building this object.

Towards this, we first define the abstraction of *correlated garbling*. This abstraction allows for generating multiple garbled circuits from a shared random string. More specifically, it comprises of two algorithms: CorrGarb and CorrEval. The correlated garbling algorithm CorrGarb takes as input circuit $C$, input $x$, a random string $R$ (not necessarily uniformly generated) and outputs a garbled circuit GC and appropriate wire labels $\mathbf{K}_x$. The evaluation algorithm CorrEval takes as input $(\mathsf{GC}, \mathbf{K}_x)$ and outputs $C(x)$. We require that all the different correlated garbled circuits $\{\mathsf{GC}_i \leftarrow \mathsf{CorrGarb}(C_i, x, R)$ produced using the *same string $R$* do not reveal any information about $x$ beyond $\{(C_i, C_i(x))\}$.

We use this abstraction to transform $\Pi_{\mathsf{NC}^1}$ (recall, $\Pi_{\mathsf{NC}^1}$ is a reusable dynamic protocol for $\mathsf{NC}^1$) into a reusable dynamic for P/Poly as follows:

- Offline Phase: to encode an input $x$, generate a random string $R$ (as dictated by correlated garbling) and then encode $(x, R)$ using the offline phase of $\Pi_{\mathsf{NC}^1}$ to obtain $N$ input encodings.
- Online Phase: in the $i^{th}$ session, let $C_i$ be the circuit delegated by the client. The client generates the online phase of $\Pi_{\mathsf{NC}^1}$ on the circuit $\mathsf{CorrGarb}(C_i, \cdot, \cdot)$ to obtain $N$ circuit encodings and sends one encoding to each of the servers. A subset of the servers perform local computation of $\Pi_{\mathsf{NC}^1}$ and each of them output a single message. The value $C_i(x)$ can be recovered from the outputs of the servers in two steps: (i) run the decoding procedure of $\Pi_{\mathsf{NC}^1}$ to obtain the correlated garbled circuit-wire keys pair $(\mathsf{GC}_i, \mathbf{K}_x^i)$ of $(C_i, x)$ and then, (ii) run $\mathsf{CorrEval}$ on the correlated garbled circuit to recover the answer.

In order to implement the above construction, it is required that $\mathsf{CorrGarb}$ is representable by an $\mathsf{NC}^1$ circuit: this is because $\Pi_{\mathsf{NC}^1}$ only allows for delegating computations in $\mathsf{NC}^1$. The security of the above construction follows from the fact that the different correlated garbled circuits along with wire keys $\{(\mathsf{GC}_i, \mathbf{K}_x^i)\}$ can be simulated using $\{(C_i, C_i(x))\}$: note that all the correlated garbled circuits are computed as a function of the same random string $R$. In Sect. 5, we give a direct construction of client-server protocol from correlated garbling; in particular we do not assume that a client-server protocol for $\mathsf{NC}^1$ as implicitly proposed in [GVW12a].

All that remains is to construct a correlated garbling scheme with the garbling function in $\mathsf{NC}^1$. We introduce novel techniques in this construction and this is the main technical contribution of the paper.

*Construction of Correlated Garbling.* The main hurdle in constructing a correlated garbling scheme is to ensure the security of different correlated garbled circuits computed using the same randomness. As a first attempt, we use the classical garbling scheme of Yao [Yao86]:

- Let $s$ be the number of wires in the circuit to be garbled. For every wire $w$ in the circuit, generate a large (i.e., $\mathrm{poly}(\lambda, Q)$) number of uniformly random keys, denoted by the vector $\overrightarrow{\mathbf{K}_w^0}$, associated with bit 0 and $\lambda$ number of keys $\overrightarrow{\mathbf{K}_w^1}$ for bit 1. Similarly, for every gate $G$ in the circuit, generate a large (i.e., $\mathrm{poly}(\lambda, Q)$) number of random strings, denoted by $\overrightarrow{\mathbf{R}_G}$. The collection of all the strings form the random string $R$ that will be input to $\mathsf{CorrGarb}$.
- To garble a circuit $C$, $\mathsf{CorrGarb}$ performs the following steps:
    - **Generation of wire keys and randomness for encryption**: It chooses a *random* $\lambda$-sized subset $S$; for every wire $w$, it generates the wire key $K_w^0$ (resp., $K_w^1$) for $w$ by XOR-ing the subset $S$ of keys in $\overrightarrow{\mathbf{K}_w^0}$ (resp., $\overrightarrow{\mathbf{K}_w^1}$). Similarly, generate $R_G$ by XOR-ing the subset $S$ of random strings in $\overrightarrow{\mathbf{R}_G}$.
    - **Generating the garbled gates**: Using the wire keys and the random strings generated using the above process, we generate the garbled gates for every gate in the circuit. The generation process will be performed as

described in [Yao86]. In particular, this process will employ a private-key encryption scheme to generate four ciphertexts associated with every gate in the circuit.

- CorrEval is the same as the evaluation algorithm of the garbling scheme by [Yao86].

In addition to security, we need to argue that CorrGarb can be implemented in $NC^1$; recall that the latter property was crucially used to construct reusable dynamic MPC for P/Poly. Let us first give intuition as to why the above template satisfies security.

Suppose the string $R$ (input to CorrGarb) is reused $Q$ times to generate $Q$ different collections of wire keys and random strings, with each such collection generated using a different random set $S$. Then each collection in turn is used to generate a single garbled circuit. First we invoke a combinatorial argument to prove that the joint distribution of the $Q$ collections of wire keys and the random strings, generated as above, is identical to the product uniform distribution. Once this is proven, this proof can then be leveraged, using arguments standard in the garbling literature, to argue the security of the above correlated garbling candidate.

All is left is to show that CorrGarb can be implemented in $NC^1$. Since the procedure CorrGarb involves running the encryption algorithm of a private-key scheme, at the very least we need to start with a private-key scheme with encryption algorithm computable in $NC^1$. Unfortunately such schemes are known to exist only based on algebraic assumptions, in particular, assuming PRGs in $NC^1$. Thus, the above candidate does not work for us.

To overcome this barrier, we make the following observation: notice that the generation of the random string $R$ fed into CorrGarb is "lightweight", meaning that no cryptographic primitives are used. On the other hand, the algorithm CorrGarb is "crypto-heavy", meaning that it makes many invocations of a cryptographic primitive and specifically, a private-key encryption scheme. We design a *flipped* correlated garbling scheme, where the generation of $R$ is "crypto-heavy" while CorrGarb is "lightweight".

Specifically, we make the following changes to the above candidate.

- Instead of invoking the PRG during the execution of CorrGarb, we instead invoke this during the generation of $R$. While doing so, we observe that it is no longer necessary that PRG needs to be computable in $NC^1$, since there is no such restriction when generating $R$. As a result, we will end up generating all the keys in $\{\overrightarrow{\mathbf{K}_w^0}, \overrightarrow{\mathbf{K}_w^1}\}$ using *any* pseudorandom generator.
- To maintain correctness, we need to encrypt a subset of the seeds of the PRG as part of the garbled table. Arguing security is more challenging now. We need to argue that the joint distribution of the $Q$ collections of the wire keys and the random strings computed using $R$, is identical to the product uniform distribution, *even if some of the PRG seeds generating the wire keys are leaked* and this step is crucial to the proof of the correlated garbling lemma.

The above template is an over-simplified presentation of correlated garbling and we refer the reader to the technical sections for a precise description.

*Summarizing the First Step.* We summarize the steps to construct a bounded-key functional encryption for P/Poly.

1. We construct correlated garbling for P/Poly from one-way functions.
2. Combining correlated garbling with techniques from [GVW12a], we construct a protocol in the client-server framework (satisfying both reusability and dynamic recovery) that handles P/Poly computations.
3. Finally, we construct bounded-key FE for P/Poly from a client-server protocol and single-key functional encryption for P/Poly [SS10, GVW12a].

The ciphertext complexity in the resulting FE scheme, however, grows polynomially in $Q$.

**Second Step: Linear Dependence in Query Complexity.** In the second step, we give a generic transformation to turn the FE scheme resulting from the first step into one that satisfies linear complexity property. This transformation is remarkably simple and draws connections to the classical load balancing problem. Recall in the load balancing problem, there are $Q$ reviewers and there are $Q$ papers to review, with each reviewer having bandwidth to review at most $q$ papers. Assigning papers at random to the reviewers ensures that each reviewer has to review one paper on average. By a simple Chernoff argument coupled with union bound argument, it follows that, as long as $q$ is large enough, the probability that any reviewer has to review more than $q$ papers is small. We propose our transformation along these lines: let bfe be the FE scheme obtained from the first step and let BFE be the FE scheme with linear complexity that we wish to construct. To tolerate a query bound $Q$, we consider $Q$ instantiations of bfe in parallel, where the collusion bound (read as "load") in bfe is set to be $q$.

- To encrypt a message $x$ in BFE, encrypt $x$ in all the instantiations of bfe.
- To generate a functional key for a circuit $C$, pick an index $i$ in $[Q]$ at random and generate a bfe functional key corresponding to the $i^{th}$ instantiation. This is akin to assigning a paper to a reviewer at random.

If we set $q$ to be security parameter, we can prove (using Chernoff and union bounds) that it is highly unlikely that the number of bfe functional keys issued for any given index is greater than $q$. This allows us to invoke the security of bfe scheme to prove the security of BFE. Moreover, the ciphertext complexity of BFE is linear in $Q$, as desired! (each bfe ciphertext is of size fixed polynomial in the security parameter and in particular, independent of $Q$).

## 2    Preliminaries

We denote the security parameter by $\lambda$. Suppose $x$ and $y$ be two strings. Then, we denote $x \circ y$ to be the concatenation of $x$ and $y$.

Let $D$ be a distribution with an efficient sampler. We denote the process of sampling $v$ from $D$ to be $v \xleftarrow{\$} D$. The statistical distance between two distributions $D_0$ and $D_1$ is $\varepsilon$ if $\sum_{v \in V} |\Pr[v \xleftarrow{\$} D_0] - \Pr[v \xleftarrow{\$} D_1]| \leq 2\varepsilon$, where $V$ is the support of both $D_0$ and $D_1$. Two distributions $D_0$ and $D_1$ are computationally indistinguishable if for every probabilistic polynomial time (PPT) adversary $\mathcal{A}$, the following holds: $\left| \Pr_{v \xleftarrow{\$} D_0}[0 \leftarrow \mathcal{A}(v)] - \Pr_{v \xleftarrow{\$} D_1}[0 \leftarrow \mathcal{A}(v)] \right| \leq \mathsf{negl}(\lambda)$, for some negligible function $\mathsf{negl}$.

We assume that without loss of generality, every polynomial-sized circuit considered in this work contain only boolean gates (over any universal basis) with at most two output wires. Note that if every gate in a polynomial-sized circuit has at most one output wire then this circuit is representable as a polynomial-sized formula and thus, is in $\mathsf{NC}^1$. The class of all polynomial-sized circuits is denoted by $\mathsf{P/Poly}$.

## 2.1  Bounded-Key Functional Encryption

A public-key functional encryption scheme $\mathsf{bfe}$ associated with a class of boolean circuits $\mathcal{C}$ is defined by the following algorithms.

- **Setup,** $\mathsf{Setup}(1^\lambda, 1^Q, 1^s)$: On input security parameter $\lambda$, query bound $Q$, maximum size of the circuits $s$ for which functional keys are issued, output the master secret key $\mathsf{msk}$ and the master public key $\mathsf{mpk}$.
- **Key Generation,** $\mathsf{KeyGen}(\mathsf{msk}, C)$: On input master secret key $\mathsf{msk}$ and a circuit $C \in \mathcal{C}$, output the functional key $\mathsf{sk}_C$.
- **Encryption,** $\mathsf{Enc}(\mathsf{mpk}, x)$: On input master public key $\mathsf{mpk}$, input $x$, output the ciphertext $\mathsf{ct}$.
- **Decryption,** $\mathsf{Dec}(\mathsf{sk}_C, \mathsf{ct})$: On input functional key $\mathsf{sk}_C$, ciphertext $\mathsf{ct}$, output the value $y$.

*Remark 1.* A private-key functional encryption scheme is defined similarly, except that $\mathsf{Setup}(1^\lambda, 1^Q, 1^s)$ outputs only the master secret key $\mathsf{msk}$ and the encryption algorithm $\mathsf{Enc}$ takes as input the master secret key $\mathsf{msk}$ and the message $x$.

*Remark 2.* Henceforth, $\mathsf{Setup}$ will only take as input $(1^\lambda, 1^s)$ in the case when $Q = 1$.

A functional encryption scheme satisfies the following properties.

*Correctness.* Consider an input $x$ and a circuit $C \in \mathcal{C}$ of size $s$. We require the following to hold for every $Q \geq 1$:

$$\Pr\left[ C(x) \leftarrow \mathsf{Dec}(\mathsf{sk}_C, \mathsf{ct}) : \begin{array}{c} (\mathsf{mpk}, \mathsf{msk}) \leftarrow \mathsf{Setup}(1^\lambda, 1^Q, 1^s); \\ \mathsf{sk}_C \leftarrow \mathsf{KeyGen}(\mathsf{msk}, C); \\ \mathsf{ct} \leftarrow \mathsf{Enc}(\mathsf{mpk}, x) \end{array} \right] \geq 1 - \mathsf{negl}(\lambda),$$

for some negligible function $\mathsf{negl}$.

*Efficiency.* Setup, KeyGen, Enc and Dec run in time polynomial in their respective inputs.

We define a measure of efficiency that captures the dependance of the ciphertext complexity on the query bound. We define this formally below.

**Definition 1 (Linear Complexity).** *A functional encryption scheme* bfe = (Setup, KeyGen, Enc, Dec) *is said to have linear complexity if the following holds:*

- *The time to compute* $\mathsf{Enc}(\mathsf{mpk}, x)$ *is* $Q \cdot \mathrm{poly}(\lambda, s)$.
- *The time to compute* $\mathsf{KeyGen}(\mathsf{msk}, C)$ *for a circuit of size* $s$ *is* $Q \cdot \mathrm{poly}(\lambda, s)$.

*where* $(\mathsf{mpk}, \mathsf{msk}) \leftarrow \mathsf{Setup}(1^\lambda, 1^Q, 1^s)$.

*Security.* To define the security of a bounded-key functional encryption scheme bfe, we define two experiments $\mathsf{Expt}_0$ and $\mathsf{Expt}_1$. Experiment $\mathsf{Expt}_0$, also referred to as *real* experiment, is parameterized by PPT stateful adversary $\mathcal{A}$ and challenger Ch. Experiment $\mathsf{Expt}_1$, also referred to as *simulated* experiment, is parameterized by PPT adversary $\mathcal{A}$ and PPT stateful simulator Sim.

$\underline{\mathsf{Expt}_0^{\mathsf{bfe}, \mathcal{A}, \mathsf{Ch}}(1^\lambda)}$:

- $\mathcal{A}$ outputs the query bound $Q$ and the maximum circuit size $s$.
- Ch executes $\mathsf{bfe.Setup}(1^\lambda, 1^Q, 1^s)$ to obtain the master public key-master secret key pair $(\mathsf{mpk}, \mathsf{msk})$.
- **Circuit Queries:** $\mathcal{A}$, with oracle access to $\mathsf{bfe.KeyGen}(\mathsf{msk}, \cdot)$, outputs the challenge message $x$.
- **Challenge Message Query:** Ch outputs the challenge ciphertext ct.
- **Circuit Queries:** $\mathcal{A}$, with oracle access to $\mathsf{bfe.KeyGen}(\mathsf{msk}, \cdot)$, outputs the bit $b$.
- If the total number of oracle calls made by $\mathcal{A}$ is greater than $Q$, output $\bot$. Otherwise, output $b$.

$\underline{\mathsf{Expt}_1^{\mathsf{bfe}, \mathcal{A}, \mathsf{Sim}}(1^\lambda)}$:

- $\mathcal{A}$ outputs the query bound $Q$ and the maximum circuit size $s$.
- Sim, on input $(1^\lambda, 1^Q, 1^s)$, outputs the master public key mpk.
- **Circuit Queries:** $\mathcal{A}$, with oracle access to Sim (generating simulated functional keys), outputs the challenge message $x$.
    - Let QSet be the set of circuit queries made by $\mathcal{A}$ to Sim.
    - Construct the set $\mathcal{V}$ as follows: for every $C \in \mathsf{QSet}$, include $(C, C(x))$ in $\mathcal{V}$.
- **Challenge Message Query:** $\mathsf{Sim}(1^{|x|}, \mathcal{V})$ outputs the challenge ciphertext ct.
- **Circuit Queries:** $\mathcal{A}$, with oracle access to Sim (generating simulated functional keys), outputs bit $b$.
- If the total number of circuit queries made by $\mathcal{A}$ is greater than $Q$, output $\bot$. Otherwise, output $b$.

A public-key functional encryption scheme is adaptively secure if the output distributions of the above two experiments are computationally indistinguishable. More formally,

**Definition 2 (Adaptive Security).** *A public-key functional encryption scheme* bfe *is* **adaptively secure** *if for every large enough security parameter* $\lambda \in \mathbb{N}$, *every PPT adversary* $\mathcal{A}$, *there exists a PPT simulator* Sim *such that the following holds:*

$$\left| \mathsf{Pr}\left[ 0 \leftarrow \mathsf{Expt}_0^{\mathsf{bfe},\mathcal{A},\mathsf{Ch}}(1^\lambda) \right] - \mathsf{Pr}\left[ 0 \leftarrow \mathsf{Expt}_1^{\mathsf{bfe},\mathcal{A},\mathsf{Sim}}(1^\lambda) \right] \right| \leq \mathsf{negl}(\lambda),$$

*for some negligible function* negl.

*Remark 3.* The selective security notion can be defined by similarly formulating the real and the simulated experiments. The only difference between selective security and adaptive security notions is that in the selective security notion, the adversary is supposed to output the challenge message even before it receives the master public key or makes any circuit query.

In the private-key setting, selective and adaptive security notions can be defined similarly.

# 3   Result Statements

We prove our result in two steps. In the first step, we present a transformation that converts a bounded-key functional encryption scheme, that doesn't have linear complexity property, into one that satisfies linear complexity.

*Generic Transformation to Achieve Linear Complexity.* We prove the following theorem in Sect. 4.

**Theorem 3.** *Consider a class* $\mathcal{C}$ *of polynomial-sized circuits. If there exists a public-key (resp., private-key) bounded-key FE scheme for* $\mathcal{C}$ *then there exists a public-key (resp., private-key) bounded-key FE scheme for* $\mathcal{C}$ *that additionally satisfies linear complexity property (Definition 1).*

*Remark 4.* Our transformation does not place any restrictions on $\mathcal{C}$. In particular, our transformation works for identity-based encryption schemes, attribute-based encryption schemes, and so on.

The above theorem is restated as Theorem 6 in Sect. 4.

*Bounded key FE for* P/Poly. We prove the following theorem in Sect. 5.

**Theorem 4.** *Assuming the existence of public-key encryption (resp., one-way functions), there exists a public-key (resp., private-key) bounded-key functional encryption scheme for* P/Poly.

We prove the above theorem by first defining a client-server framework and then we construct a bounded-key FE from a client-server protocol. Finally, we instantiate client-server protocols from one-way functions.

The above theorem is restated as Theorem 7 in Sect. 5.

*Bounded Key FE for* P/Poly *satisfying Linear Complexity.* By combining the above two theorems, we achieve our main result.

**Theorem 5 (Main Theorem).** *Assuming the existence of public-key encryption (resp., one-way functions), there exists a public-key (resp., private-key) bounded-key functional encryption scheme satisfying linear complexity property for* P/Poly.

Our construction of functional encryption scheme in the above theorem makes only black box use of public-key encryption (or one-way functions).

# 4   Achieving Linear Complexity Generically

We show how to generically achieve linear complexity for any bounded-key FE scheme. In particular, we prove the following:

**Theorem 6.** *If there exists a bounded-key FE scheme, denoted by* bfe, *for* C *then there exists a bounded-key FE scheme, denoted by* BFE, *for* C *that additionally satisfies linear complexity property (Definition 1). Moreover, the following holds:*

- *If* bfe *is adaptively secure (resp., selectively secure) then* BFE *is adaptively secure (resp., selectively secure).*
- *If* bfe *is a public-key (resp., private key) scheme then* BFE *is a public-key (resp., private key) scheme.*
- *If* bfe *is simulation secure (resp., IND-secure) then* BFE *is simulation secure (resp., IND-secure).*

*Proof.* We focus on the case when bfe is adaptively secure, public-key and simulation secure. Our construction easily extends to the other cases as well.

We describe BFE below.

- Setup$(1^\lambda, 1^Q, 1^s)$: On input security parameter $\lambda$, query bound $Q$, maximum circuit size $s$ for which functional keys are issued, generate $(\mathsf{mpk}_i, \mathsf{msk}_i) \leftarrow$ bfe.Setup$(1^\lambda, 1^q, 1^s)$ for every $i \in [Q]$, where $q = \lambda$ (in fact, $q$ can even be set to be poly-logarithmic in the security parameter). Output the following:

$$\mathsf{MSK} = (\mathsf{msk}_1, \ldots, \mathsf{msk}_Q), \ \mathsf{MPK} = (\mathsf{mpk}_1, \ldots, \mathsf{mpk}_Q)$$

- KeyGen$(\mathsf{msk}, C)$: On input master secret key $\mathsf{msk}$, circuit $C \in \mathcal{C}$,
   - Sample $\boldsymbol{u} \xleftarrow{\$} [Q]$.
   - Generate $\mathsf{sk}_C \xleftarrow{\$}$ bfe.KeyGen(bfe.$\mathsf{msk}_u, C$).
   Output $\mathsf{SK}_C = (\boldsymbol{u}, \mathsf{sk}_C)$.

- Enc(MPK, $x$): On input master public key MPK, input $x$, generate $ct_i \leftarrow$ bfe.Enc($mpk_i, x$) for every $i \in [Q]$. Output $CT = (ct_1, \ldots, ct_Q)$.
- Dec($SK_C, CT$): On input functional key $SK_C = (u, sk_C)$, ciphertext $CT = (ct_1, \ldots, ct_Q)$, compute bfe.Dec($sk_C, ct_u$). Output the result.

The correctness of BFE follows directly from the correctness of bfe. We analyze the efficiency of the above scheme next.

Suppose the time taken to generate a bfe ciphertext of message $x$ is poly$(\lambda, s)$ then the time taken to generate a BFE ciphertext of message $x$ is $Q \cdot$ poly$(\lambda, s)$. Similarly, if the time taken to generate a bfe functional key of $C$ is poly$(\lambda, s)$, where $s$ is the size of $C$, then the time taken to generate a BFE functional key of $f$ is $Q \cdot$ poly$(\lambda, s)$. Thus, the resulting scheme BFE satisfies linear complexity property.

The only property left to be proved is the security property, which we prove next.

*Security.* Let sim be the stateful simulator of the bfe scheme. Since we invoke bfe scheme $Q$ times in the scheme, we consider $Q$ instantiations of the stateful simulator, denoted by $sim_1, \ldots, sim_Q$. We construct a simulator SIM associated with the BFE scheme. We denote the PPT adversary to be $\mathcal{A}$.

The simulator SIM proceeds as follows:

1. It receives the query bound $Q$ and the maximum circuit size $s$ from $\mathcal{A}$.
2. For every $i \in [Q]$, execute $sim_i(1^\lambda, 1^Q, 1^s)$ to obtain the $i^{th}$ master public key $mpk_i$. Set MPK $= (mpk_1, \ldots, mpk_Q)$. Send MPK to $\mathcal{A}$.
3. Initialize the sets $qset_i = \emptyset$, for every $i \in [Q]$. For every circuit query $C$ made by $\mathcal{A}$, do the following:

   Sample $u \xleftarrow{\$} [Q]$ and then generate $sk_C \leftarrow sim_u(C)$. Add $C$ to $qset_u$. If $|qset_u| > q$ then output $\perp$. Otherwise, send $SK_C = (u, sk_C)$.
   $\mathcal{A}$ finally outputs the challenge message $x$.
4. For every $i \in [Q]$, construct the set $\mathcal{V}_i$ as follows: for every $C \in qset_i$, include $(C, C(x))$ in $\mathcal{V}_i$. For every $i \in [Q]$, compute $sim_i(1^{|x|}, \mathcal{V}_i)$ to obtain $ct_i$. Set $CT = (ct_1, \ldots, ct_Q)$. Send CT to $\mathcal{A}$.
5. In the next phase, $\mathcal{A}$ makes circuit queries. For every circuit query $C$ made by the adversary, do the following:

   Sample $u \xleftarrow{\$} [Q]$ and then generate $sk_C \leftarrow sim_u(C, C(x))$. Add $C$ to $qset_u$. If $|qset_u| > q$ then output $\perp$. Otherwise, send $SK_C = (u, sk_C)$.

Consider the following hybrids. The changes are marked in red.

**Hyb$_1$:** This corresponds to the real experiment. For completeness, we describe the real experiment here.

1. The challenger Ch receives the query bound $Q$ and the maximum circuit size $s$ from $\mathcal{A}$.
2. Execute bfe.Setup$(1^\lambda, 1^Q, 1^s)$ for $Q$ times to obtain $\{(msk_i, mpk_i)\}_{i \in [Q]}$. Set MPK $= (mpk_1, \ldots, mpk_Q)$. Send MPK to $\mathcal{A}$.

3. Initialize the sets $\mathsf{qset}_i = \emptyset$, for every $i \in [Q]$. For every circuit query $C$ made by $\mathcal{A}$, Ch does the following:

   Sample $\boldsymbol{u} \xleftarrow{\$} [Q]$ and then generate $\mathsf{sk}_C \leftarrow \mathsf{bfe.KeyGen}(\mathsf{msk}_{\boldsymbol{u}}, C)$. Add $C$ to $\mathsf{qset}_{\boldsymbol{u}}$. Send $\mathsf{SK}_C = (\boldsymbol{u}, \mathsf{sk}_C)$ to $\mathcal{A}$. $\mathcal{A}$ finally outputs the challenge message $x$.
4. For every $i \in [Q]$, generate $\mathsf{ct}_i \leftarrow \mathsf{bfe.Enc}(\mathsf{mpk}_i, x)$. Set $\mathsf{CT} = (\mathsf{ct}_1, \ldots, \mathsf{ct}_Q)$. Send $\mathsf{CT}$ to $\mathcal{A}$.
5. In the next phase, $\mathcal{A}$ makes circuit queries. For every circuit query $C$ made by $\mathcal{A}$, do the following:

   Sample $\boldsymbol{u} \xleftarrow{\$} [Q]$ and then generate $\mathsf{sk}_C \leftarrow \mathsf{bfe.KeyGen}(\mathsf{msk}_{\boldsymbol{u}}, C)$. Add $C$ to $\mathsf{qset}_{\boldsymbol{u}}$. Send $\mathsf{SK}_C = (\boldsymbol{u}, \mathsf{sk}_C)$ to $\mathcal{A}$.
6. Let $b$ be the output of $\mathcal{A}$. If $\left| \bigcup_{i=1}^{Q} \mathsf{qset}_i \right| > Q$, output $\perp$. Otherwise, output $b$.

*Remark 5.* Note that the experiment described above is phrased differently from the real experiment of the bounded-key FE scheme. In the real experiment, the challenger only keeps track of the total number of BFE circuit queries made by the adversary but in $\mathbf{Hyb}_1$, the challenger keeps track of the set of bfe functional keys issued per index. Since ultimately the challenger only aborts if the size of the union of all these sets exceeds $Q$, the output distribution of $\mathbf{Hyb}_1$ is the same as the output distribution of the real experiment.

$\mathbf{Hyb}_2$: This hybrid is the same as the previous hybrid except that the real experiment outputs $\perp$ if there exists an index $\boldsymbol{u} \in [Q]$ such that $|\mathsf{qset}_{\boldsymbol{u}}| > q$.

In particular, we make the following changes to bullets 3 and 5 in the experiment described in $\mathbf{Hyb}_1$.

3. Initialize the sets $\mathsf{qset}_i = \emptyset$, for every $i \in [Q]$. For every circuit query $C$ made by $\mathcal{A}$, Ch does the following:

   Sample $\boldsymbol{u} \xleftarrow{\$} [Q]$ and then generate $\mathsf{sk}_C \leftarrow \mathsf{bfe.KeyGen}(\mathsf{msk}_{\boldsymbol{u}}, C)$. Add $C$ to $\mathsf{qset}_{\boldsymbol{u}}$. If $|\mathsf{qset}_{\boldsymbol{u}}| > q$ then output $\perp$. Otherwise, send $\mathsf{SK}_C = (\boldsymbol{u}, \mathsf{sk}_C)$ to $\mathcal{A}$. $\mathcal{A}$ finally outputs the challenge message $x$.
5. In the next phase, $\mathcal{A}$ makes circuit queries. For every circuit query $C$ made by $\mathcal{A}$, do the following:

   Sample $\boldsymbol{u} \xleftarrow{\$} [Q]$ and then generate $\mathsf{sk}_C \leftarrow \mathsf{bfe.KeyGen}(\mathsf{msk}_{\boldsymbol{u}}, C)$. Add $C$ to $\mathsf{qset}_{\boldsymbol{u}}$. If $|\mathsf{qset}_{\boldsymbol{u}}| > q$ then output $\perp$. Otherwise, send $\mathsf{SK}_C = (\boldsymbol{u}, \mathsf{sk}_C)$ to $\mathcal{A}$.

*Claim.* The statistical distance between the output distributions of $\mathbf{Hyb}_1$ and $\mathbf{Hyb}_2$ is at most $Q \cdot e^{-\frac{(q-1)^2}{1+q}}$ and thus, negligible in $\lambda$.

*Proof.* Define $\mathbf{X}_{\boldsymbol{u},j}$, for every $\boldsymbol{u} \in [Q], j \in [Q]$, to be a random variable such that $\mathbf{X}_{\boldsymbol{u},j} = 1$ if in the $j^{th}$ circuit query $C$ made by the adversary, the challenger responds with $\mathsf{SK}_C = (\boldsymbol{u}, \mathsf{sk}_C)$; that is, the challenger responds with the functional key corresponding to the $\boldsymbol{u}^{th}$ instantiation of bfe. Let $\mathbf{X}_{\boldsymbol{u}} = \sum_{j=1}^{Q} \mathbf{X}_{\boldsymbol{u},j}$.

Note that $\Pr[\mathbf{X}_{\boldsymbol{u},j} = 1] = \frac{1}{Q}$. By linearity of expectation, $\mathbb{E}[\mathbf{X}_{\boldsymbol{u}}] = 1$.

By Chernoff bound, we have the following: for every $u \in Q$,

$$\Pr[\mathbf{X}_u > q] = \Pr[\mathbf{X}_u > q \cdot \mathbb{E}[\mathbf{X}_u]]$$

$$\leq \frac{1}{e^{\frac{(q-1)^2}{2+(q-1)} \cdot \mathbb{E}[\mathbf{X}_u]}}$$

Thus for any fixed $u \in [Q]$, the probability that the number of bfe functional keys per index $u$ issued by the challenger is greater than $q$ is at most $e^{-\frac{(q-1)^2}{1+q}}$. By union bound, the probability that there exists an index $u$ such that the challenger issues more than $q$ functional keys with respect to $u$ is at most $Q \cdot e^{-\frac{(q-1)^2}{1+q}}$.

Next, we consider a sequence of intermediate hybrids.

**Hyb$_{3.j}$, for all $j \in [Q]$:** In this intermediate hybrid, the first $u$ instantiations, with $u < j$ are simulated. The rest of the instantiations are honestly computed. We consider $j$ instantiations of the stateful simulator, denoted by $\mathsf{sim}_1, \ldots, \mathsf{sim}_j$. We describe the hybrid experiment below.

1. The challenger Ch receives the query bound $Q$ and the maximum circuit size $s$ from $\mathcal{A}$.
2. For $i < j$, execute $\mathsf{sim}_i(1^\lambda, 1^Q, 1^s)$ to obtain the $i^{th}$ master public key $\mathsf{mpk}_i$. For $i \geq j$, execute $\mathsf{bfe.Setup}(1^\lambda, 1^Q, 1^s)$ to obtain $(\mathsf{msk}_i, \mathsf{mpk}_i)$. Set $\mathsf{MPK} = (\mathsf{mpk}_1, \ldots, \mathsf{mpk}_Q)$. Send $\mathsf{MPK}$ to $\mathcal{A}$.
3. Initialize the sets $\mathsf{qset}_i = \emptyset$, for every $i \in [Q]$. For every circuit query $C$ made by $\mathcal{A}$, Ch does the following:
   Sample $u \xleftarrow{\$} [Q]$ and then generate $\mathsf{sk}_C$ as follows:
   – If $u < j$, generate $\mathsf{sk}_C \leftarrow \mathsf{sim}_u(C)$.
   – If $u \geq j$, generate $\mathsf{sk}_C \leftarrow \mathsf{bfe.KeyGen}(\mathsf{msk}_u, C)$.
   Add $C$ to $\mathsf{qset}_u$. If $|\mathsf{qset}_u| > q$ then output $\perp$. Otherwise, send $\mathsf{SK}_C = (u, \mathsf{sk}_C)$ to $\mathcal{A}$.
   $\mathcal{A}$ finally outputs the challenge message $x$.
4. For every $i \in [Q]$, construct the set $\mathcal{V}_i$ as follows: for every $C \in \mathsf{qset}_i$, include $(C, C(x))$ in $\mathcal{V}_i$. Compute $\mathsf{CT}$ as follows:
   – If $i < j$, compute $\mathsf{sim}_i(1^{|x|}, \mathcal{V}_i)$ to obtain $\mathsf{ct}_i$.
   – If $i \geq j$, compute $\mathsf{ct}_i \leftarrow \mathsf{bfe.Enc}(\mathsf{mpk}_i, x)$.
   Set $\mathsf{CT} = (\mathsf{ct}_1, \ldots, \mathsf{ct}_Q)$. Send $\mathsf{CT}$ to $\mathcal{A}$.
5. In the next phase, $\mathcal{A}$ makes circuit queries. For every circuit query $C$ made by $\mathcal{A}$, do the following:
   Sample $u \xleftarrow{\$} [Q]$ and then generate $\mathsf{sk}_C$ as follows:
   – If $u < j$, generate $\mathsf{sk}_C \leftarrow \mathsf{sim}_u(C, C(x))$.
   – If $u \geq j$, generate $\mathsf{sk}_C \leftarrow \mathsf{bfe.KeyGen}(\mathsf{msk}_u, C)$.
   Add $C$ to $\mathsf{qset}_u$. If $|\mathsf{qset}_u| > q$ then output $\perp$. Otherwise, send $\mathsf{SK}_C = (u, \mathsf{sk}_C)$ to $\mathcal{A}$.
6. Let $b$ be the output of $\mathcal{A}$. If $\left|\bigcup_{i=1}^Q \mathsf{qset}_i\right| > Q$, output $\perp$. Otherwise, output $b$.

The following two claims are immediate.

*Claim.* The output distributions of $\mathbf{Hyb}_2$ and $\mathbf{Hyb}_{3.1}$ are identically distributed.

*Claim.* For every $\mathbf{j} \in [Q - 1]$, the security of bfe implies that the output distributions of $\mathbf{Hyb}_{3.j}$ and $\mathbf{Hyb}_{3.j+1}$ are computationally indistinguishable.

$\mathbf{Hyb}_4$: This corresponds to the simulated experiment.
The proof of the following claim is immediate.

*Claim.* The security of bfe implies that the output distributions of $\mathbf{Hyb}_{3.Q}$ and $\mathbf{Hyb}_4$ are computationally indistinguishable.

## 5   Construction of Bounded-Key FE for P/Poly

We construct a bounded-key FE scheme for P/Poly as follows:

- First we define a client-server framework and show how to construct a bounded-key FE for P/Poly from a protocol in this client-server framework.
- We then show, in the full version [AV19], how to construct a protocol in the client-server framework from one-way functions.

We begin by describing the client-server framework.

### 5.1   Client-Server Framework

The client-server framework consists of a single client and $N = N(\lambda, Q)$ servers, where $\lambda$ is the security parameter. It is additionally parameterized by $n = n(\lambda, Q)$ and $t = t(\lambda, Q)$. The framework consists of the following two phases:

- **Offline Phase:** In this phase, the client takes as input the number of sessions $Q$, size of the circuit delegated $s$, input $x$ and executes a PPT algorithm InpEnc that outputs correlated input encodings $(\widehat{x}^1, \ldots, \widehat{x}^N)$. It sends the encoding $\widehat{x}^u$ to the $u^{th}$ server.
- **Online Phase:** This phase is executed for $Q$ sessions. In each session, the client delegates the computation of a circuit $C$ on $x$ to the servers. This is done in the following steps:
    - **Client Delegation:** This is performed by the client computing a PPT algorithm CktEnc on input $(1^\lambda, 1^Q, 1^s, C)$ to obtain $(\widehat{C}^1, \ldots, \widehat{C}^N)$. It sends the circuit encoding $\widehat{C}^u$ to the $u^{th}$ server. Note that CktEnc is executed independently of the offline phase and in particular, does not depend on the randomness used in the offline phase[2].
    - **Local Computation by Servers:** Upon receiving the circuit encodings from the client, a subset $\mathbf{S}$ of servers come online and the $u^{th}$ server in this set $\mathbf{S}$ computes $\mathsf{Local}(\widehat{C}^u, \widehat{x}^u)$ to obtain the $u^{th}$ output encoding $\widehat{y}^u$.
    - **Decoding:** Finally, the output is recovered by computing a PPT algorithm Decode on $\left(\{\widehat{y}^u\}_{u \in \mathbf{S}}, \mathbf{S}\right)$.

We describe the properties below. We start with correctness.

---

[2] We could define a notion where CktEnc takes as input the randomness of the offline phase. It is however not clear how to build FE from such a notion.

*Correctness.* A protocol $\Pi$ in the client-server framework is said to be correct if the following holds:

- Suppose the client computes encodings of input $x$ by computing $(\widehat{x}^1, \ldots, \widehat{x}^N) \leftarrow \mathsf{InpEnc}(1^\lambda, 1^Q, 1^s, x)$.
- In the online phase, let $C$ be the circuit that the client wants to delegate. The client computes $(\widehat{C}^1, \ldots, \widehat{C}^N) \leftarrow \mathsf{CktEnc}(1^\lambda, 1^Q, 1^s, C)$ and distributes the circuit encodings to all the servers. A subset of servers $\mathbf{S} \subseteq [N]$, of size $n$, then locally compute on the circuit encodings. That is, for every $u \in \mathbf{S}$, the $u^{th}$ server computes $\widehat{y}^u = \mathsf{Local}(\mathsf{gc}, \widehat{x}^u)$. Finally, the output can be recovered by computing $\mathsf{Decode}(\{\widehat{y}^u\}_{u \in \mathbf{S}}, \mathbf{S})$ to obtain $y$.

We require that $y = C(x)$.

**Security.** We allow the adversary to be able to corrupt a subset of servers. Once the server is corrupted, the entire state of the server is leaked to the adversary. The adversary, however, is not allowed to corrupt the client. In every session, since $n$ servers can recover the output, the number of servers that can be corrupted has to be less than $n^3$.

Informally, we require the following guarantee: even if the adversary can corrupt a subset of servers, he cannot learn anything beyond the outputs of the computation $(C_1(x), \ldots, C_Q(x))$ in every session, where $C_1, \ldots, C_Q$ are the circuits delegated by the client. However, the circuits $(C_1, \ldots, C_Q)$ are not hidden from the adversary. Since our end goal is to build FE for P/Poly, we need to suitably define the security property that would enable us to prove the security of FE. Towards this, we incorporate the following in the security definition of the client-server framework:

- We not only allow the adversary to choose the servers to corrupt but also allow it to decide the subsets of servers $\mathbf{S}_1, \ldots, \mathbf{S}_Q$ participating in the $Q$ sessions.
- In every session, the adversary is provided all the $N$ circuit encodings. Moreover, the outputs of the local computation of all the servers, including the honest servers, are visible to the adversary.

To define the security notion formally, we first state the following experiments. The first experiment $\mathsf{Expt}_0$ is parameterized by a PPT adversary $\mathcal{A}$ and PPT challenger $\mathsf{Ch}$ and the second experiment $\mathsf{Expt}_1$ is parameterized by $\mathcal{A}$ and PPT stateful simulator $\mathsf{Sim}_{\mathsf{csf}}$.

$\underline{\mathsf{Expt}_0^{\mathcal{A},\mathsf{Ch}}(1^\lambda):}$

---

[3] If $n$ or more servers can be corrupted then the corrupted set can recover $C(x)$ for any circuit $C$: this is because the corrupted servers can execute $\mathsf{CktEnc}$ on input $C$, run the local computation procedure and then decode their outputs. Thus, such a notion would imply program obfuscation.

- $\mathcal{A}$ outputs the query bound $Q$, maximum circuit size $s$, total number of parties $N$, number of parties $n$ participating in any session, threshold $t$, corruption set $\mathcal{S}_{\mathsf{corr}} \subseteq [N]$ and the input $x$. If $|\mathcal{S}_{\mathsf{corr}}| > t$ then the experiment aborts. It also outputs the sets $\mathbf{S}_1, \ldots, \mathbf{S}_Q \subseteq [N]$ such that $|\mathbf{S}_i| = n$, where $\mathbf{S}_i$ is the set of parties participating in the $i^{th}$ session.
- **Circuit Queries**: $\mathcal{A}$ is allowed to make a total of $Q$ circuit queries. First, it makes $Q_1 \leq Q$ adaptive[4] circuit queries $C_1, \ldots, C_{Q_1}$.
  For the $i^{th}$ circuit query $C_i$, Ch computes $\left(\widehat{C_i}^1, \ldots, \widehat{C_i}^N\right) \leftarrow \mathsf{CktEnc}(1^\lambda, 1^Q,$ $1^s, C_i)$ and sends $\left(\widehat{C_i}^1, \ldots, \widehat{C_i}^N\right)$.
- **Challenge Input Query**: $\mathcal{A}$ submits the input $x$. Ch generates $\mathsf{InpEnc}(1^\lambda, 1^Q, 1^s, x)$ to obtain $(\widehat{x}^1, \ldots, \widehat{x}^N)$.
  Ch sends $\left(\{\widehat{x}^u\}_{u \in \mathcal{S}_{\mathsf{corr}}}, \left\{\mathsf{Local}\left(\widehat{C_i}^u, \widehat{x}^u\right)\right\}_{i \in [Q_1], u \in \mathbf{S}_i}\right)$. That is, the challenger sends the input encodings of the corrupted set of servers along with the outputs of $\mathsf{Local}$ on the circuit encodings received so far.
- **Circuit Queries**: $\mathcal{A}$ then makes $Q_2 = Q - Q_1$ adaptive circuit queries $C_{Q_1+1}, \ldots, C_Q$.
  Ch computes $\left(\widehat{C_i}^1, \ldots, \widehat{C_i}^N\right) \leftarrow \mathsf{CktEnc}(1^\lambda, 1^Q, 1^s, C_i)$ and sends
  $$\left\{\left(\left(\widehat{C_i}^1, \ldots, \widehat{C_i}^N\right), \mathsf{Local}\left(\widehat{C_i}^u, \widehat{x}^u\right)\right)\right\}_{i \in \{Q_1+1, \ldots, Q\}, u \in [\mathbf{S}_i]}.$$
- $\mathcal{A}$ outputs a bit $b$. The output of the experiment is $b$.

$\underline{\mathsf{Expt}_1^{\mathcal{A}, \mathsf{Sim}_{\mathsf{csf}}}(1^\lambda)}:$

- $\mathcal{A}$ outputs the query bound $Q$, maximum circuit size $s$, total number of parties $N$, number of parties $n$ participating in any session, threshold $t$, corruption set $\mathcal{S}_{\mathsf{corr}} \subseteq [N]$ and the input $x$. If $|\mathcal{S}_{\mathsf{corr}}| > t$ then the experiment aborts. It also outputs the sets $\mathbf{S}_1, \ldots, \mathbf{S}_Q \subseteq [N]$ such that $|\mathbf{S}_i| = n$, where $\mathbf{S}_i$ is the set of parties participating in the $i^{th}$ session.
- **Circuit Queries**: $\mathcal{A}$ makes a total of $Q$ adaptive queries. First it makes $Q_1 \leq Q$ adaptive circuit queries. For the $i^{th}$ circuit query $C_i$, the simulator computes $\left(\widehat{C_i}^1, \ldots, \widehat{C_i}^N\right) \leftarrow \mathsf{Sim}_{\mathsf{csf}}(C_i)$ and sends $\left(\widehat{C_i}^1, \ldots, \widehat{C_i}^N\right)$.
- **Challenge Input Query**: $\mathcal{A}$ submits the input $x$. Construct $\mathcal{V}$ as follows: $\mathcal{V} = \{C_i, C_i(x) : i \in [Q_1]\}$.
  $\mathsf{Sim}_{\mathsf{csf}}$ on input $(1^{|x|}, \mathcal{S}_{\mathsf{corr}}, \mathcal{V})$ (and in particular, it does not get $x$ as input) outputs the simulated encodings $(\{\widehat{x}^u\}_{u \in \mathcal{S}_{\mathsf{corr}}})$ and the encodings of outputs $\{\widehat{y}_i^u\}_{i \in [Q_1], u \in \mathbf{S}_i}$ such that $\widehat{y}_i^u = \mathsf{Local}\left(\widehat{C_i}^u, \widehat{x}^u\right)$ for every $u \in \mathbf{S}_i \cap \mathcal{S}_{\mathsf{corr}}$.
- **Circuit Queries**: $\mathcal{A}$ then makes $Q_2 = Q - Q_1$ adaptive circuit queries $C_{Q_1+1}, \ldots, C_Q$. The simulator $\mathsf{Sim}_{\mathsf{csf}}$ on input $(i, C_i, C_i(x))$, for $i \in \{Q_1 + 1, \ldots, Q\}$, sends $\left(\left(\widehat{C_i}^1, \ldots, \widehat{C_i}^N\right), \widehat{y}_i^u\right)$.
- $\mathcal{A}$ outputs a bit $b$. The output of the experiment is $b$.

---

[4] By adaptive, we mean that the adversary can decide each circuit query as a function of all the previous circuit queries.

We formally define the security property below.

**Definition 3 (Security).** *A protocol $\Pi$ is secure if for every PPT adversary $\mathcal{A}$, there exists a PPT simulator $\mathsf{Sim}_{\mathsf{csf}}$ such that the following holds:*

$$\left| \Pr[0 \leftarrow \mathsf{Expt}_0^{\mathcal{A},\mathsf{Ch}}(1^\lambda)] - \Pr[0 \leftarrow \mathsf{Expt}_1^{\mathcal{A},\mathsf{Sim}_{\mathsf{csf}}}(1^\lambda)] \right| \leq \mathsf{negl}(\lambda),$$

*for some negligible function* $\mathsf{negl}$.

## 5.2    Bounded-Key FE for P/Poly from Client-Server Framework

We now present a construction of a bounded-key functional encryption for all polynomial-sized circuits from a protocol in the client-server framework.

**Theorem 7.** *There exists a public-key (resp., private-key) adaptively secure bounded-key functional encryption scheme* BFE *for* P/Poly *assuming,*

- *A public-key (resp., private-key) adaptively secure single-key functional encryption scheme* 1fe *for* P/Poly *and,*
- *A protocol for* P/Poly *in the client-server framework, denoted by* $\Pi = (\mathsf{InpEnc}, \mathsf{CktEnc}, \mathsf{Local}, \mathsf{Decode})$.

*Proof.* We focus on the public-key setting; the construction and the analysis for the private-key setting is identical. We describe the algorithms of BFE below. Let the protocol in the client-server framework be parameterized by $t = \Theta(Q\lambda)$, $N = \Theta(Q^2 t^2)$ and $n = \Theta(t)$, where $Q$ is the query bound defined as part of the scheme.

- $\underline{\mathsf{Setup}(1^\lambda, 1^Q, 1^s)}$: On input security parameter $\lambda$, query bound $Q$, circuit size $s$, generate $(\mathsf{msk}_i, \mathsf{mpk}_i) \leftarrow \mathsf{1fe.Setup}(1^\lambda, 1^s)$ for $i \in [N]$. Output the following:

$$\mathsf{MSK} = (\mathsf{msk}_1, \ldots, \mathsf{msk}_N), \quad \mathsf{MPK} = (Q, \mathsf{mpk}_1, \ldots, \mathsf{mpk}_N)$$

- $\underline{\mathsf{KeyGen}(\mathsf{MSK}, C)}$: On input master secret key MSK, circuit $C$,

   • Sample a set $\mathbf{S} \xleftarrow{\$} [N]$, of size $n$, uniformly at random.
   • Compute $\left( \widehat{C}^1, \ldots, \widehat{C}^N \right) \leftarrow \mathsf{CktEnc}(1^\lambda, 1^Q, 1^s, C)$.
   • Let $\mathsf{E}^u(\cdot) = \mathsf{Local}(\widehat{C}^u, \cdot)$. Generate a functional key for $\mathsf{E}^u$; that is, compute $\mathsf{sk}_{\mathsf{E}^u} \leftarrow \mathsf{1fe.KeyGen}(\mathsf{msk}_u, \mathsf{E}^u)$ for every $u \in \mathbf{S}$.

   Output $\mathsf{SK}_C = \left( \mathbf{S}, \{\mathsf{sk}_{\mathsf{E}^u}\}_{u \in \mathbf{S}} \right)$.

- $\underline{\mathsf{Enc}(\mathsf{MPK}, x)}$: On input master public key MPK,
   • Compute $(\widehat{x}^1, \ldots, \widehat{x}^N) \leftarrow \mathsf{InpEnc}\left(1^\lambda, 1^Q, 1^s, x\right)$.
   • For every $i \in [N]$, compute $\mathsf{ct}_i \leftarrow \mathsf{FE.Enc}\left(\mathsf{mpk}_i, \widehat{x}^i\right)$.

   Output $\mathsf{CT} = (\mathsf{ct}_1, \ldots, \mathsf{ct}_N)$.

- $\underline{\mathsf{Dec}(\mathsf{SK}_C, \mathsf{CT})}$: On input functional key $\mathsf{SK}_C = \left( \mathbf{S}, \{\mathsf{sk}_{\mathsf{E}^u}\}_{u \in \mathbf{S}} \right)$, ciphertext $\mathsf{CT} = (\mathsf{ct}_1, \ldots, \mathsf{ct}_N)$,
   • For every $u \in \mathbf{S}$, compute $\widehat{y}^u \leftarrow \mathsf{1fe.Dec}(\mathsf{sk}_{\mathsf{E}^u}, \mathsf{ct}_u)$.
   • Compute $\mathsf{Decode}\left( \{\widehat{y}^u\}_{u \in \mathbf{S}}, \mathbf{S} \right)$ to obtain $y$.

   Output $y$.

*Correctness.* Consider a circuit $C$ and an input $x$. Suppose $\mathsf{CT} \leftarrow \mathsf{Enc}(\mathsf{MPK}, x)$ and $\mathsf{SK}_C \leftarrow \mathsf{KeyGen}(\mathsf{MSK}, C)$. Let $\mathsf{CT} = (\mathsf{ct}_1, \ldots, \mathsf{ct}_N)$ and $\mathsf{SK}_C = (\mathbf{S}, \{\mathsf{sk}_{\mathsf{E}^u}\}_{u \in \mathbf{S}})$. By the correctness of 1fe, $\mathsf{1fe.Dec}(\mathsf{sk}_{\mathsf{E}^u}, \mathsf{ct}^u) = \mathsf{Local}(\widehat{C}^u, \widehat{x}^u)$ for every $u \in \mathbf{S}$. From the correctness of $\Pi$, it follows that $\mathsf{Decode}\left(\left\{\mathsf{Local}(\widehat{C}^u, \widehat{x}^u)\right\}_{u \in \mathbf{S}}, \mathbf{S}\right) = C(x)$.

We present the proof of security in the full version [AV19].

*Instantiation.* The bounded-key functional encryption scheme described above makes black box usage of $\mathsf{InpEnc}(\cdot)$ algorithm of $\Pi$. Moreover, in the construction of $\Pi$ (described in the full version [AV19]), pseudorandom generators are only used in $\mathsf{InpEnc}(\cdot)$. Furthermore, $\mathsf{InpEnc}(\cdot)$ only makes black box calls to the pseudorandom generator. Thus, assuming that 1fe makes black box usage of public-key encryption, the bounded-key functional encryption scheme described above, when instantiated with $\Pi$, yields a bounded-key scheme that makes only oracle calls to cryptographic primitives (public-key encryption and pseudorandom generators). All that is left is to demonstrate the feasibility of a single-key adaptively-secure public-key functional encryption that makes black box usage of public-key encryption.

To show this, we first present an informal description of single-key public-key FE 1fe for P/Poly from [SS10].

- $\mathsf{1fe.Setup}\left(1^\lambda, 1^s\right)$: Sample $2s$ public keys $pk_{i,b}$ ($i \in [s], b \in \{0,1\}$) and secret keys $sk_{i,b}$ ($i \in [s], b \in \{0,1\}$) corresponding to a public-key encryption scheme. Call the master public key $\mathsf{mpk} = (pk_{i,b})_{i \in [s], b \in \{0,1\}}$ and the master secret key $\mathsf{msk} = (sk_{i,b})_{i \in [s], b \in \{0,1\}}$.
- $\mathsf{1fe.KeyGen}(\mathsf{msk}, C)$: Output $\mathsf{sk}_C = (sk_{i,C_i})$, where $C_i$ denotes the $i^{th}$ bit in the description of $C$. Output $\mathsf{sk}_C$.
- $\mathsf{1fe.Enc}(\mathsf{msk}, x)$: Generate a garbling of $U_x(\cdot)$, where $U_x(\cdot)$ is a universal circuit that takes as input a circuit $C$ of size $s$ and outputs $C(x)$. Call the resulting garbled circuit to be $\mathsf{GC}$. Encrypt the $(i, b)^{th}$ wire label, for $i \in [s], b \in \{0,1\}$, using $pk_{i,b}$; call this ciphertext $ct_{i,b}$. Output $\mathsf{ct} = \left(\mathsf{GC}, (ct_{i,b})_{i \in [s], b \in \{0,1\}}\right)$.
- $\mathsf{1fe.Dec}(\mathsf{sk}_C, \mathsf{ct})$: Decrypt $ct_{i,C_i}$ using $sk_{i,C_i}$ to obtain the $(i, C_i)^{th}$ wire label. Using all the wire labels recovered, evaluate the garbled circuit to obtain $C(x)$.

The above construction only guarantees selective security; this construction was upgraded to adaptive security by [GVW12a]. This construction is described in Sect. 4.3 (page 14) of the ePrint version of [GVW12a] ([GVW12b], version posted on 06-Sep-2012 17:57:14 UTC). The ONEQFE scheme (that allows a single function query and adaptive simulation security) described in Sect. 4.3 is constructed from randomized encodings for P/poly (which can be based on one-way functions) along with BFFE scheme described in Sect. 4.2. Moreover, the BFFE scheme described in Sect. 4.2 can be based on any PKE scheme (see the first para of Sect. 4.2).

BFFE scheme makes black box usage of PKE. Also, the ONEQFE scheme makes black-box usage of the one-way function (used for randomized encoding) and the underlying procedures of the BFFE scheme.

# References

[ABT18]   Applebaum, B., Brakerski, Z., Tsabary, R.: Perfect secure computation in two rounds. In: Beimel, A., Dziembowski, S. (eds.) TCC 2018. LNCS, vol. 11239, pp. 152–174. Springer, Cham (2018). https://doi.org/10.1007/978-3-030-03807-6_6

[ACGJ18]   Ananth, P., Choudhuri, A.R., Goel, A., Jain, A.: Round-optimal secure multiparty computation with honest majority. In: Shacham, H., Boldyreva, A. (eds.) CRYPTO 2018. LNCS, vol. 10992, pp. 395–424. Springer, Cham (2018). https://doi.org/10.1007/978-3-319-96881-0_14

[Agr17]   Agrawal, S.: Stronger security for reusable garbled circuits, general definitions and attacks. In: Katz, J., Shacham, H. (eds.) CRYPTO 2017. LNCS, vol. 10401, pp. 3–35. Springer, Cham (2017). https://doi.org/10.1007/978-3-319-63688-7_1

[AJ15]   Ananth, P., Jain, A.: Indistinguishability obfuscation from compact functional encryption. In: Gennaro, R., Robshaw, M. (eds.) CRYPTO 2015. LNCS, vol. 9215, pp. 308–326. Springer, Heidelberg (2015). https://doi.org/10.1007/978-3-662-47989-6_15

[AJS15]   Ananth, P., Jain, A., Sahai, A.: Achieving compactness generically: indistinguishability obfuscation from non-compact functional encryption. IACR Cryptology ePrint Archive 2015:730 (2015)

[AR17]   Agrawal, S., Rosen, A.: Functional encryption for bounded collusions, revisited. In: TCC, pp. 173–205 (2017)

[AV19]   Ananth, P., Vaikuntanathan, V.: Optimal bounded-collusion secure functional encryption. Cryptology ePrint Archive, Report 2019/314 (2019). https://eprint.iacr.org/2019/314

[BL18]   Benhamouda, F., Lin, H.: $k$-round multiparty computation from $k$-round oblivious transfer via garbled interactive circuits. In: Nielsen, J.B., Rijmen, V. (eds.) EUROCRYPT 2018. LNCS, vol. 10821, pp. 500–532. Springer, Cham (2018). https://doi.org/10.1007/978-3-319-78375-8_17

[BLSV18]   Brakerski, Z., Lombardi, A., Segev, G., Vaikuntanathan, V.: Anonymous IBE, leakage resilience and circular security from new assumptions. In: Nielsen, J.B., Rijmen, V. (eds.) EUROCRYPT 2018. LNCS, vol. 10820, pp. 535–564. Springer, Cham (2018). https://doi.org/10.1007/978-3-319-78381-9_20

[BNPW16]   Bitansky, N., Nishimaki, R., Passelègue, A., Wichs, D.: From cryptomania to obfustopia through secret-key functional encryption. In: Hirt, M., Smith, A. (eds.) TCC 2016. LNCS, vol. 9986, pp. 391–418. Springer, Heidelberg (2016). https://doi.org/10.1007/978-3-662-53644-5_15

[BOGW88]   Ben-Or, M., Goldwasser, S., Wigderson, A.: Completeness theorems for non-cryptographic fault-tolerant distributed computation. In: STOC (1988)

[BSW11] Boneh, D., Sahai, A., Waters, B.: Functional encryption: definitions and challenges. In: Ishai, Y. (ed.) TCC 2011. LNCS, vol. 6597, pp. 253–273. Springer, Heidelberg (2011). https://doi.org/10.1007/978-3-642-19571-6_16

[BV15] Bitansky, N., Vaikuntanathan, V.: Indistinguishability obfuscation from functional encryption. In: IEEE 56th Annual Symposium on Foundations of Computer Science, FOCS 2015, Berkeley, CA, USA, 17–20 October, 2015, pp. 171–190 (2015)

[CHH+07] Cramer, R., et al.: Bounded CCA2-secure encryption. In: Kurosawa, K. (ed.) ASIACRYPT 2007. LNCS, vol. 4833, pp. 502–518. Springer, Heidelberg (2007). https://doi.org/10.1007/978-3-540-76900-2_31

[CVW+18] Chen, Y., Vaikuntanathan, V., Waters, B., Wee, H., Wichs, D.: Traitor-tracing from lwe made simple and attribute-based. Cryptology ePrint Archive, Report 2018/897 (2018). https://eprint.iacr.org/2018/897

[DG17a] Döttling, N., Garg, S.: From selective IBE to full IBE and selective HIBE. In: TCC, pp. 372–408 (2017)

[DG17b] Döttling, N., Garg, S.: Identity-based encryption from the Diffie-Hellman assumption. In: Katz, J., Shacham, H. (eds.) CRYPTO 2017. LNCS, vol. 10401, pp. 537–569. Springer, Cham (2017). https://doi.org/10.1007/978-3-319-63688-7_18

[DKXY02] Dodis, Y., Katz, J., Xu, S., Yung, M.: Key-insulated public key cryptosystems. In: Knudsen, L.R. (ed.) EUROCRYPT 2002. LNCS, vol. 2332, pp. 65–82. Springer, Heidelberg (2002). https://doi.org/10.1007/3-540-46035-7_5

[GIS18] Garg, S., Ishai, Y., Srinivasan, A.: Two-round MPC: information-theoretic and black-box. In: Beimel, A., Dziembowski, S. (eds.) TCC 2018. LNCS, vol. 11239, pp. 123–151. Springer, Cham (2018). https://doi.org/10.1007/978-3-030-03807-6_5

[GKP+13] Goldwasser, S., Kalai, Y.T., Popa, R.A., Vaikuntanathan, V., Zeldovich, N.: Reusable garbled circuits and succinct functional encryption. In: STOC (2013)

[GLW12] Goldwasser, S., Lewko, A.B., Wilson, D.A.: Bounded-collusion IBE from key homomorphism. In: TCC 2012

[GS16] Garg, S., Srinivasan, A.: Single-key to multi-key functional encryption with polynomial loss. In: TCC, pp. 419–442 (2016)

[GS18] Garg, S., Srinivasan, A.: Two-round multiparty secure computation from minimal assumptions. In: Nielsen, J.B., Rijmen, V. (eds.) EUROCRYPT 2018. LNCS, vol. 10821, pp. 468–499. Springer, Cham (2018). https://doi.org/10.1007/978-3-319-78375-8_16

[GVW12a] Gorbunov, S., Vaikuntanathan, V., Wee, H.: Functional encryption with bounded collusions via multi-party computation. In: Safavi-Naini, R., Canetti, R. (eds.) CRYPTO 2012. LNCS, vol. 7417, pp. 162–179. Springer, Heidelberg (2012). https://doi.org/10.1007/978-3-642-32009-5_11

[GVW12b] Gorbunov, S., Vaikuntanathan, V., Wee, H.: Functional encryption with bounded collusions via multi-party computation. Cryptology ePrint Archive, Report 2012/521 (2012). https://eprint.iacr.org/2012/521

[HK04] Heng, S.-H., Kurosawa, K.: k-resilient identity-based encryption in the standard model. In: Okamoto, T. (ed.) CT-RSA 2004. LNCS, vol. 2964, pp. 67–80. Springer, Heidelberg (2004). https://doi.org/10.1007/978-3-540-24660-2_6

[ISV+17]  Itkis, G., Shen, E., Varia, M., Wilson, D., Yerukhimovich, A.: Bounded-collusion attribute-based encryption from minimal assumptions. In: Fehr, S. (ed.) PKC 2017. LNCS, vol. 10175, pp. 67–87. Springer, Heidelberg (2017). https://doi.org/10.1007/978-3-662-54388-7_3

[KNT18]  Kitagawa, F., Nishimaki, R., Tanaka, K.: Obfustopia built on secret-key functional encryption. In: Nielsen, J.B., Rijmen, V. (eds.) EUROCRYPT 2018. LNCS, vol. 10821, pp. 603–648. Springer, Cham (2018). https://doi.org/10.1007/978-3-319-78375-8_20

[LM16]  Li, B., Micciancio, D.: Compactness vs collusion resistance in functional encryption. In: Hirt, M., Smith, A. (eds.) TCC 2016. LNCS, vol. 9986, pp. 443–468. Springer, Heidelberg (2016). https://doi.org/10.1007/978-3-662-53644-5_17

[SS10]  Sahai, A., Seyalioglu, H.: Worry-free encryption: functional encryption with public keys. In: Proceedings of the 17th ACM Conference on Computer and Communications Security, pp. 463–472. ACM (2010)

[SW05]  Sahai, A., Waters, B.: Fuzzy identity-based encryption. In: Cramer, R. (ed.) EUROCRYPT 2005. LNCS, vol. 3494, pp. 457–473. Springer, Heidelberg (2005). https://doi.org/10.1007/11426639_27

[SW14]  Sahai, A., Waters, B.: How to use indistinguishability obfuscation: deniable encryption, and more. In: STOC (2014)

[Yao86]  Yao, A.C.-C.: How to generate and exchange secrets (extended abstract). In: FOCS, pp. 162–167 (1986)

# From FE Combiners to Secure MPC
# and Back

Prabhanjan Ananth[1]([✉]), Saikrishna Badrinarayanan[2], Aayush Jain[2],
Nathan Manohar[2], and Amit Sahai[2]

[1] UCSB, Santa Barbara, USA
prabhanjan@cs.ucsb.edu
[2] UCLA, Los Angeles, USA
{saikrishna,aayushjain,nmanohar,sahai}@cs.ucla.edu

**Abstract.** Cryptographic combiners allow one to combine many candidates for a cryptographic primitive, possibly based on different computational assumptions, into another candidate with the guarantee that the resulting candidate is secure as long as at least one of the original candidates is secure. While the original motivation of cryptographic combiners was to reduce trust on existing candidates, in this work, we study a rather surprising implication of combiners to constructing secure multiparty computation protocols. Specifically, we initiate the study of functional encryption combiners and show its connection to secure multiparty computation.

Functional encryption (FE) has incredible applications towards computing on encrypted data. However, constructing the most general form of this primitive has remained elusive. Although some candidate constructions exist, they rely on nonstandard assumptions, and thus, their security has been questioned. An FE combiner attempts to make use of these candidates while minimizing the trust placed on any individual FE candidate. Informally, an FE combiner takes in a set of FE candidates and outputs a secure FE scheme if at least one of the candidates is secure.

Another fundamental area in cryptography is secure multi-party computation (MPC), which has been extensively studied for several decades. In this work, we initiate a formal study of the relationship between functional encryption (FE) combiners and secure multi-party computation (MPC). In particular, we show implications in both directions between these primitives. As a consequence of these implications, we obtain the following main results.

- A two-round semi-honest MPC protocol in the plain model secure against up to $n-1$ corruptions with communication complexity proportional only to the depth of the circuit being computed assuming learning with errors (LWE). Prior two round protocols based on standard assumptions that achieved this communication complexity required trust assumptions, namely, a common reference string.

- A functional encryption combiner based on pseudorandom generators (PRGs) in $\mathsf{NC}^1$. This is a weak assumption as such PRGs are implied by many concrete intractability problems commonly used in

© International Association for Cryptologic Research 2019
D. Hofheinz and A. Rosen (Eds.): TCC 2019, LNCS 11891, pp. 199–228, 2019.
https://doi.org/10.1007/978-3-030-36030-6_9

cryptography, such as ones related to factoring, discrete logarithm, and lattice problems [11]. Previous constructions of FE combiners, implicit in [7], were known only from LWE. Using this result, we build a universal construction of functional encryption: an explicit construction of functional encryption based only on the assumptions that functional encryption exists and PRGs in $NC^1$.

**Keywords:** Functional encryption · Cryptographic combiners · Multi-party computation

# 1 Introduction

The foundations of several cryptographic primitives rely upon computational assumptions. The last few decades have seen the birth of many assumptions, such as factoring, quadratic residuosity, decisional Diffie-Hellman, learning with errors, and many more. Understanding the security of these assumptions is still very much an active research area. Despite years of research, very little is known in terms of how different cryptographic assumptions compare with each other. For instance, its not known whether decisional Diffie-Hellman is a weaker or a stronger assumption than learning with errors. This leads us to the following unsatisfactory scenario: suppose a cryptographic primitive (say, public key encryption) has many candidate constructions based on different assumptions, and we want to pick the most secure candidate. In this scenario, it is unclear which one we should pick.

*Cryptographic Combiners.* The notion of cryptographic combiners was introduced to resolve this dilemma. Given many candidates of a cryptographic primitive, possibly based on different assumptions, a cryptographic combiner churns these candidates into another candidate construction for the same primitive with the guarantee that the resulting construction is secure as long as at least *one* of the original candidates are secure. For instance, a combiner for public key encryption can be used to transform two candidates based on decisional Diffie-Hellman and learning with errors into a different public-key encryption candidate that is secure as long as *either* decisional Diffie-Hellman *or* learning with errors is secure.

While combiners were originally introduced to reduce trust on existing cryptographic constructions, in this work, we study a rather surprising implication from combiners to secure multi-party computation. Secure multi-party computation [19,50,79], one of the fundamental notions in cryptography, allows many parties, who don't necessarily trust each other, to come together and compute a function on their private inputs. We consider the primitive of functional encryption and study the implications of functional encryption combiners to secure multi-party computation. But first, we recall the notion of functional encryption.

*Functional Encryption.* Functional encryption (FE), introduced by [28,73,78], is one of the core primitives in the area of computing on encrypted data. This notion allows an authority to generate and distribute constrained keys associated with functions $f_1, \ldots, f_q$, called *functional keys*, which can be used to learn the values $f_1(x), \ldots, f_q(x)$ given an encryption of $x$. Intuitively, the security notion states that the functional keys associated with $f_1, \ldots, f_q$ and an encryption of $x$ reveal nothing beyond the values $f_1(x), \ldots, f_q(x)$. While this notion is interesting on its own, several works have studied its connections to other areas in cryptography and beyond, including reusable garbled circuits [51], indistinguishability obfuscation [8,9,23,68,69], adaptive garbling [57], verifiable random functions [14,21,54], deniable encryption [52], hardness olf Nash equilibrium [45,46], and many more.

Currently, we know how to construct only restricted versions[1] of functional encryption from well studied cryptographic assumptions. However, constructing the most general form of functional encryption has been an active research area and has intensified over the past few years given its implication to indistinguishability obfuscation [8,23]. In fact, if we are willing to tolerate a subexponential security loss, then even secret-key FE is enough to imply indistinguishability obfuscation [22,62,63]. All the candidates [10,43,65,66,70,71] we know so far are either based on assumptions pertaining to the tool of graded encodings [29,42], or on other new and relatively unstudied assumptions [1,5,67]. Recent cryptanalytic attacks [35,36,38,39,60] on assumptions related to graded encodings have prompted scrutiny of the security of schemes that use this tool as the building block. Given this, we should hope to minimize the trust we place on any individual FE candidate. The notion of a functional encryption combiner achieves this purpose. Roughly speaking, a functional encryption combiner allows for combining many functional encryption candidates in such a way that the resulting FE candidate is secure as long as any one of the initial FE candidates is secure. In other words, a functional encryption combiner says that it suffices to place trust collectively on multiple FE candidates, instead of placing trust on any specific FE candidate.

*Our Work.* We initiate a systematic study of functional encryption combiners. In particular, we study implications from FE combiners to secure multi-party computation (and vice versa), and by doing so, we achieve interesting consequences that were previously unknown. We detail our contributions next.

## 1.1  Our Contributions

Our results can be classified into two parts. The first part shows how to translate constructions of functional encryption combiners into secure MPC protocols. The second part studies the other direction.

---

[1] For instance, we can restrict the adversary to only ask for one functional key in the security experiment. A functional encryption scheme satisfying this property can be based on public key encryption schemes [53,77] (or one-way functions if one can settle for the secret key version).

*From Combiners for Single-key FE to Secure MPC:* Our first result shows how to construct a passively secure multi-party computation protocol that is both round-optimal (two rounds) and communication efficient (depends only on circuit depth). Recall that in a passively secure MPC protocol, corrupted parties follow the instructions of the protocol, but try to learn about honest party inputs from their combined view of the protocol execution. Moreover, our resulting protocol is in the plain model and can tolerate all but one corruption[2]. Prior round-optimal passively-secure MPC protocols were either communication inefficient, that is communication complexity was proportional to circuit size [20,30,47,48], based on strong assumptions such as indistinguishability obfuscation [40] or were based on trust assumptions [32,33,37,72,74] (for instance, a common reference string). Independently of our work, [76] formulated the notion of laconic function evaluation, which is quite different from combiners for functional encryption. However, subsequent to our work, [76] showed that laconic function evaluation can also be used to build 2-round semi-honest MPC with communication that is sub-linear in the circuit size.

We prove the following theorem.

**Theorem 1 (Informal).** *Consider an n-party functionality f computable by a poly-sized circuit of depth d, for any $n \geq 2$. Assuming LWE, there is a construction of a passively secure (semi-honest) n-party computation protocol for f in the plain model secure against $n - 1$ corruptions. The number of rounds in this protocol is 2, and the communication complexity is $\mathsf{poly}(\lambda, n, d, L_{in}, L_{out})$, where $L_{in}$ is the input length of this circuit computing f, $L_{out}$ is its output length and $\lambda$ is the security parameter.*

We summarize the state of art in the Fig. 1.

| | Communication Complexity | Assumptions | Model |
|---|---|---|---|
| [37,72,74,33] | $\mathsf{poly}(\lambda, n, d, L_{in}, L_{out})$ | LWE | CRS |
| [40] | $\mathsf{poly}(\lambda, n, d, L_{in}, L_{out})$ | piO and lossy encryption | Plain |
| [47] | $\mathsf{poly}(\lambda, n, |f|)$ | Bilinear maps | Plain |
| [20,48] | $\mathsf{poly}(\lambda, n, |f|)$ | Two-round OT | Plain |
| **Our Work,** [76] | $\mathsf{poly}(\lambda, n, d, L_{in}, L_{out})$ | LWE | Plain |

**Fig. 1.** State of the art in terms of communication complexity of two-round passively secure n-party protocols in the all-but-one corruption model. We denote by $|f|$ and $d$ the size and depth of the circuit representing the MPC functionality $f$, respectively. Moreover, $L_{in}$ and $L_{out}$, respectively, denote the input and output lengths of the circuit. CRS stands for common reference string and piO stands for probabilistic indistinguishability obfuscation [34].

---

[2] Unless otherwise specified, we only consider MPC protocols tolerating all but one corruption.

Central to proving the above theorem is a transformation from a functional encryption combiner to passively secure MPC. We only require a combiner for functional encryption schemes where the adversary only receives one functional key. We require the functional encryption combiner to have some structural properties. Namely, the functional key for $f$ associated with the combined candidate needs to be of the form $(f, sk_f^1, \ldots, sk_f^n)$, where (i) decomposability: $sk_f^i$ is produced by the $i^{th}$ FE candidate and, (ii) succinctness: the length of $sk_f^i$ is $\mathsf{poly}(\lambda, d, L_{out})$, where $d$ is the depth of the circuit computing $f$ and $L_{out}$ is its output length. As part of the succinctness property, we also require that the encryption complexity is $\mathsf{poly}(\lambda, d, L_{in})$, where $L_{in}$ is the length of the message to be encrypted. We show how to construct such an FE combiner assuming LWE.

An intermediate tool we use in this implication is a communication inefficient passively secure MPC protocol. By communication inefficient, we mean that the communication complexity is proportional to the size of the circuit representing $f$. We note that such protocols [20,47,48] exist in the literature[3] based on just the assumption of round-optimal passively secure oblivious transfer.

**Lemma 1 (Informal).** *Consider a $n$-party functionality $f$, for any $n \geq 2$. There is a passively secure $n$-party computation protocol for $f$ in two rounds with communication complexity $\mathsf{poly}(\lambda, n, d, L_{in}, L_{out})$ secure against $n-1$ corruptions, where $d$ is the depth of circuit computing $f$, $L_{in}$ is the input length of the circuit and $L_{out}$ is its output length. Moreover, we assume (i) a decomposable and succinct functional encryption combiner and (ii) a communication inefficient (as defined above) two-round secure $n$-party computation protocol secure against $n-1$ corruptions.*

By plugging in the recent round-optimal secure MPC protocols [20,47,48] that can be based on two-round oblivious transfer, which in turn can be based on learning with errors [75], and our new decomposable and succinct FE combiner from LWE, we get Theorem 1. We note that MPC with malicious security requires at least 4 rounds [4,15,32,44,55], and thus, we do not consider MPC with malicious security in this work.

*From Secure MPC to Combiners for Unbounded-Key FE:* In the other direction, we show how to transform existing secure multi-party computation protocols into constructions of functional encryption combiners. However, we note that the FE combiners we construct from MPC here do not satisfy decomposability or succinctness. In particular, we show how to transform specific constant round passively secure MPC protocols based on low degree randomized encodings [17] into functional encryption combiners. By instantiating low degree randomized encodings from pseudorandom generators in $\mathsf{NC}^1$, we get the following result.

---

[3] These protocols are inherently communication inefficient. The reason is that they present a compiler that turns any arbitrary interactive MPC protocol into a two-round MPC protocol. The communication complexity in the resulting two-round MPC protocol is at least the computational complexity of the original MPC protocol. However, the computational complexity of the resulting protocol has to be proportional to the size of the circuit representing the functionality $f$.

**Theorem 2 (Informal).** *Assuming pseudorandom generators in* $\mathsf{NC}^1$*, there is a construction of a combiner for unbounded-key functional encryption.*

By unbounded-key functional encryption, we mean that there is no a priori bound on the number of functional keys the adversary can request in the security experiment. We note that such pseudorandom generators in $\mathsf{NC}^1$ are implied by most concrete intractability assumptions commonly used in cryptography, such as ones related to factoring, discrete logarithm, and lattice problems [11]. Furthermore, such PRGs are also implied by the existence of one-way permutations in $\mathsf{NC}^1$ or one-way functions in $\mathsf{NC}^1$ with efficiently computable entropy [11].

Next, we present a generic reduction that can transform two-round passively secure MPC protocols into functional encryption combiners. For this transformation to hold, the MPC protocol must satisfy two properties: (i) delayed function-dependence: the first round of the MPC protocol should be independent of the functionality being securely computed and (ii) reusability: the first round can be reused by the parties to securely compute many functionalities (but on the same inputs fixed by the first round).

**Theorem 3 (Informal).** *Assuming a delayed function-dependent and reusable round-optimal secure MPC protocol, there is a construction of an unbounded-key decomposable functional encryption combiner.*

We then observe that existing two-round secure MPC protocols [33,72,74], based on learning with errors, already satisfy delayed function-dependence and reusability. We note that it is not necessary for the round-optimal protocols to be in the plain model (indeed, the protocols [33,72,74] are in the common reference string (CRS) model).

Prior to this work, the only polynomial hardness assumption known to imply an FE combiner was the learning with errors assumption [7][4]. While Theorem 2 already gives a construction of a functional encryption combiner from learning with errors (pseudorandom generators in $\mathsf{NC}^1$ can be based on learning with errors [16]), the functional encryption combiner constructed in Theorem 3 arguably provides a more efficient transformation. In particular, the efficiency of the functional keys in the combined scheme from Theorem 3 is linear in the efficiency of the functional keys in the FE candidates. However, the efficiency in the combined scheme from Theorem 2 degrades polynomially in the efficiency of the original FE candidates. Furthermore, the FE combiner from Theorem 3 is *decomposable*, a property needed by an FE combiner as a building block in the proof of Theorem 1. On the other hand, the FE combiner from Theorem 2 is inherently not decomposable, since it is based on an "onion-layered" approach – this means that the keys generated with respect to one FE candidate make oracle calls to other FE candidates (see [56] for a related discussion on black-box combiners). Furthermore, the FE combiner from Theorem 3 makes only black-box use of the underlying FE candidates, whereas the FE combiner from Theorem 2 is inherently non-black-box.

---

[4] Note that [7] required sub-exponential hardness only for constructing iO combiners, not for constructing FE combiners.

In terms of techniques, we introduce mechanisms to emulate a MPC protocol using functional encryption candidates. This is remiscient of "MPC-in-the-head" paradigm introduced by Ishai et al. [61] and more relevant to the context of FE is the work of Gorbunov et al. [53] who used information-theoretic MPC protocols to construct single-key FE. However, we encounter new challenges to implement the "MPC-in-the-head" paradigm in our context.

*Universal Functional Encryption:* We strengthen our constructions of FE combiners by showing how to transform them into combiners that also work when the insecure candidates don't necessarily satisfy correctness (of course, we still require that the secure candidate is correct). Such combiners are called *robust combiners*. To do this, we present correctness amplification theorems based on previous works on indistinguishability obfuscation [7,24] and, in particular, our correctness amplification assumes only one-way functions (unlike [24,25]). Robust combiners have been useful in universal constructions [6,7]. Roughly speaking, a universal construction of FE is a concrete construction of FE that is secure as long as any secure and correct construction exists. We show how to build universal functional encryption from robust FE combiners.

**Theorem 4 (Universal Functional Encryption).** *Assuming pseudorandom generators in* $NC^1$*, there is a universal unbounded-key functional encryption scheme.*

Our construction will be parameterized by $T$, where $T$ is an upper bound on the running time of all the algorithms associated with the secure candidate. This was a feature even in the universal iO construction of [6].

*Related Work:* The notion of combiners has been studied in the context of many cryptographic primitives. Asmuth and Blakely [13] studied combiners for encryption schemes. Levin proposed a universal construction of one-way functions [64]. Later, a systematic study of combiners and their relation to universal constructions was proposed by Harnik et al. [56] (also relevant are the constructions in [58,59]). Recently, Ananth et al. [6] designed universal constructions of indistinguishability obfuscation (iO). Concurrently, Fischlin et al. also proposed combiners in the context of program obfuscation [41]. Ananth et al. [7] then proposed the concept of transforming combiners that transforms many candidates of a primitive $X$, with at least one of them being secure and, into a secure candidate of primitive $Y$. In particular, they construct iO-to-functional encryption transforming combiners.

As mentioned previously, independently of our work, [76] formulated the notion of laconic function evaluation, and, subsequent to our work, showed that laconic function evaluation can also be used to build 2-round semi-honest MPC with communication that is sub-linear in the circuit size. [76]'s protocol consists of pre-processing, online, and post-processing phases. Additionally, they note that the computation complexity of the online phase is also independent of the size of the function being computed. After seeing their work, we observe that our protocol also satisfies this property. In particular, in the construction in Sect. 5, steps 1–3 in round 1 can be made the preprocessing phase. The resulting protocol will now have online computation complexity independent of the size of the function being computed.

## 1.2 Technical Overview

We begin by tackling the problem of constructing secure multi-party computation with depth-proportional communication complexity, i.e, proportional only to the depth of the circuit being securely computed, starting from a functional encryption combiner.

*Round-Optimal MPC with Depth-Proportional Communication:* Let's start by recalling prior known two-round secure MPC protocols [33,72,74] with depth-proportional communication in the CRS model. The basic template is as follows: in the first round, the $i^{th}$ party broadcasts an encryption of its input $x_i$. These ciphertexts are computed with respect to public keys that are derived from the CRS. All the $n$ parties then homomorphically compute on the encryptions of $(x_1, \ldots, x_n)$ to obtain a ciphertext of $f(x_1, \ldots, x_n)$, where $f$ is the function they wish to securely compute. The resulting ciphertext is then partially decrypted, and every party broadcasts its partially decrypted value in the second round. These values can be combined to recover the output of the functionality.

One could imagine getting rid of the CRS in the above protocol using the recent round-optimal MPC protocols in the plain model [20,47]. If this were possible, then it would yield a round-optimal MPC in the plain model that has depth-proportional communication complexity. However, the issue is that the messages in the first round of [33,72,74] are computed as functions of the CRS and thus, such an approach would inherently require three rounds.

To overcome this, we introduce a mechanism to parallelize the evaluation and the encryption processes. The output of the evaluation in our approach is the output of the functionality and not a partially decrypted value, as was the case in [33,72,74], and thus, we save one round. To implement this high level idea, we use a functional encryption combiner. Before we describe the high level template, we require that the underlying functional encryption combiner satisfies the *decomposability property:* Suppose we have FE candidates $\mathsf{FE}_1, \ldots, \mathsf{FE}_n$. Then, a functional key for a circuit $C$ in the combined scheme is just a concatenation of the functional keys for $C$, $(sk_1^C, \ldots, sk_n^C)$, where $sk_i^C$ is computed with respect to the $i^{th}$ FE candidate.

The template of our depth-proportional communication secure MPC construction from an FE combiner satisfying this decomposability property is in Fig. 2. As an intermediate tool, we use a size-proportional communication secure MPC protocol (henceforth, also referred to as a communication inefficient protocol). By this, we mean that the communication complexity of the secure MPC protocol grows polynomially with the size of the circuit being securely computed.

At the end of second round, every party has an encryption of $(x_1, \ldots, x_n)$ with respect to the combined candidate and functional keys for $f$ with respect

---

**Our Approach**

**Goal**: $t$-round depth-proportional communication secure MPC from $t$-round size-proportional communication secure MPC using decomposable FE combiners.

- Suppose the input of the $i^{th}$ party is $x_i$ and $f$ is the function to be securely computed. All the parties execute the $t$-round (communication-inefficient) MPC protocol to obtain an encryption of $(x_1, \ldots, x_n)$ with respect to the combined FE scheme.
- Simultaneously, the $i^{th}$ party computes the functional key of $f$ with respect to the $i^{th}$ candidate and sends it to everyone.

---

**Fig. 2.** Our approach to construct round-optimal depth-proportional communication secure MPC from decomposable functional encryption combiners.

to every candidate. From the decomposability property, this is equivalent to generating a functional key for $f$ with respect to the combined candidate. Each party can separately execute the FE combiner decryption algorithm to obtain $f(x_1, \ldots, x_n)$, as desired. Here, we crucially rely on the fact that all the FE candidates are correct. This completes the high level description of the template.

In the first bullet in Fig. 2, we instantiate the secure MPC protocol with size-proportional communication with [20,47,48]. The works of [20,47,48] are two-round protocols in the plain model and by suitably instantiating the FE combiners (described later), our approach yields a two-round MPC protocol with depth-proportional communication.

To argue security of our MPC protocol, the idea is to start with the assumption of a secure FE scheme and instantiate all the candidates using the same FE scheme. If the adversary corrupts all but the $j^{th}$ party, this means that he can obtain all the master secret keys of the FE scheme except the $j^{th}$ one. This is effectively the same as all except the $j^{th}$ candidate being broken. At this point, we can use the security of the $j^{th}$ FE scheme to argue the security of the MPC protocol. This shows that the above template yields a secure two-round MPC protocol assuming a secure FE scheme.

Note that we also assume a two-round (communication-inefficient) MPC protocol. Without showing that our protocol has depth-proportional communication, the above protocol doesn't achieve anything new. Indeed, it is unclear why our protocol should have depth-proportional communication. There are two sources of concern: (i) we are still using a communication *inefficient* MPC protocol and, (ii) the functional key of $f$ could be proportional to the size of the circuit computing $f$. Suppose we had a secure (magical) FE scheme satisfying the following two properties: (1) the encryption complexity of this FE scheme is proportional only to the depth of $f$, and (2) the functional key of $f$ is of the form $(f, \mathsf{aux})$, where $|\mathsf{aux}|$ only depends on the depth of the circuit computing $f$. We claim that this would immediately show that our protocol has communication complexity proportional only to the depth. Concern (i) is addressed by the fact the communication-inefficient MPC protocol is used only to evaluate the encryption circuit of the underlying FE scheme. Since the underlying FE scheme is succinct, the size of the encryption circuit only depends on the depth of the functionality $f$. Therefore, the communication complexity of the communication-inefficient MPC protocol does not affect our construction. Concern (ii) is handled by the fact that the parties only have to send the "aux" part of the function keys to the other parties, which is only proportional to the depth of $f$.

We next observe that the functional encryption scheme of Goldwasser et al. [51] can be used to satisfy both properties (1) and (2). We recall the functional encryption construction of Goldwasser et al.: the building blocks in this construction are attribute based encryption (ABE) for circuits, fully homomorphic encryption (FHE), and garbling schemes.

- To encrypt a message $x$, first encrypt $x$ using a (leveled) FHE scheme. Suppose the maximum output length of the functions for which we generate functional keys is $L_{out}$. Generate $\mathsf{poly}(L_{out})$ ABE encryptions of the FHE ciphertext, for some fixed polynomial $\mathsf{poly}$, along with wire keys of a garbled circuit. The garbled circuit is associated with the FHE decryption circuit.
- A functional key of $f$ consists of $\mathsf{poly}(L_{out})$ ABE keys associated with the circuit that computes the FHE evaluation of $f$.

If we instantiate the ABE scheme with the scheme of Boneh et al. [27] and the leveled FHE scheme with any of the schemes proposed in [31,49], we achieve both properties (1) and (2) described above. The schemes of [27] and [31,49] have encryption complexity proportional only to the depth of the circuit. In terms of the structure of the functional key, we note that the ABE scheme of [27] satisfies this nice property: you can express the ABE key of a function $f$ as $(f, \mathsf{aux})$, where $|\mathsf{aux}|$ is a polynomial in depth and $L_{out}$. This can be used to argue that the above FE scheme satisfies property (2).

Thus starting from an FE combiner, we have constructed a communication-efficient two-round MPC. We note that the FE combiner is required to satisfy simulation security in order to prove that the resulting MPC is simulation secure. The security proof of the resulting MPC directly follows from the simulation security of the FE combiner and the simulation security of the underlying communication inefficient MPC.

Next, we show how to construct such an FE combiner.

*Constructing the FE Combiner:* As in the works of [6,7], we view the FE candidates as analogous to parties in a secure MPC protocol. Suppose we want to construct an FE combiner for $n$ candidates. We start with a two-round (semi-honest) secure $n$-party MPC protocol in the plain model. To encrypt a message $x$, first additively secret share $x$ into shares $(x_1, \ldots, x_n)$. Compute the first round messages of all the parties, where the $i^{th}$ party's input is $x_i$. Finally, for every $i \in [n]$, encrypt the first round messages of all the parties along with the local state of the $i^{th}$ party using $i^{th}$ FE candidate. All the $n$ encryptions will form the ciphertext corresponding to the FE combiner scheme.

To generate a functional key for $f$, we generate $n$ functional keys with each key associated with an FE candidate. The $i^{th}$ functional key computes the next message function of the $i^{th}$ party. In this context, we define the next message function to be a deterministic algorithm that takes as input the state of the party along with the messages received so far and produces the next message. Moreover, the MPC functionality associated with the next message function is as follows: it takes as input $n$ shares of $x$, reconstructs $x$, and computes $f(x)$. The functional key of $f$ corresponding to the FE combiner is the collection of all these $n$ functional keys.

The decryption in the FE combiner scheme proceeds by recovering the first and second round messages of all the parties. The reconstruction algorithm of the secure MPC protocol is then executed to recover the output of the functionality. An issue here is that the reconstruction part need not be publicly computable. Meaning that it might not be possible to recover the output of the functionality from the transcript of the protocol alone. This can be resolved by revealing the local state of one of the parties to the FE evaluator who can then use this to recover the output. We implement this by considering an $(n + 1)$-party MPC protocol with the FE evaluator corresponding to one of the parties in the MPC protocol.

Without restricting ourselves to a specific type of two-round secure MPC protocols, the above template could be ill defined for two reasons:

- *Function-Dependence*: The first round messages of the MPC protocol we start off with could depend on the functionality being securely computed. This means that the FE encryptor needs to be aware of the function $f$ when it is encrypting the message $x$. Hence, we need to enforce a delayed function-dependence property on the underlying MPC protocol. Roughly, this property states that the first round messages of the MPC protocol are independent of the functionality being securely computed.

- *Reusability*: Suppose we wish to construct a *collusion-resistant* FE combiner, meaning that the FE combiner is secure even if the adversary obtains multiple functional keys during the security experiment. Even if one of the candidates is secure in the collusion-resistant setting, the above template doesn't necessarily yield a collusion-resistant FE combiner. This is because the first round MPC messages are "reused" across different FE evaluations. The security of MPC, as is, doesn't necessarily guarantee any security if the first round messages are reused for secure computation of multiple functionalities. Hence, we need to enforce a corresponding reusability property on the underlying MPC protocol to make it work in the collusion resistant setting.

Once we start with a delayed function-dependent and reusable secure MPC protocol, we can implement an FE combiner using the above template. We observe that the schemes of [33, 72, 74] are both delayed function-dependent and reusable. As a corollary, we obtain an FE combiner based on learning with errors.

We note that this would give an FE combiner that satisfies indistinguishability security. This is inherent since collusion-resistant FE that is also simulation secure was shown to be impossible [2]. Thus, for our application of communication efficient MPC, we construct a simulation secure FE combiner in the single-key setting (i.e., the adversary can only submit one function query) starting from a threshold fully homomorphic encryption scheme.

*FE Combiner from Weaker Assumptions:* The above constructions and previous constructions of FE combiners [7] relied on the learning with errors assumption. However, it would be interesting to try to construct an FE combiner from weaker assumptions. Our first observation is that there is a simple construction of an FE combiner for two FE candidates. In this case, one can simply "nest" the two candidates. That is, if the candidates are denoted $FE_1$ and $FE_2$, we encrypt a message $x$ by first encrypting $x$ under $FE_1$ and then encrypting the resulting ciphertext under $FE_2$. To construct a function key for $f$, we first construct the function key $SK_1$ for $f$ using $FE_1$ and then construct the function key $SK_2$ for the decryption circuit of $FE_1$, with $SK_1$ hardcoded as the function key, using $FE_2$. $SK_2$ is then the function key for $f$ in the nested scheme. In fact, this nested approach works to combine any constant $d$ number of candidates. However, this approach does not scale polynomially in the number of candidates, and therefore, does not give us an FE combiner for a polynomial number of candidates.

Using the above observation, we note that we can evaluate circuits over a constant number of inputs. In particular, we can evaluate constant-sized products. If we could compute the sum of various constant-sized products, then we could compute constant-degree polynomials, which would allow us to apply known bootstrapping techniques to go from FE for constant degree polynomials to FE for arbitrary functions via randomized encodings. Such randomized encodings can be constructed assuming a PRG in $NC^1$ [11]. But how do we go about computing the sums of constant degree polynomials? To reason about this, we will view this as an MPC problem, where each FE candidate is associated with a party. Given an input $x$, we bitwise secret share $x$ amongst all the parties. This effectively gives us an MPC problem where each party/candidate has a secret input (their share of $x$). For simplicity, let's consider the case where each candidate is given a single bit (the $i$th candidate is given the bit $x_i$). As an example, suppose we wished to evaluate the polynomial

$$x_1^2 + x_1 x_2 + x_1 x_3 + x_2 x_3.$$

Using the simple nested combiner for two candidates, we could evaluate each monomial and then sum the resulting monomial evaluations to compute the polynomial. However, this approach is flawed, since it will leak the values of each of the monomials, whereas functional encryption requires *only* the value of the polynomial to be computable and nothing else. We resolve this issue by masking each of the monomial evaluations by secret shares of 0 such that summing all these values gives the correct polynomial evaluation, but the individual computed monomial evaluations hide the true values of the monomials. To illustrate this, for the above polynomial, candidate 1 has its secret input in 3 monomials $x_1^2, x_1x_2$, and $x_1x_3$. We secret share 0 across 3 shares. Let $\mathsf{Share}_{1,1}, \mathsf{Share}_{1,2}, \mathsf{Share}_{1,3}$ denote these values, where

$$\mathsf{Share}_{1,1} + \mathsf{Share}_{1,2} + \mathsf{Share}_{1,3} = 0.$$

Similarly, candidates 2 and 3 have their secret inputs in 2 monomials: $x_1x_2, x_2x_3$ for candidate 2 and $x_1x_3, x_2x_3$ for candidate 3. We secret share 0 across 2 shares for each of these candidates. These shares are denoted $\mathsf{Share}_{2,1}, \mathsf{Share}_{2,2}$ for candidate 2 and $\mathsf{Share}_{3,1}, \mathsf{Share}_{3,2}$ for candidate 3. We then place a total ordering on the monomials of the polynomial in order to assign the shares to the monomials. Suppose our ordering was

$$x_1^2 < x_1x_2 < x_1x_3 < x_2x_3.$$

Then, we would see that $x_1^2$ was the first monomial containing $x_1$ and assign $\mathsf{Share}_{1,1}$ to this monomial. For $x_1x_2$, we see that it is the second monomial containing $x_1$ and the first monomial containing $x_2$. Therefore, we assign the shares $\mathsf{Share}_{1,2}$ and $\mathsf{Share}_{2,1}$ to the monomial $x_1x_2$. In a similar manner, we assign the shares $\mathsf{Share}_{1,3}, \mathsf{Share}_{3,1}$ to $x_1x_3$ and the shares $\mathsf{Share}_{2,2}, \mathsf{Share}_{3,2}$ to $x_2x_3$. When generating the function key to evaluate the monomial $x_1^2$, we actually give out a function key that evaluates $x_1^2 + \mathsf{Share}_{1,1}$. Similarly, when generating a function key to evaluate the monomial $x_1x_2$, we actually give out a function key that evaluates $x_1x_2 + \mathsf{Share}_{1,2} + \mathsf{Share}_{2,1}$.

By proceeding in this manner, we have made it so that each monomial evaluation hides the actual monomial value, but the sum of the monomial evaluations gives the polynomial value. However, this approach still raises several concerns: (i) how can we ensure that our secret sharing procedure hides intermediate sums of monomials, and (ii) how can we coordinate the randomness needed to generate the secret shares amongst the various monomials. To illustrate the first issue, suppose that the polynomial to evaluate was $x_1 + x_2$. In this instance, we would not add any secret shares, which would reveal $x_1$ and $x_2$. Fortunately, the first issue is not an issue at all, since such problematic polynomials will not occur. This is because we begin by secret sharing the bits of the input $x$ amongst the candidates. Therefore, every monomial will be broken into the sum of new monomials, such that each candidate contains a private bit in one of these new monomials. Since one of the candidates is secure, the secret sharing amongst the monomials with bits corresponding to the secure candidate ensures that nothing except the actual polynomial evaluation can be learned. To solve issue (ii), we utilize a PRF and generate a random PRF key for each candidate. This PRF key is then used to generate the secret shares of 0 associated with that candidate.

*Organization:* We begin by defining the notion of functional encryption and secure multi-party computation in Sect. 2. In Sect. 3, we define the notion of a functional encryption combiner. In Sect. 4, we show how to build a decomposable FE combiner that will be used as a building block in the construction of our round-optimal and communication efficient MPC protocol and how to instantiate it from [51]. In Sect. 5, we give the construction of our round-optimal and communication efficient MPC protocol. In Sect. 6, we show how to build an FE combiner assuming the existence of a PRG in $\mathsf{NC}^1$. In Sect. 7, we demonstrate how to convert a delayed function-dependent and reusable round-optimal secure MPC protocol into an FE combiner. Finally, in Sect. 8, we show how to convert an FE combiner into a robust FE combiner and build a universal functional encryption scheme.

## 2    Preliminaries

We denote the security parameter by $\lambda$. For an integer $n \in \mathbb{N}$, we use $[n]$ to denote the set $\{1, 2, \ldots, n\}$. We use $\mathcal{D}_0 \cong_c \mathcal{D}_1$ to denote that two distributions $\mathcal{D}_0, \mathcal{D}_1$ are computationally indistinguishable. We use $\mathsf{negl}(\lambda)$ to denote a function that is negligible in $\lambda$. We use $x \leftarrow \mathcal{A}$ to denote that $x$ is the output of a randomized algorithm $\mathcal{A}$, where the randomness of $\mathcal{A}$ is sampled from the uniform distribution.

### 2.1    Functional Encryption

We define the notion of a (secret key) functional encryption candidate and a (secret key) functional encryption scheme. A functional encryption candidate is associated with the correctness requirement, while a secure functional encryption scheme is associated with both correctness and security.

*Syntax of a Functional Encryption Candidate/Scheme.* A functional encryption (FE) candidate/scheme FE for a class of circuits $\mathcal{C} = \{\mathcal{C}_\lambda\}_{\lambda \in \mathbb{N}}$ consists of four polynomial time algorithms (Setup, Enc, KeyGen, Dec) defined as follows. Let $\mathcal{X}_\lambda$ be the input space of the circuit class $\mathcal{C}_\lambda$ and let $\mathcal{Y}_\lambda$ be the output space of $\mathcal{C}_\lambda$. We refer to $\mathcal{X}_\lambda$ and $\mathcal{Y}_\lambda$ as the input and output space of the candidate/scheme, respectively.

- **Setup**, $\mathsf{MSK} \leftarrow \mathsf{FE.Setup}(1^\lambda)$: It takes as input the security parameter $\lambda$ and outputs the master secret key $\mathsf{MSK}$.
- **Encryption**, $\mathsf{CT} \leftarrow \mathsf{FE.Enc}(\mathsf{MSK}, m)$: It takes as input the master secret key $\mathsf{MSK}$ and a message $m \in \mathcal{X}_\lambda$ and outputs $\mathsf{CT}$, an encryption of $m$.
- **Key Generation**, $\mathsf{SK}_C \leftarrow \mathsf{FE.KeyGen}(\mathsf{MSK}, C)$: It takes as input the master secret key $\mathsf{MSK}$ and a circuit $C \in \mathcal{C}_\lambda$ and outputs a function key $\mathsf{SK}_C$.
- **Decryption**, $y \leftarrow \mathsf{FE.Dec}(\mathsf{SK}_C, \mathsf{CT})$: It takes as input a function secret key $\mathsf{SK}_C$, a ciphertext $\mathsf{CT}$ and outputs a value $y \in \mathcal{Y}_\lambda$.

Throughout this work, we will only be concerned with *uniform* algorithms. That is, (Setup, Enc, KeyGen, Dec) can be represented as Turing machines (or equivalently uniform circuits).

We describe the properties associated with the above candidate.

*Approximate Correctness*

**Definition 1 (Approximate Correctness).** *A functional encryption candidate* FE = (Setup, KeyGen, Enc, Dec) *is said to be $\alpha$-correct if it satisfies the following property: for every $C : \mathcal{X}_\lambda \to \mathcal{Y}_\lambda \in \mathcal{C}_\lambda, m \in \mathcal{X}_\lambda$ it holds that:*

$$\Pr \left[ \begin{array}{c} \mathsf{MSK} \leftarrow \mathsf{FE.Setup}(1^\lambda) \\ \mathsf{CT} \leftarrow \mathsf{FE.Enc}(\mathsf{MSK}, m) \\ \mathsf{SK}_C \leftarrow \mathsf{FE.KeyGen}(\mathsf{MSK}, C) \\ C(m) \leftarrow \mathsf{FE.Dec}(\mathsf{SK}_C, \mathsf{CT}) \end{array} \right] \geq \alpha,$$

*where the probability is taken over the coins of the algorithms.*

*We refer to FE candidates that satisfy the above definition of correctness with $\alpha = 1 - \mathsf{negl}(\lambda)$ for a negligible function $\mathsf{negl}(\cdot)$ as (almost) correct candidates.*

Except for Sect. 8, we will only deal with correct candidates. Unless explicitly stated otherwise, all FE candidates throughout this paper satisfy (almost) correctness.

*IND-Security.* We recall indistinguishability-based selective security for FE. This security notion is modeled as a game between a challenger $\mathcal{C}$ and an adversary $\mathcal{A}$ where the adversary can request functional keys and ciphertexts from $\mathcal{C}$. Specifically, $\mathcal{A}$ can submit function queries $C$ and $\mathcal{C}$ responds with the corresponding functional keys. $\mathcal{A}$ can also submit message queries of the form $(x_0, x_1)$ and receives an encryption of messages $x_b$ for some bit $b \in \{0, 1\}$. The adversary $\mathcal{A}$ wins the game if she can guess $b$ with probability significantly more than $1/2$ and if for all function queries $C$ and message queries $(x_0, x_1)$, $C(x_0) = C(x_1)$. That is to say, any function evaluation that is computable by $\mathcal{A}$ gives the same value regardless of $b$. It is required that the adversary must declare the challenge messages at the beginning of the game.

**Definition 2 (IND-secure FE).** *A secret-key FE scheme* FE *for a class of circuits $\mathcal{C} = \{\mathcal{C}_\lambda\}_{\lambda \in [\mathbb{N}]}$ and message space $\mathcal{X} = \{\mathcal{X}_\lambda\}_{\lambda \in [\mathbb{N}]}$ is selectively secure if for any PPT adversary $\mathcal{A}$, there exists a negligible function $\mu(\cdot)$ such that for all sufficiently large $\lambda \in \mathbb{N}$, the advantage of $\mathcal{A}$ is*

$$\mathsf{Adv}_{\mathcal{A}}^{\mathsf{FE}} = \left| \Pr[\mathsf{Expt}_{\mathcal{A}}^{\mathsf{FE}}(1^\lambda, 0) = 1] - \Pr[\mathsf{Expt}_{\mathcal{A}}^{\mathsf{FE}}(1^\lambda, 1) = 1] \right| \leq \mu(\lambda),$$

*where for each $b \in \{0, 1\}$ and $\lambda \in \mathbb{N}$, the experiment $\mathsf{Expt}_{\mathcal{A}}^{\mathsf{FE}}(1^\lambda, b)$ is defined below:*

1. **Challenge message queries:** *$\mathcal{A}$ submits message queries,*

$$\left\{ (x_0^i, x_1^i) \right\}$$

*with $x_0^i, x_1^i \in \mathcal{X}_\lambda$ to the challenger $\mathcal{C}$.*
2. *$\mathcal{C}$ computes $\mathsf{MSK} \leftarrow \mathsf{FE.Setup}(1^\lambda)$ and then computes $\mathsf{CT}_i \leftarrow \mathsf{FE.Enc}(\mathsf{MSK}, x_b^i)$ for all $i$. The challenger $\mathcal{C}$ then sends $\{\mathsf{CT}_i\}$ to the adversary $\mathcal{A}$.*

3. **Function queries:** *The following is repeated an at most polynomial number of times: $A$ submits a function query $C \in C_\lambda$ to $C$. The challenger $C$ computes $\mathsf{SK}_C \leftarrow \mathsf{FE.KeyGen}(\mathsf{MSK}, C)$ and sends it to $A$.*

4. *If there exists a function query $C$ and challenge message queries $(x_0^i, x_1^i)$ such that $C(x_0^i) \neq C(x_1^i)$, then the output of the experiment is set to $\perp$. Otherwise, the output of the experiment is set to $b'$, where $b'$ is the output of $A$.*

*Adaptive Security.* The above security notion is referred to as selective security in the literature. One can consider a stronger notion of security, called *adaptive security*, where the adversary can interleave the challenge messages and the function queries in any arbitrary order. Analogous to Definition 2, we can define an adaptively secure FE scheme. In this paper, we only deal with selectively secure FE schemes. However, the security of these schemes can be upgraded to adaptive with no additional cost [3].

*Simulation Security.* We can also consider a different notion of security, called (single-key) simulation security.

**Definition 3** *(SIM-Security).* *Let $\mathsf{FE}$ denote a functional encryption scheme for a circuit class $C$. For every PPT adversary $\mathsf{A} = (\mathsf{A}_1, \mathsf{A}_2)$ and a PPT simulator $\mathsf{Sim}$, consider the following two experiments:*

| $\mathsf{Exp}_{\mathsf{FE},\mathsf{A}}^{\mathsf{real}}(1^\lambda)$ | $\mathsf{Exp}_{\mathsf{FE},\mathsf{A},\mathsf{Sim}}^{\mathsf{ideal}}(1^\lambda)$ |
|---|---|
| $\{\mathsf{FE.Setup}(1^\lambda) \to \mathsf{MSK}\}$ | $\{\mathsf{FE.Setup}(1^\lambda) \to \mathsf{MSK}\}$ |
| $\mathsf{A}_1 \to (C, \mathsf{state}_{\mathsf{A}_1})$ | $\mathsf{A}_1 \to (C, \mathsf{state}_{\mathsf{A}_1})$ |
| $\{\mathsf{SK}_C \leftarrow \mathsf{FE.KeyGen}(\mathsf{MSK}, C)\}$ | $\{\mathsf{SK}_C \leftarrow \mathsf{FE.KeyGen}(\mathsf{MSK}, C)\}$ |
| $\mathsf{A}_2(\mathsf{state}_{\mathsf{A}_1}, \mathsf{SK}_C) \to (m, \mathsf{state}_{\mathsf{A}_2})$ | $\mathsf{A}_2(\mathsf{state}_{\mathsf{A}_1}, \mathsf{SK}_C) \to (m, \mathsf{state}_{\mathsf{A}_2})$ |
| $\mathsf{FE.Enc}(\mathsf{MSK}, m) \to \mathsf{CT}$ | $\mathsf{Sim}(\mathsf{MSK}, C, \mathsf{SK}_C, C(m)) \to \mathsf{\tilde{CT}}$ |
| *Output* $(\mathsf{CT}, \mathsf{state}_{\mathsf{A}_2})$ | *Output* $(\mathsf{\tilde{CT}}, \mathsf{state}_{\mathsf{A}_2})$ |

*The scheme is said to be (single-key) SIM-secure if there exists a PPT simulator $\mathsf{Sim}$ such that for all PPT adversaries $(\mathsf{A}_1, \mathsf{A}_2)$, the outcomes of the two experiments are computationally indistinguishable:*

$$\{\mathsf{Exp}_{\mathsf{FE},\mathsf{A}}^{\mathsf{real}}(1^\lambda)\}_{\lambda \in \mathbb{N}} \approx_c \{\mathsf{Exp}_{\mathsf{FE},\mathsf{A},\mathsf{Sim}}^{\mathsf{ideal}}(1^\lambda)\}_{\lambda \in \mathbb{N}}$$

*Collusions.* We can parameterize the FE candidate by the number of function secret key queries that the adversary can make in the security experiment. If the adversary can only submit an a priori upper bounded $q$ secret key queries, we say that the scheme is $q$-key or $q$-collusion secure. We say that the functional encryption scheme unbounded-key or unbounded-collusion secure if the adversary can make an unbounded (polynomial) number of function secret key queries. In this work, unless otherwise stated, we will allow the adversary to make an arbitrary polynomial number of function secret key queries.

*Succinctness*

**Definition 4 (Succinctness).** *A functional encryption candidate* FE = (Setup, Enc, KeyGen, Dec) *for a circuit class* $\mathcal{C}$ *containing circuits that take inputs of length* $\ell_{in}$, *outputs strings of length* $\ell_{out}$ *bits and are of depth at most* $d$ *is said to be succinct if the following holds: For any circuit* $C \in \mathcal{C}$,

- *Let* MSK $\leftarrow$ FE.Setup($1^\lambda$). *The size of the circuit* FE.Enc(MSK, $\cdot$) < poly($\lambda, d$, $\ell_{in}, \ell_{out}$) *for some polynomial* poly.
- *The function key* $SK_C \leftarrow$ FE.KeyGen(MSK, $C$) *is of the form* ($C$, aux) *where* |aux| $\leq$ poly($\lambda, d, \ell_{out}$) *for some polynomial* poly.

In general, an FE candidate/scheme need not satisfy succinctness. However, we will need to utilize succinct FE candidates when constructing depth-proportional communication MPC (Sects. 4 and 5). In such cases, we will explicitly state that the FE candidates are succinct.

*FE Candidates vs. FE Schemes.* As defined above, an FE scheme must satisfy *both* correctness and security, while an FE candidate is simply the set of algorithms. Unless otherwise specified, we will be dealing with FE candidates that satisfy correctness. We will only refer to FE constructions as FE schemes if it is known that the construction satisfies both correctness and security.

## 2.2 Secure Multi-party Computation

The syntax and security definitions for secure multi-party computation can be found in the full version. Since we are dealing throughout this paper with the efficiency of MPC protocols, we give the definition of a succinct MPC protocol below.

**Definition 5 (Succinct MPC protocol).** *Consider an* $n$-*party semi-honest secure MPC protocol* $\Pi$ *for a functionality* $f$, *represented by a polynomial-sized circuit* $C$. *We define the communication complexity of* $\Pi$ *to be the total length of all the messages exchanged in the protocol.*

*We define* $\Pi$ *to be succinct if the communication complexity of* $\Pi$ *is* poly($\lambda, d, n$), *where* $\lambda$ *is the security parameter and* $d$ *is the depth of the circuit* $C$.

## 2.3 Additional Preliminaries

In this work, we will also make occasional use of threshold leveled fully homomorphic encryption [12,26,72] and garbling schemes [18,79]. Formal definitions of these primitives can be found in the full version.

## 3 FE Combiners: Definition

In this section, we give a formal definition of an FE combiner. Intuitively, an FE combiner FEComb takes $n$ FE candidates, $FE_1, \ldots, FE_n$ and compiles them into a new FE candidate with the property that FEComb is a secure FE scheme provided that at least one of the $n$ FE candidates is a secure FE scheme.

*Syntax of a Functional Encryption Combiner.* A functional encryption combiner FEComb for a class of circuits $\mathcal{C} = \{\mathcal{C}_\lambda\}_{\lambda \in \mathbb{N}}$ consists of four polynomial time algorithms (Setup, Enc, KeyGen, Dec) defined as follows. Let $\mathcal{X}_\lambda$ be the input space of the circuit class $\mathcal{C}_\lambda$ and let $\mathcal{Y}_\lambda$ be the output space of $\mathcal{C}_\lambda$. We refer to $\mathcal{X}_\lambda$ and $\mathcal{Y}_\lambda$ as the input and output space of the combiner, respectively. Furthermore, let $FE_1, \ldots, FE_n$ denote the descriptions of $n$ FE candidates.

- **Setup,** $FEComb.Setup(1^\lambda, \{FE_i\}_{i \in [n]})$: It takes as input the security parameter $\lambda$ and the descriptions of $n$ FE candidates $\{FE_i\}_{i \in [n]}$ and outputs the master secret key MSK.
- **Encryption,** $FEComb.Enc(MSK, \{FE_i\}_{i \in [n]}, m)$: It takes as input the master secret key MSK, the descriptions of $n$ FE candidates $\{FE_i\}_{i \in [n]}$, and a message $m \in \mathcal{X}_\lambda$ and outputs CT, an encryption of $m$.
- **Key Generation,** $FEComb.Keygen\left(MSK, \{FE_i\}_{i \in [n]}, C\right)$: It takes as input the master secret key MSK, the descriptions of $n$ FE candidates $\{FE_i\}_{i \in [n]}$, and a circuit $C \in \mathcal{C}_\lambda$ and outputs a function key $SK_C$.
- **Decryption,** $FEComb.Dec\left(\{FE_i\}_{i \in [n]}, SK_C, CT\right)$: It is a deterministic algorithm that takes as input the descriptions of $n$ FE candidates $\{FE_i\}_{i \in [n]}$, a function secret key $SK_C$, and a ciphertext CT and outputs a value $y \in \mathcal{Y}_\lambda$.

*Remark 1.* In the formal definition above, we have included $\{FE_i\}_{i \in [n]}$, the descriptions of the FE candidates, as input to all the algorithms of FEComb. For notational simplicity, we will often forgo these inputs and assume that they are implicit.

We now define the properties associated with an FE combiner. The three properties are correctness, polynomial slowdown, and security. Correctness is analogous to that of an FE candidate, provided that the $n$ input FE candidates are all valid FE candidates. Polynomial slowdown says that the running times of all the algorithms of FEComb are polynomial in $\lambda$ and $n$. Finally, security intuitively says that if at least one of the FE candidates is also secure, then FEComb is a secure FE scheme. We provide the formal definitions below.

*Correctness*

**Definition 6 (Correctness).** *Suppose* $\{FE_i\}_{i \in [n]}$ *are correct FE candidates. We say that an FE combiner is correct if for every circuit* $C : \mathcal{X}_\lambda \to \mathcal{Y}_\lambda \in \mathcal{C}_\lambda$, *and message* $m \in \mathcal{X}_\lambda$ *it holds that:*

$$\Pr\left[\begin{array}{c} MSK \leftarrow FEComb.Setup(1^\lambda, \{FE_i\}_{i \in [n]}) \\ CT \leftarrow FEComb.Enc(MSK, \{FE_i\}_{i \in [n]}, m) \\ SK_C \leftarrow FEComb.Keygen(MSK, \{FE_i\}_{i \in [n]}, C) \\ C(m) \leftarrow FEComb.Dec(\{FE_i\}_{i \in [n]}, SK_C, CT) \end{array}\right] \geq 1 - negl(\lambda),$$

*where the probability is taken over the coins of the algorithms and* $negl(\lambda)$ *is a negligible function in* $\lambda$.

*Polynomial Slowdown*

**Definition 7 (Polynomial Slowdown).** *An FE combiner* FEComb *satisfies polynomial slowdown if on all inputs, the running times of* FEComb.Setup, FEComb.Enc, FEComb.Keygen, *and* FEComb.Dec *are at most* $\text{poly}(\lambda, n)$, *where n is the number of FE candidates that are being combined.*

*IND-Security*

**Definition 8 (IND-Secure FE Combiner).** *An FE combiner* FEComb *is selectively secure if for any set* $\{\mathsf{FE}_i\}_{i \in [n]}$ *of correct FE candidates, it satisfies Definition 2, where the descriptions of* $\{\mathsf{FE}_i\}_{i \in [n]}$ *are public and implicit in all invocations of the algorithms of* FEComb, *if at least one of the FE candidates* $\mathsf{FE}_1, \ldots, \mathsf{FE}_n$ *also satisfies Definition 2.*

Note that *Definition 2* is the IND-security definition for FE. Unless otherwise specified, when we say a *secure* FE combiner, we refer to one that satisfies IND-security.

*Simulation Security.* Similarly to FE candidates, we can also consider a different notion of security called (single-key) simulation security.

**Definition 9.** *An FE combiner* FEComb *is single-key simulation secure if for any set* $\{\mathsf{FE}_i\}_{i \in [n]}$ *of correct FE candidates, it satisfies Definition 3, where the descriptions of* $\{\mathsf{FE}_i\}_{i \in [n]}$ *are public and implicit in all invocations of the algorithms of* FEComb, *if at least one of the FE candidates* $\mathsf{FE}_1, \ldots, \mathsf{FE}_n$ *also satisfies Definition 3.*

Note that *Definition 3* is the simulation security definition for FE.

*Succinctness.* Similarly to FE candidates, we can also define the notion of a succinct FE combiner. An FE combiner is not required to satisfy succinctness, but we will utilize a succinct FE combiner when construction low communication MPC (Sects. 4 and 5).

**Definition 10.** *An FE combiner* FEComb = (Setup, Enc, KeyGen, Dec) *for a circuit class* $\mathcal{C}$ *containing circuits that take inputs of length* $\ell_{\mathsf{in}}$, *outputs strings of length* $\ell_{\mathsf{out}}$ *bits and are of depth at most d is succinct if for every set of succinct FE candidates* $\mathsf{FE}_1, \ldots, \mathsf{FE}_n$, *the following holds: For any circuit* $C \in \mathcal{C}$,

- *Let* MSK $\leftarrow$ FEComb.Setup$(1^\lambda, \{\mathsf{FE}_i\}_{i \in [n]})$. *The size of the circuit* FEComb.Enc$(\mathsf{MSK}, \cdot) \leq \text{poly}(\lambda, d, \ell_{\mathsf{in}}, \ell_{\mathsf{out}}, n)$ *for some polynomial* poly.
- *The function key* $\mathsf{SK}_C \leftarrow$ FEComb.KeyGen$(\mathsf{MSK}, C)$ *is of the form* $(C, \mathsf{aux})$ *where* $|\mathsf{aux}| \leq \text{poly}(\lambda, d, \ell_{\mathsf{out}}, n)$ *for some polynomial* poly.

*Robust FE Combiners and Universal FE*

*Remark 2.* We also define the notion of a robust FE combiner. An FE combiner FEComb is robust if it is an FE combiner that satisfies the three properties (correctness, polynomial slowdown, and security) associated with an FE combiner when given any set of FE candidates $\{\mathsf{FE}_i\}_{i \in [n]}$, provided that one is a correct and secure FE candidate. No restriction is placed on the other FE candidates. In particular, they need not satisfy correctness at all.

Robust FE combiners can be used to build a universal functional encryption scheme defined below.

**Definition 11 (T-Universal Functional Encryption).** *We say that an explicit Turing machine $\Pi_{\mathsf{univ}} = (\Pi_{\mathsf{univ}}.\mathsf{Setup}, \Pi_{\mathsf{univ}}.\mathsf{Enc}, \Pi_{\mathsf{univ}}.\mathsf{KeyGen}, \Pi_{\mathsf{univ}}.\mathsf{Dec})$ is a universal functional encryption scheme parametrized by $T$ if $\Pi_{\mathsf{univ}}$ is a correct and secure FE scheme assuming the existence a correct and secure FE scheme with runtime $< T$.*

## 4    Succinct Single-Key Simulation Secure Decomposable FE Combiner

In this section, we define and construct a succinct single-key simulation secure decomposable FE combiner (DFEComb for short) that will be useful later for our communication-efficient MPC result. This section can be found in the full version.

## 5    Round Optimal MPC with Depth-Proportional Communication from an FE Combiner

In this section, using any succinct single-key simulation secure decomposable FE combiner (see Sect. 4), we show how to compile any two round semi-honest secure MPC protocol into one where the communication complexity is proportional only to the depth of the circuit being evaluated.

Let $\mathsf{Comm.Compl}(\pi)$ denote the communication complexity of any protocol $\pi$. Let $\lambda$ denote the security parameter, $n$ denote the number of parties, and $\ell$ denote the size of the input to each party. Formally, we show the following theorem:

**Theorem 5.** *Assuming the existence of*

- *A succinct single-key single-ciphertext simulation secure decomposable FE combiner (AND)*
- *Succinct FE candidates (AND)*
- *A two round semi-honest MPC in the plain model (that may not be communication efficient) that is secure against up to all but one corruption,*

*there exists a two round semi-honest MPC protocol $\pi$ in the plain model that is secure against up to all but one corruption for any boolean circuit $C$, where the communication complexity of the protocol $\pi$ is independent of the size of the circuit. That is,* Comm.Compl$(\pi) =$ poly$($Depth$(C), n, \ell, \lambda)$.

We know how to construct a succinct single-key simulation secure decomposable FE combiner based on the learning with errors (LWE) assumption (see Sect. 4). Further, in Sect. 4, we saw that the construction in [51] is a succinct FE candidate. Also, two round semi-honest MPC protocols secure against up to all but one corruption can be based on the LWE assumption [20,48,75][5]. Instantiating the primitives in the above theorem, we get the following corollary:

**Corollary 1.** *Assuming LWE, there exists a two round semi-honest MPC protocol $\pi$ in the plain model that is secure against up to all but one corruption for any boolean circuit $C$ with* Comm.Compl$(\pi) =$ poly$($Depth$(C), n, \ell, \lambda)$.

Furthermore, if we allow our protocol to have a preprocessing phase, we can obtain a two round semi-honest MPC protocol with depth-proportional communication complexity and with the computational complexity of each party in the online phase independent of the size of the circuit, matching the result of [76]. By simply making steps 1–3 in round 1 of our construction the preprocessing phase, we arrive at the following corollary:

**Corollary 2.** *Assuming LWE, there exists a two round semi-honest MPC protocol $\pi$ in the plain model that is secure against up to all but one corruption for any boolean circuit $C$ with* Comm.Compl$(\pi) =$ poly$($Depth$(C), n, \ell, \lambda)$ *and with the computational complexity of the online phase* poly$($Depth$(C), n, \ell, \lambda)$.

### 5.1   Construction

*Notation:*

- Consider $n$ parties $P_1, \ldots, P_n$ with inputs $x_1, \ldots, x_n$, respectively, who wish to evaluate a boolean circuit $C$ on their joint inputs. Let $\lambda$ denote the security parameter and without loss of generality, let's assume $|x_i| = \lambda$ for all $i \in [n]$. Also, let's denote the randomness of each party $P_i$ as $r_i = (r_i^{\mathsf{Setup}}, r_i^{\mathsf{Enc}}, r_i^{\mathsf{SH}}, r_i^{\mathsf{KeyGen}})$.
- Let DFEComb = (DFEComb.Setup, DFEComb.Enc, DFEComb.Keygen, DFEComb.Dec, DFEComb.Partition) be a succinct single-key simulation secure decomposable FE combiner (see Sect. 4) for $n$ FE candidates $\mathsf{FE}_1, \ldots, \mathsf{FE}_n$.
- Let $\pi^{\mathsf{SH}}$ be a two round semi-honest secure MPC protocol (not necessarily communication efficient). Let $(\pi^{\mathsf{SH}}.\mathsf{Round}_1, \pi^{\mathsf{SH}}.\mathsf{Round}_2)$ denote the algorithms used by any party to compute the messages in each of the two rounds and $\pi^{\mathsf{SH}}.\mathsf{Out}$ denote the algorithm to compute the final output. Further, let

---

[5] [20,48] showed how to construct two round semi-honest MPC in the plain model from any two round semi-honest OT in the plain model and [75] show that the latter can be constructed from LWE.

$\pi^{\mathsf{SH}}.\mathsf{Sim} = (\pi^{\mathsf{SH}}.\mathsf{Sim}_1, \pi^{\mathsf{SH}}.\mathsf{Sim}_2)$ denote the simulator for this protocol - that is, $\pi^{\mathsf{SH}}.\mathsf{Sim}_i$ is the simulator's algorithm to compute the $i^{th}$ round's messages.

*Protocol.* We now describe the construction of our protocol $\pi$ with depth-proportional communication complexity.

- **Round 1:** Each party $\mathsf{P}_i$ does the following:
  1. Generate $\mathsf{MSK}_i \leftarrow \mathsf{FE}_i.\mathsf{Setup}(1^\lambda)$ using randomness $r_i^{\mathsf{Setup}}$.
  2. Compute $(C_1, \ldots, C_n) \leftarrow \mathsf{DFEComb.Partition}(1^\lambda, C)$.
  3. Compute $\mathsf{SK}_i = \mathsf{FE}_i.\mathsf{KeyGen}(\mathsf{MSK}_i, C_i)$ using randomness $r_i^{\mathsf{KeyGen}}$.
  4. Participate in an execution of protocol $\pi^{\mathsf{SH}}$ with the remaining $(n-1)$ parties using input $y_i = (x_i, \mathsf{MSK}_i, r_i^{\mathsf{Enc}})$ and randomness $r_i^{\mathsf{SH}}$ to compute the deterministic circuit $C_{\mathsf{CT}}$ defined in Fig. 3. That is, compute the first round message $\mathsf{msg}_{1,i} \leftarrow \pi^{\mathsf{SH}}.\mathsf{Round}_1(y_i; r_i^{\mathsf{SH}})$.
  5. Output $(\mathsf{msg}_{1,i}, \mathsf{SK}_i)$.
- **Round 2:** Each party $\mathsf{P}_i$ does the following:
  1. Let $\tau_1$ denote the transcript of protocol $\pi^{\mathsf{SH}}$ after round 1.
  2. Compute the second round message $\mathsf{msg}_{2,i} \leftarrow \pi^{\mathsf{SH}}.\mathsf{Round}_2(y_i, \tau_1; r_i^{\mathsf{SH}})$ where $y_i = (x_i, \mathsf{MSK}_i, r_i^{\mathsf{Enc}})$.
  3. Output $(\mathsf{msg}_{2,i})$.
- **Output Computation:** Each party $\mathsf{P}_i$ does the following:
  1. Let $\tau_2$ denote the transcript of protocol $\pi^{\mathsf{SH}}$ after round 2.
  2. Compute the output of $\pi^{\mathsf{SH}}$ as $\mathsf{CT} \leftarrow \pi^{\mathsf{SH}}.\mathsf{Out}(y_i, \tau_2; r_i^{\mathsf{SH}})$.
  3. Let $\mathsf{SK}_C = (\mathsf{SK}_1, \ldots, \mathsf{SK}_n)$.
  4. Output $\mathsf{DFEComb.Dec}(\mathsf{SK}_C, \mathsf{CT})$.

---

**Input:** $\{(x_i, \mathsf{MSK}_i, r_i^{\mathsf{Enc}})\}_{i=1}^n$

- Let $\mathsf{MSK} = (\mathsf{MSK}_1, \ldots, \mathsf{MSK}_n)$, $x = (x_1, \ldots, x_n)$ and $r = (r_1^{\mathsf{Enc}}, \ldots, r_n^{\mathsf{Enc}})$.
- Output $\mathsf{DFEComb.Enc}(\mathsf{MSK}, x)$ using randomness $r$.

---

**Fig. 3.** Circuit $C_{\mathsf{CT}}$

*Correctness and Efficiency:* Correctness follows immediately from the construction. In particular, at the end of the protocol, each party possesses $\mathsf{CT}$, an encryption of $x = (x_1, \ldots, x_n)$ under the FE combiner, and $\mathsf{SK}_C$, the function key for $C$. This ciphertext can then be decrypted using $\mathsf{SK}_C$ to yield $C(x)$, as desired.

Now, let's analyze the communication complexity of the protocol. First, observe that each circuit $C$ that is of depth $d$ and outputs a single bit is partitioned into $n$ circuits $C_1, \ldots, C_n$ by running the $\mathsf{DFEComb.Partition}$ algorithm.

The circuit $C_i$ just computes a partial decryption of $\mathsf{TFHE.Eval}(C, \cdot)$. Now, even though $C$ is a boolean circuit, the output length of $C_i$ might not be 1. However, this is not an issue for us. Indeed, observe that from the compactness of the $\mathsf{TFHE}$ scheme, the length of the partial decryption is just $\mathsf{poly}(\lambda, d)$ for some fixed polynomial $\mathsf{poly}$ for all circuits $C$ with depth $d$ and output length 1. Thus, the size of the output length of $C_i$ for all $i \in [n]$ is at most $\mathsf{poly}(\lambda, d)$ bits. Thus, from Sect. 4, we know that $|\mathsf{SK}_i| = \mathsf{poly}(d, n, \lambda)$ and $|\mathsf{CT}| = \mathsf{poly}(d, n, \lambda)$. Recall that $\mathsf{CT}$ is the ciphertext that is the output of the protocol $\pi^{\mathsf{SH}}$ (computed during decryption). In fact, from Sect. 4, we also know that the size of the circuit computing the ciphertext $\mathsf{CT}$ is also bounded by $\mathsf{poly}(d, n, \lambda)$. Then, for the protocol $\pi^{\mathsf{SH}}$ recall that the input is $y_i = (x_i, \mathsf{MSK}_i, r_i^{\mathsf{Enc}})$ and so $|y_i| = \mathsf{poly}(\lambda, d)$ for some polynomial. Therefore, for each party $\mathsf{P}_i$, $|\mathsf{msg}_{1,i}| = \mathsf{poly}(d, n, \lambda)$ and $|\mathsf{msg}_{2,i}| = \mathsf{poly}(d, n, \lambda)$.

Therefore, in our two round protocol $\pi$, in each round the size of the message sent by any party is $\mathsf{poly}(n, d, \lambda)$. Thus, $\mathsf{Comm.Compl}(\pi) = \mathsf{poly}(n, d, \lambda)$.

The above analysis was for circuits with boolean output. For circuits that output multi-bit strings, the communication complexity of our MPC protocol $\pi$ is bounded by $\mathsf{poly}(n, d, \lambda) \cdot \ell_{\mathsf{out}}$, where $\ell_{\mathsf{out}}$ is the output length of the circuit. This follows immediately by viewing the multi-bit output circuit as $\ell_{\mathsf{out}}$ different boolean circuits and running in parallel.

### 5.2  Security Proof

The security proof can be found in the full version.

## 6  Construction of an FE Combiner from Weaker Assumptions

In this section, we employ a tool extensively used in the secure multi-party computation literature, namely, randomized encodings to construct an FE combiner. Roughly speaking, a randomized encoding is a mechanism to "efficiently" encode a function $f$ and an input $x$ such that the encoding reveals $f(x)$ and nothing more. A randomized encoding scheme is said to be low degree if the encoding algorithm can be represented as a low degree polynomial. Low degree randomized encodings have been used to achieve constant-round secure multi-party computation [17]. We show how to use this tool to obtain functional encryption combiners. The underlying assumption used to instantiate the low degree randomized encoding is the existence of a PRG in $\mathsf{NC}^1$. Formally, we show the following theorem.

**Theorem 6.** *Assuming the existence of a PRG in* $\mathsf{NC}^1$, *there exists an unbounded-key FE combiner for polynomial-sized circuits.*

The rest of this section can be found in the full version.

# 7    From MPC to FE Combiners

In this section, we show how to build an FE combiner from any semi-honest MPC protocol $\pi$ that satisfies a property called delayed function-dependence. This section can be found in the full version.

# 8    From an FE Combiner to a Robust FE Combiner

The FE combiners constructed previously are not *robust*. By this, we mean that the constructions provide no guarantee of correctness or security if any of the underlying FE candidates do not satisfy correctness. However, determining the correctness of FE candidates may be difficult since a candidate FE may be correct with overwhelming probability on certain message, circuit pairs $(m, C)$ and not others. With no worst-case guarantees, it can be challenging to reason about the correctness of an FE candidate especially if the function space $\mathcal{C}$ is say all poly-sized circuits, where sampling uniformly over the space is difficult.

We can mitigate this issue by making our FE combiners robust. A *robust FE combiner* is an FE combiner that satisfies correctness and security provided that at least one FE candidate, $\mathsf{FE}_i$, satisfies both correctness and security. No restrictions are placed on the other FE candidates. In particular, they may satisfy neither correctness nor security. In this section, we show how to transform any FE combiner into a robust FE combiner. Formally, we show the following.

**Theorem 7.** *If there exists an FE combiner, then there exists a robust FE combiner.*

Combining Theorem 7 with Theorem 6, we obtain the following corollary.

**Corollary 3.** *Assuming the existence of a PRG in* $\mathsf{NC}^1$, *there exists an unbounded-key robust FE combiner.*

This is done, at a high level, via the following steps.

1. Transform each FE candidate $\mathsf{FE}_i$ into a new FE candidate $\mathsf{FE}_i'$ such that
   (a) If $\mathsf{FE}_i$ is correct and secure, then $\mathsf{FE}_i'$ is also correct and secure.
   (b) If $\mathsf{FE}_i'$ is correct for any fixed message, circuit pair $(m, C)$ with probability $\alpha$, then it is at least $\alpha'$-correct for all other message, circuit pairs $(m', C')$ where $\alpha' = \alpha - \mathsf{negl}(\lambda)$.
2. Fix a message $m$ and a circuit $C$ and test each candidate repeatedly on $(m, C)$ to determine if each candidate is $\alpha$-correct for $\alpha \geq 1 - \frac{1}{\lambda}$. Discard those that are not.
3. Using standard techniques of BPP correctness amplification, transform the $\alpha$-correct candidates into (almost) correct candidates.
4. Instantiate constructions of FE combiners from previous sections with these (almost) correct candidates.

We defer the construction and proof of Theorem 7 to the full version.

*Universal Functional Encryption:* Robust FE combiners are closely related to the notion of universal functional encryption. Universal functional encryption is a construction of functional encryption satisfying the following simple guarantee. If there exists a Turing Machine with running time bounded by some $T(n) = \mathsf{poly}(n)$ that implements a correct and secure FE scheme, then the universal functional encryption construction is itself a correct and secure FE scheme. Using the existence of a robust FE combiner (Theorem 7) and the results of [6], we observe the following.

**Theorem 8.** *Assuming the existence of a robust FE combiner, there exists a universal functional encryption scheme.*

Using the above theorem and Corollary 3, we arrive at the following corollary.

**Corollary 4.** *Assuming the existence of a PRG in $\mathsf{NC}^1$, there exists a universal unbounded-key functional encryption scheme.*

**Acknowledgements.** We thank the anonymous TCC reviewers for their helpful comments.

Saikrishna Badrinarayanan, Aayush Jain, Nathan Manohar and Amit Sahai were supported in part from a DARPA/ARL SAFEWARE award, NSF Frontier Award 1413955, and NSF grant 1619348, BSF grant 2012378, a Xerox Faculty Research Award, a Google Faculty Research Award, an equipment grant from Intel, and an Okawa Foundation Research Grant. Saikrishna Badrinarayanan is also supported by an IBM PhD fellowship. Aayush Jain is also supported by a Google PhD fellowship award in Privacy and Security. This material is based upon work supported by the Defense Advanced Research Projects Agency through the ARL under Contract W911NF-15-C-0205. The views expressed are those of the authors and do not reflect the official policy or position of the Department of Defense, the National Science Foundation, the U.S. Government, IBM, or Google.

# References

1. Agrawal, S.: New Methods for Indistinguishability Obfuscation: Bootstrapping and Instantiation. Cryptology ePrint Archive, Report 2018/633 (2018). https://eprint.iacr.org/2018/633
2. Agrawal, S., Gorbunov, S., Vaikuntanathan, V., Wee, H.: Functional encryption: new perspectives and lower bounds. In: Canetti, R., Garay, J.A. (eds.) CRYPTO 2013. LNCS, vol. 8043, pp. 500–518. Springer, Heidelberg (2013). https://doi.org/10.1007/978-3-642-40084-1_28
3. Ananth, P., Brakerski, Z., Segev, G., Vaikuntanathan, V.: From selective to adaptive security in functional encryption. In: Gennaro, R., Robshaw, M. (eds.) CRYPTO 2015. LNCS, vol. 9216, pp. 657–677. Springer, Heidelberg (2015). https://doi.org/10.1007/978-3-662-48000-7_32
4. Ananth, P., Choudhuri, A.R., Jain, A.: A new approach to round-optimal secure multiparty computation. In: Katz, J., Shacham, H. (eds.) CRYPTO 2017. LNCS, vol. 10401, pp. 468–499. Springer, Cham (2017). https://doi.org/10.1007/978-3-319-63688-7_16

5. Ananth, P., Jain, A., Khurana, D., Sahai, A.: Indistinguishability Obfuscation Without Multilinear Maps: iO from LWE, Bilinear Maps, and Weak Pseudorandomness. Cryptology ePrint Archive, Report 2018/615 (2018). https://eprint.iacr.org/2018/615

6. Ananth, P., Jain, A., Naor, M., Sahai, A., Yogev, E.: Universal constructions and robust combiners for indistinguishability obfuscation and witness encryption. In: Robshaw, M., Katz, J. (eds.) CRYPTO 2016. LNCS, vol. 9815, pp. 491–520. Springer, Heidelberg (2016). https://doi.org/10.1007/978-3-662-53008-5_17

7. Ananth, P., Jain, A., Sahai, A.: Robust transforming combiners from indistinguishability obfuscation to functional encryption. In: Coron, J.-S., Nielsen, J.B. (eds.) EUROCRYPT 2017. LNCS, vol. 10210, pp. 91–121. Springer, Cham (2017). https://doi.org/10.1007/978-3-319-56620-7_4

8. Ananth, P., Jain, A.: Indistinguishability obfuscation from compact functional encryption. In: Gennaro, R., Robshaw, M. (eds.) CRYPTO 2015. LNCS, vol. 9215, pp. 308–326. Springer, Heidelberg (2015). https://doi.org/10.1007/978-3-662-47989-6_15

9. Ananth, P., Jain, A., Sahai, A.: Indistinguishability Obfuscation from Functional Encryption for Simple Functions. Cryptology ePrint Archive, Report 2015/730 (2015)

10. Ananth, P., Sahai, A.: Projective arithmetic functional encryption and indistinguishability obfuscation from degree-5 multilinear maps. In: Coron, J.-S., Nielsen, J.B. (eds.) EUROCRYPT 2017. LNCS, vol. 10210, pp. 152–181. Springer, Cham (2017). https://doi.org/10.1007/978-3-319-56620-7_6

11. Applebaum, B., Ishai, Y., Kushilevitz, E.: Computationally private randomizing polynomials and their applications (extended abstract). In: CCC, June 2005

12. Asharov, G., Jain, A., López-Alt, A., Tromer, E., Vaikuntanathan, V., Wichs, D.: Multiparty computation with low communication, computation and interaction via threshold FHE. In: Pointcheval, D., Johansson, T. (eds.) EUROCRYPT 2012. LNCS, vol. 7237, pp. 483–501. Springer, Heidelberg (2012). https://doi.org/10.1007/978-3-642-29011-4_29

13. Asmuth, C., Blakley, G.: An efficient algorithm for constructing a cryptosystem which is harder to break than two other cryptosystems. Comput. Math. Appl. 7(6), 447–450 (1981)

14. Badrinarayanan, S., Goyal, V., Jain, A., Sahai, A.: A note on VRFs from Verifiable Functional Encryption. IACR Cryptology ePrint Archive 2017, 51 (2017)

15. Badrinarayanan, S., Goyal, V., Jain, A., Kalai, Y.T., Khurana, D., Sahai, A.: Promise zero knowledge and its applications to round optimal MPC. In: Shacham, H., Boldyreva, A. (eds.) CRYPTO 2018. LNCS, vol. 10992, pp. 459–487. Springer, Cham (2018). https://doi.org/10.1007/978-3-319-96881-0_16

16. Banerjee, A., Peikert, C., Rosen, A.: Pseudorandom functions and lattices. In: Pointcheval, D., Johansson, T. (eds.) EUROCRYPT 2012. LNCS, vol. 7237, pp. 719–737. Springer, Heidelberg (2012). https://doi.org/10.1007/978-3-642-29011-4_42

17. Beaver, D., Micali, S., Rogaway, P.: The round complexity of secure protocols. In: STOC (1990)

18. Bellare, M., Hoang, V.T., Rogaway, P.: Foundations of garbled circuits. In: CCS (2012)

19. Ben-Or, M., Goldwasser, S., Wigderson, A.: Completeness theorems for non-cryptographic fault-tolerant distributed computation. In: STOC (1988)

20. Benhamouda, F., Lin, H.: $k$-round multiparty computation from $k$-round oblivious transfer via garbled interactive circuits. In: Nielsen, J.B., Rijmen, V. (eds.) EURO-CRYPT 2018. LNCS, vol. 10821, pp. 500–532. Springer, Cham (2018). https://doi.org/10.1007/978-3-319-78375-8_17

21. Bitansky, N.: Verifiable random functions from non-interactive witness-indistinguishable proofs. In: TCC (2017)

22. Bitansky, N., Nishimaki, R., Passelègue, A., Wichs, D.: From cryptomania to obfustopia through secret-key functional encryption. In: TCC Part II (2016)

23. Bitansky, N., Vaikuntanathan, V.: Indistinguishability obfuscation from functional encryption. In: FOCS (2015)

24. Bitansky, N., Vaikuntanathan, V.: Indistinguishability obfuscation: from approximate to exact. In: Kushilevitz, E., Malkin, T. (eds.) TCC 2016. LNCS, vol. 9562, pp. 67–95. Springer, Heidelberg (2016). https://doi.org/10.1007/978-3-662-49096-9_4

25. Bitansky, N., Vaikuntanathan, V.: A note on perfect correctness by derandomization. In: Coron, J.-S., Nielsen, J.B. (eds.) EUROCRYPT 2017. LNCS, vol. 10211, pp. 592–606. Springer, Cham (2017). https://doi.org/10.1007/978-3-319-56614-6_20

26. Boneh, D., et al.: Threshold Cryptosystems From Threshold Fully Homomorphic Encryption. IACR Cryptology ePrint Archive **2017** (2017)

27. Boneh, D., et al.: Fully key-homomorphic encryption, arithmetic circuit ABE and compact garbled circuits. In: Nguyen, P.Q., Oswald, E. (eds.) EUROCRYPT 2014. LNCS, vol. 8441, pp. 533–556. Springer, Heidelberg (2014). https://doi.org/10.1007/978-3-642-55220-5_30

28. Boneh, D., Sahai, A., Waters, B.: Functional encryption: definitions and challenges. In: Ishai, Y. (ed.) TCC 2011. LNCS, vol. 6597, pp. 253–273. Springer, Heidelberg (2011). https://doi.org/10.1007/978-3-642-19571-6_16

29. Boneh, D., Silverberg, A.: Applications of multilinear forms to cryptography. Contemp. Math. **324**(1), 71–90 (2003)

30. Boyle, E., Gilboa, N., Ishai, Y., Lin, H., Tessaro, S.: Foundations of homomorphic secret sharing. In: LIPIcs-Leibniz International Proceedings in Informatics, vol. 94. Schloss Dagstuhl-Leibniz-Zentrum fuer Informatik (2018)

31. Brakerski, Z., Gentry, C., Vaikuntanathan, V.: (Leveled) fully homomorphic encryption without bootstrapping. ACM Trans. Comput. Theory **6**(3), 13:1–13:36 (2014)

32. Brakerski, Z., Halevi, S., Polychroniadou, A.: Four round secure computation without setup. In: Kalai, Y., Reyzin, L. (eds.) TCC 2017. LNCS, vol. 10677, pp. 645–677. Springer, Cham (2017). https://doi.org/10.1007/978-3-319-70500-2_22

33. Brakerski, Z., Perlman, R.: Lattice-based fully dynamic multi-key FHE with short ciphertexts. In: Robshaw, M., Katz, J. (eds.) CRYPTO 2016. LNCS, vol. 9814, pp. 190–213. Springer, Heidelberg (2016). https://doi.org/10.1007/978-3-662-53018-4_8

34. Canetti, R., Lin, H., Tessaro, S., Vaikuntanathan, V.: Obfuscation of probabilistic circuits and applications. In: Dodis, Y., Nielsen, J.B. (eds.) TCC 2015. LNCS, vol. 9015, pp. 468–497. Springer, Heidelberg (2015). https://doi.org/10.1007/978-3-662-46497-7_19

35. Cheon, J.H., Han, K., Lee, C., Ryu, H., Stehlé, D.: Cryptanalysis of the multilinear map over the integers. In: Oswald, E., Fischlin, M. (eds.) EUROCRYPT 2015. LNCS, vol. 9056, pp. 3–12. Springer, Heidelberg (2015). https://doi.org/10.1007/978-3-662-46800-5_1

36. Cheon, J.H., Jeong, J., Lee, C.: An Algorithm for CSPR Problems and Cryptanalysis of the GGH Multilinear Map without an encoding of zero. Technical report, Cryptology ePrint Archive, Report 2016/139 (2016)
37. Clear, M., McGoldrick, C.: Multi-identity and multi-key leveled FHE from learning with errors. In: Gennaro, R., Robshaw, M. (eds.) CRYPTO 2015. LNCS, vol. 9216, pp. 630–656. Springer, Heidelberg (2015). https://doi.org/10.1007/978-3-662-48000-7_31
38. Coron, J.S., et al.: Zeroizing without low-level zeroes: new MMAP attacks and their limitations. In: Gennaro, R., Robshaw, M. (eds.) CRYPTO 2015. LNCS, vol. 9215, pp. 247–266. Springer, Heidelberg (2015). https://doi.org/10.1007/978-3-662-47989-6_12
39. Coron, J.S., Lee, M.S., Lepoint, T., Tibouchi, M.: Cryptanalysis of GGH15 Multilinear Maps. Cryptology ePrint Archive, Report 2015/1037 (2015)
40. Dodis, Y., Halevi, S., Rothblum, R.D., Wichs, D.: Spooky encryption and its applications. In: Robshaw, M., Katz, J. (eds.) CRYPTO 2016. LNCS, vol. 9816, pp. 93–122. Springer, Heidelberg (2016). https://doi.org/10.1007/978-3-662-53015-3_4
41. Fischlin, M., Herzberg, A., Bin-Noon, H., Shulman, H.: Obfuscation combiners. In: Robshaw, M., Katz, J. (eds.) CRYPTO 2016. LNCS, vol. 9815, pp. 521–550. Springer, Heidelberg (2016). https://doi.org/10.1007/978-3-662-53008-5_18
42. Garg, S., Gentry, C., Halevi, S.: Candidate multilinear maps from ideal lattices. In: Johansson, T., Nguyen, P.Q. (eds.) EUROCRYPT 2013. LNCS, vol. 7881, pp. 1–17. Springer, Heidelberg (2013). https://doi.org/10.1007/978-3-642-38348-9_1
43. Garg, S., Gentry, C., Halevi, S., Zhandry, M.: Fully secure functional encryption without obfuscation. IACR Cryptology ePrint Archive **2014**, 666 (2014)
44. Garg, S., Mukherjee, P., Pandey, O., Polychroniadou, A.: The exact round complexity of secure computation. In: Fischlin, M., Coron, J.-S. (eds.) EUROCRYPT 2016. LNCS, vol. 9666, pp. 448–476. Springer, Heidelberg (2016). https://doi.org/10.1007/978-3-662-49896-5_16
45. Garg, S., Pandey, O., Srinivasan, A.: Revisiting the cryptographic hardness of finding a nash equilibrium. In: Robshaw, M., Katz, J. (eds.) CRYPTO 2016. LNCS, vol. 9815, pp. 579–604. Springer, Heidelberg (2016). https://doi.org/10.1007/978-3-662-53008-5_20
46. Garg, S., Pandey, O., Srinivasan, A., Zhandry, M.: Breaking the sub-exponential barrier in obfustopia. In: Coron, J.-S., Nielsen, J.B. (eds.) EUROCRYPT 2017. LNCS, vol. 10212, pp. 156–181. Springer, Cham (2017). https://doi.org/10.1007/978-3-319-56617-7_6
47. Garg, S., Srinivasan, A.: Garbled protocols and two-round MPC from bilinear maps. In: FOCS (2017)
48. Garg, S., Srinivasan, A.: Two-round multiparty secure computation from minimal assumptions. In: Nielsen, J.B., Rijmen, V. (eds.) EUROCRYPT 2018. LNCS, vol. 10821, pp. 468–499. Springer, Cham (2018). https://doi.org/10.1007/978-3-319-78375-8_16
49. Gentry, C., Sahai, A., Waters, B.: Homomorphic encryption from learning with errors: conceptually-simpler, asymptotically-faster, attribute-based. In: Canetti, R., Garay, J.A. (eds.) CRYPTO 2013. LNCS, vol. 8042, pp. 75–92. Springer, Heidelberg (2013). https://doi.org/10.1007/978-3-642-40041-4_5
50. Goldreich, O., Micali, S., Wigderson, A.: How to play any mental game. In: STOC, pp. 218–229. ACM (1987)
51. Goldwasser, S., Kalai, Y.T., Popa, R.A., Vaikuntanathan, V., Zeldovich, N.: Reusable garbled circuits and succinct functional encryption. In: STOC (2013). https://doi.org/10.1145/2488608.2488678

52. Goldwasser, S., Klein, S., Wichs, D.: The edited truth. In: Kalai, Y., Reyzin, L. (eds.) TCC 2017. LNCS, vol. 10677, pp. 305–340. Springer, Cham (2017). https://doi.org/10.1007/978-3-319-70500-2_11

53. Gorbunov, S., Vaikuntanathan, V., Wee, H.: Functional encryption with bounded collusions via multi-party computation. In: Safavi-Naini, R., Canetti, R. (eds.) CRYPTO 2012. LNCS, vol. 7417, pp. 162–179. Springer, Heidelberg (2012). https://doi.org/10.1007/978-3-642-32009-5_11

54. Goyal, R., Hohenberger, S., Koppula, V., Waters, B.: A generic approach to constructing and proving verifiable random functions. In: Kalai, Y., Reyzin, L. (eds.) TCC 2017. LNCS, vol. 10678, pp. 537–566. Springer, Cham (2017). https://doi.org/10.1007/978-3-319-70503-3_18

55. Halevi, S., Hazay, C., Polychroniadou, A., Venkitasubramaniam, M.: Round-optimal secure multi-party computation. In: Shacham, H., Boldyreva, A. (eds.) CRYPTO 2018. LNCS, vol. 10992, pp. 488–520. Springer, Cham (2018). https://doi.org/10.1007/978-3-319-96881-0_17

56. Harnik, D., Kilian, J., Naor, M., Reingold, O., Rosen, A.: On robust combiners for oblivious transfer and other primitives. In: Cramer, R. (ed.) EUROCRYPT 2005. LNCS, vol. 3494, pp. 96–113. Springer, Heidelberg (2005). https://doi.org/10.1007/11426639_6

57. Hemenway, B., Jafargholi, Z., Ostrovsky, R., Scafuro, A., Wichs, D.: Adaptively secure garbled circuits from one-way functions. In: Robshaw, M., Katz, J. (eds.) CRYPTO 2016. LNCS, vol. 9816, pp. 149–178. Springer, Heidelberg (2016). https://doi.org/10.1007/978-3-662-53015-3_6

58. Herzberg, A.: On tolerant cryptographic constructions. In: Menezes, A. (ed.) CT-RSA 2005. LNCS, vol. 3376, pp. 172–190. Springer, Heidelberg (2005). https://doi.org/10.1007/978-3-540-30574-3_13

59. Herzberg, A.: Folklore, practice and theory of robust combiners. J. Comput. Secur. 17(2), 159–189 (2009)

60. Hu, Y., Jia, H.: Cryptanalysis of GGH Map. IACR Cryptology ePrint Archive 2015, 301 (2015)

61. Ishai, Y., Kushilevitz, E., Ostrovsky, R., Sahai, A.: Zero-knowledge from secure multiparty computation. In: Proceedings of the Thirty-Ninth Annual ACM Symposium on Theory of Computing, pp. 21–30. ACM (2007)

62. Kitagawa, F., Nishimaki, R., Tanaka, K.: Obfustopia built on secret-key functional encryption. In: Nielsen, J.B., Rijmen, V. (eds.) EUROCRYPT 2018. LNCS, vol. 10821, pp. 603–648. Springer, Cham (2018). https://doi.org/10.1007/978-3-319-78375-8_20

63. Komargodski, I., Segev, G.: From minicrypt to obfustopia via private-key functional encryption. In: Coron, J.-S., Nielsen, J.B. (eds.) EUROCRYPT 2017. LNCS, vol. 10210, pp. 122–151. Springer, Cham (2017). https://doi.org/10.1007/978-3-319-56620-7_5

64. Levin, L.A.: One-way functions and pseudorandom generators. Combinatorica 7, 357–363 (1987)

65. Lin, H.: Indistinguishability obfuscation from constant-degree graded encoding schemes. In: Fischlin, M., Coron, J.-S. (eds.) EUROCRYPT 2016. LNCS, vol. 9665, pp. 28–57. Springer, Heidelberg (2016). https://doi.org/10.1007/978-3-662-49890-3_2

66. Lin, H.: Indistinguishability obfuscation from SXDH on 5-linear maps and locality-5 PRGs. In: Katz, J., Shacham, H. (eds.) CRYPTO 2017. LNCS, vol. 10401, pp. 599–629. Springer, Cham (2017). https://doi.org/10.1007/978-3-319-63688-7_20

67. Lin, H., Matt, C.: Pseudo Flawed-Smudging Generators and Their Application to Indistinguishability Obfuscation. Cryptology ePrint Archive, Report 2018/646 (2018). https://eprint.iacr.org/2018/646
68. Lin, H., Pass, R., Seth, K., Telang, S.: Indistinguishability obfuscation with non-trivial efficiency. In: Cheng, C.-M., Chung, K.-M., Persiano, G., Yang, B.-Y. (eds.) PKC 2016. LNCS, vol. 9615, pp. 447–462. Springer, Heidelberg (2016). https://doi.org/10.1007/978-3-662-49387-8_17
69. Lin, H., Pass, R., Seth, K., Telang, S.: Output-compressing randomized encodings and applications. In: Kushilevitz, E., Malkin, T. (eds.) TCC 2016. LNCS, vol. 9562, pp. 96–124. Springer, Heidelberg (2016). https://doi.org/10.1007/978-3-662-49096-9_5
70. Lin, H., Tessaro, S.: Indistinguishability obfuscation from trilinear maps and block-wise local PRGs. In: Katz, J., Shacham, H. (eds.) CRYPTO 2017. LNCS, vol. 10401, pp. 630–660. Springer, Cham (2017). https://doi.org/10.1007/978-3-319-63688-7_21
71. Lin, H., Vaikuntanathan, V.: Indistinguishability obfuscation from DDH-like assumptions on constant-degree graded encodings. In: FOCS (2016)
72. Mukherjee, P., Wichs, D.: Two round multiparty computation via multi-key FHE. In: Fischlin, M., Coron, J.-S. (eds.) EUROCRYPT 2016. LNCS, vol. 9666, pp. 735–763. Springer, Heidelberg (2016). https://doi.org/10.1007/978-3-662-49896-5_26
73. O'Neill, A.: Definitional issues in functional encryption. IACR Cryptology ePrint Archive 2010, 556 (2010)
74. Peikert, C., Shiehian, S.: Multi-key FHE from LWE, revisited. In: Hirt, M., Smith, A. (eds.) TCC 2016. LNCS, vol. 9986, pp. 217–238. Springer, Heidelberg (2016). https://doi.org/10.1007/978-3-662-53644-5_9
75. Peikert, C., Vaikuntanathan, V., Waters, B.: A framework for efficient and compos-able oblivious transfer. In: Wagner, D. (ed.) CRYPTO 2008. LNCS, vol. 5157, pp. 554–571. Springer, Heidelberg (2008). https://doi.org/10.1007/978-3-540-85174-5_31
76. Quach, W., Wee, H., Wichs, D.: Laconic Function Evaluation and Applications. Cryptology ePrint Archive, Report 2018/409 (2018). https://eprint.iacr.org/2018/409
77. Sahai, A., Seyalioglu, H.: Worry-free encryption: functional encryption with public keys. In: CCS, pp. 463–472. ACM (2010)
78. Sahai, A., Waters, B.: Fuzzy identity-based encryption. In: Cramer, R. (ed.) EURO-CRYPT 2005. LNCS, vol. 3494, pp. 457–473. Springer, Heidelberg (2005). https://doi.org/10.1007/11426639_27
79. Yao, A.C.C.: How to generate and exchange secrets (extended abstract). In: FOCS, pp. 162–167 (1986)

# (Pseudo) Random Quantum States
# with Binary Phase

Zvika Brakerski[1]([⊠]) and Omri Shmueli[2]

[1] Weizmann Institute of Science, Rehovot, Israel
zvika.brakerski@weizmann.ac.il
[2] Tel-Aviv University, Tel-Aviv, Israel
omrishmueli@mail.tau.ac.il

**Abstract.** We prove a quantum information-theoretic conjecture due to Ji, Liu and Song (CRYPTO 2018) which suggested that a uniform superposition with random *binary* phase is statistically indistinguishable from a Haar random state. That is, any polynomial number of copies of the aforementioned state is within exponentially small trace distance from the same number of copies of a Haar random state.

As a consequence, we get a provable elementary construction of *pseudorandom* quantum states from post-quantum pseudorandom functions. Generating pseudorandom quantum states is desirable for physical applications as well as for computational tasks such as quantum money. We observe that replacing the pseudorandom function with a $(2t)$-wise independent function (either in our construction or in previous work), results in an explicit construction for *quantum state $t$-designs* for all $t$. In fact, we show that the circuit complexity (in terms of both circuit size and depth) of constructing $t$-designs is bounded by that of $(2t)$-wise independent functions. Explicitly, while in prior literature $t$-designs required linear depth (for $t > 2$), this observation shows that polylogarithmic depth suffices for all $t$.

We note that our constructions yield pseudorandom states and state designs with only real-valued amplitudes, which was not previously known. Furthermore, generating these states require quantum circuit of restricted form: applying one layer of Hadamard gates, followed by a sequence of Toffoli gates. This structure may be useful for efficiency and simplicity of implementation.

The full version of this paper is available at https://arxiv.org/abs/1906.10611.

Supported by the Israel Science Foundation (Grant No. 468/14), Binational Science Foundation (Grants No. 2016726, 2014276), and by the European Union Horizon 2020 Research and Innovation Program via ERC Project REACT (Grant 756482) and via Project PROMETHEUS (Grant 780701).

Supported by the Zevulun Hammer Scholarship from the Council for Higher Education in Israel, and by Israel Science Foundation Grant No. 18/484, and by Len Blavatnik and the Blavatnik Family Foundation.

D. Hofheinz and A. Rosen (Eds.): TCC 2019, LNCS 11891, pp. 229–250, 2019.
https://doi.org/10.1007/978-3-030-36030-6_10

# 1    Introduction

Randomness is one of the most fundamental resources for computation, and is indispensable for algorithms, complexity theory and cryptography. It is also a foundational tool for science in general, for purposes of describing and modeling natural phenomena. As our understanding of nature expands to quantum phenomena, the importance of understanding the uniform distribution over quantum states, and being able to sample from it, naturally emerges.

Quantum states can be described as unit vectors in a high-dimensional complex Hilbert space. Thus, a random quantum state is just a random unit vector on this abstract sphere. This distribution is also referred to as the Haar measure over quantum states. We note that this is a continuous distribution, even if the Hilbert space is finite dimensional (i.e. can be described by a finite number of qubits). Since quantum states cannot be duplicated, the ability to generate random quantum states refers to the ability to generate multiple copies of the same random state vector. (In fact, a single copy of a quantum random state is identical to a classical random state.) Haar random quantum states have numerous computational and physical applications. The former includes optimal quantum communication channels [8], efficient quantum POVM measurements [14] which are in turn useful in quantum state tomography, and gate fidelity estimation [4]. The latter includes constructing physical models of quantum thermalization [13].

Since random states have infinitely long descriptions (and super-exponential even if restricting to some finite precision), there is extensive literature studying approximate notions and specifically the notion of $\epsilon$-approximate $t$-designs. These are distributions whose $t$-tensor (i.e. taking $t$ copies of a sample from this distribution) are $\epsilon$ indistinguishable from (a $t$-tensor of) Haar (using the standard notion for statistical indistinguishability known as trace distance). We adopt the standard asymptotic convention and require by default that $\epsilon$ is negligible in our "security parameter", which we associate with the logarithm of the dimension of the Hilbert space. In this work we focus on quantum states over $n$ qubits (i.e. $2^n$ dimensional Hilbert space), so we associate our security parameter with $n$. However, our methods are extendable to any finite-dimensional space (with efficient representation). There is extensive literature studying (approximate) designs with bounded $t$, which also carry physical significance, see e.g. [2,4,5,7,9,10]. Indeed, it is possible to efficiently generate $t$-designs using quantum circuits of size $\mathrm{poly}(t, n)$. Up to asymptotics, this matches the information theoretic bound (however, the important aspect of the depth complexity of generating $t$-designs remained open, to the best of our knowledge), and one cannot hope to efficiently generate $t$-designs for super-polynomial $t$.

**Asymptotically Random States, Pseudorandom States and the JLS Conjecture.** Ji, Liu and Song [6] (henceforth JLS) recently proposed to extend the notion of approximate designs. They proposed the notion of a *pseudorandom quantum state* (PRS) which has a finite description but is *computationally indistinguishable* from Haar given a $t$-tuple, for *any* $t = \mathrm{poly}(n)$. Thus, for any computationally bounded purpose (experiment, naturally occurring process) a PRS is indistinguishable from a Haar state, regardless of the number of copies. They also showed that PRS are useful for cryptographic applications such as quantum money.

Furthermore, [6] proposed an insightful template for constructing PRS. They start by showing that given quantum RAM access to exponentially many classical random bits, it is possible to construct a negl($n$)-approximate $n^{\omega(1)}$-design. Let us call such a distribution ARS, for Asymptotically Random State.[1] An ARS is a statistical notion of PRS which has asymptotic limitations but no computational restrictions. Then, replacing the exponential random string with a quantum-query-resistant classically-computable pseudorandom function (PRF), the PRS construction naturally follows from ARS. The existence of such PRF is implied by the existence of quantum secure one-way functions [15].

The ARS construction of JLS is quite straightforward to describe. Generate a uniform superposition over all strings $x \in \{0,1\}^n$. This is described in the standard Dirac notation as $\sum_x |x\rangle$ (with some normalization factor). Then, assign a random quantum phase to each component $x$, i.e. generate $\sum_x \alpha_x |x\rangle$ for random independent roots of unity $\alpha_x$. To cope with finite precision, $\alpha_x$ is taken to a finite but exponential resolution $\alpha_x = \omega_{2^n}^{f(x)}$, where $f : \{0,1\}^n \to [2^n]$ is a random function and $\omega_{2^n}$ is the $2^n$-th root of unity. Given RAM access to the truth table of $f$, this state can be efficiently computed using Quantum Fourier Transform (QFT) modulo $2^n$.

JLS then conjecture (but were unable to prove) that a much simpler construction, where $\alpha_x = (-1)^{f(x)}$, should also imply ARS. That is, replacing the "high-resolution" random phase, by the simplest binary phase. While this is only one of a few conjectures made in that work, it is the only one relevant to our work and we thus refer to it simply as the JLS conjecture.

*Conjecture 1.1 ([6], restated).* The distribution over $n$-qubit quantum states defined by

$$2^{-n/2} \sum_{x \in \{0,1\}^n} (-1)^{f(x)} |x\rangle$$

where $f : \{0,1\}^n \to \{0,1\}$ is a random function, is an ARS.

To highlight the gap between the conjecture and the provable ARS construction of JLS, let us describe a crucial point in the analysis of JLS. The analysis is based on an equivalence relation between $t$-tuples of $n$-bit strings, which naturally arises from the expression for statistical distance from Haar. The tuples $(x_1, \ldots, x_t)$, $(y_1, \ldots, y_t)$ are equivalent if their histograms (i.e. the number of times each $n$-bit string appears) are equal modulo $2^n$. Since $t < 2^n$ this condition is equivalent to requiring that the tuples are permutations of each other, which makes it possible to analyze the equivalence classes of this relation and for the analysis to go through.

---

[1] Actually, their ARS, as well as the one proven in this work, is even stronger: they show that for all $t$, their distribution is $O(t^2)/2^n$-approximate $t$-design.

In the binary setting, the equivalence relates tuples whose histograms are equal modulo 2. Thus the equivalence classes can no longer be described simply as a set and all of its permutations, and they don't even have the same size anymore. This creates many additional terms in the so called density matrix of the state (which is a complex matrix of exponential dimensions $2^{tn} \times 2^{tn}$). In order to prove the conjecture, one will have to show that the effect of these exponentially many new terms on the spectrum of the matrix is negligible and there seems to be no straightforward handle for this analysis. We resolve this problem in this work.

**Our Results – Proving the Conjecture.** We prove the JLS conjecture, in fact we prove that the binary ARS implied by the conjecture has comparable properties to the prior construction (that used complex phase).

**Theorem 1.2 (Main Result).** *The distribution over $n$-qubit quantum states defined by*

$$2^{-n/2} \sum_{x \in \{0,1\}^n} (-1)^{f(x)} |x\rangle$$

*where $f : \{0,1\}^n \to \{0,1\}$ is a random function, is a $\frac{4t^2}{2^n}$-approximate $t$-design for all $t$, and thus an ARS.*

This result has various implications that we describe below. We furthermore hope that our techniques will be useful for analyzing similarly complicated quantum states.

We make two additional observations that refer to the requirement from a function $f$ to be plugged into either our theorem or that of JLS in order to imply PRS and quantum $t$-designs.

1. If we wish to obtain a PRS, the requirement of using a full-fledged quantum secure PRF can be relaxed. In fact, it is sufficient to have a function $f$ that is indistinguishable from random while allowing only uniform superposition queries (as opposed to arbitrary superposition queries). This leads to a quantum notion which is somewhat analogous to the classical notion of weak pseudorandom functions [11], an object that can be of interest for independent investigation and possibly more efficient constructions than PRFs.

2. If we only wish to obtain a $t$-design, it is sufficient to replace $f$ with a $(2t)$-wise independent function, using the fact that given $t$-quantum-query access, a $(2t)$-wise independent function is perfectly indistinguishable from a completely random function [15].

**Implications.** We find the JLS conjecture compelling from aesthetic, conceptual and perhaps even practical reasons. In terms of aesthetics, it is bothersome that one would need to go into exponentially fine-grained resolution on the phase in order to generate an ARS/PRS, being able to achieve the same parameters with a more coarse resolution (and as we show next without compromising on parameters) seems to be a more desirable state of affairs. Conceptually, the result shows that ARS, which is for all efficiently observable purposes identical to a Haar random state, can be generated using only real-valued phases. Recalling that the Haar distribution is defined over complex vectors, it appears not obvious that it can be approximated for all observable purposes by real-valued vectors.

In terms of computational complexity, our construction uses circuits with restricted structure known in the literature as **HT** [12]. Concretely, the circuit contains a single parallel layer of Hadamard gates, followed by a circuit of Toffoli gates. This model is considered fairly weak, and in particular **HT** circuits are weakly classically simulatable (i.e. any distribution samplable by an **HT** circuit followed by measurement is also classically samplable). Result shows that even such a restricted model of quantum computation is enough to approximate the Haar measure.

Lastly, from a practical standpoint, replacing the function $f$ by an efficient quantum-resilient PRF yields a very simple construction of a PRS, requiring only an **HT** circuit with the same circuit size and depth (up to asymptotics) as that of the PRF. Prior provable PRS candidates do not enjoy this property and appear to require a more complicated implementation (that in particular seem to need performing the Quantum Fourier Transform modulo $2^n$, or a similar procedure) to allow for the high-resolution of complex phase.

In the context of generating $t$-designs, using our aforementioned observation and replacing $f$ with a $(2t)$-wise independent function (in either our theorem or JLS) implies a $t$-design construction with circuit size $poly(t, n)$ and depth $O(\log t \cdot \log n)$. We are not aware of prior constructions of $t$ designs with $o(n)$ depth for $t > 2$ in the literature. Moreover, the $t$-design construction which is implied by our result can be implemented by an **HT** circuit with the same circuit size and depth (up to asymptotics) as that of the $(2t)$-wise independent function.

**Proof High-Level Overview.** Formally speaking, the proof follows by bounding the trace norm of the difference between the density matrix of $t$-copies of the state with binary phase, and the density matrix of $t$-copies of the state with $2^n$ roots of unity. However, one needs not know much about density matrices, it suffices to say that we have a complex Hermitian matrix of dimensions $2^{tn} \times 2^{tn}$, where the sum of all eigenvalues is 0, and we want to bound the sum of all absolute values of eigenvalues. It is thus sufficient to consider only positive or only negative eigenvalues.

Each row of the matrix corresponds to a tuple $(x_1, \ldots, x_t) \in (\{0,1\}^n)^t$ and each column corresponds to a tuple $(y_1, \ldots, y_t) \in (\{0,1\}^n)^t$. The entry in location $(x_1, \ldots, x_t), (y_1, \ldots, y_t)$ is nonzero if the aforementioned "histogram condition" holds on the tuples.[2] In a bit more detail, up to a global $2^{-tn}$ scaling factor, if the modulo-2 histogram condition holds but the modulo-$2^n$ condition

---

[2] Recall that the (modulo-2) histogram condition states that $(x_1, \ldots, x_t), (y_1, \ldots, y_t)$ are equivalent if for all $z$, the number of times $z$ appears in the first tuple and the number of times it appears in the second tuple have the same parity.

(i.e. permutation) does not hold then the entry will be 1, but if both hold then there is a cancellation and the entry will be 0.

We start by observing that the matrix can be decomposed into "combinatorial blocks", each representing an equivalence class of the histogram relation. We analyze the properties of these blocks. We then provide two structural lemmas that together imply the theorem:

1. We provide a non-trivial upper bound on the rank of the matrix. While it is tempting to disregard the cancellations and just count the number of nonzero blocks and their respective rank, this implies an upper bound that is too coarse. We must therefore carefully take into account the cancellations induced by permutations in order to obtain a usable bound.
2. We provide an upper bound on the absolute value of each negative eigenvalue. We do this by computing the characteristic polynomial of the matrix (the polynomial whose roots are the eigenvalues), which amounts to a product of the characteristic polynomials of the blocks. Within each block we obtain a closed form formula for the characteristic polynomial and show that its root cannot exceed a bound that is determined by the cardinality of the respective equivalence class (properly normalized).

Combining the two lemmas by multiplying the rank bound with the eigenvalue absolute value bound implies the theorem.

**Paper Organization.** We use standard quantum and cryptographic notations and definitions, essentially following [6], see short summary in Sect. 2. Our construction is presented in Sect. 3 and proven in Sect. 4.

## 2    Preliminaries

For $m \in \mathbb{N}$, we denote $[m] := \{1, \cdots, m\}$. For a natural number $N$, denote by $\omega_N := e^{\frac{2\pi i}{N}}$ the complex root of unity of order $N$. Also for $N$, denote by $\mathcal{S}(N)$ the set of unit vectors in $\mathbb{C}^N$, by $\mathcal{D}(N)$ the set of $N \times N$ density matrices over $\mathbb{C}$, and by $\mathcal{U}(N)$ the set of $N \times N$ unitary matrices over $\mathbb{C}$. Note that for $n \in \mathbb{N}$, $\mathcal{S}(2^n)$ is the set of $n$-qubit pure quantum states, $\mathcal{D}(2^n)$ is the set of $n$-qubit mixed states, and $\mathcal{U}(2^n)$ is the set of $n$-qubit unitaries. When we consider quantum algorithms, we usually think of them as a uniform family of quantum circuits.

When we consider eigenvalues and singular values of matrices throughout this paper, we implicitly refer to eigenvalues and singular values that possibly repeat, e.g. $\lambda_1 \geq \lambda_2 \geq \cdots \geq \lambda_n$ for matrix with $n$, possibly identical eigenvalues.

The trace distance, defined below, is a generalization of statistical distance to the quantum setting and represents the maximal distinguishing probability between quantum states.

**Definition 2.1 (Trace distance).** *Let $\rho_1, \rho_2 \in \mathcal{D}(2^n)$ be two density matrices of $n$-qubit mixed states. The trace distance between them is*

$$\mathrm{TD}(\rho_1, \rho_2) := \frac{1}{2} \left\| \rho_1 - \rho_2 \right\|_1 \ ,$$

*where for a hermitian matrix $M$, $\|M\|_1 = \sum_i |\lambda_i|$, where $\lambda_i$ are the eigenvalues of $M$.*

The following is a basic fact that shows that classical circuits are a subset of quantum circuits. Recall that the Toffoli gate implements the 3-qubit unitary defined by $|x, y, z\rangle \to |x, y, z \oplus xy\rangle$.

**Proposition 2.2 (Toffoli gate is universal for classical computation).** *Let $f : \{0,1\}^n \to \{0,1\}^m$ be a function and let $C$ be a classical circuit that computes $f$. Define the unitary $U_f : |x\rangle|y\rangle \to |x\rangle|y \oplus f(x)\rangle$. Then there exists a quantum circuit of size $O(|C|)$ consisting only of Toffoli gates that computes $U_f$ (possibly using auxiliary $|0\rangle$ qubits).*

HT circuits are quantum circuits of a restricted structure, defined as follows.

**Definition 2.3 (HT Circuit).** *A quantum circuit $C$ is an **HT** circuit if the first layer of the circuit consists of only Hadamard gates on a subset of the qubits, and the rest of the circuit consists of only Toffoli gates.*

## 2.1 Pseudorandom Functions and $k$-Wise Independent Functions

Here we define pseudorandom functions with quantum security (QPRFs).

**Definition 2.4 (Quantum-Secure Pseudorandom Function (QPRF)).** *Let $\mathcal{K} = \{\mathcal{K}_n\}_{n \in \mathbb{N}}$ be an efficiently samplable key distribution, and let $\mathsf{PRF} = \{\mathsf{PRF}_n\}_{n \in \mathbb{N}}$, $\mathsf{PRF}_n : \mathcal{K}_n \times \{0,1\}^n \to \{0,1\}^n$ be an efficiently computable function. We say that $\mathsf{PRF}$ is a quantum-secure pseudorandom function if for every efficient non-uniform quantum algorithm $A$ that can make quantum queries there exists a negligible function $\mathrm{negl}(\cdot)$ s.t. for every $n \in \mathbb{N}$,*

$$\left| \Pr_{k \leftarrow \mathcal{K}_n} [A^{\mathsf{PRF}(k, \cdot)}() = 1] - \Pr_{f \leftarrow (\{0,1\}^n)^{(\{0,1\}^n)}} [A^f() = 1] \right| \le \mathrm{negl}(n) \ .$$

In [15], QPRFs were proved to exist under the assumption that post-quantum one-way functions exist.

We define $k$-wise independent functions are keyed functions s.t. when the key is sampled uniformly at random, then any $k$ different inputs to the function generate $k$-wise independent random variables.

**Definition 2.5 ($k(n)$-Wise Independent Function).** *Let $k(n) : \mathbb{N} \to \mathbb{N}$ be a function, $\mathcal{K} = \{\mathcal{K}_n\}_{n \in \mathbb{N}}$ be a key distribution, and let $f = \{f_n\}_{n \in \mathbb{N}}$, $f_n : \mathcal{K}_n \times \{0,1\}^n \to \{0,1\}^n$ be a function. Thus, $f$ is a $k(n)$-wise independent function if for all $n$, for every distinct $k(n)$ input values $x_1, \cdots, x_{k(n)} \in \{0,1\}^n$,*

$$\forall y_1, \cdots, y_{k(n)} \in \{0,1\}^n : \Pr_{s \leftarrow \mathcal{K}_n} [f(s, x_1) = y_1 \wedge \cdots \wedge f(s, x_{k(n)}) = y_{k(n)}] = 2^{-n \cdot k(n)} \ .$$

It is not a part of the standard definition, but it is usually the case that we consider $\mathcal{K}$ to be efficiently samplable and $f$ to be efficiently computable.

## 2.2   Quantum Randomness and Pseudorandomness

**The Haar Measure on Quantum States.** Intuitively, the Haar measure on quantum states is the quantum analogue of the classical uniform distribution over bit strings, that is, we can think of it as the uniform (continuous) probability distribution on quantum states. Recall that an $n$-qubit quantum state can be viewed as a unit vector in $\mathbb{C}^{2^n}$, thus the Haar measure on $n$ qubits is the uniform distribution over all unit vectors in $\mathbb{C}^{2^n}$.

Formally, the density matrix representing the distribution of drawing a random Haar vector and outputting $t$ copies of it is given below.

**Definition 2.6 ($n$-Qubits, $t$-Copy Random Haar State).** *Let $t, n \in \mathbb{N}$, we define the $n$-qubits $t$-copy random Haar mixed state to be*

$$\rho_{(t,n,H)} := \mathbb{E}_{|\psi\rangle \leftarrow \mu(2^n)} \left[ (|\psi\rangle\langle\psi|)^{\otimes t} \right] \; ,$$

*where $\mu(2^n)$ is the continuous distribution over $\mathbb{C}^{2^n}$ that is invariant under unitary transformations (it is known that there is only one such distribution).*

**Approximate Quantum State $t$-Designs.** Approximate $t$-designs are quantum distributions that are approximately random when the number of output copies of the sampled state is restricted. The formal definition follows.

**Definition 2.7 ($n$-Qubits, $\varepsilon$-Approximate State $t$-Design).** *Let $\varepsilon \in [0,1], t \in \mathbb{N}$, and let $\mathcal{Q}$ be a quantum distribution over $n$-qubit states. We say that $\mathcal{Q}$ is an $\varepsilon$-approximate state $t$-design if*

$$\mathrm{TD}\big(\mathbb{E}_{|\psi\rangle \leftarrow \mathcal{Q}}[(|\psi\rangle\langle\psi|)^{\otimes t}], \; \rho_{(t,n,H)}\big) \leq \varepsilon \; .$$

For the sake of completeness, we give a definition for quantum state $t$-design generators.

**Definition 2.8 ($\varepsilon(n)$-Approximate State $t(n)$-Design Generator).** *Let $\varepsilon(n) : \mathbb{N} \to [0,1]$, $t(n) : \mathbb{N} \to \mathbb{N}$ be functions. We say that a pair of quantum algorithms $(K, G)$ is an $\varepsilon(n)$-approximate state $t(n)$-design generator if the following holds:*

- *Key Generation. For all $n$, $K(1^n)$ always outputs a classical key $k$.*
- *State Generation. For all $n$ and for all $k$ in the image of $K(1^n)$, there exists an $n$-qubit pure state $|\phi_k\rangle$ s.t. $G(1^n, k) = |\phi_k\rangle$.*
- *Approximate Quantum Randomness. For all $n$, the distribution $|\phi_k\rangle_{k \leftarrow K(1^n)}$ is an $n$-qubit, $\varepsilon(n)$-approximate state $t(n)$-design.*

Note that we define the generator as two algorithms instead of one, to highlight the fact that a state that is sampled can be generated multiple times on demand.

For the purposes of this work it is convenient to define the notion of Asymptotically Random States (ARS) as follows.

**Definition 2.9 (Asymptotically Random State (ARS)).** *An Asymptotically Random State (ARS) is shorthand for an asymptotic sequence of $\mathrm{negl}(n)$-approximate $n^{\omega(1)}$-designs.*

**Quantum Pseudorandomness.** The notion of pseudorandom quantum states was introduced in [6], was shown to be implied by QPRFs, and is defined below.

**Definition 2.10 (Pseudorandom Quantum State (PRS)).** *A pair of quantum polynomial-time algorithms $(K, G)$ is a Pseudorandom State Generator (PRS Generator) if the following holds:*

- **Key Generation.** *For all $n$, $K(1^n)$ always outputs a classical key $k$.*
- **State Generation.** *For all $n$ and for all $k$ in the image of $K(1^n)$, there exists an $n$-qubit pure state $|\phi_k\rangle$ s.t. $G(1^n, k) = |\phi_k\rangle$.*
- **Security.** *For any polynomial $t(\cdot)$ and a non-uniform efficient quantum algorithm $A$ there exists a negligible function $\mathrm{negl}(\cdot)$ such that for all $n \in \mathbb{N}$,*

$$\left| \Pr_{k \leftarrow K(1^n)}[A(|\phi_k\rangle^{\otimes t(n)}) = 1] - \Pr_{|\psi\rangle \leftarrow \mu}[A(|\psi\rangle^{\otimes t(n)}) = 1] \right| \leq \mathrm{negl}(n) \ ,$$

*where $\mu$ is the Haar measure on $\mathcal{S}(2^n)$.*

*If the above holds, we say that the ensemble $\mathsf{PRS} = \{\mathsf{PRS}_n\}_{n \in \mathbb{N}}$, where $\mathsf{PRS}_n$ is the distribution $|\phi_k\rangle_{k \leftarrow K(1^n)}$, is a Pseudorandom Quantum State (PRS) which is generated by $(K, G)$.*

In the above definition, the number of qubits in the pseudorandom states can also be parameterized (i.e. $G(1^n, k)$ can output $m(n)$-qubit states and not necessarily $n$-qubit states), but in the current work we will ignore this.

## 3   Construction

The following construction will be the base of both our pseudorandom state and quantum state $t$-design constructions.

**Definition 3.1 (Binary Phase State Generator for $F$).** *Let $\mathcal{K} = \{\mathcal{K}_n\}_{n \in \mathbb{N}}$ be a key space and let $F = \{F_n\}_{n \in \mathbb{N}}$ be a keyed (boolean) function $F_n : \mathcal{K}_n \times \{0,1\}^n \to \{0,1\}$. $\mathsf{G}_{\mathrm{bin}}^F$ is the procedure that takes as input a $k \in \mathcal{K}_n$ and outputs the superposition*

$$|\phi_k\rangle := 2^{-n/2} \sum_{x \in \{0,1\}^n} (-1)^{F_k(x)} |x\rangle \ .$$

The following claim establishes that $\mathsf{G}_{\mathrm{bin}}^F$ is efficiently implementable when $F$ is.

*Claim.* If $F$ is computable by a classical circuit of size $s(n)$ and depth $d(n)$, then $\mathsf{G}_{\mathrm{bin}}^F$ is computable by an **HT** circuit of size $O(s(n))$ and depth $d(n) + 1$.

*Proof.* The algorithm of $\mathsf{G}_{\mathrm{bin}}^F$ will get as input a key $k$ and generate the state $|+\rangle^{\otimes n}|-\rangle$ by performing $(n + 1)$ Hadamard gates (in parallel) $H^{\otimes(n+1)}$ on the ancillary classical state $|0\rangle^{\otimes n}|1\rangle$, then execute the $F_k$ circuit (which can be realized quantumly by Toffoli gates) on the state $|+\rangle^{\otimes n}|-\rangle$. After the execution of $F_k$, the state is

$$2^{-n/2} \sum_{x \in \{0,1\}^n} (-1)^{F_k(x)} |x\rangle|-\rangle,$$

thus by tracing out the last qubit we get the output state $|\phi_k\rangle$.

We note that previous candidates required a more involved generation process which required applying quantum Fourier transform modulo $2^n$, or a similar procedure.

### 3.1 Our Pseudorandom Quantum State (PRS) Generator and Its Properties

Recall the definition of a PRS (see Definition 2.10) and of a QPRF (Defintion 2.4). We present our construction of a PRS candidate with binary phase as follows.

*Claim.* If $F$ is a QPRF then $\mathsf{G}_{\mathrm{bin}}^F$ (along with the key generation algorithm of $F$) is a secure PRS generator.

*Proof.* First, it's clear that the key generation algorithm $K$ of our PRS is the key generation algorithm of $F$ (that for input $1^n$, samples $k \leftarrow \mathcal{K}_n$), and that the state generation algorithm $G$ of our PRS is $\mathsf{G}_{\mathrm{bin}}^F$.

Now, we argue that by the quantum-security of $F$, for any polynomial number of copies $t(n)$, the distribution $|\phi_k\rangle_{k \leftarrow \mathcal{K}_n}$ is computationally indistinguishable (by quantum adversaries) from a random binary phase state, that is, the distribution over $n$-qubit quantum states defined by

$$2^{-n/2} \sum_{x \in \{0,1\}^n} (-1)^{f(x)} |x\rangle \ ,$$

where $f : \{0,1\}^n \to \{0,1\}$ is a truly random function.

By Theorem 1.2, a random binary phase state is an ARS (Definition 2.9), which in particular means that a random Haar state and a random binary phase state are computationally indistinguishable for any polynomial number of copies. By the the triangle inequality of computational indistinguishability, we deduce that for any polynomial number of copies, the quantum distribution $|\phi_k\rangle_{k \leftarrow \mathcal{K}_n}$ and the Haar distribution are computationally indistinguishable, which completes our proof.

*Remark 3.2.* We note that in our security proof we did not use the full power of quantumly secure PRFs. Indeed, if we consider the QPRF unitary $U_{\mathsf{PRF}_k}$ : $|x\rangle|y\rangle \to |x\rangle|y \oplus \mathsf{PRF}_k(x)\rangle$, then in order for the PRS to be secure, it is only needed that the QPRF will be secure when the input register is in the uniform superposition $|+\rangle^{\otimes n}$ (and moreover, the output register is $|-\rangle$). In particular, we don't even need the QPRF to be secure against chosen classical queries. This can be thought of as a quantum analog of the classical notion of weak PRFs [11]. In the classical setting, it is conjectured that weak PRFs reside in a lower complexity class than full fledged PRFs [1]. If similar behavior can be shown in the quantum case it could improve the efficiency of PRS constructions.

We leave the investigation of this new notion (which we propose to call quantumly weak PRFs) to future works.

We conclude with observing that by our result, the complexity of PRSs is no greater than that of QPRFs, and is moreover implementable by **HT** circuits.

**Corollary 3.3.** *Let* PRF $= \{$PRF$_n\}_{n \in \mathbb{N}}$ *be a QPRF. Thus there is a PRS generator construction* $(K, G)$ *implemented by* **HT** *circuits, where* $K$ *is implemented by circuits of the same size and depth as that of the key sampling algorithm of* PRF, *and* $G$ *is implemented by circuits of the same size and depth (up to asymptotics) as that of* PRF.

## 3.2    Shallow-Circuit Approximate $t$-Design Generators

We note that by a simple observation, we can replace the truly random function $f$ in Theorem 1.2 with a $2t$-wise independent function to gain an elementary and efficient construction of quantum state approximate $t$-designs. Formally, we use the following fact.

**Fact 3.4 ([15], Fact 2).** *The behavior of any quantum algorithm making at most $q$ queries to a $2q$-wise independent function is identical to its behavior when the queries are made to a random function.*

This implies that when $f$ is a $2t$-wise independent function, then the state from Theorem 1.2 is a $\frac{4t^2}{2^n}$-approximate $t$-design. We note that this observation can also be applied to the ARS from [6], and it would imply a different (but seemingly less efficient) construction of $t$-designs.

**Corollary 3.5.** *The distribution over $n$-qubit quantum states defined by*

$$2^{-n/2} \sum_{x \in \{0,1\}^n} (-1)^{f(x)} |x\rangle$$

*where* $f : \{0,1\}^n \rightarrow \{0,1\}$ *is a $2t$-wise independent function, is a $\frac{4t^2}{2^n}$-approximate $t$-design.*

More explicitly, combining the above with Claim 3 implies that that when $f$ is a $2t$-wise independent function, $\mathsf{G}^f_{\mathrm{bin}}$ is an approximate $t$-design generator (along with the key generation algorithm of $f$). The following corollary relates the complexity of $t$-design generators with that of the $2t$-wise independent functions.

**Corollary 3.6.** *Let* $t(n) : \mathbb{N} \rightarrow \mathbb{N}$ *be a function and let* $f = \{f_n\}_{n \in \mathbb{N}}$, $f_n : \mathcal{K}_n \times \{0,1\}^n \rightarrow \{0,1\}$ *be a $(2t(n))$-wise independent function. Thus there is an $\frac{O(t(n)^2)}{2^n}$-approximate quantum state $t(n)$-design generator $(K, G)$ implemented* by **HT** *circuits, where $K$ is implemented by circuits of the same size and depth as that of the key sampling algorithm of $f$, and $G$ is implemented by circuits of the same size and depth (up to asymptotics) as that of $f$.*

Finally, we can instantiate with known construction of $k$-wise independent functions to obtain the following.

**Corollary 3.7.** *For every function $t(n) : \mathbb{N} \to \mathbb{N}$, there exists a $\frac{O(t(n)^2)}{2^n}$-approximate quantum state $t(n)$-design generator, implemented by* **HT** *circuits of $\mathrm{poly}(t(n), n)$ size and $O(\log t(n) \cdot \log n)$ depth.*

*Proof.* We recall the most elementary construction of $k$-wise independent distributions over $2^n$ variables. Consider the field $\mathbb{F} = \mathbb{F}_{2^n}$ and recall that $\mathbb{F}$ elements correspond to degree $(n-1)$ formal polynomials with binary coefficients. Thus there is a natural bijection between $\mathbb{F}$ and $\{0,1\}^n$ that allows to represent $\mathbb{F}$ elements as elements in $\{0,1\}^n$. This representation allows to perform field arithmetic operations using circuits of size $\mathrm{poly}(n)$ and depth $O(\log n)$.

A $k$-wise independent distribution over $\mathbb{F}^{\mathbb{F}}$ is defined by the evaluations of a random degree $(k-1)$ polynomial over $\mathbb{F}$, on all elements in $\mathbb{F}$. The computational complexity of evaluating such a polynomial is $\mathrm{poly}(k, n)$ and its depth is $O(\log k \cdot \log n)$. Plugging in $k = 2t$ completes the proof (note that we only require $2t$-wise independence over $\{0,1\}^{\mathbb{F}}$ so our instantiation is actually a slight overkill). ∎

## 4    Proof of Theorem 1.2

We introduce the following notation.

**Notation 4.1 (Complex phase state by $f$).** *For a function $f : \{0,1\}^n \to [2^n]$ we denote*

$$|f\rangle_{(2^n)} := 2^{-n/2} \sum_{x \in \{0,1\}^n} \omega_{2^n}^{f(x)} |x\rangle .$$

*when it is clear from the context, the subscript $2^n$ will be dropped from $|f\rangle_{(2^n)}$.*

**Notation 4.2 (Binary phase state by $f$).** *For a function $f : \{0,1\}^n \to \{0,1\}$ we denote*

$$|f\rangle_{(2)} := 2^{-n/2} \sum_{x \in \{0,1\}^n} (-1)^{f(x)} |x\rangle .$$

*when it is clear from the context, the subscript $2$ will be dropped from $|f\rangle_{(2)}$.*

**Notation 4.3 ($t$-copy random complex phase mixed state).** *For $t, n \in \mathbb{N}$, denote*

$$\rho_{(t,n,2^n)} := \mathbb{E}_f [(|f\rangle_{(2^n)} \langle f|_{(2^n)})^{\otimes t}] ,$$

*where the expectation is taken over a uniformly random function $f : \{0,1\}^n \to [2^n]$.*

**Notation 4.4 (t-copy random binary phase mixed state).** *For* $t, n \in \mathbb{N}$, *denote*

$$\rho_{(t,n,2)} := \mathbb{E}_f\left[(|f\rangle_{(2)}\langle f|_{(2)})^{\otimes t}\right],$$

*where the expectation is taken over a uniformly random function* $f : \{0,1\}^n \rightarrow \{0,1\}$.

In [6] It is shown that the random complex phase state is an ARS.

**Lemma 4.5 ([6], Lemma 2).** *Let* $n, t \in \mathbb{N}$, *then*

$$\mathrm{TD}\big(\rho_{(t,n,2^n)}, \rho_{(t,n,H)}\big) = \prod_{i \in [t-1]} \left(1 - \frac{i}{2^n}\right) - \prod_{i \in [t-1]} \left(1 - \frac{2 \cdot i}{2^n + i}\right).$$

We will show that a random binary phase state is asymptotically statistically close to a random complex phase state. More precisely, we will prove the following lemma.

**Lemma 4.6.** *Let* $n, t \in \mathbb{N}$, *then*

$$\mathrm{TD}\big(\rho_{(t,n,2)}, \rho_{(t,n,2^n)}\big) \leq \prod_{i \in [t-1]} \left(1 + \frac{i}{2^n}\right) - \prod_{i \in [t-1]} \left(1 - \frac{i}{2^n}\right).$$

Using the triangle inequality of trace distance and Lemmas 4.5 and 4.6 (below, in the first inequality), we show that a random binary phase state is an ARS. In the following, assume that $t < \frac{\sqrt{2^n}}{2}$, otherwise the upper bound on the trace distance trivially holds:

$$\mathrm{TD}\big(\rho_{(t,n,2)}, \rho_{(t,n,H)}\big) \leq \prod_{i \in [t-1]} \left(1 + \frac{i}{2^n}\right) - \prod_{i \in [t-1]} \left(1 - \frac{2 \cdot i}{2^n + i}\right)$$

$$\leq \left(1 + \frac{t}{2^n}\right)^t - \left(1 - \frac{2 \cdot t}{2^n + t}\right)^t \leq \left(1 + \frac{t}{2^n}\right)^t - \left(1 - \frac{2 \cdot t}{2^n}\right)^t$$

$$\underset{(*)}{\leq} 1 + \frac{2 \cdot t^2}{2^n} - \left(1 - \frac{2 \cdot t}{2^n}\right)^t \underset{(**)}{\leq} 1 + \frac{2 \cdot t^2}{2^n} - \left(1 - \frac{2 \cdot t^2}{2^n}\right) = \frac{4 \cdot t^2}{2^n},$$

where $(*)$ is due to one variant of Bernoulli's inequality $(\forall r > 1, x \in [0, \frac{1}{2(r-1)}) :$ $(1+x)^r \leq 1 + 2rx)$, and $(**)$ follows from the more popular variant of Bernoulli's inequality $(\forall r \notin (0,1), x \geq -1 : (1+x)^r \geq 1 + rx)$.

Therefore, all that remains is to prove Lemma 4.6, which will require most technical effort.

## 4.1   Proof of Lemma 4.6

Denote the difference matrix $\rho_n := \rho_{(t,n,2)} - \rho_{(t,n,2^n)}$. The proof of the lemma contains two main components. First, an upper bound on the number of non-zero eigenvalues of $\rho_n$.

**Lemma 4.7.** *Let $n \in \mathbb{N}$ and let $t \in \{1, 2, \cdots, 2^n - 1\}$, thus the number of non-zero eigenvalues of $\rho_n$ is upper bounded by*

$$\binom{2^n + t - 1}{t} - \binom{2^n}{t}.$$

Second, a lower bound on the minimal (as in most negative) eigenvalue of $\rho_n$.

**Lemma 4.8.** *Let $n \in \mathbb{N}$ and let $t \in \{1, 2, \cdots, 2^n - 1\}$, thus for all eigenvalues $\lambda$ of $\rho_n$ we have $-\frac{t!}{2^{tn}} \leq \lambda$.*

Note that this will give an upper bound on the absolute values of all negative eigenvalues of $\rho_n$.

Given the last two lemmas, we can prove Lemma 4.6.

*Proof.* Let $n \in \mathbb{N}$ and let $t \in \{1, 2, \cdots, 2^n - 1\}^3$. $\rho_n$ is a difference between two density matrices, and because that trace is linear and density matrices have a trace of 1, the trace of $\rho_n$ is 0. Also recall that the sum of eigenvalues of a matrix is equal to its trace, so, the positive and negative eigenvalues of $\rho_n$ balance each other to 0, and thus, a bound on the sum of absolute values of all eigenvalues of $\rho_n$ can be obtained by bounding the sum of the absolute values of its negative eigenvalues. Formally:

$$\mathrm{TD}\big(\rho_{(t,n,2)}, \rho_{(t,n,2^n)}\big) = \frac{1}{2} \, \|\rho_n\|_1 =$$

$$\frac{1}{2} \cdot \sum_{\lambda \text{ eigenvalue of } \rho_n} |\lambda| = \sum_{\lambda \text{ negative eigenvalue of } \rho_n} |\lambda| \ .$$

Using Lemmas 4.7 and 4.8, we obtain an upper bound on the last sum, which yields the wanted inequality.

$$\sum_{\lambda \text{ negative eigenvalue of } \rho_n} |\lambda| \leq \left( \binom{2^n + t - 1}{t} - \binom{2^n}{t} \right) \frac{t!}{2^{tn}}$$

$$= \frac{(2^n + t - 1)!}{2^{tn}(2^n - 1)!} - \frac{(2^n)!}{2^{tn}(2^n - t)!} = \frac{(2^n)! \big( \prod_{i \in [t-1]} (2^n + i) \big)}{2^{tn}(2^n - 1)!} - \frac{(2^n)! \big( \prod_{i \in [t-1]} (2^n - i) \big)}{2^{tn}(2^n - 1)!}$$

$$= \frac{\prod_{i \in [t-1]} (2^n + i)}{2^{(t-1)n}} - \frac{\prod_{i \in [t-1]} (2^n - i)}{2^{(t-1)n}} = \prod_{i \in [t-1]} \frac{2^n + i}{2^n} - \prod_{i \in [t-1]} \frac{2^n - i}{2^n}$$

$$= \prod_{i \in [t-1]} \left( 1 + \frac{i}{2^n} \right) - \prod_{i \in [t-1]} \left( 1 - \frac{i}{2^n} \right) \ .$$

---

[3] For $t \geq 2^n$ the bound trivially holds: Note that for $t \geq 2^n$ the bound's expression is minimized for $t = 2^n$ and $n = 1$, which yields 1 as a trivial bound on any trace distance.

## 4.2    The Structure of the Matrix $\rho_n$

We identify the structure of $\rho_n$ in order to prove Lemma 4.13, which will be used in both proofs of Lemmas 4.7 and 4.8. We do this by first describing $\rho_{(t,n,2^n)}$ and $\rho_{(t,n,2)}$. More precisely, we will derive combinatorial expressions for $\rho_{(t,n,2^n)}$ and $\rho_{(t,n,2)}$, and as a consequence we'll have an expression for their difference $\rho_n$.

**The Structure of** $\rho_{(t,n,2^n)}$. We will start with a formula for the entries of $\rho_{(t,n,2^n)}$ (a similar analysis was done for this matrix in [6]); for convenience, the definition is restated:

$$\rho_{(t,n,2^n)} = \mathbb{E}_{f \leftarrow [2^n]^{\{0,1\}^n}} \left[ (|f\rangle\langle f|)^{\otimes t} \right] = \mathbb{E}_{f \leftarrow [2^n]^{\{0,1\}^n}} \left[ |f\rangle^{\otimes t} \langle f|^{\otimes t} \right] .$$

Observe that for a function $f : \{0,1\}^n \rightarrow [2^n]$,

$$|f\rangle^{\otimes t} = \left( 2^{-n/2} \sum_{x \in \{0,1\}^n} \omega_{2^n}^{f(x)} |x\rangle \right)^{\otimes t} = 2^{-tn/2} \sum_{\mathbf{x}=(x_1,\cdots,x_t) \in \{0,1\}^{n \times t}} \omega_{2^n}^{(\sum_{i \in [t]} f(x_i))} |\mathbf{x}\rangle .$$

Now we can compute $\rho_{(t,n,2^n)}$:

$$\rho_{(t,n,2^n)} = \mathbb{E}_f \left[ |f\rangle^{\otimes t} \langle f|^{\otimes t} \right]$$

$$= \mathbb{E}_f \left[ \left( 2^{-tn/2} \sum_{\mathbf{x}=(x_1,\cdots,x_t) \in \{0,1\}^{n \times t}} \omega_{2^n}^{(\sum_{i \in [t]} f(x_i))} |\mathbf{x}\rangle \right) \cdot \right.$$

$$\left. \left( 2^{-tn/2} \sum_{\mathbf{y}=(y_1,\cdots,y_t) \in \{0,1\}^{n \times t}} \omega_{2^n}^{(-\sum_{i \in [t]} f(y_i))} \langle \mathbf{y}| \right) \right]$$

$$= 2^{-tn} \sum_{\mathbf{x},\mathbf{y} \in \{0,1\}^{n \times t}} |\mathbf{x}\rangle\langle\mathbf{y}| \cdot \mathbb{E}_f \left[ \omega_{2^n}^{(\sum_{i \in [t]} f(x_i) - \sum_{i \in [t]} f(y_i))} \right] ,$$

So, for $\mathbf{x},\mathbf{y} \in \{0,1\}^{n \times t}$, the $(\mathbf{x},\mathbf{y})$-th entry of $\rho_{(t,n,2^n)}$ is

$$2^{-tn} \cdot \mathbb{E}_f \left[ \omega_{2^n}^{(\sum_{i \in [t]} f(x_i) - \sum_{i \in [t]} f(y_i))} \right] .$$

Now, define:

**Definition 4.9 ($(t,n)$ permutations).** *Let* $\mathbf{x},\mathbf{y} \in \{0,1\}^{t \times n}$, *and denote* $\mathbf{x} = (x_1,\cdots,x_t), \mathbf{y} = (y_1,\cdots,y_t)$, *where* $\forall i \in [t] : x_i, y_i \in \{0,1\}^n$. *We say that* $\mathbf{x},\mathbf{y}$, *are $(t,n)$ permutations of each other (or just permutations of each other) if there exists a permutation* $\pi \in S_t$ *s.t.*

$$(x_1,\cdots,x_t) = (y_{\pi(1)},\cdots,y_{\pi(t)}) .$$

Note that an equivalent convenient characterization of the two strings $\mathbf{x}, \mathbf{y}$ being permutations of each other is that the multisets $\{x_1, \cdots, x_t\}, \{y_1, \cdots, y_t\}$ are equal.

Observe that when $\mathbf{x}$ and $\mathbf{y}$ are permutations of each other, then for every $f$ we have $\sum_{i\in[t]} f(x_i) = \sum_{i\in[t]} f(y_i)$ and thus the expected value is 1 and the entry's value is $2^{-tn}$. We would like to also claim that if $\mathbf{x}, \mathbf{y}$ are not permutations of each other then the entry is 0, and it turns out we indeed can. Observe that if $\mathbf{x}, \mathbf{y}$ are not permutations of each other then there exists a string $s \in \{0,1\}^n$ that appears a different number of times in $\mathbf{x}$ and $\mathbf{y}$, and we can say that the $(\mathbf{x}, \mathbf{y})$-th entry is

$$2^{-tn} \cdot \mathbb{E}_f \left[ \omega_{2^n}^{(\sum_{i\in[t]} f(x_i) - \sum_{i\in[t]} f(y_i))} \right] = 2^{-tn} \cdot \beta \cdot \mathbb{E}_f \left[ \omega_{2^n}^{a\cdot f(s)} \right] ,$$

where $\beta \in \mathbb{R}$ is some real number (which we won't care about) and $a \in \{-t, \cdots, -1, 1, \cdots, t\}$ is the (non-zero) difference between the number of appearances of $s$ in $\mathbf{x}$ and $\mathbf{y}$ (last equality follows from the fact that the expectation of a product of independent random variables is the product of expectations). Now we will use our restriction on $t$, which is that $t$ is strictly smaller then $2^n$. Combined with the fact that $a \neq 0$, it is necessarily the case that $\omega_{2^n}^a \neq 1$ (if $t$ could be as big as $2^n$ then $a$ will be able to be $2^n$ or some integer multiple of it, which will yield $\omega_{2^n}^a = 1$). After this restriction we obtain:

$$\mathbb{E}_f \left[ \omega_{2^n}^{a\cdot f(s)} \right] = \sum_{i\in\{0,1,\cdots,2^n-1\}} 2^{-n} \cdot \omega_{2^n}^{a\cdot i} = 2^{-n} \cdot \left( \frac{\omega_{2^n}^{a\cdot 2^n} - 1}{\omega_{2^n}^a - 1} \right) = 0 ,$$

Finally, the above yields a combinatorial description of $\rho_{(t,n,2^n)}$:

$$\forall \mathbf{x}, \mathbf{y} \in \{0,1\}^{n\times t} : \rho_{(t,n,2^n)}[\mathbf{x}, \mathbf{y}] = \begin{cases} 2^{-tn} & \mathbf{x}, \mathbf{y} \text{ are permutations} \\ 0 & \mathbf{x}, \mathbf{y} \text{ are not permutations} \end{cases} .$$

**The Structure of $\rho_{(t,n,2)}$.** By the same reasoning as in the case of $\rho_{(t,n,2^n)}$, we obtain that the $(\mathbf{x}, \mathbf{y})$-th entry of $\rho_{(t,n,2)}$ is

$$2^{-tn} \cdot \mathbb{E}_f \left[ (-1)^{(\sum_{i\in[t]} f(x_i) - \sum_{i\in[t]} f(y_i))} \right] ,$$

where this time $f$ is a random function from $\{0,1\}^n$ to $\{0,1\}$ (rather than from $\{0,1\}^n$ to $[2^n]$). Because $(-1) = (-1)^{-1}$, the entry is simplified to

$$2^{-tn} \cdot \mathbb{E}_f \left[ (-1)^{(\sum_{i\in[t]} f(x_i) + \sum_{i\in[t]} f(y_i))} \right] .$$

Like in the case of $\rho_{(t,n,2^n)}$, we would like a nice and clean combinatorial predicate to describe the entries of the matrix, and as we'll see in a bit, the matrix $\rho_{(t,n,2)}$ indeed have the same general structure as $\rho_{(t,n,2^n)}$ but with different predicate on $\mathbf{x}, \mathbf{y}$.

First, define the following:

**Definition 4.10** $((t,n)$ **stabilizations**)**.** *Let* $\mathbf{x}, \mathbf{y} \in \{0,1\}^{t \times n}$, *and denote* $\mathbf{x} = (x_1, \cdots, x_t), \mathbf{y} = (y_1, \cdots, y_t)$, *where* $\forall i \in [t] : x_i, y_i \in \{0,1\}^n$. *We say that* $\mathbf{x}, \mathbf{y}$, *are* $(t,n)$ *stabilizations of each other (or just stabilizations of each other) if in the concatenated string* $(\mathbf{x} \ \mathbf{y}) = (x_1, \cdots, x_t, y_1, \cdots, y_t)$, *for every* $s \in \{0,1\}^n$, $s$ *appears an even number of times (this, of course, includes appearing 0 times).*

We note that the stabilization relation (which is all pairs that stabilize each other) is an equivalence relation over the set $\{0,1\}^{n \times t}$ (just like the permutation relation, which we didn't mention it being an equivalence relation, but it can easily be seen as one). It is clear that the stabilization relation is reflexive ($\mathbf{x}$ is always stabilizing $\mathbf{x}$), and it is also easy to verify that it is symmetric. To see why it is also transitive, we will use an additional characterization:

**Definition 4.11.** *For a string* $\mathbf{z} = (z_1, \cdots, z_t) \in \{0,1\}^{n \times t}$ *with* $\forall i \in [t] : z_i \in \{0,1\}^n$, $\mathrm{Odd}(\mathbf{z})$ *is the set of strings from* $\{0,1\}^n$ *that appear an odd number of times in the sequence* $(z_1, \cdots, z_t)$.

For example, if $n = 3$ and $t = 7$ then $\mathrm{Odd}(101, 111, 101, 000, 011, 111, 111) = \{111, 000, 011\}$.

We claim that two strings $\mathbf{x}, \mathbf{y}$ are stabilizations of each other if and only if $\mathrm{Odd}(\mathbf{x}) = \mathrm{Odd}(\mathbf{y})$. It is easy to verify the correctness of this claim, and also the fact that this claim implies the transitivity of the stabilization relation.

To identify the elements of $\rho_{(t,n,2)}$ it remains to observe that when $\mathbf{x}, \mathbf{y}$ are stabilizations of each other then the entry is $2^{-tn}$, and when they are not, then we have $\mathrm{Odd}(\mathbf{x}) \neq \mathrm{Odd}(\mathbf{y})$ and it can be verified that the entry is 0, which yields the following description of $\rho_{(t,n,2)}$:

$$\forall \mathbf{x}, \mathbf{y} \in \{0,1\}^{n \times t} : \rho_{(t,n,2)}[\mathbf{x}, \mathbf{y}] = \begin{cases} 2^{-tn} & \mathbf{x}, \mathbf{y} \text{ are stabilizations} \\ 0 & \mathbf{x}, \mathbf{y} \text{ are not stabilizations} \end{cases}.$$

**Conclusion.** Note that if $\mathbf{x}, \mathbf{y}$ are permutations then they necessarily stabilize each other, but the opposite is not true generally, furthermore, it is fairly easy to find stabilizing pairs that are not permutations, for instance $(111, 000, 101, 101, 000)$ and $(110, 111, 111, 111, 110)$. We'll call a pair of strings that suffice this demand (i.e. stabilize each other but are not permutations) remotely stabilized, that is:

**Definition 4.12** $((t,n)$ **remote stabilizations**)**.** *Let* $\mathbf{x}, \mathbf{y} \in \{0,1\}^{t \times n}$, *we say that* $\mathbf{x}, \mathbf{y}$ *are* $(t,n)$ *remote stabilizations of each other (or just remote stabilizations of each other) if they are stabilizations of each other but are not permutations of each other.*

In contrast to the cases of permutation and stabilization, remote stabilization is not an equivalence relation, and thus (generally speaking) it is harder to work with it. The stabilization relation is symmetric, but it is not reflexive, and in fact it is anti-reflexive, because a string is always a permutation of itself (and thus not a remote stabilization of itself), and it is also not transitive, because a (non-empty) relation which is symmetric and anti-reflexive can't be transitive.

As said above, two strings that are permutations of each other are necessarily stabilizations of each other (in other words, the permutation relation is a refinement of the stabilization relation), and we deduce that $\rho_n$ has no negative terms and is also binary (scaled by $2^{-tn}$). Finally, this proves the characterization lemma of $\rho_n$.

**Lemma 4.13.** *Let* $n \in \mathbb{N}$ *and let* $t \in \{1, 2, \cdots, 2^n - 1\}$, *then the entries of* $\rho_n$ *can be given by the following formula:*

$$\forall \mathbf{x}, \mathbf{y} \in \{0, 1\}^{n \times t} : \rho_n[\mathbf{x}, \mathbf{y}] = \begin{cases} 2^{-tn} & \mathbf{x}, \mathbf{y} \text{ are remote stabilizations} \\ 0 & \mathbf{x}, \mathbf{y} \text{ are not remote stabilizations} \end{cases}.$$

## 4.3    Proof of Lemma 4.7

*Proof.* We will give an upper bound on the number of non-zero eigenvalues of $\rho_n$. $\rho_n$ is hermitian (and in particular diagonalizable) and thus the sum of dimensions of its eigenspaces sums up to the order of the matrix, which is $2^{tn}$. Also recall that the 0-eigenspace of $\rho_n$ is its kernel, thus by the rank-nullity theorem, the dimension of the 0-eigenspace plus the rank of $\rho_n$ equals the order of the matrix, $2^{tn}$. This means that the rank of $\rho_n$ equals the sum of dimensions of non-zero eigenspaces of $\rho_n$, which is exactly the number of non-zero (possibly identical) eigenvalues of $\rho_n$, thus, by giving an upper bound of rank($\rho_n$), we get an upper bound on the number of non-zero eigenvalues of $\rho_n$.

It is a well known fact in linear algebra that elementary row operations does not change the rank of a matrix, it is also known that the rank of a matrix is bounded from above by the number of non-zero rows (the rank is the dimension of the row space, which in turn cannot be more than the number of non-zero rows), thus our bound on the rank of $\rho_n$ will come from looking at $\rho_n'$, a row-equivalent matrix to $\rho_n$, and bounding its number of non-zero rows.

$\rho_n'$ is obtained by the following procedure: Recall that the permutation relation and the stabilization relation are both equivalence relations on $\{0, 1\}^{t \times n}$ and thus induce equivalence classes. It will be useful (also for the proof of the next lemma) to define the following:

**Definition 4.14 (Sentinel of an Equivalence Class).** *Let* $C$ *be an equivalence class of one of the two equivalence relations above (either the permutation relation or the stabilization relation). We define* $\mathbf{x}_C \in \{0, 1\}^{tn}$ *the sentinel of* $C$ *to be the element in* $C$ *with the largest lexicographic order (where the lexicographic order of strings is as usual, with the most significant bit on the left, and least significant bit on the right).*

**Observation 1.** *Let* $P$ *be a permutation class of* $\{0, 1\}^{tn}$. *Then, every pair in it* $\mathbf{x}, \mathbf{y} \in P$ *have the same set of remote stabilizers, and thus have identical rows in* $\rho_n$.

This means we can erase a bunch of redundant rows from $\rho_n$; for each permutation class $P$, take the sentinal row $\mathbf{x}_P$ of $P$ and subtract it from all other rows of strings from $P$. In the obtained matrix $\rho'_n$, the only non-zero rows are of sentinels.

The number of sentinels is exactly the number of equivalence classes of the permutation relation, which in turn is the number of different multisets of $t$ elements from $\{0,1\}^n$ (note that a permutaion class can be defined by a multiset from $\{0,1\}^n$ of size $t$), and that number is known as common knowledge in combinatorics, usually referred to as "n multichoose k", in our case, $\binom{2^n+t-1}{t}$.

**Observation 2.** *Let $P$ be a permutation class of a multiset of $t$ distinct elements (essentially, a permutation class of a set of size $t$ with elements from $\{0,1\}^n$), then each of its elements have no remote stabilizers.*

The above observation basically says that strings of $t$ distinct elements are a special case where every stabilizer of them is also a permutation of them. This observation is useful to us because it means that for every permutation class $P$ of $t$ distinct elements, all rows of $P$ are zero-rows in the original $\rho_n$ (and thus so in $\rho'_n$).

Furthermore, the reason that Observation 2 is important to our proof comes from the fact that there are $\binom{2^n}{t}$ such permutation classes, which is an overwhelming precentage from the total number of permutation classes $\binom{2^n+t-1}{t}$. To conclude, we said that in $\rho'_n$, only the sentinels can possibly have non-zero rows, and that there are $\binom{2^n+t-1}{t}$ sentinels in total, but now we add the information that out of these $\binom{2^n+t-1}{t}$ sentinels, $\binom{2^n}{t}$ have zero rows, and thus, there are at most

$$\binom{2^n+t-1}{t} - \binom{2^n}{t}$$

non-zero rows in $\rho'_n$ (and as a side note, there are in fact more zero-rows, for instance, for permutation classes of a multisets of the same element appearing $t$ times, but we won't care about these as their precentage is negligible). This concludes our proof of Lemma 4.7.

## 4.4   Proof of Lemma 4.8

We will give a lower bound on the most negative eigenvalue of $\rho_n$. Recall that $\rho_n$ is hermitian and thus has only real eigenvalues. Let $\lambda \in \mathbb{R}$, we know that $\lambda$ is an eigenvalue $\rho_n$ if and only if $\det(\rho_n - \lambda I) = 0$. Denote by $\mathcal{A}$ the set of negative relative sizes of the permutation classes (along with 0),

$$\mathcal{A} := \left\{ -\frac{|P|}{2^{tn}} \;\middle|\; P \text{ is a permutation class} \right\} \cup \{0\} \;,$$

where for a permutation class, its size is the number of different possible permutations of it, e.g. if $P$ is a permutation class of a multiset of the same element $t$

times, then $|P| = 1$, if $P$ is a permutation class of a multiset of $t$ distinct elements (in this specific case it is also a set) then $|P| = t!$, and if $P$ is a permutation class of a multiset of $(t-2)$ distinct elements plus an additional distinct element that appears twice, then $|P| = \binom{t}{2} \cdot (t-2)!$. We will show that there are no eigenvalues of $\rho_n$ smaller then all elements of $\mathcal{A}$, which will give us a lower bound of $(-\frac{t!}{2^{tn}})$ on the minimal eigenvalue of $\rho_n$ (as this is the minimal element in $\mathcal{A}$).

We prove the eigenvalue lower bound by calculating the determinant $\det(\rho_n - \lambda I)$ for $\lambda \in \mathbb{R} \setminus \mathcal{A}$, and showing that it cannot be 0. Recall that the permutation relation is a refinement of the stabilization relation, which means that every stabilization class can be divided into a bunch of permutation classes, also recall that in the proof of Lemma 4.7 we saw that for some stabilization classes, they are exactly a single permutation class and not a few (for example, according to the second observation in the proof, this is the case for permutation classes of sets of size $t$) - we'll call such stabilization classes *trivial stabilization classes*.

By the observations from Lemma 4.7 and by the restriction $\lambda \notin \mathcal{A}$, the calculation of the determinant is enabled and we obtain that for every $\lambda \in (\mathbb{R} \setminus \mathcal{A})$, the value of the determinant $\det(\rho_n - \lambda \cdot I)$ is,

$$\prod_{\substack{S \text{ trivial stabilization class}}} (-\lambda)^{|S|} \cdot \prod_{\substack{S \text{ non-trivial stabilization class}}} \left( \alpha_S \cdot \beta_S \cdot \gamma_S \right) ,$$

where,

$$\alpha_S = \prod_{\mathbf{x} \text{ non-sentinel in } S} (-\lambda) ,$$

$$\beta_S = \prod_{\substack{P \text{ permutation class in } S \text{ with } P \neq P_S}} \left( -\lambda - \frac{|P|}{2^{tn}} \right) ,$$

$$\gamma_S = -\lambda + \left( \lambda + \frac{|P_S|}{2^{tn}} \right) \cdot \sum_{\substack{P \text{ permutation class in } S \text{ with } P \neq P_S}} \left( \frac{\frac{|P|}{2^{tn}}}{(\lambda + \frac{|P|}{2^{tn}})} \right) .$$

The full version of this calculation is in [3].

**Using The Determinant to Show The Lower Bound.** Given the above determinant result, we can now finally prove Lemma 4.8.

*Proof.* Assume towards contradiction that there is a real number $\lambda' < -\frac{t!}{2^{tn}}$ (note that this implies $\lambda' \notin \mathcal{A}$) such that it is an eigenvalue of $\rho_n$, thus $\det(\rho_n - \lambda' \cdot I) = 0$ and thus it is necessarily the case that one of the terms in the above product (of the determinant) has to be 0. Due to $\lambda' \notin \mathcal{A}$, it can be seen that the only terms that can possibly be 0 in the above product are the terms $\gamma_S$ for non-trivial $S$, so let's check what happens in these terms.

Let $S$ be a non-trivial stabilization class, and consider the term $\gamma_S$ in the product above:

$$-\lambda' + \left( \lambda' + \frac{|P_S|}{2^{tn}} \right) \cdot \sum_{\substack{P \text{ permutation class in } S \text{ with } P \neq P_S}} \left( \frac{\frac{|P|}{2^{tn}}}{(\lambda' + \frac{|P|}{2^{tn}})} \right) .$$

We have,

$$\forall P \text{ permutation class in } S, \text{ including } P_S : \lambda' < -\frac{|P|}{2^{tn}} \,,$$

and thus

$$\left(\lambda' + \frac{|P_S|}{2^{tn}}\right) < 0, \qquad \sum_{P \text{ permutation class in } S \text{ with } P \neq P_S} \left(\frac{\frac{|P|}{2^{tn}}}{(\lambda' + \frac{|P|}{2^{tn}})}\right) < 0 \,,$$

which implies

$$\left(\lambda' + \frac{|P_S|}{2^{tn}}\right) \cdot \sum_{P \text{ permutation class in } S \text{ with } P \neq P_S} \left(\frac{\frac{|P|}{2^{tn}}}{(\lambda' + \frac{|P|}{2^{tn}})}\right) > 0 \,.$$

Finally, due to $-\lambda'$ being in particular positive, the term has to be positive as well:

$$-\lambda' + \left(\lambda' + \frac{|P_S|}{2^{tn}}\right) \cdot \sum_{P \text{ permutation class in } S \text{ with } P \neq P_S} \left(\frac{\frac{|P|}{2^{tn}}}{(\lambda' + \frac{|P|}{2^{tn}})}\right) > 0 \,,$$

in contradiction to $\det(\rho_n - \lambda' I) = 0$.

**Acknowledgments.** We thank Henry Yuen and Vinod Vaikuntanathan for insightful discussions. In particular thanks to Henry for pointing us to the [6] result. We thank the anonymous reviewers for their useful comments. We also thank Aram Harrow for providing advice regarding the state of the art.

# References

1. Akavia, A., Bogdanov, A., Guo, S., Kamath, A., Rosen, A.: Candidate weak pseudorandom functions in ac0 mod2. In: Electronic Colloquium on Computational Complexity (ECCC), vol. 21, p. 33 (2014)
2. Ambainis, A., Emerson, J.: Quantum t-designs: t-wise independence in the quantum world. In: Twenty-Second Annual IEEE Conference on Computational Complexity (CCC 2007), pp. 129–140. IEEE (2007)
3. Brakerski, Z., Shmueli, O.: (pseudo) random quantum states with binary phase. CoRR, abs/1906.10611 (2019)
4. Dankert, C., Cleve, R., Emerson, J., Livine, E.: Exact and approximate unitary 2-designs and their application to fidelity estimation. Phys. Rev. A **80**(1), 012304 (2009)
5. Harrow, A.W., Low, R.A.: Random quantum circuits are approximate 2-designs. Commun. Math. Phys. **291**(1), 257–302 (2009)
6. Ji, Z., Liu, Y.-K., Song, F.: Pseudorandom quantum states. In: Shacham, H., Boldyreva, A. (eds.) CRYPTO 2018. LNCS, vol. 10993, pp. 126–152. Springer, Cham (2018). https://doi.org/10.1007/978-3-319-96878-0_5
7. Kueng, R., Gross, D.: Qubit stabilizer states are complex projective 3-designs. arXiv preprint arXiv:1510.02767 (2015)

8. Lloyd, S.: Capacity of the noisy quantum channel. Phys. Rev. A **55**(3), 1613 (1997)
9. Nakata, Y., Koashi, M., Murao, M.: Generating a state t-design by diagonal quantum circuits. New J. Phys. **16**(5), 053043 (2014)
10. Nakata, Y., Murao, M.: Diagonal-unitary 2-design and their implementations by quantum circuits. Int. J. Quantum Inf. **11**(07), 1350062 (2013)
11. Naor, M., Reingold, O.: Synthesizers and their application to the parallel construction of pseudo-random functions. J. Comput. Syst. Sci. **58**(2), 336–375 (1999)
12. Nest, M.: Classical simulation of quantum computation, the gottesman-knill theorem, and slightly beyond. arXiv preprint arXiv:0811.0898 (2008)
13. Popescu, S., Short, A.J., Winter, A.: Entanglement and the foundations of statistical mechanics. Nat. Phys. **2**(11), 754 (2006)
14. Renes, J.M., Blume-Kohout, R., Scott, A.J., Caves, C.M.: Symmetric informationally complete quantum measurements. J. Math. Phys. **45**(6), 2171–2180 (2004)
15. Zhandry, M.: How to construct quantum random functions. In: 2012 IEEE 53rd Annual Symposium on Foundations of Computer Science, pp. 679–687. IEEE (2012)

# General Linear Group Action on Tensors: A Candidate for Post-quantum Cryptography

Zhengfeng Ji[1(✉)], Youming Qiao[1(✉)], Fang Song[2(✉)], and Aaram Yun[3(✉)]

[1] Centre for Quantum Software and Information, School of Software,
Faculty of Engineering and Information Technology,
University of Technology Sydney, Ultimo, NSW, Australia
{Zhengfeng.Ji,Youming.Qiao}@uts.edu.au
[2] Department of Computer Science and Engineering, Texas A&M University,
College Station, TX, USA
fang.song@tamu.edu
[3] Department of Cyber Security, Division of Software Science and Engineering,
Ewha Womans University, Seoul, Korea
aaramyun@ewha.ac.kr

**Abstract.** Starting from the one-way group action framework of Brassard and Yung (Crypto'90), we revisit building cryptography based on group actions. Several previous candidates for one-way group actions no longer stand, due to progress both on classical algorithms (e.g., graph isomorphism) and quantum algorithms (e.g., discrete logarithm).

We propose the *general linear group action on tensors* as a new candidate to build cryptography based on group actions. Recent works (Futorny–Grochow–Sergeichuk *Lin. Alg. Appl.*, 2019) suggest that the underlying algorithmic problem, the *tensor isomorphism problem*, is the hardest one among several isomorphism testing problems arising from areas including coding theory, computational group theory, and multivariate cryptography. We present evidence to justify the viability of this proposal from comprehensive study of the state-of-art heuristic algorithms, theoretical algorithms, hardness results, as well as quantum algorithms.

We then introduce a new notion called *pseudorandom group actions* to further develop group-action based cryptography. Briefly speaking, given a group $G$ acting on a set $S$, we assume that it is hard to distinguish two distributions of $(s, t)$ either uniformly chosen from $S \times S$, or where $s$ is randomly chosen from $S$ and $t$ is the result of applying a random group action of $g \in G$ on $s$. This subsumes the classical Decisional Diffie-Hellman assumption when specialized to a particular group action. We carefully analyze various attack strategies that support instantiating this assumption by the general linear group action on tensors.

Finally, we construct several cryptographic primitives such as digital signatures and pseudorandom functions. We give quantum security

---

Full version of this paper is available at ia.cr/2019/687.

© International Association for Cryptologic Research 2019
D. Hofheinz and A. Rosen (Eds.): TCC 2019, LNCS 11891, pp. 251–281, 2019.
https://doi.org/10.1007/978-3-030-36030-6_11

proofs based on the one-way group action assumption and the pseudo-random group action assumption.

# 1   Introduction

Modern cryptography has thrived thanks to the paradigm shift to a formal approach: precise *definition* of security and mathematically sound *proof* of security of a given construction based on accurate *assumptions*. Most notably, computational assumptions originated from specific algebraic problem such as factoring and discrete logarithm have enabled widely deployed cryptosystems.

Clearly, it is imperative to base cryptography on diverse problems to reduce the risk that some problems turn out to be easy. One such effort was by Brassard and Yung soon after the early development of modern cryptography [17]. They proposed an approach to use a *group action* to construct a *one-way function*, from which they constructed cryptographic primitives such as bit commitment, identification and digital signature. The abstraction of one-way group actions (OWA) not only unifies the assumptions from factoring and discrete logarithm, but more importantly Brassard and Yung suggested new problems to instantiate it such as the graph isomorphism problem (GI). Since then, many developments fall in this framework [26,46,65,70]. In particular, the work of Couveignes [26] can be understood as a specific group action based on isogenies between elliptic curves, and it has spurred the development of *isogeny-based* cryptography [28].

However, searching for concrete group actions to support this approach turns out to be a tricky task, especially given the potential threats from attackers capable of quantum computation. For graph isomorphism, there are effective heuristic solvers [63,64] as well as efficient *average-case* algorithms [7], not to mention Babai's recent breakthrough of a *quasipolynomial*-time algorithm [5]. Shor's celebrated work solves discrete logarithm and factoring in polynomial time on a *quantum* computer [79], which would break a vast majority of public-key cryptography. The core technique, *quantum Fourier sampling*, has proven powerful and can be applied to break popular symmetric-key cryptosystems as well [54]. A *subexponential-time* quantum algorithm was also found for computing isogenies in ordinary curves [23], which attributes to the shift to *super-singular* curves in the recent development of isogeny-based cryptography [40]. In fact, there is a considerable effort developing *post-quantum* cryptography that can resist quantum attacks. Besides isogeny-based, there are popular proposals based on discrete *lattices*, *coding* problems, and *multivariate equations* [10,22].

## 1.1   Overview of Our Results

In this paper, we revisit building cryptography via the framework of group actions and aim to provide new candidate and tools that could serve as *quantum-safe* solutions. Our contribution can be summarized below.

First, we propose a family of group actions on *tensors* of order at least three over a finite field as a new candidate for one-way actions. We back up its viability by comparison with other group actions, extensive analysis from heuristic algorithms, provable algorithmic and hardness results, as well as demonstrating its resistance to a standard quantum Fourier sampling technique.

Second, we propose the notion of *pseudorandom group actions* (PRA) that extends the scope of the existing group-action framework. The PRA assumption can be seen as a natural generalization of the Decisional Diffie-Hellman (DDH) assumption. We again instantiate it with the group action on tensors, and we provide further evidence (in addition to those for one-wayness) by analyzing various state-of-art attacking strategies.

Finally, based on any PRA, we show realization of several primitives in *Minicrypt* such as digital signatures via the Fiat-Shamir transformation and pseudorandom functions. We give complete security proofs against *quantum* adversaries, thanks to recent advances in analyzing quantum *superposition* attacks and the quantum random oracle model [81,82,85], which is known to be a tricky business. Our constructions based on PRA are more efficient than known schemes based on one-way group actions. As a side contribution, we also describe formal *quantum-security* proofs for several OWA-based schemes including identification and signatures, which are incomplete in the literature and deserve some care.

In what follows, we elaborate on our proposed group action based on tensors and the new pseudorandom group action assumption. Readers interested in the cryptographic primitives supported by PRA are referred to the full version of this paper [53].

*The General Linear Group Action on Tensors.* The candidate group action we propose is based on *tensors*, a central notion in quantum theory. In this paper, a $k$-tensor $T$ is a multidimensional array with $k$ indices $i_1, i_2, \ldots, i_k$ over a field $\mathbb{F}$, where $i_j \in \{1, 2, \ldots, d_j\}$ for $j = 1, 2, \ldots, k$. For a tuple of indices $(i_1, i_2, \ldots, i_k)$, the corresponding component of $T$ denoted as $T_{i_1, i_2, \ldots, i_k}$ is an element of $\mathbb{F}$. The number $k$ is called the order of the tensor. A matrix over field $\mathbb{F}$ can be regarded as a tensor of order two.

We consider a natural group action on $k$-tensors that represents a local change of basis. Let $G = \prod_{j=1}^{k} \mathrm{GL}(d_j, \mathbb{F})$ be the direct product of general linear groups. For $M = \left(M^{(j)}\right)_{j=1}^{k} \in G$, and a $k$-tensor $T$, the action of $M$ on $T$ is given by

$$\alpha : (M, T) \mapsto \widehat{T}, \text{ where } \widehat{T}_{i_1, i_2, \ldots, i_k} = \sum_{l_1, l_2, \ldots, l_k} \left(\prod_{j=1}^{k} M_{i_j, l_j}^{(j)}\right) T_{l_1, l_2, \ldots, l_k}.$$

We shall refer to the above group action as the *general linear group action on tensors* (GLAT) of dimensions $(d_1, \ldots, d_k)$ over $\mathbb{F}$, or simply GLAT when there is no risk of confusion. We will consider group actions on tensors of order at least three, as the problem is usually easy for matrices. In fact, in most of the cases, we focus on 3-tensors which is most studied and believed to be hard.

*General Linear Actions on Tensors as a Candidate for One-Way Group Actions.* We propose to use GLAT as an instantiation of one-way group actions. Roughly speaking, a group action is called a *one-way group action* (OWA in short), if for a random $s \in S$, a random $g \in G$, $t = g \cdot s$, and any polynomial-time adversary $\mathcal{A}$ given $s$ and $t$ as input, $\mathcal{A}$ outputs a $g' \in G$ such that $t = g' \cdot s$ only with negligible probability.

Breaking the one-wayness can be identified with solving some isomorphism problem. Specifically, two $k$-tensors $T$ and $\widehat{T}$ are said to be isomorphic if there exists an $M \in G$ such that $\widehat{T} = \alpha(M, T)$. We define the decisional tensor isomorphism problem (DTI) as deciding if two given $k$-tensors are isomorphic; and the search version (TI) is tasked with computing an $M \in G$ such that $\widehat{T} = \alpha(M, T)$ if there is one. Clearly, our assumption that GLAT is a one-way group action is equivalent to assuming that TI is hard for random $M \in G$, random $k$-tensor $S$, and $T := \alpha(M, S)$. We focus on the case when the order $k$ of the tensor equals three and the corresponding tensor isomorphism problem is abbreviated as 3TI. We justify our proposal from multiple routes; see Sect. 3 for a more formal treatment.

1. The 3-tensor isomorphism problem can be regarded as "the most difficult" one among problems about testing isomorphism between objects, such as polynomials, graphs, linear codes, and groups, thanks to the recent work of Futorny, Grochow, and Sergeichuk [39]. More specifically, it was proven in [39] that several isomorphism problems, including graph isomorphism, quadratic polynomials with 2 secrets from multivariate cryptography [70], $p$-group isomorphism from computational group theory [59,69], and linear code permutation equivalence from coding theory [73,77], all reduce to 3TI; cf. Observation 2. Note that testing isomorphism of quadratic polynomials with two secrets has been studied in multivariate cryptography for more than two decades [70]. Isomorphism testing of $p$-groups has been studied in computational group theory and theoretical computer science at least since the 1980's (cf. [59,69]). Current status of these two problems then could serve as evidence for the difficulty of 3TI.
2. Known techniques that are effective on GI, including the combinatorial techniques [83] and the group-theoretic techniques [3,60], are difficult to translate to 3TI. Indeed, it is not even clear how to adapt a basic combinatorial technique for GI, namely individualizing a vertex [7], to the 3TI setting. It is also much harder to work with matrix groups over finite fields than to work with permutation groups. Also, techniques in computer algebra, including those that lead to the recent solution of isomorphism of quadratic polynomials with one secret [50], seem not applicable to 3TI.
3. Finally, there is negative evidence that quantum algorithmic techniques involving the most successful quantum Fourier sampling may not be able to solve GI and code equivalence [34,45]. It is expected that the same argument holds with respect to 3TI as well. Loosely speaking, this is because the group underlying 3TI is a direct product of general linear groups, which also has irreducible representations of high dimensions.

*A New Assumption: Pseudorandom Group Actions.* Inspired by the Decisional Diffie-Hellman assumption, which enables versatile cryptographic constructions, we propose the notion of *pseudorandom group actions*, or PRA in short.

Roughly speaking, we call a group action $\alpha : G \times S \to S$ *pseudorandom*, if any quantum polynomial-time algorithm $\mathcal{A}$ cannot distinguish the following two distributions except with negligible probability: $(s, t)$ where $s, t \in_R S$, and the other distribution $(s, \alpha(g, s))$, where $s \in_R S$ and $g \in_R G$. A precise definition can be found in Sect. 4.

Note that if a group action is transitive, then the pseudorandom distribution trivially coincides with the random distribution. Unless otherwise stated, we will consider *intransitive* group actions when working with pseudorandom group actions. In fact, we can assume that $(s, t)$ from the random distribution are in different orbits with high probability, while $(s, t)$ from the pseudorandom distribution are always in the same orbit.

Also note that PRA is a stronger assumption than OWA. To break PRA, it is enough to solve the isomorphism testing problem *on average* in a relaxed sense, i.e., on $1/\text{poly}(n)$ fraction of the input instances instead of all but $1/\text{poly}(n)$ fraction, where $n$ is the input size.

The Decisional Diffie-Hellman (DDH) assumption [13,32] can be seen as the PRA initiated with a certain group action; see Observation 4. However, DDH is broken on a quantum computer. We resort again to GLAT as a quantum-safe candidate of PRA. We investigate the hardness of breaking PRA from various perspectives and provide further justification for using the general linear action on 3-tensors as a candidate for PRA.

1. Easy instances on 3-tensors seem scarce, and average-case algorithms do not speed up dramatically. Indeed, the best known average-case algorithm, while improves over worst-case somewhat due to the birthday paradox, still inherently enumerate all vectors in $\mathbb{F}_q^n$ and hence take exponential time [15,59].
2. For 3-tensors, there have not been non-trivial and easy-to-compute isomorphism invariants, i.e., those properties that are preserved under the action. For example, a natural isomorphism invariant, the tensor rank, is well-known to be NP-hard [47]. Later work suggests that "most tensor problems are NP-hard" [49].
3. We propose and analyze several attack strategies from group theory and geometry. While effective on some non-trivial actions, these attacks do not work for the general linear action on 3-tensors. For instance, we notice that breaking our PRA from GLAT reduces to the orbit closure intersection problem, which has received considerable attention in optimization, and geometric complexity theory. Despite recent advances [1,19,20,29,52,66], any improvement towards a more effective attack would be a breakthrough.

Recently, De Feo and Galbraith proposed an assumption in the setting of supersingular isogeny-based cryptography, which can be viewed as another instantiation of PRA [36, Problem 4]. This gives more reason to further explore PRA as a basic building block in cryptography.

## 1.2   Discussions

In this paper, we further develop and extend the scope of group action based cryptography by introducing the *general linear group actions on tensors* (GLAT) and formulating the pseudorandom assumption, generalizing the DDH assumption. We construct and prove the quantum security of various cryptographic primitives such as signatures and pseudorandom functions in this framework.

There are two key features of GLAT that are worth mentioning explicitly. First, the general linear action is *non-commutative* simply because the general linear group is non-abelian. This is, on the one hand, an attractive property that enabled us to argue the quantum hardness and the infeasibility of quantum Fourier sampling type of attacks. On the other hand, however, this also makes it challenging to extend many attractive properties of discrete-logarithm and decisional Diffie-Hellman to the more general framework of group action cryptography. For example, while it is known that the worst-case DDH assumption reduces to the average-case DDH assumption [68], the proof relies critically on commutativity. Second, the general linear action is *linear* and the space of tensors form a linear space. Linearity seems to be responsible for the supergroup attacks on the PRA($d$) assumption discussed in Sect. 5.1. It also introduces the difficulty for building more efficient PRF constructions analogous to the DDH-based ones proposed in [68].

Our work leaves a host of basic problems about group action based cryptography as future work. First, we have been focusing on the general *linear* group actions on tensors. A mixture of different types of group actions on different indices of the tensor may enable more efficient constructions or other appealing structural properties. It will be interesting to investigate how the hardness varies with the group actions on tensors, and identify group actions for practicability considerations. Second, it is appealing to recover the average-case to worst-case reduction, at least to some extent, for the general group actions framework. Finally, it is an important open problem to build quantum-secure public-key encryption schemes based on hard problems about GLAT or its close variations.

## 2   The Group Action Framework

In this section, we formally describe the framework for group action based cryptography to be used in this paper. While such general frameworks were already proposed by Brassard and Yung [17] and Couveignes [26], there are delicate differences in several places, so we will have to still go through the details. This section should be considered as largely expository.

### 2.1   Group Actions and Notations

Let us first formally define group actions. Let $G$ be a group, $S$ be a set, and id the identity element of $G$. A *(left) group action* of $G$ on $S$ is a function $\alpha : G \times S \to S$ satisfying the following: (1) $\forall s \in S$, $\alpha(\mathrm{id}, s) = s$; (2) $\forall g, h \in G$,

$s \in S$, $\alpha(gh, s) = \alpha(g, \alpha(h, s))$. The group operation is denoted by $\circ$, e.g. for $g, h \in G$, we can write their product as $g \circ h$. We shall use $\cdot$ to denote the left action, e.g. $g \cdot s = \alpha(g, s)$. We may also consider the right group action $\beta : S \times G \to S$, and use the exponent notation for right actions, e.g. $s^g = \beta(s, g)$.

Later, we will use a special symbol $\perp \notin G \cup S$ to indicate that a bit string does not correspond to an encoding of an element in $G$ or $S$. We extend the operators $\circ$ and $\cdot$ to $\circ : G \cup \{\perp\} \times G \cup \{\perp\} \to G \cup \{\perp\}$ and $\cdot : G \cup \{\perp\} \times S \cup \{\perp\} \to S \cup \{\perp\}$, by letting $g \circ h = \perp$ whenever $g = \perp$ or $h = \perp$, and $g \cdot s = \perp$ whenever $g = \perp$ or $s = \perp$.

Let $\alpha : G \times S \to S$ be a group action. For $s \in S$, the *orbit* of $s$ is $O_s = \{t \in S : \exists g \in G, g \cdot s = t\}$. The action $\alpha$ partitions $S$ into a disjoint union of orbits. If there is only one orbit, then $\alpha$ is called transitive. Restricting $\alpha$ to any orbit $O$ gives a transitive action. In this case, take any $s \in O$, and let $\mathrm{Stab}(s, G) = \{g \in G : g \cdot s = s\}$ be the stabilizer group of $s$ in $G$. For any $t \in O$, those group elements sending $s$ to $t$ form a coset of $\mathrm{Stab}(s, G)$. We then obtain the following easy observation.

**Observation 1.** Let $\alpha : G \times S \to S$, $s$, and $O$ be as above. The following two distributions are the same: the uniform distribution of $t \in O$, and the distribution of $g \cdot s$ where $g$ is sampled from a uniform distribution over $G$.

## 2.2   The Computational Model

For computational purposes, we need to model the algorithmic representations of groups and sets, as well as basic operations like group multiplication, group inverse, and group actions. We review the group action framework as proposed in Brassard and Yung [17]. A variant of this framework, with a focus on restricting to abelian (commutative) groups, was studied by Couveignes [26]. However, it seems to us that some subtleties are present, so we will propose another version, and compare it with those by Brassard and Yung, and Couveignes, later.

- Let $n$ be a parameter which controls the instance size. Therefore, polynomial time or length in the following are with respect to $n$.
- (Representing group and set elements.) Let $G$ be a group, and $S$ be a set. Let $\alpha : G \times S \to S$ be a group action. Group elements and set elements are represented by bit strings $\{0, 1\}^*$. There are polynomials $p(n)$ and $q(n)$, such that we only work with group elements representable by $\{0, 1\}^{p(n)}$ and set elements representable by $\{0, 1\}^{q(n)}$. There are functions $F_G$ and $F_S$ from $\{0, 1\}^*$ to $G \cup \{\perp\}$ and $S \cup \{\perp\}$, respectively. Here, $\perp$ is a special symbol, designating that the bit string does not represent a group or set element. $F_G$ and $F_S$ should be thought of as assigning bit strings to group elements.
- (Unique encoding of group and set elements.) For any $g \in G$, there exists a unique $b \in \{0, 1\}^*$ such that $F_G(b) = g$. In particular, there exists a unique bit string, also denoted by id, such that $F_G(\mathrm{id}) = \mathrm{id}$. Similarly, for any $s \in S$, there exists a unique $b \in \{0, 1\}^*$ such that $F_S(b) = s$.

- (Group operations.) There are polynomial-time computable functions $\mathrm{PROD} : \{0,1\}^* \times \{0,1\}^* \to \{0,1\}^*$ and $\mathrm{INV} : \{0,1\}^* \to \{0,1\}^*$, such that for $b, c \in \{0,1\}^*$, $F_G(\mathrm{PROD}(b,c)) = F_G(b) \circ F_G(c)$, and $F_G(\mathrm{INV}(b)) \circ F_G(b) = \mathrm{id}$.
- (Group action.) There is a polynomial-time function $a : \{0,1\}^* \times \{0,1\}^* \to \{0,1\}^*$, such that for $b \in \{0,1\}^*$ and $c \in \{0,1\}^*$, satisfies $F_S(a(b,c)) = \alpha(F_G(b), F_S(c))$.
- (Recognizing group and set elements.) There are polynomial-time computable functions $C_G$ and $C_S$, such that $C_G(b) = 1$ iff $F_G(b) \neq \perp$, and $C_S(b) = 1$ iff $F_S(b) \neq \perp$.
- (Random sampling of group and set elements.) There are polynomial-time computable functions $R_G$ and $R_S$, such that $R_G$ uniformly samples a group element $g \in G$, represented by the unique $b \in \{0,1\}^{p(n)}$ with $F_G(b) = g$, and $R_S$ uniformly samples a set element $s \in S$, represented by some $b \in \{0,1\}^{q(n)}$ with $F_S(b) = s$.

*Remark 1.* Some remarks are due for the above model.

1. The differences with Brassard and Yung are: (1) allowing infinite groups and sets; (2) adding random sampling of set elements. Note that in the case of infinite groups and sets, the parameters $p(n)$ and $q(n)$ are used to control the bit lengths for the descriptions of legitimate group and set elements. This allows us to incorporate e.g. the lattice isomorphism problem [48] into this framework. In the rest of this article, however, we will mostly work with finite groups and sets, unless otherwise stated.
2. The main reason to consider infinite groups is the uses of lattice isomorphism and equivalence of integral bilinear forms in the cryptographic setting.
3. The key difference with Couveignes lies in Couveignes's focus on transitive abelian group actions with trivial stabilizers.
4. It is possible to adapt the above framework to use the black-box group model by Babai and Szemerédi [8], whose motivation was to deal with non-unique encodings of group elements (like quotient groups). For our purposes, it is more convenient and practical to assume that the group elements have unique encodings.
5. Babai [4] gives an efficient Monte Carlo algorithm for sampling a group element of a finite group in a very general setting which is applicable to most of our instantiations with finite groups.

## 2.3    The Isomorphism Problem and the One-Way Assumption

Now that we have defined group actions and a computational model, let us examine the isomorphism problems associated with group actions.

**Definition 1 (The isomorphism problem).** *Let $\alpha : G \times S \to S$ be a group action. The isomorphism problem for $\alpha$ is to decide, given $s, t \in S$, whether $s$ and $t$ lie in the same orbit under $\alpha$. If they are, the search version of the isomorphism problem further asks to compute some $g \in G$, such that $\alpha(g, s) = t$.*

If we assume that there is a distribution on $S$ and we require the algorithm to succeed for $(s, t)$ where $s$ is sampled from this distribution and $t$ is arbitrary, then this is the *average-case* setting of the isomorphism problem. For example, the first average-case efficient algorithm for the graph isomorphism problem was designed by Babai, Erdős and Selkow in the 1970's [7].

The hardness of the isomorphism problem provides us with the basic intuition for its use in cryptography. But for cryptographic uses, the *promised* search version of the isomorphism problem is more relevant, as already observed by Brassard and Yung [17]. That is, suppose we are given $s, t \in S$ with the promise that they are in the same orbit, the problem asks to compute $g \in G$ such that $g \cdot s = t$. Making this more precise and suitable for cryptographic purposes, we formulate the following problem.

**Definition 2 (The group-action inversion (GA-Inv) problem).** *Let $G$ be a group action family, such that for a security parameter $\lambda$, $\mathcal{G}(1^\lambda)$ consists of descriptions of a group $G$, a set $S$ with $\log(|G|) = \text{poly}(\lambda)$, $\log(|S|) = \text{poly}(\lambda)$, and an group action $\alpha : G \times S \to S$ that can be computed efficiently, which we denote as a whole as a public parameter params. Generate random $s \leftarrow S$ and $g \leftarrow G$, and compute $t := \alpha(g, s)$. The group-action inversion (GA-Inv) problem is to find $g$ given $(s, t)$.*

**Definition 3 (Group-action inversion game).** *The group-action inversion game is the following game between a challenger and an arbitrary adversary $\mathcal{A}$:*

1. *The challenger and adversary $\mathcal{A}$ agree on the public parameter params by choosing it to be $\mathcal{G}(1^\lambda)$ for some security parameter $\lambda$.*
2. *Challenger samples $s \leftarrow S$ and $g \leftarrow G$ using $R_S$ and $R_G$, computes $t = g \cdot s$, and gives $(s, t)$ to $\mathcal{A}$.*
3. *The adversary $\mathcal{A}$ produces some $g'$ and sends it to the challenger.*
4. *We define the output of the game $\text{GA-Inv}_{\mathcal{A}, \mathcal{G}}(1^\lambda) = 1$ if $g' \cdot s = t$, and say $\mathcal{A}$ wins the game if $\text{GA-Inv}_{\mathcal{A}, \mathcal{G}}(1^\lambda) = 1$.*

**Definition 4.** *We say that the group-action inversion (GA-Inv) problem is hard relative to $\mathcal{G}$, if for any polynomial time quantum algorithm $\mathcal{A}$,*

$$\Pr\left[\text{GA-Inv}_{\mathcal{A}, \mathcal{G}}(1^\lambda)\right] \leq \text{negl}(\lambda).$$

We propose our first cryptographic assumption in the following. It generalizes the one in [17].

**Assumption 1 (One-way group action (OWA) assumption).** There exists a family $\mathcal{G}$ relative to which the GA-Inv problem is hard.

We informally call the group action family $\mathcal{G}$ in Assumption 1 a one-way group action. Its name comes from the fact that, as already suggested in [17], this assumption immediately implies that we can treat $\Gamma_s : G \to S$ given by $\Gamma_s(g) = \alpha(g, s)$ as a one-way function for a random $s$. In fact, OWA assumption is equivalent to the assertion that the function $\Gamma : G \times S \to S \times S$ given by $\Gamma(g, s) = (g \cdot s, s)$ is one-way in the standard sense.

Note that the OWA assumption comes with the promise that $s$ and $t$ are in the same orbit. The question is to compute a group element that sends $s$ to $t$. Comparing with Definition 1, we see that the OWA assumption is stronger than the assumption that the search version of the isomorphism problem is hard for a group action, while incomparable with the decision version. Still, most algorithms for the isomorphism problem we are aware of do solve the search version.

*Remark 2.* Note that Assumption 1 has a slight difference with that of Brassard and Yung as follows. In [17], Brassard and Yung asks for the *existence* of some $s \in S$ as in Definition 2, such that for a random $g \in G$, it is not feasible to compute $g'$ that sends $s$ to $\alpha(g, s)$. Here, we relax this condition, namely a *random* $s \in S$ satisfies this already. One motivation for Brassard and Yung to fix $s$ was to take into account of graph isomorphism, for which Brassard and Crepéau defined the notion of "hard graphs" which could serve as this starting point [16]. However, by Babai's algorithm [5] we know that hard graphs could not exist. Here we use a stronger notion by allowing a random $s$, which we believe is a reasonable requirement for some concrete group actions discussed in Sect. 3.

A useful fact for the GA-Inv problem is that it is *self-reducible* to random instances within the orbit of the input pair. For any given $s$, let $O_s$ be the orbit of $s$ under the group action $\alpha$. If there is an efficient algorithm $\mathcal{A}$ that computes $g$ from $(t, t')$ where $t' = \alpha(g, t)$ for at least $1/\operatorname{poly}(\lambda)$ fraction of the pairs $(t, t') \in O_s \times O_s$, then the GA-Inv problem can be computed for any $(t, t') \in O_s \times O_s$ with probability $1 - e^{-\operatorname{poly}(\lambda)}$. On input $(t, t')$, the algorithm samples random group elements $h, h'$ and calls $\mathcal{A}$ with $(\alpha(h, t), \alpha(h', t'))$. If $\mathcal{A}$ successfully returns $g$, the algorithm outputs $h^{-1} g h'$ and otherwise repeats the procedure for polynomial number of times.

The one-way assumption leads to several basic cryptographic applications as described in the literature. First, it gives a identification scheme by adapting the zero-knowledge proof system for graph isomorphism [42]. Then via the celebrated Fiat-Shamir transformation [37], one also obtains a signature scheme. Proving quantum security of these protocols, however, would need more care. Detailed proofs may be found in the full version of this paper [53].

# 3    General Linear Actions on Tensors: The One-Way Group Action Assumption

In this section, we propose the general linear actions on tensors, i.e., the tensor isomorphism problem, as our choice of candidate for the OWA assumption. We first reflect on what would be needed for a group action to be a good candidate.

## 3.1    Requirements for a Group Action to Be One-Way

Naturally, the hardness of the GA-Inv problem for a specific group action needs to be examined in the context of the following four types of algorithms.

- Practical algorithms: implemented algorithms with practical performance evaluations but no theoretical guarantees;
- Average-case algorithms: for some natural distribution over the input instances, there is an algorithm that are efficient for most input instances from this distribution with provable guarantees;
- Worst-case algorithms: efficient algorithms with provable guarantees for all input instances;
- Quantum algorithms: average-case or worst-case efficient algorithms in the quantum setting.

Here, efficient means sub-exponential, and most means $1 - 1/\text{poly}(n)$ fraction. It is important to keep in mind all possible attacks by these four types of algorithms. Past experience suggests that one problem may look difficult from one viewpoint, but turns out to be easy from another.

The graph isomorphism problem has long been thought to be a difficult problem from the worst-case viewpoint. Indeed, a quasipolynomial-time algorithm was only known very recently, thanks to Babai's breakthrough [5]. However, it has long been known to be effectively solvable from the practical viewpoint [63,64]. This shows the importance of practical algorithms when justifying a cryptographic assumption.

Patarin proposed to use polynomial map isomorphism problems in his instantiation of the identification and signature schemes [70]. He also proposed the one-sided version of such problems, which has been studied intensively, mostly from the viewpoint of practical cryptanalysis [11,14,15,35,41,55,61,71,72,74]. However, the problem of testing isomorphism of quadratic polynomials with one secret was recently shown to be solvable in randomized polynomial time [50], using ideas including efficient algorithms for computing the algebra structure, and the $*$-algebra structure underlying such problems. Hence, the investigation of theoretical algorithms is also valuable.

Considering of quantum attacks is necessary for security in the quantum era. Shor's algorithm, for example, invalidates the hardness assumption of the discrete logarithm problems.

Guided by the difficulty met by the hidden subgroup approach on tackling graph isomorphism [45], Moore, Russell, and Vazirani proposed the code equivalence problem as a candidate for the one-way assumption [65]. However, this problem turns out to admit an effective practical algorithm by Sendrier [77].

**One-Way Group Action Assumption and the Hidden Subgroup Approach.** From the post-quantum perspective, a general remark can be made on the OWA assumption and the hidden subgroup approach in quantum algorithm design.

Recall that the hidden subgroup approach is a natural generalization of Shor's quantum algorithms for discrete logarithm and factoring [79], and can accommodate both lattice problems [75] and isomorphism testing problems [45]. The survey paper of Childs and van Dam [24] contains a nice introduction to this approach.

A well-known approach to formulate GA-Inv as an HSP problem is the following [24, Sec. VII.A]. Let $\alpha : G \times S \to S$ be a group action. Given $s, t \in S$ with the promise that $t = g \cdot s$ for some $g \in G$, we want to compute $g$. To cast this problem as an HSP instance, we first formulate it as an automorphism type problem. Let $\tilde{G} = G \wr S_2$, where $S_2$ is the symmetric group on two elements, and $\wr$ denotes the wreath product. The action $\alpha$ induces an action $\beta$ of $\tilde{G}$ on $S \times S$ as follows. Given $(g, h, i) \in \tilde{G} = G \wr S_2$ where $g, h \in G, i \in S_2$, if $i$ is the identity, it sends $(s, t) \in S \times S$ to $(g \cdot s, h \cdot t)$; otherwise, it sends $(s, t)$ to $(h \cdot t, g \cdot s)$. Given $(s, t) \in S \times S$, we define a function $f_{(s,t)} : \tilde{G} \to S \times S$, such that $f_{(s,t)}$ sends $(g, h, i)$ to $(g, h, i) \cdot (s, t)$, defined as above. It can be verified that $f_{(s,t)}$ hides the coset of the stabilizer group of $(s, t)$ in $\tilde{G}$. Since $s$ and $t$ lie in the same orbit, any generating set of the stabilizer group of $(s, t)$ contains an element of the form $(g, h, i)$, where $i$ is not the identity element in $S_2$, $g \cdot s = t$, and $h \cdot t = s$. In particular, $g$ is the element required to solve the GA-Inv problem. In the above reduction to the HSP problem, the ambient group is $G \wr S_2$ instead of the original $G$. In some cases like the graph isomorphism problem, because of the polynomial-time reduction from isomorphism testing to automorphism problem, we can retain the ambient group to be $G$. However, such a reduction is not known for GLAT.

There has been notable progress on the HSP problems for various ambient groups, but the dihedral groups and the symmetric groups have withstood the attacks so far. Indeed, one source of confidence on using lattice problems in post-quantum cryptography lies in the lack of progress in tackling the hidden subgroup problem for dihedral groups [75]. There is formal negative evidence for the applicability of this approach for certain group actions where the groups have high-dimensional representations, like $S_n$ and $GL(n, q)$ in the case of the graph isomorphism problem [45] and the permutation code equivalence problem [34]. The general lesson is that current quantum algorithmic technologies seem incapable of handling groups which have irreducible representations of high dimensions.

As mentioned, the OWA assumption has been discussed in post-quantum cryptography with the instantiation of the permutation code equivalence problem [33,34,65,78]. Though this problem is not satisfying enough due to the existence of effective practical algorithms [77], the following quoted from [65] would be applicable to our choice of candidate to the discussed below.

*The design of efficient cryptographic primitives resistant to quantum attack is a pressing practical problem whose solution can have an enormous impact on the practice of cryptography long before a quantum computer is physically realized. A program to create such primitives must necessarily rely on insights into the limits of quantum algorithms, and this paper explores consequences of the strongest such insights we have about the limits of quantum algorithms.*

## 3.2   The Tensor Isomorphism Problem and Others

We now formally define the tensor isomorphism problem and other isomorphism testing problems. For this we need some notation and preparations.

**Notation and Preliminaries.** We usually use $\mathbb{F}$ to denote a field. The finite field with $q$ elements and the real number field are denoted by $\mathbb{F}_q$ and $\mathbb{R}$, respectively. The linear space of $m$ by $n$ matrices over $\mathbb{F}$ is denoted by $\mathrm{M}(m, n, \mathbb{F})$, and $\mathrm{M}(n, \mathbb{F}) := \mathrm{M}(n, n, \mathbb{F})$. The identity matrix in $\mathrm{M}(n, \mathbb{F})$ is denoted by $I_n$. For $A \in \mathrm{M}(m, n, \mathbb{F})$, $A^t$ denotes the transpose of $A$. The group of $n$ by $n$ invertible matrices over $\mathbb{F}$ is denoted by $\mathrm{GL}(n, \mathbb{F})$. We will also meet the notation $\mathrm{GL}(n, \mathbb{Z})$, the group of $n$ by $n$ integral matrices with determinant $\pm 1$. We use a slightly non-standard notation $\mathrm{GL}(m, n, \mathbb{F})$ to denote the set of rank $\min(m, n)$ matrices in $\mathrm{M}(m, n, \mathbb{F})$. We use $\langle \cdot \rangle$ to denote the linear span; for example, given $A_1, \ldots, A_k \in \mathrm{M}(m, n, \mathbb{F})$, $\langle A_1, \ldots, A_k \rangle$ is a subspace of $\mathrm{M}(m, n, \mathbb{F})$.

We will meet some subgroups of $\mathrm{GL}(n, \mathbb{F})$ as follows. The symmetric group $\mathrm{S}_n$ on $n$ objects is embedded into $\mathrm{GL}(n, \mathbb{F})$ as permutation matrices. The orthogonal group $\mathrm{O}(n, \mathbb{F})$ consists of those invertible matrices $A$ such that $A^t A = I_n$. The special linear group $\mathrm{SL}(n, \mathbb{F})$ consists of those invertible matrices $A$ such that $\det(A) = 1$. Finally, when $n = \ell^2$, there are subgroups of $\mathrm{GL}(\ell^2, \mathbb{F})$ isomorphic to $\mathrm{GL}(\ell, \mathbb{F}) \times \mathrm{GL}(\ell, \mathbb{F})$. This can be seen as follows. First we fix an isomorphism of linear spaces $\phi : \mathbb{F}^{\ell^2} \to \mathrm{M}(\ell, \mathbb{F})$[1]. Then $\mathrm{M}(\ell, \mathbb{F})$ admits an action by $\mathrm{GL}(\ell, \mathbb{F}) \times \mathrm{GL}(\ell, \mathbb{F})$ by left and right multiplications, e.g. $(A, D) \in \mathrm{GL}(\ell, \mathbb{F}) \times \mathrm{GL}(\ell, \mathbb{F})$ sends $C \in \mathrm{M}(\ell, \mathbb{F})$ to $ACD^t$. Now use $\phi^{-1}$ and we get one subgroup of $\mathrm{GL}(\ell^2, \mathbb{F})$ isomorphic to $\mathrm{GL}(\ell, \mathbb{F}) \times \mathrm{GL}(\ell, \mathbb{F})$.

**Definitions of Several Group Actions.** We first recall the concept of tensors and the group actions on the space of $k$-tensors as introduced in Sect. 1.

**Definition 5 (Tensor).** *A $k$-tensor $T$ of local dimensions $d_1, d_2, \ldots, d_k$ over $\mathbb{F}$, written as*

$$T = (T_{i_1, i_2, \ldots, i_k}),$$

*is a multidimensional array with $k$ indices and its components $T_{i_1, i_2, \ldots, i_k}$ chosen from $\mathbb{F}$ for all $i_j \in \{1, 2, \ldots, d_j\}$. The set of $k$-tensors of local dimensions $d_1, d_2, \ldots, d_k$ over $\mathbb{F}$ is denoted as*

$$\mathrm{T}(d_1, d_2, \ldots, d_k, \mathbb{F}).$$

*The integer $k$ is called the order of tensor $T$.*

---

[1] For example, we can let the first $\ell$ components be the first row, the second $\ell$ components be the second row, etc.

**Group Action 1** (The general linear group action on tensors). Let $\mathbb{F}$ be a field, $k$, $d_1, d_2, \ldots, d_k$ be integers.

- Group $G$: $\prod_{j=1}^{k} \mathrm{GL}(d_j, \mathbb{F})$.
- Set $S$: $\mathrm{T}(d_1, d_2, \ldots, d_k, \mathbb{F})$.
- Action $\alpha$: for a $k$-tensor $T \in S$, a member $M = (M^{(1)}, M^{(2)}, \ldots, M^{(k)})$ of the group $G$,

$$\alpha(M, T) = \left( \bigotimes_{j=1}^{k} M^{(j)} \right) T = \sum_{l_1, l_2, \ldots, l_k} \left( \prod_{j=1}^{k} M_{i_j, l_j}^{(j)} \right) T_{l_1, l_2, \ldots, l_k}.$$

We refer to the general linear group action on tensors in Action 1 as GLAT. In the following, let us formally define several problems which have been referred to frequently in the above discussions.

As already observed by Brassard and Yung [17], the discrete logarithm problem can be formulated using the language of group actions. More specifically, we have:

**Group Action 2** (Discrete Logarithm in Cyclic Groups of Prime Orders). Let $p$ be a prime, $\mathbb{Z}_p$ the integer.

- Group $G$: $\mathbb{Z}_p^*$, the multiplicative group of units in $\mathbb{Z}_p$.
- Set $S$: $C_p \setminus \{\mathrm{id}\}$, where $C_p$ is a cyclic group of order $p$ and id is the identity element.
- Action $\alpha$: for $a \in \mathbb{Z}_p^*$, and $s \in S$, $\alpha(a, s) = s^a$.

Note that in the above, we refrained from giving a specific realization of the cyclic group $C_p$ for the sake of clarify; the reader may refer to Boneh's excellent survey [13] for concrete proposals that can support the security of the Decisional Diffie-Hellman assumption.

The linear code permutation equivalence (LCPE) problem asks to decide whether two linear codes (i.e. linear subspaces) are the same up to a permutation of the coordinates. It has been studied in the coding theory community since the 1990's [73, 77].

**Group Action 3** (Group action for Linear Code Permutation Equivalence problem (LCPE)). Let $m, d$ be integers, $m \leq d$, and let $\mathbb{F}$ be a field.

- Group $G$: $\mathrm{GL}(m, \mathbb{F}) \times S_d$.
- Set $S$: $\mathrm{GL}(m, d, \mathbb{F})$.
- Action $\alpha$: for $A \in S$, $M = (N, P) \in G$, $\alpha(M, A) = NAP^t$.

The connection with coding theory is that $A$ can be viewed as the generating matrix of a linear code (a subspace of $\mathbb{F}_q^n$), and $N$ is the change of basis matrix taking care of different choices of bases. Then, $P$, as a permutation matrix, does not change the weight of a codeword— that is a vector in $\mathbb{F}^n$. (There are other operations that preserve weights [78], but we restrict to consider this setting for simplicity.) The GA-Inv problem for this group action is called the linear code permutation equivalence (LCPE) problem, which has been studied in the coding theory community since the 1980's [57], and we can dodge the only successful attack [77] by restricting to self-dual codes.

The following group action induces a problem called the polynomial isomorphism problems proposed by Patarin [70], and has been studied in the multivariate cryptography community since then.

**Group Action 4** (Group action for the Isomorphism of Quadratic Polynomials with two Secrets problem (IQP2S)). Let $m, d$ be integers and $\mathbb{F}$ a finite field.

- Group $G$: $GL(d, \mathbb{F}) \times GL(m, \mathbb{F})$.
- Set $S$: The set of tuples of homogeneous polynomials $(f_1, f_2, \ldots, f_m)$ for $f_i \in \mathbb{F}[x_1, x_2, \ldots, x_d]$ the polynomial ring of $d$ variables over $\mathbb{F}$.
- Action $\alpha$: for $f = (f_1, f_2, \ldots, f_m) \in S$, $M = (C, D) \in G$, $C' = C^{-1}$, define $\alpha(M, f) = (g_1, g_2, \ldots, g_m)$ by $g_i(x_1, x_2, \ldots, x_d) = \sum_{j=1}^{m} D_{i,j} f_i(x'_1, \ldots, x'_d)$, where $x'_i = \sum_{j=1}^{d} C'_{i,j} x_j$.

The GA-Inv problem for this group action is essentially the isomorphism of quadratic polynomials with two secrets (IQP2S) assumption. The algebraic interpretation here is that the tuple of polynomials $(f_1, \ldots, f_n)$ is viewed as a polynomial map from $\mathbb{F}^n$ to $\mathbb{F}^m$, by sending $(a_1, \ldots, a_n)$ to $(f_1(a_1, \ldots, a_n), \ldots, f_m(a_1, \ldots, a_n))$. The changes of bases by $C$ and $D$ then are naturally interpreted as saying that the two polynomial maps are essentially the same.

Finally, the GA-Inv problem for the following group action originates from computational group theory, and is basically equivalent to a bottleneck case of the group isomorphism problem (i.e. $p$-groups of class 2 and exponent $p$) [59,69].

**Group Action 5** (Group action for alternating matrix space isometry (AMSI)). Let $d, m$ be integers and $\mathbb{F}$ be a finite field.

- Group $G$: $GL(m, \mathbb{F})$.
- Set $S$: the set of all linear spans $\mathcal{A}$ of $d$ alternating[2] matrices $A_i$ of size $m \times m$.
- Action $\alpha$: for $\mathcal{A} = \langle A_1, A_2, \ldots, A_d \rangle \in S$, $C \in G$, $\alpha(C, \mathcal{A}) = \langle B_1, B_2, \ldots, B_d \rangle$ where $B_i = C A_i C^t$ for all $i = 1, 2, \ldots, d$.

### 3.3 General Linear Actions on Tensors as One-Way Action Candidates

**The Central Position of 3-tensor Isomorphism.** As mentioned, the four problems, linear code permutation equivalence (LCPE), isomorphism of polynomials with two secrets (IQP2S), and alternating matrix space isometry (AMSI), have been studied in coding theory, multivariate cryptography, and computational group theory, respectively, for decades. Only recently we begin to see connections among these problems which go through the 3TI problem thanks to the work of Futorny, Grochow, and Sergeichuk [39]. We spell out this explicitly.

---

[2] An $m \times m$ matrix $A$ is alternating if for any $v \in \mathbb{F}^n$, $v^t A v = 0$.

**Observation 2** ([39,43]). IQP2S, AMSI, GI, and LCPE reduce to 3TI.

*Proof.* Note that the set underlying Group Action 5 consists of $d$-tuples of $m \times m$ alternating matrices. We can write such a tuple $(A_1, \ldots, A_d)$ as a 3-tensor $A$ of dimension $m \times m \times d$, such that $A_{i,j,k} = (A_k)_{i,j}$. Then AMSI asks to test whether two such 3-tensors are in the same orbit under the action of $(M, N) \in \mathrm{GL}(m, \mathbb{F}) \times \mathrm{GL}(d, \mathbb{F})$ by sending a 3-tensor $A$ to the result of applying $(M, M, N)$ to $A$ as in the definition of GLAT.

Such an action belongs to the class of actions on 3-tensors considered in [39] under the name *linked actions*. This work constructs a function $r$ from 3-tensors to 3-tensors, such that $A$ and $B$ are in the same orbit under $\mathrm{GL}(m, \mathbb{F}) \times \mathrm{GL}(d, \mathbb{F})$ if and only if $r(A)$ and $r(B)$ are in the same orbit under $\mathrm{GL}(m, \mathbb{F}) \times \mathrm{GL}(m, \mathbb{F}) \times \mathrm{GL}(d, \mathbb{F})$. This function $r$ can be computed efficiently [39, Remark 1.1].

This explains the reduction of the isomorphism problem for Group Action 5 to the 3-tensor isomorphism problem. For Group Action 4, by using the classical correspondence between homogeneous quadratic polynomials and symmetric matrices, we can cast it in a form similar to Group Action 5, and then apply the above reasoning using again [39].

Finally, to reduce the graph isomorphism problem (GI) and the linear code permutation equivalent problem (LCPE) to the 3-tensor isomorphism problem, we only need to take care of LCPE as GI reduces to LCPE [73]. To reduce LCPE to 3TI, we can reduce it to the matrix Lie algebra conjugacy problem by [43], which reduces to 3TI by [39] along the linked action argument, though this time linked in a different way. □

This put 3TI at a central position of these difficult isomorphism testing problems arising from multivariate cryptography, computational group theory, and coding theory. In particular, from the worst-case analysis viewpoint, 3TI is the hardest problem among all these. This also allows us to draw experiences from previous research in various research communities to understand 3TI.

**Current Status of the Tensor Isomorphism Problem and Its One-Way Action Assumption.** We now explain the current status of the tensor isomorphism problem to support it as a strong candidate for the OWA assumption. Because of the connections with isomorphism of polynomials with two secrets (IQP2S) and alternating matrix space isometry (AMSI), we shall also draw results and experiences from the multivariate cryptography and the computational group theory communities.

For convenience, we shall restrict to finite fields $\mathbb{F}_q$, though other fields are also interesting. That is, we consider the action of $\mathrm{GL}(\ell, \mathbb{F}_q) \times \mathrm{GL}(n, \mathbb{F}_q) \times \mathrm{GL}(m, \mathbb{F}_q)$ on $T \in \mathrm{T}(\ell, n, m, \mathbb{F}_q)$. Without loss of generality, we assume $\ell \geq n \geq m$. The reader may well think of the case when $\ell = n = m$, which seems to be the most difficult case in general. Correspondingly, we will assume that the instances for IQP2S are $m$-tuples of homogeneous quadratic polynomials in $n$ variables over $\mathbb{F}_q$, and the instances for AMSI are $m$-tuples of alternating matrices of size $n \times n$ over $\mathbb{F}_q$.

To start, we note that 3TI over finite fields belongs to NP ∩ coAM, following the same coAM-protocol for graph isomorphism.

For the worst-case time complexity, it can be solved in time $q^{m^2}$ · poly$(\ell, m, n, \log q)$, by enumerating $GL(m, q)$, and then solving an instance of the matrix tuple equivalence problem, which asks to decide whether two matrix tuples are the same under the left-right multiplications of invertible matrices. This problem can be solved in deterministic polynomial time by reducing [50] to the module isomorphism problem, which in turn admits a deterministic polynomial-time solution [18, 25, 51]. It is possible to reduce the complexity to $q^{cm^2}$ · poly$(\ell, m, n, \log q)$ for some constant $0 < c < 1$, by using some dynamic programming technique as in [59]. But in general, the worst-case complexity could not go beyond this at present, which matches the experiences of IQP2S and AMSI as well; see [50].

For the average-case time complexity, it can be solved in time $q^{O(m)}$ · poly$(\ell, n)$, by adapting the average-case algorithm for AMSI in [59]. This also matches the algorithm for IQP2S which has an average-case running time of $q^{O(n)}$ [15].

For practical algorithms, we draw experiences from the computational group theory community and the multivariate cryptography community. In the computational group theory community, the current status of the art is that one can hope to handle 10-tuples of alternating matrices of size $10 \times 10$ over $\mathbb{F}_{13}$, but absolutely not, for 3-tensors of local dimension say 100, even though in this case the input can still be stored in only a few megabytes.[3] In the multivariate cryptography community, the Gröbner basis technique [35] and certain combinatorial technique [15] have been studied to tackle IQF2S problem. However, these techniques are not effective enough to break it [15][4].

For quantum algorithms, 3TI seems difficult for the hidden subgroup approach, due to the reasons presented in Sect. 3.1.

Finally, let us also elaborate on the prospects of using those techniques for graph isomorphism [5] and for isomorphism of quadratic polynomials with one secret [50] to tackle 3TI. In general, the difficulties of applying these techniques seem inherent.

We first check out the graph isomorphism side. Recall that most algorithms for graph isomorphism, including Babai's [5], are built on two families of techniques: group-theoretic, and combinatorial. To use the group-theoretic techniques, we need to work with matrix groups over finite fields instead of permutation groups. Algorithms for matrix groups over finite fields are in general far harder than those for permutation groups. For example, the basic membership problem is well-known to be solvable by Sims's algorithm [80], while for

---

[3] We thank James B. Wilson, who maintains a suite of algorithms for $p$-group isomorphism testing, for communicating this insight to us from his hands-on experience. We of course maintain responsibility for any possible misunderstanding, or lack of knowledge regarding the performance of other implemented algorithms.

[4] In particular, as pointed out in [15], one needs to be careful about certain claims and conjectures made in some literature on this research line.

matrix groups over finite fields of odd order, this was only recently shown to be efficiently solvable with a number-theoretic oracle and the algorithm is much more involved [6]. To use the combinatorial techniques, we need to work with linear or multilinear structures instead of combinatorial structures. This shift poses severe limitations on the use of most combinatorial techniques, like individualizing a vertex. For example, it is quite expensive to enumerate all vectors in a vector space over a finite field, while this is legitimate to go over all elements in a set.

We then check out the isomorphism of quadratic polynomials with one secret side. The techniques for settling this problem as in [50] are based on those developed for the module isomorphism problem [18,25,51], involutive algebras [84], and computing algebra structures [38]. The starting point of that algorithm solves an easier problem, namely testing whether two matrix tuples are equivalent under the left-right multiplications. That problem is essentially linear, so the techniques for the module isomorphism problem can be used. After that we need to utilize the involutive algebra structure [84] based on [38]. However, for 3TI, there is no such easier linear problem to start with, so it is not clear how those techniques can be applied.

To summarize, the 3-tensor isomorphism problem is difficult from all the four types of algorithms mentioned in Sect. 3.1. Furthermore, the techniques in the recent breakthrough on graph isomorphism [5], and the solution of the isomorphism of quadratic polynomials with one secret [50], seem not applicable to this problem. All these together support this problem as a strong candidate for the one-way assumption.

**Choices of the Parameters.** Having reviewed the current status of the tensor isomorphism problem, we lay out some principles of choosing the parameters for the security, namely the order $k$, the dimensions $d_i$, and the underlying field $\mathbb{F}$.

Let us first explain why we focus on $k = 3$, namely 3-tensors. Of course, $k$ needs to be $\geq 3$ as most problems about 2-tensors, i.e. matrices, are easy. Recently, Grochow and the third author show that $k$-tensor isomorphism reduces to 3-tensor isomorphism [44]. This justifies our choice of $k = 3$ from the worst-case analysis viewpoint. From the practical viewpoint though, it will be interesting to investigate into the tradeoff between the local dimensions $d_i$ and $k$.

After fixing $k = 3$, it is suggested to set $d_1 = d_2 = d_3$. This is because of the argument when examining the worst-case time complexity in the above subsection.

Then for the underlying finite field $\mathbb{F}_q$, the intuition is that setting $q$ to be a large prime would be more secure. Note that we can still store an exponentially large prime using polynomially-many bits. This is because, if $q$ is small, then the "generic" behaviors as ensured by the Lang–Weil type theorems [56] may not be that generic. So some non-trivial properties may arise which then help with isomorphism testing. This is especially important for the pseudorandom assumption to be discussed Sect. 4. We then examine whether we want to set $q$ to be a large prime, or a large field with a small characteristic. The former one is preferred, because the current techniques in computer algebra and computational group theory, cf. [50] and [6], can usually work efficiently with large fields of small characteristics.

However, let us emphasize that even setting $q$ to be a constant, we do not have any concrete evidence for breaking GLAT as a one-way group action candidate. Furthermore, there are certain problems that are easy over large fields, while NP-hard over small fields; one such example is the maximum rank problem for matrix spaces [21]. To summarize, the above discussion on the field size issue is rather hypothetical and conservative.

# 4   The Pseudorandom Action Assumption

In this section, we introduce the new security assumption for group actions, namely pseudorandom group actions, which generalizes the Decisional Diffie-Hellman assumption. In Sect. 5, we shall study the prospect of using the general linear action on tensors as a candidate for this assumption. In the full version of this paper [53], the reader can find the cryptographic uses of this assumption including signatures and pseudorandom functions.

**Definition 6.** *Let $\mathcal{G}$ be a group family as specified before. Choose public parameters params $= (G, S, \alpha)$ to be $\mathcal{G}(1^\lambda)$. Sample $s \leftarrow S$ and $g \leftarrow G$. The group action pseudorandomness (GA-PR) problem is that given $(s, t)$, where $t = \alpha(g, s)$ or $t \leftarrow S$, decide which case $t$ is sampled from.*

**Definition 7 (Pseudorandom group action game).** *The pseudorandom group action game is the following game between a challenger and an adversary $\mathcal{A}$:*

- *The challenger and the adversary $\mathcal{A}$ agree on the public parameters params $= (G, S, \alpha)$ by choosing it to be $\mathcal{G}(1^\lambda)$ for some security parameter $\lambda$.*
- *Challenger samples random bit $b \in \{0, 1\}$, $s \leftarrow S$, $g \leftarrow G$, and chooses $t \leftarrow S$ if $b = 0$ and $t = g \cdot s$ if $b = 1$.*
- *Give $(s, t)$ to $\mathcal{A}$ who produces a bit $a \in \{0, 1\}$.*
- *We define the output of the game $GA\text{-}PR_{\mathcal{A}, \mathcal{G}}(1^\lambda) = 1$ and say $\mathcal{A}$ wins the game if $a = b$.*

**Definition 8.** *We say that the group-action pseudorandomness (GA-PR) problem is hard relative to $\mathcal{G}$, if for any polynomial-time quantum algorithm $\mathcal{A}$,*

$$\Pr[GA\text{-}PR_{\mathcal{A}, \mathcal{G}}(1^\lambda) = 1] = \mathrm{negl}(\lambda).$$

Some remarks on this definition are due here.

*For Transitive and Almost Transitive Actions.* In the case of transitive group actions, as an easy corollary of Observation 1, we have the following.

**Observation 3.** GA-PR problem is hard, if the group action $\alpha$ is transitive.

Indeed, when $\alpha$ is transitive, the two distributions in Definition 6 are the same, so in fact statistically impossible to distinguish.

Slightly generalizing the transitive case, it is not hard to see that GA-PR problem is hard, if there exists a "dominant" orbit $O \subseteq S$. Intuitively, this means that $O$ is too large such that random $s$ and $t$ from $S$ would both lie in $O$ with high probability. For example, consider the action of $\mathrm{GL}(n, \mathbb{F}) \times \mathrm{GL}(n, \mathbb{F})$ on $\mathrm{M}(n, \mathbb{F})$ by the left and right multiplications. The orbits are determined by the ranks of matrices in $\mathrm{M}(n, \mathbb{F})$, and the orbit of matrices of full-rank is dominant. But again, such group actions do not seem very useful for cryptographic purposes. Indeed, we require the orbit structure to satisfy that random $s$ and $t$ do not fall into the same orbit. Let us formally put forward this condition.

**Definition 9.** *We say that a group action $\alpha$ of $G$ on $S$ does not have a dominant orbit, if*

$$\Pr_{s,t \leftarrow S} [s, t \text{ lie in the same orbit}] = \mathrm{negl}(\lambda).$$

This definition is closely related to a classical question in geometry, namely classifying representations with a Zariski-dense orbit. When the group is a connected linear algebraic group over $\mathbb{C}$ and the representation is irreducible, this question has been settled by Sato and Kimura [76].

We now put forward a key assumption.

**Assumption 2** (Pseudorandom group action (PRA) assumption). There exists an $\mathcal{G}$ outputting a group action without a dominant orbit, relative to which the GA-PR problem is hard.

The name comes from the fact that the PRA assumption says 'in spirit' that the function $\Gamma : G \times S \to S \times S$ given by $\Gamma(g, s) = (g \cdot s, s)$ is a secure PRG. Here, it is only 'in spirit', because the PRA assumption does not include the usual expansion property of the PRG. Rather, it only includes the inexistence of a dominant orbit.

The applications of the PRA assumption including more efficient quantum-secure digital signature schemes and pseudorandom function constructions are given in the full version of this paper [53].

*Subsuming the Classical Diffie-Hellman Assumption.* We now formulate the classical decisional Diffie-Hellman (DDH) assumption as an instance of the pseudorandom group action assumption. To see this, we need the following definition.

**Definition 10.** *Let $\alpha : G \times S \to S$ be a group action. The $d$-diagonal action of $\alpha$, denoted by $\alpha^{(d)}$, is the group action of $G$ on $S^d$, the Cartesian product of $d$ copies of $S$, where $g \in G$ sends $(s_1, \ldots, s_d) \in S^d$ to $(g \cdot s_1, \ldots, g \cdot s_d)$.*

The following observation shows that the classical DDH can be obtained by instantiating GA-PR with a concrete group action.

**Observation 4.** Let $\alpha$ be the group action in Group Action 2. The classical Decisional Diffie-Hellman assumption is equivalent to the PRA assumption instantiated with $\alpha^{(2)}$, the 2-diagonal action of $\alpha$.

*Proof.* Recall from Group Action 2 defines an action $\alpha$ of $G \cong \mathbb{Z}_p^*$ on $S = C_p \backslash \{\text{id}\}$ where $C_p$ is a cyclic group of order $p$. The 2-diagonal action $\alpha^{(2)}$ is defined by $a \in \mathbb{Z}_p^*$ sending $(s,t) \in S \times S$ to $(s^a, t^a)$. Note that while $\alpha$ is transitive, $\alpha^{(2)}$ is not, and in fact it does not have a dominant orbit.

PRA instantiated with $\alpha^{(2)}$ then asks to distinguish between the following two distributions. The first distribution is $((s,t),(s',t'))$ where $s,t,s',t' \in_R S$. Since $\alpha$ is transitive, by Observation 1, this distribution is equivalent to $((s,s^a),(s^b,s^c))$, where $s \in_R S$ and $a,b,c \in_R G$. The second distribution is $((s,t),(s^b,t^b))$, where $s,t \in_R S$, and $b \in_R G$. Again, by Observation 1, this distribution is equivalent to $((s,s^a),(s^b,s^{ab}))$, where $s \in_R S$, and $a,b \in_R G$.

We then see that this is just the Decisional Diffie-Hellman assumption[5].    $\square$

As will be explained in Sect. 5.1, the pseudorandom assumption is a strong one, in a sense much stronger than the one-way assumption. Therefore, Observation 4 is important because, by casting the classical Diffie-Hellman assumption as an instance of the pseudorandom assumption, it provides a non-trivial and well-studied group action candidate for this assumption.

Of course, the DDH assumption is no longer secure under quantum attacks. Recently, this assumption in the context of supersingular isogeny based cryptography has been proposed by De Feo and Galbraith in [36]. We will study the possibility for the 3-tensor isomorphism problem as a pseudorandom group action candidate in Sect. 5

*The d-Diagonal Pseudorandomness Assumption.* Motivated by Observation 4, it will be convenient to specialize GA-PR to diagonal actions, and make the following assumption.

**Definition 11.** *The d-diagonal pseudorandomness (GA-PR(d)) problem for a group action $\alpha$, is defined to be the pseudorandomness problem for the d-diagonal group action $\alpha^{(d)}$.*

We emphasize that GA-PR(d) is just GA-PR applied to group actions of a particular form, so a special case of GA-PR. Correspondingly, we define PRA(d) to be the assumption that GA-PR(d) is hard relative to some $\mathcal{G}$.

Given a group action $\alpha : G \times S \to S$, let $F_\alpha = \{f_g : S \to S \mid g \in G, f_g(s) = g \cdot s\}$. It is not hard to see that PRA(d) is equivalent to say that $F_\alpha$ is a d-query weak PRF in the sense of Maurer and Tessaro [62]. This gives a straightforward cryptographic use of the PRA(d) assumption.

Given $d, e \in \mathbb{Z}^+$, $d < e$, it is clear that PRA(e) is no weaker than PRA(d). Indeed, given an algorithm $A$ that distinguishes between

$$((s_1, \ldots, s_d), (g \cdot s_1, \ldots g \cdot s_d)) \text{ and } ((s_1, \ldots, s_d), (t_1, \ldots, t_d)),$$

where $s_i, t_j \leftarrow S$, and $g \leftarrow G$, one can use $A$ to distinguish between $((s_1, \ldots, s_e), (g \cdot s_1, \ldots g \cdot s_e))$ and $((s_1, \ldots, s_e), (t_1, \ldots, t_e))$, by just looking at the

---

[5] Here we use the version of DDH where the generator of the cyclic group is randomly chosen as also used in [27]. A recent discussion on distinction between fixed generators and random generators can be found in [9].

first $d$ components in each tuple. It is an interesting question whether PRA($e$) is strictly stronger than PRA($d$). Note though that in the following, we will exhibit some group actions, for which PRA($d$) does not hold for large enough $d$.

# 5    General Linear Actions on Tensors: The Pseudorandom Action Assumption

## 5.1    Requirements for a Group Action to Be Pseudorandom

Clearly, a first requirement for a group action to be pseudorandom is that it should be one-way. Further requirements naturally come from certain attacks. We have devised the following attack strategies. These attacks suggest that the pseudorandom assumption is closely related to the orbit closure intersection problem which has received considerable attention recently.

*Isomorphism Testing in the Average-Case Setting.* To start with, we consider the impact of an average-case isomorphism testing algorithm on the pseudorandom assumption. Recall that for a group action $\alpha : G \times S \rightarrow S$, an average-case algorithm is required to work for instances $(s, t)$ where $s \leftarrow S$ and $t$ is arbitrary. Let $n$ be the input size to this algorithm. The traditional requirement for an average-case algorithm is that it needs to work for *all but at most* $1/\mathrm{poly}(n)$ fraction of $s \in S$, like such algorithms for graph isomorphism [7] and for alternating matrix space isometry [59]. However, in order for such an algorithm to break the pseudorandom assumption, it is enough that it works for a non-negligible, say $1/\mathrm{poly}(n)$, fraction of the instances. This is quite relaxed compared to the traditional requirement.

*The Supergroup Attack.* For a group action $\alpha : G \times S \rightarrow S$, a supergroup action of $\alpha$ is another group action $\beta : H \times S \rightarrow S$, such that (1) $G$ is a subgroup of $H$, (2) the restriction of $\beta$ to $G$, $\beta|_G$, is equal to $\alpha$. If it further holds that (3.1) the isomorphism problem for $H$ is easy, and (3.2) $\beta$ is not dominant, we will then have the following so-called *supergroup attack.* Give input $s, t \in S$, the adversary for the GA-PR problem of $\alpha$ will use the solver for the isomorphism problem for $H$ to check if $s, t$ are from the same orbit induced by $H$ and return 1 if they are from the same orbit and 0 otherwise. If $s, t$ are from the same orbit induced by $G$, the adversary always returns the correct answer as $G$ is a subgroup of $H$. In the case that $s, t$ are independently chosen from $S$, by the fact that $\beta$ is not dominant, the adversary will return the correct answer 0 with high probability.

*The Isomorphism Invariant Attack.* Generalizing the condition (3) above, we can have the following more general strategy as follows. We now think of $G$ and $H$ as defining equivalence relations by their orbit structures. Let $\sim_G$ (resp. $\sim_H$) be the equivalence relation defined by $G$ (resp. $H$). By the conditions (1) and (2), we have (a) $\sim_H$ is coarser than $\sim_G$. By the condition (3.1), we have (b) $\sim_H$ is easy to decide. By the condition (3.2), we have (c) $\sim_H$ have enough equivalence classes.

Clearly, if a relation $\sim$, not necessarily defined by a supergroup $H$, satisfies (a), (b), and (c), then $\sim$ can also be used to break the PRA assumption for $G$.

Such an equivalence relation is more commonly known as an isomorphism invariant, namely those properties that are preserved under isomorphism. The sources of isomorphism invariants can be very versatile. The supergroup attack can be thought of as a special case of category where the equivalence relation is defined by being isomorphic under a supergroup action. Another somewhat surprising and rich "invariant" comes from geometry, as we describe now.

*The Geometric Attack.* In the case of matrix group actions, the underlying vector spaces usually come with certain geometry which can be exploited for the attack purpose. Let $\alpha$ be a group action of $G$ on $V \cong \mathbb{F}^d$. For an orbit $O \subseteq V$, let its Zariski closure be $\overline{O}$. Let $\sim$ be the equivalence relation on $V$, such that for $s, t \in O$, $s \sim t$ if and only if $\overline{O_s} \cap \overline{O_t} \neq \emptyset$. It is obvious that $\sim$ is a coarser relation than $\sim_G$. Furthermore, except some degenerate settings when $m$ or $n$ are very small, there would be enough equivalence classes defined by $\sim$, because of the dimension reason. So (a) and (c) are satisfied. Therefore, if we could test efficiently whether the orbit closures of $s$ and $t$ intersect, (b) would be satisfied and we could break the PRA for $\alpha$. This problem, known as the orbit closure intersection problem, has received considerable attention recently.

Another straightforward approach based on this viewpoint is to recall that the geometry of orbit closures is determined by the ring of invariant polynomials [67]. More specifically, the action of $G$ on $V$ induces an action on $\mathbb{F}[V]$, the ring of polynomial functions on $V$. As $V \cong \mathbb{F}^d$, $\mathbb{F}[V] \cong \mathbb{F}[x_1, \ldots, x_d]$. Those polynomials invariant under this induced action form a subring of $\mathbb{F}[V]$, denoted as $\mathbb{F}[V]^G$. If there exists one easy-to-compute, non-trivial, invariant polynomial $f$ from $\mathbb{F}[V]^G$, we could then use $f$ to evaluate on the input instances and distinguish between the random setting (where $f$ is likely to evaluate differently) and the pseudorandom setting (where $f$ always evaluates the same).

**Example Attacks.** We now list some examples to illustrate the above attacks.

*An Example of Using the Isomorphism Invariant Attack.* We first consider the isomorphism invariant attack in the graph isomorphism case. Clearly, the degree sequence, consisting of vertex degrees sorted from large to small, is an easy to compute isomorphism invariant. A brief thought suggests that this invariant is already enough to break the pseudorandom assumption for graph isomorphism.

*An Example of Using the Geometric Attack.* We consider a group action similar to the 3-tensor isomorphism case (Group Action 1), inspired by the quantum marginal problem [19]. Given a 3-tensor of size $\ell \times n \times m$, we can "slice" this 3-tensor according to the third index to obtain a tuple of $m$ matrices of size $\ell$ by $n$. Consider the action of $G = \mathrm{O}(\ell, \mathbb{F}) \times \mathrm{O}(n, \mathbb{F}) \times \mathrm{SL}(m, \mathbb{F})$ on matrix tuples $\mathrm{M}(\ell \times n, \mathbb{F})^m$, where the three direct product factors act by left multiplication, right multiplication, and linear combination of the $m$ components, respectively.

For a matrix tuple $(A_1, \ldots, A_m)$ where $A_i \in M(\ell \times n, \mathbb{F})$, form an $\ell n \times m$ matrix $A$ where the $i$-th column of $A$ is obtained by straightening $A_i$ according to columns. Then $A^t A$ is an $m$ by $m$ matrix. The polynomial $f = \det(A^t A)$ is then a polynomial invariant for this action. For this note that the group $O(\ell, \mathbb{F}) \times O(n, \mathbb{F})$ can be embedded as a subgroup of $O(\ell n, \mathbb{F})$, so its action becomes trivial on $A^t A$. Then the determinant is invariant under the $SL(m, \mathbb{F})$. When $m < \ell n$, which is the interesting case, $\det(A^t A)$ is non-zero. It follows that we have a non-trivial, easy-to-compute, polynomial invariant which can break the PRA assumption for this group action.

*An Example of Using the Supergroup Attack.* We then explain how the supergroup attack invalidates the PRA($d$) assumption for certain families of group actions with $d > 1$.

Let $\alpha$ be a linear action of a group $G$ on a vector space $V \cong \mathbb{F}^N$. We show that as long as $d > N$, PRA($d$) does not hold. To see this, the action of $G$ on $V$ gives a homomorphism $\phi$ from $G$ to $GL(V) \cong GL(N, \mathbb{F})$. For any $g \in G$, and $v_1, \ldots, v_d \in V$, we can arrange an $N \times d$ matrix $S = [v_1, \ldots, v_d]$, such that $T = [\phi(g)v_1, \ldots, \phi(g)v_d] = \phi(g)[v_1, \ldots, v_d]$. On the other hand, for $u_1, \ldots, u_d \in V$, let $T' = [u_1, \ldots, u_d]$. Let us consider the row spans of $S$, $T$ and $T'$, which are subspaces of $\mathbb{F}^d$ of dimension $\leq N < d$. Clearly, the row spans of $S$ and $T$ are the same. On the other hand, when $u_i$'s are random vectors, the row span of $T'$ is unlikely to be the same as that of $S$. This gives an efficient approach to distinguish between $T$ and $T'$.

We can upgrade the above attack even further as follows. Let $\alpha$ be a linear action of $G$ on the linear space of matrices $M = M(m \times n, \mathbb{F})$. Recall that $GL(m, \mathbb{F}) \times GL(n, \mathbb{F})$ acts on $M$ by left and right multiplications. Suppose $\alpha$ gives rise to a homomorphism $\phi : G \to GL(m, \mathbb{F}) \times GL(n, \mathbb{F})$. For $g \in G$, if $\phi(g) = (A, B) \in GL(m, \mathbb{F}) \times GL(n, \mathbb{F})$, we let $\phi_1(g) := A \in GL(m, \mathbb{F})$, and $\phi_2(g) = B \in GL(n, \mathbb{F})$. We now show that when $d > (m^2 + n^2)/(mn)$, PRA($d$) does not hold for $\alpha$. To see this, for any $g \in G$, and $S = (A_1, \ldots, A_d) \in M(m \times n, \mathbb{F})^d$, let

$$T = (\phi_1(g)^t A_1 \phi_2(g), \ldots, \phi_1(g)^t A_d \phi_2(g)).$$

On the other hand, let $T' = (B_1, \ldots, B_d) \in M^d$. Since $\dim(S) = \dim(GL(m \times n, \mathbb{F})^d) = mnd > m^2 + n^2 = \dim(GL(m, \mathbb{F}) \times GL(n, \mathbb{F}))$, $\alpha$ does not have a dominant orbit (cf. Definition 9) This means that, when $B_i$'s are sampled randomly from $S$, $T'$ is unlikely to be in the same orbit as $S$. Now we use the fact that, the isomorphism problem for the action of $GL(m, \mathbb{F}) \times GL(n, \mathbb{F})$ on $S$ can be solved in deterministic polynomial time [50, Proposition 3.2]. This gives an efficient approach to distinguish between $T$ and $T'$.

Note that the set up here captures the Group Actions 3 and 4 in Sect. 3.2. For example, suppose for Group Action 3, we consider linear codes which are $n/2$-dimensional subspaces of $\mathbb{F}_q^n$. Then we have $m = n/2$, so PRA(3) for this action does not hold, as $3 > (m^2 + n^2)/(mn) = 5/2$.

On the other hand, when $d \leq (m^2 + n^2)/(mn)$, such an attack may fail, simply because of the existence of a dominant orbit.

## 5.2    The General Linear Action on Tensors as a Pseudorandom Action Candidate

We have explained why the general linear action on tensors is a good candidate for the one-way assumption in Sect. 3. We now argue that, to the best of our knowledge, it is also a candidate for the pseudorandom assumption.

We have described the current status of average-case algorithms for 3-tensor isomorphism problem in Sect. 3.3. One may expect that, because of the relaxed requirement for the average-case setting as discussed in Sect. 5.1, the algorithms in [15,59] may be accelerated. However, this is not the case, because these algorithms inherently enumerate all vectors in $\mathbb{F}_q^n$, or improve somewhat by using the birthday paradox.

We can also explain why the relaxed requirement for the average-case setting is still very difficult, by drawing experiences from computational group theory, because of the relation between GLAT and Group Action 5, which in turn is closely related to the group isomorphism problem as explained in Sect. 3.2. In group theory, it is known that the number of non-isomorphic $p$-groups of class 2 and exponent $p$ of order $p^\ell$ is bounded as $p^{\frac{2}{27}\ell^3 + \Theta(\ell^2)}$ [12]. The relaxed average-case requirement in this case then asks for an algorithm that could test isomorphism for a subclass of such groups containing non-isomorphic groups as many as $p^{\frac{2}{27}\ell^3 + \Theta(\ell^2)}/\operatorname{poly}(\ell, \log p) = p^{\frac{2}{27}\ell^3 + \Theta(\ell^2)}$. This is widely regarded as a formidable task in computational group theory: at present, we only know of a subclass of such groups with $p^{O(\ell^2)}$ many non-isomorphic groups that allows for an efficient isomorphism test [58].

The supergroup attack seems not useful here. The group $G = \mathrm{GL}(\ell, \mathbb{F}) \times \mathrm{GL}(n, \mathbb{F}) \times \mathrm{GL}(m, \mathbb{F})$ naturally lives in $\mathrm{GL}(\ell n m, \mathbb{F})$. However, by Aschbacher's classification of maximal subgroups of finite classical groups [2], there are few natural supergroups of $G$ in $\mathrm{GL}(\ell n m, \mathbb{F})$. The obvious ones include subgroups isomorphic to $\mathrm{GL}(\ell n, \mathbb{F}) \times \mathrm{GL}(m, \mathbb{F})$, which is not useful because it has a dominant orbit (Definition 9).

The geometric attack seems not useful here either. The invariant ring here is trivial [31][6]. For the orbit closure intersection problem, despite some recent exciting progress in [1,19,20,29,52], the current best algorithms for the corresponding orbit closure intersection problems still require exponential time.

Finally, for the most general isomorphism invariant attack, the celebrated paper of Hillar and Lim [49] is just titled "Most Tensor Problems Are NP-Hard." This suggests that getting one easy-to-compute and useful isomorphism invariant for GLAT is already a challenging task. Here, useful means that the invariant does not lead to an equivalence relation with a dominant class in the sense of Definition 9.

---

[6] If instead of $\mathrm{GL}(\ell, \mathbb{F}) \times \mathrm{GL}(n, \mathbb{F}) \times \mathrm{GL}(m, \mathbb{F})$ we consider $\mathrm{SL}(\ell, \mathbb{F}) \times \mathrm{SL}(n, \mathbb{F}) \times \mathrm{SL}(m, \mathbb{F})$, the invariant ring is non-trivial – also known as the ring of semi-invariants for the corresponding GL action – but highly complicated. When $\ell = m = n$, we do not even know one single easy-to-compute non-trivial invariant. It further requires exponential degree to generate the whole invariant ring [30].

The above discussions not only provide evidence for GLAT to be pseudorandom, but also highlight how this problem connects to various mathematical and computational disciplines. We believe that this could serve a further motivation for all these works in various fields.

**Acknowledgement.** Y.Q. would like to thank Joshua A. Grochow for explaining the results in [39] to him. The authors would like to thank an anonymous reviewer for careful reading and suggesting several interesting questions and references. Y.Q. was partially supported by Australian Research Council DE150100720. F.S. was partially supported by the U.S. National Science Foundation under CCF-1816869. Any opinions, findings, and conclusions or recommendations expressed in this material are those of the author(s) and do not necessarily reflect the views of the National Science Foundation. A.Y. was supported by Institute of Information & Communications Technology Planning & Evaluation (IITP) grant funded by the Korea government (MSIT) (No. 2017-0-00616, Development of lattice-based post-quantum public-key cryptographic schemes).

# References

1. Allen-Zhu, Z., Garg, A., Li, Y., de Oliveira, R.M., Wigderson, A.: Operator scaling via geodesically convex optimization, invariant theory and polynomial identity testing. In: Proceedings of the 50th Annual ACM SIGACT Symposium on Theory of Computing, STOC 2018, Los Angeles, CA, USA, 25–29 June 2018, pp. 172–181 (2018)
2. Aschbacher, M.: On the maximal subgroups of the finite classical groups. Inven. Math. **76**(3), 469–514 (1984)
3. Babai, L.: Monte-Carlo algorithms in graph isomorphism testing. Technical report 79–10, Dép. Math. et Stat., Université de Montréal (1979)
4. Babai, L.: Local expansion of vertex-transitive graphs and random generation in finite groups. In: Proceedings of the 23rd Annual ACM Symposium on Theory of Computing, New Orleans, Louisiana, USA, 5–8 May 1991, pp. 164–174 (1991)
5. Babai, L.: Graph isomorphism in quasipolynomial time [extended abstract]. In: Proceedings of the 48th Annual ACM SIGACT Symposium on Theory of Computing, STOC 2016, Cambridge, MA, USA, 18–21 June 2016, pp. 684–697 (2016)
6. Babai, L., Beals, R., Seress, Á.: Polynomial-time theory of matrix groups. In: Proceedings of the 41st Annual ACM Symposium on Theory of Computing, STOC 2009, Bethesda, MD, USA, May 31 – June 2, 2009, pp. 55–64 (2009). https://doi.org/10.1145/1536414.1536425
7. Babai, L., Erdős, P., Selkow, S.M.: Random graph isomorphism. SIAM J. Comput. **9**(3), 628–635 (1980)
8. Babai, L., Szemerédi, E.: On the complexity of matrix group problems I. In: 25th Annual Symposium on Foundations of Computer Science, West Palm Beach, Florida, USA, 24–26 October 1984, pp. 229–240 (1984)
9. Bartusek, J., Ma, F., Zhandry, M.: The distinction between fixed and random generators in group-based assumptions. IACR Cryptology ePrint Archive 2019, 202 (2019). https://eprint.iacr.org/2019/202
10. Bernstein, D.J., Buchmann, J., Dahmen, E.: Post-Quantum Cryptography. Springer, Heidelberg (2009). https://doi.org/10.1007/978-3-540-88702-7

11. Berthomieu, J., Faugère, J., Perret, L.: Polynomial-time algorithms for quadratic isomorphism of polynomials: the regular case. J. Complexity **31**(4), 590–616 (2015)
12. Blackburn, S.R., Neumann, P.M., Venkataraman, G.: Enumeration of Finite Groups. Cambridge University Press, Cambridge (2007)
13. Boneh, D.: The Decision Diffie-Hellman problem. In: Buhler, J.P. (ed.) ANTS 1998. LNCS, vol. 1423, pp. 48–63. Springer, Heidelberg (1998). https://doi.org/10.1007/BFb0054851
14. Bouillaguet, C., Faugère, J.-C., Fouque, P.-A., Perret, L.: Practical cryptanalysis of the identification scheme based on the isomorphism of polynomial with one secret problem. In: Catalano, D., Fazio, N., Gennaro, R., Nicolosi, A. (eds.) PKC 2011. LNCS, vol. 6571, pp. 473–493. Springer, Heidelberg (2011). https://doi.org/10.1007/978-3-642-19379-8_29
15. Bouillaguet, C., Fouque, P.-A., Véber, A.: Graph-theoretic algorithms for the "Isomorphism of Polynomials" problem. In: Johansson, T., Nguyen, P.Q. (eds.) EUROCRYPT 2013. LNCS, vol. 7881, pp. 211–227. Springer, Heidelberg (2013). https://doi.org/10.1007/978-3-642-38348-9_13
16. Brassard, G., Crépeau, C.: Non-transitive transfer of confidence: a perfect zero-knowledge interactive protocol for SAT and beyond. In: 27th Annual Symposium on Foundations of Computer Science, FOCS 1986, Toronto, Canada, October 1986, pp. 188–195 (1986)
17. Brassard, G., Yung, M.: One-way group actions. In: Menezes, A.J., Vanstone, S.A. (eds.) CRYPTO 1990. LNCS, vol. 537, pp. 94–107. Springer, Heidelberg (1991). https://doi.org/10.1007/3-540-38424-3_7
18. Brooksbank, P.A., Luks, E.M.: Testing isomorphism of modules. J. Algebr. **320**(11), 4020–4029 (2008). https://doi.org/10.1016/j.jalgebra.2008.07.014
19. Bürgisser, P., Franks, C., Garg, A., de Oliveira, R.M., Walter, M., Wigderson, A.: Efficient algorithms for tensor scaling, quantum marginals, and moment polytopes. In: 59th IEEE Annual Symposium on Foundations of Computer Science, FOCS 2018, Paris, France, 7–9 October 2018, pp. 883–897 (2018). https://doi.org/10.1109/FOCS.2018.00088
20. Bürgisser, P., Garg, A., de Oliveira, R.M., Walter, M., Wigderson, A.: Alternating minimization, scaling algorithms, and the null-cone problem from invariant theory. In: 9th Innovations in Theoretical Computer Science Conference, ITCS 2018, Cambridge, MA, USA, 11–14 January 2018, pp. 24:1–24:20 (2018)
21. Buss, J.F., Frandsen, G.S., Shallit, J.O.: The computational complexity of some problems of linear algebra. J. Comput. Syst. Sci. **58**(3), 572–596 (1999)
22. Chen, L.: Report on post-quantum cryptography. NIST.GOV (2016)
23. Childs, A., Jao, D., Soukharev, V.: Constructing elliptic curve isogenies in quantum subexponential time. J. Math. Cryptol. **8**(1), 1–29 (2014)
24. Childs, A.M., van Dam, W.: Quantum algorithms for algebraic problems. Rev. Mod. Phys. **82**, 1–52 (2010). https://doi.org/10.1103/RevModPhys.82.1
25. Chistov, A., Ivanyos, G., Karpinski, M.: Polynomial time algorithms for modules over finite dimensional algebras. In: Proceedings of the 1997 International Symposium on Symbolic and Algebraic Computation, pp. 68–74. ACM (1997)
26. Couveignes, J.M.: Hard homogeneous spaces. IACR Cryptology ePrint Archive (2006). http://eprint.iacr.org/2006/291
27. Cramer, R., Shoup, V.: A practical public key cryptosystem provably secure against adaptive chosen ciphertext attack. In: Krawczyk, H. (ed.) CRYPTO 1998. LNCS, vol. 1462, pp. 13–25. Springer, Heidelberg (1998). https://doi.org/10.1007/BFb0055717

28. De Feo, L., Jao, D., Plût, J.: Towards quantum-resistant cryptosystems from super-singular elliptic curve isogenies. J. Math. Cryptol. **8**(3), 209–247 (2014)
29. Derksen, H., Makam, V.: Algorithms for orbit closure separation for invariants and semi-invariants of matrices. CoRR abs/1801.02043 (2018). http://arxiv.org/abs/1801.02043
30. Derksen, H., Makam, V.: An exponential lower bound for the degrees of invariants of cubic forms and tensor actions (2019)
31. Derksen, H., Weyman, J.: Semi-invariants of quivers and saturation for Littlewood-Richardson coefficients. J. Am. Math. Soc. **13**(3), 467–479 (2000)
32. Diffie, W., Hellman, M.: New directions in cryptography. IEEE Trans. Inf. Theory **22**(6), 644–654 (1976)
33. Dinh, H., Moore, C., Russell, A.: McEliece and Niederreiter cryptosystems that resist quantum Fourier sampling attacks. In: Rogaway, P. (ed.) CRYPTO 2011. LNCS, vol. 6841, pp. 761–779. Springer, Heidelberg (2011). https://doi.org/10.1007/978-3-642-22792-9_43
34. Dinh, H.T., Moore, C., Russell, A.: Limitations of single coset states and quantum algorithms for code equivalence. Quantum Inf. Comput. **15**(3&4), 260–294 (2015)
35. Faugère, J.-C., Perret, L.: Polynomial equivalence problems: algorithmic and theoretical aspects. In: Vaudenay, S. (ed.) EUROCRYPT 2006. LNCS, vol. 4004, pp. 30–47. Springer, Heidelberg (2006). https://doi.org/10.1007/11761679_3
36. De Feo, L., Galbraith, S.D.: SeaSign: compact isogeny signatures from class group actions. In: Ishai, Y., Rijmen, V. (eds.) EUROCRYPT 2019. LNCS, vol. 11478, pp. 759–789. Springer, Cham (2019). https://doi.org/10.1007/978-3-030-17659-4_26
37. Fiat, A., Shamir, A.: How To prove yourself: practical solutions to identification and signature problems. In: Odlyzko, A.M. (ed.) CRYPTO 1986. LNCS, vol. 263, pp. 186–194. Springer, Heidelberg (1987). https://doi.org/10.1007/3-540-47721-7_12
38. Friedl, K., Rónyai, L.: Polynomial time solutions of some problems of computational algebra. In: Proceedings of the Seventeenth Annual ACM Symposium on Theory of Computing, pp. 153–162. ACM (1985)
39. Futorny, V., Grochow, J.A., Sergeichuk, V.V.: Wildness for tensors. Linear Algebr. Appl. **566**, 212–244 (2019). https://doi.org/10.1016/j.laa.2018.12.022
40. Galbraith, S.D., Vercauteren, F.: Computational problems in supersingular elliptic curve isogenies. Quantum Inf. Process. **17**(10), 265 (2018)
41. Geiselmann, W., Meier, W., Steinwandt, R.: An attack on the isomorphisms of polynomials problem with one secret. Int. J. Inf. Sec. **2**(1), 59–64 (2003)
42. Goldreich, O., Micali, S., Wigderson, A.: Proofs that yield nothing but their validity or all languages in np have zero-knowledge proof systems. J. ACM **38**(3), 691–729 (1991). https://doi.org/10.1145/116825.116852
43. Grochow, J.A.: Matrix isomorphism of matrix Lie algebras. In: Proceedings of the 27th Conference on Computational Complexity, CCC 2012, Porto, Portugal, 26–29 June 2012, pp. 203–213 (2012). https://doi.org/10.1109/CCC.2012.34
44. Grochow, J.A., Qiao, Y.: Isomorphism problems for tensors, groups, and cubic forms: completeness and reductions (2019). arXiv:1907.00309 [cs.CC]
45. Hallgren, S., Moore, C., Rötteler, M., Russell, A., Sen, P.: Limitations of quantum coset states for graph isomorphism. J. ACM **57**(6), 34:1–34:33 (2010). https://doi.org/10.1145/1857914.1857918
46. Hartung, R.J., Schnorr, C.-P.: Public key identification based on the equivalence of quadratic forms. In: Kučera, L., Kučera, A. (eds.) MFCS 2007. LNCS, vol. 4708, pp. 333–345. Springer, Heidelberg (2007). https://doi.org/10.1007/978-3-540-74456-6_31

47. Håstad, J.: Tensor rank is NP-complete. J. Algorithms **11**(4), 644–654 (1990). https://doi.org/10.1016/0196-6774(90)90014-6

48. Haviv, I., Regev, O.: On the lattice isomorphism problem. In: Proceedings of the Twenty-Fifth Annual ACM-SIAM Symposium on Discrete Algorithms, SODA 2014, Portland, Oregon, USA, 5–7 January 2014, pp. 391–404 (2014)

49. Hillar, C.J., Lim, L.: Most tensor problems are NP-hard. J. ACM **60**(6), 45:1–45:39 (2013). https://doi.org/10.1145/2512329

50. Ivanyos, G., Qiao, Y.: Algorithms based on *-algebras, and their applications to isomorphism of polynomials with one secret, group isomorphism, and polynomial identity testing. SIAM J. Comput. **48**(3), 926–963 (2019). https://doi.org/10.1137/18M1165682

51. Ivanyos, G., Karpinski, M., Saxena, N.: Deterministic polynomial time algorithms for matrix completion problems. SIAM J. Comput. **39**(8), 3736–3751 (2010). https://doi.org/10.1137/090781231

52. Ivanyos, G., Qiao, Y., Subrahmanyam, K.V.: Constructive non-commutative rank computation is in deterministic polynomial time. In: 8th Innovations in Theoretical Computer Science Conference, ITCS 2017, Berkeley, CA, USA, 9–11 January 2017, pp. 55:1–55:19 (2017)

53. Ji, Z., Qiao, Y., Song, F., Yun, A.: General linear group action on tensors: a candidate for post-quantum cryptography. Cryptology ePrint Archive, Report 2019/687 (2019). https://eprint.iacr.org/2019/687

54. Kaplan, M., Leurent, G., Leverrier, A., Naya-Plasencia, M.: Breaking symmetric cryptosystems using quantum period finding. In: Robshaw, M., Katz, J. (eds.) CRYPTO 2016. LNCS, vol. 9815, pp. 207–237. Springer, Heidelberg (2016). https://doi.org/10.1007/978-3-662-53008-5_8

55. Kayal, N.: Efficient algorithms for some special cases of the polynomial equivalence problem. In: Proceedings of the Twenty-Second Annual ACM-SIAM Symposium on Discrete Algorithms, SODA 2011, San Francisco, California, USA, 23–25 January 2011, pp. 1409–1421 (2011)

56. Lang, S., Weil, A.: Number of points of varieties in finite fields. Am. J. Math. **76**(4), 819–827 (1954)

57. Leon, J.S.: Computing automorphism groups of error-correcting codes. IEEE Trans. Inf. Theory **28**(3), 496–510 (1982)

58. Lewis, M.L., Wilson, J.B.: Isomorphism in expanding families of indistinguishable groups. Groups Complex. Cryptol. **4**(1), 73–110 (2012)

59. Li, Y., Qiao, Y.: Linear algebraic analogues of the graph isomorphism problem and the Erdős-Rényi model. In: 58th IEEE Annual Symposium on Foundations of Computer Science, FOCS 2017, Berkeley, CA, USA, 15–17 October 2017, pp. 463–474 (2017)

60. Luks, E.M.: Isomorphism of graphs of bounded valence can be tested in polynomial time. J. Comput. Syst. Sci. **25**(1), 42–65 (1982). https://doi.org/10.1016/0022-0000(82)90009-5

61. Macario-Rat, G., Plut, J., Gilbert, H.: New insight into the isomorphism of polynomial problem IP1S and its use in cryptography. In: Sako, K., Sarkar, P. (eds.) ASIACRYPT 2013. LNCS, vol. 8269, pp. 117–133. Springer, Heidelberg (2013). https://doi.org/10.1007/978-3-642-42033-7_7

62. Maurer, U., Tessaro, S.: Basing PRFs on constant-query weak PRFs: minimizing assumptions for efficient symmetric cryptography. In: Pieprzyk, J. (ed.) ASIACRYPT 2008. LNCS, vol. 5350, pp. 161–178. Springer, Heidelberg (2008). https://doi.org/10.1007/978-3-540-89255-7_11

63. McKay, B.D.: Practical graph isomorphism. Congr. Numer, pp. 45–87 (1980)
64. McKay, B.D., Piperno, A.: Practical graph isomorphism. II. J. Symb. Comput. **60**, 94–112 (2014)
65. Moore, C., Russell, A., Vazirani, U.: A classical one-way function to confound quantum adversaries. arXiv preprint quant-ph/0701115 (2007)
66. Mulmuley, K.D.: Geometric complexity theory V: efficient algorithms for Noether normalization. J. Am. Math. Soc. **30**(1), 225–309 (2017)
67. Mumford, D., Fogarty, J., Kirwan, F.: Geometric Invariant Theory. Springer, Heidelberg (1994)
68. Naor, M., Reingold, O.: Number-theoretic constructions of efficient pseudo-random functions. J. ACM **51**(2), 231–262 (2004). https://doi.org/10.1145/972639.972643
69. O'Brien, E.A.: Isomorphism testing for $p$-groups. J. Symb. Comput. **17**(2), 133–147 (1994)
70. Patarin, J.: Hidden Fields Equations (HFE) and Isomorphisms of Polynomials (IP): two new families of asymmetric algorithms. In: Maurer, U. (ed.) EUROCRYPT 1996. LNCS, vol. 1070, pp. 33–48. Springer, Heidelberg (1996). https://doi.org/10.1007/3-540-68339-9_4
71. Patarin, J., Goubin, L., Courtois, N.: Improved algorithms for isomorphisms of polynomials. In: Nyberg, K. (ed.) EUROCRYPT 1998. LNCS, vol. 1403, pp. 184–200. Springer, Heidelberg (1998). https://doi.org/10.1007/BFb0054126
72. Perret, L.: A fast cryptanalysis of the isomorphism of polynomials with one secret problem. In: Cramer, R. (ed.) EUROCRYPT 2005. LNCS, vol. 3494, pp. 354–370. Springer, Heidelberg (2005). https://doi.org/10.1007/11426639_21
73. Petrank, E., Roth, R.M.: Is code equivalence easy to decide? IEEE Trans. Inf. Theory **43**(5), 1602–1604 (1997)
74. Plût, J., Fouque, P., Macario-Rat, G.: Solving the "isomorphism of polynomials with two secrets" problem for all pairs of quadratic forms. CoRR abs/1406.3163 (2014). http://arxiv.org/abs/1406.3163
75. Regev, O.: Quantum computation and lattice problems. SIAM J. Comput. **33**(3), 738–760 (2004). https://doi.org/10.1137/S0097539703440678
76. Sato, M., Kimura, T.: A classification of irreducible prehomogeneous vector spaces and their relative invariants. Nagoya Math. J. **65**, 1–155 (1977)
77. Sendrier, N.: Finding the permutation between equivalent linear codes: the support splitting algorithm. IEEE Trans. Inf. Theory **46**(4), 1193–1203 (2000)
78. Sendrier, N., Simos, D.E.: The hardness of code equivalence over $\mathbb{F}_q$ and its application to code-based cryptography. In: Gaborit, P. (ed.) PQCrypto 2013. LNCS, vol. 7932, pp. 203–216. Springer, Heidelberg (2013). https://doi.org/10.1007/978-3-642-38616-9_14
79. Shor, P.W.: Algorithms for quantum computation: discrete logarithms and factoring. In: 35th Annual Symposium on Foundations of Computer Science, Santa Fe, New Mexico, USA, 20–22 November 1994, pp. 124–134 (1994)
80. Sims, C.C.: Some group-theoretic algorithms. In: Newman, M.F., Richardson, J.S. (eds.) Topics in Algebra. LNM, vol. 697, pp. 108–124. Springer, Heidelberg (1978). https://doi.org/10.1007/BFb0103126
81. Song, F., Yun, A.: Quantum security of NMAC and related constructions. In: Katz, J., Shacham, H. (eds.) CRYPTO 2017. LNCS, vol. 10402, pp. 283–309. Springer, Cham (2017). https://doi.org/10.1007/978-3-319-63715-0_10
82. Unruh, D.: Post-quantum security of Fiat-Shamir. In: Takagi, T., Peyrin, T. (eds.) ASIACRYPT 2017. LNCS, vol. 10624, pp. 65–95. Springer, Cham (2017). https://doi.org/10.1007/978-3-319-70694-8_3

83. Weisfeiler, B., Lehman, A.A.: A reduction of a graph to a canonical form and an algebra arising during this reduction. Nauchno-Technicheskaya Informatsia **2**(9), 12–16 (1968)
84. Wilson, J.B.: Decomposing $p$-groups via Jordan algebras. J. Algebr. **322**(8), 2642–2679 (2009)
85. Zhandry, M.: How to construct quantum random functions. In: 2012 IEEE 53rd Annual Symposium on Foundations of Computer Science, pp. 679–687. IEEE (2012)

# Composable and Finite Computational Security of Quantum Message Transmission

Fabio Banfi$^{(\boxtimes)}$ , Ueli Maurer, Christopher Portmann , and Jiamin Zhu

Department of Computer Science, ETH Zurich, 8092 Zurich, Switzerland
{fbanfi,maurer,chportma,zhujia}@inf.ethz.ch

**Abstract.** Recent research in quantum cryptography has led to the development of schemes that encrypt and authenticate quantum messages with computational security. The security definitions used so far in the literature are asymptotic, game-based, and not known to be composable. We show how to define finite, composable, computational security for secure quantum message transmission. The new definitions do not involve any games or oracles, they are directly operational: a scheme is secure if it transforms an insecure channel and a shared key into an ideal secure channel from Alice to Bob, i.e., one which only allows Eve to block messages and learn their size, but not change them or read them. By modifying the ideal channel to provide Eve with more or less capabilities, one gets an array of different security notions. By design these transformations are composable, resulting in composable security.

Crucially, the new definitions are *finite*. Security does not rely on the asymptotic hardness of a computational problem. Instead, one proves a finite reduction: if an adversary can distinguish the constructed (real) channel from the ideal one (for some fixed security parameters), then she can solve a finite instance of some computational problem. Such a finite statement is needed to make security claims about concrete implementations.

We then prove that (slightly modified versions of) protocols proposed in the literature satisfy these composable definitions. And finally, we study the relations between some game-based definitions and our composable ones. In particular, we look at notions of quantum authenticated encryption and QCCA2, and show that they suffer from the same issues as their classical counterparts: they exclude certain protocols which are arguably secure.

## 1 Introduction

At its core, a security definition is a set of mathematical conditions, and a security proof consists in showing that these conditions hold for a given protocol. Given various security definitions, one may analyze which are stronger and weaker by proving reductions or finding separating examples. This however does not tell us which definitions one should use, since too weak definitions

© International Association for Cryptologic Research 2019
D. Hofheinz and A. Rosen (Eds.): TCC 2019, LNCS 11891, pp. 282–311, 2019.
https://doi.org/10.1007/978-3-030-36030-6_12

may have security issues and too strong definitions may exclude protocols that are arguably secure. For example, IND-CCA2 is often considered an unnecessarily strong security definition, since taking a scheme which is IND-CCA2 and appending a bit to the ciphertext results in a new encryption scheme that is arguably as secure as the original scheme, but does not satisfy IND-CCA2 [15,17]. In this work we take a more critical approach to defining security. We ask what criteria a security definition needs to satisfy that are both necessary and sufficient conditions to call a protocol "secure". We then apply them to the problem of encrypting and authenticating quantum messages with computational security in the symmetric-key setting.

## 1.1   A Security Desideratum

*Operational Security.* Common security definitions for encryption and authentication found in the literature are *game-based*, i.e., they require that an adversary cannot win a game such as guessing what message has been encrypted given access to certain oracles, see, e.g., [8] and [24] for comparisons of various such games in the public-key and private-key settings, respectively. These have been adapted for transmitting quantum messages: a definition for QCPA has been proposed in [11], QCCA1 in [1], and QCCA2 as well as notions of quantum unforgeability and quantum authenticated encryption in [2]. These are just some of the security games one can imagine—in the classical, symmetric-key setting, [24] analyzes 18 different security notions. A natural question is then to ask which of these games are the relevant ones, for which ones is it both necessary and sufficient that an adversary cannot win them. And the general answer is: we do not know.

Through such cryptographic protocols one wishes to prevent an adversary from learning some part of a message or modifying a message undetected. But it is generally unclear how such game-based security definitions relate to these operational notions—we refer to [32] for a more in-depth critique of game-based security. Instead, one should directly define security *operationally*.[1] In this work we follow the constructive paradigm of [28,30,31], and define a protocol to be secure if it constructs a channel with the desired properties, e.g., only leaks the message size or only allows the adversary to block the message, but not change it or insert new messages.

*Composable Security.* A second drawback of the definitions proposed so far in the literature for computational security of quantum message transmission [1,2,11] is that they are not (proven to be) *composable*. A long history of work on composable security has shown that analyzing a protocol in an isolated setting does not imply that it is actually secure when one considers the environment in which it is used. When performing such a composable security analysis,

---

[1] Note that once a game-based definition has been proven to capture operational notions such as confidentiality or authenticity (e.g., via a reduction), then the game-based criterion may become a benchmark for designing schemes with the desired security; see the discussion in Sect. 1.6.

one sometimes finds that the definitions used are inappropriate but the protocols are actually secure like for quantum key distribution [10,25,39], that the definitions are still secure (up to a loss of security parameter) like for delegated quantum computation [18], or that not only the definitions but also the protocols are insecure like in relativistic and bounded storage bit commitment and (biased) coin tossing [44].[2] It is thus necessary for a protocol to be proven to satisfy a composable security definition before it may be considered (provably) secure and safely used in an arbitrary environment.

*Finite Security.* A third problem with the aforementioned security definitions is that they are all *asymptotic*. This means that the protocols have a security parameter $k \in \mathbb{N}$—formally, one considers a sequence of protocols $\{\Pi_k\}_{k \in \mathbb{N}}$— and security is defined in the limit when $k \to \infty$. An implementation of a protocol will however always be finite, e.g., the honest players choose a specific parameter $k_0$ which they consider to be sufficient and run $\Pi_{k_0}$. A security proof for $k \to \infty$ does not tell us anything about security for any specific parameter $k_0$ and thus does not tell us anything about the security of $\Pi_{k_0}$, which is run by the honest players. To resolve this issue, some works consider what is called *concrete security* [7], i.e., instead of hiding parameters in $O$-notation, security bounds and reductions are given explicitly. This is a first step at obtaining finite security, but it still considers the security of a sequence $\{\Pi_k\}_{k \in \mathbb{N}}$ instead of security of the individual elements $\Pi_{k_0}$ in this sequence. For example, one still considers adversaries that are polynomial in $k$, simulators that must be efficient in $k$, and errors that are negligible in $k$. But the security definition of some $\Pi_{k_0}$ should not depend on any other elements in the sequence, on how the sequence is defined or whether it is defined at all. Hence notions such as poly-time, efficiency, or negligibility should not be part of a security definition for some specific $\Pi_{k_0}$. We call the security paradigm that analyzes individual elements $\Pi_{k_0}$ *finite security*, and show in this work how to define it for computational security of quantum message transmission.

## 1.2  Overview of Results

Our contributions are threefold. We first provide definitions for encryption and authentication of quantum messages that satisfy the desideratum expressed above. In particular, we show how to define finite security in the computational case. In Sect. 1.3 below we explain the intuition behind this security paradigm.

We then show that (slightly modified) protocols from the literature [1,2] satisfy these definitions. These protocols use the quantum one-time pad and quantum information-theoretic authentication as subroutine [6,36], but run them with keys that are only computationally secure to encrypt multiple messages. We explain the constructions and what is achieved in more detail in Sect. 1.4.

---

[2] Note that a negative result in a composable framework only proves that a protocol does not construct the desired ideal functionality. This does not exclude that the protocol may construct some other ideal functionality or may be secure given some additional set-up assumptions.

Now that we have security definitions that satisfy our desideratum, we revisit some game-based definitions from the literature, and compare them to our own notions of security. An overview of these results is given in Sect. 1.5.

### 1.3   Finite Computational Security

In traditional asymptotic security, a cryptographic protocol is parameterized by a single value $k \in \mathbb{N}$—any other parameters must be expressed as a function of $k$—and one studies a sequence of objects $\{\Pi_k\}_{k \in \mathbb{N}}$. In composable security, one uses this to define a parameterized real world $\mathbb{R} = \{\mathsf{R}_k\}_{k \in \mathbb{N}}$ and ideal world $\mathbb{S} = \{\mathsf{S}_k\}_{k \in \mathbb{N}}$, and argues that no polynomial distinguisher $\mathbb{D} = \{\mathsf{D}_k\}_{k \in \mathbb{N}}$ can distinguish one from the other with non-negligible advantage. At first glance the notions of polynomial distinguishers and negligible functions might seem essential, because an unbounded distinguisher can obviously distinguish the two, and without a notion of negligibility, how can one define what is a satisfactory bound on the distinguishability.

The latter problem is the simpler to address: instead of categorizing distinguishability as black or white (negligible or not), we give explicit bounds. The former issue is resolved by observing that we never actually prove that the real and ideal world are indistinguishable (except in the case of information-theoretic security), since in most cases that would amount to solving a problem such as $\mathsf{P} \neq \mathsf{NP}$. What one actually proves is a *reduction*, which is a finite statement, not an asymptotic one. More precisely, one proves that if $\mathsf{D}_k$ can distinguish $\mathsf{R}_k$ from $\mathsf{S}_k$ with advantage $p_k$, then some (explicit) $\mathsf{D}'_k$ can solve some problem $W_k$ with probability $p'_k$—if one believes that $W_k$ is asymptotically hard to solve, then this implies that $\mathbb{D}$ cannot distinguish $\mathbb{R}$ from $\mathbb{S}$.

A finite security statement stops after the reduction. We prove that for any $k_0$ and any $\mathsf{D}_{k_0}$,

$$d^{\mathsf{D}_{k_0}}(\mathsf{R}_{k_0}, \mathsf{S}_{k_0}) \leq f(\mathsf{D}_{k_0}), \tag{1}$$

where $d^{\mathsf{D}_{k_0}}(\cdot, \cdot)$ denotes the advantage $\mathsf{D}_{k_0}$ has in distinguishing two given systems, and $f(\cdot)$ is some arbitrary function, e.g., the probability that $\mathsf{D}'_{k_0}$ (which is itself some function of $\mathsf{D}_{k_0}$) can solve some problem $W_{k_0}$.

Equation 1 does not require systems to be part of a sequence with a single security parameter $k \in \mathbb{N}$. There may be no security parameter at all, or multiple parameters. Information-theoretic security corresponds to the special case where one can prove that $f(\mathsf{D}_{k_0})$ is small for all $\mathsf{D}_{k_0}$.

### 1.4   Constructing Quantum Channels

As mentioned in Sect. 1.1, we use the Abstract and Constructive Cryptography (AC) framework of Maurer and Renner [28,30,31] in this work. To define the security of a message transmission protocol, we need to first define the type of channel we wish to achieve—for simplicity, we always consider channels going from Alice to Bob.

The strongest channel we construct in this work is an ordered secure quantum channel, OSC, which allows Eve to decide which messages that Alice sent will be delivered to Bob and which ones get discarded. But it does not reveal any information about the messages (except their size and number) to Eve and guarantees that the delivered messages arrive in the same order in which they were sent. A somewhat weaker channel, a secure channel SC, also allows Eve to block or deliver each message, but additionally allows her to jumble their order of arrival at Bob's.

Our first result shows that a modified version of a protocol from [2] constructs the strongest channel, OSC, from an insecure channel and a short key that is used to select a function from a pseudo-random family (PRF). Security holds for any distinguisher that cannot distinguish the output of the PRF from the output of a uniform function. We also show how one can construct OSC from SC by simply appending a counter to the messages.

The two channels described above are labeled "secure", because they are both confidential (Eve does not learn anything about the messages) and authentic (Eve cannot change or insert any messages). If we are willing to sacrifice authenticity, we can define weaker channels that allow Eve to modify or insert messages in specific ways. We define a non-malleable confidential channel, NMCC—which does not allow Eve to change a message sent by Alice, but does allow her to insert a message of her choice—and a Pauli-malleable channel, PMCC—which allows Eve to apply bit and phase flips to Alice's messages or insert a fully mixed state.

Our second construction modifies a protocol from [1] to construct PMCC from an insecure channel and a short key that is used to select a function from a pseudo-random family (PRF). Here too, security holds for any distinguisher that cannot distinguish the PRF from uniform.

## 1.5  Comparison to Game-Based Definitions

In the last part of this work, we relate existing game-based security definitions for quantum encryption with our new proposed security definitions phrased in constructive cryptography. More concretely, we focus on the notions of *quantum ciphertext indistinguishability under adaptive chosen-ciphertext attack* (QCCA2) and *quantum authenticated encryption* (QAE), both introduced in [2].

We first note that encryption schemes are defined to be stateless in [1,2,11] and the proposed game-based definitions are tailored to such schemes. The restricted class of encryption protocols analyzed can thus not construct ordered channels, because the players need to remember tags numbering the messages to be able to preserve this ordering. The strongest notion of encryption from these works, namely QAE, is thus closest to constructing a SC. In fact, we show that QAE is *strictly* stronger than constructing a SC: a scheme satisfying QAE constructs a SC, however there are (stateless) schemes constructing a SC that would be considered insecure by the QAE game. These schemes are obtained in the same way as the ones showing that classical IND-CCA2 is unnecessarily strong: one starts with a scheme satisfying QAE and appends a bit to the ciphertext, resulting in a new scheme that still constructs a SC, but is not QAE-secure. Our proof shows that QAE may be seen as constructing a SC with a *fixed* simulator that is hard-coded in the game. A composable security definition only requires the existence of a simulator, and the separation between the two notions is obtained by considering schemes that can be proven secure using a different simulator than the one hard-coded in the game.

For QCCA2, we first propose an alternative game-based security notion that captures the same intuition, but which we consider more natural than the one suggested in [2]. In particular, its classical analogue is easily shown to be equivalent to a standard IND-CCA2 notion, whereas the notion put forth in [2], when cast to a classical definition, incurs a concrete constant factor loss when compared to IND-CCA2, and requires a complicated proof of this fact. We then show that for a restricted class of protocols (which includes all the ones for which a security proof is given in previous work), our new game-based notion indeed implies that the protocol constructs a NMCC. The same separation holds here as well: QCCA2 definitions are unnecessarily strong, and exclude protocols that naturally construct a NMCC. Note that in the classical case, the IND-RCCA game [15] that was developed to avoid the problems of IND-CCA2 has been shown to be exactly equivalent to constructing a classical non-malleable confidential channel in the case of large message spaces [17].

## 1.6 Alternative Security Notions

Common security definitions often capture properties of (encryption) schemes, e.g., let $M$ be a plaintext random variable, let $C$ be the corresponding ciphertext, $H$ is the entropy function, $M'$ is the received plaintext, and accept is the event that the message is accepted by the receiver, then

$$H(M|C) = H(M) \qquad \text{and} \qquad \Pr\left[M \neq M' \text{ and accept}\right] \leq \varepsilon \qquad (2)$$

are simple notions of confidentiality and authenticity, respectively. But depending on how schemes satisfying these equations are used—e.g., encrypt-then-authenticate or authenticate-then-encrypt—one gets drastically different results.[3] The equations in (2) may be regarded as crucial security properties of encryption schemes, but before schemes satisfying these may be safely used, one needs to consider the context and prove what is actually achieved by such constructs (in an operational sense).

The same applies to security definitions proposed for quantum key distribution. The accessible information[4] and the trace distance criterion[5] capture

---

[3] Encrypt-then-authenticate is always secure, but one can find examples of schemes satisfying (2) following the authenticate-then-encrypt paradigm that are insecure [9, 26,33].

[4] $I_{\text{acc}}(K; E) := \max_{\Gamma} I(K; \Gamma(E))$, where $\rho_{KE}$ is the joint state of the secret key $K$ and the adversary's information $E$, and $\Gamma(E)$ is the random variable resulting from measuring the $E$ system with a POVM $\Gamma$.

[5] $\|\rho_{KE} - \tau_K \otimes \rho_E\|$, where $\rho_{KE}$ is the joint state of the secret key $K$ and the adversary's information $E$ and $\tau_K$ is a fully mixed state.

different properties of a secret key. If a scheme satisfying the former is used with an insecure quantum channel, then the resulting key could be insecure, but if the channel only allows the adversary to measure and store classical information, then the key has information-theoretic security [25,38]. A scheme satisfying the latter notion—the trace distance criterion—constructs a secure key even when the quantum channel used is completely insecure [10,38,39]. Neither criterion is a satisfactory security definition on its own, they both require a further analysis to prove whether a protocol satisfying them does indeed distribute a secure key. But now that this has been done [10,38], the trace distance criterion has become a reference for what a quantum key distribution scheme must satisfy [40,42].

Previous work on computational security of quantum message transmission [1,2,11] as well as the new definition of QCCA2 proposed on this paper may be viewed in the same light. These game-based definitions capture properties of encryption schemes. But before a scheme satisfying these definitions may be safely used, one needs to analyze how the scheme is used and what is achieved by it. The constructive definitions introduced in this work and the reductions from the game-based definitions do exactly this. As a result of this, QAE or QCCA2 may be used as a benchmark for future schemes—though unlike the trace distance criterion, they are only sufficient criteria, not necessary ones.

## 1.7    Other Related Work

The desideratum expressed in Sect. 1.1 is the fruit of many different lines of research that go back to the late 90's. We give an incomplete overview of some of this work in this section.

Composable security was introduced independently by Pfitzmann and Waidner [3,4,34,35] and Canetti [12–14], who each defined their own framework, dubbed *reactive simulatability* and *universal composability* (UC), respectively. Unruh adapted UC to the quantum setting [43], whereas Maurer and Renner's AC applies to any model of computation, classical or quantum [30]. Quantum UC may however not be used for finite security without substantial modifications, since it hard-codes asymptotic security in the framework: machines are defined by sequences of operators $\left\{\mathcal{E}^{(k)}\right\}_k$, where $k \in \mathbb{N}$ is a security parameter, and distinguishability between networks of machines is then defined asymptotically in $k$.[6]

Concrete security [7] addresses the issues of reductions and parameters being hidden in $O$-notation by requiring them to be explicit. Theses works consider distinguishing advantages (or game winning probabilities) as a function of the allowed complexity or running time of the distinguisher, and aim at proving as

---

[6] The object about which ones makes a security statement is quite different in an asymptotic and a finite framework. In the former it is an infinite sequence of behaviors (e.g., a *machine* in UC), whereas in the later it is an element in such a sequence (the sequence itself is not necessarily well-defined). One thus composes different objects in the two models, and a composition theorem in one model does not immediately translate to a composition theorem in the other.

tight statements a possible. In such an approach, one would have to define a precise computational model. This, however, is avoided, meaning that any model in a certain class of meaningful models is considered equivalent. This unavoidably means that the security statements are asymptotic, at least with an unspecified linear or sublinear term. In contrast, the objects we consider, including distinguishers, are discrete systems and are directly composed as such, without need for considering a computational model for implementing the systems.

In the classical case, a model of discrete systems that may be used for finite security is *random systems* [27,29]. Generalizations to the quantum case have been proposed by Gutoski and Watrous [19,20]—and called *quantum strategies*—by Chiribella, D'Ariano and Perinotti [16]—called *quantum combs*—and by Hardy [21–23]—*operator tensors*. A model for discrete quantum systems that can additionally model time and superpositions of causal structures is the *causal boxes* framework [37].

None of the previous works on computational security of quantum message transmission satisfy any of the three criteria outlined in Sect. 1.1. These criteria are however standard by now for quantum key distribution [38,42]. In the classical case, they have also been used for computational security, e.g., [17,32].

## 1.8  Structure of This Paper

In Sect. 2 we introduce the elements needed from AC [28,30,31], and from the discrete system model with which we instantiate AC, namely quantum combs [16]. This allows us to define the notion of a finite construction of a resource (e.g., a secure channel) from another resource (e.g., an insecure channel and a key). In Sect. 3 we first define the channels and other resources needed in this work. Then we give protocols and prove that they construct various confidential and secure channels, as outlined in Sect. 1.4. Finally, in Sect. 4 we compare our security definitions to some game-based ones from the literature [2] and prove the results described in Sect. 1.5.

## 2  Abstract and Constructive Cryptography

In this section we give a brief overview of the Abstract and Constructive Cryptography (AC) framework, which is sufficient to understand the main claims of this work. A more extended introduction to AC is provided in the full version [5], which is needed to understand the proofs. We refer to [28,30,31,38] for further reading.

The AC framework views cryptography as a resource theory in which a protocol is a transformation between resources. Players may share certain resources— e.g., secret key, an authentic channel, a public-key infrastructure, common reference strings, etc.—and use these to construct other resources—e.g., an authentic channel, a secure channel, secret key, a bit commitment resource, an idealization of a multipartite function, etc. More abstractly, a protocol $\pi$ uses some resource R (the *assumed* resource) to construct some other resource S (the *constructed* resource) within $\varepsilon$, where $\varepsilon$ may be thought of as the error of the construction. We denote this

$$R \xrightarrow{\pi, \varepsilon} S. \tag{3}$$

A formal definition of Eq. (3) is provided in the full version [5].

Such a security statement is *composable*, because if $\pi_1$ constructs S from R within $\varepsilon_1$ and $\pi_2$ constructs T from S within $\varepsilon_2$, the composition of the two protocols, $\pi_2\pi_1$, constructs T from R within $\varepsilon_1 + \varepsilon_2$, i.e.,

$$\left. \begin{array}{c} R \xrightarrow{\pi_1, \varepsilon_1} S \\ S \xrightarrow{\pi_2, \varepsilon_2} T \end{array} \right\} \implies R \xrightarrow{\pi_2\pi_1, \varepsilon_1 + \varepsilon_2} T. \tag{4}$$

In this work, resources R, S or T are instantiated with a model of quantum interactive systems called *quantum strategies* [19,20] or *quantum combs* [16] in the literature. We use the term *interface* to denote the inputs and outputs accessible to a specific player, e.g., most resources considered in this work have 3 interfaces for Alice, Bob and Eve. In the following we often provide pseudo-code describing a resource. However, this always corresponds to a specific quantum strategy/comb. When multiple resources $R_1, \ldots, R_n$ are accessible to players, we write $[R_1, \ldots, R_n]$ for the new resource resulting from combining the individual $R_i$ in parallel. The mathematical meaning of this expression is explained in the full version [5].

We often write a protocol $\pi = (\pi_A, \pi_B)$ as a tuple, where each element $\pi_A$ corresponds to the operations of a specific player (e.g., $A$ for Alice), and only interacts at the corresponding interface of the shared resources. Formally, these are functions mapping a resource to another resource. Running several protocols then corresponds to the composition of the functions as in Eq. (4).

Finally, the error of a construction $\varepsilon$ that appears in Eq. (3) is a function mapping distinguishers to real numbers. In information-theoretic security, one has that $\varepsilon(D)$ is small for all distinguishers D. In computational security this might not be the case, since security does not hold against all adversaries, only efficient ones. More precisely, let D[R] be the random variable corresponding to the distinguisher's output when interacting with R. Then the functions

$$\Delta^D(R, S) := |\Pr[D[R] = 0] - \Pr[D[S] = 0]| \quad \text{and} \quad d^{\mathcal{D}}(R, S) := \sup_{D \in \mathcal{D}} \Delta^D(R, S)$$

are pseudo-metrics for any set of distinguishers $\mathcal{D}$. We define the error of a construction using one particular set $\mathcal{D}$, namely the set of distinguishers obtained from some distinguisher D by adding or removing converters between D and the measured resources.[7] Thus, for any distinguisher D, we define the class

$$\mathcal{B}(D) := \left\{ D' \middle| \exists \alpha \text{ such that } D\alpha = D' \text{ or } D'\alpha = D \right\}, \tag{5}$$

where $\Delta^{D\alpha}(R, S) = \Delta^D(\alpha R, \alpha S)$. Abusing somewhat notation, we often write D instead of $\mathcal{B}(D)$. In the following, $d^D(\cdot, \cdot)$ always refers to the pseudo-metric using the class of distinguishers generated from D as in Eq. (5).

---

[7] For more details on this, we refer to the full version [5].

We now formalize the notion of (secure) resource construction in the three party setting, with honest Alice and Bob and dishonest Eve.

**Definition 1 (Cryptographic security [30]).** *Let $\varepsilon$ be a function from distinguishers to real numbers. We say that a protocol $\pi_{AB} = (\pi_A, \pi_B)$ constructs a resource S from a resource R within $\varepsilon$ if there exists a converter $\mathrm{sim}_E$ (called a simulator) such that for all D,*

$$d^D(\pi_{AB}\mathsf{R}, \mathrm{sim}_E\mathsf{S}) \leq \varepsilon(D).$$

*If this holds, then we write*

$$\mathsf{R} \xrightarrow{\pi, \varepsilon} \mathsf{S}.$$

*When the resources R, S are clear from the context, we say that $\pi$ is $\varepsilon$-secure.*

$\pi_{AB}\mathsf{R}$ is often referred to as the *real* system, and $\mathrm{sim}_E\mathsf{S}$ as the *ideal* one. We emphasis that an ideal (or *constructed*) resource S will be used as the real (or *assumed*) resource in the next construction, so the terms *real* and *ideal* are relative. The details may be found in the full version [5].

# 3   Constructing Quantum Cryptographic Channels

In Sect. 3.1 we introduce the notations for Pauli operators and Bell basis. In Sects. 3.2 and 3.3 we formalize the resources used in our constructions. Then, starting from the insecure quantum channel IC, a shared secret key KEY and local pseudo random function PRF, we show how to construct (1) the ordered secure quantum channel OSC in Sect. 3.4 and (2) the Pauli-malleable confidential quantum channel PMCC in Sect. 3.5. A construction of the ordered secure quantum channel OSC from one which is secure but not ordered (SC) is also presented in the full version [5].

## 3.1   Quantum Operators and States

*Pauli Operators.* We write $P_k$ or $P_{x,z}$ to denote a Pauli operator on $m$ qubits, where $k = (x, z)$ are concatenation of two $m$-bits strings indicating in which qubit bit flips and phase flips occur.

$$P_k = P_{x,z} = \bigotimes_{i=1}^{m} P_{x_i z_i}, \qquad \text{where} \quad P_{ab} = \begin{cases} I & a = 0, b = 0, \\ X & a = 1, b = 0, \\ Z & a = 0, b = 1, \\ XZ & a = 1, b = 1. \end{cases}$$

Note that $P_k = P_k^\dagger$, therefore we simply write $P_k \rho P_k$ when applying a Pauli-operator $P_k$ on state $\rho$. To undo Pauli-operator $P_k$, we simply apply $P_k$ again, namely, $P_k P_k \rho P_k P_k = \rho$.

*Bell Basis.* We write $|\phi_0\rangle$ as the maximum entangled state of $2m$ qubits, $|\phi_0\rangle :=$ $\left(\frac{|00\rangle + |11\rangle}{\sqrt{2}}\right)^{\otimes m}$, and $|\phi_k\rangle := I^{\otimes m} \otimes P_k |\phi_0\rangle$ as the result of applying $P_k$ to half of the qubits. Then $\{|\phi_k\rangle\}_{k \in \{0,1\}^{2m}}$ forms the Bell basis for $2\,m$ qubits.

## 3.2  Key Resources

A (shared) secret key resource corresponds to a system that provides a key $k$ to the honest players, but nothing to the adversary.

**Definition 2 (Symmetric (Classical) Key KEY).** *The resource* KEY *is associated with a probability distribution* $P_K$ *for (classical) key space* $\mathcal{K}$*. A key* $k \in \mathcal{K}$ *is drawn according to* $P_K$ *and stored in the resource.*

– **Interface** $A$: *On input* getKey, $k$ *is output at interface* $A$.
– **Interface** $B$: *On input* getKey, $k$ *is output at interface* $B$.
– **Interface** $E$: *Inactive.*

In the computational setting, instead of sharing a long key, players often share a short key which is used as seed in a local key expansion scheme. On such key expansion scheme which we use in this work is a so-called *pseudo random function*. It is essentially a family of functions which looks random.

**Definition 3 (Pseudo Random Function PRF$^{r,\nu,\mu}$).** *The resource* PRF$^{r,\nu,\mu}$ *is associated to a family of functions* $\{f_k : \{0,1\}^\nu \rightarrow \{0,1\}^\mu | k \in \{0,1\}^r\}$ *and has an internal variable* seed *of length* $r$*. The functions in the family have input length* $\nu$ *and output length* $\mu$*. The resource is local to one party only. Let this party's interface be labeled* $X$.

– **Interface** $X$:
  • *On input* seed($s$), *set variable* seed *to* $s$.
  • *On input* input($x$), *output* $f_{\mathsf{seed}}(x)$ *at interface* $X$.

The above definition of a PRF does not contain any criterion for what it means to "look random". This is defined in a second step as distinguishability from a uniform random function.

**Definition 4 (Uniform Random Function URF$^{\nu,\mu}$).** *The resource* URF$^{\nu,\mu}$ *picks a function* $f$ *from all functions* $\{0,1\}^\nu \rightarrow \{0,1\}^\mu$ *uniformly at random.*

– **Interface** $A$: *On input* input($x$), *output* $f(x)$ *at interface* $A$.
– **Interface** $B$: *On input* input($x$), *output* $f(x)$ *at interface* $B$.
– **Interface** $E$: *Inactive.*

Let $\pi^{\mathsf{PRF}}$ be the trivial protocol which uses a (short) shared key (from a KEY resource) and plugs it as seed in a PRF resource, and let $\varepsilon^{\mathsf{PRF}}(\mathsf{D})$ be the advantage the distinguisher D has in distinguishing such a construction from a URF, i.e., for all D

$$d^{\mathsf{D}}(\pi^{\mathsf{PRF}}[\mathsf{KEY}^r, \mathsf{PRF}_A^{r,\nu,\mu}, \mathsf{PRF}_B^{r,\nu,\mu}], \mathsf{URF}^{\nu,\mu}) \leq \epsilon^{\mathsf{PRF}}(\mathsf{D}),$$

where $d^D(\cdot, \cdot)$ is the distinguisher pseudo-metric as defined in Sect. 2. In terms of AC construction, this means that

$$[\text{KEY}^r, \text{PRF}_A^{r,\nu,\mu}, \text{PRF}_B^{r,\nu,\mu}] \xrightarrow{\pi^{\text{PRF}}, \epsilon^{\text{PRF}}} \text{URF}^{\nu,\mu}. \tag{6}$$

Concrete constructions of PRFs proven secure in the presence of quantum adversaries may be found in [45].

### 3.3  Channel Resources

We consider three-party channels in this work: the sending party Alice has access to interface $A$, the receiving party Bob to interface $B$, and the adversary Eve to interface $E$. We model all our channels in the following way: upon an input at interface $A$, an output is generated at interface $E$, while upon an input at interface $E$, an output is generated at interface $B$. Moreover, we consider multi-message channels parameterized by $\ell$, that is, Alice and Eve can provide at most $\ell$ inputs at their respective interfaces. These inputs can be entangled with each other. We model quantum channels, therefore inputs and outputs to and from the channels' interfaces are quantum systems. The channels are also parameterized by $m$, the size of each message in qubits.

In the following we introduce the formal description of the channels considered in this work by specifying the behavior they assume upon inputs at their $A$ and $E$ interfaces. First, we consider the weakest possible channel, that is, the *insecure* one, which gives full control to the adversary Eve. Eve receives all the message that Alice inputs to the channel. Bob receives all the messages that Eve inputs to the channel.

### Definition 5 (Insecure Quantum Channel $\text{IC}^{\ell,m}$)

- **Interface $A$:** *On receiving an input system in some state $\rho$, perform an identity map and output the same system at interface $E$.*
- **Interface $E$:** *On receiving an input system in some state $\rho'$, perform an identity map and output the same system at interface $B$.*

*Interface $A$ and $E$ will receive at most $\ell$ inputs and ignore the rest. The quantum systems input at interface $A$ and $E$ and output at interface $B$ have length $m$ in qubits.*

Next, we enhance the insecure channel by providing some form of confidentiality on the states input by Alice. More precisely, we allow Eve to only get a notification that a new message has arrived in interface $A$, but still, Eve will retain the capability to *modify* each input $\rho^{A_i}$ (held in register $A_i$).

Here, one may consider different ways in which Eve is allowed to modify the messages. The first channel we consider grants Eve the power to insert fully mixed states on the channel, as well as performing Pauli operators (bit flips and phase flips) on Alice's message and decide when each message gets delivered. This is modeled by keeping registers $A_i$ for each new input at interface $A$, and allowing Eve to input indices specifying which register should be modified and output at interface $B$. Along with the index, Eve also inputs a string of length $2\,\mathrm{m}$, indicating on which qubits of the message to apply Pauli operators. If Eve wants a fully mixed state to be output at Bob's, she inputs $\perp$ at her interface and the channel generates the corresponding state.

**Definition 6 (Pauli-Malleable    Confidential    Quantum    Channel PMCC$^{\ell,m}$).** *The channel keeps registers $A_1, A_2, \ldots, A_\ell$, initially set to $\perp$.*

- **Interface $A$:** *Upon receiving the $i$-th input in some state $\rho$, this system is stored in register $A_i$, and* newMsg *is output at interface $E$.*
- **Interface $E$:**
  - *On input $(j, k) \in [l] \times \{0, 1\}^{2m}$, output system in state $P_k \rho^{A_j} P_k$ at interface $B$, where $\rho^{A_j}$ is the state of the system held in register $A_j$ and $P_k$ is the Pauli operator defined by the string $k$. If the tuple is invalid or $\rho^{A_j}$ is $\perp$, the input is considered as $\perp$. After the output, the state in register $A_j$ becomes $\perp$.*
  - *On input $\perp$, output a fully mixed stated $\frac{1}{2^m} I_{2^m}$ at interface $B$.*

*Interface $A$ and $E$ will receive at most $\ell$ inputs and ignore the rest. The quantum systems input at interface $A$ and output at interface $B$ always have length $m$ in qubits.*

Another type of confidential channel we consider is obtained by removing Eve's capability to modify Alice's messages, while giving her the ability to *inject* any system (instead of only systems in the fully mixed state).

**Definition 7 (Non-Malleable    Confidential    Quantum    Channel NMCC$^{\ell,m}$).** *The channel keeps registers $A_1, A_2, \ldots, A_\ell$, initially set to $\perp$.*

- **Interface $A$:** *Upon receiving the $i$-th input in some state $\rho$, this system is stored in register $A_i$, and* newMsg *is output at interface $E$.*
- **Interface $E$:**
  - *On receiving an input system in some state $\rho'$, perform an identity map and output the same system at interface $B$.*
  - *On input index $j \in [\ell]$, output the system in state $\rho^{A_j}$ held in register $A_j$ at interface $B$. After the output, the state of register $A_j$ becomes $\perp$.*

*Interface $A$ and $E$ will receive at most $\ell$ inputs and ignore the rest. The quantum systems input at interface $A$ and output at interface $B$ always have length $m$ in qubits.*

The next property to consider is authenticity: recall that in the quantum setting, authenticity implies confidentiality, thus it does not make sense to consider a "non-confidential authentic channel", since a state cannot be cloned to be given to both Bob and Eve. An authentic channel will automatically also be a confidential one [6]. Therefore, as a next channel we directly consider the *secure* one – by secure we mean both authentic and confidential. Eve only knows a new message has arrived but cannot read, modify, nor inject messages. Eve still has the power to block and reorder Alice's message.

**Definition 8 (Secure Quantum Channel $\mathsf{SC}^{\ell,m}$).** *The channel keeps registers $A_1, A_2, \ldots, A_\ell$, initially set to $\bot$.*

- **Interface A:** *Upon receiving the $i$-th input in some state $\rho$, this system is stored in register $A_i$, and* newMsg *is output at interface E.*
- **Interface E:** *On input index $j \in [\ell]$, output the system in state $\rho^{A_j}$ held in register $A_j$ at interface B. After the output, the state in register $A_j$ becomes $\bot$.*

*Interface A and E will receive at most $\ell$ inputs and ignore the rest. The quantum systems input at interface A and output at interface B always have length $m$ in qubits.*

Finally, we consider an even stronger version of the secure channel which preserves the *order* of the transmitted messages. In particular, the adversary now only retains the power to delete messages, but cannot change the order in which they are transmitted. This is enforced by replacing the capability to input indices by the ability of only inputting either send or skip.

**Definition 9 (Ordered Secure Quantum Channel $\mathsf{OSC}^{\ell,m}$).** *The channel keeps registers $A_1, A_2, \ldots, A_\ell$, initially set to $\bot$.*

- **Interface A:** *Upon receiving the $i$-th input in some state $\rho$, this system is stored in register $A_i$, and* newMsg *is output at interface E.*
- **Interface E:** *On $i$-th input* send *or* skip: *If the input is* send, *output the system in state $\rho^{A_i}$ held in register $A_i$ at interface B. If the input is* skip, *then output $\bot$ at interface B. After the output, the state in register $A_i$ becomes $\bot$.*

*Interface A and E will receive at most $\ell$ inputs and ignore the rest. The quantum systems input at interface A and output at interface B always have length $m$ in qubits.*

### 3.4 Constructing an Ordered Secure Quantum Channel

As shown in [36], there is a construction of one time secure quantum channel from one time insecure quantum channel resource and a uniform key resource within $\epsilon^{\text{q-auth}}$, i.e.

$$\left[ \mathsf{IC}^{1,n}, \mathsf{KEY}^\mu, \mathsf{QC}_A^{1,m,n}, \mathsf{QC}_B^{1,m,n} \right] \xrightarrow{\pi_{AB}^{\text{q-auth}}, \epsilon^{\text{q-auth}}} \left[ \mathsf{SC}^{1,m}, \mathsf{QC}_E^{2,m,n} \right].$$

Here, $\mathsf{IC}$, $\mathsf{SC}$ and $\mathsf{KEY}$ are channel and key resources, as defined above. $\mathsf{QC}_{A/B/E}$ denote a resource that does quantum computation for Alice, Bob or Eve, and allows them to perform encryption and decryption operations (we informally refer to such resources as *quantum computers* in the following). These appear in the construction statement since for finite security one makes all computational operations explicit—see the full version [5] for more details.

We denote the encoding and decoding CPTP maps in this construction by $\mathsf{enc}^{\text{q-auth}} : \mathcal{K} \times \mathcal{L}(\mathcal{H}_A) \to \mathcal{L}(\mathcal{H}_C)$ and $\mathsf{dec}^{\text{q-auth}} : \mathcal{K} \times \mathcal{L}(\mathcal{H}_{\tilde{C}}) \to \mathcal{L}(\mathcal{H}_B \oplus |\bot\rangle\langle\bot|)$. We also denote by $\mathcal{E}$ the CPTP map that always discards the state and replaces it with error state $|\bot\rangle\langle\bot|$. In this section, we build on top of these encoding and

$\boxed{\quad \pi_A \quad \pi_B \quad \mathsf{QC}_A \quad \mathsf{QC}_B \quad}$

1. $\pi_A$: Alice inputs a message $\rho^A$ and requests her computer to encrypt $\rho^A$.
2. $\mathsf{QC}_A$: On the $i$-th input $\rho^A$, the computer requests (through $\pi_A$) $k_i = \mathsf{input}(i)$ from URF, computes ciphertext $\sigma^C = \mathsf{enc}_{k_i}^{\text{q-auth}}(\rho^A)$, appends index $|i\rangle\langle i|$ on the ciphertext and outputs $\psi^{CT} = \sigma^C \otimes |i\rangle\langle i|^T$ to Alice.
3. $\pi_A$: Alice sends ciphertext $\psi^{CT}$ to Bob through insecure quantum channel IC.
4. $\pi_B$: Bob receives ciphertext $\tilde{\psi}^{\tilde{C}\tilde{T}}$ and requests his computer to decrypt $\tilde{\psi}^{\tilde{C}\tilde{T}}$.
5. $\mathsf{QC}_B$: On the $i$-th input $\tilde{\psi}^{\tilde{C}\tilde{T}}$, the computer takes first $n$ qubits as $\tilde{\sigma}^C$, measures last $\log \ell$ qubits and obtains the measurement result $\tilde{\imath}$. If $\tilde{\imath} = i$, the computer requests (through $\pi_B$) $k_i = \mathsf{input}(i)$ from resource URF, computes plaintext $\tilde{\rho} = \mathsf{dec}_{k_i}^{\text{q-auth}}(\tilde{\sigma})$. If it decrypts successfully, the computer outputs $\tilde{\rho}$ to Bob. If $\tilde{\imath} \neq i$ or it does not decrypt successfully, the computer outputs $\perp$ to Bob.
6. $\pi_B$: Bob outputs the decrypted message $\tilde{\rho}^B$.

**Fig. 1.** Converters and computing resources to construct $\mathsf{OSC}^{\ell,m}$ from $\mathsf{IC}^{\ell,n+\log \ell}$. $\mathsf{QC}_A^{\ell,m,n+\log \ell}$ and $\mathsf{QC}_B^{\ell,m,n+\log \ell}$ will be queried $\ell$ times. The plaintext has length $m$ and the ciphertext has length $n + \log \ell$. $\mathsf{URF}^{\log \ell,\mu}$ has input length $\log \ell$ and output length $\mu$.

decoding maps to construct a multi-message ordered secure quantum channel from a multi-message insecure quantum channel, with a shared uniform random function resource $\mathsf{URF}^{\log \ell,\mu}$. The real system is drawn in Fig. 2 and the components are described in Fig. 1.

**Theorem 1.** *Let* $\pi_{AB} = (\pi_A, \pi_B), \mathsf{QC}_A^{\ell,m,n+\log \ell}, \mathsf{QC}_B^{\ell,m,n+\log \ell}$ *and* $\mathsf{URF}^{\log \ell,\mu}$ *denote converters and computing resources as described in Fig. 1, corresponding to Alice and Bob both applying the following CPTP maps with increasing index* $i$:

$$\Lambda_i^{A \to CT}(\cdot) = \mathsf{enc}_{k_i}^{\text{q-auth}}(\cdot) \otimes |i\rangle\langle i|^T$$

$$\Lambda_i^{\tilde{C}\tilde{T} \to B}(\cdot) = \mathsf{dec}_{k_i}^{\text{q-auth}}\left( (I^{\tilde{C}} \otimes \langle i|^{\tilde{T}})(\cdot)(I^{\tilde{C}} \otimes |i\rangle^{\tilde{T}}) \right) + \mathcal{E}\left( \bar{P}_i^{\tilde{T}}(\cdot)\bar{P}_i^{\tilde{T}} \right),$$

*where* $\bar{P}_i = I - |i\rangle\langle i|$, *and* $k_i$ *is the output of* $\mathsf{URF}^{\log \ell,\mu}$ *with input* $i$. *Let* $\mathsf{QC}_E^{2\ell,m,n+\log \ell}$ *be the computing resource of Eve capable of doing* $\ell$ *encryption operations and* $\ell$ *decryption operations. Let* $\epsilon^{\text{q-auth}}$ *be the upper bound on the distinguishing advantage of the one time secure quantum channel construction. Then,*

$$\left[ \mathsf{IC}^{\ell,n+\log \ell}, \mathsf{URF}^{\log \ell,\mu}, \mathsf{QC}_A^{\ell,m,n+\log \ell}, \mathsf{QC}_B^{\ell,m,n+\log \ell} \right]$$

$$\xrightarrow{\pi_{AB}, \ell\epsilon^{\text{q-auth}}} \left[ \mathsf{OSC}^{\ell,m}, \mathsf{QC}_E^{2\ell,m,n+\log \ell} \right].$$

*Proof.* The proof of Theorem 1 appears in the full version [5].

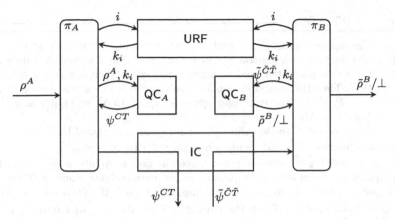

**Fig. 2.** The real system consisting of the shared resources $\mathsf{IC}^{\ell,n+\log\ell}$ and $\mathsf{URF}^{\log\ell,\mu}$, Alice and Bob's computing resources $\mathsf{QC}_A^{\ell,m,n+\log\ell}\mathsf{QC}_B^{\ell,m,n+\log\ell}$, and the protocol converters $\pi_A$ and $\pi_B$.

*Remark 1.* Theorem 1 is meaningful only if the protocol is also *correct*, i.e., if the distinguisher always puts back the same ciphertext on the insecure channel in the right order, then Bob always successfully decrypts. This follows trivially from the correctness of the underlying quantum authentication protocol, so we omit a formal discussion of it.

Suppose now that one has a PRF resource and a bound $\epsilon^{\mathsf{PRF}}$ satisfying Eq. (6), that is, indistinguishable from URF within $\epsilon^{\mathsf{PRF}}$, the following corollary follows trivially from the composition theorem.

**Corollary 1**

$$\left[\mathsf{IC}^{\ell,n+\log\ell}, \mathsf{KEY}^r, \mathsf{PRF}_A^{r,\log\ell,\mu}, \mathsf{PRF}_B^{r,\log\ell,\mu}, \mathsf{QC}_A^{\ell,m,n+\log\ell}, \mathsf{QC}_B^{\ell,m,n+\log\ell}\right]$$

$$\xrightarrow{\;\pi'_{AB},\epsilon\;} \left[\mathsf{OSC}^{\ell,m}, \mathsf{QC}_E^{2\ell,m,n+\log\ell}\right],$$

*where* $\pi'_{AB} = (\pi_{AB}, \pi^{\mathsf{PRF}})$, $\epsilon(\mathsf{D}) = \epsilon^{\mathsf{PRF}}(\mathsf{DC}) + \ell\epsilon^{\mathsf{q\text{-}auth}}$ *and* $\mathsf{C}$ *is the system including* $\pi_{AB}, \mathsf{IC}^{\ell,n+\log\ell}, \mathsf{QC}_A^{\ell,m,n+\log\ell}, \mathsf{QC}_B^{\ell,m,n+\log\ell}$.

### 3.5 Constructing a Pauli-Malleable Confidential Quantum Channel

In this section, we construct a Pauli-malleable confidential quantum channel $\mathsf{PMCC}^{\ell,m}$ from an insecure quantum channel $\mathsf{IC}^{\ell,m+\nu}$. In the Pauli-malleable confidential channel, the adversary can only get a notification of a new message arriving but has no access to the message. The adversary has the ability to block, reorder and modify the message via Pauli operators (bit flip and phase flip), as well as ask the channel to output a fully mixed state at Bob's interface, as defined in Definition 6.

Now we present the protocol in the multi-message case, described in Fig. 3. In the protocol, Alice's computer will generate a new random string $x$ of length $\nu$

---

$\pi_A$    $\pi_B$    $QC_A$    $QC_B$

1. $\pi_A$: Alice inputs a message $\rho^{A_i}$ and requests her computer to encrypt it.
2. $QC_A$: On input $\rho^{A_i}$, it generates a new random string $x$ of length $\nu$ different from previously generated random strings, requests (through $\pi_A$) $k = \text{input}(x)$ from URF. Then the computer applies Pauli operator $P_k$ on the state $\rho^{A_i}$ and gets $\sigma^C = P_k \rho^{A_i} P_k$. The computer appends $|x\rangle\langle x|^T$ to $\sigma^C$ and outputs $\psi^{CT} = \sigma^C \otimes |x\rangle\langle x|^T$ to Alice.
3. $\pi_A$: Alice sends $\psi^{CT}$ to Bob through secure quantum channel $\text{IC}^{\ell,m+\nu}$.
4. $\pi_B$: Bob receives $\tilde{\psi}^{\tilde{C}\tilde{T}}$ and requests his computer to decrypt it.
5. $QC_B$: On input $\tilde{\psi}^{\tilde{C}\tilde{T}}$, the computer takes the first $m$ qubits as $\tilde{\sigma}^{\tilde{C}}$. Then the computer measures the last $\nu$ qubits and get measurement result $\tilde{x}$. Then the computer requests (through $\pi_B$) $\tilde{k} = \text{input}(\tilde{x})$ from URF. Then the computer applies Pauli operator $P_{\tilde{k}}$ on the state $\tilde{\sigma}^{\tilde{C}}$. Then the computer outputs $\tilde{\rho}^B = P_{\tilde{k}} \tilde{\sigma} P_{\tilde{k}}$ to Bob.
6. $\pi_B$: Bob outputs the decrypted message $\tilde{\rho}^B$.

**Fig. 3.** Converters and computer resources to construct $\text{PMCC}^{\ell,m}$ from $\text{IC}^{\ell,m+\nu}$. $QC_A^{\ell,m,m+\nu}$ and $QC_B^{\ell,m,m+\nu}$ will be queried $\ell$ times. The plaintext has length $m$ and ciphertext has length $m + \nu$. $\text{URF}^{\nu,2m}$ has input length $\nu$ and output length $2m$.

for each message different from previous random strings and input it to $\text{URF}^{\nu,2m}$, a key $k$ is returned by $\text{URF}^{\nu,2m}$, the Pauli-operator $P_k$ is applied to the message and $x$ is appended to the ciphertext. Bob's computer will do the measurement on the last $\nu$ qubits to get $\tilde{x}$, which is input to $\text{URF}^{\nu,2m}$, from which $\tilde{k}$ is obtained and finally the Pauli operator $P_{\tilde{k}}$ is applied to the ciphertext. The real system is drawn in Fig. 4.

**Theorem 2.** *Let* $\pi_{AB} = (\pi_A, \pi_B)$, $QC_A^{\ell,m,m+\nu}$ *and* $QC_B^{\ell,m,m+\nu}$ *denote converters and computing resources, described in Fig. 3, corresponding to Alice and Bob applying the following CPTP maps,*

$$\Lambda^{A_i \to CT}(\cdot) = \frac{1}{2^\nu} \sum_x P_{k_x}(\cdot)P_{k_x} \otimes |x\rangle\langle x|^T$$

$$\Lambda^{\tilde{C}\tilde{T} \to B}(\cdot) = \sum_x (P_{k_x} \otimes \langle x|^{\tilde{T}})(\cdot)(P_{k_x} \otimes |x\rangle^{\tilde{T}}),$$

*where* $k_x$ *is the output of* $\text{URF}^{\nu,2m}$ *with input* $x$. *Let* $QC_E^{2\ell,m,m+\nu}$ *be the computing resource of Eve capable of doing* $\ell$ *encryption operations and* $\ell$ *decryption operations. Then* $\pi_{AB}$ *constructs a Pauli-malleable confidential quantum channel* $\text{PMCC}^{\ell,m}$ *from an insecure quantum channel resource* $\text{IC}^{\ell,m+\nu}$, *a shared uniform random function resource* $\text{URF}^{\nu,2m}$ *within* $\ell^2 \cdot 2^{-\nu}$, *i.e.,*

$$\left[ \text{IC}^{\ell,m+\nu}, \text{URF}^{\nu,2m}, QC_A^{\ell,m,m+\nu}, QC_B^{\ell,m,m+\nu} \right]$$

$$\xrightarrow{\pi_{AB}, \ell^2 2^{-\nu}} \left[ \text{PMCC}^{\ell,m}, QC_E^{2\ell,m,m+\nu} \right].$$

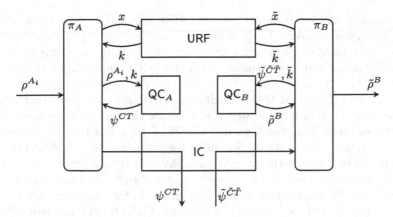

**Fig. 4.** The real system consisting of shared resources $IC^{\ell,m+\nu}$ and $URF^{\nu,2m}$, Alice and Bob's computing resources $QC_A^{\ell,m,m+\nu}$ and $QC_B^{\ell,m,m+\nu}$, and the protocol converters $\pi_A$ and $\pi_B$.

*Proof.* The proof of Theorem 2 appears in the full version [5].

*Remark 2.* The protocol given in Theorem 2 also has to satisfy correctness, i.e., when the distinguisher always puts back the same state Bob should decrypt correctly. One can easily see that this holds, since in the real world, the state will be flipped on Alice's side and be flipped back on Bob side, thus the distinguisher will get the same state back at interface $B$.

Suppose now that one has a PRF resource and a bound $\epsilon^{PRF}$ satisfying Eq. (6), that is, indistinguishable from URF within $\epsilon^{PRF}$, the following corollary follows trivially from the composition theorem.

**Corollary 2**

$$\left[IC^{\ell,m+\nu}, KEY^r, PRF^{r,\nu,2m}, PRF^{r,\nu,2m}, QC_A^{\ell,m,m+\nu}, QC_B^{\ell,m,m+\nu}\right]$$

$$\xrightarrow{\pi'_{AB},\epsilon} \left[PMCC^{\ell,m}, QC_E^{2\ell,m,m+\nu}\right].$$

where $\pi'_{AB} = (\pi_{AB}, \pi^{PRF})$, $\epsilon(D) = \epsilon^{PRF}(DC) + \ell^2 2^{-\nu}$ and C *is the system including* $\pi_{AB}, IC^{\ell,m+\nu}, QC_A^{\ell,m,m+\nu}, QC_B^{\ell,m,m+\nu}$.

## 4 Relations to Game-Based Security Definitions

In this section we explore the relations between our constructive security definitions and two game based security definitions for (specific protocols making use of) symmetric quantum encryption schemes, both introduced in [2]. The two notions we consider are those of *quantum ciphertexts indistinguishability under adaptive chosen-ciphertext attack* (AGM-QCCA2) and *quantum authenticated encryption* (QAE). Both definitions are inspired by classical security notions which intrinsically require the ability to copy data, which in [2] were successfully translated into quantum analogue by circumventing the no-cloning theorem.

We will first show that QAE security exactly implies the constructive cryptography security notion of *constructing a secure channel from an insecure one and a shared secret key*, which we call CC-QSEC (but is actually stronger, and thus we also show a separation). Secondly, we will relate the AGM-QCCA2 security definition to the constructive cryptography security notion of *constructing a confidential channel from an insecure one and a shared secret key*, which we call CC-QCNF, but the implication will be less direct. In fact, we introduce two new (intermediate) game-based security definitions, RRC-QCCA2 and RRO-QCCA2, and show that:

1. The classical versions of AGM-QCCA2 and RRC-QCCA2 are asymptotically equivalent;
2. For a restricted class of schemes, RRC-QCCA2 implies RRO-QCCA2 (they are actually equivalent);
3. RRO-QCCA2 implies CC-QCNF (but is actually stronger).

We leave open the question whether it is possible to generalize (2.) to general schemes. Throughout this section we will assume that both the plaintext and the ciphertext spaces comprise elements of the same length, an thus ignore the corresponding superscripts for channels and quantum computers.

## 4.1  Background and Notation

In [6], a characterization of any *symmetric quantum encryption schemes* (SQES) was given, which states that encryption works by attaching some (possibly) key-dependent auxiliary state, and applying a unitary operator, and decryption undoes the unitary, and then checks whether the support of the state in the auxiliary register has changed. Thus, as pointed out in [2], for key-generation function Gen (inducing a probability distribution over some key-space $\mathcal{K}$), encryption function Enc, and decryption function Dec, we can characterize a SQES $\mathfrak{S} := (\text{Gen}, \text{Enc}, \text{Dec})$ as follows.

**Lemma 1** ([2, Corollary 1]). *Let $\mathfrak{S} = (\text{Gen}, \text{Enc}, \text{Dec})$ be a SQES. Then for every $k \in \mathcal{K}$ there exists a probability distribution $p_k : \mathcal{R} \to [0,1]$ and a family of quantum states $\{|\psi_{k,r}\rangle^T\}_{r \in \mathcal{R}}$, with $\Pi_{k,r}^T := |\psi_{k,r}\rangle\langle\psi_{k,r}|^T$, such that:*

- $\text{Enc}_k(\varrho^M) := V_k \left( \varrho^M \otimes \Pi_{k,r}^T \right) V_k^\dagger$, *where $r$ is sampled according to $p_k$;*
- $\text{Dec}_k(\sigma^C) := \text{Tr}_T \left( P_{\omega_k}^T (V_k^\dagger \sigma^C V_k) P_{\omega_k}^T \right) + \hat{D}_k \left( \bar{P}_{\omega_k}^T (V_k^\dagger \sigma^C V_k) \bar{P}_{\omega_k}^T \right);$

*where $P_{\omega_k}^T$ and $\bar{P}_{\omega_k}^T$ are the orthogonal projectors onto the support of*

$$\omega_k^T := \sum_{r \in \mathcal{R}} p_k(r) \cdot \Pi_{k,r}^T = \sum_{r \in \mathcal{R}} p_k(r) \cdot |\psi_{k,r}\rangle\langle\psi_{k,r}|^T.$$

For a SQES $\mathfrak{S}$, we define a security notion XXX in terms of the advantage $\mathbf{Adv}_{\mathfrak{S},D}^{XXX}$ of a distinguisher D in solving some (usually distinction) problem involving $\mathfrak{S}$. In the asymptotic setting, security of $\mathfrak{S}$ according to notion XXX should be interpreted as $\mathbf{Adv}_{\mathfrak{S},D}^{XXX}$ being negligible for every D from some class $\mathbb{D}$ of distinguishers (usually, efficient distinguishers). Following the finite security approach, here we are just interested in relating advantages of different notions, making use of black-box reductions. Therefore, for a second notion YYY, we say that XXX *(security) implies* YYY *(security)* if and only if $\mathbf{Adv}_{\mathfrak{S},D}^{YYY} \leq c \cdot \mathbf{Adv}_{\mathfrak{S},DC}^{XXX}$, for some $c \geq 1$, where C denotes the black-box reduction that uses the distinguisher D for YYY to make a new distinguisher DC for XXX.

When describing experiments involving interaction between a distinguisher[8] D and a game system G, we use pseudo-code from G's perspective, that is, the **return** statement indicates what is output by the latter. Note that this implies that for distinction problems we always make the game system output the bit output by the distinguisher. In this case we use the expression D[G] to denote the bit output by D after interacting with G. On the other hand, if the output bit is decided by G (as is the case for the AGM-QCCA2 definition, which is *not* a distinction problem), we use the expression G[D]. Moreover, we use both expressions not only for the returned value, but also for denoting the whole random experiments. When specifying that a distinguisher D has access to a list of oracles, e.g. $O_1(\cdot)$ and $O_2(\cdot)$, we write $x \leftarrow D^{O_1(\cdot), O_2(\cdot)}$, where the variable $x$ holds the value output by D after the interaction with the oracles. We denote the application of a two-outcome projective measurement, e.g. $\{P_{\omega_k}^T, \mathbb{1} - P_{\omega_k}^T\}$, as $\{P_{\omega_k}^T, \mathbb{1} - P_{\omega_k}^T\} \Rightarrow b$, where $b \in \{0,1\}$ is the result of the measurement (we associate 0 to the the first outcome and 1 to the second). The state $|\phi_0\rangle$ is the EPR pair (one of the Bell state), to which we associate the two-outcome projective measurement $\{\Pi_+, \mathbb{1} - \Pi_+\}$. Furthermore, by $XY \leftarrow |\phi_0\rangle$ we mean that the EPR pair has been prepared on registers $XY$, and we use $\tau^X$ as a shorthand for the reduced state in register $X$, that is, half of a maximally-entangled state.

## 4.2    Relating QAE and CC-QSEC

In this section we first present the quantum authenticated encryption security definition introduced in [2], and then show that it directly implies our constructive security notion CC-QSEC of constructing a secure channel from an insecure one and a shared secret key.

**QAE Security Definition ([2]).** We begin by restating what it means for a SQES $\mathfrak{S}$ to be secure in the QAE sense according to [2]. On a high level, a distinguisher D must not be able to distinguish between two scenarios: in the first (the real one), it has access to regular encryption and decryption oracles, whereas in the second (the ideal one), it has access to an encryption oracle which replaces its queried plaintexts by random ones (half of a maximally-entangled

---

[8] We understand the distinguisher D as stateful, which can therefore be invoked multiple times (without making explicit the various updated states).

state), and a decryption oracle that normally decrypts ciphertext not returned by the encryption oracle, but answers with the originally queried plaintexts otherwise (thus not really performing correct decryption). Note that this security notion, as shown in [2], when phrased classically is equivalent to the canonical notion of authenticated encryption (dubbed IND-CCA3 by Shrimpton in [41]). The only difference with the latter, is that the decryption oracle returns $\perp$ when queried on ciphertexts previously returned by the encryption oracle. But crucially, this detail is what would not make it possible to adapt IND-CCA3 into a quantum definition: returning $\perp$ would require the game to *copy data* (store the ciphertexts returned by the encryption oracle, and then compare them to each query to the decryption oracle), which is not allowed in general in the quantum world. Nevertheless, the formulation of QAE introduced in [2] works quantumly because, intuitively, *"it is possible to compare random states generated as half of a maximally-entangled state"*: the trick consists of first ignoring (but storing) each plaintext submitted by the adversary to the encryption oracle, and then, for each plaintext, prepare an EPR pair $|\phi_0\rangle$, encrypt just half of it, and store the other half (as well as the involved randomness) together with the original plaintext submitted by the distinguisher; then the decryption oracle normally decrypts each ciphertext, and subsequently applies a projective measurement on the support of $|\phi_0\rangle$ to the obtained plaintext against each stored half, and the associated original plaintext can thus be easily retrieved. We now restate the definition from [2] (Definition 10 therein), adapted to our notation, and in the concrete setting (as opposed to the asymptotic one).

**Definition 10 (QAE Security [2]).** *For SQES* $\mathfrak{S} := (\mathsf{Gen}, \mathsf{Enc}, \mathsf{Dec})$ *(implicit in all defined systems) we define the* QAE-*advantage of* $\mathfrak{S}$ *for distinguisher* $\mathsf{D}$ *as*

$$\mathbf{Adv}^{\mathsf{qae}}_{\mathfrak{S},\mathsf{D}} := \Pr\left[\mathsf{D}[\mathsf{G}^{\mathsf{qae\text{-}real}}] = 1\right] - \Pr\left[\mathsf{D}[\mathsf{G}^{\mathsf{qae\text{-}ideal}}] = 1\right],$$

*where the interactions of* $\mathsf{D}$ *with game systems* $\mathsf{G}^{\mathsf{qae\text{-}real}}$ *and* $\mathsf{G}^{\mathsf{qae\text{-}ideal}}$ *are defined in Fig. 5.*

**QAE Implies QSEC.** Here we denote by $\mathsf{G}^{\mathsf{qae\text{-}real},\ell}$ and $\mathsf{G}^{\mathsf{qae\text{-}ideal},\ell}$ the games $\mathsf{G}^{\mathsf{qae\text{-}real}}$ and $\mathsf{G}^{\mathsf{qae\text{-}ideal}}$ where the distinguisher is allowed to make at most $\ell$ queries to each oracle (and analogously for $\mathbf{Adv}^{\mathsf{qae},\ell}_{\mathfrak{S},\mathsf{D}}$).

**Theorem 3.** *Let* $\mathfrak{S} := (\mathsf{Gen}, \mathsf{Enc}, \mathsf{Dec})$ *be a SQES (implicit in all defined systems). Then with protocol* $\pi^{\mathsf{q\text{-}enc}}_{AB} = (\pi^{\mathsf{q\text{-}enc}}_A, \pi^{\mathsf{q\text{-}enc}}_B)$ *making use of quantum computers* $\mathsf{QC}^\ell_A$ *and* $\mathsf{QC}^\ell_B$ *as defined in Fig. 6, simulator* $\mathsf{sim}^{\mathsf{qae}}_E$ *making use of quantum computer* $\mathsf{QC}^\ell_E$ *as defined in Fig. 7 (until the dashed line), and (trivial) reduction system* $\mathsf{C}$ *as specified in the proof, for any distinguisher* $\mathsf{D}$ *we have*

$$\Delta^{\mathsf{D}}(\pi^{\mathsf{q\text{-}enc}}_{AB}[\mathsf{KEY}, \mathsf{IC}^\ell, \mathsf{QC}^\ell_A, \mathsf{QC}^\ell_B], \mathsf{sim}^{\mathsf{qae}}_E[\mathsf{SC}^\ell, \mathsf{QC}^\ell_E]) \leq \mathbf{Adv}^{\mathsf{qae},\ell}_{\mathfrak{S},\mathsf{DC}}.$$

*Proof.* The proof of Theorem 3 appears in the full version [5].

---

Experiments $D[G^{\text{qae-real}}]$ and $D[G^{\text{qae-ideal}}]$ for SQES $\mathfrak{G} := (\text{Gen}, \text{Enc}, \text{Dec})$

| | |
|---|---|
| | $k \leftarrow \text{Gen}()$ |
| | $\mathcal{M} \leftarrow \varnothing$ |
| | $\text{return } D^{\text{Enc}(\cdot), \text{Dec}(\cdot)}$ |
| | **oracle Enc**$(\varrho^M)$: |
| | $\quad \hat{r} \xleftarrow{p_k} \mathcal{R}$ |
| | $\quad \hat{M}\tilde{M} \leftarrow |\phi_0\rangle$ |
| $k \leftarrow \text{Gen}()$ | $\quad \hat{\sigma}^{\hat{C}} \leftarrow V_k(\varrho^{\hat{M}} \otimes \Pi^T_{k,\hat{r}})V_k^\dagger \qquad \triangleright \textit{Ignore } \varrho^M$ |
| $\text{return } D^{\text{Enc}_k(\cdot), \text{Dec}_k(\cdot)}$ | $\quad \mathcal{M} \leftarrow \mathcal{M} \cup \{(\hat{r}, \tilde{M}, M)\}$ |
| | $\quad \text{return } \hat{\sigma}^{\hat{C}}$ |
| | **oracle Dec**$(\sigma^C)$: |
| | $\quad \hat{M}T \leftarrow V_k^\dagger \sigma^C V_k$ |
| | $\quad \textbf{for each } (\hat{r}, \tilde{M}, M) \in \mathcal{M} \textbf{ do}$ |
| | $\quad\quad \textbf{if } \{\Pi_{k,\hat{r}}, \mathbb{1} - \Pi_{k,\hat{r}}\}(\omega^T) \Rightarrow 0 \textbf{ then}$ |
| | $\quad\quad\quad \textbf{if } \{\Pi_+, \mathbb{1} - \Pi_+\}(\varphi^{\hat{M}\tilde{M}}) \Rightarrow 0 \textbf{ then}$ |
| | $\quad\quad\quad\quad \text{return } \varrho^M$ |
| | $\quad \text{return } |\bot\rangle\langle\bot|$ |

**Fig. 5.** QAE security games $G^{\text{qae-real}}$ (**left**) and $G^{\text{qae-ideal}}$ (**right**).

**Corollary 3.** *With* $\varepsilon(D) := \sup_{D' \in \mathcal{B}(D)} \mathbf{Adv}^{\text{qae},\ell}_{\mathfrak{G},D'}$, *we have*

$$\left[ \text{KEY}, \text{IC}^\ell, \text{QC}^\ell_A, \text{QC}^\ell_B \right] \xrightarrow{\pi^{\text{q-enc}}_{AB}, \varepsilon} \left[ \text{SC}^\ell, \text{QC}^\ell_E \right],$$

*where the class* $\mathcal{B}(D)$ *is defined in Eq. (5).*

**QAE is Stronger than QSEC.** We remark that even though QAE implies CC-QSEC, the converse is not true. In particular, we find that QAE is an (unnecessarily) stronger notion than CC-QSEC. We can in fact show that there are SQESs that satisfy CC-QSEC, but not QAE. Following [15], in order to show this fact it suffices to take any SQES $\mathfrak{G}$ which is QAE secure, and slightly modify it

---

$\pi^{\text{q-enc}}_A$ QC$^\ell_A$

1. QC$^\ell_A$ request the key $k$ from KEY and stores it in its memory.
2. For the $i$-th input $\varrho^M$ at the outside interface, QC$^\ell_A$ samples randomness $r \xleftarrow{p_k} \mathcal{R}$, computes the ciphertext $\sigma^C \leftarrow V_k(\varrho^M \otimes \Pi^T_{k,r})V_k^\dagger$, and outputs $\sigma^C$ at the inside interface to IC$^\ell$.

---

$\pi^{\text{q-enc}}_B$ QC$^\ell_B$

1. QC$^\ell_B$ request the key $k$ from KEY and stores it in its memory.
2. For the $i$-th input $\sigma^C$ at the inside interface from IC$^\ell$, QC$^\ell_B$ computes $MT \leftarrow V_k\sigma^C V_k^\dagger$, and if $\{P^T_{\omega_k}, \mathbb{1} - P^T_{\omega_k}\}(\omega^T) \Rightarrow 0$, outputs the plaintext message $\varrho^M$ at the outside interface.

**Fig. 6.** Encryption and decryption protocols.

---

$\text{sim}_E^{\text{qae},\ell} \text{QC}_E^{\ell} \; / \; \text{sim}_E^{\text{qcca2},\ell} \text{QC}_E^{\ell}$

1. $\text{QC}_E^{\ell}$ generates a key $k \leftarrow \text{Gen}()$, stores it in its memory, and sets $\mathcal{M} \leftarrow \varnothing$.
2. $\text{QC}_E^{\ell}$ performs the following two tasks in parallel:
   (a) For the $i$-th input newMsg at the inside interface from $\text{SC}^{\ell}$, $\text{QC}_E^{\ell}$ samples randomness $\hat{r} \xleftarrow{p_k} \mathcal{R}$, prepares $\hat{M}\tilde{M} \leftarrow |\phi_0\rangle$, computes $\sigma^C \leftarrow V_k(\hat{\varrho}^{\hat{M}} \otimes \Pi_{k,\hat{r}}^T)V_k^{\dagger}$, and outputs the ciphertext $\sigma^C$ at the outside interface. Finally, it performs the update $\mathcal{M} \leftarrow \mathcal{M} \cup \{(\hat{r}, \tilde{M}, i)\}$.
   (b) For the $i$-th input $\sigma^C$ at the outside interface, $\text{QC}_E^{\ell}$ computes $\hat{M}T \leftarrow V_k^{\dagger}\sigma^C V_k$. Then for each $(\hat{r}, \tilde{M}, j) \in \mathcal{M}$, it computes $\{\Pi_{k,\hat{r}}, \mathbb{1} - \Pi_{k,\hat{r}}\}(\omega^T)$; if the result of the measurement is 0, then it computes $\{\Pi_+, \mathbb{1} - \Pi_+\}(\varphi^{\hat{M}\tilde{M}})$; if the result of the measurement is again 0, then it outputs the index $j$ at the inside interface to $\text{SC}^{\ell}$.

   - - - - - - - - - - - - - - - - - - - - - - - - - - - - - - - - - - -

   Otherwise, it computes $\{P_{\omega_k}^T, \mathbb{1} - P_{\omega_k}^T\}(\omega^T)$, and if the result of the measurement is 0, then it outputs the message $\hat{\varrho}^{\hat{M}}$ at the inside interface to $\text{SC}^{\ell}$.

---

**Fig. 7.** QAE (until the dashed line) and QCCA2 (until the end) simulators.

into a new SQES $\mathfrak{S}'$ so that a classical 0-bit is appended to every encryption, which is then ignored upon decryption. Now an adversary can flip the bit of a ciphertext that it got from the encryption oracle, and then query the decryption oracle on the new ciphertext: in the real setting it will get back the original message, while in the ideal setting it will get back $|\bot\rangle\langle\bot|$, and can thus perfectly distinguish between the two, hence $\mathfrak{S}'$ cannot be QAE secure. On the other hand, $\mathfrak{S}'$ is still CC-QSEC secure because it can still be used to achieve the construction of a secure channel from an insecure one and a shared secret key. This is possible by using a simulator which works essentially as $\text{sim}_E^{\text{qae},\ell}\text{QC}_E^{\ell}$ from Fig. 7, but which ignores the bit.

## 4.3   Relating QCCA2 and CC-QCNF

The goal of this section is to present and relate several QCCA2 security definitions. We begin by introducing a new definition, RRC-QCCA2 (where RRC stands for *"real-or-random challenge"*), which is similar to AGM-QCCA2. Both notions define a challenge phase, and thus we introduce a third variant, RRO-QCCA2 (where RRO stands for *"real-or-random oracles"*), in which there is no real-or-random challenge, but rather access to real-or-random oracles. Crucially, the latter is identical to QAE as introduced by [2], up to a small detail: *upon decryption, if the ciphertext was not generated by the encryption oracle, instead of returning* $|\bot\rangle\langle\bot|$, *return the decrypted plaintext*. Finally, we show that for a restricted class of SQESs, RRC-QCCA2 implies RRO-QCCA2, and for any SQESs, RRO-QCCA2 implies CC-QCNF.

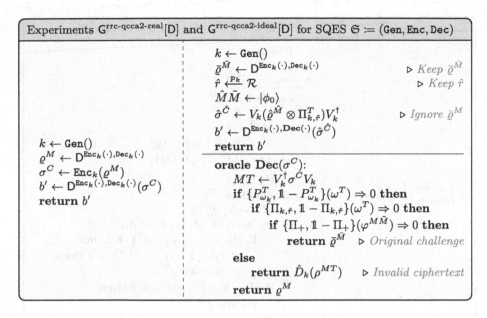

**Fig. 8.** RRC-QCCA2 games $\mathsf{G}^{\mathrm{rrc\text{-}qcca2\text{-}real}}$ (**left**) and $\mathsf{G}^{\mathrm{rrc\text{-}qcca2\text{-}ideal}}$ (**right**).

**RRC-QCCA2 Security Definition.** We now introduce an alternative game-based security definition that seems more natural than AGM-QCCA2. This notion is defined in terms of a distinction problem (as opposed to AGM-QCCA2), and essentially it is analogous to the test setting of the latter, but where the decryption oracle provided to the distinguisher behaves differently: after the real-or-random challenge phase, upon querying the challenge ciphertext, it will respond with the plaintext originally submitted by the distinguisher, in both the real and ideal settings. Note that this is possible in the ideal setting, because we make use of the same trick as in the fake setting of AGM-QCCA2, but we do not just set a flag whenever we detect that the adversary is cheating, but rather return the original message that it submitted as challenge. Since a similar behavior is implemented in the real setting, the adversary must really be able to distinguish between ciphertexts in order to win.

**Definition 11 (RRC-QCCA2 Security).** *For SQES* $\mathfrak{S} := (\mathsf{Gen}, \mathsf{Enc}, \mathsf{Dec})$ *(implicit in all defined systems) we define the* RRC-QCCA2-*advantage of* $\mathfrak{S}$ *for distinguisher* D *as*

$$\mathbf{Adv}^{\mathrm{rrc\text{-}qcca2}}_{\mathfrak{S}, \mathsf{D}} := \Pr\left[\mathsf{D}[\mathsf{G}^{\mathrm{rrc\text{-}qcca2\text{-}real}}] = 1\right] - \Pr\left[\mathsf{D}[\mathsf{G}^{\mathrm{rrc\text{-}qcca2\text{-}ideal}}] = 1\right],$$

*where the interactions of* D *with game systems* $\mathsf{G}^{\mathrm{rrc\text{-}qcca2\text{-}real}}$ *and* $\mathsf{G}^{\mathrm{rrc\text{-}qcca2\text{-}ideal}}$ *are defined in Fig. 8.*

---

**Experiments** $D[G^{\text{rro-qcca2-real}}]$ **and** $D[G^{\text{rro-qcca2-ideal}}]$ **for SQES** $\mathfrak{S} := (\text{Gen}, \text{Enc}, \text{Dec})$

| | |
|---|---|
| $k \leftarrow \text{Gen}()$<br>$\textbf{return } D^{\text{Enc}_k(\cdot), \text{Dec}_k(\cdot)}$ | $k \leftarrow \text{Gen}()$<br>$\mathcal{M} \leftarrow \varnothing$<br>$\textbf{return } D^{\text{Enc}(\cdot), \text{Dec}(\cdot)}$ |

$$
\begin{aligned}
&\textbf{oracle } \text{Enc}(\varrho^M): \\
&\quad \hat{r} \xleftarrow{p_k} \mathcal{R} \\
&\quad \hat{M}\tilde{M} \leftarrow |\phi_0\rangle \\
&\quad \hat{\sigma}^{\hat{C}} \leftarrow V_k(\hat{\varrho}^{\hat{M}} \otimes \Pi^T_{k,\hat{r}})V_k^\dagger \qquad \triangleright \textit{Ignore } \varrho^M \\
&\quad \mathcal{M} \leftarrow \mathcal{M} \cup \{(\hat{r}, \tilde{M}, M)\} \\
&\quad \textbf{return } \hat{\sigma}^{\hat{C}}
\end{aligned}
$$

$$
\begin{aligned}
&\textbf{oracle } \text{Dec}(\sigma^C): \\
&\quad \hat{M}T \leftarrow V_k^\dagger \sigma^C V_k \\
&\quad \textbf{for each } (\hat{r}, \tilde{M}, M) \in \mathcal{M} \textbf{ do} \\
&\quad\quad \textbf{if } \{\Pi_{k,\hat{r}}, \mathbb{1} - \Pi_{k,\hat{r}}\}(\omega^T) \Rightarrow 0 \textbf{ then} \\
&\quad\quad\quad \textbf{if } \{\Pi_+, \mathbb{1} - \Pi_+\}(\varphi^{\hat{M}\tilde{M}}) \Rightarrow 0 \textbf{ then} \\
&\quad\quad\quad\quad \textbf{return } \varrho^M \\
&\quad\quad\quad \textbf{if } \{P^T_{\omega_k}, \mathbb{1} - P^T_{\omega_k}\}(\omega^T) \Rightarrow 0 \textbf{ then} \\
&\quad\quad\quad\quad \textbf{return } \hat{\varrho}^M \\
&\quad\quad\quad \textbf{else} \\
&\quad\quad\quad\quad \textbf{return } \hat{D}_k(\rho^{\hat{M}T}) \qquad \triangleright \textit{Invalid ciphertext}
\end{aligned}
$$

**Fig. 9.** RRO-QCCA2 games $G^{\text{rro-qcca2-real}}$ (**left**) and $G^{\text{rro-qcca2-ideal}}$ (**right**).

**RRO-QCCA2 Security Definition.** In order to relate the latter definition with a constructive notion of confidentiality, it is helpful to have a game-based security definition which analogously to QAE defines a real and an ideal setting (by specifying real-or-random oracles, and in particular, not only a real-or-random challenge). We do this by introducing the notion RRO-QCCA2, which can be seen as a natural extension of RRC-QCCA2.

**Definition 12 (RRO-QCCA2 Security).** *For SQES* $\mathfrak{S} := (\text{Gen}, \text{Enc}, \text{Dec})$ *(implicit in all defined systems) we define the* RRO-QCCA2*-advantage of* $\mathfrak{S}$ *for distinguisher* D *as*

$$\mathbf{Adv}^{\text{rro-qcca2}}_{\mathfrak{S},D} := \Pr\left[D[G^{\text{rro-qcca2-real}}] = 1\right] - \Pr\left[D[G^{\text{rro-qcca2-ideal}}] = 1\right],$$

*where the interactions of* D *with game systems* $G^{\text{rro-qcca2-real}}$ *and* $G^{\text{rro-qcca2-ideal}}$ *are defined in Fig. 9.*

**Relating AGM-QCCA2 and RRC-QCCA2.** We feel that RRC-QCCA2 is a much simpler and more natural definition than AGM-QCCA2. In fact, in [2] the authors claim that AGM-QCCA2 is a "natural" security definition based on the fact that its classical analogon is shown to be equivalent to (a variation of) the standard classical IND-CCA2 security definition. We claim that our RRC-QCCA2 is more natural in the sense that it is formulated as a normal distinction problem (as opposed to AGM-QCCA2), and its classical analogon can be shown to be equivalent to standard classical IND-CCA2 security much more directly (in particular, with no concrete security loss, as opposed to AGM-QCCA2, where it is shown that the concrete reduction has a factor 2 security loss).

Similarly as done in [2] for QAE, whose classical restriction was shown to be equivalent to the common classical notion of authenticated encryption IND-CCA3 from [41], we now show that our RRC-QCCA2 security notion, when casted to a classical definition, dubbed RRC-CCA2, is equivalent (in particular, with no loss factors, as opposed to AGM-QCCA2) to a common classical notion of IND-CCA2. The latter definition is the same mentioned in [2], and comprises a real-or-random challenge, but the decryption oracle returns $\perp$ upon submitting the challenge ciphertext. On the other hand, RRC-CCA2 behaves exactly the same as IND-CCA2, except that it always returns the challenge plaintext as originally submitted by the adversary upon querying the challenge ciphertext, independently from the (real or ideal) setting.

**Lemma 2.** RRC-CCA2 *and* IND-CCA2 *are equivalent.*

*Proof.* To transform RRC-CCA2 into IND-CCA2, the reduction simply stores the challenge ciphertext $\hat{c}$, and returns $\perp$ whenever the decryption oracle is queried upon $\hat{c}$. To transform IND-CCA2 into RRC-CCA2, the reduction simply stores the challenge plaintext $\hat{m}$ and the challenge ciphertext $\hat{c}$, and returns $\hat{m}$ whenever the decryption oracle is queried upon $\hat{c}$.

**RRC-QCCA2 Implies RRO-QCCA2.** As above, here we add as superscript the parameter $\ell$ to games and advantages to denote that the distinguisher is allowed to make at most $\ell$ queries to the oracles. Note that we relate RRC-QCCA2 and RRO-QCCA2 for only the subclass of SQESs which satisfy the following condition.

**Condition 1.** *SQES* $\mathfrak{S}$ *is such that the auxiliary state does not depend on the key (but possibly on the randomness), and it appends explicitly the randomness to the ciphertext, that is:*

$$\mathrm{Enc}_k(\varrho^M) = U_{k,r}(\varrho^M \otimes \Pi_r^T)U_{k,r}^\dagger \otimes |r\rangle\langle r|^R,$$

*for some unitary* $U_{k,r}$ *depending on both the key* $k$ *and the randomness* $r$.

We remark that this restriction still captures all the explicit protocols considered in [2].

**Lemma 3.** *Let* $\mathfrak{S}$ *be a SQES satisfying Condition 1. Then for reduction system* $C_I$ *as specified in the proof, for any distinguisher* D *we have*

$$\mathbf{Adv}_{\mathfrak{S},\mathsf{D}}^{\mathrm{rro\text{-}qcca2},\ell} \leq \ell \cdot \mathbf{Adv}_{\mathfrak{S},\mathsf{DC}_I}^{\mathrm{rrc\text{-}qcca2},\ell-1}.$$

*Proof.* The proof of Lemma 3 appears in the full version [5].

It is easy to show that the other direction of Lemma 3 also holds (for the same class of SQES), that is, RRO-QCCA2 implies RRC-QCCA2. For this, the reduction C flips a bit $\tilde{B}$ and uses the RRO-QCCA2 security game to emulate the RRC-QCCA2 game, resulting in perfect emulation with probability $\frac{1}{2}$, and perfect unguessability otherwise. Thus, with DC outputting 1 if and only if D correctly guesses $\tilde{B}$, we have $\mathbf{Adv}_{\mathfrak{S},D}^{\mathrm{rrc\text{-}qcca2},\ell} \leq 2 \cdot \mathbf{Adv}_{\mathfrak{S},DC}^{\mathrm{rro\text{-}qcca2},\ell-1}$, and therefore the two notions are asymptotically equivalent, as we formalize in the following lemma.

**Lemma 4.** *For SQES satisfying Condition 1, RRC-QCCA2 and RRO-QCCA2 are asymptotically equivalent.*

Just as we casted RRC-QCCA2 into the classical definition RRC-CCA2, we can cast RRO-QCCA2 into RRO-CCA2. Then it is possible to obtain analogous results as above for the classical notions (without restrictions on the (classical) encryption scheme).

**Corollary 4.** *RRC-CCA2 and RRO-CCA2 are asymptotically equivalent.*

**RRO-QCCA2 Implies CC-QCNF.** We can now finally relate QCCA2 game-based security definitions to the constructive cryptography notion of confidentiality, CC-QCNF. We do that by showing that RRO-QCCA2 security implies CC-QCNF, and therefore, by Lemma 3, so does RRC-QCCA2 (with concrete security loss factor $\ell$).

**Theorem 4.** *Let* $\mathfrak{S} := (\mathsf{Gen}, \mathsf{Enc}, \mathsf{Dec})$ *be a SQES (implicit in all defined systems). Then with protocol* $\pi_{AB}^{\mathrm{q\text{-}enc}} = (\pi_A^{\mathrm{q\text{-}enc}}, \pi_B^{\mathrm{q\text{-}enc}})$ *making use of quantum computers* $\mathsf{QC}_A^\ell$ *and* $\mathsf{QC}_B^\ell$ *(already defined in Fig. 6 for Theorem 3), simulator* $\mathsf{sim}_E^{\mathrm{qcca2}}$ *making use of quantum computer* $\mathsf{QC}_E^\ell$ *as defined in Fig. 7 (until the end), and (trivial) reduction system* C *as specified in the proof, for any distinguisher* D *we have*

$$\Delta^D(\pi_{AB}^{\mathrm{q\text{-}enc}}[\mathsf{KEY}, \mathsf{IC}^\ell, \mathsf{QC}_A^\ell, \mathsf{QC}_B^\ell], \mathsf{sim}_E^{\mathrm{qcca2}}[\mathsf{NMCC}^\ell, \mathsf{QC}_E^\ell]) \leq \mathbf{Adv}_{\mathfrak{S},DC}^{\mathrm{rro\text{-}qcca2},\ell}.$$

*Proof.* The proof of Theorem 4 appears in the full version [5]. 

**Corollary 5.** *With* $\varepsilon(D) := \sup_{D' \in \mathcal{B}(D)} \mathbf{Adv}_{\mathfrak{S},D'}^{\mathrm{rro\text{-}qcca2},\ell}$, *we have*

$$\left[\mathsf{KEY}, \mathsf{IC}^\ell, \mathsf{QC}_A^\ell, \mathsf{QC}_B^\ell\right] \xrightarrow{\pi_{AB}^{\mathrm{q\text{-}enc}}, \varepsilon} \left[\mathsf{NMCC}^\ell, \mathsf{QC}_E^{\mathrm{qcca2},\ell}\right],$$

*where the class* $\mathcal{B}(D)$ *is defined in Eq. (5).*

Using Lemma 3, we finally obtain the following corollary.

**Corollary 6.** *With* $\varepsilon(D) := \sup_{D' \in \mathcal{B}(D)} \mathbf{Adv}_{\mathfrak{S},D'}^{\mathrm{rrc\text{-}qcca2},\ell}$, *we have*

$$\left[\mathsf{KEY}, \mathsf{IC}^\ell, \mathsf{QC}_A^\ell, \mathsf{QC}_B^\ell\right] \xrightarrow{\pi_{AB}^{\mathrm{q\text{-}enc}}, (\ell+1)\cdot\varepsilon} \left[\mathsf{NMCC}^\ell, \mathsf{QC}_E^{\mathrm{qcca2},\ell}\right],$$

*where the class* $\mathcal{B}(D)$ *is defined in Eq. (5).*

**RRO-QCCA2 is Stronger than CC-QCNF .** We remark that even though RRO-QCCA2 implies CC-QCNF, the converse is not true for the same reason outlined above for QAE and CC-QSEC: it is possible to show that there are SQESs that satisfy CC-QCNF but not RRO-QCCA2 by applying the same principle of extending a RRO-QCCA2 secure scheme into one which is not anymore RRO-QCCA2, but still satisfies CC-QCNF.

**Acknowledgments.** CP acknowledges support from the Zurich Information Security and Privacy Center.

# References

1. Alagic, G., Broadbent, A., Fefferman, B., Gagliardoni, T., Schaffner, C., Jules, M.S.: Computational security of quantum encryption. In: International Conference on Information Theoretic Security. pp. 47–71. Springer (2016)
2. Alagic, Gorjan, Gagliardoni, Tommaso, Majenz, Christian: Unforgeable Quantum Encryption. In: Nielsen, Jesper Buus, Rijmen, Vincent (eds.) EUROCRYPT 2018. LNCS, vol. 10822, pp. 489–519. Springer, Cham (2018). https://doi.org/10.1007/978-3-319-78372-7_16
3. Backes, Michael, Pfitzmann, Birgit, Waidner, Michael: A General Composition Theorem for Secure Reactive Systems. In: Naor, Moni (ed.) TCC 2004. LNCS, vol. 2951, pp. 336–354. Springer, Heidelberg (2004). https://doi.org/10.1007/978-3-540-24638-1_19
4. Backes, M., Pfitzmann, B., Waidner, M.: The reactive simulatability (RSIM) framework for asynchronous systems. Information and Computation 205(12), 1685–1720 (2007), extended version of [35]
5. Banfi, F., Maurer, U., Portmann, C., Zhu, J.: Composable and finite computational security of quantum message transmission. IACR Cryptology ePrint Archive **2019**, 914 (2019)
6. Barnum, H., Crépeau, C., Gottesman, D., Smith, A., Tapp, A.: Authentication of quantum messages. In: Proceedings of the 43rd Symposium on Foundations of Computer Science, FOCS '02. pp. 449–458. IEEE (2002)
7. Bellare, M., Desai, A., Jokipii, E., Rogaway, P.: A concrete security treatment of symmetric encryption. In: Proceedings of the 38th Annual Symposium on Foundations of Computer Science. pp. 394–403. FOCS '97, IEEE Computer Society (1997)
8. Bellare, M., Desai, A., Pointcheval, D., Rogaway, P.: Relations among notions of security for public-key encryption schemes. In: Advances in Cryptology - CRYPTO '98. pp. 26–45. Springer (1998)
9. Bellare, Mihir, Namprempre, Chanathip: Authenticated Encryption: Relations among Notions and Analysis of the Generic Composition Paradigm. In: Okamoto, Tatsuaki (ed.) ASIACRYPT 2000. LNCS, vol. 1976, pp. 531–545. Springer, Heidelberg (2000). https://doi.org/10.1007/3-540-44448-3_41
10. Ben-Or, Michael, Horodecki, Michał, Leung, Debbie W., Mayers, Dominic, Oppenheim, Jonathan: The Universal Composable Security of Quantum Key Distribution. In: Kilian, Joe (ed.) TCC 2005. LNCS, vol. 3378, pp. 386–406. Springer, Heidelberg (2005). https://doi.org/10.1007/978-3-540-30576-7_21

11. Broadbent, Anne, Jeffery, Stacey: Quantum Homomorphic Encryption for Circuits of Low T-gate Complexity. In: Gennaro, Rosario, Robshaw, Matthew (eds.) CRYPTO 2015. LNCS, vol. 9216, pp. 609–629. Springer, Heidelberg (2015). https://doi.org/10.1007/978-3-662-48000-7_30

12. Canetti, R.: Universally composable security: A new paradigm for cryptographic protocols. In: Proceedings of the 42nd Symposium on Foundations of Computer Science, FOCS '01. pp. 136–145. IEEE (2001)

13. Canetti, R.: Universally composable security: A new paradigm for cryptographic protocols. Cryptology ePrint Archive, Report 2000/067 (2013), http://eprint.iacr.org/2000/067, updated version of [12]

14. Canetti, Ran, Dodis, Yevgeniy, Pass, Rafael, Walfish, Shabsi: Universally Composable Security with Global Setup. In: Vadhan, Salil P. (ed.) TCC 2007. LNCS, vol. 4392, pp. 61–85. Springer, Heidelberg (2007). https://doi.org/10.1007/978-3-540-70936-7_4

15. Canetti, Ran, Krawczyk, Hugo, Nielsen, Jesper B.: Relaxing Chosen-Ciphertext Security. In: Boneh, Dan (ed.) CRYPTO 2003. LNCS, vol. 2729, pp. 565–582. Springer, Heidelberg (2003). https://doi.org/10.1007/978-3-540-45146-4_33

16. Chiribella, G., D'Ariano, G.M., Perinotti, P.: Theoretical framework for quantum networks. Physical Review A **80**, 022339 (2009)

17. Coretti, S., Maurer, U., Tackmann, B.: Constructing confidential channels from authenticated channels–public-key encryption revisited. In: Sako, K., Sarkar, P. (eds.) Advances in Cryptology - ASIACRYPT 2013. pp. 134–153. Springer (2013)

18. Dunjko, Vedran, Fitzsimons, Joseph F., Portmann, Christopher, Renner, Renato: Composable Security of Delegated Quantum Computation. In: Sarkar, Palash, Iwata, Tetsu (eds.) ASIACRYPT 2014. LNCS, vol. 8874, pp. 406–425. Springer, Heidelberg (2014). https://doi.org/10.1007/978-3-662-45608-8_22

19. Gutoski, G.: On a measure of distance for quantum strategies. Journal of Mathematical Physics **53**(3), 032202 (2012)

20. Gutoski, G., Watrous, J.: Toward a general theory of quantum games. In: Proceedings of the 39th Symposium on Theory of Computing, STOC '07. pp. 565–574. ACM (2007)

21. Hardy, L.: Reformulating and reconstructing quantum theory (2011), http://www.arxiv.org/abs/1104.2066, eprint

22. Hardy, L.: The operator tensor formulation of quantum theory. Philosophical Transactions of the Royal Society of London A: Mathematical, Physical and Engineering Sciences **370**(1971), 3385–3417 (2012)

23. Hardy, L.: Quantum theory with bold operator tensors. Philosophical Transactions of the Royal Society of London A: Mathematical, Physical and Engineering Sciences **373**(2047) (2015)

24. Katz, J., Yung, M.: Characterization of security notions for probabilistic private-key encryption. Journal of Cryptology **19**(1), 67–95 (2006)

25. König, R., Renner, R., Bariska, A., Maurer, U.: Small accessible quantum information does not imply security. Physical Review Letters **98**, 140502 (2007)

26. Krawczyk, H.: The order of encryption and authentication for protecting communications (or: How secure is SSL?). In: Advances in Cryptology - CRYPTO 2001. Lecture Notes in Computer Science, vol. 2139, pp. 310–331. Springer (2001). DOI: https://doi.org/10.1007/3-540-44647-8_19

27. Maurer, U.: Indistinguishability of random systems. In: International Conference on the Theory and Applications of Cryptographic Techniques. pp. 110–132. Springer (2002)

28. Maurer, U.: Constructive cryptography–a new paradigm for security definitions and proofs. In: Proceedings of Theory of Security and Applications, TOSCA 2011. Lecture Notes in Computer Science, vol. 6993, pp. 33–56. Springer (2012)

29. Maurer, U., Pietrzak, K., Renner, R.: Indistinguishability amplification. In: Annual International Cryptology Conference. pp. 130–149. Springer (2007)

30. Maurer, U., Renner, R.: Abstract cryptography. In: Proceedings of Innovations in Computer Science, ICS 2011. pp. 1–21. Tsinghua University Press (2011)

31. Maurer, Ueli, Renner, Renato: From Indifferentiability to Constructive Cryptography (and Back). In: Hirt, Martin, Smith, Adam (eds.) TCC 2016. LNCS, vol. 9985, pp. 3–24. Springer, Heidelberg (2016). https://doi.org/10.1007/978-3-662-53641-4_1

32. Maurer, U., Rüedlinger, A., Tackmann, B.: Confidentiality and integrity: A constructive perspective. In: Cramer, R. (ed.) Theory of Cryptography, pp. 209–229. Springer, Berlin Heidelberg, Berlin, Heidelberg (2012)

33. Maurer, U., Tackmann, B.: On the soundness of authenticate-then-encrypt: Formalizing the malleability of symmetric encryption. In: Proceedings of the 17th ACM Conference on Computer and Communication Security. pp. 505–515. ACM (2010)

34. Pfitzmann, B., Waidner, M.: Composition and integrity preservation of secure reactive systems. In: Proceedings of the 7th ACM Conference on Computer and Communications Security, CSS '00. pp. 245–254. ACM (2000)

35. Pfitzmann, B., Waidner, M.: A model for asynchronous reactive systems and its application to secure message transmission. In: IEEE Symposium on Security and Privacy. pp. 184–200. IEEE (2001)

36. Portmann, Christopher: Quantum Authentication with Key Recycling. In: Coron, Jean-Sébastien, Nielsen, Jesper Buus (eds.) EUROCRYPT 2017. LNCS, vol. 10212, pp. 339–368. Springer, Cham (2017). https://doi.org/10.1007/978-3-319-56617-7_12

37. Portmann, C., Matt, C., Maurer, U., Renner, R., Tackmann, B.: Causal boxes: Quantum information-processing systems closed under composition. IEEE Transactions on Information Theory **63**(5), 3277–3305 (2017)

38. Portmann, C., Renner, R.: Cryptographic security of quantum key distribution (2014), http://www.arxiv.org/abs/1409.3525, eprint

39. Renner, R.: Security of Quantum Key Distribution. Ph.D. thesis, Swiss Federal Institute of Technology (ETH) Zurich (Sep 2005)

40. Scarani, V., Bechmann-Pasquinucci, H., Cerf, N.J., Dušek, M., Lütkenhaus, N., Peev, M.: The security of practical quantum key distribution. Reviews of Modern Physics **81**, 1301–1350 (2009)

41. Shrimpton, T.: A characterization of authenticated-encryption as a form of chosen-ciphertext security. IACR Cryptology ePrint Archive **2004**, 272 (2004)

42. Tomamichel, M., Leverrier, A.: A largely self-contained and complete security proof for quantum key distribution. Quantum **1**, 14 (2017)

43. Unruh, Dominique: Universally Composable Quantum Multi-party Computation. In: Gilbert, Henri (ed.) EUROCRYPT 2010. LNCS, vol. 6110, pp. 486–505. Springer, Heidelberg (2010). https://doi.org/10.1007/978-3-642-13190-5_25

44. Vilasini, V., Portmann, C., del Rio, L.: Composable security in relativistic quantum cryptography. New J. Phys. **21**, 043057 (2019). https://doi.org/10.1088/1367-2630/ab0e3b

45. Zhandry, M.: How to construct quantum random functions. In: Proceedings of the 43rd Symposium on Foundations of Computer Science, FOCS '12. pp. 679–687. IEEE (2012)

# On Fully Secure MPC with Solitary Output

Shai Halevi[1], Yuval Ishai[2], Eyal Kushilevitz[2], Nikolaos Makriyannis[2(✉)], and Tal Rabin[1]

[1] Algorand Foundation, New York City, USA
[2] Department of Computer Science, Technion, Haifa, Israel
{yuvali,eyalk}@cs.technion.ac.il, n.makriyannis@gmail.com

**Abstract.** We study the possibility of achieving *full security*, with guaranteed output delivery, for secure multiparty computation of functionalities where only one party receives output, to which we refer as *solitary functionalities*. In the standard setting where all parties receive an output, full security typically requires an honest majority; otherwise even just achieving fairness is impossible. However, for solitary functionalities, fairness is clearly not an issue. This raises the following question: Is full security with no honest majority possible for *all* solitary functionalities?

We give a negative answer to this question, by showing the existence of solitary functionalities that cannot be computed with full security. While such a result cannot be proved using fairness-based arguments, our proof builds on the classical proof technique of Cleve (STOC 1986) for ruling out fair coin-tossing and extends it in a nontrivial way.

On the positive side, we show that full security against any number of malicious parties is achievable for many natural and useful solitary functionalities, including ones for which the multi-output version cannot be realized with full security.

## 1 Introduction

Secure multiparty computation (MPC) [7,9,19,32] allows a set of mutually distrusting parties to compute any function of their local inputs while guaranteeing (to the extent possible) the privacy of the inputs and the correctness of the outputs. Security is formulated by requiring that a real execution of a protocol is indistinguishable from an ideal execution in which the parties hand their inputs to a trusted party who computes the function and returns the outputs.

The strongest level of security one could hope for is so-called "full security" [8,19]. Full security ensures *guaranteed output delivery* in the sense of

---

S. Halevi and T. Rabin—Work done while at IBM Research.

Y. Ishai and N. Makriyannis—Research supported by ERC grant 742754.

Y. Ishai and E. Kushilevitz—Research supported by ISF grant 1709/14, NSF-BSF grant 2015782, and a grant from the Ministry of Science and Technology, Israel and Department of Science and Technology, Government of India.

D. Hofheinz and A. Rosen (Eds.): TCC 2019, LNCS 11891, pp. 312–340, 2019.
https://doi.org/10.1007/978-3-030-36030-6_13

allowing all parties to learn their outputs without revealing additional information about other inputs. In particular, it implies *fairness*: malicious parties cannot learn their outputs while preventing honest parties from learning their outputs. This level of security is achievable in the presence of an honest majority, either unconditionally [4,7,9,31] (assuming secure point-to-point channels and a broadcast channel) or under standard cryptographic assumptions [18,19] (assuming a public-key infrastructure).

Without an honest majority, a classical result of Cleve [11] shows that full security, or *even fairness alone*, is generally impossible. Concretely, there are many natural functionalities such that in *every protocol* for computing them, malicious parties can gain a significant advantage over honest parties in learning information about the output. Thus, when no honest majority is assumed, it is common to settle for weaker notions of security such as "security with abort" [5, 19–21,32].

In this paper, we consider the possibility of achieving full security for functionalities that deliver output to a single party, to which we refer as "functionalities with solitary output" or "solitary functionalities" for short. Such functionalities capture many realistic use-cases of MPC in which different participants play different roles. For instance, consider a (single) employer who wishes to learn some aggregate private information about a group of employees, where the output should remain hidden from the employees. This type of functionalities is commonly considered in the non-interactive setting, including the Private Simultaneous Messages (PSM) model of secure computation [15] and its robust variants [1,6].

Beyond being a natural class of functionalities, the class of solitary functionalities is also interesting because it bypasses all fairness-based impossibility results. Indeed, fairness is not an issue when only one party receives an output, and thus Cleve's impossibility result does not have any consequences for such functionalities. Therefore, the first question that we ask is a very basic feasibility question in the theory of MPC:

Do *all* functionalities with solitary output admit a fully secure protocol?

This feasibility question can be contrasted with the state of affairs in other ongoing lines of work on characterizing the functionalities that admit protocols with *information-theoretic* security, or *UC security*, or *fairness* [3,10,13,23,28], where the high-order bit is already known and the current efforts are focused on trying to fully characterize the realizable functionalities.

We make two main contributions. On the negative side, we settle the high-order bit by proving that some solitary functionalities *cannot* be computed with full security. This is conceptually intriguing because, as mentioned above, solitary functionalities do not introduce "fairness" problems. So what is the source of difficulty in achieving full security? Our impossibility proof extends Cleve's original attack in a rather subtle way. In Cleve's attack, the adversary gains advantage over honest parties by aborting the protocol at a point where it knows significantly more information about the output than the honest parties do. Our new attack, dubbed the "double-dipping attack", is based on the following rough intuition. (The following simplified description of the attack ignores important subtleties; see Sects. 1.2 and 3 for a more precise version.) The adversary controls a majority of the parties that includes the output party. It instructs one of the parties it controls to abort the protocol just when learning enough (but not all) information about the output. Intuitively, in such a case, the protocol must be run again with default values (in particular, the original inputs cannot be recovered as the aborting parties form a majority). In the end of the protocol, the adversary learns the output of $f$ on *two* inputs, with the same input values for honest parties. This is an information that the adversary cannot obtain in the ideal world, hence security fails.

On the positive side, we make progress towards full characterization of the solitary functionalities that admit fully secure protocols. We present such protocols for several natural and useful families of solitary functionalities, including variants of commonly studied MPC problems such as Private Set Intersection. Our positive results apply in many cases where negative results are known for the multi-output variant. We elaborate on both our positive and negative results below.

## 1.1   Our Results

For our negative result, we present a family $\Omega$ of solitary functionalities for which no fully secure protocol exists. A representative example of such a functionality, first considered in the context of "best of both worlds" security [25] (see below), is the following 3-party functionality $f_{\mathsf{eq}}$ with two parties $P_1$ and $P_2$ receiving inputs $x, y \in \{1, 2, 3\}$, respectively, and an output-receiving party $Q$. The output of $f_{\mathsf{eq}}$ is defined as $f_{\mathsf{eq}}(x, y) = x$ if $x = y$ and $f_{\mathsf{eq}}(x, y) = \bot$ otherwise. We sketch below how "double dipping" is applied to this functionality, and present the family $\Omega$ and the formal impossibility proof in Sect. 3.

Next, in Sect. 4, we present several positive results. We start by proving that fairness implies full security in the following sense: if $f$ is an $n$-party function, where all parties receive the output, and $f$ can be computed with fairness, then the $(n + 1)$-party solitary functionality $f'$, with inputs given to $P_1, \ldots, P_n$, as in $f$, and with the output delivered to the output party $Q$, can be computed with full security. Our next positive result shows that we can go much beyond fairness positive results; specifically, we consider a family of $n$-party functionalities that we call functions with "forced output distribution". Described for the 3-party case, this family includes all functions $f(x, y)$ (with inputs $x, y$ to $P_1, P_2$, respectively, and output to $Q$) such that for at least one of the input parties, say $P_1$, there is a distribution on its input, where the output $f(x, y)$ is distributed the same, no matter what the other input is. Note that such (non-trivial) functions $f$ cannot be computed with fairness, as this would imply fair coin-tossing, which is impossible [11]. Finally, as a third positive result, we consider a family of functionalities that we term "functionalities with fully revealing input". Described in the 3-party setting above, this family includes all functionalities where one of the parties, say $P_1$, has an input for which the function $f$ becomes injective.

We stress that these results fall short of providing a full characterization of the fully secure solitary functionalities, as we give an example of a function that does not fall into any of the families of positive results but nevertheless can be computed with full security. Interestingly, we compute this function using a variant of the GHKL protocol [23] for computing fair two-party functionalities, yet—viewed as a symmetric two-party functionality—it is inherently unfair. We leave the question of finding a full characterization as an intriguing open question for future work.

*Example.* To demonstrate the usefulness of the above positive and negative results, we consider some variants of the Private Set Intersection (PSI) problem. In this problem, the inputs $x, y$ of $P_1, P_2$ correspond to subsets $S_1, S_2$ of some domain $[m]$ and the output is the intersection $S = S_1 \cap S_2$. It follows from our negative result that if $|S_1| = |S_2| = k$, for some fixed $k$, then this function cannot be computed with full security (in fact, the function $f_{eq}$ mentioned above is exactly the case $k = 1$). On the other hand, for the same inputs, if the required output is only the intersection size, i.e. $|S|$, then this becomes a functionality with a forced output distribution (e.g., by choosing $S_1$ as a uniformly random set of size $k$) and so this functionality can be computed with full security. Similarly, if we allow $|S_1|, |S_2|$ to be anywhere between $k$ and $m$ then PSI with full security becomes possible (using $[m]$ as a revealing input) and, if we allow $|S_1|, |S_2|$ to be anywhere between $0$ and $k$, this is also possible (using a degenerate version of the forced output distribution, where $\emptyset$ is selected with probability 1). Other interesting cases, like the case where $|S_1|, |S_2|$ are between 1 and $k$, are left as an open problem. (See the full version of the present paper [24] for an analysis of additional variants of PSI, including additional variants where the output is just the intersection size $|S|$, or just a bit indicating whether $S = \emptyset$, sometimes referred to as the *disjointness* function. The full version also includes similar analyses for different natural flavors of Oblivious Transfer (OT)).

Finally, as an additional contribution, we analyse the round complexity of computing solitary functionalities with full security. We observe that some of the protocols presented in our positive results are constant-round protocols, while others use super-logarithmic number of rounds. We prove that, for certain solitary functionalities, full security actually requires super-constant round complexity (see Sect. 5). We leave the question of figuring out the exact round-complexity for any solitary functionality as an intriguing open question for future work.

*Feasibility Landscape of Boolean Solitary Functionalities.* We conclude this section with a few sentences regarding the "feasibility" landscape of solitary MPC. We focus on functions with Boolean output where the output receiving party does not provide input; this case is interesting as it is readily comparable to the non-solitary Boolean two-party case (the most well understood instance of fully secure MPC with dishonest majority). We distinguish two cases depending of the size of the input domains. From the fairness criterion, if one party has a strictly bigger input domain than the other, then almost all functionalities

Classification of PSI variants

Define $\mathsf{PSI}_m^g : (S_1, S_2) \mapsto g(S_1 \cap S_2)$, for some $m \in \mathbb{N}$ and function $g$, where $S_1, S_2 \subseteq [m]$ are drawn from a predetermined input space (specified below). Let $k < \ell$ denote some arbitrary fixed numbers different than 0 or $m$ such that $k + \ell + 1 \leq m$.

| Input restriction. \ Function $g$ | $S \mapsto S$ | $S \mapsto \lvert S \rvert$ | $S \mapsto \begin{cases} 1 & \text{if } S \neq \emptyset \\ 0 & \text{otherwise} \end{cases}$ |
|---|---|---|---|
| $\lvert S_1 \rvert, \lvert S_2 \rvert = k < m/2$ | Impossible | Forced | Forced |
| $\lvert S_1 \rvert, \lvert S_2 \rvert \in \{0, \ldots, k\}$ | Forced | Forced | Forced & Fairness |
| $\lvert S_1 \rvert, \lvert S_2 \rvert \in \{k, \ldots, m\}$ | Revealing | Open | Forced & Fairness |
| $\lvert S_1 \rvert, \lvert S_2 \rvert \in \{k, \ldots, \ell\}$ | Open | Open | Open |
| $\lvert S_1 \rvert \in \{k, \ldots, \ell\}$ and $\lvert S_2 \rvert \in \{k, \ldots, \ell+1\}$ | Open | Open | Fairness |

**Fig. 1.** Table summarizing our results vis-à-vis the PSI problem

are computable with full security, because almost all two-party Boolean functions admit fair protocols in this case [3]. On the other hand, when the parties have exactly the same number of inputs, the fairness criterion does *not* apply, because almost all two-party Boolean functions are *not* computable with fairness.[1] However, by excluding the functions that are computable using a variant of the forced criterion, we can succinctly describe the set of functions whose status is unknown: $\{M \in \{0,1\}^{n \times n} \mid \exists \mathbf{x} \in \mathbb{R}^n \text{ s.t. } M\mathbf{x} = \mathbf{1}_n \wedge \sum_i \mathbf{x}_i \leq 0\}$. In words, the set corresponds to 0–1 matrices (viewed as matrices over the reals) whose columns span $\mathbf{1}_n$ with coefficient that have a negative sum. While we could not rigorously analyze the measure of this set, we conjecture that it represents a vanishing fraction of the entire space, i.e. relative to $\{0,1\}^{n \times n}$; experimental evidence for $n \leq 300$ strongly supports our conjecture (see [24], Appendix A). Thus, the following picture emerges for functionalities with equal-sized input domains: almost all 2-party functionalities *cannot* be computed fairly, while almost all solitary 3-party functionalities (two inputs and one output) *can* be computed with full security.

## 1.2   Our Techniques

Next, we elaborate on some of the techniques that we use.

**(i) Impossibility result.** As mentioned above, for our impossibility result, we use a technique inspired by Cleve's seminal "biasing" attack on coin-tossing [11]. In Cleve's attack, the adversary is trying to bias the output of a fair coin-flip. The adversary picks a random round $i$, and plays honestly until that round. Then, the adversary computes the corrupted party's backup value for that round,

---

[1] The reason being that most such functions can be used to implement the coin-tossing functionality [29] – which does not admit a fair protocol.

i.e. the output prescribed by the protocol in case the other party aborted at that round. The adversary aborts the corrupted party at that round or the next round depending on the "direction" it is attempting to bias the output to. Intuitively, because the protocol is inherently unfair, the adversary has an advantage in learning the output. Therefore, by aborting prematurely, the adversary alters the distribution of the honest party's output.

Translating the above attack to our setting is not straightforward, given that the above gives an attack on correctness while we aim for an attack on privacy. For concreteness, we now explain how our impossibility applies to the 3-party functionality $f_{eq}$ described above. Notice that, in an ideal execution, if $P_1$ chooses its input at random, then the other two colluding parties can only be sure of $P_1$'s input with probability at most $1/3$ (i.e. by guessing the right value). In the real-world however, there must be some round of the protocol where the joint backup value of $P_2$ and $Q$ (i.e. the output prescribed by the protocol in case $P_1$ aborted at that round) contains information about $P_1$'s input, while the joint backup value of $P_1$ and $Q$ does not contain information about $P_2$'s input. By aborting $P_2$ at that round, the adversary can effectively compute the output on two different inputs of $P_2$ and thus guess $P_1$'s input with probability noticeably greater than $1/3$.

Rather crudely, the above can be summarized as follows: We define a coin-toss between $\{P_1, Q\}$ and $\{P_2, Q\}$ such that the outcome of the "coin-toss" is tied to some privacy event. By "biasing" the coin-toss, the adversary effectively increases its chance that the privacy event occurs, which results in a privacy breach. It should be noted that this picture is not accurate since, in our setting, the direction of bias is very important and this cannot be guaranteed by Cleve's attack.

**(ii) Protocols.** Our transformation from $n$-party fair protocols (with output to all) to $(n + 1)$-party fully secure protocols with solitary output to $Q$ describes a compiler that takes a fair protocol $\Pi$ and transforms it into a fully secure protocol $\Pi'$ with solitary output. The idea is to emulate $\Pi$ by sharing the view of each party $P_i$ in the original protocol $\Pi$ between $P_i$ and $Q$ in $\Pi'$. This way, an adversary corrupting a subset of parties not including $Q$ learns nothing, while an adversary corrupting a subset of parties that includes $Q$ only learns the views of the corresponding parties in $\Pi$. The latter cannot be used to mount an attack, given the presumed security of the original protocol. Our protocols for the forced output distribution class and for the fully revealing input class are very different. Interestingly, these two cases are symmetric in some sense, where each has "problematic" parties. In the former (forced output distribution) case, the problematic party is the one that does not have a forced output distribution. The protocol we propose in this case funnels the communication through the others parties. Thus, by design, the problematic party only contributes to the computation once. For the latter (fully revealing input) case, the problematic parties are the ones without fully revealing input. The protocol we propose for this case funnels the communication through the party with a revealing input, say $P_1$. Thus, by design, unless $P_1$ is corrupt (in which case there are no secrets), computation only occurs once.

*Related Work.* Below, we discuss some related work that deals with full security and other related security notions (in particular, fairness).

In the two-party case, it is known that fairness is equivalent to full security (with guaranteed output delivery), since if an honest party aborts it can safely replace the input of the corrupted party by a default value and compute the resulting output locally. In contrast, Cohen and Lindell [12] show that in the multiparty case there are functionalities that admit fair protocols but do not admit fully secure protocols.

Since the work of Cleve [11], it is known that full security, or even fairness, cannot be achieved in general unless there is an honest majority. This led to a rich line of work [2,3,14,23,30] attempting to characterize *which* functions can be computed with full security. Most works along this line focused on the two-party case, starting with the results of [23], and culminating in a full characterization for the class of fair Boolean functions with the same output for both parties [3].

Less is known for the multi-party case. Examples of multi-output functions for which fair protocols exist (specifically, $n$-party OR and 3-party majority) are given in [22]. In [25,27] (see also [26]), the notion of "Best-of-both-worlds security" is introduced as a hybrid between full security and security with abort. A protocol satisfies this definition, if there is one protocol that *simultaneously* provides full security if there is an honest majority and otherwise it guarantees security with abort. Note that, in the context of best-of-both-worlds, [25] already gives an example of a 3-party solitary function for which no constant-round protocol exists (concretely, the function $f_{eq}$ mentioned above). This was improved to $\log n$ rounds in [27].

*Open Problems.* As mentioned above, the most obvious open problems are obtaining a characterization or at least reducing the gap between the positive and negative results, and working out the exact round complexity for fully secure computation of solitary functionalities. Less obviously, we identify the following interesting open questions.

1. Our attack in Sect. 3 crucially relies on the *rushing* capability of the adversary. It would be interesting to show that this is inherent for impossibility or to extend the negative result to the case of a non-rushing adversary.
2. In this work, we are mainly concerned with the feasibility questions of solitary MPC. Therefore, for obtaining malicious security, our protocols use a generic step that we have not tried to optimize. We leave the interesting question of improving concrete efficiency for future work, or designing concretely efficient fully secure protocols for useful special cases such as PSI.
3. As explained in subsequent sections, broadcast is necessary for solitary MPC. However, *some* functionalities do not require broadcast. While the question is orthogonal to the goal of the paper, it would be interesting to understand which functionalities require broadcast in the solitary setting.

# 2   Preliminaries

The following models and definitions are adapted from [12,17].

## 2.1   Models

In this section we outline the definition of secure computation, following Canetti's definition approach for the standalone model [8], and highlight some details that are important for our purposes. The following version of the definition is somewhat simplified. We refer the reader to [8] for more complete definitions.

*Communication Model.* We consider a network of $n$ processors, usually denoted $P_1, \ldots, P_n$ and referred to as *parties*. Each pair of parties is connected via a private, authenticated point-to-point channel. In addition, all parties share a common *broadcast* channel, which allows each party to send an identical message to *all* other parties. In some sense, the broadcast channel can be viewed as a medium which "commits" the party to a specific value.[2]

*Functionality.* A secure computation task is defined by some $n$-party functionality $f : X_1 \times \ldots \times X_n \to \Sigma^n$, specifying the desired mapping from the parties' inputs to their final outputs. Party $P_i$'s input domain is denoted by $X_i$, for each $i \in [n]$, and the outputs of the parties are assumed to belong to some alphabet $\Sigma$. When $n = 3$, the parties' input domains will be denoted $X, Y$ and $Z$ to make the distinction more explicit. One may also consider *randomized* functionalities, which take an additional random input; however, in this work we focus on the deterministic case.

*Functionality with Solitary Output.* A $n$-party functionality $f : X_1 \times \ldots \times X_n \to \Sigma^n$ admits solitary output if it delivers output to (the same) one party alone, i.e. $f$ is of the form $(x_1, \ldots, x_n) \mapsto (\emptyset, \ldots, \emptyset, \sigma, \emptyset, \ldots, \emptyset)$, where the index of $\sigma$ does not depend on the input. The output-receiving party will be denoted by, $Q$, and, unless stated otherwise, will be identified with $P_n$. If no confusion arises, we simply write $f : X_1 \times \ldots \times X_n \to \Sigma$ or $f : (x_1, \ldots, x_n) \mapsto \sigma$.

*Some Notations.* Denote by $\mathcal{P} = \{P_1, \ldots, P_n\}$ the set of all parties. If no confusion arises, we sometimes identify $\mathcal{P}$ with the numbers in $[n] = \{1, \ldots, n\}$. Subsets of these parties are denoted by calligraphic letters $(\mathcal{S}, \mathcal{T}, \ldots)$, and their complements will be denoted by $(\overline{\mathcal{S}}, \overline{\mathcal{T}}, \ldots)$. Random variables are denoted by lower-case boldface $(\mathbf{x}, \mathbf{y}, \ldots)$ and distributions by upper-case boldface $(\mathbf{X}, \mathbf{Y}, \ldots)$. For a functionality $f$ taking input from $X_1 \times \ldots \times X_n$ we will write $x_\mathcal{S}$ to denote

---

[2] We remark that our assumption regarding broadcast is in fact necessary for fully secure computation of solitary functionalities. This observation follows from the fact that "convergecast" implies broadcast [16]. We also sketch a simpler direct argument in the full version [24].

an element of the subspace $\times_{i \in S} X_i$ and, abusing notation, $f(x_S, x_{\overline{S}})$ denotes the value of $f(x_1, x_2, \ldots, x_n)$. Furthermore, for integers $m$ and $k$, we let $\binom{[m]}{k}$ denote the subsets of $[m]$ of size exactly $k$ and $2^{[m]}$ the set of all subsets of $[m]$. For set $S$ and distribution $\mathbf{S}$, we write $s \leftarrow S$ and $s \leftarrow \mathbf{S}$ to denote that element $s$ is sampled uniformly at random from $S$ or according to distribution $\mathbf{S}$, respectively.

*Protocol.* Initially, each party $P_i$ holds an input $x_i$, a random input $\rho_i$ and, possibly, a common *security parameter* $\kappa$. The parties are restricted to (expected) polynomial time in $\kappa$. The protocol proceeds in *rounds*, where in each round each party $P_i$ may send a "private" message to each party $P_j$ (including itself) and may broadcast a "public" message, to be received by all parties. The messages $P_i$ sends in each round may depend on all its inputs ($x_i$, $\rho_i$ and $\kappa$) and the messages it received in previous rounds. Without loss of generality, we assume that each $P_i$ sends $x_i, \rho_i, \kappa$ to itself in the first round, so that the messages it sends in each subsequent round may be *determined* from the messages received in previous rounds. We assume that the protocol terminates after a fixed number of rounds, denoted $r$ (that may depend on the security parameter $\kappa$), and that honest parties never halt prematurely, i.e. honest parties are active at any given round of the protocol. Finally, each party locally computes some output based on its view. We note that our negative results extend to protocols that have *expected polynomial* number of rounds (in $\kappa$) via a simple Markov inequality argument.

*Fail-Stop Adversary.* We consider a *fail-stop $t$-adversary* $\mathcal{A}$, where the parameter $t$ is referred to as the *security threshold*. The adversary is an efficient interactive algorithm,[3] which is initially given the security parameter $\kappa$ and a random input $\rho$. Based on these, it may choose a set $\mathcal{T}$ of *at most $t$* parties to corrupt. The adversary then starts interacting with a protocol (either a "real" protocol as above, or an *ideal-process* or *hybrid-process* protocol to be defined below), where it takes control of all parties in $\mathcal{T}$. In particular, it can read their inputs, random inputs, and received messages and, contrary to the *malicious* case (see below), it can control the messages that parties in $\mathcal{T}$ send only by deciding whether to send them or to abort. We assume by default that the adversary has a *rushing* capability: at any round it can first wait to hear all messages sent by uncorrupted parties to parties in $\mathcal{T}$, and use these to make its decisions whether to abort or continue (some of) the parties he corrupts. Corrupted parties that do not abort send their prescribed messages for the present round, while corrupted parties that abort send a special abort symbol to *all parties*.[4]

---

[3] It is usually assumed that the adversary is given an "advice" string $a$, or is alternatively modeled by a nonuniform algorithm. In fact, the proofs of our negative results are formulated in this nonuniform setting, but can be modified to apply to the uniform one as well.

[4] This assumption implies that an abort is detected by all parties, even one that occurred on a private channel. This assumption can be enforced via a dispute resolution mechanism, thanks to the broadcast channel.

*Malicious Adversaries.* Adversaries that deviate arbitrarily from the protocol are not discussed in the present paper. Using the GMW compiler [19], our positive results can be extended to malicious adversaries. Negative results trivially extend to such adversaries (since fail-stop is a special kind of malicious adversary).

*Security.* We consider two types of security known as *full security* and *security with identifiable abort*. The former is the focus of the paper, i.e. it corresponds to the security notion we want to realize or rule out. The latter is a weaker security notion that is useful towards realizing our positive results. Informally, a protocol computing $f$ is said to be $t$-secure if whatever a $t$-adversary can "achieve" by attacking the protocol, it could have also achieved (by corrupting the same set of parties) in an ideal process in which $f$ is evaluated using a trusted party. To formalize this definition, we have to define what "achieve" means and what the ideal process is. The *ideal process* for evaluating the functionality $f$ is a protocol $\pi_f$ involving the $n$ parties and an additional, incorruptible, trusted party TP.

*Ideal Model with Full Security.* The protocol proceeds as follows: (1) each party $P_i$ sends its input $x_i$ to TP; (2) TP computes $f$ on the inputs (using its own random input in the randomized case), and sends to each party its corresponding output. Note that when the adversary corrupts parties $\mathcal{T}$ in the ideal process, it can pick the inputs sent by parties in $\mathcal{T}$ to TP (possibly, based on their original inputs) and then output an arbitrary function of its view (including the outputs it received from TP). Honest parties always output the message received from the trusted party and the corrupted parties output nothing.

*Ideal Model with Identifiable Abort.* In this case, an adversary can abort the computation in the ideal model after learning its outputs, at the cost of revealing to the honest parties the identity of at least one of the corrupted parties. The protocol proceeds as follows: (1) each $P_i$ sends its input $x_i$ to TP; (2) TP computes $f$ on the inputs (using its own random input in the randomized case), and sends to each of the *corrupted* parties its corresponding output. (3) By sending to TP either (continue, $\emptyset$) or (abort, $P_i$), for some $P_i$ in $\mathcal{T}$, according to whether the adversary continues the execution, or aborts the execution at the cost of revealing one corrupted party. (4) TP sends the outputs to the honest parties if the adversary continues, or the identity of the corrupted $P_i$ together with a special abort-symbol, if the adversary aborted the computation. Similarly to the previous case, when an adversary corrupts parties in the ideal process, it can pick the inputs sent by parties in $\mathcal{T}$ to TP (possibly, based on their original inputs) and then output an arbitrary function of its view (including the outputs it received from TP). Honest parties always output the message received from the trusted party and the corrupted parties output nothing.

## 2.2 Security Definition

To formally define security, we capture what the adversary "achieves" by a random variable concatenating the adversary's output together with the *outputs* and the *identities* of the uncorrupted parties. For a protocol $\Pi$, adversary $\mathcal{A}$, input vector $x$, and security parameter $\kappa$, let $exec_{\Pi,\mathcal{A}}(\kappa, x)$ denote the above random variable, where the randomness is over the random inputs of the uncorrupted parties, the trusted party (if $f$ is randomized), and the adversary. The security of a protocol $\Pi$ (also referred to as a *real-life* protocol) is defined by comparing the *exec* variable of the protocol $\Pi$ to that of the ideal process $\pi_f^{\text{type}}$, where type $\in$ {full_sec, id_abort} specifies the ideal process to be compared with (either full security or identifiable abort). Formally:

**Definition 2.1.** *We say that a protocol $\Pi$ $t$-securely computes $f$ if, for any (real-life) $t$-adversary $\mathcal{A}$, there exists (an ideal-process) $t$-adversary $\mathcal{A}'$ such that the distribution ensembles $exec_{\Pi,\mathcal{A}}(\kappa, x)$ and $exec_{\pi_f^{\text{type}},\mathcal{A}'}(\kappa, x)$ are indistinguishable. The security is referred to as perfect, statistical, or computational according to the notion of indistinguishability being achieved. For instance, in the computational case it is required that for any family of polynomial-size circuits $\{C_\kappa\}$ there exists some negligible functionality* neg, *such that for any $x$,*

$$|C_\kappa(exec_{\Pi,\mathcal{A}}(\kappa, x)) - C_\kappa(exec_{\pi_f^{\text{type}},\mathcal{A}'}(\kappa, x))| \leq \mathsf{neg}(\kappa).$$

An equivalent form of Definition 2.1 quantifies over all *input distributions* $X$ rather than specific input vectors $x$. This equivalent form is convenient for proving our negative results.

*Intuitive Discussion.* Definition 2.1 asserts that for any *real-life* $t$-adversary $\mathcal{A}$ attacking the real protocol there is an *ideal-process* $t$-adversary $\mathcal{A}'$ which can "achieve" in the ideal process as much as $\mathcal{A}$ does in the real life. The latter means that the output produced by $\mathcal{A}'$ together with the inputs and outputs of uncorrupted parties in the ideal process is indistinguishable from the output (wlog, the entire view) of $\mathcal{A}$ concatenated with the inputs and outputs of uncorrupted parties in the real protocol. This concatenation captures both *privacy* and *correctness* requirements. On the one hand, it guarantees that the view of $\mathcal{A}$ does not allow it to gain more information about inputs and outputs of uncorrupted parties than is possible in the ideal process and, on the other hand, it ensures that the inputs and outputs of the uncorrupted parties in the real protocol be consistent with some correct computation of $f$ in the ideal process. We stress that ideal-world adversary can indeed choose whatever input it likes, and it need not restrict itself to the input chosen by the real-world adversary.

*Default Security Threshold.* Throughout the paper, we assume that the security threshold is $t = n - 1$, namely an arbitrary strict subset of the parties can be corrupted. We therefore do not mention the parameter $t$ in the rest of the paper.

## 2.3 Hybrid Model and Composition

*Hybrid Model.* The hybrid model extends the real model with a trusted party that provides ideal computation for predetermined functionalities. In more detail, the parties communicate with this trusted party as per the specifications of the ideal models described above (either fully secure or identifiable abort, to be specified). Let Fn be a functionality. Then, an execution of a protocol $\Pi$ computing a functionality $f$ in the Fn-hybrid model involves the parties interacting as per the real model and, in addition, having access to a trusted party computing Fn. The protocol proceeds in rounds such that, at any given round, the parties send normal messages as in the standard model, or, make a single invocation of the functionality Fn. Security is defined analogously to Definition 2.1 by replacing the real protocol with the hybrid one. The model in question is referred to as the (Fn, type)-hybrid model, depending on the specification of the ideal functionality.

*Composition.* The hybrid model is useful because it allows cryptographic tasks to be divided into subtasks. In particular, a fully secure hybrid protocol making ideal invocations to an ideal functionality with identifiable abort can be transformed into a fully secure real protocol, if there exists a real protocol for the ideal functionality that is secure with identifiable abort. This technique is captured by Canneti's sequential composition theorem.

**Theorem 2.1 (Canetti [8]).** *Suppose that protocol $\Pi$ securely computes $f$ in the (Fn, id_abort)-hybrid model with full security, and suppose that $\Psi$ securely computes $f$ in the real model. Then, protocol $\Pi^{\Psi}$ securely computes $f$ in the real model, where $\Pi^{\Psi}$ is obtained by replacing ideal invocations of Fn with real executions of $\Psi$. Furthermore, the quality of the security (computational, statistical or perfect) of the resulting protocol is the weakest among the security of $\Pi$ and $\Psi$.*

Finally, we define the notion of *backup values*. It is immediate from the security definition that any fully secure protocol admits well defined backup values.

**Definition 2.2 (Backup values).** *The following definitions are with respect to a fixed honest execution of an n-party, r-round correct protocol (determined by the parties' random coins) for solitary functionality $f$. The $i^{\text{th}}$ round backup value of a subset of parties $\mathcal{Q} = \{Q\} \cup \mathcal{S} \subseteq \mathcal{P}$ at round $i \in [r]$, denoted Backup($\mathcal{Q}, i$), is defined as the value $Q$ would output, if all parties in $\mathcal{P} \setminus \mathcal{Q}$ abort at round $i + 1$ and no other party aborts. For consistency, we let Backup($\mathcal{Q}, r$) denote the output of the protocol if no parties abort (i.e Backup($\mathcal{Q}, r$) = Backup($\mathcal{Q}', r$), for every $\mathcal{Q}$ and $\mathcal{Q}'$).*

# 3    Impossibility: The Double-Dipping Attack

In this section we prove our main negative result. Namely, we show impossibility of achieving full security for a number of solitary functionalities, including the following natural families:

- Equality testing with leakage of input (including $f_{\text{eq}}$ from the introduction).

- Private Set Intersection for fixed input size (i.e. PSI as defined in Definition 3.1).

**Definition 3.1.** *Let* $\mathsf{PSI}^{\mathrm{id}}_{m,k} : \binom{[m]}{k} \times \binom{[m]}{k} \to 2^{[m]}$ *be such that* $\mathsf{PSI}^{\mathrm{id}}_{m,k}(S_1, S_2) = S_1 \cap S_2$. *As a three party functionality,* $\mathsf{PSI}^{\mathrm{id}}_{m,k}$ *receives inputs from* $P_1$ *and* $P_2$ *and delivers output to an additional party* $Q$.

Namely, $\mathsf{PSI}^{\mathrm{id}}_{m,k}$ takes as input two sets of size $k$ and outputs their intersection. We point out that $f_{\mathsf{eq}} \equiv \mathsf{PSI}^{\mathrm{id}}_{m,1}$. In this section, we show impossibility for a class of functions that includes $\mathsf{PSI}^{\mathrm{id}}_{m,k}$, for every $0 < k < m/2$. As a warm-up, we sketch our impossibility result for the specific functionality $f_{\mathsf{eq}}$; the general case is essentially an extrapolation of this case. We will be using the following notation.

**Notation 3.1.** *Let* $\Pi$ *be a three-party, $r$-round protocol for computing a function* $f : X \times Y \times Z \to \Sigma$ *with solitary output. Define random variables* $\mathbf{a}_0, \dots, \mathbf{a}_r$ *and* $\mathbf{b}_0, \dots, \mathbf{b}_r$ *such that* $\mathbf{a}_i$ *is the value of* $\mathsf{Backup}(\{Q, P_1\}, i)$ *in a random execution of* $\Pi$ *and, similarly,* $\mathbf{b}_i$ *is the value of* $\mathsf{Backup}(\{Q, P_2\}, i)$ *in a random execution of* $\Pi$, *where* $\mathsf{Backup}(\mathcal{Q}, i)$ *is according to Definition 2.2.*

### 3.1  Warm up

Let $\Pi$ be a three-party protocol for computing $f_{\mathsf{eq}}$. Let $\mathbf{X}$ and $\mathbf{Y}$ denote the uniform distribution for the inputs of $P_1$ and $P_2$ respectively. We proceed under the following simplifying assumptions for $\Pi$: for every $i \in [r]$, it holds that $\mathrm{Pr}_{x \leftarrow \mathbf{X}}[\mathbf{a}_i = x] = 1/3$ and $\mathrm{Pr}_{y \leftarrow \mathbf{Y}}[\mathbf{b}_i = y] = 1/3$. In words, if $P_1$ (resp. $P_2$) chooses its input uniformly at random, then the backup output of $Q$ and $P_1$ (resp. $Q$ and $P_2$) at round $i$ is equal to the aforementioned input with probability exactly $1/3$, regardless of $P_2$'s (resp. $P_1$'s) choice of input. For the purposes of the present warm up, we will further assume that $\mathbf{a}_0$ and $\mathbf{b}_0$ are independent random variables. Next, we rule out fully secure computation for $f_{\mathsf{eq}}$ under these simplifying assumptions. When we tackle the general case in the next subsection, we get rid of these simplifying assumptions, by showing additional attacks (adversaries) where the aforementioned properties do no to hold.

We show that there exists an adversary that can guess the honest party's input with probability noticeably greater than what the ideal model allows. First, in the ideal model with full security, notice that when an honest party $P_\ell$ chooses his input uniformly at random, then an adversary corrupting $\{P_{3-\ell}, Q\}$ may guess (with certainty) the honest party's input with probability at most $1/3$ (by using the right input for the corrupted party). We show that for any real protocol, there exists an adversary that can guess the input with noticeably greater probability, thus violating security.

Consider two adversaries $A^{P_1}$ and $A^{P_2}$ corrupting $\{Q, P_1\}$ and $\{Q, P_2\}$, respectively, acting as follows. The honest party and corrupted party choose their inputs uniformly at random; write $x$ and $y$ for the inputs chosen by $P_1$ and $P_2$. The adversary $A^{P_1}$ chooses a round $i$ uniformly at random. Then, before sending its messages for round $i$, if $\mathbf{a}_i \neq x$, the adversary aborts party $P_1$ without sending further messages and instructs $Q$ to continue honestly with $P_2$; otherwise, it sends its messages for round $i$ and aborts $P_1$ alone. The adversary $A^{P_2}$ chooses a round $i$ uniformly at random. Then, after sending its messages for round $i$, if $\mathbf{b}_i \neq y$, the adversary aborts $P_2$ without sending further messages and instructs $Q$ to continue honestly with $P_1$; otherwise, it sends its messages for round $i+1$ and aborts $P_2$ alone. Adversary $A^{P_1}$ outputs $\mathbf{b}_{i-1}$ or $\mathbf{b}_i$ (depending on the round $P_1$ aborted) and $A^{P_2}$ outputs $\mathbf{a}_i$ or $\mathbf{a}_{i+1}$ (depending on the round $P_2$ aborted). We show that at least one of the adversaries outputs the honest party's input with probability noticeably greater than $1/3$, in violation of privacy. Next, we compute each of the relevant probabilities.

$$\Pr\left[A^{P_1} \text{ outputs } y\right] = \frac{1}{r} \cdot \sum_{i=1}^{r} \left( \Pr_{\substack{x \leftarrow \mathbf{X} \\ y \leftarrow \mathbf{Y}}}[\mathbf{a}_i \neq x \wedge \mathbf{b}_{i-1} = y] + \Pr_{\substack{x \leftarrow \mathbf{X} \\ y \leftarrow \mathbf{Y}}}[\mathbf{a}_i = x \wedge \mathbf{b}_i = y] \right)$$

$$\Pr\left[A^{P_2} \text{ outputs } x\right] = \frac{1}{r} \cdot \sum_{i=0}^{r-1} \left( \Pr_{\substack{x \leftarrow \mathbf{X} \\ y \leftarrow \mathbf{Y}}}[\mathbf{b}_i \neq y \wedge \mathbf{a}_i = x] + \Pr_{\substack{x \leftarrow \mathbf{X} \\ y \leftarrow \mathbf{Y}}}[\mathbf{b}_i = y \wedge \mathbf{a}_{i+1} = x] \right)$$

Next, we compute the average of the two quantities above.

$$\left(\Pr\left[A^{P_1} \text{ outputs } y\right] + \Pr\left[A^{P_2} \text{ outputs } x\right]\right)/2$$

$$= \frac{1}{2r} \left( \Pr_{\substack{x \leftarrow \mathbf{X} \\ y \leftarrow \mathbf{Y}}}[\mathbf{b}_0 \neq y \wedge \mathbf{a}_0 = x] + \Pr_{\substack{x \leftarrow \mathbf{X} \\ y \leftarrow \mathbf{Y}}}[\mathbf{a}_r = x \wedge \mathbf{b}_r = y] + \sum_{i=1}^{r-1} \Pr_{\substack{x \leftarrow \mathbf{X} \\ y \leftarrow \mathbf{Y}}}[\mathbf{a}_i = x] + \sum_{i=0}^{r-1} \Pr_{\substack{x \leftarrow \mathbf{X} \\ y \leftarrow \mathbf{Y}}}[\mathbf{b}_i = y] \right)$$

By correctness of the protocol and simplifying assumptions,

$$\left(\Pr\left[A^{P_1} \text{ outputs } y\right] + \Pr\left[A^{P_2} \text{ outputs } x\right]\right)/2 = \frac{1}{2r} \cdot \Pr_{\substack{x \leftarrow \mathbf{X} \\ y \leftarrow \mathbf{Y}}}[\mathbf{b}_0 \neq y \wedge \mathbf{a}_0 = x] + \frac{1}{3}$$

$$= \frac{1}{3} + \frac{1}{2r} \cdot \frac{2}{9}$$

We conclude that at least one of the adversaries can guess with certainty the opponent's input with probability noticeably greater than $1/3$, thus violating privacy.

## 3.2   General Case

We define a class $\Omega$ of 3-party functions, and we show that no function in this class admits a fully secure realization. Intuitively, this class of functions satisfies the following requirement: For both $\ell \in \{1,2\}$, there is a (non-trivial) partition of the inputs of $P_\ell$ and a distribution over the inputs of $P_\ell$ such that if $P_\ell$ samples its input according to the specified distribution then, with some fixed probability bounded away from 0 or 1, the output alone[5] fully determines what set of the

---

[5] Without knowledge of the inputs of $Q$ and $P_{3-\ell}$.

partition $P_\ell$'s chosen input belongs to, *no matter* how the inputs of $Q$ and $P_{3-\ell}$ were chosen. Furthermore, if both parties sample their inputs according to their respective distributions, then either for both inputs their sets in the partitions are determined from the output alone, or for neither. Formally,

**Definition 3.2.** *The class of functions $\Omega$ consists of all functions $f$ satisfying the following conditions, for some $\gamma_1, \gamma_2 \in (0,1)$. There exist distributions $\mathbf{X}$ and $\mathbf{Y}$ over $X$ and $Y$, respectively, such that $\mathrm{supp}(\mathbf{X}) = X$ and $\mathrm{supp}(\mathbf{Y}) = Y$, and partitions $X_1 \ldots X_k$ and $Y_1 \ldots Y_\ell$ of $X$ and $Y$, respectively, such that*

1. *For every distribution $\Delta_1$ over $X \times Z$,*
   $$\Pr_{\substack{(x_0,z_0)\leftarrow\Delta_1 \\ \tilde{y}\leftarrow\mathbf{Y}}} [\exists j \text{ s.t. } \Pr_{y'\leftarrow\mathbf{Y}} [y' \in Y_j \mid f(x_0, \tilde{y}, z_0) = f(x_0, y', z_0)] = 1] = \gamma_1$$
2. *For every distribution $\Delta_2$ over $Y \times Z$,*
   $$\Pr_{\substack{\tilde{x}\leftarrow\mathbf{X} \\ (y_0,z_0)\leftarrow\Delta_2}} [\exists j \text{ s.t. } \Pr_{x'\leftarrow\mathbf{X}} [x' \in X_j \mid f(\tilde{x}, y_0, z_0) = f(x', y_0, z_0)] = 1] = \gamma_2$$
3. *There exists $z_0 \in Z$ such that, for every $\sigma \in \Sigma$,*
   *$\exists j$ s.t. $\Pr[\tilde{x} \in X_j \mid f(\tilde{x}, \tilde{y}, z_0) = \sigma] = 1$ if and only if*
   *$\exists j$ s.t. $\Pr_{\substack{\tilde{x}\leftarrow\mathbf{X} \\ \tilde{y}\leftarrow\mathbf{Y}}} [\tilde{y} \in Y_j \mid f(\tilde{x}, \tilde{y}, z_0) = \sigma] = 1$*

Note that $\mathsf{PSI}^{\mathrm{id}}_{m,k}$, with $0 < k < m/2$, satisfies the above definition: define $\mathbf{X} = \mathbf{Y}$ as the uniform distribution and define partitions $\{X_x = \{x\}\}_{x \in X}$ and $\{Y_y = \{y\}\}_{y \in Y}$.

*Remark 3.1.* The class of functions $\Omega$ can be generalized in few ways that we omitted, for the sake of presentation. The first generalization considers functions that take more than three inputs and can be reduced to functions in $\Omega$ by grouping parties together. The second generalization relaxes the requirement on the support of the distributions $\mathbf{X}$ and $\mathbf{Y}$ (allowing $\mathrm{supp}(\mathbf{X}) \subsetneq X$ or $\mathrm{supp}(\mathbf{Y}) \subsetneq Y$). The proof for the latter is almost identical to the one below.

**Theorem 3.2.** *For any $f \in \Omega$ and for any protocol $\Pi$ computing $f$, at least one of the following holds.*

- *There exists an adversary corrupting either $P_1$ or $P_2$ that can violate correctness.*
- *There exists an adversary corrupting either $Q$ and $P_1$, or $Q$ and $P_2$ that can violate privacy.*

Hereafter, fix a function $f$, real numbers $\gamma_1, \gamma_2 \in (0,1)$, distributions $\mathbf{X}$ and $\mathbf{Y}$ and partitions $X_1 \ldots X_k$ and $Y_1 \ldots Y_\ell$, and $z_0$ satisfying Definition 3.2. It is immediate that $\gamma_1 = \gamma_2$, hence we simply write $\gamma$ $(= \gamma_1 = \gamma_2)$. We define $4r + 1$ adversaries $\{A_i^{P_1}\}_{i=1}^r$, $\{A_i^{P_2}\}_{i=0}^{r-1}$, $\{C_i^{P_\ell}\}_{i=1}^r$ and $\tilde{A}_0^{P_1}$ (See Fig. 2). Let $\Sigma' \subset \Sigma$ denote all the elements $\sigma \in \Sigma$ such that there exists $j$ for which $\Pr_{\substack{\tilde{x}\leftarrow\mathbf{X} \\ \tilde{y}\leftarrow\mathbf{Y}}} [\tilde{y} \in Y_j \mid f(\tilde{x}, \tilde{y}, z_0) = \sigma] = 1$. Such a $\Sigma'$ is guaranteed to exist by Item 2 of Definition 3.2.

---

### Adversaries $\{C_i^{P_\ell}\}_{i=1}^r$, $\widetilde{A}_0^{P_1}$, $\{A_i^{P_1}\}_{i=1}^r$ and $\{A_i^{P_2}\}_{i=0}^{r-1}$

- Each $C_i^{P_1}$ corrupts party $P_1$ and uses input sampled according to $\mathbf{X}$. Party $P_1$ aborts at round $i$.
- Each $C_i^{P_2}$ corrupts party $P_2$ and uses input sampled according to $\mathbf{Y}$. Party $P_2$ aborts at round $i$.
- Adversary $\widetilde{A}_0^{P_1}$ corrupts $P_1$ and $Q$ and is *non-rushing*. The adversary instructs $P_1$ to use an input sampled according to $\mathbf{X}$ and $Q$ to use input $z_0$. The adversary computes $a_0$ using the aforementioned inputs and $P_1$ and $Q$'s random input. If $a_0 \in \Sigma'$, the adversary aborts $P_1$ alone without sending the first message and computes $b_0$ with the honest party. It outputs 1 if $b_0 \in \Sigma'$; otherwise, it continues honestly till the end and computes $b_r$ with the honest party. The adversary outputs 1 if $b_r \in \Sigma'$.
- Each $A_i^{P_1}$ corrupts $P_1$ and $Q$ and is *rushing*. The adversary instructs $P_1$ to use an input sampled according to $\mathbf{X}$ and $Q$ to use input $z_0$. At round $i$, before sending the $i$-th round message, the adversary computes the backup value $a_i$ and checks whether $a_i \in \Sigma'$ i.e. whether the backup value leaks its own input. If so, the adversary aborts $P_1$ alone at round $i + 1$ and computes $b_i$ with the honest party, or the adversary aborts $P_1$ alone at round $i$ and computes $b_{i-1}$ with the honest party. The adversary outputs 1 if $b_i \in \Sigma'$ (or $b_{i-1} \in \Sigma'$).
- Each $A_i^{P_2}$ corrupts $P_2$ and $Q$ and is *non-rushing*. The adversary instructs $P_2$ to use an input sampled according to $\mathbf{Y}$ and $Q$ to use input $z_0$. At round $i$, after sending the $i$-th round message, the adversary computes the backup $b_i$ and checks whether $b_i \in \Sigma'$ i.e. he checks whether the backup leaks his own input. If so, the adversary aborts at round $i + 2$ (i.e. sends one more message) and learns $a_{i+1}$, or the adversary aborts at round $i + 1$ learns $a_i$. The adversary outputs 1 if $a_i \in \Sigma'$ (or $a_{i+1} \in \Sigma'$), and 0 otherwise.

**Fig. 2.** Description of the adversaries

*Proof.* Define $\widetilde{a}_0, \ldots, \widetilde{a}_r$ and $\widetilde{b}_0, \ldots, \widetilde{b}_r$ such that $\widetilde{a}_i = 1$ (resp. $\widetilde{b}_i = 1$) if and only if $\mathbf{a}_i \in \Sigma'$ (resp. $\mathbf{b}_i \in \Sigma'$) and 0 otherwise. In the following, we consider an execution of the protocol where $Q$ uses $z_0$ as input, $P_1$ uses input sampled according to $\mathbf{X}$ and $P_2$ uses input sampled according to $\mathbf{Y}$, regardless of whether the parties are corrupted or not.

**Claim 3.1.** *Unless $C_i^{P_1}$ or $C_i^{P_2}$ violate correctness, it holds that $|\Pr[\widetilde{\mathbf{b}}_i = 1] - \gamma|$, $|\Pr[\widetilde{\mathbf{a}}_i = 1] - \gamma| \leq \mathrm{neg}(\kappa)$, for every $i \in \{0, \ldots, r-1\}$.*

Next, we analyze the probability that $A_i^{P_1}$ and $A_i^{P_2}$ output 1. Observe that, by correctness, with all but negligible probability, whenever $A_i^{P_1}$ (resp. $A_i^{P_2}$) outputs 1, the adversary succeeds in guessing the "bucket" the honest party's input belongs to, with certainty. To prove our theorem, we show that one of the adversaries $A_i^{P_\ell}$ or $\widetilde{A}_0^{P_1}$ outputs 1 with probability greater than $\gamma$, violating privacy.

$$\Pr\left[A_i^{P_1} \text{ outputs } 1\right] = \Pr\left[\widetilde{\mathbf{a}}_i = 0 \wedge \widetilde{\mathbf{b}}_{i-1} = 1\right] + \Pr\left[\widetilde{\mathbf{a}}_i = 1 \wedge \widetilde{\mathbf{b}}_i = 1\right]$$

$$\Pr\left[A_i^{P_2} \text{ outputs } 1\right] = \Pr\left[\widetilde{\mathbf{b}}_i = 0 \wedge \widetilde{\mathbf{a}}_i = 1\right] + \Pr\left[\widetilde{\mathbf{b}}_i = 1 \wedge \widetilde{\mathbf{a}}_{i+1} = 1\right]$$

Therefore,

$$\sum_{i=1}^{r} \Pr\left[A_i^{P_1} \text{ outputs } 1\right] + \sum_{i=0}^{r-1} \Pr\left[A_i^{P_2} \text{ outputs } 1\right] \tag{1}$$

$$= \Pr\left[\widetilde{\mathbf{b}}_0 = 0 \wedge \widetilde{\mathbf{a}}_0 = 1\right] + \sum_{i=1}^{r-1} \Pr\left[\widetilde{\mathbf{a}}_i = 1\right] + \sum_{i=0}^{r-1} \Pr\left[\widetilde{\mathbf{b}}_i = 1\right] + \Pr\left[\widetilde{\mathbf{a}}_r = 1 \wedge \widetilde{\mathbf{b}}_r = 1\right]$$

Thus

$$\sum_{i=1}^{r} \Pr\left[A_i^{P_1} \text{ outputs } 1\right] + \sum_{i=0}^{r-1} \Pr\left[A_i^{P_2} \text{ outputs } 1\right] = \Pr\left[\widetilde{\mathbf{b}}_0 = 0 \wedge \widetilde{\mathbf{a}}_0 = 1\right] + 2r \cdot \gamma \tag{2}$$

The last equation follows by correctness and Items 1 to 3 of Definition 3.2. Next, we argue that $\Pr[\widetilde{\mathbf{b}}_0 = 0 \wedge \widetilde{\mathbf{a}}_0 = 1]$ is a noticeable quantity. If not, then we claim that adversary $\widetilde{A}_0^{P_1}$ can violate privacy. Suppose that $\Pr[\widetilde{\mathbf{b}}_0 = 0 \wedge \widetilde{A}_0^{P_1} = 1] \leq \mathsf{neg}(\kappa)$ and let $\rho$ denote the (joint) randomness of parties $P_1$ and $Q$. In the presence of adversary $\widetilde{A}_0^{P_1}$, we claim that the events $\mathbf{a}_0 \notin \Sigma'$ and $\mathbf{a}_r \notin \Sigma'$ are independent of each other. To prove it, first notice that $\mathbf{a}_0$ may be viewed as deterministic function of the inputs of $P_1$ and $Q$ and $\rho$, and $\mathbf{a}_r$ may be viewed as a deterministic function of the inputs of $f$ (the latter assumption holds by correctness, with all but negligible probability). We write $\mathbf{a}_0(x, z_0; \rho)$ and $\mathbf{a}_r(x, y, z_0)$ to make the dependency explicit and compute:

$$\Pr_{x \leftarrow \mathbf{X}, y \leftarrow \mathbf{Y}, \rho \leftarrow \mathbf{R}}\left[\mathbf{a}_0(x, z_0; \rho) \notin \Sigma' \wedge \mathbf{a}_r(x, y, z_0) \notin \Sigma'\right]$$

$$= \sum_{x_0 \in X} \Pr_{y \leftarrow \mathbf{Y}, \rho \leftarrow \mathbf{R}}\left[\mathbf{a}_0(x, z_0; \rho) \notin \Sigma' \wedge \mathbf{a}_r(x, y, z_0) \notin \Sigma' \mid x = x_0\right] \cdot \Pr_{x \leftarrow \mathbf{X}}\left[x = x_0\right]$$

Observe that for any fixed $x_0$, the random variables $\mathbf{a}_0(x_0, y; \rho)$ and $\mathbf{a}_r(x_0, y, z_0)$ are independent random variables. Therefore,

$$\Pr_{x \leftarrow \mathbf{X}, y \leftarrow \mathbf{Y}, \rho \leftarrow \mathbf{R}}\left[\mathbf{a}_0(x, z_0; \rho) \notin \Sigma' \wedge \mathbf{a}_r(x, y, z_0) \notin \Sigma'\right]$$

$$= \sum_{x_0 \in X} \Pr_{\rho \leftarrow \mathbf{R}}\left[\mathbf{a}_0(x, z_0; \rho) \notin \Sigma' \mid x = x_0\right] \cdot \Pr_{y \leftarrow \mathbf{Y}}\left[\mathbf{a}_r(x, y, z_0) \notin \Sigma' \mid x = x_0\right] \cdot \Pr_{x \leftarrow \mathbf{X}}\left[x = x_0\right]$$

Finally, by correctness and Item 2 of Definition 3.2

$$\Pr_{x \leftarrow \mathbf{X}, y \leftarrow \mathbf{Y}, \rho \leftarrow \mathbf{R}}\left[\mathbf{a}_0(x, z_0; \rho) \notin \Sigma' \wedge \mathbf{a}_r(x, y, z_0) \notin \Sigma'\right]$$

$$= \sum_{x_0 \in X} \Pr_{\rho \leftarrow \mathbf{R}}\left[\mathbf{a}_0(x, z_0; \rho) \notin \Sigma' \mid x = x_0\right] \cdot (1 - \gamma) \cdot \Pr_{x \leftarrow \mathbf{X}}\left[x = x_0\right]$$

$$= (1 - \gamma) \cdot \Pr_{x \leftarrow \mathbf{X}, \rho \leftarrow \mathbf{R}}\left[\mathbf{a}_0(x, z_0; \rho) \notin \Sigma'\right] = (1 - \gamma)^2$$

The last equality follows from correctness and Item 1 of Definition 3.2. Thus, if $\Pr[\widetilde{\mathbf{b}}_0 = 0 \wedge \widetilde{\mathbf{a}}_0 = 1] \leq \operatorname{neg}(\kappa)$, then adversary $\widetilde{A}_0^{P_1}$ outputs 1 with probability $1 - (1 - \gamma)^2 > \gamma$, in violation of privacy. In conclusion, using an averaging argument in Eq. 2, at least one of $\{A_i^{P_1}\}_{i=1}^r$, $\{A_i^{P_2}\}_{i=0}^{r-1}$ outputs 1 with probability noticeably greater than $\gamma$ and, thus, violates privacy.

## 4   Positive Results

In this section, we present our positive results. First, we give a generic transformation from a fully secure $n$-party protocol with non-solitary output to a fully secure $(n+1)$-party protocol with solitary output; The latter protocol computes the associated functionality that delivers output to an additional auxiliary party that doesn't provide input. In light of the positive results for fair two-party computation, our transformation enables fully secure computation for (almost all) Boolean functions with unequal domain size. For instance, it yields a secure protocol for the following PSI variant that escapes our other criteria: From a universe of size $n$, party $P_1$ picks a set of size between 1 and $k$, for some arbitrary fixed $k \leq n - 2$, party $P_2$ picks a set size between 1 and $k + 1$ (i.e. one party has more inputs to pick than the other), and Party $Q$ receives value 1 if the sets intersect and 0 if not.[6] Interestingly, this technique yields protocols with super-constant (in fact, super-logarithmic) round complexity since, with few exceptions, super-logarithmic number of rounds is necessary for fair computation. In Sect. 5, we show that super-constant round complexity is inherent for fully secure MPC with solitary output.

Then, we present a generic protocol for functionalities that satisfy the "forced output distribution" criterion. Intuitively, these are functionalities where (almost) all parties can "force" the distribution of the output to be invariant of the other parties' choice of input. These functionalities should be contrasted with the above fair ones, since they are utterly unfair viewed as non-solitary functionalities (they imply coin-tossing). Interestingly, every functionality in this class can be computed in a constant number of rounds.

We also present a generic protocol for functionalities that satisfy the "fully revealing input" criterion. Intuitively, these are functionalities where at least one party has a choice of input that reveals all other parties' inputs. While this family may appear somewhat pathological from a cryptographic point of view, it contains several natural examples. In particular, it contains a PSI variant where one party may choose the entire universe as input. Similarly to the previous case, every functionality in this class can be computed in constant number of rounds.

Finally, for a functionality that escapes the above criteria, we design a fully secure protocol that runs in superlogarithmic number of rounds. This protocol is inspired by the GHKL protocol [23]. We emphasize that the feasibility of

---

[6] Viewed as a two-party non-solitary functionality, the fact that it can be computed with full security (fairness) follows from the criteria of [3].

this functionality does *not* follow from the fairness criterion since, viewed as a non-solitary functionality, it cannot be computed fairly. Furthermore, in the next section, we show that superconstant round complexity is inherent for this function.

## 4.1   Security via Fairness

Let $f : X_1 \times \ldots \times X_n \to \Sigma$ be an $n$-party functionality that delivers the same output to all parties. Let $\Pi$ be a fully secure protocol for $f$. Write $m_i^{(\ell,\ell')} \in \{0,1\}^{\mu_\kappa}$ for the message sent by $P_\ell$ to $P_{\ell'}$ at round $i$. Let $M_\kappa = \mu_\kappa \cdot n$ denote the total length of messages received by party $P_\ell$ in a single round (without loss of generality $\mu_\kappa$ and $M_\kappa$ do not depend on $i$, $\ell'$ or $\ell$). In this section, we show how to transform protocol $\Pi$ into a protocol $\Pi'$ that computes the associated solitary functionality that delivers the output to one of the parties, or to an additional auxiliary party. We note that the transformation and analysis of the two cases are the same, therefore we only focus on the latter transformation (i.e. from $n$-party to $n+1$-party protocol, where the output receiving party does not provide input). The rest of this sub-section is dedicated to the proof of the following theorem.

**Theorem 4.1.** *Let $\Pi$ be a protocol for computing non-solitary functionality $f$ with full security. Then, there exist a protocol $\Pi'$ that computes with full security the associated $(n + 1)$-party solitary functionality that delivers the output to an additional auxiliary party.*

At a high level, to transform the $n$-party non-solitary protocol $\Pi$ into an $(n + 1)$-party solitary protocol $\Pi'$, we have each party $P_\ell$ in $\Pi'$ share the view of the party $P_\ell$ in the original protocol $\Pi$ between himself and the auxiliary party $Q$. To do so, we begin by defining protocol's $\Pi$ message function $\mathsf{NxtMsg}_\Pi$ that deterministically maps each party $P_\ell$'s view until some round $i$ (a view that includes its identity, its input, its private coins and all incoming messages until that round) to all messages that $P_\ell$ sends at the upcoming round.

**Definition 4.1.** *Let $\mathsf{NxtMsg}_\Pi$ denote the next message function of $r$-round protocol $\Pi$. Formally, $\mathsf{NxtMsg}_\Pi$ maps $\mathsf{view}_i^{P_\ell} \mapsto (m_{i+1}^{(\ell,1)}, \ldots, m_{i+1}^{(\ell,n)})$ such that*

1. *$\mathsf{view}_i^{P_\ell} \in \{0,1\}^{i \cdot M_\kappa}$ corresponds to the view of party $P_\ell$ up to and including round $i$ (wlog, we assume that the value of $i$ and the identity of $P_\ell$ are contained in its view).*
2. *If $i \neq r$, then $m_{i+1}^{(\ell,\ell')} \in \{0,1\}^{\mu_\kappa}$ corresponds to $P_\ell$'s prescribed message to $P_{\ell'}$ at round $i + 1$ according to $\Pi$. If $i = r$ then $m_{i+1}^{(\ell,\ell')} \in \{0,1\}^{\mu_\kappa}$ corresponds to $P_\ell$'s prescribed output.*

In our protocol design, all messages will be additively-shared between party $P$ and a helper party $Q$. That is, a message $m$ will be randomly split into $m_1$, $m_2$ such that $m = m_1 \oplus m_2$ and party $P$ will hold $m_1$ and $Q$ will hold $m_2$. In the following functionality $\mathsf{ShrNxtMsg}_\Pi$ (Fig. 3) we describe how the messages of the protocol are created to deliver this sharing. Party $P$ and $Q$ hold $\mathsf{view}_i^P$, $P$'s view up to and including round $i$, in shared form as $v_P, v_Q$ and they receive the next round messages of $P$ also in shared form.

---

**Functionality $\mathsf{ShrNxtMsg}_\Pi$**

- **Input:** Party $P$ holds $v_P \in \{0,1\}^{i \cdot M_\kappa}$ and party $Q$ holds $v_Q \in \{0,1\}^{i \cdot M_\kappa}$, $v_P \oplus v_Q = \mathsf{view}_i^P$.
- **Output:**
  1. **Case $i \neq r$.** Party $P$ receives random $m_1 \leftarrow \{0,1\}^{M_\kappa}$ and $Q$ receives $m_2 = m_1 \oplus \mathsf{NxtMsg}(v_P \oplus v_Q)$.
  2. **Case $i = r$.** Party $P$ receives $m_1 = 0^{M_\kappa}$ and $Q$ receives $m_2 = \mathsf{NxtMsg}(v_P \oplus v_Q)$.

---

**Fig. 3.** Two-party functionality $\mathsf{ShrNxtMsg}_\Pi$ for parties $P$ and $Q$.

We describe the protocol for computing a function with an auxiliary party $Q$ that receives the solitary output. The idea is that each party $P_\ell$ will invoke with party $Q$ the protocol for creating the messages that $P_\ell$ needs to send to all the other parties in the upcoming round. This is done by utilizing the functionality $\mathsf{ShrNxtMsg}_\Pi$. The result is that $P_\ell$ and $Q$ receive the set of messages $(m_{i+1}^{(\ell,1)}, \ldots, m_{i+1}^{(\ell,n)})$ in shared form. Then, $P_\ell$ send to each other party $P_j$ its share of the message $m^{(\ell,j)}$. The auxiliary party $Q$ holds in a string $\mathsf{view}_i^{Q_\ell}$ its share of the view of the messages of party $P_\ell$ up to and including round $i$ (a different string for each $P_\ell$). If (some) parties abort, then proceed under the specifications of the original protocol $\Pi$, while maintaining the invariant that each $P_\ell$'s view from the original protocol is shared between $P_\ell$ and $Q$. At the end of the execution, $Q$ together with one of the $P_\ell$'s that hasn't aborted reconstruct the output (which is a deterministic function of their joint views).

The above protocol is described where the output is delivered to the auxiliary party $Q$ (not one of the $P_1 \ldots P_n$). However, as noted at the beginning of this section, this party can be one of the $n$ original parties and simply serves both as himself and as party $Q$. Observe that, in this case, $Q$ will simply see all the messages that it sends and receives (as it holds both shares of the messages).

*Proof of Theorem 4.1.* We prove the claim by showing that protocol $\Pi'$ from Fig. 4 is fully secure in the $\mathsf{ShrNxtMsg}_\Pi$-hybrid model with identifiable abort. Then, the theorem follows from composition [8]. Let $A$ be an adversary corrupting up to $n$ parties (of the $n+1$ parties). Observe that, if party $Q$ is not among the corrupted parties, then $A$'s view can be trivially simulated since it

---

### $(n+1)$-Party Solitary Protocol from $n$-party Non-Solitary Protocol

**Input:**  Each party $P_\ell$ holds input $x_\ell$, random input $\rho_\ell$ and security parameter $1^\kappa$.
Party $Q$ holds security parameter $1^\kappa$ and does not hold any private input.

**Protocol:**

1. $Q$ sets $\{\text{view}_0^{Q\ell} = 0^{M_\kappa}\}_{\ell \in [n]}$ and every other party sets $\text{view}_0^{P_\ell} = (1^\kappa, x_\ell, \rho_\ell)$
2. For $i = 1, \ldots, r$
   (a) Each $P_\ell$ and $Q$ invoke $\mathsf{ShrNxtMsg}_\Pi$ on input $\text{view}_{i-1}^{Q\ell}$ and $\text{view}_{i-1}^{P_\ell}$.
   (b) Each party $P_\ell$ (other than $Q$) is instructed to send his share of message $m_i^{\ell,\ell'}$ to $P_{\ell'}$.
   (c) Each $P_\ell$ (other than $Q$) computes $\text{view}_i^{P_\ell}$ by concatenating $\text{view}_{i-1}^{P_\ell}$ with the (shares of the) messages they received at Step 2b. Party $Q$ computes each $\text{view}_i^{Q\ell}$ by concatenating $\text{view}_{i-1}^{Q\ell}$ with the (shares of the) messages he received from the invocations at Step 2a (collating them appropriately).

   **Abort scenarios:**

   – If $Q$ aborts, then all parties halt.
   – If any of the $P_j$ abort, then each remaining $P_\ell$ and $Q$ update $\text{view}_i^{P_\ell}$ and $\text{view}_i^{Q\ell}$, respectively, such that the latter jointly reflect that $P_j$ stopped sending messages from that round onward (since the original protocol $\Pi$ is fully secure, the remaining parties will be able to continue with the execution).

3. Initialize $\mathsf{ctr} = 1$.
   (a) As long as $\mathsf{ctr} \leq n$ and $P_{\mathsf{ctr}}$ is not alive or aborted, then increment $\mathsf{ctr}$.
   (b) If $\mathsf{ctr} \leq n$, then $P_{\mathsf{ctr}}$ and $Q$ invoke $\mathsf{ShrNxtMsg}_\Pi$ on input $\text{view}_r^{Q\mathsf{ctr}}$ and $\text{view}_r^{P_{\mathsf{ctr}}}$. Party $Q$ outputs whatever he receives from the invocation, and notifies all parties to halt. Otherwise, if $\mathsf{ctr} = n+1$, then $Q$ outputs $f(\widetilde{x}_1, \ldots, \widetilde{x}_n)$ where $(\widetilde{x}_1, \ldots, \widetilde{x}_n)$ is chosen uniformly at random from $X_1 \times \ldots \times X_n$.

**Output:**  Party $Q$'s output is determined at Step 3b. Other parties output nothing.

---

**Fig. 4.** $(n+1)$-party protocol for solitary $f$ in the $\mathsf{ShrNxtMsg}_\Pi$-hybrid model with identifiable abort

is just a uniform random string, and it is not hard to see that he cannot affect correctness. It remains to prove that the protocol is secure when $Q$ is among the corrupted parties. Let $\mathcal{C}$ denote the set of corrupt parties, assuming that $Q \in \mathcal{C}$. For adversary $A$ attacking $\Pi'$ corrupting parties in $\mathcal{C}$, we construct an adversary $\widetilde{A}$ attacking $\Pi$ (on the same input distribution and auxiliary information) and corrupting parties $\widetilde{\mathcal{C}} = \mathcal{C} \setminus \{Q\}$ (there are at most $n-1$ such parties). Since $A$'s and $\widetilde{A}$'s views are identically distributed (modulo a 2-out-of-2 secret sharing), and since the latter can be simulated in the ideal model with full security, it follows that the former can be simulated as well. Formally, let $\widetilde{S}$ denote the simulator for $\widetilde{A}$ and define simulator $S$ for $A$ as follows:

1. $S$ runs $\widetilde{S}$ on the relevant inputs, security parameter and auxiliary information. Write $(v_{P_i})_{P_i \in \widetilde{C}}$ for $\widetilde{S}$'s output corresponding to the joint simulated view of the parties.
2. $S$ samples $(\nu_{P_i})_{P_i \in \widetilde{C}}$ uniformly at random from the relevant space and outputs $(v_{P_i} \oplus \nu_{P_i})_{P_i \in \widetilde{C}}$ (the simulated views of parties in $\widetilde{C}$) and $(\nu_{P_i})_{P_i \in \widetilde{C}}$ (the simulated view of $Q$).

$\square$

## 4.2    Functions with Forced Output Distribution

In this section, we present the "Forced Output Distribution" criterion. First, we define the notion.

**Definition 4.2.** *A party $P_i \neq Q$ admits a* forced output distribution *for $f$ if there exists a distribution $\Delta_i$ over $X_i$ such that the distribution of the random variable $f(x_1, \dots, x_{i-1}, \hat{x}_i, x_{i+1}, \dots, x_n)|_{\hat{x}_i \leftarrow \Delta_i}$ is independent of the $(n-1)$-tuple $(x_1, \dots, x_{i-1}, x_{i+1}, \dots, x_n)$.*

Intuitively, a party admits a *forced output distribution* if it can choose its input in a way that "forces" the output, i.e. it makes the output distribution independent of the other parties' inputs. The theorem below states that if all-but-one parties, not including $Q$, admit a forced output distribution, then the functionality is computable with perfect full security in a constant number of rounds in a hybrid model with ideal access with identifiable abort to functionality $\mathsf{ShrGn}_f$ (to be specified below). As a corollary, assuming OT, functions with a forced output distribution admit fully secure protocol in the plain model.

**Theorem 4.2.** *Assume that at least $n - 1$ of the parties in $\mathcal{P} \setminus \{Q\}$ admit a forced output distribution for functionality $f$. Then, $f$ is computable with perfect full security in the $\mathsf{ShrGn}_f$-hybrid model with identifiable abort. Furthermore, the computation runs in a constant number of rounds.*

We now introduce functionality $\mathsf{ShrGn}_f$ (Fig. 5) and we will prove our theorem in the $\mathsf{ShrGn}_f$-hybrid model with identifiable abort. This functionality provides the following. It shares the output of the function $f$ between the parties that invoke it, by obliviously choosing a random input for the parties that do not provide input. That is, it provides uniform random shares to all-parties-but-one, and that last party gets the *xor* of these shares with the output of the function. We emphasize that this functionality may be invoked by a *subset* of the $n$ parties, and, as per the ideal model with identifiable abort, the invocation can be aborted by any single party in that set (at the cost of revealing its identity).

Without loss of generality, if it exists, suppose that $P_1$ is the party without forced output distribution (the protocol and our analysis remains sound if all parties have a forced output distribution). The protocol (see Fig. 6) proceeds as follows: the parties invoke the trusted party for computing $\mathsf{ShrGn}_f$, and obtain shares of the output. Then, in two distinct steps (1) $P_1$ sends its share of the

---

### Functionality ShrGn$_f$

- **Input:**   Each $P_i \in \mathcal{P}$ provides input $x_i$.

- **Computation:**

1. If parties in $\mathcal{T}$ do not provide input then $x_{\mathcal{T}} \leftarrow \underset{P_i \in \mathcal{T}}{\times} X_i$ is chosen uniformly at random.
   Write $S_1, \ldots, S_\ell$ for the parties in $\mathcal{S} = \mathcal{P} \setminus \mathcal{T}$.
2. Compute $\left\{ \sigma_{S_j} \in \Sigma \right\}_{S_j \in \mathcal{S}}$ such that
   (a) $\sigma_{S_j} \leftarrow \Sigma$ independently and uniformly at random, for each $S_j \neq S_1$ (i.e., $2 \leq j \leq \ell$).
   (b) $\sigma_{S_1} = f(x_{\mathcal{S}}, x_{\mathcal{T}}) \oplus \sigma_{S_2} \oplus \ldots \oplus \sigma_{S_\ell}$.

- **Output:**   Each $S_j \in \mathcal{S}$ receives $\sigma_{S_j}$.

---

**Fig. 5.** $n$-party functionality ShrGn$_f$.

output to $Q$ and (2) all other parties send their shares to $Q$. In case of abort, there are two scenarios; either $P_1$ aborts alone, in which case the process starts again without $P_1$, or, if anyone else aborts at this iteration or the next, the computation halts and $Q$ outputs a value from the forced distribution. Intuitively, the protocol maintains security because it is not useful to abort any of the parties; aborting any party but $P_1$ halts the execution, while aborting $P_1$ does not reveal anything about the output (since the honest party will not send its share before $P_1$ sends his).

*Proof of Theorem* 4.2. First note that distribution **D** in Fig. 6 is well defined since it is unique. Let $A$ denote an adversary corrupting a subset of parties. Like in the previous proof, it is straightforward that if $A$ does not corrupt $Q$ then it cannot affect correctness and its view can be trivially simulated. Let $\mathcal{C}$ be the set of corrupted parties. Define simulator $S$ that does the following: $S$ invokes the trusted party on the inputs of the corrupted parties and receives output out form the trusted party. Then, $S$ samples $|\mathcal{C}|$ random elements $\{\sigma'_C\}_{C \in \mathcal{C}}$ and hands them to the adversary.

- If $P_1$ alone aborts, $S$ samples $|\mathcal{C}| - 1$ fresh random values $\{\sigma''_C\}_{C \in \mathcal{C} \setminus \{P_1\}}$, and hands them to the adversary.
- If any other party aborts (at any point in the simulation), $S$ samples $d' \leftarrow \mathbf{D}$, hands $d$ to the adversary, and outputs whatever $A$ outputs.
- If no other party aborts, $S$ hands out to the adversary and outputs whatever $A$ outputs.    $\square$

---

### n-Party Protocol $\Pi$ for Computing $f$ with Forced Output Distribution

Recall that $P_1$ denotes the party that does not admit a forced output distribution (if there is such party). Write **D** for the distribution induced by (any of) the forced distributions.

**Input:**  Each party $P_\ell$ holds input $x_\ell$ (Recall that $Q$ is one of the $P_\ell$'s).
**Protocol:**

1. Set $\mathcal{S} = \mathcal{P}$.
2. Invoke the oracle computing $\mathsf{ShrGn}_f$. If parties in $\mathcal{T} \subset \mathcal{S}$ abort the computation, then the parties set $\mathcal{S} = \mathcal{S} \setminus \mathcal{T}$ and repeat the current step. If the computation is not aborted then each $P \in \mathcal{S}$ receives $\sigma_P$.
3. If $P_1$ is still alive,
   (a) $P_1$ sends $\sigma_{P_1}$ to $Q$.
   (b) Parties in $\mathcal{S} \setminus \{P_1\}$ send their shares to $Q$.
   **Abort scenarios:**
   - If $Q$ aborts, then the computation halts.
   - If $P_1$ aborts at Step 3a, then the parties set $\mathcal{S} = \mathcal{S} \setminus \mathcal{T}$ and go back to Step 2.
   - If parties in $\mathcal{T} \subseteq \mathcal{S} \setminus \{Q, P_1\}$ abort, then $Q$ outputs $d \leftarrow \mathbf{D}$ and the computation halts.
4. If $P_1$ already aborted,
   (a) Parties in $\mathcal{S}$ send their shares to $Q$.
   **Abort scenarios:**
   - If $Q$ aborts, then the computation halts.
   - If parties in $\mathcal{T} \subseteq \mathcal{S} \setminus \{Q\}$ abort the computation, then $Q$ outputs $d \leftarrow \mathbf{D}$ and the computation halts.

**Output:**  If $Q$'s output hasn't been determined yet, then $Q$ outputs $\bigoplus\limits_{P \in \mathcal{S}} \sigma_P$. All other parties output nothing.

---

**Fig. 6.** $n$-Party Protocol $\Pi$ for $f$ with Ideal Access to $\mathsf{ShrGn}_f$ with Identifiable Abort

## 4.3   Functions with Fully Revealing Input

In this section, we present the "Fully Revealing Input" criterion. First, we define the notion.

**Definition 4.3.** *Let $\mathcal{S} \subsetneq \mathcal{P}$. We say that the parties in $\mathcal{S}$ admit a fully revealing input, if there exists $x_{\mathcal{S}} \in \underset{P_i \in \mathcal{S}}{\times} X_i$ such that the following function is injective*

$$f_{x_{\mathcal{S}}} : x_{\overline{\mathcal{S}}} \mapsto f(x_{\mathcal{S}}, x_{\overline{\mathcal{S}}}).$$

The theorem below states that if there exists a fixing of the inputs of $P_1$ and $Q$ (or any $P_i$ and $Q$) that yields an injective function, then the overlying functionality $f$ is computable with full security in a constant number of rounds in the $\mathsf{ShrGn}_f$-hybrid model. Similarly to the previous section, assuming OT, it follows as an immediate corollary that functions with fully revealing input admit fully secure protocol in the plain model.

**Theorem 4.3.** *Assume there exists $i$ such that $\{P_i, Q\}$ admit a fully revealing input. Then, functionality $f$ is computable with perfect full security in the $\mathsf{ShrGn}_f$-hybrid model with identifiable abort. Furthermore, the computation runs in a constant number of rounds.*

Without loss of generality, suppose that $P_1, Q$ admit a fully revealing input. The protocol (Fig. 7) proceeds as follows: the parties invoke the trusted party for computing $\mathsf{ShrGn}_f$, and obtain shares of the output. Then, in two distinct steps (1) All-parties-but-$P_1$ send their shares of the output to $Q$ and (2) $P_1$ sends its share to $Q$. In case of abort, the process is repeated until it succeeds. Intuitively, the protocol maintains security because the only way to extract more information from the protocol is to corrupt both $P_1$ and $Q$. In that case however, $P_1$ and $Q$ can provide input in the ideal model that reveals everything about the inputs of the honest parties.

*Proof of Theorem* 4.3. Let $A$ denote the adversary corrupting a subset of parties. Like in the previous proof, it is straightforward that if $A$ does not corrupt both $Q$ and $P_1$ then it cannot affect correctness and its view can be trivially simulated. If $A$ corrupts both $P_1$ and $Q$, then by instructing the simulator to send the fully revealing input in the ideal model, the adversary's view can be simulated perfectly, no matter what is its course of action.[7]                                    □

## 4.4   Outliers

In this section, we present protocol for a function that escapes the above criteria but is nevertheless computable with full security. Due to space constraints, we only give here a brief overview of the protocol. For the formal description and security analysis, the reader is refered to the full version of the present paper [24]. Define functionality $f$ that takes inputs $x \in \{0,1,2\}$ from $P_1$ and $y \in \{0,1,2\}$ from $P_2$ and delivers $f(x,y)$ to $Q$ such that

$$f(x,y) = \begin{cases} 1 & \text{if } x = y \in \{0,1\} \\ 2 & \text{if } x = y = 2 \\ 0 & \text{otherwise} \end{cases}$$

In this section, we show that the functionality $f$ is computable with full security in $\omega(\log(\kappa))$ rounds. In what follows, we identify $\{0,1,2\}$ with $\{x_0, x_1, x_2\}$ or $\{y_0, y_1, y_2\}$ to make the distinction between the parties' input-spaces explicit.

Our protocol is inspired by the GHKL protocol and proceeds as follows. Formal descriptions and more detailed security analysis appear in the full version

---

[7] We stress that honest-but-curious adversaries can be simulated without having recourse to the fully revealing input, conforming to the standard definition. We have omitted the analysis here, since it is straightforward.

---

**$n$-Party Protocol for Computing $f$ with Fully Revealing Input**

Recall that $P_1$ denotes the party such that $\{P_1, Q\}$ admit a fully revealing input.

- **Input:**  Each party $P_\ell$ holds input $x_\ell$ (recall that here $Q$ is one of the $P_\ell$'s).

1. The parties invoke the oracle computing $\mathsf{ShrGn}_f$ and each $P_i \in S$ receives $\sigma_{P_i}$.
   **Abort scenarios:**
   - If $Q$ aborts, then the computation halts.
   - If parties in $\mathcal{T} \subsetneq S \setminus \{Q\}$ abort the computation, then the remaining parties set $S = S \setminus \mathcal{T}$ and repeat the present step.
   - If parties in $\mathcal{T} = S \setminus \{Q\}$ abort the computation, then $Q$ outputs $f(x_{\{Q\}}, x_{\mathcal{T}})$ where $x_{\mathcal{T}} \leftarrow \underset{P_i \neq Q}{\times} X_i$ is sampled uniformly at random.

2. If $P_1$ is still alive then
   (a) All parties except $P_1$ send their shares to $Q$.
   (b) $P_1$ sends $\sigma_{P_1}$ to $Q$.
   **Abort scenarios:**
   - If $Q$ aborts, then the computation halts.
   - If parties in $\mathcal{T} \subsetneq S \setminus \{Q\}$ abort at Steps 3a or 2a, then the parties update $S = S \setminus \mathcal{T}$ and go back to Step 1.
   - If parties in $\mathcal{T} = S \setminus \{Q\}$ abort the computation, then $Q$ outputs $f(x_{\{Q\}}, x_{\mathcal{T}})$ where $x_{\mathcal{T}} \leftarrow \underset{P_i \neq Q}{\times} X_i$ is sampled uniformly at random.

3. If $P_1$ already aborted then
   (a) Remaining parties send their shares to $Q$.
   **Abort scenarios:**
   - If $Q$ aborts, then the computation halts.
   - If parties in $\mathcal{T} \subsetneq S \setminus \{Q\}$ abort at Step 2a, then the parties update $S = S \setminus \mathcal{T}$ and go back to Step 1.
   - If parties in $\mathcal{T} = S \setminus \{Q\}$ abort the computation, then $Q$ outputs $f(x_{\{Q\}}, x_{\mathcal{T}})$ where $x_{\mathcal{T}} \leftarrow \underset{P_i \neq Q}{\times} X_i$ is sampled uniformly at random.

- **Output:**  If $Q$'s output hasn't been determined yet, then $Q$ outputs $\underset{P_i \in S}{\oplus} \sigma_{P_i}$. All other parties output nothing.

---

**Fig. 7.** $n$-Party Protocol $\Pi$ for $f$ in the $\mathsf{ShrGn}_f$-Hybrid Model with Identifiable Abort

of the present paper [24]. In the remainder of this section, we only give a high level overview. Write $x$ and $y$ for the inputs used by the parties. In a share generation phase, the parties obliviously generate two sequences of values $(a_0, \ldots, a_r)$ and $(b_0, \ldots, b_r)$ and an integer $i^* \in [r]$ such that every value $a_i$ and $b_i$ is equal to $f(x, y)$ for indices succeeding $i^*$, and, for indices preceding $i^*$, $a_i$ is computed by obliviously choosing a fresh input from $\{y_0, y_1\}$ for $P_2$, and using input $x$ for $P_1$ and, similarly, $b_i$ is computed by obliviously choosing a fresh input from $\{x_0, x_1\}$ for $P_1$, and using input $y$ for $P_2$. The value of $i^*$ is chosen according to a suitable distribution. The two sequences are then shared in a 3-out-of-3 additive (modulo 3) secret sharing among the parties. Then, in the share exchange phase, in $r$ iterations, $P_1$ is instructed to send its share of $b_i$ to $Q$, and $P_2$ is instructed to send its share of $a_i$ to $Q$. If party $P_1$ aborts at round $i$, then $P_2$ sends its share of $b_{i-1}$ to $Q$, and, similarly, if $P_2$ aborts at round $i$, then $P_1$ sends its share of $a_i$ to $Q$. Party $Q$ is instructed to output the value it can reconstruct from the shares.

We crucially observe that, prior to $i^*$, the obliviously chosen input for each party is sampled from $\{0, 1\}$, and *not* $\{0, 1, 2\}$. This seemingly superficial technicality is what enables the protocol to be secure.

We conclude with the following theorem which immediately yields full security for $f$, assuming a protocol for OT.

**Theorem 4.4.** *Protocol $\Pi$ computes $f$ with statistical full security in the* $\mathsf{ShrGn}_f^*$*-hybrid model with identifiable abort.*

## 5  Lower-Bound on Round-Complexity

In this section, we present a lower bound for the functionality $f$ from the previous section. Let $f$ be the three-party solitary functionality from Sect. 4.4. In what follows, let $\Pi$ denote a protocol for $f$, let $\kappa$ denote the security parameter, and assume the round-complexity of $\Pi$ is set to some value $r$ that is independent of $\kappa$. It follows as an immediate corollary of the theorem below that no such protocol can be fully secure.

**Theorem 5.1.** *Using the notation above, there exists $i \in [r]$ such that at least one of the following is true:*

1. *An adversary corrupting $P_2$ and $Q$ violates $P_1$'s privacy by aborting $P_2$ at round $i$.*
2. *An adversary corrupting $P_1$ and $Q$ violates $P_2$'s privacy by aborting $P_1$ at round $i$.*
3. *An adversary corrupting $P_1$ violates correctness by aborting at round $i$.*
4. *An adversary corrupting $P_2$ violates correctness by aborting at round $i$.*

For the proof of the above, the reader is referred to the full version [24] of the present paper.

**Acknowledgments.** We are grateful to Noam Mazor, Matan Orland and Jad Silbak for helpful discussions.

## References

1. Agarwal, N., Anand, S., Prabhakaran, M.: Uncovering algebraic structures in the MPC landscape. In: Ishai, Y., Rijmen, V. (eds.) EUROCRYPT 2019, Part II. LNCS, vol. 11477, pp. 381–406. Springer, Cham (2019). https://doi.org/10.1007/978-3-030-17656-3_14

2. Asharov, G.: Towards characterizing complete fairness in secure two-party computation. In: Lindell, Y. (ed.) TCC 2014. LNCS, vol. 8349, pp. 291–316. Springer, Heidelberg (2014). https://doi.org/10.1007/978-3-642-54242-8_13
3. Asharov, G., Beimel, A., Makriyannis, N., Omri, E.: Complete characterization of fairness in secure two-party computation of boolean functions. In: Dodis, Y., Nielsen, J.B. (eds.) TCC 2015, Part I. LNCS, vol. 9014, pp. 199–228. Springer, Heidelberg (2015). https://doi.org/10.1007/978-3-662-46494-6_10
4. Beaver, D.: Multiparty protocols tolerating half faulty processors. In: Brassard, G. (ed.) CRYPTO 1989. LNCS, vol. 435, pp. 560–572. Springer, New York (1990). https://doi.org/10.1007/0-387-34805-0_49
5. Beaver, D., Goldwasser, S.: Multiparty computation with faulty majority. In: Proceedings of the 30th Annual Symposium on Foundations of Computer Science (FOCS), pp. 468–473 (1989)
6. Beimel, A., Gabizon, A., Ishai, Y., Kushilevitz, E., Meldgaard, S., Paskin-Cherniavsky, A.: Non-interactive secure multiparty computation. In: Garay, J.A., Gennaro, R. (eds.) CRYPTO 2014, Part II. LNCS, vol. 8617, pp. 387–404. Springer, Heidelberg (2014). https://doi.org/10.1007/978-3-662-44381-1_22
7. Ben-Or, M., Goldwasser, S., Wigderson, A.: Completeness theorems for non-cryptographic fault-tolerant distributed computation (extended abstract). In: Proceedings of the 29th Annual Symposium on Foundations of Computer Science (FOCS), pp. 1–10 (1988)
8. Canetti, R.: Security and composition of multiparty cryptographic protocols. J. Cryptol. 13(1), 143–202 (2000)
9. Chaum, D., Crépeau, C., Damgard, I.: Multiparty unconditionally secure protocols (extended abstract). In: Proceedings of the 10th Annual ACM Symposium on Theory of Computing (STOC), pp. 11–19 (1988)
10. Chor, B., Kushilevitz, E.: A zero-one law for boolean privacy. SIAM J. Discrete Math. 4(1), 36–47 (1991)
11. Cleve, R.: Limits on the security of coin flips when half the processors are faulty. In: Proceedings of the 18th Annual ACM Symposium on Theory of Computing (STOC), pp. 364–369 (1986)
12. Cohen, R., Lindell, Y.: Fairness versus guaranteed output delivery in secure multiparty computation. J. Cryptol. 30(4), 1157–1186 (2017)
13. Data, D., Prabhakaran, M.: Towards characterizing securely computable two-party randomized functions. In: Abdalla, M., Dahab, R. (eds.) PKC 2018. LNCS, vol. 10769, pp. 675–697. Springer, Cham (2018). https://doi.org/10.1007/978-3-319-76578-5_23
14. Daza, V., Makriyannis, N.: Designing fully secure protocols for secure two-party computation of constant-domain functions. In: Kalai, Y., Reyzin, L. (eds.) TCC 2017, Part I. LNCS, vol. 10677, pp. 581–611. Springer, Cham (2017). https://doi.org/10.1007/978-3-319-70500-2_20
15. Feige, U., Kilian, J., Naor, M.: A minimal model for secure computation (extended abstract). In: Proceedings of the Twenty-Sixth Annual ACM Symposium on Theory of Computing, Montréal, Québec, Canada, 23–25 May 1994, pp. 554–563 (1994)
16. Fitzi, M., Garay, J.A., Maurer, U.M., Ostrovsky, R.: Minimal complete primitives for secure multi-party computation. J. Cryptol. 18(1), 37–61 (2005)
17. Gennaro, R., Ishai, Y., Kushilevitz, E., Rabin, T.: On 2-round secure multiparty computation. In: Yung, M. (ed.) CRYPTO 2002. LNCS, vol. 2442, pp. 178–193. Springer, Heidelberg (2002). https://doi.org/10.1007/3-540-45708-9_12
18. Goldreich, O.: Foundations of Cryptography — Basic Applications. Cambridge University Press, Cambridge (2004)

19. Goldreich, O., Micali, S., Wigderson, A.: How to play any mental game or a completeness theorem for protocols with honest majority. In: Proceedings of the 19th Annual ACM Symposium on Theory of Computing (STOC), pp. 218–229 (1987)

20. Goldwasser, S., Levin, L.: Fair computation of general functions in presence of immoral majority. In: Menezes, A.J., Vanstone, S.A. (eds.) CRYPTO 1990. LNCS, vol. 537, pp. 77–93. Springer, Heidelberg (1991). https://doi.org/10.1007/3-540-38424-3_6

21. Goldwasser, S., Lindell, Y.: Secure multi-party computation without agreement. J. Cryptol. **18**(3), 247–287 (2005)

22. Gordon, S.D., Katz, J.: Complete fairness in multi-party computation without an honest majority. In: Reingold, O. (ed.) TCC 2009. LNCS, vol. 5444, pp. 19–35. Springer, Heidelberg (2009). https://doi.org/10.1007/978-3-642-00457-5_2

23. Dov Gordon, S., Hazay, C., Katz, J., Lindell, Y.: Complete fairness in secure two-party computation. J. ACM **58**(6), 24:1–24:37 (2011)

24. Halevi, S., Ishai, Y., Kushilevitz, E., Makriyannis, N., Rabin, T.: On fully secure MPC with solitary output. Cryptology ePrint Archive, Report 2019/1032 (2019). https://eprint.iacr.org/2019/1032

25. Ishai, Y., Kushilevitz, E., Lindell, Y., Petrank, E.: On combining privacy with guaranteed output delivery in secure multiparty computation. In: Dwork, C. (ed.) CRYPTO 2006. LNCS, vol. 4117, pp. 483–500. Springer, Heidelberg (2006). https://doi.org/10.1007/11818175_29

26. Ishai, Y., Katz, J., Kushilevitz, E., Lindell, Y., Petrank, E.: On achieving the "best of both worlds" in secure multiparty computation. SIAM J. Comput. **40**(1), 122–141 (2011)

27. Katz, J.: On achieving the "best of both worlds" in secure multiparty computation. In: Proceedings of the 39th Annual ACM Symposium on Theory of Computing (STOC), pp. 11–20 (2007)

28. Kushilevitz, E.: Privacy and communication complexity. SIAM J. Discrete Math. **5**(2), 273–284 (1992)

29. Lindell, Y., Rabin, T.: Secure two-party computation with fairness - a necessary design principle. In: Kalai, Y., Reyzin, L. (eds.) TCC 2017, Part I. LNCS, vol. 10677, pp. 565–580. Springer, Cham (2017). https://doi.org/10.1007/978-3-319-70500-2_19

30. Makriyannis, N.: On the classification of finite boolean functions up to fairness. In: Abdalla, M., De Prisco, R. (eds.) SCN 2014. LNCS, vol. 8642, pp. 135–154. Springer, Cham (2014). https://doi.org/10.1007/978-3-319-10879-7_9

31. Rabin, T., Ben-Or, M.: Verifiable secret sharing and multiparty protocols with honest majority (extended abstract). In: Proceedings of the 30th Annual Symposium on Foundations of Computer Science (FOCS), pp. 73–85 (1989)

32. Yao, A.C.-C.: How to generate and exchange secrets. In: Proceedings of the 27th Annual Symposium on Foundations of Computer Science (FOCS), pp. 162–167 (1986)

# Secure Computation with Preprocessing via Function Secret Sharing

Elette Boyle[1]([✉]), Niv Gilboa[2], and Yuval Ishai[3]

[1] IDC, Herzliya, Israel
eboyle@alum.mit.edu
[2] Ben Gurion University, Beersheba, Israel
gilboan@bgu.ac.il
[3] Technion, Haifa, Israel
yuvali@cs.technion.ac.il

**Abstract.** We propose a simple and powerful new approach for secure computation with input-independent preprocessing, building on the general tool of *function secret sharing* (FSS) and its efficient instantiations. Using this approach, we can make efficient use of correlated randomness to compute any type of gate, as long as a function class naturally corresponding to this gate admits an efficient FSS scheme. Our approach can be viewed as a generalization of the "TinyTable" protocol of Damgård et al. (Crypto 2017), where our generalized variant uses FSS to achieve exponential efficiency improvement for useful types of gates.

By instantiating this general approach with efficient PRG-based FSS schemes of Boyle et al. (Eurocrypt 2015, CCS 2016), we can implement useful nonlinear gates for equality tests, integer comparison, bit-decomposition and more with optimal online communication and with a relatively small amount of correlated randomness. We also provide a unified and simplified view of several existing protocols in the preprocessing model via the FSS framework.

Our positive results provide a useful tool for secure computation tasks that involve secure integer comparisons or conversions between arithmetic and binary representations. These arise in the contexts of approximating real-valued functions, machine-learning classification, and more. Finally, we study the necessity of the FSS machinery that we employ, in the simple context of secure string equality testing. First, we show that any "online-optimal" secure equality protocol implies an FSS scheme for point functions, which in turn implies one-way functions. Then, we show that *information-theoretic* secure equality protocols with relaxed optimality requirements would follow from the existence of big families of "matching vectors." This suggests that proving strong lower bounds on the efficiency of such protocols would be difficult.

## 1 Introduction

The power of correlated randomness in secure computation has recently been an active area of research. In the setting of *secure computation with preprocessing*,

© International Association for Cryptologic Research 2019
D. Hofheinz and A. Rosen (Eds.): TCC 2019, LNCS 11891, pp. 341–371, 2019.
https://doi.org/10.1007/978-3-030-36030-6_14

two or more parties receive correlated random inputs from a trusted dealer in an offline phase, before the inputs are known. In a subsequent online phase, once the inputs are known, the parties use this correlated randomness to obtain significant speedup over similar protocols in the plain model, either unconditionally or under weaker cryptographic assumptions. Alternatively, in the absence of a trusted dealer, the correlated randomness can be generated via an interactive secure protocol that is executed offline, before the inputs are known, and only the outputs of this protocol need to be stored for later use. For simplicity, we focus in this work on the case of secure *two-party* computation with security against *semi-honest* adversaries.[1]

Originating from the work of Beaver [2], who showed how to use "multiplication triples" for secure arithmetic computation with no honest majority, many current protocols for secure computation make extensive use of correlated randomness. Commonly used types of two-party correlations include garbled circuit correlations, OT and OLE correlations, multiplication ("Beaver") triples and their authenticated version, and one-time truth-tables [2,4,11,13,14,22].

Motivated by secure computation applications that involve integer comparisons or conversions between arithmetic and boolean values, we introduce a simple and powerful new approach for secure computation in the preprocessing model. Our approach is based on the general tool of *function secret sharing* (FSS) [7] and its efficient instantiations from any pseudorandom generator. Informally, a (2-party) FSS scheme splits a function $f : \mathbb{G}^{\mathsf{in}} \to \mathbb{G}^{\mathsf{out}}$ from a function class $\mathcal{F}$, where $\mathbb{G}^{\mathsf{in}}$ and $\mathbb{G}^{\mathsf{out}}$ are finite Abelian[2] groups, into two functions, $f_0$ and $f_1$, such that (1) each $f_\sigma$ is represented by a compact key $k_\sigma$ that allows its efficient evaluation; (2) each key $k_\sigma$ hides the function $f$; and (3) for any input $x \in \mathbb{G}^{\mathsf{in}}$ we have $f(x) = f_0(x) + f_1(x)$.

**The Idea in a Nutshell.** Our FSS-based approach for secure computation with preprocessing is very simple. Denote the two parties by $P_0$ and $P_1$. We represent the function being evaluated as a circuit $C$, in which inputs internal wires take values from (possibly distinct) groups. The circuit nodes are labeled by gates, where each gate $g$ maps an input from a group $\mathbb{G}^{\mathsf{in}}$ into an output from a group $\mathbb{G}^{\mathsf{out}}$. Note that we can use product groups to capture a gate with multiple input or output wires. To securely evaluate $C$ in the preprocessing model, the dealer generates and distributes the following type of correlated randomness. First, for every wire $j$ in $C$, the dealer picks a random mask $r_j$ from the corresponding group. Each party $P_\sigma$ receives the random masks of the input wires it owns. The online phase evaluates the circuit gate-by-gate in a topological order, maintaining the following invariant: for every wire value $w_j$ in $C$, *both* parties learn the masked

---

[1] Our techniques naturally generalize to the multi-party setting, though typically with reduced efficiency benefits over alternative approaches. Moreover, most of our protocols can be extended to the malicious security model by employing simple authentication techniques (as in [4,14]).

[2] Unlike previous applications of FSS, here it is important that the *input* domain additionally be endowed with group structure. From here on, the term "group" will always refer to a finite Abelian group.

value $w_j + r_j$. This is easy to achieve at the inputs level: if input $x_i$ is owned by party $P_\sigma$, this party can simply compute and send $x_i + r_i$ to the other party.

The key idea is the following FSS-based gate evaluation procedure. For each gate $g : \mathbb{G}^{\mathsf{in}} \to \mathbb{G}^{\mathsf{out}}$, the dealer uses an FSS scheme for the class of *offset* functions $\mathcal{G}$ that includes all functions of the form $g_{r^{\mathsf{in}}, r^{\mathsf{out}}}(x) = g(x - r^{\mathsf{in}}) + r^{\mathsf{out}}$. If the input to gate $g$ is wire $i$ and the output is wire $j$, the dealer uses the FSS scheme for $\mathcal{G}$ to split the function $g_{r_i, r_j}$ into two functions with keys $k_0, k_1$, and delivers each key $k_\sigma$ to party $P_\sigma$. Now, evaluating their FSS shares on the common masked input $w_i + r_i$, the parties obtain additive shares of the masked output $w_j + r_j$, which they can exchange and maintain the invariant for wire $j$. Finally, the outputs are reconstructed by having the dealer reveal to both parties the masks of the output wires.

The above protocol is not only simple, but in a sense is implicit in the literature. It can be viewed as a generalization of the "TinyTable" protocol of Damgård et al. [13], where the novel idea is to use efficient FSS for achieving exponential compression (and speedup[3]) for natural types of gates that are useful in applications. We discuss several useful instances of this approach below.

While the correlated randomness in the above protocol depends on the topology of $C$, we also present a *circuit-independent* variant where the input and output masks of different gates are independent of each other. In this variant, for each gate $g$ the dealer chooses additive $r^{\mathsf{in}}$ offsets only for the *input* wires of $g$, and provides FSS shares for the function $g_{r^{\mathsf{in}}, 0}(x) = g(x - r^{\mathsf{in}}) + 0$, together with *additive shares* of $r^{\mathsf{in}}$. During the online phase, the parties can "match up" the offsets for adjacent gates, and non-interactively emulate FSS shares of $g_{r^{\mathsf{in}}, r^{\mathsf{out}}}(x) = g(x - r^{\mathsf{in}}) + r^{\mathsf{out}}$ using the additive shares, where $r^{\mathsf{out}}$ is defined to be $(r^{\mathsf{in}})'$ for the appropriate next gate $g'$. The resulting online communication is one element per *wire*, as opposed to only one element per computed wire *value* as in the circuit-dependent version (where circuit fan-out introduces extra wires but not new wire values).

Finally, one could alternatively consider a variant of our protocols in which FSS is used to convert *secret-shared* inputs to secret-shared outputs rather than common *masked* inputs to masked outputs. Whereas in the above protocol both parties first apply FSS on the common masked input and then exchange their output shares to obtain a masked output, in the alternative variant they start by reconstructing a common masked input from their input shares, and then apply FSS to directly obtain the output shares.

**Application: Simple Derivation of Existing Protocols.** By using simple information-theoretic FSS schemes for truth-tables and low-degree polynomials, our FSS-based approach can be used to derive in a simple and unified way several previous protocols for secure computation in the preprocessing model. For instance, protocols from [2, 11, 13, 22, 23] can be easily cast in this framework.

---

[3] A general method for compressing truth-table correlations was recently suggested in [6]. However, the *running time* still grows linearly with the truth-table size, or exponentially with the gate input length.

We also present useful generalizations of such protocols to broader classes of algebraic computations.

**Application: Online-Optimal Secure Equality, Comparison, Bit Decomposition, and More.** Our FSS-based technique yields a simple new approach for securely performing useful nonlinear operations on masked or secret-shared values. We first describe the types of nonlinear operations we can efficiently support, and then the efficiency features of our FSS-based solution.

When performing secure arithmetic computations, it is often useful to switch between an *arithmetic* representation, where the values are secret-shared over a big modulus $\mathbb{Z}_q$, and a Boolean representation, where the values are secret shared bit-by-bit over $\mathbb{Z}_2$. Other useful nonlinear operations include zero-testing of a shared value or equality testing of two shared values, comparing between different integer values (i.e., the "greater than" predicate), or checking if an integer value is in an interval. For all of the above predicates, the input is secret-shared over $\mathbb{Z}_q$ and the 0/1 output is secret-shared for further computations over either $\mathbb{Z}_2$, $\mathbb{Z}_q$, or another group. A more general class of nonlinear computations are *spline functions* that output a different polynomial on each interval. A useful special case is the ReLU function $g(x) = \max(0, x)$ that is commonly used as an activation function in neural networks. Finally, one can also consider a garbling-compatible variant of the above operations, where the bits of the output select between pairs of secret keys that can be fed to a garbled circuit.

In all of the above cases, we can use computationally secure FSS schemes based on one-way functions [7, 8, 19] to efficiently realize the corresponding offset classes $\mathcal{G}$ using only symmetric cryptography. Concretely, for all the above types of gates we can use efficient preprocessing to convert shares of an input into shares of an output with optimal online communication that only involves a *single round* of exchanging masked input shares and no further interaction. Each party can then directly compute its share of the output given its part of the correlated randomness and the message received from the other party.

The above types of nonlinear "FSS gates" can provide a valuable toolbox for the large body of work on secure machine learning classification, secure implementation of bounded-precision arithmetic, and secure approximations of real-valued functions. In fact, they can even be useful for evaluating standard Boolean circuits. For instance, evaluating an AND/OR gate with fan-in $m$ reduces to a secure equality of $m$-bit strings.

**Comparison with Prior Approaches.** There is a long line of work on secure implementation of useful nonlinear computations such as bit-decomposition in different models (see [10, 12, 15, 25] and references therein). As discussed above, our FSS-based technique has an *optimal online cost* of converting secret-shared inputs to secret-shared outputs. Compared to the commonly used "ABY framework" [15] for performing such operations using garbled circuits, our approach has better round complexity (1 instead of 2 rounds) and, more importantly, it avoids the big overhead of sending a key for each bit of the input. In concrete terms, this improves the online communication complexity by two orders of magnitude. Even in the relatively simple cases of equality testing and integer

**Table 1.** Comparison of the performance of our protocols to the ABY framework by Demmler, Schneider and Zohner [15] and protocols of Couteau [10] (bit-decomposition is not directly supported by [10]). The inputs are taken from a group $\mathbb{G}^{in}$ with $m = \lceil \log |\mathbb{G}^{in}| \rceil$ (e.g., $\mathbb{G}^{in} = \mathbb{Z}_{2^m}$). We let $\lambda$ denote the seed length of a length-doubling PRG ($\lambda = 128$ for an AES-based implementation) and use big-$O$ notation to hide small constants that are strictly bigger than 1. Online rounds allow one message per party per round. The specified complexity refers to converting secret-shared input to secret-shared output, where the input sharing is over $\mathbb{G}^{in}$ and the output sharing is over $\mathbb{Z}_2$ (for zero test or comparison) or $\mathbb{Z}_2^m$ (for bit-decomposition). The online computational cost of our protocols is dominated by roughly $s/\lambda$ invocations of the PRG, where $s$ is the offline storage in bits.

| Gate type | Protocol | Online communication (bits per party) | Online rounds | Offline storage (bits) |
|---|---|---|---|---|
| Zero test | [10] | $m + o(m)$ | $\geq 3$ | $2m + o(m)$ |
| | ABY [15] | $O(\lambda m)$ | 2 | $O(\lambda m)$ |
| | **Proposition 2** | $m$ | 1 | $\approx \lambda m$ |
| Zero test example $m = 64$ | [10] | 77 | 3 | 152 |
| | **Proposition 2** | 64 | 1 | 8384 |
| Integer comparison | [10] SC1 | $O(m)$ | $O(\log \log m)$ | $3m + o(m)$ |
| | ABY [15] | $O(\lambda m)$ | 2 | $O(\lambda m)$ |
| | **Proposition 3** | $m$ | 1 | $\approx \lambda m$ |
| Comparison example $m = 64$ | [10] SC1 | 1120 | 12 | $\approx 300$ |
| | **Proposition 3** | 64 | 1 | 8512 |
| Bit decomposition | ABY [15] | $O(\lambda m)$ | 2 | $O(\lambda m)$ |
| | **Proposition 5** | $m$ | 1 | $\approx \lambda m^2/2$ |
| Spline over $\mathbb{Z}_{2^m}$ $k + 1$ deg.-$d$ polynomials | ABY [15] | $O(m(\lambda k + d))$ | 2 | $O(m(\lambda k + d))$ |
| | **Proposition 4** | $m$ | 1 | $\approx 2\,km(\lambda + d)$ |

comparison, where improved special-purpose protocols are known (see [10] and references therein), our FSS-based approach has significant advantages over the best previous protocols.

The low online cost of our FSS-based protocols is inherited from the efficiency of recent constructions of FSS schemes for point functions, intervals, and decision trees [7,8,19]. These constructions make a black-box use of any pseudorandom generator, which can be instantiated by AES in practice. Thus, for the type of "gates" supported by such simple FSS schemes, our protocols significantly improve the online communication complexity and round complexity of prior approaches while still being very computationally efficient in the online phase. See Table 1 for comparison.

**Realizing the Dealer.** We turn to discuss the offline cost of securely generating and storing the correlated randomness. The amount of correlated randomness used by our protocols is dominated by the size of the FSS keys. For equality and comparison gates, this includes a linear number of PRG seeds (e.g., AES keys) in the bit-length of the inputs, and for bit-decomposition it involves a quadratic number of PRG seeds. When the input domain is not too big, the distributed generation of this correlated randomness can be done with good concrete efficiency using a distributed FSS key generation protocol of Doerner and Shelat [16]. Otherwise one can use concretely efficient general-purpose secure computation protocols (such as [24]) for emulating the dealer. Finally, one can avoid the cost of securely distributing the correlated randomness by using a third party as a dealer and settling for security against a single corrupted party. This is similar to the 3-party ABY$^3$ framework from [25], except that here the third party is only used to generate correlated randomness and can remain offline during the actual computation.

**Is FSS Necessary?** Our most useful positive results make use of symmetric cryptography. Given that most protocols in the preprocessing model are *information-theoretic*, one may ask if it is possible to obtain similar results in the information-theoretic model with a polynomial amount of correlated randomness. For simplicity, we consider a *shared equality* protocol with optimal online complexity. In such a protocol, the parties hold $n$-bit strings $x_0$ and $x_1$, and in a single round of interaction they send an $n$-bit message to each other. These messages should hide their inputs. Following this interaction, they each locally output a single output bit such that the exclusive-or of the two bits is 1 if and only if $x_0 = x_1$. We show that our FSS machinery is not only sufficient for obtaining this type of protocols, but is also necessary. In particular, any protocol as above implies the existence of a one-way function. (This implication is more subtle than it may seem since unlike our simple FSS-based protocol, a general shared equality protocol may correlate the randomness used to mask the inputs with the randomness used to compute the output shares.) On the other hand, we show that efficient *information-theoretic* shared equality protocols with constant-size output shares would follow from the existence of big families of "matching vectors" [17,18,21], a longstanding open problem in extremal combinatorics. This suggests that strong lower bounds on the efficiency of information-theoretic shared equality protocols would be difficult to obtain.

*Organization.* In Sect. 2, we provide necessary preliminaries. In Sect. 3, we present our general framework for secure computation with preprocessing via FSS. In Sect. 4, we present applications, instantiating the necessary FSS schemes for specific motivated computation tasks. We conclude in Sect. 5 by exploring negative results and barriers.

## 2 Preliminaries

### 2.1 Representing Functions

In order to seamlessly handle both arithmetic and Boolean operations, we will consider all functions to be defined over Abelian groups. For instance, a Boolean function $f : \{0,1\}^n \to \{0,1\}^m$ will be viewed as a mapping from the group $\mathbb{Z}_2^n$ to the group $\mathbb{Z}_2^m$. Given our heavy use of function secret sharing, we use a similar convention for function representation to the one used in [8] (the only difference being that here we also endow the input domain with a group structure).

**Definition 1 (Function families).** *A function family is defined by $\mathcal{F} = (P_\mathcal{F}, E_\mathcal{F})$, where $P_\mathcal{F} \subseteq \{0,1\}^*$ is an infinite collection of function descriptions $\hat{f}$ and $E_\mathcal{F} : P_\mathcal{F} \times \{0,1\}^* \to \{0,1\}^*$ is a polynomial-time algorithm defining the function described by $\hat{f}$. Concretely, $\hat{f} \in P_\mathcal{F}$ describes a corresponding function $f : D_f \to R_f$ defined by $f(x) = E_\mathcal{F}(\hat{f}, x)$. We require $D_f$ and $R_f$ to be finite Abelian groups, denoted by $\mathbb{G}^{in}$ and $\mathbb{G}^{out}$ respectively. We will typically let $\mathbb{G}^{in}$ and $\mathbb{G}^{out}$ be product groups, which can capture the case of multiple inputs and outputs. When there is no risk of confusion, we will sometimes write $f$ instead of $\hat{f}$ and $f \in \mathcal{F}$ instead of $\hat{f} \in P_\mathcal{F}$. We assume that $\hat{f}$ includes an explicit description of $\mathbb{G}^{in}$ and $\mathbb{G}^{out}$.*

By convention, we denote by $0 \in \mathbb{G}$ the identity element of $\mathbb{G}$. We will use the notation $1 \in \mathbb{G}$ to denote a fixed canonical nonzero element of $\mathbb{G}$; when $\mathbb{G}$ is additionally endowed with a multiplicative structure, e.g., when $\mathbb{G}$ is the additive group of a finite *ring*, 1 will be set to the multiplicative identity.

### 2.2 Secure Computation with Preprocessing

We follow the standard definitional framework for secure computation (cf. [9,20]), except that we allow a trusted input-independent setup phase that distributes correlated secret randomness to the parties. This setup phase can be securely emulated by an interactive preprocessing protocol that can be carried out before the inputs are known. We focus here on protocols with security against a *semi-honest* adversary who may non-adaptively corrupt any strict subset of parties. For simplicity, we explicitly spell out the definitions for the two-party case, and later explain the (straightforward) extension to the multi-party case.

*Functionalities.* We denote the two parties by $P_0$ and $P_1$ and a party index by $\sigma \in \{0, 1\}$. We consider by default protocols for *deterministic* functionalities that deliver the *same output* to the two parties. The general case (of randomized functionalities with different outputs) can be reduced to this case via a standard reduction [9, 20]. A two-party functionality $f$ is described by a bit-string $\hat{f}$ via a function family $\mathcal{F}$, as in Definition 1. We assume that the input domain $\mathbb{G}^{in}$ is split into $\mathbb{G}^{in} = \mathbb{G}_0^{in} \times \mathbb{G}_1^{in}$, capturing the inputs of the two parties.

*Protocols with Preprocessing.* A two-party protocol is defined by a pair of PPT algorithms $\Pi = (\mathsf{Setup}, \mathsf{NextMsg})$. The setup algorithm $\mathsf{Setup}(1^\lambda, \hat{f})$, given a security parameter $\lambda$ and functionality description $\hat{f}$, outputs a pair of correlated random strings $(r_0, r_1)$. We also consider protocols with *function-independent preprocessing*, in which $\mathsf{Setup}$ only receives a bound $1^S$ on the size of $\hat{f}$ instead of $\hat{f}$ itself. The *next-message function* $\mathsf{NextMsg}$ determines the messages sent by the two parties. Concretely, the function $\mathsf{NextMsg}$, on input $(\sigma, j, \hat{f}, x_\sigma, r_\sigma, \mathbf{m})$, specifies the message sent by party $P_\sigma$ in Round $j$ depending on the functionality description $\hat{f}$, input $x_\sigma$, random input $r_\sigma$, and vector $\mathbf{m}$ of previous messages received from $P_{1-\sigma}$. We assume both parties can speak to each other in the same round. (In the semi-honest model, one can eliminate this assumption by at most doubling the number of rounds.) If the output of $\mathsf{NextMsg}$ is of the form $(\mathsf{Out}, y)$ then party $P_\sigma$ terminates the protocol with output $y$. We denote by $\mathsf{Out}_{\Pi,\sigma}(\lambda, \hat{f}, (x_0, x_1))$ and $\mathsf{View}_{\Pi,\sigma}(\lambda, \hat{f}, (x_0, x_1))$ the random variables containing the output and view of party $P_\sigma$ (respectively) in the execution of $\Pi$ on inputs $(x_0, x_1)$, where the view includes $r_\sigma$ and messages received from $P_{1-\sigma}$.

*Security Definition.* We require both *correctness* and *security*, where security is captured by the existence of a PPT algorithm $\mathsf{Sim}$ that simulates the view of a party given its input and output alone. We formalize this below.

**Definition 2 (Secure computation with preprocessing).** *We say that* $\Pi = (\mathsf{Setup}, \mathsf{NextMsg})$ *securely realizes a function family* $\mathcal{F}$ *in the preprocessing model if the following holds:*

- Correctness: *For all* $\hat{f} \in P_{\mathcal{F}}$ *describing* $f : \mathbb{G}_0^{in} \times \mathbb{G}_1^{in} \to \mathbb{G}^{out}$, $(x_0, x_1) \in \mathbb{G}_0^{in} \times \mathbb{G}_1^{in}$, $\lambda \in \mathbb{N}$, $\sigma \in \{0, 1\}$, *we have* $\Pr[\mathsf{Out}_{\Pi,\sigma}(\lambda, \hat{f}, (x_0, x_1)) = f(x_0, x_1)] = 1$.
- Security: *For each corrupted party* $\sigma \in \{0, 1\}$ *there exists a PPT algorithm* $\mathsf{Sim}_\sigma$ *(simulator), such that for every infinite sequence* $(\hat{f}_\lambda)_{\lambda \in \mathbb{N}}$ *of polynomial-size function descriptions from* $P_{\mathcal{F}}$ *and polynomial-size input sequence* $(x_0^\lambda, x_1^\lambda)_{\lambda \in \mathbb{N}}$ *for* $f_\lambda$, *the outputs of the following experiments* Real *and* Ideal *are computationally indistinguishable:*
  - Real$_\lambda$: *Output* $\mathsf{View}_{\Pi,\sigma}(\lambda, \hat{f}_\lambda, (x_0^\lambda, x_1^\lambda))$
  - Ideal$_\lambda$: *Output* $\mathsf{Sim}_\sigma(1^\lambda, \hat{f}_\lambda, x_\sigma^\lambda, f_\lambda(x_0^\lambda, x_1^\lambda))$

*We say that* $\Pi$ *realizes* $\mathcal{F}$ *with* statistical *(resp., perfect) security if the above security requirement holds with statistical (resp., perfect) indistinguishability instead of computational indistinguishability.*

## 2.3    Function Secret Sharing

We follow the definition of function secret sharing (FSS) from [8]. Intuitively, a (2-party) FSS scheme is an efficient algorithm that splits a function $f \in \mathcal{F}$ into two *additive* shares $f_0, f_1$, such that: (1) each $f_\sigma$ hides $f$; (2) for every input $x$, $f_0(x) + f_1(x) = f(x)$. The main challenge is to make the descriptions of $f_0$ and $f_1$ compact, while still allowing their efficient evaluation. As in [7,8], we insist on an additive representation of the output rather than settle for an arbitrary compact output representation. The additive representation is critical for the applications we consider in this work and is achieved by existing constructions.

We now formally define the notion of FSS. While in this work we consider the 2-party case for simplicity, the definitions and the applications can be extended in a natural way to the $k$-party case.

**Definition 3 (FSS: Syntax).**    *A (2-party) function secret sharing (FSS) scheme is a pair of algorithms* (Gen, Eval) *with the following syntax:*

- Gen$(1^\lambda, \hat{f})$ *is a PPT key generation algorithm, which on input $1^\lambda$ (security parameter) and $\hat{f} \in \{0,1\}^*$ (description of a function $f$) outputs a pair of keys $(k_0, k_1)$. We assume that $\hat{f}$ explicitly contains descriptions of input and output groups $\mathbb{G}^{in}, \mathbb{G}^{out}$.*
- Eval$(\sigma, k_\sigma, x)$ *is a polynomial-time evaluation algorithm, which on input $\sigma \in \{0,1\}$ (party index), $k_\sigma$ (key defining $f_\sigma : \mathbb{G}^{in} \to \mathbb{G}^{out}$) and $x \in \mathbb{G}^{in}$ (input for $f_\sigma$) outputs a group element $y_\sigma \in \mathbb{G}^{out}$ (the value of $f_\sigma(x)$, the $\sigma$-th share of $f(x)$).*

**Definition 4 (FSS: Correctness and Security).**    *Let $\mathcal{F} = (P_\mathcal{F}, E_\mathcal{F})$ be a function family (as defined in Definition 1) and* Leak *be a polynomial-time computable function specifying the allowable leakage about $\hat{f}$. When* Leak *is omitted, it is understood to output only $\mathbb{G}^{in}$ and $\mathbb{G}^{out}$. We say that* (Gen, Eval) *as in Definition 3 is an FSS scheme for the function family $\mathcal{F}$ (with respect to leakage* Leak*) if it satisfies the following requirements.*

- **Correctness:** *For all $\hat{f} \in P_\mathcal{F}$ describing $f : \mathbb{G}^{in} \to \mathbb{G}^{out}$, and every $x \in \mathbb{G}^{in}$, if $(k_0, k_1) \leftarrow$ Gen$(1^\lambda, \hat{f})$ then $\Pr[\text{Eval}(0, k_0, x) + \text{Eval}(1, k_1, x) = f(x)] = 1$.*
- **Security:** *For each $\sigma \in \{0,1\}$ there is a PPT algorithm* Sim$_\sigma$ *(simulator), such that for every infinite sequence $(\hat{f}_\lambda)_{\lambda \in \mathbb{N}}$ of polynomial-size function descriptions from $P_\mathcal{F}$ and polynomial-size input sequence $x_\lambda$ for $f_\lambda$, the outputs of the following experiments* Real *and* Ideal *are computationally indistinguishable:*
  - Real$_\lambda$: $(k_0, k_1) \leftarrow$ Gen$(1^\lambda, \hat{f}_\lambda)$; *Output* $k_\sigma$.
  - Ideal$_\lambda$: *Output* Sim$_\sigma(1^\lambda, \text{Leak}(\hat{f}_\lambda))$.

*We refer to the FSS scheme as being statistical (resp., perfect) if the above holds with statistical (resp., perfect) indistinguishability instead of computational indistinguishability.*

**Definition 5 (Distributed Point Function (DPF)).** *A point function $f_{\alpha,\beta}$, for $\alpha \in \mathbb{G}^{in}$ and $\beta \in \mathbb{G}^{out}$, is defined to be the function $f : \mathbb{G}^{in} \to \mathbb{G}^{out}$ such that $f(\alpha) = \beta$ and $f(x) = 0$ for $x \neq \alpha$. A* Distributed Point Function *(DPF) is an FSS scheme for the family of all point functions, with the default leakage (i.e., $\mathsf{Leak}(\hat{f}) = (\mathbb{G}^{in}, \mathbb{G}^{out}))$.*

**Definition 6 (Distributed Interval Function (DIF)).** *An interval function $f_{(a,b),\beta}$, for $a, b \in \mathbb{G}^{in}$, and $\beta \in \mathbb{G}^{out}$, and given an arbitrary total order $\leq$ on $\mathbb{G}^{in}$, is defined to be the function $f : \mathbb{G}^{in} \to \mathbb{G}^{out}$ such that $f(x) = \beta$ for $x \in \mathbb{G}^{in}, a \leq x \leq b$, while $f(x) = 0$ for $x < a$ or $x > b$. If $a = 0$ (the minimal element of $\mathbb{G}^{in}$) or $b = |\mathbb{G}^{in}| - 1$ (the maximal element) then we say that $f_{(a,b),\beta}$ is a* special interval *function. A* Distributed Interval Function *(DIF) is an FSS scheme for the family of all interval functions, with the default leakage (i.e., $\mathsf{Leak}(\hat{f}) = (\mathbb{G}^{in}, \mathbb{G}^{out})$) and a similar definition holds for Distributed Special Interval Functions.*

The following theorem captures the complexity of the best known constructions of DPF and distributed interval functions from a PRG.

**Theorem 1 (Concrete complexity of DPF and DIF schemes [8]).** *Given a PRG $G : \{0,1\}^\lambda \to \{0,1\}^{2\lambda+2}$, there exists a DPF for $f_{\alpha,\beta} : \mathbb{G}^{in} \to \mathbb{G}^{out}$ with key size $m \cdot (\lambda + 2) + \lambda + \ell$ bits, where $m = \lceil \log_2 |\mathbb{G}^{in}| \rceil$ and $\ell = \lceil \log_2 |\mathbb{G}^{out}| \rceil$. For $\ell' = \lceil \frac{\ell}{\lambda+2} \rceil$, the key generation algorithm $\mathsf{Gen}$ invokes $G$ at most $2(m + \ell')$ times and the evaluation algorithm $\mathsf{Eval}$ invokes $G$ at most $m + \ell'$ times. For special (resp., general) DIF, the above costs are multiplied by at most 2 (resp., 4).*

## 3 Secure Computation with Preprocessing from FSS

In this section, we develop our primary general transformation for using FSS to obtain secure 2PC with preprocessing. We then demonstrate how this approach captures and generalizes existing techniques within this regime.

### 3.1 Circuit and Offset-Family Notation

We begin by introducing some notation for modeling circuits of computation gates.

**Definition 7 (Computation Gate).** *A computation gate is a function family $\mathcal{G}$ (Definition 1), where each function describes a pair of Abelian groups $(\mathbb{G}^{in}, \mathbb{G}^{out})$, and a mapping $g : \mathbb{G}^{in} \to \mathbb{G}^{out}$. In some cases it will be convenient to interpret $\mathbb{G}^{in}$ and $\mathbb{G}^{out}$ explicitly as product groups, of the form $\mathbb{G}^{in} = \prod_{i \in [\ell]} \mathbb{G}_i^{in}$ and $\mathbb{G}^{out} = \prod_{i \in [m]} \mathbb{G}_i^{out}$.*

For example, one may consider a *zero-test gate*, corresponding to the family of zero-test functions parameterized by different input and output groups.

For syntactic purposes, it will be useful to define notation for the following type of (trivial) *input and output gates*.

**Definition 8 (Input and Output Gates).** *An* input *gate is a gate $\mathcal{G}_{\mathsf{Inp}}$ which syntactically receives no input from other gates ($\mathbb{G}^{\mathsf{in}} = \emptyset$), and outputs a single value. An* output *gate is a gate $\mathcal{G}_{\mathsf{Out}}$ which syntactically sends no output to further gates ($\mathbb{G}^{\mathsf{out}} = \emptyset$), and receives as input a single value.*

We now define a *circuit* of input, output, and computation gates, via two parts: (1) the circuit syntax, dictating its topological connectivity amongst gates, and (2) the circuit instantiation, selecting a specific function for each gate, such that the choices of input/output groups are consistent across edges. For example, given multiplication gates followed by a zero-test gate (each corresponding to a family of functions), these gates could be instantiated over any arithmetic ring $R$ followed by zero-test from $\mathbb{G}^{\mathsf{in}} = R$ to any other space $\mathbb{G}^{\mathsf{out}}$ with canonical 0 and 1 values.

The syntax of the circuit will be modeled by the structure of a directed acyclic graph, with nodes serving as gates and edges serving as wires. In order to model fan-out, each gate will be associated with both an *out-degree* (dictated by the graph) and an *out-arity* $\ell^{\mathsf{out}}$, which may not be the same. The out-arity corresponds to the number of values output by the gate computation. Each outgoing edge from the gate corresponds to a wire carrying the value of one of these outputs to another gate, and is labeled with the corresponding index $j \in [\ell^{\mathsf{out}}]$.

**Definition 9 (Circuit syntax).** *Let $\mathcal{B}$ be a finite set ("basis") of gates. A circuit $C$ over basis $\mathcal{B}$ specifies a directed acyclic graph $(V, E)$, where each node $v \in V$ is labeled with an input and output arity $(\ell_v^{\mathsf{in}}, \ell_v^{\mathsf{out}})$, and a gate type $\mathcal{G}_v \in \mathcal{B}$, such that:*

- *Each source node is labeled by an* input *gate and every sink an* output *gate (as per Definition 8). We sometimes denote the set of input and output gates of $C$ by* Inp *and* Out.
- *The in-arity $\ell_v^{\mathsf{in}}$ of each node $v \in V$ is equal to its in-degree; each incoming edge into $v$ is associated with a distinct index $i \in [\ell_v^{\mathsf{in}}]$. Each outgoing edge from $v$ is labeled with an index $j \in [\ell_v^{\mathsf{out}}]$, possibly with repetition (representing fan-out).*
- *The depth of $C$, denoted* depth$(C)$, *is defined as the length of the longest directed path in $C$.*

**Definition 10 (Circuit instantiation).** *Let $C$ be a circuit over basis $\mathcal{B}$ with graph $(V, E)$. An instantiation $C_g$ of $C$ is a selection for each $v \in V$ of a function $g_v : \mathbb{G}_v^{\mathsf{in}} \to \mathbb{G}_v^{\mathsf{out}}$ from the gate function family $\mathcal{G}_v$, subject to the following constraints:*

1. *$\mathbb{G}_v^{\mathsf{in}} = \prod_{i \in [\ell_v^{\mathsf{in}}]} \mathbb{G}_{(v,i)}^{\mathsf{in}}$ and $\mathbb{G}_v^{\mathsf{out}} = \prod_{j \in [\ell_v^{\mathsf{out}}]} \mathbb{G}_{(v,j)}^{\mathsf{out}}$ for some abelian groups $\mathbb{G}_{(v,i)}^{\mathsf{in}}, \mathbb{G}_{(v,j)}^{\mathsf{out}}$, where $\ell_v^{\mathsf{in}}, \ell_v^{\mathsf{out}}$ are the arity of $v$.*
2. *For every edge $(u, v) \in E$ labeled by $i \in [\ell_u^{\mathsf{out}}]$ and $j \in [\ell_v^{\mathsf{in}}]$, it holds that $\mathbb{G}_{(u,i)}^{\mathsf{out}} = \mathbb{G}_{(v,j)}^{\mathsf{in}}$.*
   *We will sometimes refer to edges $(u, v) \in E$ as wires $w \in C$, denoting $\mathbb{G}_w :=$ $\mathbb{G}_{(u,i)}^{\mathsf{out}} = \mathbb{G}_{(v,j)}^{\mathsf{in}}$.*

*Remark 1 (Instantiation-dependent topology).* In some cases, the circuit topology cannot be completely decoupled from the instantiation. For example, instantiating a bit-decomposition gate with $\mathbb{G}^{in} = \mathbb{Z}_{2^k}$ would yield output $\mathbb{G}^{out} = \mathbb{Z}_2^k$ of arity $k$. However, we will attempt to keep syntax and instantiation separate whenever possible for sake of modularity.

Our approach for preprocessing a gate computation relies on FSS sharing of a corresponding family of functions, formed by allowing different additive offset values to both the input and output value. In our application to 2PC, these will serve as the values of random wire masks.

**Definition 11 (Offset function family).** *Let $\mathcal{G}$ be a computation gate. The family of offset functions $\hat{\mathcal{G}}$ of $\mathcal{G}$ is given by*

$$\hat{\mathcal{G}} := \left\{ g^{[r^{in}, r^{out}]} : \mathbb{G}^{in} \to \mathbb{G}^{out} \,\middle|\, \begin{array}{l} g : \mathbb{G}^{in} \to \mathbb{G}^{out} \in \mathcal{G}, \\ r^{in} \in \mathbb{G}^{in}, r^{out} \in \mathbb{G}^{out} \end{array} \right\}, \quad where$$

$$g^{[r^{in}, r^{out}]}(x) := g(x - r^{in}) + r^{out},$$

*and where each $g^{[r^{in}, r^{out}]}$ contains an explicit description of $r^{in}, r^{out}$.*

## 3.2   Secure 2-Party Computation with Preprocessing from FSS

We now demonstrate how to apply the ideas from the introduction to obtain a secure 2-party computation protocol in the preprocessing model with cheap online complexity. We restrict our protocol descriptions to the 2-party setting, both for purposes of simplicity, and since this is currently the setting of most efficient FSS constructions. However, the statements generalize to the multi-party case (given corresponding multi-party FSS) with any number of corrupted parties.

The following statement constitutes our core protocol, which leverages the structure of the circuit to provide tailored preprocessing information. Later, in Theorem 3, we extend the approach to support circuit-independent preprocessing, at small extra offline and communication cost. Roughly, the extra communication corresponds to an element communicated for every *wire* as opposed to every *gate output* value; note that multiple wires may correspond to the same gate output, in the case of circuit fanout.

**Theorem 2 (Circuit-Dependent Preprocessing).** *Let $C$ be a circuit over basis $\mathcal{B}$. For each $\mathcal{G} \in \mathcal{B}$, let $(\mathsf{Gen}_{\hat{\mathcal{G}}}, \mathsf{Eval}_{\hat{\mathcal{G}}})$ be an FSS for the offset-function family $\hat{\mathcal{G}}$ with key size $\mathsf{size}_{\hat{\mathcal{G}}}(\lambda, |\mathbb{G}^{in}|, |\mathbb{G}^{out}|)$. Then for any instantiation $C_g$ of $C$, there exists a 2-party protocol for securely computing $C_g$ with the following properties:*

- *Preprocessing. Given circuit $C$ with gate ("vertex") indices $v \in C$, denote the set of gates by $\mathcal{G}_v$ and their instantiations by $g_v$, which in particular specify input/output groups $\mathbb{G}_v^{in}, \mathbb{G}_v^{out}$. The preprocessing phase executes $\mathsf{Gen}_{\hat{\mathcal{G}}_v}$ for each $g_v$ and produces output of size $\sum_{v \in C} \mathsf{size}_{\hat{\mathcal{G}}_v}(\lambda, |\mathbb{G}_v^{in}|, |\mathbb{G}_v^{out}|)$.*

- Online. *The online protocol requires local execution of* $\mathsf{Eval}_{\hat{G}}$ *for each gate, yielding the following properties:*
  - *Rounds:* $\mathsf{depth}_{\mathcal{B}}(C)$.
  - *Communication:* $\sum_{v \in C} \log |\mathbb{G}_v^{\mathsf{out}}|$ *bits per party.*

*If the FSS schemes are perfectly (resp., statistically) secure, then the resulting protocol is perfectly (resp., statistically) secure in the preprocessing model.*

The proof of Theorem 2 follows the high-level description from the Introduction and appears in the full version.

*Remark 2 (Compressing preprocessing output).* In some cases, the size of the offline preprocessing information can be compressed, when e.g. FSS keys of neighboring gates contain redundant information. This will be the case, for example, when generating FSS keys for neighboring gates which are each instantiated by degree-2 functions. (Here, the output mask $r_w$ of the first gate will be identical to the input mask of the second, as they correspond to the same wire; thus including secret shares of $r_w$ as part of both FSS keys is unnecessary.) See discussion in the following section for further cases.

*Circuit-Independent Preprocessing.* The protocol construction in Theorem 2 used preprocessing information that was *tailored* to the topology of the given circuit $C$. More concretely, we were able to "match up" the input/output offset masks $r_v$ of every pair of gates sharing a wire, hardcoding the same offset into the FSS keys for the respective functions. In particular, this enabled "for free" a direct translation from masked output of one gate to appropriate masked input to *all* gates in the next level which accepted this value as input (via fan-out).

In some cases, it may be advantageous to produce generic preprocessing information that depends on the individual gate structure, but which can be used for any circuit built from such gates (independent of the topology linking the gates together). Our approach generalizes to this circuit-independent setting with a small amount of additional overhead, via a few small changes, which we now describe.

The only difference between the two constructions is that the circuit-dependent correlation could directly "match up" the outgoing mask $r^{\mathsf{out}}$ for a gate to be equal to the incoming mask $r^{\mathsf{in}}$ of any gate to which it enters. In contrast, when the structure of the circuit $C$ is not a priori known, this can be effectively emulated as follows.

- For each gate $g$, we will sample a random *input* offset mask $r^{\mathsf{in}}$ (but not $r^{\mathsf{out}}$), and provide FSS shares for the offset function $g^{[r^{\mathsf{in}},0]} = g(x - r^{\mathsf{in}}) + 0$, together with *additive secret shares* of the mask $r^{\mathsf{in}}$ (which was not needed previously). Note that a mask per input corresponds directly to a mask per *wire* in the circuit.
- Then, once the structure of the circuit $C$ is known (during the protocol), a party $P_\sigma$ can locally convert his overall collection of preprocessing information over all gates $(k_v^\sigma, (r_v^{\mathsf{in}})^\sigma)_{v \in C}$ into FSS shares for the desired "matched up"

$g^{[r^{in}, r^{out}]}$ (where $r^{out}$ is equal to the input mask $r^{in}$ for the next gate that the gate $v$ output value will enter into), by leveraging the additive secret shares of all wire masks $r^{in}$ together with linearity of FSS reconstruction: i.e., outputting $\mathsf{Eval}(\sigma, k_v^\sigma, x) + (r_v^{out})^\sigma$.

This effectively reduces us back to the circuit-dependent version, in terms of correctness and security. Observe, however, that whereas in the circuit-dependent version, $r^{in}$ values of all target gates for fan-out wires of the same value could a priori be coordinated, in this setting (when this structure is not a priori known), the parties must send a separate element per fan-out wire. We also must provide the additive shares of the input masks $r^{in}$ as part of the correlated randomness.

**Theorem 3 (Circuit-Independent Preprocessing).** *Let $\mathcal{B}$ be a finite gate basis; for each $\mathcal{G} \in \mathcal{B}$, let $(\mathsf{Gen}_{\hat{\mathcal{G}}}, \mathsf{Eval}_{\hat{\mathcal{G}}})$ be an FSS for the offset-function family $\hat{\mathcal{G}}$ with key size $\mathsf{size}_{\hat{\mathcal{G}}}(\lambda, |\mathbb{G}^{in}|, |\mathbb{G}^{out}|)$. Then there exists a 2-party protocol for securely computing any $\mathcal{B}$-circuit instantiation $C_g$ consisting of $s_{\mathcal{G}} \in \mathbb{N}$ gates $g$ of type $\mathcal{G}$ for each $\mathcal{G} \in \mathcal{B}$, with the following complexity:*

- Preprocessing. *(Independent of $C_g$) The preprocessing phase executes $s_{\mathcal{G}}$ executions of $\mathsf{Gen}_{\hat{\mathcal{G}}}$ for each gate $\mathcal{G} \in \mathcal{B}$ and produces output size*

$$\sum_{\mathcal{G} \in \mathcal{B}} s_{\mathcal{G}} \cdot \left( \mathsf{size}_{\hat{\mathcal{G}}}(\lambda, |\mathbb{G}^{in}|, |\mathbb{G}^{out}|) + \log |\mathbb{G}^{in}| \right).$$

- Online. *The online execution takes $\mathsf{depth}(C)$ rounds (as before), but requires communication $\sum_{v \in C} \log |\mathbb{G}_v^{in}|$ bits per party (vs. $\sum_{v \in C} \log |\mathbb{G}_v^{out}|$). Equivalently, one element is communicated per wire, as opposed to only one element per value (where fan-out introduces extra wires but not values).*

The proof of Theorem 3 appears in the full version.

## 3.3   Recasting and Generalizing Existing Protocols

We begin by briefly demonstrating that common existing approaches to 2PC with preprocessing (and even useful extensions) can be cast as instances of the FSS-based framework, for special simple cases of FSS.

**Low-Degree Gates.** The first category is FSS of low-degree polynomials, which can be attained simply by providing additive secret shares of each coefficient. More broadly:

**Observation 4 (FSS via Coefficient-Sharing).** *For any module $M$ over coefficient ring $R$, and family of functions of the form $\mathcal{F} = \{\sum_{i=1}^m \alpha_i F_i(x) \mid \alpha_i \in R\}$ for public functions $(F_i)_{i \in [m]} : \mathbb{G}^{in} \to M$, there exists an FSS scheme for $\mathcal{F}$ with perfect security and correctness, as follows:*

- Gen($1^\lambda, f$): *Parse the description of $f \in \mathcal{F}$ as secret coefficients $(\alpha_i)_{i \in [m]} \in R^m$. The output FSS keys are additive secret shares of each $\alpha_i$ over $R$, yielding key size $m \log |R|$.*
- Eval($\sigma, k_\sigma, x$): *Parse $k_\sigma = (\alpha_i^\sigma)_{i \in [m]}$. Output $\sum_{i \in [m]} \alpha_i^\sigma F_i(x)$.*

Note that FSS keys perfectly hide the coefficients $\alpha_i$, and thus $f$. Correctness holds by the distributive law within the module $M$.

As an example of "public functions" $F_i$, one can consider, e.g., input monomials of a certain degree. Indeed, we can use this approach to instantiate FSS schemes for offset-function classes $\hat{\mathcal{G}}$ for the following types of low-degree gates.

**Definition 12 (Low-Degree Gates).**

1. *The* degree-$d$ *gate* $\mathcal{G}_{\text{deg-}d}$ *is the class of functions* $g_{\text{deg-}d} : R^n \to R^m$ *parameterized by a ring $R$ and $n, m \in \mathbb{N}$, such that for each $i \in [m]$, the $i$th output function $(g_{\text{deg-}d})_i(x_1, \ldots, x_n)$ is a polynomial over $R$ of degree no greater than $d$.*
2. *The* bilinear map *gate* $\mathcal{G}_{\text{blin}}$ *is the class of functions* $g_{\text{blin}} : \mathbb{G}_1^{\text{in}} \times \mathbb{G}_2^{\text{in}} \to \mathbb{G}^{\text{out}}$ *such that* $\mathbb{G}^{\text{in}} = \mathbb{G}_1^{\text{in}} \times \mathbb{G}_2^{\text{in}}, \mathbb{G}^{\text{out}}$ *are Abelian groups, and $g_{\text{blin}}$ is a bilinear map.*

Note that these two classes are incomparable: $\mathcal{G}_{\text{deg-}d}$ addresses higher-order polynomials, beyond degree 2. On the other hand, $\mathcal{G}_{\text{blin}}$ captures bilinear operations across different structures beyond a single ring $R$: e.g., multiplication of non-square matrices, $\mathbb{G}_1^{\text{in}} = R^{m_1 \times m_2}$, $\mathbb{G}_2^{\text{in}} = R^{m_2 \times m_3}$, and $\mathbb{G}^{\text{out}} = R^{m_1 \times m_3}$.

**Proposition 1 (Information-Theoretic FSS for Low-Degree Gates).** *Let $d \in N$. Then there exists perfectly secure FSS for the following offset-function families, with the given complexities:*

- $\hat{\mathcal{G}}_{\text{deg-}d}$*: For $\mathbb{G}^{\text{in}} = R^n$, $\mathbb{G}^{\text{out}} = R^m$, key size is $m\binom{n+d}{d}(\log |R|)$ bits.*
- $\hat{\mathcal{G}}_{\text{blin}}$*: For $\mathbb{G}^{\text{in}} = \mathbb{G}_1^{\text{in}} \times \mathbb{G}_2^{\text{in}}, \mathbb{G}^{\text{out}}$, key size is $(\log |\mathbb{G}^{\text{in}}| + \log |\mathbb{G}^{\text{out}}|)$ bits.*

*Proof.* Consider the following FSS constructions.

- For $\hat{\mathcal{G}}_{\text{deg-}d}$: Recall we are sharing offset functions of the form $g_{\text{deg-}d}^{[r^{\text{in}}, r^{\text{out}}]}$, where $g = (g_1, \ldots, g_m)$ is a degree-$d$ polynomial $g : R^n \to R^m$, and with offsets $r^{\text{in}} = (r_1^{\text{in}}, \ldots, r_n^{\text{in}}) \in R^n$ and $r^{\text{out}} = (r_1^{\text{out}}, \ldots r_m^{\text{out}}) \in R^m$. By definition, for each $i \in [m]$,

$$(g_{\text{deg-}d}^{[r^{\text{in}}, r^{\text{out}}]})_i(x_1, \ldots, x_n) = g_i(x_1 - r_1^{\text{in}}, \ldots, x_m - r_m^{\text{in}}) + r_i^{\text{out}}.$$

In particular, each $(g_{\text{deg-}d}^{[r^{\text{in}}, r^{\text{out}}]})_i$ itself is a degree-$d$ polynomial in the inputs, where the coefficients of each degree $\leq d$ monomial in the variables $x_i$ depends on the secret values $r^{\text{in}}, r^{\text{out}}$. By Observation 4, we can thus obtain secure FSS by giving additive secret shares of each of these coefficients. There are $\binom{n+d}{d}$ distinct monomials of degree $\leq d$ in the $n$ input variables; for each output $i \in [m]$, the FSS key will contain an additive share of size $\log |R|$ for each monomial.

– For $\hat{\mathcal{G}}_{\mathsf{blin}}$: Given an offset function of the form $g_{\mathsf{blin}}^{[r^{\mathsf{in}}, r^{\mathsf{out}}]}$, parse as a *bilinear* function $g : \mathbb{G}_1^{\mathsf{in}} \times \mathbb{G}_2^{\mathsf{in}} \to \mathbb{G}^{\mathsf{out}}$, and $r^{\mathsf{in}} = (r_1^{\mathsf{in}}, r_2^{\mathsf{in}}) \in \mathbb{G}_1^{\mathsf{in}} \times \mathbb{G}_2^{\mathsf{in}}$, and $r^{\mathsf{out}} \in \mathbb{G}^{\mathsf{out}}$. By definition,

$$
\begin{aligned}
g_{\mathsf{blin}}^{[r^{\mathsf{in}}, r^{\mathsf{out}}]}(x_1, x_2) &= g(x_1 - r_1^{\mathsf{in}}, x_2 - r_2^{\mathsf{in}}) + r^{\mathsf{out}} \\
&= g(x_1, x_2) - g(r_1^{\mathsf{in}}, x_2) - g(x_1, r_2^{\mathsf{in}}) + g(r_1^{\mathsf{in}}, r_2^{\mathsf{in}}) + r^{\mathsf{out}}.
\end{aligned}
$$

Consider the following observations: (1) $g(x_1, x_2)$ is publicly computable. (2) $r_3 := g(r_1^{\mathsf{in}}, r_2^{\mathsf{in}}) + r^{\mathsf{out}}$ is a fixed additive term, independent of the input $x$. (3) Bilinearity of $g$ implies the functions $g(\cdot, x_2)$ and $g(x_1, \cdot)$ are *linear* in the corresponding second position.

We can thus achieve FSS for this function class by giving out *additive secret shares* of the values $r_1^{\mathsf{in}}, r_2^{\mathsf{in}}$, and $r_3 := g(r_1^{\mathsf{in}}, r_2^{\mathsf{in}}) + r^{\mathsf{out}}$. The corresponding FSS key size is $\log |\mathbb{G}_1^{\mathsf{in}}| + \log |\mathbb{G}_2^{\mathsf{in}}| + \log |\mathbb{G}^{\mathsf{out}}| = (\log |\mathbb{G}^{\mathsf{in}}| + \log |\mathbb{G}^{\mathsf{out}}|)$ bits.

Plugging these FSS constructions into our protocols from the previous section (Theorems 2 and 3), we obtain secure computation protocols isomorphic to existing protocols from the literature. In addition, the FSS abstraction extends directly to broader classes: e.g., directly supporting general bilinear gates over different rings $R_i$ (such as matrix multiplications), as well as arbitrary low-degree gates over a ring $R$.

Note that a degree-$d$ mapping can have circuit complexity $\sim n^d$. In the corresponding approach, this increases only the size of the FSS preprocessing information (corresponding to more coefficients) whereas the online communication scales just with the input and output size of the gate. Similarly, bilinear operations such as matrix multiplication when expressed as circuits over the base ring $R$ require significantly more small gates as compared to a single matrix input and output when viewed as a single large bilinear gate.

**Corollary 1 (2PC with Preprocessing: Low-Degree and Bilinear Gates).** *Applying our FSS framework (Theorems 2 and 3) for circuits of degree-$d$ and bilinear gates $\mathcal{G}_{\mathsf{deg}\text{-}d}, \mathcal{G}_{\mathsf{blin}}$ as above yields perfectly secure protocols in the preprocessing model isomorphic to (and generalizing) the following:*

– Beaver Triples [2]: *Applying Theorem 3, yielding circuit-independent preprocessing 2PC for low-degree and bilinear gates.*
– Circuit-Dependent Beaver (e.g., [3,11,13,23]): *Applying Theorem 2, yielding circuit-dependent preprocessing 2PC for low-degree and bilinear gates.*

*Proof.* Consider the two approaches.

(Circuit-independent). Applying the protocol framework of Theorem 3, we obtain the following structure. We describe for the case of multiplication gates over a ring $R$ to illustrate the Beaver triple structure (but observe that the construction extends directly to more general degree-$d$ and bilinear gates).

– For each multiplication gate $v$ with input wires $(w_1, w_2)$ and output wire $w_3$, sampling random $r_1, r_2 \leftarrow R$, and generating FSS shares for the gate-offset function will correspond to sharing the function

$$g_v^{[(r_1, r_2), 0]}(x_1, x_2) = (x_1 - r_1)(x_2 - r_2)$$
$$= x_1 x_2 - r_1 x_2 - x_2 r_1 + r_1 r_2.$$

Note that $x_1 x_2$ is always with coefficient 1 and publicly computable. Applying Observation 4 for the remaining (secret) coefficients yields FSS keys that are additive secret shares of 3 values: $r_1, r_2$, and $r_1 r_2$.

- The circuit-independent 2PC preprocessing included FSS keys of each such gate offset function, as well as additive shares of the input masks themselves. In this case, additive shares of the input masks are *already* included as part of the FSS keys. Thus, the final resulting correlation corresponds directly to Beaver triples: for each gate, additive shares of random $r_1, r_2$, and $r_1 r_2$.

(Circuit-dependent). Applying Theorem 2 results in an optimization of this approach, as in [11,13,23], where the offset masks are correlated across gates.

**Truth-Table Gates.** The second category is a straightforward FSS of arbitrary functions of polynomial-size domain, formed by simply providing additive secret shares of each element of the truth table. Perfect secrecy and evaluation with additive reconstruction follow in a trivial manner.

**Observation 5 (FSS via Shared Truth Table).** *Let $\mathcal{F}$ be any family of functions where for a given $(\mathbb{G}^{in}, \mathbb{G}^{out})$, the truth table of a function $f \in \mathcal{F}$ can be described by $s = s(\mathbb{G}^{in}, \mathbb{G}^{out})$ elements of the output space $\mathbb{G}^{out}$. Then there exists an FSS scheme for $\mathcal{F}$ with perfect security and correctness, with key size $s \cdot \log |\mathbb{G}^{out}|$ bits.*

Note that one can *always* express the truth table of a function $g : \mathbb{G}^{in} \rightarrow \mathbb{G}^{out}$ using $|\mathbb{G}^{in}|$ many elements of $\mathbb{G}^{out}$. However, for some interesting function classes, this can be made even smaller. For example, functions with bounded locality: where $\mathbb{G}^{in} = \prod_{i=1}^{n} \widetilde{\mathbb{G}^{in}}$, and each output of the function depends only on a bounded number $\ell(\mathbb{G}^{in}, \mathbb{G}^{out})$ of fixed coordinates of the input; in such case, the full truth table of the function can be expressed given just $|\widetilde{\mathbb{G}^{in}}|^{\ell} \cdot \log |\mathbb{G}^{out}|$ bits, as opposed to $|\mathbb{G}^{in}| \cdot \log |\mathbb{G}^{out}| = |\widetilde{\mathbb{G}^{in}}|^{n} \cdot \log |\mathbb{G}^{out}|$ bits.

In a straightforward way, this translates to the *offset-function* family $\hat{\mathcal{F}}$ of any such function family $\mathcal{F}$.

Analogous to the case of low-degree functions, plugging these general truth table FSS constructions into our 2PC protocols from Theorems 2 and 3 yields secure computation protocols that reproduce existing protocols from the literature.

**Corollary 2 (2PC with Preprocessing: Truth Table Gates).** *Applying our FSS framework (Theorems 2 and 3) for circuits of arbitrary gates $\mathcal{G}$ as above rederives perfectly secure protocols in the preprocessing model isomorphic to the following:*

- One-Time Truth Tables [13,22]: *Applying Theorem 3 together with Observation 5 for arbitrary truth tables.*
- Leveled circuits, with sublinear online communication [11]: *Applying Theorem 2, together with Observation 5 for circuits with bounded locality.*

*Proof.* (One-Time Truth Tables). For a given gate function $g$, the truth table of the offset-function $g^{[r^{in},0]}$ (recall in the circuit-independent setting, we take $r^{out} = 0$) is simply a randomly shifted version of the original truth table, and FSS shares of this function will be precisely additive shares of the shifted truth table.

(Leveled Circuits). The core technical insight in [11] is that a leveled circuit of size $s$ can be partitioned into large "gates" of depth $\log \log s$, whose input locality are each bounded by $\log s$, and thus whose truth tables can each be described in polynomial size. Applying Theorem 2 to such circuit decomposition yields a comparable protocol, with polynomial-size preprocessing information, and where parties need only communicate $O(s/\log \log s)$ elements, corresponding to just inputs and outputs of these gates, in $\mathsf{depth}(C)/\log \log s$ rounds.

# 4  Applications

In this section we explore applications of our technique to useful types of gates for which we can obtain significant improvements over the current state of the art.

## 4.1  Zero Test/Equality

We start with gates that either compare a single group element to 0 or check that two group elements are equal.

### Definition 13 (Equality-Type Gates).

1. *The* zero-test gate $\mathcal{G}_{zt}$ *is the class of functions* $g_{zt} : \mathbb{G}^{in} \to \mathbb{G}^{out}$ *parameterized by Abelian groups* $\mathbb{G}^{in}, \mathbb{G}^{out}$ *and given by*

$$g_{zt}(x) = \begin{cases} 0 \in \mathbb{G}^{out} & \text{if } x = 0 \in \mathbb{G}^{in} \\ 1 \in \mathbb{G}^{out} & \text{else} \end{cases}.$$

2. *The* equality-test gate $\mathcal{G}_{eq}$ *is the class of functions* $g_{eq} : \mathbb{G}^{in} \times \mathbb{G}^{in} \to \mathbb{G}^{out}$ *parameterized by* $\mathbb{G}^{in}, \mathbb{G}^{out}$ *and given by*

$$g_{eq}(x, x') = \begin{cases} 0 \in \mathbb{G}^{out} & \text{if } x = x' \in \mathbb{G}^{in} \\ 1 \in \mathbb{G}^{out} & \text{else} \end{cases}.$$

Note that the offset function class of the zero-test gate is precisely the class of point functions, where the special input $\alpha$ corresponds to the input offset and the output value $\beta$ to the output offset. Hence, realizing a zero-test gate (on a masked input) reduces to a single DPF evaluation.

**Proposition 2 (Zero Test from DPF).** *There is an FSS scheme* $(\mathsf{Gen}_{zt}, \mathsf{Eval}_{zt})$ *for the offset function family* $\hat{\mathcal{G}}_{zt}$ *making black-box use of a PRG. The scheme has the same key size and number of PRG invocations as a DPF with input domain* $\mathbb{G}^{in}$ *and output domain* $\mathbb{G}^{out}$.

*Proof.* Consider the following construction, where $(\mathsf{Gen}_{DPF}, \mathsf{Eval}_{DPF})$ is a distributed point function.

- $\mathsf{Gen}_{zt}(1^\lambda, g_{zt}^{[r^{in}, r^{out}]})$: Parse $g_{zt}^{[r^{in}, r^{out}]}$ to recover $\mathbb{G}^{in}, \mathbb{G}^{out}, r^{in}, r^{out}$. Sample and output keys $(k_0', k_1') \leftarrow \mathsf{Gen}_{DPF}(1^\lambda, f_{\alpha,\beta})$, for $\alpha = r^{in} \in \mathbb{G}^{in}$ and $\beta = 1 \in \mathbb{G}^{out}$. Sample random additive secret shares $\langle r_0, r_1 \rangle$ of $r^{out} \in \mathbb{G}^{out}$. Output keys $k_0 = (k_0', r_0)$ and $k_1 = (k_1', r_1)$.
- $\mathsf{Eval}_{zt}(\sigma, k_\sigma, x)$: Output $\mathsf{Eval}_{DPF}(\sigma, k_\sigma', x) + r_\sigma$.

Correctness and security can be easily seen to follow from those of the DPF. Moreover, the construction does not involve additional cryptographic operations beyond making a single call to the DPF.

The case of comparing two group elements can be easily reduced to the above case of a zero-test. Indeed, by taking the difference between the two masked inputs, the problem reduces to a zero-test of a masked input whose mask is the difference between the two masks, where the latter are known to the key generation algorithm. We provide an explicit description of the corresponding FSS scheme below.

**Theorem 6 (Equality Test from DPF).** *There is an FSS scheme* $(\mathsf{Gen}_{eq}, \mathsf{Eval}_{eq})$ *for the offset function family* $\hat{\mathcal{G}}_{eq}$ *making black-box use of a PRG. The scheme has the same key size and number of PRG invocations as a DPF with input domain* $\mathbb{G}^{in}$ *and output domain* $\mathbb{G}^{out}$.

*Proof.* Consider the following construction, where $(\mathsf{Gen}_{DPF}, \mathsf{Eval}_{DPF})$ is a distributed point function.

- $\mathsf{Gen}_{eq}(1^\lambda, g_{eq}^{[r^{in}, r^{out}]})$: Parse $g_{eq}^{[r^{in}, r^{out}]}$ to recover $\mathbb{G}^{in} = (\mathbb{G}_1^{in} \times \mathbb{G}_2^{in}), \mathbb{G}^{out}, r^{in}, r^{out}$, where $r^{in} = (r_1^{in}, r_2^{in}) \in \mathbb{G}^{in}$. Sample and output keys $(k_0', k_1') \leftarrow \mathsf{Gen}_{DPF}(1^\lambda, f_{\alpha,\beta})$, for $\alpha = (r_1^{in} - r_2^{in}) \in \mathbb{G}^{in}$ and $\beta = 1 \in \mathbb{G}^{out}$. Sample random additive secret shares $\langle r_0, r_1 \rangle$ of $r^{out} \in \mathbb{G}^{out}$. Output keys $k_0 = (k_0', r_0)$ and $k_1 = (k_1', r_1)$.
- $\mathsf{Eval}_{eq}(\sigma, k_\sigma, (x_1, x_2))$: Output $\mathsf{Eval}_{DPF}(\sigma, k_\sigma, (x_1 - x_2)) + r_\sigma$.

Security follows directly. Correctness holds since the point function $f_{\alpha,\beta}(x)$ evaluates to $\beta = 1$ exactly when $(x_1 - x_2) = \alpha = (r_1^{in} - r_2^{in})$, or equivalently, when $(x_1 - r_1^{in}) = (x_2 - r_2^{in})$. As before, the only cryptographic operations involve a single call to the DPF.

## 4.2   Integer Comparison, Interval Membership, and Splines

We turn from equality-type gates to the slightly more involved case of gates related to integer comparisons. The offset functions of such gates can be easily expressed in terms of distributed *interval* functions (DIFs) as constructed in [8]. See Definition 6 and Theorem 1.

**Definition 14 (Comparison-Type Gates).**

1. *The* interval-containment gate $\mathcal{G}_{(a,b)}$ *is the class of functions* $g_{(a,b)} : \mathbb{G}^{in} \to \mathbb{G}^{out}$ *parameterized by Abelian groups* $\mathbb{G}^{in}, \mathbb{G}^{out}$ *endowed with a total ordering* $a \leq b \in \mathbb{G}^{in}$, *and given by*

$$g_{(a,b)}(x) = \begin{cases} 0 \in \mathbb{G}^{out} & \text{if } a \leq x \leq b \in \mathbb{G}^{in} \\ 1 \in \mathbb{G}^{out} & \text{else} \end{cases}.$$

   *We also sometimes consider the sub-family of "special" (one-sided) intervals, in which* $a = 0$ *is set to the minimum element of* $\mathbb{G}^{in}$ *(or, alternatively, the family wherein* $b$ *is set to the maximum element of* $\mathbb{G}^{in}$*). For these sub-families,* Leak *is amended to include this information.*

2. *The* comparison gate $\mathcal{G}_{\leq}$ *is the class of functions* $g_{\leq} : \mathbb{G}^{in} \times \mathbb{G}^{in} \to \mathbb{G}^{out}$ *parameterized by Abelian groups* $\mathbb{G}^{in}, \mathbb{G}^{out}$ *endowed with a total ordering, and given by*

$$g_{\leq}(x, x') = \begin{cases} 0 \in \mathbb{G}^{out} & \text{if } x \leq x' \in \mathbb{G}^{in} \\ 1 \in \mathbb{G}^{out} & \text{else} \end{cases}.$$

3. *The* spline gate $\mathcal{G}_{\text{spline}}$ *is the class of functions* $g_{(a,f)} : \mathbb{G}^{in} \to \mathbb{G}^{out}$ *parameterized by Abelian groups* $\mathbb{G}^{in}, \mathbb{G}^{out}$ *endowed with a total ordering, a list* $\boldsymbol{a} = a_1 < a_2 < \cdots < a_k \in \mathbb{G}^{in}$, *and a list of functions* $\boldsymbol{f} = f_0, \ldots, f_k : \mathbb{G}^{in} \to \mathbb{G}^{out}$, *given by*

$$g_{(\boldsymbol{a},\boldsymbol{f})}(x) = \begin{cases} f_0(x) \in \mathbb{G}^{out} & \text{if } x \leq a_1 \in \mathbb{G}^{in} \\ f_1(x) \in \mathbb{G}^{out} & \text{if } a_1 < x \leq a_2 \in \mathbb{G}^{in} \\ \quad \vdots & \\ f_k(x) \in \mathbb{G}^{out} & \text{if } a_k < x \end{cases}.$$

   *By default, we consider the case where* $\mathbb{G}^{in}$ *and* $\mathbb{G}^{out}$ *are the additive groups of the same finite ring (e.g.,* $R = \mathbb{Z}_{2^m}$*), and each* $f_i$ *is a degree-d univariate polynomial over* $R$. *This is useful in the context of approximating real-valued functions.*

We start with the case of interval containment. The key observation is that the offset function of an interval $(a, b)$ is can be expressed as the sum of two *special* intervals.

**Proposition 3 (Interval-Containment from FSS for Intervals).** *There exists an FSS scheme* $(\mathsf{Gen}_{(a,b)}, \mathsf{Eval}_{(a,b)})$ *for the offset function family* $\hat{\mathcal{G}}_{(a,b)}$ *making black-box use of a PRG. The scheme has the same cost (in key size and number of PRG invocations) as* two *instances of a special DIF with input domain* $\mathbb{G}^{\mathsf{in}}$ *and output domain* $\mathbb{G}^{\mathsf{out}}$*, except that each key includes an additional element of* $\mathbb{G}^{\mathsf{out}}$*. Moreover, there is an FSS scheme with the same parameters for the offset function family* $\hat{\mathcal{G}}_{\leq}$ *of comparison gates.*

*Proof.* We argue that each function in the offset family $\hat{\mathcal{G}}_{(a,b)}$ can be expressed as the sum of two special intervals plus the constant offset $r^{\mathsf{out}}$. Indeed, the effect of the input offset $r^{\mathsf{in}}$ is cyclically shifting the interval function $f_{(a,b),1}$ to the right. There are two possible cases:

1. There is no wrap-around, namely we get another standard interval of the form $f_{(a',b'),1}$. If $a' = 0$, this is a special interval. Otherwise it can be expressed as the sum of two special intervals: $f_{(a',b'),1} = f_{(0,b'),1} + f_{(0,a'-1),-1}$.
2. There is a wrap-around, in which case we get a sum of two disjoint special intervals: one starting with $a + r^{\mathsf{in}}$ and one ending with $(b + r^{\mathsf{in}}) \mod |\mathbb{G}^{\mathsf{in}}|$.

We can now realize FSS for the offset function by letting $\mathsf{Gen}$ generate independent keys for the two instances of a DIF, and $\mathsf{Eval}$ output the sum of the two output shares. Finally, given additive shares of the output offset $r^{\mathsf{out}}$ as part of the key, $\mathsf{Eval}$ can add $r^{\mathsf{out}}$ to the output. We can obtain an analogous statement for comparison gates $\hat{\mathcal{G}}_{\leq}$ similarly to the reduction of $\hat{\mathcal{G}}_{\mathsf{eq}}$ to $\hat{\mathcal{G}}_{\mathsf{zt}}$.

We turn to the case of spline functions, starting with the default case where $\mathbb{G}^{\mathsf{in}}$ and $\mathbb{G}^{\mathsf{out}}$ are the same finite ring $R$ and each function $f_i(x)$ is a degree-$d$ univariate polynomial over $R$. Here the high level idea is to use $2(k+1)$ instances of special DIF to additively share, for each interval, the $d + 1$ *coefficients* of either the degree-$d$ polynomial $f_i'(x') = f_i(x' - r^{\mathsf{in}}) + r^{\mathsf{out}}$ in case the input $x'$ is in the shifted $i$-th interval or the 0 polynomial if $x'$ is not in this interval. The $2(k+1)(d+1)$ coefficients can then be linearly combined with public coefficients to yield additive output shares.

**Proposition 4 (Splines from FSS for Intervals).** *There exists an FSS scheme* $(\mathsf{Gen}_{(a,f)}, \mathsf{Eval}_{(a,f)})$ *for the offset function family* $\hat{\mathcal{G}}_{\mathsf{spline}}$*, where* $\mathbb{G}^{\mathsf{in}} = \mathbb{G}^{\mathsf{out}} = R$ *and each* $f_i$*,* $0 \leq i \leq k$*, is a polynomial of degree at most* $d$ *over* $R$*, making black-box use of a PRG. The scheme has the same cost (in key size and number of PRG invocations) as* $2(k + 1)$ *instances of a special DIF with input domain* $R$ *and output domain* $R^{d+1}$*.*

*Proof.* We express the shifted spline function as the sum of $k + 1$ cyclically shifted interval functions. As before, each shifted interval can be expressed as the sum of two special intervals. For the shifted interval $i$, $0 \leq i \leq k$, the payload $\beta_i \in R^{d+1}$ is the coefficient vector of the univariate polynomial $f_i'$, where $f_i'(x') = f_i(x' - r^{\mathsf{in}}) + r^{\mathsf{out}}$. Note that if $x$ is *not* in the shifted interval, the output of the shifted interval function will be $\beta_i = (0, 0, \ldots, 0) \in R^{d+1}$. Finally, given the $k + 1$ additively-shared coefficient vectors $\beta_i$, the parties can homomorphically evaluate $\langle \sum_{i=0}^{k} \beta_i \,, (1, x', (x')^2, \ldots, (x')^d) \rangle = g_{(a,f)}^{[r^{in}, r^{out}]}(x')$, where $\langle \cdot, \cdot \rangle$ denotes inner product over $R$. Since $x'$ is public, this can be done via a local linear combination of the $(k+1)(d+1)$ ring elements included in the payloads $\beta_i$.

We note that, with some loss of concrete efficiency, the spline construction can be generalized to accommodate any functions $f_i$ from a class that supports efficient FSS. Such a construction can be obtained by using the general tensoring operator for FSS from [8] (Theorem 3.2 of full version) to obtain an FSS scheme for functions that output the same output as $f_i$ on a shifted interval and 0 outside the interval.

## 4.3   Bit Decomposition

As a concluding item, we turn our attention to the more involved task of bit decomposition.

**Definition 15 (Bit-Decomposition Gate).** *The bit-decomposition gate $\mathcal{G}_{\text{bit}}$ is the class of functions $g_{\text{bit}} : \mathbb{Z}_M \to \mathbb{Z}_2^m$ parameterized by $M \in \mathbb{N}$ (and $m := \lceil \log M \rceil$), given by*

$$g_{\text{bit}}(a) = (a_{m-1}, \ldots, a_0) \in \mathbb{Z}_2^m \quad \text{such that} \quad \sum_{i=0}^{m-1} 2^i a_i = a \in \mathbb{Z}_M.$$

We now describe how to obtain the required FSS for these gates.

*Remark 3 (Bit Decomposition for Special Modulus).* For the sake of simplicity, we present in Proposition 5 a construction of bit decomposition for the special case of $\mathbb{Z}_M$ for $M = 2^m$. In this setting, modular arithmetic over $M$ does not incur wraparound carries. The same construction and analysis covers also a promise setting where $M$ is arbitrary, but both the input $x \in \mathbb{Z}_M$ and the secret offset $r^{in} \in \mathbb{Z}_M$ are guaranteed to be of low magnitude (bounded by e.g. $\sqrt{M}$), as stated in Corollary 3. The general case of $\mathbb{Z}_M$ with arbitrary inputs and offsets requires a slightly more sophisticated treatment. We discuss the extension of our construction in Remark 4 below.

**Proposition 5 (Bit-Decomposition for $M = 2^m$).**   *There exists an FSS $(\text{Gen}_{\text{bit}}, \text{Eval}_{\text{bit}})$ for the offset function family $\hat{\mathcal{G}}_{\text{bit}}$ (restricted to $\mathbb{Z}_M$ with $M = 2^m$) making black-box use of a pseudorandom generator $\text{PRG} : \{0,1\}^\lambda \to \{0,1\}^{2(\lambda+1)}$ with the following complexities.*

– $\text{Gen}_{\text{bit}}$ *for function $g_{\text{bit}} : \mathbb{Z}_M \to \mathbb{Z}_2^m$ (with $M = 2^m$) makes $m(m-1)$ calls to PRG. It outputs keys $k_0, k_1$ each of size $(\lambda + 4)m(m-1)/2 + m$ bits.*
– $\text{Eval}_{\text{bit}}$ *makes $m(m-1)/2$ calls to PRG.*

*Proof.* Consider the following construction, making use of an FSS for special intervals $(\mathsf{Gen}_{\mathsf{SI}}, \mathsf{Eval}_{\mathsf{SI}})$. Recall the goal is to recover shares of the ($r^{\mathsf{out}}$-shifted) bit representation of $x + (-r^{\mathsf{in}}) \in \mathbb{Z}_M$, where $r^{\mathsf{in}}, r^{\mathsf{out}}$ are known at time of FSS generation. Let $\boldsymbol{r} = (r_{m-1}, \ldots, r_0) \in \mathbb{Z}_2^m$ denote the bit representation of $(-r^{\mathsf{in}}) \in \mathbb{Z}_M$ (note the additive inverse for notational convenience). For (public) input $x \in \mathbb{Z}_M$, we similarly denote its bit representation as $(x_{m-1}, \ldots, x_0)$.

Given public input $x$, we will compute (shares of) each bit of $(x + (-r^{\mathsf{in}}))$ over $\mathbb{Z}_M$ by computing "grade-school" addition on the bits. Each desired output bit $y_i, i \in \{0, \ldots, m-1\}$ can be expressed as a sum *over* $\mathbb{Z}_2$: $y_i = x_i \oplus r_i \oplus \mathsf{carry}_{i,r}(x)$, where $\mathsf{carry}_{i,r}(x) \in \{0,1\}$ is equal to 1 precisely when there is a carry entering into bit $i$ from the lower-order bits, indexes $j < i$. Note that for $M = 2^m$, there are no wraparound carries.

The function $x_i \oplus r_i$ is linear over the output space $\mathbb{Z}_2$ and can thus be directly evaluated given the public input $x$ and additive secret shares of $r_i$ (over $\mathbb{Z}_2$). The challenge is in implementing the nonlinear function $\mathsf{carry}_{i,r}(x)$, while hiding the value of $\boldsymbol{r}$. To do so, we make a simple observation: $\mathsf{carry}_{i,r}(x) = 1$ if and only if $(\sum_{j=0}^{i-1} 2^j x_j) \geq 2^i - (\sum_{j=0}^{i-1} 2^j r_j) \in \mathbb{Z}_{2^i}$. That is, there is a carry exactly if the numbers formed by the two truncated bit strings $(x_{i-1}, \ldots, x_0)$ and $(r_{i-1}, \ldots, r_0)$ sum to greater than $2^i$ (note they will never reach $2^{i+1}$). For each index $i \in \{0, \ldots, m-1\}$, we can thus implement FSS for $\mathsf{carry}_{i,r}(x)$ directly by one FSS for a *special (one-sided) interval* $f_{(a, 2^i-1)} : \mathbb{Z}_{2^i} \to \{0,1\}$, which evaluates to 1 on input $x' \in \mathbb{Z}_{2^i}$ precisely if $x' > a$.

We thus achieve the desired FSS with the following construction.

- $\mathsf{Gen}_{\mathsf{bit}}(1^\lambda, g_{\mathsf{bit}}^{[r^{\mathsf{in}}, r^{\mathsf{out}}]})$:
  1. Parse $g_{\mathsf{bit}}^{[r^{\mathsf{in}}, r^{\mathsf{out}}]}$ to recover $M, r^{\mathsf{in}} \in \mathbb{Z}_M, r^{\mathsf{out}} \in \mathbb{Z}_2^m$. Parse $r^{\mathsf{in}}$ as its bit representation $\boldsymbol{r} = (r_{m-1}, \ldots, r_0)$.
  2. For each $i \in \{0, \ldots, m-1\}$, do the following.
     (a) Sample special interval FSS keys $(k_0^i, k_1^i) \leftarrow \mathsf{Gen}_{\mathsf{SI}}(1^\lambda, f_{(a, 2^i-1)})$, for
     $$f_{(a, 2^i-1)} : \mathbb{Z}_{2^i} \to \{0,1\}, \text{ with } a = 2^i - (\textstyle\sum_{j=0}^{i-1} 2^j r_j) \in \mathbb{Z}_{2^i}.$$
     (b) Sample random additive secret shares $\langle z_0^i, z_1^i \rangle$ of $(r_i \oplus r_i^{\mathsf{out}})$ over $\mathbb{Z}_2$.
  3. Output keys $k_0 = (k_0^i, z_0^i)_{i=0}^{m-1}$ and $k_1 = (k_1^i, z_1^i)_{i=0}^{m-1}$.
- $\mathsf{Eval}_{\mathsf{bit}}(\sigma, k_\sigma, x)$: Parse $k_\sigma = (k_\sigma^i, z_\sigma^i)_{i=0}^{m-1}$ and $x = (x_{m-1}, \ldots, x_0)$ For each $i \in \{0, \ldots, m-1\}$, do the following.
  1. Execute $\mathsf{carry}_\sigma^i = \mathsf{Eval}_{\mathsf{SI}}\left(\sigma, k_\sigma^i, \sum_{j=0}^{i-1} 2^j x_j\right)$.
  2. Let $y_\sigma^i = \sigma \cdot x_i \oplus \mathsf{carry}_\sigma^i \oplus z_\sigma^i \in \mathbb{Z}_2$. Note that a single party will contribute $x_i$. (Recall $z_\sigma^i$ incorporates party $\sigma$'s shares of both the $r_i$ bit itself, as well as output offset bit $r_i^{\mathsf{out}}$.)
- Output $(y_\sigma^{m-1}, \ldots, y_\sigma^0) \in \mathbb{Z}_m^2$ as party $\sigma$'s output share.

Correctness of the construction holds as argued above; FSS security holds directly by the security of the underlying FSS scheme for special intervals (and additive secret sharing).

As mentioned, this case extends beyond just $\mathbb{Z}_M$ for $M = 2^m$, if we are in a promise setting of small inputs as compared to the modulus size. This can be useful within applications, e.g., in order to emulate computations over a non-$2^m$ modulus by emulating over $\mathbb{Z}_M$ for an artificially large $M$.

**Corollary 3 (Bit Decomposition for Small Inputs).** *There is an FSS scheme for the family of bit-decomposition functions with small inputs*

$$\hat{\mathcal{G}}_{\mathsf{bit}}^{\mathsf{small\text{-}input}} := \left\{ g^{[r^{\mathsf{in}}, r^{\mathsf{out}}]} : \mathbb{Z}_M \to \mathbb{Z}_2^m \; \middle| \; \begin{array}{c} g_{\mathsf{bit}} : \mathbb{Z}_M \to \mathbb{Z}_2^m \in \mathcal{G}_{\mathsf{bit}}, \\ r^{\mathsf{in}} \in \mathbb{Z}_M, |r^{\mathsf{in}}| \le \sqrt{M}, r^{\mathsf{out}} \in \mathbb{Z}_2^m \end{array} \right\},$$

*where the FSS guarantees correctness for inputs $x \in \mathbb{Z}_M$ of small magnitude $|x| \le \sqrt{M}$. The complexities of the FSS are as in Proposition 5.*

*Remark 4 (Bit Decomposition for General Modulus).* Our bit-arithmetic approach can be extended to the setting of general modulus $M$, by combining with an additional branch that either computes the same function as in the $M = 2^m$ case (if no wraparound occurs), or the function with an additional additive offset of $2^m - M$ (if a wraparound does occur). Ultimately, the computation of each $\mathsf{carry}_{i,r}$ can be expressed by the linear combination of two different functions, each an AND of two special intervals (namely, [> value to wraparound] $\wedge$ [> value to induce carry given wraparound] as well as [< value to wraparound] $\wedge$ [> value to induce carry without wraparound]).

This can be instantiated via FSS for 2-dimensional intervals, as described in [8]. We leave optimization of such scheme to future work.

### 4.4 Garbling-Compatible Variants

For the purpose of minimizing round complexity, it can be beneficial to combine FSS-based gate evaluation with garbled circuits, where the outputs of FSS gates are fed into a garbled circuit. This motivates garbling-compatible variants of the above types of gates, where the bits of the output select between pairs of secret keys that correspond to inputs of the garbled circuit.

We can realize this modified functionality with a low additional cost for almost all of the above types of gates (the only exception is spline gates, whose output is not binary). This is done in the following way. The secret keys are incorporated into the function families as part of the function description. The key selection is done by incorporating the keys in the DPF or DIF payload $\beta$. For instance, in the case of interval membership, the input domain is partitioned into intervals, where for each interval a DIF whose payload is the corresponding key is used to produce an additive secret-sharing of the key corresponding to membership in the (shifted) interval.

## 5    Negative Results and Barriers

In this section we rule out information-theoretic protocols that achieve the efficiency features of our FSS-based protocols, showing that the machinery we use is in a sense necessary. This should be contrasted with the fact that most positive results on secure computation given a trusted source of correlated randomness are information-theoretic.

We also give evidence that ruling out information-theoretic protocols with slightly relaxed efficiency features is difficult, by establishing a link with the existence of big matching vector families, a well known open problem in extremal combinatorics.

## 5.1  Online-Optimal Shared Equality Implies DPF

One of the simplest nontrivial instances of our positive results is a secure protocol for *string equality* with preprocessing and with secret-shared output. Concretely, we consider a protocol that given a pair of $n$-bit strings $(x_0, x_1)$ and correlated randomness $(r_0, r_1)$ outputs a *secret-sharing* of a single bit that indicates whether $x_0 = x_1$.

We define an *online-optimal protocol* to be one that has a single online round in which the message sent by each party is of the same length as its input. (By the perfect correctness requirement, the message length cannot be shorter than the input.) Note that this optimality feature is indeed satisfied by our DPF-based protocol, whose existence can be based on any OWF. We show that any online-optimal protocol can be used to build a DPF, though possibly with an exponential computation overhead in the input length. The latter suffices to prove that an online-optimal shared equality protocol implies a OWF.

Given the very restricted nature of an online-optimal protocol, this converse direction of showing that it implies a DPF may appear to be a mere syntactic translation. However, there are two main challenges that complicate this proof. First, the mapping of the inputs to messages does not necessarily rely on just additive masking. We get around this by requiring this masking to be efficiently invertible. (This requirement is not needed in case the input domain size is polynomial in the security parameter.) Second, the class of online-optimal protocols can deviate from the template of first masking the inputs using a pair of independent random strings and then *independently* applying an FSS scheme to the offset class defined by mapping the masked inputs to the secret-shared output. Indeed, a general protocol allows an arbitrary dependence between the two parts. As a result of these subtleties, it is not clear how to extend our argument from equality to general functions. Even in the case of equality, we need to assume the protocol to have the extra "efficient inversion" property mentioned above, unless the input domain is small.

We now formalize the notion of an online-optimal shared equality protocol and prove that it implies a DPF.

**Definition 16 (Online-optimal shared equality protocol).** *A protocol* $\Pi = (\mathsf{Setup}, \mathsf{Msg}, \mathsf{Out})$ *is an* online-optimal shared equality protocol *with inversion algorithm* $\mathsf{Inv}$ *if it satisfies the following requirements:*

– **Syntax**: *The protocol has the following structure.*

1. $\mathsf{Setup}(1^\lambda, 1^n)$ *outputs correlated randomness* $(r_0, r_1)$ *of size* $\mathsf{poly}(\lambda, n)$.
2. *In the online phase party* $P_\sigma$, *on input* $x_\sigma \in \{0,1\}^n$, *sends a single message* $m_\sigma = \mathsf{Msg}(\sigma, r_\sigma, x_\sigma)$ *to* $P_{1-\sigma}$, *where* $m_\sigma \in \{0,1\}^n$.
3. *Party* $P_\sigma$ *outputs* $y_\sigma \in \{0,1\}$ *where* $y_\sigma = \mathsf{Out}(\sigma, r_\sigma, x_\sigma, m_{1-\sigma})$.

- **Correctness:** *For any* $x_0, x_1 \in \{0,1\}^n$, *the resulting outputs* $y_0, y_1$ *always satisfy* $y_0 \oplus y_1 = EQ(x_0, x_1)$, *where* $EQ$ *outputs* 1 *if the two inputs are equal and outputs* 0 *otherwise.*
- **Security:** *The protocol* $\Pi$ *computationally hides from* $P_\sigma$ *the input* $x_{1-\sigma}$. *Formally, it satisfies the security requirement of Definition 2 with respect to the constant function* $f(x_0, x_1) = 0$.
- **Inversion:** *The algorithm* $\mathsf{Inv}$ *extracts the input from the corresponding randomness and message. That is, for any* $\sigma \in \{0,1\}$ *and* $r_\sigma, x_\sigma, m_\sigma$ *consistent with an execution of* $\Pi$, *we have* $\mathsf{Inv}(\sigma, 1^\lambda, r_\sigma, m_\sigma) = x_\sigma$.

Note that the correctness requirement implies that $x_\sigma$ is uniquely determined by $r_\sigma$ and $m_\sigma$. Moreover, whenever $n = O(\log \lambda)$, one can implement $\mathsf{Inv}$ in polynomial-time via brute-force search. This will suffice for constructing a DPF on a polynomial-size input domain, which implies a OWF. In our DPF-based shared equality protocol, however, the message is obtained by simply adding (or XORing) the input and a part of the randomness, and thus $\mathsf{Inv}$ can be implemented in linear time.

We now construct a DPF given oracle access to $\Pi$ and $\mathsf{Inv}$ as in Definition 16. The intuition for the construction is the following. Given $\mathsf{Inv}$, the output of each party $\sigma$ can be computed from $r_\sigma, m_0, m_1$ alone (without relying on the input $x_\sigma$). The correlated randomness $(r_0, r_1)$ then defines a pair of tables $T_\sigma^{r_\sigma}$, where $T_\sigma^{r_\sigma}[m_0, m_1]$ contains the output of $P_\sigma$ on randomness $r_\sigma$ and messages $(m_0, m_1)$. The two tables can be viewed as shares of a shifted identity matrix $T = T_0^{r_0} \oplus T_1^{r_1}$, where the location $\Delta$ of the 1-entry in the first row of $T$ is masked by randomness of both parties. To convert this into a DPF for a point function $f_{\alpha, 1}$, we include $\alpha \oplus \Delta$ in both keys. This does not reveal $\alpha$ to either party and yet effectively allows the parties to convert the first row of $T$ into one that contains 1 only in position $\alpha$ and 0 elsewhere, as required for sharing $f_{\alpha, 1}$. Finally, to guarantee security even in the case of super-polynomial input domains, we need to replace the first row with a random row $\rho$, where $\rho$ is included in both DPF keys.

The construction is formally described in Fig. 1.

**Theorem 7.** *If* $(\mathsf{Setup}, \mathsf{Msg}, \mathsf{Out}, \mathsf{Inv})$ *form an online-optimal shared equality protocol as in Definition 16, then* $(\mathsf{Gen}, \mathsf{Eval})$ *defined in Fig. 1 is a DPF.*

*Proof.* We separately argue correctness and security.

---

$\mathsf{Gen}(1^\lambda, \alpha)$:                    $\triangleright$ We assume here that $\mathbb{G}^{in} = \mathbb{Z}_2^{|\alpha|}$, $\mathbb{G}^{out} = \mathbb{Z}_2$, and $\beta = 1$

1: $n \leftarrow |\alpha|$; Sample random $\rho \leftarrow \{0,1\}^n$;
2: $(r_0, r_1) \leftarrow \mathsf{Setup}(1^\lambda, 1^n)$;
3: Let $\pi_0, \pi_1 : \{0,1\}^n \to \{0,1\}^n$ defined by $\pi_\sigma(x_\sigma) = \mathsf{Msg}(\sigma, r_\sigma, x_\sigma)$;
4: $\Delta \leftarrow \pi_1(\pi_0^{-1}(\rho))$;          $\triangleright$ Use $\mathsf{Msg}$ to compute $\pi_1$ and $\mathsf{Inv}$ to compute $\pi_0^{-1}$
5: Output $(k_0, k_1)$ where $k_\sigma = (r_\sigma, \rho, \alpha \oplus \Delta)$;

$\mathsf{Eval}(\sigma, k_\sigma, x)$:

1: $n \leftarrow |x|$;
2: Parse $k_\sigma$ as $(r_\sigma, \rho, \alpha')$;
3: Let $x_\sigma \leftarrow \mathsf{Inv}(\sigma, 1^\lambda, r_\sigma, \rho)$ if $\sigma = 0$ or $\mathsf{Inv}(\sigma, 1^\lambda, r_\sigma, \alpha' \oplus x)$ if $\sigma = 1$;
4: Let $y_\sigma \leftarrow \mathsf{Out}(\sigma, r_\sigma, x_\sigma, \alpha' \oplus x)$ if $\sigma = 0$ or $\mathsf{Out}(\sigma, r_\sigma, x_\sigma, \rho)$ if $\sigma = 1$;
5: Output $y_\sigma$                        $\triangleright$ $y_\sigma = T_\sigma^{r_\sigma}[\rho, \alpha' \oplus x]$

---

**Fig. 1.** DPF from online-optimal shared equality protocol ($\mathsf{Setup}, \mathsf{Msg}, \mathsf{Out}, \mathsf{Inv}$).

For correctness, letting $\pi_\sigma, T_\sigma^{r_\sigma}$ be as in Fig. 1 and $T = T_0^{r_0} \oplus T_1^{r_1}$, we can write:

$$y_0 \oplus y_1 = T[\rho, \alpha' \oplus x] \tag{1}$$

$$= EQ(\pi_0^{-1}(\rho), \pi_1^{-1}(\alpha' \oplus x)) \tag{2}$$

$$= EQ(\pi_1(\pi_0^{-1}(\rho)), \alpha' \oplus x) \tag{3}$$

$$= EQ(\Delta, \alpha' \oplus x) \tag{4}$$

$$= EQ(\Delta, (\alpha \oplus \Delta) \oplus x) \tag{5}$$

$$= EQ(\alpha, x) \tag{6}$$

as required, where (1) follows from Lines 3–4 of $\mathsf{Eval}$, (2) from the correctness of the equality protocol, (3) from applying $\pi_1$ to both sides from the left, (4) from Line 4 of $\mathsf{Gen}$, (5) from Line 5 of $\mathsf{Gen}$ and Line 2 of $\mathsf{Eval}$, and (6) by masking both sides with $\alpha \oplus \Delta$.

We turn to argue security. A key $k_\sigma$ produced by $\mathsf{Gen}$ is of the form $k_\sigma = (r_\sigma, \rho, \alpha \oplus \Delta)$, where $\Delta = \pi_1(\pi_0^{-1}(\rho))$. From the (computational) security of the equality protocol against $P_0$, it follows that $(r_0, \rho, \pi_1(\rho)) \approx (r_0, \rho, \pi_1(\rho'))$, where $\rho'$ is distributed uniformly over $\{0,1\}^n$ independently of $\rho$, and since $\pi_1$ is a permutation we have

$$(r_0, \rho, \pi_1(\rho)) \approx (r_0, \rho, \rho'). \tag{7}$$

Similarly, from the security against $P_1$ it follows that

$$(r_1, \rho, \pi_0(\rho)) \approx (r_1, \rho, \rho'). \tag{8}$$

It follows from (7) that

$$(r_0, \rho, \pi_1(\pi_0^{-1}(\rho))) \equiv (r_0, \pi_0(\rho), \pi_1(\rho)) \approx (r_0, \pi_0(\rho), \pi_1(\rho')) \equiv (r_0, \rho, \rho')$$

and hence $k_0 = (r_0, \rho, \alpha \oplus \Delta) \approx (r_0, \rho, \rho')$ as required. Similarly, it follows from (8) and from $(\rho, \pi_0^{-1}(\rho)) \equiv (\pi_0(\rho), \rho)$ that $k_1 = (r_1, \rho, \alpha \oplus \Delta) \approx (r_1, \rho, \rho')$ as required.

**Corollary 4.** *If there exists an online-optimal shared equality protocol as in Definition 16 with efficient* (Setup, Msg, Out) *(but possibly without an efficient inversion algorithm* Inv*) then a one-way function exists.*

*Proof.* The algorithm Inv can be implemented in time $\mathsf{poly}(\lambda, 2^n)$ via a brute-force search that enumerates over all possible choices of $x_\sigma$. Suppose that the DPF described in Fig. 1 (with oracle to Inv) has key size $|k_\sigma| = O((\lambda + n)^c)$ for a positive integer $c$. Then, letting $n(\lambda) = (c+1)\log \lambda$, we get a DPF with domain size $N(\lambda) = \lambda^{c+1}$ and asymptotically smaller key size $|k_\sigma| = O(\lambda^c)$. Using Theorem 5 from [19], this implies a one-way function.

## 5.2 Matching Vectors Imply Shared Equality

In the previous section we have shown that any shared equality protocol that has *optimal* online complexity implies a DPF, which in turn implies a one-way function. This raises the following question: suppose we relax the optimality requirement by, say, allowing each online message to be of length $10n$ or even $\mathsf{poly}(n)$ rather than $n$. Does such a protocol still imply a DPF? Alternatively, can we get an information-theoretic protocol with this complexity?

We do not know the answer to the above question. However, we show that if we slightly relax the output sharing requirement by allowing a constant-size (rather than single-bit) shares, then the problem of shared equality reduces to finding big families of *matching vectors* modulo a composite [5,17,18,21], a well studied problem in combinatorics. Given known constructions of matching vectors, this connection implies some unexpected (but rather weak) upper bounds. Perhaps more interestingly, the lack of progress on ruling out much bigger matching vector families suggests that proving strong lower bounds on information-theoretic shared equality protocols would be difficult.

**Definition 17 (Matching vectors).** *[17] Let $m$ be a positive integer and $S \subseteq \mathbb{Z}_m \setminus \{0\}$. We say that subsets $U = \{u_1, \ldots, u_N\}$ and $V = \{v_1, \ldots, v_N\}$ of vectors in $\mathbb{Z}_m^h$ form an $S$-matching family if the following two conditions are satisfied:*

- *For all $i \in [N]$, $\langle u_i, v_i \rangle = 0$, where $\langle \cdot, \cdot \rangle$ denotes inner product over $\mathbb{Z}_m$;*
- *For all $i, j \in [N]$ such that $i \neq j$, $\langle u_i, v_j \rangle \in S$.*

The best known constructions of matching vectors over a constant composite modulus $m$ are of quasi-polynomial size. For instance, for $m = 6$ the best known construction is of size $N = h^{O(\log h / \log \log h)}$ [21]. Whether bigger sets of matching vectors exist is a well known open problem, and only weak upper bounds are known; see [5] for the current state of the art.

We now show how to use families of matching vectors over a constant-size modulus $m$ to obtain an information-theoretic shared equality protocol that has a single online round and constant-size output shares.

**Theorem 8.** *Let $n$ be a positive integer and $N = 2^n$. Suppose there is a family of matching vectors with parameters $m, h, N$ as in Definition 17. Then there is a perfectly secure shared equality protocol* (Setup, Msg, Out) *for n-bit inputs with the following efficiency features:*

- Setup *outputs correlated randomness $(r_0, r_1)$ consisting of $O(h)$ elements of $\mathbb{Z}_m$;*
- Msg$(\sigma, r_\sigma, x_\sigma)$ *outputs a message in $\mathbb{Z}_m^h$;*
- Out$(\sigma, r_\sigma, x_\sigma, m_{1-\sigma})$ *outputs an output share in $\mathbb{Z}_m$.*

*Moreover, the two output shares produced by* Out *are equal if and only if $x_0 = x_1$.*

*Proof.* The protocol first encodes each input into a corresponding matching vector, and then computes shares of the inner product using the correlated randomness. In more detail, Setup generates a pair of random masks $R_0, R_1 \in \mathbb{Z}_m^h$ and additive shares of their inner product (this can be viewed as a generalized Beaver triple, or an instance of our FSS-based construction for a bilinear gate). Msg first encodes $x_\sigma$ into a corresponding matching vector $X_\sigma$ (where $x_0$ is encoded using $U$ and $x_1$ using $V$) and outputs $X_\sigma + R_\sigma$. Finally, Out uses the correlated randomness and the two messages to compute *subtractive* shares of the inner product of $X_0$ and $X_1$ (namely, the difference between the outputs is the inner product). Security follows from the masking, and correctness from the definition of a matching vector family.

Generalizing Theorem 8 to other useful predicates beyond equality seems challenging. Indeed, there are strong limitations on the existence of big sets of matching vectors with respect predicates other than equality, even for simple ones such as the "greater than" predicate [1]. This should be contrasted with our (computational) FSS-based protocols, which are not only more efficient for the simple case of equality but also apply almost as efficiently to the "greater than" predicate and other types of simple predicates.

**Acknowledgements.** Research supported by ERC Project NTSC (742754). E. Boyle additionally supported by ISF grant 1861/16 and AFOSR Award FA9550-17-1-0069. N. Gilboa additionally supported by ISF grant 1638/15, ERC grant 876110, and a grant by the BGU Cyber Center. Y. Ishai additionally supported by ISF grant 1709/14, NSF-BSF grant 2015782, and a grant from the Ministry of Science and Technology, Israel and Department of Science and Technology, Government of India.

# References

1. Bauer, B., Vihrovs, J., Wee, H.: On the inner product predicate and a generalization of matching vector families. In: 38th IARCS Annual Conference on Foundations of Software Technology and Theoretical Computer Science, FSTTCS 2018, 11–13 December 2018, Ahmedabad, India, pp. 41:1–41:13 (2018)
2. Beaver, D.: Efficient multiparty protocols using circuit randomization. In: Feigenbaum, J. (ed.) CRYPTO 1991. LNCS, vol. 576, pp. 420–432. Springer, Heidelberg (1992). https://doi.org/10.1007/3-540-46766-1_34

3. Ben-Efraim, A., Nielsen, M., Omri, E.: Turbospeedz: double your online SPDZ! Improving SPDZ using function dependent preprocessing. In: Deng, R.H., Gauthier-Umaña, V., Ochoa, M., Yung, M. (eds.) ACNS 2019. LNCS, vol. 11464, pp. 530–549. Springer, Cham (2019). https://doi.org/10.1007/978-3-030-21568-2_26

4. Bendlin, R., Damgård, I., Orlandi, C., Zakarias, S.: Semi-homomorphic encryption and multiparty computation. In: Paterson, K.G. (ed.) EUROCRYPT 2011. LNCS, vol. 6632, pp. 169–188. Springer, Heidelberg (2011). https://doi.org/10.1007/978-3-642-20465-4_11

5. Bhowmick, A., Dvir, Z., Lovett, S.: New bounds for matching vector families. SIAM J. Comput. 43(5), 1654–1683 (2014)

6. Boyle, E., Couteau, G., Gilboa, N., Ishai, Y., Kohl, L., Scholl, P.: Efficient pseudorandom correlation generators: silent OT extension and more. In: Boldyreva, A., Micciancio, D. (eds.) CRYPTO 2019. LNCS, vol. 11694, pp. 489–518. Springer, Cham (2019). https://doi.org/10.1007/978-3-030-26954-8_16

7. Boyle, E., Gilboa, N., Ishai, Y.: Function secret sharing. In: Oswald, E., Fischlin, M. (eds.) EUROCRYPT 2015. LNCS, vol. 9057, pp. 337–367. Springer, Heidelberg (2015). https://doi.org/10.1007/978-3-662-46803-6_12

8. Boyle, E., Gilboa, N., Ishai, Y.: Function secret sharing: improvements and extensions. In: Proceedings of the ACM Conference on Computer and Communications Security, pp. 1292–1303 (2016). Full version: ePrint report 2018/707

9. Canetti, R.: Security and composition of multiparty cryptographic protocols. J. Cryptol., 143–202 (2000)

10. Couteau, G.: New protocols for secure equality test and comparison. In: Preneel, B., Vercauteren, F. (eds.) ACNS 2018. LNCS, vol. 10892, pp. 303–320. Springer, Cham (2018). https://doi.org/10.1007/978-3-319-93387-0_16

11. Couteau, G.: A note on the communication complexity of multiparty computation in the correlated randomness model. In: Ishai, Y., Rijmen, V. (eds.) EUROCRYPT 2019. LNCS, vol. 11477, pp. 473–503. Springer, Cham (2019). https://doi.org/10.1007/978-3-030-17656-3_17

12. Damgård, I., Fitzi, M., Kiltz, E., Nielsen, J.B., Toft, T.: Unconditionally secure constant-rounds multi-party computation for equality, comparison, bits and exponentiation. In: Halevi, S., Rabin, T. (eds.) TCC 2006. LNCS, vol. 3876, pp. 285–304. Springer, Heidelberg (2006). https://doi.org/10.1007/11681878_15

13. Damgård, I., Nielsen, J.B., Nielsen, M., Ranellucci, S.: The TinyTable protocol for 2-party secure computation, or: gate-scrambling revisited. In: Katz, J., Shacham, H. (eds.) CRYPTO 2017. LNCS, vol. 10401, pp. 167–187. Springer, Cham (2017). https://doi.org/10.1007/978-3-319-63688-7_6

14. Damgård, I., Pastro, V., Smart, N., Zakarias, S.: Multiparty computation from somewhat homomorphic encryption. In: Safavi-Naini, R., Canetti, R. (eds.) CRYPTO 2012. LNCS, vol. 7417, pp. 643–662. Springer, Heidelberg (2012). https://doi.org/10.1007/978-3-642-32009-5_38

15. Demmler, D., Schneider, T., Zohner, M.: ABY - a framework for efficient mixed-protocol secure two-party computation. In: NDSS 2015 (2015)

16. Doerner, J., Shelat, A.: Scaling ORAM for secure computation. In: Proceedings of the 2017 ACM SIGSAC Conference on Computer and Communications Security, CCS 2017, Dallas, TX, USA, 30 October–03 November, pp. 523–535 (2017)

17. Dvir, Z., Gopalan, P., Yekhanin, S.: Matching vector codes. SIAM J. Comput. 40(4), 1154–1178 (2011)

18. Efremenko, K.: 3-query locally decodable codes of subexponential length. SIAM J. Comput. 41(6), 1694–1703 (2012)

19. Gilboa, N., Ishai, Y.: Distributed point functions and their applications. In: Nguyen, P.Q., Oswald, E. (eds.) EUROCRYPT 2014. LNCS, vol. 8441, pp. 640–658. Springer, Heidelberg (2014). https://doi.org/10.1007/978-3-642-55220-5_35
20. Goldreich, O.: Foundations of Cryptography - Basic Applications. Cambridge University Press, New York (2004)
21. Grolmusz, V.: On set systems with restricted intersections modulo a composite number. In: Jiang, T., Lee, D.T. (eds.) COCOON 1997. LNCS, vol. 1276, pp. 82–90. Springer, Heidelberg (1997). https://doi.org/10.1007/BFb0045075
22. Ishai, Y., Kushilevitz, E., Meldgaard, S., Orlandi, C., Paskin-Cherniavsky, A.: On the power of correlated randomness in secure computation. In: Sahai, A. (ed.) TCC 2013. LNCS, vol. 7785, pp. 600–620. Springer, Heidelberg (2013). https://doi.org/10.1007/978-3-642-36594-2_34
23. Katz, J., Kolesnikov, V., Wang, X.: Improved non-interactive zero knowledge with applications to post-quantum signatures. In: Proceedings of the ACM Conference on Computer and Communications Security, pp. 525–537 (2018)
24. Katz, J., Ranellucci, S., Rosulek, M., Wang, X.: Optimizing authenticated garbling for faster secure two-party computation. In: Shacham, H., Boldyreva, A. (eds.) CRYPTO 2018. LNCS, vol. 10993, pp. 365–391. Springer, Cham (2018). https://doi.org/10.1007/978-3-319-96878-0_13
25. Mohassel, P., Rindal, P.: ABY³: a mixed protocol framework for machine learning. In: Proceedings of the ACM Conference on Computer and Communications Security, pp. 35–52 (2018)

# Efficient Private PEZ Protocols
# for Symmetric Functions

Yoshiki Abe[✉], Mitsugu Iwamoto, and Kazuo Ohta

The University of Electro-Communications,
1–5–1 Chofugaoka, Chofushi, Tokyo 182–8585, Japan
{yoshiki,mitsugu,kazuo.ohta}@uec.ac.jp

**Abstract.** A private PEZ protocol is a variant of secure multi-party computation performed using a (long) PEZ dispenser. The original paper by Balogh et al. presented a private PEZ protocol for computing an arbitrary function with $n$ inputs. This result is interesting, but no follow-up work has been presented since then, to the best of our knowledge. We show herein that it is possible to shorten the *initial string* (the sequence of candies filled in a PEZ dispenser) and the number of *moves* (a player pops out a specified number of candies in each move) drastically if the function is *symmetric*. Concretely, it turns out that the length of the initial string is reduced from $\mathcal{O}(2^n!)$ for general functions in Balogh et al.'s results to $\mathcal{O}(n \cdot n!)$ for symmetric functions, and $2^n$ moves for general functions are reduced to $n^2$ moves for symmetric functions. Our main idea is to utilize the recursive structure of symmetric functions to construct the protocol recursively. This idea originates from a *new* initial string we found for a private PEZ protocol for the three-input majority function, which is different from the one with the same length given by Balogh et al. without describing how they derived it.

**Keywords:** Private PEZ protocol · Multi-party computation · Symmetric functions · Threshold functions

## 1 Introduction

### 1.1 Background and Motivation

A private PEZ protocol is a type of implementation of secure multi-party computation (MPC, [5]) that employs a (long) PEZ dispenser.[1] The private PEZ protocol is interesting not only because MPC can be implemented by physical tools[2] such as a PEZ dispenser but also because the protocol does not require randomness for executing MPC.[3] The original paper by Balogh et al. [1] presented a model of the PEZ protocol for computing a function $f_n$ with $n$ inputs

---

This work was supported by JSPS KAKENHI Grant Numbers JP17H01752, JP18K19780, JP18K11293, JP18H05289, and JP18H03238.

[1] An ordinary PEZ dispenser can store 12 candies.

[2] The other examples are card-based protocols [2,3].

[3] Several card-based protocols, e.g., [4], do not require any randomness, either.

D. Hofheinz and A. Rosen (Eds.): TCC 2019, LNCS 11891, pp. 372–392, 2019.
https://doi.org/10.1007/978-3-030-36030-6_15

**Table 1.** Comparison of the lengths of initial strings

| $n$ | 2 | 3 | 4 | 5 | 6 | 7 |
|---|---|---|---|---|---|---|
| Balogh et al. [1] | 7 | 72 | 6941 | $6.3 \cdot 10^7$ | $5.3 \cdot 10^{15}$ | $3.8 \cdot 10^{31}$ |
| Recursive construction (Sect. 4) | 7 | 31 | 165 | 1,031 | 7,423 | 60,621 |
| Efficient $\mathrm{maj}_n^{\lceil n/2 \rceil}$ (Sect. 5) | 3 | 13 | 21 | 131 | 223 | 1,821 |

without privacy, and they extended it to a model of the private PEZ protocol. The paper also proposed a method for constructing private PEZ protocols for a general function $f_n$.

There are two major efficiency measures of a private PEZ protocol: the length of the *initial string* and the number of *moves*. An initial string is a sequence of candies filled in a PEZ dispenser at the beginning of the protocol. A move refers to the execution step in which each player reads the candies according to the protocol. The shorter the initial string and the smaller the number of moves, the better. Unfortunately, Balogh et al.'s protocol is very inefficient in terms of both measures although the proposed protocol can compute an *arbitrary* function $f_n$.

The length of an initial string for computing $f_n$ presented in [1] is $\mathcal{O}(2^n!)$, which does not depend on $f_n$ itself but depends only on $n$. The numbers of candies for specific $n \leq 7$ are provided in Table 1. For instance, for $n = 7$, almost $3.8 \times 10^{31}$ candies are required for the initial string, which is far from practical. The other efficiency measure is also impractical because the number of moves in [1] is $2^n - 1$.

Although the initial strings are *very long* for computing the general function $f_n$, Balogh et al.'s paper also presented a private PEZ protocol with a *very short* initial string for the majority function with three inputs, which is denoted by $\mathrm{maj}_3^2$ in this paper. Surprisingly, only 13 candies are shown to be sufficient for the initial string in this protocol, whereas 72 candies are required for an arbitrary $f_3$. Unfortunately, nothing was mentioned about why and how the authors obtained this protocol, and no follow-up work on private PEZ protocols has been presented after Balogh et al.'s original paper.

## 1.2 Our Contributions

**Efficient Protocols for Symmetric Functions (Section 4):** Our motivation is to propose a more efficient private PEZ protocol. A shorter length for the initial string and a smaller number of moves are desirable, but it is not easy to realize these for a general function $f_n$. We instead succeeded in making the length of the initial strings shorter and the number of moves smaller by restricting the class of functions to be computed to *symmetric* functions.

The impact of the restriction is so great that the length of the initial string is reduced from $\mathcal{O}(2^n!)$ for general functions in [1] to $\mathcal{O}(n \cdot n!)$ for symmetric functions. For instance, the case where $n = 7$ in Table 1 shows us that the length of the initial string is almost $3.8 \times 10^{31}$ for a general function, but it is reduced to only $60,621$ for symmetric function. Furthermore, $2^n - 1$ moves in [1] for general functions are considerably reduced to $n^2$ moves for symmetric functions.

**Why Are 13 Candies Sufficient for maj$_3^2$?** (**Sections 3 and 5**): Our main idea for constructing a private PEZ protocol for a symmetric function $f_n$ is to utilize the recursive structure of $f_n$ to construct the protocol recursively. This idea is suggested by observation of the *new* initial string with length 13 for computing maj$_3^2$, which is different from the initial string with the same length presented in [1]. We will explain how we obtained such a short initial string in Sect. 3 as a preliminary step before proposing a general protocol for symmetric functions.

As is explained in Sect. 4, observation of our new initial string suggests how private PEZ protocols with much shorter initial strings for arbitrary symmetric functions can be constructed. Furthermore, our new initial string also suggests that the initial string of majority functions can be further shortened, which will be explained in Sect. 5. The difference between the constructions of initial strings for symmetric functions in Sect. 4 and for majority functions in Sect. 5 is that instead of constructing the initial string completely recursively, we use the initial string for and/or functions in the middle of the recursions because these functions can be implemented by very short initial strings. As seen from Table 1, we can further shorten the initial strings compared to the case of recursive construction proposed in Sect. 4. For $n = 7$, only $1,821$ candies are sufficient: i.e., our new construction requires initial strings with a length of only $4.8 \times 10^{-27}\%$ of Balogh et al.'s result!

## 1.3   Organization of the Paper

The remaining part of this paper is organized as follows: In Sect. 2, the notations and models of PEZ protocols with/without privacy [1] are provided. Section 3 is devoted to finding initial strings of private PEZ protocols for computing maj$_3^2$ and maj$_4^2$, which suggests how private PEZ protocols can be constructed recursively. Then, we propose the recursive construction of a private PEZ protocol for computing arbitrary symmetric functions in Sect. 4. Section 5 revisits a private PEZ protocol for computing majority functions. We show how to further shorten the (short) initial strings presented in Sect. 4. Section 6 concludes this paper. Technical lemma and proofs are provided in Appendix A.

## 2   Preliminaries

### 2.1   Notations

- For integers $a$ and $b$ such that $a \leq b$, $[a : b] := \{a, a+1, \ldots, b\}$.
- For a bit $b \in \{0, 1\}$, define $\bar{b} := 1 - b$.
- For two strings $a, b \in \Gamma^*$, $|a|$ denotes the length of $a$, and $a \prec b$ means that the string $a$ is a prefix of the string $b$.
- $\lambda$ is the empty string. Note that $|\lambda| = 0$.
- For two strings $a, b \in \Gamma^*$, $a \circ b$ is the concatenation of $a$ and $b$. Concatenations of $n$ identical strings of $a$ are expressed as $[a]^n := \underbrace{a \circ \cdots \circ a}_{n \text{ times}}$.

**Table 2.** A PEZ protocol for a function $f_n$

| Move | Player to move | # of symbols to be read | | |
|------|----------------|------------------------|---|---|
| | | $x_{i_j} = \sigma_1$ | $\cdots$ | $x_{i_j} = \sigma_k$ |
| $M_1$ | $P_{i_1}$ | $\mu_1(\sigma_1)$ | $\cdots$ | $\mu_1(\sigma_k)$ |
| $M_2$ | $P_{i_2}$ | $\mu_2(\sigma_1)$ | $\cdots$ | $\mu_2(\sigma_k)$ |
| $\vdots$ | $\vdots$ | $\vdots$ | $\ddots$ | $\vdots$ |
| $M_m$ | $P_{i_m}$ | $\mu_m(\sigma_1)$ | $\cdots$ | $\mu_m(\sigma_k)$ |

- For a binary string $a$, $\mathsf{hw}(a)$ is the Hamming weight of $a$.
- For a binary string $a$ of length $n$, $\mathsf{and}_n(a)$ and $\mathsf{or}_n(a)$ are the results of the conjunction and disjunction of all the elements of $a$, respectively.
- For two sets $X$ and $Y$, the difference set is defined as $X \setminus Y := X \cap Y^c$, where $Y^c$ is the complement set of $Y$.

## 2.2 PEZ Protocols

Suppose that there are $n(\geq 2)$ semi-honest players $P_1, P_2, \ldots, P_n$. Each player $P_i$ has an input $x_i \in \Sigma$, and the players wish to compute a function $f_n : \Sigma^n \to \Gamma$ while hiding their inputs from each other. The PEZ protocol for computing $f_n$ consists of the following three steps:

**Initialization** Prepare a public fixed string, called an *initial string*, $\alpha \in \Gamma^*$ depending on only $f_n$.

**Execution** Follow a sequence of *moves* $M_1, M_2, \ldots, M_m$: at each move $M_j$, player $P_{i_j}$ reads the next $\mu_j(x_{i_j})$ symbols of $\alpha$ privately, where $\mu_j(\sigma)$ indicates the number of symbols read at the $j$-th move with input $\sigma \in \Sigma$. The sequence $i_1, i_2, \ldots, i_m$ is called the *move order*.

**Output** Read the first symbol of the unread string in $\alpha$.

By defining in advance the one-to-one correspondence between the colors of candies and symbols in $\alpha$, the PEZ protocol can be interpreted as follows: Initialization consists of filling a sequence of candies represented by $\alpha$ into a PEZ dispenser. Execution consists of popping out $\mu_j(x_{i_j})$ candies from the dispenser privately. Finally, we output the topmost candy left in the PEZ dispenser, which indicates the result of $f_n(x_1, x_2, \ldots, x_n)$.

We define a PEZ protocol with an initial string $\alpha$ that computes a function $f_n : \Sigma^n \to \Gamma$, where $n$ is the number of players of this protocol. When we denote an initial sequence by $\alpha(f_n)$, it means an initial sequence of the PEZ protocol for computing the function $f_n$.

**Definition 1 (PEZ protocol [1]).** Let $\alpha \in \Gamma^*$ be an initial string and $f_n : \Sigma^n \to \Gamma$ be a function to be computed. A PEZ protocol $\Pi_{\alpha, f_n}$ is defined by an initial string $\alpha$ and a sequence of $m$ moves $(M_1, M_2, \ldots, M_m)$. Each move $M_j$ consists of a pair $(i_j, \mu_j)$, where $i_j$ is a player index specifying who moves (i.e., reads symbols from $\alpha$) and $\mu_j : \Sigma \to \{0, 1, \ldots, |\alpha| - 1\}$ maps each input of players to the number of symbols to be read.

Table 2 indicates how many candies are popped out by the $i_j$-th player at the $j$-th move.

## 2.3    Private PEZ Protocols

**Definition 2 (Private PEZ protocol [1]).** For an initial string $\alpha$ and a function $f_n$ with $n$ inputs, a PEZ protocol $\Pi_{\alpha,f_n}$ is called *private* if there exists a mapping $\nu : \{1, 2, \ldots, m\} \times \Sigma \to \Gamma^*$ that satisfies the following two conditions[4]:

1. For all $j \in \{1, 2, \ldots, m\}$, and for all $\sigma \in \Sigma$, the following holds:

$$|\nu(j, \sigma)| = \mu_j(\sigma).$$

2. For any $x := (x_1, x_2, \ldots, x_n) \in \Sigma^n$, the following holds:

$$\nu(1, x_{i_1}) \circ \nu(2, x_{i_2}) \circ \cdots \circ \nu(m, x_{i_m}) \circ f_n(x) \prec \alpha.$$

Intuitively, Definition 2 can be explained as follows: Condition 1 means that the number of candies read by player $P_{i_j}$ at the $j$-th move is specified by $j$ and the input $x_{i_j}$ of $P_{i_j}$. Condition 2 requires that if we read the candies with the number specified by Condition 1, the output becomes $f_n(x)$, which implies *correctness*.

Condition 2 simultaneously requires that if every player reads the candies by following Condition 1, player $P_{i_j}$ with input $x_{i_j}$ at the $j$-th move must eventually read the same sequence $\nu(j, x_{i_j})$, which guarantees *privacy*. In other words, the substrings to be read by $P_i$, i.e., the view of $P_i$, in each move depends on $x_i$ only, so that the view contains no information about the other players' inputs.

**Definition 3 (Round in a private PEZ protocol).** In a private PEZ protocol for computing $f_n$, we call a series of $n$ moves a *round* if the $n$ moves satisfy the following conditions. The $\ell$-th round is denoted by $R_\ell$, $\ell \geq 0$.

1. Every player $P_i$ moves only once in the $n$ moves.[5]
2. During the same round, every $P_i$ reads the same sequence if the input of $P_i$ is the same.

If a sequence of moves consists of rounds, the move order in each round does not affect the output.

**Example 1 (Private PEZ protocols for $\mathsf{and}_n$ and $\mathsf{or}_n$ [1]).** We show private PEZ protocols for computing AND and OR of $n$ binary inputs which are denoted by $\mathsf{and}_n$ and $\mathsf{or}_n$, respectively. The private PEZ protocols for $\mathsf{and}_n$ and $\mathsf{or}_n$ are useful for constructing efficient private PEZ protocols discussed hereafter.

A private PEZ protocol for $\mathsf{and}_n$ uses the $(n+1)$-bit initial string $\alpha(\mathsf{and}_n) := [0]^n \circ 1$ and has $n$ moves: each player $P_i$ reads one candy of "0" from $\alpha(\mathsf{and}_n)$

---

[4] In [1], $\beta$ was used instead of $\nu$, but in this paper, we use $\beta$ to express a string.
[5] If $f_n$ is symmetric, the move order in a round does not affect the output.

**Table 3.** A private PEZ protocol $\Pi_{\alpha,\mathsf{and}_n}$ where $\alpha := \alpha(\mathsf{and}_n) = [0]^n \circ 1$

| Round | Player to move | # of bits to be read | | Substring to be read | |
|---|---|---|---|---|---|
| | | $x_i = 0$ | $x_i = 1$ | $x_i = 0$ | $x_i = 1$ |
| $R_0$ | $\{P_i\}_{i=1}^n$ | 0 | 1 | – | 0 |

**Table 4.** A private PEZ protocol $\Pi_{\alpha,\mathsf{or}_n}$ where $\alpha := \alpha(\mathsf{or}_n) = [1]^n \circ 0$

| Round | Player to move | # of bits to be read | | Substring to be read | |
|---|---|---|---|---|---|
| | | $x_i = 0$ | $x_i = 1$ | $x_i = 0$ | $x_i = 1$ |
| $R_0$ | $\{P_i\}_{i=1}^n$ | 1 | 0 | 1 | – |

if the input value of $P_i$ is 1, otherwise each $P_i$ does not read any candy. After round $R_0$, i.e., $n$ moves by $P_1, P_2$, and $P_n$, the first remaining candy of $\alpha(\mathsf{and}_n)$ becomes "1" only when all the input values of $P_i$ are 1, otherwise it becomes "0". This protocol $\Pi_{\alpha(\mathsf{and}_n),\mathsf{and}_n}$ is summarized in Table 3. A private PEZ protocol for $\mathsf{or}_n$ can be specified analogously by letting $\alpha(\mathsf{or}_n) := [1]^n \circ 0$ and following the moves in Table 4.

The privacy of $\mathsf{and}_n$ is easy to see because every player reads "0" during $R_0$ if $P_i$ inputs 1, and hence, no information leaks until the output phase. The privacy of $\mathsf{or}_n$ is also easy to understand.

**Example 2 (Private PEZ protocol for $\mathsf{maj}_3^2$).** Consider the case of a majority function with three inputs denoted by $\mathsf{maj}_3^2$, which outputs 1 if two or more inputs are 1. The initial string for $\mathsf{maj}_3^2$ is given by $\alpha(\mathsf{maj}_3^2) = 0010010010001$, and the protocol works as shown in Table 5.

In this example, correctness is easy to check. Privacy is easy to see as well because every player who inputs 1 reads "001" and "0" in rounds $R_0$ and $R_1$, respectively, and nothing is read by the player who inputs 0.

*Remark.* Note that a private PEZ protocol for $\mathsf{maj}_3^2$ with an initial string with length 13 was presented in [1], which is different from the one in Example 2. Unfortunately, however, no description was given in [1] regarding why and how the protocol was derived. On the other hand, in this paper, we will explain how we derived the protocol in Example 2, which is insightful for constructing a private PEZ protocol for symmetric functions and its improvement for $\mathsf{maj}_n^t$ that are proposed in Sects. 4 and 5, respectively.

**Table 5.** A private PEZ protocol $\Pi_{\alpha,\mathsf{maj}_3^2}$ where $\alpha := \alpha(\mathsf{maj}_3^2) = 0010010010001$

| Round | Players to move | # of bits to be read | | Substring to be read | |
|---|---|---|---|---|---|
| | | $x_i = 0$ | $x_i = 1$ | $x_i = 0$ | $x_i = 1$ |
| $R_0$ | $\{P_i\}_{i=1}^3$ | 0 | 3 | – | 001 |
| $R_1$ | $\{P_i\}_{i=1}^3$ | 0 | 1 | – | 0 |

## 2.4   Symmetric Functions

**Definition 4 (Symmetric functions).** A function $f_n : \{0,1\}^n \to \Gamma$ is called *symmetric* if

$$f_n(x_1, x_2, \ldots, x_n) = f_n(x_{\sigma(1)}, x_{\sigma(2)}, \ldots, x_{\sigma(n)}) \tag{1}$$

holds for all $(x_1, x_2, \ldots, x_n) \in \{0,1\}^n$ and an arbitrary permutation $\sigma : [n] \to [n]$.

Since the symmetric function does not depend on the order of $x_1, x_2, \ldots, x_n$, we will sometimes regard $f_n$ as a function taking a multiset as an input. For instance, a symmetric function $f_2(x_1, x_2) = f_2(x_2, x_1)$ is also written as $f_2^{\mathsf{m}}(\{x_1, x_2\}) := f_2(x_1, x_2) = f_2(x_2, x_1)$. Furthermore, if $f_n$ takes $n$ binary inputs, $f_n$ depends only on the Hamming weight of the $n$ binary inputs. Summarizing, we use the following equivalent expressions for symmetric functions.

**Definition 5 (Equivalent expressions for symmetric functions).** For a symmetric function $f_n : \{0,1\}^n \to \Gamma$, define $f_n^{\mathsf{m}} : \{\{x_1, x_2, \ldots, x_n\} \mid x_i \in \{0,1\}\} \to \Gamma$ and $f_n^{\mathsf{w}} : [0:n] \to \Gamma$ as

$$f_n^{\mathsf{m}}(\{x_1, x_2, \ldots, x_n\}) := f_n(x_1, x_2, \ldots, x_n), \tag{2}$$

$$f_n^{\mathsf{w}}(w) := f_n(x_1, x_2, \ldots, x_n), \tag{3}$$

where $\{x_1, x_2, \ldots, x_n\}$ is a multiset and $x_1, x_2, \ldots, x_n$ are the binary inputs satisfying $w = \mathsf{hw}(x_1, x_2, \ldots, x_n)$ .

Hereafter, we choose an appropriate expression for a symmetric function from (1)–(3) depending on the context. The superscripts $\mathsf{m}$ and $\mathsf{w}$ will be omitted if they are clear from the context.

# 3   Warm-Up: Private PEZ Protocols for Majority Voting

Before presenting our construction of private PEZ protocols for general symmetric functions, we show private PEZ protocols for $n$-input majority voting ($n \geq 3$).

**Definition 6 (Majority function with threshold).** Let $n$ and $t$ be positive integers with $n \geq t$. For $x_1, x_2, \ldots, x_n \in \{0,1\}$, define a majority function with threshold $t$ by

$$\mathsf{maj}_n^t(x_1, x_2, \ldots, x_n) := \begin{cases} 1, & \text{if } \sum_{i=1}^n x_i \geq t \\ 0, & \text{otherwise.} \end{cases} \tag{4}$$

For $t = \lceil n/2 \rceil$, $\mathsf{maj}_n^t$ reduces to the ordinary majority voting.

In this section, for intuitive understanding, we construct private PEZ protocols from the perspective of each player's view and do not explicitly prove that proposed protocols satisfy Definition 2. Later, we directly prove that the proposed private PEZ protocols for symmetric functions satisfies Definition 2.

**Table 6.** Truth table of $\mathsf{maj}_3^2$ classified by $x_3$

| $x_1$ | $x_2$ | $x_3 = 0$ | $x_3 = 1$ |
|---|---|---|---|
| 0 | 0 | 0 | 0 |
| 0 | 1 | 0 | 1 |
| 1 | 0 | 0 | 1 |
| 1 | 1 | 1 | 1 |

**Example 3 (A private PEZ protocol for three-input majority voting).**
Table 6 is the truth table of $\mathsf{maj}_3^2$ classified by the value of $x_3 \in \{0, 1\}$. Observing
the input values of $x_1$ and $x_2$, and the output values for $x_3 = 0$ in Table 6, we
can see that $\mathsf{maj}_3^2(\{x_1, x_2, 0\})$ can be regarded as $\mathsf{and}_2(\{x_1, x_2\})$: i.e.,

$$\mathsf{maj}_3^2(\{x_1, x_2, 0\}) = \mathsf{maj}_2^2(\{x_1, x_2\}) = \mathsf{and}_2(\{x_1, x_2\}). \tag{5}$$

We can also find

$$\mathsf{maj}_3^2(\{x_1, 0, x_3\}) = \mathsf{maj}_2^2(\{x_1, x_3\}) = \mathsf{and}_2(\{x_1, x_3\}), \tag{6}$$

$$\mathsf{maj}_3^2(\{0, x_2, x_3\}) = \mathsf{maj}_2^2(\{x_2, x_3\}) = \mathsf{and}_2(\{x_2, x_3\}). \tag{7}$$

(5)–(7) imply that if there exists at least one input with value 0, $\mathsf{maj}_3^2$ can
be computed by $\mathsf{and}_2$ with two inputs obtained by fixing one input to 0 in three
inputs of $\mathsf{maj}_3^2$. Only when $x_1 = x_2 = x_3 = 1$, $\mathsf{maj}_3^2$ is not representable by $\mathsf{and}_2$.
Therefore, $\mathsf{maj}_3^2$ can be represented as follows:

$$\mathsf{maj}_3^2(\{x_1, x_2, x_3\})$$
$$= \begin{cases} \mathsf{maj}_3^2(\{1, 1, 1\}), & \text{if } x_1 = x_2 = x_3 = 1, \\ \mathsf{maj}_2^2(\{x_1, x_2, x_3\} \setminus \{0\}) = \mathsf{and}_2(\{x_1, x_2, x_3\} \setminus \{0\}), & \text{otherwise.} \end{cases} \tag{8}$$

Equivalently, for $w \in [0 : 3]$,[6]

$$\mathsf{maj}_3^2(w) = \begin{cases} \mathsf{maj}_3^2(3), & \text{if } w = 3, \\ \mathsf{maj}_2^2(w - 0) = \mathsf{and}_2(w - 0), & \text{otherwise.} \end{cases} \tag{9}$$

We construct a private PEZ protocol for $\mathsf{maj}_3^2$ based on (8). Let $\alpha(\mathsf{maj}_3^2)$ be
an initial string for $\mathsf{maj}_3^2$.

Let $\beta_0$ and $\beta_1$ be strings used for computing $\mathsf{and}_2(\{x_1, x_2, x_3\} \setminus \{0\})$ and
$\mathsf{maj}_3^2(\{1, 1, 1\})$, in (8), respectively. The actual sequence of $\beta_0$ and $\beta_1$ are undetermined so far, but will be specified below. Note here that the cases in (8) are
classified by the results of $\mathsf{and}_3$. From Example 1, the initial string for computing
$\mathsf{and}_3$ is given by $\alpha(\mathsf{and}_3) = 0001$, and we replace 0 and 1 in $\alpha(\mathsf{and}_3)$ with $\beta_0$ and
$\beta_1$, respectively. Then we obtain

$$\alpha(\mathsf{maj}_3^2) = \beta_0 \circ \beta_0 \circ \beta_0 \circ \beta_1 \tag{10}$$

---

[6] "$-0$" means that the weight does not change, which is used to aid in understanding.

as the initial string for computing $\mathsf{maj}_3^2$. The reason of these replacements will be explained later more clearly.

Using the initial string $\alpha(\mathsf{maj}_3^2)$ in (10), the private PEZ protocol for computing $\mathsf{maj}_3^2$ can be described as follows: In round $R_0$, each player $P_i$ who inputs $x_i = 1$ reads $|\beta_0|$ bits: otherwise ($x_i = 0$), $P_i$ does not read any bit. The following shows the remaining string $\alpha'$ after round $R_0$.

$$\alpha' \succ \begin{cases} \beta_1, & \text{if } x_1 = x_2 = x_3 = 1 \\ \beta_0, & \text{otherwise.} \end{cases} \tag{11}$$

After $R_0$, several moves are added to compute $\mathsf{maj}_3^2$ using $\beta_0$ or $\beta_1$, which will specify $\beta_0$ and $\beta_1$.

The correctness ((11) holds) and privacy (no player obtains information about other players' inputs) in $R_0$ are guaranteed by the correctness and privacy of the private PEZ protocol for $\mathsf{and}_3$, which is the reason why we replaced 0 and 1 in $\alpha(\mathsf{and}_3)$ with $\beta_0$ and $\beta_1$, respectively, to obtain (10). Therefore, to construct the private PEZ protocol for $\mathsf{maj}_3^2$, the additional moves have to satisfy the following requirements:

**Correctness of the additional moves**
  **C-1** Compute $\mathsf{and}_2(\{x_1, x_2, x_3\} \setminus \{0\})$ using $\beta_0(\prec \alpha')$.
  **C-2** Compute $\mathsf{maj}_3^2(\{1, 1, 1\})$ using $\beta_1(\prec \alpha')$.
**Privacy of the additional moves**
  **P-1** Computation of $\mathsf{and}_2(\{x_1, x_2, x_3\} \setminus \{0\})$ is private.
  **P-2** Computation of $\mathsf{maj}_3^2(\{1, 1, 1\})$ is private.
  **P-3** Each string read by each player for $\mathsf{and}_2(\{x_1, x_2, x_3\} \setminus \{0\})$ is the same as the one for $\mathsf{maj}_3^2(\{1, 1, 1\})$.

First, we discuss **C-1** and **P-1** to specify $\beta_0$ and the additional moves. Since $0 \in \{x_1, x_2, x_3\}$, $\mathsf{and}_2(\{x_1, x_2, x_3\} \setminus \{0\})$ can be computed in the same way as the private PEZ protocol for $\mathsf{and}_2$. That is, using the string $\beta_0 := 001$, each player $P_i$, $1 \leq i \leq 3$, reads one bit represented by "0" if $x_i = 1$, otherwise $P_i$ does not read any bit. Note that there exists a bit in $\beta_0$ to be output when three players execute the move in the private PEZ protocol for $\mathsf{and}_2$ with $\alpha(\mathsf{and}_2) = 001$, because there exists at least one player $P_j$ whose input $x_j = 0$ and does not read any bit. Therefore, $\mathsf{and}_2(\{x_1, x_2, x_3\} \setminus \{0\})$ can be computed using $\beta_0 = 001$. In addition, no player can obtain information about other players' inputs because one bit read by a player is always "0" regardless of other players' inputs. Hence, in summary, to satisfy **C-1** and **P-1**, we should use $\beta_0 = 001$ and add three moves as round $R_1$; each player $P_i$, $1 \leq i \leq 3$, reads one bit from $\beta_0$ if $x_i = 1$, which is always "0", otherwise the player does nothing.

Next, we discuss **C-2**, **P-2**, and **P-3**, to specify $\beta_1$. To satisfy **P-3**, we must follow the moves in round $R_1$ in the same manner as when $\{x_1, x_2, x_3\}$ contains at least one 0. To be specific, every player $P_i$, $1 \leq i \leq 3$, reads one bit "0" in round $R_1$, which determines the prefix of $\beta_1$ as 000, i.e., $000 \prec \beta_1$. These three moves also satisfy **P-2**. Since the remaining one bit is read as output after round

**Table 7.** Truth tables of $\mathsf{maj}_4^2$ and $\mathsf{maj}_4^3$ classified by $x_4$

<table>
<tr><td colspan="5" align="center">(a) $\mathsf{maj}_4^2$</td><td colspan="5" align="center">(b) $\mathsf{maj}_4^3$</td></tr>
<tr><td>$x_1$</td><td>$x_2$</td><td>$x_3$</td><td>$x_4 = 0$</td><td>$x_4 = 1$</td><td>$x_1$</td><td>$x_2$</td><td>$x_3$</td><td>$x_4 = 0$</td><td>$x_4 = 1$</td></tr>
<tr><td>0</td><td>0</td><td>0</td><td>0</td><td>0</td><td>0</td><td>0</td><td>0</td><td>0</td><td>0</td></tr>
<tr><td>0</td><td>0</td><td>1</td><td>0</td><td>1</td><td>0</td><td>0</td><td>1</td><td>0</td><td>0</td></tr>
<tr><td>0</td><td>1</td><td>0</td><td>0</td><td>1</td><td>0</td><td>1</td><td>0</td><td>0</td><td>0</td></tr>
<tr><td>1</td><td>0</td><td>0</td><td>0</td><td>1</td><td>1</td><td>0</td><td>0</td><td>0</td><td>1</td></tr>
<tr><td>1</td><td>1</td><td>0</td><td>1</td><td>1</td><td>1</td><td>1</td><td>0</td><td>0</td><td>1</td></tr>
<tr><td>1</td><td>0</td><td>1</td><td>1</td><td>1</td><td>1</td><td>0</td><td>1</td><td>0</td><td>1</td></tr>
<tr><td>0</td><td>1</td><td>1</td><td>1</td><td>1</td><td>0</td><td>1</td><td>1</td><td>0</td><td>1</td></tr>
<tr><td>1</td><td>1</td><td>1</td><td>1</td><td>1</td><td>1</td><td>1</td><td>1</td><td>1</td><td>1</td></tr>
</table>

**Table 8.** A private PEZ protocol $\Pi_{\alpha,\mathsf{maj}_4^2}$ where $\alpha := \alpha(\mathsf{maj}_4^2) = 111011101110$ $111011110$

| Round | Players to move | # of bits to read | | Substring of read bits | |
|-------|-----------------|---------|---------|---------|---------|
|       |                 | $x_i = 0$ | $x_i = 1$ | $x_i = 0$ | $x_i = 1$ |
| $R_0$ | $\{P_i\}_{i=1}^4$ | 4 | 0 | 1110 | – |
| $R_1$ | $\{P_i\}_{i=1}^4$ | 1 | 0 | 1 | – |

$R_1$, the next bit of 000 in $\beta_1$ is determined as $1(= \mathsf{maj}_3^2(\{1,1,1\}))$ to satisfy **C-2**. As a result, we obtain $\beta_1 = 0001$.

Summarizing the above discussion, a private PEZ protocol for $\mathsf{maj}_3^2$ is shown in Table 5, which can be implemented with the 13-bit initial string $\alpha = \beta_0 \circ \beta_0 \circ \beta_0 \circ \beta_1 = 0010010010001$ and six moves.

Throughout Example 3, the input of a function is written as a multiset such as $\mathsf{maj}_3^2(\{x_1, x_2, x_3\})$. Hereafter, an input of a symmetric function is represented by the Hamming weight of the input such as $\mathsf{maj}_3^2(3) \ (= \mathsf{maj}_3^2(\{1,1,1\}))$. This is because the Hamming weight of the input is sufficient information to compute the symmetric function.

### Example 4 (Private PEZ protocols for four-input majority voting). 

In Table 7, (a) and (b) are the truth tables of $\mathsf{maj}_4^2$ and $\mathsf{maj}_4^3$, respectively. Note that the truth values in these tables are classified by the value of $x_4 \in \{0, 1\}$. In the following, we mainly explain the construction of a private PEZ protocol for $\mathsf{maj}_4^2$ in the same way as for $\mathsf{maj}_3^2$ in the Example 3, but a protocol for $\mathsf{maj}_4^3$ is obtained analogously.

Let $w \in [0 : 4]$ be the Hamming weight of the four inputs of $\mathsf{maj}_4^2$.

When $w \neq 0$, i.e., when there exists at least one input whose value is 1, the outputs of $\mathsf{maj}_4^2(w)$ is equal to the outputs of $\mathsf{or}_3$ with input $w - 1$, i.e., three inputs obtained by fixing one input to 1 in four inputs of $\mathsf{maj}_4^2$. Actually, the right column of the outputs in Table 7(a) shows the case when $x_4$ is fixed to 1, and it can be regarded as $\mathsf{maj}_3^1(w - 1) = \mathsf{or}_3(w - 1)$.

Together with the case where $w = 0$, the following holds:

$$\mathsf{maj}_4^2(w) = \begin{cases} \mathsf{maj}_4^2(0), & \text{if } w = 0 \\ \mathsf{maj}_3^1(w-1) = \mathsf{or}_3(w-1), & \text{otherwise } (w \neq 0). \end{cases} \quad (12)$$

We can construct a private PEZ protocol for $\mathsf{maj}_4^2$ based on (12) similar to how the private PEZ protocol for $\mathsf{maj}_3^2$ was constructed in Example 3. Let $\tilde{\beta}_0$ and $\tilde{\beta}_1$ be the undetermined strings which are used for computing $\mathsf{maj}_4^2(0)$ and $\mathsf{or}_3(w-1)$, respectively.

Let $\alpha(\mathsf{maj}_4^2)$ be an initial string for computing $\mathsf{maj}_4^2$. In the same way as Example 3, set $\alpha(\mathsf{maj}_4^2) := [\tilde{\beta}_1]^4 \circ \tilde{\beta}_0$, which is obtained by replacing "0" and "1" in $\alpha(\mathsf{or}_4) = 1110$ with $\tilde{\beta}_0$ and $\tilde{\beta}_1$, respectively. In round $R_0$, each player $P_i$, $1 \leq i \leq 4$, reads $|\tilde{\beta}_1|$ bits if the input $x_i = 0$, otherwise the player does not read any bit. Then, at the end of round $R_0$, the remaining string $\tilde{\alpha}'$ satisfies

$$\tilde{\alpha}' \succ \begin{cases} \tilde{\beta}_0, & \text{if } w = 0 \\ \tilde{\beta}_1, & \text{otherwise.} \end{cases} \quad (13)$$

In round $R_1$, we will add four moves for computing $\mathsf{maj}_4^2(0)$ and $\mathsf{or}_3(w-1)$ by using $\tilde{\beta}_0$ and $\tilde{\beta}_1$, respectively.

The function $\mathsf{or}_3(w-1)$ can be computed in the same way as the private PEZ protocol for $\mathsf{or}_3$. That is, by using a string $\tilde{\beta}_1 := 1110$ in round $R_1$, each player $P_i$, $1 \leq i \leq 4$, reads one bit represented by "1" if $x_i = 0$, otherwise the player does not read any bit. Then, every move is specified as shown in Table 8.

Now we are prepared to compute $\mathsf{maj}_4^2(0)$ privately; the first four bits of $\tilde{\beta}_0$ have to be 1111, which is the string read in round $R_1$. Since the next bit of 1111 becomes the output, $\tilde{\beta}_0$ is obtained by appending $0(= \mathsf{maj}_4^2(0))$ to the rightmost part of 1111. Therefore, we obtain $\tilde{\beta}_0 := 11110$. In summary, Table 8 shows a private PEZ protocol for $\mathsf{maj}_4^2$, which uses the 21-bit initial string $\alpha := \alpha(\mathsf{maj}_4^2) = 111011101110111011110$, and has eight moves.

The private PEZ protocol for computing $\mathsf{maj}_4^3$ can be derived in the same manner starting from the truth table (b) in Table 7 and based on

$$\mathsf{maj}_4^3(w) = \begin{cases} \mathsf{maj}_4^3(4), & \text{if } w = 4 \\ \mathsf{maj}_3^3(w) = \mathsf{and}_3(w), & \text{otherwise } (w \neq 4). \end{cases} \quad (14)$$

and the private PEZ protocol for $\mathsf{and}_4$. The protocol is shown in Table 9, with eight moves and the initial string $\alpha := \alpha(\mathsf{maj}_4^3) = 000100010001000100001$.

## 4   A Private PEZ Protocol for Symmetric Functions

### 4.1   Recursive Structure of Symmetric Functions

We generalize the discussion in Sect. 3 for a general symmetric function $f_n$ with $n$ inputs. First, we generalize the relations (8), (12) and (14) as follows.

**Table 9.** A private PEZ protocol $\Pi_{\alpha,\mathsf{maj}_4^3}$ where $\alpha := \alpha(\mathsf{maj}_4^3) = 0001000100$ 01000100001

| Round | Players to move | # of bits to read | | Substring of read bits | |
|---|---|---|---|---|---|
| | | $x_i = 0$ | $x_i = 1$ | $x_i = 0$ | $x_i = 1$ |
| $R_0$ | $\{P_i\}_{i=1}^4$ | 0 | 4 | – | 0001 |
| $R_1$ | $\{P_i\}_{i=1}^4$ | 0 | 1 | – | 0 |

**Theorem 1.** Let $f_n : \{0,1\}^n \to \Gamma$ be an arbitrary symmetric function with $n$ binary inputs. Then, we recursively define the symmetric functions $g_k : \{0,1\}^k \to \Gamma$ and $h_k : \{0,1\}^k \to \Gamma$, for $1 \le k \le n$, by $g_n := f_n, h_n := f_n$, and

$$g_{k-1}^m(\{x_1, x_2, \ldots, x_k\} \setminus \{0\}) := g_k^m(\{x_1, x_2, \ldots, x_k\}),$$
$$\text{if } \{x_1, x_2, \ldots, x_k\} \text{ contains at least one } 0, \quad (15)$$

$$h_{k-1}^m(\{x_1, x_2, \ldots, x_k\} \setminus \{1\}) := h_k^m(\{x_1, x_2, \ldots, x_k\}).$$
$$\text{if } \{x_1, x_2, \ldots, x_k\} \text{ contains at least one } 1. \quad (16)$$

Then, the following holds for $w \in [0 : k]$:

$$g_k^w(w) = \begin{cases} g_k^w(k) = f_n^w(k) & \text{if } w = k \\ g_{k-1}^w(w) & \text{otherwise,} \end{cases} \quad (17)$$

$$h_k^w(w) = \begin{cases} h_k^w(0) = f_n^w(n-k) & \text{if } w = 0 \\ h_{k-1}^w(w-1) & \text{otherwise,} \end{cases} \quad (18)$$

where $g_n^w(0) := f_n^w(0)$ and $h_0^w(0) := f_n^w(n)$.

The proof is provided in Appendix A.2.

**Example 5.** We revisit the case of Example 4. Let $f_4 = h_4 = \mathsf{maj}_4^2$. Then, it is easy to see that $h_3 = \mathsf{or}_3$ from Table 7(a). On the other hand, for $f_4 = g_4 = \mathsf{maj}_4^3$, we can choose $g_3 = \mathsf{and}_3$ from Table 7(b). This is the reason why (12), and (14) hold.

## 4.2   Proposed Construction for General Symmetric Functions

We propose the construction of a private PEZ protocol for computing a symmetric function $f_n$. Let $\alpha(f_n)$ be an initial sequence of the private PEZ protocol for computing the function $f_n$. There are two ways of constructing $\alpha(f_n)$, as shown below.

**Construction 1.** Assume that a symmetric function $f_n$ is recursively decomposed into two cases by either (17) or (18). For $1 \le k \le n$, $\alpha(g_k)$ and $\alpha(h_k)$

**Table 10.** A private PEZ protocol for $f_n$ using $\alpha(g_n)$ as the initial string

| Round | Players to move | # of bits to read | | Substring of read bits | |
|---|---|---|---|---|---|
| | | $x_i = 0$ | $x_i = 1$ | $x_i = 0$ | $x_i = 1$ |
| $R_0$ | $\{P_i\}_{i=1}^n$ | 0 | $|\alpha(g_{n-1})|$ | – | $\alpha(g_{n-1})$ |
| $R_1$ | $\{P_i\}_{i=1}^n$ | 0 | $|\alpha(g_{n-2})|$ | – | $\alpha(g_{n-2})$ |
| $\vdots$ | $\vdots$ | $\vdots$ | $\vdots$ | $\vdots$ | $\vdots$ |
| $R_{n-1}$ | $\{P_i\}_{i=1}^n$ | 0 | $|\alpha(g_0)|$ | – | $\alpha(g_0)$ |

**Table 11.** A private PEZ protocol for $f_n$ using $\alpha(h_n)$ as the initial string

| Round | Players to move | # of bits to read | | Substring of read bits | |
|---|---|---|---|---|---|
| | | $x_i = 0$ | $x_i = 1$ | $x_i = 0$ | $x_i = 1$ |
| $R_0$ | $\{P_i\}_{i=1}^n$ | $|\alpha(h_{n-1})|$ | 0 | $\alpha(h_{n-1})$ | – |
| $R_1$ | $\{P_i\}_{i=1}^n$ | $|\alpha(h_{n-2})|$ | 0 | $\alpha(h_{n-2})$ | – |
| $\vdots$ | $\vdots$ | $\vdots$ | $\vdots$ | $\vdots$ | $\vdots$ |
| $R_{n-1}$ | $\{P_i\}_{i=1}^n$ | $|\alpha(h_0)|$ | 0 | $\alpha(h_0)$ | – |

are the initial strings for computing $g_k$ and $h_k$, respectively. From (17) and (18), $\alpha(g_k)$ and $\alpha(h_k)$ can be recursively constructed as follows:

$$\alpha(g_k) := [\alpha(g_{k-1})]^k \circ [\alpha(g_{k-2})]^k \circ \cdots \circ [\alpha(g_0)]^k \circ g_k^{\mathrm{w}}(k), \tag{19}$$

$$\alpha(h_k) := [\alpha(h_{k-1})]^k \circ [\alpha(h_{k-2})]^k \circ \cdots \circ [\alpha(h_0)]^k \circ h_k^{\mathrm{w}}(0), \tag{20}$$

where $\alpha(g_0) := g_0 = f_n^{\mathrm{w}}(0)$ and $g_k^{\mathrm{w}}(k) = f_n^{\mathrm{w}}(k)$ in (19), and $\alpha(h_0) := h_0 = f_n^{\mathrm{w}}(n)$ and $h_k^{\mathrm{w}}(0) = f_n^{\mathrm{w}}(n-k)$ in (20). Finally, we obtain two types of the initial string $\alpha(g_n)$ and $\alpha(h_n)$ recursively from (19) and (20). Then, we have

$$\alpha(f_n) := \alpha(g_n), \tag{21}$$

$$\alpha(f_n) := \alpha(h_n). \tag{22}$$

Note that the sequences of $\alpha(f_n)$ obtained from (21) and (22) are not in general the same.

First, we describe the private PEZ protocol for $f_n$ using $\alpha(f_n)$ obtained from (21) as the initial string. In this protocol, the sequence of $n^2$ moves $(M_1, M_2, \ldots, M_{n^2})$ for computing $f_n$ is determined as follows: Each move $M_j$ consists of $((j \bmod n) + 1, \mu_j)$ where $\mu_j : \{0,1\} \to \{0, |\alpha(g_0)|, |\alpha(g_1)|, \cdots, |\alpha(g_{n-1})|\}$ and $\mu_j(0) = 0, \mu_j(1) = |\alpha(g_{n-\lceil j/n \rceil})|$. These moves can be represented as $n$ rounds $(R_0, R_1, \ldots, R_{n-1})$, and each player $P_i$ reads $\mu_{rn+i}(x_i)$ bits in the $r$-th round. These $n$ rounds are shown in Table 10.

Second, the private PEZ protocol for $f_n$ using $\alpha(f_n)$ obtained from (22) as the initial string is similar to the protocol for $\alpha(f_n)$ obtained from (21) and is shown in Table 11.

**Theorem 2.** The private PEZ protocol obtained from Construction 1 satisfies Definition 2.

The proof is provided in Appendix A.3.

## 4.3    Evaluation of the Length of Initial Strings

For a symmetric function $f_n$, let $a_n := |\alpha(f_n)|$ for simplicity.

**Theorem 3.** The length of the initial string of a private PEZ protocol for computing a symmetric function $f_n$ is computed as

$$a_n = n \cdot n! \sum_{i=1}^{n} \frac{1}{i!} + 1, \tag{23}$$

from which we can conclude that $a_n = \mathcal{O}(n \times n!)$.

The proof is provided in Appendix A.4.

# 5    A More Efficient Private PEZ Protocol for the Majority Function $\mathsf{maj}_n^t$

By restricting the functions to be computed to $\mathsf{maj}_n^t$, the length of the initial string $\alpha$ becomes much shorter than that for computing symmetric functions.

Consider the case $t = 1$ and $t = n$ for $\mathsf{maj}_n^t$. Since $\mathsf{maj}_n^1$ and $\mathsf{maj}_n^n$ are equivalent to $\mathsf{or}_n$ and $\mathsf{and}_n$, respectively, they can be computed with only $(n + 1)$-bit strings $[1]^n \circ 0$ and $[0]^n \circ 1$ as shown in Example 1. Therefore, $|\alpha(\mathsf{and}_n)| = |\alpha(\mathsf{or}_n)| = \mathcal{O}(n)$ while $|\alpha(f_n)| = \mathcal{O}(n \times n!)$ as shown in Theorem 3 for a symmetric function $f_n$.

In Examples 3 and 4, $\alpha(\mathsf{maj}_3^2) = 13$ and $\alpha(\mathsf{maj}_4^2) = \alpha(\mathsf{maj}_4^3) = 21$, whereas $|\alpha(f_3)| = 31$ and $|\alpha(f_4)| = 165$ in Construction 1. The reason for this difference is the number of times decomposition is performed by either (17) or (18). In Construction 1, $\alpha(f_3)$, and $\alpha(f_4)$ are obtained by decomposing two times and three times, respectively, to the end. On the other hand, in Examples 3 and 4, $\alpha(\mathsf{maj}_3^2)$, $\alpha(\mathsf{maj}_4^2)$ and $\alpha(\mathsf{maj}_4^3)$ are obtained by decomposing only once. After the one-time decomposition by (17) or (18), the functions $\alpha(\mathsf{maj}_3^2)$, $\alpha(\mathsf{maj}_4^2)$ and $\alpha(\mathsf{maj}_4^3)$ can be computed using $\mathsf{and}_2$, $\mathsf{or}_3$, and $\mathsf{and}_3$, respectively.

In general, we can construct private PEZ protocols for majority functions $\mathsf{maj}_n^t$ using the initial strings for $\{\mathsf{and}_i\}_{i=2}^n$ or $\{\mathsf{or}_n\}_{i=2}^n$. Therefore, the initial string becomes shorter by reducing the number of decompositions using a private PEZ protocol for $\mathsf{and}_n$ or $\mathsf{or}_n$ rather than by recursively decomposing to the end.

Let $s$ be the number of times $\mathsf{maj}_n^t$ is decomposed by (17) where $0 \leq s \leq n-1$. From observation of (17), we can learn that if $\mathsf{maj}_n^t$ is decomposed by (17), $\mathsf{maj}_n^t$ becomes $\mathsf{maj}_{n-1}^t$. Therefore, after $s$ decompositions by (17), $\mathsf{maj}_n^t$ becomes $\mathsf{maj}_{n-s}^t$. In addition, if $n - s = t$, i.e., $s = n - t$, then $\mathsf{maj}_{n-s}^t = \mathsf{maj}_{n-s}^{n-s}$ is identical to $\mathsf{and}_{n-s}$. Similarly, when (18) is used for $s$ decompositions, $\mathsf{maj}_n^t$

**Table 12.** A private PEZ protocol for $\mathsf{maj}_n^t$ for $t \geq (n+1)/2$

| Round | Players to move | # of bits to read | | Substring of read bits | |
|-------|-----------------|-------------------|---|------------------------|---|
| | | $x_i = 0$ | $x_i = 1$ | $x_i = 0$ | $x_i = 1$ |
| $R_0$ | $\{P_i\}_{i=1}^n$ | 0 | $|\alpha(\mathsf{maj}_{n-1}^t)|$ | – | $\alpha(\mathsf{maj}_{n-1}^t)$ |
| $R_1$ | $\{P_i\}_{i=1}^n$ | 0 | $|\alpha(\mathsf{maj}_{n-2}^t)|$ | – | $\alpha(\mathsf{maj}_{n-2}^t)$ |
| $\vdots$ | $\vdots$ | $\vdots$ | $\vdots$ | $\vdots$ | $\vdots$ |
| $R_s$ | $\{P_i\}_{i=1}^n$ | 0 | $|\alpha(\mathsf{maj}_{n-s-1}^t)|$ | – | $\alpha(\mathsf{maj}_{n-s-1}^t)$ |

becomes $\mathsf{maj}_{n-s}^{t-s}$ and if $t - s = 1$, i.e., $s = t - 1$, then $\mathsf{maj}_{n-s}^t = \mathsf{maj}_{n-s}^1$ is identical to $\mathsf{or}_{n-s}$.

To reduce the number of decompositions, $s$ should be as small as possible. Thus, if $n - t \leq t - 1$, i.e., $t \geq (n+1)/2$, $\mathsf{maj}_n^t$ should be decomposed by (17). On the other hand, if $n - t \geq t - 1$, i.e., $t \leq (n+1)/2$, $\mathsf{maj}_n^t$ should be decomposed by (18).

**Construction 2.** Assume that $\mathsf{maj}_n^t$ is decomposed $s$ times by either (17) or (18), where

$$s = \begin{cases} n - t & \text{if } t \geq (n+1)/2, \\ t - 1 & \text{if } t \leq (n+1)/2, \end{cases}$$

and we define $\alpha(\mathsf{maj}_k^t)$, where $n - s \leq k \leq n$, as follows:

$$\alpha(\mathsf{maj}_k^t) :=$$
$$\begin{cases} [\alpha(\mathsf{maj}_{k-1}^t)]^k \circ [\alpha(\mathsf{maj}_{k-2}^t)]^k \circ \cdots \circ [\alpha(\mathsf{maj}_{n-s}^t)]^k \circ [\alpha(\mathsf{maj}_{n-s-1}^t)]^k \circ \mathsf{maj}_k^t(k), \\ \qquad\qquad\qquad\qquad\qquad\qquad\qquad\qquad \text{if } t \geq (n+1)/2, \\ [\alpha(\mathsf{maj}_{k-1}^{t-1})]^k \circ [\alpha(\mathsf{maj}_{k-2}^{t-2})]^k \circ \cdots \circ [\alpha(\mathsf{maj}_{n-s}^1)]^k \circ [\alpha(\mathsf{maj}_{n-s-1}^0)]^k \circ \mathsf{maj}_k^t(0), \\ \qquad\qquad\qquad\qquad\qquad\qquad\qquad\qquad \text{if } t \leq (n+1)/2, \end{cases}$$
$$(24)$$

where $\alpha(\mathsf{maj}_{n-s-1}^t) := 0$ and $\alpha(\mathsf{maj}_{n-s-1}^0) := 1$. Then, we obtain the initial string $\alpha(\mathsf{maj}_n^t)$ by substituting $n$ for $k$ in (24). Note that if $n$ is odd, we can use either equation.

If $t \leq (n+1)/2$, the sequence of $n(s+1)$ moves $(M_1, M_2, \ldots, M_{n(s+1)})$ for computing $\mathsf{maj}_n^t$ is determined as follows: each move $M_j$ consists of $((j \bmod n) + 1, \mu_j')$, where $\mu_j' : \{0,1\} \to \{0, |\alpha(\mathsf{maj}_{n-s-1}^1)|, |\alpha(\mathsf{maj}_{n-s}^2)|, \ldots, |\alpha(\mathsf{maj}_{n-1}^{t-1})|\}$ and $\mu_j'(0) = |\alpha(\mathsf{maj}_{n-\lceil j/n \rceil}^{t-\lceil j/n \rceil})|, \mu_j'(1) = 0$. These moves can be represented as $s + 1$ rounds $(R_0, R_1, \ldots, R_s)$, and each player $P_i$ reads $\mu_{rn+i}'(x_i)$ bits in the $r$-th round. These $s + 1$ rounds are shown in Table 13. The sequences of moves for $t \geq (n+1)/2$ are similar to those for $t \leq (n+1)/2$ and are shown in Table 12.

**Table 13.** A private PEZ protocol for $\mathsf{maj}_n^t$ for $t \le (n+1)/2$

| Round | Players to move | # of bits to read | | Substring of read bits | |
|-------|-----------------|-------------------|-------------|------------------------|-------------|
| | | $x_i = 0$ | $x_i = 1$ | $x_i = 0$ | $x_i = 1$ |
| $R_0$ | $\{P_i\}_{i=1}^n$ | $|\alpha(\mathsf{maj}_{n-1}^{t-1})|$ | 0 | $\alpha(\mathsf{maj}_{n-1}^{t-1})$ | − |
| $R_1$ | $\{P_i\}_{i=1}^n$ | $|\alpha(\mathsf{maj}_{n-2}^{t-2})|$ | 0 | $\alpha(\mathsf{maj}_{n-2}^{t-2})$ | − |
| $\vdots$ | $\vdots$ | $\vdots$ | $\vdots$ | $\vdots$ | $\vdots$ |
| $R_s$ | $\{P_i\}_{i=1}^n$ | $|\alpha(\mathsf{maj}_{n-s-1}^1)|$ | 0 | $\alpha(\mathsf{maj}_{n-s-1}^1)$ | − |

**Example 6.** Consider the case of $\mathsf{maj}_4^2$ in Example 4. In this case, since $t = 2 < 5/2 = (n+1)/2$, $s = t - 1 = 1$. Therefore, we decompose $\mathsf{maj}_4^2$ once by using (17). Then, we obtain $\alpha(\mathsf{maj}_4^2) = [\alpha(\mathsf{maj}_3^1)]^4 \circ [1]^4 \circ \mathsf{maj}_4^2(0)$ and $\alpha(\mathsf{maj}_3^1) = [1]^3 \circ \mathsf{maj}_3^1(0) = 1110$, which yields

$$\alpha(\mathsf{maj}_4^2) = [1110]^4 \circ [1]^4 \circ 0. \tag{25}$$

Therefore, this initial string $\alpha(\mathsf{maj}_4^2)$ coincides with the initial string obtained in Example 4. We can also see that the moves (rounds) of this protocol obtained by Construction 2 coincide with the rounds of the protocol for $\mathsf{maj}_4^2$ in Table 8, which is obtained in Example 4.

**Theorem 4.** The private PEZ protocol obtained from Construction 2 satisfies Definition 2.

The proof is omitted since it is similar to the proof of Theorem 2.

Finally, let $a_{n,t}$ be the length of the initial string of a private PEZ protocol for computing $\mathsf{maj}_n^t$ obtained from Construction 2. From (24), for $n - s \le k \le n$, the following holds:

$$a_{k,t} = \begin{cases} ka_{k-1,t} + ka_{k-2,t} + \cdots + ka_{n-s,t} + ka_{n-s-1,t} + 1 & \text{if } t \le (n+1)/2 \\ ka_{k-1,t-1} + ka_{k-2,t-2} + \cdots + ka_{n-s,1} + ka_{n-s-1,0} + 1 & \text{if } t \ge (n+1)/2 \end{cases}$$

$$= \begin{cases} k\sum_{i=1}^{s+1} a_{n-i,t} + 1 & \text{if } t \le (n+1)/2 \\ k\sum_{i=1}^{s+1} a_{n-i,t-i} + 1 & \text{if } t \ge (n+1)/2 \end{cases} \tag{26}$$

where $a_{n-s-1,t} = 1$ and $a_{n-s-1,0} = 1$. Then, the theorem below immediately follows from Lemma 1 in Appendix A.1 and (24), and hence, the proof is omitted.

**Theorem 5.** The length of the initial string of a private PEZ protocol for computing $\mathsf{maj}_n^t$ is computed as

$$a_{n,t} = n \sum_{i=n-s}^n \frac{n!}{i!} + 1, \quad \text{where } s = \begin{cases} t - 1 & \text{if } t \le (n+1)/2 \\ n - t & \text{if } t \ge (n+1)/2 \end{cases} \tag{27}$$

from which we can conclude that $a_n = \mathcal{O}(n \times n^s)$.

## 6   Conclusion

In the previous work [1], a general, but inefficient private PEZ protocol was presented. By restricting our attention to the symmetric functions, we achieved the exponential improvement on a private PEZ protocol for symmetric functions using the recursive structure of symmetric functions. Specifically, the double exponential length of initial string is reduced to exponential length, and the exponential number of moves is reduced to polynomial moves. Furthermore, in the case of threshold functions, the length of an initial string and the number of moves are further reduced compared with the ones for symmetric functions. These results resolve a part of open problems suggested in [1].

Finally, we mention the relationship between our construction for symmetric functions and the general construction [1]. A general function $f_n$ with $n$ inputs can be easily computed by applying our construction for symmetric function $g_{2^n-1}$ with $2^n - 1$ inputs in the following manner.

- For $w \in [0 : 2^n - 1]$, $g_{2^n-1}(w) := f_n(w)$
- For $i \in [0 : n-1]$, each player $P_i$ behaves as if $P_i$ were $P_j, j \in [2^i - 1 : 2^{i+1} - 2]$ in the protocol for $g_{2^n-1}$.

However, the private PEZ protocol obtained from this method is different from the one obtained from the general construction in [1] although the *order* of an initial string is the same: $\mathcal{O}((2^n - 1) \times (2^n - 1)!) = \mathcal{O}(2^n!)$. For instance, for $n = 3$, $|\alpha(g_{2^n-1})| = |\alpha(g_7)| = 60,621$ for the above protocol, whereas $|\alpha(f_n)| = |\alpha(f_3)| = 72$ for original protocol in [1], as you can see in Table 1. Therefore, it seems that the general protocol in [1] cannot be directly obtained from our construction.

**Acknowledgements.** The authors would like to thank the reviewers for their helpful comments and suggestions. They are also grateful to Mr. Shota Yamamoto for insightful discussions.

## A   Technical Lemma and Proofs

### A.1   Technical Lemma

**Lemma 1.** *Let $n$ and $s$ $(n \geq s)$ be nonnegative integers such that $n - s - 1 \geq 0$. For $k \in [0 : n]$, let*

$$a_{n-s-1} = 1 \quad and \quad a_k = k \sum_{i=n-s-1}^{k-1} a_i + 1, \tag{28}$$

*be a recurrence relation with respect to $(a_i)_{i=n-s-1}^{k-1}$. Then, the following holds:*

$$a_n = n \cdot n! \sum_{i=n-s}^{n} \frac{1}{i!} + 1. \tag{29}$$

*Proof of Lemma 1:* For fixed $s$ and $n$, let

$$S_k := \sum_{i=n-s-1}^{k} a_i. \tag{30}$$

Then, we have $S_{n-s-1} = a_{n-s-1} = 1$ and

$$a_k = kS_{k-1} + 1. \tag{31}$$

We also have

$$S_k - S_{k-1} = a_k = kS_{k-1} + 1, \tag{32}$$

where the first and the second equalities are due to (30) and (31), respectively.

Equation (32) can be rearranged as $S_k = (k+1)S_{k-1} + 1$. Dividing both sides of this equality by $(k+1)!$, we obtain

$$T_k = T_{k-1} + \frac{1}{(k+1)!}, \quad \text{and} \quad T_{n-s-1} = \frac{1}{(n-s)!}, \tag{33}$$

where $T_k := S_k/(k+1)!$. Equation (33) is easy to solve. That is,

$$
\begin{aligned}
T_k &= T_{k-1} + \frac{1}{(k+1)!} \\
&= T_{k-2} + \frac{1}{(k+1)!} + \frac{1}{k!} \\
&\quad \cdots \\
&= T_{n-s-1} + \frac{1}{(k+1)!} + \cdots \frac{1}{(n-s+1)!} \\
&= \sum_{i=n-s}^{k+1} \frac{1}{i!}.
\end{aligned}
\tag{34}
$$

Therefore, we have $S_k = (k+1)! \, T_k = (k+1)! \sum_{i=n-s}^{k+1} 1/i!$. Substituting this into (31), we obtain (29). $\qquad\square$

## A.2    Proof of Theorem 1

We prove (17). Equation (18) can be proved similarly.

For the weight $w \in [0:k]$, fix the input $(x_1, x_2, \ldots, x_k)$ arbitrarily such that $\mathsf{hw}(x_1, x_2, \ldots, x_k) = w$. Then, $g_k^{\mathsf{w}}(w) = g_k(x_1, x_2, \ldots, x_k)$ holds. If $w = k$, the following holds:

$$g_k^{\mathsf{w}}(w) = g_k^{\mathsf{w}}(k) = g_k^{\mathsf{m}}(\{\underbrace{1,1,\ldots,1}_{k}\}) \overset{(a)}{=} g_n^{\mathsf{m}}(\{\underbrace{1,1,\ldots,1}_{k},\underbrace{0,0,\ldots,0}_{n-k}\}) \overset{(b)}{=} f_n^{\mathsf{w}}(k) \tag{35}$$

where the marked equalities are due to the following reasons:

(a): From (15), the value of $g_k$ equals to the value of $g_n$ if the Hamming weights of inputs are equal.

(b): Definition of $g_n$: $g_n := f_n$, given in Theorem 1.

If $w \neq k$, there exists an index $i \in [0 : k-1]$ such that $x_i = 0$, and we have

$$g_k^{\mathrm{w}}(w) = g_k(x_1, x_2, \ldots, x_k)$$

$$= x_k g_k(x_1, x_2, \ldots, \overset{i}{0}, \ldots, x_{k-1}, 1) + \overline{x}_k g_k(x_1, x_2, \ldots, x_{k-1}, 0)$$

$$\overset{(c)}{=} x_k g_k(x_1, x_2, \ldots, \overset{i}{1}, \ldots, x_{k-1}, 0) + \overline{x}_k g_k(x_1, x_2, \ldots, x_{k-1}, 0)$$

$$\overset{(d)}{=} x_k g_{k-1}(x_1, x_2, \ldots, \overset{i}{1}, \ldots, x_{k-1}) + \overline{x}_k g_{k-1}(x_1, x_2, \ldots, x_{k-1})$$

$$\overset{(e)}{=} g_{k-1}^{\mathrm{w}}(w), \tag{36}$$

where the marked equalities are due to the following reasons:

(c): Symmetry of $g_k$.

(d): Definition of $g_{k-1}$ given by (15).

(e): For $x_k = 1$, $\mathrm{hw}(x_1, x_2, \ldots, \overset{i}{1}, \ldots, x_{k-1}) = w$ holds, otherwise $\mathrm{hw}(x_1, x_2, \ldots, x_{k-1}) = w$ holds. □

## A.3   Proof of Theorem 2

We show the proof for the private PEZ protocol constructed by using (19) in Construction 1. If (20) is used, the proof is similar to that for (19).

Let $\Sigma = \{0, 1\}$. Let $\nu : \{1, 2, \ldots, n^2\} \times \{0, 1\} \to \Gamma^*$ be a mapping such that $\nu(j, 0) = \lambda$, and $\nu(j, 1) = \alpha(g_{n - \lceil j/n \rceil})$ for all $j \in \{1, 2, \ldots, n^2\}$. From the definition of $\nu$ and $\mu$, we obtain for all $j \in \{1, 2, \cdots, n^2\}$,

$$|\nu(j, 0)| = |\lambda| = 0 = \mu_j(0) \tag{37}$$

$$|\nu(j, 1)| = |\alpha(g_{n - \lceil j/n \rceil})| = \mu_j(1) \tag{38}$$

Therefore, $\nu$ satisfies the first condition in Definition 2.

Next, we show that $\nu$ also satisfies the second condition in Definition 2. Let $w$ be a Hamming weight of $n$ inputs where $0 \leq w \leq n$, and $N(w)$ be the substring read by players throughout $n$ rounds when the Hamming weight of $n$ inputs is $w$. Since the substring read in the $j$-th round can be represented by $[\alpha(g_{n-j})]^w$, we have

$$N(w) = [\alpha(g_{n-1})]^w \circ [\alpha(g_{n-2})]^w \circ \cdots \circ [\alpha(g_0)]^w. \tag{39}$$

Note that it is not necessary to care about the move order in each round, but it is necessary to care about the Hamming weight of $n$ inputs. Using $N(w)$, the second condition in Definition 2 can be rewritten as follows: For all $w \in \{0, 1, \ldots, n\}$,

$$N(w) \circ f_n^{\mathrm{w}}(w) = [\alpha(g_{n-1})]^w \circ [\alpha(g_{n-2})]^w \circ \cdots \circ [\alpha(g_0)]^w \circ f_n^{\mathrm{w}}(w) \prec \alpha(g_n). \tag{40}$$

Noting that $g_w^w(w) = f_n^w(w)$ and (19), we have

$$\alpha(g_w) = [\alpha(g_{w-1})]^w \circ [\alpha(g_{w-2})]^w \circ \cdots \circ [\alpha(g_0)]^w \circ f_n^w(w). \tag{41}$$

Hence, $N(w) \circ f_n^w(w)$ is written as follows:

$$
\begin{aligned}
&N(w) \circ f_n^w(w) \\
&= [\alpha(g_{n-1})]^w \circ [\alpha(g_{n-2})]^w \circ \cdots \circ [\alpha(g_{w+1})]^w \circ [\alpha(g_w)]^w \circ \alpha(g_w) \\
&= [\alpha(g_{n-1})]^w \circ [\alpha(g_{n-2})]^w \circ \cdots \circ [\alpha(g_{w+1})]^w \circ [\alpha(g_w)]^{(w+1)} \\
&\prec [\alpha(g_{n-1})]^w \circ [\alpha(g_{n-2})]^w \circ \cdots \circ [\alpha(g_{w+1})]^w \circ [\alpha(g_w)]^{(w+1)} \\
&\quad \circ [\alpha(g_{w-1})]^{(w+1)} \circ \cdots \circ [\alpha(g_0)]^{(w+1)} \circ f_n^w(w+1) \\
&= [\alpha(g_{n-1})]^w \circ [\alpha(g_{n-2})]^w \circ \cdots \circ [\alpha(g_{w+2})]^w \circ [\alpha(g_{w+1})]^w \circ \alpha(g_{w+1}) \\
&\cdots \\
&\prec [\alpha(g_{n-1})]^w \circ \alpha(g_{n-1}) \\
&= [\alpha(g_{n-1})]^{w+1}, \tag{42}
\end{aligned}
$$

where the first and the third equalities are due to (41). Therefore, for all $w \in [0 : n-1]$, $N(w) \circ f_n^w(w) \prec [\alpha(g_{n-1})]^{w+1} \prec [\alpha(g_{n-1})]^n \prec \alpha(g_n)$ holds. In addition, for $w = n$, $N(w) \circ f_n^w(w) = \alpha(g_n)$. Thus, for all $w \in [0 : n]$, $N(w) \circ f_n^w(w) \prec \alpha(g_n)$.

Therefore, there exists a mapping $\nu$ for a PEZ protocol of Construction 1 using an initial string $\alpha(g_n)$ such that $\nu$ satisfies the two condition in Definition 2. □

## A.4    Proof of Theorem 3

From (19) and (20), we obtain the length of the initial string $|\alpha(g_n)|$ and $|\alpha(h_n)|$ as follows:

$$
\begin{aligned}
|\alpha(g_n)| &= n|\alpha(g_{n-1})| + n|\alpha(g_{n-2})| + \cdots + n|\alpha(g_0)| + 1 \\
&= n \sum_{i=0}^{n-1} |\alpha(g_i)| + 1, \tag{43}
\end{aligned}
$$

$$
\begin{aligned}
|\alpha(h_n)| &= n|\alpha(h_{n-1})| + n|\alpha(h_{n-2})| + \cdots + n|\alpha(h_0)| + 1 \\
&= n \sum_{i=0}^{n-1} |\alpha(h_i)| + 1, \tag{44}
\end{aligned}
$$

where $|\alpha(g_0)| = |f_n^w(0)| = 1$ and $|\alpha(h_0)| = |f_n^w(n)| = 1$. Therefore, we obtain the same relation between $|\alpha(g_n)|$ and $|\alpha(h_n)|$. Summarizing the above, and noting that $a_n = |\alpha(f_n)| = |\alpha(g_n)| = |\alpha(h_n)|$, $\{a_i\}_{i=0}^n$ satisfies the following recurrence relation:

$$a_0 = 1, \quad a_n = n \sum_{i=0}^{n-1} a_i + 1, \tag{45}$$

which is a special case of (28) in Lemma 1 with $s = n - 1$. Thus, we obtain (23).

In addition, the following relations hold:

$$\sum_{i=1}^n \frac{1}{i!} < \sum_{i=0}^{n-1} \frac{1}{2^i} = 2 - (1/2)^n < 2 \tag{46}$$

Therefore, $a_n < 2n \cdot n! + 1$, which yields $a_n = \mathcal{O}(n \times n!)$.    □

# References

1. Balogh, J., Csirik, J.A., Ishai, Y., Kushilevitz, E.: Private computation using a PEZ dispenser. Theoret. Comput. Sci. **306**(13), 69–84 (2003). https://doi.org/10.1016/S0304-3975(03)00210-X. http://linkinghub.elsevier.com/retrieve/pii/S030439750300210X
2. Boer, B.: More efficient match-making and satisfiability *The Five Card Trick*. In: Quisquater, J.-J., Vandewalle, J. (eds.) EUROCRYPT 1989. LNCS, vol. 434, pp. 208–217. Springer, Heidelberg (1990). https://doi.org/10.1007/3-540-46885-4_23
3. Nishida, T., Hayashi, Y., Mizuki, T., Sone, H.: Card-based protocols for any boolean function. In: Jain, R., Jain, S., Stephan, F. (eds.) TAMC 2015. LNCS, vol. 9076, pp. 110–121. Springer, Cham (2015). https://doi.org/10.1007/978-3-319-17142-5_11
4. Watanabe, Y., Kuroki, Y., Suzuki, S., Koga, Y., Iwamoto, M., Ohta, K.: Card-based majority voting protocols with three inputs using three cards. In: 2018 International Symposium on Information Theory and Its Applications (ISITA), pp. 218–222. IEEE (2018)
5. Yao, A.C.: Protocols for secure computations. In: 23rd Annual Symposium on Foundations of Computer Science (FOCS 1982), pp. 160–164. IEEE, November 1982. https://doi.org/10.1109/SFCS.1982.38, http://ieeexplore.ieee.org/document/4568388/

# The Function-Inversion Problem: Barriers and Opportunities

Henry Corrigan-Gibbs and Dmitry Kogan[(✉)]

Stanford University, Stanford, USA
{henrycg,dkogan}@cs.stanford.edu

**Abstract.** The task of function inversion is central to cryptanalysis: breaking block ciphers, forging signatures, and cracking password hashes are all special cases of the function-inversion problem. In 1980, Hellman showed that it is possible to invert a random function $f \colon [N] \to [N]$ in time $T = \widetilde{O}(N^{2/3})$ given only $S = \widetilde{O}(N^{2/3})$ bits of precomputed advice about $f$. Hellman's algorithm is the basis for the popular "Rainbow Tables" technique (Oechslin 2003), which achieves the same asymptotic cost and is widely used in practical cryptanalysis.

Is Hellman's method the best possible algorithm for inverting functions with preprocessed advice? The best known lower bound, due to Yao (1990), shows that $ST = \widetilde{\Omega}(N)$, which still admits the possibility of an $S = T = \widetilde{O}(N^{1/2})$ attack. There remains a long-standing and vexing gap between Hellman's $N^{2/3}$ upper bound and Yao's $N^{1/2}$ lower bound. Understanding the feasibility of an $S = T = N^{1/2}$ algorithm is cryptanalytically relevant since such an algorithm could perform a key-recovery attack on AES-128 in time $2^{64}$ using a precomputed table of size $2^{64}$.

For the past 29 years, there has been no progress either in improving Hellman's algorithm or in strengthening Yao's lower bound. In this work, we connect function inversion to problems in other areas of theory to (1) explain why progress may be difficult and (2) explore possible ways forward.

Our results are as follows:

- We show that *any* improvement on Yao's lower bound on function-inversion algorithms will imply new lower bounds on depth-two circuits with arbitrary gates. Further, we show that proving strong lower bounds on *non-adaptive* function-inversion algorithms would imply breakthrough circuit lower bounds on linear-size log-depth circuits.
- We take first steps towards the study of the *injective* function-inversion problem, which has manifold cryptographic applications. In particular, we show that improved algorithms for breaking PRGs with preprocessing would give improved algorithms for inverting injective functions with preprocessing.
- Finally, we show that function inversion is closely related to well-studied problems in communication complexity and data structures. Through these connections we immediately obtain the best known algorithms for problems in these domains.

© International Association for Cryptologic Research 2019
D. Hofheinz and A. Rosen (Eds.): TCC 2019, LNCS 11891, pp. 393–421, 2019.
https://doi.org/10.1007/978-3-030-36030-6_16

# 1    Introduction

A central task in cryptanalysis is that of *function inversion*. That is, given a function $f\colon [N] \to [N]$ and a point $y \in [N]$, find a value $x \in [N]$ such that $f(x) = y$, if one exists. The hardness of function inversion underpins the security of almost every cryptographic primitive we use in practice: block ciphers, hash functions, digital signatures, and so on. Understanding the exact complexity of function inversion is thus critical for assessing the security of our most important cryptosystems.

We are particularly interested in function-inversion algorithms that only make *black-box* use of the function $f$—or formally, that have only oracle access to $f$—since these algorithms invert *all* functions. A straightforward argument shows that any black-box inversion algorithm that makes at most $T$ queries to its $f$-oracle succeeds with probability at most $O(T/N)$, over the randomness of the adversary and the random choice of the function. This argument suggests that an attacker running in $o(N)$ time cannot invert a black-box function on domain $[N]$ with good probability.

When the inversion algorithm may use *preprocessing*, this logic breaks down. An algorithm with preprocessing runs in two phases: In the preprocessing phase, the algorithm repeatedly queries $f$ and then outputs an "advice string" about $f$. In the subsequent online phase, the algorithm takes as input its preprocessed advice string and a challenge point $y \in [N]$. It must then produce a value $x \in [N]$ such that $f(x) = y$. When using these algorithms for cryptanalysis, the attacker typically seeks to jointly minimize the bit-length $S$ of the advice string and the running time $T$ of the online algorithm. The computation required to construct the advice string, though usually expensive, can often be amortized over a large number of online inversions.

A trivial preprocessing algorithm stores a table of $f^{-1}$ in its entirety as its advice string using $S = \widetilde{O}(N)$ bits and can then invert the function on all points using a single lookup into the table. In contrast, constructing algorithms that simultaneously achieve sublinear advice and online time $S = T = o(N)$ is non-trivial.

In a seminal paper, Hellman [46] introduced time-space tradeoffs as a tool for cryptanalysis and gave a black-box preprocessing algorithm that inverts a function $f\colon [N] \to [N]$ using only $S = \widetilde{O}(N^{2/3})$ bits of advice and online time $T = \widetilde{O}(N^{2/3})$, where the algorithm is guaranteed to succeed only on a constant fraction of functions. (More precisely, the algorithm has a constant success probability over the uniformly random choice of the function $f$.) Fiat and Naor [27,28] later gave a rigorous analysis of Hellman's algorithm and extended it to invert all possible functions, albeit with a slightly worse trade-off of the form $S^3 T = \widetilde{O}(N^3)$ for any choice of $N^{3/4} \le S \le N$. Hellman's trade-off is the best known today, and his algorithm is a fundamental tool in real-world cryptanalysis [7,8,59,61].

In this work, we investigate the following question:

*Is it possible to improve upon Hellman's time-space trade-off?*

Yao first asked this question in 1990 [77] and proved that any preprocessing algorithm for function inversion that uses $S$ bits of advice and $T$ online queries must satisfy $ST = \widetilde{\Omega}(N)$. (Counting only queries—and not online computation—only strengthens lower bounds in this model.) Notably, this lower bound does not rule out an algorithm that achieves $S = T = \widetilde{O}(N^{1/2})$. In contrast, Hellman's algorithm only gives an upper bound of $S = T = \widetilde{O}(N^{2/3})$, even for the slightly easier case of inverting a random function. The question resurfaces in the work of Fiat and Naor [28], Barkan, Biham, and Shamir [5] (who show that Hellman's method is optimal for a certain natural but restricted class of algorithms), De, Trevisan and Tulsiani [21], and Abusalah et al. [1].

In addition to the problem's theoretical appeal, determining the best possible time-space trade-offs for function inversion is relevant to practice, since the difference between an online attack time of $N^{2/3}$ and an $N^{1/2}$ becomes crucial when dealing with 128-bit block ciphers, such as the ubiquitous AES-128. Hellman's algorithm gives the best known preprocessing attack against AES-128, with $S = T \approx 2^{86}$. If we could improve Hellman's algorithm to achieve $S = T = N^{1/2}$, matching Yao's lower bound, we could break AES-128 in time $2^{64}$ with a data structure of size $2^{64}$, albeit after an expensive preprocessing phase. While today's $S = T = 2^{86}$ attack is likely far beyond the power of any realistic adversary, an improved $S = T = 2^{64}$ attack would leave us with an alarmingly narrow security margin.

Recent work proves new lower bounds on preprocessing algorithms for various cryptographic problems, using both incompressibility arguments [1,23,32] and the newer presampling method [19,65]. While this progress might give hope for an improved lower bound for function inversion as well, both techniques mysteriously fail to break the $ST = \widetilde{\Omega}(N)$ barrier.

**Non-adaptive Algorithms.** Another avenue for study is to explore the role of *parallelism* or *adaptivity* in preprocessing algorithms for function inversion. All non-trivial algorithms for function inversion, including Hellman's algorithm and Rainbow-table methods [61], critically use the adaptivity of their queries. It would be very interesting to construct a highly parallelizable preprocessing algorithm for function inversion. Such an algorithm would achieve the same advice and time complexity $S = T = \widetilde{O}(N^{2/3})$ as Hellman's algorithm, but would make all $\widetilde{O}(N^{2/3})$ of its queries to the $f$-oracle in one non-adaptive batch. Such a non-adaptive inversion algorithm could speed up function inversion on cryptanalytic machines with a very large number of parallel processing cores.

We do not even know if there exists a non-adaptive algorithm with $S = T = o(N)$. Can we find new non-adaptive inversion algorithms, or is adaptivity necessary for good time-space trade-offs? Proving lower bounds in this more restricted model could be a stepping stone to improving the general lower bounds on function inversion.

## 1.1    Our Results

This work establishes new connections between the function-inversion problem and well-studied problems in cryptography, complexity theory, and data structures. These connections are useful in two directions.

First, they shed new light on the function-inversion problem: a connection to circuit complexity suggests that improving on the known lower bounds for function-inversion will be difficult. In particular, we show that new lower bounds for function inversion will imply new circuit lower bounds and could even resolve complexity-theoretic questions that predate Hellman's results [66]. Moreover, a new connection to the problem of breaking PRGs with preprocessing suggests a new avenue for better inversion algorithms for *injective functions*. For many of the cryptanalytic applications, progress on this variant of function inversion would in fact be sufficient.

Second, these connections, together with classic cryptanalytic algorithms, give rise to better algorithms for problems in the other areas of theory. For example, a connection to communication complexity leads to the best known algorithm for the multiparty pointer-jumping problem, improving upon a twenty-year-old upper bound [63]. Similarly, a connection to data structures leads to a new upper bound for the systematic substring-search problem, resolving an open question [29].

We now state our results in detail.

**Proving Better Lower Bounds for Function-Inversion Implies New Circuit Lower Bounds.** A major question in circuit complexity, open since the 1970s [66,67], is to give an explicit family of functions $F_n \colon \{0,1\}^n \to \{0,1\}^n$ that cannot be computed by fan-in-two circuits of size $O(n)$ and depth $O(\log n)$. Following ideas of Brody and Larsen [13], we demonstrate a close connection between this classic problem in circuit complexity and non-adaptive preprocessing algorithms for function inversion.

Specifically, we show that proving that every *non-adaptive* black-box function-inversion algorithm that uses $S = N \log N / \log \log N$ bits of advice requires at least $T = \Omega(N^\epsilon)$ oracle queries, for some constant $\epsilon > 0$, would give an explicit family of functions that cannot be computed by linear-size log-depth Boolean circuits. This, in turn, would resolve a long-standing open problem in circuit complexity. Though we cannot prove it, we suspect that the above lower bound holds even for $\epsilon = 1$.

This connection implies that proving lower bounds against non-adaptive function-inversion algorithms that use the relatively large amount of advice $S = N \log N / \log \log N$ should be quite difficult. A much more modest goal would be to rule out any non-adaptive algorithm using $S = T = \widetilde{O}(N^{1/2+\epsilon})$, for some $\epsilon > 0$. This would represent only a slight strengthening of Yao's $ST = \widetilde{\Omega}(N)$ bound for adaptive algorithms. However, we show that achieving even this far-more-modest goal would improve the best known lower bound for circuits in Valiant's common-bits model [66,67]. This, in turn, would represent substantial progress towards proving lower bounds against linear-size log-depth circuits. In particular, since any lower bound against algorithms without a restriction on adaptivity would only be more general, *improving the $ST = \widetilde{\Omega}(N)$ lower* *bound for function inversion would imply new circuit lower bounds in Valiant's common-bits model.*

We believe that the difficulty of proving such a circuit lower bound suggests that beating the square-root barrier exhibited by both the compression [33,77] and presampling [19,65] techniques might prove more difficult than previously expected.

**One-to-One Function Inversion from PRG Distinguishers.** Many cryptanalytic applications of Hellman tables (cryptanalysis of block ciphers, password cracking, etc.) only require inverting *injective* functions. Does there exist a better-than-Hellman algorithm for inverting injective functions with preprocessing?

One reason to hope for a better algorithm for injective functions is that for the very special case of *permutations*, there exists an inversion algorithm with preprocessing that achieves the improved trade-off $ST = \widetilde{O}(N)$ (i.e., $S = T = N^{1/2}$) [77]. Can we achieve the same trade-off for injective functions?

While we have not been able to answer this question yet, we do open one possible route to answering it. In particular, we show that the problem of inverting injective functions with preprocessing has a close connection to the problem of breaking pseudorandom generators (PRGs) with preprocessing [2,19,21,23,24]. Specifically, De, Trevisan, and Tulsiani [21] show that black-box PRG distinguishers with preprocessing can realize the trade-off $S = \widetilde{O}(\epsilon^2 N)$, for $T = \widetilde{O}(1)$ and for any choice of distinguishing advantage $\epsilon$.

We show that achieving a more general trade-off of the form $ST = \widetilde{O}(\epsilon^2 N)$, for any constant $\epsilon$, would imply a better-than-Hellman algorithm for inverting injective functions. Thus, improving the known PRG distinguishers with preprocessing can improve the known injective inversion algorithms.

**New Protocols for Multiparty Pointer Jumping.** We show that algorithms for the black-box function-inversion problem are useful in designing new communication protocols for a well-studied problem in communication complexity. In particular, any black-box preprocessing algorithm for inverting permutations yields a protocol for the permutation variant of the "$k$-party pointer-jumping" problem ($\mathsf{MPJ}_{N,k}^{\mathsf{perm}}$) [10,11,14,20,56,63,70] in the number-on-the-forehead model of communication complexity [15].

Then, by instantiating the permutation-inversion algorithm with a variant of Hellman's method, we obtain the *best known protocol* for $\mathsf{MPJ}_{N,k}^{\mathsf{perm}}$ for $k = \omega(\log N/\log \log N)$ players (this regime is in fact the most consequential for the original motivation for studying this problem), improving the previous best upper bound of $O(N \log \log N/\log N)$, by Pudlák et al. [63], to $\widetilde{O}(N/k + \sqrt{N})$. We thus make progress on understanding the communication complexity of multiparty pointer jumping, a problem with significance to $\mathsf{ACC}^0$ circuit lower bounds [6,47,78].

Beyond the quantitative improvement, our protocol is different from all previous approaches to the problem and is an unexpected application of a cryptanalytic algorithm to a communication-complexity problem. While the use of a cryptanalytic algorithm in this context appears new, prior work has found application of results in communication complexity to lower bounds [44] and constructions [12] in the cryptographic setting.

This connection presents a path forward for proving non-adaptive lower bounds for permutation inversion. In particular, we show that for every non-adaptive black-box permutation-inversion algorithm using $S$ bits of advice and $T$ online queries, it must hold that $\max\{S, T\}$ is at least as large as the communication complexity of $\mathsf{MPJ}_{N,3}^{\mathsf{perm}}$. Any improvement on the lower bound for $\mathsf{MPJ}_{N,3}^{\mathsf{perm}}$ would give an improved lower bound for non-adaptive black-box permutation-inversion algorithms. The best lower bound for $\mathsf{MPJ}_{N,3}^{\mathsf{perm}}$ is $\Omega(\sqrt{N})$ [3,73]. Interestingly, this matches the best lower-bound for black-box permutation-inversion algorithms, regardless of their adaptivity.

**New Time-Space Trade-Off for Systematic Substring Search.** Finally, we show that improved algorithms for function inversion will also imply improved data structures for the *systematic substring-search problem* [22,29,30,40,41]. In particular, we prove that there is a preprocessing algorithm for the function-inversion problem using few bits of advice and few online queries if and only if there is a space- and time-efficient data structure for systematic substring search in the cell-probe model [75]. In the systematic substring-search problem, we are given a bitstring of length $N$ (the "text"), and from it we must construct an $S$-bit data structure (the "index"). Given a query string, we should be able to determine whether the query string appears as a substring of the text by reading the index and by inspecting at most $T$ bits of the original text.

This connection is fruitful in two directions: First, we show that instantiating this connection with the Fiat-Naor algorithm for function inversion [28] yields an $S^3T = \widetilde{O}(N^3)$ systematic data structure, which is the best known in the parameter regime $S = \widetilde{O}(N^\alpha)$ for $\alpha < 1$. Gál and Miltersen [29] ask whether a very strong $S + T = \widetilde{\Omega}(N)$ lower bound on this problem is possible. By beating this hypothetical lower bound, our algorithm answers their open question in the negative.

Second, Gál and Miltersen prove an $ST = \widetilde{\Omega}(N)$ lower bound for systematic substring search. Our barrier to proving lower bounds against black-box algorithms for function inversion implies that improving this lower bound would also imply new lower bounds in Valiant's circuit model and therefore may be quite challenging.

## 1.2  Related Work

We now recall a few salient related results on function inversion, and we discuss additional related work at relevant points throughout the text.

Fiat and Naor [27,28] proved that Hellman's algorithm [46] achieves a trade-off of the form $S^2T = \widetilde{O}(N^2)$, when the algorithm needs only to invert a random function with constant probability (i.e., in the cryptanalytically interesting case). For the worst-case problem of inverting arbitrary functions, Fiat and Naor give an algorithm that achieves a trade-off of the form $S^3T = O(N^3)$. De, Trevisan, and Tulsiani [21] improve the Fiat-Naor trade-off when the algorithm needs only to invert the function at a sub-constant fraction of points.

For inverting functions, Yao [77] proved that every algorithm that uses $S$ bits of advice and makes $T$ online queries must satisfy $ST = \widetilde{\Omega}(N)$ lower bound. Impagliazzo gives a short alternative proof [48]. Dodis et al. [23], building on prior work [21, 33], extended the lower bound to capture algorithms that invert only a sub-constant fraction of functions $f$.

Barkan, Biham, and Shamir [5] show that, for a *restricted class of preprocessing algorithms*, a Hellman-style trade-off of the form $S^2T = \widetilde{O}(N^2)$ is the best possible. Their lower bound is powerful enough to capture the known inversion schemes, including Hellman's algorithm and Oechslin's practically efficient "Rainbow tables" technique [61]. At the same time, this restricted lower bound leaves open the possibility that an entirely new type of algorithm could subvert their lower bound.

For inverting *permutations*, Yao [77] observed that a Hellman-style algorithm can achieve the $ST = \widetilde{O}(N)$ upper bound and proved a matching lower bound. Gennaro and Trevisan [33], Wee [71], and De, Trevisan, and Tulsiani [21] extend this lower bound to handle randomized algorithms and those that succeed with small probability.

Two recent works [39, 52] use the function-inversion algorithm of Fiat and Naor to obtain new algorithms for the preprocessing version of the 3-SUM problem.

## 1.3   Preliminaries

*Notation.* Through this paper, $\mathbb{Z}^{\geq 0}$ denotes the non-negative integers, and $\mathbb{Z}^{>0}$ denotes the positive integers. For any $N \in \mathbb{Z}^{>0}$ we write $[N] = \{1, 2, \ldots, N\}$. We often identify every element $x \in [N]$ with the binary representation of $x - 1$ in $\{0, 1\}^{\lceil \log N \rceil}$. We use $x \leftarrow 4$ to denote assignment and, for a finite set $\mathcal{X}$, we use $x \xleftarrow{\text{R}} \mathcal{X}$ to denote a uniform random draw from $\mathcal{X}$. For a function $f : A \to B$ and $y \in B$, we define the preimage set of $y$ as $f^{-1}(y) := \{x \in A \mid f(x) = y\}$. All logarithms are base-two unless stated otherwise. Parameters $S$ and $T$ are always implicit functions of the parameter $N$, and to simplify the bounds, we always implicitly take $S = T = \Omega(1)$. The notation $\widetilde{\Omega}(\cdot)$ and $\widetilde{O}(\cdot)$ hides factors polynomial in $\log N$.

**Definition 1 (Black-box inversion algorithm with preprocessing).** Let $N \in \mathbb{Z}^{>0}$. A black-box inversion algorithm with preprocessing for functions on $[N]$ is a pair $(\mathcal{A}_0, \mathcal{A}_1)$ of oracle algorithms, such that $\mathcal{A}_0$ gets oracle access to a function $f : [N] \to [N]$, takes no input, and outputs an *advice string* $\mathsf{st}_f \in \{0, 1\}^*$. Algorithm $\mathcal{A}_1$ gets oracle access to a function $f : [N] \to [N]$, takes as input a string $\mathsf{st}_f \in \{0, 1\}^*$ and a point $y \in [N]$, and outputs a point $x \in [N]$. Moreover, for every $x \in [N]$, it holds that $\mathcal{A}_1^f(\mathcal{A}_0^f(), f(x)) \in f^{-1}(f(x))$.

We can define a black-box inversion algorithm *for permutations* analogously by restricting the oracle $f : [N] \to [N]$ to implement an injective function. In this case, we will often denote the oracle as $\pi$ instead of $f$.

**Definition 2 (Adaptivity).** We say that an oracle algorithm is $k$-round adaptive if the algorithm's oracle queries consist of $k$ sets, such that each set of queries depends on the advice string, the input, and the replies to the previous rounds of queries. We call a 1-round adaptive algorithm *non-adaptive*. Finally, we say that an algorithm is *strongly non-adaptive* if it issues a single set of queries that only depends on the algorithm's input, but not on the advice string. In all of the above cases, when referring to the number of queries made by the algorithm, we account for the sum over all rounds.

**Worst Case Versus Average Case.** The algorithms in Definition 1 are deterministic and successfully invert all functions on all points. It is also interesting to consider algorithms that invert successfully only with probability $\epsilon < 1$, over the random choice of: the function $f: [N] \to [N]$, the point to invert, and/or algorithm's randomness. As most of the results in this paper deal with *barriers for improving lower bounds*, restricting ourselves to deterministic algorithms that always succeed in inverting only makes these results *stronger*. In any case, assume that all algorithms we consider halt with probability 1.

**Running Time Versus Query Complexity.** For the purposes of proving lower bounds, and reductions towards proving lower bounds, it suffices to consider the query complexity of a preprocessing algorithm's online phase. Counting only queries (and not computation time) only strengthens lower bounds proved in this model. The algorithms we construct can be made to use only $\widetilde{O}(N)$ preprocessing time in a suitable RAM model, when they are allowed to fail with small probability. Furthermore, the running time of our algorithms' $T$-query online phase is $\widetilde{O}(T)$.

**Non-uniformity.** Our definition allows for "free" non-uniformity in the parameter $N$. Nevertheless, in a model that only "charges" the online algorithm for queries to the oracle and ignores the actual running time, non-uniformity makes little difference since a uniform algorithm can simply search for the optimal choice of non-uniform advice without increasing its query complexity.

**Shared Randomness.** We allow the preprocessing and online phases to access a common stream of random bits. Allowing the adversary to access correlated randomness in both phases only strengthens the lower bounds. Only one of our upper bounds (Theorem 8) makes use of this correlated randomness.

## 2   Lower Bounds on Inversion Imply Circuit Lower Bounds

The motivating question of this work is whether Hellman's $S = T = \widetilde{O}(N^{2/3})$ algorithm for inverting random functions is optimal. In this section, we show that resolving this question will require proving significant new lower bounds in Valiant's "common bits" model of circuits [66]. We also show that proving strong lower bounds on *non-adaptive* algorithms for function inversion would imply new lower bounds against linear-sized logarithmic-depth circuits.

We obtain these connections by observing that the function-inversion problem is an example of a class of so called "succinct" static data-structure problems [4,17,30,31,40,41,43,45,49,58,64]. We show a barrier to proving lower bounds against *systematic* data structures, which are a special case of succinct data structures.

**Related Work.** Brody and Larsen [13] showed that proving certain lower bounds against *linear* data structures for *dynamic* problems would imply strong lower bounds on the wire complexity of linear depth-two circuits. We follow their general blueprint, but we instead focus on *arbitrary* algorithms for solving *static* data-structure problems (e.g., function inversion), and our connection is to Valiant's common-bits model of circuits, rather than to linear depth-two circuits.

In recent independent work, Viola [69, Theorem 3] shows that lower bounds against a large class of static data-structures problems imply circuit lower bounds. In his work, Viola considers an incomparable circuit model that, on the one hand, admits circuits of depth larger than two, but, on the other hand, restricts the number of wires connected to the common bits. As a result, Viola's work does not seem to apply to the function-inversion problem within the relevant parameter regime (namely, in the gap between Hellman's upper bound and Yao's lower bound).

In another recent independent work, Dvir, Golovnev, and Weinstein [26] connect data-structure lower bounds to matrix rigidity and circuit lower bounds. Their focus is on *linear* data structures, whereas the function inversion problem, considered in our work, does not have an apparent linear structure.

Boyle and Naor [9] make a surprising connection between cryptographic algorithms and circuit lower bounds. They show that proving the non-existence of certain "offline" oblivious RAM algorithms (ORAMs) [34,38,62] would imply new lower bounds on the size of Boolean circuits for sorting lists of integers. Larsen and Nielsen [54] recently skirted this barrier by proving a lower bound against ORAMs in the "online" setting. Following that, Weiss and Wichs [72] showed that a variant of the Boyle-Naor barrier still holds against "online read-only" ORAMs.

## 2.1 Systematic Data Structures and Low-Depth Circuits

A major open question in circuit complexity is whether there exists an explicit family of Boolean functions (from $n$ bits to one bit) that cannot be computed by fan-in-two circuits of size $O(n)$ and depth $O(\log n)$. An easier problem, which is still famously difficult, is to find an explicit family of functions $F_n \colon \{0,1\}^n \to \{0,1\}^n$ with $n$-bit output—often called *Boolean operators*—that cannot be computed by this same class of circuits. Even this question has been open since the 1970s [51,66,67].

More precisely, we say that a family of Boolean operators $\{F_n\}_{n \in \mathbb{Z}^{>0}}$, for $F_n \colon \{0,1\}^n \to \{0,1\}^n$, is an *explicit operator* if the decision problem associated with each bit of the output of $F_n$ is in the complexity class NP.

The main result of this section is that proving a certain type of data-structure lower bound implies the existence of an explicit Boolean operator on $n$ bits that cannot be computed by fan-in-two circuits of size $O(n)$ and depth $O(\log n)$.

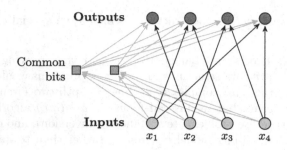

**Fig. 1.** Common-bits circuit with $n = 4$ inputs, degree $d = 2$, and width $w = 2$.

We then show that a lower bound on function-inversion algorithms can be cast as a data-structure lower bound, and therefore a function-inversion lower bound implies a circuit lower bound.

We now give the necessary background on data-structure problems. A *systematic* data structure of size $s$ and query complexity $t$ for an operator $F_n$ is a pair of algorithms:

- a preprocessing algorithm, which takes as input the data $x \in \{0,1\}^n$ and outputs a string $\mathsf{st} \in \{0,1\}^s$ of length $s = o(n)$, and
- a query algorithm, which takes as input the string $\mathsf{st}$, and an index $i \in [n]$, may probe (read) $t$ bits of the input $x$, and then outputs the $i$th bit of $F_n(x)$.

A systematic data structure is *non-adaptive* if the query algorithm probes a set of bits of the input data $x$ whose location depends only on the index $i$ and not on the input data $x$.

The following theorem is the main result of this section.

**Theorem 3.** *If an explicit operator $\{F_n\}_{n \in \mathbb{Z}^{>0}}$ has fan-in-two Boolean circuits of size $O(n)$ and depth $O(\log n)$ then, for every $\epsilon > 0$, then this operator admits a non-adaptive systematic data structure of size $O(n/\log \log n)$ and query complexity $O(n^\epsilon)$.*

To prove this, we first recall Valiant's common-bits model of circuits [66,67].

**Valiant's Common-Bits Model.** A circuit in the common-bits model of width $w$ and degree $d$ computing a Boolean operator $F_n : \{0,1\}^n \to \{0,1\}^n$ contains an input layer, a middle layer, and output layer (Fig. 1). The input layer consists of $n$ input bits $x_1, \ldots, x_n \in \{0,1\}$, and the output layer consists of $n$ output gates. There are $w$ gates in the middle layer of the circuit (the "common bits"); each input feeds into each of these $w$ middle gates, and the output of each of the $w$ middle gates feeds into each output gate. Further, each output gate reads from at most $d$ of the inputs. Unlike in a standard circuit, the gates in the middle and output layers of the circuit compute *arbitrary* functions of their inputs. The output of the circuit is the $n$-bit string formed at the output gates.

It is immediate that any Boolean operator $F_n : \{0,1\}^n \to \{0,1\}^n$ has common-bits circuits of width $n$ and degree $0$ or, alternatively, of width $0$ and degree $n$.

A non-trivial question is: For a given operator $F_n$ and choice of degree (e.g., $d = n^{1/3}$), what is minimal width of a common-bits circuit that computes $F_n$?

**Lemma 4.** *If there exists a circuit in the common-bits model of width $w$ and degree $d$ that computes an operator $F\colon \{0,1\}^n \to \{0,1\}^n$, then there exists a non-adaptive systematic data structure for $F$ of size $w$ and query complexity $d$.*

*Proof.* Let $\mathcal{C}$ be a circuit in the common-bits model as in the statement of the lemma. The data structure consists of the outputs of the $w$ middle-layer gates in the circuit $\mathcal{C}$ (i.e., the circuit's common bits). On input $i \in [n]$, the algorithm reads all the input bits connected to the $i$th output gate of $\mathcal{C}$ and computes the value of the output gate. Since each output gate in the circuit is connected to at most $d$ input bits, the query complexity of the systematic data structure is at most $d$. $\qquad\square$

Theorem 3 then follows from Lemma 4 and the following result of Valiant:

**Theorem 5 (Valiant [66,67]).** *If every explicit operator has fan-in-two Boolean circuits of size $O(n)$ and depth $O(\log n)$, then for every constant $\epsilon > 0$, every explicit operator has circuits in the common-bits model of width $O(n/\log\log n)$ and degree $n^\epsilon$.*

Viola [68, Section 3] and Jukna [50, Chapter 13] give detailed proofs of Theorem 5.

## 2.2  Consequences for Function Inversion

Observe that every function $f\colon [N] \to [N]$ can be described using $O(N \log N)$ bits, so there is a trivial strongly non-adaptive algorithm that inverts every function using $O(N \log N)$ bits of advice and no queries to the function in the online phase. We know of no non-adaptive function-inversion algorithm that inverts with constant probability using $o(N \log N)$ bits of advice and $o(N)$ queries. The following theorem states that ruling out the existence of such a non-adaptive algorithm is as hard as proving lower bounds against linear-size logarithmic-depth Boolean circuits.

**Theorem 6.** *If, for some $\epsilon > 0$, every family of strongly non-adaptive black-box algorithms for inverting functions $f\colon [N] \to [N]$ that uses $O(N^\epsilon)$ queries requires $\omega(N \log N/\log\log N)$ bits of advice, then there exists an explicit operator that cannot be computed by fan-in-two Boolean circuits of size $O(n)$ and depth $O(\log n)$.*

The theorem considers a restricted class of inversion algorithms that: (i) may only use strongly non-adaptive queries (the most restrictive type of query), (ii) are only allowed, for example, $O(N^{0.0001})$ queries (very few queries), and (iii) must invert arbitrary functions with probability one (the most difficult variant of the inversion problem).

So, even though we may suspect that there are no algorithms for inverting functions $f\colon [N] \to [N]$ using $O(N \log N/\log\log N)$ bits of advice and $O(N^{0.0001})$ non-adaptive queries, proving such an assertion seems very challenging.

*Proof of Theorem* 6. Let $n = N \log N$, where $N \in \mathbb{Z}^{>0}$ is a power of two. (For all other values of $n$, define the inversion operator trivially as the identity mapping.) We define the *inversion operator* $F_n^{\mathsf{inv}} \colon \{0,1\}^n \to \{0,1\}^n$ as follows. Let $x \in \{0,1\}^n$ be an input to $F_n^{\mathsf{inv}}$, and view $x$ as the concatenation of $N$ blocks of length $\log N$ bits each: $x = x_1 \| x_2 \| \cdots \| x_N$. For each $i \in [N]$, let $y_i \in [N]$ be the least $j \in [N]$ such that $x_j = i$, if one such $j$ exists. If no such $j$ exists, set $y_i = 0$. We define $F_n^{\mathsf{inv}}(x) = (y_1 \| y_2 \| \cdots \| y_N)$.

Observe that a systematic data structure for $F_n^{\mathsf{inv}}$ gives a strongly non-adaptive preprocessing algorithm that inverts every function $f \colon [N] \to [N]$. The preprocessing phase constructs the data structure for operator $F_n^{\mathsf{inv}}$ on input $f(1) \| f(2) \| \cdots \| f(N)$ and outputs this data structure as the advice string.

In the online phase, on input $i \in [N]$, the algorithm uses the data structure in the advice string and its oracle access to $f$ to compute all $\log N$ bits of the $i$th output block $y_i$ of $F_n^{\mathsf{inv}}$, which is enough to recover some inverse of $i$ under $f$, if it exists.

The theorem now follows from Theorem 3, instantiated with $F_n^{\mathsf{inv}}$. For $n$ of the form $n = N \log N$, where $N > 0$ is a power of two, we get that the length of the advice string is $O(N \log N / \log \log(N \log N)) = O(N \log N / \log \log N)$ and the online query complexity is $\log N \cdot O\left((N \log N)^\epsilon\right) = O(N^{\epsilon'})$, for any $\epsilon' > \epsilon$. $\square$

Theorem 6 suggests the hardness of proving stronger lower bounds for non-adaptive inversion algorithms, but it applies only to algorithms that use a relatively long advice string, of length $O(N \log N / \log \log N)$. We might still hope to improve upon Yao's $ST = \widetilde{\Omega}(N)$ lower bound for function inversion without breaking the aforementioned barrier.

The following corollary shows that ruling out function-inversion algorithms using advice and time $S = T = \widetilde{O}(N^{1/2+\epsilon})$, for any $\epsilon > 0$, would imply the existence of an explicit operator that cannot be computed by circuits of width $O(n^{1/2+\epsilon'})$ and degree $O(n^{1/2+\epsilon'})$ in the common-bits model, for some $\epsilon' > 0$. As we will discuss, no such lower bound in the common-bits model is known, so proving the optimality of Hellman's $\widetilde{O}(N^{2/3})$ algorithm, or even showing that inverting functions with preprocessing is marginally harder than inverting permutations with preprocessing, would imply an advance in the state of lower bounds on circuits in the common-bits model.

**Corollary 7.** *If, for some $\epsilon > 0$, there does not exist a family of strongly non-adaptive algorithms for inverting functions $f \colon [N] \to [N]$ using $O(N^{1/2+\epsilon})$ bits of advice and $O(N^{1/2+\epsilon})$ queries, then there exists an explicit operator that does not have circuits in the common-bits model of width $O(n^{1/2+\epsilon'})$ and degree $O(n^{1/2+\epsilon'})$, for every $\epsilon'$ satisfying $0 < \epsilon' < \epsilon$.*

*Proof.* We prove the contrapositive. Assume that for every $\epsilon' > 0$, every explicit operator has common-bits circuits of width $O(n^{1/2+\epsilon'})$ and depth $O(n^{1/2+\epsilon'})$. Then, as in the proof of Theorem 6, we can apply Lemma 4 to operator $F_n^{\mathsf{inv}}$ to show that, for $n = N \log N$, there exists a strongly non-adaptive preprocessing algorithm that inverts functions $f \colon [N] \to [N]$ using $O(n^{1/2+\epsilon'}) = O((N \log N)^{1/2+\epsilon'}) = O(N^{1/2+\epsilon'} \log N)$ bits of advice and $O(n^{1/2+\epsilon'} \log N) = O((N \log N)^{1/2+\epsilon'} \log N)$ online queries. Then, for any $\epsilon > \epsilon'$, the advice usage and number of online queries is $O(N^{1/2+\epsilon})$. $\square$

Notice that while the hypothesis of Corollary 7 considers a lower bound against strongly non-adaptive inversion algorithms, this only *strengthens* the statement. This is true because proving a lower bound against adaptive inversion algorithms implies a lower bound against strongly non-adaptive algorithms as well.

If we instantiate Corollary 7 with $\epsilon = 1/6$, we find that ruling out function-inversion algorithms using $S = T = o(N^{2/3})$, even against the restricted class of strongly non-adaptive algorithms, would give an explicit operator that does not have common-bits circuits of width $w$ and degree $d$ satisfying $w = d = o(n^{2/3-\delta})$, for any $\delta > 0$.

Proving such a lower bound on common-bits circuits is *not* strong enough to yield a lower bound against linear-size log-depth circuits via Valiant's method (Theorem 5). However, this lower bound *would* improve the best known lower bound against circuits in the common-bits model. The best known bound, due to Pudlák, Rödl, and Sgall, gives $d = \Omega(\frac{n}{w} \cdot \log(\frac{n}{w}))$, for a common-bits circuit of width $w$ and degree $d$ [63]. In particular, they construct an explicit operator that does not have common-bits circuits satisfying $w = d = \widetilde{O}(n^{1/2})$. By Corollary 7, ruling out function-inversion algorithms with $S = T = \widetilde{O}(N^{1/2+\epsilon})$, for any $\epsilon > 0$, would thus improve the best lower bounds on common-bits circuits.

## 2.3    Consequences for Other Succinct Data-Structure Problems

Theorem 3 and Lemma 4 together imply that proving strong lower bounds for *any* systematic data-structure problem—not only for the function-inversion problem—will be challenging. To explain how this barrier applies to a completely different data-structure problem, we recall the systematic variant of the standard data-structure problem of *polynomial evaluation with preprocessing* [57]. We give an informal description of the problem, and the transformation into a formal systematic data-structure problem (as in Sect. 2.1) is straightforward.

The problem of polynomial evaluation with preprocessing is parameterized by an integer $N \in \mathbb{Z}^{>0}$ and a finite field $\mathbb{F}$ of size $\Theta(N)$. The input data is a polynomial $p \in \mathbb{F}[X]$ of degree at most $N - 1$, represented as its vector of coefficients $\bar{c} = (c_0, c_1, \ldots, c_{N-1}) \in \mathbb{F}^N$. The preprocessing algorithm reads this input (the entire polynomial $p$) and produces a preprocessed $S$-bit string st. In a subsequent online phase, the query algorithm takes as input a point $x_0 \in \mathbb{F}$, and must output the evaluation $p(x_0) \in \mathbb{F}$ of the polynomial $p$ at point $x_0$. To produce its answer, the query algorithm may read the entire preprocessed string st, query at most $T$ coordinates of the coefficient vector $\bar{c}$, and perform an unlimited amount of computation.

For what choices of space usage $S$ and query complexity $T$ does there exist a systematic data structure for polynomial evaluation with preprocessing?

The two naïve approaches to solving this problem are:

1. Have the preprocessing algorithm store in the string st the evaluation of the polynomial $p$ on every point in the field $\mathbb{F}$, using $S = \Omega(N)$ space.

2. Have the online-phase algorithm read the entire coefficient vector $\bar{c}$, using $T = \Omega(N)$ queries, and then evaluate $p(x_0) = \sum_i c_i x_0 \in \mathbb{F}$ directly.

These solutions both have $S + T = \widetilde{\Omega}(N)$.

It seems very difficult to construct an algorithm that simultaneously uses a data structure of size $S = N^\delta$ and query complexity $T = N^\delta$, for some $\delta < 1$. And yet, the best lower bound we have for this problem, implied by a bound of Gál and Miltersen [30], is of the form $ST = \widetilde{\Omega}(N)$. A variant of Corollary 7 implies that proving stronger lower bounds for this problem—or proving any lower bound better than $ST = \widetilde{\Omega}(N)$ for *any* systematic or succinct data-structure problem, for that matter—will also imply new lower bounds in Valiant's common-bits model. Proving even a stronger lower bound could, via Theorem 3, imply a lower bound against linear-size log-depth fan-in-two circuits.

# 3   Breaking PRGs Is as Hard as Inverting Injective Functions

Many cryptanalytic applications of Hellman tables only require inverting *injective* functions. That is given a *injective* function $f : [N] \to [M]$ and a point $y \in [M]$, find a value $x \in [N]$ such that $f(x) = y$, if one exists.

For example, consider the classic application of Hellman tables to plaintext attacks on block ciphers: Let $E : \{0,1\}^k \times \{0,1\}^n \to \{0,1\}^n$ be a block cipher, where $k$ is the key size and $n$ is the block size. If we define $f_E : \{0,1\}^k \to \{0,1\}^n$ such that $f_E(x) = E(x, m_0)$ for some fixed plaintext $m_0$, then an algorithm with preprocessing for the function $f_E$ essentially gives a known-plaintext attack on the block cipher $E$. We can (heuristically) expect the resulting function $f_E$ to behave similar to a random function, and therefore be injective only beyond the birthday bound $k \gtrsim 2n$. However, even for shorter keys, we can reduce a known-plaintext attack to the problem of inverting an injective function by considering the encryption of multiple known plaintexts $m_0, m_1, m_2$. For example, if $k = n$, then we expect $f_{E \times 3} : \{0,1\}^n \to \{0,1\}^{3n}$, defined as $f_{E \times 3}(x) = E(x, m_0) \| E(x, m_1) \| E(x, m_2)$, to have no collisions.

A function-inversion algorithm can invert an injective function $f : [N] \to [M]$ without taking any advantage of the fact that it is injective, so Hellman's $S^2 T = \widetilde{O}(N^2)$ upper bound for function inversion [46] applies in this setting as well. However, the fact that for the case of random permutations (i.e., an injective function $f : [N] \to [N]$), Hellman's algorithm gives a significantly better upper bound of $ST = \widetilde{O}(N)$, gives hope that a similar improvement—or at least some improvement—is possible for injective length-increasing functions.

To the best of our knowledge, the injective variant of the function-inversion problem has not been studied directly so far, even though it is a special case with wide cryptanalytic applications. As a first step, we connect the injective inversion problem to the problem of breaking pseudorandom generators (PRGs) with preprocessing [2,19,21,23,24]. In that problem, we model a "black-box" PRG as an oracle $G : [N] \to [M]$, with $N < M$. A PRG distinguisher with preprocessing first makes arbitrarily many queries to $G$ and outputs an $S$-bit advice string. In the online phase, the distinguisher can then use its advice string, along with $T$ queries to $G$, to distinguish whether a given sample $y \in [M]$ has been drawn from the distribution $\{G(x) \mid x \xleftarrow{\text{R}} [N]\}$ or the distribution $\{y \mid y \xleftarrow{\text{R}} [M]\}$.

In their work, De, Trevisan, and Tulsiani [21] give a distinguisher with $S = O(\epsilon^2 N)$ and $T = \widetilde{O}(1)$ that achieves a distinguishing advantage $\epsilon \leq 1/\sqrt{N}$. They ask whether it is possible to realize the trade-off $ST = \widetilde{O}(\epsilon^2 N)$ for other parameter settings as well. The following theorem shows that a PRG distinguisher that achieves constant distinguishing advantage at points on this trade-off (e.g., $\epsilon = 1/100$, $S = N^{1/4}$, and $T = N^{3/4}$) would imply a better-than-Hellman algorithm for inverting injective functions.

**Theorem 8.** *Suppose that there is a black-box PRG distinguisher that uses $S$ bits of advice, makes $T$ online queries to a PRG $G \colon [N] \to [M]$, and achieves distinguishing advantage $\epsilon$. Then there exists a black-box algorithm that inverts any injective function $f \colon [N] \to [M]$ using $\widetilde{O}(\epsilon^{-2}S)$ bits of advice and $\widetilde{O}(\epsilon^{-2}T)$ online queries, and that inverts $f$ with probability $1 - 1/\log N$ (over the algorithm's randomness).*

*Furthermore, if the preprocessing and online phase algorithms have access to a common random oracle, the online phase also runs in time $\widetilde{O}(T)$.*

*Remark 9 (Relation to Goldreich-Levin).* A classic line of results [36,37,55,76] shows how to use any injective one-way function $f : [N] \to [M]$ to construct an efficient PRG $G_f : [N^2] \to [2N^2]$ which makes black-box use of $f$. The proof uses the Goldreich-Levin theorem [37] to show that any efficient distinguisher for $G_f$ yields an inversion algorithm for $f$. (Consult Goldreich's textbook [35, Section 3.5] for the details.) It is not clear to us whether a non-uniform generalization of these classic results directly implies Theorem 8. The problem is that the domain of the PRG $G_f$ has size $N^2$, whereas the domain of the original function $f$ has size $N$. Since we are interested in the exact exponent of the advice and time usage of function-inversion algorithms (i.e., $S = N^{3/4}$ versus $S = N^{1/2}$), we are sensitive to this polynomial expansion in the domain size. For example, say that we were able to construct a black-box PRG distinguisher that achieves $S = T = \widetilde{O}(\sqrt{N})$. Applying the classic reduction directly to $G_f$ would only imply the existence of an inverter for the function $f$ that uses the trivial advice and time complexity $S = T = \widetilde{O}(\sqrt{N^2}) = \widetilde{O}(N)$. In contrast, Theorem 8 implies that an $S = T = \widetilde{O}(\sqrt{N})$ distinguisher yields an $S = T = \widetilde{O}(\sqrt{N})$ inverter.

*Proof Idea for Theorem 8.* Given a distinguisher for any length-increasing generator $G \colon [N] \to [M]$, we construct an inversion algorithm for injective functions $f \colon [N] \to [M]$ in two steps. First, for each $i \in [n]$, we construct a bit-recovery algorithm $\mathcal{B}_i$ that, given $f(x)$, achieves a non-trivial advantage in recovering the $i$th bit of $x$. We then use the algorithms $(\mathcal{B}_1, \dots, \mathcal{B}_n)$ to construct an inversion algorithm $\mathcal{I}$ that, given $f(x)$, recovers the full preimage $x$ with good probability.

To give the intuition behind the bit-recovery algorithm $\mathcal{B}_i$: Given a function $f\colon [N] \to [M]$ to invert, we construct a function $G_i\colon [N] \to [M]$ such that a point $y = f(x)$ is in the image of $G_i$ if and only if the $i$th bit of $x$ is 1. Then, we can apply the PRG distinguisher to $G_i$ and recover the $i$th bit of $y$'s preimage.

This simple algorithm does not quite work when the PRG distinguisher has small distinguishing advantage $\epsilon$, since the distinguisher may fail on the point $y$. To fix this, we give $\mathcal{B}_i$ access to two random permutations $\pi\colon [N] \to [N]$ and $\sigma\colon [M] \to [M]$ that allow $\mathcal{B}_i$ to essentially randomize the point it gives as input to the PRG distinguisher.

We then can run $\mathcal{B}_i$ many times with different random permutations and then take the majority vote of the outputs of these runs. This majority vote will yield the $i$th bit of the $x$ with high probability. To complete the construction, we instantiate the permutations $\pi$ and $\sigma$ using correlated randomness between the preprocessing and online algorithms. The full description of the construction appears in the full version of this paper. $\qquad\square$

# 4    From Cryptanalysis to New Communication Protocols

Communication complexity [53, 74] quantifies the number of bits that a set of players need to communicate amongst themselves in order to compute a function on an input that is split between the players. One of the major open problems in communication complexity is to obtain a non-trivial lower bound for some problem for a super-poly-logarithmic number of players. Such a bound would in turn lead to a breakthrough circuit lower bound for the complexity class $\mathsf{ACC}^0$ [6, 47, 78].

In this section, we develop connections between the function-inversion problem and the multiparty pointer-jumping problem in the number-on-the-forehead (NOF) model of communication complexity [15]. By combining these new connections with the classic cycle-walking algorithm for permutation inversion, we obtain the best known NOF protocols for the permutation variant of the pointer-jumping problem. Since pointer jumping is a candidate hard problem in the $k$-party NOF setting, understanding the exact communication complexity of pointer jumping for a super-poly-logarithmic number of players is an important step towards the eventual goal of proving circuit lower bounds [10, 11, 14, 20, 56, 63, 70].

## 4.1    Multiparty Pointer-Jumping in the NOF Model

A classical problem in the NOF model is the *pointer-jumping* problem. We describe the *permutation* variant of the problem, and then discuss the general case. In the pointer-jumping problem $\mathsf{MPJ}^{\mathsf{perm}}_{N,k}$, there are $k$ computationally-unbounded players, denoted $P_0, P_1, \ldots, P_{k-1}$, and each has an input "written on her forehead." The first player $P_0$ has a point $x \in [N]$ written on her forehead, the last player $P_{k-1}$ has a Boolean mapping $\beta\colon [N] \to \{0, 1\}$ written on her forehead, and each remaining player $P_i$, for $i = 1, \ldots, k-2$, has a permutation $\pi_i\colon [N] \to [N]$ written on her forehead. Each player can see all $k-1$

inputs except the one written on her own forehead. The goal of the players is to compute the value $\beta \circ \pi_{k-2} \circ \cdots \circ \pi_1(x)$, which loosely corresponds to "following a trail of pointers" defined by the permutations, starting from $x$ (Fig. 2). The players can communicate by writing messages on a public blackboard. The communication complexity of a protocol is the total number of bits written on the blackboard for a worst-case input.

A *one-way* protocol is a protocol in which each player writes a single message on the blackboard in the fixed order $P_0, \ldots, P_{k-1}$, and the last player's message must be the output. The one-way communication complexity of a function $f$, denoted $\mathsf{CC}^1(f)$, is the minimum communication complexity of all one-way protocols that successfully compute $f$. Without the "one-way" restriction, there are protocols for $\mathsf{MPJ}^{\mathsf{perm}}_{N,k}$ that require only $O(\log N)$ bits of communication.

*Known Bounds.* The best upper bound for $\mathsf{MPJ}^{\mathsf{perm}}_{N,k}$ is due to Pudlák et al. [63], who showed that $\mathsf{CC}^1(\mathsf{MPJ}^{\mathsf{perm}}_{N,k}) = O(N \log \log N / \log N)$. More recently, Brody and Sanchez [14] showed that this upper bound applies to the more general pointer-jumping problem, in which we replace the permutations $\pi_1, \ldots, \pi_{k-2}$ with arbitrary functions. In this general case, Wigderson [73] proved an $\Omega(\sqrt{N})$ lower bound for $k = 3$ players (see also [3]), and Viola and Wigderson [70] proved an $\widetilde{\Omega}(N^{\frac{1}{k-1}})$ lower bound for $k \geq 3$ players.

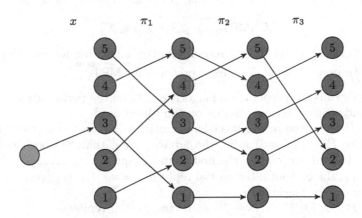

**Fig. 2.** A pointer-jumping instance for $\widehat{\mathsf{MPJ}}^{\mathsf{perm}}_{k=4, N=5}$ with $\pi_1 = (1\,2\,4\,5\,3)$, $\pi_2 = (2\,3)(4\,5)$, $\pi_3 = (2\,3\,4\,5)$ and $x = 2$. Lemma 11 reduces this instance to inverting the permutation $\pi_1^{-1}\pi_2^{-1}\pi_3^{-1} = (1\,3\,5\,4)$ on the point $x = 2$.

## 4.2   A New Communication Protocol from Permutation Inversion

We obtain the best known communication protocol for the *permutation* variant of the pointer-jumping game on parameter $N$ for $k = \omega(\log N / \log \log N)$ players. Our result improves the previously best known upper bound of $\widetilde{O}(N)$ to $\widetilde{O}(N/k + \sqrt{N})$. Extending our upper bound to the *general* multiparty pointer-jumping problem remains an open problem, which we discuss in Remark 13.

On the lower-bound side, this connection suggests a path to prove lower bounds against *partially adaptive* permutation-inversion algorithms, as in Definition 2. In contrast, the techniques of Sect. 2 can only prove lower bounds against strongly non-adaptive algorithms.

In this section, we prove the following new upper bound on $\mathsf{CC}^1(\mathsf{MPJ}^{\mathsf{perm}}_{N,k})$:

**Theorem 10.** $\mathsf{CC}^1(\mathsf{MPJ}^{\mathsf{perm}}_{N,k}) \leq O\left((N/k + \sqrt{N})\log N\right).$

To prove Theorem 10, as we do later in this section, we use the integer-valued version the pointer-jumping problem, commonly denoted $\widehat{\mathsf{MPJ}}^{\mathsf{perm}}_{N,k}$. In this version, the last player $P_{k-1}$ holds a permutation $\pi_{k-1} : [N] \to [N]$, instead of a boolean mapping, so the output of the problem is a value in $[N]$. The following technical lemma, which we prove in Appendix A, shows that the boolean-valued version of the pointer-jumping problem has communication complexity that is not much larger than that of the integer-valued pointer-jumping problem.

**Lemma 11.** $\mathsf{CC}^1(\mathsf{MPJ}^{\mathsf{perm}}_{N,k}) \leq \mathsf{CC}^1(\widehat{\mathsf{MPJ}}^{\mathsf{perm}}_{N,k}) + \lceil \log N \rceil.$

Then, our main lemma technical uses an arbitrary permutation-inversion algorithm with preprocessing to solve the integer-valued problem $\widehat{\mathsf{MPJ}}^{\mathsf{perm}}_{N,k}$:

**Lemma 12.** *If there exists a $(k-2)$-round adaptive algorithm for inverting permutations $\pi : [N] \to [N]$ that uses advice $S$ and time $T$, then*

$$\mathsf{CC}^1(\widehat{\mathsf{MPJ}}^{\mathsf{perm}}_{N,k}) \leq S + T\lceil \log N \rceil.$$

*Proof.* Let $(\mathcal{A}_0, \mathcal{A}_1)$ be a $(k-2)$-round adaptive algorithm for inverting permutations with preprocessing. We give a protocol for $\widehat{\mathsf{MPJ}}^{\mathsf{perm}}_{N,k}$.

- Player $P_0$ runs the preprocessing algorithm $\mathcal{A}_0$ on the permutation $\pi_1^{-1} \circ \cdots \circ \pi_{k-1}^{-1}$ and writes the advice string on the blackboard.
- Player $P_1$ runs the online inversion algorithm $\mathcal{A}_1$ on the input $x$ (written on player $P_0$'s forehead) using the advice string that has been written on the blackboard, to produce the first round of queries $q_{1,1}, \ldots, q_{1,t_1}$. For each query $q_{1,\ell}$, she computes the partial reply $p_{1,\ell} = \pi_2^{-1}(\ldots(\pi_{k-1}^{-1}(q_{1,\ell}))\ldots)$ and writes it on the blackboard.
- Player $P_i$, for $i \in \{2, \ldots, k-2\}$, reads the partial replies $p_{i-1,1}, \ldots, p_{i-1,t_{i-1}}$ written by the previous player, computes the (complete) query replies $r_{i-1,1}, \ldots, r_{i-1,t_{i-1}}$ by computing $r_{i-1,\ell} = \pi_1^{-1}(\ldots(\pi_{i-1}^{-1}(p_{i-1,\ell}))\ldots)$. Player $P_i$ then runs (in her head) the first $i-1$ rounds of the online inversion algorithm on input $x$, using the advice string and the replies to the first $i-1$ rounds of queries, all of which, she can compute using the partial replies written on the blackboard. Player $P_i$ then produces the $i^{\text{th}}$ round of queries, on which, similarly to Player $P_1$, she computes the partial replies and writes them on the blackboard.
- Player $P_{k-1}$ completes the evaluation of round $k-2$ of the queries by evaluating the remaining permutations $\pi_1^{-1} \circ \cdots \circ \pi_{k-2}^{-1}$ on the partial replies written by $P_{k-2}$. Player $P_{k-1}$ then runs in her head all $k-2$ rounds of the online inversion algorithm and writes the output on the blackboard.

By definition, the output $y$ of the algorithm satisfies $\pi_1^{-1} \circ \cdots \circ \pi_{k-1}^{-1}(y) = x$. Since all $\pi_i$ are permutations, it must hold $\pi_{k-1} \circ \cdots \circ \pi_1(x) = y$ and so $y$ is the correct output for $\widehat{\mathsf{MPJ}}_{N,k}^{\mathsf{perm}}$.

The communication consists of the advice string written by Player $P_0$ and a partial reply for each query, giving a total of $S + T\lceil \log N \rceil$. (The last player writes the $\lceil \log N \rceil$-bit output, but does not need to write the response to the $T$-th query). $\qquad\qquad\qquad\qquad\qquad\qquad\qquad\qquad\qquad\qquad\qquad\qquad\qquad\square$

*Proof of Theorem 10.* To prove Theorem 10, we instantiate Lemma 12 using Hellman's cycle-walking algorithm [46], which we recall in the full version of this paper. The algorithm inverts permutations using $T$ queries and $S$ bits of advice, for every choice of $S$ and $T$ such that $ST \geq 2N\lceil \log N + 1 \rceil$. Furthermore the algorithm is $T$-round adaptive. Specifically, for $k \leq \sqrt{N} + 2$, using Hellman's algorithm with $T = k - 2$ and $S = \lceil (2N \log N)/T \rceil$ gives a protocol with communication $O((N/k) \log N)$. For $k > \sqrt{N} + 2$, we use Hellman's algorithm with $T = \sqrt{N}$ and $S = 2\sqrt{N}(\lceil \log N \rceil + 1)$ to find that $\mathsf{CC}^1(\widehat{\mathsf{MPJ}}_{N,k}^{\mathsf{perm}}) \leq O(\sqrt{N} \log N)$. Then, applying Lemma 11 lets us conclude that $\mathsf{CC}^1(\mathsf{MPJ}_{N,k}^{\mathsf{perm}}) \leq O(\sqrt{N} \log N)$. $\qquad\square$

*Remark 13 (The function case).* We might hope to show that a good function-inversion algorithm, such as that of Fiat and Naor [28], implies a good protocol for the *general* multiparty pointer-jumping problem, in which each player $i$ has an arbitrary function $f_i$ (which may not be a permutation) written on her forehead. We do not know how to prove such a result. The problem is that the reduction of Lemma 12 requires that the composition $f_1^{-1} \circ f_2^{-1} \circ \cdots \circ f_{k-1}^{-1}$ is a function, and this is not true in the general case. (In contrast, when $f_1, \ldots, f_k$ are all permutations it holds that $f_1^{-1} \circ f_2^{-1} \circ \cdots \circ f_{k-1}^{-1}$ is a permutation.) Since several upper bounds for the permutation variant of the pointer-jumping problem [11,20,63] have led to subsequent upper bounds for the unrestricted case [11,14], there is still hope to generalize the result.

# 5   From Cryptanalysis to Data-Structures

In this section, we show how to apply the Fiat-Naor algorithm for function inversion [28] to obtain the best known data structure for the *systematic substring-search* problem [22,29,30,40,41], in a wide range of parameter regimes. As a consequence of this connection, we show that the open problem of improving the known lower bounds on function inversion is equivalent to the open problem in the data-structure literature of whether it is possible to improve the known lower bounds for systematic substring search.

In the systematic substring-search problem, we are given a bitstring of length $N$ ("the text") and a bitstring of length $P \ll N$ ("the pattern"). If the pattern appears in the text, we must output an index $i \in [N]$ into the text at which the pattern begins. We take the pattern length to be $P = \Theta(\log N)$.

An algorithm for systematic substring search is a two-part algorithm $\mathcal{A} = (\mathcal{A}_0, \mathcal{A}_1)$. The preprocessing algorithm $\mathcal{A}_0$ takes as input only the text, may perform arbitrary computation on it, and then outputs an $S$-bit "index" into the text. The online algorithm $\mathcal{A}_1$ takes as input the index and the pattern, queries $T$ bits of the text, and then outputs the location of pattern in the text, if one exists.

By applying the Fiat-Naor function inversion algorithm [28], we obtain the *best known algorithm* for systematic substring search on texts of length $N$ when using an index of size $O(N^\epsilon)$ bits, for any $\epsilon < 1$. Gál and Miltersen [30] asked for a strong lower bound against search algorithms using an $O(N/\text{polylog } N)$-bit index, and we answer this question by giving an upper bound that beats their hypothetical lower bound. This connection also gives evidence that finding a faster algorithm for systematic substring search will require a cryptanalytic breakthrough.

*Known Lower Bounds.* Demaine and López-Ortiz [22] prove that on texts of length $N$ with pattern length $P = \Theta(\log N)$, any algorithm that uses an $S$-bit index and makes $T = o(P^2/\log P)$ queries in the online phase must satisfy $ST = \Omega(N \log N)$. Golynski [40,41] gives a stronger version of this bound that applies even for larger $T = o(\sqrt{N}/\log N)$. Gál and Miltersen prove a slightly weaker bound but that holds for all values of $T$. They show that for certain pattern lengths $P = \Theta(\log N)$, and any choice of $T$, any algorithm must satisfy $ST = \Omega(N/\log N)$.[1]

The main technical result of this section is the following theorem, which we prove in the full version of this paper.

**Theorem 14.** *For any integer $N \in \mathbb{Z}^{>0}$ and integral constant $c > 2$, if there is an algorithm for systematic substring search on texts of length $cN \cdot \lceil \log N \rceil$ with pattern length $c \cdot \lceil \log N \rceil$ that uses an $S$-bit index and reads $T$ bits of the text in its online phase, then there is a black-box algorithm for inverting functions $f\colon [N] \to [N]$ that uses $S$ bits of advice and makes $T$ online queries.*

*For any integer $N \in \mathbb{Z}^{>0}$, if there is a black-box algorithm for inverting functions $f\colon [2N] \to [2N]$ that uses $S$ bits of advice and $T$ queries, then, for any integral constant $c > 1$, there is an algorithm for systematic substring search on texts of length $N$ with pattern length $c \cdot \lceil \log N \rceil$ that uses an $\widetilde{O}(S)$-bit index and reads $\widetilde{O}(T)$ bits of the text in its online phase.*

*Remark 15.* It is possible to make the preprocessing time $\widetilde{O}(N)$ by allowing the algorithm to fail with probability $O(1/N)$ over the randomness of the preprocessing phase. Similarly, the online running time (in addition to the query complexity) is $\widetilde{O}(T)$.

---

[1] Gál and Miltersen in fact prove their lower bound against algorithms that solve the *decision* version of the problem, rather than the *search* version that we describe here. Using an argument similar to that of Theorem 8, which treats the case of black-box PRG distinguishers, we can show that these problems are equivalent up to log factors when we demand constant success probability.

*Proof Idea.* The full proof appears in the full version of this paper. In the first part, we must use a substring-search algorithm to invert a function $f\colon [N] \to [N]$. The idea is to construct a text $\tau$ of length $\Theta(N \log N)$ by writing out the evaluation of $f$ at all points in its domain, in order, with a few extra bits added as delimiters. To invert a point $y \in [N]$, we use the substring search algorithm to find the location at which $y$ appears in the text $\tau$. This location immediately yields a preimage of $y$ under $f$. Demaine and López-Ortiz [22] use a similar—but more sophisticated encoding—on the way to proving a data-structure lower bound for systematic substring search. Their encoding maps a function $f\colon [N] \to [N]$ into a string of length $(1 + o(1))N \log N$, while ours maps $f$ into a string of length $3N \log N$.

In the second part, we must use a function-inversion algorithm to solve substring search on a text $\tau$ of length $N$ with pattern length $P = c \cdot \lceil \log N \rceil$, for some constant $c > 1$. To do so, we define a function $f'\colon [N] \to [N^c]$ such that $f'(i)$ is equal to the length-$P$ substring that starts from the $i$th bit of the text $\tau$. Given a pattern string $\sigma = \{0,1\}^P$, finding the inverse of $y$ under $f'$ is enough to locate the position of the pattern string $\sigma$ in the text $\tau$. The only remaining challenge is that $f'$ is length-increasing, rather than length-preserving. We then use universal hashing to reduce the problem of inverting length-increasing functions to the problem of inverting length-preserving functions, which completes the proof.                                                                 □

We now apply Theorem 14 to construct a new algorithm for systematic substring search that resolves an open question of Gál and Miltersen. In their 2007 paper, Gál and Miltersen say that "it would be nice to prove a lower bound of, say, the form," $T < N/\text{polylog}\, N \Rightarrow S > N/\text{polylog}\, N$ (using our notation) for systematic substring search [30]. Goyal and Saks [42] use an elegant argument to show that the specific technique of Gál and Miltersen cannot prove this lower bound. As a corollary of Theorem 14, we construct an algorithm for substring search that beats the hypothetical lower bound.

**Corollary 16.** *For any integral constant $c > 1$ there is an algorithm for systematic substring search on texts of length $N$ with pattern length $c \cdot \lceil \log N \rceil$, that uses an $S$-bit index, reads $T$ bits of the text in its online phase, and achieves the trade-off $S^3 T = \widetilde{O}(N^3)$.*

*Proof.* Theorem 14 shows that systematic substring search on strings of length $N$ with pattern length $\Theta(\log N)$ reduces to the problem of inverting arbitrary functions $f\colon [N] \to [N]$. The inversion algorithm of Fiat and Naor [28] inverts such functions $f$ achieving the desired complexity bounds.                                 □

In particular, we get an algorithm that solves systematic substring search using an index size and time satisfying $S = T = \widetilde{O}(N^{3/4})$, for strings of length $N$ and patterns of length $\Theta(\log N)$. Furthermore, this connection, along with the results of Sect. 2.2, shows that improving on the $ST = \widetilde{\Omega}(N)$ bound of Gál and Miltersen will require advances in techniques for proving lower bounds on the power of depth-two circuits.

# 6  Discussion and Future Directions

In this final section, we discuss a few directions for future work.

## 6.1  Which Lower-Bound Techniques Can Work?

In Sect. 2, we showed that improving Yao's lower bound on function-inversion algorithms requires new circuit lower bounds in the common-bits model. What potential approaches do we have to prove such a lower bound?

**Function Inversion and Yao's "Box Problem."** Yao's "box problem" [60,77] is a preprocessing problem that is closely related to the function-inversion problem. In the box problem, we are given oracle access to a function $f\colon [N] \to \{0,1\}$. First, we get to look at all of $f$ and write down an $S$-bit advice string $\mathsf{st}_f$. Later on, we are given our advice string $\mathsf{st}_f$ and a point $x \in [N]$. We may then make $T$ queries to $f$, provided that we do not query $f(x)$, and we must then output a value $y \in \{0,1\}$ such that $y = f(x)$.

The box problem is in some sense the dual of the function-inversion problem: we are given an $f$-oracle and we must compute $f$ in the *forward* direction, rather than in the *inverse* direction. The same $ST = \widetilde{\Omega}(N)$ lower bound applies to both problems [77]. However, in contrast to the inversion problem, for which we suspect that good parallel (i.e., non-adaptive) algorithms do not exist, the natural algorithm for the box problem is *already* non-adaptive and achieves $ST = O(N \log N)$.[2]

Puzzlingly, the two main techniques for proving time-space lower bounds *do not distinguish* between the function-inversion problem and Yao's box problem. In particular, the known lower bounds use compression [21,23,33,77] or bit-fixing [18,19,65]. Both techniques essentially look at the information that the oracle queries and their replies give on the pair $(x, f(x))$ induced by the challenge, regardless of whether the actual challenge is $x$, and the algorithm has to find $f(x)$ (as in the case of Yao's box problem), or the challenge is $y = f(x)$, and the algorithm has to find $x = f^{-1}(y)$ (as in the case of the inversion problem).

Since there is an $ST = \widetilde{O}(N)$ *upper bound* for Yao's box problem, then any method that proves a lower bound better than $ST = \Omega(N)$ for function inversion must not apply to the box problem. Therefore, a "sanity check" for any improved lower bound for the function-inversion problem is to verify that the same proof technique does not apply to Yao's box problem.

**Strong-Multiscale-Entropy.** Drucker [25] shows, at the very least, that improving lower bounds in the common-bits model will require new types of arguments. In particular, Jukna [50, Chapter 13], generalizing earlier arguments of Cherukhin [16] defined the "strong multiscale entropy" (SME) property of

---

[2] Divide $[N]$ into disjoint blocks of (at most) $T + 1$ points each. For each block, store the sum of the values of the function over all points in the block. In the online phase, query all the other points in the block given by the challenge point, and use the stored sum to recover the value of the function over the given challenge point.

Boolean Operators. Jukna proved that an operator on $n$ bits with the SME property cannot be computed by common-bits circuits of width $o(n^{1/2})$ and degree $o(n^{1/2})$. (These results are actually phrased in terms of the wire complexity of depth-two circuits with arbitrary gates, but the implications to the common-bits model are straightforward.)

Strengthening Jukna's lower bound on the circuit complexity of SME operators appeared to be one promising direction for progress on lower bounds. Thwarting this hope, Drucker constructs an explicit operator with the SME property that has circuits in the common-bits model of width $O(n^{1/2})$ and degree $O(n^{1/2})$. Thus, SME-type arguments alone are not strong enough to prove that an operator cannot be computed by circuits of width $O(n^{1/2+\epsilon})$ and degree $O(n^{1/2+\epsilon})$ for $\epsilon > 0$.

### 6.2 One-to-One Functions

Prompted by the fact that many cryptanalytic applications of function inversion only require inverting injective function, we initiated in Sect. 3 the study of injective function inversion. Though we take the first step by connecting this problem to the problem of distinguishing PRGs, the basic question remains: is it easier to invert a random injective function $f \colon [N] \to [M]$, for $N \ll M$, than it is to invert a random length-preserving function $f \colon [N] \to [N]$? A better-than-Hellman attack against injective functions would be remarkable. Or, can we prove that inverting injective functions is as hard as inverting random functions?

### 6.3 Barriers for Upper Bounds

Is there a barrier to getting an $S = T = o(N^{2/3})$ algorithm for function inversion? Barkan, Biham, and Shamir [5] prove a lower bound against a certain *restricted* class of Hellman-like algorithms, which suggests that better algorithms must use new techniques. It would be satisfying to show at least that improving Hellman's upper bound would result in a dramatic algorithmic improvement for a well-studied problem in another domain.

**Acknowledgments.** We would like to thank Dan Boneh for encouraging us to investigate whether Hellman's method can be improved and for his continued advice as we undertook this project. Iftach Haitner gave us meaningful guidance on our research process early on and, along with Ronen Shaltiel, suggested many possible approaches towards proving new lower bounds. Joshua Brakensiek, Joshua Brody, Clément Canonne, Andrew Drucker, Michael Kim, Peter Bro Miltersen, Ilya Mironov, Omer Reingold, Avishay Tal, Li-Yang Tan, and David Wu made a number of suggestions that improved the presentation of our results. Finally, we would like to thank the anonymous TCC reviewers for their many constructive comments. This work was supported by CISPA, DARPA, NSF, ONR, and the Simons Foundation.

## A    Proof of Lemma 11

The first step is to define a permutation $\pi_\beta \colon [N] \to [N]$, for every function $\beta \colon [N] \to \{0, 1\}$. We then use this permutation $\pi_\beta$ to convert a

Boolean-valued pointer-jumping instance $(x, \pi_1, \ldots, \pi_{k-1}, \beta)$ to an integer-valued pointer-jumping instance $(x, \pi_1, \ldots, \pi_{k-1}, \pi_\beta)$. Solving the integer-valued instance using a protocol for $\widehat{\mathsf{MPJ}}_{N,k}^{\mathsf{perm}}$ is then enough—with a few extra bits of communication—to solve the Boolean-valued instance of $\mathsf{MPJ}_{N,k}^{\mathsf{perm}}$.

**Table 1.** Example of the encoding procedure of Lemma 11. $N = 2^3$, and $\beta \colon [N] \to \{0,1\}$. Note that the last column is a permutation over the elements of $[N]$. Also note how $\beta$ can be recovered from $\pi_\beta(x)$ for all $x \neq 0$.

| $x$ | $\beta(x)$ | $(x\|_3, x\|_2, x\|_1)$ | $\beta(x\|_3)\beta(x\|_2)\beta(x\|_1)$ | $y = \pi_\beta(x)$ |
|---|---|---|---|---|
| 000 | 1 | $(100, 010, 001)$ | 001 | 100 |
| 001 | 1 | $(101, 011, 001)$ | 011 | 101 |
| 010 | 0 | $(110, 010, 001)$ | 101 | 000 |
| 011 | 1 | $(111, 011, 001)$ | 111 | 011 |
| 100 | 0 | $(100, 010, 001)$ | 001 | 010 |
| 101 | 0 | $(101, 011, 001)$ | 011 | 001 |
| 110 | 1 | $(110, 010, 001)$ | 101 | 100 |
| 111 | 1 | $(111, 011, 001)$ | 111 | 111 |

Towards constructing $\pi_\beta$, consider first the case when $N$ is a power of two. For $N = 2^n$, consider the following mapping from $\{0,1\}^N$ to permutations on $\{0, 1, \ldots, N-1\} = \{0,1\}^n$. On $\beta \colon \{0,1\}^n \to \{0,1\}$ we construct a permutation $\pi_\beta$ on $\{0,1\}^n$ as follows: let $x \in \{0,1\}^n$ and let $x = x_n x_{n-1} \ldots x_1$ be the binary representation of $x$. Set $\pi_\beta(x) = y = y_n y_{n-1} \ldots y_1$ defined by $y_i = \beta(x\|_i) \oplus x_i \oplus 1$ where $x\|_i = 0 \ldots 0 1 x_{i-1} x_{i-2} \ldots x_1$. The following two properties hold:

- The mapping $\pi_\beta$ defined above is a permutation. To see this let $x \neq x'$ be two distinct elements in $\{0,1\}^n$, and let $y = \pi_\beta(x)$ and $y' = \pi_\beta(x')$. Let $i \in [n]$ be the rightmost bit position on which $x$ and $x'$ differ. Then $x_i \neq x'_i$ but $x\|_i = x'\|_i$. Therefore $y_i = \beta(x\|_i) \oplus x_i \oplus 1 \neq \beta(x'\|_i) \oplus x'_i \oplus 1 = y'_i$, so $y \neq y'$.
- For any $x \in \{0,1\}^n$ such that $x = x_n \ldots x_1 \neq 0$, let $i$ be the leftmost bit position such that $x_i = 1$. It then holds that $\beta(x)$ is equal to the $i$th bit of $\pi_\beta(x)$.

Note that the latter property guarantees that the value of $\beta(x)$ for every $x \neq 0$ can be recovered from a single bit of $\pi_\beta(x)$.

For $N$ which is not a power of 2, we can view $N$ as a sum $\sum_{j=1}^{\ell} 2^{n_j}$ of at most $\lceil \log N \rceil$ powers of 2, and construct a permutation $\pi_\beta$ on $\{0, \ldots, N-1\} = \{0,1\}^{n_1} \cup \cdots \cup \{0,1\}^{n_\ell}$ as a union of permutations on $\{0,1\}^{n_j}$. By the properties above, for all but $\ell = \lceil \log N \rceil$ *bad* points, the value of $\beta$ can be recovered from the corresponding value of $\pi_\beta$. Note that the set of bad points depends only on $N$ and not on $\beta$. We give an example of this encoding procedure in Table 1.

Therefore, given a communication protocol for $\widehat{\mathsf{MPJ}}_{N,k}^{\mathsf{perm}}$, we construct a protocol for $\mathsf{MPJ}_{N,k}^{\mathsf{perm}}$ as follows. Let $\beta \in \{0,1\}^N$ be the input (on the forehead) of the last player. Each of the first $k-1$ players computes the permutation $\pi_\beta$ from $\beta$ according to the mapping above. The first player also writes on the blackboard the value of $\beta$ evaluated on all of the bad points of $\pi_\beta$. The players then run the protocol for $\widehat{\mathsf{MPJ}}_{N,k}^{\mathsf{perm}}$ on the instance $(x, \pi_1, \ldots, \pi_{k-2}, \pi_\beta)$.

The last player computes the output of the original protocol $\pi_\beta \circ \pi_{k-2} \circ \cdots \circ \pi_1(x) = \pi_\beta(\hat{x}) \in \{0, 1, \ldots, N-1\}$ where $\hat{x} = \pi_{k-2} \circ \cdots \circ \pi_1(x)$. If $\hat{x}$ is not a bad point she can recover and output $\beta \circ \pi_{k-2} \circ \cdots \circ \pi_1(x) = \beta(\hat{x}) \in \{0, 1\}$ from $\pi_\beta(\hat{x})$. Otherwise, if $\hat{x}$ is a bad point, she outputs the value $\beta(\hat{x})$, which the first player wrote on the blackboard.

The new protocol increases the communication complexity of the original protocol by $\lceil \log N \rceil$.

# References

1. Abusalah, H., Alwen, J., Cohen, B., Khilko, D., Pietrzak, K., Reyzin, L.: Beyond Hellman's time-memory trade-offs with applications to proofs of space. In: Takagi, T., Peyrin, T. (eds.) ASIACRYPT 2017. LNCS, vol. 10625, pp. 357–379. Springer, Cham (2017). https://doi.org/10.1007/978-3-319-70697-9_13
2. Alon, N., Goldreich, O., Håstad, J., Peralta, R.: Simple construction of almost k-wise independent random variables. Random Struct. Algorithms 3(3), 289–304 (1992). https://doi.org/10.1002/rsa.3240030308
3. Babai, L., Hayes, T.P., Kimmel, P.G.: The cost of the missing bit: communication complexity with help. Combinatorica 21(4), 455–488 (2001). https://doi.org/10.1007/s004930100009
4. Barbay, J., He, M., Munro, J.I., Satti, S.R.: Succinct indexes for strings, binary relations and multilabeled trees. ACM Trans. Algorithms 7(4), 52:1–52:27 (2011). https://doi.org/10.1145/2000807.2000820
5. Barkan, E., Biham, E., Shamir, A.: Rigorous bounds on cryptanalytic time/memory tradeoffs. In: Dwork, C. (ed.) CRYPTO 2006. LNCS, vol. 4117, pp. 1–21. Springer, Heidelberg (2006). https://doi.org/10.1007/11818175_1
6. Beigel, R., Tarui, J.: On ACC. Comput. Complex. 4, 350–366 (1994). https://doi.org/10.1007/BF01263423
7. Biryukov, A., Shamir, A.: Cryptanalytic time/memory/data tradeoffs for stream ciphers. In: Okamoto, T. (ed.) ASIACRYPT 2000. LNCS, vol. 1976, pp. 1–13. Springer, Heidelberg (2000). https://doi.org/10.1007/3-540-44448-3_1
8. Biryukov, A., Shamir, A., Wagner, D.: Real time cryptanalysis of A5/1 on a PC. In: Goos, G., Hartmanis, J., van Leeuwen, J., Schneier, B. (eds.) FSE 2000. LNCS, vol. 1978, pp. 1–18. Springer, Heidelberg (2001). https://doi.org/10.1007/3-540-44706-7_1
9. Boyle, E., Naor, M.: Is there an oblivious RAM lower bound? In: ITCS (2016). https://doi.org/10.1145/2840728.2840761
10. Brody, J.: The maximum communication complexity of multi-party pointer jumping. In: CCC (2009). https://doi.org/10.1109/CCC.2009.30
11. Brody, J., Chakrabarti, A.: Sublinear communication protocols for multi-party pointer jumping and a related lower bound. In: STACS (2008). https://doi.org/10.4230/LIPIcs.STACS.2008.1341

12. Brody, J., Dziembowski, S., Faust, S., Pietrzak, K.: Position-based cryptography and multiparty communication complexity. In: Kalai, Y., Reyzin, L. (eds.) TCC 2017. LNCS, vol. 10677, pp. 56–81. Springer, Cham (2017). https://doi.org/10.1007/978-3-319-70500-2_3

13. Brody, J., Larsen, K.G.: Adapt or die: polynomial lower bounds for non-adaptive dynamic data structures. Theory Comput. **11**(19), 471–489 (2015). https://doi.org/10.4086/toc.2015.v011a019

14. Brody, J., Sanchez, M.: Dependent random graphs and multi-party pointer jumping. In: APPROX/RANDOM (2015). https://doi.org/10.4230/LIPIcs.APPROX-RANDOM.2015.606

15. Chandra, A.K., Furst, M.L., Lipton, R.J.: Multi-party protocols. In: STOC (1983). https://doi.org/10.1145/800061.808737

16. Cherukhin, D.Y.: Lower bounds for the complexity of Boolean circuits of finite depth with arbitrary elements. Discret. Math. Appl. **23**(4), 39–47 (2011). https://doi.org/10.1515/dma.2011.031

17. Clark, D.R., Munro, J.I.: Efficient suffix trees on secondary storage. In: SODA (1996)

18. Coretti, S., Dodis, Y., Guo, S.: Non-uniform bounds in the random-permutation, ideal-cipher, and generic-group models. In: Shacham, H., Boldyreva, A. (eds.) CRYPTO 2018. LNCS, vol. 10991, pp. 693–721. Springer, Cham (2018). https://doi.org/10.1007/978-3-319-96884-1_23

19. Coretti, S., Dodis, Y., Guo, S., Steinberger, J.: Random oracles and non-uniformity. In: Nielsen, J.B., Rijmen, V. (eds.) EUROCRYPT 2018. LNCS, vol. 10820, pp. 227–258. Springer, Cham (2018). https://doi.org/10.1007/978-3-319-78381-9_9

20. Damm, C., Jukna, S., Sgall, J.: Some bounds on multiparty communication complexity of pointer jumping. Comput. Complex. **7**(2), 109–127 (1998). https://doi.org/10.1007/PL00001595

21. De, A., Trevisan, L., Tulsiani, M.: Time space tradeoffs for attacks against one-way functions and PRGs. In: Rabin, T. (ed.) CRYPTO 2010. LNCS, vol. 6223, pp. 649–665. Springer, Heidelberg (2010). https://doi.org/10.1007/978-3-642-14623-7_35

22. Demaine, E.D., López-Ortiz, A.: A linear lower bound on index size for text retrieval. J. Algorithms **48**(1), 2–15 (2003). https://doi.org/10.1016/S0196-6774(03)00043-9

23. Dodis, Y., Guo, S., Katz, J.: Fixing cracks in the concrete: random oracles with auxiliary input, revisited. In: Coron, J.-S., Nielsen, J.B. (eds.) EUROCRYPT 2017. LNCS, vol. 10211, pp. 473–495. Springer, Cham (2017). https://doi.org/10.1007/978-3-319-56614-6_16

24. Dodis, Y., Steinberger, J.: Message authentication codes from unpredictable block ciphers. In: Halevi, S. (ed.) CRYPTO 2009. LNCS, vol. 5677, pp. 267–285. Springer, Heidelberg (2009). https://doi.org/10.1007/978-3-642-03356-8_16

25. Drucker, A.: Limitations of lower-bound methods for the wire complexity of Boolean operators. In: CCC (2012). https://doi.org/10.1109/CCC.2012.39

26. Dvir, Z., Golovnev, A., Weinstein, O.: Static data structure lower bounds imply rigidity. In: STOC (2019). https://doi.org/10.1145/3313276.3316348

27. Fiat, A., Naor, M.: Rigorous time/space tradeoffs for inverting functions. In: STOC (1991). https://doi.org/10.1145/103418.103473

28. Fiat, A., Naor, M.: Rigorous time/space trade-offs for inverting functions. SIAM J. Comput. **29**(3), 790–803 (1999). https://doi.org/10.1137/S0097539795280512

29. Gál, A., Miltersen, P.B.: The cell probe complexity of succinct data structures. In: ICALP (2003). https://doi.org/10.1007/3-540-45061-0_28

30. Gál, A., Miltersen, P.B.: The cell probe complexity of succinct data structures. Theoret. Comput. Sci. **379**(3), 405–417 (2007). https://doi.org/10.1016/j.tcs.2007.02.047

31. Geary, R.F., Raman, R., Raman, V.: Succinct ordinal trees with level-ancestor queries. ACM Trans. Algorithms **2**(4), 510–534 (2006). https://doi.org/10.1145/1198513.1198516

32. Gennaro, R., Gertner, Y., Katz, J., Trevisan, L.: Bounds on the efficiency of generic cryptographic constructions. SIAM J. Comput. **35**(1), 217–246 (2005). https://doi.org/10.1137/S0097539704443276

33. Gennaro, R., Trevisan, L.: Lower bounds on the efficiency of generic cryptographic constructions. In: FOCS (2000). https://doi.org/10.1109/SFCS.2000.892119

34. Goldreich, O.: Towards a theory of software protection and simulation by oblivious RAMs. In: STOC (1987). https://doi.org/10.1145/28395.28416

35. Goldreich, O.: Foundations of Cryptography, vol. 1. Cambridge University Press, New York (2006)

36. Goldreich, O., Krawczyk, H., Luby, M.: On the existence of pseudorandom generators. SIAM J. Comput. **22**(6), 1163–1175 (1993). https://doi.org/10.1137/0222069

37. Goldreich, O., Levin, L.A.: A hard-core predicate for all one-way functions. In: STOC (1989). https://doi.org/10.1145/73007.73010

38. Goldreich, O., Ostrovsky, R.: Software protection and simulation on oblivious RAMs. J. ACM **43**(3), 431–473 (1996). https://doi.org/10.1145/233551.233553

39. Golovnev, A., Guo, S., Horel, T., Park, S., Vaikuntanathan, V.: 3SUM with preprocessing: algorithms, lower bounds and cryptographic applications. arXiv:1907.08355 [cs.DS] (2019). http://arxiv.org/abs/1907.08355

40. Golynski, A.: Stronger lower bounds for text searching and polynomial evaluation (2007). https://cs.uwaterloo.ca/research/tr/2007/CS-2007-25.pdf

41. Golynski, A.: Cell probe lower bounds for succinct data structures. In: SODA (2009). https://doi.org/10.1137/1.9781611973068.69

42. Goyal, N., Saks, M.: A parallel search game. Random Struct. Algorithms **27**(2), 227–234 (2005). https://doi.org/10.1002/rsa.20068

43. Grossi, R., Orlandi, A., Raman, R.: Optimal trade-offs for succinct string indexes. In: ICALP (2010). https://doi.org/10.1007/978-3-642-14165-2_57

44. Haitner, I., Mazor, N., Oshman, R., Reingold, O., Yehudayoff, A.: On the communication complexity of key-agreement protocols. In: ITCS (2019). https://doi.org/10.4230/LIPIcs.ITCS.2019.40

45. He, M., Munro, J.I., Satti, S.R.: Succinct ordinal trees based on tree covering. ACM Trans. Algorithms **8**(4), 42:1–42:32 (2012). https://doi.org/10.1145/2344422.2344432

46. Hellman, M.: A cryptanalytic time-memory trade-off. IEEE Trans. Inf. Theory **26**(4), 401–406 (1980). https://doi.org/10.1109/TIT.1980.1056220

47. Håstad, J., Goldmann, M.: On the power of small-depth threshold circuits. Comput. Complex. **1**, 113–129 (1991). https://doi.org/10.1007/BF01272517

48. Impagliazzo, R.: Relativized separations of worst-case and average-case complexities for NP. In: CCC (2011). https://doi.org/10.1109/CCC.2011.34

49. Jacobson, G.: Space-efficient static trees and graphs. In: FOCS (1989). https://doi.org/10.1109/SFCS.1989.63533

50. Jukna, S.: Boolean Function Complexity. Algorithms and Combinatorics, vol. 27. Springer, Heidelberg (2012). https://doi.org/10.1007/978-3-642-24508-4

51. Jukna, S., Schnitger, G.: Min-rank conjecture for log-depth circuits. J. Comput.Syst. Sci. **77**(6), 1023–1038 (2011). https://doi.org/10.1016/j.jcss.2009.09.003

52. Kopelowitz, T., Porat, E.: The strong 3SUM-INDEXING conjecture is false. arXiv:1907.11206 [cs.DS] (2019). http://arxiv.org/abs/1907.11206
53. Kushilevitz, E., Nisan, N.: Communication Complexity. Cambridge University Press, New York (1997)
54. Larsen, K.G., Nielsen, J.B.: Yes, there is an oblivious RAM lower bound!. In: Shacham, H., Boldyreva, A. (eds.) CRYPTO 2018. LNCS, vol. 10992, pp. 523–542. Springer, Cham (2018). https://doi.org/10.1007/978-3-319-96881-0_18
55. Levin, L.A.: One-way functions and pseudorandom generators. Combinatorica **7**(4), 357–363 (1987). https://doi.org/10.1007/BF02579323
56. Liang, H.: Optimal collapsing protocol for multiparty pointer jumping. Theory Comput. Syst. **54**(1), 13–23 (2014). https://doi.org/10.1007/s00224-013-9476-x
57. Miltersen, P.B.: On the cell probe complexity of polynomial evaluation. Theoret. Comput. Sci. **143**(1), 167–174 (1995). https://doi.org/10.1016/0304-3975(95)80032-5
58. Munro, J.I., Raman, R., Raman, V., Rao, S.S.: Succinct representations of permutations and functions. Theoret. Comput. Sci. **438**, 74–88 (2012). https://doi.org/10.1016/j.tcs.2012.03.005
59. Narayanan, A., Shmatikov, V.: Fast dictionary attacks on passwords using time-space tradeoff. In: CCS (2005). https://doi.org/10.1145/1102120.1102168
60. Nayebi, A., Aaronson, S., Belovs, A., Trevisan, L.: Quantum lower bound for inverting a permutation with advice. Quantum Inf. Comput. **15**(11–12), 901–913 (2015)
61. Oechslin, P.: Making a faster cryptanalytic time-memory trade-off. In: Boneh, D. (ed.) CRYPTO 2003. LNCS, vol. 2729, pp. 617–630. Springer, Heidelberg (2003). https://doi.org/10.1007/978-3-540-45146-4_36
62. Ostrovsky, R.: Efficient computation on oblivious RAMs. In: STOC (1990). https://doi.org/10.1145/100216.100289
63. Pudlák, P., Rödl, V., Sgall, J.: Boolean circuits, tensor ranks, and communication complexity. SIAM J. Comput. **26**(3), 605–633 (1997). https://doi.org/10.1137/S0097539794264809
64. Sadakane, K., Grossi, R.: Squeezing succinct data structures into entropy bounds. In: SODA (2006). https://doi.org/10.1145/1109557.1109693
65. Unruh, D.: Random oracles and auxiliary input. In: Menezes, A. (ed.) CRYPTO 2007. LNCS, vol. 4622, pp. 205–223. Springer, Heidelberg (2007). https://doi.org/10.1007/978-3-540-74143-5_12
66. Valiant, L.G.: Graph-theoretic arguments in low-level complexity. In: Gruska, J. (ed.) MFCS 1977. LNCS, vol. 53, pp. 162–176. Springer, Heidelberg (1977). https://doi.org/10.1007/3-540-08353-7_135
67. Valiant, L.G.: Why is Boolean complexity theory difficult. In: London Mathematical Society Lecture Note Series, vol. 169, pp. 84–94 (1992). https://doi.org/10.1017/cbo9780511526633.008
68. Viola, E.: On the power of small-depth computation. Found. Trends Theoret. Comput. Sci. **5**(1), 1–72 (2009). https://doi.org/10.1561/0400000033
69. Viola, E.: Lower bounds for data structures with space close to maximum imply circuit lower bounds. Electronic Colloquium on Computational Complexity (ECCC), Report 2018/186 (2018)
70. Viola, E., Wigderson, A.: One-way multiparty communication lower bound for pointer jumping with applications. Combinatorica **29**(6), 719–743 (2009). https://doi.org/10.1007/s00493-009-2667-z
71. Wee, H.: On obfuscating point functions. In: STOC (2005). https://doi.org/10.1145/1060590.1060669

72. Weiss, M., Wichs, D.: Is there an oblivious RAM lower bound for online reads? Cryptology ePrint Archive, Report 2018/619 (2018)
73. Weiss, M., Wichs, D.: Is there an oblivious RAM lower bound for online reads? In: Beimel, A., Dziembowski, S. (eds.) TCC 2018. LNCS, vol. 11240, pp. 603–635. Springer, Cham (2018). https://doi.org/10.1007/978-3-030-03810-6_22
74. Yao, A.C.: Some complexity questions related to distributive computing (preliminary report). In: STOC (1979). https://doi.org/10.1145/800135.804414
75. Yao, A.C.: Should tables be sorted? J. ACM **28**(3), 615–628 (1981). https://doi.org/10.1145/322261.322274
76. Yao, A.C.: Theory and applications of trapdoor functions. In: FOCS (1982). https://doi.org/10.1109/SFCS.1982.45
77. Yao, A.C.: Coherent functions and program checkers (extended abstract). In: STOC (1990). https://doi.org/10.1145/100216.100226
78. Yao, A.C.: On ACC and threshold circuits. In: FOCS (1990). https://doi.org/10.1109/FSCS.1990.89583

# On the Complexity of Collision Resistant Hash Functions: New and Old Black-Box Separations

Nir Bitansky[1][(⊠)] and Akshay Degwekar[2]

[1] Tel Aviv University, Tel Aviv, Israel
nirbitan@tau.ac.il
[2] MIT, Cambridge, MA, USA
akshayd@alum.mit.edu

**Abstract.** The complexity of collision-resistant hash functions has been long studied in the theory of cryptography. While we often think about them as a Minicrypt primitive, black-box separations demonstrate that constructions from one-way functions are unlikely. Indeed, theoretical constructions of collision-resistant hash functions are based on rather structured assumptions.

We make two contributions to this study:

1. *A New Separation:* We show that collision-resistant hashing does not imply hard problems in the class Statistical Zero Knowledge in a black-box way.
2. *New Proofs:* We show new proofs for the results of Simon, ruling out black-box reductions of collision-resistant hashing to one-way permutations, and of Asharov and Segev, ruling out black-box reductions to indistinguishability obfuscation. The new proofs are quite different from the previous ones and are based on simple *coupling arguments*.

## 1 Introduction

*Collision-resistant hash functions* (CRHFs) are perhaps one of the most studied and widely used cryptographic primitives. Their applications range from basic ones like "hash-and-sign" [Dam87, Mer89] and statistically hiding commitments [DPP93, HM96] to more advanced ones like verifiable delegation of data and computation [Kil92, BEG+94] and hardness results in complexity theory [MP91, KNY17].

**Constructions.** Collision resistance is trivially satisfied by random oracles and in common practice, to achieve it, we heuristically rely on unstructured hash functions like SHA. Accordingly, we often think of CRHFs as a creature of *Minicrypt*, the realm of symmetric key cryptography [Imp95]. However, when considering theoretical constructions with formal reductions, collision resistance is only known based on problems with some algebraic structure, like Factoring, Discrete Log, and different short vector and bounded distance decoding

© International Association for Cryptologic Research 2019
D. Hofheinz and A. Rosen (Eds.): TCC 2019, LNCS 11891, pp. 422–450, 2019.
https://doi.org/10.1007/978-3-030-36030-6_17

problems (in lattices or in binary codes) [Dam87, GGH96, PR06, LM06, AHI+17, YZW+17, BLVW19]. Generic constructions are known from claw-free permutations [Dam87, Rus95], homomorphic primitives [OK91, IKO05], and private information retrieval [IKO05], which likewise are only known from similar structured assumptions. An exception is a recent work by Holmgren and Lombardi [HL18] which constructs CRHFs from a new assumption called *one-way product functions*. These are functions where efficient adversaries succeed in inverting two random images with probability at most $2^{-n-\omega(\log n)}$. Indeed, this assumption does not explicitly require any sort of algebraic structure.

**Understanding the Complexity of CRHFs.** In light of the above, it is natural to study what are the minimal assumptions under which CRHFs can be constructed, and whether they require any sort of special structure. Here Simon [Sim98] provided an explanation for our failure to base CRHFs on basic Minicrypt primitives like one-way functions or one-way permutations. He showed that there are no black-box reductions of CRHFs to these primitives. In fact, Asharov and Segev [AS15] demonstrated that the difficulty in constructing CRHFs from general assumptions runs far deeper. They showed that CRHFs cannot be black-box reduced even to *indistinguishability obfuscation* (and one-way permutations), and accordingly not to anyone of the many primitives it implies, like public key encryption, oblivious transfer, or functional encryption.

**CRHFs and SZK.** An aspect common to many CRHF constructions is that they rely on assumptions that imply hardness in the class SZK. Introduced by Goldwasser, Micali and Rackoff [GMR85], SZK is the class of *promise problems* with statistical zero-knowledge proofs. Indeed, SZK hardness is known to follow from various algebraic problems that lead to CRHFs, such as Discrete Logarithms [GK93], Quadratic Residuosity [GMR85], and Lattice Problems [GG98, MV03], as well as from generic primitives that lead to CRHFs such as homomorphic encryption [BL13], lossy functions [PVW08], and computational private information retrieval [LV16].

The formal relation between SZK and CRHFs is still not well understood. As possible evidence that SZK hardness may be sufficient to obtain collision resistance, Komargodski and Yogev [KY18] show that average-case hardness in SZK implies a relaxations of CRHFs known as *distributional* CRHFs. Applebaum and Raykov [AR16] show that CRHFs are implied by average-case hardness in a subclass of SZK of problems that have a *perfect randomized encoding*. Berman et al. [BDRV18] showed that average-case hardness of a variant of entropy approximation, a complete problem for the class of Non-Interactive SZK (NISZK), suffices to construct yet a different relaxation known as *multi-collision resistance*.

Is hardness in SZK necessary for CRHFs? Our perception of CRHFs as a Minicrypt primitive, as well as the result by Holmgren and Lombardi mentioned above, suggest that this should not be the case. However, we do not know how to prove this. Meaningfully formalizing a statement of the form "CRHFs do not require SZK hardness" requires care—it is commonly believed that SZK *does* contain hard problems, and if this is the case then formally, CRHFs (or any other assumption for that matter) imply hardness in SZK. To capture this statement we again resort to the methodology of black-box separations; that is, we aim to prove that hard problems in SZK cannot be obtained from CRHFs in a black-box way.

Recent work by Bitansky, Degwekar, and Vaikuntanathan [BDV17] showed that a host of primitives, essentially, all primitives known to follow from IO, do not lead to hard problems in SZK through black-box reductions. Their separation, however, does not imply a separation from CRHFs; indeed, CRHFs are not known to follow from IO, and in fact according to Asharov and Segev [AS15], cannot in a black-box way.

## 1.1  This Work

In this work, we close the above gap, proving that CRHFs do not imply hardness in SZK through black-box reductions.

**Theorem 1.1.** *There are no fully black-box reductions of any (even worst-case) hard problem in* SZK *to CRHFs.*

Here by *fully* black box we mean reductions where both the construction and the security proof are black box in the CRHF and the attacker, respectively. This is the common type of reductions used in cryptography. We refer the reader to the technical overview in Sect. 2 for more details.

**New Proofs of Simon and Asharov and Segev.** Our second contribution is new proofs for the results of Simon [Sim98], ruling out fully black-box reductions of CRHFs to OWPs,[1] and of Asharov and Segev [AS15], ruling out black-box reductions of CRHFs to OWPs and IO. The new proofs draw from ideas used in [BDV17]. They are based mostly on simple *coupling arguments* and are quite different from the original proofs.

## 1.2  More Related Work on Black-Box Separations

Following the seminal work of Impagliazzo and Rudich [IR89], black-box separations in cryptography have been thoroughly studied (see, e.g., [Rud88, KST99, GKM+00, GT00, GMR01, BT03, RTV04, HR04, GGKT05, Pas06, GMM07, BM09, HH09, BKSY11, DLMM11, KSS11, GKLM12, DHT12, Fis12, BBF13, Pas13, BB15, GHMM18]). Most of this study has been devoted to establishing separations between different cryptographic primitives and some of it to putting limitations on basing cryptographic primitives on NP-hardness [GG98, AGGM06, MX10, BL13, BB15, LV16].

Perhaps most relevant to our works are the works of Simon [Sim98], Asharov and Segev [AS15] and [BDV17] mentioned above, as well as the work by Haitner et al. [HHRS15] who gave an alternative proof for the Simon result (and extended it to the case of statistically-hiding commitments of low round complexity).

---

[1] Simon also ruled out a stronger type of reductions known as semi-black-box reductions [RTV04]. We only rule out the notion of fully black-box reductions described above.

We also note that [KNY18] claim to show that distributional CRHFs cannot be reduced to multi-collision resistant hash functions in a black box way, which given the black-box construction of distributional CRHFs from SZK hardness [KY18], would imply that SZK hardness cannot be obtained from multi-collision resistance in a black box way. However, for the time being there seems to be a gap in the proof of this claim [Per].

## 2    Techniques

We now give an overview of the techniques behind our results.

**Ruling Out Black-Box Reductions.** Most constructions in cryptography are fully black-box [RTV04], in the sense that both the construction and (security) reduction are black box. In a bit more detail, a fully black-box construction of a primitive $\mathcal{P}'$ from another primitive $\mathcal{P}$ consists of two algorithms: a construction C and a reduction R. The construction $C^{\mathcal{P}}$ implements $\mathcal{P}'$ for any valid oracle $\mathcal{P}$. The reduction $R^{A,\mathcal{P}}$, given oracle-access to any adversary A that breaks $C^{\mathcal{P}}$, breaks the underlying $\mathcal{P}$. Hence, breaking the instantiation $C^{\mathcal{P}}$ of $\mathcal{P}'$ is at least as hard as breaking $\mathcal{P}$ itself.

A common methodology to rule out fully black black-box constructions of a primitive $\mathcal{P}'$ from primitive $\mathcal{P}$ (see e.g., [Sim98,HR04,HHRS15]), is to demonstrate oracles $(\Gamma, A)$ such that:

- relative to $\Gamma$, there exists a construction $C^{\Gamma}$ realizing $\mathcal{P}$ that is secure in the presence of A,
- but *any* construction $C'^{\Gamma}$ realizing $\mathcal{P}'$ can be broken in the presence of A.

Indeed, if such oracles $(\Gamma, A)$ exist, then no efficient reduction will be able to use (as a black-box) the attacker A against $\mathcal{P}'$ to break $\mathcal{P}$ (as the construction of $\mathcal{P}$ is secure in the presence of A).

We now move on to explain how each of our results is shown in this framework.

### 2.1    Collision Resistance When SZK Is Easy

Our starting point is the work by [BDV17] who showed oracles relative to which Indistinguishability Obfuscation (IO) and One-Way Permutations (OWPs) exist and yet SZK is easy. We next recall their approach and explain why it falls short of separating CRHFs from SZK. We then explain the approach that we take in order to bridge this gap.

**Black-box Constructions of SZK Problems.** The [BDV17] modeling of problems in SZK follows the characterization of SZK by Sahai and Vadhan [SV03] through its complete Statistical Difference Problem (SDP). SDP is a promise problem, where given circuit samplers $(C_0, C_1)$, the task is to determine if the statistical distance between their respective output distributions is large ($>2/3$)

or small ($<1/3$). Accordingly, we can model a black-box construction of a statistical distance problem $\text{SDP}^{\Psi}$, relative to an oracle $\Psi$, defined by

$$\text{SDP}_Y^{\Psi} = \left\{ (C_0, C_1) : \text{SD}(C_0^{\Psi}, C_1^{\Psi}) \geq \frac{2}{3} \right\},$$

$$\text{SDP}_N^{\Psi} = \left\{ (C_0, C_1) : \text{SD}(C_0^{\Psi}, C_1^{\Psi}) \leq \frac{1}{3} \right\}.$$

Jumping ahead, our eventual goal will be construct an oracle $\Gamma = (\Psi, \mathsf{A})$ such that $\text{SDP}^{\Psi}$ is easy in the presence of $\mathsf{A}$, and yet $\Psi$ can be used to securely realize a CRHF, in the presence of $\mathsf{A}$. Here we naturally choose $\Psi$ to be a random shrinking function $f$, and for the SZK breaker $\mathsf{A}$ adopt the oracle $\text{SDO}^f$ from [BDV17]. $\text{SDO}^f$ is a randomized oracle that takes as input a pair of oracle-aided circuits $(C_0^{(\cdot)}, C_1^{(\cdot)})$, computes the statistical distance $s = \text{SD}(C_0^f, C_1^f)$, samples a random value $t \leftarrow (1/3, 2/3)$, and outputs:

$$\text{SDO}^f(C_0, C_1; t) := \begin{cases} N & \text{If } s < t \\ Y & \text{If } s \geq t \end{cases}.$$

This oracle is clearly sufficient to break (or rather, decide) $\text{SDP}^f$. The challenge is in showing that CRHFs exist in the presence of the oracle $\text{SDO}^f$, which may make exponentially many queries to $f$ when computing the statistical distance.

**One-Way Permutations in the Presence of SDO.** Toward proving the existence of CRHFs in the presence of SDO, we first recall the argument from [BDV17] as to why one-way permutations exist relative to SDO, and then explain why it falls short of establishing the existence of CRHFs.

Consider the oracle $\Gamma = (f, \text{SDO}^f)$, where $f$ is a random permutation. Showing that $f(x)$ is hard to invert for an adversary $\mathsf{A}^{f,\text{SDO}^f}(f(x))$ with access to $f$ and $\text{SDO}^f$ relies on two key observations:

1. Inverting $f$ requires detecting random *local changes*. Indeed, imagine an alternative experiment where we replace $f$ with a slightly perturbed function $f_{x' \to f(x)}$, which diverts a random $x'$ to $f(x)$. In this experiment, the attacker would not be able to distinguish $x$ from $x'$ and would output them with the exact same probability. Note, however, that if the attacker can invert $f$ in the real experiment (namely, output $x$) with noticeable probability, then this means that the probabilities of outputting $x$ and $x'$ in the original experiment must noticeably differ. Indeed, in the original experiment $x'$ is independent of the attacker's view. It is not hard to show that without access to the oracle $\text{SDO}^f$, such perturbations cannot be detected (this can be shown for example via a coupling argument, as we explain in more detail in Sect. 2.2).

2. The $\text{SDO}^f$ oracle itself, and thus $\mathsf{A}^{f,\text{SDO}^f}$, can be made oblivious to random, local changes. Hence, even given access to the $\text{SDO}^f$ oracle, the adversary cannot invert with non-trivial probability. This is shown based on the idea of "smoothening": any two circuits $(C_0^f, C_1^f)$ can be transformed into new

circuits that do not make any specific query $x$ with high probability. This allows arguing that even if we perturb $f$ at a given point, their statistical distance $s$ does not change by much. In particular, if $s$ is moderately far from the random threshold $t$, chosen by SDO, $s'$ the statistical distance of the perturbed circuits remains on the same side of $t$, which means that SDO's answer will remain invariant. Indeed, such "farness" holds with overwhelming probability over SDO's choice of $t$.

**What About Collision Resistance?** The above approach is not sufficient to argue that collisions are hard to find (when $f$ is replaced with a shrinking function). The reason is that collisions are "non-local" — they are abundant, and it is impossible to eliminate all of them in a shrinking function. In fact, as we shall show later on, a similar argument to the one above can be made to work relative to an oracle that trivially breaks CRHFs (this leads to our new proofs of the separations of CRHFs from OWPs and IO [Sim98, AS15]). Accordingly, a different approach is required.

**Our Approach: Understanding What Statistical Difference Oracles Reveal.** At high level, to show that collisions in $f$ are hard to find, we would like to argue that queries to $SDO^f$ leak no information about any $f(x)$, except for inputs $x$, which the adversary had already explicitly revealed by querying $f$ itself. This would essentially reduce the argument to the standard argument showing that random oracles are collision resistant—each new query collides with any previous query with probability at most $2^{-m}$, where $m$ is $f$'s output length. Overall, an attacker making $q$ queries cannot find a collision except with negligible probability $q^2 2^{-m}$.

However, showing that $SDO^f$ reveals nothing is too good to be true. Rather, we show that this is the case with overwhelming probability. That is, with overwhelming probability on any partial execution, the value $f(x)$ of any $x$ not explicitly queried within the execution is uniformly random. Roughly speaking, the property that such partial executions should satisfy is that all queries to $SDO^f$ satisfy smoothness and farness conditions similar to those discussed above. The essential observation is that when such conditions hold the answer of $SDO^f$ remains invariant not only to a random local change, but to *any* local change. In particular, a partial execution transcript satisfying these conditions would remain invariant if we change the value $f(x)$ for any $x$ not explicitly queried to any particular $y \neq f(x)$.

**A Note on Leakage from Random Oracles.** Our approach is in part inspired by the works of Unruh [Unr07] and Coretti et al. [CDGS18] on *random oracles with auxiliary information*. They show that revealing short auxiliary information about $f$ (so called leakage), essentially has the effect of fixing $f$ on a small set of values, while the rest of $f$ remains hidden. This does not suffice for us, because it does not restrict in any way which values are fixed. We need to ensure that *all* values not explicitly queried remain hidden even under the leakage from the oracle SDO. (Our argument is restricted though to the specific oracle SDO and does not say anything about arbitrary leakage.)

## 2.2  Proving Simon and Asharov-Segev: A Coupling-Based Approach

Next, we sketch the main ideas underlying the new proofs of Simon's result that OWPs do not imply CRHFs through fully black-box constructions, and the extended result by Asharov and Segev, which consider not only OWPs, but also IO. In this overview, we focus on the simpler result by Simon. We refer the reader to the full version of this paper for the extension to IO.

**Simon's Collision Finding Oracle.** The oracle $\Gamma = (f, \mathsf{Coll}^f)$ introduced by Simon consists of a random permutation $f$ and a collision finding oracle $\mathsf{Coll}^f$. The oracle $\mathsf{Coll}^f$ given a circuit $C^f$ returns a random $w$ along with a random element that collides with $w$; namely a random $w'$ in the preimage of $y = C^f(w)$. In particular, if the circuit $C$ is compressing, then the oracle will output a collision $w \neq w'$ with high probability, meaning that CRHFs cannot exist in its presence.

**Our Proof.** To prove that $\mathsf{Coll}$ does not help inverting $f$, Simon used careful conditional probability arguments, whereas Haitner et al. [HHRS15], and then Asharov and Segev [AS15] adding also IO to the picture, relied on a *compression and reconstruction argument*, originally due to Gennaro and Trevisan [GT00]. Our proof is inspired by the [BDV17] proof that the statistical distance oracle SDO does not help inverting permutations (discussed above). At high level, we would like to argue that the collision-finding oracle $\mathsf{Coll}$, like the oracle SDO, is oblivious to random local changes. Following the intuition outlined for SDO, an attacker that fails to detect random local changes will also fail in inverting random permutations.

**Punctured Collision Finders.** To fulfil this plan, we consider a *punctured* version $\mathsf{PColl}$ of the oracle $\mathsf{Coll}$, where the function $f$ can be erased at a given set of values $S$. Roughly speaking, $\mathsf{PColl}$ will allow us to argue that $\mathsf{Coll}$ is not particularly sensitive to the value $f(x)$ of almost any $x$. To define $\mathsf{PColl}$, we first give a more concrete description of $\mathsf{Coll}$ and then explain how we change it.

The oracle $\mathsf{Coll}$, for any circuit $C : \{0,1\}^k \to \{0,1\}^*$, assigns a random input $w \in \{0,1\}^k$ and a random permutation $\pi$ of $\{0,1\}^k \simeq [2^k]$. It then returns $(w, w')$, where $w'$ is the first among $\pi(1), \pi(2), \dots$ such that $C^f(w) = C^f(w')$. The oracle $\mathsf{PColl}_S^f$ is parameterized by a set of punctured inputs $S \subseteq \{0,1\}^n$. Like $\mathsf{Coll}$, for any $C$, it samples a random input $w$ and a permutation $\pi$. Differently from $\mathsf{Coll}$, if $C^f(w)$ queries any $x \in S$, the oracle returns $\bot$. Else, it iterates over the inputs $\{0,1\}^k$ according to $\pi$ and finds the first value $w'$ such that (1) $C^f(w')$ makes no queries to any $x \in S$, and (2) $C^f(w) = C^f(w')$. The oracle outputs the collision $(w, w')$.

The $\mathsf{PColl}$ oracle satisfies the following essential property. Let $\tau$ be a transcript generated by the attacker $\mathsf{A}^{f, \mathsf{Coll}^f}$ and assume that for all $\mathsf{Coll}$ answers $(w, w')$ in $\tau$, neither $C^f(w)$ nor $C^f(w')$ query any $x \in S$. Then $\mathsf{A}^{f, \mathsf{PColl}_S^f}$ generates the exact same transcript $\tau$. Indeed, this follows directly from the definition of the punctured oracle $\mathsf{PColl}$.

**Proving Hardness of Inversion by Smoothening and Coupling.** Equipped with the punctured oracle, we now explain how it can be used argue the hardness of inversion. We first consider a smoothening process analogous to the one considered in the statistical distance separation discussed above. That is, we make sure that (with overwhelming probability) all queries $C$ made to Coll are smooth in the sense that $C^f(w)$ does not query any specific input with high probability when $w$ is chosen at random. We then make a few small perturbations to our oracles, and argue that they are undetectable by a coupling argument. Finally, we deduce univertability.

**Step 1:** Let $x$ be the preimage that $\mathsf{A}^{f,\mathsf{Coll}^f}(f(x))$ aims to find. We first consider, instead of Coll, the punctured oracle $\mathsf{PColl}^f_{\{x\}}$. Due to smoothness, almost every transcript produced by $\mathsf{A}^{f,\mathsf{Coll}^f}(f(x))$ is such that $x$ is not queried by $C^f(w), C^f(w')$ for any query $C$ and answer $(w, w')$ returned by Coll. Any transcript satisfying the latter can be coupled with an identical transcript generated by $\mathsf{A}^{f,\mathsf{PColl}^f_{\{x\}}}(f(x))$, and deduce that the probability of inversion (outputting $x$) in this new experiment $E_1$ is close to the probability in the original experiment $E_0$.

**Step 2:** We perturb the oracle again. We sample a random $x' \leftarrow \{0,1\}^n$ and make the following two changes: (1) we change the oracle $f$ to $f_{x' \to f(x)}$, which diverts $x'$ to $f(x)$, and (2) we puncture at $x'$, namely, we consider $\mathsf{PColl}^f_{\{x,x'\}}$.

We next observe that in this new experiment $E_2$, $x$ and $x'$ are symmetric. Accordingly, $x$ and $x'$ are output with the same probability in the experiment $E_2$. To complete the proof, we apply a coupling argument to show that $x$ and $x'$ are output with *almost* the same probability also in the previous experiment $E_1$. This is enough as in $E_1$ the view of the attacker is independent of $x'$, which will allows us to deduce that the probability of inversion is negligible overall.

Let us describe the coupling argument more explicitly. Both experiments $E_1$ and $E_2$ are determined by the choice of $f, x, x'$ and randomness $R = \{w, \pi\}$ for Coll. We can look at the events $X_1 = X_1(f, x, x', R)$ and $X_2 = X_2(f, x, x', R)$, where $X_1$ occurs when the attacker outputs $x$ in the experiment $E_1$ and $X_2$ occurs when it outputs $x$ in $E_2$. Similarly, we can look at $X_1'$ and $X_2'$, which describe the events that $x'$ is output in each of the experiments. Then by coupling, we know that

$$\left| \Pr[X_1] - \Pr[X_2] \right| \leq \Pr_{f,x,x',R}[I_{X_1} \neq I_{X_2}],$$

where $I_{X_1}, I_{X_2}$ are the corresponding indicators. The same holds for $X_1'$, $X_2'$. Thus, we can bound:

$$\left| \Pr[X_1] - \Pr[X_1'] \right| \leq \left| \Pr[X_1] - \Pr[X_2] \right| + \left| \Pr[X_2] - \Pr[X_2'] \right| + \left| \Pr[X_1'] - \Pr[X_2'] \right|$$

$$\leq \Pr_{f,x,x',R}[I_{X_1} \neq I_{X_2}] + 0 + \Pr_{f,x,x',R}\left[I_{X_1'} \neq I_{X_2'}\right].$$

It is left to see that when fixing $f, x, R$ the outputs in the two experiments $E_1, E_2$ (and thus also $X_1, X_2$ and $X_1', X_2'$) are identical as long as $x'$ does not coincide with any of the queries to $f$, nor with any of the queries induced by any $\mathsf{PColl}_{\{x\}}$ answer $(w, w')$. Since the number of such queries is bounded and $x'$ is chosen independently at random, this will almost surely be the case.

## Organization

In Sect. 3, we provide relevant preliminaries. In Sect. 4, we prove that there are no fully black-box reductions of SZK hardness to CRHFs. In Sect. 5, we reprove Simon's result that there are no fully black-box reductions of CRHFs to OWPs. The extension of this result to IO can be found in the full version of this paper.

# 3   Preliminaries

In this section, we introduce the basic definitions and notation used throughout the paper.

## 3.1   Conventions

For a distribution $D$, we denote the process of sampling from $D$ by $x \leftarrow D$. A function $\mathsf{negl} : \mathbb{N} \to \mathbb{R}^+$ is negligible if for every constant $c$, there exists a constant $n_c$ such that for all $n > n_c$ $\mathsf{negl}(n) < n^{-c}$.

**Randomized Algorithms.** As usual, for a random algorithm A, we denote by $\mathsf{A}(x)$ the corresponding output distribution. When we want to be explicit about the algorithm using randomness $r$, we shall denote the corresponding output by $\mathsf{A}(x; r)$. We refer to uniform probabilistic polynomial-time algorithms as PPT algorithms.

**Oracles.** We consider *oracle-aided algorithms (or circuits)* that make repeated calls to an oracle $\Gamma$. Throughout, we will consider deterministic oracles $\Gamma$ that are a-priori sampled from a distribution $\Gamma$ on oracles. More generally, we consider infinite oracle ensembles $\Gamma = \{\Gamma_n\}_{n \in \mathbb{N}}$, one distribution $\Gamma_n$ for each security parameter $n \in \mathbb{N}$ (each defined over a finite support). For example, we may consider an ensemble $f = \{f_n\}$ where each $f_n : \{0, 1\}^n \to \{0, 1\}^n$ is a random function. For such an ensemble $\Gamma$ and an oracle aided algorithm (or circuit) A with finite running time, we will often abuse notation and denote by $\mathsf{A}^\Gamma(x)$ and execution of A on input $x$ where each of (finite number of) oracle calls that $A$ makes is associated with a security parameter $n$ and is answered by the corresponding oracle $\Gamma_n$. When we write $\mathsf{A}_1^\Gamma, \ldots, \mathsf{A}_k^\Gamma$ for $k$ algorithms, we mean that they all access the same realization of $\Gamma$.

## 3.2   Coupling and Statistical Distance

**Definition 3.1 (Coupling).** *Given two random variables $X, Y$ over $\mathcal{X}, \mathcal{Y}$, a coupling of $X, Y$ is defined to be any distribution $P_{X'Y'}$ on $\mathcal{X} \times \mathcal{Y}$ such that, the marginals of $P_{X'Y'}$ on $\mathcal{X}$ and $\mathcal{Y}$ are the distributions $X, Y$ respectively.*
 *Denote by $\mathcal{P}_{XY}$ the set of all couplings of $X, Y$.*

**Lemma 3.2.** *Given any two distributions $X, Y$ supported on $\mathcal{X}$,*

$$\mathrm{SD}(X, Y) = \inf_{P_{X'Y'} \in \mathcal{P}_{XY}} \Pr_{(x,y) \leftarrow P_{X'Y'}} [x \neq y].$$

*Furthermore, for distributions over a discrete domain $\mathcal{X}$ the infimum is attained: that is, there exists a coupling $P_{XY}$ such that $\mathrm{SD}(X, Y) = \Pr_{(x,y) \leftarrow P_{XY}} [x \neq y]$.*

The lemma allows us to bound the statistical distance between two random variables (hybrid experiments in our case) by setting up a coupling between two experiments and bounding the probability of them giving a different outcome. Looking ahead, in Lemma 5.6, we describe an explicit coupling for the Simon's collision finder oracle, of the form above that allows us to bound the statistical distance between hybrids.

# 4 Separating SZK and CRHFs

## 4.1 Fully Black-Box Constructions of SZK Problems

The class of problems with Statistical Zero Knowledge Proofs (SZK) [GMR85, Vad99] can be characterized by complete promise problems [SV03], particularly statistical difference, and the transformation is black-box. In order to consider black-box constructions of hard problems in SZK, we start by defining statistical difference problem relative to oracles. This modelling follows [BDV17].

In the following definition, for an oracle-aided (sampler) circuit $C^{(\cdot)}$ with $n$-bit input and an oracle $\Psi$, we denote by $\mathbf{C}^\Psi$ the output distribution $C^\Psi(r)$ where $r \leftarrow \{0, 1\}^n$. We denote statistical distance by SD: for two distributions $X$ and $Y$ $\mathrm{SD}(X, Y) = \frac{1}{2} \sum_x |\Pr[X = x] - \Pr[Y = x]|$.

**Definition 4.1 (Statistical Difference Problem relative to oracles).** *For an oracle $\Psi$, the statistical difference promise problem relative to $\Psi$, denoted as $\mathrm{SDP}^\Psi = (\mathrm{SDP}_Y^\Psi, \mathrm{SDP}_N^\Psi)$, is given by*

$$\mathrm{SDP}_Y^\Psi = \left\{ (C_0, C_1) : \mathrm{SD}(\mathbf{C}_0^\Psi, \mathbf{C}_1^\Psi) \geq \frac{2}{3} \right\},$$

$$\mathrm{SDP}_N^\Psi = \left\{ (C_0, C_1) : \mathrm{SD}(\mathbf{C}_0^\Psi, \mathbf{C}_1^\Psi) \leq \frac{1}{3} \right\}.$$

Next, we define formally define fully black-box reductions from CRHFs to SZK.

**Definition 4.2 (Black-Box Construction of SZK-hard Problems).** *A fully black-box construction of a hard statistical distance problems (SDP) from CRHFs consists of*

- **Black-box construction:** *A collection of oracle-aided circuit pairs $\Pi^{(\cdot)} = \left\{ \Pi_n^{(\cdot)} \right\}_{n \in \mathbb{N}}$ where $\Pi_n = \left\{ (C_0^{(\cdot)}, C_1^{(\cdot)}) \in \{0, 1\}^{n \times 2} \right\}$ such that each $(C_0, C_1)$ defines an SDP instance.*

– **Black-box security proof:** *A probabilistic oracle-aided reduction* R *with functions* $q_R(\cdot), \varepsilon_R(\cdot)$ *such that the following holds: Let* $f$ *be any distribution on functions. For any probabilistic oracle-aided* A *that decides* $\Pi$ *in the worst-case, namely, for all* $n \in \mathbb{N}$,

$$\Pr\left[ A^f(C_0, C_1) = B \quad \text{for all} \quad \begin{array}{c} (C_0, C_1) \in \Pi_n, B \in \{Y, N\} \\ \text{such that } (C_0, C_1) \in \mathrm{SDP}_B^f \end{array} \right] = 1$$

*the reduction breaks collision resistance of* $f$, *namely, for infinitely many* $n \in \mathbb{N}$,

$$\Pr_f\left[ f_n(x) = f_n(x') \text{ where } (x, x') \leftarrow R^{f,A} \right] \geq \varepsilon_R(n),$$

*where* R *makes at most* $q_R(n)$ *queries to any of its oracles* $(A, f)$ *where each query to* A *consists of circuits* $C_0, C_1$ *each of which makes at most* $q_R(n)$ *queries to* $f$.

Next, we state the main result of this section: that any fully black-box construction of SDP problems from CRHFs has to either run in time exponential in the security parameter or suffer exponential security loss.

**Theorem 4.3.** *For any fully black-box construction* $(\Pi, R, q_R, \varepsilon_R)$ *of SDPs from CRHFs, the following holds:*

1. *(The reduction runs in exponential time.)* $q_R(n) \geq 2^{n/10}$. *Or,*
2. *(Reduction succeeds with exponentially small probability.)* $\varepsilon_R(n) \leq 2^{-n/10}$.

We prove the theorem by describing an oracle $\Gamma = (f, A)$ such that, A solves $\mathrm{SDP}^f$ but $f$ is a CRHF relative to $\Gamma$. The rest of the section is devoted to describing this oracle and proving the theorem. We start by describing the adversary that breaks SDP: the statistical distance oracle.

## 4.2   The Statistical Distance Oracle

Next we describe the statistical distance oracle SDO from [BDV17] that solves SZK instances.

**Definition 4.4 (Oracle $\mathrm{SDO}^\Psi$).** *The oracle consists of* $t = \{t_n\}_{n \in \mathbb{N}}$ *where* $t_n : \{0,1\}^{2n} \to (\frac{1}{3}, \frac{2}{3})$ *is a uniformly random function. Given n-bit descriptions of oracle-aided circuits* $C_0, C_1 \in \{0,1\}^n$, *let* $t^* = t_n(C_0, C_1)$, *and let* $s = \mathrm{SD}(\mathbf{C}_0^\Psi, \mathbf{C}_1^\Psi)$, *return*

$$\mathrm{SDO}^\Psi(C_0, C_1; t) := \begin{cases} 0 & \text{If } s < t^* \\ 1 & \text{If } s \geq t^* \end{cases}$$

It is immediate to see that $\mathrm{SDO}^\Psi$ decides $\mathrm{SDP}^\Psi$ in the worst-case.

**Claim 4.4.1.** For any oracle $\Psi$,

$$\mathsf{SDP}^\Psi \in \mathsf{P}^{\Psi,\mathsf{SDO}^\Psi}.$$

*Remark 4.5 (On the Oracle Used).* Our separation is sensitive to the oracle used. Subsequent to [BDV17, KY18] observed that the Simon's collision finding oracle Coll can be used to decide SZK. Clearly, no separation between CRHFs and SZK holds relative to the Simon's oracle. It turns out that Simon's oracle can be used to estimate a different measure of distance between distributions, the Triangular Discrimination,[2] which like statistical distance also gives an SZK-complete promise problem [BDRV19]. Our separation does hold with a variant of Coll and SDO that measures triangular discrimination, but does not output a collision.

## 4.3   Insensitivity to Local Changes

Next, we recall the notions of smoothness and farness from [BDV17] that are used to argue that the $\mathsf{SDO}^\Psi$ oracle is insensitive to local changes. Roughly speaking *farness* says that the random threshold $t$ used for a query $(C_0, C_1)$ to $\mathsf{SDO}^\Psi$ is "far" from the actual statistical distance. [BDV17] show that with high probability over the choice of random threshold $t$, farness holds for all queries $(C_0, C_1)$ made to $\mathsf{SDO}^\Psi$ by any (relatively) efficient adversary. This intuitively means that changing the distributions $(\mathbf{C}_0^\Psi, \mathbf{C}_1^\Psi)$, on sets of small density, will not change the oracle's answer.

**Definition 4.6 $((\Psi, t, \varepsilon)$-Farness).** *Two oracle-aided circuits $(C_0, C_1) \in \{0,1\}^n$ satisfy $(\Psi, t, \varepsilon)$-farness if the statistical difference $s = \mathrm{SD}(\mathbf{C}_0^\Psi, \mathbf{C}_1^\Psi)$ and threshold $t$ are $\varepsilon$-far:*

$$|s - t| \geq \varepsilon.$$

*For an adversary A, we denote by* $\mathsf{farness}(\mathsf{A}, \Psi, \varepsilon)$ *the event that every* SDO *query $(C_0, C_1)$ made by $\mathsf{A}^{\Psi,\mathsf{SDO}^\Psi}$ satisfies $(\Psi, t, \varepsilon)$-farness, where $t = t_n(C_0, C_1)$ is the threshold sampled by* SDO.

**Lemma 4.7 ([BDV17](Claim 3.7)).** *Fix any $\Psi$ and any oracle-aided adversary A such that $\mathsf{A}^{\Psi,\mathsf{SDO}^\Psi}$ makes at most $q$ queries to $\mathsf{SDO}^\Psi$. Then*

$$\Pr_t\left[\mathsf{farness}(\mathsf{A}, \Psi, \varepsilon)\right] \geq 1 - 6q\varepsilon,$$

*where the probability is over the choice $t$ of random thresholds by* SDO.

We now turn to define the notion of *smoothness*. Roughly speaking we will say that an oracle-aided circuit $C$ is smooth with respect to some oracle $\Psi$ if any specific oracle query is only made with small probability. In particular, for a pair of smooth circuits $(C_0, C_1)$, local changes to the oracle $\Psi$ should not change significantly the statistical distance $s = \mathrm{SD}(\mathbf{C}_0^\Psi, \mathbf{C}_1^\Psi)$.

---

[2] The triangular discrimination is defined as $\mathrm{TD}(X, Y) = \frac{1}{2} \sum_x \frac{(\Pr[X=x] - \Pr[Y=x])^2}{(\Pr[X=x] + \Pr[Y=x])}$. This measure also lies in the interval $[0, 1]$ and is a metric.

**Definition 4.8 (($\Psi, \varepsilon$)-Smoothness).** *A circuit $C^{(\cdot)}$ is $(\Psi, \varepsilon)$-smooth, if every location $x \in \{0,1\}^*$ is queried with probability at most $\varepsilon$. That is,*

$$\max_x \Pr_w \left[ C^{\Psi}(w) \text{ queries } \Psi \text{ at } x \right] < \varepsilon.$$

*For an adversary* A, *we denote by* smooth(A, $\Psi, \varepsilon$) *the event that in every* SDO *query $(C_0, C_1)$ made by* $\mathsf{A}^{\Psi, \mathsf{SDO}^{\Psi}}$ *both circuits are $(\Psi, \varepsilon)$-smooth.*

**Lemma 4.9 ([BDV17](Claim 3.9)).** *Let $\Psi, \Psi'$ be oracles that differ on at most $c$ values in the domain. Let $C_0$ and $C_1$ be $(\Psi, \varepsilon)$-smooth. Let $s = \mathrm{SD}(C_0^{\Psi}, C_1^{\Psi})$ and $s' = \mathrm{SD}(C_0^{\Psi'}, C_1^{\Psi'})$ then $|s - s'| \leq 2c\varepsilon$.*

The above roughly means that (under the likely event that farness holds) making smooth queries should not help the adversary detect local changes in the oracle $\Psi$. [BDV17] show that we can always "smoothen" the adversary's circuit at the expense of making (a few) more queries to $\Psi$, which intuitively deems the statistical difference oracle $\mathsf{SDO}^{\Psi}$ useless altogether for detecting local changes in $\Psi$.

In what follows, a $(q', q)$-query algorithm A makes at most $q'$ queries to the oracle $\Psi$ and $q$ queries to $\mathsf{SDO}^{\Psi}$ such that for each query $(C_0, C_1)$ to SDO, the circuits $C_0, C_1$ themselves make at most $q$ queries to $\Psi$ on any input.

**Lemma 4.10 (Smoothing Lemma for SDO [BDV17](Lemma 3.10)).** *For any $(q, q)$-query algorithm A and $\beta \in \mathbb{N}$, there exists a $(q + 2\beta q^2, q)$-query algorithm S such that for any input $z \in \{0,1\}^*$ and oracles $\Psi, \mathsf{SDO}^{\Psi}$:*

1. $\mathsf{S}^{\Psi, \mathsf{SDO}^{\Psi}}(z)$ *perfectly simulates the output of* $\mathsf{A}^{\Psi, \mathsf{SDO}^{\Psi}}(z)$,
2. $\mathsf{S}^{\Psi, \mathsf{SDO}^{\Psi}}(z)$ *only makes queries $(C_0, C_1)$ where both $C_0, C_1$ are $(\Psi, \varepsilon)$-smooth queries to* $\mathsf{SDO}^{\Psi}$ *with probability:*

$$\Pr_{\mathsf{S}} \left[ \mathsf{smooth}(\mathsf{S}, \Psi, \varepsilon) \right] \geq 1 - 2^{-\varepsilon\beta + \log(2q^2/\varepsilon)},$$

*over its own random coin tosses.*

## 4.4   Collision Resistance in the Presence of SDO Oracle

In this section, we prove the oracle separation between collision resistant hash functions and SZK.

Let $\mathcal{F}_n$ be the set of all functions from $\{0,1\}^n$ to $\{0,1\}^{m(n)}$ where $m(n) < n$ is a shrinking function. Let $\mathcal{F} = \{\mathcal{F}_n\}_{n \in \mathbb{N}}$ denote the family of these sets of functions. Let $\mathcal{T} = \{\mathcal{T}_n\}_{n \in \mathbb{N}}$ where $\mathcal{T}_n$ denotes the set of threshold functions $t : \{0,1\}^n \to (1/3, 2/3)$. [3]

---

[3] While we describe the threshold function as a real valued function, it can be safely discretized because statistical distance for any pair of circuits $C_0, C_1 : \{0,1\}^m \to \{0,1\}^*$, takes values that are multiples of $2^{-(m+1)}$. We omit the details here.

**Definition 4.11 (The Oracle $f$).** *The oracle $f = \{f_n\}_{n \in \mathbb{N}}$ on input $x \in \{0,1\}^n$ returns $f_n(x)$ where $f_n : \{0,1\}^n \to \{0,1\}^m$ is a random function from $\mathcal{F}_n$.*

The oracle we consider is $\Gamma = (f, \mathsf{SDO}^f)$. It is easy to see that all $\mathsf{SDP}^f \in \mathsf{P}^{f,\mathsf{SDO}^f}$. What remains to show is that $f$ is still collision resistant in the presence of the $\mathsf{SDO}^f$ oracle. We do so next.

**Theorem 4.12.** *Let $\mathsf{A}$ be a $(q,q)$query adversary for $q = O(2^{m/10})$. Then,*

$$\Pr\left[f_n(x) = f_n(x') \text{ where } (x,x') \leftarrow \mathsf{A}^{f,\mathsf{SDO}^f}(1^n)\right] \leq 2^{-m/10}.$$

*Proof.* Fix oracle $f_{-n} = \{f_k\}_{k \neq n}$ arbitrarily. Consider the $(q + 2\beta q^2, q)$query smooth version $\mathsf{S}$, of $\mathsf{A}$ given by Lemma 4.10 for $\beta = 2^{m/5} \cdot m$ and $\varepsilon = 2^{-m/5}$. We assume w.l.o.g that $\mathsf{S}$ makes no repeated oracle queries and that whenever $\mathsf{S}$ outputs a collision $(x,x')$, $x$ is its last oracle query and $x'$ is a previous query (both to the $f$ oracle).

The first assumption is w.l.o.g because $\mathsf{S}$ may store a table of previously made queries and answers. The second is w.l.o.g because $\mathsf{S}$ may halt once its $f$-queries include a collision and output that collision; also, if one, or both, outputs $x, x'$ have not been queried, $\mathsf{S}$ can query it at the end (and if needed change the order of the output so that $x$ is queries last). The latter costs at most two additional queries, and does not affect the smoothness of $\mathsf{S}$.

Next, we define some notation about transcripts generated in the process.

**Transcripts.** A transcript $\pi$ consists of all queries asked and answers received by $\mathsf{S}$ to the oracle $(f, \mathsf{SDO}^f)$. Let $x_i$ denote the $i$-th query to the $f$-oracle. We say that $x \notin \pi$ if the location $x$ is not among the queries explicitly made in $\pi$.

**The Underlying Joint Distribution.** The proof infers properties of the joint distribution $(f, t, \pi)$ consisting of the oracle $f$, the $\mathsf{SDO}$ oracle's random thresholds $t$ and the transcript generated by $\mathsf{S}$. The distribution is generated as follows: $f \leftarrow \mathcal{F}$ and $t \leftarrow \mathcal{T}$ and $\pi \leftarrow \mathsf{S}^{f,\mathsf{SDO}^{f;t}}$ where $\mathsf{SDO}^{f;t}$ denotes running the $\mathsf{SDO}$ oracle with random thresholds $t$. Denote this distribution by $P_{FT\Pi}$.

Note that given $f, t$, the transcript $\pi$ is generated in a deterministic manner as $\mathsf{S}$ is deterministic and the oracle's behavior is completely specified. Furthermore, we also consider partial transcripts obtained by running $\mathsf{S}$ and stopping after $i$ queries. This transcript is denoted by $\pi_{<i}, x_i$: that is the $\pi_{<i}$ consists of queries and responses received and $x_i$ is the next query to the oracle $f$. Note that $x_i$ is a deterministic function of $\pi_{<i}$. Given the distribution $P_{FT\Pi}$, the conditional distributions $P_{FT|\Pi=\pi}$ or $P_{FT|\Pi=\pi_{<i}}$ are well defined: these consist of uniform distribution on pairs $(f, t)$ that when run using $\mathsf{S}$ result in the transcript being $\pi$ (or $\pi_{<i}$).

**The Good Event.** We define the concept of Good transcripts. Roughly speaking, these are transcripts $\pi$ that satisfy sufficient smoothness and farness so to guarantee that the value $f(x)$ at any $x \notin \pi$ is completely hidden.

**Definition 4.13 (Good).** *A tuple* $(f, t, \pi, x, \varepsilon)$ *is* good, *denoted by* good$(f, t, \pi, x, \varepsilon)$ *if the following hold:*

1. $\pi = \mathsf{S}^{f_{x \to \perp}, \mathsf{SDO}^{f_{x \to \perp};t}}(1^n)$, *where* $f_{x \to \perp}$ *is the function equal to* $f$ *everywhere except at* $x$ *where it takes the value* $\perp$.
2. *(x is not explicitly queried:)* $x \notin \pi$.
3. *(Transcript is smooth:)* *Every* SDO-*query made by* $\mathsf{S}^{f_{x \to \perp}, \mathsf{SDO}^{f_{x \to \perp};t}}(1^n)$ *is* $(f_{x \to \perp}, 2\varepsilon)$-*smooth. Denote this event by* smooth$(f_{x \to \perp}, t, \pi, 2\varepsilon)$.
4. *(Transcript is far:)* *Every* SDO-*query* $(C_0, C_1)$ *made by* $\mathsf{S}^{f_{x \to \perp}, \mathsf{SDO}^{f_{x \to \perp};t}}(1^n)$, *satisfies* $(f_{x \to \perp}, t, 12\varepsilon)$-*farness where* $t = t(C_0, C_1)$. *Denote this by* far$(f, t, \pi, 12\varepsilon)$.

The key reason for using $f_{x \to \perp}$ instead of $f$ in the definition is that when an execution of $\mathsf{S}^{f_{x \to \perp}, \mathsf{SDO}^{f_{x \to \perp};t}}$ generates a transcript $\pi$ while making only smooth and far queries, all executions of $\mathsf{S}^{f_{x \to z}, \mathsf{SDO}^{f_{x \to z};t}}$ for all $z$, *also generate* $\pi$ while not necessarily being smooth or far themselves.

A tuple $(f, t, \pi, \varepsilon)$ is good if for all $x \notin \pi$, good$(f, t, \pi, x, \varepsilon)$ holds.

**Lemma 4.14.** *Let* $P_{FT\Pi}$ *as defined above. Then,*

$$\Pr_{(f, t, \pi) \leftarrow P_{FT\Pi}} [\text{good}(f, t, \pi, \varepsilon)] \geq 1 - 16q\varepsilon - 2^{-\beta\varepsilon + \log(2q^2/\varepsilon)}$$

*The same holds for* $i$-*length partial transcripts generated as well, for all* $i$.

**Lemma 4.15.** *For any transcript* $\pi$ *and query* $x \notin \pi$ *such that*

$$\Pr_{(f, t, \pi) \leftarrow P_{FT\Pi}} [\text{good}(f, t, \pi, x, \varepsilon)] > 0,$$

*it holds that,*

$$\{f(x) : (f, t) \leftarrow P_{FT | \Pi = \pi, \text{good}(f, t, \pi, x, \varepsilon)}\} \equiv U_m .$$

Next, we prove Theorem 4.12 assuming Lemmas 4.14 and 4.15. Then, we prove the two lemmas.

Let hit$(\pi)$ denote the event that $\pi$ contains two queries $x, x'$ such that $f_n(x) = f_n(x')$. Then,

$$\Pr_{f, t} \left[ f_n(x) = f_n(x') \wedge (x, x') = \mathsf{S}^{f, \mathsf{SDO}^{f;t}}(1^n) \right] = \Pr_{f, t, \pi} [\text{hit}(\pi)]$$

$$\leq \Pr_{f, t, \pi} [\text{hit}(\pi) \wedge \text{good}(f, t, \pi, \varepsilon)]$$

$$+ \Pr_{f, t, \pi} \left[ \overline{\text{good}(f, t, \pi, \varepsilon)} \right].$$

We will bound the two terms separately. The first term will involve using Lemma 4.15 while the second term is bound using Lemmas 4.7 and 4.10.

We begin by bounding the first term. This is done by decomposing the probability of hitting a collision by the first query that hits a collision:

$$\Pr_{f,t}\left[\mathsf{hit}(\pi) \wedge \mathsf{good}(f,t,\pi,\varepsilon)\right]$$

$$\leq \sum_i \Pr_{f,t}\left[\mathsf{hit}(\pi_{\leq i}) \wedge \overline{\mathsf{hit}(\pi_{<i})} \wedge \mathsf{good}(f,t,\pi_{<i},\varepsilon)\right]$$

$$= \sum_i \Pr_{f,t}\left[f(x_i) \in \mathsf{hitSet}(\pi_{<i}) \wedge \overline{\mathsf{hit}(\pi_{<i})} \wedge \mathsf{good}(f,t,\pi_{<i},\varepsilon)\right],$$

where $x_i \notin \pi$ denotes the $i$-th $f$ query made by S and $\mathsf{hitSet}(\pi_{<i})$ denotes the answers to $f$-queries in $\pi_{<i}$,

$$= \sum_i \sum_{\pi_{<i},x_i} \Pr_{f,t}\left[(\pi_{<i},x_i) = \mathsf{S}^{f,\mathsf{SDO}^{f;t}}(1^n) \wedge \mathsf{good}(f,t,\pi_{<i},x_i,\varepsilon)\right]$$

$$\cdot \Pr_{f,t \leftarrow P_{FT}|\Pi=\pi_{<i},\mathsf{good}}\left[f(x_i) \in \mathsf{hitSet}(\pi_{<i})\right]$$

The last equality follows from the definition of conditional probability. At this point, we can use Lemma 4.15 to argue that

$$\Pr_{f,t \leftarrow P_{FT}|\Pi=\pi_{<i},\mathsf{good}(f,t,\pi_{<i},x_i,\varepsilon)}\left[f(x_i) \in \mathsf{hitSet}(\pi_{<i})\right] \leq \frac{i}{2m}$$

because $f(x_i)$ is uniformly random and $|\mathsf{hitSet}(\pi_{<i})| \leq i$. Hence, we get that,

$$\leq \sum_i \frac{i}{2m} \cdot \sum_{\pi_{<i},x_i} \Pr_{f,t}\left[(\pi_{<i},x_i) = \mathsf{S}^{f,\mathsf{SDO}^{f;t}}(1^n) \wedge \mathsf{good}(f,t,\pi_{<i},x_i,\varepsilon)\right]$$

$$\leq \sum_{i=1}^{q'} \frac{i}{2m} \leq \frac{q'^2}{2m},$$

where $q' = q + 2\beta q^2 + 2$, the number queries that S makes to $f$.

Hence, by Lemma 4.14, the algorithm's success probability is bounded by

$$\Pr_{f,t}\left[f_n(x) = f_n(x') \wedge (x,x') = \mathsf{S}^{f,\mathsf{SDO}^{f;t}}(1^n)\right] \leq \Pr_{f,t}\left[\mathsf{hit}(\pi) \wedge \mathsf{good}(f,t,\pi)\right] + \Pr_{f,t}\left[\overline{\mathsf{good}(f,t,\pi)}\right]$$

$$\leq \frac{(q + 2\beta q^2 + 2)^2}{2m} + 16q\varepsilon + 2^{-\beta\varepsilon+\log(2q^2/\varepsilon)}$$

$$\leq O(q^4\beta^2 2^{-m} + 16q\varepsilon + q^2/\varepsilon 2^{-\varepsilon\beta})$$

$$\leq O(2^{-m/10}) .$$

when substituting $\varepsilon = 2^{-m/5}$, $\beta = 2^{m/5} \cdot m$, and $q \leq 2^{m/10}$.

*Proof (of Lemma 4.14).* The proof follows from the observation if $\mathsf{S}^{f,\mathsf{SDO}^f}$ outputs $\pi$ with all the queries being both smooth, and far, then, the same holds for $\mathsf{S}^{f_x \to \perp,\mathsf{SDO}^{f_x \to \perp}}$ with slightly degraded parameters. That is,

$$\Pr_{(f,t,\pi)\leftarrow P_{FT\Pi}}[\mathsf{good}(f,t,\pi,\varepsilon)] = \Pr_{f,t,\pi}[\wedge_{x\notin\pi}\mathsf{good}(f,t,\pi,x,\varepsilon)]$$

$$\geq \Pr_{f,t,\pi}[\mathsf{smooth}(f,t,\pi,\varepsilon) \wedge \mathsf{farness}(f,t,\pi,8\varepsilon)]$$

$$\geq 1 - 16\varepsilon q - 2^{-\beta\varepsilon+\log(2q^2/\varepsilon)}$$

Hence, to complete the proof, we need to show that, for any $(f,t)$ if $\mathsf{S}^{f,\mathsf{SDO}^f}(1^n)$ outputs $\pi$ with all the queries being $(f,\varepsilon)$-smooth, and $(f,t,16\varepsilon)$-far, then, $\mathsf{S}^{f_{x\to\perp},\mathsf{SDO}^{f_{x\to\perp}}}(1^n)$ generates $\pi$ with all the queries being $(f,2\varepsilon$-smooth and $(f,t,12\varepsilon)$-far.

First observe that by Lemma 4.9, since $16\varepsilon$-farness and $\varepsilon$-smoothness hold, answers by $\mathsf{SDO}^{f_{x\to\perp}}$ are identical to those by $\mathsf{SDO}^f$. Accordingly, the transcript $\pi = \mathsf{S}^{f_{x\to\perp},\mathsf{SDO}^{f_{x\to\perp}}}(1^n)$.

Next, we show that $2\varepsilon$-smoothness holds with respect to $\mathsf{SDO}^{f_{x\to\perp}}$. Indeed, any SDO-query $(C_0^{(\cdot)},C_1^{(\cdot)})$ is $\varepsilon$-smooth with respect to $f$, accordingly the probability that either circuit $C_b$ queries any individual $z$ is bounded by

$$\Pr\left[C_b^{f_{x\to\perp}} \text{ queries } z\right] \leq \Pr\left[C_b^{f_{x\to\perp}} \text{ queries } x\right] + \Pr\left[C_b^f \text{ queries } z\right] \leq 2\varepsilon .$$

Finally, to conclude the proof, we show that $12\varepsilon$-farness holds with respect to $f_{x\to\perp}$. Indeed, for any query $(C_0,C_1)$, let $s = \mathsf{SD}(C_0^f,C_1^f)$ be the statistical distance with respect to $f$, then by $\varepsilon$-smoothness with respect to $f$, the statistical distance $s^x = \mathsf{SD}(C_0^{f_{x\to\perp}},C_1^{f_{x\to\perp}})$ with respect to $f_{x\to\perp}$ is at most $2\varepsilon$-far from $s$. Letting $t = t(C_0,C_1)$ be the threshold chosen by SDO, we know by $16\varepsilon$-farness that $|s - t| \geq 16\varepsilon$ and thus $|s^x - t| \geq 12\varepsilon$, which implies the require farness with respect to $f_{x\to\perp}$.

The above argument holds unaltered for partial transcripts output by S as well. Even there, when a partial transcript is output by $\mathsf{S}^{f,\mathsf{SDO}^f}$ with all queries being $(f,\varepsilon)$-smooth and $(f,t,16\varepsilon)$-far, then, $\mathsf{S}^{f_{x\to\perp},\mathsf{SDO}^{f_{x\to\perp}}}(1^n)$ generates the same partial transcript with all the queries being $(f,2\varepsilon)$-smooth and $(f,t,12\varepsilon)$-far. $\qquad\square$

*Proof (of Lemma 4.15).* Given $\pi, x \notin \pi$, for any $y$

$$\Pr_{f,t\leftarrow P_{FT|\Pi=\pi,\mathsf{good}(f,t,\pi,x,\varepsilon)}}[f(x) = y] = \frac{\Pr_{f,t}\left[\pi = \mathsf{S}^{f,\mathsf{SDO}^{f;t}}(1^n) \wedge f(x) = y \wedge \mathsf{good}(f,t,\pi,x,\varepsilon)\right]}{\Pr_{f,t}\left[\pi = \mathsf{S}^{f,\mathsf{SDO}^t}(1^n) \wedge \mathsf{good}(f,t,\pi,x,\varepsilon)\right]}$$

In order to show that, the distribution $\{f(x) : f \leftarrow P_{F|\Pi=\pi,\mathsf{good}}\}$ is uniform, it suffices to show that for all $y_1,y_2 \in \{0,1\}^m$,

$$\Pr_{f,t}\left[\pi = \mathsf{S}^{f,\mathsf{SDO}^{f;t}}(1^n) \wedge f(x) = y_1 \wedge \mathsf{good}(f,t,\pi,x,\varepsilon)\right]$$

$$= \Pr_{f,t}\left[\pi = \mathsf{S}^{f,\mathsf{SDO}^{f;t}}(1^n) \wedge f(x) = y_2 \wedge \mathsf{good}(f,t,\pi,x,\varepsilon)\right]$$

To prove this, it suffices to show that for every $(f,t)$ where $f(x) = y_1$,

$$\pi = \mathsf{S}^{f,\mathsf{SDO}^{f;t}}(1^n) \wedge \mathsf{good}(f,t,\pi,x,\varepsilon) = 1 \iff \pi = \mathsf{S}^{f_{x\to y_2},\mathsf{SDO}^{f_{x\to y_2};t}}(1^n) \wedge \mathsf{good}(f_{x\to y_2},t,\pi,x,\varepsilon)$$

This follows because as $\mathsf{good}(f,t,\pi,x,\varepsilon)$ holds, $\pi = \mathsf{S}^{f_{x\to\perp},\mathsf{SDO}^{f_{x\to\perp};t}}(1^n)$ and every query made to $\mathsf{SDO}^{f_{x\to\perp};t}$ is both $12\varepsilon$-far and $2\varepsilon$-smooth. Hence, when we change the oracle to $(f_{x\to y_2},\mathsf{SDO}^{x\to y_2})$, each query is answered identically to $f_{x\to\perp},\mathsf{SDO}^{f_{x\to\perp};t}$. Indeed, for any query $(C_0,C_1)$, let $s = \mathrm{SD}(C_0^{f_{x\to\perp}},C_1^{f_{x\to\perp}})$ be their statistical distance with respect to $f_{x\to\perp}$, then by $2\varepsilon$-smoothness with respect to $f_{x\to\perp}$, the statistical distance $s' = \mathrm{SD}(C_0^{f_{x\to y_2}},C_1^{f_{x\to y_2}})$ is at most $4\varepsilon$-far from $s$. As the threshold $t = t(C_0,C_1)$ is more than $12\varepsilon$ far by farness, the answer will be unchanged to this query.

Hence, $\mathsf{S}^{(f_{x\to y_2},\mathsf{SDO}^{x\to y_2})}$ will also return $\pi$ as the answer. Also, by definition, $\mathsf{good}(f_{x\to y_2},t,\pi,x,\varepsilon)$ will hold because $\pi = \mathsf{S}^{f_{x\to\perp},\mathsf{SDO}^{f_{x\to\perp};t}}(1^n)$ and every query made to $\mathsf{SDO}^{f_{x\to\perp};t}$ is both $12\varepsilon$-far and $2\varepsilon$-smooth. Hence, the claim follows.

□

This completes the proof of Theorem 4.12.    □

# 5   A New Proof of an Old Separation

In this section, we give a new proofs of a result by Simon [Sim98] ruling out fully black-box reductions of collision-resistant hash functions to one-way permutations.

**Fully Black Box Constructions of CRHFs from OWPs.** We begin by defining oracle-aided constructions of CRHFs and then specialize it to the setting of OWPs.

**Definition 5.1 (Oracle-Aided Collision-Resistant Function Families).** *A pair of polynomial-time oracle-aided algorithms* (Gen, Hash) *is a collision-resistant function family relative to an oracle $\Gamma$ if it satisfies the following properties:*

- *The index-generation algorithm* Gen *is a probabilistic algorithm that on input $1^n$ and oracle access to $\Gamma$ outputs a function index $\sigma \in \{0,1\}^{m(n)}$.*
- *The evaluation algorithm* Hash *is a deterministic algorithm that takes as input a function index $\sigma \in \{0,1\}^{m(n)}$ and a string $x \in \{0,1\}^n$, has oracle access to $\Gamma$, and outputs a string $y = \mathsf{Hash}^{\Gamma}(\sigma,x) \in \{0,1\}^{n-1}$.*

**Definition 5.2 (Black-Box Construction of CRHFs from OWPs).** *A* fully black-box construction of a Collision Resistant Hash Functions (CRHFs) from One-Way Permutations *consists of a pair of PPT oracle-aided algorithms* (Gen, Hash), *an oracle-reduction* R *along with functions $q_R(n)$, $\varepsilon_R(n)$ such that the following two conditions hold:*

- **Correctness:** *For any $n \in \mathbb{N}$, for any permutation $f$, and for any function index $\sigma$ produced by $\mathsf{Gen}^f(1^n)$, it holds that $\mathsf{Hash}^f(\sigma, \cdot) : \{0,1\}^n \to \{0,1\}^{n-1}$.*
- **Black-box security proof:** *For any permutation $f$ and probabilistic oracle-aided algorithm $\mathsf{A}$ , if*

$$\Pr\left[\mathsf{Hash}^f(\sigma, x) = \mathsf{Hash}^f(\sigma, x') \wedge x \neq x'\right] \geq \frac{1}{2}$$

*where the experiment is $\sigma \leftarrow \mathsf{Gen}^f(1^n)$ and $(x, x') \leftarrow \mathsf{A}^f(1^n, \sigma)$, for infinitely many $n$, then the reduction breaks $f$, namely, for infinitely many $n \in \mathbb{N}$ either*

$$\Pr_{\substack{x \leftarrow \{0,1\}^n \\ f, \mathsf{A}}} \left[\mathsf{R}^{\mathsf{A}, f}(f_n(x)) = x\right] \geq \varepsilon_{\mathsf{R}}(n),$$

*for infinitely many values of $n$ where $\mathsf{R}$ makes at most $q_{\mathsf{R}}(n)$ queries to the oracles $\mathsf{A}, f$ and for every circuit $D^{(\cdot)}$ queried to $\mathsf{A}$ makes at most $q_{\mathsf{R}}(n)$ queries to $f$ on any input.*

We remark that ruling out black-box reductions as defined above where the reduction has to break the OWP given an adversary that breaks CRHFs w.p. over $1/2$ only makes our result stronger. In the standard setting, the reduction has to break OWP given an adversary that succeeds with any noticeable probability.

## 5.1   Simon's Collision Finding Oracle and Puncturing

Recall that the Simon's collision finding oracle is defined as follows:

**Definition 5.3 (Simon's Oracle $\mathsf{Coll}^\Psi$).**   *Given any description of a circuit $C$ with $m$-bit inputs, the oracle's randomness contains a random input $w_C \in \{0,1\}^m$ and a random permutation $\pi_C : \{0,1\}^m \to \{0,1\}^m$. The $\mathsf{Coll}^\Psi$ oracle returns the following:*

$\mathsf{Coll}^\Psi(C) := (w_C, w'_C)$ *where $w'_C = \pi_C(i)$ for the smallest $i$ such that $C^\Psi(w_C) = C^\Psi(\pi_C(i))$.*

*W.l.o.g, along with $(w_C, w'_C)$, let $\mathsf{Coll}$ also return the queries made to $\Psi$, and their answers, when evaluating $C^\Psi(w_C)$ and $C^\Psi(w'_C)$.*

The collision-finding oracle breaks any oracle-aided collision resistant hash function.

**Lemma 5.4 ([Sim98]).**   *Let $\Gamma = (\Psi, \mathsf{Coll}^\Psi)$. Let $C^{(\cdot)} : \{0,1\}^n \to \{0,1\}^{n-1}$ be any candidate construction of CRHFs. Then,*

$$\Pr\left[C^\Psi(w) = C^\Psi(w') \wedge w \neq w' \text{ where, } (w, w') \leftarrow \mathsf{Coll}^\Psi(C)\right] \geq \frac{1}{2}$$

*where the randomness is over the randomness of $\mathsf{Coll}$.*

*Proof.* Fix $\Psi$ and omit it from the notation. For any string $y \in \{0,1\}^{n-1}$, let $a_y = |\{x : C(x) = y\}|$. Then,

$$
\Pr[w \neq w'] = \sum_{y \in \mathrm{Supp}(C)} \Pr_{w,w' \leftarrow C^{-1}(y)} [w \neq w'] \cdot \Pr_w [C(w) = y]
$$

$$
= \sum_{y \in \mathrm{Supp}(C)} \frac{a_y - 1}{a_y} \cdot \frac{a_y}{2^n}
$$

$$
= \sum_{y \in \mathrm{Supp}(C)} \frac{a_y}{2^n} - \sum_{y \in \mathrm{Supp}(C)} \frac{1}{2^n} \geq 1 - \frac{2^{n-1}}{2^n},
$$

where the second inequality follows from the fact that $\Pr_{w,w' \leftarrow C^{-1}(y)} [w \neq w'] = \Pr_{w' \leftarrow C^{-1}(y)} [w' \neq w] = \frac{a_y - 1}{a_y}$. $\square$

Next we define a variant of the Simon's oracle, dubbed as the punctured Simon's oracle. This collision finding oracle allows $\Psi$ to be punctured, that is, a set of values in $\Psi$ are erased. As we will show later, this oracle returns the same answers as $\mathsf{Coll}^\Psi$ most of the time, and we can characterize when it does not.

**Definition 5.5 (Punctured Simon's Oracle $\mathsf{PColl}_S^\Psi$).** *Let* $\Psi : \{0,1\}^* \rightarrow \{0,1\}^*$ *be an oracle. Let* $S \subseteq \{0,1\}^*$ *be a subset of inputs. The oracle $\mathsf{PColl}$'s randomness contains for any circuit $C$ with $m$-bit inputs, a random input $w_C \in \{0,1\}^m$ and a random permutation $\pi_C : \{0,1\}^m \rightarrow \{0,1\}^m$. The $\mathsf{PColl}_S^\Psi$ oracle returns the following:*

$$
\mathsf{PColl}_S^\Psi(C) = \perp, \text{ if } C^\Psi(w_C) \text{ queries any } x \in S.
$$

*Else,*

$$
\mathsf{PColl}_S^\Psi(C) := (w_C, w_C')
$$

*where $w_C' = \pi_C(i)$ for the smallest $i$ such that $C^\Psi(w_C) = C^\Psi(\pi_C(i))$ and $C^\Psi(\pi_C(i))$ does not query any $x \in S$. Along with $(w_C, w_C')$, let it also return the queries made to $\Psi$ when evaluating $C^\Psi(w_C)$ and $C^\Psi(w_C')$. We refer to these queries as $\Psi$ queries induced by the $\mathsf{Coll}$ oracle.*

There are two key properties of the punctured oracle: (1) The answers of $\mathsf{PColl}_S^\Psi$ are independent of the values of the oracle $\Psi$ on all of $S$; and (2) there is a natural coupling between $\mathsf{Coll}^\Psi$ and $\mathsf{PColl}_S^\Psi$ such that, as long as there is no *explicit* query $x \in S$ to $\Psi$, the two oracles return identical answers. This is captured by the following lemma.

**Lemma 5.6.** *Let $\Psi : \{0,1\}^* \rightarrow \{0,1\}^*$ be an oracle, let $S \subseteq \{0,1\}^*$. Consider the coupling of $\mathsf{Coll}^\Psi$ and $\mathsf{PColl}_S^\Psi$ that instantiates the two oracles with identical randomness. Let $A$ be any deterministic oracle-aided algorithm. Let $\tau$ be the transcript generated by $A^{\Psi, \mathsf{Coll}^\Psi}$. Then,*

$$
A^{\Psi, \mathsf{PColl}_S^\Psi} = \tau \text{ if and only if, } \Psi\text{-set}(\tau) \cap S = \emptyset,
$$

*where $\Psi$-set$(\tau)$ is the set of all queries made to $\Psi$ in the execution. This includes the queries to $\Psi$ returned by the $\mathsf{Coll}$ oracle.*

*Proof.* Every direct query to $\Psi$ by A is returned identically in both the executions. Furthermore, in any transcript $\tau$, such that $\Psi\text{-set}(\tau) \cap S = \emptyset$, all queries to $\mathsf{Coll}^\Psi$ and $\mathsf{PColl}_S^\Psi$ are answered identically. This follows from the definition of PColl because for every query $C$ to Coll and response $(w_C, w'_C)$, all the queries made to $\Psi$ when evaluating $C^\Psi(w_C)$ and $C^\Psi(w'_C)$ are explicitly made directly to $\Psi$, and are thus in $\Psi$-set. In more detail, for any query $C^\Psi$ made to $\mathsf{Coll}^\Psi$ with answer $(w_C, w'_C)$, $C^\Psi(w_C)$ does not make any queries in $S$, and thus PColl, will also return $w_C$. In addition, any $w''$ that is lexicographically prior to $w'_C$ will not be returned because it either induces queries in $S$, or if it does then it is such that $C^\Psi(w'') \neq C^\Psi(w_C)$. In contrast, $C(w'_C)$ does not make any queries to $S$, and is such that $C(w'_C) = C(w_C)$. Hence $w'_C$ will also be returned by PColl (and likewise the queries to $\Psi$ induced by $w_C, w'_C$). $\qquad\square$

**A Word of Caution.** In Lemma 4.15, we showed that the distribution $f(x)$ when conditioned on a transcript $\tau$ is close to uniformly random.[4]

$$\left\{ f(x) : f \leftarrow P_{F|\Pi=\pi,\text{good}} \right\} \equiv U_m$$

Lemma 5.6 seems to suggest the same for the collision finding oracle. That is, the oracle reveals no information about $f(x)$ for any location $x$ not explicitly queried in $\tau$. Unfortunately, we do not know how to show this. The key reason for this is that the probability of seeing this transcript $\tau$ could itself depend on the value of $f(x)$. This issue is not new: it also comes up with the SDO oracle. We are able to remedy this issue in the case of the SDO oracle in part because of its short output: it allows us to define the notion of farness which shows that the SDO oracle is robust to *any* small changes to the SDO oracle. Puncturing only allows us to erase a value, and not set it to a different one.

## 5.2   Smoothening for the Collision Finding Oracle

Similar to Lemma 4.10, we can show that any algorithm $\mathsf{A}^{\Psi,\mathsf{Coll}^\Psi}$ can be transformed to a smoothened algorithm $\mathsf{S}^{\Psi,\mathsf{Coll}^\Psi}$ that with high probability makes only smooth queries to the $\mathsf{Coll}^\Psi$ oracle.

A $(q', q)$-query algorithm A makes at most $q'$ queries to the oracle $f$ and $q$ queries to $\mathsf{Coll}^f$ such that each for each query $C$ to Coll, the circuit $C$ makes at most $q$ queries to $f$ on any input.

**Lemma 5.7 (Smoothing Lemma for Coll).** *For any $(q, q)$-query algorithm A and $\beta \in \mathbb{N}$, there exists a $(q + \beta q^2, q)$-query algorithm S such that for any input $z \in \{0,1\}^*$ and oracles $\Psi, \mathsf{Coll}^\Psi$:*

*1. $\mathsf{S}^{\Psi,\mathsf{Coll}^\Psi}(z)$ perfectly simulates the output of $\mathsf{A}^{\Psi,\mathsf{Coll}^\Psi}(z)$,*

---

[4] We are using $\tau$ for transcript here to avoid the ambiguity with the Coll oracle randomness $\pi$.

2. $S^{\Psi,\text{Coll}^{\Psi}}(z)$ *only makes queries that are* $(\Psi, \varepsilon)$-*smooth queries to* $\text{Coll}^{\Psi}$ *with probability:*

$$\Pr_{S}\left[\text{smooth}(S, \Psi, \varepsilon)\right] \geq 1 - 2^{-\varepsilon\beta + \log(q^2/\varepsilon)},$$

*over its own random coin tosses.*

The proof of the lemma is identical to that of Lemma 4.10, the bound differs in a factor of 2: $(q + \beta q^2)$ instead of $(q + 2\beta q^2)$ in case of Lemma 4.10 because Coll oracle takes only one circuit as input.

## 5.3     One Way Permutations in the Presence of Coll

In this section, we show that CRHFs cannot be constructed from OWPs in a black-box manner (Definition 5.2). That is, we show,

**Theorem 5.8.** *Let* $(\text{Gen}, \text{Eval}, R, q_R, \varepsilon_R)$ *be a fully black-box construction of CRHFs from OWPs. Then, either*

1. *(Large Running Time)* R *makes at least* $q_R(n) \geq 2^{n/6}$ *queries. Or,*
2. *(Large Security Loss)* $\varepsilon_R(n) \leq 2^{-n/6}$.

To prove the theorem, we consider the oracle $\Gamma = (f, \text{Coll}^f)$ where $f$ is a random permutation. We show that a random permutation $f$ is hard to invert even given access to $\text{Coll}^f$. We start by defining the oracle. In what follows, $\mathcal{P}_n$ denotes the set of permutations of $\{0, 1\}^n$.

**Definition 5.9 (The Oracle $f$).** $f = \{f_n\}_{n \in \mathbb{N}}$ *on input* $x \in \{0, 1\}^n$ *answers with* $f_n(x)$ *where* $f_n$ *is a random permutation* $f_n \leftarrow \mathcal{P}_n$.

It is clear that $\text{Coll}^f$ breaks any potential CRHF construction with probability at least $1/2$. Our main result states that $f$ cannot be inverted, except with exponentially small probability, even given an exponential number of oracle queries to $f$ and $\text{Coll}^f$. Here, consistently with the previous subsection, we say that an adversary A is $q$-query if $A^{f,\text{Coll}^f}$ makes at most $q$ queries to $f$ and $q$ queries to $\text{Coll}^f$, and any query made to $\text{Coll}^f$ consists of oracle-aided circuit $C$ that makes at most $q$ queries to $f$, on any specific input.

**Theorem 5.10.** *Let* $q \leq O(2^{n/6})$. *Then for any* $(q, q)$-*query adversary* A,

$$\Pr_{f,\text{Coll},x}\left[A^{f,\text{Coll}^f}(f(x)) = x\right] \leq O(2^{-n/6}).$$

*Proof.* We, in fact, prove a stronger statement: the above holds when fixing the oracles $f_{-n} := \{f_k\}_{k \neq n}$. Let $\varepsilon = 2^{-n/3}$ and $\beta = 2^{n/3} \cdot n$. Fix a $q$-query adversary A and let S be its smooth $(q + \beta q^2 + 2q^2, q)$ query simulator given by Lemma 4.10. The extra $2q^2$ queries are incurred by the fact that along with each collision $w, w'$ from $\text{Coll}^f(C)$, the queries made to $f$ in computing $C^f(w)$ and $C^f(w')$ are also returned. Since S perfectly emulates A, it is enough to bound the probability that S successfully inverts. To bound S's inversion probability, we consider six hybrid experiments $\{H_i\}_{i\in[6]}$ given in Table 1. Throughout, for a permutation $f \in \mathcal{P}_n$ and $x, y \in \{0,1\}^n$, we denote by $f_{x\to y}$ the function that maps $x$ to $y$ and is identical to $f$ on all other inputs (in particular, $f_{x\to y}$ is no longer a permutation when $x \neq f^{-1}(y)$).

**Table 1.** The hybrid experiments.

| Hybrid | $H_1$ (Real) | $H_2$ | $H_3$ | $H_4$ | $H_5$ | $H_6$ (Ideal) |
|---|---|---|---|---|---|---|
| Permutation | $f_n \leftarrow \mathcal{P}_n$ | | | | | |
| Preimage | $x \leftarrow \{0,1\}^n$ | | | | | |
| 2nd Preimage | $z \leftarrow \{0,1\}^n$ | | | | | |
| Planted Image | $y \leftarrow \{0,1\}^n$ | | | | | |
| Challenge | $f(x)$ | | | $y$ | | |
| Oracle | $f, \text{Coll}^f$ | $f, \text{PColl}^f_{\{x\}}$ | $f_{z\to f(x)}, \text{PColl}^f_{\{x,z\}}$ | $f_{x\to y}, \text{PColl}^f_{\{f^{-1}(y),x\}}$ | $f, \text{PColl}^f_{\{f^{-1}(y)\}}$ | $f, \text{Coll}^f$ |
| Winning Condition | Find $x$ | | | | | |

Hybrid $H_1$ is identical to the real world where S wins if it successfully inverts the permutation at a random output. We show that the probability that the adversary wins in any of the experiments is roughly the same, and that in hybrid $H_6$ the probability that S wins is tiny.

**Claim 5.10.1.** $|\Pr[\text{S wins in } H_1] - \Pr[\text{S wins in } H_2]| \leq O(2^{-n/6})$

*Proof.* The difference between the two hybrids is in the collision finding oracle: in $H_1$, S gets the standard $\text{Coll}^f$ oracle, while in $H_2$, punctured oracle $\text{PColl}^f_{\{x\}}$, punctured at $x$. Note that by coupling the two experiments, we can bound the statistical distance (and hence the winning probabilities) in $H_1$ and $H_2$ as follows:

$$\left|\Pr[\text{S wins in } H_1] - \Pr[\text{S wins in } H_2]\right| \leq \Pr_{\substack{f,x,z \\ \text{Coll}}}\left[\text{S}^{f,\text{Coll}^f}(f(x)) \neq \text{S}^{f,\text{PColl}^f_{\{x\}}}(f(x))\right]$$

Let $\text{smooth} = \text{smooth}(\text{S}(f(x)), f, \varepsilon)$ be the event that all Coll-queries made by $\text{S}^{f,\text{Coll}^f}(f(x))$ are $(f, \varepsilon)$-smooth (Definition 4.8). And let $\text{collHit} = \text{collHit}(\text{S}, f, x, z)$ denote the event that the collision finder oracle $\text{Coll}^f$ for some query $C$ returns an answer $(w, w')$ such that $C^f(w)$ or $C^f(w')$ queries $x$ during the evaluation. Note that collHit does not occur when $f$ is queried at $x$ by S, but only when its indirectly queried by $\text{Coll}^f$.

Observe that by Lemma 5.6, as long as punctured set $\{x\}$ is not queried by a collision returned, that is as long as collHit event does not occur, the two oracles $\text{Coll}^f$ and $\text{PColl}^f_{\{x\}}$ would return identical answers. Hence,

$$\Pr_{\substack{f,x,z \\ \text{Coll}}}\left[\text{S}^{f,\text{Coll}^f}(f(x)) \neq \text{S}^{f,\text{PColl}^f_{\{x\}}}(f(x))\right] \leq \Pr_{\substack{f,x,z \\ \text{Coll}}}[\text{collHit}]$$

We bound the probability of collHit as:

$$\Pr\left[\text{collHit}\right] \le \Pr\left[\overline{\text{smooth}}\right] + \Pr\left[\text{smooth} \wedge \text{collHit}\right]$$

By the smoothness Lemma 5.7,

$$\Pr\left[\overline{\text{smooth}}\right] \le 2^{-\varepsilon\beta + \log(2q^2/\varepsilon)} \ ,$$

and, when smooth holds, we can bound the probability of a collHit.

$$\Pr\left[\text{smooth} \wedge \text{collHit}\right] \le 2q\varepsilon$$

This follows from the fact that for any $(f, \varepsilon)$-smooth circuit $C$, and any $x$, the following holds:

$$\Pr_r\left[C^f(r) \text{ queries } x\right] \le \varepsilon$$

Hence, as the marginal of each coordinate of a collision returned by the Coll oracle is uniformly random, by a union bound, the probability of collHit occurring for this particular Coll query $C$ is at most $2 \cdot \varepsilon$. Hence the total probability is bounded by $q \cdot (2\varepsilon)$ as desired.

Hence, we can bound the difference between $\mathbf{H}_1$ and $\mathbf{H}_2$ by

$$2^{-\varepsilon\beta + \log(2q^2/\varepsilon)} + 2q\varepsilon \le O(2^{-n/6})$$

when setting $\varepsilon = 2^{-n/3}$, $\beta = 2^{n/3} \cdot n$ and recalling that $q \le O(2^{n/6})$. $\qquad\square$

**Claim 5.10.2.** $|\Pr\left[S \text{ wins in } \mathbf{H}_2\right] - \Pr\left[S \text{ wins in } \mathbf{H}_3\right]| \le O(2^{-n/6})$.

*Proof.* The difference between the two hybrids is that in $\mathbf{H}_2$, $S$ receives the normal $f$ oracle, while in $\mathbf{H}_3$, it receives the planted oracle $f_{z \to f(x)}$. And it receives $\text{PColl}^f_{\{x\}}$ in $\mathbf{H}_2$ while receiving $\text{PColl}^f_{\{x,z\}}$ in $\mathbf{H}_3$. In what follows, we denote by $\text{zHit} = \text{zHit}(S, f, x, z)$ the event that $S^{f, \text{PColl}^f_{\{x\}}}(f(x))$ queries $f$ on $z$, either directly or indirectly through a collision returned.

Consider the execution of $S^{f, \text{PColl}^f_{\{x\}}}$ in $\mathbf{H}_2$, every query $S$ makes to the oracle is answered identically in $\mathbf{H}_3$, unless the event zHit occurs. This follows because the $f$ oracle itself differs only at $z$ in the two hybrids, and the PColl oracle returns the same value by Lemma 5.6 unless zHit occurs. Hence, as $S$ receives the same answers and hence asks the same questions in both hybrids, it would have the same output, unless zHit occurs. As $z$ is picked uniformly at random, independent of everything else in $\mathbf{H}_2$,

$$\Pr\left[\text{zHit}\right] \le 2^{-n} \cdot |\text{total } f\text{-queries made by } S| \le 2^{-n} \cdot (q + \beta q^2 + 2q^2) \le O(2^{-n/6})$$

when setting $\varepsilon = 2^{-n/3}$, $\beta = 2^{n/3} \cdot n$ and recalling that $q \le O(2^{n/6})$. $\qquad\square$

**Claim 5.10.3.** $\Pr\left[S \text{ wins in } \mathbf{H}_3\right] = \Pr\left[S \text{ wins in } \mathbf{H}_4\right]$.

*Proof.* First, by symmetry, observe that in $\mathbf{H}_3$, the probability of S outputting $x$ is the same as that of S outputting $z$, because they are completely symmetrical in this hybrid. Then observe that these two hybrids $\mathbf{H}_3$ and $\mathbf{H}_4$ are relabellings of each other: $z \leftrightarrow x$, $f(x) \leftrightarrow y$ and $x \leftrightarrow f^{-1}(y)$. This implies that the probability of the probability of S outputting $z$ in $\mathbf{H}_3$ is the same as that of S outputting $x$ in $\mathbf{H}_4$. This completes the argument.    □

**Claim 5.10.4.** $|\Pr[\mathsf{S} \text{ wins in } \mathbf{H}_4] - \Pr[\mathsf{S} \text{ wins in } \mathbf{H}_5]| \leq O(2^{-n/6})$.

The difference between the two hybrids is two fold: the $f$ and PColl oracles differs at $x$ and are identical otherwise. Note that $x$ is independent of the adversary's view in $\mathbf{H}_5$. The proof of this claim is identical to that of Claim 5.10.2 and is omitted.

**Claim 5.10.5.** $|\Pr[\mathsf{S} \text{ wins in } \mathbf{H}_5] - \Pr[\mathsf{S} \text{ wins in } \mathbf{H}_6]| \leq O(2^{-n/6})$.

The only difference between the two hybrids is that the Coll oracle from $\mathbf{H}_6$ is punctured at $f^{-1}(y)$ in $\mathbf{H}_5$. The proof of this claim is identical to that of Claim 5.10.1, relies on smoothness, and is omitted.

To conclude the proof of Theorem 5.10, we observe that

**Claim 5.10.6.** $\Pr[\mathsf{S} \text{ wins in } \mathbf{H}_6] \leq 2^{-n}$.

*Proof.* The view of S in this hybrid is completely independent of the random choice of $x$.    □

This completes the proof of Theorem 5.10.    □

**Acknowledgements.** Nir Bitansky is a member of the Check Point Institute of Information Security. Supported by the Alon Young Faculty Fellowship, by Len Blavatnik and the Blavatnik Family foundation, and an ISF grant 18/484. Akshay Degwekar did part of this work while visiting the FACT Center in IDC Herzliya, supported in part by ISF grant 1861/16 and AFOSR Award FA9550-17-1-0069. Also supported in part by NSF Grants CNS-1413920 and CNS-1350619, and by the Defense Advanced Research Projects Agency (DARPA) and the U.S. Army Research Office under contracts W911NF-15-C-0226 and W911NF-15-C-0236.

# References

[AGGM06] Akavia, A., Goldreich, O., Goldwasser, S., Moshkovitz, D.: On Basing One-way Functions on NP-hardness. In: STOC (2006)

[AHI+17] Applebaum, B., Haramaty, N., Kushilevitz, E., Vaikuntanathan, V.: Low-complexity cryptographic hash functions. In: ITCS, Yuval Ishai (2017)

[AR16] Applebaum, B., Raykov, P.: On the relationship between statistical zero-knowledge and statistical randomized encodings. In: Robshaw, M., Katz, J. (eds.) CRYPTO 2016. LNCS, vol. 9816, pp. 449–477. Springer, Heidelberg (2016). https://doi.org/10.1007/978-3-662-53015-3_16

[AS15] Asharov, G., Segev, G.: Limits on the power of indistinguishability obfuscation and functional encryption. In: FOCS (2015)

[BB15]    Bogdanov, A., Brzuska, C.: On basing size-verifiable one-way functions on NP-hardness. In: Dodis, Y., Nielsen, J.B. (eds.) TCC 2015. LNCS, vol. 9014, pp. 1–6. Springer, Heidelberg (2015). https://doi.org/10.1007/978-3-662-46494-6_1

[BBF13]   Baecher, P., Brzuska, C., Fischlin, M.: Notions of black-box reductions, revisited. In: Sako, K., Sarkar, P. (eds.) ASIACRYPT 2013. LNCS, vol. 8269, pp. 296–315. Springer, Heidelberg (2013). https://doi.org/10.1007/978-3-642-42033-7_16

[BDRV18]  Berman, I., Degwekar, A., Rothblum, R.D., Vasudevan, P.N.: Multi-collision resistant hash functions and their applications. In: Nielsen, J.B., Rijmen, V. (eds.) EUROCRYPT 2018. LNCS, vol. 10821, pp. 133–161. Springer, Cham (2018). https://doi.org/10.1007/978-3-319-78375-8_5

[BDRV19]  Berman, I., Degwekar, A., Rothblum, R.D., Vasudevan, P.N.: Statistical Difference Beyond the Polarizing Regime. In: ECCC (2019)

[BDV17]   Bitansky, N., Degwekar, A., Vaikuntanathan, V.: Structure vs. hardness through the obfuscation lens. In: Katz, J., Shacham, H. (eds.) CRYPTO 2017. LNCS, vol. 10401, pp. 696–723. Springer, Cham (2017). https://doi.org/10.1007/978-3-319-63688-7_23

[BEG+94]  Blum, M., Evans, W.S., Gemmell, P., Kannan, S., Naor, M.: Checking the correctness of memories. Algorithmica 12(2/3), 225–244 (1994)

[BKSY11]  Brakerski, Z., Katz, J., Segev, G., Yerukhimovich, A.: Limits on the power of zero-knowledge proofs in cryptographic constructions. In: Ishai, Y. (ed.) TCC 2011. LNCS, vol. 6597, pp. 559–578. Springer, Heidelberg (2011). https://doi.org/10.1007/978-3-642-19571-6_34

[BL13]    Bogdanov, A., Lee, C.H.: Limits of provable security for homomorphic encryption. In: Canetti, R., Garay, J.A. (eds.) CRYPTO 2013. LNCS, vol. 8042, pp. 111–128. Springer, Heidelberg (2013). https://doi.org/10.1007/978-3-642-40041-4_7

[BLVW19]  Brakerski, Z., Lyubashevsky, V., Vaikuntanathan, V., Wichs, D.: Worst-case hardness for LPN and cryptographic hashing via code smoothing. In: Ishai, Y., Rijmen, V. (eds.) EUROCRYPT 2019. LNCS, vol. 11478, pp. 619–635. Springer, Cham (2019). https://doi.org/10.1007/978-3-030-17659-4_21

[BM09]    Barak, B., Mahmoody-Ghidary, M.: Merkle puzzles are optimal—an $O(n^2)$-query attack on any key exchange from a random oracle. In: Halevi, S. (ed.) CRYPTO 2009. LNCS, vol. 5677, pp. 374–390. Springer, Heidelberg (2009). https://doi.org/10.1007/978-3-642-03356-8_22

[BT03]    Bogdanov, A., Trevisan, L.: On worst-case to average-case reductions for NP problems. In: FOCS (2003)

[CDGS18]  Coretti, S., Dodis, Y., Guo, S., Steinberger, J.: Random oracles and non-uniformity. In: Nielsen, J.B., Rijmen, V. (eds.) EUROCRYPT 2018. LNCS, vol. 10820, pp. 227–258. Springer, Cham (2018). https://doi.org/10.1007/978-3-319-78381-9_9

[Dam87]   Damgård, I.B.: Collision free hash functions and public key signature schemes. In: Chaum, D., Price, W.L. (eds.) EUROCRYPT 1987. LNCS, vol. 304, pp. 203–216. Springer, Heidelberg (1988). https://doi.org/10.1007/3-540-39118-5_19

[DHT12]   Dodis, Y., Haitner, I., Tentes, A.: On the instantiability of hash-and-sign RSA signatures. In: Cramer, R. (ed.) TCC 2012. LNCS, vol. 7194, pp. 112–132. Springer, Heidelberg (2012). https://doi.org/10.1007/978-3-642-28914-9_7

[DLMM11]  Dachman-Soled, D., Lindell, Y., Mahmoody, M., Malkin, T.: On the black-box complexity of optimally-fair coin tossing. In: Ishai, Y. (ed.) TCC 2011. LNCS, vol. 6597, pp. 450–467. Springer, Heidelberg (2011). https://doi.org/10.1007/978-3-642-19571-6_27

[DPP93]  Damgård, I.B., Pedersen, T.P., Pfitzmann, B.: On the existence of statistically hiding bit commitment schemes and fail-stop signatures. In: Stinson, D.R. (ed.) CRYPTO 1993. LNCS, vol. 773, pp. 250–265. Springer, Heidelberg (1994). https://doi.org/10.1007/3-540-48329-2_22

[Fis12]  Fischlin, M.: Black-box reductions and separations in cryptography. In: Mitrokotsa, A., Vaudenay, S. (eds.) AFRICACRYPT 2012. LNCS, vol. 7374, pp. 413–422. Springer, Heidelberg (2012). https://doi.org/10.1007/978-3-642-31410-0_26

[GG98]  Goldreich, O., Goldwasser, S.: On the Possibility of basing Cryptography on the assumption that P $\neq$ NP. IACR Cryptology ePrint Archive (1998)

[GGH96]  Goldreich, O., Goldwasser, S., Halevi, S.: Collision-free hashing from lattice problems. IACR Cryptology ePrint Archive, 1996:9 (1996)

[GGKT05]  Gennaro, R., Gertner, Y., Katz, J., Trevisan, L.: Bounds on the efficiency of generic cryptographic constructions. SIAM J. Comput. **35**(1), 217–246 (2005)

[GHMM18]  Garg, S., Hajiabadi, M., Mahmoody, M., Mohammed, A.: Limits on the power of garbling techniques for public-key encryption. In: Shacham, H., Boldyreva, A. (eds.) CRYPTO 2018. LNCS, vol. 10993, pp. 335–364. Springer, Cham (2018). https://doi.org/10.1007/978-3-319-96878-0_12

[GK93]  Goldreich, O., Kushilevitz, E.: A perfect zero-knowledge proof system for a problem equivalent to the discrete logarithm. J. Cryptol. **6**(2), 97–116 (1993)

[GKLM12]  Goyal, V., Kumar, V., Lokam, S., Mahmoody, M.: On black-box reductions between predicate encryption schemes. In: Cramer, R. (ed.) TCC 2012. LNCS, vol. 7194, pp. 440–457. Springer, Heidelberg (2012). https://doi.org/10.1007/978-3-642-28914-9_25

[GKM+00]  Gertner, Y., Kannan, S., Malkin, T., Reingold, O., Viswanathan, M.: The relationship between public key encryption and oblivious transfer. In: FOCS (2000)

[GMM07]  Gertner, Y., Malkin, T., Myers, S.: Towards a separation of semantic and CCA security for public key encryption. In: Vadhan, S.P. (ed.) TCC 2007. LNCS, vol. 4392, pp. 434–455. Springer, Heidelberg (2007). https://doi.org/10.1007/978-3-540-70936-7_24

[GMR85]  Goldwasser, S., Micali, S., Rackoff, C.: The knowledge complexity of interactive proof-systems (Extended Abstract). In: STOC (1985)

[GMR01]  Gertner, Y., Malkin, T., Reingold, O.: On the impossibility of basing trapdoor functions on trapdoor predicates. In: FOCS (2001)

[GT00]  Gennaro, R., Trevisan, L.: Lower bounds on the efficiency of generic cryptographic constructions. In: FOCS (2000)

[HH09]  Haitner, I., Holenstein, T.: On the (im)possibility of key dependent encryption. In: Reingold, O. (ed.) TCC 2009. LNCS, vol. 5444, pp. 202–219. Springer, Heidelberg (2009). https://doi.org/10.1007/978-3-642-00457-5_13

[HHRS15]  Haitner, I., Hoch, J.J., Reingold, O., Segev, G.: Finding collisions in interactive protocols-tight lower bounds on the round and communication complexities of statistically hiding commitments. SIAM J. Comput. **44**(1), 193–242 (2015)

[HL18]  Holmgren, J., Lombardi, A.: Cryptographic hashing from strong one-way functions (or: one-way product functions and their applications). In: FOCS (2018)

[HM96]  Halevi, S., Micali, S.: Practical and provably-secure commitment schemes from collision-free hashing. In: Koblitz, N. (ed.) CRYPTO 1996. LNCS, vol. 1109, pp. 201–215. Springer, Heidelberg (1996). https://doi.org/10. 1007/3-540-68697-5_16

[HR04]  Hsiao, C.-Y., Reyzin, L.: Finding collisions on a public road, or do secure hash functions need secret coins? In: Franklin, M. (ed.) CRYPTO 2004. LNCS, vol. 3152, pp. 92–105. Springer, Heidelberg (2004). https://doi.org/ 10.1007/978-3-540-28628-8_6

[IKO05]  Ishai, Y., Kushilevitz, E., Ostrovsky, R.: Sufficient conditions for collision-resistant hashing. In: Kilian, J. (ed.) TCC 2005. LNCS, vol. 3378, pp. 445–456. Springer, Heidelberg (2005). https://doi.org/10.1007/978-3-540-30576-7_24

[Imp95]  Impagliazzo, R.: A personal view of average-case complexity. In: CCC (1995)

[IR89]  Impagliazzo, R., Rudich, S.: Limits on the provable consequences of one-way permutations. In: STOC (1989)

[Kil92]  Kilian, J.: A note on efficient zero-knowledge proofs and arguments (extended abstract). In: STOC (1992)

[KNY17]  Komargodski, I., Naor, M., Yogev, E.: White-box vs. black-box complexity of search problems: ramsey and graph property testing. In: FOCS (2017)

[KNY18]  Komargodski, I., Naor, M., Yogev, E.: Collision resistant hashing for paranoids: dealing with multiple collisions. In: Nielsen, J.B., Rijmen, V. (eds.) EUROCRYPT 2018. LNCS, vol. 10821, pp. 162–194. Springer, Cham (2018). https://doi.org/10.1007/978-3-319-78375-8_6

[KSS11]  Kahn, J., Saks, M.E., Smyth, C.D.: The dual BKR inequality and rudich's conjecture. Comb. Probab. Comput. **20**(2), 257–266 (2011)

[KST99]  Kim, J.H., Simon, D.R., Tetali, P.: Limits on the efficiency of one-way permutation-based hash functions. In: FOCS (1999)

[KY18]  Komargodski, I., Yogev, E.: On distributional collision resistant hashing. In: Shacham, H., Boldyreva, A. (eds.) CRYPTO 2018. LNCS, vol. 10992, pp. 303–327. Springer, Cham (2018). https://doi.org/10.1007/978-3-319-96881-0_11

[LM06]  Lyubashevsky, V., Micciancio, D.: Generalized compact knapsacks are collision resistant. In: Bugliesi, M., Preneel, B., Sassone, V., Wegener, I. (eds.) ICALP 2006. LNCS, vol. 4052, pp. 144–155. Springer, Heidelberg (2006). https://doi.org/10.1007/11787006_13

[LV16]  Liu, T., Vaikuntanathan, V.: On basing private information retrieval on NP-hardness. In: Kushilevitz, E., Malkin, T. (eds.) TCC 2016. LNCS, vol. 9562, pp. 372–386. Springer, Heidelberg (2016). https://doi.org/10.1007/978-3-662-49096-9_16

[Mer89]  Merkle, R.C.: A certified digital signature. In: Brassard, G. (ed.) CRYPTO 1989. LNCS, vol. 435, pp. 218–238. Springer, New York (1990). https://doi.org/10.1007/0-387-34805-0_21

[MP91]  Megiddo, N., Papadimitriou, C.H.: On total functions, existence theorems and computational complexity. Theor. Comput. Sci. **81**(2), 317–324 (1991)

[MV03]   Micciancio, D., Vadhan, S.P.: Statistical zero-knowledge proofs with efficient provers: lattice problems and more. In: Boneh, D. (ed.) CRYPTO 2003. LNCS, vol. 2729, pp. 282–298. Springer, Heidelberg (2003). https://doi.org/10.1007/978-3-540-45146-4_17

[MX10]   Mahmoody, M., Xiao, D.: On the power of randomized reductions and the checkability of SAT. In: CCC (2010)

[OK91]   Ogata, W., Kurosawa, K.: On claw free families. In: Imai, H., Rivest, R.L., Matsumoto, T. (eds.) ASIACRYPT 1991. LNCS, vol. 739, pp. 111–123. Springer, Heidelberg (1993). https://doi.org/10.1007/3-540-57332-1_9

[Pas06]   Pass, R.: Parallel repetition of zero-knowledge proofs and the possibility of basing cryptography on NP-hardness. In: CCC (2006)

[Pas13]   Pass, R.: Unprovable security of perfect NIZK and non-interactive non-malleable commitments. In: Sahai, A. (ed.) TCC 2013. LNCS, vol. 7785, pp. 334–354. Springer, Heidelberg (2013). https://doi.org/10.1007/978-3-642-36594-2_19

[Per]   Personal communication with the authors of [KNY18]

[PR06]   Peikert, C., Rosen, A.: Efficient collision-resistant hashing from worst-case assumptions on cyclic lattices. In: Halevi, S., Rabin, T. (eds.) TCC 2006. LNCS, vol. 3876, pp. 145–166. Springer, Heidelberg (2006). https://doi.org/10.1007/11681878_8

[PVW08]   Peikert, C., Vaikuntanathan, V., Waters, B.: A framework for efficient and composable oblivious transfer. In: Wagner, D. (ed.) CRYPTO 2008. LNCS, vol. 5157, pp. 554–571. Springer, Heidelberg (2008). https://doi.org/10.1007/978-3-540-85174-5_31

[RTV04]   Reingold, O., Trevisan, L., Vadhan, S.: Notions of reducibility between cryptographic primitives. In: Naor, M. (ed.) TCC 2004. LNCS, vol. 2951, pp. 1–20. Springer, Heidelberg (2004). https://doi.org/10.1007/978-3-540-24638-1_1

[Rud88]   Rudich, S.: Limits on the Provable Consequences of One-Way Functions. Ph.D. thesis, University of California, Berkeley (1988)

[Rus95]   Russell, A.: Necessary and sufficient condtions for collision-free hashing. J. Cryptol. 8(2), 87–100 (1995)

[Sim98]   Simon, D.R.: Finding collisions on a one-way street: can secure hash functions be based on general assumptions? In: Nyberg, K. (ed.) EUROCRYPT 1998. LNCS, vol. 1403, pp. 334–345. Springer, Heidelberg (1998). https://doi.org/10.1007/BFb0054137

[SV03]   Sahai, A., Vadhan, S.: A complete problem for statistical zero knowledge. J. ACM (JACM) 50(2), 196–249 (2003)

[Unr07]   Unruh, D.: Random oracles and auxiliary input. In: Menezes, A. (ed.) CRYPTO 2007. LNCS, vol. 4622, pp. 205–223. Springer, Heidelberg (2007). https://doi.org/10.1007/978-3-540-74143-5_12

[Vad99]   Vadhan, S.P.: A study of statistical zero-knowledge proofs. Ph.D. thesis, Massachusetts Institute of Technology (1999)

[YZW+17]   Yu, Y., Zhang, J., Weng, J., Guo, C., Li, X.: Collision resistant hashing from learning parity with noise. IACR Cryptology ePrint Archive, 2017:1260 (2017)

# Characterizing Collision and Second-Preimage Resistance in Linicrypt

Ian McQuoid[✉], Trevor Swope, and Mike Rosulek

Oregon State University, Corvallis, USA
{mcquoidi,swopet,rosulekm}@oregonstate.edu

**Abstract.** Linicrypt (Carmer & Rosulek, Crypto 2016) refers to the class of algorithms that make calls to a random oracle and otherwise manipulate values via fixed linear operations. We give a characterization of collision-resistance and second-preimage resistance for a significant class of Linicrypt programs (specifically, those that achieve domain separation on their random oracle queries via nonces). Our characterization implies that collision-resistance and second-preimage resistance are equivalent, in an asymptotic sense, for this class. Furthermore, there is a polynomial-time procedure for determining whether such a Linicrypt program is collision/second-preimage resistant.

## 1 Introduction

Collision resistance and second-preimage resistance are fundamental properties of hash functions, and are the basis of security for hash-based signature schemes [4,7,10,11], which are a promising approach for post-quantum security.

We give a new way to reason about and characterize the collision resistance and second-preimage resistance of a large, natural class of programs, in the random oracle model. Specifically, we characterize these properties for the class of **Linicrypt programs**, introduced by Carmer and Rosulek [5]. Roughly speaking, a Linicrypt program is one where all intermediate values are field elements, and the only operations possible are fixed linear combinations, sampling uniformly from the field, and calling a random oracle (whose outputs are field elements). Many of the most practical cryptographic constructions are captured by this model: hash-based signatures and block cipher modes, to name a few.

Carmer and Rosulek showed that such programs admit an algebraic representations that is amenable to reasoning about programs' cryptographic properties. Specifically, they showed a polynomial-time algorithm for deciding whether two Linicrypt programs induce computationally indistinguishable distributions. They also demonstrated the feasibility of using a SAT solver to *automatically synthesize* Linicrypt programs that satisfy given correctness & security constraints, by successfully synthesizing secure Linicrypt constructions of garbled circuits.

Authors partially supported by NSF award #1617197.

Our work follows a similar path, showing that collision properties can also be characterized cleanly in terms of the algebraic representation for Linicrypt programs. Our characterization holds for programs in which distinct oracle queries have the form $H(t_1; \cdot), H(t_2; \cdot), \ldots$ for *distinct nonces* $t_i$.

We introduce an algebraic property of Linicrypt programs called a *collision structure*, which completely characterizes both second-preimage resistance and collision resistance. The presence of a collision structure in a program $\mathcal{P}$ can be detected in polynomial time (in the size of $\mathcal{P}$'s algebraic representation).

**Theorem 1 (Main Theorem).** *Let $\mathcal{P}$ be a deterministic Linicrypt program with distinct nonces, making $n$ oracle queries. Let $\mathbb{F}$ be the underlying field (and range of the random oracle). Then the following are equivalent:*

1. *There is an adversary $\mathcal{A}$ making $q$ oracle queries that finds collisions with probability more than $(q/n)^{2n}/|\mathbb{F}|$.*
2. *There is an adversary $\mathcal{A}$ making $q$ oracle queries that finds second preimages with probability more than $(q/n)^n/|\mathbb{F}|$.*
3. *There is an adversary $\mathcal{A}$ making at most $2n$ oracle queries that finds second preimages with probability 1.*
4. *$\mathcal{P}$ either has a collision structure or is degenerate. (See main text for definitions)*

We emphasize that the theorem statement refers to **standard security properties** (*i.e.*, security against arbitrary, computationally unbounded algorithms that make only a polynomial number of queries to the random oracle) of Linicrypt constructions. We are **not** in a heuristic model that considers Linicrypt *adversaries*.

Our results show that second-preimage resistance and collision resistance are equivalent, *in an asymptotic sense* (i.e., considering only whether a quantity is negligible or not). However, as might be expected, it is quadratically easier to find collisions than second preimages, due to birthday attacks. Our concrete bounds reflect this. In practice, reducing security to second-preimage resistance rather than collision resistance can result in constructions with 50% smaller parameters; e.g., [2,6,8].

## 1.1   Related Work and Comparison

Bellare and Micciancio [1] discuss the collision resistance of the function $H^*(x_1, \ldots, x_n) = H(1; x_1) \oplus \cdots \oplus H(n; x_n)$, where $H$ is collision-resistant. Indeed, this function is naturally modeled in Linicrypt over a field $GF(2^\lambda)$. They show that this function fails to be collision-resistant if $n$ is allowed to vary with the input (in particular, when $n \geq \lambda + 1$). Our characterization shows that an adversary making $q$ oracle queries breaks collision resistance with probability bounded by $(q/n)^{2n}/2^\lambda$ since the function lacks a "collision structure." These two results are not in conflict, since our bound is meaningless when $n \geq \lambda + 1$. In short, the Linicrypt model is best suited for programs whose only dependence on the security parameter is the choice of field, but where (in particular) the number of inputs and calls to $H$ are fixed constants.

Another related work is that of Wagner [13], who gives an algorithm for a generalized birthday problem. The problem (translated to our notation) is to find $x_1, \ldots, x_k$ such that $H(x_1) \oplus \cdots \oplus H(x_k) = 0$. The case of $k = 2$ corresponds to the well-known birthday problem. One can see that by generating a list $L_i$ of roughly $2^{\lambda/k}$ candidates for each $x_i$ (i.e., so $|L_1 \times \cdots \times L_k| \geq 2^\lambda$), there is likely to exist some solution to the problem. Wagner's focus is on the *algorithmic* aspect of actually identifying the appropriate candidates. In Linicrypt, all adversaries are considered to be computationally unbounded but bounded in the number of queries to the random oracle $H$. As such, our results do not provide any upper/lower bounds on attack complexity (other than in random oracle query complexity).

Black, Rogaway and Shrimpton [3] categorize 64 ways to construct a compression function (suitable for Merkle-Damgård hashing) from an ideal cipher, building on prior work by Preneel, Govaerts and Vandewalle [12]. These constructions can be thought of as $GF(2^\lambda)$-Linicrypt programs that use only XOR (e.g., linear combinations with coefficients of 0 or 1 only). However, the reasoning is tied to the ideal cipher model rather than the random oracle model, as in Linicrypt (see Sect. B.3 for more information). We leave it as interesting future work to extend results in Linicrypt to the ideal cipher model, and potentially re-derive the characterization of BRS from a linear-algebraic perspective.

## 2   Preliminaries

We write scalar field elements as lowercase non-bold letters (e.g., $v \in \mathbb{F}$). We write vectors as lowercase bold letters (e.g., $\boldsymbol{q} \in \mathbb{F}^n$). We write matrices as uppercase bold letters (e.g., $\boldsymbol{M} \in \mathbb{F}^{n \times m}$). We write vector inner product as $\boldsymbol{q} \cdot \boldsymbol{v}$, and matrix-vector multiplication as $\boldsymbol{M} \times \boldsymbol{v}$ or $\boldsymbol{M}\boldsymbol{v}$.

### 2.1   Linicrypt

The Linicrypt model was introduced in [5]. We present a brief summary of the model and its important properties.

A Linicrypt program (over field $\mathbb{F}$) is one in which every intermediate value is an element of $\mathbb{F}$, and the program is a fixed, straight-line sequence of the following kinds of operations:

- Call a random oracle (whose inputs/outputs are field elements).
- Sample a random field element.
- Combinine existing values using a fixed linear combination.

The sequence of operations (including choice of arguments to the oracle, coefficients of linear combinations, etc.) is entirely fixed. In particular, these cannot depend on intermediate values in the computation.

The only source of cryptographic power in Linicrypt is the random oracle, whose outputs are $\mathbb{F}$-elements. We therefore require the size of the field $|\mathbb{F}|$ to be exponential in the security parameter $\lambda$. Since the field depends on the security parameter, we sometimes write $\mathbb{F} = \mathbb{F}_\lambda$ to make the association explicit.

If the field depends on the security parameter, then the program does too (since it is parameterized by specific coefficients of linear combinations). One can either consider a Linicrypt program to be a non-uniform family of programs (one for each choice of field/security parameter), or one can fix all coefficients in the program from $\widetilde{\mathbb{F}}$ which is a subfield of every $\mathbb{F}_\lambda$ (for example, a program that uses only $\{0, 1\}$ coefficients can be instantiated over any field $GF(2^\lambda)$). Our treatment of security is concrete (not asymptotic), so these distinctions are not important in this work.

We can reason about Linicrypt programs in the following *algebraic* way. Let $\mathcal{P}$ be such a program, and let $v_1, \ldots, v_n$ denote all of its intermediate variables. Say the first $k$ of them are $\mathcal{P}$'s input and the last $l$ of them are $\mathcal{P}$'s output. We say that $v_i$ is a **base variable** if $v_i$ is either an input variable, the result of a call to the oracle, or the result of sampling a field element. All variables can therefore be expressed as a fixed linear combination of base variables.

Let $\boldsymbol{v}_{\mathsf{base}}$ denote the vector of all base variables. For each variable $v_i$, let $\boldsymbol{r}_i$ denote the vector such that $v_i = \boldsymbol{r}_i \cdot \boldsymbol{v}_{\mathsf{base}}$. For example, for base variables, $\boldsymbol{r}_i$ is a canonical basis vector (0s everywhere except 1 in one component).

Suppose the output of $\mathcal{P}$ consists of $v_{n-l+1}, \ldots, v_n$. Then the **output matrix** of $\mathcal{P}$ is defined as: $\boldsymbol{M} \stackrel{\text{def}}{=} \begin{bmatrix} \boldsymbol{r}_{n-l+1} \\ \vdots \\ \boldsymbol{r}_n \end{bmatrix}$. This matrix captures the fact that $\mathcal{P}$'s output can be expressed as $\boldsymbol{M} \times \boldsymbol{v}_{\mathsf{base}}$.

Each oracle query in $\mathcal{P}$ is of the form "$v_i := H(t; v_{i_1}, \ldots, v_{i_m})$," where $t$ is a string (e.g., *nonce*) and $i_1, \ldots, i_m < i$ are indices, all *fixed* as part of $\mathcal{P}$. For each such query we define an associated **oracle constraint** $c = \left( t, \begin{bmatrix} \boldsymbol{r}_{i_1} \\ \vdots \\ \boldsymbol{r}_{i_m} \end{bmatrix}, \boldsymbol{r}_i \right)$. In other words, an oracle constraint $(t, \boldsymbol{Q}, \boldsymbol{a})$ captures the fact that if the oracle is queried as $H(t; \boldsymbol{Q} \times \boldsymbol{v}_{\mathsf{base}})$, then the response is $\boldsymbol{a} \cdot \boldsymbol{v}_{\mathsf{base}}$. When $t$ is the empty string, we often omit it from our notation and simply write $H(\cdot)$ instead of $H(\epsilon; \cdot)$.

The **algebraic representation** of $\mathcal{P}$ is $\mathcal{P} = (\boldsymbol{M}, \mathcal{C})$, where $\boldsymbol{M}$ is the output matrix of $\mathcal{P}$ and $\mathcal{C}$ is the set of all oracle constraints. Indeed, these two pieces of information completely characterize the behavior of $\mathcal{P}$ (as established in [5]).

*Example.* In this work we focus on deterministic Linicrypt programs. One such example is given below. Its base variables are $(v_1, \ldots, v_5, v_7)$.

$$
\begin{array}{|l|}
\hline
\mathcal{P}^H(v_1, v_2, v_3): \\
\hline
\quad v_4 := H(\texttt{foo}; v_1) \\
\quad v_5 := H(\texttt{bar}; v_3) \\
\quad v_6 := v_4 + v_5 + v_2 \\
\quad v_7 := H(\texttt{foo}; v_6) \\
\quad v_8 := v_7 + v_1 \\
\quad \text{return } (v_8, v_5) \\
\hline
\end{array}
\Rightarrow
\begin{bmatrix} v_1 \\ v_2 \\ v_3 \\ v_4 \\ v_5 \\ v_6 \\ v_7 \\ v_8 \end{bmatrix}
=
\begin{bmatrix}
1 & 0 & 0 & 0 & 0 & 0 \\
0 & 1 & 0 & 0 & 0 & 0 \\
0 & 0 & 1 & 0 & 0 & 0 \\
0 & 0 & 0 & 1 & 0 & 0 \\
0 & 0 & 0 & 0 & 1 & 0 \\
0 & 1 & 0 & 1 & 1 & 0 \\
0 & 0 & 0 & 0 & 0 & 1 \\
1 & 0 & 0 & 0 & 0 & 1
\end{bmatrix}
\begin{bmatrix} v_1 \\ v_2 \\ v_3 \\ v_4 \\ v_5 \\ v_7 \end{bmatrix}
$$

Hence, the algebraic representation of $\mathcal{P}$ is:

$$
M = \begin{bmatrix} 1 & 0 & 0 & 0 & 0 & 1 \\ 0 & 0 & 0 & 0 & 1 & 0 \end{bmatrix}; \qquad
C = \left\{
\begin{array}{l}
(\texttt{foo}, [1\ 0\ 0\ 0\ 0], [0\ 0\ 1\ 0\ 0]), \\
(\texttt{bar}, [0\ 0\ 1\ 0\ 0], [0\ 0\ 0\ 1\ 0]), \\
(\texttt{foo}, [0\ 1\ 0\ 1\ 1\ 0], [0\ 0\ 0\ 0\ 0\ 1])
\end{array}
\right\}
$$

## 2.2  Security Definitions

The Linicrypt model is meant to capture a special class of *construction*, but not adversaries. In this work we characterize **standard security definitions**, against arbitrary (i.e., not necessarily Linicrypt) adversaries. As in Impagliazzo's "Minicrypt" [9] we consider computationally unbounded adversaries that are *bounded-query:* they make only at most $p(\lambda)$ queries to the random oracle, for some polynomial $p$.

**Definition 2.** *Let $\mathcal{P}$ be a Linicrypt program over a family of fields $\mathbb{F} = (\mathbb{F}_\lambda)_\lambda$. Then $\mathcal{P}$ is $(q, \epsilon)$-**collision-resistant (in the random oracle model)** if for all $q$-query adversaries $\mathcal{A}$, $\Pr[\mathsf{ColGame}(\mathcal{P}, \mathcal{A}, \lambda) = 1] \leq \epsilon$, where:*

$$
\begin{array}{|l|}
\hline
\mathsf{ColGame}(\mathcal{P}, \mathcal{A}, \lambda): \\
\hline
\quad \text{instantiate a random oracle } H : \{0,1\}^* \times (\mathbb{F}_\lambda)^* \to \mathbb{F}_\lambda \\
\quad (\boldsymbol{x}, \boldsymbol{x}') \leftarrow \mathcal{A}^H(\lambda) \\
\quad \text{return } (\boldsymbol{x} \neq \boldsymbol{x}') \wedge (\mathcal{P}^H(\boldsymbol{x}) = \mathcal{P}^H(\boldsymbol{x}')) \\
\hline
\end{array}
$$

**Definition 3.** *Let $\mathcal{P}$ be as above (with $k$ inputs). $\mathcal{P}$ is $(q, \epsilon)$-**2nd-preimage-resistant (in the random oracle model)** if for all $q$-query adversaries $\mathcal{A}$, $\Pr[\mathsf{2PlGame}(\mathcal{P}, \mathcal{A}, \lambda) = 1] \leq \epsilon$, where:*

$$
\begin{array}{|l|}
\hline
\mathsf{2PlGame}(\mathcal{P}, \mathcal{A}, \lambda): \\
\hline
\quad \text{instantiate a random oracle } H : \{0,1\}^* \times (\mathbb{F}_\lambda)^* \to \mathbb{F}_\lambda \\
\quad \boldsymbol{x} \leftarrow (\mathbb{F}_\lambda)^k \\
\quad \boldsymbol{x}' \leftarrow \mathcal{A}^H(\lambda, \boldsymbol{x}) \\
\quad \text{return } (\boldsymbol{x} \neq \boldsymbol{x}') \wedge (\mathcal{P}^H(\boldsymbol{x}) = \mathcal{P}^H(\boldsymbol{x}')) \\
\hline
\end{array}
$$

## 3    Characterizing Collision-Resistance in Linicrypt

We now present our main technical result, which is a characterization of collision-resistance for Linicrypt programs.

In order to simplify the notation, we present the results for the **special case** of Linicrypt programs that make 1-ary calls to $H$. That is, every call to $H$ is of the form $H(t; v)$ for a *single* $v \in \mathbb{F}$ (note that Linicrypt supports more general calls of the form $H(t; v_1, \ldots, v_k)$). With this simplification, every oracle constraint has the form $(t, q, a)$ where $q$ is a simple vector (rather than a matrix as in the most general form).

This special case simplifies the notation required to express our theorems/proofs, but does not gloss over any meaningful complexity. Later in Sect. B.1 we discuss what minor changes are necessary to extend these results to the unrestricted general case.

### 3.1    Easy Case: Degeneracy

Some Linicrypt programs allow easy collisions. Consider the program $\mathcal{P}^H(x, y) = H(x + y)$. An obvious collision in $\mathcal{P}$ is $\mathcal{P}^H(x, y) = \mathcal{P}^H(x + z, y - z)$ for any $z \neq 0$. What makes this program particularly easy to attack is that not only do the two computations give the same *output*, but they *query $H$ on exactly the same points*. In other words, the input of $\mathcal{P}$ is not uniquely determined by its sequence of oracle queries along with its outputs.

**Definition 4.** *Let $\mathcal{P} = (M, \mathcal{C})$ be a Linicrypt program with $k$ inputs. In the algebraic representation, $\mathcal{P}$'s inputs are associated with canonical basis vectors $e_1, \ldots, e_k$ ($e_i$ has 0s everywhere except a 1 in the ith component). We say that $\mathcal{P}$ is degenerate if*

$$\mathsf{span}(e_1, \ldots, e_k) \not\subseteq \mathsf{span}\Big(\{q \mid (t, q, a) \in \mathcal{C}\} \cup \mathsf{rows}(M)\Big)$$

**Lemma 5.** *If $\mathcal{P}$ is degenerate, then second preimages can be found with probability 1.*

*Proof.* Given an input $x$ for $\mathcal{P}$ in the second preimage game, compute the base variables $v$ in the computation of $\mathcal{P}^H(x)$. If $\mathcal{P}$ is degenerate, there must exist two (actually, at least $|\mathbb{F}_\lambda|$) solutions for the input $x'$ that are consistent with $\{q \cdot v \mid (t, q, a) \in \mathcal{C}\} \cup \{r \cdot v \mid r \in \mathsf{rows}(M)\}$. Such an $x'$ will clearly lead $\mathcal{P}^H$ to make the same oracle queries and give the same output.

### 3.2    Running Example: An Interesting Second-Preimage Attack

Consider the example program below. In fact, it is the example from Sect. 2.1 but with the nonces omitted and most intermediate variables unnamed:

$$\boxed{\begin{array}{l} \mathcal{P}^H(x, y, z): \\ \hline \quad w := H(x) + H(z) + y \\ \quad \text{return } \big(H(w) + x, \ H(z)\big) \end{array}}$$

Suppose we are given $x, y, z$ and are asked to find a second preimage $x', y', z'$ with $\mathcal{P}^H(x, y, z) = \mathcal{P}^H(x', y', z')$. Here is how to do it:

1. The second component of $\mathcal{P}$'s output is $H(z)$. Since we cannot hope to find a second preimage directly in $H$, we must set $z' = z$.
2. The key insight is to now set $w' \neq w$ arbitrarily (hence, why we gave this value a name). We make a promise to choose $x', y'$ so that $w' = H(x') + H(z') + y'$.
3. To have a collision, we must have $H(w') + x' = H(w) + x$. Importantly, $x'$ is the only unknown value in this expression, and it is possible to simply solve for $x'$.
4. It is time to fulfill the promise that $w' = H(x') + H(z') + y'$. Since $w', x', z'$ are already fixed, we can solve for $y'$.

Note that we are guaranteed that $(x, y, z) \neq (x', y', z')$ since the two computations of $\mathcal{P}$ lead to different intermediate values $w \neq w'$ (and $\mathcal{P}$ is deterministic).

*Perspective.* This example is representative of how second preimages can be computed in arbitrary Linicrypt programs. Given an input $\boldsymbol{x}$ for $\mathcal{P}^H$, we compute a second preimage $\boldsymbol{x}'$ by focusing on the oracle queries that $\mathcal{P}^H(\boldsymbol{x})$ and $\mathcal{P}^H(\boldsymbol{x}')$ will make:

1. Designate some of the oracle queries to take the same values in both $\mathcal{P}^H(\boldsymbol{x})$ and $\mathcal{P}^H(\boldsymbol{x}')$. In our example, we decided that the oracle query $H(z)$ would take the same values in both computations.
2. Identify the first query that we will assign different values in the two computations. Set the input to this query arbitrarily in $\mathcal{P}^H(\boldsymbol{x}')$. In our example, we identify the $H(w)$ query to take on different values and set $w' \neq w$ arbitrarily.
3. Repeatedly make followup oracle queries as they become possible, while using linear algebra to solve for other intermediate values. In our example, we call $H(w')$, which allows us to solve for $x'$, which allows us to call $H(x')$, which allows us to solve for $y'$.

## 3.3   Collision Structures for Finding Second Preimages

We have given a rough outline of how (we claim) Linicrypt second preimages must be found. The next step is to formalize what is required of $\mathcal{P}$ in terms of its algebraic representation.

In step 2 above, we identify a query whose input will be chosen arbitrarily. Suppose that query corresponds to constraint $(t, \boldsymbol{q}, \boldsymbol{a})$. Since this is the first value that is fixed differently in $\mathcal{P}^H(\boldsymbol{x})$ and $\mathcal{P}^H(\boldsymbol{x}')$, we must have $\boldsymbol{q}$ linearly independent of the vectors that are already fixed by step 1. Otherwise it would not be possible to find two consistent values for this query.

In steps 2 and 3 above, we repeatedly query $H$, and we have written the attack outline to suggest we never get "stuck." One way we could get stuck is to make some query $H(x')$ for the first time, when we have already fixed (either directly or indirectly) what $H(x')$ must be. If this is the case, then we cannot succeed with probability better than $1/|\mathbb{F}_\lambda|$. To avoid this case, every query we make in steps 2 & 3 of the outline must correspond to a constraint $(t, \boldsymbol{q}, \boldsymbol{a})$ where $\boldsymbol{a}$ is linearly independent of the values that have already been fixed.

The following definition formalizes these algebraic intuitions:

**Definition 6.** *Let $\mathcal{P} = (\boldsymbol{M}, \mathcal{C})$ be a Linicrypt program. A **collision structure** for $\mathcal{P}$ is a tuple $(i^*; c_1, \ldots, c_n)$, where:*

1. *$c_1, \ldots, c_n$ is an ordering of $\mathcal{C}$, and we write $c_i = (t_i, \boldsymbol{q}_i, \boldsymbol{a}_i)$.*
2. *$\boldsymbol{q}_{i^*} \notin \text{span}\Big( \{\boldsymbol{q}_1, \ldots, \boldsymbol{q}_{i^*-1}\} \cup \{\boldsymbol{a}_1, \ldots, \boldsymbol{a}_{i^*-1}\} \cup \text{rows}(\boldsymbol{M}) \Big)$*
3. *For $j \geq i^*$: $\boldsymbol{a}_j \notin \text{span}\Big( \{\boldsymbol{q}_1, \ldots, \boldsymbol{q}_j\} \cup \{\boldsymbol{a}_1, \ldots, \boldsymbol{a}_{j-1}\} \cup \text{rows}(\boldsymbol{M}) \Big)$*

Connecting to the previous intuition, a collision-finding attack will let oracle queries $c_1, \ldots, c_{i^*-1}$ be the same in both executions $\mathcal{P}^H(\boldsymbol{x})$ and $\mathcal{P}^H(\boldsymbol{x}')$. Then $c_{i^*}$ is the first oracle query that the attack fixes differently for the two executions. Property (2) of the definition ensures that it is possible to find 2 query values that are consistent with the previously fixed values. Property (3) captures the fact that from this point forward, no query should be forced to result in an output value that has already been fixed.

*Running Example.* We now revisit the running example from before, to illustrate a collision structure for it. The base variables of this program are $x$, $y$, $z$, $H(x)$, $H(z)$, $H(w)$. Below is the algebraic representation of this program, with the oracle constraints arranged to show a collision structure (we do not write the empty nonces of the oracle constraints):

$$
\begin{array}{r}
\\
\boldsymbol{M} = \\
\\
\boldsymbol{q}_1 = \\
\boldsymbol{a}_1 = \\
\boldsymbol{q}_{i^*} = \boldsymbol{q}_2 = \\
\boldsymbol{a}_{i^*} = \boldsymbol{a}_2 = \\
\boldsymbol{q}_3 = \\
\boldsymbol{a}_3 =
\end{array}
\begin{array}{cccccc}
x & y & z & H(x) & H(z) & H(w) \\
\hline
1 & 0 & 0 & 0 & 0 & 1 \\
0 & 0 & 0 & 0 & 1 & 0 \\
\hline
0 & 0 & 1 & 0 & 0 & 0 \\
0 & 0 & 0 & 0 & 1 & 0 \\
\hline
0 & 1 & 0 & 1 & 1 & 0 \\
0 & 0 & 0 & 0 & 0 & 1 \\
\hline
1 & 0 & 0 & 0 & 0 & 0 \\
0 & 0 & 0 & 1 & 0 & 0
\end{array}
$$

$H(z)$

$H(w) = H(y + H(x) + H(z))$

$H(x)$

This ordering of queries is indeed a collision structure since:

- $\boldsymbol{q}_2$ is linearly independent of all vectors above it in this diagram.
- $\boldsymbol{a}_2$ is linearly independent of all vectors above it in this diagram.
- $\boldsymbol{a}_3$ is linearly independent of all vectors above it in this diagram.

*Second-Preimage-Finding Algorithm.* In Fig. 1 we give an algorithm that finds second preimages by following the intuitive strategy above, from a given collision structure.

---

FindSecondPreimage$\left(\mathcal{P} = (M, \mathcal{C}), (i^*; c_1, \ldots, c_n), x\right)$:

---

compute $v$, the set of base variables in computation $\mathcal{P}^H(x)$
initialize an empty set of linear constraints on unknowns $v'$

add constraint $Mv = Mv'$
for $i = 1$ to $i^* - 1$:
    add constraints $q_i \cdot v = q_i \cdot v'$ and $a_i \cdot v = a_i \cdot v'$

choose a value $v^* \in \mathbb{F}_\lambda$ arbitrarily, with $v^* \neq q_{i^*} \cdot v$
add constraint $v^* = q_{i^*} \cdot v'$

for $i = i^*$ to $n$:
    if $q_i \cdot v'$ is not already uniquely determined by current constraints:
        choose $r \in \mathbb{F}_\lambda$ arbitrarily and add constraint $r = q_i \cdot v'$
    call $s := H(t_i, q_i \cdot v')$    // $q_i \cdot v'$ guaranteed to be uniquely determined here
    add constraint $s = a_i \cdot v'$

return $(e_1 \cdot v', \ldots, e_k \cdot v')$

---

**Fig. 1.** Method for computing second preimages

**Lemma 7.** *If a collision structure $(i^*; c_1, \ldots, c_n)$ exists for $\mathcal{P}$, and $\mathcal{P}$ is not degenerate, then the second-preimage resistance of $\mathcal{P}$ is comprehensively broken. Specifically, let $\mathcal{A}$ refer to* FindSecondPreimage$(\mathcal{P}, (i^*; c_1, \ldots, c_n), \cdot)$. *Then:*

$$\Pr\left[\text{2PIGame}(\mathcal{P}, \mathcal{A}, \lambda) = 1\right] = 1$$

*Proof.* Given $x$, the goal is to compute a second preimage $x'$. The computation of $\mathcal{P}^H(x')$ has a certain set of base variables $v'$, and it suffices to compute those instead since $x' = (e_1 \cdot v', \ldots, e_k \cdot v')$. The attack FindSecondPreimage fixes one linear constraint of $v'$ at a time, until $v'$ is completely determined.

It suffices to show the following about the behavior of FindSecondPreimage:

1. It computes a different set of base variables $v'$ than those of $\mathcal{P}^H(x)$.
2. It never adds incompatible (unsatisfiable) linear constraints on $v'$.
3. Values $v'$ are consistent with $H$. Namely, if $(t, q, a) \in \mathcal{C}$, then $H(t; q \cdot v') = a \cdot v'$.
4. By the end of the computation, enough constraints have been added to completely determine $v'$.

Property 1 holds since $q_{i^*} \cdot v \neq q_{i^*} \cdot v'$ by design. Regarding property 2:

- The constraints on $v'$ that are added for $M$ and in the first for-loop are self-consistent—by construction they already have a valid solution in $v$.
- The constraint involving $q_{i^*}$ is compatible with the previous constraints since $q_{i^*}$ is linearly independent of the previous constraint vectors $\{q_1, \ldots, q_{i^*-1}\} \cup \{a_1, \ldots, a_{i^*-1}\} \cup \text{rows}(M)$, by the collision structure property.

- Similarly, a constraint involving $q_i$ for $i \geq i^*$ (if-statement within last for-loop) is only added in the case that $q_i$ is linearly independent of the previous constraint vectors.
- The constraint involving $a_i$ in the second for-loop is consistent since $a_i$ is linearly independent of existing constraint vectors, again by the collision structure property.

---

FindColStruct($\mathcal{P} = (\boldsymbol{M}, \mathcal{C})$):

LEFT := $\mathcal{C}$
RIGHT := empty stack
$V := \{\boldsymbol{q} \mid (t, \boldsymbol{q}, \boldsymbol{a}) \in \mathcal{C}\} \cup \{\boldsymbol{a} \mid (t, \boldsymbol{q}, \boldsymbol{a}) \in \mathcal{C}\} \cup \mathsf{rows}(\boldsymbol{M})$, as a **multi-set**

// below: "$V \setminus \{\boldsymbol{a}\}$" means "$V$ with multiplicity of $\boldsymbol{a}$ reduced by 1"
while $\exists (t, \boldsymbol{q}, \boldsymbol{a}) \in$ LEFT such that $\boldsymbol{a} \notin \mathsf{span}(V \setminus \{\boldsymbol{a}\})$:
    remove $(t, \boldsymbol{q}, \boldsymbol{a})$ from LEFT
    push $(t, \boldsymbol{q}, \boldsymbol{a})$ to RIGHT
    reduce multiplicity of $\boldsymbol{q}, \boldsymbol{a}$ in $V$ by 1

while $\exists (t, \boldsymbol{q}, \boldsymbol{a}) \in$ RIGHT such that $\boldsymbol{q} \in \mathsf{span}(V)$:
    remove $(t, \boldsymbol{q}, \boldsymbol{a})$ from RIGHT
    add $(t, \boldsymbol{q}, \boldsymbol{a})$ to LEFT
    increase multiplicity of $\boldsymbol{q}, \boldsymbol{a}$ in $V$ by 1

if RIGHT is nonempty:
    set $i^* := |\text{LEFT}| + 1$
    write LEFT $= (c_1, \ldots, c_{i^*-1})$, where order doesn't matter
    write RIGHT $= (c_{i^*}, \ldots, c_n)$ in reverse order of insertion
    return $(i^*; c_1, \ldots, c_n)$
else: return $\perp$

---

**Fig. 2.** Method for finding collision structures in a Linicrypt program.

Regarding property 3: for oracle constraints $c_i$ with $i < i^*$, consistency with $H$ is ensured by agreeing with the existing values $v$. For constraints $c_i$ with $i \geq i^*$, consistency is guaranteed since the second for-loop actually calls $H$ to determine the consistent way to constrain $a_i \cdot v'$.

Property 4 follows from the fact that $\mathcal{P}$ is not degenerate. We can see that $\boldsymbol{M} \times v'$ and $\boldsymbol{q} \cdot v'$ are fixed/determined by the end of the computation, for all $(t, \boldsymbol{q}, \boldsymbol{a}) \in \mathcal{C}$. Non-degeneracy implies that the input of $\mathcal{P}$ (and hence all base variables) is uniquely determined.

### 3.4    Efficiently Finding Collision Structures

In this section we show that it is possible to efficiently determine whether a Linicrypt program has a collision structure, by analyzing its algebraic representation. The algorithm for finding a collision structure is given in Fig. 2.

**Lemma 8.** *FindColStruct($\mathcal{P}$) (Fig. 2) outputs a collision structure for $\mathcal{P}$ if and only if one exists. Furthermore, the running time of FindColStruct is polynomial (in the size of $\mathcal{P}$'s algebraic representation).*

In the interest of space, the proof is deferred to Appendix A.

### 3.5 Breaking Collision Resistance Implies Collision Structure

So far our discussion has centered around the relationship between collision structures and second-preimage resistance. We now show that if $\mathcal{P}$ fails to be even *collision resistant* (in the random oracle model), then it has a collision structure. The main approach is to observe the oracle queries made by an arbitrary attacker (who computes a collision), and "extract" a collision structure from these queries.

The results in this subsection hold only for the following subclass of Linicrypt programs. In Sect. B.2 we discuss specifically why the results are restricted to this subclass.

**Definition 9.** *Let $\mathcal{P} = (M, C)$ be a Linicrypt program, with $C = \{(t_1, q_1, a_1), \ldots, (t_n, q_n, a_n)\}$. If all of $\{t_1, \ldots, t_n\}$ are distinct then we say that $\mathcal{P}$ has **distinct nonces**.*

**Lemma 10.** *Let $\mathcal{P}$ be a deterministic Linicrypt program with distinct nonces that makes $n$ oracle queries. Let $\mathcal{A}$ be an oracle program that makes at most $N$ oracle queries. If*

$$\Pr[ColGame(\mathcal{P}, \mathcal{A}, \lambda) = 1] > \left(\frac{N}{n}\right)^{2n} / |\mathbb{F}_\lambda|$$

$$\text{or if } \Pr[2PIGame(\mathcal{P}, \mathcal{A}, \lambda) = 1] > \left(\frac{N}{n}\right)^{n} / |\mathbb{F}_\lambda|$$

*then $\mathcal{P}$ either has a collision structure or is degenerate.*

*Proof.* Without loss of generality, we can assume the following about $\mathcal{A}$:

- Let $(x, x')$ be the two preimages from the games (in 2PIGame $\mathcal{A}$ gets $x$ as input and gives $x'$ as output; in ColGame $\mathcal{A}$ outputs both $x$ and $x'$). We assume that $\mathcal{A}^H$ has made the oracle queries that $\mathcal{P}^H(x)$ and $\mathcal{P}^H(x')$ will make. In ColGame this can be achieved by modifying $\mathcal{A}$ to run these two computations as its last action. In 2PIGame this can be achieved by having $\mathcal{A}$ run $\mathcal{P}^H(x)$ as its *first* action and $\mathcal{P}^H(x')$ as its last action.
- $\mathcal{A}$ never repeats a query to $H$. This can be achieved by simple memoization. Note that when $\mathcal{A}$ runs, say, $\mathcal{P}^H(x')$ as its last action, some of those oracle queries may have been made previously.
- $\mathcal{A}^H$ can actually output $(v, v')$, where $v$ is the set of *base variables* in the computation of $\mathcal{P}^H(x)$, and $v'$ the base variables in $\mathcal{P}^H(x')$. This is because the base variables are computed during the process of running $\mathcal{P}^H(x)$ and $\mathcal{P}^H(x')$.

Note that the base variables have the following property. Let $c = (t, q, a)$ be one of the oracle constraints of $\mathcal{P}$. Then the computation $\mathcal{P}^H(x)$ (and hence $\mathcal{A}^H$ as well) at some point makes an oracle query $H(t, q \cdot v)$ and gets a response $a \cdot v$.

From these assumptions, whenever $\mathcal{A}$ outputs a successful collision there exist well-defined mappings $T, T' : \mathcal{C} \to \mathbb{N}$ such that:

- For every constraint $c = (t, q, a) \in \mathcal{C}$, the $T(c)$th query made by $\mathcal{A}^H$ is the one corresponding to oracle constraint $c$ in the computation of $\mathcal{P}^H(x)$. In other words, it is the query in which $\mathcal{A}^H$ "decided" what $q \cdot v$ should be (and learned what $a \cdot v$ was as a result of the query).
- Similarly, the $T'(c)$th query made by $\mathcal{A}^H$ is the one corresponding to oracle constraint $c$ in the computation of $\mathcal{P}^H(x')$. This is the query in which $q \cdot v'$ was determined.

How many possible mappings $(T, T')$ are there if $\mathcal{A}$ makes $N$ oracle queries? Let $N_i$ be the number of oracle queries that $\mathcal{A}$ makes which have nonce $t_i$. Since the nonces are distinct, we have $\sum_i N_i \leq N$. There are only $N_i$ choices for how $T$ or $T'$ can map $T(c_i)$. Hence there are at most $\prod_{i=1}^n N_i^2$ possible $(T, T')$ mappings. However, in the 2PIGame, the mapping $T$ is completely fixed since we assume $\mathcal{A}$ performs the computation $\mathcal{P}^H(x)$ as its first action. In that case, there are only $\prod_{i=1}^n N_i$ choices of the mapping $T'$. These products are maximized when each $N_i = N/n$, so we get an upper bound of $(N/n)^{2n}$ possible $(T, T')$ mappings in the ColGame and $(N/n)^n$ mappings in the 2PIGame.

Applying the pigeonhole principle and uniting both cases from the statement of the lemma (collision game and second preimage game), there is a *specific* $(T, T')$ such that:

$$\Pr[\mathcal{A}^H \text{ outputs a valid collision while using mappings } (T, T')] > 1/|\mathbb{F}_\lambda|$$

For the rest of the proof, we condition on the event that $\mathcal{A}$ computes a collision while using this *specific* mapping $(T, T')$. This is without loss of generality by making $\mathcal{A}$, as its final action, output $\perp$ if it observes that some different mapping is used. Hence we can view the association between oracle calls of $\mathcal{P}$ and $\mathcal{A}$ as fixed *a priori*. That is, we can know in advance that a particular oracle call of $\mathcal{A}$ will determine the value of $q \cdot v$ (or $q \cdot v'$) for a specific $q$.

For some $c \in \mathcal{C}$, if $T(c) = T'(c)$, then we call $c$ **convergent**. In this case, $\mathcal{P}^H(x)$ and $\mathcal{P}^H(x')$ make the same $c$-query and receive the same output. In other words, under such a mapping $T, T'$, adversary $\mathcal{A}^H$ will choose that $q \cdot v = q \cdot v'$. If $T(c) \neq T'(c)$, we call $c$ **divergent**—$\mathcal{P}^H(x)$ and $\mathcal{P}^H(x')$ make different $c$-queries, i.e., $q \cdot v \neq q \cdot v'$.

If *all* $c \in \mathcal{C}$ are convergent, then two distinct inputs $x$ and $x'$ cause $\mathcal{P}$ to make identical oracle queries and give identical output. Hence $\mathcal{P}$ is degenerate, and we are done. We continue assuming that some query is divergent, and will conclude that $\mathcal{P}$ has a collision structure.

Define $\mathsf{finish}(c) = \max\{T(c), T'(c)\}$. Note that since $\mathcal{P}$ has distinct nonces, an oracle query made by $\mathcal{A}$ cannot be associated with more than one $c \in \mathcal{C}$. Hence $\mathsf{finish}$ is an injective function.

We obtain a collision structure for $\mathcal{P}$ as follows. Order the oracle constraints in $\mathcal{C}$ as $(c_1, \ldots, c_n)$, where all of the convergent queries come first, followed by the divergent queries ordered by increasing finish time. Let $i^*$ be the index of the divergent query with earliest finish time. Then:

- $i^* \leq i \Leftrightarrow c_i$ is divergent
- $i^* \leq i < j \Leftrightarrow \mathsf{finish}(i) < \mathsf{finish}(j)$

*Claim.* $(i^*; c_1, \ldots, c_n)$ is a collision structure for $\mathcal{P}$.

In the following, we write each oracle constraint $c_i$ as $c_i = (t_i, \boldsymbol{q}_i, \boldsymbol{a}_i)$.

For $j < i^*$, the query $c_j$ is convergent so we have $\boldsymbol{q}_j \cdot \boldsymbol{v} = \boldsymbol{q}_j \cdot \boldsymbol{v}'$ and $\boldsymbol{a}_j \cdot \boldsymbol{v} = \boldsymbol{a}_j \cdot \boldsymbol{v}'$. Since the outputs of the two executions of $\mathcal{P}$ are also identical, we also have $\boldsymbol{M}\boldsymbol{v} = \boldsymbol{M}\boldsymbol{v}'$. Since $c_{i^*}$ is divergent, we have $\boldsymbol{q}_{i^*} \cdot \boldsymbol{v} \neq \boldsymbol{q}_{i^*} \cdot \boldsymbol{v}'$. From this we conclude that:

$$\boldsymbol{q}_{i^*} \notin \mathsf{span}\Big(\{\boldsymbol{q}_1, \ldots, \boldsymbol{q}_{i^*-1}\} \cup \{\boldsymbol{a}_1, \ldots, \boldsymbol{a}_{i^*-1}\} \cup \mathsf{rows}(\boldsymbol{M})\Big).$$

This is the first property required of a collision structure.

It remains to show that for all $i > i^*$,

$$\boldsymbol{a}_i \notin \mathsf{span}\Big(\{\boldsymbol{q}_1, \ldots, \boldsymbol{q}_i\} \cup \{\boldsymbol{a}_1, \ldots, \boldsymbol{a}_{i-1}\} \cup \mathsf{rows}(\boldsymbol{M})\Big).$$

Suppose for contradiction that the above is false, and that we actually have:

$$\boldsymbol{a}_i = \sum_{j \leq i} \alpha_j \boldsymbol{q}_j + \sum_{j < i} \beta_j \boldsymbol{a}_j + \gamma \boldsymbol{M}$$

Focus on the moment when $\mathcal{A}$ has asked its $\mathsf{finish}(c_i)$th query and is awaiting the response from $H$. By symmetry, suppose $\mathsf{finish}(c_i) = T'(c_i)$, so that this query is on $\boldsymbol{q}_i \cdot \boldsymbol{v}'$; the result of the query will be assigned to $\boldsymbol{a}_i \cdot \boldsymbol{v}'$. At this moment:

- All queries $c_j$ for $i^* \leq j < i$ are finished. This means that the oracle queries of $\mathcal{A}^H$ have already determined $\boldsymbol{q}_j \cdot \boldsymbol{v}$, $\boldsymbol{a}_j \cdot \boldsymbol{v}$, $\boldsymbol{q}_j \cdot \boldsymbol{v}'$, and $\boldsymbol{a}_j \cdot \boldsymbol{v}'$. Further, the queries (but not responses) of oracle constraint $c_i$ have been fixed as well—these values are $\boldsymbol{q}_i \cdot \boldsymbol{v}$ and $\boldsymbol{q}_i \cdot \boldsymbol{v}'$.
- $\boldsymbol{a}_i \cdot \boldsymbol{v}$ has already been fixed, since this happened at time $T(c_i) < T'(c_i)$. But $\boldsymbol{a}_i \cdot \boldsymbol{v}'$ is about to be chosen as a uniform field element.

Now consider the expression $\boldsymbol{a}_i \cdot (\boldsymbol{v}' - \boldsymbol{v})$:

$$\boldsymbol{a}_i \cdot (\boldsymbol{v}' - \boldsymbol{v}) = \sum_{j \leq i} \alpha_j \boldsymbol{q}_j \cdot (\boldsymbol{v}' - \boldsymbol{v}) + \sum_{j < i} \beta_j \boldsymbol{a}_j \cdot (\boldsymbol{v}' - \boldsymbol{v}) + \gamma \boldsymbol{M}(\boldsymbol{v}' - \boldsymbol{v})$$

For $j < i^*$ we know that query $c_j$ is convergent. This implies that $\boldsymbol{q}_j \cdot (\boldsymbol{v}' - \boldsymbol{v}) = 0$ and $\boldsymbol{a}_j \cdot (\boldsymbol{v}' - \boldsymbol{v}) = 0$. We also know that $\boldsymbol{M}(\boldsymbol{v}' - \boldsymbol{v}) = 0$, in the case that $\mathcal{A}^H$ is successful generating a collision. Cancelling these terms gives:

$$\boldsymbol{a}_i \cdot (\boldsymbol{v}' - \boldsymbol{v}) = \sum_{j=i^*}^{i} \alpha_j \boldsymbol{q}_j \cdot (\boldsymbol{v}' - \boldsymbol{v}) + \sum_{j=i^*}^{i-1} \beta_j \boldsymbol{a}_j \cdot (\boldsymbol{v}' - \boldsymbol{v})$$

Isolating $a_i \cdot v'$ gives:

$$a_i \cdot v' = -a_i \cdot v + \sum_{j=i^*}^{i} \alpha_j q_j \cdot (v' - v) + \sum_{j=i^*}^{i-1} \beta_j a_j \cdot (v' - v)$$

But all terms on the right-hand side have already been fixed, while the term on the left is chosen uniformly in $\mathbb{F}$. So equality holds with probability $1/|\mathbb{F}_\lambda|$. This contradicts the assumption that $\mathcal{A}$ succeeds with strictly greater probability.

### 3.6    Putting Everything Together

Our main characterization shows that second-preimage resistance and collision resistance coincide for this class of Linicrypt programs, in a very strong sense:

**Theorem 11.** *Let $\mathcal{P}$ be a deterministic Linicrypt program with distinct nonces, making $n$ oracle queries. Then the following are equivalent:*

*1. There is an adversary $\mathcal{A}$ making $N$ oracle queries such that*

$$\Pr[\mathsf{ColGame}(\mathcal{P}, \mathcal{A}, \lambda) = 1] > \left(\frac{N}{n}\right)^{2n} / |\mathbb{F}_\lambda|.$$

*2. There is an adversary $\mathcal{A}$ making $N$ oracle queries such that*

$$\Pr[\mathsf{2PI}(\mathcal{P}, \mathcal{A}, \lambda) = 1] > \left(\frac{N}{n}\right)^{n} / |\mathbb{F}_\lambda|.$$

*3. There is an adversary $\mathcal{A}$ making at most $2n$ oracle queries such that*

$$\Pr[\mathsf{2PIGame}(\mathcal{P}, \mathcal{A}, \lambda) = 1] = 1.$$

*4. $\mathcal{P}$ either has a collision structure or is degenerate*

**Corollary 12.** *The collision resistance (equivalently, second-preimage resistance) of deterministic, distinct-nonce Linicrypt programs $\mathcal{P}$ can be decided in polynomial time (in the size of $\mathcal{P}$'s algebraic representation).*

*Proof.* Using standard linear algebraic operations (e.g., Gaussian elimination), one can check $\mathcal{P}$ for degeneracy or for the existence of a collision structure in polynomial time.

## 4    A Simple Application

We can illustrate the use of our main theorem with a simple example application. Suppose we have access to a random oracle which is compressing by a factor of 2-to-1. In the Linicrypt notation, this would be an oracle that takes 2 field elements (and the oracle nonce) as input and produces one field element as output—$H : \{0,1\}^* \times \mathbb{F}^2 \to \mathbb{F}$. If we require a collision resistant function that compresses by $k$-to-1 (for some fixed $k$), the following natural Merkle-Damgård-style iterative hash comes to mind:

$$
\begin{array}{l}
\mathcal{P}^H(x_1, x_2, \ldots, x_k): \\[4pt]
\quad y_1 := x_1 \\
\quad y_2 := H(2; y_1, x_2) \\
\quad y_3 := H(3; y_2, x_3) \\
\quad \vdots \\
\quad y_k := H(k; y_{k-1}, x_k) \\
\quad \text{return } y_k
\end{array}
$$

The algebraic representation of this program is:

$$
\begin{array}{c}
\begin{array}{ccccccccccc}
 & x_2 & x_3 & \cdots & x_k & y_1 & y_2 & y_3 & \cdots & y_{k-1} & y_k
\end{array} \\
\boldsymbol{M} = \begin{bmatrix} 0 & 0 & \cdots & 0 & 0 & 0 & 0 & \cdots & 0 & 1 \end{bmatrix} \\
\boldsymbol{Q}_2 = \begin{bmatrix} 0 & 0 & \cdots & 0 & 1 & 0 & 0 & \cdots & 0 & 0 \\ 1 & 0 & \cdots & 0 & 0 & 0 & 0 & \cdots & 0 & 0 \end{bmatrix} \\
\boldsymbol{a}_2 = \begin{bmatrix} 0 & 0 & \cdots & 0 & 0 & 1 & 0 & \cdots & 0 & 0 \end{bmatrix} \\
\boldsymbol{Q}_3 = \begin{bmatrix} 0 & 0 & \cdots & 0 & 0 & 1 & 0 & \cdots & 0 & 0 \\ 0 & 1 & \cdots & 0 & 0 & 0 & 0 & \cdots & 0 & 0 \end{bmatrix} \\
\boldsymbol{a}_3 = \begin{bmatrix} 0 & 0 & \cdots & 0 & 0 & 0 & 1 & \cdots & 0 & 0 \end{bmatrix} \\
\vdots \\
\boldsymbol{Q}_k = \begin{bmatrix} 0 & 0 & \cdots & 0 & 0 & 0 & 0 & \cdots & 1 & 0 \\ 0 & 0 & \cdots & 1 & 0 & 0 & 0 & \cdots & 0 & 0 \end{bmatrix} \\
\boldsymbol{a}_k = \begin{bmatrix} 0 & 0 & \cdots & 0 & 0 & 0 & 0 & \cdots & 0 & 1 \end{bmatrix}
\end{array}
$$

We have numbered the oracle constraints so that constraint $(i, \boldsymbol{Q}_i, \boldsymbol{a}_i)$ corresponds to the statement "$y_i := H(i; y_{i-1}, x_i)$" in $\mathcal{P}$.

To determine whether this program is collision-resistant, we execute the FindColStruct algorithm.[1] Initially all oracle constraints start in the set LEFT, and RIGHT starts out empty. The first loop in FindColStruct moves oracle constraints from LEFT to RIGHT whenever their $\boldsymbol{a}_i$ value is linearly independent of all other vectors appearing in LEFT (the multiset of vectors is represented as the variable $V$ in FindColStruct).

In this program, every $\boldsymbol{a}_i$ vector is zeroes everywhere except for a 1 corresponding to the "$y_i$" column. Also note that $\boldsymbol{a}_k$ is identical to $\boldsymbol{M}$, and $\boldsymbol{a}_i$ (for $i < k$) appears as the first row of $\boldsymbol{Q}_{i+1}$ (see the example with $\boldsymbol{a}_2$ and $\boldsymbol{Q}_3$ above). In other words, every $\boldsymbol{a}_i$ is always in the span of other vectors appearing in LEFT, so no oracle constraint will ever be added to RIGHT.

Hence, FindColStruct will terminate with RIGHT $= \emptyset$ and return $\perp$. From our main characterization, this proves that the function is collision-resistant.

---

[1] Look ahead to Appendix B.1 to see how the characterization and FindColStruct are modified to support a random oracle with arity 2, as we have in this case.

# 5    Extensions, Limitations, Future Work

In Appendix B we discuss several extensions and limitations of our techniques:

- How the results generalize to oracle calls that take several field elements as input (results as stated in previous sections consider a random oracle of the form $H : \{0,1\}^* \times \mathbb{F} \to \mathbb{F}$).
- Why the restriction to distinct nonces is significant, and how repeated nonces make the picture more complicated.
- Extending the work to support the ideal cipher model instead of the random oracle model.

# A    Proofs

*Proof (Proof of Lemma 8).* Some useful invariants in FindColStruct are that at any time, LEFT $\cup$ RIGHT $= \mathcal{C}$ and $V$ is a multiset of the vectors appearing in rows($M$) and LEFT. Note that FindColStruct works in two phases: it starts with all oracle queries in LEFT and in the first phase moves some to RIGHT. In the second phase, it moves some of the oracle queries back into LEFT.

($\Rightarrow$) First, we argue that if FindColStruct($\mathcal{P}$) $= (i^*; c_1, \ldots, c_n) \neq \bot$, then this output is indeed a collision structure. Write each oracle constraint $c_i$ as $c_i = (t_i, \boldsymbol{q}_i, \boldsymbol{a}_i)$.

- At the time the second while-loop terminates, we must have $\boldsymbol{q}_{i^*} \notin$ span($V$) since otherwise $c_{i^*}$ would have been moved to LEFT. But $V = \{\boldsymbol{q}_1, \ldots, \boldsymbol{q}_{i^*-1}\} \cup \{\boldsymbol{a}_1, \ldots, \boldsymbol{a}_{i^*-1}\} \cup$ rows($M$), so this establishes one of the required properties of a collision structure.
- For $j \geq i^*$, consider the time at which $c_j$ is about to be added to RIGHT in the first while-loop (i.e., the point that the while loop body is entered). At that point, LEFT $= \{c_1, \ldots, c_j\}$, so $V$ contains $\{\boldsymbol{q}_1, \ldots, \boldsymbol{q}_j\} \cup \{\boldsymbol{a}_1, \ldots, \boldsymbol{a}_j\} \cup$ rows($M$). Since the while-loop condition is fulfilled, we have

$$\boldsymbol{a}_j \notin \text{span}(V \setminus \{\boldsymbol{a}_j\}) = \text{span}\Big(\{\boldsymbol{q}_1, \ldots, \boldsymbol{q}_j\} \cup \{\boldsymbol{a}_1, \ldots, \boldsymbol{a}_{j-1}\} \cup \text{rows}(M)\Big)$$

which is the other condition required for a collision structure.

($\Leftarrow$) For the other direction, suppose $(i^*, c_1, \ldots, c_n)$ is some collision structure for $\mathcal{P}$. We will show that the algorithm adds $c_{i^*}, \ldots, c_n$ to RIGHT in the first phase, but does *not* move $c_{i^*}$ back to LEFT in the second phase. This implies that the algorithm terminates with $|\text{RIGHT}| \neq \emptyset$, so by the previous reasoning it outputs some valid collision structure (perhaps different than the collision structure we are assuming exists).

The fact that $c_{i^*}, \ldots, c_n$ are added to RIGHT in the first phase is essentially the converse of what was shown above. For example, the collision structure property is that $\boldsymbol{a}_n \notin \text{span}\Big(\{\boldsymbol{q}_1, \ldots, \boldsymbol{q}_n\} \cup \{\boldsymbol{a}_1, \ldots, \boldsymbol{a}_{n-1}\} \cup \text{rows}(M)\Big)$, implying that $c_n$ can trigger the while-loop and be added to RIGHT immediately.

Note that even if other constraints are added to RIGHT in this phase, it only makes $V$ smaller, so only causes the condition to check a *smaller* span than in the collision-property definition. A simple inductive argument establishes that $c_{i^*}, \ldots, c_n$ are eventually added to RIGHT.

Since $\{c_{i^*}, \ldots, c_n\} \subseteq$ RIGHT after the first phase, we must have LEFT $\subseteq \{c_1, \ldots, c_{i^*-1}\}$ after the first phase. We want to show that $c_{i^*}$ is never placed back into LEFT. For the sake of contradiction, suppose not. Define $S$ to be a set of indices such that LEFT $= \{c_i \mid i \in S\}$ at the time $c_{i^*}$ is about to be moved into LEFT. Then $q_{i^*} \in \mathsf{span}(\mathsf{rows}(M) \cup \{q_i, a_i \mid i \in S\})$. We can then write:

$$q_{i^*} = \sum_{j \in S} \alpha_j q_j + \sum_{j \in S} \beta_j a_j + \gamma M$$

For $j > i^*$, the constraint $c_j$ was previously in RIGHT and was moved back into LEFT. The only way to be moved back into LEFT is for $q_j$ to be in the span of other vectors already in LEFT (and hence already on the right-hand side of this expression). Hence, without loss of generality we can remove the terms involving $q_j$ for $j > i^*$, to obtain:

$$q_{i^*} = \sum_{j \in S \setminus \{i^*, \ldots, n\}} \alpha'_j q_j + \sum_{j \in S} \beta'_j a_j + \gamma' M$$

Let $j^*$ be the highest $j \in S$ for which $\beta'_j \neq 0$. There are two cases.

Case $j^* < i^*$: Then all of the nonzero terms $q_j, a_j$ on the right-hand side have subscript less than $i^*$. This contradicts the fact (from the original collision structure) that $q_{i^*} \notin \mathsf{span}(\mathsf{rows}(M) \cup \{q_j, a_j \mid j < i^*\})$.

Case $j^* > i^*$: We can solve for $a_{j^*}$ in the above expression, yielding:

$$a_{j^*} = -\frac{1}{\beta'_{j^*}} \left( \sum_{j \in S \setminus \{i^*, \ldots, n\}} \alpha'_j q_j - q_{i^*} + \sum_{j \in S \setminus \{j^*\}} \beta'_j a_j + \gamma' M \right)$$

But now all nonzero $q_j$ and $a_j$ terms on the right-hand side have subscript less than $j^*$. This contradicts the fact (from the original collision structure) that $a_{j^*} \notin \mathsf{span}(\{q_j \mid j < j^*\} \cup \{a_j \mid j < j^*\} \cup \mathsf{rows}(M))$.

In either case we have a contradiction to the claim that $c_{i^*}$ is moved back into LEFT. Since the algorithm terminates with at least $c_{i^*} \in$ RIGHT, it outputs some valid collision structure.

## B    Extensions, Limitations, Future Work

### B.1    Generalizing to Higher Arity

For simplicity our results were proven for Linicrypt programs in which all oracle calls have arity 1. That is, $H : \{0,1\}^* \times \mathbb{F} \to \mathbb{F}$, and all oracle constraints have the form $(t, q, a)$ where $q$ is a single row. This reflects a program that always queries the oracle as $H(t; v)$ where $v$ is a *single* field element.

More generally, Linicrypt allows calls to $H$ with multiple field elements as arguments. This leads to oracle constraints of the form $(t, Q, a)$ where $Q$ is now a matrix. We briefly discuss the changes necessary to support such programs. Basically, whenever the definitions (of degeneracy & collision structure) or algorithms (to find a second preimage or to find a collision structure) refer to $q$, the analogous condition should hold with respect to all rows of $Q$.

The generalized definition of degeneracy (Definition 4) is that:

$$\text{span}(e_1, \ldots, e_k) \not\subseteq \text{span}\left( \bigcup_{(t, Q, a) \in \mathcal{C}} \text{rows}(Q) \cup \text{rows}(M) \right)$$

The generalized definition of collision structure (Definition 6) requires the following change:

2. $\text{rows}(Q_{i*}) \not\subseteq \text{span}\left( \text{rows}(Q_1) \cup \cdots \cup \text{rows}(Q_{i*-1}) \cup \{a_1, \ldots, a_{i*-1}\} \cup \text{rows}(M) \right)$

3. For $j \geq i^*$: $a_j \notin \text{span}\left( \text{rows}(Q_1) \cup \cdots \cup \text{rows}(Q_j) \cup \{a_1, \ldots, a_{j-1}\} \cup \text{rows}(M) \right)$

Specifically, for item (2) it is enough if *any row* of $Q_{i*}$ is not in the given span.

In the FindSecondPreimage algorithm (Fig. 1), there are times when the algorithm chooses $q_j \cdot v'$ arbitrarily. This happens when such a constraint would be linearly independent of the existing constraints on $v'$. In the analogous generalized case, we might have *only some of the rows* of $Q_j$ linearly independent of the existing constraints. In that case, some of the components of $Q_j \times v'$ are already fixed. We obviously cannot choose these arbitrarily—only the unconstrained positions in $Q_j \times v'$ are fixed arbitrarily. One can verify that the algorithm only attempts to arbitrarily fix some values if there is some row of $Q_j$ linearly independent with existing constraints on $v'$.

In the FindColStruct algorithm (Fig. 2) we let $V$ now contain $Q$-matrices as well as simple $a$-vectors. Then we overload notation so that $\text{span}(V)$ considers the span of all of the rows of all matrices/vectors in $V$. The second "while" condition is modified as follows:

$$\text{while } \exists (t, Q, a) \in \mathsf{RIGHT} \text{ such that } \text{rows}(Q) \subseteq \text{span}(V)$$

In other words, $(t, Q, a)$ is moved from LEFT to RIGHT if *all rows of $Q$* are spanned by $V$.

With these modifications, all proofs in Sect. 3 go through with straightforward modifications.

## B.2    Why the Restriction to Distinct Nonces?

The main characterization holds for Linicrypt programs with distinct nonces. It is instructive to understand why the results are limited in this way. Specifically, where do we use the property of distinct nonces?

Suppose $\mathcal{A}$ breaks the collision-resistance of $\mathcal{P}$. We observe the oracle queries made by $\mathcal{A}$ and obtain a mapping between these queries and the ones made in

$\mathcal{P}^H(x)$ and $\mathcal{P}^H(x')$. When the nonces are distinct, a query made by $\mathcal{A}$ can only be associated with a unique oracle constraint $c \in \mathcal{C}$. When the nonces are not distinct, a single query of $\mathcal{A}$ can serve double-duty and correspond to two oracle constraints of $\mathcal{P}$. This indeed causes the argument to break down.

We illustrate with the two example Linicrypt programs:

$$\mathcal{P}_1^H(x, y) = H(2, H(1, x)) - H(3, y)$$
$$\mathcal{P}_2^H(x, y) = H(\quad H(\quad x)) - H(\quad y)$$

The first has distinct nonces and is indeed collision resistant (it has no collision structure). The second program is not collision-resistant, because $\mathcal{P}_2^H(x, H(x)) = 0$ for all $x$. In other words, $(x, H(x))$ and $(x', H(x'))$ constitute a collision.

When given inputs of this form, $\mathcal{P}_2$ makes duplicate queries—both $H(H(x))$ (the outermost $H$-call) and $H(y)$ receive the same argument. In our previous proofs, we would observe the adversary making such a query, which would have to be associated with two distinct oracle constraints.

Another way of seeing what happens is that in the *algebraic representation* of $\mathcal{P}_2$, the base variables $H(x)$ and $y$ correspond to independent vectors. In this case, the adversary's choice of inputs causes these vectors to coincide, and this has the effect of "collapsing" two oracle queries.

Interestingly, it is possible to give an ad-hoc argument that $\mathcal{P}_2$ is second-preimage resistant. When $x$ and $y$ are chosen uniformly, this has the effect of keeping the vectors (in the algebraic representation) corresponding to $H(x)$ and $y$ independent. We can then argue that the adversary doesn't make any oracle query that is associated with two distinct queries of $\mathcal{P}_2$, so the reasoning of our main theorem also applies in this case. Hence, $\mathcal{P}_2$ demonstrates that our main characterization is different for Linicrypt programs with non-distinct nonces.

## B.3    Random Oracle vs Ideal Cipher

A natural application of collision resistance would be the constructions of collision-resistant hash functions from an ideal cipher [3,12]. It should be possible to use Linicrypt to reason about constructions in the ideal cipher model, although it would require non-trivial modifications. We could interpret $E(k, m)$ as $H(\mathsf{E}, k, m)$ and $D(k, c)$ as $H(\mathsf{D}, k, c)$. The constraint that $D(k, E(k, m)) = m$ adds some extra structure that must be reflected in the algebraic representation. For example, if a program $\mathcal{P}$ makes a query $c = E(k, m)$, we must consider the adversary's ability to make this forward query but also its ability to make the corresponding backwards query $D(k, c)$. Both forward/backwards queries must be considered before deeming the *pair* of queries $E(k, m)$ and $D(k, c)$ unreachable.

We do not foresee the transition to ideal cipher model to be particularly problematic. However, the specific analysis of [3] shows several constructions of hash functions from ideal ciphers where the *round functions are not collision-resistant*, and yet their use in a Merkle-Damgård construction gives a collision-resistant result. So far, the theory of Linicrypt is not developed enough to reason about programs with looping constructs, as in an iterated hash function (despite the fact that such reasoning happens to be tractable for the specific example in Sect. 4).

# References

1. Bellare, M., Micciancio, D.: A new paradigm for collision-free hashing: incremental-ity at reduced cost. In: Fumy, W. (ed.) EUROCRYPT 1997. LNCS, vol. 1233, pp. 163–192. Springer, Heidelberg (1997). https://doi.org/10.1007/3-540-69053-0_13

2. Bernstein, D.J., et al.: SPHINCS: practical stateless hash-based signatures. In: Oswald, E., Fischlin, M. (eds.) EUROCRYPT 2015. LNCS, vol. 9056, pp. 368–397. Springer, Heidelberg (2015). https://doi.org/10.1007/978-3-662-46800-5_15

3. Black, J., Rogaway, P., Shrimpton, T.: Black-box analysis of the block-cipher-based hash-function constructions from PGV. In: Yung, M. (ed.) CRYPTO 2002. LNCS, vol. 2442, pp. 320–335. Springer, Heidelberg (2002). https://doi.org/10.1007/3-540-45708-9_21

4. Bos, J.N.E., Chaum, D.: Provably unforgeable signatures. In: Brickell, E.F. (ed.) CRYPTO 1992. LNCS, vol. 740, pp. 1–14. Springer, Heidelberg (1993). https://doi.org/10.1007/3-540-48071-4_1

5. Carmer, B., Rosulek, M.: Linicrypt: a model for practical cryptography. In: Robshaw, M., Katz, J. (eds.) CRYPTO 2016. LNCS, vol. 9816, pp. 416–445. Springer, Heidelberg (2016). https://doi.org/10.1007/978-3-662-53015-3_15

6. Dahmen, E., Okeya, K., Takagi, T., Vuillaume, C.: Digital signatures out of second-preimage resistant hash functions. In: Buchmann, J., Ding, J. (eds.) PQCrypto 2008. LNCS, vol. 5299, pp. 109–123. Springer, Heidelberg (2008). https://doi.org/10.1007/978-3-540-88403-3_8

7. Even, S., Goldreich, O., Micali, S.: On-line/off-line digital schemes. In: Brassard, G. (ed.) CRYPTO'89. LNCS, vol. 435, pp. 263–275. Springer, Heidelberg (1990)

8. Hülsing, A.: W-OTS+ - shorter signatures for hash-based signature schemes. In: Youssef, A., Nitaj, A., Hassanien, A.E. (eds.) AFRICACRYPT 13. LNCS, vol. 7918, pp. 173–188. Springer, Heidelberg (2013)

9. Impagliazzo, R.: A personal view of average-case complexity. In: Proceedings of the Tenth Annual Structure in Complexity Theory Conference, Minneapolis, Minnesota, USA, 19–22 June, 1995, pp. 134–147. IEEE Computer Society (1995)

10. Lamport, L.: Constructing digital signatures from a one-way function. Technical report SRI-CSL-98, SRI International Computer Science Laboratory, October 1979

11. Merkle, R.C.: A digital signature based on a conventional encryption function. In: Pomerance, C. (ed.) CRYPTO 1987. LNCS, vol. 293, pp. 369–378. Springer, Heidelberg (1988). https://doi.org/10.1007/3-540-48184-2_32

12. Preneel, B., Govaerts, R., Vandewalle, J.: Hash functions based on block ciphers: a synthetic approach. In: Stinson, D.R. (ed.) CRYPTO 1993. LNCS, vol. 773, pp. 368–378. Springer, Heidelberg (1994). https://doi.org/10.1007/3-540-48329-2_31

13. Wagner, D.: A generalized birthday problem. In: Yung, M. (ed.) CRYPTO 2002. LNCS, vol. 2442, pp. 288–304. Springer, Heidelberg (2002). https://doi.org/10.1007/3-540-45708-9_19

# Efficient Information-Theoretic Secure Multiparty Computation over $\mathbb{Z}/p^k\mathbb{Z}$ via Galois Rings

Mark Abspoel[1,2(✉)], Ronald Cramer[1,3], Ivan Damgård[4], Daniel Escudero[4], and Chen Yuan[1]

[1] Centrum Wiskunde & Informatica (CWI), Amsterdam, The Netherlands
abspoel@cwi.nl
[2] Philips Research, Eindhoven, The Netherlands
[3] Mathematisch Instituut, Leiden University, Leiden, The Netherlands
[4] Aarhus University, Aarhus, Denmark

**Abstract.** At CRYPTO 2018, Cramer et al. introduced a secret-sharing based protocol called SPDZ$_{2^k}$ that allows for secure multiparty computation (MPC) in the dishonest majority setting over the ring of integers modulo $2^k$, thus solving a long-standing open question in MPC about secure computation over rings in this setting. In this paper we study this problem in the information-theoretic scenario. More specifically, we ask the following question: Can we obtain information-theoretic MPC protocols that work over rings with comparable efficiency to corresponding protocols over fields? We answer this question in the affirmative by presenting an efficient protocol for robust Secure Multiparty Computation over $\mathbb{Z}/p^k\mathbb{Z}$ (for *any* prime $p$ and positive integer $k$) that is perfectly secure against active adversaries corrupting a fraction of at most 1/3 players, and a robust protocol that is statistically secure against an active adversary corrupting a fraction of at most 1/2 players.

## 1 Introduction

Secure Multiparty Computation (MPC) is a technique that allows several parties to compute any functionality in secret inputs, while revealing nothing more than the output, even if an adversary corrupts $t$ of the $n$ parties.

Several flavors of MPC exist, depending on the desired security level and threat model considered. A protocol is perfectly secure if an adversary's view of the protocol can be simulated given only his inputs and outputs, and where the simulated view follows exactly the same distribution as the real view. It is statistically secure if the statistical distance between the views is negligible in a security parameter. We will say that a protocol is information-theoretically secure if it is either perfectly or statistically secure.

MPC has been a very active area of research since the 1980s, beginning with the seminal work of Yao on garbled circuits. Since then, many theoretical and practical results have been found by the community, extending the knowledge about what is possible, and increasing efficiency. However, almost all the progress

© International Association for Cryptologic Research 2019
D. Hofheinz and A. Rosen (Eds.): TCC 2019, LNCS 11891, pp. 471–501, 2019.
https://doi.org/10.1007/978-3-030-36030-6_19

has focused on arithmetic circuits over finite fields (even Boolean circuits are a special case of this). On the other hand, it is clearly also interesting to securely compute functions that are defined over other rings, such as $\mathbb{Z}/p^k\mathbb{Z}$, the ring of integers modulo $p^k$, where $p$ is a prime and $k$ is a positive integer. From a practical point of view, for instance, computing modulo $2^{32}$ or $2^{64}$ is close to what standard CPUs do. Closely matching the data format used by CPUs is an advantage since one expects that when programming secure computation one can reuse some of the techniques that CPUs use to run efficiently. Additionally, bitwise operations like comparison or bit decomposition are expressed more naturally modulo powers of 2, and are very fast when computed over these rings [1].

This observation has been confirmed in practice [13]. For example, for replicated secret sharing, protocols over rings like $\mathbb{Z}/2^{64}\mathbb{Z}$ can provide up to $8\times$ savings in runtime and memory usage with respect to the field counterpart for some specific applications like neural network evaluation, which are heavy in terms of comparisons [2].

Thus, the natural question is: *can we design protocols that work directly over* $\mathbb{Z}/p^k\mathbb{Z}$ *and have efficiency close to what we can obtain for fields?*

This question was solved recently in the setting of dishonest majority (i.e. $t \leq n-1$), where cryptography is required to provide security, with the introduction of the SPD$\mathbb{Z}_{2^k}$ protocol [8]. This protocol computes with computational security circuits defined over the ring $\mathbb{Z}/2^k\mathbb{Z}$ (in fact, 2 can be replaced by any prime). This is achieved mainly by the introduction of information-theoretic MACs that work over rings with zero divisors and non-invertible elements, like $\mathbb{Z}/p^k\mathbb{Z}$. The efficiency is similar to the SPDZ and MASCOT protocols [12,14] which are state-of-the-art for dishonest majority MPC over finite fields.

However, the question has remained open for the case of honest majority where we can hope to get better (information-theoretic) security. It is also expected that in this setting the computational efficiency improves due to the fact that the computation needed for information-theoretically secure protocols tends to be simpler, as it is independent of a computational security parameter.

## 1.1   Our Contributions

In this work we resolve the above open question. Our solution relies on several key ingredients, which may be interesting in their own right. We give an overview below.

The first ingredient is a new secret sharing scheme that allows us to do "Shamir-style" sharing of elements in $\mathbb{Z}/p^k\mathbb{Z}$. We begin by noticing that Shamir secret sharing works over $\mathbb{Z}/p^k\mathbb{Z}$ as long as the secret is shared by at most $p-1$ players. In order to accomodate more players whilst maintaining a constant $p$, our key solution is to move to a Galois ring $R = (\mathbb{Z}/p^k\mathbb{Z}[x])/(f(x))$, where $f(x) \in (\mathbb{Z}/p^k\mathbb{Z})[x]$ is a monic polynomial of degree $d$ such that $\overline{f}(x) \in \mathbb{F}_p[x]$, its reduction modulo $p$, is irreducible. We get a secret-sharing scheme over $R$ using polynomial interpolation that works with $p^d - 1$ parties, so using the fact that $R$ is a free module over $\mathbb{Z}/p^k\mathbb{Z}$ of rank $d$, we can embed $\mathbb{Z}/p^k\mathbb{Z}$ into the first coordinate of $R$ and get an arithmetic secret-sharing scheme for $\mathbb{Z}/p^k\mathbb{Z}$.

Since we need that $p^d$ is at least the number of players $n$, this incurs an overhead of $\log_p(n)$. To secret-share an element in $\mathbb{Z}/p^k\mathbb{Z}$ in this manner, each player gets an element in $R$ as his share, which can be represented as $\log(n)$ elements in $\mathbb{Z}/p^k\mathbb{Z}$.

In terms of computational complexity, sharing an element requires $O(n^2\text{polylog}(n))$ ring operations which is an improvement over the black-box approach from [10]. It is known that the FFT-algorithms for operations over degree-$d$ finite field extensions, as well as operations on polynomials over such fields, carry over to degree-$d$ Galois rings, preserving quasi-linear (in $d$) computational complexity when working over our ring $R$ [6].

For the remaining key ingredients, we distinguish between two models of MPC: perfectly secure MPC with $t < n/3$ assuming secure channels, and statistically secure MPC with $t < n/2$ in a setting where broadcast is given.

In the setting of perfectly secure MPC with $t < n/3$, we show that we can efficiently perform robust reconstruction in the presence of errors, we show that the hyperinvertible matrices needed in the protocol can be obtained over $R$ can be obtained by lifting them from the residue field, and we show how to get MPC over $\mathbb{Z}/p^k\mathbb{Z}$ by efficient verification of the inputs, using techniques from [7]. We give the modifications needed to the protocol of [4], to obtain MPC over $\mathbb{Z}/p^k\mathbb{Z}$ with the communication complexity for a circuit $C$ of size $|C|$ of $O(n\log(n)|C|)$ elements in $\mathbb{Z}/p^k\mathbb{Z}$.

For the setting where $t < n/2$ and broadcast is given, we develop a way to reduce the soundness error when checking whether values are secret-shared correctly.[1] We also show a packing technique that allows us to reduce the overhead to obtain a total communication complexity $O(|C|n^2\log n)$ ring elements, plus some term that does not depend on the size of the circuit. Finally, to get MPC over $\mathbb{Z}/p^k\mathbb{Z}$ rather than $R$, we show how to efficiently sample $R$-sharings of random elements of $\mathbb{Z}/p^k\mathbb{Z}$ with statistical security. These ideas allow us to adapt the protocol of Beerliova and Hirt [3]. We chose to adapt this protocol rather than the state-of-the-art of [5], because it allows for a simpler exposition of our novel techniques.

The protocols we get for the two settings are both a $\log(n)$ factor away from their original results due to the extension of $\mathbb{Z}/p^k\mathbb{Z}$ to $R$. Follow-up work by some of the authors provides a way to amortize away this factor, by using so-called "reverse multiplication-friendly embeddings" from algebraic geometric codes over rings with asymptotically good parameters [11].

## 1.2 Outline of the Document

In Sect. 2 we introduce the preliminaries for the rest of the work. This includes basic notation, Shamir secret-sharing over commutative rings, and the notion

---

[1] A problem that arises here is that the error probability of the protocol is not automatically negligible even if $p^k$ is large. This is in contrast to the case of finite fields where the error probability usually is $1/|\mathbb{F}|$, where $|\mathbb{F}|$ is the order of the field. As we shall explain, by taking an extension of Galois rings $R \subset \hat{R}$ (where $R$ is a subring), we can reduce the error.

of Galois rings. Then, in Sect. 3 we present our protocol for perfectly secure MPC over $\mathbb{Z}/p^k\mathbb{Z}$ with a corruption threshold of $t < n/3$. Section 4 discusses our protocol for statistically secure MPC over $\mathbb{Z}/p^k\mathbb{Z}$ in the honest majority setting. Finally, in Sect. 5 we present some conclusions and future work.

# 2   Preliminaries

## 2.1   Notation

$\mathbb{Z}$ denotes the ring of integers. For $m \in \mathbb{Z}$, $m\mathbb{Z}$ denotes the ideal $\{m \cdot n \mid n \in \mathbb{Z}\}$, and $\mathbb{Z}/m\mathbb{Z}$ denotes the quotient ring, which we regard as the ring of integers modulo $m$. For a ring $R$, let $R[X]$ denote the ring of polynomials in the variable $X$ with coefficients in $R$. For an integer $m \geq 0$, let $R[X]_{\leq m} \subset R[X]$ denote the set of polynomials in $R[X]$ of degree at most $m$; it is an $R$-module. We denote by $R^*$ the multiplicative subgroup of invertible elements in $R$.

## 2.2   Polynomial Interpolation over Commutative Rings

In this section, we will construct secret-sharing schemes over an arbitrary commutative ring. It will be the building block for the MPC protocols presented in this article. We begin by recalling some notions on polynomial interpolation, and on how it follows from the Chinese Remainder Theorem for rings; we follow the approach of Part II of [9].

Throughout this section, $R$ will denote a commutative ring with multiplicative identity 1. Recall that an *ideal* of $R$ is an additive subgroup $I \subseteq R$ such that $r \cdot x \in I$ for any $r \in R$, $x \in I$, i.e., an $R$-submodule. For $x \in R$, $(x)$ denotes the ideal generated by $x$, i.e., $(x) := \{r \cdot x \mid r \in R\}$. Given two ideals $I, I'$, their product is defined as the ideal $II'$ given by finite sums of products $xy$ with $x \in I$, $y \in I'$, and their sum $I + I'$ is defined as the ideal given by all elements of the from $x + y$, where $x \in I$, $y \in I'$.

Now we state the Chinese Reminder Theorem over rings.

**Theorem 1.** *Let $I_1, \ldots, I_m$ be $m$ ideals of $R$ that are pairwise co-maximal, i.e., for each pair $I, I'$ we have $I + I' = R$. Then, the map*

$$
\begin{aligned}
R/(I_1 \cdots I_m) &\to & R/I_1 \times \cdots \times R/I_m \\
r \bmod I_1 \cdots I_m &\mapsto & (r \bmod I_1, \ldots, r \bmod I_m)
\end{aligned}
$$

*is a ring isomorphism.*

We now recall some notions and results on polynomials over rings.

**Theorem 2.** *Let $g(X), h(X) \in R[X]$ be two polynomials, with $h(X)$ monic (i.e., its leading coefficient is equal to 1). Then, there are two unique polynomials $q(X), r(X) \in R[X]$ such that*

- *$g(X) = h(X)q(X) + r(X)$, and*
- *$\deg r(X) < \deg h(X)$.*

**Corollary 1.** *We have the following:*

1. *For any monic $h(X) \in R[X]$ where $\deg h(X) = d$, we have an $R$-module isomorphism*

$$R[X]_{\leq d-1} \xrightarrow{\sim} R[X]/(h(X))$$
$$g(X) \mapsto g(X) \bmod (h(X)).$$

2. *If $h(X) = X - \alpha$ for some $\alpha \in R$, then*

$$R[X]/(X - \alpha) \xrightarrow{\sim} R$$
$$g(X) \bmod (X - \alpha) \mapsto g(\alpha)$$

   *is an isomorphism of $R$-modules.*

The above properties lead to the following result:

**Theorem 3.** *Let $\alpha_1, \ldots, \alpha_m \in R$ be such that $\alpha_i - \alpha_j$ is invertible for every pair of indices $i \neq j$. We then have that the map*

$$R[X]_{\leq m-1} \rightarrow R \times \cdots \times R$$
$$f(X) \mapsto (f(\alpha_1), \ldots, f(\alpha_m))$$

*is an $R$-module isomorphism. Hence, for any $x_1, \ldots, x_m \in R$, there exists a unique interpolating polynomial of degree at most $m-1$ such that $f(\alpha_i) = x_i$ for each $i$.*

*Proof.* Let $h(X) := (X - \alpha_1) \cdot \ldots \cdot (X - \alpha_m)$. By Corollary 1, we have that the map $R[X]_{\leq m-1} \rightarrow R[X]/(h(X))$ given by $f(X) \mapsto f(X) \bmod (h(X))$ is an $R$-module isomorphism.

Notice that since $\alpha_i - \alpha_j$ is invertible for every $i \neq j$, we have that the ideals $(X - \alpha_i)$ and $(X - \alpha_j)$ are co-maximal for every $i \neq j$; thus by Theorem 1 we have that the map

$$R[X]/(h(X)) \rightarrow R[X]/(X - \alpha_1) \times \cdots \times R[X]/(X - \alpha_m)$$
$$f(X) \bmod h(X) \mapsto (f(X) \bmod X - \alpha_1, \ldots, f(X) \bmod X - \alpha_m)$$

is an $R$-module isomorphism.

Finally, again by Corollary 1, we have that the map $R[X]/(X - \alpha_i) \rightarrow R$ given by $f(X) \bmod X - \alpha_i \mapsto f(\alpha_i)$ is an isomorphism for every $i = 1, \ldots, m$. $\square$

The above theorem thus shows that polynomial interpolation extends from the field to the ring case, provided that the evaluation points are not only pairwise distinct, but that their pairwise differences are invertible.

**Definition 1.** *Let $\alpha_1, \ldots, \alpha_n \in R$. We say that these points form an exceptional sequence if for each pair of integers $1 \leq i, j \leq n$ with $i \neq j$ it holds that $\alpha_i - \alpha_j \in R^*$. We define the Lenstra constant of $R$ to be the maximum length of an exceptional sequence in $R$.*

We the theory seen this far we can already define Shamir-secret sharing over an arbitrary ring $R$.

**Construction 1 (Shamir-secret sharing over $R$).** Let $R$ be a finite ring, and let $\alpha_0, \ldots, \alpha_n \in R$ be an exceptional sequence. Let $t$ be any positive integer such that $t \leq n$. We define the $R$-module of *share vectors* $C = \{(f(\alpha_0), \ldots, f(\alpha_n)) \mid f \in R[X]_{\leq t}\}$. To secret-share an element $x \in R$, pick a uniformly random share vector $\mathbf{x} \leftarrow \{(x_0, \ldots, x_n) \in C \mid x_0 = x\}$, and set the $i$-th share to be $f(\alpha_i)$ for $i = 1, \ldots, n$. If $x$ is secret-shared with each player $P_i$ having a share $x_i$, we denote the share vector $\mathbf{x}$ by $[x]$.

Note that the number of players the secret-sharing scheme admits is bounded by the Lenstra constant minus 1. Combining Construction 1 with Theorem 3 we have the following.

**Proposition 1.** *Construction 1 provides $t$-privacy and $(t+1)$-reconstruction.*

## 2.3    Galois Rings

We now restrict our attention to *Galois rings*, which are very well suited to our setting, since they contain $\mathbb{Z}/p^k\mathbb{Z}$ as a subring and have a relatively high Lenstra constant. For proofs of the assertions in this subsection, we refer the reader to [16].

**Definition 2.** *A Galois ring is a ring of the form $R := (\mathbb{Z}/p^k\mathbb{Z})[Y]/(h(Y))$, where $p$ is a prime number, $k$ is a positive integer, and $h(Y) \in (\mathbb{Z}/p^k\mathbb{Z})[Y]$ is a non-constant, monic polynomial such that its reduction modulo $p$ is an irreducible polynomial in $\mathbb{F}_p[Y]$.*

**Proposition 2.** *Let $R$ as in the above definition. It has the following properties:*

1. *$R$ is a local ring, i.e. it has a unique maximal ideal $(p) \subsetneq R$. We have that $R/(p) \cong \mathbb{F}_{p^d}$, where $d$ denotes the degree of $h$. In particular, we have a homomorphism $\pi : R \to \mathbb{F}_{p^d}$ that is "reduction modulo $p$".*
2. *The Lenstra constant of $R$ is $p^d$.*
3. *For any prime $p$, positive integer $k$, and positive integer $d$ there exists a Galois ring as defined above, and any two of them with identical parameters $p, k, d$ are isomorphic. We may therefore write $R = GR(p^k, d)$.*
4. *If $e$ is any positive integer, then $R$ is a subring of $\hat{R} = GR(p^k, d \cdot e)$. There is a non-constant monic polynomial $\hat{h} \in R[X]$ that is irreducible modulo $p$, such that $\hat{R} = R[X]/(\hat{h}(X))$.*

*Remark 1.* Let $R = GR(p^k, d)$ be a Galois ring. Then there exists an $\mathbb{Z}/p^k\mathbb{Z}$-module isomorphism $(\mathbb{Z}/p^k\mathbb{Z})^d \to R$, that sends each element $\mathbf{e}_j = (0, \ldots, 1, \ldots, 0)$ of the canonical basis of $(\mathbb{Z}/p^k\mathbb{Z})^d$ to $Y^j \bmod (h(Y))$. Also, we have a natural ring embedding $\mathbb{Z}/p^k\mathbb{Z} \hookrightarrow R$, given by $x \mapsto x \bmod h(Y)$.

Moreover, there is another way to uniquely represent the elements of $R$. We have $R/(p) \cong \mathbb{F}_{p^d}$ and there exists a non-zero element $\xi \in R^*$ of multiplicative order $p^d - 1$. By defining the subset $\mathcal{I} = \{0, 1, \xi, \ldots, \xi^{p^d-2}\} \subset R$, it turns out that any element $a \in R$ can be uniquely written as $a = \sum_{i=0}^{k-1} a_i \cdot p^i$ where $a_0, \ldots, a_{k-1} \in \mathcal{I}$. Note that the homomorphism $\pi : R \to \mathbb{F}_{p^d}$ that is reduction modulo $p$ from Item 1 in Proposition 2 is defined by $\pi(a) = a_0$.

This decomposition also allows us to define "division by powers of $p$". Indeed, notice that given an element $a = a_0 + a_1 p + a_2 p^2 + \cdots + a_{k-1} p^{k-1} \in R$ and a positive integer $u$, we have that $p^u$ divides $a$ if and only if $a_i = 0$ for all $i < u$. If this is the case, we then define $a/p^u := a_u + a_{u+1}p + \cdots + a_{k-1}p^{k-u-1}$; notice that $a/p^u \equiv a_u \pmod{p}$. If $u$ is maximal and $a$ is non-zero in $R$, then $a/p^u \in R^*$.

## 3  Perfectly Secure MPC for $t < n/3$ over Galois Rings

We assume that the computation is performed by $n$ players, connected by a complete network of secure and authenticated channels. Let $p$ be a prime number and $k$ a positive integer; $t$ players are under the control of a malicious, computationally unbounded adversary, where $t < n/3$. The adversary can be adaptive and rushing.

We adapt the protocol of [4], which uses three algebraic tools: the interpolation of a polynomial, hyper-invertible matrices and efficient error correction in Reed-Solomon codes. In the original protocol, these tools are defined over finite fields. In this section, we provide analogues of these tools over Galois rings. Note that the first tool, polynomial interpolation, is already given in Construction 1.

With these new tools, we obtain secure computation over any Galois ring $R$ that has a Lenstra constant of at least $n + 1$. By taking the Galois ring to be large enough, we can accommodate any number of players. In Sect. 3.4, we show how to we obtain secure computation over $\mathbb{Z}/p^k\mathbb{Z}$ from computation over $R$. For passive security this is automatic, but for active security this requires verification of the inputs.

### 3.1  Hyper-Invertible Matrices

Hyper-invertible matrices are introduced in [4] to efficiently obtain secret-shared randomness in MPC protocols with active security. Here we summarize their definition and fundamental properties, generalized to hold over rings.

**Definition 3.** *A matrix* $\mathbf{M} \in R^{u \times u'}$ *is hyper-invertible if for any row index set* $I \subseteq \{1, \ldots, u\}$ *and column index set* $J \subseteq \{1, \ldots, u'\}$ *with* $|I| = |J| > 0$, *the matrix* $\mathbf{M}_I^J$ *is invertible, where* $\mathbf{M}_I$ *denotes the submatrix of* $\mathbf{M}$ *with rows in* $I$, $\mathbf{M}^J$ *denotes the submatrix of* $\mathbf{M}$ *with columns in* $J$, *and* $\mathbf{M}_I^J := (\mathbf{M}_I)^J$.

**Construction 2.** Let $n$ and $k$ be positive integers, and let $p$ be a prime number. Further, let $R = GR(p^k, d)$ with $p^d \geq 2n$, and let $\alpha_1, \ldots, \alpha_{2n}$ be an exceptional sequence in $R$. Applying Theorem 3 twice, we get an $R$-module isomorphism from $R^n$ to $R^n$, sending $(f(\alpha_1), \ldots, f(\alpha_n)) \mapsto (f(\alpha_{n+1}), f(\alpha_{n+2}), \ldots, f(\alpha_{2n}))$. It is represented by an $n \times n$ matrix over $R$ which is hyper-invertible. The proof of this fact follows the lines of its analogous proof over fields, and we refer the reader to [4] for details.

Hyper-invertible matrices have the following key property. The proof from [4] carries over, given the properties that we have shown for $R$.

**Lemma 1.** *Let $\mathbf{M} \in R^{n \times n}$ be an $n$-by-$n$ hyper-invertible matrix, and let $I, J \subseteq \{1, \ldots, n\}$ be index sets such that $|I| + |J| = n$. Then, there exists a linear isomorphism $\varphi = \varphi_{I,J} : R^n \to R^n$ such that for any $\mathbf{x}, \mathbf{y} \in R^n$ it holds that $\varphi(\mathbf{x}_J, \mathbf{y}_I) = (\mathbf{x}_{\bar{J}}, \mathbf{y}_{\bar{I}})$, where $\bar{R}$ and $\bar{C}$ denote the complements $\{1, \ldots, n\} \setminus R$ and $\{1, \ldots, n\} \setminus C$, respectively.*

### 3.2    Robust Reconstruction

Recall from Construction 1 we have an $R$-module $C = \{(f(\alpha_1), \ldots, f(\alpha_n)) \mid f \in R[X]_{\leq t}\}$ of share vectors. We wish to have *robust reconstruction*: a party $P$ that receives shares $x_i$ for $i = 1, \ldots, n$, where $x_i = f(\alpha_i)$ for "most" values of $i$, should be able to reconstruct the correct secret $f(\alpha_0)$ even some shares are corrupted, e.g., they contain arbitrary elements of $R$.

This is also known as the *decoding problem* of linear codes. When $R$ is a finite field, $R$-vector spaces of the form $C$ as above are known as (generalized) *Reed-Solomon codes*. We want an algorithm that does the following. As input we give a vector $(x_1, \ldots, x_n) \in (R \cup \{\perp\})^n$ such that there exists some $f \in R[X]_{\leq t}$ with $x_i = f(\alpha_i)$ for all $i = 1, \ldots, n$ except for at most $\lfloor \frac{n-t-1}{2} \rfloor$ positions. As output, the algorithm has to produce $f$.

We assume black-box access to a decoding algorithm for Reed-Solomon codes (i.e. for vector spaces of the form $C$ as above when $R$ is a finite field), such as the Berlekamp-Massey algorithm [15]. We show how to obtain a decoding algorithm for $C$ over a Galois ring $R = GR(p^k, d)$ that makes $k$ calls to the algorithm over fields.

We fix an exceptional sequence $\alpha_1, \ldots, \alpha_n \in R$. Recall from Remark 1 that any element $a \in R$ can be uniquely written as

$$a = a_0 + a_1 p + a_2 p^2 + \cdots + a_{k-1} p^{k-1}$$

where $a_0, \ldots, a_{k-1} \in \mathcal{I} = \{0, 1, \xi, \ldots, \xi^{p^d - 2}\}$. It follows that for $f(X) \in R[X]_{\leq t}$, we can uniquely write $f(X)$ as $f(X) = f_0(X) + p f_1(X) + \cdots + p^{k-1} f_{k-1}(X)$, where $f_0(X), \ldots, f_{k-1}(X) \in \mathcal{I}[X]_{\leq t}$. Moreover, we have

$$f(\alpha_i) \equiv \sum_{i=0}^{j-1} p^i f_i(\alpha_i) \pmod{p^j}.$$

Since $\alpha_1, \ldots, \alpha_n$ have their pairwise differences invertible, this means they map to distinct elements modulo $p$. For each $i = 1, \ldots, n$ let $\beta_i = \pi(\alpha_i) \in \mathbb{F}_{p^d}$ where $\pi : R \to \mathbb{F}_{p^d}$ is the reduction modulo $p$ from Item 1 of Proposition 2. Notice that $\pi$ gives this one-to-one correspondence between $\mathcal{I}$ and $\mathbb{F}_{p^d}$. In particular, the inverse $\pi^{-1}$ is a well-defined function onto $\mathcal{I}$.

**Theorem 4.** *The protocol of Fig. 1 can correct up to $\lfloor \frac{n-t-1}{2} \rfloor$ errors with $k$ calls to the decoding algorithm over $\mathbb{F}_{p^d}$.*

---

**Decoding Reed-Solomon Codes over a Galois Ring $R$**

- Input: $\mathbf{x} = (x_1, \ldots, x_n) \in (R \cup \{\bot\})^n$.
- Let $\mathbf{y} \leftarrow \mathbf{x}$. For $i = 0, \ldots, k-1$ perform the following operations:
  1. $\mathbf{y} \leftarrow \pi(\mathbf{y}/p^i)$, applied element-wise.
  2. Run the decoding algorithm the input $\mathbf{y}$ and let the $\bar{f}_i(X)$ be the output polynomial. Let $f_i(X) = \pi^{-1}(\bar{f}_i(X)) \in \mathcal{I}[X]_{\leq t}$.
  3. Let $t_j = \sum_{\ell=0}^i p^\ell f_\ell(\alpha_j)$ for $j = 1, \ldots, n$ and $\mathbf{y} \leftarrow (x_1 - t_1, \ldots, x_n - t_n)$.
  4. If there exists $j$ such that $x_j - t_j$ is not divisible by $p^{i+1}$, we claim an error in index $j$ and set $\bot$ on the $j$-th component of $\mathbf{y}$.
- Output: $f(X) = f_0(X) + pf_1(X) + \cdots + p^{k-1}f_{k-1}(X)$.

---

**Fig. 1.** Decoding Reed-Solomon Codes over a Galois Ring $R$

*Proof.* Let us justify this decoding algorithm. We start with $i = 0$. Note that $\bar{f}_0(X) = \pi(f_0(X)) \in \mathbb{F}_{p^d}[X]_{\leq t}$. Thus,

$$\mathbf{c}_f = (\bar{f}_0(\beta_1), \ldots, \bar{f}_0(\beta_n))$$

is a vector in the corresponding Reed-Solomon code over $\mathbb{F}_{p^d}$. Since $\mathbf{y} = \pi(\mathbf{x})$ is a corrupted vector in $\mathbb{F}_{p^d}^n$ differing in at most $\lfloor \frac{n-t-1}{2} \rfloor$ positions from $\mathbf{c}_f$, the decoding algorithm over $\mathbb{F}_{p^d}$ will recover $\bar{f}_0(X)$ and then $f_0(X)$. Now, assume that we have already recovered $f_0(X), \ldots, f_i(X)$. Let us fix $x_j$, the $j$-th component of $\mathbf{x}$. Assume that $x_j$ is not corrupted, i.e., $x_j = f(\alpha_j)$. Then, we have

$$x_j - t_j = f(\alpha_j) - \sum_{\ell=0}^i p^\ell f_\ell(\alpha_j) = p^{i+1} \sum_{\ell=0}^{k-i-2} p^\ell f_{\ell+i+1}(\alpha_j).$$

This implies $x_j - t_j$ is divisible by $p^{i+1}$. Moreover, $\pi((x_j - t_j)/p^{i+1}) = \pi((f_{i+1}(\alpha_j)) = \bar{f}_{i+1}(\beta_j)$. Thus $\pi(\mathbf{y}/p^i)$ agrees with $(\bar{f}_{i+1}(\beta_1), \ldots, \bar{f}_{i+1}(\beta_N))$ in the position that is not corrupted. It follows that $\pi(\mathbf{y}/p^i)$ differs in at most $\lfloor \frac{n-t-1}{2} \rfloor$ positions from $(\bar{f}_{i+1}(\beta_1), \ldots, \bar{f}_{i+1}(\beta_N))$. Running the decoding algorithm over $\mathbb{F}_{p^d}$ on $\pi(\mathbf{y}/p^i)$ will output the polynomial $f_{i+1}(X)$. The desired result follows as we only invoke the decoding algorithm over the finite field $k$ times. $\square$

### 3.3   MPC over $R$

Let $d$ be the smallest positive integer with $p^d \geq 2n$, and write $R = GR(p^k, d)$. Let $(\alpha_0, \alpha_1, \ldots, \alpha_n)$ and $(\beta_1, \ldots, \beta_{2n})$ be exceptional sequences of $R$ of respective lengths $n+1$ and $2n$.

We replace some of the components of [4] to extend this protocol over rings. We use the $n$-player Shamir-like secret-sharing scheme obtained in Construction 1, where $\alpha_i$ is assigned to each player $P_i$. Thus both the share and secret lie in $R$. Also, we use the hyper-invertible matrices from Construction 2, with evaluation points $\beta_1, \ldots, \beta_{2n}$; and we recover secrets from $n' \leq n$ shares with $t'$ corruptions, provided that $t < n' - 2t'$, using the procedure in Fig. 1.

With these tools in place, the remainder of the protocol from [4] can be used to obtain MPC over $R$, as encapsulated in the following theorem.

**Theorem 5.** *There exists an efficient MPC protocol over the Galois Ring $R = GR(p^k, d)$ with $p^d \geq 2n$, for $n$ parties, that is secure against the maximal number of active corruptions $\lfloor (n - 1)/3 \rfloor$, and that has an amortized communication complexity of $O(n)$ ring elements per gate.*

### 3.4   MPC over $\mathbb{Z}/p^k\mathbb{Z}$

From Theorem 5, we get MPC over $R = GR(p^k, d)$ with $p^d \geq 2n$, but this does not give us MPC over $\mathbb{Z}/p^k\mathbb{Z}$ for an arbitrary number of players. We can embed inputs in $\mathbb{Z}/p^k\mathbb{Z}$ into $R$, but we do need to verify that the original inputs are actually in $\mathbb{Z}/p^k\mathbb{Z}$.

Proving that a secret-shared value $[a]$ is in $\mathbb{Z}/p^k\mathbb{Z}$ reduces to sampling a secret-shared random element $[r] \leftarrow \mathbb{Z}/p^k\mathbb{Z}$, as follows: to check that $a \in \mathbb{Z}/p^k\mathbb{Z}$ we simply locally compute $[a + r]$ and open the result. We have that $a \in \mathbb{Z}/p^k\mathbb{Z}$ if and only if $a + r \in \mathbb{Z}/p^k\mathbb{Z}$. Also, since $r$ is a uniformly random element in $\mathbb{Z}/p^k\mathbb{Z}$, $a + r$ does not reveal any information about $a$ (if $a$ is in fact in $\mathbb{Z}/p^k\mathbb{Z}$).

We use an idea from [7] to generate these sharings of random elements in $\mathbb{Z}/p^k\mathbb{Z}$. Since $R$ is a free module over $\mathbb{Z}/p^k\mathbb{Z}$ of rank $d$, we can write down a basis of $R$. In fact, a power basis $1, \xi, \ldots, \xi^{d-1}$ exists. After fixing $\xi$, an element $b \in R$ can thus be uniquely written $b = b_0 + b_1\xi + \cdots + b_{d-1}\xi^{d-1}$, and we can identify $b$ with its coefficient vector $(b_0, \ldots, b_{d-1})$. The map $\phi : R \to (\mathbb{Z}/p^k\mathbb{Z})^d$ such that $\phi(b) = (b_0, \ldots, b_{d-1})$ is a $\mathbb{Z}/p^k\mathbb{Z}$-module isomorphism.

Let $\lambda \in R$. Multiplication by $\lambda$ in $R$ defines an $R$-module endomorphism $R \to R$, which is in particular an $\mathbb{Z}/p^k\mathbb{Z}$-module homomorphism $(\mathbb{Z}/p^k\mathbb{Z})^d \to (\mathbb{Z}/p^k\mathbb{Z})^d$. Thus, this operation can be seen be represented as a $d \times d$ matrix $M_\lambda$ with entries in $\mathbb{Z}/p^k\mathbb{Z}$ such that for any $b \in R$ it holds that $\phi(\lambda b) = M_\lambda \phi(b)$. This is similar to how elements in a field extension can be seen as matrices over the base field.

Now, let $A$ be an $n \times n$ matrix with entries in $R$, for arbitrary $n \geq 1$, and let $(x_1, \ldots, x_n) \in R^n$ be a vector. Each entry $x_i$ can in turn be represented as a vector $(x_{i,1}, \ldots, x_{i,d})$ with entries in $\mathbb{Z}/p^k\mathbb{Z}$ such that $x_i = \phi((x_{i,1}, \ldots, x_{i,d}))$. The action of $A$ on $R^n$ is $R$-linear so in particular $\mathbb{Z}/p^k\mathbb{Z}$-linear. If we let $(y_1, \ldots, y_n)^T = A(x_1, \ldots, x_n)^T$ then each entry $y_i$ is the $R$-linear combination $y_i = a_{i,1}x_1 + \cdots + a_{i,n}x_n$, where $(a_{i,1}, \ldots, a_{i,n}) \in R^n$ is the $i$-th row of $A$. Applying $\phi^{-1}$ to this equation we see that the $\mathbb{Z}/p^k\mathbb{Z}$-linear action of $A$ on the elements $x_{i,j}$ is as follows

$$(y_{i,1}, \ldots, y_{i,d})^T = M_{a_{i,1}}(x_{1,1}, \ldots, x_{1,d})^T + \cdots + M_{a_{i,n}}(x_{n,1}, \ldots, x_{n,d})^T.$$

In Fig. 2, we present a protocol for constructing sharings over $R$ of random elements in $\mathbb{Z}/p^k\mathbb{Z}$. The function of $\mathsf{RandEl}(\mathbb{Z}/p^k\mathbb{Z})$ is to amortize away the cost of generating sharings of random elements in $\mathbb{Z}/p^k\mathbb{Z}$ and meanwhile to verify if the shares correspond to a random element in $\mathbb{Z}/p^k\mathbb{Z}$ instead of $R$. Our protocol is similar to $\mathsf{RandElSub}(V)$ in [7]. Using player elimination, we assume that

---

**RandEl($\mathbb{Z}/p^k\mathbb{Z}$)**

**Fixed public parameters:** $1 \leq T \leq n' - 2t'$, $M$ an $n' \times n'$ hyper-invertible matrix over $R$ given in Construction 2.

**Processing:** 1. For $i = 1, \ldots, n'$, $P_i$ selects $d$ uniformly random elements $s_{i,1}, \ldots, s_{i,d} \in \mathbb{Z}/p^k\mathbb{Z}$ and secret-shares each of them in parallel using the secret-sharing scheme in Construction 1 over $R$ with $n'$ players and $t'$-privacy. This can be interpreted as each party secret-sharing a vector of $d$ elements, and we write $[\![\mathbf{s}_i]\!] := ([s_{i,1}], \ldots, [s_{i,d}])$. This constitutes a secret-sharing where the *correct* secrets are elements of $(\mathbb{Z}/p^k\mathbb{Z})^d$ and the shares are elements of $R^d$.

2. Players locally compute $([\![\mathbf{r}_1]\!], \ldots, [\![\mathbf{r}_{n'}]\!]) = M([\![\mathbf{s}_1]\!], \ldots, [\![\mathbf{s}_{n'}]\!])$. Note that the matrix $M$ is defined over $R$; the action on the individual $R$-sharings is defined via the matrices $M_{m_{i,j}}$ where $M = (m_{i,j})$.

3. For $i = T+1, \ldots, n'$, every party $P_j$ sends its share of $[\![\mathbf{r}_i]\!]$ to $P_i$. $P_i$ then verifies the values received if the secret is indeed a vector in $(\mathbb{Z}/p^k\mathbb{Z})^d$, and if not, gets unhappy.

**Output:** If all honest players are happy, the $d \cdot T$ sharings $[r_{1,1}], \ldots, [r_{1,d}], [r_{2,1}], \ldots, [r_{T,d}]$ are sharings over $R$ with each secret an independent uniformly random element from $\mathbb{Z}/p^k\mathbb{Z}$.

---

**Fig. 2.** Protocol for Generating Sharings of Random Elements in Subring

there are currently $n'$ parties taking part in the computation (labeled $P_1, \ldots, P_{n'}$ without loss of generality) and at most $t'$ of them are corrupted. Note that $t < n' - 2t'$. If a party is unhappy, player elimination ensures that we can find a pair of players that contains at least one corrupted player. Like Proposition 4 in [7], we only need to communicate $O(n)$ elements in $R$ per sharing of a random element in $\mathbb{Z}/p^k\mathbb{Z}$.

**Proposition 3.** *If all honest players are happy after the execution of RandEl($\mathbb{Z}/p^k\mathbb{Z}$), then the output is correct, i.e. the $d \cdot T$ sharings $[r_{1,1}], \ldots, [r_{1,d}], [r_{2,1}], \ldots, [r_{T,d}]$ are correct sharings of uniformly random elements in $\mathbb{Z}/p^k\mathbb{Z}$, and the adversary has no information about these values, other than the fact that they belong to $\mathbb{Z}/p^k\mathbb{Z}$.*

With the help of Proposition 3 and our above analysis, we obtain the following theorem.

**Theorem 6.** *There exists an efficient n-party MPC protocol for circuits defined over $\mathbb{Z}/p^k\mathbb{Z}$, that is secure against the maximal number of active corruptions $\lfloor (n-1)/3 \rfloor$, and that has an amortized communication complexity of $O(n \log n)$ ring elements per gate.*

# 4   Statistically Secure MPC for Honest Majority over Galois Rings

In this section we present a protocol for secure computation over the Galois ring $R = GR(p^k, d)$ that is statistically secure against active adversaries. The protocol tolerates a number of corrupted parties $t < n/2$, which is optimal in this setting.

Our protocol is largely based on the dispute control protocol from [3]. However, some of their techniques explicitly use properties about fields, which do not apply to our setting directly. In this section we show that, due to some special properties of the Galois ring $R$ (mostly the fact that $R$ is local), most of these techniques actually apply to this setting as well, at the expense of having a higher failure probability than in the field case. More explicitly, when working over a field $\mathbb{F}$ it can be shown that the failure probability is roughly $1/|\mathbb{F}|$, but in our setting this probability is close to $1/p^d$, which is potentially far from $1/|R| = 1/p^{k \cdot d}$. In particular, this implies that $d$ must be as large as the security parameter $\kappa$.

However, if we have our computation over $R = GR(p^k, d)$ with $p^d \geq n + 1$, so that we have enough interpolation points for each player, we can avoid much of the overhead. We do this by moving to an extension Galois ring $\hat{R} = GR(p^k, d \cdot \hat{d}) \supset R$ (see Proposition 2). For many subprotocols where the error depends on $p^d$, we can pack $\hat{d}$ values of $R$ into $\hat{R}$ (since $\hat{R} \cong R^{\hat{d}}$ as $R$-modules), and keep the same amortized complexity. In particular, we do not get a total complexity that is linear in both the size of the circuit *and* the security parameter $\kappa$, which is what one would get if $d$ were as large as $\kappa$.

To get computation over $\mathbb{Z}/p^k\mathbb{Z}$ where $p \leq n$, we embed $\mathbb{Z}/p^k\mathbb{Z} \hookrightarrow R$, but we do need to verify that the inputs are actually in $\mathbb{Z}/p^k\mathbb{Z}$, like we saw in Sect. 3.3. We will develop the machinery needed for this in Sect. 4.7.

## 4.1   Overview of Our Techniques

We begin by presenting a summary of the main novel techniques used to achieve the results in this section. The details of these, and their specific usage in the context of our protocol, are explained thoroughly in subsequent sections.

**Error Checking.** To guarantee correctness of the computation, we need a process that checks whether values are secret-shared correctly, with negligible error. Suppose we have secret-shared values $[x_1], \ldots, [x_\ell]$ and we want to check whether the players have consistent shares, i.e. each reconstructing set of honest players jointly have shares that reconstruct to the same secret value. A trick commonly used over fields is to fix a random linear combination $y = r_1 x_1 + \cdots + r_\ell x_\ell$, for publicly known uniformly random values $r_1, \ldots, r_\ell$, and to have the players broadcast the shares of $y$. They can then check whether their shares are consistent, e.g. for Shamir's secret-sharing scheme they check whether the shares are on a polynomial of degree of at most $t$.

This approach works over a finite field $\mathbb{F}$ since the inner product of any non-zero vector (an "error vector") with a uniformly random vector is zero with probability $1/|\mathbb{F}|$. Therefore any inconsistency in some value $x_i$ is very likely to give an inconsistency in $y$. In other rings, this does not necessarily apply, and the product of a non-zero value times a random value is not necessarily random: for example, in $\mathbb{Z}/2^k\mathbb{Z}$ we have $\Pr[r \cdot 2^{k-1} = 0] = 1/2$ for uniformly random $r$.

For the Galois ring $R$, it turns out the above procedure does work, but only with error probability $p^{-d}$, i.e. it only scales in the *degree* of the Galois ring, not in its order $p^{k \cdot d}$. We illustrate this with the following protocol.

Consider the setting where we have a single dealer that secret-shares a single secret value $[x] \in R$ and a single verifier that wants to check whether $[x]$ is secret-shared correctly. To ensure privacy towards the verifier, the dealer also secret-shares a random value $[u] \in R$. The protocol runs as follows:

1. The dealer samples $u \in R$ and secret-shares $[x], [u]$ among the players.
2. The verifier samples $r \in R$ and broadcasts it to all players.
3. All players reconstruct $y = rx + u$ towards the verifier.
4. The verifier accepts if all received shares of $y$ are consistent, and rejects otherwise.

This protocol is private because $u$ is chosen uniformly random by the dealer. We shall now analyze the soundness error. It is useful to take a more general view, and let $C \subseteq R^n$ denote the set of vectors of consistent shares; recall $C$ from Construction 1. More generally, let $C$ be any free $R$-module, i.e. it has a basis. Note that the verifier accepts if $y \in C$, and the dealer cheats successfully if the verifier accepts and $x \notin C$.

We analyze the soundness error using a fact about roots of polynomials over $R$:

**Lemma 2.** *Let $f \in R[X]$ be a polynomial of arbitrary degree $\ell > 0$. Then $\Pr_{x \leftarrow R}[f(x) = 0] \leq \ell/p^d$, where $x$ is drawn uniformly from $R$.*

*Proof.* Write $f(X) = a_0 + a_1 X + \cdots + a_\ell X^\ell$. Let $u$ be the highest power of $p$ such that $p^u$ divides each coefficient $a_0, \ldots, a_\ell$ of $f$. Then, $f(X)/p^u$ has at least one coefficient invertible, hence its reduction $g := \overline{f(X)/p^u}$ modulo $p$ is a nonzero polynomial of degree $\leq \ell$ over the field $R/(p)$ of order $p^d$. Clearly, if $f(x) = 0$ then $\overline{x} := x \bmod (p)$ is a root of $g$. Since $g$ has at most $\ell$ roots, $g(\overline{x}) = 0$ with probability $\leq \ell/p^d$ for uniformly random $\overline{x}$. Since reduction modulo $(p)$ is a homomorphism, in particular it has pre-images of equal size, hence given that $x$ is uniformly random in $R$, $\overline{x}$ is uniformly random in $R/(p)$. $\square$

**Lemma 3.** *Let $C \subseteq R^n$ be a free $R$-module. For all $x \notin C$ and $u \in R^n$, we have that*

$$\Pr_{r \leftarrow R}[rx + u \in C] \leq 1/p^d,$$

*where $r$ is chosen uniformly at random from $R$.*

*Proof.* Let $g : R^n \to R$ be an $R$-module homomorphism such that $g(c) = 0$ for all $c \in C$, and such that $g(x) \neq 0$. Such a homomorphism in particular exists because $C$ is free, and it is therefore a direct summand of $R^n$.

If $rx + u \in C$, then $0 = g(rx + u) = rg(x) + g(u)$, so $r$ is a root of the linear polynomial $g(x)X + u$, which by the previous lemma occurs with probability $\leq 1/p^d$.                                                                                      $\square$

**Packing.** To get a negligible correctness error for MPC over $R$, our solution is to move from $R$ to an extension $R \subset \hat{R}$, where $\hat{R} = GR(p^k, d \cdot \hat{d})$ for an integer $\hat{d} > 1$ with $p^{d \cdot \hat{d}} \geq 2^\kappa$. However, the efficiency is unfavorable since communication and computation is $\Omega(\kappa n^2)$ per multiplication gate.

To improve efficiency, we observe that $\hat{R}$ is a free $R$-module of rank $\hat{d}$, i.e. $\hat{R} \cong R^{\hat{d}}$. Therefore, we can interpret an element of $\hat{R}$ as a vector of elements of $R$ of length $\hat{d}$. This allows us to check $\hat{d}$ elements of $R$ in parallel, by checking one element of $\hat{R}$. In $\hat{R}$ our correctness check has error probability $p^{-d \cdot \hat{d}} \leq 2^{-\kappa}$, and thus by moving to the extension we can both achieve the desired soundness error while getting no amortized overhead.

Let $g(Y)$ be a monic polynomial over $R$ of degree $\hat{d}$ which is irreducible when taken modulo $p$, and let $\hat{R} = R[Y]/(g(Y))$. Let $w_1, \ldots, w_{\hat{d}}$ be a basis of $\hat{R}$ over $R$ as a module and consider the natural isomorphism of modules $\psi : R^{\hat{d}} \to \hat{R}$ given by $\psi(x_1, \ldots, x_{\hat{d}}) = \sum_{i=1}^{\hat{d}} x_i \cdot w_i$.

Finally, consider $y \in \hat{R}$ with $\psi(y_1, \ldots, y_{\hat{d}}) = y$ and assume that $y$ is secret-shared via a polynomial $F \in \hat{R}[X]$ and that the exceptional sequence $\alpha_1, \ldots, \alpha_n$ of evaluation points is in $R$. This polynomial can be written uniquely as $F(X) = \sum_{i=1}^m f_i(X) \cdot w_i$ where $f_i$ are polynomials in $R[X]$. Moreover, we notice that for all $r \in R$ it holds that $F(r) = \psi(f_1(r), \ldots, f_{\hat{d}}(r))$, so in particular the polynomial $f_i$ defines shares of $y_i$, for $i = 1, \ldots, \hat{d}$. Conversely, if we have shares of $y_1, \ldots, y_{\hat{d}}$ using polynomials $f_1, \ldots, f_{\hat{d}}$ over $R$, then we can define a share of $\psi(y_1, \ldots, y_{\hat{d}})$ over $\hat{R}$ which is given by the polynomial $F = \sum_{i=1}^{\hat{d}} f_i \cdot w_i$. We abuse notation and write $\psi([y]_{\hat{R}}) = ([y_1]_R, \ldots, [y_m]_R)$ to denote the situation above.

We then have the following:

**Lemma 4.** *Let $y \in \hat{R}$ and $(y_1, \ldots, y_m) = \psi^{-1}(y)$, and suppose that $\psi([y]_{\hat{R}}) = ([y_1]_R, \ldots, [y_m]_R)$. Then $[y]_{\hat{R}}$ is correctly shared if and only if each $[y_i]_R$ is correctly shared.*

*Proof.* Let $F$ be the polynomial over $\hat{R}$ interpolating $y$ and let $f_i$ be the polynomial over $R$ interpolating $y_i$, for $i = 1, \ldots, m$. We know that $F = \sum_{i=1}^m f_i \cdot w_i$, and since $w_1, \ldots, w_i$ is a basis for $\hat{R}$ over $R$ it follows that $\deg(F) = \max\{\deg(f_1), \ldots, \deg(f_m)\}$. Therefore, in particular $\deg(F) \leq t$ if and only if $\deg(f_i) \leq t$ for all $i$. The desired result follows.                         $\square$

**MPC over $\mathbb{Z}/p^k\mathbb{Z}$.** Like in Sect. 3.4, checking the membership of a secret-shared value in a Galois subring $S \subset R$ can be reduced to sampling a random secret-shared $[s]$, where $s \leftarrow S$ and the secret-sharing is over $R$. To check whether an input $[x]$ is in $S$, we can simply mask and open $x + s$, and check whether it is in $S$. This holds for any $x \in S$, since $S$ is additively closed.

To get a random sharing $[s]$, a straightforward solution is to let each player $P_i$ sample a random element $s_i$ and secret-share it (over $R$). The players then compute $[s] = \sum_{i=1}^{n}[s_i]$. We can check the correctness of $[s]$ by using the method of Sect. 4.1, where we check a batch of many different values at once. However, in this situation, we are only allowed to take $S$-linear combinations. In particular, for $S = \mathbb{Z}/p^k\mathbb{Z}$, Lemma 3 only gives an error probability of $1/p$.

To reduce the error probability, we do the following. Let $C$ be the set of share vectors $[s] = (s_1, \ldots, s_n)$ of secrets $s \in S$, with shares $s_1, \ldots, s_n \in R$. Note that $C$ is an $S$-module but not an $R$-module in general. Since $R$ is a free module over $S$, we have $R \cong S^e$ where $e = \operatorname{rank} R$. We may now take the extension of scalars of $C$ to $R$ via the following tensor product of $S$-modules:

$$\hat{C} := C \otimes_S R \cong C \otimes_S S^e$$

In contrast to $C$, we have that $\hat{C}$ *is* an $R$-module, and in fact an $R$-submodule of $R^n \otimes_S R \cong R^{n \cdot e}$. A dealer will secret-share a vector of $e$ random elements of $S$ in parallel over $R$. Each player thus obtains a vector of shares (with each entry in $R$), which can be interpreted as one element of $R \otimes_S R \cong R^e$. All of the players' shares together form a vector in $R^{n \cdot e}$, which is in $\hat{C}$ if indeed the $e$ secret-shared elements are in $S$. We can now apply the methods from Sect. 4.1 to batch check these values with error probability $1/p^d$.

## 4.2  Computation over Fields

As a base for our protocol for statistically secure MPC in the honest majority setting, we choose the protocol from [3]. It maintains the invariant that every wire of the circuit is secret-shared using Shamir's secret-sharing scheme. Linear gates are given for free by the secret-sharing scheme, and multiplication gates are handled by means of some preprocessed data known as multiplication triples, which are generated themselves using a technique known as resharing. The protocol follows the traditional offline/online paradigm where the multiplication triples are generated during the so-called offline phase that is independent from the inputs, and these triples are subsequently used in the online phase to perform the actual secure computation.

With the secret-sharing scheme over rings from Sect. 2.2, adapting the basic resharing based protocol to the ring setting is straight-forward. Therefore, an efficient protocol for statistically secure computation with honest majority *with abort* and *over rings* can be easily developed at this point. However, in this work we aim for full security, and in order to provide robustness we need to adapt the tools introduced by the dispute control technique, and this becomes much more involved since these highly exploit the fact that the underlying structure is a field.

While we do not have the nice structural properties of fields, we are able to exploit properties of Galois rings to obtain sub-protocols with comparable efficiency to those over fields. In the rest of the section we will focus only on the algebraic aspects of dispute control that must be modified in order to adapt them to work over Galois rings. A second part of dispute control uses more "combinatorial" arguments which are independent of the underlying algebraic structure and therefore they apply directly to our setting. In these cases we refer the reader to the appropriate references.

## 4.3   Dispute Control

Dispute control is a technique used in [3] in order to provide guaranteed output delivery. Here the parties keep track of a publicly known dispute set $\Delta$ of unordered pairs $\{P_i, P_j\}$ of parties that are in dispute. We write $P_i \not\leftrightarrow P_j$ if $\{P_i, P_j\} \in \Delta$, and $P_i \leftrightarrow P_j$ otherwise. At a very high level, a new dispute $P_i \not\leftrightarrow P_j$ is generated whenever $P_i$ thinks that $P_j$ has cheated, or vice versa, and the protocol will guarantee that whenever a new dispute is generated then at least one of the two parties involved is corrupt (i.e. an honest party will never go in dispute with another honest party).

We let $\Delta_i$ denote the set of parties $P_j$ such that $P_i \not\leftrightarrow P_j$. Let $\mathcal{X} \subseteq \mathcal{P}$ denote the set of parties $P_i$ that have $|\Delta_i| > t$, i.e. parties that have a dispute with more than $t$ other parties. They are universally known as corrupt, because no honest party can have a dispute with more than $t$ other parties.

At a very high level, the way in which dispute control is used in the protocol is the following. The computation is divided into segments such that at the end of each segment there is a consistency check. If the check fails, the parties run a dispute control protocol that results in a new pair of players that are not yet in dispute, such that one of them is guaranteed to be corrupt.

Once the dispute has been identified, the segment is re-run. There can be at most $t(t+1)$ disputes. By dividing the computation into $n^2$ segments of approximately equal length, the overhead of repeating failed segments is at most a factor of 2. In this work we will not focus on the details of dispute control and we only introduce it as we will need the notation. For the details of dispute control see [3].

## 4.4   1D, 2D and 2D* Sharings

As before, let $h(Y) \in (\mathbb{Z}/p^k\mathbb{Z})[Y]$ be a monic polynomial of degree $d$ such that its reduction mod $p$ is irreducible, and let $R$ be the Galois ring $(\mathbb{Z}/p^k\mathbb{Z})[Y]/(h(Y))$. We assume that $d \geq \log_p(1+n)$, so that there is an exceptional sequence $0, \alpha_1, \ldots, \alpha_n \in R$.

Given $r \in R$, we write $[r]_R$ to denote the situation in which $r$ is secret-shared using our secret-sharing scheme from Construction 1 over the ring $R$ (if $R$ is obvious we omit it, as we have done until now). Recall from Sect. 2.2 that this means that there is a polynomial $f$ over $R$ of degree at most $t$ such that party $P_i$ has the share $r_i = f(\alpha_i)$ for $i = 1, \ldots, n$, and $r = f(0)$. We shall call this a 1D-sharing of $r$, and refer to the shares $r_1, \ldots, r_n$ as level-one shares.

If each level-one share $r_i$ is itself 1D-shared as $[r_i]_R$ we say we have a *2D-sharing* of $r$, and we denote this by $[[r]]$. We refer to the entries of the share vector $[r_i]$ as *level-two shares*.

Finally, we denote by $\langle r \rangle$ the situation in which $r$ is 2D-shared and additionally the parties hold authentication tags on $r$. We will call this a *2D\*-sharing* of $r$, and it will be explained in detail in Sect. 4.5.

## 4.5  Sub-protocols for Secure Computation over Galois Rings

The overall protocol for secure computation follows the offline/online phase paradigm, which is typical from other secret-sharing based protocols, like these from [3–5,8,12,14]. Essentially, the parties preprocess some material in the offline phase which is used in the online phase to perform the computation, after sharing the inputs. The building blocks to achieve this include procedures for sharing values, generating signatures, checking correctness of triples, and some others. In this section we describe the pieces required to build our protocol, and also the protocol itself. We prove their security and analyze their communication complexity.

For the rest of the section we let $\kappa$ denote the statistical security parameter.

**Dispute Control Broadcast.** This protocol allows a set of senders to broadcast a set of values among all the parties such that, with overwhelming probability, all the parties receive the same value which is the one sent initially if the sender is honest. Also, this broadcast is "compatible" with the dispute control mechanism, in the sense that it detects cheaters and generates new disputes. We remark that our model assumes a network with broadcast which may not provide dispute control by default.[2]

Even though the protocol for dispute control broadcast of [3] uses fields, no arithmetic properties of the input values are used. We may therefore just serialize elements of $R$ as bit strings, map them to a finite field of suitable size, and use their protocol verbatim.

*Complexity Analysis.* The protocol communicates $O(\ell n d + \kappa n^2) = O(\ell n \log n + \kappa n^2)$ bits and broadcasts $O(n\kappa)$ bits. Here $\ell$ is the number of values in $R$ being broadcasted, $n$ is the number of players, and $\kappa$ the security parameter.[3]

**Verifiable 1D-Sharings.** This protocol allows one party $P_D$ to 1D-share some value $x \in R$ with the guarantee that the shares of the honest parties are consistent with a degree-$t$ polynomial over $R$.[4] Note that we make no guarantees

---

[2] Assuming broadcast is necessary for $t \geq n/3$ since it is known that unconditional broadcast is not possible in this settting.

[3] Throughout this work we consider $p$ and $k$ as constants for the asymptotic complexity analysis. We also ignore the dispute control layer, as our complexity closely matches the one from [3] for the fault localization.

[4] Notice that if there are exactly $t + 1$ honest parties then this is trivial since any set of $t + 1$ values is consistent with a degree-$t$ polynomial. However, VSS1D is needed for the general case.

beyond this; in particular, we do not guarantee robustness of shares. With the protocol, we can verify many different sharings at once, by opening a masked linear combination of the shares and checking correctness on the combination.

For this protocol we will make use of the packing technique as detailed in Sect. 4.1. Recall we move to an extension ring $\hat{R} \supset R$ with $\hat{R} = GR(p^k, d \cdot \hat{d})$. We denote a 1D-sharing over $\hat{R}$ as $[x]_{\hat{R}}$, which corresponds to sharing a vector of $\hat{d}$ elements of $R$ via Lemma 4.

The protocol can be found in Fig. 3.

---

**VSS1D**

A party $P_D$ will distribute $\ell$ values $a^{(1)}, \ldots, a^{(\ell)} \in R$ among all parties.

- $P_D$ partitions $a^{(1)}, \ldots, a^{(\ell)} \in R$ into $L = \ell/\hat{d}$ vectors of length $\hat{d}$: $\mathbf{s}^{(j)} = (a^{(1,j)}, \ldots, a^{(\hat{d},j)}) \in R^{\hat{d}}$, for $j = 1, \ldots, L$.
- Let $s^{(j)} = \psi(\mathbf{s}^{(j)}) \in \hat{R}$ for $j = 1, \ldots, L$.

**Private Computation:** $P_D$ samples at random $s^{(L+1)}, \ldots, s^{(L+n)} \in \hat{R}$ and deals $[s^{(1)}]_{\hat{R}}, \ldots, [s^{(L+n)}]_{\hat{R}}$ to all parties.

**Fault Detection:** Every verifier $P_V \in \mathcal{P} \setminus \mathcal{X}$ executes the following steps (in parallel).
  1. $P_V$ samples a challenge vector $(r_1, \ldots, r_L) \in \hat{R}^L$ and broadcasts this value using protocol DCBroadcast.
  2. All the parties reconstruct $\sum_{i=1}^{L} r_i [s^{(i)}]_{\hat{R}} + [s^{(L+V)}]_{\hat{R}}$ towards $P_V$, who then checks correctness of the shares, i.e., $P_V$ checks that these shares lie on a polynomial of degree at most $t$.
  3. $P_V$ broadcasts a bit indicating whether or not the check succeeded.

**Fault Localization:** See Section 3.2 of [3].

If no verifier $P_V$ complained in the previous step, the output is defined to be $[a^{(1)}]_R, \ldots, [a^{(\ell)}]_R = \psi^{-1}([s^{(1)}]_{\hat{R}}), \ldots, \psi^{-1}([s^{(L)}]_{\hat{R}})$.

---

**Fig. 3.** Protocol for Verifiable Secret-Sharing

**Proposition 4.** *If the protocol VSS1D from Fig. 3 succeeds then, with probability at least $1 - p^{-\kappa}$, each $[a^{(m)}]_R$ is correctly 1D-shared for $m = 1, \ldots, \ell$. If the protocol aborts then a new dispute is generated. Input-privacy is guaranteed during the whole protocol (even if it fails).*

*Proof.* It is clear that the shared values remain secret since the random masks $s^{(L+V)}$ prevent them from being revealed.

Now, for soundness we consider the setting of an honest verifier $P_V$ checking the shares of the dealer. Let $C$ denote the $\hat{R}$-module of correct share vectors (see Construction 1). The adversary successfully cheats if for some $i$ we have $[s^{(i)}] \notin C$ and the check passes, i.e. $\sum_{i=1}^{L} r_i [s^{(i)}]_{\hat{R}} + [s^{(L+V)}]_{\hat{R}} \in C$. Since the adversary knows which values they cheat on, we may take $i = 1$ without loss of generality. We can apply Lemma 3 and see that the probability of successfully cheating is at most $1/p^{d\hat{d}} \leq 1/p^{\kappa}$.

Finally, since each $[s^{(1)}]_{\hat{R}}, \ldots, [s^{(L)}]_{\hat{R}}$ is correctly shared, it follows from Lemma 4 that the shares $[a^{(1)},]_R \ldots, [a^{(\ell)}]_R$ output by the protocol are correct. For the case in which a dispute is generated see Lemma 2 in [3]. $\qquad\square$

*Complexity Analysis.* The protocol communicates $O\left(n^2\kappa + \ell n \frac{\log n}{\kappa}\right)$ bits and broadcasts $O(n)$ bits.

**Reconstruct 1D.** Here we consider the setting in which a set of dealers $\mathcal{P}_D \subseteq \mathcal{P} \setminus \mathcal{X}$ have 1D-shared some values $[s^{(1,D)}], \ldots, [s^{(\ell,D)}]$, $P_D \in \mathcal{P}_D$. The goal is to reconstruct the values $s^{(m)} = \sum_{P_D \in \mathcal{P}_D} s^{(m,D)}$ for $m = 1, \ldots, \ell$ to a set of recipients $\mathcal{P}_R \subseteq \mathcal{P} \setminus \mathcal{X}$. This is achieved by letting each player $P_i \in \mathcal{P}$ compute its share of the sum $s_i^{(m)} = \sum_{P_D \in \mathcal{P}_D} s_i^{(m,D)}$ and send it to each player in $\mathcal{P}_R$. Then a dispute control layer makes sure that all parties agree that the reconstruction was done successfully.

**Proposition 5.** *There is a protocol Reconstruct1D such that, on input some values $[s^{(1,D)}], \ldots, [s^{(\ell,D)}]$ correctly shared by each $P_D \in \mathcal{P} \setminus \mathcal{X}$, the protocol either fails or each party in $\mathcal{P} \setminus \mathcal{X}$ receives $s^{(m)} = \sum_{P_D \in \mathcal{P}_D} s^{(m,D)}$ for $m = 1, \ldots, \ell$. Moreover, if the protocol aborts a new pair of players in dispute is identified.*

For the description of the protocol and its proof of security see Lemma 3 in Sect. 3.2 of [3]. The main observation is that their argument applies directly to our setting since it only relies on polynomial interpolation, which works for $R$ in essentially the same way as it does for a field as long as the base points are chosen to form an exceptional sequence.

*Complexity Analysis.* The protocol communicates $O(\ell n^2 d)$ bits and broadcasts $O(nd)$ bits, where $d$ is the degree of the Galois ring $R$ over $\mathbb{Z}/p^k\mathbb{Z}$.

**Generating Random Challenges.** An essential tool needed for statistically secure MPC is the generation of publicly known random elements. This is achieved by a protocol GenerateChallenges which operates as follows.

1. Each party $P_i \in \mathcal{P} \setminus \mathcal{X}$ samples some random values $s^{(1,i)}, \ldots, s^{(\ell,i)} \in R$ and uses VSS1D to distribute correct shares of it.
2. The parties compute $[s^{(m)}] = \sum_{P_i \in \mathcal{P} \setminus \mathcal{X}} [s^{(m,i)}]$ and open $s^{(m)}$ to all parties in $\mathcal{P} \setminus \mathcal{X}$ using Reconstruct1D, for $m = 1, \ldots, \ell$.

Since the additive group of $R$ is abelian, if each $s^{(m,i)}$ is independent and there is at least one that is uniformly random, then $s^{(m)}$ is random. Now, the $s^{(m,i)}$ are independent from each other since they are secret-shared, so one player cannot choose its share conditioned on the other players' shares.

*Complexity Analysis.* The protocol communicates $O(n^3\kappa + \ell n^2 d)$ bits and broadcasts $O(nd)$ bits where $d$ is the degree of the Galois ring $R$ over $\mathbb{Z}/p^k\mathbb{Z}$.

**Upgrading 1D-Sharings to 2D-Sharings.** The goal of this protocol is to upgrade a 1D-sharing $[a]$ of $a \in R$ to a 2D-sharing $[\![a]\!]$. In fact, several values $a^{(1)}, \ldots, a^{(\ell)} \in R$ will be upgraded in one go, and moreover, sums of 1D-shares instead of individual 1D-shares will be upgraded due to our use-case.

More precisely, let $\mathcal{P}_D \subseteq \mathcal{P} \setminus \mathcal{X}$ be some subset of dealers. Each $P_D \in \mathcal{P}_D$ has a list of values $a^{(1,D)}, \ldots, a^{(\ell,D)} \in R$ it has secret-shared. The goal of the Upgrade1Dto2D sub-protocol is to let each party $P_i$ distribute shares of its share $a_i^{(m)}$ of $a^{(m)} = \sum_{P_D \in \mathcal{P}_D} a^{(m,D)}$ for $m = 1, \ldots, \ell$. At the end of the protocol it is guaranteed that all shares (both, the shares of each $a^{(m)}$ and the shares of their shares) are correct.

---

### Upgrade1Dto2D

Let $a^{(1,D)}, \ldots, a^{(\ell,D)} \in R$ such that each $a^{(m,D)}$ has been 1D-shared by $P_D \in \mathcal{P}_D$.

- The parties partition $[a^{(1,D)}]_R, \ldots, [a^{(\ell,D)}]_R$ into $L = \ell/\hat{d}$ vectors of length $\hat{d}$:
  $$\mathbf{s}^{(j,D)} = ([a^{(1,j,D)}]_R, \ldots, [a^{(\hat{d},j,D)}]_R) \in R^{\hat{d}}, \text{ for } j = 1, \ldots, L.$$
- Let $[s^{(j)}]_{\hat{R}} = \sum_{P_D \in \mathcal{P}_D} \psi(\mathbf{s}^{(j,D)}) \in \hat{R}$ for $j = 1, \ldots, L$.

**Private Computation:**  1. Each $P_D \in \mathcal{P}_D$ shares a random value $s^{(L+1,D)} \in \hat{R}$.
2. Each player $P_i$ 1D-shares each of its shares $s_i^{(m)} \in \hat{R}$ for $m = 1, \ldots, L+1$. We denote by $s_{ij}^{(m)} \in \hat{R}$ the share of $s_i^{(m)}$ received by $P_j$.

**Fault Detection:** Using the protocol GenerateChallenges, the parties jointly generate random values $(r_1, \ldots, r_L) \in \hat{R}^L$. Then the following is executed for every verifier $P_V \in \mathcal{P} \setminus \mathcal{X}$.

  1. Every $P_j$ with $P_j \leftrightarrow P_V$ computes the share $s_{ij} = \sum_{m=1}^{L} r_m \cdot s_{ij}^{(m)} + s_{ij}^{(L+1)}$ for every $P_i$ with $P_i \leftrightarrow P_j$, and sends these to $P_V$ (notice that these are shares of $s_i = \sum_{m=1}^{L} r_m \cdot s_i^{(m)} + s_i^{(L+1)}$).
  2. For every $P_i$ with $P_i \leftrightarrow P_V$, $P_V$ checks that $(s_{i1}, \ldots, s_{in})$ lie in a polynomial over $\hat{R}$ of degree at most $t$. Then broadcasts accept or reject depending on the case.
  3. If $P_V$ accepted in the previous step, then interpolate $s_1, \ldots, s_n$ and check whether or not these lie in a polynomial of degree at most $t$.

**Fault Localization:** See protocol Upgrade1Dto2D in Section 3.4 of [3].

If no verifier $P_V$ complained in the previous step, the output is defined to be $[\![a^{(1)}]\!]_R, \ldots, [\![a^{(L)}]\!]_R = \psi^{-1}([s^{(1)}]_{\hat{R}}), \ldots, \psi^{-1}([s^{(L)}]_{\hat{R}})$.

---

**Fig. 4.** Protocol for upgrading 1D-shares to 2D-shares

**Proposition 6.** *If Upgrade1Dto2D aborts, then a new conflicting pair of parties is detected. Otherwise, it is guaranteed with probability at least $1 - p^{-d}$ that the values $s^{(m)} \in R$ for $m = 1, \ldots, \ell$ are correctly 2D-shared, meaning that for each $m$ there are polynomials $f^{(m)}, f_1^{(m)}, \ldots, f_n^{(m)} \in R[X]$ of degree at most $t$ such that each party $P_j$ has shares $s_j^{(m)}, s_{ij}^{(m)} \in R$ with $s_j^{(m)} = f^{(m)}(j)$, $s_{ij}^{(m)} = f_i^{(m)}(j)$, $s_i^{(m)} \equiv_k f_i^{(m)}(0)$ and $s^{(m)} = f^{(m)}(0)$.*

*Proof.* The proof of this proposition follows the lines of the proof of Proposition 4.                                                                    □

*Complexity Analysis.* The protocol communicates $O(n^3\kappa + \ell n^2)$ bits and broadcasts $O(n\kappa)$ bits.

**Information-Checking Signatures with Dispute Control.** The goal of information-checking signatures, or IC signatures for short, is to provide a way for one party $P_R$ to prove to another party $P_V$ that it received some specific shares from some other party $P_S$. This will be used in the online phase to detect cheaters when revealed shares happen to be inconsistent. The idea is that whenever a player sends his share, he is "committed" to it by means of the authentication tags and therefore, if he sends an incorrect share, this can be detected by checking the tags.

For the IC signatures in this work we follow a similar approach to [3], which at a very high level consists of finding a polynomial $f$ that interpolates a set of messages as well as the point $(0, y)$ for a randomly chosen $y$. The value $y$ will be referred to as the *authentication tag*. The *authentication key* will be a random point $(u, f(u))$ on this polynomial where $u$ is not an evaluation point corresponding to any of the messages. To check correctness, the key is used to interpolate the polynomial and then it is checked that its evaluation at zero matches the presented tag. Intuitively, if any message is modified then the polynomial will be different, and the only way in which an attacker can make the check pass is by presenting the right tag, which is equivalent to guessing point used as authentication key. If there are enough points to choose from, this happens only with low probability.

In more detail, the protocol IC-Distr allows a sender $P_S$ to send $\ell$ values $m_1, \ldots, m_\ell \in R$ to a receiver $P_R$ along with authentication tags, and to send an authentication key to a verifier $P_V$. At a later point the protocol IC-Reveal can be called to verify correctness of these tags. In this protocol, party $P_R$ sends the messages and their tags to $P_V$, who can then verify their correctness using its authentication key.

**Theorem 7 (Lemma 6 from [3]).** *If IC-Distr succeeds and $P_V, P_R$ are honest, then with overwhelming probability $P_V$ accepts the message $m$ in IC-Reveal (completeness). If IC-Distr fails, then the localized pair in dispute contains at least one corrupted player. If $P_S$ and $P_V$ are honest, then with overwhelming probability, $P_V$ rejects any fake message $m' \neq m$ in IC-Reveal (correctness). If $P_S$ and $P_R$ are honest, then $P_V$ obtains no information about $m$ in IC-Distr (even if it fails) (privacy).*

---

**IC-Distr**

A sender $P_S$ has $\ell$ messages $m^{(1)}, \ldots, m^{(\ell)} \in R$.

- Let $\hat{d}$ be such that $d \cdot \hat{d} \geq \kappa$. let $L = \ell/\hat{d}$, and assume that $\hat{d}$ is large enough so $p^\kappa \geq L + \kappa + 1$, i.e. $\hat{d} \geq \ell/(p^\kappa - \kappa - 1)$.
- $P_S$ partitions $m^{(1)}, \ldots, m^{(\ell)} \in R$ into $\ell/\hat{d}$ vectors of length $\hat{d}$: $\mathbf{s}^{(j)} = (m^{(1,j)}, \ldots, m^{(\hat{d},j)}) \in R^{\hat{d}}$, for $j = 1, \ldots, L$.
- Let $s^{(j)} = \psi(\mathbf{s}^{(j)}) \in \hat{R}$ for $j = 1, \ldots, L$.

**Private Computation:**  1. Let $B = \{\beta_1, \ldots, \beta_L\} \subseteq \hat{R}$ be an exceptional sequence. $P_S$ selects $\kappa$ random authentication tags $y_1, \ldots, y_\kappa \in \hat{R}$ and random points $u_1, \ldots, u_\kappa \in \hat{R} \setminus (B \cup \{0\})$ such that $B \cup \{0, u_1, \ldots, u_\kappa\} \subseteq \hat{R}$ forms an exceptional sequence.

2. For $i = 1, \ldots, \kappa$, $P_S$ computes the polynomial $f_i$ over $\hat{R}$ of degree at most $L$ interpolating $(0, y_i), (\beta_1, s^{(1)}), \ldots, (\beta_L, s^{(L)})$, and computes $v_i = f_i(u_i)$.

3. $P_S$ sends the messages $m^{(1)}, \ldots, m^{(\ell)}$ to $P_R$, along with the authentication tags $y_1, \ldots, y_k$. It also sends the authentication keys $(u_1, v_1), \ldots, (u_\kappa, v_\kappa)$ to $P_V$.

**Fault Detection:** $P_V$ reveals a random half of the keys to $P_R$. Then $P_R$ checks the validity of these keys, who then broadcast accept or reject depending on the case. If the check passes then the remaining, unrevealed half of the keys is kept as the actual keys.

**Fault Localization:** See Section 3.5 of [3].

**Fig. 5.** Protocol for Distributing IC Signatures

---

**IC-Reveal**

A receiver $P_R$ has $\ell$ messages $m^{(1)}, \ldots, m^{(\ell)} \in R$ and $\kappa' = \kappa/2$ authentication tags $y_1, \ldots, y_{\kappa'} \in \hat{R}$. A verifier $P_V$ has $\kappa'$ authentication keys $(u_1, v_1), \ldots, (u_{\kappa'}, v_{\kappa'})$ corresponding to these messages.

- $P_R$ partitions $m^{(1)}, \ldots, m^{(\ell)} \in R$ into $L = \ell/\hat{d}$ vectors of length $\hat{d}$: $\mathbf{s}^{(j)} = (m^{(1,j)}, \ldots, m^{(\hat{d},j)}) \in R^{\hat{d}}$, for $j = 1, \ldots, L$.
- Let $s^{(j)} = \psi(\mathbf{s}^{(j)}) \in \hat{R}$ for $j = 1, \ldots, L$.

1. $P_R$ sends the messages and the authentication tags to $P_V$

2. $P_V$ checks the validity of the tags using its authentication keys by checking that, for at least one $i$, the points $(0, y_i), (\beta_1, s^{(1)}), \ldots, (\beta_L, s^{(L)}), (u_i, v_i)$ lie on a polynomial of degree at most $L$ over $\hat{R}$.

**Fig. 6.** Protocol for Revealing and Checking IC Signatures

*Proof.* Regarding completeness, notice that if the randomly chosen $\kappa/2$ tags are correct, then it holds that at least one of the remaining authentication tags is valid with probability at least $1 - \kappa/2^{\kappa}$.

For correctness, consider the scenario of an honest $P_V$ and a corrupt $P_R$. Suppose that $P_R$ manages to make the check pass whilst presenting a different set of messages. Let $f_i$ be the polynomial of degree at most $L$ over $\hat{R}$ interpolating $(\beta_1, s'^{(1)}), \ldots, (\beta_L, s'^{(L)}), (u_i, v_i)$, then $P_R$ must have sent a tag $y'_i$ that is equal to one of the elements in $\{f_1(0), \ldots, f_\kappa(0)\}$. This can be done only if $P_R$ guesses at least one of the authentication keys $(u_i, v_i)$. Recall that $\hat{R}$ has a Lenstra constant of at least $p^\kappa$, so there are at least $p^\kappa - L - 1$ possibilities for each $u_i$. This means that the probability of guessing *at least one* $u_i$ is at most $\kappa/(p^\kappa - L - 1)$.

For the proof of the other properties see the proof of Lemma 6 in [3].    □

**Upgrading 2D-Sharings to 2D\*-Sharings.** Recall that in Sect. 4.4 we mentioned the concept of 2D\*-shares, but we did not explicitly define it since we did not have the concept of IC signatures. We begin by defining what a 2D\*-share is. Given $a \in R$, we say that $a$ is 2D\*-shared, written as $\langle a \rangle$, if it holds that $[\![a]\!]$ and also, for every set of three players $P_R, P_S, P_V$ such that $P_R \leftrightarrow P_S, P_S \leftrightarrow P_V$ and $P_R \leftrightarrow P_V$ it holds that $P_R$ has authentication tags of the level-two share of $P_S$'s share, and $P_V$ has the corresponding authentication keys.

Protocol Upgrade2Dto2D\* takes as input some 2D-shared values $s^{(1)}, \ldots,$ $s^{(\ell)} \in R$, and upgrades them to 2D\*-shares. The protocol works by calling IC-Distr for every set of three players $P_R, P_S, P_V$ such that $P_R \leftrightarrow P_S, P_S \leftrightarrow P_V$ and $P_R \leftrightarrow P_V$, where the message $m$ are the shares $s_{SR}^{(1)}, \ldots, s_{SR}^{(\ell)}$.

For the dispute control layer of the protocol and its security proof see Sect. 3.6 of [3].

*Complexity Analysis.* The protocol communicates $O(\kappa^2 n^3)$ bits and broadcasts $O(n\kappa)$ bits.

**Triple-Checking Protocol.** The protocol SacrificeTriple, described in Fig. 7, allows the parties to check that some given shares $[a], [b], [c]$ satisfy $c = a \cdot b$. This is achieved by generating some shares $[a'], [c']$ where $c' = a' \cdot b$, and "sacrificing" $([a'], [b], [c'])$ to check correctness of $([a], [b], [c])$.

For the security of the SacrificeTriple protocol we need to argue about the number of roots of a polynomial over a ring. In general, not much can be said since over a ring with zero divisors a polynomial can have many more roots than its degree. However, we have the following lemma, which bounds the number of roots that constitute an exceptional sequence.

---

**Sacrifice Triple**

The inputs are 1D-shared values $[a_k^{(m)}]_R, [b_k^{(m)}]_R, [c^{(m,k)}]_R$ for $m = 1, \ldots, \ell$, where $a_k^{(m)}, b_k^{(m)}, c^{(m,k)}$ were dealt by party $P_k \in \mathcal{P} \setminus \mathcal{X}$.

1. Every player $P_k \in \mathcal{P} \setminus \mathcal{X}$ verifiably 1D-shares random values $\bar{a}_k^{(m)} \in \hat{R}$ and $\bar{c}^{(m,k)} \in \hat{R}$ with $\bar{c}^{(m,k)} = \bar{a}_k^{(m)} \cdot b_k^{(m)}$ for $m = 1, \ldots, \ell$ as follows:
   (a) For $m = 1, \ldots, \ell$, player $P_k \in \mathcal{P} \setminus \mathcal{X}$ samples $\bar{a}_k^{(m)}$ and $\bar{c}^{(m,k)}$ as specified above. Let $\psi^{-1}(\bar{a}_k^{(m)}) = (\bar{a}_{k,1}^{(m)}, \ldots, \bar{a}_{k,\hat{d}})^{(m)} \in R^{\hat{d}}$ and $\psi^{-1}(\bar{c}^{(m,k)}) = (\bar{c}_1^{(m,k)}, \ldots, \bar{c}_{\hat{d}}^{(m,k)}) \in R^{\hat{d}}$.
   (b) $P_k$ 1D-shares the $2\ell\hat{d}$ values $\bar{a}_{k,1}^{(m)}, \ldots, \bar{a}_{k,\hat{d}}^{(m)} \in R$ and $\bar{c}_1^{(m,k)}, \ldots, \bar{c}_{\hat{d}}^{(m,k)} \in R$ using the VSS1D protocol, for $m = 1, \ldots, \ell$. This implies that $\bar{a}_k^{(m)} \in \hat{R}$ and $\bar{c}^{(m,k)}\hat{R}$ are verifiably 1D-shared over $\hat{R}$.
2. Parties jointly sample a random value $r \in \hat{R}$ using protocol GenerateChallenges.
3. Each player $P_k \in \mathcal{P} \setminus \mathcal{X}$ sends $\tilde{a}_k^{(m)} = r \cdot a_k^{(m)} + \bar{a}_k^{(m)} \in \hat{R}$ to all parties $P_i$ with $P_i \leftrightarrow P_k$, for $m = 1, \ldots, \ell$.
4. Parties jointly sample a random value $s \in \hat{R}$ using protocol GenerateChallenges.[a]
5. Parties invoke Reconstruct1D to reconstruct $[z^{(k)}]_{\hat{R}} = \sum_{m=1}^{\ell} s^{m-1}[z_k^{(m)}]_{\hat{R}}$, where $[z_k^{(m)}]_{\hat{R}} = \tilde{a}_k^{(m)}[b_k^{(m)}]_R - r[c^{(m,k)}]_R - [\bar{c}^{(m,k)}]_R$, for $k = 1, \ldots, n$.[b]
6. The parties check that $z^{(k)} = 0$ for all $k$. If this fails for some $k_0$ then new disputes $P_i \not\leftrightarrow P_{k_0}$ are generated for all $P_i \in \mathcal{P} \setminus \mathcal{X}$.

---

[a] We could choose $\ell$ independent challenges instead, but we use this optimization to save in communication. Notice that a similar optimization can be applied to the protocol from [3]
[b] Some extra step is needed to ensure players are committed to their $\tilde{a}$. See [3] for the details.

---

**Fig. 7.** Protocol for Verifying Multiplications

**Lemma 5.** *Let $f(X) \in R[X]$ be a non-zero polynomial of degree at most $\ell$. If $\{\alpha_1, \ldots, \alpha_m\} \subseteq R$ are different roots of $f$ that form an exceptional sequence, then $m \leq \ell$.*

*Proof.* This follows from Theorem 3. Suppose that $\ell < m$, so $\ell \leq m - 1$. We know that there is a unique polynomial of degree at most $m - 1$ that interpolates the points $(\alpha_1, 0), \ldots, (\alpha_m, 0)$, but both the zero polynomial and $f$ satisfy this condition, so $f$ is the zero polynomial, which is a contradiction. Therefore, we conclude that $m \leq \ell$. $\square$

We proceed to the proof of security of the protocol SacrificeTriple.

**Proposition 7.** *Assume all shares $[a_k^m], [b_k^m], [c^{(m,k)}]$ are correctly 1D-shared. If the protocol SacrificeTriple succeeds, then with probability at least $1 - \ell/p^\kappa$ it holds that $c^{(m.k)} = a_k^m \cdot b_k^m$ for all $P_k \in \mathcal{P} \setminus \mathcal{X}$ and $m = 1, \ldots, \ell$. If the protocol aborts then it generates a new dispute.*

*Proof.* Consider a corrupt player $P_k$ for which $\bar{c}^{(m,k)} = \bar{a}_k^{(m)} b_k^{(m)} + \gamma_k^{(m)}$ and $c^{(m,k)} = a_k^{(m)} b_k^{(m)} + \delta_k^{(m)}$ with $\delta_k^{(m)} \neq 0$ for some $m$, say $m = 1$. Now, suppose the protocol succeeds, then $z^{(k)} = 0$. However, we see that this value is equal to[5]

$$z^{(k)} = \sum_{m=1}^{\ell} s^{m-1}(\tilde{a}_k^{(m)} b_k^{(m)} - r c^{(m,k)} - \bar{c}^{(m,k)})$$

$$= \sum_{m=1}^{\ell} s^{m-1}((ra_k^{(m)} + \bar{a}_k^{(m)}) b_k^{(m)} - r(a_k^{(m)} b_k^{(m)} + \delta_k^{(m)}) - (\bar{a}_k^{(m)} b_k^{(m)} + \gamma_k^{(m)}))$$

$$= -\sum_{m=1}^{\ell} s^{m-1}(r\delta_k^{(m)} + \gamma_k^{(m)}) = 0.$$

Now, since $\delta_k^{(1)} \neq 0$, it follows from Lemma 2 that $r\delta_k^{(1)} + \gamma_k^{(1)}$ is non-zero with probability at least $1 - p^{-\kappa}$ (over the choice of $r$).

Applying Lemma 5 we see that conditioned on $r\delta_k^{(1)} + \gamma_k^{(1)} \neq 0$ the event $r\delta_k^{(1)} + \gamma_k^{(1)} + \sum_{m=2}^{\ell} s^{m-1}(r\delta_k^{(m)} + \gamma_k^{(m)}) = 0$ holds with probability at most $(\ell - 1)/p^\kappa$. Furthermore, using the same lemma we see that the probability that $r\delta_k^{(1)} + \gamma_k^{(1)} = 0$ is at most $1/p^\kappa$. Therefore, putting these together we obtain that the adversary can only successfully cheat with probability at most $\ell/p^\kappa$.

Regarding privacy, we observe that the value $r \cdot a_k^{(m)} \in \hat{R}$, which contains information about $a_k^{(m)}$, is masked by the element $\bar{a}_k^{(m)} \in \hat{R}$. Since this element is uniformly random for an honest $P_k$, and given that $\hat{R}$ is an additive group, we conclude that the private value $a_k^{(m)}$ of $P_k$ remains hidden.

For the arguments related to dispute control see Lemma 8 in [3]. □

*Complexity Analysis.* Assuming that $n \log(n) \leq \kappa^2$, the protocol transmits $O(n^3\kappa + n^2\kappa\ell)$ bits, and broadcasts $O(n\kappa)$ bits.

### 4.6  Final Protocol

**Offline Phase.** In the offline phase the parties generate a number $M$ of multiplication triples $(\langle a \rangle, \langle b \rangle, \langle c \rangle)$, where $c = a \cdot b$ and $a, b$ are random. This phase is totally independent of the circuit to be computed (parties only need to make sure to generate as many triples as multiplication gates in the circuit), and therefore it can be executed at a totally different time than the evaluation of the circuit itself, thus the name "offline".

To compute these sharings, a technique known as re-sharing is used to obtain $[a \cdot b]$ from $[a]$ and $[b]$. This works by letting the parties locally compute degree $2t$−sharings of $a \cdot b$ by taking the local product of their shares on $a$ and $b$.

---

[5]  We use the equality $\tilde{a}_k^{(m)} = ra_k^{(m)} + \bar{a}_k^{(m)}$, which follows from the extra step we omitted in the protocol.

Then these shares are distributed and an appropriate linear combination is taken to obtain $[a \cdot b]$.

Assume for simplicity that $n^2$ divides $M$. To produce the $M$ triples, the parties produce $n^2$ batches of $L = M/n^2$ triples each. To generate the $L$ triples of each batch (or *segment*), the parties run the protocol from Fig. 8. Notice that each segment may fail due to the dispute control, in which case a new dispute is identified and the segment must be repeated. Since there are most $n^2$ different disputes that can occur, there may be up to $n^2$ repetitions of segments overall, and since there are at most $n^2$ segments we see that there are at most $2n^2$ segment executions.

**Proposition 8.** *The preprocessing protocol generates correctly 2D\*-shared multiplication triples with overwhelming probability.*

*Proof.* The proof follows from the properties of Upgrade1Dto2D, VSS1D and Upgrade2Dto2D\*. See Lemma 10 in [3] for the details.    □

*Complexity Analysis.* Suppose that there are $M$ triples to be processed. The preprocessing phase communicates $O(Mn^2 \log n + \kappa^2 n^5)$ bits and broadcasts $O(n^3 \kappa)$ bits.

---

### Preprocessing Protocol

Since this is the first protocol to be executed, initially the dispute set and the set of identified corrupt parties are $\Delta, \mathcal{X} = \{\}$. The following is executed for each segment, and each time a new dispute pair $P_i \nleftrightarrow P_j$ is identified, it is added to $\Delta$ and the segment is repeated.

1. Each player $P_k$ 1D-shares $2L$ random values $a^{(m,k)}, b^{(m,k)} \in R$ for $m = 1, \ldots, L$.
2. Upgrade1Dto2D is called on $a^{(m,i)}$ for $m = 1, \ldots, L$ and $P_i \in \mathcal{P} \backslash \mathcal{X}$ to obtain correct 2D-shares $[\![a^{(m)}]\!]$ and $[\![b^m]\!]$ for $m = 1, \ldots, L$, where $a^{(m)} = \sum_{P_i \in \mathcal{P} \backslash \mathcal{X}} a^{(m,i)}$ and similarly $b^{(m)} = \sum_{P_i \in \mathcal{P} \backslash \mathcal{X}} b^{(m,i)}$.
3. The players invoke VSS1D to let each $P_k \in \mathcal{P} \backslash \mathcal{X}$ 1D-share the values $c^{(m,k)} = a_k^{(m)} \cdot b_k^{(m)}$ for $m = 1, \ldots, L$.
4. Invoke the protocol SacrificeTriple to prove that the value $[c^{(m,k)}]$ shared on the previous step is the product of $[a_k^{(m)}]$ and $[b_k^{(m)}]$ (recall that $a^{(m)}$ and $b^{(m)}$ are 2D-shared), for $m = 1, \ldots, L$.
5. Let $\lambda_1, \ldots, \lambda_n \in R$ be such that $f(0) = \sum_{i=1}^n \lambda_i \cdot f(i)$ for any polynomial $f$ over $R$ of degree at most $2t$. The parties use Upgrade1Dto2D to compute $[\![c^{(m)}]\!] \leftarrow \sum_{k=1}^n \lambda_k \cdot [c^{(m,k)}]$ for $m = 1, \ldots, L$.
6. Parties use Upgrade2Dto2D\* to upgrade all shares to 2D\*-shares.

---

**Fig. 8.** Protocol for Preparing Multiplication Triples

**Online Phase.** In the online phase is where the parties actually compute the circuit securely, using the triples that were preprocessed in the offline phase. We present here the online phase without the dispute control layer, which takes care of executing only certain amount of steps within a segment and checking correctness within that segment, repeating it if something was found to be inconsistent. We refer the reader to [3] for the details of how this is done.

This phase starts by the parties sharing their inputs. This is done by letting $P_i$, for each $i$, share its input $s^{(i)} \in R$ to the other parties. For this $P_i$ begins by 1D-sharing $s^{(i)}$ and then the parties invoke the procedures Upgrade1Dto2D and Upgrade2Dto2D* to obtain 2D*-sharings of $s^{(i)}$. Then the parties process the gates in topological order. For the addition gates, all the 2D-shares of the inputs are simply added locally, thus requiring no interaction. However, when two shared values $[\![x]\!]$ and $[\![y]\!]$ need to be multiplied, the parties must make use of a preprocessed triple $([\![a]\!], [\![b]\!], [\![c]\!])$ with $c = a \cdot b$. The multiplication is then achieved by computing $[\![x - a]\!] = [\![x]\!] - [\![a]\!]$ and opening it as $\epsilon$, and similarly $[\![y - b]\!] = [\![y]\!] - [\![b]\!]$ and opening it as $\delta$, and then computing $[\![x \cdot y]\!] = [\![c]\!] + \delta[\![x]\!] + \epsilon[\![y]\!] + \epsilon\delta$.

As we mentioned at the beginning of the section, the details about how to handle consistency are exactly the same as discussed in [3], so we omit some of the details of such procedure. See Sect. 6 in the aforementioned reference to see how this is done precisely. Something to point out is that consistency is eventually checked by means of the IC signatures from Sect. 4.5. This tool is used in dispute control so that some party $P_S$ can prove to some verifier $P_V$ that certain values were indeed sent by some other party $P_R$.

*Complexity Analysis.* The input phase communicates $O(c_I n^2 \log n + \kappa n^5)$ bits where $c_I$ is the number of input gates, and broadcasts $O(\kappa n^3)$ bits. The computation phase communicates $O(|C|n^2 \log n + n^4\kappa^2)$ bits where $|C|$ is the size of the circuit, and broadcasts $O(n^3\kappa)$ bits.

## 4.7   Computation over $\mathbb{Z}/p^k\mathbb{Z}$

Summing up, we have seen so far how to perform unconditional secure computation over the Galois ring $R = (\mathbb{Z}/p^k\mathbb{Z}[Y])/(h(Y))$. However, we wish to obtain unconditional secure computation over $\mathbb{Z}/p^k\mathbb{Z}$ itself. We can embed $\mathbb{Z}/p^k\mathbb{Z}$ into $R$ in the natural way, and as seen in Sect. 3.4 this works for passive adversaries, but if an active adversary manages to share values that are in $R \setminus \mathbb{Z}/p^k\mathbb{Z}$, correctness and security could be broken. As discussed in Sect. 3.4 and Sect. 4.1 this reduces to securely sampling an $R$-sharing of a random element $[s]$ where $s \leftarrow \mathbb{Z}/p^k\mathbb{Z}$.

Here we present a protocol RandElStat($S$) in Fig. 9 for sampling this element $[s] \in S$ efficiently. Here $S \subseteq R$ denotes an arbitrary subring; for our use case $S = \mathbb{Z}/p^k\mathbb{Z}$. We have made the protocol to be explicit and removed any mention of tensor products, but the intuition for this was given already in Sect. 4.1. The protocol succeeds with overwhelming probability.

---

### RandElStat($S$)

OUTPUT: sharings $[x_j^{(i)}]$ for $j = 0, \ldots, d-1$ and $i = 1, \ldots, L$ for a total of $dL$ random elements, where the shares are in $R$ and the secrets $x_j^{(i)}$ are in $S$.

PUBLIC INFORMATION: fix $\xi \in R$ such that $\{1, \xi, \xi^2, \ldots, \xi^{d-1}\}$ is an $S$-basis for $R$ as an $S$-module. With respect to this basis, multiplication by an element $r \in R$ can be represented by a $d \times d$ matrix $M_r$ with entries in $S$.

**Private Computation:** Each player $P_k \in \mathcal{P} \setminus \mathcal{X}$ samples $d(L+1)$ uniformly random values $x_j^{(i,k)} \leftarrow S$ for $j = 0, \ldots, d-1$ and $i = 1, \ldots, L+1$, and 1D-shares each of them over $R$. The players compute $[x_j^{(i)}] = \sum_{P_k \in \mathcal{P} \setminus \mathcal{X}}^{n} [x_j^{(i,k)}]$

**Fault Detection:** The players run GenerateChallenges to sample uniformly random $r_1, \ldots, r_L$ in $\hat{R}$, with associated matrices as mentioned above. Then the following is executed for every verifier $P_V \in \mathcal{P} \setminus \mathcal{X}$.

1. The players interpret the random elements $[x_j^{(i)}]$ as $L+1$ column vectors of length $d$, i.e. for each $i = 1, \ldots, L+1$ we have $[\mathbf{x}^{(i)}] = ([x_0^{(i)}], \ldots, [x_{d-1}^{(i)}])^T$. Then, they compute the sum $[\mathbf{y}] = M_{r_1}[\mathbf{x}^{(1)}] + \cdots + M_{r_L}[\mathbf{x}^{(L)}] + [\mathbf{x}^{(L+1)}]$ and send the shares of $\mathbf{y}$ to $P_V$.

2. $P_V$ checks if it holds that all the entries of $\mathbf{y}$ are in $S$, and broadcast a bit indicating which is the case.

If all verifiers $P_V \in \mathcal{P} \setminus \mathcal{X}$ accepted in the previous step then output the shares $[x_j^{(i)}]$.

**Fault Localization:** Run the following for the smallest $P_V \in \mathcal{P} \setminus \mathcal{X}$ that complained in the fault detection phase.

1. Every player $P_k$ with $P_k \leftrightarrow P_V$ sends their shares of each $x_j^{(i,\ell)}$ to $P_V$, for $j = 0, \ldots, d-1$, $i = 1, \ldots, L$ and $P_\ell \leftrightarrow P_k$.

2. $P_V$ checks that all the shares for $P_\ell \leftrightarrow P_V$ interpolate correctly.

3. If they do interpolate correctly then $P_V$ gets $x_j^{(i,\ell)}$ for $j = 0, \ldots, d-1$, $i = 1, \ldots, L$ and $P_\ell \in \mathcal{P} \setminus \mathcal{X}$. $P_V$ broadcasts the smallest index $\ell$ of the party for which $x_j^{(i,\ell)} \notin S$ and the protocol fails with $P_V \not\leftrightarrow P_k$.[a]

4. If they do not interpolate correctly then $P_V$ broadcasts the smallest indexes $\ell, i, j$ for which interpolation of $x_j^{(i,\ell)}$ failed.

5. Each party $P_k \in \mathcal{P} \setminus \mathcal{X}$ with $P_k \leftrightarrow P_\ell$ broadcasts its share of $x_j^{(i,\ell)}$.

6. If the broadcasted shares interpolate correctly then $P_V$ broadcasts the index $k$ of a party $P_k$ with $P_k \leftrightarrow P_V$ that broadcasted a share different than the one it sent to $P_V$ before and the protocol fails with $P_V \not\leftrightarrow P_k$.

7. Otherwise, the accused party $P_\ell$ broadcasts the index of the party $P_k$ who broadcasted a wrong share and the protocol fails with $P_\ell \not\leftrightarrow P_k$.

---

[a] Such party exists with overwhelming probability, as we argue in Proposition 9

**Fig. 9.** Statistically secure protocol for generating sharings of random elements in a Galois subring $S \subset R$

With this protocol in hand, the input phase from the previous section is modified slightly in order to make sure that underlying inputs lie in $\mathbb{Z}/p^k\mathbb{Z}$. This is done as follows:

1. Party $P_i \in \mathcal{P} \setminus \mathcal{X}$ shares its input $x \in \mathbb{Z}/p^k\mathbb{Z}$ as $[x]_R$.
2. The parties use $\mathsf{RandElStat}(\mathbb{Z}/p^k\mathbb{Z})$ to obtain shares $[s]_R$ of a random element $s \in \mathbb{Z}/p^k\mathbb{Z}$. Then use $\mathsf{Reconstruct1D}$ to open $[s+x]_R$.
3. If $s + x \notin \mathbb{Z}/p^k\mathbb{Z}$ then add $P_i \in \mathcal{X}$, i.e. mark $P_i$ as corrupt.

It is clear that if the check is sound since $x \notin \mathbb{Z}/p^k\mathbb{Z}$ iff $s + x \notin \mathbb{Z}/p^k\mathbb{Z}$. Regarding the security of $\mathsf{RandElStat}$, we have the following proposition.

**Proposition 9.** *If $\mathsf{RandElStat}$ succeeds, then, with probability at least $1 - p^{-\kappa}$, each value $s_j^{(l)}$ is uniformly random in $S$. If it fails then a new dispute pair is generated.*

*Proof.* Suppose the check succeeds for an honest verifier $P_V$ and the adversary cheats successfully, i.e. there is an element $x_j^{(i_*)}$ which is not in $S$. Recall $\{1, \xi, \ldots, \xi^{d-1}\}$ is an $S$-basis for $R$, so we may without loss of generality assume that the $\xi^m$-coefficient of $x_j(i_*)$ is non-zero. We have

$$[\mathbf{y}] = M_{r_1}[\mathbf{x}^{(1)}] + \cdots + M_{r_L}[\mathbf{x}^{(L)}] + [\mathbf{x}^{(L+1)}] \tag{1}$$

where each element of $\mathbf{y}$ is in $S$, but note that the shares are actually vectors in $R^d$. On both sides of Eq. 1, we first take the coefficients of $\xi^m$ *for each $R$-element*, and then interpret the resulting $S$-vectors and matrices $M_r$ as elements of $R$. Both of these operations are $S$-linear. The result is the equation $0 = r_1 u_1 + \cdots + r_L u_L + u_{L+1}$, where $u_i = \phi\left(x_0^{(i)}\right) + \phi\left(x_1^{(i)}\right)\xi + \cdots + \phi\left(x_{d-1}^{(i)}\right)\xi^{d-1}$ for each $i$, and $\phi : R \to S$ maps an element in $R$ to its coefficient of $\xi^m$. Similarly to the proof of Proposition 4, we apply Lemma 2 to conclude that this equation holds with probability at most $p^{-d}$, since each $r_i$ is uniformly random. $\square$

## 5   Conclusions

In this work, we have answered the open question *"Can we design protocols that work directly over $\mathbb{Z}/p^k\mathbb{Z}$?"* in the affirmative. We have developed novel machinery that allows us to adapt existing protocols for information-theoretic MPC to work over the ring $\mathbb{Z}/p^k\mathbb{Z}$, for any prime $p$ and any positive integer $k$. In fact, by using CRT, this implies information-theoretic MPC over the ring $\mathbb{Z}/N\mathbb{Z}$ for *any* integer $N$. The communication complexity of our techniques introduce an overhead of only $\log n$ compared to the corresponding protocols over fields, where $n$ is the number of parties. This overhead comes from the fact that we need to work over a larger structure (a Galois ring) in order to obtain algebraic properties that resemble those on fields, and that can be used for multiparty computation. A similar approach is taken in the SPDZ$_{2^k}$ protocol [8] for computation over $\mathbb{Z}/2^k\mathbb{Z}$ by using the larger ring $\mathbb{Z}/2^{k+s}\mathbb{Z}$. In that work it is conjectured that this is an inherent price to pay for working over an algebraic structure with less nice properties than a field, and our current approach to information-theoretic MPC over $\mathbb{Z}/p^k\mathbb{Z}$ seems to support this claim, at least in the setting of a single circuit execution.

We consider as future work improving the complexity of the protocols presented here (specially the one from Sect. 4 for honest majority) by adapting more efficient protocols over fields like [5], whose complexity is almost-linear in the number of parties.

**Acknowledgements.** This work has been supported by the European Research Council (ERC) under the European Unions's Horizon 2020 research and innovation programme under grant agreement No. 669255 (MPCPRO) and ERC ADG grant No. 74079 (ALGSTRONGCRYPTO).

# References

1. Araki, T., et al.: Generalizing the SPDZ compiler for other protocols. In: Proceedings of the 2018 ACM SIGSAC Conference on Computer and Communications Security, pp. 880–895. ACM (2018)
2. Barak, A., Escudero, D., Dalskov, A., Keller, M.: Secure evaluation of quantized neural networks. Cryptology ePrint Archive, Report 2019/131 (2019). https://eprint.iacr.org/2019/131
3. Beerliová-Trubíniová, Z., Hirt, M.: Efficient multi-party computation with dispute control. In: Halevi, S., Rabin, T. (eds.) TCC 2006. LNCS, vol. 3876, pp. 305–328. Springer, Heidelberg (2006). https://doi.org/10.1007/11681878_16
4. Beerliová-Trubíniová, Z., Hirt, M.: Perfectly-secure MPC with linear communication complexity. In: Canetti, R. (ed.) TCC 2008. LNCS, vol. 4948, pp. 213–230. Springer, Heidelberg (2008). https://doi.org/10.1007/978-3-540-78524-8_13
5. Ben-Sasson, E., Fehr, S., Ostrovsky, R.: Near-linear unconditionally-secure multiparty computation with a dishonest minority. In: Safavi-Naini, R., Canetti, R. (eds.) CRYPTO 2012. LNCS, vol. 7417, pp. 663–680. Springer, Heidelberg (2012). https://doi.org/10.1007/978-3-642-32009-5_39
6. Cantor, D.G., Kaltofen, E.: On fast multiplication of polynomials over arbitrary algebras. Acta Inf. **28**(7), 693–701 (1991)
7. Cascudo, I., Cramer, R., Xing, C., Yuan, C.: Amortized complexity of information-theoretically secure MPC revisited. In: Shacham, H., Boldyreva, A. (eds.) CRYPTO 2018. LNCS, vol. 10993, pp. 395–426. Springer, Cham (2018). https://doi.org/10.1007/978-3-319-96878-0_14
8. Cramer, R., Damgård, I., Escudero, D., Scholl, P., Xing, C.: SPDZ$_{2^k}$: efficient MPC mod $2^k$ for dishonest majority. In: Shacham, H., Boldyreva, A. (eds.) CRYPTO 2018. LNCS, vol. 10992, pp. 769–798. Springer, Cham (2018). https://doi.org/10.1007/978-3-319-96881-0_26
9. Cramer, R., Damgård, I., Nielsen, J.B.: Secure Multiparty Computation and Secret Sharing. Cambridge University Press, Cambridge (2015)
10. Cramer, R., Fehr, S., Ishai, Y., Kushilevitz, E.: Efficient multi-party computation over rings. In: Biham, E. (ed.) EUROCRYPT 2003. LNCS, vol. 2656, pp. 596–613. Springer, Heidelberg (2003). https://doi.org/10.1007/3-540-39200-9_37

11. Cramer, R., Rambaud, M., Xing, C.: Asymptotically-good arithmetic secret sharing over $\mathbb{Z}/p^\ell\mathbb{Z}$ with strong multiplication and its applications to efficient MPC. IACR Cryptology ePrint Archive 2019/832 (2019)
12. Damgard, I., Keller, M., Larraia, E., Pastro, V., Scholl, P., Smart, N.P.: Practical covertly secure MPC for dishonest majority - or: Breaking the SPDZ limits. Cryptology ePrint Archive, Report 2012/642 (2012)
13. Damgård, I., Escudero, D., Frederiksen, T., Keller, M., Scholl, P., Volgushev, N.: New primitives for actively-secure MPC over rings with applications to private machine learning. In: 2019 2019 IEEE Symposium on Security and Privacy (SP), pp. 1325–1343. IEEE Computer Society, Los Alamitos (2019)
14. Keller, M., Orsini, E., Scholl, P.: MASCOT: faster malicious arithmetic secure computation with oblivious transfer. Cryptology ePrint Archive, Report 2016/505 (2016). http://eprint.iacr.org/2016/505
15. Massey, J.: Shift-register synthesis and BCH decoding. IEEE Trans. Inf. Theory **15**(1), 122–127 (1969)
16. Wan, Z.-X.: Lectures on Finite Fields and Galois Rings. World Scientific Publishing Company, Singapore (2003)

# Is Information-Theoretic Topology-Hiding Computation Possible?

Marshall Ball[1]([✉]), Elette Boyle[2], Ran Cohen[3,4], Tal Malkin[1], and Tal Moran[2]

[1] Columbia University, New York, USA
{marshall,tal}@cs.columbia.edu
[2] IDC Herzliya, Herzliya, Israel
{elette.boyle,talm}@idc.ac.il
[3] Boston University, Boston, USA
[4] Northeastern University, Boston, USA
rancohen@ccs.neu.edu

**Abstract.** Topology-hiding computation (THC) is a form of multi-party computation over an incomplete communication graph that maintains the privacy of the underlying graph topology. Existing THC protocols consider an adversary that may corrupt an arbitrary number of parties, and rely on cryptographic assumptions such as DDH.

In this paper we address the question of whether *information-theoretic* THC can be achieved by taking advantage of an *honest majority*. In contrast to the standard MPC setting, this problem has remained open in the topology-hiding realm, even for simple "privacy-free" functions like broadcast, and even when considering only semi-honest corruptions.

We uncover a rich landscape of both positive and negative answers to the above question, showing that what types of graphs are used and how they are selected is an important factor in determining the feasibility of hiding topology information-theoretically. In particular, our results include the following.

- We show that topology-hiding broadcast (THB) on a *line* with four nodes, secure against a single semi-honest corruption, implies *key agreement*. This result extends to broader classes of graphs, e.g., THB on a *cycle* with two semi-honest corruptions.
- On the other hand, we provide the first feasibility result for information-theoretic THC: for the class of *cycle* graphs, with a single semi-honest corruption.

Given the strong impossibilities, we put forth a weaker definition of *distributional*-THC, where the graph is selected from some distribution (as opposed to worst-case).

- We present a formal separation between the definitions, by showing a distribution for which information theoretic distributional-THC is possible, but even topology-hiding broadcast is not possible information-theoretically with the standard definition.
- We demonstrate the power of our new definition via a new connection to adaptively secure low-locality MPC, where distributional-THC enables parties to "reuse" a secret low-degree communication graph even in the face of adaptive corruptions.

© International Association for Cryptologic Research 2019
D. Hofheinz and A. Rosen (Eds.): TCC 2019, LNCS 11891, pp. 502–530, 2019.
https://doi.org/10.1007/978-3-030-36030-6_20

# 1 Introduction

In the setting of secure multiparty computation (MPC) [8,15,21,33], a set of mutually distrusting parties wish to jointly perform a computation, such that no coalition of cheating parties can learn more information than their outputs (privacy) or affect the outputs of the computation any more than by choosing their own inputs (correctness). Seminal results initiated in the 1980s [8,15,21,33], showed feasibility of MPC for general functions in many settings. The original definitions—and most works in the rich field of research they gave rise to— assume the participants are connected via a complete graph: i.e., any pair of parties can communicate directly with each other. However, in many settings the communication graph is in fact partial (either by design or by necessity). Moreover, as we discuss below, the network topology itself may be sensitive information to be hidden.

Several lines of work have studied secure computation over incomplete networks, in different contexts, but without attempting to hide the communication graph. For example, beginning with classical results in Byzantine agreement [17,20], a line of work studied the feasibility of reliable communication over (known) incomplete networks (cf. [4–6,9,13,18,19,28]). More recent lines of work study secure computation with restricted interaction patterns, motivated by improving efficiency, latency, scalability, usability, or security, including [7,10,11, 14,22–24]. Some of these works utilize a secret communication subgraph of the complete graph that is available to the parties as a tool to achieve their goal; e.g., [10,11,14] use this idea in order to achieve communication locality.

*Topology-Hiding Computation.* Moran et al. [31] initiated the study of *Topology-Hiding Computation (THC)*, addressing the setting where the communication graph is incomplete and *sensitive*. Here, the goal is to allow parties who see only their immediate neighborhood (and possibly know that the graph belongs to some class), to securely compute arbitrary functions without revealing any other information about the graph topology. THC is of theoretical interest, but is also motivated by real-world settings where it is desired to keep the underlying communication graph private. These include social networks, ISP networks, vehicle-to-vehicle communications, wireless and ad-hoc sensor networks, and other Internet of Things networks.

THC protocols have been studied within two adversarial settings. In the *semi-honest* setting, the adversary follows the prescribed protocol but attempts to extrapolate disallowed information. In the *fail-stop* setting, the adversary may additionally abort the computation of parties at any point. Most existing THC protocols focus on the former, semi-honest setting, and this will also be our focus in this paper. We mention that in the fail-stop setting, Moran et al. [31] showed that THC is not possible except for extremely limited graphs/adversarial corruption patterns, and Ball et al. [3] and LaVigne et al. [29] showed how to achieve it with small leakage, assuming a secure hardware setup assumption, and assuming the hardness of decisional Diffie-Hellman (DDH), quadratic residuosity (QR), or learning with errors (LWE).

For the rest of this paper we assume the semi-honest setting (although some of our results could potentially be extended to fail-stop or malicious settings). In this regime, after several protocols achieving THC for various subclasses of graphs (log-diameter, cycles, trees, etc.) [1,26,31] from different cryptographic assumptions, Akavia et al. [2] showed how to achieve THC for all graphs from the DDH or QR assumptions, and LaVigne et al. [29] from LWE.

*Our Question: Information-Theoretic THC.* Existing topology-hiding computation protocols provide a strong notion of hiding *all* information about the graph against an adversary who can corrupt an arbitrary number of parties. On the other hand, these existing protocols use structured cryptographic assumptions such as DDH, oblivious transfer (OT), or public-key encryption (PKE) with special properties, or even stronger assumptions such as a secure hardware box [3] to achieve more practical efficiency.

In this paper, we ask whether we can hide topology *information theoretically*, against a computationally unbounded adversary (in the plain model, with no correlated randomness or other trusted setup). A similar question, albeit only for (non-private) communication, was considered by Hinkelmann and Jakoby [25]. They claim an impossibility result for the class of all graphs, as well as a positive result showing an information-theoretic all-to-all communication protocol that leaks specific information about the graph (routing tables) but no other information. In contrast, here we are interested in (positive and negative) results for subclasses of graphs, as it is typically the case in applications of THC that the graph belongs to a certain known class. Looking ahead, we will see that what graphs are allowed and how they are chosen plays a crucial role for the feasibility of information-theoretic THC.

Ball et al. [3] have also considered this question, and showed that in their setting—semi-honest, arbitrary number of corruptions—the answer is negative. Specifically, they prove that even semi-honest secure topology-hiding *broadcast* for four parties or more, implies OT. Note that standard information-theoretic MPC for broadcast (where topology can be revealed) is trivial in the semi-honest setting, since there is nothing to hide: simply "flooding"—i.e., forwarding received messages to all neighbors—for sufficiently many rounds, works. Their proof crucially depends on the adversary corrupting at least half of the parties, namely no honest majority. This brings up a natural question, which we study in this paper:

Can we take advantage of a low corruption threshold to achieve information-theoretic topology-hiding computation?

This question is particularly natural when we consider how fruitful this approach had been in the realm of standard (topology-revealing) secure computation. Indeed, classical results [8,15,32] show information-theoretic protocols for secure computation of general functions with an honest majority. However, in the topology-hiding realm, this question remained open (and explicitly mentioned in previous works such as [3]). In fact, the question was open even for the special case of topology-hiding broadcast (THB), where no privacy of inputs is required.

In this paper, we prove several results answering the above question, both negatively and positively, in different settings. All our positive results hold for general THC and all our negative results hold even for THB. Below we first describe our results for the standard definition of THC. We then discuss a new weaker definition of *distributional*-topology-hiding computation that we put forward, together with our results for this definition (as well as motivation and applications of this relaxation). Our results deepen our understanding of the nature of topology hiding, and point to a rich terrain of possibilities and applications of THC.

## 1.1  Our Results: Standard (Strong) Topology Hiding

We start by presenting both feasibility and infeasibility results of information-theoretic THC according to the standard definition from [30].

*Broadcast on a Line Implies Key Agreement.* We identify a large class of graphs for which information-theoretic THC is not possible, even when the semi-honest adversary can corrupt just a single party, and even without relying on input privacy.

Theorem (informal): Topology-hiding broadcast for a graph with four parties on a line, resilient to one semi-honest corruption, implies key agreement.

Note that this theorem is for THB. Information-theoretic THC is trivially not possible here because the graph is only 1-connected, hence no privacy is possible with one corruption [18] (recall that we do not have any setup or correlated randomness).

At a high level, our key-agreement protocol considers two permutations of the four nodes: $G_0 = (1 - 2 - 3 - 4)$ and $G_1 = (2 - 3 - 4 - 1)$ (see Fig. 1), with party 1 acting as the broadcaster. In this setting, a corrupted party 3 cannot distinguish which topology is being used: namely, whether 1 is a neighbor of 2 or of 4. This gap can be used to achieve a two-party key-agreement protocol. Consider an execution of the THB where Alice emulates parties 1, 2, and 3 while Bob emulates party 4, and another execution where Alice emulates parties 2 and 3 while Bob emulates parties 4 and 1. In both cases the messages that are exchanged by Alice and Bob—and so can be heard by an eavesdropper—consist of a partial view of party 3 in the THB protocol.

The key-agreement protocol now comprises of repeated phases, where in each phase Alice and Bob run two executions of the THB protocol. Each party tosses a private coin to decide whether to emulate the broadcaster party 1 in the first execution or the second. If Alice and Bob toss *different* coins, then either both emulate party 1 or nobody does. In this case they simply discard this phase and continue to the next one. However, if they toss the *same* coin, an eavesdropper will not be able to guess with more than negligible probability whether Alice emulated 1 in the first run and Bob in the second, or vice versa; hence, Alice and Bob can agree on this bit.

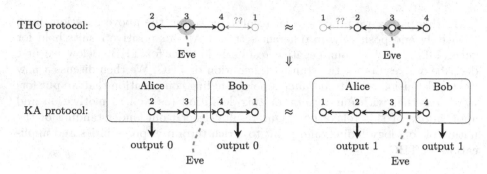

**Fig. 1.** Four-party THB implies two-party key agreement. At the top are two configurations of the line, where party 3 is connected to party 2 on the left and to party 4 on the right. Party 3 does not know the location of party 1. At the bottom is the induced KA protocol, where Alice and Bob simulate executions of the THB protocol. The transcript visible to Eve forms a partial view of party 3's view in the THB; hence, Eve cannot distinguish between both scenarios.

*Extension to Broader Classes of Graphs.* Clearly, this theorem holds for any class of graphs that includes all lines over $n \geq 4$ parties (topology-hiding here means that the order of the parties on the line, other than the two neighbors of the corrupted party, is not known, and in particular, the location of the broadcaster is hidden).

Our theorem further extends by a standard player-partitioning argument to more general classes of graphs, namely, any graph that can be partitioned into 4 "subsets" on a line. An example for such a class, most relevant to our positive result (below), are cycles of seven parties or more and with two corruptions (see Fig. 2).

*Information-Theoretic THC on a Cycle.* Our negative result rules out information-theoretic THC on cycles with two corruptions. Does a similar result hold even when we have a single corruption? Our next result shows that the answer is no. We construct a perfectly secure THC protocol on cycles, resilient to a single corruption.

> Theorem (informal): THC on a cycle with one corruption can be achieved information theoretically, with perfect correctness.

Note that this does not contradict the negative result claimed by Hinkelmann and Jakoby [25]. While that result precludes information-theoretic THC for the class of all graphs, here the parties know they are on a cycle (but do not know in which order the parties are arranged on the cycle).

The proof consists of two parts. Initially, we show how to realize anonymous and private pairwise communication. That is, each party can send a message to any other party on the cycle, but without knowing to whom he is sending, and from whom he is receiving messages. Instead, the sender can send the messages to the *relative location* on the cycle, i.e., he can send one message to a party that

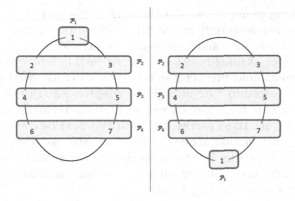

**Fig. 2.** Reducing a seven-node cycle to a four-node line. Consider the partition of the seven nodes into $\mathcal{P}_1 = \{1\}$, $\mathcal{P}_2 = \{2,3\}$, $\mathcal{P}_3 = \{4,5\}$, and $\mathcal{P}_4 = \{6,7\}$. The cycle on the left yields $(\mathcal{P}_1 - \mathcal{P}_2 - \mathcal{P}_3 - \mathcal{P}_4)$ and the cycle on the right yields $(\mathcal{P}_2 - \mathcal{P}_3 - \mathcal{P}_4 - \mathcal{P}_1)$.

is 2 hops to his right, another message to a party that is 3 hops to his left, and so on. To send a message to a party that is $j$ hops to his right (i.e., $n-j$ hops to his left), the sender secret shares the message and sends one share to his right neighbor and the second to his left neighbor. A party that receives a message from one of his neighbors forwards the message to his other neighbor. As there are $n-1$ hops in the cycle, sending a message takes $n-1$ rounds, and the sender (that is sending to the party that is $j$ hops to his right) starts sending the right share after $n-j$ rounds and the left share after $j$ rounds. This way, after $n-1$ rounds, the receiver obtains both shares and can reconstruct the message.

Once establishing private pairwise channels, the parties can compute any function using the BGW protocol [8]. However, BGW cannot be executed immediately over an anonymous network, since to process input wires the real identities should be known, rather than the alias IDs (e.g., for computing $(x_1+x_2)\cdot x_3$). To overcome this obstacle, we first observe that *symmetric* functions $f$ can be implemented immediately via BGW over an anonymous communication network. Then, we generically reduce arbitrary $f$ to the symmetric case, by having parties submit their real ID as part of their input $(i, x_i)$, and computing the modified *symmetric* function $f'$ which acts equivalently on all input pairs via multiplexing.

### 1.2 Our Results: Distributional-Topology Hiding

Having shown that information-theoretic THC is impossible for a large class of graphs even in the honest-majority setting, a natural question is whether we can construct weaker—but still useful—variants of THC for such settings. In particular, suppose we do not aim to hide everything about the graph, but rather just hide *something* about the graph, which will allow us to use the protocol as a building block in other applications.

As a motivating example, consider the work of Boyle et al. [11], who showed a protocol achieving adaptively secure MPC, where the actual communication graph has a sublinear cut, and thus is not an expander. Their protocol is in the so-called *hidden-channel model*, introduced in [14], where the adversary is unaware of the communication between honest parties (otherwise a trivial attack would separate the graph).[1] Intuitively, the adaptive security of their protocol hinges on the fact that the adversary cannot find which parties are on the small cut; if it could corrupt those parties, the security would be compromised. Thus, although hiding information about the topology was not their goal, it seems that the main tool used by [11] to prove their result is that something about the topology (where the sublinear cut is) is hidden. Intuitively, their protocol captures some notion of topology hiding.

Trying to formalize this claim and prove it within the existing framework of THC quickly fails. Indeed, the standard definition of THC (considered in Sect. 1.1 and in all prior work) captures security in "worst-case" graphs; hence, the communication graph is chosen by the environment. Since the environment can choose which parties to corrupt in a correlated way, it can simply corrupt the parties on the cut and break security of the protocol (even with static corruptions). This motivates us to define a weaker notion:

We define *distributional* topology-hiding computation, where, informally, the environment only knows the distribution from which the graph is chosen, not the specific graph.

*Defining Distributional-Topology Hiding.* Formalizing this definition poses some subtleties. In its most intuitive form, this definition resembles the *hidden-graph model* from [14]. In this model, the graph is sampled according to some predefined distribution, and each party learns its local neighborhood. Chandran et al. [14] used this model to construct adaptively secure MPC with sublinear communication locality; however, their protocol was *not* meant to hide topology, and indeed each graph was only valid for a one-time use. In the distributional-topology-hiding case, we wish to construct protocols that *do* hide the topology, and so can reuse the same graph.

To support hidden topology during the computation along with strong composition capabilities, we allow the environment to receive the communication graph from the ideal functionality (either the communication-graph functionality in the real world, or the graph-information functionality in the ideal world), before announcing its decision-bit: real or ideal. Once the environment has learned the graph, we fall back to a similar state as in the classical THC setting, and we cannot base the security of the protocol on the graph's entropy. For this reason, after the environment receives the graph, the ideal functionality

---

[1] This is in fact the communication model that is considered in the topology-hiding setting, since if the communication is over standard private channels, the adversary would learn information about the graph just by observing with whom honest parties communicate.

will stop processing any further messages, and in a sense, the communication network enters an "out of order" state.

However, the environment might still attempt to misuse this additional power, and after receiving the communication graph, corrupt a set of parties in a way that will break security (e.g., corrupt the entire sublinear cut in the example above). This attack is quite subtle, since essentially, after learning the graph the environment has the capability to learn all of the inputs that were used in the protocol just from the messages received by a small set of parties (recall that we consider information-theoretic protocols in the plain model). Clearly, the simulator will not be able to simulate such an attack. One way to protect against this attack is to rely on *secure data erasures* and instruct every party to erase all of the received and sent messages as soon as the network goes out of order. However, since secure erasures form a strong assumption that cannot always be realized, and thus limit the model, we resort to an alternative, more general, solution. To overcome this subtlety, once the environment receives the graph the ideal functionality will provide the simulator with all of the input messages it received from honest parties. This new information will allow the simulator to simulate additional corruption requests that are issued as a function of the graph, and will balance the additional advantage the environment gained.

In a sense, the new definition guarantees privacy of the communication network *as long as it is active*; however, if the network enters an "out of order" state, it does not retain the privacy of the protocols that used it, unless secure data erasure are employed.

We note that since the new definition hides the communication graph from the environment while it is active, computation that depend on the communication graph itself (e.g., finding shortest paths) cannot be supported - this is another weakening of the original definition.

*Relation to Classical THC.* Having formalized distributional-THC, one may ask whether this definition can be used to achieve meaningful computations, and whether it implies standard THC. We show that this definition can capture the intuitive topology-hiding property of the protocol in [11], discussed above. In fact, we modify their protocol to show a strong separation between the definitions. We construct a distribution $\mathcal{D}$ which, on the one hand, can be used for computing any function while hiding a sublinear cut between two cliques (tolerating a linear number of adaptive corruptions), and on the other hand, even broadcast cannot be computed in a topology-hiding manner (in the classical sense) using any graph in the support of $\mathcal{D}$ (tolerating merely a sublinear number of static corruptions).

> Theorem (informal): We show a distribution $\mathcal{D}$ over graphs with $n$ nodes such that:
> - Distributional-THC of every function can be achieved with respect to $\mathcal{D}$, with information-theoretic security, against an adaptive semi-honest adversary.

- For any class of graphs $\mathcal{C}$ with $\mathcal{C} \cap \mathsf{supp}(\mathcal{D}) \neq \emptyset$, even broadcast cannot be computed information theoretically in the strong THC setting, even with static semi-honest corruptions (as it implies key agreement).

*Connection to Adaptively Secure Low-Locality MPC.* Finally, we demonstrate the power of our new definition via a new connection to adaptively secure low-locality MPC, where distributional-THC enables parties to "reuse" a secret low-degree communication graph even in the face adaptive corruptions. Concretely, this will enable sequential composition of the adaptively secure MPC protocol from [14] while maintaining sublinear locality. The starting point of [14] was any adaptively secure MPC protocol over pairwise private channels. They used the hidden-graph model to sample an Erdős-Rényi graph $G$ (with sublinear degree and polylog diameter) and showed how to emulate pairwise private communication over the graph $G$. In addition, an elegant distributed sampling algorithm for a Erdős-Rényi graph was given in [14] (based on [13,27]).

However, as discussed above, their protocol does not hide the topology of $G$, and so a fresh graph is used for every communication round. For this reason, their protocol can be used for executing MPC protocols with sublinear many communication rounds, and maintains sequential composition of sublinear many computations (otherwise the locality will blow up).

We show that if the private pairwise communication can be instantiated in a distributional-THC manner, the adaptively secure MPC protocol from [14] will be able to reuse the *same* secret Erdős-Rényi communication graph for polynomially many rounds, and so will remain secure under arbitrary sequential composition.

Theorem (informal): If there exists an adaptively secure distributional-THC protocol for private pairwise communication with respect to the Erdős-Rényi distribution from [14] (tolerating a linear number of semi-honest corruptions), then there exists an honest-majority adaptively secure MPC protocol with sublinear locality (tolerating the same corruptions) that remains secure under polynomially many sequential executions.

We note that this theorem does not present a new feasibility result, as we do not yet know how to implement the required underlying adaptively secure distributional-THC protocol. We leave this as an interesting open problem. Instead, the theorem demonstrates the power and usefulness of our definition (despite its weakness compared to the original).

## 1.3  Open Problems

Our results from Sect. 1.1 characterize the feasibility of information-theoretic THC over *lines* and *cycles*. Ultimately, the desire is to provide a similar characterization for all graphs. An interesting starting point is to extend our understanding in broader classes of graph, e.g., wheel graphs or 3-regular graphs.

Another intriguing question to come up with more distributions over graphs that can be computed in a distributional-THC manner.

Finally, as mentioned above, it is not clear whether private pairwise communication can be realized with distributional-THC security with respect to the Erdős-Rényi distribution. Answering this question will have implications on low-locality adaptively secure MPC.

*Additional Related Work.* In an independent and concurrent work, Damgård et al. [16] investigate the feasibility of information-theoretic THC. Their setting is different from ours, as they consider a trusted setup phase to generate correlated randomness for the parties.

*Organization of the Paper.* The preliminaries can be found in Sect. 2. Initially, we consider the standard THC definition and present our lower bound in Sect. 3, followed by the positive results in Sect. 4. We proceed to define distributional-THC in Sect. 5, show a separation between the definitions in Sect. 6. Due to space limit, some of the proofs and the connection to low-locality MPC are deferred to the full version.

## 2 Preliminaries

*Notations.* For $n \in \mathbb{N}$ let $[n] = \{1, \cdots, n\}$. We denote by $\kappa$ the security parameter, by $n$ the number of parties, and by $t$ an upper bound on the number of corrupted parties. The empty string is denoted by $\epsilon$.

*UC Framework.* We consider the UC framework of Canetti [12]. Unless stated otherwise, we will consider computationally unbounded and semi-honest adversaries and environments. We will consider both *static* corruptions (where the corrupted parties are chosen before the protocol begins) and *adaptive* corruptions (where parties can get corrupted dynamically during the course of the computation), and explicitly mention which type of corruption is considered in every section.

We will consider the standard *secure function evaluation* (SFE) functionality, denoted $\mathcal{F}_{\mathsf{sfe}}^{f}$. Informally, the functionality is parametrized by an efficiently computable function $f : (\{0,1\}^*)^n \to \{0,1\}^*$. Every honest party forwards its input received from the environment to the ideal functionality, and the simulator sends the corrupted parties' inputs. The functionality computes $y = f(x_1, \ldots, x_n)$ and returns $y$ to every party. *Broadcast* is a special case of SFE for the function that receives an input from a single party, named *the broadcaster*, (formally, every other party gives the empty string $\epsilon$ as input) and delivers this value to every party as the output. We denote the broadcast functionality by $\mathcal{F}_{\mathsf{bc}}$.

*Topology-Hiding Computation (THC).* We recall the definition of topology-hiding computation from [31]. The real-world protocol is defined in a model where all communication is transmitted via the $\mathcal{F}_{\mathsf{graph}}^{\mathcal{G}}$ functionality (described in Fig. 3). The functionality $\mathcal{F}_{\mathsf{graph}}^{\mathcal{G}}$ is parametrized by a family of graphs $\mathcal{G}$. Initially, before the protocol begins, $\mathcal{F}_{\mathsf{graph}}^{\mathcal{G}}$ receives the network communication graph $G$ from a special graph party $P_{\text{graph}}$, makes sure that $G \in \mathcal{G}$, and provides to each party his local neighbor-set. Next, during the protocol's execution, the functionality receives a message to be delivered from a sender $P_v$ to a receiver $P_w$ and delivers the message if the edge $(v, w)$ appears in the graph.

An ideal-model computation of a functionality $\mathcal{F}$ is augmented to provide the corrupted parties with the information that is leaked about the graph; namely, every ideal (dummy) party should learn his neighbor-set. To capture this, we define the wrapper-functionality $\mathcal{W}^{\mathcal{G}}_{\text{graph-info}}(\mathcal{F})$, that runs internally a copy of the functionality $\mathcal{F}$. The wrapper receives the graph $G = (V, E)$ from $P_{\text{graph}}$, makes sure that $G \in \mathcal{G}$, and upon receiving an initialization message from a party $P_i$ responds with its neighbor set $\mathcal{N}_G[i]$ (just like $\mathcal{F}^{\mathcal{G}}_{\text{graph}}$). All other input messages are forwarded to $\mathcal{F}$ and every message from $\mathcal{F}$ is delivered to its recipient.

---

**The functionality $\mathcal{F}^{\mathcal{G}}_{\text{graph}}$**

The $n$-party functionality $\mathcal{F}^{\mathcal{G}}_{\text{graph}}$ is parametrized by a family of graphs $\mathcal{G}$ and proceeds with parties $P_1, \ldots, P_n$ and a special graph party $P_{\text{graph}}$ as follows.

**Initialization Phase:**
    **Input:** $\mathcal{F}^{\mathcal{G}}_{\text{graph}}$ waits to receive the graph $G = (V, E)$ from $P_{\text{graph}}$. If $G \notin \mathcal{G}$, abort.
    **Output:** $\mathcal{F}^{\mathcal{G}}_{\text{graph}}$ outputs $\mathcal{N}_G[v]$ to each $P_v$.
**Communication Phase:**
    **Input:** $\mathcal{F}^{\mathcal{G}}_{\text{graph}}$ receives from a party $P_v$ a destination/data pair $(w, m)$ where
        $w \in \mathcal{N}_G[v]$ and $m$ is the message $P_v$ wants to send to $P_w$. (If $w$ is not a
        neighbor of $v$, $\mathcal{F}^{\mathcal{G}}_{\text{graph}}$ ignores this input.)
    **Output:** $\mathcal{F}^{\mathcal{G}}_{\text{graph}}$ gives output $(v, m)$ to $P_w$ indicating that $P_v$ sent the message
        $m$ to $P_w$.

---

**Fig. 3.** The communication graph functionality

**Definition 1 (Topology-hiding computation).** *We say that a protocol $\pi$ securely realizes a functionality $\mathcal{F}$ in a* **topology-hiding manner** *with respect to $\mathcal{G}$ tolerating semi-honest $t$-adversaries if $\pi$ securely realizes $\mathcal{W}^{\mathcal{G}}_{\text{graph-info}}(\mathcal{F})$ in the $\mathcal{F}^{\mathcal{G}}_{\text{graph}}$-hybrid model tolerating semi-honest $t$-adversaries.*

We note a few technical changes in the definition above compared to [31]. First, we let the graph functionality $\mathcal{F}_{\text{graph}}$ and the wrapper $\mathcal{W}_{\text{graph-info}}$ be parametrized by a family of graphs $\mathcal{G}$. This captures the fact that certain properties of the graphs might be inherently leaked e.g., the diameter of the graph [31] or that the graph is a cycle or a tree [1]. This technical adjustment has also been considered in [26]. A second difference is that we define the graph-information as a *wrapper functionality* around $\mathcal{F}$ rather than a separate functionality that is composed with $\mathcal{F}$. Although this difference is only syntactic with respect to the definition above, it will enable a cleaner definition of *distributional THC* in Sect. 5.

# 3   TH-Broadcast on a Line Implies Key Agreement

In this section, we show that a topology-hiding broadcast protocol of four parties (or more) connected in a line that tolerates one semi-honest corruption, implies the existence of two-party key-agreement protocols.

We define the following class of graphs $\mathcal{G}_{line} = \{G_0, G_1\}$, where each graph has four nodes on a line: $G_0 = (1 - 2 - 3 - 4)$ and $G_1 = (2 - 3 - 4 - 1)$ (see Fig. 1). Consider party 1 to be the broadcaster, then a corrupted party 3 will not know whether 1 is a neighbor of 2 or of 4. We next show how to utilize this property to achieve a two-party key-agreement protocol. The high-level idea is that either Alice will emulate parties $1, 2$, and 3 and Bob will emulate party 4, or that Alice will emulate parties 2 and 3, and Bob will emulate parties 4 and 1. An eavesdropper listening to their communication will in fact hear all the messages exchanged between party 3 and party 4 in the THB protocol, and therefore will not be able to guess with more than negligible probability who emulates party 1.

**Theorem 1.** *The existence of four-party topology-hiding broadcast with respect to class $\mathcal{G}_{line}$ secure against semi-honest adversaries that may make a single corruption implies the existence of key agreement.*

*High-Level Idea.* Our key-agreement protocol proceeds in phases. In a given phase, Alice and Bob will jointly simulate the topology-hiding broadcast protocol on a line graph of nodes 1, 2, 3, 4. Alice will always simulate nodes 2 and 3 and Bob will always simulate node 4. Alice and Bob will flip private coins to determine if they simulate 1. Note that it may be that neither or both of them simulate node 1. It will always be the case that node 2 has an edge to node 3 which is in turn has an edge to node 4. If Alice's coin is heads she will simulate node 1 with a unique edge to node 2. Similarly, if Bob's coin is heads, he will simulate node 1 with a unique edge to node 4. The node 1 will always be broadcaster, and will correspond to the bit agreed upon. The eavesdropper, Eve, will of course see the messages between 3 and 4 as Alice and Bob communicate to simulate the protocol execution. We will design our protocol so that Alice and Bob can identify when both or neither are controlling node 1 so they can throw them out, as the protocol will have no guarantees in this case. In the other cases, whether Alice or Bob controls 1 will indicate the bit agreed upon. This bit will be obvious to both Alice and Bob; however, it will be obscured from Eve. In particular, any advantage Eve has in guessing the bit can be used to break the topology hiding of the protocol. To increase the probability of successfully agreeing on a bit the protocol can simply be repeated. However, for simplicity we will specify and analyze the low-success version.

*Proof.* Let $\pi$ be a topology-hiding broadcast protocol with respect to $\mathcal{G}_{line}$, where node 1 is the broadcaster. Via sequential composition, we may assume $\pi$ is a $\kappa$-bit broadcast protocol without. We use $\pi$ to construct the following key-agreement protocol.

## Protocol 2 (Two-party key agreement)

1. *Alice sends two random $\kappa$-bit strings, $r_1$ and $r_2$, to Bob. These will be the strings broadcasted in the simulations of $\pi$.*
2. *Alice and Bob each flips a coin: $c_A, c_B \leftarrow \{0, 1\}$, respectively. They will jointly simulate the protocol twice.*
   - *If $c_A = 1$, Alice will first simulate nodes 1 (broadcasting $r_1$), 2, and 3 in $\pi$. The second time, Alice will just simulate nodes 2 and 3. If $c_A = 0$, Alice will just simulate nodes 2 and 3 the first time and additionally simulate node 1 (broadcasting $r_2$), the second time.*
   - *If $c_B = 1$, Bob will first simulate nodes 1 (broadcasting $r_1$) and 4 in $\pi$. The second time, Bob will just simulate node 4. If $c_B = 0$, Bob will just simulate node 4 the first time, and additionally simulate node 1 (broadcasting $r_2$), the second time.*
3. *Alice and Bob jointly simulate $\pi$ twice according to the roles designated above, communicating messages between 3 and 4 as needed.*
   - *If node 2 did not output either $r_1$ in the first simulation of $\pi$ or $r_2$ in the second simulation of $\pi$, Alice outputs $\perp$. Otherwise, Alice outputs $c_A$.*
   - *If node 4 did not output either $r_1$ in the first simulation of $\pi$ or $r_2$ in the second simulation of $\pi$, Bob outputs $\perp$. Otherwise, Bob outputs $1 - c_B$.*

There are 4 cases for how $(c_A, c_B)$ is chosen (each occurring with probability $1/4$. We will divide them into two sets (each occurring with probability $1/2$): $c_A = c_B$ and $c_A \neq c_B$. We claim that in the first case both Alice and Bob output $\perp$ with probability $\geq 1 - 2^{1-\kappa}$. In the second case, we claim that both Alice and Bob output $c_A$ with overwhelming probability and that Eve's output can be at most negligibly correlated with $c_A$. Thus, conditioned on Alice and Bob not outputting $\perp$ (which happens with probability negligibly close to $1/2$), Alice and Bob will agree on a bit (with overwhelming probability) that is negligibly correlated with any bit outputted by an efficient eavesdropper. Therefore, it suffices to prove the claim for each case.

*The case of $c_A = c_B$.* If both $c_A = 1$ and $c_B = 1$, then neither Alice nor Bob is simulating the broadcasting node 1 in the second simulation. In which case, all outputs of $\pi$ in this simulation is independent of $r_2$. Thus, the probability that either node 2 or node 4 outputs $r_2$ in the simulation is at most $2/2^\kappa$. Conversely, if both $c_A = 0$ and $c_B = 0$, then neither party is simulating node 1 in the first simulation and all outputs are independent of $r_1$. And similarly the probability that either node 2 or node 4 outputs $r_1$, in this case, is at most $2/2^\kappa$.

In either case there is a simulation where both node 2 and node 4 fail to output the chosen string with probability at least $1 - 2^{1-\kappa}$. Thus, both Alice and Bob will output $\perp$ with probability at least $1 - 2^{1-\kappa}$.

*The case of $c_A \neq c_B$.* In this case, in each simulation exactly one of Alice and Bob is simulating node 1, the broadcaster. By correctness, all nodes (including nodes 2 and 4) will output the string $r_1$ in the first simulation and $r_2$ in the second simulation with overwhelming probability. Thus, both Alice and Bob will output $c_A$ (note that $c_A = 1 - c_B$, in this case) with overwhelming probability.

On the other hand, suppose Eve outputs a bit $b$ such that $\Pr[b = c_A] = 1/2 + \alpha$. Note that Eve only sees the correspondence between nodes 3 and 4. We can use such an Eve to distinguish between running $\pi$ on $G_0$ or $G_1$ with advantage at least $\alpha/3$. Moreover, it will distinguish with respect to a *specific* distribution of broadcast messages and topology: the one where both message and topology are chosen uniformly and independently.

A semi-honest adversary that has corrupted node 3 will wait until the protocol has completed and the output $r$ has been received before simulating Eve. The adversary will flip a bit $b'$: effectively guessing the opposite topology of actual execution 1-2-3-4 (in the case that $b' = 0$) or 2-3-4-1 (in the case that $b' = 1$). After the protocol has completed, the adversary will sample a random string $r'$ and run Eve on a transcript comprised of $r$, $r'$, the actual communication between nodes 3 and 4, and a communication between nodes 3 and 4 in a simulated execution where $r'$ is broadcasted over the guessed topology. The simulated Eve will output a bit $b$. If $b = 1$, the adversary will output the 1-2-3-4 topology, and the 2-3-4-1 topology otherwise.

In the case that the adversary guessed correctly (which happens with probability $1/2$), the transcript Eve is given is identically distributed to the that of the key-agreement protocol. In this case, the simulated Eve's bit will be $\alpha$-correlated with the actual topology. In the other case, when Eve is given two independent invocations of the protocol on the same graph, Eve's output must be negligibly close to $1/2$ and the security of $\pi$. Therefore, the probability the adversary outputs the correct topology is at least

$$1/4 - \mathsf{negl}(\kappa) + 1/4 + \alpha/2 > 1/2 + \alpha/3.$$

So, by the topology-hiding property, $\alpha$ must be negligible.

This concludes the proof of Theorem 1.                                        □

Next, we extend the lower bound to more classes of graphs using the player-partitioning technique.

**Corollary 1.** *Let $\mathcal{G}$ be a class of (connected) graphs with $n$ nodes such that there exists a partition of the nodes into four subsets $\mathcal{P}_1, \mathcal{P}_2, \mathcal{P}_3, \mathcal{P}_4$, and there exists graphs $\tilde{G}_0, \tilde{G}_1 \in \mathcal{G}$ such that:*

- *In $\tilde{G}_0$: there are no edges $(i,j) \in \mathcal{P}_1 \times \mathcal{P}_3$, or $(i,j) \in \mathcal{P}_2 \times \mathcal{P}_4$, or $(i,j) \in \mathcal{P}_1 \times \mathcal{P}_4$,*
- *In $\tilde{G}_1$: there are no edges $(i,j) \in \mathcal{P}_1 \times \mathcal{P}_3$, or $(i,j) \in \mathcal{P}_2 \times \mathcal{P}_4$, or $(i,j) \in \mathcal{P}_1 \times \mathcal{P}_2$.*

*Let $t = |\mathcal{P}_3|$. Then, a THB protocol with respect to $\mathcal{G}$ tolerating semi-honest, static $t$-adversaries, implies the existence of key agreement.*

*Proof.* Let $\pi$ be such a THB protocol, and without loss of generality assume that the broadcaster is in $\mathcal{P}_1$. We will construct the following four-party broadcast protocol on a line with respect to the class of two graphs $\mathcal{G}_{\mathsf{line}} = (G_0, G_1)$, where

- $G_0 = (1 - 2 - 3 - 4)$,
- $G_1 = (2 - 3 - 4 - 1)$.

To define the protocol, every party $i$, for $i \in [4]$, emulates in its head the parties in $\mathcal{P}_i$ executing protocol $\pi$. Whenever a party $P_j \in \mathcal{P}_i$ wishes to send a message $m$ to a party $P_{j'}$, proceed as follows: (1) If $P_{j'} \in \mathcal{P}_i$, party $i$ simulates in its head party $P_{j'}$ receiving the message $m$ from party $P_j$. (2) If $P_{j'} \in \mathcal{P}_{i'}$ for some $i' \neq i$, send the message $(j, j', m)$ to party $i'$; in this case, party $i'$ simulates party $P_{j'}$ receiving the message $m$ from party $P_j$.

Note that for $b \in \{0, 1\}$, an execution of the four-party THB over $G_b$ corresponds to an execution of the protocol $\pi$ over $\tilde{G}_b$. Since $|\mathcal{P}_3| = t$ and $\pi$ is $t$-secure, it holds that the new protocol is secure tolerating a single corruption of party $P_3$. The proof now follows from Theorem 1.    □

An example for a family of graphs that satisfies the above requirements are cycles of seven nodes tolerating two corruptions. Indeed, consider the partition

$$\mathcal{P}_1 = \{1\}, \quad \mathcal{P}_2 = \{2, 3\}, \quad \mathcal{P}_3 = \{4, 5\}, \quad \mathcal{P}_4 = \{6, 7\}.$$

Then, the two cycle-graphs $\tilde{G}_0 = (2 - 1 - 3 - 4 - 6 - 7 - 5)$ and $\tilde{G}_1 = (2 - 3 - 4 - 6 - 1 - 7 - 5)$ satisfy the properties of the corollary, as illustrated in Fig. 2.

## 4   Perfect THC on a Cycle

In this section, we show a *perfectly secure* topology-hiding *computation* protocol tolerating a single semi-honest corruption with respect to cycles. Note that in this setting we are only hiding a permutation of the nodes.

**Theorem 3.** *Let $n > 2$, and let $f$ be an efficiently computable $n$-party function. Then, $\mathcal{F}_{\mathsf{sfe}}^f$ can be securely realized in a topology-hiding manner with respect to the class of graphs that includes all cycles on $n$ nodes, tolerating a single, semi-honest corruption. Moreover, the protocol is perfectly correct and perfectly secure.*

To prove Theorem 3, we will first show how to realize anonymous secure channels without revealing the topology of the cycle. Given anonymous secure channels, it is not difficult to realize general THC on a cycle.

**Private Anonymous Communication over a Cycle.** We begin by defining the anonymous communication functionality. This randomized functionality initially assigns aliases to all parties based on their location, so that the parties can address each other by these aliases. Specifically, the functionality will choose a random party to be assigned with the alias '1', and will choose a random orientation of "left" and "right" for its outgoing edges. This will define an alias for each other party, in an increasing order going to the left. Each party will receive its alias and orientation (hence allowing it to compute the alias of any party that is a certain number of hops away in each direction). Then, each party can privately send messages to any alias of their choice. The party associated with the alias will receive the message along with the alias of the sender. A full description is provided in Fig. 4.

---

**The functionality $\mathcal{F}_{\mathsf{anon}}$**

The $n$-party randomized reactive functionality $\mathcal{F}_{\mathsf{anon}}$ proceeds with parties $P_1, \ldots, P_n$ as follows.

**Initialization Phase:**

   **Input:** Each party invokes the functionality by providing his neighbor-set (i.e., the pair of neighbors).

   **Alias assignment:** Upon invocation, the functionality reconstructs the cycle. The functionality proceeds by selecting $u \in [n]$ at random, setting $\mathrm{id}_u = 1$, and randomly selecting an orientation of the two neighbors of $P_u$ as either "left" or "right." This defines the orientation of the rest of the cycle edges for each other party.

   **Output:** Each $P_v$ receives an alias $\mathrm{id}_v \in [n]$ such that if $P_v$ is $k \in \{0, \ldots, n-1\}$ hops to the left of $P_u$, then $\mathrm{id}_v = k + 1$. Further, each $P_v$ receives a bit pointing out which of its two neighbors is "left" (increasing alias order).

**Communication Phase:**

   **Input:** Each party $P_v$ (with alias $\mathrm{id}_v$) specifies a set of messages to all other parties $\{(\mathrm{id}_v, j, m_j^{\mathrm{id}_v})\}_{j \neq \mathrm{id}_v}$, where $m_j^{\mathrm{id}_v}$ is a message from the party with alias $\mathrm{id}_v$ intended for the party with alias $j$.

   **Output:** Each party $P_v$ assigned the alias $\mathrm{id}_v$ in the initialization phase receives a set of messages from every other alias $\{(j, \mathrm{id}_v, m_{\mathrm{id}_v}^j)\}_{j \neq \mathrm{id}_v}$ indicating the party assigned with alias $j$ sent to the party with $\mathrm{id}_v$ the message $m_{\mathrm{id}_v}^j$ (for all $j \neq \mathrm{id}_v$).

---

**Fig. 4.** The anonymous communication functionality

Let $\mathcal{G}_{\mathsf{cycle}}(n)$ be the class of cycles over $n$ nodes. Next, we show how to perfectly securely realize $\mathcal{W}_{\mathsf{graph\text{-}info}}^{\mathcal{G}_{\mathsf{cycle}}(n)}(\mathcal{F}_{\mathsf{anon}})$ in the $\mathcal{F}_{\mathsf{graph}}^{\mathcal{G}_{\mathsf{cycle}}(n)}$-hybrid model.

*High-Level Idea.* At a high level, our protocol proceeds in two phases. In the first phase, a fixed designated party $P^*$, will randomly assign an alias in $[n]$ for itself, as well as an orientation of left and right. This defines aliases for the rest of the parties based on their distance from $P^*$ and its randomly chosen alias. A protocol is then performed to securely provide all parties with their alias and orientation. In the communication phase, parties use their output from the initialization phase and the 2-connectedness of the cycle to securely communicate with other parties (specified via their aliases, indicating how many hops away they are). Before specifying the full protocol in Fig. 5, we give some intuition.

To begin, suppose that $n = 2k$ is even, and that a party $P_v$ wishes to send a message $m$ to the party directly opposite it on the cycle (denote that party as $P_u$, although $P_v$ does not know $P_u$'s identity, just location). This can be done easily by uniformly sampling $r$ and forwarding $m \oplus r$ to the right and $r$ to the left (where right and left are from some arbitrary orientation). If other parties forward received messages in the same direction, after exactly $k$ rounds, $P_u$ will receive $m \oplus r$ and $r$ simultaneously and can compute $(m \oplus r) \oplus r = m$. Because every other party sees either $m \oplus r$ or $r$, but not both, this will be uniformly distributed ensuring privacy of the message. By delaying timing of messages to left and right appropriately, we can adjust the protocol to allow any party to deliver a message to any other party that is a given number of hops away.

Once aliases have been agreed upon by all parties, the above will in fact suffice for the communication phase, as there will be nothing more to hide. However, for the initialization phase, if the designated party $P^*$ simply uses the above to deliver aliases to other parties, this will leak the distance from the sender $P^*$. Hence, we will have all parties perform the above secure message sending protocol to all other parties, in parallel. The designated party $P^*$ will send the actual aliases to each other party, while all other parties will perform the above as if sending 0 to all other parties. Note that message privacy here is only being used to hide the location of the designated party.

To perform the above in parallel, in each round parties will take the message received from the left in the previous round, XOR it with what they should send to the right themselves according to the secure message passing above, and then send the result to the right. They behave identically with respect to messages travelling in the other direction. In the final round, all parties simply XOR what they received from the left and right to receive their own alias. Moreover, because up to that point the view of any single party is simply a sequence of random messages, the location of $P^*$ remains hidden. (The final messages of $P^*$ will not be uniform, but XOR to 0.)

**Lemma 1.** *Let $n > 2$. Protocol $\pi_{\mathsf{anon\text{-}cycle}}$ perfectly securely realizes $\mathcal{F}_{\mathsf{anon}}$ in a topology-hiding manner with respect to the class of graphs that includes all cycles on $n$ nodes, tolerating a single semi-honest adversary.*

*Proof (sketch).* Let $\pi : [n] \to [n]$ denote the map such that $\mathrm{id}_i \mapsto i$ for the id's implicitly defined by $P^*$. Let $\alpha : [n] \to [n]$ denote the cyclic permutation such that $i \mapsto i+1$ for $i < n$ and $n \mapsto 1$. Additionally, let $\alpha^{(k)}$ denote $k$ sequential applications of $\alpha$. We take left and right to denote the orientation selected by $P^*$ in the initialization phase.

For correctness, consider the sequence of messages: the message sent left by the party left of $P_u$ in the first round, the message send left by the party two nodes left of $P_u$, and so on until the message that is delivered to $P_u$ from the right in final round. Each subsequent message is formed by XORing with the previous message in the sequence. Because all parties other than $P^*$ behave identically with respect to each direction in this phase, we may assume they all chose an orientation consistent with $P^*$. Then, we can observe that $P_u$ receives $\pi^{-1}(u) \oplus \bigoplus_{j=1}^{n-1} r_j^{\pi(\alpha^{(j)}(\pi^{-1}(u)))}$ on the right in the final round of the initialization phase. Via the same argument, we can see $P_u$ receives $r_j^{\pi(\alpha^{(j)}(\pi^{-1}(u)))}$ on the left of the initialization phase.

For security, note that if we view the $r_j^i$ values each party sends to the right and left as traveling around the cycle in either direction (having values XORed with them), the only other party that sees both is the one that they arrive at simultaneously in the last round. Thus, to all other parties, they are uniformly distributed.

---

**Protocol** $\pi_{\text{anon-cycle}}$

**Hybrid Model:** The $n$ party protocol is defined in the $\mathcal{F}_{\text{graph}}$-hybrid model.

**Common Input:** A designated party $P^* \in \{P_1, \ldots, P_n\}$ responsible for selecting the aliases.

**The Protocol:**

**Initialization Phase:** In the initialization phase the parties establish their aliases.

- Party $P^* = P_{j^*}$ picks a random orientation of its neighbors as "left" and "right." It samples a random alias $\sigma \in [n]$ for itself. Then, for $i = 0, \ldots, n - \sigma$, sets $m_i^{j^*} = \sigma + i$, and for $i = n - \sigma + 1, \ldots, n - 1$ sets $m_i^{j^*} = i - \sigma$. (Thus, for all $i$, $m_i^{j^*}$ is the alias of whichever party is $i$ hops left of $P^*$)
- Each other party $P_k \neq P^*$ arbitrarily picks an orientation of its neighbors as "left" and "right," and sets $m_i^k = 0$ for $i = 0, \ldots, n - 1$.
- Every party $P_\ell$ (including $P^*$) additionally samples $n-1$ independent uniform random values $r_1^\ell, \ldots, r_{n-1}^\ell$.
- For rounds $i = 1, \ldots, n - 1$, every party $P_\ell$ samples random $r_i^\ell$ and sends $m_i^\ell \oplus r_i^\ell \oplus (p_R^\ell)$ to the left and $r_{n-i}^\ell \oplus p_L^\ell$ to the right, where $p_L^\ell$ and $p_R^\ell$ are the messages received by $P_\ell$ in the previous round from the left and right, respectively.
- Party $P^*$ outputs alias $\sigma$. Every other party $P_k \neq P^*$ outputs $p_L^k \oplus p_R^k$, where $p_L^k$ and $p_R^k$ are the messages received by $P_k$ from the left and right (respectively) in the last round.

  Additionally, parties exchange aliases with their neighbors to get a consistent orientation. We take right to denote direction of decreasing id's. (Notice that, relative to alias $j$, alias $i$ is distance $i - j$ (mod $n$) to the left. Therefore, we can simply assume all parties subsequently share the same orientation as that chosen by $P^*$.)

**Communication Phase:** Each "round" of the communication phase is performed in $n$ sub-phases, each corresponding to a different alias responsible for sending. Each subphase lasts exactly $n - 1$ rounds. (The subphases can be performed in parallel, but the sequential presentation is simpler.)

- **Private input:** Each party $P_i$ has input of the form $\{(\text{id}_i, \ell, m_\ell^{\text{id}_i})\}_{\ell \neq \text{id}_i}$ (where $\ell$ denotes an alias and $m_\ell^{\text{id}_i}$ the message to be sent to the party with alias $\ell$ by the party with alias $\text{id}_i$). We take $\text{id}_i$ to denote the alias output by $P_i$ in the initialization phase.
- **Protocol:** For sub-phases $j = 1, \ldots, n$:
  - Party $P_i$ with $\text{id}_i = j$ samples $n - 1$ independent uniform random values $r_1, \ldots, r_{n-1}$.
  - For rounds $k = 1, \ldots, n - 1$:
    * $P_i$ sends $m_{j-k \pmod{n}}^j \oplus r_k$ to the left and $r_{n-k}$ to the right.
    * All other parties forward messages received from the left in the previous round to the right, and messages received from the right in the previous round to the left.
  - After receiving in the final round, each party $P_\ell$ with an alias $\text{id}_\ell \neq j$ (locally) sets $\hat{m}_\ell^j$ as the XOR of the last message received from the left and right.
- **Output:** Each party $P_i$ outputs $\{(j, \text{id}_i, \hat{m}_{\text{id}_i}^j)\}_{j \neq \text{id}_i}$.

**Fig. 5.** Securely realizing $\mathcal{F}_{\text{anon}}$ in a topology-hiding manner, for cycles

Therefore, the view of the corrupted party $P_c$ is simply uniformly distributed messages in each round, until the last. In the last round, if $P_c \neq P^*$, party $P_c$ receives two random messages (one from each side) that XOR to a random $i \in [n]$. If $P_c = P^*$, party $P_c$ receives two random messages that XOR to zero. This can be simulated by simply sending random messages until the last round, where the messages XOR to a uniformly drawn $i \leftarrow [n]$ if $P_c \neq P^*$ and 0 otherwise. Because of this simulation the view of any party is clearly independent of the ordering of parties outside that party's immediate neighborhood.

The correctness and security of the communication phase proceed similarly, except here we will use the fact that the relative positions of $id_c$ and the $id_i$ to start simulating via uniformly random values on a given side. The full simulator is described below.

**Initialization Phase:**
- Let $P_u$ be the corrupted party. Get $\mathcal{N}_G[u]$ from $\mathcal{W}^{\mathcal{G}}_{\text{graph-info}}(\mathcal{F}_{\text{anon}})$.
- Invoke $\mathcal{W}^{\mathcal{G}}_{\text{graph-info}}(\mathcal{F}_{\text{anon}})$ with $\mathcal{N}_G[u]$ (as the input to $\mathcal{F}_{\text{anon}}$) and receive back $id_u$ and the orientation.
- If $P_u \neq P^*$, deliver uniformly random messages from neighbors for first $n-2$ rounds. In final round, deliver uniformly random messages conditioned on them XORing to $id_u$.
  Otherwise, deliver uniformly random messages from neighbors to either side for the first $n-2$ rounds. In the final round, deliver uniformly random messages that XOR to 0.

**Communication Phase:** In each communication "round," get from the environment the tuples $\{(id_u, i, m^i_{id_u})\}_{i \neq u}$ (as the input of $P_u$).
  In the $i$'th sub-phase of each "round,"
- From round $id_u - i \pmod{n}$ of the sub-phase until the penultimate round, give $P_u$ uniformly random messages from the right.
- From round $i - id_u \pmod{n}$ of the sub-phase until the penultimate round, give $P_u$ uniformly random messages from the left.
- In the final round if $id_u \neq i$, give $P_u$ random messages conditioned on them XORing to $m^i_{id_u}$.
  If $id_u = i$, $P_u$ doesn't receive anything throughout the phase.

$\square$

**THC from Secure Anonymous Channels.** Equipped with secure anonymous point-to-point channels, we can now use standard honest-majority MPC techniques to achieve general THC.

**Lemma 2.** *Let $n \in \mathbb{N}$, let $t \leq n/2$, and let $f$ be an efficiently computable $n$-party function. Then, $\mathcal{F}^f_{\text{sfe}}$ can be UC-realized with perfect security in $\mathcal{F}_{\text{anon}}$-hybrid model, tolerating $t$ semi-honest corruptions.*

*Proof (sketch).* Without loss of generality, it suffices to consider functionalities that give the same output to all parties. Let $f'$ denote the *symmetric* functionality that takes in $n$ tuples of the form $(i, x_i) \in [n] \times \{0,1\}^n$ and outputs

$f(x_1, \ldots, x_n)$ if all $i$ are distinct, and $\perp$ otherwise. Note that for any permutation $\pi$ of $[n]$ (describing $i \mapsto \mathrm{id}_i$, the alias of $P_i$), it holds that

$$f'\left((\pi^{-1}(1), x_{\pi^{-1}(1)}), \ldots, (\pi^{-1}(n), x_{\pi^{-1}(n)})\right) \equiv f(x_1, \ldots, x_n).$$

So, to complete the proof, parties simply securely evaluate $f'$ under their aliases, where the input of $P_i$ with alias $\mathrm{id}_i$ is $(i, x_i)$, using the BGW protocol [8] over secure anonymous channels (between aliased identities) provided by $\mathcal{F}_{\mathsf{anon}}$.    $\square$

Putting together Lemmas 1 and 2, and using UC-composition, completes the proof of Theorem 3, our positive result for cycles with one corruption.

## 5    Distributional-Topology-Hiding Computation

In this section, we present a relaxed notion of topology-hiding computation. Namely, it is not required that *all* of the topology of the graph will remain hidden, but only certain properties of the graph. The crucial difference to THC is that the functionality does not receive the graph from a graph party; rather, the communication-graph functionality is parametrized by a distribution over graphs and locally samples a graph from this distribution. As a result of this modification, the environment is ignorant of the actual graph that is used during the communication phase.

As discussed in Sect. 1.2, we require strong composition capabilities from this definition. Therefore, the environment is allowed to ask for the graph. This is

---

**The functionality $\mathcal{F}_{\mathsf{dist\text{-}graph}}^{\mathcal{D}}$**

The $n$-party functionality $\mathcal{F}_{\mathsf{dist\text{-}graph}}^{\mathcal{D}}$, parametrized by a distribution $\mathcal{D}$ over graphs of $n$ nodes, proceeds with parties $P_1, \ldots, P_n$ and a special graph party $P_{\mathsf{graph}}$ as follows.

**Initialization Phase:**
   **Input:** $\mathcal{F}_{\mathsf{dist\text{-}graph}}^{\mathcal{D}}$ receives an initialization input from every party $P_v$. Upon receiving the first input, $\mathcal{F}_{\mathsf{dist\text{-}graph}}^{\mathcal{D}}$ samples a graph $G = (V, E) \leftarrow \mathcal{D}$.
   **Output:** $\mathcal{F}_{\mathsf{dist\text{-}graph}}^{\mathcal{D}}$ outputs $\mathcal{N}_G[v]$ to each $P_v$.
**Communication Phase:**
   **Input:** $\mathcal{F}_{\mathsf{dist\text{-}graph}}^{\mathcal{D}}$ receives from a party $P_v$ a destination/data pair $(w, m)$ where $w \in \mathcal{N}_G[v]$ and $m$ is the message $P_v$ wants to send to $P_w$. (If $w$ is not a neighbor of $v$, $\mathcal{F}_{\mathsf{dist\text{-}graph}}^{\mathcal{D}}$ ignores this input.)
   **Output:** $\mathcal{F}_{\mathsf{dist\text{-}graph}}^{\mathcal{D}}$ gives output $(v, m)$ to $P_w$ indicating that $P_v$ sent the message $m$ to $P_w$.
**Termination Phase:**
   **Input:** $\mathcal{F}_{\mathsf{dist\text{-}graph}}^{\mathcal{D}}$ receives a termination input from $P_{\mathsf{graph}}$.
   **Output:** $\mathcal{F}_{\mathsf{dist\text{-}graph}}^{\mathcal{D}}$ outputs the graph $G$ to $P_{\mathsf{graph}}$ and stops processing further messages.

---

**Fig. 6.** The distributional-graph-communication functionality

done via a special graph party $P_{\text{graph}}$. Unlike in classical THC, where $P_{\text{graph}}$ is used to give the graph to the functionality, here $P_{\text{graph}}$ is used to ask the graph from the functionality. Once the environment asks for the graph, the communication functionality enters an "out of order" state and stops processing other messages (Fig. 6).

As before, the ideal-model computation of a functionality $\mathcal{F}$ needs to be augmented to provide the simulator with the appropriate leakage on the graph, i.e., the neighbor-set of each corrupted party. Toward this purpose, we define a graph-information wrapper functionality around $\mathcal{F}$, denoted $\mathcal{W}^{\mathcal{D}}_{\text{dist-graph-info}}(\mathcal{F})$. Initially, the wrapper samples a graph from the distribution and provides every corrupted party with the neighbor-set. All subsequent input messages are forwarded to $\mathcal{F}$ and all messages from $\mathcal{F}$ are delivered to their recipients.

To keep the graph hidden from the environment during the computation phase, $\mathcal{W}^{\mathcal{D}}_{\text{dist-graph-info}}(\mathcal{F})$ does not send the neighbor-set to honest parties. The environment can adaptively issue corruption requests, and upon any such adaptive corruption $\mathcal{W}^{\mathcal{D}}_{\text{dist-graph-info}}(\mathcal{F})$ outputs the neighbor-set of the newly corrupted party.

As before, the environment can request the communication graph via a special graph party $P_{\text{graph}}$. After receiving this request from $P_{\text{graph}}$, the wrapper functionality stops processing further messages, other than corruption requests. As explained in Sect. 1.2, to balance the advantage given to the environment, that now can corrupt parties as a function of the graph, after giving the graph to $P_{\text{graph}}$, the wrapper gives the simulator all of the input messages it received (Fig. 7).

---

**The wrapper functionality $\mathcal{W}^{\mathcal{D}}_{\text{dist-graph-info}}(\mathcal{F})$**

The $n$-party wrapper functionality $\mathcal{W}^{\mathcal{D}}_{\text{dist-graph-info}}$, parametrized by a distribution $\mathcal{D}$ over graphs of $n$ nodes, internally runs a copy of $\mathcal{F}$ and proceeds with parties $P_1, \ldots, P_n$ and a special graph party $P_{\text{graph}}$ as follows.

**Initialization Phase:**
    **Input:** $\mathcal{W}^{\mathcal{D}}_{\text{dist-graph-info}}(\mathcal{F})$ receives an initialization input from every party $P_v$.
        Upon receiving the first input, $\mathcal{W}^{\mathcal{D}}_{\text{dist-graph-info}}(\mathcal{F})$ samples a graph $G = (V, E) \leftarrow \mathcal{D}$.
    **Output:** $\mathcal{W}^{\mathcal{D}}_{\text{dist-graph-info}}(\mathcal{F})$ outputs $N_G[v]$ to each corrupted $P_v$.
**Computation Phase:**
    **Input:** $\mathcal{W}^{\mathcal{D}}_{\text{dist-graph-info}}(\mathcal{F})$ forwards every message it receives to $\mathcal{F}$.
    **Output:** Whenever $\mathcal{F}$ sends a message, $\mathcal{W}^{\mathcal{D}}_{\text{dist-graph-info}}(\mathcal{F})$ forwards the message to the recipient.
**Termination Phase:**
    **Input:** $\mathcal{W}^{\mathcal{D}}_{\text{dist-graph-info}}(\mathcal{F})$ receives a termination input from $P_{\text{graph}}$.
    **Output:** $\mathcal{W}^{\mathcal{D}}_{\text{dist-graph-info}}(\mathcal{F})$ sends a termination message to the simulator, including all input messages sent to $\mathcal{F}$, outputs the graph $G$ to $P_{\text{graph}}$ and stops processing further messages, except for corruption requests.
**Corruption request:** Once a party $P_v$ gets corrupted, $\mathcal{W}^{\mathcal{D}}_{\text{dist-graph-info}}(\mathcal{F})$ sends $N_G[v]$ to $P_v$.

---

**Fig. 7.** The distributional-graph-information wrapper functionality

**Definition 2 (Distributional topology hiding).** *Let $\mathcal{D}$ be a distribution over graphs with $n$ nodes. A protocol $\pi$ securely realizes a functionality $\mathcal{F}$ in a* distributional-topology-hiding manner with respect to *$\mathcal{D}$ tolerating semi-honest $t$-adversaries, if $\pi$ securely realizes $\mathcal{W}^{\mathcal{D}}_{\text{dist-graph-info}}(\mathcal{F})$ in the $\mathcal{F}^{\mathcal{D}}_{\text{dist-graph}}$-hybrid model tolerating semi-honest $t$-adversaries.*

*The Relation Between the Definitions.* We show that Definition 2 is indeed a relaxation of Definition 1. We start by showing that every protocol that satisfies Definition 1 will also satisfy Definition 2, at least as long as the functionality does not depend on the graph. Next, in Sect. 6, we will show a separation between the definitions.

Consider an environment $\mathcal{Z}$ of the form $\mathcal{Z} = (\mathcal{Z}_1, \mathcal{Z}_2)$, where $\mathcal{Z}_1$ invokes $P_{\text{graph}}$ with a graph $G \in \mathcal{G}$ and receives back its output, and $\mathcal{Z}_2$ interacts with the parties and the adversary (without knowing the output received by $\mathcal{Z}_1$) and outputs the decision bit. We say that an $n$-party functionality $\mathcal{F}$ does not depend on the communication graph if for every family $\mathcal{G}$ of graphs with $n$ nodes and every environment $\mathcal{Z} = (\mathcal{Z}_1, \mathcal{Z}_2)$ as described above, the output of $\mathcal{Z}$ (i.e., the output of $\mathcal{Z}_2$) in an ideal computation of $\mathcal{W}^{\mathcal{G}}_{\text{graph-info}}(\mathcal{F})$ is identically distributed as the output of $\mathcal{Z}$ in an ideal computation of $\widetilde{\mathcal{W}}^{\mathcal{G}}_{\text{graph-info}}(\mathcal{F})$, where $\widetilde{\mathcal{W}}^{\mathcal{G}}_{\text{graph-info}}$ acts like $\mathcal{W}^{\mathcal{G}}_{\text{graph-info}}$ with the exception that it ignores the graph $G$ it receives and chooses an arbitrary graph from $\mathcal{G}$ instead. In the modified functionality, the input provided by the environment is independent of the communication graph; hence, if the output of the functionality is identically distributed in both cases, it can't be dependent on the graph structure.

**Theorem 4.** *Let $\mathcal{F}$ be functionality that does not depend on the communication graph and let $\mathcal{D}$ be an efficiently sampleable distribution over graphs with $n$ nodes. If $\mathcal{F}$ can be securely realized in a topology-hiding manner with respect to $\mathsf{supp}(\mathcal{D})$, then $\mathcal{F}$ can be securely realized in a distributional-topology-hiding manner with respect to $\mathcal{D}$.*

*Proof.* Assume that $\mathcal{F}$ cannot be securely realized in a distributional-topology-hiding manner with respect to $\mathcal{D}$, i.e., for every protocol and every simulator for the dummy adversary, there exists an environment $\mathcal{Z}$ that can create a non-negligible distinguishing advantage. Note that initially, $\mathcal{Z}$ knows only the distribution $\mathcal{D}$ but not the actual graph, but at any point can invoke $P_{\text{graph}}$ to obtain the graph. We will show that $\mathcal{F}$ cannot be securely realized in a topology-hiding manner with respect to $\mathsf{supp}(\mathcal{D})$.

We use $\mathcal{Z}$ to construct an environment $\mathcal{Z}'$ as follows. Initially, $\mathcal{Z}'$ samples a graph $G \leftarrow \mathcal{D}$ and sends it to $P_{\text{graph}}$ to initialize the communication graph functionality (or the graph-information functionality). Next, $\mathcal{Z}'$ invokes $\mathcal{Z}$ and forwards any message from $\mathcal{Z}$ to the parties or the adversary, and vice versa. Once an honest party receives its neighbor-set from the functionality, $\mathcal{Z}'$ does not forward the message to $\mathcal{Z}$, but upon a corruption of a party $\mathcal{Z}'$ provides its neighbor-set to $\mathcal{Z}$. If $\mathcal{Z}$ asks $P_{\text{graph}}$ to get the graph, $\mathcal{Z}'$ responds with the graph $G$ and proceed to process only corruption requests from $\mathcal{Z}$. Finally, $\mathcal{Z}'$ outputs the output of $\mathcal{Z}$ and halts. Clearly, $\mathcal{Z}'$ has the same distinguishing probability as $\mathcal{Z}$, and the proof follows. $\qquad\square$

# 6   Distributional-THC with Hidden Sublinear Cuts

In this section, we show a distributional-THC protocol that hides sublinear cuts between two linear-size cliques in the communication graph, and tolerates a linear number of adaptive semi-honest corruptions. The protocol is based on a recent work by Boyle et al. [11], that constructed an adaptively secure MPC protocol in the dynamic-graph setting (where every party can talk to every other party, but dynamically decides on its neighbor-set).

In Sect. 6.1, we present the protocol in the distributional-THC setting that can hide sublinear cuts against adaptive corruptions, and in Sect. 6.2 we show that a similar result cannot be achieved in the classical THC setting.

## 6.1   Feasibility in the Distributional-THC Model

We start by defining the distribution of potential communication graphs in the $n$-party protocol.

**Definition 3.** *Let $n = 4m + 1$ for $m \in \mathbb{N}$, and let $n' = \log^c n$ for a constant $c > 1$. Denote*

$$\mathcal{P}_1 = \{1, \ldots, m\}, \quad \mathcal{P}_2 = \{m+1, \ldots, 2m\}, \quad \mathcal{P}_3 = \{2m+1, \ldots, 3m\}, \quad \mathcal{P}_4 = \{3m+1, \ldots, 4m\}.$$

*Given a bit $b \in \{0, 1\}$ and two vectors $\boldsymbol{i} = (i_1, \ldots, i_{n'})$ and $\boldsymbol{j} = (j_1, \ldots, j_{n'})$ in $[m]^{n'}$ with distinct coordinates, i.e., $i_k \neq i_{k'}$ and $j_k \neq j_{k'}$ for $k \neq k'$, define the graph $G_n(b; \boldsymbol{i}; \boldsymbol{j})$ as follows:*

- *Two cliques of size $2m$, $\mathcal{P}_1 \cup \mathcal{P}_2$ and $\mathcal{P}_3 \cup \mathcal{P}_4$.*
- *The edges $(m + i_k, 2m + j_k)$ for every $k \in [n']$ (i.e., a sublinear cut between $\mathcal{P}_2$ to $\mathcal{P}_3$).*
- *The edges $(4m + 1, i)$, for every $i \in \mathcal{P}_1$ if $b = 0$, or for every $i \in \mathcal{P}_4$ if $b = 1$ (i.e., connecting $4m + 1$ to either $\mathcal{P}_1$ or $\mathcal{P}_4$).*

*We define the distribution $\mathcal{D}_{\mathsf{cut}}(n, c)$ over graphs of $n$ nodes by uniformly sampling a bit $b \in \{0, 1\}$ and $\boldsymbol{i}, \boldsymbol{j} \leftarrow [m]^{n'}$ with distinct coordinates, and returning $G_n(b; \boldsymbol{i}; \boldsymbol{j})$ (Fig. 8).*

**Theorem 5.** *Let $n \in \mathbb{N}$, let $\beta < 1/4$ and $c > 1$ be constants, and let $f$ be an efficiently computable n-party function. Then, $\mathcal{F}_{\mathsf{sfe}}^f$ can be securely realized in a distributional-topology-hiding manner with respect to $\mathcal{D}_{\mathsf{cut}}(n, c)$ with statistical security tolerating an adaptive, semi-honest, computationally unbounded $\beta n$-adversary.*

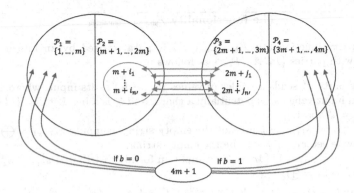

**Fig. 8.** A graph $G_n(b; i; j)$ with $n = 4m + 1$ nodes in support of the distribution $\mathcal{D}_{\text{cut}}(n, c)$.

To prove Theorem 5, we construct a protocol $\pi_{\text{hide-cuts}}$ in the $\mathcal{F}^{\mathcal{D}_{\text{cut}}(n,c)}_{\text{dist-graph}}$-hybrid model that securely realizes $\mathcal{W}^{\mathcal{D}_{\text{cut}}(n,c)}_{\text{dist-graph-info}}(\mathcal{F}^f_{\text{sfe}})$ (see Fig. 12). More specifically, the protocol is defined in a hybrid model with the additional ideal functionalities $\mathcal{F}_{\text{share-to-committee}}$, $\mathcal{F}_{\text{recon-compute}}$, and $\mathcal{F}_{\text{out-dist}}$ (all functionalities are explained and formally defined in Sect. 6.1). These functionalities need *not* be defined and realized in a topology-hiding manner, since each such functionality will be called by a pre-defined subsets of parties that forms a clique in the communication graph, and so they can be instantiated using a "standard" MPC protocol such as BGW.

In Lemma 3 (below) we prove that the protocol $\pi_{\text{hide-cuts}}$ securely realizes $\mathcal{F}^f_{\text{sfe}}$ in a distributional-topology-hiding manner with respect to $\mathcal{D}_{\text{cut}}(n, c)$. We start by defining the ideal functionalities that are used to define the protocol.

### Ideal Functionalities Used in the Construction

*The Share-to-Committee Functionality.* In the share-to-committee $m$-party functionality, $\mathcal{F}_{\text{share-to-committee}}$, every party $P_i \in \{P_1, \ldots, P_{2m}\}$ sends his input $x_i \in \{0, 1\}^*$, a share $s_i$ (that can be the empty string), and a bit $b_i \in \{0, 1\}$ indicating whether $P_i$ has a neighbor in $\{P_{2m+1}, \ldots, P_{3m}\}$. The functionality first tries to reconstruct the value $x_{4m+1}$ from the shares $s_1, \ldots, s_m$. Next, each party secret shares its input value $x_i$ and sends the shares to the parties with $b_i = 1$. The formal description of the functionality can be found in Fig. 9.

*The Reconstruct-and-Compute Functionality.* The reconstruct-and-compute functionality, $\mathcal{F}_{\text{recon-compute}}$, is a $2m$-party functionality. Denote the party-set by $\{P_{2m+1}, \ldots, P_{4m}\}$. Every party $P_{2m+i}$ has an input value $x_{2m+i} \in \{0, 1\}^*$, and additional values consisting of shares of $(x_1, \ldots, x_{2m}, x_{4m+1})$. The functionality starts by using the additional inputs to reconstruct $(x_1, \ldots, x_{2m}, x_{4m+1})$. Next, the functionality computes $y = f(x_1, \ldots, x_{4m+1})$ and hands $y$ as the output for every party. The formal description of the functionality can be found in Fig. 10.

---

**The functionality $\mathcal{F}_{\text{share-to-committee}}$**

The $2m$-party functionality $\mathcal{F}_{\text{share-to-committee}}$ is parametrized by an integer $n'$ and proceeds with parties $\{P_1, \ldots, P_{2m}\}$ as follows.

1. Every party $P_i$ sends a triplet of values $(x_i, s_i, b_i)$ as its input, where $x_i$ is the actual input value, $s_i$ is potentially a share, and $b_i$ is a bit. Let $\mathcal{C} = \{i \mid b_i = 1\}$. If $|\mathcal{C}| \neq n'$ abort.
2. If the shares $s_1, \ldots, s_m$ are not the empty string, compute $x_{4m+1} = \bigoplus_{i \in [m]} s_i$; otherwise set $x_{4m+1} = \epsilon$ to be the empty string.
3. For every $i \in [2m] \cup \{4m+1\}$, sample uniformly distributed $s_i^1, \ldots, s_i^{n'}$ conditioned on $x_i = \bigoplus_{j \in [n']} s_i^j$.
4. Denote $\mathcal{C} = \{i_1, \ldots, i_{n'}\}$. For every $i_j \in \mathcal{C}$, set $s_{i_j} = (s_1^j, \ldots, s_{2m}^j, s_{4m+1}^j)$.
5. For every $i_j \in \mathcal{C}$, set the output of $P_{i_j}$ to be $s_{i_j}$ (other parties don't get an output).

---

**Fig. 9.** The share-to-committee functionality

*The Output-Distribution Functionality.* The $2m$-party output-distribution functionality receives input values from (some) of the parties and sends one of them as output to all the parties (looking ahead, in the protocol there will be a single input value). The formal description of the functionality can be found in Fig. 11.

**The Protocol.** We now describe the protocol $\pi_{\text{hide-cuts}}$ and prove its security.

---

**The functionality $\mathcal{F}_{\text{recon-compute}}$**

The $2m$-party functionality $\mathcal{F}_{\text{recon-compute}}$ is parametrized by an integer $n'$ and proceeds with parties $\{P_{2m+1}, \ldots, P_{4m}\}$ as follows.

1. Every party $P_{2m+i}$ (for $i \in [2m]$) sends a pair of values $(x_{2m+i}, z_{2m+i})$ as its input, where $x_{2m+i}$ is the actual input value, $z_{2m+i} = s_{2m+i}$ for some $i \in [m]$, and potentially $z_{2m+i} = s_i$ for $i \in [2m] \setminus [m]$ (all other values are the empty string $\epsilon$).
2. Let $\mathcal{C}_2 = \{i \in [m] \mid z_{2m+i} \neq \epsilon\}$. If $|\mathcal{C}_2| \neq n'$ then abort. Otherwise, denote $\mathcal{C}_2 = \{i_1 \ldots, i_{n'}\}$. For every $i_j \in \mathcal{C}_2$, let $s_{2m+i_j} = (s_1^j, \ldots, s_{2m}^j, s_{4m+1}^j)$ be the input provided by $P_{2m+i_j}$.
3. If the inputs $z_{3m+i} = s_i$ are not empty for $i \in [m]$, then compute $x_{4m+1} = \bigoplus_{i \in [m]} s_i$. Otherwise compute $x_{4m+1} = \bigoplus_{j \in [n']} s_{4m+1}^j$.
4. For every $i \in [2m]$, reconstruct $x_i = \bigoplus_{j \in [n']} s_i^j$.
5. Compute $y = f(x_1, \ldots, x_{4m+1})$.
6. Output $y$ to every $P_{2m+i}$ for $i \in [2m]$.

---

**Fig. 10.** The reconstruct-and-compute functionality

---

**The functionality $\mathcal{F}_{\text{out-dist}}$**

The $2m$-party functionality $\mathcal{F}_{\text{out-dist}}$ proceeds with parties $\{P_1, \ldots, P_{2m}\}$ as follows.

1. Every party $P_i$, gives (a potentially empty) input value $y_i$.
2. Let $i$ be the minimal value such that $y_i \neq \epsilon$. Denote $y = y_i$.
3. Output $y$ to every $P_i$.

---

**Fig. 11.** The output-distribution functionality

**Lemma 3.** *Protocol $\pi_{\text{hide-cuts}}$ UC-realizes the wrapped functionality $\mathcal{W}_{\text{dist-graph-info}}^{\mathcal{D}_{\text{cut}}(n,c)}(\mathcal{F}_{\text{sfe}}^f)$ in the $(\mathcal{F}_{\text{dist-graph}}^{\mathcal{D}_{\text{cut}}(n,c)}, \mathcal{F}_{\text{share-to-committee}}, \mathcal{F}_{\text{recon-compute}}, \mathcal{F}_{\text{out-dist}})$-hybrid model tolerating an adaptive, semi-honest, computationally unbounded $\beta n$-adversary, for any constant $\beta < 1/4$.*

The proof of Lemma 3 can be found in the full version.

### 6.2 Impossibility in the Classical THC Model

The protocol $\pi_{\text{hide-cuts}}$ was defined in the weaker distributional-THC model. To justify the weaker model, we show that a similar result cannot be achieved in the stronger (classical) THC model. The reason is that according to this model (Definition 1) the environment, who chooses the communication graph, knows exactly which parties are on the cut and can corrupt them. This means that without relying on cryptographic assumptions or some correlated-randomness setup phase, two honest parties from opposite sides of the cut cannot communicate privately [18].

We prove this intuition using our lower bound from Sect. 3.

**Theorem 6.** *Let $c > 1$ be a constant and let $t = \log^c(n)$. Then, $\mathcal{F}_{\text{bc}}$ cannot be securely computed in a topology-hiding manner with respect to $\text{supp}(\mathcal{D}_{\text{cut}}(n,c))$ tolerating computationally unbounded, semi-honest, static $t$-adversaries.*

*Proof.* Let $n = 4m + 1$ and let $\pi$ be an $n$-party $t$-resilient broadcast protocol where party $P_{4m+1}$ is the broadcaster. Let $\boldsymbol{i} = (i_1, \ldots, i_{n'})$ and $\boldsymbol{j} = (j_1, \ldots, j_{n'})$ in $[m]^{n'}$ with distinct coordinates, and consider the following partition of the nodes:

$$\mathcal{P}_1 = \{4m+1\} \quad \mathcal{P}_2 = \{1, \ldots, 2m\} \setminus \{i_1, \ldots, i_{n'}\},$$
$$\mathcal{P}_3 = \{i_1, \ldots, i_{n'}\}, \mathcal{P}_4 = \{2m+1, \ldots, 4m\}.$$

For $b \in \{0, 1\}$, consider the graph $\tilde{G}_b = G(b; \boldsymbol{i}; \boldsymbol{j}) \in \text{supp}(\mathcal{D}_{\text{cut}}(n,c))$. By definition, it holds that

- In $\tilde{G}_0$: there are no edges $(i, j) \in \mathcal{P}_1 \times \mathcal{P}_3$, or $(i, j) \in \mathcal{P}_2 \times \mathcal{P}_4$, or $(i, j) \in \mathcal{P}_1 \times \mathcal{P}_4$,
- In $\tilde{G}_1$: there are no edges $(i, j) \in \mathcal{P}_1 \times \mathcal{P}_3$, or $(i, j) \in \mathcal{P}_2 \times \mathcal{P}_4$, or $(i, j) \in \mathcal{P}_1 \times \mathcal{P}_2$.

Since $t = |\mathcal{P}_3|$, by Corollary 1 there is no THB protocol with respect to $\mathcal{G}$ tolerating semi-honest, static $t$-adversaries with information-theoretic security. $\square$

---

**Protocol $\pi_{\text{hide-cuts}}$**

- **Hybrid Model:** The protocol is defined in the $(\mathcal{F}^{\mathcal{D}_{\text{cut}}(n,c)}_{\text{dist-graph}}, \mathcal{F}_{\text{share-to-committee}},$ $\mathcal{F}_{\text{recon-compute}}, \mathcal{F}_{\text{out-dist}})$-hybrid model.
- **Common Input:** A partition of the party-set $\mathcal{P}_1 = \{1, \ldots, m\}$, $\mathcal{P}_2 = \{m + 1, \ldots, 2m\}$, $\mathcal{P}_3 = \{2m+1, \ldots, 3m\}$, $\mathcal{P}_4 = \{3m+1, \ldots, 4m\}$, and $\mathcal{P}_5 = \{4m+1\}$.
- **Private Input:** Every party $P_i$, for $i \in [n]$, has private input $x_i \in \{0,1\}^*$.
- **The Protocol:**

1. Every party $P_i$ sends an initialization input to $\mathcal{F}^{\mathcal{D}_{\text{cut}}(n,c)}_{\text{dist-graph}}$ and receives the neighbor-set $\mathcal{N}_G[i]$.
2. Party $P_{4m+1}$ samples random $s_1, \ldots, s_m$ conditioned on $x_{4m+1} = \bigoplus_{i \in [m]} s_i$ and sends one share to each of its neighbors (either in $\mathcal{P}_1$ or in $\mathcal{P}_4$).
3. Every party $P_i \in \mathcal{P}_1 \cup \mathcal{P}_2$ sets the bit $b_i = 1$ if he has a neighbor in $\mathcal{P}_3$, and $b_i = 0$ otherwise. In addition, if $P_i$ did not receive a value $s_i$ from $P_{4n+1}$ in Step 2 he sets $s_i = \epsilon$. The parties in $\mathcal{P}_1 \cup \mathcal{P}_2$ invoke $\mathcal{F}_{\text{share-to-committee}}$, where every $P_i \in \mathcal{P}_1 \cup \mathcal{P}_2$ sends input $(x_i, s_i, b_i)$. Every $P_i = P_{i_j}$ (for some $j \in [n']$) with $b_{i_j} = 1$ receives back output consisting of a vector $s_{i_j} = (s_1^j, \ldots, s_{2m}^j, s_{4m+1}^j)$.
4. Every party $P_i$ with $b_i = 1$ sends the value received $s_i$ to his neighbor in $\mathcal{P}_3$ (via $\mathcal{F}^{\mathcal{D}_{\text{cut}}(n,c)}_{\text{dist-graph}}$).
5. If a party $P_{2m+i} \in \mathcal{P}_3 \cup \mathcal{P}_4$ has a neighbor in $\mathcal{P}_2$ he sets $z_{2m+i}$ to be the value received in Step 4, If the party received a value $s_i$ from $P_{4n+1}$ in Step 2 he sets $z_{2m+i} = s_i$; otherwise set $z_{2m+i} = \epsilon$. The parties in $\mathcal{P}_3 \cup \mathcal{P}_4$ invoke $\mathcal{F}_{\text{recon-compute}}$, where $P_{2m+i} \in \mathcal{P}_3 \cup \mathcal{P}_4$ sends input $(x_{2m+i}, z_{2m+i})$. Every party in $\mathcal{P}_3 \cup \mathcal{P}_4$ receives back output $y$.
6. If a party $P_{2m+i} \in \mathcal{P}_3$ has a neighbor in $\mathcal{P}_2$, he sends $y$ to his neighbor (via $\mathcal{F}^{\mathcal{D}_{\text{cut}}(n,c)}_{\text{dist-graph}}$).
7. The parties in $\mathcal{P}_1 \cup \mathcal{P}_2$ invoke $\mathcal{F}_{\text{out-dist}}$, where party $P_i$, with $b_i = 1$, sends the value $y$ he received in Step 6 as his input. Every party in $\mathcal{P}_1 \cup \mathcal{P}_2$ receives output $y$.
8. Every party that received a value from party $P_{4m+1}$ in Step 2 send $y$ to $P_{4m+1}$.
9. Every party outputs $y$ and halts.

**Fig. 12.** Hiding low-weight cuts in the $(\mathcal{F}_{\text{share-to-committee}}, \mathcal{F}_{\text{recon-compute}}, \mathcal{F}_{\text{out-dist}})$-hybrid model

**Acknowledgements.** We thank Mike Rosulek for his graphical support, and the anonymous reviewers of TCC'19 for useful comments.

M. Ball's research supported by an IBM Research PhD Fellowship. Part of this work was completed while M. Ball was visiting IDC Herzliya's FACT center. M. Ball and T. Malkin's research is based upon work supported in part by the Office of the Director of National Intelligence (ODNI), Intelligence Advanced Research Projects Activity (IARPA) via Contract No. 2019-1902070006. E. Boyle's research supported by ISF grant 1861/16 and AFOSR Award FA9550-17-1-0069. R. Cohen's research supported by the Northeastern University Cybersecurity and Privacy Institute Post-doctoral fellowship, NSF grant TWC-1664445, NSF grant 1422965, and by the NSF MACS project. This work was supported in part by the Intelligence Advanced Research Project Activity (IARPA) under contract number 2019-19-020700009. T. Moran's research supported by the Bar-Ilan Cyber Center. The views and conclusions contained herein are those

# References

1. Akavia, A., Moran, T.: Topology-hiding computation beyond logarithmic diameter. In: Coron, J.-S., Nielsen, J.B. (eds.) EUROCRYPT 2017. LNCS, vol. 10212, pp. 609–637. Springer, Cham (2017). https://doi.org/10.1007/978-3-319-56617-7_21
2. Akavia, A., LaVigne, R., Moran, T.: Topology-hiding computation on all graphs. In: Katz, J., Shacham, H. (eds.) CRYPTO 2017. LNCS, vol. 10401, pp. 447–467. Springer, Cham (2017). https://doi.org/10.1007/978-3-319-63688-7_15
3. Ball, M., Boyle, E., Malkin, T., Moran, T.: Exploring the boundaries of topology-hiding computation. In: Nielsen, J.B., Rijmen, V. (eds.) EUROCRYPT 2018. LNCS, vol. 10822, pp. 294–325. Springer, Cham (2018). https://doi.org/10.1007/978-3-319-78372-7_10
4. Beimel, A.: On private computation in incomplete networks. Distrib. Comput. 19(3), 237–252 (2007)
5. Beimel, A., Franklin, M.K.: Reliable communication over partially authenticated networks. Theor. Comput. Sci. 220(1), 185–210 (1999)
6. Beimel, A., Malka, L.: Efficient reliable communication over partially authenticated networks. Distrib. Comput. 18(1), 1–19 (2005)
7. Beimel, A., Gabizon, A., Ishai, Y., Kushilevitz, E., Meldgaard, S., Paskin-Cherniavsky, A.: Non-interactive secure multiparty computation. In: Garay, J.A., Gennaro, R. (eds.) CRYPTO 2014. LNCS, vol. 8617, pp. 387–404. Springer, Heidelberg (2014). https://doi.org/10.1007/978-3-662-44381-1_22
8. Ben-Or, M., Goldwasser, S., Wigderson, A.: Completeness theorems for non-cryptographic fault-tolerant distributed computation (extended abstract). In: STOC, pp. 1–10 (1988)
9. Bläser, M., Jakoby, A., Liśkiewicz, M., Manthey, B.: Private computation: k-connected versus 1-connected networks. J. Cryptol. 19(3), 341–357 (2006)
10. Boyle, E., Goldwasser, S., Tessaro, S.: Communication locality in secure multiparty computation. In: Sahai, A. (ed.) TCC 2013. LNCS, vol. 7785, pp. 356–376. Springer, Heidelberg (2013). https://doi.org/10.1007/978-3-642-36594-2_21
11. Boyle, E., Cohen, R., Data, D., Hubáček, P.: Must the communication graph of MPC protocols be an expander? In: Shacham, H., Boldyreva, A. (eds.) CRYPTO 2018. LNCS, vol. 10993, pp. 243–272. Springer, Cham (2018). https://doi.org/10.1007/978-3-319-96878-0_9
12. Canetti, R.: Security and composition of multiparty cryptographic protocols. J. Cryptol. 13(1), 143–202 (2000)
13. Chandran, N., Garay, J., Ostrovsky, R.: Edge fault tolerance on sparse networks. In: Czumaj, A., Mehlhorn, K., Pitts, A., Wattenhofer, R. (eds.) ICALP 2012. LNCS, vol. 7392, pp. 452–463. Springer, Heidelberg (2012). https://doi.org/10.1007/978-3-642-31585-5_41
14. Chandran, N., Chongchitmate, W., Garay, J.A., Goldwasser, S., Ostrovsky, R., Zikas, V.: The hidden graph model: communication locality and optimal resiliency with adaptive faults. In: ITCS, pp. 153–162 (2015)
15. Chaum, D., Crépeau, C., Damgård, I.: Multiparty unconditionally secure protocols (extended abstract). In: STOC, pp. 11–19 (1988)

16. Damgård, I., Meyer, P., Tschudi, D.: Information-theoretic topology-hiding computation with setup (2019). http://perso.ens-lyon.fr/pierre.meyer/docs/m2.pierre.meyer.pdf
17. Dolev, D.: The Byzantine generals strike again. J. Algorithms **3**(1), 14–30 (1982)
18. Dolev, D., Dwork, C., Waarts, O., Yung, M.: Perfectly secure message transmission. J. ACM **40**(1), 17–47 (1993)
19. Dwork, C., Peleg, D., Pippenger, N., Upfal, E.: Fault tolerance in networks of bounded degree. SICOMP **17**(5), 975–988 (1988)
20. Fischer, M.J., Lynch, N.A., Merritt, M.: Easy impossibility proofs for distributed consensus problems. In: PODC, pp. 59–70 (1985)
21. Goldreich, O., Micali, S., Wigderson, A.: How to play any mental game or a completeness theorem for protocols with honest majority. In: STOC, pp. 218–229 (1987)
22. Gordon, S.D., Malkin, T., Rosulek, M., Wee, H.: Multi-party computation of polynomials and branching programs without simultaneous interaction. In: Johansson, T., Nguyen, P.Q. (eds.) EUROCRYPT 2013. LNCS, vol. 7881, pp. 575–591. Springer, Heidelberg (2013). https://doi.org/10.1007/978-3-642-38348-9_34
23. Halevi, S., Lindell, Y., Pinkas, B.: Secure computation on the web: computing without simultaneous interaction. In: Rogaway, P. (ed.) CRYPTO 2011. LNCS, vol. 6841, pp. 132–150. Springer, Heidelberg (2011). https://doi.org/10.1007/978-3-642-22792-9_8
24. Halevi, S., Ishai, Y., Jain, A., Kushilevitz, E., Rabin, T.: Secure multiparty computation with general interaction patterns. In: ITCS, pp. 157–168 (2016)
25. Hinkelmann, M., Jakoby, A.: Communications in unknown networks: preserving the secret of topology. Theor. Comput. Sci. **384**(2–3), 184–200 (2007)
26. Hirt, M., Maurer, U., Tschudi, D., Zikas, V.: Network-hiding communication and applications to multi-party protocols. In: Robshaw, M., Katz, J. (eds.) CRYPTO 2016. LNCS, vol. 9815, pp. 335–365. Springer, Heidelberg (2016). https://doi.org/10.1007/978-3-662-53008-5_12
27. King, V., Lonargan, S., Saia, J., Trehan, A.: Load balanced scalable byzantine agreement through quorum building, with full information. In: Aguilera, M.K., Yu, H., Vaidya, N.H., Srinivasan, V., Choudhury, R.R. (eds.) ICDCN 2011. LNCS, vol. 6522, pp. 203–214. Springer, Heidelberg (2011). https://doi.org/10.1007/978-3-642-17679-1_18
28. Kumar, M.V.N.A., Goundan, P.R., Srinathan, K., Rangan, C.P.: On perfectly secure communication over arbitrary networks. In: PODC, pp. 193–202 (2002)
29. LaVigne, R., Liu-Zhang, C.-D., Maurer, U., Moran, T., Mularczyk, M., Tschudi, D.: Topology-hiding computation beyond semi-honest adversaries. In: Beimel, A., Dziembowski, S. (eds.) TCC 2018. LNCS, vol. 11240, pp. 3–35. Springer, Cham (2018). https://doi.org/10.1007/978-3-030-03810-6_1
30. Micali, S., Ohta, K., Reyzin, L.: Accountable-subgroup multisignatures: extended abstract. In: ACM CCS, pp. 245–254 (2001)
31. Moran, T., Orlov, I., Richelson, S.: Topology-hiding computation. In: Dodis, Y., Nielsen, J.B. (eds.) TCC 2015. LNCS, vol. 9014, pp. 159–181. Springer, Heidelberg (2015). https://doi.org/10.1007/978-3-662-46494-6_8
32. Rabin, T., Ben-Or, M.: Verifiable secret sharing and multiparty protocols with honest majority (extended abstract). In: FOCS, pp. 73–85 (1989)
33. Yao, A.C.: Protocols for secure computations (extended abstract). In: FOCS, pp. 160–164 (1982)

# Channels of Small Log-Ratio Leakage and Characterization of Two-Party Differentially Private Computation

Iftach Haitner[1], Noam Mazor[1(✉)], Ronen Shaltiel[2], and Jad Silbak[1(✉)]

[1] School of Computer Science, Tel Aviv University, Tel Aviv-Yafo, Israel
iftachh@cs.tau.ac.il, noammaz@gmail.com, jadsilbak@gmail.com
[2] Department of Computer Science, University of Haifa, Haifa, Israel
ronen@cs.haifa.ac.il

**Abstract.** Consider a PPT two-party protocol $\Pi = (\mathsf{A}, \mathsf{B})$ in which the parties get no private inputs and obtain outputs $O^\mathsf{A}, O^\mathsf{B} \in \{0,1\}$, and let $V^\mathsf{A}$ and $V^\mathsf{B}$ denote the parties' individual views. Protocol $\Pi$ has $\alpha$-*agreement* if $\Pr[O^\mathsf{A} = O^\mathsf{B}] = \frac{1}{2} + \alpha$. The *leakage* of $\Pi$ is the amount of information a party obtains about the event $\{O^\mathsf{A} = O^\mathsf{B}\}$; that is, the *leakage* $\epsilon$ is the maximum, over $\mathsf{P} \in \{\mathsf{A}, \mathsf{B}\}$, of the distance between $V^\mathsf{P}|_{O^\mathsf{A}=O^\mathsf{B}}$ and $V^\mathsf{P}|_{O^\mathsf{A} \neq O^\mathsf{B}}$. Typically, this distance is measured in *statistical distance*, or, in the computational setting, in *computational indistinguishability*. For this choice, Wullschleger [TCC '09] showed that if $\epsilon \ll \alpha$ then the protocol can be transformed into an OT protocol.

We consider measuring the protocol leakage by the *log-ratio distance* (which was popularized by its use in the differential privacy framework). The log-ratio distance between $X, Y$ over domain $\Omega$ is the minimal $\epsilon \geq 0$ for which, for every $v \in \Omega$, $\log \frac{\Pr[X=v]}{\Pr[Y=v]} \in [-\epsilon, \epsilon]$. In the computational setting, we use computational indistinguishability from having log-ratio distance $\epsilon$. We show that a protocol with (noticeable) accuracy $\alpha \in \Omega(\epsilon^2)$ can be transformed into an OT protocol (note that this allows $\epsilon \gg \alpha$). We complete the picture, in this respect, showing that a protocol with $\alpha \in o(\epsilon^2)$ does not necessarily imply OT. Our results hold for both the information theoretic and the computational settings, and can be viewed as a "fine grained" approach to "weak OT amplification".

We then use the above result to *fully* characterize the complexity of differentially private two-party computation for the XOR function, answering the open question put by Goyal, Khurana, Mironov, Pandey, and Sahai, [ICALP '16] and Haitner, Nissim, Omri, Shaltiel, and Silbak [22] [FOCS '18]. Specifically, we show that for any (noticeable) $\alpha \in \Omega(\epsilon^2)$, a two-party protocol that computes the XOR function with $\alpha$-accuracy and $\epsilon$-differential privacy can be transformed into an OT protocol. This improves upon Goyal et al. that only handle $\alpha \in \Omega(\epsilon)$, and upon Haitner et al. who showed that such a protocol implies (infinitely-often) key agreement (and not OT). Our characterization is tight since OT does not follow from protocols in which $\alpha \in o(\epsilon^2)$, and extends to

I. Haitner—Member of the Check Point Institute for Information Security.
R. Shaltiel—Research supported by ISF grant 1628/17.
J. Silbak—Research supported by ERC starting grant 638121.

D. Hofheinz and A. Rosen (Eds.): TCC 2019, LNCS 11891, pp. 531–560, 2019.
https://doi.org/10.1007/978-3-030-36030-6_21

functions (over many bits) that "contain" an "embedded copy" of the XOR function.

**Keywords:** Oblivious transfer · Differential privacy · Hardness amplification

# 1  Introduction

Oblivious transfer (OT), introduced by Rabin [37], is one of the most fundamental primitives in cryptography and a complete primitive for secure multiparty computation [14,43]. Oblivious transfer protocols are known to exist assuming (several types of) *families of trapdoor permutations* [12,18], *learning with errors* [35], *decisional Diffie-Hellman* [1,33], *computational Diffie-Hellman* [4] and *quadratic residuosity* [28]. While in some of the constructions of OT in the literature, the construction immediately yields a full-fledged OT, in others it only yields a "weak" form of OT, that is later "amplified" into a full-fledged one.

In this paper we introduce a new notion for a "weak form of OT", and show how to amplify this "weak OT" into full-fledged OT. This notion is more "fine grained" than some previously suggested notions, which allows us to obtain OT in scenarios that could not be handled by previous works. Our approach is suitable for the computational and for the information theoretic settings (i.e., the dishonest parties are assumed to be computationally bounded or not).

## 1.1  Our Results

We start with presenting our results in the information theoretic setting, and then move to the computation one.

### 1.1.1  The Information Theoretic Setting

The information theoretic analogue of a two-party protocol between parties A and B, is a "channel": namely, a quadruple of random variables $C = ((V^A, O^A), (V^B, O^B))$, with the interpretation that when "activating" (or "calling") the channel $C$, party $P \in \{A, B\}$ receives his "output" $O^P$ and his "view" $V^P$. In other words, "activating a channel" is analogous to running a two-party protocol with fresh randomness. (We assume that the view $V^P$ contains the output $O^P$).

*Log-Ratio Leakage (Channels).* We are interested in the special case where the channel $C = ((V^A, O^A), (V^B, O^B))$ has Boolean outputs (i.e., $O^A, O^B \in \{0,1\}$), and assume for simplicity that the channel is *balanced*, meaning that for both $P \in \{A, B\}$, $O^P$ is uniformly distributed. Such channels are parameterized by their *agreement* and *leakage*:

- A channel $C$ has $\alpha$-*agreement* if $\Pr[O^A = O^B] = \frac{1}{2} + \alpha$. (Without loss of generality, $\alpha \geq 0$, as otherwise one of the parties can flip his output).
- The *leakage* of party B in $C$ is the distance between the distributions $V^A|_{O^A=O^B}$ and $V^A|_{O^A\neq O^B}$. (Note that these two distributions are well defined if $\alpha \in [0, \frac{1}{2})$). The leakage of party A is defined in an analogous way, and the leakage of $C$ is the maximum of the two leakages.

This approach (with somewhat different notation) was taken by past work [40,41], using *statistical distance* as the distance measure.

Loosely speaking, leakage measures how well can a party distinguish the case $\{O^A = O^B\}$ from the case $\{O^A \neq O^B\}$. As each party knows his output, this can be thought of as the "amount of information" on the input of one party that *leaks* to the other party.[1]

We will measure leakage using a *different distance measure*, which we refer to as "log-ratio distance".

**Definition 1.1 (Log-Ratio distance).** *Two numbers* $p_0, p_1 \in [0,1]$ *satisfy* $p_0 \overset{R}{\approx}_{\epsilon,\delta} p_1$ *if for both* $b \in \{0,1\}$: $p_b \leq e^\epsilon \cdot p_{1-b} + \delta$. *Two distributions* $D_0, D_1$ *over the same domain* $\Omega$, *are* $(\epsilon, \delta)$ *-log-ratio-close (denoted* $D_0 \overset{R}{\approx}_{\epsilon,\delta} D_1$) *if for every* $A \subseteq \Omega$:

$$\Pr[D_0 \in A] \overset{R}{\approx}_{\epsilon,\delta} \Pr[D_1 \in A].$$

We use the notation $D_0 \overset{S}{\approx}_\delta D_1$ to say that the *statistical distance* between $D_0$ and $D_1$ is at most $\delta$. Log-ratio distance is a generalization of statistical distance as $\overset{S}{\approx}_\delta$ is the same as $\overset{R}{\approx}_{0,\delta}$. This measure of distance was popularized by its use in the *differential privacy* framework [10] (that we discuss in Sect. 1.1.3).

Loosely speaking, log-ratio distance considers the "log-ratio function" $L_{D_0 \| D_1}(x) := \log \frac{\Pr[D_0 = x]}{\Pr[D_1 = x]}$, and the two distribution are $(\epsilon, \delta)$-log-ratio-close if this function is in the interval $[-\epsilon, \epsilon]$ with probability $1 - \delta$. As such, it can be seen as a "cousin" of *relative entropy* (also known as, *Kullback–Leibler (KL) divergence*) that measures the expectation of the log-ratio function.

Note that for $\epsilon \in [0,1]$, $D_0 \overset{R}{\approx}_{\epsilon,0} D_1$ implies $D_0 \overset{R}{\approx}_{0,2\epsilon} D_1$, but the converse is not true, and the condition $(D_0 \overset{R}{\approx}_{\epsilon,0} D_1)$ gives tighter handle on the distance between independent samples of distributions (as we explain in detail in Sect. 2.1).

We use the log-ratio distance to measure leakage in channels. This leads to the following definition (in which we substitute "log-ratio distance" as a distance measure).

**Definition 1.2 (Log-ratio leakage, channels, informal).** *A channel* $C = ((V^A, O^A), (V^B, O^B))$ *has* log-ratio leakage $(\epsilon, \delta)$, *denoted* $(\epsilon, \delta)$-leakage *if for both* $P \in \{A, B\}$:

$$V^P|_{O^A = O^B} \overset{R}{\approx}_{\epsilon,\delta} V^P|_{O^A \neq O^B}.$$

This definition is related (and inspired by) the *differential privacy* framework [10]. In the terminology of differential privacy, this can be restated as

---

[1] We remark that one should be careful with this intuition. Consider a "binary symmetric channel": a channel in which $V^A = O^A$ and $V^B = O^B$ (i.e., the parties receive no additional view except their outputs), $O^A$ is uniformly distributed, and $O^B = O^A \oplus U_p$ (where $U_p$ is an independent biased coin which is one with probability $p$). The leakage of this channel is zero, for every choice of $p$, whereas each party can predict the output of the other party with probability $1 - p$ by using his own output as a prediction.

follows: let $E$ be the indicator variable for the event $\{O^A = O^B\}$. For both $P \in \{A, B\}$, the "mechanism" $V^P$ is $(\epsilon, \delta)$-differentially private with regards to the "secret"/"database" $E$.

*Channels of Small Log-Ratio Leakage Imply OT.* Wullschleger [41] considered channels with small leakage (measured by statistical distance). Using our terminology, he showed for $\alpha \in [0, \frac{1}{2})$ and $\epsilon \in [0, 1]$ with $\epsilon$ "sufficiently smaller than" $\alpha^2$, a channel with $\alpha$-agreement and $(0, \epsilon)$-leakage yields OT. This can be interpreted as saying that if the leakage $\epsilon$ is sufficiently *smaller* than the agreement $\alpha$, then the channel yields OT. We prove the following "fine grained" amplification result, which is restated with precise notation in Theorem 4.2.

**Theorem 1.3 (Channels of small log-ratio leakage imply OT, infromal).** *There exists a constants $c_1 > 0$ such that the following holds for every $\epsilon, \delta, \alpha$ with $c_1 \cdot \epsilon^2 \leq \alpha < 1/8$ and $\delta \leq \epsilon^2$: a channel $C$ that has $\alpha$-agreement and $(\epsilon, \delta)$-leakage yields OT (of statistical security).*

For simplicity, let us focus on Theorem 1.3 in the case that $\delta = 0$. Two distributions that are $(\epsilon, 0)$-log-ratio close, may have statistical distance $\epsilon$, and so, a channel with $(\epsilon, 0)$-leakage, can only be assumed to have $(0, \epsilon)$-leakage (when measuring leakage in statistical distance). Nevertheless, in contrast to [41], Theorem 1.3 allows the leakage parameter $\epsilon$ to be *larger* than the agreement parameter $\alpha$.[2]

The above can be interpreted as saying that when the leakage is "well behaved" (that is the $\delta$ parameter in log-ratio distance is sufficiently small), OT can be obtained even from a channel whose leakage $\epsilon$ is *much larger* than the agreement $\alpha$. This property will be the key for our applications in Sect. 1.1.3.

*Triviality of Channels with Large Leakage.* We now observe that the relationship between $\epsilon$ and $\alpha$ in Theorem 1.3 is best possible (up to constants). Namely, a channel with agreement that is asymptotically smaller than the one allowed in Theorem 1.3 does not necessarily yield OT.

**Theorem 1.4 (Triviality of channels with large leakage, informal).** *There exists a constant $c_2 > 0$, such that the following holds for every $\epsilon > 0$: there exists a two-party protocol (with no inputs) that when it ends, party $P \in \{A, B\}$ outputs $O^P$ and sees view $V^P$, and the induced channel $C = ((V^A, O^A), (V^B, O^B))$ has $(c_2 \cdot \epsilon^2)$-agreement and $(\epsilon, 0)$-leakage.*

---

[2] To make this more concrete, consider the following channel $C = ((V^A, O^A), (V^B, O^B))$: $O^A \leftarrow U_{1/2}$, $O^B \leftarrow O^A \oplus U_{1/2-\alpha}$, $V^A \leftarrow O^B \oplus U_{1/2-\epsilon}$, $V^B \leftarrow O^A \oplus U_{1/2-\epsilon}$ (where $U_p$ denotes a biased coin which is one with probability $p$, and the three "noise variables" are independent). This channel is balanced, has $\alpha$-agreement, and $(O(\epsilon), 0)$-leakage. However, if we were to measure leakage using statistical distance, then we would report that it has $(0, O(\epsilon))$-leakage. We are assuming that $\epsilon > \alpha$, and it will be critical that leakage is measured by log-ratio distance, as we do not know how to amplify leakage that is measured by statistical distance in this range.

Together, the two theorems say that our characterization of "weak-OT" using agreement $\alpha$ and $(\epsilon, 0)$-log-ratio leakage has a "threshold behavior" at $\alpha \approx \epsilon^2$: if $\alpha \geq c_1 \cdot \epsilon^2$ then the channel yields OT, and if $\alpha \leq c_2 \cdot \epsilon^2$ then such a channel can be simulated by a two-party protocol with no inputs (and thus cannot yield OT with information theoretic security). The proof of Theorem 1.4 uses a variant of the well-known randomized response approach of Warner [38].

### 1.1.2  The Computational Setting

We consider a no-input, Boolean output, two-party protocol $\Pi = (\mathsf{A}, \mathsf{B})$. Namely, both parties receive a security parameter $1^\kappa$ as a common input, get no private input, and both output one bit. We denote the output of party $\mathsf{P}$ by $O_\kappa^\mathsf{P}$, and its view by $V_\kappa^\mathsf{P}$. In other words, an instantiation of $\Pi(1^\kappa)$ can be thought of as inducing a channel $C_\kappa = ((V_\kappa^\mathsf{A}, O_\kappa^\mathsf{A}), (V_\kappa^\mathsf{B}, O_\kappa^\mathsf{B}))$. Similar to the information theoretic setting, protocol $\Pi$ has $\alpha$-agreement if for every $\kappa \in \mathbb{N}$: $\Pr\left[O_\kappa^\mathsf{A} = O_\kappa^\mathsf{B}\right] = 1/2 + \alpha(\kappa)$.

*Log-Ratio Leakage (Protocols).* We extend the definition of log-ratio leakage to the computational setting (where adversaries are PPT machines). We will use the simulation paradigm to extend the information theoretic definition to the computational setting.

**Definition 1.5 (Log-ratio leakage, protocols, informal).** *A two-party no-input Boolean output protocol* $\Pi = (\mathsf{A}, \mathsf{B})$ *has* Comp-log-ratio *leakage* $(\epsilon, \delta)$, *denoted* $(\epsilon, \delta)$-comp-leakage, *if there exists an "ideal channel" ensemble* $\widetilde{C} = \left\{\widetilde{C}_\kappa = ((V_\kappa^{\widetilde{\mathsf{A}}}, O_\kappa^{\widetilde{\mathsf{A}}}), (V_\kappa^{\widetilde{\mathsf{B}}}, O_\kappa^{\widetilde{\mathsf{B}}}))\right\}_{\kappa \in \mathbb{N}}$ *such that the following holds:*

- *For every $\kappa \in \mathbb{N}$: the channel $\widetilde{C}_\kappa$ has $(\epsilon(\kappa), \delta(\kappa))$-leakage.*
- *For every $\mathsf{P} \in \{\mathsf{A}, \mathsf{B}\}$: the ensembles $\left\{V_\kappa^\mathsf{P}, O_\kappa^\mathsf{A}, O_\kappa^\mathsf{B}\right\}_{\kappa \in \mathbb{N}}$ and $\left\{V_\kappa^{\widetilde{\mathsf{P}}}, O_\kappa^{\widetilde{\mathsf{A}}}, O_\kappa^{\widetilde{\mathsf{B}}}\right\}_{\kappa \in \mathbb{N}}$ are* computationally indistinguishable.[3]

*Protocols of Small Log-Ratio Leakage Imply OT.* We prove the following computational analogue of Theorem 1.3.

**Theorem 1.6 (Amplification of protocols with small log-ratio leakage, informal).** *There exists a constant $c_1 > 0$ such that the following holds for every function $\epsilon, \delta, \alpha$ with $c_1 \cdot \epsilon(\kappa)^2 \leq \alpha(\kappa) < 1/8$, $\delta(\kappa) \leq \epsilon(\kappa)^2$ and $1/\alpha(\kappa) \in$ poly$(\kappa)$: a PPT protocol that has $\alpha$-agreement and $(\epsilon, \delta)$-comp-leakage yields OT (of computational security).*

*Triviality of Protocols with Large Leakage.* An immediate corollary of Theorem 1.4 is the relationship between $\epsilon$ and $\alpha$ in Theorem 1.6 is best possible (up to constants).

---

[3] In the technical section, we consider computational indistinguishability by both *uniform* and *nonuniform* PPT machines. We ignore this issue in the introduction.

**Corollary 1.7 (Triviality of protocols with large leakage, informal).**
*There exists a constant $c_2 > 0$, such that the following holds for every function $\epsilon$ with $\epsilon(\kappa) > 0$: there exists a PPT protocol that has $(c_2 \cdot \epsilon^2)$-agreement and $(\epsilon, 0)$-leakage.*

### 1.1.3  Application: Characterization of Two-Party Differentially Private Computation.

We use our results to characterize the complexity of differentially private two-party computation for the XOR function, answering the open question put by [17,22]. The framework of differential privacy typically studies a "one-party" setup, where a "curator" wants to answer statistical queries on a database without compromising the privacy of individual users whose information is recorded as rows in the database [10]. In this paper, we are interested in *two-party* differentially-private computation (defined in [32]). This setting is closely related to the setting of secure function evaluation: the parties A and B have private inputs $x$ and $y$, and wish to compute some functionality $f(x, y)$ without compromising the privacy of their inputs. In secure function evaluation, this intuitively means that parties do not learn any information about the other party's input, that cannot be inferred from their own inputs and outputs. This guarantee is sometimes very weak: For example, for the XOR function $f(x, y) = x \oplus y$, secure function evaluation completely reveals the inputs of the parties (as a party that knows $x$ and $f(x, y)$ can infer $y$). Differentially private two-party computation aims to give some nontrivial security even in such cases (at the cost of compromising the *accuracy* of the outputs).

**Definition 1.8 (Differentially private computation [32]).** *A PPT two-party protocol $\Pi = (\mathsf{A}, \mathsf{B})$ over input domain $\{0,1\}^n \times \{0,1\}^n$ is $\epsilon$-DP, if for every PPT nonuniform machines $\mathsf{B}^*$ and $\mathsf{D}$, and every $x, x' \in \{0,1\}^n$ with $\mathrm{Ham}(x, x') = 1$: let $V_\kappa^{\mathsf{B}^*}(x)$ be the view of $\mathsf{B}^*$ in a random execution of $(\mathsf{A}(x), \mathsf{B}^*)(1^\kappa))$, then*

$$\Pr\left[\mathsf{D}(V_\kappa^{\mathsf{B}^*}(x)) = 1\right] \le e^{\epsilon(\kappa)} \cdot \Pr\left[\mathsf{D}(V_\kappa^{\mathsf{B}^*}(x')) = 1\right] + \mathrm{neg}(\kappa),$$

*and the same hold for the secrecy of $\mathsf{B}$.*

*Such a protocol is* semi-honest $\epsilon$-DP, *if the above is only guaranteed for semi-honest adversaries (i.e., for $\mathsf{B}^* = \mathsf{B}$).*

In this paper, we are interested in functionalities $f$, in which outputs are single bits (as in the case of the XOR function). In this special case, the accuracy of a protocol can be measured as follows:

**Definition 1.9 (accuracy).** *A PPT two-party protocol $\Pi = (\mathsf{A}, \mathsf{B})$ over input domain $\{0,1\}^n \times \{0,1\}^n$ with outputs $O^{\mathsf{A}}(x, y), O^{\mathsf{B}}(x, y) \in \{0,1\}$ has* perfect agreement *if for every $x, y \in \{0,1\}^n \times \{0,1\}^n$, and every $\kappa \in \mathbb{N}$, in a random execution of the protocol $(\mathsf{A}(x), \mathsf{B}(y))(1^\kappa)$, it holds that $\Pr[O^{\mathsf{A}}(x, y) = O^{\mathsf{B}}(x, y)] = 1$.*

*The protocol implements a functionality $f$ over input domain $\{0,1\}^n \times \{0,1\}^n$ with $\alpha$-accuracy, if for $\kappa \in \mathbb{N}$, every $\mathsf{P} \in \{\mathsf{A}, \mathsf{B}\}$, and every $x, y \in \{0,1\}^n \times \{0,1\}^n$, in a random execution of the protocol $(\mathsf{A}(x), \mathsf{B}(y))(1^\kappa)$, it holds that $\Pr[O^{\mathsf{P}}(x, y) = f^{\mathsf{P}}(x, y)] = \frac{1}{2} + \alpha(\kappa)$.*

A natural question is what assumptions are needed for two-party differentially private computation achieving a certain level of accuracy/privacy (for various functionalities). A sequence of works showed that for certain tasks, achieving high accuracy requires one-way functions [3,6,16,31]; some cannot even be instantiated in the random-oracle model [21]; and some cannot be black-box reduced to key agreement [29]. See Sect. 1.2 for more details on these results. In this work we fully answer the above question for the XOR function.

Consider the functionality $f_\alpha(x, y)$ which outputs $x \oplus y \oplus U_{1/2-\alpha}$ (where $U_{1/2-\alpha}$ is an independent biased coin which is one with probability $1/2 - \alpha$). Assuming OT, there exists a two-party protocol that securely implement $f_\alpha$, and this protocol is $\epsilon$-DP, for $\epsilon = \Theta(\alpha)$. This is the best possible differential privacy that can be achieved for accuracy $\alpha$. On the other extreme, an $\Theta(\epsilon^2)$-accurate, $\epsilon$-differential private, protocol for computing XOR can be constructed (with information theoretic security) using the so-called *randomized response* approach of Warner [38], as shown in [16]. Thus, it is natural to ask whether OT *follows* from $\alpha$-accurate, $\epsilon$-DP computation of XOR, for intermediate choices of $\epsilon^2 \ll \alpha \ll \epsilon$. In this paper, we completely resolve this problem and prove that OT is implied for any intermediate $\epsilon^2 \ll \alpha \ll \epsilon$.

*Differentially Private XOR to OT, a Tight Characterization.*

**Theorem 1.10.** *[Differentially private XOR to OT, informal] There exists a constant $c_1 > 0$ such that the following holds for every function $\epsilon, \alpha$ with $\alpha \geq c_1 \cdot \epsilon^2$ such that $1/\alpha \in$ poly: the existence of a perfect agreement, $\alpha$-accurate, semi-honest $\epsilon$-DP PPT protocol for computing XOR implies OT (of computational security).*

The above improves upon Goyal et al. [17], who gave a positive answer if the accuracy $\alpha$ is the best possible: if $\alpha \geq c \cdot \epsilon$ for a constant $c$. It also improves (in the implication) upon Haitner et al. [22], who showed that $c \cdot \epsilon^2$-correct $\epsilon$-DP XOR implies (infinitely-often) key agreement. Finally, our result allows $\epsilon$ and $\alpha$ to be function of the security parameter (and furthermore, allow $\alpha$ and $\epsilon$ to be polynomially small in the security parameter) whereas previous reductions [17,22] only hold for constant values of $\epsilon$ and $\alpha$. Our characterization is tight as OT does not follow from protocols with $\alpha \in o(\epsilon^2)$.

**Theorem 1.11 (Triviality of differentially private XOR with large leakage. Folklore, see [16]).** *There exists a constant $c_2 > 0$ such that for every functions $\epsilon$ there exists a PPT protocol for computing XOR with information-theoretic $\epsilon$-DP, perfect agreement and accuracy $c_2 \cdot \epsilon^2$.*[4]

*Perspective.* Most of the work in differentially private mechanisms/protocols is in the information theoretic setting (using the addition of random noise). There are, however, examples where using computational definitions of differential privacy

---

[4] The protocol is the randomized response one, and the proof is very similar to that of Theorem 1.4 (see Sect. 4).

together with cryptographic assumptions, yield significantly improved accuracy and privacy compared to those that can be achieved in the information theoretic setting (e.g., the inner product and the Hamming distance functionalities [31], see more references in the related work section below). Understanding the minimal assumptions required in this setting is a fundamental open problem. In this paper, we completely resolve this problem for the special case of the XOR function. We stress that the XOR function is the canonical example of a function $f(x, y)$ where the security guarantee given by secure function evaluation is very weak. More precisely, for $f(x, y) = x \oplus y$, the security guaranteed by secure function evaluation is meaningless, and the protocol in which both parties reveal their private inputs is considered secure. Differential privacy can be used to provide a meaningful definition of security in such cases, and we believe that the tools that we developed for the XOR function, can be useful to argue about the minimal assumptions required for other functionalities. As a first step, we provide a sufficient condition under which our approach applies to other functionalities $g : \{0, 1\}^n \times \{0, 1\}^n \to \{0, 1\}$.

*Extending the Result to any Function that Is Not Monotone Under Relabeling.* We can use our results on the XOR function to achieve OT from differentially private, and sufficiently accurate computation of a wide class of functions that are not "monotone under relabeling". A function $g : \{0, 1\}^n \times \{0, 1\}^n \to \{0, 1\}$ is monotone under relabeling if there exist two bijective functions $\sigma_x, \sigma_y : [2^n] \to \{0, 1\}^n$ such that for every $x \in \{0, 1\}^n$ and $i \leq j \in [2^n]$:

$$g(x, \sigma_y(i)) \leq g(x, \sigma_y(j)),$$

and, for every $y \in \{0, 1\}^n$ and $i \leq j \in [2^n]$:

$$g(\sigma_x(i), y) \leq g(\sigma_x(j), y).$$

We observe that every function $g$ that is not monotone under relabeling has an "embedded XOR", meaning that there exist $x_0, x_1, y_0, y_1 \in \{0, 1\}^n$ such that for every $b, c \in \{0, 1\}$, $g(x_b, y_c) = b \oplus c$. This gives that a two-party protocol that computes $g$ can be used to give a two-party protocol that computes XOR (with some losses in privacy) and these yield OT by our earlier results.

## 1.2   Related Work

*Information-Theoretic OT.* Oblivious transfer protocols are also widely studies in their information theoretic forms [7,8,34,36,39]. In this form, and OT is simply a pair of jointly distributed random variable $(V_A, V_B)$ (a "channel"). A pair of unbounded parties $(A, B)$, having access to independent samples from this pair (from each sample $(v_A, v_B)$, party P gets the value $v_P$). Interestingly, in the information theoretic form, we do have a "simple" notion of weak OT, that is complete: such a pair can either be used to construct full-fledged (information theoretically secure) OT, or is trivial—there exists a protocol that generates these views. Unfortunately, these reductions are inherently inefficient: the parties wait till an event that might be of arbitrary small probability to occur, and thus, at least not in the most general form, cannot be translated into the computational setting.

*Hardness Amplification.* Amplifying the security of weak primitives into "fully secure" ones is an important paradigm in cryptography as well as other key fields in theoretical computer science. Most notable such works in cryptography are amplification of one-way functions [15, 20, 42], key-agreement protocols [26], and interactive arguments [19, 25]. Among the above, amplification of key-agreement protocols (KA) is the most similar to the OT amplification we consider in this paper. In particular, we do have a "simple" (non distributional) notion of weak KA [26]. This is done by reduction to the information theoretic notion of key-agreement. What enables this reduction to go through, is that unlike the case of the information theoretic OT, the amplification of information theoretic KA is efficient, since it only use the designated output of the (weak) KA (and not the parties' view).

*Minimal Assumptions for Differentially Private Symmetric Computation.* An accuracy parameter $\alpha$ is *trivial* with respect to a given functionality $f$ and differential privacy parameter $\epsilon$, if a protocol computing $f$ with such accuracy and privacy exists information theoretically (i.e., with no computational assumptions). The accuracy parameter is called *optimal*, if it matches the bound achieved in the client-server model. Gaps between the trivial and optimal accuracy parameters have been shown in the multiparty case for count queries [3, 6] and in the two-party case for inner product and Hamming distance functionalities [31]. [21] showed that the same holds also when a random oracle is available to the parties, implying that non-trivial protocols (achieving non-trivial accuracy) for computing these functionalities cannot be black-box reduced to one-way functions.

[16] initiated the study of Boolean functions, showing a gap between the optimal and trivial accuracy for the XOR or the AND functionalities, and that non-trivial protocols imply one-way functions. [27] showed that non-interactive randomised response is optimal among all the information theoretic protocols. [29] have shown that optimal protocols for computing the XOR or AND, cannot be black-box reduced to key agreement.

[17] showed that an optimal protocol (with best possible parameters) computing the XOR can be viewed as a form of weak OT, which according to Wullschleger [41] yields full fledged OT. Whereas for our choice of parameters the security guarantee is too weak, and it is essential that we correctly amplify the security.

Very recently, [22] showed that a non-trivial protocol for computing XOR (i.e., accuracy better than $\epsilon^2$) implies infinitely often key-agreement protocols. Their reduction, however, only holds for constant value of $\epsilon$, and is non black box. Finally, [2, 24] gave a criteria that proved the necessity of OT for computationally secure function evaluation, for a select class of functions.

**Paper Organization**
Due to space limitations, some of the technical details appear in the full version of this paper [23]. In Sect. 2 we give an overview of the main ideas used in the proof. In Sect. 3 we give some preliminaries and state some earlier work that we use. In Sect. 4 we give our amplification results, that convert protocols with small log-ratio leakage into OT. The proofs of our results on two-party differentially private computation of the XOR function, and on functions that are not monotone under relabeling omitted from this version.

# 2  Our Technique

In this section we give a high level overview of our main ideas and technique.

## 2.1  Usefulness of Log-Ratio Distance

Recall that the *leakage* we considered is measured using *log-ratio distance*, and not *statistical distance*. We survey some advantages of log-ratio distance over statistical distance.

As is common in "hardness amplification", our construction will apply the original channel/protocol many times (using fresh randomness). Given a distribution $X$, let $X^\ell$ denote the distribution of $\ell$ independent samples from $X$. A natural question is how does the distance between $X^\ell$ and $Y^\ell$ relate to the distance between $X$ and $Y$. For concreteness, assume that $\mathrm{SD}(X,Y) = \epsilon$ (where SD denotes statistical distance) and that we are interested in taking $\ell = c/\epsilon^2$ repetitions where $c > 0$ is a very small constant. Consider the following two examples (in the following we use $U_p$ to denote a coin which is one with probability $p$):

- $X_1 = U_0$ and $Y_1 = U_\epsilon$. In this case, $\mathrm{SD}(X_1^\ell, Y_1^\ell) = 1 - (1 - \epsilon)^\ell \approx 1 - e^{-c/\epsilon}$ which approaches one for small $\epsilon$.
- $X_2 = U_{1/2}$ and $Y_2 = U_{1/2+\epsilon}$, in this case $\mathrm{SD}(X_2^\ell, Y_2^\ell) = \eta$, where $\eta \approx \sqrt{c}$ is a small constant that is independent of $\epsilon$, and can be made as small as we want by decreasing $c$.

There is a large gap in the behavior of the two examples. In the first, the distance is very close to one, while in the second it is very close to zero. This means that when we estimate $\mathrm{SD}(X^\ell, Y^\ell)$ in terms of $\mathrm{SD}(X,Y)$, we have to take a *pessimistic* bound corresponding to the first example, which is far from the truth in case our distributions behave like in the second example.

Loosely speaking, log-ratio distance provides a "fine grained" view that distinguishes the above two cases. Note that $X_2 \overset{R}{\approx}_{O(\epsilon),0} Y_2$, whereas there is no finite $c$ for which $X_1 \overset{R}{\approx}_{c,0} Y_1$. For $X, Y$ such that $X \overset{R}{\approx}_{\epsilon,\delta} Y$ for $\delta = 0$ (or more generally, for $\delta \ll \epsilon$) we get the behavior of the second example under repetitions, yielding a better control on the resulting statistical distance. More precisely, it is not hard to show that if $X \overset{\mathrm{R}}{\approx}_\epsilon Y$ then for $\ell = c/\epsilon^2$ it holds that $X^\ell \overset{\mathrm{S}}{\approx}_{O(\sqrt{c \cdot \ln(1/c)})} Y^\ell$.[5] A more precise statement and proof are given in Theorem 3.5.[6]

## 2.2  The Amplification Protocol

In this section we give a high level overview of the proof of Theorem 1.3. The starting point is a channel $C = ((V^A, O^A), (V^B, O^B))$ that has $\alpha$-agreement, and $(\epsilon, \delta)$-leakage. (A good example to keep in mind is the channel from Footnote 2). For simplicity of exposition, let us assume that $\delta = 0$ (the same proof will go through if $\delta$ is sufficiently small). Our goal is to obtain OT if $\alpha \geq c_1 \cdot \epsilon^2$ for some constant $c_1$, which we will choose to be sufficiently large.

Wullschleger [41] showed that a balanced channel with $\alpha'$-agreement, and $(0, \epsilon')$-leakage (that is $\epsilon'$ leakage in statistical distance) implies OT if $\epsilon' \leq c_{\mathsf{Wul}} \cdot (\alpha')^2$ for some constant $c_{\mathsf{Wul}} > 0$. Thus, we are looking for a protocol, that starts with a channel that has $(\epsilon, 0)$-leakage and $\alpha$-agreement, where $\epsilon$ is *larger* than $\alpha$, and produces a channel with $(0, \epsilon')$-leakage, and $\alpha'$-agreement where $\epsilon'$ is *smaller* than $\alpha'$. We will use the following protocol achieving $\alpha' \geq 1/5$ and an arbitrarily small constant $\epsilon' > 0$.[7]

**Protocol 2.1 ($\Delta_\ell^C = (\widetilde{A}, \widetilde{B})$, amplification of log-ratio leakage)**
*Channel: $C = ((V^A, O^A), (V^B, O^B))$.*
*Prameter: Number of samples $\ell$.*
*Operation: Do until the protocol produces output:*

1. *The parties activate the channel $C$ for $\ell$ times. Let $\overline{O}^A$ and $\overline{O}^B$ be the ($\ell$-bit) outputs.*

---

[5] Let us explain the intuition behind the above phenomenon. The maximum value of both $L_{X||Y}(s) = \log \frac{\Pr[X=s]}{\Pr[Y=s]}$ and $L_{Y||X}(s) = \log \frac{\Pr[Y=s]}{\Pr[X=s]}$, is at most $\epsilon$. The relative entropy (also known as, KL divergence) $D(X||Y)$ measures the expectation of $L_{X||Y}(s)$ according to $s \leftarrow X$, and is therefore smaller than $\epsilon$. But in fact it is easy to show that both $D(X||Y)$ and $D(Y||X)$ are bounded by $\epsilon \cdot (e^\epsilon - 1)$ which is approximately $\epsilon^2$ for small $\epsilon$. It follows that $D(X^\ell||Y^\ell) = \ell \cdot D(X||Y) \approx \ell\epsilon^2 = c$. In other words, the expectation of $L_{X^\ell||Y^\ell} = D(X^\ell||Y^\ell) = c$. The random variable $L_{X^\ell||Y^\ell}$ can be seen as the sum of $\ell$ independent copies of $L_{X||Y}$, and we know that each of these variables lies in the interval $[-\epsilon, \epsilon]$. By a standard Hoeffding bound it follows that the probability that $L_{X||Y}$ deviates from the expectation $c$, by say some quantity $\eta$ is at most $e^{-\Omega(\frac{\eta^2}{\ell\epsilon^2})} = e^{-\Omega(\eta^2/c)}$ and this means that we can choose $\eta$ to be roughly $\sqrt{c \cdot \ln(1/c)}$ and obtain that the probability of deviation is bounded by $\eta$. Overall, this gives that $X^\ell \overset{\mathrm{R}}{\approx} \eta + c, \eta Y^\ell$, meaning that except for an $\eta$ fraction of the space, the ratio is bounded by $\eta + c$, and therefore, the statistical distance is also bounded by $O(\eta + c) = O(\sqrt{c \cdot \ln(1/c)})$.

[6] This phenomenon is the rationale behind the differential privacy boosting result of [9], and can be derived from the proof in that paper. In our setting, however, the proof is straightforward as outlined here, and shown in the proof of Theorem 3.5.

[7] Similar protocols were used in the context of key-agreement amplification [5,30].

2. $\widetilde{\mathsf{A}}$ *sends the (unordered) set* $\mathcal{S} = \{\overline{O}^{\mathsf{A}}, \overline{O}^{\mathsf{A}} \oplus 1^{\ell}\}$ *to* $\widetilde{\mathsf{B}}$.
3. $\widetilde{\mathsf{B}}$ *informs* $\widetilde{\mathsf{A}}$ *whether* $\overline{O}^{\mathsf{B}} \in \mathcal{S}$.

*If positive, party* $\widetilde{\mathsf{A}}$ *outputs zero if* $\overline{O}^{\mathsf{A}}$ *is the (lex.) smallest element in* $\mathcal{S}$, *and one otherwise. Party* $\widetilde{\mathsf{B}}$ *does the same with respect to* $\overline{O}^{\mathsf{B}}$. *(And the protocol halts.)*

Let $\Delta = \Delta_{\ell}^{C}$ for $\ell = 1/4\alpha$. We first observe that $\Delta$ halts in a given iteration iff the event $E = \{\overline{O}^{\mathsf{A}} \oplus \overline{O}^{\mathsf{B}} \in \{0^{\ell}, 1^{\ell}\}\}$ occurs. Note that $\Pr[E] \geq 2^{-\ell}$, and thus the expected running time of $\Delta$ is $O(2^{\ell}) = 2^{O(1/\alpha)}$ (jumping ahead, the expected running time can be improved to $\mathrm{poly}(1/\alpha)$, see Sect. 2.2.1).

We also observe that the outputs of the two parties agree, iff in the final (halting) iteration it holds that $\overline{O}^{\mathsf{A}} = \overline{O}^{\mathsf{B}}$. Thus, the agreement of $\Delta$ is given by:

$$\Pr[\overline{O}^{\mathsf{A}} = \overline{O}^{\mathsf{B}} | E] = \frac{(\frac{1}{2} + \alpha)^{\ell}}{(\frac{1}{2} + \alpha)^{\ell} + (\frac{1}{2} - \alpha)^{\ell}} = \left(1 + \left(\frac{\frac{1}{2} - \alpha}{\frac{1}{2} + \alpha}\right)^{\ell}\right)^{-1}$$

$$\approx \frac{1}{1 + e^{-4\alpha\ell}} \geq \frac{1}{1 + e^{-1}} \geq \frac{1}{2} + \alpha',$$

for $\alpha' \geq 1/5$.

In order to understand the leakage of $\Delta$, we examine the views of the parties in the *final* iteration of $\Delta$ (it is clear that the views of the previous iteration yields no information). Let us denote these part of a view $v$ by $\mathrm{final}(v)$. We are interested in understanding the log-ratio distance between $\mathrm{final}(V^{\widetilde{\mathsf{A}}}|_{O^{\widetilde{\mathsf{A}}} = O^{\widetilde{\mathsf{B}}}})$ and $\mathrm{final}(V^{\widetilde{\mathsf{A}}}|_{O^{\widetilde{\mathsf{A}}} \neq O^{\widetilde{\mathsf{B}}}})$. Observe that $\mathrm{final}(V^{\widetilde{\mathsf{A}}}|_{O^{\widetilde{\mathsf{A}}} = O^{\widetilde{\mathsf{B}}}})$ is a (deterministic) function of $\ell$ independent samples from $V^{\mathsf{A}}|_{O^{\mathsf{A}} = O^{\mathsf{B}}}$ (i.e., the function that appends $\{\overline{O}^{\mathsf{A}}, \overline{O}^{\mathsf{A}} \oplus 1^{\ell}\}$ to the view), and $\mathrm{final}(V^{\widetilde{\mathsf{A}}}|_{O^{\widetilde{\mathsf{A}}} \neq O^{\widetilde{\mathsf{B}}}})$ is the *same* deterministic function of $\ell$ independent samples from $V^{\mathsf{A}}|_{O^{\mathsf{A}} \neq O^{\mathsf{B}}}$. Thus, by data processing, it suffices to bound the distance of $\ell$ independent samples from $V^{\mathsf{A}}|_{O^{\mathsf{A}} = O^{\mathsf{B}}}$ from $\ell$ independent samples from $V^{\mathsf{A}}|_{O^{\mathsf{A}} \neq O^{\mathsf{B}}}$. By assumption, $C$ has $(\epsilon, 0)$-leakage, which means that

$$V^{\mathsf{A}}|_{O^{\mathsf{A}} = O^{\mathsf{B}}} \overset{\mathrm{R}}{\approx}_{\epsilon, 0} V^{\mathsf{A}}|_{O^{\mathsf{A}} \neq O^{\mathsf{B}}}.$$

In the previous section we showed that by choosing a sufficiently small constant $c > 0$ and taking $\ell = c/\epsilon^2$ repetitions of a pair of distributions with $(\epsilon, 0)$-log ratio distance, we obtain two distributions with statistical distance that is an arbitrary small constant $\epsilon' > 0$. Here we consider $\ell = 1/(4\alpha) = 1/(4c_1 \cdot \epsilon^2)$ repetitions, and therefore

$$\mathrm{final}(V^{\widetilde{\mathsf{A}}}|_{O^{\widetilde{\mathsf{A}}} = O^{\widetilde{\mathsf{B}}}}) \overset{\mathrm{S}}{\approx}_{\epsilon'} \mathrm{final}(V^{\widetilde{\mathsf{A}}}|_{O^{\widetilde{\mathsf{A}}} \neq O^{\widetilde{\mathsf{B}}}}).$$

By picking $c_1$ to be sufficiently large, we can obtain that the leakage in $\Delta$ is $\epsilon' \leq c_{\mathsf{Wul}} \cdot (\alpha')^2$ as required.

### 2.2.1    Efficient Amplification

The (expected) running time of $\Delta_\ell$ is $2^{O(\ell)}$ that for the above choice of $\ell = \Theta(1/\alpha)$ equals $2^{O(1/\alpha)}$. To be useful in a setting when the running time is limited, e.g., in the computational setting, this dependency restricts us to "large" values of $\alpha$. Fortunately, Protocol 2.1 can be modified so that its (expected) running time is only polynomial in $1/\alpha$.

Intuitively, rather than making $\ell$ invocations of $C$ at once, and hope that the tuple of invocations happens to be *useful*: $\overline{O}^{\mathsf{A}} \oplus \overline{O}^{\mathsf{B}} \in \{0^\ell, 1^\ell\}$, the efficient protocol combines smaller tuples of useful invocations, i.e., $\overline{O}^{\mathsf{A}} \oplus \overline{O}^{\mathsf{B}} \in \{0^{\ell'}, 1^{\ell'}\}$, for some $\ell' < \ell$, into a useful tuple of $\ell$ invocations. The advantage is that failing to generate the smaller useful tuples, only "wastes" $\ell'$ invocations of $C$. By recursively sampling the $\ell'$ tuples via the same approach, we get a protocol whose expected running time is $O(\ell^2)$ (rather than $2^{O(\ell)}$).

The actual protocol implements the above intuition in the following way: on parameter $d$, protocol $\Lambda_d$ mimics the interaction of the inefficient protocol $\Delta_{2^d}$ (i.e., the inefficient protocols with sample parameter $2^d$). It does so by using $\Delta_2$ to combines the outputs of two of execution of $\Lambda_{d-1}$. Effectively, this call to $\Delta_2$ combines the two $2^{d-1}$ useful tuples produced by $\Lambda_{d-1}$, into a single $2^d$ useful tuple.

Let $\Lambda_0^C = C$, and recursively define $\Lambda_d$, for $d > 0$, as follows:

**Protocol 2.2** ($\Lambda_d^C = (\widehat{\mathsf{A}}, \widehat{\mathsf{B}})$, **efficient amplification of log-ratio leakage**)
*Channel: $C$.*
*Prameter: log number of sample $d$.*
*Operation: The parties interact in $\Delta_2^{(\Lambda_{d-1}^C)}$.*

By induction, the expected running time of $\Lambda_d^C$ is $4^d$. A more careful analysis yields that the view of $\Lambda_d^C$ can be *simulated* by the view of $\Delta_{2^d}^C$. Indeed, there are exactly $2^d$ useful invocations of $C$ in an execution of $\Lambda_d^C$: invocations whose value was not ignored by the parties, and their distribution is exactly the same as the $2^d$ useful invocations of $C$ in $\Delta_{2^d}^C$. Hence, using $\Lambda_d^C$ with $d = \log 1/4\alpha$, we get a protocol whose expected running time is polynomial in $1/\alpha$ and guarantees the same level of agreement and security as of $\Delta_{1/4\alpha}$.

### 2.3    The Computational Case

So far, we considered information theoretic security. In order to prove Theorem 1.6 (that considers security against PPT adversaries) we note that Definition 1.5 (of computational leakage) is carefully set up to allow the argument of the previous section to be extended to the computational setting. Using the efficient protocol above, the reduction goes through as long as $\alpha$ is a noticeable function of the security parameter.

### 2.4    Two-Party Differentially Private XOR Implies OT

In this section we explain the main ideas that are used in the proof of Theorem 1.10. Our goal is to show that a perfect completeness, $\alpha$-accurate, semi-honest $\epsilon$-DP protocol for computing XOR, implies OT, if $\alpha \geq c \cdot \epsilon^2$ for a sufficiently large constant $c$. In order to prove this, we will show that such a protocol can be used to give a two-party protocol that has $\alpha$-agreement and (computational) $(\epsilon, 0)$-leakage. Such a protocol yields OT by our earlier results.[8]

We remark that there are two natural definitions of "computational differential privacy" in the literature using either *computational indistinguishability* or *simulation* [32]. Definition 1.8 is using indistinguishability, while for our purposes, it is more natural to work with simulation (as using simulation enables us to "'switch back and forth" between the information theoretic setting and the computational setting). In general, these two definitions are not known to be equivalent. For functionalities like XOR, where the inputs of both parties are single bits, however, the two definitions are equivalent by the work of [32]. This means that when considering differential privacy of the XOR function, we can imagine that we are working in an information theoretic setting, in which there is a trusted party, that upon receiving the inputs $x, y$ of the parties, provides party P, with its output $O^P$ and view $V^P$. We will use the following protocol to obtain a "channel" with $\alpha$-agreement and $(\epsilon, 0)$-leakage.

**Protocol 2.3 (DP-XOR to channel)**
1. *A samples $X \leftarrow \{0, 1\}$ and B samples $Y \leftarrow \{0, 1\}$.*
2. *The parties apply the differentially private protocol for computing XOR, using inputs $X$ and $Y$ respectively, and receive outputs $O^A_{DP}, O^B_{DP}$ respectively.*
3. *A sends $R \leftarrow \{0, 1\}$ to B.*
4. *A outputs $O^A = X \oplus R$ and B outputs $O^B_{DP} \oplus Y \oplus R$.*

The intuition behind this protocol is that if $O^B_{DP} = X \oplus Y$, then $O^B = (X \oplus Y) \oplus Y \oplus R = X \oplus R = O^A$. This means that the channel induced by this protocol inherits $\alpha$-agreement from the $\alpha$-accuracy of the original protocol. In Sect. 4 we show that this channel "inherits" log-ratio leakage of $(\epsilon, 0)$ from the fact that the original protocol is $\epsilon$-DP.

## 3  Preliminaries

### 3.1  Notation

We use calligraphic letters to denote sets, uppercase for random variables and functions, lowercase for values. For $a, b \in \mathbb{R}$, let $a \pm b$ stand for the interval $[a - b, a + b]$. For $n \in \mathbb{N}$, let $[n] = \{1, \ldots, n\}$ and $(n) = \{0, \ldots, n\}$. The Hamming distance between two strings $x, y \in \{0, 1\}^n$, is defined by $\mathrm{Ham}(x, y) = \sum_{i \in [n]} x_i \neq y_i$. Let poly denote the set of all polynomials, let PPT stand for probabilistic polynomial time and PPTM denote a PPT TM (Turing machine)

---

[8] We believe that our results extend to the case of $(\epsilon, \delta)$-differential privacy, as long as $\delta = o(\epsilon^2)$, and then we obtain $(\epsilon, \delta)$-leakage, which is sufficient to yield OT. Proving this requires a careful examination of some of the previous work (which was stated for $\delta = 0$) and extending it to nonzero $\delta$, as well as a more careful analysis on our part. We will not do this in this paper.

and let ppt$^{NU}$ stands for a *non-uniform* PPTM. A function $\nu \colon \mathbb{N} \to [0, 1]$ is *negligible*, denoted $\nu(n) = \mathrm{neg}(n)$, if $\nu(n) < 1/p(n)$ for every $p \in$ poly and large enough $n$.

## 3.2   Distributions and Random Variables

Given a distribution, or random variable, $D$, we write $x \leftarrow D$ to indicate that $x$ is selected according to $D$. Given a finite set $\mathcal{S}$, let $s \leftarrow \mathcal{S}$ denote that $s$ is selected according to the uniform distribution over $\mathcal{S}$. The support of $D$, denoted $\mathrm{Supp}(D)$, be defined as $\{u \in \mathcal{U} : D(u) > 0\}$. We will use the following distance measures.

*Statistical Distance.*

**Definition 3.1 (statistical distance).** *The* statistical distance *between two distributions* $P, Q$ *over the same domain* $\mathcal{U}$, *(denote by* $\mathrm{SD}(P, Q)$*) is defined to be:*

$$SD(P, Q) = max_{A \subseteq \mathcal{U}} |\Pr[P \in \mathcal{A}] - \Pr[Q \in \mathcal{A}]|.$$

*We say that* $P, Q$ *are* $\epsilon$-close *(denoted by* $P \overset{S}{\approx}_\epsilon Q$*) if* $\mathrm{SD}(P, Q) \leq \epsilon$.

We use the following fact, see [23] for the proof.

**Proposition 3.2.** *Let* $0 < \epsilon < \mu < 1$, *and let* $(X, Y), (\tilde{X}, \tilde{Y})$ *be two pairs of random variables over the same domain* $\mathcal{X} \times \mathcal{Y}$, *such that* $\mathrm{SD}((X, Y), (\tilde{X}, \tilde{Y})) \leq \epsilon$. *Let* $E_0, E_1 \subseteq \mathcal{X} \times \mathcal{Y}$ *be two sets such that for every* $b \in \{0, 1\}$, $\Pr[(X, Y) \in E_b] \geq \mu$. *Then* $\mathrm{SD}(\tilde{X}|_{\{(\tilde{X}, \tilde{Y}) \in E_0\}}, \tilde{X}|_{\{(\tilde{X}, \tilde{Y}) \in E_1\}}) \leq \mathrm{SD}(X|_{\{(X, Y) \in E_0\}}, X|_{\{(X, Y) \in E_1\}}) + 4\epsilon/\mu$.

**Log-Ratio Distance.** We will also be interested in the following natural notion of "log-ratio distance" which was popularized by the literature on differential privacy.

**Definition 3.3 (Log-Ratio distance).** *Two numbers* $p_0, p_1 \geq 0$ *satisfy* $p_0 \overset{R}{\approx}_{\epsilon, \delta} p_1$ *if for both* $b \in \{0, 1\}$: $p_b \leq e^\epsilon \cdot p_{1-b} + \delta$. *Two distributions* $P, Q$ *over the same domain* $\mathcal{U}$, *are* $(\epsilon, \delta)$-log-ratio-close *(denoted* $P \overset{R}{\approx}_{\epsilon, \delta} Q$*) if for every* $\mathcal{A} \subseteq \mathcal{U}$:

$$\Pr[P \in \mathcal{A}] \overset{R}{\approx}_{\epsilon, \delta} \Pr[Q \in \mathcal{A}].$$

*We let* $\overset{R}{\approx}_\epsilon$ *stands for* $\overset{R}{\approx}_{\epsilon, 0}$.

It is immediate that $D_0 \overset{S}{\approx}_\delta D_1$ iff $D_0 \overset{R}{\approx}_{0, \delta} D_1$, and that $D_0 \overset{R}{\approx}_{\epsilon, \delta} D_1$ implies $D_0 \overset{S}{\approx}_{(e^\epsilon - 1) + \delta} D_1$, and note that for $\epsilon \in [0, 1]$, $e^\epsilon - 1 = O(\epsilon)$. It is also immediate that the log-ratio distance respects data processing.

**Fact 3.4.** *Assume* $P \overset{R}{\approx}_{\epsilon, \delta} Q$, *then* $f(P) \overset{R}{\approx}_{\epsilon, \delta} f(Q)$ *for any (possibly randomized) function* $f$.

*Log-Ratio Distance Under Independent Repetitions.* As demonstrated by the framework of differential privacy, working with this notion of "relative distance" is often a very convenient distance measure between distributions, as it behaves nicely when considering independent executions. Specifically, let $D^\ell$ denote $\ell$ independent copies from $D$, the following follows:

**Theorem 3.5 (Relative distance under independent repetitions).** *If* $D_0 \overset{R}{\approx}_{\epsilon,\delta} D_1$ *then for every* $\ell \geq 1$, *and every* $\delta' \in (0,1)$

$$D_0^\ell \overset{R}{\approx}_{(\eta(\epsilon,\ell,\delta'),\ell\delta+\delta')} D_1^\ell,$$

*where* $\eta(\epsilon, \ell, \delta') = \ell \cdot \epsilon(e^\epsilon - 1) + \epsilon \cdot \sqrt{2\ell \cdot \ln(1/\delta')}$.

We remark that Theorem 3.5 can also be derived by the (much more complex) result on "boosting differential privacy" [11]. However, it can be easily derived directly by a Hoeffding bound, as is done in the full version of this paper.

**Definition 3.6 (Computational indistinguishability).** *Two distribution ensembles* $X = \{X_\kappa\}_{\kappa \in \mathbb{N}}$, $Y = \{Y_\kappa\}_{\kappa \in \mathbb{N}}$ *are [resp non-uniformly] computationally indistinguishable, denoted* $X \overset{C}{\approx} Y$ *[resp.,* $X \overset{nuC}{\approx} Y$*] if for every* PPT *[resp.,* ppt$^{NU}$*]* D:

$$|\Pr[\mathsf{D}(1^\kappa, X_\kappa) = 1] - \Pr[\mathsf{D}(1^\kappa, Y_\kappa) = 1]| \leq \mathrm{neg}(\kappa).$$

### 3.3   Protocols

Let $\Pi = (\mathsf{A}, \mathsf{B})$ be a two-party protocol. Protocol $\Pi$ is PPT if both $\mathsf{A}$ and $\mathsf{B}$ running time is polynomial in their input length. We denote by $(\mathsf{A}(x_\mathsf{A}), \mathsf{B}(x_\mathsf{B}))(z)$ a random execution of $\Pi$ with private inputs $(x_\mathsf{A}, y_\mathsf{A})$, and common input $z$. At the end of such an execution, party $\mathsf{P} \in \{\mathsf{A}, \mathsf{B}\}$ obtains his view $V^\mathsf{P}(x_\mathsf{A}, x_\mathsf{B}, z)$, which may also contain a "designated output" $O^\mathsf{P}(x_\mathsf{A}, x_\mathsf{B}, z)$ (if the protocol specifies such an output). A protocol has Boolean output, if each party outputs a bit.

### 3.4   Two-Output Functionalities and Channels

A two-output *functionality* is just a random function that outputs a tuple of two values in a predefined domain. In the following we omit the two-output term from the notation.

*Channels.* A *channel* is simply a no-input functionality with designated output bits. We naturally identify channels with the random variable characterizes their output.

**Definition 3.7 (Channels).** *A* channel *is a no-input Boolean functionality whose output pair is of the from* $((V^\mathsf{A}, O^\mathsf{A}), (V^\mathsf{B}, O^\mathsf{B}))$ *and for both* $\mathsf{P} \in \{\mathsf{A}, \mathsf{B}\}$, $O^\mathsf{P}$ *is Boolean and determined by* $V^\mathsf{P}$. *A channel has* agreement $\alpha$ *if* $\Pr[O^\mathsf{A} = O^\mathsf{B}] = \frac{1}{2} + \alpha$. *A channel ensemble* $\{C_\kappa\}_{\kappa \in \mathbb{N}}$ *has agreement* $\alpha$ *if* $C_\kappa$ *has agreement* $\alpha(\kappa)$ *for every* $\kappa$.

It is convenient to view a channel as the experiment in which there are two parties A and B. Party A receives "output" $O^A$ and "view" $V^A$, and party B receives "output" $O^B$ and "view" $V^B$.

We identify a no-input Boolean output protocol with the channel "induced" by its semi-honest execution.

**Definition 3.8 (The protocol's channel).** *For a no-input Boolean output protocol $\Pi$, we define the channel* $\mathrm{CHN}(\Pi)$ *by* $\mathrm{CHN}(\Pi) = ((V^A, O^A), (V^B, O^B))$, *for $V^P$ and $O^P$ being the view and output of party P in a random execution of $\Pi$. Similarly, for protocol $\Pi$ whose only input is a security parameter, let* $\mathrm{CHN}(\Pi) = \{\mathrm{CHN}(\Pi)_\kappa = \mathrm{CHN}(\Pi(1^\kappa))\}_{\kappa \in \mathbb{N}}$.

All protocols we construct in this work are *oblivious*, in the sense that given oracle access to a channel, the parties only make use of the channel output (though the channel's view becomes part of the party view).[9]

## 3.5 Secure Computation

We use the standard notion of securely computing a functionality, cf., [13].

**Definition 3.9 (Secure computation).** *A two-party protocol securely computes a functionality $f$, if it does so according to the real/ideal paradigm. We add the term perfectly/statistically/computationally/non-uniform computationally, if the the simulator output is perfect/statistical/computationally indistinguishable/ non-uniformly indistinguishable from the real distribution. The protocol have the above notions of security* against semi-honest adversaries, *if its security only guaranteed to holds against an adversary that follows the prescribed protocol. Finally, for the case of perfectly secure computation, we naturally apply the above notion also to the non-asymptotic case: the protocol with no security parameter perfectly compute a functionality $f$.*

*A two-party protocol securely computes a functionality ensemble $f$ in the $g$-*hybrid model, *if it does so according to the above definition when the parties have access to a trusted party computing $g$. All the above adjectives naturally extend to this setting.*

## 3.6 Oblivious Transfer

The (one-out-of-two) oblivious transfer functionality is defined as follows.

**Definition 3.10 (oblivious transfer functionality $f_{\mathrm{OT}}$).** *The oblivious transfer functionality over $\{0,1\} \times (\{0,1\}^*)^2$ is defined by $f_{\mathrm{OT}}(i, (\sigma_0, \sigma_1)) = (\bot, \sigma_i)$.*

A protocol is $*$ secure OT, for $* \in \{$semi-honest statistically/computationally/ computationally non-uniform$\}$, if it compute the $f_{\mathrm{OT}}$ functionality with $*$ security.

---

[9] This is in accordance with definition of channels in the literature in which the view component of the channel is only accessible to the eavesdropper (and not to the honest parties using the channel).

## 3.7   Two-Party Differential Privacy

We consider differential privacy in the 2-party setting.

**Definition 3.11 (Differentially private functionality).** *A functionality f over input domain $\{0,1\}^n \times \{0,1\}^n$ is $\epsilon$-DP, if the following holds: let $(V_{x,y}^A, V_{x,y}^B) = f(x,y)$, then for every $x, x'$ with $\mathrm{Ham}(x,x') = 1$, $y \in \{0,1\}^n$ and $v \in \mathrm{Supp}(V_{x,y}^B)$:*

$$\Pr\left[V_{x,y}^B = v\right] \le e^\epsilon \cdot \Pr\left[V_{x',y}^B = v\right],$$

*and the for every $y, y'$ with $\mathrm{Ham}(y,y') = 1$, $x \in \{0,1\}^n$ and $v \in \mathrm{Supp}(V_{x,y}^A)$:*

$$\Pr\left[V_{x,y}^A = v\right] \le e^\epsilon \cdot \Pr\left[V_{x,y'}^A = v\right].$$

Note that the above definition is equivalence to asking that $V_{x,y}^B \overset{R}{\approx}_\epsilon V_{x',y}^B$ for any $x, x'$ with $\mathrm{Ham}(x,x') = 1$ and $y$, and analogously for the view of A, for $\overset{R}{\approx}_\epsilon$ being the log-ratio according to Definition 3.3.

We also remark that a more general definition allows also an additive error $\delta$ in the above, making the functionality $(\epsilon, \delta)$-DP. However, for the sake simplicity, we focus on the simpler notion of $\epsilon$-DP stated above.

**Definition 3.12 (Differentially private computation).** *A PPT two-output protocol $\Pi = (A, B)$ over input domain $\{0,1\}^n \times \{0,1\}^n$ is $\epsilon$-IND-DP if the following holds for every $\mathrm{ppt}^{NU}$ B\*, D and $x, x' \in \{0,1\}^n$ with $\mathrm{Ham}(x,x') = 1$: let $V_x^{B^*}$ be the view of B\* in a random execution of $(A(x), B^*)(1^\kappa)$, then*

$$\Pr\left[D(V_x^{B^*}) = 1\right] \le e^{\epsilon(\kappa)} \cdot \Pr\left[D(V_{x'}^{B^*}) = 1\right] + \mathrm{neg}(\kappa),$$

*and the same hold for the secrecy of B.*

*Such a protocol is* semi-honest $\epsilon$-IND-DP, *if the above is only guaranteed to hold for semi-honest adversaries (i.e., for B\* = B).*

## 3.8   Passive Weak Binary Symmetric Channels

We rely on the work of Wullschleger [41] that shows that certain channels imply oblivious transfer. The following notion, adjusted to our formulation, of a "Passive weak binary symmetric channel" was studied in [41].

**Definition 3.13 (Passive weak binary symmetric channels, WBSC, [41]).** *An $(\mu, \epsilon_0, \epsilon_1, p, q)$-WBSC is a channel $C = ((V^A, O^A), (V^B, O^B))$ such that the following holds:*

- *Correctness:* $\Pr\left[O^A = 0\right] \in [\frac{1}{2} - \mu/2, \frac{1}{2} + \mu/2]$
  *and for every $b_A \in \{0,1\}$, $\Pr\left[O^B \neq O^A \mid O^A = b_A\right] \in [\epsilon_0, \epsilon_1]$.*

- *Receiver security:* $(V^A, O^A)|_{O^B=O^A} \overset{S}{\approx}_p (V^A, O^A)|_{O^B \neq O^A}$.[10]
- *Sender security: for every* $b_B \in \{0,1\}$, $V^B|_{O^B=b_B, O^A=0} \overset{S}{\approx}_q V^B|_{O^B=b_B, O^A=1}$.

The following was proven in [41].

**Theorem 3.14 (WBSC implies oblivious transfer).** *There exist a protocol* $\Delta$ *such that the following holds. Let* $\epsilon, \epsilon_0 \in (0, 1/2), p \in (0,1)$ *be such that* $150(1 - (1-p)^2) < (1 - \frac{2\epsilon^2}{\epsilon^2 + (1-\epsilon)^2})^2$, *and* $\epsilon_0 \leq \epsilon$. *Let* $C$ *be a* $(0, \epsilon_0, \epsilon_0, p, p)$-*WBSC. Then* $\Delta(1^\kappa, \epsilon)$ *is a semi-honest statistically secure OT in the C-hybrid model, and its running time is polynomial in* $\kappa$, $1/\epsilon$ *and* $1/(1-2\epsilon)$. *Furthermore, the parties in* $\Delta$ *only makes use of the output bits of the channel.*

Theorem 3.14 considers channels with $\mu = 0$, and $\epsilon_0 = \epsilon_1$. This is equivalent to saying that the channel is balanced (i.e., each of the output bits is uniform) and has $\alpha$-agreement, for $\alpha = \frac{1}{2} - \epsilon_0$. When stated in this form, Theorem 3.14 says that such a channel implies OT if $p = O(\alpha^2)$, and in particular, it is required that $p < \alpha$.

### 3.8.1 Specialized Passive Weak Binary Symmetric Channels

We will be interested in a specific choice of parameters for passive WBSC's, and for this choice, it will be more convenient to work with the following stronger notion of a channel (that is easier to state and argue about, as security is defined in the same terms for both parties).

**Definition 3.15 (Specialized passive weak binary symmetric channels).** *An* $(\epsilon_0, p)$-*SWBSC is a channel* $C = ((V^A, O^A), (V^B, O^B))$ *such that the following holds:*

- *Correctness:* $\Pr[O^A = 0] = \frac{1}{2}$, *and for every* $b_A \in \{0,1\}$,
  $\Pr[O^B \neq O^A \mid O^A = b_A] = \epsilon_0$.
- *Receiver security:* $V^A|_{O^A=O^B} \overset{S}{\approx}_p V^A|_{O^A \neq O^B}$.
- *Sender security:* $V^B|_{O^B=O^A} \overset{S}{\approx}_p V^B|_{O^B \neq O^A}$.

**Proposition 3.16.** *An* $(\epsilon_0, p)$-*SWBSC is a* $(0, \epsilon_0, \epsilon_0, 2p, 2p)$-*WBSC.*

The proof for Proposition 3.16 appears in the full version.

### 3.9 Additional Inequalities

The following fact is proven in the full version of this paper.

**Proposition 3.17.** *The following holds for every* $b \in (0, 1/2)$ *and* $\ell \in \mathbb{N}$ *such that* $b\ell < 1/4$.

$$\frac{(1/2+b)^\ell}{(1/2+b)^\ell + (1/2-b)^\ell} \in [\tfrac{1}{2}(1+b\ell), \tfrac{1}{2}(1+3b\ell)].$$

---

[10] In the requirement above, one can replace $(V^A, O^A)$ with $V^A$ (as by our conventions the latter determines the former). We remark that [41] does not use this convention, and this is why we explicitly include the random variable $O^A$.

# 4    Amplification of Channels with Small Log-Ratio Leakage

In this section we formally define log-ratio leakage and prove our amplification results. We start in Sect. 4.1 with the information theoretic setting, in which we restate and prove Theorems 1.3 and 1.4. In the full version of this paper we extend our result to the computational setting, restating and proving Theorem 1.6.

## 4.1    The Information Theoretic Setting

We start with a definition of log-ratio leakage (restating Definition 1.2 with more formal notation).

**Definition 4.1 (Log-ratio leakage).** *A channel* $((O^A, V^A), (O^B, V^B))$ *has* $(\epsilon, \delta)$-*leakage if*

- *Receiver security:* $V^A|_{O^A=O^B} \overset{R}{\approx}_{\epsilon,\delta} V^A|_{O^A \neq O^B}$.
- *Sender security:* $V^B|_{O^A=O^B} \overset{R}{\approx}_{\epsilon,\delta} V^B|_{O^A \neq O^B}$.

The following theorem is a formal restatement of Theorem 1.3

**Theorem 4.2 (Small log-ratio leakage implies OT).** *There exists an (oblivious)* PPT *protocol* $\Delta$ *and constant* $c_1 > 0$ *such that the following holds. Let* $\epsilon, \delta \in [0,1]$ *be such that* $\delta \leq \epsilon^2$, *and let* $\alpha \leq \alpha_{\max} < 1/8$ *be such that* $\alpha \geq \max\{c_1 \cdot \epsilon^2, \alpha_{\max}/2\}$. *Then for any channel* $C$ *with* $(\epsilon, \delta)$-*leakage and* $\alpha$-*agreement, protocol* $\Delta^C(1^\kappa, 1^{\lfloor 1/\alpha_{\max} \rfloor})$ *is a semi-honest statistically secure OT in the* $C$-*hybrid model.*

Before proving Theorem 4.2, we first show that it is tight. The proof of the following theorem is given in the full paper.

**Theorem 4.3 (Triviality of channels with large leakage).** *There exists a constant* $c_2 > 0$, *such that for every* $\epsilon > 0$ *there is a two-party protocol (with no inputs) where at the end of the protocol, every party* $P \in \{A, B\}$ *has output* $O^P$ *and view* $V^P$. *Moreover, the induced channel* $C = ((V^A, O^A), (V^B, O^B))$ *has* $\alpha$-*agreement, and* $(\epsilon, 0)$-*leakage, for* $\alpha \geq c_2 \cdot \epsilon^2$.

Together, the two theorems show that if $\alpha \geq c_1 \cdot \epsilon^2$ then the channel yields OT, and if $\alpha \leq c_2 \cdot \epsilon^2$ then such a channel can be simulated by a two-party protocol with no inputs (and thus cannot yield OT with information theoretic security).

The proof of Theorem 4.2 is an immediate consequence of the following two lemmata.

Recall (Definition 3.8) that $\text{CHN}(\Pi)$ denotes the channel induced by a random execution of the no-input, Boolean output protocol $\Pi$.

**Lemma 4.4 (Gap amplification).** *There exists an (oblivious)* PPT *protocol $\Delta$ and constant $c_1 > 0$ such that the following holds. Let $\epsilon, \delta, \alpha, \alpha_{\max}$ be parameters satisfying requirements in Theorem 4.2 with respect to $c_1$. Let $C$ be a channel with $(\epsilon, \delta)$-leakage and $\alpha$-agreement, let $\ell = 2^{(\lfloor \log 1/\alpha_{\max} \rfloor - 2)}$ and let $\widetilde{C} = \mathrm{CHN}(\Delta^C(1^\ell))$. Then*

- *$\widetilde{C}$ has $\widetilde{\alpha} \in [1/32, 3/8]$-agreement.*
- *For any $\delta' \in (0,1)$: $\widetilde{C}$ has $(\widetilde{\epsilon}, \widetilde{\delta})$-leakage for $\widetilde{\epsilon} = 2\ell\epsilon^2 + \epsilon\sqrt{2\ell \ln(1/\delta')}$ and $\widetilde{\delta} = \delta' + \ell\delta$.*

**Definition 4.5 (Bounded execution).** *Given Boolean output protocol $\Pi$ and $n \in \mathbb{N}$, let $\mathrm{bound}_n(\Pi)$ be the variant of $\Pi$ that if the protocol does not halt after $n$ steps, it halts and the parties output uniform independent bits.*

**Lemma 4.6 (Large Gap to OT).** *There exist an (oblivious)* PPT *protocol $\Delta$ and constants $n, c > 0$ such that the following holds: let $\Pi$ be a protocol of expected running time at most $t$ that induces a channel $C$ with $\alpha \in [1/32, 3/8]$-agreement, and $(\epsilon, \delta)$-leakage for $\epsilon, \delta \leq c$.*

*Then $\Delta^C(1^\kappa)$ is a semi-honest statistically secure OT in the $C' = \mathrm{CHN}(\mathrm{bound}_{n \cdot t}(\Pi))$ hybrid model.*

We prove the above two Lemmas in the following subsections, but first we will prove Theorem 4.2.

*Proof (Proof of Theorem 4.2).* Let $\ell = 2^{(\lfloor \log 1/\alpha_{\max} \rfloor - 2)}$. By Lemma 4.4, there exists an expected polynomially time protocol $\Lambda$ such that $\Lambda^C(1^\ell)$ induces a channel $\widetilde{C}$ of $\widetilde{\alpha} \in [1/32, 3/8]$-agreement, and $(\widetilde{\epsilon}, \widetilde{\delta})$-leakage for $\widetilde{\epsilon} = 2\ell\epsilon^2 + \epsilon\sqrt{2\ell \ln(1/\delta')}$ and $\widetilde{\delta} = \delta' + \ell\delta$, for any $\delta' \in (0,1)$.

Let $t \in \mathrm{poly}$ be a polynomial that bounds the expected running time of $\Lambda$. By Lemma 4.6, there exist universal constants $n, c$ and PPT protocol $\Delta$, such that if

$$\widetilde{\epsilon} = 2\ell\epsilon^2 + \epsilon\sqrt{2\ell \ln(1/\delta')} \leq c \qquad \text{and} \qquad \widetilde{\delta} = \delta' + \ell\delta \leq c \qquad (1)$$

then the protocol $\Gamma$, defined by $\Gamma^C(1^\kappa, 1^{\lfloor 1/\alpha_{\max} \rfloor}) = \Delta^{C'}(1^\kappa)$ for $C' = \mathrm{CHN}(\mathrm{bound}_{n \cdot t(\ell)}(\Lambda^C(1^\ell)))$, is a semi-honest statistically secure OT. Hence, we conclude the proof noting that Eq. (1) holds by setting $\delta' = \ell\delta$ and choosing $c_1$ (the constant in Theorem 4.2) to be sufficiently large.

Lemma 4.6 is proved in Sect. 4.1.3 using the amplification result of [41]. Toward proving Lemma 4.4, our main technical contribution, we start in Sect. 4.1.1 by presenting an inefficient protocol implementing the desired channel. In Sect. 4.1.2 we show how to bootstrap the the above protocol into an efficient one.

### 4.1.1 Inefficient Amplification

The following protocol implements the channel stated in Lemma 4.4, but its running time is *exponential* in $1/\alpha_{max}$.

**Protocol 4.7 (Protocol $\Delta^C = (\widetilde{A}, \widetilde{B})$)**

*Oracle: channel $C = ((V^A, O^A), (V^B, O^B))$.*
*Input: $1^\ell$.*
*Operation: The parties repeat the following process until it produces outputs:*

1. *The parties (jointly) call the channel $C$ for $\ell$ times. Let $\overline{o}^A = (o_1^A, \ldots, o_\ell^A), \overline{o}^B = (o_1^B, \ldots, o_\ell^B)$ be the outputs.*
2. *$\widetilde{A}$ computes and sends $\mathcal{S} = \{\overline{o}^A, 1^\ell \oplus \overline{o}^A\}$ according to their lexical order to $\widetilde{B}$.*
3. *$\widetilde{B}$ inform $\widetilde{A}$ whether $\overline{o}^B \in \mathcal{S}$.*
   *If positive, both parties output the index of their tuple in $\mathcal{S}$ (and the protocol ends).*

We show that the channel induced by protocol $\Delta^C(1^\ell)$ satisfies all the requirement of Lemma 4.4 apart from its expected running time (which is exponential in $\ell$).

Let $\widetilde{C} = \text{CHN}(\Delta^C(\ell)) = ((V^{\widetilde{A}}, O^{\widetilde{A}}), ((V^{\widetilde{B}}, O^{\widetilde{B}}))$. The following function outputs the calls to $C$ made in the final iteration in $\widetilde{C}$.

**Definition 4.8 (Final calls).** *For $c \in \text{Supp}(\widetilde{C})$ let $\text{final}(c)$ denote the output of the $\ell$ calls to $C$ made in the final iteration in $c$.*

We make the following observation about the final calls.

**Claim 4.9.** *The following holds for $((\cdot, \overline{O}^A), (\cdot, \overline{O}^B)) = \text{final}(\widetilde{C} = ((\cdot, O^{\widetilde{A}}), (\cdot, O^{\widetilde{B}})))$.*

- *$O^{\widetilde{A}} = O^{\widetilde{B}}$ iff $\overline{O}^A = \overline{O}^B$.*
- *Let $C^\ell = ((\cdot, (O^A)^\ell), (\cdot, (O^B)^\ell))$ be the random variable induced by taking $\ell$ copies of $C$ and let $E$ be the event that $(O^B)^\ell \in \{(O^A)^\ell, (O^A)^\ell \oplus 1^\ell\}$. Then $\text{final}(\widetilde{C}) \equiv C^\ell|_E$.*

*Proof.* Immediate by construction. ∎

*Agreement.*

**Claim 4.10 (Agreement).** $\Pr\left[O^{\widetilde{A}} = O^{\widetilde{B}}\right] \in [17/32, 7/8]$.

*Proof.* By Claim 4.9,

$$\Pr\left[O^{\widetilde{A}} = O^{\widetilde{B}}\right] = \frac{\Pr\left[(O^A)^\ell = (O^B)^\ell \mid E\right]}{\Pr\left[(O^A)^\ell = (O^B)^\ell \mid E\right] + \Pr\left[(O^A)^\ell \oplus (O^B)^\ell = 1^\ell \mid E\right]} \tag{2}$$

$$= \frac{\Pr\left[(O^A)^\ell = (O^B)^\ell\right]}{\Pr\left[(O^A)^\ell = (O^B)^\ell\right] + \Pr\left[(O^A)^\ell \oplus (O^B)^\ell = 1^\ell\right]}$$

$$= \frac{(1/2 + \alpha)^\ell}{(1/2 + \alpha)^\ell + (1/2 - \alpha)^\ell}.$$

Since, $\ell = 2^{(\lfloor \log 1/\alpha_{max} \rfloor - 2)}$ and $\alpha_{max}/2 \leq \alpha \leq \alpha_{max}$, we get that $1/4 \geq \ell \cdot \alpha \geq 1/16$. By Proposition 3.17,

$$\frac{(1/2 + \alpha)^\ell}{(1/2 + \alpha)^\ell + (1/2 - \alpha)^\ell} \in [\tfrac{1}{2}(1 + \alpha\ell), \tfrac{1}{2}(1 + 3\alpha\ell)] \tag{3}$$

Thus, $\Pr\left[O^{\widetilde{A}} = O^{\widetilde{B}}\right] \in [17/32, 7/8]$, which concludes the proof.

*Leakage.*

**Claim 4.11 (Leakage).** $\widetilde{C}$ *has* $(\widetilde{\epsilon}, \widetilde{\delta})$-*leakage, where* $\widetilde{\epsilon} = 2\ell\epsilon^2 + \epsilon\sqrt{2\ell \ln(1/\delta')}$ *and* $\widetilde{\delta} = \delta' + \ell\delta$ *for every* $\delta' \in (0, 1)$.

*Proof.* We need to prove that for both $\mathsf{P} \in \{\mathsf{A}, \mathsf{B}\}$:

$$V^{\widetilde{\mathsf{P}}}|_{O^{\widetilde{A}} = O^{\widetilde{B}}} \overset{\mathsf{R}}{\approx}_{(\widetilde{\epsilon}, \widetilde{\delta})} V^{\widetilde{\mathsf{P}}}|_{O^{\widetilde{A}} \neq O^{\widetilde{B}}} \tag{4}$$

By assumption $C$ has $(\epsilon, \delta)$-leakage. Thus, by Theorem 3.5,

$$(V^{\mathsf{P}})^\ell|_{(O^{\mathsf{A}})^\ell = (O^{\mathsf{B}})^\ell} \overset{\mathsf{R}}{\approx}_{(\widetilde{\epsilon}, \widetilde{\delta})} (V^{\mathsf{P}})^\ell|_{(O^{\mathsf{A}})^\ell = (O^{\mathsf{B}})^\ell \oplus 1^\ell} \tag{5}$$

Let $((\overline{V}^{\mathsf{A}}, \overline{O}^{\mathsf{A}}), (\overline{V}^{\mathsf{B}}, \overline{O}^{\mathsf{B}})) = \mathrm{final}(\widetilde{C})$. By the above and Claim 4.9,

$$\overline{V}^{\mathsf{P}}|_{O^{\widetilde{A}} = O^{\widetilde{B}}} \overset{\mathsf{R}}{\approx}_{(\widetilde{\epsilon}, \widetilde{\delta})} \overline{V}^{\mathsf{P}}|_{O^{\widetilde{A}} \neq O^{\widetilde{B}}} \tag{6}$$

Equation (4) now follows by a data processing argument: let $f$ be the randomized function that on input $v \in \mathrm{Supp}(\overline{V}^{\mathsf{P}})$ outputs a random sample from $V^{\widetilde{\mathsf{P}}}|_{\overline{V}^{\mathsf{P}} = v}$. It easy to verify that $f(\overline{V}^{\mathsf{P}}|_{O^{\widetilde{A}} = O^{\widetilde{B}}}) = V^{\widetilde{\mathsf{P}}}|_{O^{\widetilde{A}} = O^{\widetilde{B}}}$ and $f(\overline{V}^{\mathsf{P}}|_{O^{\widetilde{A}} \neq O^{\widetilde{B}}}) \equiv V^{\widetilde{\mathsf{P}}}|_{O^{\widetilde{A}} \neq O^{\widetilde{B}}}$. Thus Eq. (4) follows by Fact 3.4.

### 4.1.2 Efficient Amplification

We will show how to make Protocol 4.7 protocol more efficient in terms of $\alpha$. The resulting protocol will run in poly-time even if $\alpha$ is inverse polynomial. The efficient amplification protocol is defined as follows. Let $\Delta$ be the (inefficient) protocol from Protocol 4.7.

**Protocol 4.12** *[ Protocol* $\Lambda^C = (\widehat{\mathsf{A}}, \widehat{\mathsf{B}})]$

*Oracle: Channel $C$.*
*Prameter: Recursion depth $d$.*
*Operation: The parties interact in* $\Delta^{\Lambda^C(d-1)}(2)$*, letting* $\Lambda^C(0) = C$.

We show that the channel induced by protocol $\Lambda^C(d)$ satisfies all the requirement of Lemma 4.4. But we first show that the expected running time of $\Lambda^C(d)$ is $O(4^d)$, and therefore, the protocol that on input $1^\ell$ invoke $\Lambda^C(\log \ell)$, is PPT, as stated in Lemma 4.4.

*Running Time.*

**Claim 4.13 (Expected running time).** *Let $C$ be a channel, the for any $d \in \mathbb{N}$ the expected running time of $\Lambda^C(d)$ is at most $O(4^d)$.*

We will use the following claim:

**Claim 4.14.** *For any channel $C$, $\Delta^C(2)$ makes in expectation at most 4 calls to $C$.*

*Proof.* Let $C$ with a channel with agreement $\alpha \in [-1/2, 1/2]$. Let $\overline{O}^{\mathsf{A}} = (O_1^{\mathsf{A}}, O_2^{\mathsf{A}})$ and $\overline{O}^{\mathsf{B}} = (O_1^{\mathsf{B}}, O_2^{\mathsf{B}})$ denote the outputs of two invocations of $C$, respectively. By construction, $\Delta^C(2)$ concludes on the event $E = \left\{ (O_1^{\mathsf{B}}, O_2^{\mathsf{B}}) \in \{\overline{O}^{\mathsf{A}}, 1^2 \oplus \overline{O}^{\mathsf{A}}\} \right\}$. It is clear that $\Pr[E] = (\frac{1}{2} + \alpha)^2 + (\frac{1}{2} - \alpha)^2 = \frac{1}{2} + \alpha^2 \geq \frac{1}{2}$. Thus, the expected number of invocations preformed by $\Delta^C(2)$ is bounded is 4.

We now prove *Claim* 4.13 using the above claim.

*Proof. (Proof of Claim 4.13).* For $d \in \mathbb{N}$, let $T(d)$ denote the expected runtime of $\Lambda^C(d)$. By Claim 4.14,

$$T(d) = 4 \cdot T(d-1) + O(1), \tag{7}$$

letting $T(0) = 1$. Thus, $T(d) \in O(4^d)$.

Let $\widehat{C}_d = \mathrm{CHN}(\Lambda^C(d)) = ((V_d^{\widehat{\mathsf{A}}}, O_d^{\widehat{\mathsf{A}}}), ((V_d^{\widehat{\mathsf{B}}}, O_d^{\widehat{\mathsf{B}}}))$. The following function outputs the "important" calls of $C$ made in $\widehat{C}_d$, the ones used to set the final outcome.

Let $\circ$ denote vectors concatenation.

**Definition 4.15 (Important calls).** *For $d \in \mathbb{N}$ and $c \in \mathrm{Supp}(\widehat{C}_d)$, let* final$(c) = (c_0, c_1)$ *be the two calls to $\Lambda^C(d-1)$ done in final execution of $\Delta^{\Lambda^C(d-1)}(2)$ in $c$. Define* important$(c) = $ important$(c_0) \circ$ important$(c_1)$*, letting* important$(c) = c$ *for $c \in \mathrm{Supp}(\widehat{C}_0)$.*

Similarly to the analysis of inefficient protocol, the crux is the following observation about the important calls.

**Claim 4.16.** *Let $d \in \mathbb{N}$ and set $\ell = 2^d$. The following holds for $((\cdot, \overline{O}^{\mathsf{A}}), (\cdot, \overline{O}^{\mathsf{B}})) = $ important$(\widehat{C}_d = ((\cdot, O^{\widehat{\mathsf{A}}}), (\cdot, O^{\widehat{\mathsf{B}}})))$.*

- $O^{\widehat{\mathsf{A}}} = O^{\widehat{\mathsf{B}}}$ *iff $\overline{O}^{\mathsf{A}} = \overline{O}^{\mathsf{B}}$.*
- *Let $C^\ell = ((\cdot, (O^{\mathsf{A}})^\ell), (\cdot, (O^{\mathsf{B}})^\ell))$ be the random variable induced by taking $\ell$ copies of $C$ and let $E$ be the event that $(O^{\mathsf{B}})^\ell \in \{(O^{\mathsf{A}})^\ell, (O^{\mathsf{A}})^\ell \oplus 1^\ell\}$. Then* important$(\widehat{C}_d) \equiv C^\ell|_E$.

We prove Claim 4.16 below, but first use it for proving Lemma 4.4.

*Agreement.*

**Claim 4.17 (Agreement).** $\Pr\left[O^{\hat{A}} = O^{\hat{B}}\right] \in [17/32, 7/8]$.

*Proof.* The proof follows by Claim 4.16, using the same lines as the proof that Claim 4.10 follows from Claim 4.9.

*Leakage.*

**Claim 4.18 (Leakage).** $\hat{C}$ *has* $(\tilde{\epsilon}, \tilde{\delta})$-*leakage, where* $\tilde{\epsilon} = 2\ell\epsilon^2 + \epsilon\sqrt{2\ell\ln(1/\delta')}$ *and* $\tilde{\delta} = \delta' + \ell\delta$ *for every* $\delta' \in (0,1)$.

*Proof.* The proof follows by Claim 4.16 and a data processing argument, using similar lines to the proof that Claim 4.11 follows from Claim 4.9.

*Proving Lemma 4.4.*

*Proof (Proof of Lemma 4.4).* Consider the protocol $T^C(1^\ell) = \Lambda^C(\lfloor \log \ell \rfloor)$. The proof that T satisfies the requirements of Lemma 4.4 immediately follows by Claims 4.13, 4.17 and 4.18.

*Proving Claim 4.16.*

*Proof (Proof of Claim 4.16).* First note that the first item in the claim immediately follows by construction. We now prove the second item.

Let $d \in \mathbb{N}$ and let $\ell = 2^d$. For $C^\ell = ((\cdot, (O^A)^\ell), (\cdot, (O^B)^\ell))$, let $D_\ell$ be the distribution of $C^\ell|_{\{(O^B)^\ell \in \{(O^A)^\ell, (O^A)^\ell \oplus 1^\ell\}\}}$. We need to prove that

$$\text{important}(\hat{C}_d) \equiv D_\ell$$

We prove the claim by induction on $d$. The base case $d = 1$ follows by Claim 4.9.

Fix $d > 1$, for $j \in \{0,1\}$, let $\hat{C}_{d-1,j}$ be an invocations of the channel on input $d-1$ and let $((\cdot, \overline{O}_j^A), (\cdot, \overline{O}_j^B)) = \text{important}(\hat{C}_{d-1,j})$. By the induction hypothesis,

$$\text{important}(\hat{C}_{d-1,j}) \equiv D_{\ell/2} \tag{8}$$

The key observation is that by construction, the event $\text{final}(\hat{C}_d) = \hat{C}_{d-1,0} \circ \hat{C}_{d-1,1}$ occurs if and only if,

$$\overline{O}_0^B \circ \overline{O}_1^B \in \left\{\overline{O}_0^A \circ \overline{O}_1^A, 1^\ell \oplus \overline{O}_0^A \circ \overline{O}_1^A\right\} \tag{9}$$

Recall this means that,

$$\text{important}(\hat{C}_d) = \left(\text{important}(\hat{C}_{d-1,0}) \circ \text{important}(\hat{C}_{d-1,1})\right)|_{\overline{E}}$$

where $\overline{E} = \left\{\overline{O}_0^B \circ \overline{O}_1^B \in \left\{\overline{O}_0^A \circ \overline{O}_1^A, 1^\ell \oplus \overline{O}_0^A \circ \overline{O}_1^A\right\}\right\}$. The above observations yields that $\text{important}(\hat{C}_d) \equiv D_\ell$.

### 4.1.3    From Channels with Large Gap to OT

**Definition 4.19.** *A  channel*  $C = ((V^A, O^A), (V^B, O^B))$  *is  balanced  if*  $\Pr\left[O^A = 1\right] = \Pr\left[O^B = 1\right] = \frac{1}{2}.$

We use the following claim.

**Claim 4.20.** *Let*  $C = ((V^A, O^A), (V^B, O^B))$  *be a balanced channel that has*  $\alpha \in [\alpha_{\min}, \alpha_{\max}]$-*agreement and*  $(\epsilon, \delta)$-*leakage. Then*  $C$  *is a*  $(\epsilon_0, p)$-*SWBSC for some*  $\epsilon_0 \in [\frac{1}{2} - \alpha_{\max}, \frac{1}{2} - \alpha_{\min}],$  *and*  $p = 2\epsilon + \delta.$

*Proof.* For every  $\mathsf{P} \in \{\mathsf{A}, \mathsf{B}\}$  we have that,  $V^{\widetilde{\mathsf{P}}}|_{O^{\widetilde{\mathsf{A}}} = O^{\widetilde{\mathsf{B}}}} \overset{\mathsf{R}}{\approx}_{(\epsilon, \delta)} V^{\widetilde{\mathsf{P}}}|_{O^{\widetilde{\mathsf{A}}} \neq O^{\widetilde{\mathsf{B}}}}$, thus by definition it follows that,  $V^{\widetilde{\mathsf{P}}}|_{O^{\widetilde{\mathsf{A}}} = O^{\widetilde{\mathsf{B}}}} \overset{\mathsf{S}}{\approx}_{(2\epsilon + \delta)} V^{\widetilde{\mathsf{P}}}|_{O^{\widetilde{\mathsf{A}}} \neq O^{\widetilde{\mathsf{B}}}}$, and the claim holds.

The following claim, states that a given a channel with bounded leakage and agreement we can construct a new protocol using the olds one, that has the same leakage and agreement, while having the additional property of being balanced.

**Claim 4.21.** *There exists a constant-time single oracle call protocol*  $\Delta$  *such that for every channel*  $C$, *the channel*  $\widetilde{C}$  *induced by*  $\Delta^C$  *is balanced and has the same agreement and leakage as of*  $C$.

**Protocol 4.22.** *[Protocol*  $\Delta = (\widetilde{\mathsf{A}}, \widetilde{\mathsf{B}})$*]*

*Oracle: Channel*  $C$.
*Operation:*

1. *The parties (jointly) call the channel*  $C$. *Let*  $o^A$  *and*  $o^B$  *denote their output respectively.*
2.  $\widetilde{\mathsf{A}}$  *sends*  $r \leftarrow \{0, 1\}$  *to*  $\widetilde{\mathsf{B}}$.
3.  $\widetilde{\mathsf{A}}$  *outputs*  $o^A \oplus r$  *and*  $\widetilde{\mathsf{B}}$  *outputs*  $o^B \oplus r$.

*Proof (Proof of Claim 4.21).* Let  $\widetilde{C} = \mathrm{CHN}(\Delta^C)$. By construction  $\widetilde{C}$  is balanced and has  $\alpha$-agreement. Finally, by a data processing argument,  $\widetilde{C}$  has the same leakage as  $C$.

*Proving Lemma 4.6.*

*Proof (Proof of Lemma 4.6).* Set  $n = 10^8$, let  $C = \mathrm{CHN}(\Pi)$, let  $\Pi' = \mathrm{bound}_{n \cdot t}(\Pi)$  and let  $C' = \mathrm{CHN}(\Pi')$. By Markov inequality,

$$C' \overset{\mathsf{S}}{\approx}_{1/n} C \tag{10}$$

By Claim 4.21, there exist a protocol  $\Delta$  such that  $\Delta^C$  is balanced and has the same leakage and agreement as  $C$. Moreover, since  $\Delta$  only uses one call to the channel  $C$, by data processing argument,

$$\mathrm{CHN}(\Delta^{C'}) \overset{\mathsf{S}}{\approx}_{1/n} \mathrm{CHN}(\Delta^C) \tag{11}$$

By Claim 4.21, $\Delta^{C'}$ is also balanced. Claim 4.20 yields that $\Delta^C$ is a $(15/32, p)$-WBSC for $p = 2\epsilon + \delta$. Hence, using Proposition 3.2, we get that $\Delta^{C'}$ is $(\epsilon_0, \overline{p})$-WBSC, for $\epsilon_0 = \epsilon + 1/10^8$ and $\overline{p} = p + 4/10^7$.

In the following we use Theorem 3.14 to show that $\Delta^{C'}$ can be used to construct semi-honest statistically secure OT. To do this, we need to prove that

$$150(1 - (1 - 2\overline{p})^2) < (1 - \frac{2\epsilon_0^2}{\epsilon_0^2 + (1 - \epsilon_0)^2})^2 \tag{12}$$

Indeed, since $(1 - 2\frac{\epsilon_0^2}{\epsilon_0^2 + (1-\epsilon_0)^2})^2 \geq 1/100$, for $\delta' = 1/10^7$ it holds that, for small enough $c$,

$$(1 - (1 - 2\overline{p})^2) \leq 4\overline{p} \leq 4p + 2/10^6 \leq 2\epsilon + \delta + 2/10^6 \tag{13}$$
$$\leq 3c + 2/10^6$$
$$< 1/(150 \cdot 100).$$

And therefore $\Delta^{C'}$ satisfies the requirement of Theorem 3.14. Let $\Gamma$ be the protocol guaranteed in Theorem 3.14, and let $\widetilde{\Gamma}^{C'}(1^\kappa) = \Gamma^{\Delta^{C'}}(1^\kappa, 49/100)$. By Eq. (12) and Theorem 3.14, $\widetilde{\Gamma}^{C'}(1^\kappa)$ is statistically secure semi-honest OT. Since $\epsilon_0$ is a bounded from 0 and 1/2 by constants, $\widetilde{\Gamma}$ running time in polynomial in $\kappa$.

## 4.2   The Computational Setting

Due to space limitations, the remainder of this section appears in the full version of this paper [23].

### Conclusion and Open Problems

A natural open problem is to characterize the (Boolean) AND differential private functionality. That is, show a similar dichotomy that characterizes which accuracy and leakage require OT.

More generally, the task of understanding and characterizing other (non Boolean) differentially private functionalities like hamming distance and inner product remains open.

**Acknowledgement.** We are very grateful to Kobbi Nissim, Eran Omri and Ido Abulafya for helpful conversations and advice. We thank the anonymous referees for detailed and very helpful comments.

# References

1. Aiello, B., Ishai, Y., Reingold, O.: Priced oblivious transfer: how to sell digital goods. In: Pfitzmann, B. (ed.) EUROCRYPT 2001. LNCS, vol. 2045, pp. 119–135. Springer, Heidelberg (2001). https://doi.org/10.1007/3-540-44987-6_8

2. Beimel, A., Malkin, T., Micali, S.: The all-or-nothing nature of two-party secure computation. In: Wiener, M. (ed.) CRYPTO 1999. LNCS, vol. 1666, pp. 80–97. Springer, Heidelberg (1999). https://doi.org/10.1007/3-540-48405-1_6

3. Beimel, A., Nissim, K., Omri, E.: Distributed private data analysis: simultaneously solving how and what. In: Wagner, D. (ed.) CRYPTO 2008. LNCS, vol. 5157, pp. 451–468. Springer, Heidelberg (2008). https://doi.org/10.1007/978-3-540-85174-5_25

4. Bellare, M., Micali, S.: Non-interactive oblivious transfer and applications. In: Brassard, G. (ed.) CRYPTO 1989. LNCS, vol. 435, pp. 547–557. Springer, New York (1990). https://doi.org/10.1007/0-387-34805-0_48

5. Bennett, C.H., Brassard, G., Crépeau, C., Maurer, U.M.: Generalized privacy amplification. IEEE Trans. Inf. Theory **41**(6), 1915–1923 (1995)

6. Chan, T.-H.H., Shi, E., Song, D.: Optimal lower bound for differentially private multi-party aggregation. In: Epstein, L., Ferragina, P. (eds.) ESA 2012. LNCS, vol. 7501, pp. 277–288. Springer, Heidelberg (2012). https://doi.org/10.1007/978-3-642-33090-2_25

7. Crépeau, C.: Efficient cryptographic protocols based on noisy channels. In: Fumy, W. (ed.) EUROCRYPT 1997. LNCS, vol. 1233, pp. 306–317. Springer, Heidelberg (1997). https://doi.org/10.1007/3-540-69053-0_21

8. Crépeau, C., Kilian, J.: Achieving oblivious transfer using weakened security assumptions. In: 29th Annual Symposium on Foundations of Computer Science, pp. 42–52. IEEE (1988)

9. Dwork, C., Rothblum, G.N.: Concentrated differential privacy. arXiv preprint arXiv:1603.01887 (2016)

10. Dwork, C., McSherry, F., Nissim, K., Smith, A.: Calibrating noise to sensitivity in private data analysis. In: Halevi, S., Rabin, T. (eds.) TCC 2006. LNCS, vol. 3876, pp. 265–284. Springer, Heidelberg (2006). https://doi.org/10.1007/11681878_14

11. Dwork, C., Rothblum, G.N., Vadhan, S.: Boosting and differential privacy. In: Proceedings of the 51st Annual Symposium on Foundations of Computer Science (FOCS), pp. 51–60 (2010)

12. Even, S., Goldreich, O., Lempel, A.: A randomized protocol for signing contracts. Commun. ACM **28**(6), 637–647 (1985)

13. Goldreich, O.: Foundations of Cryptography - Volume 2: Basic Applications. Cambridge University Press (2004)

14. Goldreich, O., Micali, S., Wigderson, A.: How to play any mental game or a completeness theorem for protocols with honest majority. In: STOC 19, pp. 218–229 (1987)

15. Goldreich, O., Krawczyk, H., Luby, M.: On the existence of pseudorandom generators. SIAM J. Comput. **22**(6), 1163–1175 (1993)

16. Goyal, V., Mironov, I., Pandey, O., Sahai, A.: Accuracy-privacy tradeoffs for two-party differentially private protocols. In: Canetti, R., Garay, J.A. (eds.) CRYPTO 2013. LNCS, vol. 8042, pp. 298–315. Springer, Heidelberg (2013). https://doi.org/10.1007/978-3-642-40041-4_17

17. Goyal, V., Khurana, D., Mironov, I., Pandey, O., Sahai, A.: Do distributed differentially-private protocols require oblivious transfer? In: LIPIcs-Leibniz International Proceedings in Informatics, vol. 55. Schloss Dagstuhl-Leibniz-Zentrum fuer Informatik (2016)
18. Haitner, I.: Implementing oblivious transfer using collection of dense trapdoor permutations. In: Naor, M. (ed.) TCC 2004. LNCS, vol. 2951, pp. 394–409. Springer, Heidelberg (2004). https://doi.org/10.1007/978-3-540-24638-1_22
19. Haitner, I.: A parallel repetition theorem for any interactive argument. SIAM J. Comput. **42**(6), 2487–2501 (2013)
20. Haitner, I., Harnik, D., Reingold, O.: On the power of the randomized iterate. SIAM J. Comput. **40**(6), 1486–1528 (2011)
21. Haitner, I., Omri, E., Zarosim, H.: Limits on the usefulness of random oracles. J. Cryptol. **29**(2), 283–335 (2016)
22. Haitner, I., Nissim, K., Omri, E., Shaltiel, R., Silbak, J.: Computational two-party correlation. In: Proceedings of the 59th Annual Symposium on Foundations of Computer Science (FOCS) (2018)
23. Haitner, I., Mazor, N., Shaltiel, R., Silbak, J.: Channels of small log-ratio leakage and characterization of two-party differentially private computation (2019/616) (2019)
24. Harnik, D., Naor, M., Reingold, O., Rosen, A.: Completeness in two-party secure computation: a computational view. J. Cryptol. **19**(4), 521–552 (2006)
25. Håstad, J., Pass, R., Wikström, D., Pietrzak, K.: An efficient parallel repetition theorem. In: Micciancio, D. (ed.) TCC 2010. LNCS, vol. 5978, pp. 1–18. Springer, Heidelberg (2010). https://doi.org/10.1007/978-3-642-11799-2_1
26. Holenstein, T.: Pseudorandom generators from one-way functions: a simple construction for any hardness. In: Halevi, S., Rabin, T. (eds.) TCC 2006. LNCS, vol. 3876, pp. 443–461. Springer, Heidelberg (2006). https://doi.org/10.1007/11681878_23
27. Kairouz, P., Oh, S., Viswanath, P.: Differentially private multi-party computation: optimality of non-interactive randomized response. arXiv preprint arXiv:1407.1546 (2014)
28. Kalai, Y.T.: Smooth projective hashing and two-message oblivious transfer. In: Cramer, R. (ed.) EUROCRYPT 2005. LNCS, vol. 3494, pp. 78–95. Springer, Heidelberg (2005). https://doi.org/10.1007/11426639_5
29. Khurana, D., Maji, H.K., Sahai, A.: Black-box separations for differentially private protocols. In: Sarkar, P., Iwata, T. (eds.) ASIACRYPT 2014. LNCS, vol. 8874, pp. 386–405. Springer, Heidelberg (2014). https://doi.org/10.1007/978-3-662-45608-8_21
30. Maurer, U.M.: Secret key agreement by public discussion from common information. IEEE Trans. Inf. Theory **39**(3), 733–742 (1993)
31. McGregor, A., Mironov, I., Pitassi, T., Reingold, O., Talwar, K., Vadhan, S.P.: The limits of two-party differential privacy. In: Electronic Colloquium on Computational Complexity (ECCC), p. 106 (2011). Preliminary version in FOCS 10
32. Mironov, I., Pandey, O., Reingold, O., Vadhan, S.: Computational differential privacy. In: Halevi, S. (ed.) CRYPTO 2009. LNCS, vol. 5677, pp. 126–142. Springer, Heidelberg (2009). https://doi.org/10.1007/978-3-642-03356-8_8
33. Naor, M., Pinkas, B.: Efficient oblivious transfer protocols. In: Proceedings of the Twelfth Annual ACM-SIAM Symposium on Discrete Algorithms, pp. 448–457. Society for Industrial and Applied Mathematics (2001)
34. Nascimento, A.C., Winter, A.: On the oblivious-transfer capacity of noisy resources. IEEE Trans. Inf. Theory **54**(6), 2572–2581 (2008)

35. Peikert, C., Vaikuntanathan, V., Waters, B.: A framework for efficient and composable oblivious transfer. In: Wagner, D. (ed.) CRYPTO 2008. LNCS, vol. 5157, pp. 554–571. Springer, Heidelberg (2008). https://doi.org/10.1007/978-3-540-85174-5_31

36. Prabhakaran, V.M., Prabhakaran, M.M.: Assisted common information with an application to secure two-party sampling. IEEE Trans. Inf. Theory 60(6), 3413–3434 (2014)

37. Rabin, M.O.: How to exchange secrets by oblivious transfer. TR-81, Harvard (1981)

38. Warner, S.L.: Randomized response: a survey technique for eliminating evasive answer bias. J. Am. Stat. Assoc. 60(309), 63–69 (1965)

39. Wolf, S., Wultschleger, J.: Zero-error information and applications in cryptography. In: IEEE Information Theory Workshop, pp. 1–6. IEEE (2004)

40. Wullschleger, J.: Oblivious-Transfer Amplification. Ph.D. thesis, ETH Zurich (2008)

41. Wullschleger, J.: Oblivious transfer from weak noisy channels. In: Reingold, O. (ed.) TCC 2009. LNCS, vol. 5444, pp. 332–349. Springer, Heidelberg (2009). https://doi.org/10.1007/978-3-642-00457-5_20

42. Yao, A.C.: Protocols for secure computations. In: Proceedings of the 23th Annual Symposium on Foundations of Computer Science (FOCS), pp. 160–164 (1982)

43. Yao, A.C.: How to generate and exchange secrets. In: Proceedings of the 27th Annual Symposium on Foundations of Computer Science (FOCS), pp. 162–167. IEEE Computer Society (1986)

# On Perfectly Secure 2PC
# in the OT-Hybrid Model

Bar Alon[✉] and Anat Paskin-Cherniavsky

Department of Computer Science, Ariel University, Ariel, Israel
alonbar08@gmail.com, anatpc@ariel.ac.il

**Abstract.** A well known result by Kilian [22] (ACM 1988) asserts that
general secure two computation (2PC) with statistical security, can be
based on OT. Specifically, in the client-server model, where only one
party – the client – receives an output, Kilian's result shows that given
the ability to call an ideal oracle that computes OT, two parties can
securely compute an arbitrary function of their inputs with unconditional security. Ishai et al. [19] (EUROCRYPT 2011) further showed
that this can be done efficiently for every two-party functionality in $NC^1$
in a *single round*.

However, their results only achieve statistical security, namely, it is
allowed to have some error in security. This leaves open the natural question as to which client-server functionalities can be computed with perfect security in the OT-hybrid model, and what is the round complexity
of such computation. So far, only a handful of functionalities were known
to have such protocols. In addition to the obvious theoretical appeal of
the question towards better understanding secure computation, perfect,
as opposed to statistical reductions, may be useful for designing secure
multiparty protocols with high concrete efficiency, achieved by eliminating the dependence on a security parameter.

In this work, we identify a large class of client-server functionalities
$f : \mathcal{X} \times \mathcal{Y} \mapsto \{0,1\}$, where the server's domain $\mathcal{X}$ is larger than the
client's domain $\mathcal{Y}$, that have a perfect reduction to OT. Furthermore,
our reduction is 1-round using an oracle to secure evaluation of many
parallel invocations of $\binom{2}{1}$-bit-OT, as done by Ishai et al. [19] (EURO-
CRYPT 2011). Interestingly, the set of functions that we are able to
compute was previously identified by Asharov [2] (TCC 2014) in the
context of fairness in two-party computation, naming these functions
*full-dimensional*. Our result also extends to randomized non-Boolean
functions $f : \mathcal{X} \times \mathcal{Y} \mapsto \{0,\ldots,k-1\}$ satisfying $|\mathcal{X}| > (k-1) \cdot |\mathcal{Y}|$.

## 1 Introduction

In the setting of secure two-party computation (2PC), the goal is to allow two
mutually distrustful parties to compute some function of their private inputs.
The computation should preserve some security properties, even in the face

---

B. Alon—Research supported by ISF grant 152/17.

D. Hofheinz and A. Rosen (Eds.): TCC 2019, LNCS 11891, pp. 561–595, 2019.
https://doi.org/10.1007/978-3-030-36030-6_22

of adversarial behavior by one of the parties. The two most common types of adversaries are *malicious* adversaries (which may instruct the corrupted party to deviate from the prescribed protocol in an arbitrary way), and *semi-honest* adversaries (which must follow the instructions of the protocol, but may try to infer additional information based on the view of the corrupted party).

Oblivious transfer (OT) is a two-party functionality, fundamental to 2PC and the more general secure multiparty computation (MPC). It was first introduced by Rabin [28] and Even et al. [13]. In the setting of $\binom{2}{1}$-bit-OT, there is a receiver holding a bit $b \in \{0, 1\}$, and a sender holding two bit-messages $a_0, a_1 \in \{0, 1\}$. At the end of the interaction, the receiver learns $a_b$ and nothing else, and the sender learns nothing. It turns out that OT can be used in the construction of protocols, both in 2PC and MPC with various security guarantees [6, 14, 22, 33]. Moreover, giving to the parties access to an ideal process that computes OT securely, is potentially useful. Constructing protocols in this model, called the OT-hybrid model, could be used for optimizing the complexity of real-world, computationally secure protocols for several reasons. First, using the OT-precomputation paradigm of Beaver [4], the heavy computation of OT can many times be pushed back to an off-line phase. This off-line phase is performed before the actual inputs for the computation (and possibly even the function to be computed) are known. Later, as the actual computation takes place, the precomputed OTs are very cheaply converted into actual OT interactions. Furthermore, the OT-extension paradigm of [5] offers a way to efficiently implement many OTs using a relatively small number of base OTs. This can be done using only symmetric-key primitives (e.g., one-way functions, pseudorandom generators). Furthermore, it can also be used to implement $\binom{2}{1}$-$s$-string-OT using a sub-linear (in the security parameter) number of calls to $\binom{2}{1}$-bit-OT and some additional sub-linear work, assuming a strong variant of PRG [17]. Additionally, there is a variety of computational assumptions that are sufficient to realize OT [27], or even with unconditional security under physical assumptions [10, 11, 21, 26, 32].

An interesting family of two-party functionalities are the client-server functionalities, where only one party – the client – receives an output. In addition to the OT functionality mentioned earlier, client-server functionalities include many other examples. Securely computing some of theses functionalities could be useful for many interesting applications, both in theory and in practice.

For client-server, a well known result due to Kilian [22], asserts that OT is complete. That is, any two-party client-server functionality can be computed with unconditional security in the OT-hybrid model. Ishai, Prabhakaran, and Sahai [18] further showed that the protocol can be made efficient. Later, it was shown by Ishai et al. [19], that in the OT-hybrid model, every client-server functionality can be computed using a *single round*. Furthermore, the protocol's computational and communication complexity are efficient for functions in $NC^1$. However, all of the results achieve only *statistical security*, namely, it is allowed to have some error in security.

For the case of *perfect security* in this setting much less is known. Given access to (many parallel) ideal computations for $\binom{2}{1}$-bit-OT, Brassard et al. [8] showed how to compute the functionality $\binom{n}{1}$-$s$-string-OT, and Wullschleger [30] showed how to compute $\binom{2}{1}$-bit-TO, which is the same as $\binom{2}{1}$-bit-OT where the roles of the parties are reversed. Furthermore, the former protocol has a single round, in which the parties invoke the OT, and with no additional bits to be sent over the channel between the parties. The latter protocol requires an additional bit to be sent by the server.

Observe that the result of [8] implies that any client-server functionality $f$ can be computed with perfect security against *semi-honest* corruptions. Indeed, let $n$ be the number of inputs in the client's domain, and let $s$ be the number of bits required to represent an output of $f$. The server will send to the $\binom{n}{1}$-$s$-string-OT functionality all of the possible outputs with respect to its input, and the client will send its input. The client then outputs whatever it received from the OT. Clearly, the protocol is secure against semi-honest adversaries, however, in the malicious case, this is not true, in general. This is due to the fact that the server has complete control over the output of the client. For instance, for the "greater-than" function, the server can force the output of the client to be 1 if and only if $y$ is even. Therefore, we are only interested in security against malicious adversaries.

Ishai et al. [20] studied perfectly secure multiparty computation in the correlated randomness model. They showed that any multiparty client-server functionality can be computed with perfect security, when the parties have access to a correlated randomness whose correlation depends on the function to be computed by the parties.

There are also various client-server functionalities that can be computed trivially (even in the plain model). For example, the XOR functionality can be computed by having the server sending its input to the client. These simple examples suggest that fairness is not a necessary condition for being able to compute a function perfectly in the client-server model.

Thus, the state of affairs is that most two-party client-server functionalities remain unclassified as to perfect security in the OT-hybrid model. In this work we address the following natural questions.

> Which client-server functionalities can be computed with *perfect security* against malicious adversaries in the OT-hybrid model? What is the round complexity of such protocols?

The questions have an obvious theoretical appeal to it, and understanding it could help us gain a better understanding of general secure computation. In addition, perfect security may be useful for designing multiparty protocols with high concrete efficiency, achieved by eliminating the dependency on a security parameter.

We stress that, under the assumption that $NP \not\subseteq BPP$, it is impossible to achieve completeness theorems in our setting, similar to the completeness theorems of Kilian [22]. Indeed, suppose the parties want to compute an NP relation with perfect zero-knowledge and perfect soundness. Then it is impossible even when given access to any ideal functionality with no input (distributing some kind of correlated randomness) [20]. This is due to the fact that if such a protocol does exist, then one can use the simulator to decide the relation, putting it in BPP. Since OT can be perfectly reduced to a suitable no-input functionality, this implies that no such protocol exist in the OT-hybrid model.

## 1.1  Our Results

Our main result is that if the parties have access to many parallel ideal computations of $\binom{2}{1}$-bit-OT, most client-server functionalities, where the server's domain is larger than the client's domain, can be computed with perfect full-security in a single round. Interestingly, the set of functions that we are able to compute was previously identified by Asharov [2] in the context of fairness in two-party computation, naming these functions as *full-dimensional*.

Let $f : \mathcal{X} \times \mathcal{Y} \mapsto \{0,1\}$ be a function, where the server's domain size $|\mathcal{X}|$ is larger than the client's domain size $|\mathcal{Y}|$. Write $\mathcal{X} = \{x_1, \ldots, x_n\}$ and $\mathcal{Y} = \{y_1, \ldots, y_m\}$. We consider the geometric representation of $f$ as $|\mathcal{X}|$ points over $\mathbb{R}^{|\mathcal{Y}|}$, where the $j$-th coordinate of the $i$-th point is simply $f(x_i, y_j)$. We then consider the *convex polytope*[1] defined by these points. The function is called *full-dimensional* if the dimension of the polytope is exactly $|\mathcal{Y}|$, e.g., a triangle in the plane.[2] We prove the following theorem:

**Theorem 1 (Informal).** *Let $f : \mathcal{X} \times \mathcal{Y} \mapsto \{0,1\}$ be a client-server functionality. If $f$ is full-dimensional, then it can be computed with perfect full-security in the OT-hybrid model in a single round. Furthermore, the number of OT calls is $O\left(\mathrm{poly}\left(|\mathcal{Y}|\right)\right)$.*

In fact, we generalize the above theorem, and we give a similar criterion for randomized non-Boolean functions. The class of functions that our protocol can compute can be further extended by letting the client have inputs that fix the output. This class of functions includes many interesting examples, such as Yao's "millionaires' problem" (the "greater-than" function). Here the parties have inputs that ranges from 1 to $n$, and the output of the client is 1 if and only if its input is greater than or equal to the server's input. The communication complexity of our protocol is polynomial in the client's domain size, and not in its input's size. For functions with small domain, however, this does improve upon known construction that achieve statistical security (e.g., the single round protocol by Ishai et al. [19], see Sect. 7 for more details).

Its was proven by [2], that the number of full-dimensional functions tends to 1 exponentially fast as $|\mathcal{X}|$ and $|\mathcal{Y}|$ grow. Specifically, a random function with domains sizes $|\mathcal{X}| = m+1$ and $|\mathcal{Y}| = m$, will be full-dimensional with probability

---

[1] A polytope is a generalization in any number of dimensions of the two-dimensional polygon and the three-dimensional polyhedron.

[2] Observe that if $f$ is full-dimensional then $|\mathcal{X}| > |\mathcal{Y}|$, since the polytope requires at least $|\mathcal{Y}| + 1$ points to be of dimension $|\mathcal{Y}|$.

at least $1 - p_m$, where $p_m$ denotes the probability that a random Boolean $m \times m$ matrix is singular. The value $p_m$ is conjectured to be $(1/2 + o(1))^m$. Currently, the best known upper bound is $(1/\sqrt{2} + o(1))^m$ proved by [31].

Theorem 1 identifies a set of client-server functionalities that are computable with perfect full-security. It does not yield a full characterization of such functions. For example, the status of the equality function $3\mathsf{EQ} : \{x_1, x_2, x_3\} \times \{y_1, y_2, y_3\} \mapsto \{0, 1\}$, defined as $3\mathsf{EQ}(x, y) = 1$ if and only if $x = y$, is currently unknown. However, for the case of Boolean functions (even randomized), we are able to show that the protocol suggested in the proof of Theorem 1 computes *only* full-dimensional functions.

## 1.2 Our Techniques

The protocol we suggest is a variation of the protocol of Ishai et al. [19]. Viewing the protocol abstractly, in addition to the computation of some related function, the server will also send (via the OT) a proof of correct behavior. The client will use the OT functionality to learn only a few random bits from the proof so that privacy is preserved. We next give a technical overview of our construction.

In our construction, we make use of perfect randomized encoding (PRE) [1]. A PRE $\hat{f}$ of a function $f$ is a randomized function, such that for every input $x$ and a uniformly random choice of the randomness $r$, it is possible to decode $\hat{f}(x; r)$ and compute $f(x)$ with no error. In addition, the output distribution of $\hat{f}$ on input $x$ reveals no information about $x$ except what follows from $f(x)$. For our construction, we rely on a property called decomposability. A PRE is said to be decomposable, if it can be written as $\hat{f} = \left( \hat{f}_1, \ldots, \hat{f}_n \right)$. Here, each $\hat{f}_i$ can be written as one of two vectors that depends on the $i$-th bit of $x$, i.e., we can write it as $\mathbf{v}_{i, x_i}$, where $(\mathbf{v}_{i,0}, \mathbf{v}_{i,1})$ depends on the randomness $r$. This definition can be viewed as the perfect version of garbled circuits [24, 33].

Our starting point is the protocol of Ishai et al. [19], which will be dubbed the IKOPS protocol. It is a single round protocol in the OT-hybrid model that achieves statistical security. It allows the parties to compute a "certified OT" functionality. We next give a brief overview of the IKOPS protocol.

The main idea behind the IKOPS protocol is to have the server run an "MPC in the head" [18]. That is, the real server locally emulates the execution of a perfectly secure protocol $\Pi$ with many virtual servers performing the computation, and $2m$ virtual clients, denoted $\mathsf{C}_{1,0}, \mathsf{C}_{1,1}, \ldots, \mathsf{C}_{m,0}, \mathsf{C}_{m,1}$, receiving output, where $m$ is the number of bits in the real client's input $y$. The underlying protocol $\Pi$ computes (and distributes among the clients) a decomposable PRE $\hat{f} = (\hat{f}_1, \ldots, \hat{f}_m)$ of $f$. Specifically, the input of the virtual servers' are secret sharing of the real server's input $x$ and randomness $r$. The output of the virtual client $\mathsf{C}_{j,b}$ in an execution of $\Pi$, is $\hat{f}_j(b; r)$, i.e., the part of the encoding that corresponds to the $j$-th bit of $y$ being equal to $b$.

The real client can then use OT in order to recover the correct output of the PRE and reconstruct the output $f(x, y)$. As part of the "MPC in the head" paradigm, the client and server jointly set up a watchlist (the views of some of the virtual servers) allowing the client to check consistency between the virtual servers' views and the virtual clients' views. If there was an inconsistency, the client outputs $f(x_0, y)$ for some default value $x_0 \in \mathcal{X}$. However, it is unclear how to have the server send only *some* of the views according to the request of the client. Ishai et al. [19] handle this by letting the client get each view with some constant probability independently of the other views.

The security of the protocol as described so far can still be breached by a malicious server. By tampering with the outputs of the virtual clients, a malicious server could force the output of the real client to be $f(x, y)$ for some inputs $y$ and force the output to be $f(x_0, y)$ for other values of $y$, where the choice is completely determined by the adversary. To overcome this problem, the function $f$ is replaced with a function $f'$ where each bit $y_i$ is replaced with $\kappa$ random bits whose XOR equals to $y_i$, where $\kappa$ is the security parameter.[3] This modification prevents the adversary from having complete control over which inputs the client will output $f(x_0, y)$, and for which inputs it will output $f(x, y)$.

Two problems arise when trying to use the IKOPS protocol to achieve perfect security. First, a malicious client could potentially receive the views of *all virtual servers*, and as a result, it could learn the server's input. Second, with some non-zero probability, a malicious server might still be able to have the client output be $f(x_0, y)$ for some inputs $y$, but output $f(x, y)$ for other inputs $y$.

We solve the former issue, by showing how the client can request views deterministically. We would like to have the request be made using $\binom{n}{t}$-$s$-string-OT, where $t$ bounds the number of corruptions allowed in $\Pi$, namely, the client asks for exactly $t$ views. However, it is not known if implementing it in the OT-hybrid model with perfect security is even possible. Therefore, we slightly relax the security requirement, so that a malicious client will not be able to receive *more than twice* the number of views that an honest client receives. We then let the honest client ask for exactly $t/2$ of the views. The idea in constructing such a watchlist is the following. For each view of a virtual server, the real server sends (via the OT functionality) either a masking of the view, or a share of the concatenation of the maskings. That is, the server's input to the OT is $(V_i \oplus r_i, \mathbf{r}[i])$ for every view $V_i$ of a virtual server $S_i$, where $\mathbf{r} = (r_1, \ldots, r_n)$ is a vector of random strings, and $\mathbf{r}[i]$ is the $i$-th share of $\mathbf{r}$, for some threshold secret sharing scheme with sufficiently large threshold value.[4] As a result, in each invocation of the OT, the client will be able to learn either a masked view or a share, which bounds the number of views it can receive.

To solve the second issue, it will be convenient to represent the server security requirement from a geometric point of view. To simplify the explanation in this introduction, we only focus on deterministic Boolean functions. Recall that we can view the function $f$ as $|\mathcal{X}|$ points over $\mathbb{R}^{|\mathcal{Y}|}$, where the $j$-th coordinate of the $i$-th point is simply $f(x_i, y_j)$. Observe that all a simulator for a malicious server can do, is to send a random input according to some distribution $D$.

---

[3] This technique for eliminating selective failure attacks was previously used in [22,23].

[4] There are additional technical subtleties, however, for this informal introduction we ignore them.

The goal of the simulator is to force the distribution of the client's output to be equivalent to the distribution in the real-world. Thus, perfect simulation of a malicious server is possible if and only if there exists such distribution $D$ over the server's inputs in the ideal-world, such that for every input $y \in \mathcal{Y}$ of the client, $\Pr_{x \leftarrow D}[f(x,y) = 1] = q_y$, where $q_y$ is the probability the client outputs 1 in the real-world where its input is $y$. Since for every $y \in \mathcal{Y}$ the value $\Pr_{x \leftarrow D}[f(x,y) = 1]$ can be written as the same *convex combination* of the points $\{f(x_i, y)\}_{i=1}^{|\mathcal{X}|}$, the point $(\Pr_{x \leftarrow D}[f(x,y) = 1])_{y \in \mathcal{Y}}$ lie inside the *convex hull* of the points of $f$. Thus, we can state perfect security as follows. Simulation of an adversary is possible if and only if the *vector of outputs* $(q_y)_{y \in \mathcal{Y}}$ in the real-world is in the *convex-hull* of the points in $\mathbb{R}^{|\mathcal{Y}|}$ described by $f$.

Now, consider the IKOPS protocol. It could be the case that the vector of outputs has different errors in each coordinate created by an adversary, and hence is not necessarily inside the convex-hull of the points of $f$. To fix this issue, instead of having the client output according to a default value in case of an inconsistency, the client will now pick $x_0$ uniformly at random, and output $f(x_0, y)$. Stated differently, it outputs according to $c_y$, where $\mathbf{c}$ is the center of the polytope.[5] We next (roughly) explain why this results in a perfectly secure protocol. Let $p$ denote the probability of detecting an inconsistency (more precisely, for each $y$ the probability $p_y$ of detecting an inconsistency is in $[p-\varepsilon, p+\varepsilon]$, for some small $\varepsilon$). Further defined the matrix $M_f(x,y) = f(x,y)$ (i.e., each row of $M_f$ describes a point in $\mathbb{R}^{|\mathcal{Y}|}$). Thus, the output vector of the client is close to the point $\mathbf{q} = p \cdot \mathbf{c} + (1-p) \cdot M_f(x, \cdot)$, give or take $\pm \varepsilon$ in each coordinate, for some small $\varepsilon$. If $p$ is close to 1, this point $\mathbf{q}$ is close to $\mathbf{c}$, and since $\mathbf{c}$ is an internal point, $\mathbf{q}$ is also internal for a sufficiently small $\varepsilon$. Otherwise, the point $\mathbf{q}$ will be close to the boundary. As a result, it is unclear as to why perfect security holds. Here, we utilize a special property of IKOPS protocol's security. We manage to prove that $\varepsilon$ is bounded by $p \cdot \varepsilon'$, for some small $\varepsilon'$. That is, $\varepsilon$ depends on $p$, unlike the standard security requirement. This property allows us to prove that perfect security holds.

## 1.3 Related Work

In the 2PC settings, Cleve [9] showed that the functionality of coin-tossing, where the parties output the same random bit, is impossible to compute with full-security, even in the OT-hybrid model. In spite of that, in the seminal work Gordon et al. [15], and later followed by [2,3,12,25], it was discovered that in the OT-hybrid model, most two-party functionalities can be evaluated with full security by efficient protocols. In particular, [3] completes the characterization of symmetric Boolean functions (where both parties receive the same output). However, all known general protocols for such functionalities have round complexity that is super-logarithmic in the security parameter. Moreover, this was proven to be necessary for functions with embedded XOR [15].

---

[5] The same construction works for any other choice of a point $\mathbf{v}$ that is *strictly* inside the convex-hull of the points.

## 1.4    Organization

In Sect. 2 we provide some notations and definitions that we use in this work, alongside some required mathematical background. Section 3 is dedicated to expressing security in geometrical terms and the formal statement of our result. In Sects. 4 and 5 we present the proof of the main theorem. In Sect. 6 we show that the analysis of our protocol for Boolean functions is tight.Finally, in Sect. 7 we briefly discuss the efficiency of our construction.

## 2    Preliminaries

### 2.1    Notations

We use calligraphic letters to denote sets, uppercase for random variables and matrices, lowercase for values, and we use bold characters to denote vectors and points. All logarithms are in base 2. For $n \in \mathbb{N}$, let $[n] = \{1, 2 \ldots n\}$. For a set $\mathcal{S}$ we write $s \leftarrow \mathcal{S}$ to indicate that $s$ is selected uniformly at random from $\mathcal{S}$. Given a random variable (or a distribution) $X$, we write $x \leftarrow X$ to indicate that $x$ is selected according to $X$. We use poly to denote an unspecified polynomial, and we use polylog to denote an unspecified polylogarithmic function. For a randomized function (or an algorithm) $f$ we write $f(x)$ to denote the random variable induced by the function on input $x$, and write $f(x; r)$ to denote the value when the randomness of $f$ is fixed to $r$.

For a vector $\mathbf{v} \in \mathbb{R}^n$, we denote its $i$-th component with $v_i$ and we let $||\mathbf{v}||_\infty = \max_i |v_i|$ denote its $\ell_\infty$ norm. We denote by $\mathbf{1}_n$ ($\mathbf{0}_n$) the all-ones (all-zeros) vector of dimension $n$. A vector $\mathbf{p} \in \mathbb{R}^n$ is called a probability vector if $\mathbf{p}_i \geq 0$ for every $i \in [n]$ and $\sum_{i=1}^n p_i = 1$.

For a matrix $M \in \mathbb{R}^{n \times m}$, we let $M(i, \cdot)$ be its $i$-th row, we let $M(\cdot, j)$ be its $j$-th column, and we denote by $M^T$ the transpose of $M$. For a pair of matrices $M_1 \in \mathbb{R}^{n \times m_1}, M_2 \in \mathbb{R}^{n \times m_2}$, we denote by $[M_1 || M_2]$ the concatenation of $M_2$ to the right of $M_1$.

### 2.2    Cryptographic Tools

**Definition 1.** *The statistical distance between two finite random variables $X$ and $Y$ is*

$$\mathrm{SD}(X, Y) = \frac{1}{2} \sum_a |\Pr[X = a] - \Pr[Y = a]|.$$

**Secret Sharing Schemes.** A $(t+1)$-out-of-$n$ secret-sharing scheme is a mechanism for sharing data among a set of parties $\{P_1, \ldots, P_n\}$, such that every set of size $t + 1$ can reconstruct the secret, while any smaller set knows nothing about the secret. As a convention, for a secret $s$ and $i \in [n]$ we let $s[i]$ be the $i$-th share, namely, the share received by $P_i$. In this work, we rely on Shamir's secret sharing scheme [29].

In a $(t+1)$-out-of-$n$ Shamir's secret sharing scheme over a field $\mathbb{F}$, where $|\mathbb{F}| > n$, a secret $s \in \mathbb{F}$ is shared as follows: A polynomial $p(\cdot)$ of degree at most $t+1$ over $\mathbb{F}$ is picked uniformly at random, conditioned on $p(0) = s$. Each party $P_i$, for $1 \leq i \leq n$, receives a share $s[i] := p(i)$ (we abuse notation and let $i$ be the element in $\mathbb{F}$ associated with $P_i$).

**Decomposable Randomized Encoding.** We recall the definition of randomized encoding [1,33]. They are known to exists unconditionally [1,16].

**Definition 2 (Randomized Encoding).** *Let* $f : \{0,1\}^n \mapsto \mathcal{Z}$ *be some function. We say that a function* $\hat{f} : \{0,1\}^n \times \mathcal{R} \mapsto \mathcal{W}$ *is a perfect randomized encoding (PRE) of* $f$ *if the following holds.*

**Correctness:** *There exists a decoding algorithm* Dec *such that for every* $x \in \{0,1\}^n$

$$\Pr_{r \leftarrow \mathcal{R}} \left[ \mathsf{Dec}\left( \hat{f}\left(x;r\right) \right) = f(x) \right] = 1.$$

**Privacy:** *There exists a randomized algorithm* Sim *such that for every* $x \in \{0,1\}^n$ *it holds that*

$$\mathsf{Sim}\left(f(x)\right) \equiv \hat{f}\left(x;r\right),$$

*where* $r \leftarrow \mathcal{R}$.

**Definition 3 (Decomposable Randomized Encoding).** *For every* $x \in \{0,1\}^n$, *we write* $x = x_1, \ldots, x_n$, *where* $x_i$ *is the* $i$-th *bit of* $x$. *A randomized encoding* $\hat{f}$ *is said to be* decomposable *if it can be written as*

$$\hat{f}\left(x;r\right) = \left( \hat{f}_0\left(r\right), \hat{f}_1\left(x_1;r\right), \ldots, \hat{f}_n\left(x_n;r\right) \right),$$

*where each* $\hat{f}_i$, *for* $i \in [n]$, *can be written as one of two vectors that depends on* $x_i$, *i.e., we can write it as* $\mathbf{v}_{i,x_i}$, *where* $(\mathbf{v}_{i,0}, \mathbf{v}_{i,1})$ *depends on the randomness* $r$.

### 2.3 Mathematical Background

**Definition 4 (Convex Combination and Convex Hull).** *Let* $\mathcal{V} = \{\mathbf{v}_1, \ldots, \mathbf{v}_m\} \subseteq \mathbb{R}^n$ *be a set of vectors. A convex combination is a linear combination* $\sum_{i=1}^{m} \alpha_i \cdot \mathbf{v}_i$ *where* $\sum_{i=1}^{m} \alpha_i = 1$ *and* $\alpha_i \geq 0$ *for all* $1 \leq i \leq m$. *The convex hull of* $\mathcal{V}$, *denoted*

$$\mathbf{conv}\left(\mathcal{V}\right) = \left\{ \sum_{i=1}^{m} \alpha_i \cdot \mathbf{v}_i \mid \sum_{i=1}^{m} \alpha_i = 1 \text{ and } \alpha_i \geq 0 \text{ for all } i \in [m] \right\},$$

*is the set of all vectors that can be represented as a convex combination of the vectors in* $\mathcal{V}$. *For a matrix* $M = [\mathbf{v}_1 || \ldots || \mathbf{v}_m]$ *we let* $\mathbf{conv}\left(M\right) = \mathbf{conv}\left(\{\mathbf{v}_1, \ldots, \mathbf{v}_m\}\right)$.

**Definition 5 (Affine Hull).** *For a set of vectors $\mathcal{V} = \{v_1, \ldots, v_m\} \subseteq \mathbb{R}^n$, we define their* affine hull *to be the set*

$$\text{aff}(\mathcal{V}) = \left\{ \sum_{i=1}^{m} \alpha_i \cdot v_i \mid \sum_{i=1}^{m} \alpha_i = 1 \right\}.$$

*For a matrix $M = [v_1 || \ldots || v_m]$ we let $\text{aff}(M) = \text{aff}(\{v_1, \ldots, v_m\})$.*

**Definition 6 (Affine Independence).** *A set of points $v_1, \ldots, v_m \in \mathbb{R}^n$ is said to be* affinely independent *if whenever $\sum_{i=1}^{m} \alpha_i \cdot v_i = 0_n$ and $\sum_{i=1}^{m} \alpha_i = 0$, then $\alpha_i = 0$ for every $i \in [m]$. Observe that $v_1, \ldots, v_m$ are affinely independent if and only if $v_2 - v_1, \ldots, v_m - v_1$ are linearly independent.*

For a square matrix $M \in \mathbb{R}^{n \times n}$, we denote by $\det(M)$ the determinant of $M$, and we denote by $M_{i,j}$ the $(i,j)$'th cofactor of $M$, which is the $(n-1) \times (n-1)$ matrix obtained by removing the $i$'th row and $j$'th column of $M$. It is well known that:

**Fact 2.** *Let $M \in \mathbb{R}^{n \times n}$ be an invertible matrix. Then for every $i, j \in [n]$ it holds that $|M^{-1}(i,j)| = |\det(M_{j,i}) / \det(M)|$.*

## 2.4 The Model of Computation

We follow the standard *ideal vs. real* paradigm for defining security. Intuitively, the security notion is defined by describing an ideal functionality, in which both the corrupted and non-corrupted parties interact with a trusted entity. A real-world protocol is deemed secure if an adversary in the real-world cannot cause more harm than an adversary in the ideal-world. This is captured by showing that an ideal-world adversary (simulator) can simulate the full view of the real world adversary.

We focus our attention on the *client-server model*. In this model a server S holds some input $x$ and a client C holds some input $y$. At the end of the interaction the client learns the output of some function of $x$ and $y$, while the server learns nothing. We further restrict ourselves to allow only a *single round* of interaction between the two parties, however, as only trivial functionalities are computable in this setting, the parties interact in the $\mathcal{OT}$-hybrid model. We next formalize the interaction done in this model.

**The OT Functionality.** We start by formally defining the (family) of the OT functionality. The $\binom{2}{1}$-bit-OT functionality, is a two-party client-server functionality in which the server inputs a pair of bit-messages $a_0$ and $a_1$, and the client inputs a single bit $b$. The server receives $\perp$ and the client receives $a_b$. For every natural number $\ell \geq 1$, we define the functionality $\binom{2}{1}$-bit-OT$^\ell$ as follows. Let $a = (a_0^i, a_1^i)_{i=1}^{\ell}$ and let $b = (b_i)_{i=1}^{\ell}$, where $a_0^i, a_1^i, b_i \in \{0,1\}$ for every $i$. We let $a[b] := (a_{b_i}^i)_{i=1}^{\ell}$. The functionality is then defined as $(a, b) \mapsto (\perp, a[b])$. That is, it is the equivalent to computing $\binom{2}{1}$-bit-OT $\ell$ times in parallel. Finally, we let $\mathcal{OT} = \left\{ \binom{2}{1}\text{-bit-OT}^\ell \right\}_{\ell \geq 1}$.

A generalization of $\binom{2}{1}$-bit-OT is the $\binom{n}{1}$-bit-OT functionality, which lets the client pick one out of $n$ bits $a_1, a_2, \ldots, a_n$ supplied by the server, and on input $i \in [n]$ the client learns $a_i$. This can be further generalized to $\binom{n}{1}$-$s$-string-OT where the $n$ bits are replaced by strings $a_1, \ldots, a_n \in \{0,1\}^s$, and this can generalized even further to $\binom{n}{k}$-$s$-string-OT where the input $i$ of the client is replaced with $k$ inputs $i_1, \ldots, i_k \in [n]$, and it receives $a_{i_1}, \ldots, a_{i_k}$.

**The 1-Round $\mathcal{OT}$-Hybrid Model.** We next describe the execution in the *1-round $\mathcal{OT}$-hybrid model*. In the following we fix a (possibly randomized) client-server functionality $f : \mathcal{X} \times \mathcal{Y} \mapsto \{0, \ldots, k-1\}$. A protocol $\Pi$ in the *1-round $\mathcal{OT}$-hybrid model* with security parameter $\kappa$, is a triple of randomized functions $(\alpha, \beta, \varphi)$. The server and client use the function $\alpha$ and $\beta$ respectively to obtain messages to send to the OT. The client then compute some local function $\varphi$ on its view to obtain an output. Formally, the computation is done as follows.

**Inputs:** The server S holds input $x \in \mathcal{X}$ and the client C holds input $y \in \mathcal{Y}$. In addition, both parties hold the security parameter $1^\kappa$.

**Parties send inputs to the OT:** S samples $2\ell(\kappa)$ bits $\mathbf{a} = \alpha(x, 1^\kappa)$, and C samples $\ell(\kappa)$ bits $\mathbf{b} = \beta(y, 1^\kappa)$, for some $\ell(\cdot)$ determined by the protocol. S and C send $\mathbf{a}$ and $\mathbf{b}$ to the OT functionality, respectively. C then receives $\mathbf{a}[\mathbf{b}]$ from the OT.

**Outputs:** The server S outputs nothing, while the client C computes the local function $\varphi(y, \mathbf{b}, \mathbf{a}[\mathbf{b}], 1^\kappa)$ and outputs its result.

We refer to the $\ell(\kappa)$ used in the protocol as the *communication complexity* (CC) of $\Pi$.

We consider an adversary $\mathcal{A}$ that controls a single party. The adversary has access to the full view of that party. We assume the adversary is malicious, that is, it may instruct the corrupted party to deviate from the protocol in any way it chooses. The adversary is non-uniform, and is given an auxiliary input aux. For simplicity we do not concern ourselves with the efficiency of the protocols or the adversaries, namely, we assume that the parties and the adversary are unbounded.

Fix inputs $x \in \mathcal{X}$, $y \in \mathcal{Y}$, and $\kappa \in \mathbb{N}$. For an adversary $\mathcal{A}$ corrupting the *server*, we let $\text{Out}^{\text{HYBRID}}_{\mathcal{A}(x,\text{aux}),\Pi}(x, y, 1^\kappa)$ denote the output of the client in a random execution of $\Pi$. For an adversary $\mathcal{A}$ corrupting the *client*, we let $\text{View}^{\text{HYBRID}}_{\mathcal{A}(y,\text{aux}),\Pi}(x, y, 1^\kappa)$ denote the adversary's view in a random execution of $\Pi$, when it corrupts the *client*. This includes its input, auxiliary input, randomness, and the output received from the OT functionality.

**The Ideal Model.** We now describe the interaction in the ideal model, which specifies the requirements for fully secure computation of the function $f$ with security parameter $\kappa$. Let $\mathcal{A}$ be an adversary in the ideal-world, which is given an auxiliary input aux and corrupts one of the parties.

**The Ideal Model – Full-Security**

**Inputs:** The server S holds input $x \in \mathcal{X}$ and the client C holds input $y \in \mathcal{Y}$. The adversary is given an auxiliary input $\mathsf{aux} \in \{0,1\}^*$ and the input of the corrupted party. The trusted party T holds $1^\kappa$.

**Parties send inputs:** The honest party sends its input to T. The adversary sends a value $w$ from its domain as the input for corrupted party.

**The trusted party performs computation:** T selects a random string $r$ and computes $z = f(x, w; r)$ if C is corrupted and computes $z = f(w, y; r)$ if S is corrupted. T then sends $z$ to C (which is also given to $\mathcal{A}$ if C is corrupted).

**Outputs:** An honest server outputs nothing, an honest client output $z$, and the malicious party outputs nothing. The adversary outputs some function of its view.

Fix inputs $x \in \mathcal{X}$, $y \in \mathcal{Y}$, and $\kappa \in \mathbb{N}$. For an $\mathcal{A}$ corrupting the *server* we let $\mathrm{Out}^{\mathrm{IDEAL}}_{\mathcal{A}(x,\mathsf{aux}),f}(x, y, 1^\kappa)$ denote the output of the client in a random execution of the above ideal-world process. For an $\mathcal{A}$ corrupting the *client* we let $\mathrm{View}^{\mathrm{IDEAL}}_{\mathcal{A}(y,\mathsf{aux}),f}(x, y, 1^\kappa)$ be the view description being the *output* of $\mathcal{A}$ in such a process.

We next present the definition for security against malicious adversaries. The definition we present is tailored to the setting of the 1-round two-party client-server in the $\mathcal{OT}$-hybrid model.

**Definition 7 (malicious security).** *Let $\Pi = (\alpha, \beta, \varphi)$ be a protocol for computing $f$ in the 1-round $\mathcal{OT}$-hybrid model. Let $\varepsilon(\cdot)$ be a positive function of the security parameter.*

1. **Correctness:** We say that $\Pi$ is *correct* if for all $\kappa \in \mathbb{N}$, $x \in \mathcal{X}$, and $y \in \mathcal{Y}$

$$\Pr\left[\varphi(y, \mathbf{b}, \mathbf{a}[\mathbf{b}], 1^\kappa) = f(x, y)\right] = 1.$$

   Here, $\mathbf{a} = \alpha(x, 1^\kappa)$, $\mathbf{b} = \beta(y, 1^\kappa)$ and the probability is taken over the random coins of $\alpha$, $\beta$, $\varphi$, and $f$.

2. **Server Security:** We say that $\Pi$ is $\varepsilon$-*server secure*, if for any non-uniform adversary $\mathcal{A}$ corrupting the server in the $\mathcal{OT}$-hybrid world, there exists a non-uniform adversary $\mathrm{Sim}_{\mathcal{A}}$ (called the simulator) corrupting the server in the ideal-world, such that for all $\kappa \in \mathbb{N}$, $x \in \mathcal{X}$, $y \in \mathcal{Y}$, and $\mathsf{aux} \in \{0,1\}^*$ it holds that

$$\mathrm{SD}\left(\mathrm{Out}^{\mathrm{HYBRID}}_{\mathcal{A}(x,\mathsf{aux}),\Pi}(x, y, 1^\kappa),\ \mathrm{Out}^{\mathrm{IDEAL}}_{\mathrm{Sim}_{\mathcal{A}}(x,\mathsf{aux}),f}(x, y, 1^\kappa)\right) \leq \varepsilon(\kappa).$$

   We say that $\Pi$ has perfect server security if it is 0-server secure.

3. **Client Security:** We say that $\Pi$ is $\varepsilon$-*client secure*, if for any non-uniform adversary $\mathcal{A}$ corrupting the client in the $\mathcal{OT}$-hybrid world, there exists a non-uniform simulator $\mathrm{Sim}_{\mathcal{A}}$ corrupting the client in the ideal-world, such that for all $\kappa \in \mathbb{N}$, $x \in \mathcal{X}$, $y \in \mathcal{Y}$, and $\mathsf{aux} \in \{0,1\}^*$ it holds that

$$\mathrm{SD}\left(\mathrm{View}^{\mathrm{HYBRID}}_{\mathcal{A}(y,\mathsf{aux}),\Pi}(x, y, 1^\kappa),\ \mathrm{View}^{\mathrm{IDEAL}}_{\mathrm{Sim}_{\mathcal{A}}(y,\mathsf{aux}),f}(x, y, 1^\kappa)\right) \leq \varepsilon(\kappa).$$

   We say that $\Pi$ has perfect client security if it is 0-client secure.

*We say that $\Pi$ computes $f$ with $\varepsilon$-statistical full-security, if $\Pi$ is correct, is $\varepsilon$-server secure, and is $\varepsilon$-client secure. Finally, we say that $\Pi$ computes $f$ with perfect full-security, if it computes $f$ with 0-statistical full-security.*

To alleviate notation, from now on we will completely remove $1^\kappa$ from the input the functions $\alpha$, $\beta$, and $\varphi$, and remove $\kappa$ from $\ell$ and $\varepsilon$. Statistical security will now be stated as a function of $\varepsilon$ and the CC of the protocol as a function of $\ell$. Observe that aborts in this model are irrelevant. Indeed, honest server outputs nothing, and if a malicious server aborts then the client can output $f(x_0, y)$ for some default value $x_0 \in \mathcal{X}$, which can be perfectly simulated. Therefore, throughout the paper we assume without loss of generality that the adversary does not abort the execution.

We next describe the notion of *security with input-dependent abort* [19]. Generally, it is a relaxation of the standard full-security notion, which allows an adversary to learn at most 1 bit of information by causing the protocol to abort depending on the other party's inputs. We state only perfect security. Furthermore, the security notion is written with respect only to a malicious server. Since we work in the client-server model, the trusted party *does not* send to the server any output. Therefore, in this relaxation selective abort attacks [22,23] *are simulatable.*

**Definition 8.** *Fix $f : \mathcal{X} \times \mathcal{Y} \mapsto \{0, \ldots, k-1\}$. In the* input-dependent *model, we modify the ideal-world so that the malicious adversary corrupting the server, in addition to sending an input $x^* \in \mathcal{X}$, also gives the trusted party $\mathsf{T}$ a predicate $P : \mathcal{Y} \mapsto \{0, 1\}$. $\mathsf{T}$ then sends to the client $f(x^*, y)$ if $P(y) = 0$, and $\perp$ otherwise. We let $\mathrm{Out}^{\mathrm{ID}}_{\mathcal{A}(x, \mathsf{aux}), f}(x, y)$ denote the output of the client in a random execution of the above ideal-world process, with $\mathcal{A}$ corrupting the server.*

*Let $\Pi$ be a protocol that computes $f$ in the 1-round $\mathcal{OT}$-hybrid model. We say that $\Pi$ has* perfect input-dependent security, *if for every non-uniform adversary $\mathcal{A}$ corrupting the server in the $\mathcal{OT}$-hybrid world, there exists a non-uniform adversary $\mathsf{Sim}_\mathcal{A}$ corrupting the server in the input-dependent ideal-world, such that for all $x \in \mathcal{X}$, $y \in \mathcal{Y}$, and $\mathsf{aux} \in \{0, 1\}^*$ it holds that*

$$\mathrm{Out}^{\mathrm{HYBRID}}_{\mathcal{A}(x, \mathsf{aux}), \Pi}(x, y) \equiv \mathrm{Out}^{\mathrm{ID}}_{\mathsf{Sim}_\mathcal{A}(x, \mathsf{aux}), f}(x, y).$$

## 3   A Class of Perfectly Computable Client-Server Functions

In this section, we state the main result of this paper – presenting a large class of two-party client-server functions that are computable with perfect security. We start with presenting a geometric view of security in our model. We take a similar approach to that of [2] to representing the server-security requirement geometrically.

## 3.1   A Geometrical Representation of the Security Requirements

*Boolean Functions.* We start with giving the details for (randomized) Boolean functions. For any function $f : \mathcal{X} \times \mathcal{Y} \mapsto \{0, 1\}$ we associate an $|\mathcal{X}| \times |\mathcal{Y}|$ matrix $M_f$ defined as $M_f(x, y) = \Pr[f(x, y) = 1]$, where the probability is taken over $f$'s random coins (if $f$ is deterministic, then this value is Boolean). Let $\mathcal{X} = \{x_1, \ldots, x_n\}$. Observe that in the ideal-world, every strategy that is employed by a simulator corrupting the server can be encoded with a probability vector $\mathbf{p} \in \mathbb{R}^n$, where $p_i$ corresponds to the probability of sending $x_i$ to T. Therefore, if the input of the client is $y$, then the probability that the output is 1, equals to $\mathbf{p}^T \cdot M_f(\cdot, y)$. On the other hand, in the 1-round $\mathcal{OT}$-hybrid model, a malicious server can only choose a string $\mathbf{a}^* \in \{0, 1\}^{2\ell}$ and send in to the OT. Then on input $y \in \mathcal{Y}$, the probability the client outputs 1 is exactly

$$q_y^{\Pi}(\mathbf{a}^*) := \Pr[\varphi(y, \mathbf{b}, \mathbf{a}^*[\mathbf{b}]) = 1],$$

where $\mathbf{b} = \beta(y)$ and the probability is over the randomness of $\beta$ and $\varphi$. This implies that an ideal-world simulator must send a random input $x^* \in \mathcal{X}$ such that the client will output 1 with probability $q_y^{\Pi}(\mathbf{a}^*)$. Thus, *perfect security* holds if and only if for every $\mathbf{a}^* \in \{0, 1\}^{2\ell}$ there exists a probability vector $\mathbf{p} \in \mathbb{R}^n$ such that for every $y \in \mathcal{Y}$

$$\mathbf{p}^T \cdot M_f(\cdot, y) = q_y^{\Pi}(\mathbf{a}^*).$$

Equivalently, for every $\mathbf{a}^*$ the vector $\mathbf{q}^{\Pi}(\mathbf{a}^*) := (q_y^{\Pi}(\mathbf{a}^*))_{y \in \mathcal{Y}}$ is inside the *convex-hull* of the rows of $M_f$. Further observe that this holds true regardless of the auxiliary input held by a corrupt server.

*General Functions.* We now extend the above discussion to non-Boolean functions. For every function $f : \mathcal{X} \times \mathcal{Y} \mapsto \{0, \ldots, k-1\}$, and every possible output $z \in \{0, \ldots, k-1\}$, we associate an $|\mathcal{X}| \times |\mathcal{Y}|$ matrix $M_f^z$ defined as $M_f^z(x, y) = \Pr[f(x, y) = z]$. Similarly to the Boolean case, in the ideal world, every strategy that is employed by a corrupt server can be encoded with a probability vector $\mathbf{p} \in \mathbb{R}^n$, hence the probability that the client will output $z$, on input $y$, is $\mathbf{p}^T \cdot M_f^z(\cdot, y)$. In the 1-round $\mathcal{OT}$-hybrid model, for a string $\mathbf{a}^* \in \{0, 1\}^{2\ell}$ chosen by a malicious server, the probability to output $z$ equals to

$$q_{y,z}^{\Pi}(\mathbf{a}^*) := \Pr[\varphi(y, \mathbf{b}, \mathbf{a}^*[\mathbf{b}]) = z],$$

where $\mathbf{b} = \beta(y)$ and the probability is over the randomness of $\beta$ and $\varphi$. Therefore, perfect security holds if and only if for every $\mathbf{a}^* \in \{0, 1\}^{2\ell}$ there exists a probability vector $\mathbf{p} \in \mathbb{R}^n$ such that for every $y \in \mathcal{Y}$ and for every $z \in \{0, \ldots, k-1\}$

$$\mathbf{p}^T \cdot M_f^z(\cdot, y) = q_{y,z}^{\Pi}(\mathbf{a}^*). \tag{1}$$

Observe that since $\mathbf{p}$ is a probability vector and since $\sum_z M_f^z$ is the all-one matrix, it is equivalent to consider only $k - 1$ possible values for $z$ instead of all $k$ values considered in Eq. (1). We next write the perfect security formulation more succinctly.

Let $M_f = \left[ M_f^1 || \dots || M_f^{k-1} \right]$ be the concatenation of the matrices by columns, and let $\mathbf{q}^{\Pi}(\mathbf{a}^*) := \left( (q_{y,z}^{\Pi}(\mathbf{a}^*))_{y \in \mathcal{Y}} \right)_{z \in [k-1]}$. Then Eq. (1) is equivalent to saying that for every $\mathbf{a}^*$ the vector $\mathbf{q}^{\Pi}(\mathbf{a}^*)$ belongs to the *convex-hull* of the rows of $M_f$. It will be convenient to index the columns of $M_f$ with $(y, z)$, i.e., we let $M_f(x, (y, z)) = M_f^z(x, y)$.[6] We now have an equivalent definition of perfect server security.

**Lemma 1.** *Let $\Pi$ be a protocol for computing some function $f : \mathcal{X} \times \mathcal{Y} \longmapsto \{0, \dots, k - 1\}$ in the 1-round $\mathcal{OT}$-hybrid model with CC of $\ell$. Then $\Pi$ has perfect server security if and only if for every $\mathbf{a}^* \in \{0, 1\}^{2\ell}$ it holds that*

$$\mathbf{q}^{\Pi}(\mathbf{a}^*) \in \mathbf{conv}\left( M_f^T \right).$$

We next describe another for security against a corrupt server. Intuitively, it states that for a malicious server, the *less* it deviates from the prescribed protocol, the *better* it can be simulated. Moreover, instead of using the traditional $\ell_1$ distance (i.e., statistical distance) we phrase the security in terms of the $\ell_\infty$ norm. This, somewhat non-standard definition will later act as a sufficient condition for reducing perfect server-security to perfect client-security.

**Definition 9.** *Let $f : (\mathcal{X} \cup \{\bot\}) \times \mathcal{Y} \longmapsto \{\bot, 0, \dots, k - 1\}$. Assume that $f(x, y) = \bot$ if and only if $x = \bot$. Let $\Pi = (\alpha, \beta, \varphi)$ be a protocol for computing $f$ in the 1-round $\mathcal{OT}$-hybrid model. We say that $\Pi$ is strong $\varepsilon$-server secure[7] if the following holds. For every message $\mathbf{a}^*$ sent by a malicious server in the $\mathcal{OT}$-hybrid world, there exists a probability vector $\mathbf{p} = (p_x)_{x \in (\mathcal{X} \cup \{\bot\})} \in \mathbb{R}^{|\mathcal{X}|+1}$ such that*

$$\left\| \mathbf{q}^{\Pi}(\mathbf{a}^*) - M_f^T \cdot \mathbf{p} \right\|_\infty \le \varepsilon \cdot p_\bot.$$

## 3.2 Stating the Main Result

With the above representation in mind, we are now ready to state our main result. We first recall the definition of a full-dimensional function, as stated in [2].

---

[6] We may view the above presentation differently. We can apply the presentation discussed for *Boolean* functions, to the function $f' : \mathcal{X} \times (\mathcal{Y} \times [k-1]) \longmapsto \{0, 1\}$, defined as $f'(x, (y, z)) = \Pr[f(x, y) = z]$.

[7] Although this definition as stated is not actually stronger than the standard server security definition, we decide to keep this name because of the intuition behind it. Furthermore, stating simulation error with respect to the $\ell_1$ norm instead of the $\ell_\infty$ norm, is in fact stronger.

**Definition 10 (full-dimensional function).** *We say that a function* $f : \mathcal{X} \times \mathcal{Y} \mapsto \{0, \ldots, k-1\}$ *is full-dimensional if*

$$\dim \left( \mathbf{aff} \left( M_f^T \right) \right) = (k-1) \cdot |\mathcal{Y}|,$$

*namely, the affine-hull defined by the rows of $M_f$ spans the entire vector space.*

Recall that a basis for an affine space of dimension $n$ has cardinality $n+1$, and therefore it must holds that $|\mathcal{X}| > (k-1) \cdot |\mathcal{Y}|$. Thus, the assumption that $f$ is full-dimensional implies this condition. We are now ready to state our main result.

**Theorem 3.** *Let* $f : \mathcal{X} \times \mathcal{Y} \mapsto \{0, \ldots, k-1\}$ *be a full-dimensional function. Then there exists a protocol $\Pi$ in the 1-round $\mathcal{OT}$-hybrid model, that computes $f$ with perfect full-security. Furthermore, if $f$ is deterministic the CC is the following. Let $\gamma_i$ denote the size of the smallest formula for evaluating the $i$'th bit of $f(x, y)$, and let $\gamma = \max_i \gamma_i$. Then $\Pi$ has CC at most*

$$\xi \cdot \gamma^2 \cdot \log k \cdot \log |\mathcal{Y}| \cdot \mathrm{poly} \left( k \cdot |\mathcal{Y}| \right),$$

*where $\xi \in \mathbb{R}^+$ is some global constant independent of the function $f$.*

Although the communication complexity of our protocol is roughly $\mathrm{poly} \left( k \cdot |\mathcal{Y}| \right)$, for functions with small client-domain, it does yield a concrete improvement upon known protocols such as the protocol proposed by [19].

A simple corollary of Theorem 3 is that adding constant columns to a full-dimensional function, results in a functions that can still be computed with perfect security.

**Corollary 1.** *Let* $f : \mathcal{X} \times \mathcal{Y} \mapsto \{0, \ldots, k-1\}$ *be some function. Assume that there exists a subset $\mathcal{Y}' \subseteq \mathcal{Y}$ that fixes the output distribution of $f$, i.e., for all $y \in \mathcal{Y}'$ there exists a distribution $D_y$ over $\{0, \ldots, k-1\}$ such that $f(x, y) \equiv D_y$ for every $x \in \mathcal{X}$. Then if the function $f' : \mathcal{X} \times (\mathcal{Y} \setminus \mathcal{Y}') \mapsto \{0, \ldots, k-1\}$, defined as $f'(x, y) = f(x, y)$, is full-dimensional, then $f$ can be computed the 1-round $\mathcal{OT}$-hybrid model with perfect full-security and with the same communication complexity as $f'$.*

Many interesting examples of functionalities that satisfy the constraints in Theorem 3 and Corollary 1 exists. Yao's millionaires' problem is an example for such a function. Here, the server and the client each hold a number from 1 to $n$. The output is 1 if and only if the client's input is greater than or equal to the server's input. The matrix for this function has a constant column of 1's (when taking the client's input to be $n$). After removing it, the last row of the matrix will be the all 0 vector, and the other rows are linearly independent. Therefore the function satisfies the constraints in Corollary 1.

Theorem 3 clearly follows from the following two lemmata. The first lemma reduces the problem of constructing a perfectly secure protocol, to the task of constructing a protocol with perfect client security and strong statistical server security. The second lemma states that such a protocol exists.

**Lemma 2.** *Let $f : \mathcal{X} \times \mathcal{Y} \mapsto \{0, \ldots, k-1\}$ be some function. Define the function $g : (\mathcal{X} \cup \{\perp\}) \times \mathcal{Y} \mapsto \{\perp, 0, \ldots, k-1\}$ as $g(x,y) = f(x,y)$ if $x \neq \perp$ and $g(\perp, y) = \perp$, for every $y \in \mathcal{Y}$. Assume that for every $\varepsilon > 0$, there exists a protocol $\Pi_g(\varepsilon)$ in the 1-round $\mathcal{OT}$-hybrid model that computes $g$ with correctness, is strong $\varepsilon$-server secure, has perfect client security, and has CC at most $\ell(\varepsilon, |\mathcal{X}|, |\mathcal{Y}|, k)$. Then, if $f$ is full-dimensional, there exists a protocol $\Pi_f$ in the 1-round $\mathcal{OT}$-hybrid model, that computes $f$ with perfect full-security. Moreover, if $f$ is deterministic then $\Pi_f$ has CC at most*

$$\ell\left(\frac{1}{2n(n+1)!}, |\mathcal{X}|, |\mathcal{Y}|, k\right),$$

*where $n = (k-1) \cdot |\mathcal{Y}|$.*

**Lemma 3.** *Let $g : (\mathcal{X} \cup \{\perp\}) \times \mathcal{Y} \mapsto \{\perp, 0, \ldots, k-1\}$ be a function such that $g(x,y) = \perp$ if and only if $x = \perp$. Then for every $\varepsilon > 0$, there exists a protocol $\Pi_g(\varepsilon)$ in the 1-round $\mathcal{OT}$-hybrid model that computes $g$ with correctness, is strong $\varepsilon$-server secure, and has perfect client security. Furthermore, its communication complexity is the following. Let $\gamma_i$ denote the size of the smallest formula for evaluating the $i$-th bit of $g(x,y)$, and let $\gamma = \max_i \gamma_i$. Then $\Pi_g(\varepsilon)$ has CC at most*

$$\xi \cdot \gamma^2 \cdot \log k \cdot \log |\mathcal{Y}| \cdot \text{polylog}\left(\varepsilon^{-1}\right),$$

*where $\xi \in \mathbb{R}^+$ is some global constant independent of the function $g$ and of $\varepsilon$.*

We prove Lemma 2 in Sect. 4 and we prove Lemma 3 in Sect. 5.

## 4 Proof of Lemma 2

In this section, we reduce the problem of constructing a perfectly secure protocol, to the problem of constructing a protocol that has perfect client security and has strong statistical server security. The idea is to wrap the given protocol for computing $g$. Whenever the output of $\Pi_g(\varepsilon)$ is $\perp$ (for small enough $\varepsilon$), the client will choose $x_0 \in \mathcal{X}$ at random and output $f(x_0, y)$. Stated from a geometric point of view, the client outputs according to a distribution that is consistent with some point that is *strictly inside* the convex-hull of the rows of $M_f$ (e.g., the center).

*Proof (of Lemma 2).* It is easy to see that if the probability that the output of $\Pi_g(\varepsilon)$ equals $\perp$ is 0 for every $y \in \mathcal{Y}$ for some $\varepsilon > 0$, then $\Pi_g(\varepsilon)$ computes $f$ with perfect security.

Assume otherwise. Let $n = (k-1) \cdot |\mathcal{Y}|$. Since $f$ is full-dimensional there exists a subset $\mathcal{S} = \{\mathbf{x}_0, \ldots, \mathbf{x}_n\} \subseteq \mathbb{R}^n$ of the rows of $M_f$, that is affinely independent. Let $\mathbf{u}_\mathcal{S} \in \mathbb{R}^n$ be the vector associated with uniform distribution over $\mathcal{S}$ (i.e., $u_i = 1/|\mathcal{S}|$ if $i \in \mathcal{S}$ and $u_i = 0$ otherwise), and let $\mathbf{c} = (c_{y,z})_{y \in \mathcal{Y}, z \in [k-1]} := M_f^T \cdot \mathbf{u}_\mathcal{S}$ be the center of the simplex[8] defined by the points in $\mathcal{S}$. The protocol $\Pi_f$ is described as follows.

---

[8] A simplex is the convex-hull of an affinely independent set of points.

**Protocol 4** ($\Pi_f$)

   *Input: Server* S *has input* $x \in \mathcal{X}$ *and client* C *has input* $y \in \mathcal{Y}$.

1. *The parties execute protocol* $\Pi_g (\varepsilon)$ *with small enough* $\varepsilon > 0$ *to be determined by the analysis. Let* $z$ *be the output* C *receive.*
2. *If* $z \neq \perp$, *then* C *output* $z$. *Otherwise, output* $z' \in [k-1]$ *with probability* $c_{y,z'}$ *(and output 0 with the complement probability).*

Correctness and perfect client-security follows from the fact that $\Pi_g$ satisfies these properties. It remains to show that perfect server-security holds. By Lemma 1, it suffices to show that for every $\mathbf{a}^* \in \{0,1\}^{2\ell}$ sent to the OT by a malicious server, it holds that

$$\mathbf{q}^{\Pi_f} (\mathbf{a}^*) \in \mathbf{conv} \left( M_f^T \right). \tag{2}$$

Fix $\mathbf{a}^* \in \{0,1\}^{2\ell}$. For brevity, we write $\mathbf{q}^f$ and $\mathbf{q}^g$ instead of $\mathbf{q}^{\Pi_f} (\mathbf{a}^*)$ and $\mathbf{q}^{\Pi_g(\varepsilon)} (\mathbf{a}^*)$ respectively. Since $\Pi_g(\varepsilon)$ is strong $\varepsilon$-server secure, it follows that there exists a probability vector $\mathbf{p}^g \in \mathbb{R}^{|\mathcal{X}|+1}$ such that

$$\mathbf{q}^g = M_g^T \cdot \mathbf{p}^g + \mathbf{err}, \tag{3}$$

where $\mathbf{err} \in \mathbb{R}^{k \cdot |\mathcal{Y}|}$ satisfies $||\mathbf{err}||_\infty \leq \varepsilon \cdot p_\perp^g$. Let $\overline{\mathbf{p}}^g = (p_x^g)_{x \in \mathcal{X}}$ be the vector $\mathbf{p}$ with $p_\perp$ removed. We first show that Eq. (2) follows from the following two claims.

**Claim 5.** *There exists a vector* $\widehat{\mathbf{err}} \in \mathbb{R}^{k \cdot |\mathcal{Y}|}$ *satisfying* $||\widehat{\mathbf{err}}||_\infty \leq 2\varepsilon$, *such that*

$$\mathbf{q}^f = M_f^T \cdot \overline{\mathbf{p}}^g + p_\perp \cdot (\mathbf{c} + \widehat{\mathbf{err}}).$$

**Claim 6.** *There exists a small enough* $\varepsilon > 0$ *such that*

$$\mathbf{c} + \widehat{\mathbf{err}} \in \mathbf{conv} \left( M_f^T \right),$$

*where* $\widehat{\mathbf{err}}$ *is the same as in Claim 5.*

Indeed, by Claim 6 there exists a probability vector $\widehat{\mathbf{p}} \in \mathbb{R}^{|\mathcal{X}|}$ such that

$$\mathbf{c} + \widehat{\mathbf{err}} = M_f^T \cdot \widehat{\mathbf{p}}.$$

Thus, by Claim 5

$$\mathbf{q}^f = M_f^T \cdot \overline{\mathbf{p}}^g + p_\perp \cdot (\mathbf{c} + \widehat{\mathbf{err}}) = M_f^T \cdot (\overline{\mathbf{p}}^g + p_\perp \cdot \widehat{\mathbf{p}}).$$

Recall that the entries of $\overline{\mathbf{p}}$ sum up to $1 - p_\perp$. Therefore $\overline{\mathbf{p}}^g + p_\perp \cdot \widehat{\mathbf{p}}$ is a probability vector, hence Eq. (2) holds.

   To conclude the proof, we next prove Claims 5 and 6.

*Proof (of Claim 5).* Let $\mathbf{err}' = \frac{1}{p_\perp} \cdot \mathbf{err}$. Observe that for every $y \in \mathcal{Y}$ and $z \in [k-1]$ it holds that

$$
\begin{aligned}
q^f_{y,z} &= q^g_{y,z} + q^g_{y,\perp} \cdot c_{y,z} \\
&= M^T_g \left( \cdot, (y,z) \right) \cdot \mathbf{p}^g + \mathbf{err}_{y,z} + \left( M^T_g \left( \cdot, (y,\perp) \right) \cdot \mathbf{p}^g + \mathbf{err}_{y,\perp} \right) \cdot c_{y,z} \\
&= M^T_f \left( \cdot, (y,z) \right) \cdot \overline{\mathbf{p}}^g + \mathbf{err}_{y,z} + (p_\perp + \mathbf{err}_{y,\perp}) \cdot c_{y,z} \\
&= M^T_f \left( \cdot, (y,z) \right) \cdot \overline{\mathbf{p}}^g + p_\perp \cdot (c_{y,z} + \mathbf{err}'_{y,z} + \mathbf{err}'_{y,\perp} \cdot c_{y,z}),
\end{aligned}
$$

where the first equality is by the description of $\Pi_f$, the second is by Eq. (3), and the third follows from the definition of $g$. Define the vector $\widehat{\mathbf{err}}$ as follows. For every $y \in \mathcal{Y}$ and $z \in [k-1]$ let $\widehat{\mathbf{err}}_{y,z} = \mathbf{err}'_{y,z} + \mathbf{err}'_{y,\perp} \cdot c_{y,z}$. Then

$$
\mathbf{q}^f = M^T_f \cdot \overline{\mathbf{p}}^g + p_\perp \cdot (\mathbf{c} + \widehat{\mathbf{err}}).
$$

To conclude the proof, we upper-bound $\|\widehat{\mathbf{err}}\|_\infty$. It holds that

$$
\|\widehat{\mathbf{err}}\|_\infty \leq \|\mathbf{err}'\|_\infty \cdot (1 + \|\mathbf{c}\|_\infty) = \frac{1}{p_\perp} \cdot \|\mathbf{err}\|_\infty \cdot (1 + \|\mathbf{c}\|_\infty) \leq 2\varepsilon.
$$

*Proof (of Claim 6).* One approach would be to use similar techniques as in [2], namely, take a "small enough" Euclidean ball around $\mathbf{c}$ and take $\varepsilon$ to be small enough so that $\mathbf{c} + \widehat{\mathbf{err}}$ is contained inside the ball. This approach, however, only proves the existence of such an $\varepsilon$. We take a slightly different approach, which would also provide an explicit upper bound on $\varepsilon$ for deterministic functions.

For every $i \in [n]$ let $\overline{\mathbf{x}}_i = \mathbf{x}_i - \mathbf{x}_0$, let $\overline{\mathcal{S}} = \{\overline{\mathbf{x}}_1, \ldots, \overline{\mathbf{x}}_n\}$ be a basis for $\mathbb{R}^n$, and let $A = [\overline{\mathbf{x}}_1 \| \ldots \| \overline{\mathbf{x}}_n]$ be the corresponding change of basis matrix. Then

$$
\mathbf{c} = M^T_f \cdot \mathbf{u}_\mathcal{S} = \sum_{i=0}^{n} \frac{1}{n+1} \cdot \mathbf{x}_i = \mathbf{x}_0 + \sum_{i=1}^{n} \frac{1}{n+1} \cdot \overline{\mathbf{x}}_i = \mathbf{x}_0 + \frac{1}{n+1} \cdot A \cdot \mathbf{1}_n. \quad (4)
$$

Observe that a point $\mathbf{v}$ is in the convex-hull of $\mathcal{S}$ if and only if it can be written as $\mathbf{x}_0 + \sum_{i=1}^{n} p_i \cdot \overline{\mathbf{x}}_i$, where the $p_i$'s are non-negative real numbers that sum up to *at most* 1. Indeed, we can write

$$
\mathbf{x}_0 + \sum_{i=1}^{n} p_i \cdot \overline{\mathbf{x}}_i = \left( 1 - \sum_{i=1}^{n} p_i \right) \cdot \mathbf{x}_0 + \sum_{i=1}^{n} p_i \cdot \mathbf{x}_i.
$$

Next, as $\overline{\mathcal{S}}$ forms a basis, there exists a vector $\widetilde{\mathbf{err}} \in \mathbb{R}^n$ such that $\widehat{\mathbf{err}} = A \cdot \widetilde{\mathbf{err}}$. Then, if $\|\widetilde{\mathbf{err}}\|_\infty \leq \frac{1}{n(n+1)}$, by Eq. (4) it follows that

$$
\mathbf{c} + \widehat{\mathbf{err}} = \mathbf{x}_0 + A \cdot \left( \frac{1}{n+1} \cdot \mathbf{1}_n + \widetilde{\mathbf{err}} \right) = \mathbf{x}_0 + \sum_{i=1}^{n} p_i \cdot \overline{\mathbf{x}}_i,
$$

where $0 \leq p_i \leq 1/n$ for every $i \in [n]$, implying that the point is inside $\mathbf{conv}\,(\mathcal{S})$. Thus, it suffices to find $\varepsilon$ for which $||\widehat{\mathbf{err}}||_\infty \leq \frac{1}{n(n+1)}$. It holds that

$$
\begin{aligned}
||\widehat{\mathbf{err}}||_\infty &= ||A^{-1} \cdot \overline{\mathbf{err}}||_\infty \\
&= \max_{i \in [n]} \left\{ |A^{-1}(i, \cdot) \cdot \overline{\mathbf{err}}| \right\} \\
&\leq \max_{i \in [n]} \left\{ \sum_{j=1}^{n} |A^{-1}(i,j) \cdot \widehat{\mathbf{err}}_j| \right\} \\
&= \max_{i \in [n]} \left\{ \sum_{j=1}^{n} \left| \frac{\det (A_{j,i})}{\det (A)} \right| \cdot |\widehat{\mathbf{err}}_j| \right\} \\
&\leq n \cdot \frac{(n-1)!}{|\det (A)|} \cdot 2\varepsilon \\
&= \frac{2n!}{|\det (A)|} \cdot \varepsilon,
\end{aligned}
$$

where the third equality is by Fact 2, and the second inequality is due to the fact that each entry in $A$ is a real number between $-1$ and $1$. Therefore, by taking $\varepsilon = \frac{|\det(A)|}{2n(n+1)!}$ the claim will follow. Observe that if the function $f$ is deterministic, then the entries of $A$ are in $\{-1,1\}$ implying that $|\det (A)| \geq 1$, and hence taking $\varepsilon = \frac{1}{2n(n+1)!}$ suffices. Therefore the communication complexity will be at most $\ell\left(\frac{1}{2n(n+1)!}, |\mathcal{X}|, |\mathcal{Y}|, k\right)$ in this case.

## 5   Proof of Lemma 3

In this section we fix a function $g : (\mathcal{X} \cup \{\bot\}) \times \mathcal{Y} \mapsto \{\bot, 0, \ldots, k-1\}$ satisfying $g(x,y) = \bot$ if and only if $x = \bot$. We show how to construct a protocol for computing the function $g$ in the 1-round $\mathcal{OT}$-hybrid model. The protocol we construct has perfect client security, and has strong statistical server security. Our protocol is a modified version of the protocol by Ishai et al. [19], which we shall next give an overview of. Their protocol is parametrized with $\varepsilon$, and we denote this protocol by $\Pi_{\mathrm{IKOPS}}(\varepsilon)$. It is a single round protocol in the $\mathcal{OT}$-hybrid model, that has $\varepsilon$-statistical full-security. It is stated for functions computable by $\mathrm{NC}^1$ circuits, however, this is only done for improving concrete efficiency, which is not a concern in our paper. We therefore restate it for general functions, and bound its communication complexity as a function of $|\mathcal{X}|$, $|\mathcal{Y}|$, and $k$ (which are assumed to be finite in our work).

## 5.1   The Protocol $\Pi_{\mathrm{IKOPS}}$ The IKOPS Protocol

We next give the rough idea of $\Pi_{\mathrm{IKOPS}}$. First, we view the inputs $x$ and $y$ as a binary strings.[9] The parties will compute a "certified OT" functionality. We next give a brief overview of the IKOPS protocol.

The main idea behind the $\Pi_{\mathrm{IKOPS}}$ is to have the server run an "MPC in the head" [18]. That is, the real server locally emulates the execution of a perfectly secure protocol $\Pi$ with many virtual servers performing the computation, and $2m$ virtual clients, denoted $C_{1,0}, C_{1,1}, \ldots, C_{m,0}, C_{m,1}$, receiving output, where $m$ is the number of bits in the client's input $y$. The underlying protocol $\Pi$ computes a decomposable PRE $\hat{g} = (\hat{g}_0, \hat{g}_1, \ldots, \hat{g}_m)$ of $g$. Specifically, the output of client $C_{j,b}$ in an execution of $\Pi$ is the corresponds to the $j$-th bit of $y$, when the bit equals to $b$.

The real client can then use OT in order to recover the correct output of the PRE and reconstruct the output $g(x, y)$. As part of the "MPC in the head" paradigm, the client further ask the server to send a watchlist (the views of some of the virtual servers) and check consistency. If there was an inconsistency, then the client outputs $\bot$. To make sure that the client will not receive too large of a watchlist and break the privacy requirement, it will get each view with some (constant) probability independently of the other views.

Observe that although the client can use OT in order to receive the correct output from the virtual clients, the two real parties need to use string-OT, while they only have access to bit-OT. This technicality can be overcome using the perfect reduction from $\binom{n}{1}$-$s$-string-OT to OT that was put forward in the elegant work of Brassard et al. [8], which also constitutes one of the few examples of perfect reductions to $\binom{2}{1}$-bit-OT known so far. They proved the following theorem.

**Theorem 7.** *There exists a protocol $\Pi_{\mathrm{BCS}} = (\alpha_{\mathrm{BCS}}, \beta_{\mathrm{BCS}}, \varphi_{\mathrm{BCS}})$ in the 1-round OT-hybrid world that computes $\binom{n}{1}$-$s$-string-OT with perfect full-security. Furthermore, its communication complexity is at most $5s(n-1)$.*

The security of the protocol described so far can still be breached by a malicious server. By tampering with the outputs of the virtual clients, a malicious server could force the output of the real client to be $g(x, y)$ for some inputs $y$ and force the output to be $\bot$ for other values of $y$, where the choice is *completely determined* by the adversary. To overcome this problem, we replace $g$ with a function $g'$ where each bit $y_i$ is replaced with $m'$ random bit whose XOR equals

---

[9] We can assume without loss of generality that the size of $\mathcal{X}$ and $\mathcal{Y}$ are a power of 2. This is due to the fact that we can add new elements to $\mathcal{X}$ such that the new rows in $M_f$ are duplicates of existing rows. We then do the same to $\mathcal{Y}$. It is easy to see that the new function is computable with statistical (perfect) full-security if and only if the previous function is computable with statistical (perfect) full-security.

to $y_i$, for some large $m'$.[10] Here, the adversary does not have complete control over which inputs the client will output $\bot$, and for which inputs it will output $g(x, y)$. We next describe the protocol formally. We start with some notations.

*Notation.* Throughout the following section, client's input are now binary strings $\mathbf{y}$ of length $m$. Let $m' = m'(\varepsilon) = \lceil \log(\varepsilon^{-1}) \rceil + 1$ and let $\mathsf{Enc} : \{0,1\}^m \mapsto \left( \{0,1\}^{m'} \right)^m$ be a randomized function that on input $m$ bits $y_1, \ldots, y_m$, outputs $m \cdot m'$ random bits $\left( y_i^1, \ldots, y_i^{m'} \right)_{i \in [m]}$ conditioned on $\oplus_{j=1}^{m'} y_i^j = y_i$ for every $i \in [m]$. We also let $\mathsf{Dec} : \left( \{0,1\}^{m'} \right)^m \mapsto \{0,1\}^m$ be the inverse of $\mathsf{Enc}$, namely,

$$\mathsf{Dec}\left( \left( y_i^1, \ldots, y_i^{m'} \right)_{i \in [m]} \right) = \left( y_i^1 \oplus \ldots \oplus y_i^{m'} \right)_{i \in [m]}.$$

Finally, we let $g' : (\mathcal{X} \cup \{\bot\}) \times \left( \{0,1\}^{m'} \right)^m \mapsto \{\bot, 0, \ldots, k-1\}$ be defined as

$$g'\left( x, \left( y_i^1, \ldots, y_i^{m'} \right)_{i \in [m]} \right) = g\left( x, \mathsf{Dec}\left( \left( y_i^1, \ldots, y_i^{m'} \right)_{i \in [m]} \right) \right),$$

and let $\hat{g}$ be a decomposable PRE of $g'$.

**Protocol 8** ($\Pi_{\mathrm{IKOPS}}(\varepsilon)$)
    *Input: Server has input $x \in (\mathcal{X} \cup \{\bot\})$ and client has input $\mathbf{y} \in \{0,1\}^m$.*

- $\alpha(x)$:
  1. The server $\mathsf{S}$ *runs "MPC in the head" for the following functionality. There are $n = \Theta\left( \log(\varepsilon^{-1}) \right)$ virtual servers $\mathsf{S}_1, \ldots, \mathsf{S}_n$ with inputs and $2m \cdot m'$ virtual clients $\mathsf{C}_{1,0}, \mathsf{C}_{1,1}, \ldots, \mathsf{C}_{m \cdot m',0}, \mathsf{C}_{m \cdot m',1}$ receiving outputs. Each virtual server holds a share of the $\mathsf{S}$'s input and randomness, where the shares are in an $n$-out-of-$n$ secret sharing scheme. Each virtual client $\mathsf{C}_{j,b}$ will receive $\hat{g}_{j,b}(x)$, namely, it will receive the $(j,b)$-th component of the decomposable PRE where the first part of the input is fixed to $x$. In addition every virtual client will hold $\hat{g}_0(x)$ which is the value of $\hat{g}$ that depends only on $x$ and the randomness.*
  2. The virtual parties execute a multiparty protocol in order to compute $\hat{g}$. The protocol used has perfect full-security against $t = \lceil n/3 \rceil - 1$ corrupted virtual servers and any number of corrupted virtual clients. We also assume that the virtual clients receive messages at the last round of the protocol. (e.g., the BGW protocol [7]).*

---

[10] This method has the disadvantage of increasing the length of the client's input and as a result increase the communication complexity, so [19] suggested a different approach. We stick with the presented approach, as we prefer simplicity over concrete efficiency.

3. Let $V_{j,b}$ be the view of $C_{j,b}$, and let $\mathbf{a}_1 = (\alpha_{BCS}(V_{j,0}, V_{j,1}))_{j \in [m \cdot m']}$.

4. Let $V_i$ be the view of $S_i$. For each $i \in [n]$ the server creates $\tilde{\mathbf{a}}_i$ of length $\lceil 2n/t \rceil$, where $V_i$ is located in a randomly chosen entry, while the other entries are $\perp$ (this allows the server to send each $V_i$ with probability $t/2n$). Let $\mathbf{a}_2 = (\alpha_{BCS}(\tilde{\mathbf{a}}_i))_{i \in [n]}$.

5. Output $\mathbf{a} = (\mathbf{a}_1, \mathbf{a}_2)$.

- $\beta(\mathbf{y})$:

  1. The client computes $\left(y_i^1, \ldots, y_i^{m'}\right)_{i \in [m]} = \mathsf{Enc}(\mathbf{y})$.

  2. Let $\mathbf{b}_1 = \left(\beta_{BCS}\left(y_j^{j'}\right)\right)_{j \in [m], j \in [m']}$.

  3. Let $\mathbf{b}_2 = (\beta_{BCS}(1))_{i \in [\lceil 2n/t \rceil]}$ (i.e., a constant vector of length $\lceil 2n/t \rceil$).

  4. Output $\mathbf{b} = (\mathbf{b}_1, \mathbf{b}_2)$.

- $\varphi(\mathbf{y}, \mathbf{b}, \mathbf{c}')$:

  1. Let $\mathbf{c} = (\varphi_{BCS}(c_i'))_i$[11]. Write $\mathbf{c} = (\mathbf{c}_1, \mathbf{c}_2)$, where $\mathbf{c}_1$ corresponds to the outputs and $\mathbf{c}_2$ corresponds to the watchlist.

  2. For every $V_{j,b}$ in $\mathbf{c}_1$, we may write without loss of generality that $V_{j,b} = \left(V_{j,b}^i\right)_{i \in [n]}$, where $V_{j,b}^i$ is the message that $V_i$ sends to $V_{j,b}$.

  3. If there exists $V_{i_1}, V_{i_2} \in \mathbf{c}_2$ or $V_i \in \mathbf{c}_2$ and $V_{j,b}^i \in \mathbf{c}_1$ that are inconsistent, output $\perp$.

  4. Otherwise, apply the PRE decoder on $\mathbf{c}_1$ to recover the output $z$.

We summarize the properties of the protocol below.

**Theorem 9 ([19, Theorem 1]).** *For every $\varepsilon > 0$, $\Pi_{IKOPS}(\varepsilon)$ computes $g$ with $\varepsilon$-statistical full security.*[12] *Furthermore, using the PRE from [1, 16] and the BGW protocol, the CC will be the following. Let $\gamma_i$ denote the size of the smallest formula for evaluating the $i$'th bit of $g(x, y)$, and let $\gamma = \max_i \gamma_i$. Then, $\Pi_{IKOPS}$ has CC at most*

$$\ell_{IKOPS} = \xi_{IKOPS} \cdot \gamma^2 \cdot \log k \cdot \log |\mathcal{Y}| \cdot \mathrm{polylog}\left(\varepsilon^{-1}\right),$$

*where $\xi_{IKOPS} \in \mathbb{R}^+$ is some global constant independent of the function $g$ and of $\varepsilon$.*

Observe that $\Pi_{IKOPS}$ has a (small) non-zero probability of the client seeing to many views of the virtual servers (in the worst case all of them which gives him the knowledge of $x$). Thus, $\Pi_{IKOPS}$ is not perfectly client secure.

In the following section, we slightly tweak $\Pi_{IKOPS}$, making the watchlists deterministic, thereby making it perfectly client secure. The new protocol will have the desired properties as stated in Lemma 3.

---

[11] The function $\varphi$ is different when applying to recover $\mathbf{a}_1[\mathbf{b}_1]$ from when applying to recover $\mathbf{a}_2[\mathbf{b}_2]$. To keep the presentation simple we will abuse notation and write as if they are the same function.

[12] In fact, the protocol even admits strong $\varepsilon$-server security.

## 5.2   Setting up Fixed-Size Watchlists

Recall the problem with client privacy was in the fact that the client may watch the internal state of too many servers, breaching perfect security of the protocol $\Pi_{\mathrm{IKOPS}}$, and thus of the entire construction. To solve this problem, we replace the current watchlist setup with a *fixed-size watchlist* setup.

In order to achieve the fixed-size watchlist, the parties will use a perfectly secure protocol for computing $\binom{n}{t/2}$-$s$-string-OT. We do not know, however, if such a protocol even exists in the $\mathcal{OT}$-hybrid model. Instead, we relax the security notion a bit, so that we will be able to construct the protocol, and its security guarantees still suffice for the main protocol. Specifically, we show how in the $\mathcal{OT}$-hybrid model, the parties can compute $\binom{n}{t/2}$-$s$-string-OT in a single round, where a malicious client will only be able to learn at most $t$ strings rather than $t/2$. We stress that the construction we suggest *does not* achieve perfect server security. Instead, it admits perfect *input-dependent security*. As we show in Sect. 5.3, this will not affect the security properties of our final construction.

Let $t, n, s \in \mathbb{N}$ where $t < n$, and $s \geq 1$. For simplicity, we assume that $t$ is even. Let $f_1$ and $f_2$ be the $\binom{n}{t/2}$-$s$-string-OT and $\binom{n}{t}$-$s$-string-OT functionalities respectively. We next briefly explain the ideas behind the construction. The parties will use protocol $\Pi_{\mathrm{BCS}}$ in order to simulate computation of $n$ instances of $\binom{2}{1}$-$sn$-string-OT in parallel. On input $(x_1, \ldots, x_n)$, the $i$-th pair of strings the server will send (by first applying $\alpha_{\mathrm{BCS}}$) consist of a masking of the $i$-th string $x_i$, and a Shamir share of the concatenation of all of the maskings, that is, the pair will be $(x_i \oplus r_i, \mathbf{r}[i])$, where $\mathbf{r} = (r_1, \ldots, r_n)$. The client will then recover the maskings of the correct outputs alongside the shares, which will help him to reconstruct the outputs. Since for each $i$ the client will learn either a share or a masked string, a malicious client will not be able to learn to many masked strings. The protocol $\Pi_{\mathrm{ROT}} = (\alpha_{\mathrm{ROT}}, \beta_{\mathrm{ROT}}, \varphi_{\mathrm{ROT}})$ for computing $f_1$ in the 1-round $\mathcal{OT}$-hybrid model is formally described as follows.

**Construction 10 ($\Pi_{\mathrm{ROT}}$)**
*Input: Server* S *holds* $\mathbf{x} = (x_1, \ldots, x_n) \in (\{0,1\}^s)^n$, *and the client* C *holds* $\mathbf{y} = \{y_1, \ldots, y_{t/2}\} \subseteq [n]$.

- $\alpha_{\mathrm{ROT}}(\mathbf{x})$: *Samples* $n$ *random strings* $r_1, \ldots, r_n \leftarrow \{0,1\}^s$ *independently. For every* $i \in [n]$, *let* $\mathbf{r}[i] \in \{0,1\}^{sn}$ *be a share of* $\mathbf{r} = (r_1, \ldots, r_n)$ *in an* $(n-t)$-*out-of-*$n$ *Shamir's secret sharing (we pad* $\mathbf{r}[i]$ *if needed). Output* $\mathbf{a} = \left(\alpha_{\mathrm{BCS}}\left((x_i \oplus r_i, \mathbf{r}[i])\right)\right)_{i \in [n]}$ *(the* $x_i \oplus r_i$'s *are also padded accordingly).*
- $\beta_{\mathrm{ROT}}(\mathbf{y})$: *Output* $\mathbf{b} = (\beta_{\mathrm{BCS}}(b_1), \ldots, \beta_{\mathrm{BCS}}(b_n))$, *where* $b_i = 0$ *if and only if* $i \in \mathbf{y}$.
- $\varphi_{\mathrm{ROT}}(\mathbf{y}, \mathbf{b}, \mathbf{c}')$: *Let* $\mathbf{c} = (\varphi_{\mathrm{BCS}}(c_i'))_{i=1}^{n}$, *let* $\mathbf{c}_1 = (c_i)_{i \in \mathbf{y}}$, *and let* $\mathbf{c}_2 = (c_i)_{i \notin \mathbf{y}}$. *If the elements in* $\mathbf{c}_2$ *agree on a common secret* $\mathbf{r} \in \{0,1\}^{sn}$, *then output* $\mathbf{c}_1 \oplus (r_i)_{i \in \mathbf{y}}$. *Otherwise, output* $\perp$.

**Lemma 4.** $\Pi_{\mathrm{ROT}}$ *computes* $f_1$ *with CC at most* $5 \cdot sn^2$, *such that the following holds:*

- $\Pi_{\mathrm{ROT}}$ *is correct.*
- $\Pi_{\mathrm{ROT}}$ *has perfect input-dependent security.*
- *For any non-uniform adversary* $\mathcal{A}$ *corrupting the client in the* $\mathcal{OT}$-*hybrid world, there exists a non-uniform simulator* $\mathrm{Sim}_{\mathcal{A}}$ *corrupting the client in the ideal-world of* $f_2$, *such that for all* $\mathbf{x} \in (\{0,1\}^s)^n$, $\mathbf{y} \subseteq [n]$ *of size* $t/2$, *and* $\mathrm{aux} \in \{0,1\}^*$ *it holds that*

$$\mathrm{View}^{\mathrm{HYBRID}}_{\mathcal{A}(\mathbf{y},\mathrm{aux}),\Pi_{\mathrm{ROT}}}(x,\mathbf{y}) \equiv \mathrm{View}^{\mathrm{IDEAL}}_{\mathrm{Sim}_{\mathcal{A}}(\mathbf{y},\mathrm{aux}),f_2}(x,\mathbf{y}).$$

*In other words, although the simulator receives* $t/2$ *indexes as inputs, it is allowed to ask for* $t$ *strings from the server's input.*

Intuitively, a malicious server cannot force the client to reconstruct two different secrets $\mathbf{r}$ for two different inputs. This is due to the fact that for every two different inputs the set of common $b_i$'s that are 1 (i.e., the number of common shares the client will receive for both inputs) is of size at least $n - t$. This implies that up to a certain set of client-inputs that the adversary can choose, the client will receive a correct output. As for a malicious client, observe that it can ask for at most $t$ masked values, as otherwise it will not have enough shares to recover the secret $\mathbf{r}$.

We next incorporate $\Pi_{\mathrm{ROT}}$ into $\Pi_{\mathrm{IKOPS}}$ to get a protocol that is perfectly client-secure. The full proof of Lemma 4 is deferred to Sect. 5.4.

## 5.3   Upgrading $\Pi_{\mathrm{IKOPS}}$

We are finally ready to prove Lemma 3. As stated in Sect. 5.2, we replace the randomly chosen watchlist with a deterministic one using $\Pi_{\mathrm{ROT}}$. Formally, the protocol, denoted $\Pi^+_{\mathrm{IKOPS}}$, is described as follows.

**Protocol 11** $(\Pi^+_{\mathrm{IKOPS}}(\varepsilon))$
  *Input: Server has input* $x \in (\mathcal{X} \cup \{\bot\})$ *and client has input* $\mathbf{y} \in \{0,1\}^m$.

- $\alpha^+(x)$: *Output* $(\mathbf{a}_1, \mathbf{a}_2)$ *as in* $\Pi_{\mathrm{IKOPS}}$, *with the exception of* $\mathbf{a}_2$ *being equal to* $\alpha_{\mathrm{ROT}}(V_1, \dots, V_n)$ *(recall that* $V_i$ *is the view of the virtual server* $S_i$).
- $\beta^+(\mathbf{y})$: *Output* $(\mathbf{b}_1, \mathbf{b}_2)$ *as in* $\Pi_{\mathrm{IKOPS}}$, *with the exception of* $\mathbf{b}_2$ *being equal to* $\beta_{\mathrm{ROT}}(\mathcal{W})$, *where* $\mathcal{W} \subseteq [n]$ *is of size* $t/2$ *chosen uniformly at random (recall that* $t = \lceil n/3 \rceil - 1$ *bounds the number of corrupted parties in the MPC protocol).*
- $\varphi^+(\mathbf{y}, \mathbf{b}, \mathbf{c}')$: *Output same as* $\varphi(\mathbf{y}, \mathbf{b}, \mathbf{c}')$, *with the exception that we apply* $\varphi_{\mathrm{ROT}}$ *to recover the outputs and watchlist.*

Clearly, Lemma 3 follows from the following lemma, asserting the security of $\Pi^+_{\mathrm{IKOPS}}$.

**Lemma 5.** *For every $\varepsilon > 0$, $\Pi_{\mathrm{IKOPS}}^{+}(\varepsilon)$ computes $g$ with correctness, it is strong $\varepsilon$-server secure, and has perfect client security. Furthermore, using the PRE from [1,16] and the BGW protocol, the CC will be the following. Let $\gamma_i$ denote the size of the smallest formula for evaluating the $i$'th bit of $g(x,y)$, and let $\gamma = \max_i \gamma_i$. Then, $\Pi_{\mathrm{IKOPS}}^{+}$ has CC at most*

$$\ell_{\mathrm{IKOPS}}^{+} = \xi_{\mathrm{IKOPS}}^{+} \cdot \gamma^2 \cdot \log k \cdot \log |\mathcal{Y}| \cdot \mathrm{polylog}\left(\varepsilon^{-1}\right),$$

*where $\xi_{\mathrm{IKOPS}}^{+} \in \mathbb{R}^{+}$ is some global constant independent of the function and of $\varepsilon$. In comparison to $\Pi_{\mathrm{IKOPS}}$, the only difference in the CC is in the constant and the exponent of $\log\left(\varepsilon^{-1}\right)$ taken. Specifically, it holds that*

$$\frac{\ell_{\mathrm{IKOPS}}^{+}}{\ell_{\mathrm{IKOPS}}} = \frac{\xi_{\mathrm{IKOPS}}^{+}}{\xi_{\mathrm{IKOPS}}} \cdot \log^2\left(\varepsilon^{-1}\right).$$

*Proof.* Correctness trivially holds. We next prove that the protocol is strong $\varepsilon$-server secure. Consider a message $\mathbf{a}^*$ sent by a malicious server holding $x \in (\mathcal{X} \cup \bot)$ and an auxiliary input $\mathrm{aux} \in \{0,1\}^*$ in the $\mathcal{OT}$-hybrid world. We need to show the existence of a certain probability vector $\mathbf{p} \in \mathbb{R}^{|\mathcal{X}|+1}$. It will be convenient to describe the vector $\mathbf{p}$ using a simulator $\mathsf{Sim}$ that will describe the probability of sending $x^*$ to $\mathsf{T}$ as an input.

The idea is to have the simulator check the inconsistencies made by the adversary. This is done via an *inconsistency graph*, where each vertex corresponds to a virtual party, and each edge corresponds to an inconsistency. There are three cases in which the simulator will send $\bot$ to $\mathsf{T}$. The first case, is when there is a large vertex cover among the servers. In the $\mathcal{OT}$-hybrid world, the client will see an inconsistency with high probability, and hence output $\bot$. The second case, is when there are two virtual clients $\mathsf{C}_{j,0}$ and $\mathsf{C}_{j,1}$, corresponding to the same bit of $\mathsf{Enc}(\mathbf{y})$ that are both inconsistent with the same server. Observe that the real client will always see an inconsistency, regardless of its input or randomness. The final case remaining, is when for each $j \in [m \cdot m']$, the adversary tampered with exactly one of $\mathsf{C}_{j,0}$ or $\mathsf{C}_{j,1}$. Here the real client will not notice the inconsistency only if asked for the virtual clients the adversary did not tamper with, which happens with low probability. For all other cases, the probability that the real client will see an inconsistency is *independent of its input*. Therefore the simulator can compute it and send $\bot$ with this probability. When the simulator does not send $\bot$ as its input, it uses the MPC simulator to reconstruct an effective input.

We next formalize the description of the simulator. The simulator holds $\mathbf{a}^*$ and $\mathrm{aux}$ as an input.

1. Write $\mathbf{a}^* = (\mathbf{a}_1^*, \mathbf{a}_2^*)$, where $\mathbf{a}_1^*$ corresponds to the outputs and $\mathbf{a}_2^*$ corresponds to the watchlist.
2. Apply the simulator guaranteed by the security of $\Pi_{\mathrm{BCS}}$ to each pair of messages in $\mathbf{a}_1^*$ to obtain $V_{1,0}, V_{1,1}, \ldots, V_{m \cdot m',0}, V_{m \cdot m',1}$, and apply the simulator guaranteed by $\Pi_{\mathrm{ROT}}$ for each pair in $\mathbf{a}_2^*$ to obtain $V_1, \ldots, V_n$ and a predicate $P$ (if the output of the simulator is $\bot$ instead of views, then send $\bot$ to $\mathsf{T}$).

3. Generate an inconsistency graph $G'$, with $[n]$ as vertices, and where $\{i_1, i_2\}$ is an edge if and only if $V_{i_1}$ and $V_{i_2}$ are inconsistent. Let VC be a minimum vertex cover of $G'$.[13] If $|\text{VC}| > t$ then send $\perp$ to T.

4. Otherwise, pick a subset $\mathcal{W} \subseteq [n]$ of size $t/2$ uniformly at random. If there exist $i_1, i_2 \in \mathcal{W}$ with an edge between them in $G$ or $P(\mathcal{W}) = 1$, then send $\perp$ to T.

5. Otherwise, extend $G'$ into an inconsistency graph $G$, where there are new vertices $(j, b) \in [m \cdot m'] \times \{0, 1\}$, and $\{i, (j, b)\}$ is an edge if and only if $V_{j,b}^i$ is inconsistent with $V_i$ (i.e., the view $C_{j,b}$ received from $S_i$ is inconsistent with the view of $S_i$).

6. Let $\mathcal{S} \subseteq [m \cdot m'] \times \{0, 1\}$ be the set of vertices corresponding to the virtual clients, that have an edge with a vertex in $\mathcal{W}$. If there exists $j \in [m]$ such that either
   - $(m'(j-1) + j', 0), (m'(j-1) + j', 1) \in \mathcal{S}$ for some $j' \in [m']$, or
   - for every $j' \in [m']$ exactly one the vertices $(m'(j-1) + j', 0), (m'(j-1) + j', 1)$ is in $\mathcal{S}$,
   
   then send $\perp$ to T.

7. Otherwise, send $\perp$ with probability $1 - 2^{-e(\mathcal{S})}$, where $e(\mathcal{S})$ is the number of edges coming out of $\mathcal{S}$. With the complement probability, apply the (malicious) MPC simulator on the virtual servers $S_i$, where $i \in \text{VC}$, to get an input for each of virtual servers in VC. The simulator Sim can then use the inputs of the other virtual servers to get an effective input $x^* \in (\mathcal{X} \cup \{\perp\})$, and send it to T.

The vector $\mathbf{p}$ is then defined as $p_{x^*} = \Pr[\text{Sim sends } x^* \text{ to T}]$. Recall that for every $\mathbf{y} \in \mathcal{Y}$ and $z \in \{\perp, 0, \ldots, k-1\}$ we denote

$$q_{y,z}^{\Pi_{\text{IKOPS}}^+}(\mathbf{a}^*) = \Pr\left[\varphi^+(\mathbf{y}, \mathbf{b}, \mathbf{a}^*[\mathbf{b}]) = z\right],$$

where $\mathbf{b} = \beta(\mathbf{y})$ and the probability is over the randomness of $\beta$ and $\varphi$. To alleviate notations, we will write $\mathbf{q} = \mathbf{q}^{\Pi_{\text{IKOPS}}^+(\varepsilon)}(\mathbf{a}^*)$. Fix $\mathbf{y} \in \{0, 1\}^m$ and $z \in \{\perp, 0, \ldots, k-1\}$. We show that[14]

$$\left|q_{\mathbf{y},z} - M_g^T(\cdot, (\mathbf{y}, z)) \cdot \mathbf{p}\right| \le \varepsilon \cdot p_\perp. \tag{5}$$

Observe that since $\Pi_{\text{BCS}}$ and $\Pi_{\text{ROT}}$ has perfect server-security, each $V_{m'(j-1)+j',b}$ and each $V_i$ in the $\mathcal{OT}$-hybrid world is distributed exactly the same as its counterpart in the ideal world. Therefore, we may condition on the event that they are indeed the same. Furthermore, by the security of $\Pi_{\text{ROT}}$, we may also assume that the watchlist $\mathcal{W}$ is distributed the same, and that $P(\mathcal{W}) = 0$,

---

[13] Recall that we do not care about the efficiency of simulator. We stress that it is also suffices to use a 2-approximation to compute the minimum vertex-cover, while slightly tweaking $t$.

[14] In fact we can show something stronger – that the $\ell_1$ distance (i.e., statistical distance) is smaller than $\varepsilon \cdot p_\perp$, implying that the protocol has standard $\varepsilon$-server security. However, this does not improve our result and the proof is therefore omitted.

as otherwise in both worlds the client will output $\bot$. In the following we fix the views and $\mathcal{W}$. We next separate into four cases, stated in the following claims (proven below). These claims together immediately imply Eq. (5).

**Claim 12.** *If* $|\mathsf{VC}| > t$ *then Eq.* (5) *holds.*

**Claim 13.** *Assume that* $|\mathsf{VC}| \le t$ *and that for every* $i \in \mathcal{W}$ *and every* $j \in [m]$, *there exists* $j' \in [m']$ *such that either both* $V_{m'(j-1)+j',0}$ *and* $V_{m'(j-1)+j',1}$ *are consistent with* $V_i$, *or both are inconsistent with* $V_i$. *Then Eq.* (5) *holds. Moreover, the simulation is perfect.*

**Claim 14.** *Assume that* $|\mathsf{VC}| \le t$ *and that there exists* $i \in \mathcal{W}$ *and* $j \in [m]$, *such that for every* $j' \in [m']$ *exactly one of the views* $V_{m'(j-1)+j',0}$ *and* $V_{m'(j-1)+j',1}$ *are inconsistent with* $V_i$, *then Eq.* (5) *holds.*

*Proof (of Claim 12).* Intuitively, the vertex cover of the graph $G$ gives us information on which servers "misbehaved". A large vertex cover means that a lot of servers have inconsistent views, implying that there are many edges in the graph. Therefore, a random subset of the vertices would contain at least one edge with high probability. We next formalize this intuition.

Since $|\mathsf{VC}| > t$ then the maximum matching in $G'$ is of size at least $(t+1)/2$. Therefore, in the $\mathcal{OT}$-hybrid world, the expected number of edges that the client will have in its watchlist is at least $\frac{t+1}{2} \cdot \frac{\binom{n-2}{t/2-2}}{\binom{n}{t/2}} = \Theta(n)$. By applying Hoeffding's inequality,[15] with probability at least $1 - 2^{-\Theta(n)} = 1 - \varepsilon$ the client will output $\bot$. As in the ideal-world the simulator sends $\bot$ to $\mathsf{T}$ with probability 1, Eq. (5) follows.

*Proof (of Claim 13).* We separate into two cases. For the first case, assume that there exist $i \in \mathcal{W}$, $j \in [m]$, and $j' \in [m']$ such that both $V_{m'(j-1)+j',0}$ and $V_{m'(j-1)+j',1}$ are inconsistent with $V_i$. Then $(m'(j-1)+j',0), (m'(j-1)+j',1) \in \mathcal{S}$, hence the simulator always sends $\bot$ in this case. Furthermore, in the $\mathcal{OT}$-hybrid world, for every input $\mathbf{y} \in \{0,1\}^m$ the client will see an inconsistency between either $V_{m'(j-1)+j',0}$ and $V_i$, or an inconsistency between either $V_{m'(j-1)+j',1}$ and $V_i$. Thus, Eq. (5) holds with no error.

By the assumptions of the claim, for the second case we may assume that for every $i \in \mathcal{W}$ and every $j \in [m]$, there exists $j' \in [m']$ such that both $V_{m'(j-1)+j',0}$ and $V_{m'(j-1)+j',1}$ are consistent with $V_i$. In this case, in the $\mathcal{OT}$-hybrid world, the client will see an inconsistency with probability $1 - 2^{-e(\mathcal{S})}$. With the complement probability, its output is determined by whatever the virtual servers computed. The output of the client in the ideal-world is either $\bot$ with probability $1 - 2^{-e(\mathcal{S})}$ or it is determined by the MPC simulator. Since it is assumed to be perfect and $|\mathsf{VC}| \le t$ bound from above the number of corrupted servers, it follows that Eq. (5) holds with no error.

---

[15] Although Hoeffding's inequality is stated for the sum of independent random variables, it still works in our case since the sampled can be modeled as if we are picking vertices without repetitions. Sampling with repetitions only decreases the probability for an edge.

*Proof (of Claim* 14*)*. By construction, the ideal-world simulator always sends $\perp$ in this case. Additionally, in the $\mathcal{OT}$-hybrid world, the client uses Enc on its input **y** to receive $m \cdot m'$ random bits $\left(y_j^{j'}\right)_{j\in[m], j'\in[m']}$ conditioned on $\oplus_{j'=1}^{m'} y_j^{j'} = y_j$ for every $j \in [m]$. Since we assume that exactly $m'$ virtual clients, corresponding to the same input bit $y_j$, where tampered by the adversary, it follows that with probability $2^{-(m'-1)} \le \varepsilon$ the client will see only consistent views. Therefore, for every $\mathbf{y} \in \{0,1\}^m$ it holds that

$$\left|q_{\mathbf{y},\perp} - M_g^T\left(\cdot, (\mathbf{y}, \perp)\right) \cdot \mathbf{p}\right| = |q_{\mathbf{y},\perp} - p_\perp| = \Pr\left[\varphi^+\left(\mathbf{y}, \mathbf{b}, \mathbf{a}^*[\mathbf{b}]\right) \ne \perp\right] \le \varepsilon,$$

and for every $z \ne \perp$

$$\left|q_{\mathbf{y},z} - M_g^T\left(\cdot, (\mathbf{y}, z)\right) \cdot \mathbf{p}\right| = \left|\Pr\left[\varphi^+\left(\mathbf{y}, \mathbf{b}, \mathbf{a}^*[\mathbf{b}]\right) = z\right] - 0\right| \le \varepsilon.$$

Equation (5) follows.

We next show that the protocol has perfect client-security. Consider an adversary $\mathcal{A}$ corrupting the client. We construct the simulator $\mathsf{Sim}_\mathcal{A}$. The construction of the simulator is done in the natural way, namely, it will apply the simulators of $\Pi_{\mathrm{BCS}}$ and $\Pi_{\mathrm{ROT}}$, and then the decoding of the PRE, to receive an output. It can then use the MPC simulator to simulate the views of the virtual servers in its watchlist. Formally, the simulator operates as follows.

1. On input $\mathbf{y} \in \{0,1\}^m$ and auxiliary input $\mathsf{aux} \in \{0,1\}^*$, query $\mathcal{A}$ to receive a message $\mathbf{b}^*$ to be sent to the OT.
2. Write $\mathbf{b}^* = (\mathbf{b}_1^*, \mathbf{b}_2^*)$, where $\mathbf{b}_1^*$ corresponds to the outputs and $\mathbf{b}_2^*$ corresponds to the watchlist.
3. Apply the simulator guaranteed by the security of $\Pi_{\mathrm{BCS}}$ to each pair of messages in $\mathbf{b}_1^*$ to obtain $(b_j)_{j\in[m\cdot m']}$ for some $b_j \in \{0,1\}$, and apply the simulator $\mathsf{Sim}_{\mathrm{ROT}}$, guaranteed by the security of $\Pi_{\mathrm{ROT}}$, for each pair in $\mathbf{b}_2^*$ to obtain a set $\mathcal{W} \subseteq [n]$.
4. Send $\mathsf{Dec}\left((b_j)_{j\in[m\cdot m']}\right)$ to $\mathsf{T}$ to obtain an output $z$.
5. Apply the PRE simulator on $z$ to obtain outputs $(z_j)_{j\in[m\cdot m']}$ for each virtual client.
6. If $|\mathcal{W}| > t$ then output $(z_j)_{j\in[m\cdot m']}$ alongside whatever $\mathsf{Sim}_{\mathrm{ROT}}$ outputs and halt.
7. Otherwise, apply the (semi-honest) MPC simulator on the parties $\{\mathsf{S}_i\}_{i\in\mathcal{W}}$ with random strings as inputs, and on $\left\{\mathsf{C}_{j,b_j}\right\}_{j\in[m\cdot m']}$ with $z_j$ as the output respectively. Send the output of the MPC simulator to $\mathsf{Sim}_{\mathrm{ROT}}$, outputs whatever it outputs and halt.

The security of $\Pi_{\mathrm{BCS}}$ and $\Pi_{\mathrm{ROT}}$ implies that $(b_j)_{j\in[m\cdot m']}$ and $\mathcal{W}$ are distributed exactly the same in both worlds. Therefore, the output $z = g\left(x, \mathsf{Dec}\left((b_j)_{j\in[m\cdot m']}\right)\right)$ is distributed the same, hence applying the PRE simulator on $z$ will also result in the same distribution. Now, if $|\mathcal{W}| > t$ then $\mathsf{Sim}_{\mathrm{ROT}}$

is guaranteed to produce a correct view as an output. If $|\mathcal{W}| \leq t$, then the MPC simulator will perfectly generate $|\mathcal{W}|$ virtual views. Handing them over to $\mathsf{Sim}_{\mathsf{ROT}}$ would result in the view that is distributed the same as in the $\mathcal{OT}$-hybrid world.

## 5.4   Proof of Lemma 4

We first prove the following simple claim, stating that the client will always reconstruct a unique secret (if its not outputting $\perp$).

**Claim 15.** *Consider a message* $\mathbf{a}^* = ((a_{1,0}^*, a_{1,1}^*), \ldots, (a_{n,0}^*, a_{n,1}^*)) \in \{0,1\}^{2sn}$ *sent to the OT by a malicious server. Then for any different inputs* $\mathbf{y}_1 \neq \mathbf{y}_2$ *for the client, either it will output* $\perp$ *for at least one of the inputs, or there exists a common secret* $\mathbf{r}$ *that will be reconstructed.*

*Proof.* Let $\mathcal{B} = \{i \in [n] : i \notin \mathbf{y}_1 \wedge i \notin \mathbf{y}_2\}$. Then $|\mathcal{B}| \geq n - t$, hence the client – who receives the shares $(a_{i,1}^*)_{i \in \mathcal{B}}$ – can reconstruct a secret $\mathbf{r}$ in case the share are consistent. This secret will be the same for both $\mathbf{y}_1$ and $\mathbf{y}_2$.

We now prove the lemma.

*Proof (of Lemma 4).* By construction, it is not hard to see that the protocol is correct. We next prove that the protocol has perfect input-dependent security. Consider a adversary $\mathcal{A}$ corrupting the server. We construct a simulator $\mathsf{Sim}_{\mathcal{A}}$ as follows. On input $\mathbf{x}$ and auxiliary input $\mathsf{aux} \in \{0,1\}^*$, query $\mathcal{A}$ to receive a message $\mathbf{a}^* = ((a_{1,0}^*, a_{1,1}^*), \ldots, (a_{n,0}^*, a_{n,1}^*)) \in \{0,1\}^{2sn}$. If there are no $n - t$ shares from $(a_{i,1}^*)_{i \in [n]}$ that are consistent, then $\mathsf{Sim}_{\mathcal{A}}$ will send the constant 1 predicate alongside some arbitrary input $\mathbf{x}_0$ to the trusted party T. Otherwise, let $\mathcal{B}$ be the maximum set of indexes $i \in [n]$ such that the $a_{i,1}^*$ are shares consistent with single value $\mathbf{r} \in (\{0,1\}^s)^n$. Then $\mathsf{Sim}_{\mathcal{A}}$ will send to T the input $\left((a_{i,0}^* \oplus r_i)_{i \notin \mathcal{B}}, (0^s)_{i \in \mathcal{B}}\right)$ with the predicate $P_{\mathcal{B}}(\mathbf{y}) = 1$ if and only if $\mathbf{y} \cap \mathcal{B} \neq \emptyset$.

To see why the simulator works, observe that $\mathsf{Sim}_{\mathcal{A}}$ sends constant 1 predicate if and only if $\mathcal{A}$ sent at most $t$ consistent shares, forcing C to output $\perp$ in the ideal-world. Since this happens if there are too many inconsistencies, C will output $\perp$ in the $\mathcal{OT}$-hybrid world as well. Furthermore, if there are at least $n - t$ shares that are consistent, then by Claim 15, there is a unique secret $\mathbf{r}$ that can be reconstructed. Therefore, in the $\mathcal{OT}$-hybrid world, on input $\mathbf{y}$, C will output $\perp$ if $\mathbf{y} \cap \mathcal{B} \neq \emptyset$, and output $(\mathbf{a}^*[\beta_{\mathsf{ROT}}(\mathbf{y})]_i \oplus r_i)_{i \in \mathbf{y}}$ otherwise. Since $\mathcal{B}$ was chosen to be the maximum set of indexes, the same holds in the input-dependent ideal-world.

We next show that the relaxed security requirement against malicious clients holds. Let $\mathcal{A}$ be an adversary corrupting the client. The simulator $\mathsf{Sim}_{\mathcal{A}}$ works as follows. On input $\mathbf{y}$ and auxiliary input $\mathsf{aux} \in \{0,1\}^*$, query $\mathcal{A}$ to receive $\mathbf{b}^* \in \{0,1\}^n$. If there are strictly more than $t$ 0's in $\mathbf{b}^*$ then output $n$ random strings, each of length $s$. Otherwise, send $\{i \in [n] : b_i^* = 0\}$ to T to receive output $(x_i)_{i:b_i^*=0}$. $\mathsf{Sim}_{\mathcal{A}}$ samples $n$ random strings $r_1, \ldots, r_n \leftarrow \{0,1\}^s$. For $i \in [n]$, let

$\mathbf{r}[i] \in \{0,1\}^{sn}$ be a share of $\mathbf{r} = (r_1, \ldots, r_n)$ in an $(n-t)$-out-of-$n$ Shamir's secret sharing (pad $\mathbf{r}[i]$ if needed). The simulator then generates the values

$$\mathbf{a} := \Big( (\alpha_{\mathrm{BCS}}(x_i \oplus r_i, \mathbf{r}[i]))_{i:b_i^* = 0} \, , (\alpha_{\mathrm{BCS}}(0^{sn}, \mathbf{r}[i]))_{i:b_i^* = 1} \Big),$$

where the $x_i \oplus r_i$'s are padded accordingly. $\mathrm{Sim}_{\mathcal{A}}$ will then compute and output

$$\binom{2}{1}\text{-bit-OT}^\ell \left( \mathbf{a}, (\beta_{\mathrm{BCS}}(b_1^*), \ldots, \beta_{\mathrm{BCS}}(b_n^*)) \right).$$

$\mathrm{Sim}_{\mathcal{A}}$ works since in the case where there are more than $t$ 0's in $\mathbf{b}^*$, by the properties the sharing scheme, the view of C in the $\mathcal{OT}$-hybrid world consist only of random values. Otherwise, C will receive the masked $x_i$ for the indexes $i$ on which $b_i^* = 0$, and shares of the maskings for the indexes $i$ on which $b_i^* = 1$.

# 6  Tightness of the Analysis

Recall that our final protocol is a "wrapper" for an upgraded version of the protocol by Ishai et al. [19], namely, protocol $\Pi_{\mathrm{IKOPS}}^+$ from Sect. 5.3. In the following section, we prove that for any (randomized) *Boolean* function $f$ that is *not* full-dimensional, and does not satisfy the constraints in Corollary 1, no "wrapper" protocol for $\Pi_{\mathrm{IKOPS}}^+$ will compute $f$ with perfect full-security. Here, the "wrapper" protocol simply replaces the output $\perp$ that the client receive from $\Pi_{\mathrm{IKOPS}}^+$ with a random bit. Formally, any "wrapper" protocol is parametrized with a vector $\mathbf{v} \in [0,1]^{|\mathcal{Y}|}$ and an $\varepsilon > 0$, and is denoted by $\Pi_f^{\mathsf{v}}(\varepsilon)$. Let $g : (\mathcal{X} \cup \{\perp\}) \times \mathcal{Y} \mapsto \{\perp, 0, 1\}$ be defined as $g(x,y) = f(x,y)$ if $x \neq \perp$ and $g(\perp, y) = \perp$. The "wrapper" protocol $\Pi_f^{\mathsf{v}}$ is described as follows.

----

**Protocol 16 ($\Pi_f^{\mathsf{v}}(\varepsilon)$)**
  *Input: Server* S *has input* $x \in \mathcal{X}$ *and client* C *has input* $y \in \mathcal{Y}$.

1. *The parties execute protocol* $\Pi_{\mathrm{IKOPS}}^+(\varepsilon)$ *in order to compute* $g$. *Let* $z$ *be the output* C *receive.*
2. *If* $z \neq \perp$, *then* C *output* $z$. *Otherwise, output 1 with probability* $v_y$.

----

We next claim that the protocol cannot compute Boolean functions that are not full-dimensional with perfect full-security.

**Theorem 17.** *Let* $f : \mathcal{X} \times \mathcal{Y} \mapsto \{0,1\}$ *denote a (possibly randomized) Boolean function that has* no *constant columns, i.e.,* $M_f(\cdot, y)$ *is not constant for every* $y \in \mathcal{Y}$, *and is* not *full-dimensional, i.e.,* $\dim\left(\mathbf{aff}\left(M_f^T\right)\right) < |\mathcal{Y}|$. *Then for every* $\mathbf{v} \in [0,1]^{|\mathcal{Y}|}$ *and every* $\varepsilon > 0$, $\Pi_f^{\mathsf{v}}(\varepsilon)$ *does not compute* $f$ *with perfect full-security.*

*Proof.* Assume towards contradiction that $\Pi_f^{\mathbf{v}}(\varepsilon)$ has perfect server security, for some $\mathbf{v}$ and $\varepsilon$. We next construct $|\mathcal{Y}| + 1$ adversaries, such that each adversary forces the vector of outputs of the client $\mathbf{q}^{\Pi_f^{\mathbf{v}}(\varepsilon)}$, to be a different point inside the convex-hull of the rows of $M_f$. We then show that these points are affinely independent, giving us a contradiction. First, write each input of the client as a binary string $\mathbf{y}$ of length $m$. For every $\mathbf{y} \in \mathcal{Y}$ define the adversary $\mathcal{A}_\mathbf{y}$ as follows.

1. Fix an encoding $\mathbf{y}' = \left(y_j^1, \ldots, y_j^{m'}\right)_{j \in [m]} \in \mathrm{Supp}\,(\mathsf{Enc}(\mathbf{y}))$, and fix some $x_\mathbf{y}^* \in \mathcal{X}$ such that $f(x_\mathbf{y}^*, \mathbf{y}) \neq v_\mathbf{y}$. (such an $x_\mathbf{y}^*$ exists, since $M_f$ does not have constant columns).
2. Execute $\Pi_{\mathrm{IKOPS}}^+(\varepsilon)$ honestly with input $x_\mathbf{y}^*$, as fixed above, with the following one exception. For every $i \in [n]$, $j \in [m]$, and $j' \in [m']$, modify $V_{m'(j-1)+j',1-y_j^{j'}}^i$ such that it is inconsistent with $V_i$.

Finally, define the adversary $\mathcal{A}_0$ who picks an arbitrary $x_0^* \in \mathcal{X}$ as an input, and acts honestly with the exception that it tampers with all $V_{j,b}^i$'s, making them inconsistent with the corresponding $V_i$. Let $\mathbf{a}^*\left(x_\mathbf{y}^*\right)$ be the message $\mathcal{A}_\mathbf{y}$ sends to the OT.

Let us analyze the client's vector of outputs $\mathbf{q}^{\Pi_f^{\mathbf{v}}(\varepsilon)}\left(\mathbf{a}^*\left(x_\mathbf{y}^*\right)\right)$, for any adversary $\mathcal{A}_\mathbf{y}$, for $\mathbf{y} \in \mathcal{Y} \cup \{0\}$. For brevity, we write $\mathbf{q}\left(x_\mathbf{y}^*\right)$ instead. By definition, $\mathcal{A}_0$ forces the client to sample its output according to $\mathbf{v}$, hence $\mathbf{q}\left(x_0^*\right) = \mathbf{v}$. Next, fix $\mathbf{y} \in \mathcal{Y}$. Observe that for every $\hat{\mathbf{y}} \neq \mathbf{y}$, any of their encodings will differ on at least one bit, i.e., $\hat{y}_j^{j'} \neq y_j^{j'}$ for some $j \in [m]$ and $j' \in [m']$, hence on input $\hat{\mathbf{y}}$, the client will see $V_{m'(j-1)+j',1-y_j^{j'}}^i$ for every $i$. Since the inconsistency is made with every virtual server, on input $\hat{\mathbf{y}}$, the client will notice it and output $\perp$ with probability 1. By the description of $\Pi_f^{\mathbf{v}}$, it follows that

$$q_{\hat{\mathbf{y}}}\left(x_\mathbf{y}^*\right) = v_{\hat{\mathbf{y}}}, \tag{6}$$

for every $\hat{\mathbf{y}} \neq \mathbf{y}$. On the other hand, on input $\mathbf{y}$, the client outputs $\perp$ if and only if the event $\mathsf{Enc}\,(\mathbf{y}) = \mathbf{y}'$ occurs, which happens with probability $1 - 2^{-m(m'-1)}$. With the complement probability $2^{-m(m'-1)}$ it does not detect an inconsistency, and outputs $f(x_\mathbf{y}^*, \mathbf{y})$. Therefore

$$q_\mathbf{y}\left(x_\mathbf{y}^*\right) = 2^{-m(m'-1)} \cdot f(x_\mathbf{y}^*, \mathbf{y}) + (1 - 2^{-m(m'-1)}) \cdot v_\mathbf{y}. \tag{7}$$

Thus, Eqs. (6) and (7) yield that

$$\mathbf{q}\left(x_\mathbf{y}^*\right) = \mathbf{v} - 2^{-m(m'-1)}(v_\mathbf{y} - f(x_\mathbf{y}^*, \mathbf{y})) \cdot \mathbf{e}_\mathbf{y},$$

where $\mathbf{e}_\mathbf{y}$ is the $\mathbf{y}$-th unit vector in $\mathbb{R}^{|\mathcal{Y}|}$.

To conclude the proof, observe that $x_\mathbf{y}^*$ was chosen so that $f(x_\mathbf{y}^*, \mathbf{y}) \neq v_\mathbf{y}$, implying that the set of points $\left\{\mathbf{q}\left(x_\mathbf{y}^*\right)\right\}_{\mathbf{y} \in \mathcal{Y} \cup \{0\}}$ are affinely independent. Furthermore, since $\Pi_f^{\mathbf{v}}$ is assumed to have perfect server security, Lemma 1 implies that all of theses points lie inside $\mathbf{conv}\left(M_f^T\right)$. Therefore, $\mathbf{aff}\left(M_f^T\right) = \mathbb{R}^{|\mathcal{Y}|}$ contradicting the assumption that $f$ is not full-dimensional.

# 7   A Note on Efficiency

While our main goal is to understand the feasibility of perfectly secure 2PC, our construction does confer concrete efficiency benefits for certain parameter ranges. It is instructive to compare our construction with the IKOPS protocol, for deterministic functions (from the right class). Here we focus on the number of OT calls, which are the most expensive part to implement in practice (usually with computational security). Specifically, for simplicity, we consider the number of calls to a $\binom{2}{1}$-$s$-string-OT oracle, of any length $s$, rather than $\binom{2}{1}$-bit-OT. We note that the strings' length of our OT's is quite a bit larger than in IKOPS (due to the step ensuring perfect client security, where the length is multiplied by the number of servers). However, we claim that this comparison is somewhat justified when having practical efficiency in mind, since for particularly long strings, a string-OT oracle can be used to pick *short PRG seeds* instead of the strings themselves during a preprocessing phase. This will be done by having the server send $s_0$ and $s_1$ to the "short" string-OT functionality, and the client will receive $s_b$, where $b \in \{0,1\}$ as its input. Then, to implement the "long" string-OT during the protocol execution, the sender sends to the client $G(s_a) \oplus m_a$, for $a \in \{0,1\}$, where $G$ is a PRG and $m_0$ and $m_1$ are the "long" messages.

Fix a deterministic function $f : \mathcal{X} \times \mathcal{Y} \rightarrow \{0, \ldots, k-1\}$ satisfying the conditions of Corollary 1. The number of calls to string-OT in $\Pi^+_{\mathrm{IKOPS}}(\varepsilon)$ and $\Pi_{\mathrm{IKOPS}}(\varepsilon)$ is $\log(\varepsilon^{-1})(\log|\mathcal{Y}| + c)$, where $c$ is a constant circa 1400 ($c$ is roughly the same in both protocols). When considering our perfectly secure protocol, we set $\varepsilon = \frac{1}{2n(n+1)!}$, where $n = (k-1) \cdot |\mathcal{Y}|$. On the one hand, this results in communication complexity that is polynomial in $|\mathcal{Y}|$ and $k$, which may be prohibitive for functions with large client-domain or range sizes. On the other hand, for functions with a small client-domain and range sizes, we do better than IKOPS even for real-world error ranges, and the advantage grows as the allowed error $\varepsilon$ decreases. For instance, consider the greater than function $3 >: \{0,1,2\} \times \{0,1,2\} \rightarrow \{0,1\}$, with an error of $\varepsilon = 2^{-40}$. The communication complexity we obtain is bounded by a factor smaller than $40/\log(24) \approx 8.724$ than that of the IKOPS protocol.

**Acknowledgements.** We are very grateful to Yuval Ishai for suggesting this question, and for many helpful discussions. We also want to thank Eran Omri for many helpful comments.

# References

1. Applebaum, B., Ishai, Y., Kushilevitz, E.: Cryptography in nc^0. SIAM J. Comput. **36**(4), 845–888 (2006)
2. Asharov, G.: Towards characterizing complete fairness in secure two-party computation. In: Lindell, Y. (ed.) TCC 2014. LNCS, vol. 8349, pp. 291–316. Springer, Heidelberg (2014). https://doi.org/10.1007/978-3-642-54242-8_13

3. Asharov, G., Beimel, A., Makriyannis, N., Omri, E.: Complete characterization of fairness in secure two-party computation of boolean functions. In: Dodis, Y., Nielsen, J.B. (eds.) TCC 2015. LNCS, vol. 9014, pp. 199–228. Springer, Heidelberg (2015). https://doi.org/10.1007/978-3-662-46494-6_10

4. Beaver, D.: Precomputing oblivious transfer. In: Coppersmith, D. (ed.) CRYPTO 1995. LNCS, vol. 963, pp. 97–109. Springer, Heidelberg (1995). https://doi.org/10.1007/3-540-44750-4_8

5. Beaver, D.: Correlated pseudo randomness and the complexity of private computations. In: Proceedings of the Twenty-eighth Annual ACM Symposium on Theory of Computing, pp. 479–488. ACM (1996)

6. Beaver, D., Micali, S., Rogaway, P.: The round complexity of secure protocols. In: Proceedings of the Twenty-Second Annual ACM Symposium on Theory of Computing, pp. 503–513. ACM (1990)

7. Ben-Or, M., Goldwasser, S., Wigderson, A.: Completeness theorems for non-cryptographic fault-tolerant distributed computation (extended abstract). In: Proceedings of the 29th Annual Symposium on Foundations of Computer Science (FOCS), pp. 1–10 (1988)

8. Brassard, G., Crépeau, C., Santha, M.: Oblivious transfers and intersecting codes. IACR Cryptology ePrint Archive, 1996:10 (1996). http://eprint.iacr.org/1996/010

9. Cleve, R.: Limits on the security of coin flips when half the processors are faulty. In: Proceedings of the 18th Annual ACM Symposium on Theory of Computing (STOC), pp. 364–369 (1986)

10. Crépeau, C.: Efficient cryptographic protocols based on noisy channels. In: Fumy, W. (ed.) EUROCRYPT 1997. LNCS, vol. 1233, pp. 306–317. Springer, Heidelberg (1997). https://doi.org/10.1007/3-540-69053-0_21

11. Crépeau, C., Morozov, K., Wolf, S.: Efficient unconditional oblivious transfer from almost any noisy channel. In: Blundo, C., Cimato, S. (eds.) SCN 2004. LNCS, vol. 3352, pp. 47–59. Springer, Heidelberg (2005). https://doi.org/10.1007/978-3-540-30598-9_4

12. Daza, V., Makriyannis, N.: Designing fully secure protocols for secure two-party computation of constant-domain functions. In: Kalai, Y., Reyzin, L. (eds.) TCC 2017. LNCS, vol. 10677, pp. 581–611. Springer, Cham (2017). https://doi.org/10.1007/978-3-319-70500-2_20

13. Even, S., Goldreich, O., Lempel, A.: A randomized protocol for signing contracts. Commun. ACM 28(6), 637–647 (1985)

14. Goldreich, O., Micali, S., Wigderson, A.: How to play any mental game or a completeness theorem for protocols with honest majority. In: STOC19, pp. 218–229 (1987)

15. Gordon, S.D., Hazay, C., Katz, J., Lindell, Y.: Complete fairness in secure two-party computation. In: Proceedings of the 40th Annual ACM Symposium on Theory of Computing (STOC), pp. 413–422 (2008)

16. Ishai, Y., Kushilevitz, E.: Perfect constant-round secure computation via perfect randomizing polynomials. In: Widmayer, P., Eidenbenz, S., Triguero, F., Morales, R., Conejo, R., Hennessy, M. (eds.) ICALP 2002. LNCS, vol. 2380, pp. 244–256. Springer, Heidelberg (2002). https://doi.org/10.1007/3-540-45465-9_22

17. Ishai, Y., Kushilevitz, E., Ostrovsky, R., Sahai, A.: Cryptography with constant computational overhead. In: Proceedings of the Fortieth Annual ACM Symposium on Theory of Computing, pp. 433–442. ACM (2008)

18. Ishai, Y., Prabhakaran, M., Sahai, A.: Founding cryptography on oblivious transfer – efficiently. In: Wagner, D. (ed.) CRYPTO 2008. LNCS, vol. 5157, pp. 572–591. Springer, Heidelberg (2008). https://doi.org/10.1007/978-3-540-85174-5_32

19. Ishai, Y., Kushilevitz, E., Ostrovsky, R., Prabhakaran, M., Sahai, A.: Efficient non-interactive secure computation. In: Paterson, K.G. (ed.) EUROCRYPT 2011. LNCS, vol. 6632, pp. 406–425. Springer, Heidelberg (2011). https://doi.org/10.1007/978-3-642-20465-4_23

20. Ishai, Y., Kushilevitz, E., Meldgaard, S., Orlandi, C., Paskin-Cherniavsky, A.: On the power of correlated randomness in secure computation. In: Sahai, A. (ed.) TCC 2013. LNCS, vol. 7785, pp. 600–620. Springer, Heidelberg (2013). https://doi.org/10.1007/978-3-642-36594-2_34

21. Khurana, D., Maji, H.K., Sahai, A.: Secure computation from elastic noisy channels. In: Fischlin, M., Coron, J.-S. (eds.) EUROCRYPT 2016. LNCS, vol. 9666, pp. 184–212. Springer, Heidelberg (2016). https://doi.org/10.1007/978-3-662-49896-5_7

22. Kilian, J.: Founding cryptography on oblivious transfer. In: Proceedings of the 20th Annual ACM Symposium on Theory of Computing (STOC), pp. 20–31 (1988)

23. Lindell, Y., Pinkas, B.: An efficient protocol for secure two-party computation in the presence of malicious adversaries. In: Naor, M. (ed.) EUROCRYPT 2007. LNCS, vol. 4515, pp. 52–78. Springer, Heidelberg (2007). https://doi.org/10.1007/978-3-540-72540-4_4

24. Lindell, Y., Pinkas, B.: A proof of security of yao's protocol for two-party computation. J. Cryptol. **22**(2), 161–188 (2009)

25. Makriyannis, N.: On the classification of finite boolean functions up to fairness. In: Abdalla, M., De Prisco, R. (eds.) SCN 2014. LNCS, vol. 8642, pp. 135–154. Springer, Cham (2014). https://doi.org/10.1007/978-3-319-10879-7_9

26. Nascimento, A.C., Winter, A.: On the oblivious transfer capacity of noisy correlations. In: 2006 IEEE International Symposium on Information Theory, pp. 1871–1875. IEEE (2006)

27. Peikert, C., Vaikuntanathan, V., Waters, B.: A framework for efficient and composable oblivious transfer. In: Wagner, D. (ed.) CRYPTO 2008. LNCS, vol. 5157, pp. 554–571. Springer, Heidelberg (2008). https://doi.org/10.1007/978-3-540-85174-5_31

28. Rabin, M.O.: How to exchange secrets with oblivious transfer (2005). http://eprint.iacr.org/2005/187. Harvard University Technical Report 81 talr@watson.ibm.com 12955. Accessed 21 Jun 2005

29. Shamir, A.: How to share a secret. Commun. ACM **22**(11), 612–613 (1979)

30. Wolf, S., Wullschleger, J.: Oblivious transfer is symmetric. In: Vaudenay, S. (ed.) EUROCRYPT 2006. LNCS, vol. 4004, pp. 222–232. Springer, Heidelberg (2006). https://doi.org/10.1007/11761679_14

31. Wood, P.J.: On the probability that a discrete complex random matrix is singular. Ph.D. thesis, Rutgers University-Graduate School-New Brunswick (2009)

32. Wullschleger, J.: Oblivious transfer from weak noisy channels. In: Reingold, O. (ed.) TCC 2009. LNCS, vol. 5444, pp. 332–349. Springer, Heidelberg (2009). https://doi.org/10.1007/978-3-642-00457-5_20

33. Yao, A.C.: Protocols for secure computations. In Proceedings of the 23th Annual Symposium on Foundations of Computer Science (FOCS), pp. 160–164 (1982)